D1608386

EVIDENCE:
CASES, MATERIALS, AND PROBLEMS

LexisNexis Law School Publishing Advisory Board

EVIDENCE: CASES, MATERIALS, AND PROBLEMS

FOURTH EDITION

Paul F. Rothstein
Professor of Law
Georgetown University Law Center

Myrna S. Raeder
Professor of Law
Southwestern Law School

David Crump
John B. Neibel Professor of Law
University of Houston Law Center

ISBN: 978-0-7698-4889-1
Looseleaf ISBN: 978-0-7698-4890-7
Ebook ISBN: 978–0–7698–8881–1

Library of Congress Cataloging-in-Publication Data

Rothstein, Paul F., 1938- author.
Evidence : cases, materials, and problems / Paul F. Rothstein, Professor of Law Georgetown University Law Center; Myrna S. Raeder, Professor of Law Southwestern Law School; David Crump, John B. Neibel Professor of Law & Director of CLE, University of Houston Law Center. -- Fourth edition.
pages cm.
Includes index.
ISBN 978-0-7698-4889-1
1. Evidence (Law)--United States . I. Raeder, Myrna S., author. II. Crump, David, author. III. Title.
KF8935.R68 2013
347.73'6--dc23 2013030199

NOTE TO USERS

To ensure that you are using the latest materials available in this area, please be sure to periodically check the LexisNexis Law School web site for downloadable updates and supplements at www.lexisnexis.com/lawschool.

Editorial Offices
121 Chanlon Rd., New Providence, NJ 07974 (908) 464-6800
201 Mission St., San Francisco, CA 94105-1831 (415) 908-3200
www.lexisnexis.com

MATTHEW BENDER

(2013–Pub.447)

DEDICATION

To my wife without whose love, help and support this book could never have been done.

—P.F.R.

To my husband who reminds me daily to follow my dreams, and whose love and support is essential in everything I do.

—M.S.R.

To Susanne.

—D.C.

PREFACE TO THE FOURTH EDITION

Using this Book, Particularly its New Edition

The materials in this book cover a wide range of perspectives, from intensely pragmatic concerns, through deeply philosophical policy issues, to new approaches to evidentiary analysis. Included are textual explanations, rules, cases, notes, questions, problems, jury instructions, articles, proposals, legislation, and excerpted testimony. Assignments may be tailored to suit the teacher's own preferences on how to best approach Evidence in an introductory course.

The first chapter contains background-and-overview material describing Evidence and the litigation process as a whole, and evidentiary procedures in particular, including the role of the various players. It is comprised of material that one of us has been assigning regularly as reading to be done prior to the first class session. Students consistently report that this initial orientation facilitated their grasp of concepts over the entire semester.

Throughout the book we have supplied explanatory text and new cases and materials while retaining old favorites. One area requiring extensive treatment was the area of constitutional confrontation, owing to continued development of the U.S. Supreme Court's decision in *Crawford*, covered in Chapter 11, *infra.*

Burgeoning developments in scientific evidence and in the admissibility of electronic and digital information are also included.

We made room for new material by careful selection, pruning, editing, deleting less instructive cases, and summarizing some opinions or portions thereof. Except where we deemed it important for understanding, we eliminated from opinions most internal citations, extraneous passages and headings, and the plethora of ellipses one sometimes sees marking such deletions.

The new edition incorporates all recent Federal Rules of Evidence amendments, including the across-the-board restyling that went into effect in Dec., 2011. In that restyling, changes were made to nearly every rule to simplify reading. The restyling Advisory Committee said they did not intend to change any meaning or any result of any rule or ruling.

So far, the bulk of federal evidence cases involve the unrestyled rules and most of the states have not restyled their similar rules. But normally the restyling would make no difference. Therefore, except where needed for clarity, we have not changed unrestyled rule references in opinions. In the very rare instances where the restyling might be consequential, we have so noted, with an explanation of the potential effect. Where we are writing our own material, the restyled rules are used.

The book is predicated on the notion that the Federal Rules of Evidence, their state progeny, and cases arising under them, are the major factors in teaching Evidence. We include, however, interesting or informative cases or materials from other jurisdictions or the common law, when we feel they shed light on an issue or impart perspective by showing other ways of doing things. In particular we have highlighted significant differences between the California and the Federal Rules. But we think the Federal Rules provide a good organizing principle.

We have sequenced the topics in the book roughly along the same lines as the sequence of topics in the Federal Rules, with the exception of privileges and the so-called evidentiary "shortcuts" (judicial notice and presumptions), which we defer to the end for pedagogical reasons. But the book is designed to allow the teacher to adopt whatever order he or she prefers.

In the privileges chapter, we set forth verbatim, at the front of each section, the *Uniform* (not the *Federal*) Rules of Evidence codifying the particular privilege being treated, because the Federal Rules do not contain particular privileges, so the student profits from an additional "rudder" here. The Uniform Rules respecting privileges are somewhat more thorough and recent than the only Federal Rules draft that had particular privileges, the so-called Supreme Court draft, upon which the Uniform Rules are basically modeled (but with improvements more reflective of current law).

The general plan of the book is this. Each section starts out with a directive to read a particular rule or portion thereof. This may be followed by a brief background explanation of the area, if needed. Then come some essential and teachable cases and other primary materials, each usually followed by a set of expository notes (including some questions) exploring permutations and implications, and finally, some problems testing whether students can apply or critique what they have learned and integrate it with other topics and rules where necessary. Each note, question, or problem has a heading indicating what it treats, so that professors are able to identify the subjects they wish to cover, while students receive direction about the intended focus of each inquiry. All decisions cited by us in textual passages, notes, questions, and problems are followed by at least a few words describing the holding, so the student is not left to wonder or look the case up in order to get our point.

Most sections of the book bear a footnote to the relevant portion of ROTHSTEIN, RAEDER & CRUMP'S EVIDENCE IN A NUTSHELL that succinctly summarizes the principal points of the matter under study. The references are to portions of the *Nutshell* by their chapter number (Arabic numeral), chapter subdivision number (capital Roman numeral), and title (in words in quotes) of the portion within that nutshell subdivision. Thus, a citation might read: *Evidence in a Nutshell*, Chapter 1:II at "Curative and Cautionary Instructions." The reader should find the location of this entry in the Table of Contents of the *Nutshell* and go to the relevant pages of the *Nutshell*. Any future editions of the *Nutshell* will have all the same designations.

The *Nutshell* referred to is more substantive than some other concise text offerings and is entirely compatible with the present book, being written by the same authors. Any use of the *Nutshell* is completely optional, however — the present book is entirely self-sufficient. But at least one of us makes regular assignments to the *Nutshell* along with readings in the present book. Some professors leave it to the students as to whether or not to consult the *Nutshell* as a study guide during the course or before finals. Some professors assign as *Nutshell* reading, those subjects, basics, or background areas, that they do not wish to spend much class time on, thereby freeing up class time for other issues they want to treat more extensively. Or they may wish to assign foundational reading they will expand upon in class without having to lay out fundamentals.

PREFACE TO THE FOURTH EDITION

Each of us is indebted to people too numerous to mention who have provided wise counsel in the preparation of this book. They include fellow teachers and, most of all, our students who, over the years, have made valuable suggestions that we have incorporated. Any errors, however, are our own.

Our aim, as always, is to help students navigate the sometimes treacherous but always fun waters of Evidence.

P.F.R.

M.S.R.

D.C.

SUMMARY TABLE OF CONTENTS

PART I ORIENTATION

Chapter 1 BACKGROUND, THEORY, AND BASIC PROCEDURES . 1

§ 1.01 INTRODUCTION 1
§ 1.02 COURTROOM SCENARIO AND SOME BASIC PROCEDURES 9
§ 1.03 LIMIT ON JUDGE'S CONDUCT OF TRIAL: IMPARTIALITY 18
§ 1.04 PURPOSE-LIMITING INSTRUCTIONS TO THE JURY 24

PART II PRIMARILY RELEVANCY-RELATED RULES

Chapter 2 RELEVANCY AND ITS COUNTERWEIGHTS 27

§ 2.01 RELEVANCE 27
§ 2.02 FORMALISTIC LOGIC (UTILIZED BY SOME TO DETERMINE RELEVANCE) 38
§ 2.03 THE COUNTERWEIGHTS 40
§ 2.04 "OVERRIDING" RULES 401–403 BY RE-CHARACTERIZING UNDERLYING COMPONENTS OF MATERIALITY OR PROBATIVE VALUE 65
§ 2.05 JUDGE'S ROLE UNDER F.R.E. 104 69
§ 2.06 EMERGING PATTERNS OR QUASI-RULES IN APPLICATION OF RULE 403 FACTORS: PRETRIAL EXPERIMENTS AS CASE IN POINT 71

Chapter 3 RELEVANCY AND ITS COUNTERWEIGHTS CONTINUED 79

§ 3.01 CHARACTER EVIDENCE (OTHER THAN IMPEACHMENT): SPECIFIC INSTANCES 79
§ 3.02 OTHER WAYS OF PROVING CHARACTER: OPINION AND REPUTATION EVIDENCE 111
§ 3.03 CHARACTER IN CASES OF SEXUAL CRIMES AND RELATED OFFENSES 127
§ 3.04 CHARACTER VERSUS HABIT 138
§ 3.05 OTHER TRANSACTIONS, SIMILAR OCCURRENCES, AND PROFILES: CHARACTER, HABIT, OR SOMETHING ELSE? 144
§ 3.06 SUBSEQUENT REMEDIAL MEASURES 158
§ 3.07 SETTLEMENT MATTERS (COMPROMISE, OFFERS TO COMPROMISE, WITHDRAWN PLEAS, AND RELATED MATTERS) 162
§ 3.08 EVIDENCE INDICATING OR SUGGESTING INSURANCE 165

SUMMARY TABLE OF CONTENTS

PART III PRIMARILY RELIABILITY-RELATED RULES

Chapter 4 COMPETENCY, EXAMINATION, AND CREDIBILITY OF WITNESSES 173

§ 4.01 INTRODUCTION: PRESENTING WITNESS TESTIMONY AT TRIAL 173
§ 4.02 PREREQUISITES FOR WITNESS TESTIMONY: COMPETENCY AND PERSONAL KNOWLEDGE 174
§ 4.03 FORM OF QUESTIONS IN DIRECT AND CROSS-EXAMINATION . 186
§ 4.04 CROSS-EXAMINATION: OTHER ASPECTS 188
§ 4.05 IMPEACHMENT: SOME GENERAL PRECEPTS 191
§ 4.06 PRIOR INCONSISTENT STATEMENTS 194
§ 4.07 BIAS 203
§ 4.08 MISCONDUCT NOT RESULTING IN CONVICTION 211
§ 4.09 CONVICTIONS 218
§ 4.10 REPUTATION AND OPINION EVIDENCE OF CHARACTER FOR LACK OF VERACITY 224
§ 4.11 EYEWITNESS TESTIMONY 225
§ 4.12 MISCELLANEOUS CREDIBILITY ISSUES 229
§ 4.13 SEQUESTRATION OF WITNESSES 231

Chapter 5 RELIABILITY OF OPINION TESTIMONY 237

§ 5.01 LAY OPINION 237
§ 5.02 EXPERTS: THE COMMON-LAW TRADITION 247
§ 5.03 EXPERTS: FIRST WAVE OF REFORM OF THE COMMON LAW: THE ADVENT OF THE FEDERAL RULES OF EVIDENCE: EXPANSION OF WHO ARE EXPERTS? TO WHAT MAY THEY TESTIFY? 253
§ 5.04 MORE FIRST-WAVE REFORM OF THE COMMON LAW BY THE FEDERAL RULES OF EVIDENCE: EXPANSION OF ADMISSIBILITY OF (OTHERWISE INADMISSIBLE) FACTS AND DATA CONSIDERED BY EXPERT, AND OPINION BASED THEREON . . . 259

Chapter 6 SCIENTIFIC AND PROBABILISTIC EVIDENCE 265

§ 6.01 TRADITIONAL FRYE STANDARD 265
§ 6.02 CURRENT TEST UNDER RULE 702: *DAUBERT* AND ITS FALLOUT 268
§ 6.03 MINOR PREMISE — WAS TEST PROPERLY CONDUCTED? 299
§ 6.04 DNA 302
§ 6.05 PSYCHOLOGY, MENTAL HEALTH, SOCIAL SCIENCES, AND RELATED FIELDS 315
§ 6.06 CRIMINAL CASES: FORENSIC EVIDENCE OTHER THAN DNA . . 338

§ 6.07 MATHEMATICAL PROBABILITY EVIDENCE 356

Chapter 7 THE HEARSAY RULE 365

§ 7.01 CONCEPT OF HEARSAY AND ITS RATIONALE 365
§ 7.02 STATEMENTS IMPLIED FROM WORDS OR CONDUCT 374
§ 7.03 OUT-OF-COURT WORDS (OR CONDUCT) STATING OR REVEALING DECLARANT'S STATE OF MIND 382

Chapter 8 EXEMPTIONS FROM THE HEARSAY RULE 387

§ 8.01 FORMER STATEMENTS OF PRESENTLY TESTIFYING WITNESSES 387
§ 8.02 ADMISSIONS OF PARTY 404

Chapter 9 THE "STRONG" HEARSAY EXCEPTIONS 429

§ 9.01 INTRODUCTION 429
§ 9.02 EXCITED UTTERANCES AND PRESENT SENSE IMPRESSIONS . . 430
§ 9.03 DECLARATIONS OF PRESENT MENTAL, EMOTIONAL, OR PHYSICAL CONDITION 444
§ 9.04 STATEMENTS FOR PURPOSES OF MEDICAL DIAGNOSIS OR TREATMENT 459
§ 9.05 PAST RECOLLECTION RECORDED; "PRESENT MEMORY REFRESHED" DISTINGUISHED 470
§ 9.06 BUSINESS RECORDS 477
§ 9.07 PUBLIC RECORDS 508
§ 9.08 MISCELLANEOUS OTHER HEARSAY EXCEPTIONS 516

Chapter 10 THE "WEAK" HEARSAY EXCEPTIONS 519

§ 10.01 DEFINING UNAVAILABILITY OF DECLARANT 519
§ 10.02 FORMER TESTIMONY 529
§ 10.03 DYING DECLARATIONS 537
§ 10.04 DECLARATIONS AGAINST INTEREST 542
§ 10.05 "CATCHALL" OR RESIDUAL EXCEPTION 556
§ 10.06 FINAL THOUGHTS ABOUT HEARSAY — BOGUS HEARSAY RULES 570

Chapter 11 CONSTITUTIONAL CONSIDERATIONS 575

§ 11.01 INTRODUCTION 575
§ 11.02 CONFRONTATION CLAUSE APPLIED TO OUT-OF-COURT STATEMENTS BY TESTIFYING DECLARANTS 576

§ 11.03 CONFRONTATION CLAUSE APPLIED TO STATEMENTS BY NONTESTIFYING DECLARANTS 578
§ 11.04 CONFRONTATION CLAUSE APPLIED TO STATEMENTS BY NONTESTIFYING CODEFENDANTS 647
§ 11.05 WAIVER OF CONFRONTATION RIGHT: EXCEPTION FOR FORFEITURE BY WRONGDOING AND F.R.E. 804(b)(6) 650
§ 11.06 OTHER CONSTITUTIONAL RIGHTS OF DEFENDANTS THAT LIMIT APPLICATION OF EVIDENTIARY RULES: HEARSAY AND BEYOND 654

Chapter 12 WRITINGS AND EXHIBITS 667

§ 12.01 AUTHENTICATION 667
§ 12.02 BEST EVIDENCE RULE: REQUIREMENT OF ORIGINAL DOCUMENT 737
§ 12.03 COMPLETENESS 757

PART IV PURELY SOCIAL POLICY RULES

Chapter 13 PRIVILEGES 761

§ 13.01 INTRODUCTION 761
§ 13.02 ATTORNEY-CLIENT PRIVILEGE: EXAMINATION OF SOME ISSUES COMMON TO MANY PRIVILEGES 767
§ 13.03 SPOUSAL PRIVILEGES: A FURTHER STUDY IN PRIVILEGE POLICIES, INCLUDING TESTIMONIAL AND COMMUNICATION PRIVILEGES 801
§ 13.04 PHYSICIAN-PATIENT PRIVILEGE 819
§ 13.05 PSYCHOTHERAPIST AND SOCIAL WORKER PRIVILEGES 821
§ 13.06 OTHER SIMILAR PRIVILEGES 836
§ 13.07 GOVERNMENTAL AND GOVERNMENT-RELATED PRIVILEGES . 854
§ 13.08 FIFTH AMENDMENT PRIVILEGE 866

PART V SHORTCUTS

Chapter 14 JUDICIAL NOTICE 869

§ 14.01 INTRODUCTION 869
§ 14.02 JUDICIAL NOTICE OF ADJUDICATIVE FACTS 870
§ 14.03 SPECIAL CONSIDERATIONS CONCERNING JUDICIAL NOTICE OF ADJUDICATIVE FACTS IN CRIMINAL CASES 872
§ 14.04 JUDICIAL NOTICE OF LEGISLATIVE FACTS 875
§ 14.05 OTHER TYPES OF NOTICE 882
§ 14.06 LIMITS OF JURY OR JUDGE USING FACTS IN THEIR PERSONAL EXPERIENCE TO “EVALUATE” EVIDENCE 885

SUMMARY TABLE OF CONTENTS

Chapter 15 BURDENS AND PRESUMPTIONS 891

§ 15.01 BURDENS OF PROOF: PREREQUISITE TO UNDERSTANDING PRESUMPTIONS 891
§ 15.02 CIVIL PRESUMPTIONS 892
§ 15.03 CRIMINAL PRESUMPTIONS 905

Table of Cases TC-1

Table of Statutes TS-1

Index I-1

TABLE OF CONTENTS

Chapter 1 BACKGROUND, THEORY, AND BASIC PROCEDURES . 1

§ 1.01 INTRODUCTION . . . 1
[A] The Classroom and the Real World . . . 1
[B] Development and Key Concepts of Evidence Law . . . 2
§ 1.02 COURTROOM SCENARIO AND SOME BASIC PROCEDURES . . . 9
[A] Offers and Objections . . . 9
[B] Making the Record: Admitted and Excluded Evidence . . . 11
Problem 1A: Preserving Error for an Appeal when Your Evidence is Excluded: Making an Offer of Proof . . . 13
[C] How Evidence Rules Relate to the Totality of Events and Stages in Jury Trial . . . 13
Problem 1B: Indirect Implication of Insurance Matters in Voir Dire and Final Argument . . . 17
Problem 1C: The Affidavit Based on Inadmissible Hearsay — Can it Prevent Summary Judgment? . . . 17
§ 1.03 LIMIT ON JUDGE'S CONDUCT OF TRIAL: IMPARTIALITY . . . 18
Notes and Questions . . . 18
§ 1.04 PURPOSE-LIMITING INSTRUCTIONS TO THE JURY . . . 24
United States v. Washington . . . 24
Note . . . 25
Problem 1D: Limiting Instructions for Prior Convictions Offered to Impeach: Problem Based on *United States v. Lipscomb*, 702 F.2d 1049 (D.C. Cir. 1983) (en banc) . . . 25

Chapter 2 RELEVANCY AND ITS COUNTERWEIGHTS . . . 27

§ 2.01 RELEVANCE . . . 27
David Crump, *On the Uses of Irrelevant Evidence* . . . 27
Notes and Questions . . . 29
Stevenson v. Stewart . . . 30
Notes and Questions . . . 31
Carter v. Hewitt . . . 32
Notes and Questions . . . 33
Problem 2A: Ronald Shipp's Offer of "Dream Evidence" in the Trial of O.J. Simpson: Was it Relevant? . . . 36
Problem Set 2B: Illuminating the Judge's Task in Deciding Relevance . 36
§ 2.02 FORMALISTIC LOGIC (UTILIZED BY SOME TO DETERMINE RELEVANCE) . . . 38
§ 2.03 THE COUNTERWEIGHTS . . . 40

[A] The Structure and Operation of Rule 403 40
Sprint/United Management Company v. Mendelsohn 43
[B] Rule 403 Provides Judicial Options other than Admissibility/ Inadmissibility 45
United States v. Jackson 45
Note 47
[C] Some Potential Limits on Rule 403 47
Ballou v. Henri Studios, Inc. 47
Note 52
Gulf States Utilities Co. v. Ecodyne Corp. 52
United States v. Knight 53
Problem 2C: *Adamson v. California*, 332 U.S. 46, 58–59 (1947) 55
Problem 2D: Tapes of Long-Past 911 Calls in the Trial of O.J. Simpson: Applying Rule 403 56
Problem Set 2E: Illuminating the Judge's Task in Deciding Relevance and Counterweights 57
§ 2.04 "OVERRIDING" RULES 401–403 BY RE-CHARACTERIZING UNDERLYING COMPONENTS OF MATERIALITY OR PROBATIVE VALUE 65
[A] Review of the Concepts of Materiality and Probative Value 65
[B] Possible Re-Characterization 66
Montana v. Egelhoff 66
Notes and Questions 69
§ 2.05 JUDGE'S ROLE UNDER F.R.E. 104 69
Problem 2F: Impeachment of Mark Fuhrman in the O.J. Simpson Trial for Bias, but not as to Planting Evidence: Was the Judge's Ruling Correct? 70
§ 2.06 EMERGING PATTERNS OR QUASI-RULES IN APPLICATION OF RULE 403 FACTORS: PRETRIAL EXPERIMENTS AS CASE IN POINT 71
[A] Pretrial Experiments as Case in Point 71
[B] Other Emerging Categories 73
Problem 2G (End-of-Chapter Problem): "American Taliban" and Al Qaeda Evidence 76

Chapter 3 RELEVANCY AND ITS COUNTERWEIGHTS CONTINUED 79

§ 3.01 CHARACTER EVIDENCE (OTHER THAN IMPEACHMENT): SPECIFIC INSTANCES 79
[A] Specific Acts Offered to Prove "Action in Conformity": Generally Inadmissible 79
United States v. Calvert 80

Note on the Notice Provision 80
[B] Contours of Exclusion of Specific-Acts Evidence 81
[1] Evidence Whose Probativity Depends on Human Tendency to Repeat: Must Not be Characterized as Character or Propensity Reasoning . . . 81
Jones v. State 81
Huddleston v. United States 82
Notes and Questions 86
Note on the Narrow View of Other-Acts Evidence: Application of Florida's Williams Rule to the Trial of William Kennedy Smith . . 90
[2] Evidence Whose Probativity Does Not Depend on Human Tendency to Repeat (Not Character or Propensity Reasoning) 92
United States v. Peltier 92
United States v. Cunningham 93
Notes and Questions 94
[3] Revisiting Evidence Whose Probativity Depends on Human Tendency to Repeat: Is it Necessarily Doomed if We Recognize that it Is Propensity Evidence? 95
Hammann v. Hartford Accident and Indemnity Co. 95
Notes and Questions 96
Problem 3A: Is the Similarity Distinctive Enough to Admit the Prior Crime? 98
[C] Other Bad Acts More Directly in Issue 99
Old Chief v. United States 99
Notes and Questions 107
Problem 3B: The Fallout from *Old Chief* — Does Its Principle Extend Beyond Issues Oof "Status" to Affect Proof About Other Elements, Such as Intent, Etc.? 108
Problem Set 3C: What is a "Status" Element of an Offense Within the Rule of *Old Chief*? 109
Problem Set 3D: Concluding Thoughts on Evidence of Other Acts . 109
§ 3.02 OTHER WAYS OF PROVING CHARACTER: OPINION AND REPUTATION EVIDENCE 111
[A] Opinion and Reputation Character Evidence That Is NOT Related to Action in Conformity: Allowed 111
Carbo v. United States 111
Note 113
[B] Opinion and Reputation Character Evidence Allowed (in Exceptional Situations) to Show Action in Conformity 113
A Preview of the Confusing Law Here 113
Note on the Historical Development of Character Rules [The Federal Rules Compared with the Common Law] 115
United States v. Yarbrough 117

United States v. Bah . . . 120
Note on How to Read the Case of *United States v. Drapeau* . . . 121
United States v. Drapeau . . . 122
Notes and Questions . . . 125
Problem Set 3E: Reviewing and Extending Character Categories; and Some Basic Tactics . . . 127
§ 3.03 CHARACTER IN CASES OF SEXUAL CRIMES AND RELATED OFFENSES . . . 127
[A] Complainant's Sexual Character, Conduct, or Propensity: Restricted Admissibility Under F.R.E. 412's "Rape Shield" and Similar State Rules . . . 127
Olden v. Kentucky . . . 128
Notes and Questions . . . 129
[B] Broader Admissibility of Defendant's Other Conduct or Propensity in Sexual Cases: F.R.E. 413–415 . . . 130
[1] Rules 413-415: The General Principle . . . 131
United States v. Roberts . . . 131
[2] Interplay of this Sexual Misconduct Evidence, F.R.E Rule 403, and the Constitution . . . 132
United States v. Guardia . . . 134
Notes and Questions . . . 136
[C] Extending Admissibility of Propensity Evidence Beyond Sexual Offenses . . . 137
§ 3.04 CHARACTER VERSUS HABIT . . . 138
Reyes v. Missouri Pacific Railroad Company . . . 138
Notes and Questions . . . 139
Problem Set 3F: Practice in Identifying Habit or Routine Practice as Opposed to Character . . . 142
§ 3.05 OTHER TRANSACTIONS, SIMILAR OCCURRENCES, AND PROFILES: CHARACTER, HABIT, OR SOMETHING ELSE? . . . 144
Linthicum v. Richardson . . . 144
Johnson v. Gulick . . . 145
Karsun v. Kelley . . . 146
Notes and Questions . . . 149
Clark v. Stewart . . . 149
Notes and Questions . . . 151
San Antonio Traction Company v. Cox . . . 152
Notes and Questions . . . 154
John Deere Company v. May . . . 155
Haakanson v. Alaska . . . 156
Notes and Questions . . . 157
Problem 3G: Munchausen Syndrome by Proxy Evidence as Proof of

Identity and Intent to Injure: Would it Violate Rule 404(a) or (b)? . . . 158
§ 3.06 SUBSEQUENT REMEDIAL MEASURES 158
Adams v. Chevron USA, Inc. 159
Notes and Questions 160
§ 3.07 SETTLEMENT MATTERS (COMPROMISE, OFFERS TO COMPROMISE, WITHDRAWN PLEAS, AND RELATED MATTERS) 162
[A] Civil Cases 162
Ramada Development Co. v. Rauch 162
[B] Criminal Cases: Guilty Pleas and Plea Negotiations 163
United States v. Mezzanatto 163
Notes and Questions 165
§ 3.08 EVIDENCE INDICATING OR SUGGESTING INSURANCE 165
Charter v. Chleborad 166
Notes and Questions 167
Problem Set 3H: Exploring Permissible Purposes, Instructions, and Remedies 168

Chapter 4 COMPETENCY, EXAMINATION, AND CREDIBILITY OF WITNESSES 173

§ 4.01 INTRODUCTION: PRESENTING WITNESS TESTIMONY AT TRIAL 173
§ 4.02 PREREQUISITES FOR WITNESS TESTIMONY: COMPETENCY AND PERSONAL KNOWLEDGE 174
[A] General Competency Rules 174
United States v. Roach 174
United States v. Allen 175
Notes and Questions 176
[B] Dead Man's Statutes or Rules 178
Reinke v. Stewart 178
Notes and Questions 179
[C] Hypnotically Refreshed Testimony 179
Rock v. Arkansas 179
Note 182
[D] Judges and Jurors 182
Tanner v. United States 182
Notes and Questions 183
[E] Personal Knowledge 184
§ 4.03 FORM OF QUESTIONS IN DIRECT AND CROSS-EXAMINATION . 186
§ 4.04 CROSS-EXAMINATION: OTHER ASPECTS 188
[A] Right to Cross-Examine Witnesses 188
[B] Scope of Cross-Examination 189

§ 4.05 IMPEACHMENT: SOME GENERAL PRECEPTS 191
§ 4.06 PRIOR INCONSISTENT STATEMENTS 194
United States v. Meza 196
Notes and Questions 201
§ 4.07 BIAS 203
United States v. Abel 203
Notes and Questions 207
§ 4.08 MISCONDUCT NOT RESULTING IN CONVICTION 211
Carter v. Hewitt 211
Notes and Questions 214
Problem 4A Based on Nonconviction Misconduct in *United States v. Amaechi*, 991 F.2d 374 (7th Cir. 1993). 217
§ 4.09 CONVICTIONS 218
Historical Note 218
United States v. Smith 219
United States v. Estes 221
Notes and Questions 222
Problem 4B: Impeaching the Career Criminal under Rule 609 224
§ 4.10 REPUTATION AND OPINION EVIDENCE OF CHARACTER FOR LACK OF VERACITY 224
Osborne v. United States 224
§ 4.11 EYEWITNESS TESTIMONY 225
Notes and Questions 226
§ 4.12 MISCELLANEOUS CREDIBILITY ISSUES 229
§ 4.13 SEQUESTRATION OF WITNESSES 231
Selected Chapter Review Problems 4C 235

Chapter 5 RELIABILITY OF OPINION TESTIMONY 237

§ 5.01 LAY OPINION 237
[A] Common-Law Restrictions 237
State v. Thorp 237
Notes 238
[B] Lay Opinions Under Federal Rules of Evidence 239
Bohannon v. Pegelow 239
Notes and Questions 241
Asplundh Manufacturing Division v. Benton Harbor Engineering . . 244
Notes and Questions 245
§ 5.02 EXPERTS: THE COMMON-LAW TRADITION 247
Deaver v. Hickox 247
Notes and Questions 250
Pointer v. Klamath Falls Land & Transportation Co. 251

Sirico v. Cotto 252
Note 252
§ 5.03 EXPERTS: FIRST WAVE OF REFORM OF THE COMMON LAW: THE ADVENT OF THE FEDERAL RULES OF EVIDENCE: EXPANSION OF WHO ARE EXPERTS? TO WHAT MAY THEY TESTIFY? 253
United States v. Johnson 253
Notes and Questions 256
§ 5.04 MORE FIRST-WAVE REFORM OF THE COMMON LAW BY THE FEDERAL RULES OF EVIDENCE: EXPANSION OF ADMISSIBILITY OF (OTHERWISE INADMISSIBLE) FACTS AND DATA CONSIDERED BY EXPERT, AND OPINION BASED THEREON . . . 259
Wilson v. Clark 259
American Universal Insurance Co. v. Falzone 261
Notes and Questions 262
Problem 5A: Multiple Experts for the Price of One, and Insulation of the Others From Cross — Or, Is Introduction of the Hearsay "Facts And Data," Considered by the Expert under Rule 703, Necessary for the Jury to Evaluate the Opinion? 263

Chapter 6 SCIENTIFIC AND PROBABILISTIC EVIDENCE 265

§ 6.01 TRADITIONAL FRYE STANDARD 265
United States v. Brown 265
Notes and Questions 267
§ 6.02 CURRENT TEST UNDER RULE 702: *DAUBERT* AND ITS FALLOUT 268
[A] *Daubert* Decision 269
Daubert v. Merrell Dow Pharmaceuticals, Inc. 269
Notes and Questions 273
[B] *Daubert* Applies to All Experts, Not Just "Scientific" Ones 276
Kumho Tire Company, Ltd. v. Carmichael 276
Notes and Questions 282
Ho v. Michelin North America, Inc. 291
[C] How Should "Fit" and "Reliability" Factors Under *Daubert-Kumho* Be Evaluated? 295
Problem 6A: The Fifth Circuit Allows for Some Admissibility of Polygraph Evidence after *Daubert*: *United States v. Posado*, 57 F.3d 428 (5th Cir. 1995) 296
[D] Procedures for Deciding *Daubert/Kumho* Issues 298
§ 6.03 MINOR PREMISE — WAS TEST PROPERLY CONDUCTED? 299
Pruitt v. State 299
Notes and Questions 302
§ 6.04 DNA 302

State v. Whittey 302
Notes and Questions 307
§ 6.05 PSYCHOLOGY, MENTAL HEALTH, SOCIAL SCIENCES, AND RELATED FIELDS 315
[A] The Relevance and Reliability of the Expert Opinion 315
Pooshs v. Phillip Morris USA, Inc. 315
Notes and Questions 317
[B] The Inadmissibility of Opinions on Mental Elements of a Charged Crime: Rule 704(b) 319
United States v. Valle 319
Notes and Questions 322
[C] Post-Traumatic Stress Disorder, Related Syndromes, and Related Evidence 323
New Mexico v. Alberico 323
Notes and Questions 327
[D] Psychological Testimony in Child Abuse Cases 331
Problem 6B: Profile Evidence and Behavioral Syndromes after *Daubert* — What Standard Governs Expert Testimony about the Characteristics of Sexual Abusers and Battered Children? 335
[E] Perception and Memory in Adults 336
§ 6.06 CRIMINAL CASES: FORENSIC EVIDENCE OTHER THAN DNA . . 338
[A] Handwriting 338
United States v. Crisp 338
Notes and Questions 340
[B] Fingerprinting 342
United States v. Llera Plaza 342
Notes and Questions 351
United States v. Scott 352
[C] Miscellaneous Evidentiary Challenges in Criminal Cases 353
§ 6.07 MATHEMATICAL PROBABILITY EVIDENCE 356
People v. Collins 356
Notes and Questions 361

Chapter 7 THE HEARSAY RULE 365

§ 7.01 CONCEPT OF HEARSAY AND ITS RATIONALE 365
[A] Introduction 365
[B] Elements of Basic Hearsay: Statement, Other than by Witness Now Testifying, Offered to Prove Truth of Matter Asserted 366
Leake v. Hagert 366
Note 366
Creaghe v. Iowa Home Mutual Casualty Co. 366

Notes and Questions . . . 367
Ferrara v. Galluchio . . . 368
Notes and Questions . . . 369
Mahone v. Lehman . . . 370
Notes and Questions . . . 371
TOMA Problem Set 7A: Are the Following Statements Offered for the "Truth of the Matter Asserted" (TOMA)? . . . 372

§ 7.02 STATEMENTS IMPLIED FROM WORDS OR CONDUCT . . . 374
Wright v. Tatham . . . 374
Notes and Questions . . . 377
United States v. Jackson . . . 378
Notes and Questions . . . 379
Altkrug v. William Whitman Co. . . . 380
Note . . . 380
Implied Statement Problem Set 7B: Is there a "Statement"? If so, What Is the "Matter Asserted" (Does it Include Implied Matters)? . . . 380

§ 7.03 OUT-OF-COURT WORDS (OR CONDUCT) STATING OR REVEALING DECLARANT'S STATE OF MIND . . . 382
Loetsch v. New York City Omnibus Corp. . . . 382
Bridges v. State . . . 383
Notes and Questions . . . 384
Problem Set 7C: Implied Statement Theory Combined With State-of-Mind Theory. . . . 385

Chapter 8 EXEMPTIONS FROM THE HEARSAY RULE . . . 387

§ 8.01 FORMER STATEMENTS OF PRESENTLY TESTIFYING WITNESSES . . . 387
[A] Introduction . . . 387
[B] Inconsistent Statements as Non-Hearsay . . . 388
United States v. Truman . . . 388
Notes and Questions . . . 392
[C] Consistent Statements as Non-Hearsay . . . 393
Tome v. United States . . . 393
Notes and Questions . . . 400
[D] Statements of Identification . . . 400
United States v. Owens . . . 400
Notes and Questions . . . 402

§ 8.02 ADMISSIONS OF PARTY . . . 404
[A] Introduction . . . 405
[B] Basic Doctrine . . . 405
Susemiehl v. Red River Lumber Co. . . . 405

Notes and Questions 406
Problem 8A: "It Was All my Fault . . ." Offered against the Plaintiff in (1) A Survival Action; (2) A Wrongful Death Case 408
[C] Adoptive Admissions 408
United States v. Flecha 408
Notes and Questions 410
Problem 8B: "You went Through a Red Light!" 412
[D] Admissions by Agents Authorized to Speak for Principals 412
Contractor Utility Sales Co., Inc. v. Certain-Teed Products Corp. . . 412
Notes and Questions 413
[E] Admissions by Unauthorized Agents or Employees about Matters within their Scope 414
Rudzinski v. Warner Theatres, Inc. 414
Notes and Questions 419
Problem 8C: "I Am to Blame: I Dropped the Thing" 420
[F] Co-Conspirator Statements 420
Bourjaily v. United States 420
Notes and Questions 424
Problem 8D: "He asked me for a Bribe!" 425
Review Problems for Chapters 7 And 8: Hearsay Quiz: Is it Hearsay after Considering the General Definition and the Exemptions (Not the Exceptions)? 426

Chapter 9 THE "STRONG" HEARSAY EXCEPTIONS 429

§ 9.01 INTRODUCTION 429
§ 9.02 EXCITED UTTERANCES AND PRESENT SENSE IMPRESSIONS . . 430
United States v. Frost 430
Notes and Questions 436
People v. Lovett 437
Notes and Questions 438
Houston Oxygen Co. v. Davis 439
Notes and Questions 441
Problem Set 9A: Present Sense Impressions, Excited Utterances and Beyond 442
§ 9.03 DECLARATIONS OF PRESENT MENTAL, EMOTIONAL, OR PHYSICAL CONDITION 444
Notes and Questions 444
United States v. Samaniego & Baez 445
Notes and Questions 448
United States v. Pheaster 449
Notes and Questions 455

Problem 9B: "I Am King Tut": Nonhearsay, or Hearsay Subject to an Exception? . . . 457
Problem 9C: Statements of Intent or Memory About the Past, Present and Future . . . 457
§ 9.04 STATEMENTS FOR PURPOSES OF MEDICAL DIAGNOSIS OR TREATMENT . . . 459
United States v. Iron Shell . . . 459
Notes and Questions . . . 465
Problem Set 9D: Statements Relating to Medical Diagnosis or Treatment . . . 467
Note on Courts' Willingness to Expand Hearsay Exceptions in Child Abuse Cases . . . 468
§ 9.05 PAST RECOLLECTION RECORDED; "PRESENT MEMORY REFRESHED" DISTINGUISHED . . . 470
[A] Hearsay Exception: Recorded Recollection . . . 471
Hodas v. Davis . . . 471
Notes and Questions . . . 473
[B] "Present Memory Refreshed" Distinguished . . . 474
In re Thomas . . . 474
Notes and Questions . . . 476
Problem Set 9E: Concerning Refreshing Recollection and Recorded Recollection . . . 476
§ 9.06 BUSINESS RECORDS . . . 477
United States v. Hedman . . . 477
Notes and Questions . . . 480
Lorraine v. Markel American Insurance Company . . . 482
State v. Blake . . . 495
Yates v. Bair Transport, Inc. . . . 497
Notes and Questions . . . 504
Problem 9F: Comparing the Rule to the Supreme Court Draft . . . 505
Problem Set 9G: Highlighting Various Aspects of Business Records . . . 505
§ 9.07 PUBLIC RECORDS . . . 508
Beech Aircraft Corp. v. Rainey . . . 508
Notes and Questions . . . 512
Problem Set 9H: Police Officers' or Insurance Regulators' Reports in Different Case Settings . . . 515
Problem Set 9I: SEC Report, Offered Later in a Private Securities Suit . . . 516
§ 9.08 MISCELLANEOUS OTHER HEARSAY EXCEPTIONS . . . 516

Chapter 10 THE "WEAK" HEARSAY EXCEPTIONS 519

§ 10.01 DEFINING UNAVAILABILITY OF DECLARANT 519
Warren v. United States 519
United States v. Samaniego & Baez 522
Perricone v. Kansas City S. R. Co. 523
Notes and Questions 526
Problem Set 10A: Various Ways in Which Witnesses May Be Unavailable and How to Establish their Unavailability 527
§ 10.02 FORMER TESTIMONY 529
Lloyd v. American Export Lines, Inc. 529
Note 534
United States v. Salerno 535
Notes and Questions 536
Problem Set 10B: Is there Still a Requirement of Identity of Parties and Issues? 537
§ 10.03 DYING DECLARATIONS 537
Plessy v. State 538
Notes and Questions 539
Problem Set 10C: Various Aspects of Dying Declarations 541
§ 10.04 DECLARATIONS AGAINST INTEREST 542
[A] Declarations Against Pecuniary and Proprietary Interests 542
[B] Declarations Against Penal Interest 544
Williamson v. United States 544
Notes and Questions 551
United States v. Thomas 553
Notes and Questions 555
Problem 10D: A Statement Allegedly Admitting Heroin Use 555
Note 556
§ 10.05 "CATCHALL" OR RESIDUAL EXCEPTION 556
Huff v. White Motor Corp. 556
United States v. Sposito 561
Notes and Questions 563
§ 10.06 FINAL THOUGHTS ABOUT HEARSAY — BOGUS HEARSAY RULES 570
Problem Set 10E: Review Problems for Hearsay Exceptions Chapters — Hearsay Exceptions Quiz 572

Chapter 11 CONSTITUTIONAL CONSIDERATIONS 575

§ 11.01 INTRODUCTION 575
§ 11.02 CONFRONTATION CLAUSE APPLIED TO OUT-OF-COURT STATEMENTS BY TESTIFYING DECLARANTS 576

United States v. Owens 576
Problem 11A: Applying Owens Generally to Confrontation Issues Regarding Testifying Witnesses 577
§ 11.03 CONFRONTATION CLAUSE APPLIED TO STATEMENTS BY NONTESTIFYING DECLARANTS 578
[A] Intertwining Hearsay and Confrontation Clause Analysis: The *Roberts* Era 578
Ohio v. Roberts 578
Notes on Supreme Court Cases Interpreting *Roberts* 581
[B] Rejecting *Roberts*: The Testimonial Approach to the Confrontation Clause 586
[1] The Seminal Case: Relying on Alleged Historic Analysis to Discern What the Framers Intended 586
Crawford v. Washington 586
Notes and Questions 592
[2] The Domestic Violence Context: Filling in Some Unanswered Questions 597
Davis v. Washington 597
Notes and Questions 601
[3] Other Types of Emergencies: Filling in Some More of the Puzzle . . . 604
Michigan v. Bryant 604
Notes and Questions 612
[4] Affidavits, Certifications, Reports, and Other Expert Issues in the Forensic Context 614
Melendez-Diaz v. Massachusetts 614
Notes and Questions 620
Bullcoming v. New Mexico 625
Notes and Questions 629
Williams v. Illinois 632
Notes and Questions 637
Crawford Review Problems 11B: What Makes Something Said Out-of-Court "Testimonial"? 644
§ 11.04 CONFRONTATION CLAUSE APPLIED TO STATEMENTS BY NONTESTIFYING CODEFENDANTS 647
Bruton v. United States 647
Notes and Questions 648
§ 11.05 WAIVER OF CONFRONTATION RIGHT: EXCEPTION FOR FORFEITURE BY WRONGDOING AND F.R.E. 804(b)(6) 650
Notes and Questions 651
§ 11.06 OTHER CONSTITUTIONAL RIGHTS OF DEFENDANTS THAT LIMIT APPLICATION OF EVIDENTIARY RULES: HEARSAY AND BEYOND 654

Chambers v. Mississippi 654
Notes and Questions 658
United States v. Scheffer 659
Notes and Questions 662
Holmes v. South Carolina 662
Note 666

Chapter 12 WRITINGS AND EXHIBITS 667

§ 12.01 AUTHENTICATION 667
[A] Documents and Signatures 667
Alexander Dawson, Inc. v. National Labor Relations Board 667
United States v. Chin 668
Notes and Questions 670
Lorraine v. Markel American Insurance Company 674
[B] Voice Identification 708
United States v. Vitale 708
Note 709
United States v. Espinoza 709
Notes and Questions 711
Notes on Audio Recording 712
[C] Self-Authentication 713
United States v. Carriger 713
United States v. Trotter 715
Notes and Questions 716
[D] Chain of Custody 718
United States v. Coffman 718
United States v. Thomas 719
Notes and Questions 720
[E] Photographs, Videotapes, and the Like 721
Averhart v. State 721
Notes and Questions 722
State v. Swinton 723
Notes and Questions 728
[F] DEMONSTRATIONS, ANIMATIONS, AND SIMULATIONS 729
United States v. Gaskell 729
Bray v. Bi-State Development Corporation 731
Hinkle v. City of Clarksburg 732
Notes and Questions 734
[G] Electronic Communications 734
United States v. Lebowitz 734
Notes and Questions 736

§ 12.02 BEST EVIDENCE RULE: REQUIREMENT OF ORIGINAL DOCUMENT . . . 737
Meyers v. United States . . . 740
Note . . . 743
United States v. Bennett . . . 743
Notes and Questions . . . 744
United States v. Gerhart . . . 745
Notes and Questions . . . 746
United States v. Johnson . . . 749
Notes and Questions . . . 751
United States v. Evans . . . 754
Notes and Questions . . . 754
Review Problem 12A: What are the Advantages and Disadvantages of the Liberalized Authentication and Best Evidence Rules? . . . 756
§ 12.03 COMPLETENESS . . . 757
Beech Aircraft Corp. v. Rainey . . . 757
Notes and Questions . . . 758

Chapter 13 PRIVILEGES . . . 761

§ 13.01 INTRODUCTION . . . 761
§ 13.02 ATTORNEY-CLIENT PRIVILEGE: EXAMINATION OF SOME ISSUES COMMON TO MANY PRIVILEGES . . . 767
[A] Basic Privilege . . . 770
American National Watermattress Corp. v. Manville . . . 770
Notes and Questions . . . 772
[B] Corporate Setting . . . 780
Upjohn Co. v. United States . . . 780
Notes and Questions . . . 786
[C] Effect of Intentional or Unintentional Disclosure (or the Like) . . . 789
Notes and Questions . . . 789
[D] Joint Defense and Joint Consultation . . . 793
[E] Crime-Fraud Exception and Other Typically Criminal Issues . . . 794
In re Grand Jury Proceedings (*Matter of Jeffrey Fine*) . . . 794
Notes and Questions . . . 795
Attorney-Client Privilege Problem Set 13A . . . 799
§ 13.03 SPOUSAL PRIVILEGES: A FURTHER STUDY IN PRIVILEGE POLICIES, INCLUDING TESTIMONIAL AND COMMUNICATION PRIVILEGES . . . 801
[A] Testimonial Privilege Not to Testify Against One's Spouse (Which Can Include Privilege to Prevent Adverse Spousal Testimony Against One's Self) . . . 802
Trammel v. United States . . . 802

Notes and Questions 806
Problem 13B: The Trial of Warren Moon for Allegedly Assaulting Felicia Moon 808
[B] Marital Communications 809
United States v. Neal 809
Notes and Questions 814
Husband-Wife Privilege Review Problem Set 13C 818
§ 13.04 PHYSICIAN-PATIENT PRIVILEGE 819
§ 13.05 PSYCHOTHERAPIST AND SOCIAL WORKER PRIVILEGES 821
Jaffee v. Redmond 824
Notes and Questions 832
Problem 13D: Jaffee v. Redmond on Remand: Should the Privilege Protect the Relevant Communications, or Should the Evolution of Exceptions and Limits Require Disclosure? 836
§ 13.06 OTHER SIMILAR PRIVILEGES 836
[A] Introduction 836
[B] Commonly Found Privileges, and Related Attempts to Extend Them 837
[1] Clergy-Communicant Privilege 837
[2] Accountant-Client Privilege 838
[3] Journalist (Reporter, Newsperson, Newsgatherer, News Media) Privilege 839
[4] Researcher Privilege 844
[5] Trade Secrets Privilege 845
[C] Privileges Less Frequently Recognized (at Least as Yet) 846
[1] Privilege Covering Peer Review and Self-Critical Analysis 846
[2] Privilege to Withhold Information if One's Life Is Threatened 847
[3] Parent-Child Privilege 848
In re Grand Jury 850
Notes and Questions 851
[D] Miscellaneous Privileges 853
§ 13.07 GOVERNMENTAL AND GOVERNMENT-RELATED PRIVILEGES 854
§ 13.08 FIFTH AMENDMENT PRIVILEGE 866

Chapter 14 JUDICIAL NOTICE 869

§ 14.01 INTRODUCTION 869
§ 14.02 JUDICIAL NOTICE OF ADJUDICATIVE FACTS 870
Shahar v. Bowers 870
Notes and Questions 871
Problem 14A: Can You Get Food Poisoning from the E. Coli Bacteria after Properly Cooking Beef? 872

§ 14.03 SPECIAL CONSIDERATIONS CONCERNING JUDICIAL NOTICE OF ADJUDICATIVE FACTS IN CRIMINAL CASES 872
United States v. Hawkins 872
United States v. Jones 873
Note 875
§ 14.04 JUDICIAL NOTICE OF LEGISLATIVE FACTS 875
United States v. Gould 875
United States v. Hernandez-Fundora 878
Notes and Questions 879
§ 14.05 OTHER TYPES OF NOTICE 882
§ 14.06 LIMITS OF JURY OR JUDGE USING FACTS IN THEIR PERSONAL EXPERIENCE TO "EVALUATE" EVIDENCE 885

Chapter 15 BURDENS AND PRESUMPTIONS 891

§ 15.01 BURDENS OF PROOF: PREREQUISITE TO UNDERSTANDING PRESUMPTIONS 891
§ 15.02 CIVIL PRESUMPTIONS 892
McNulty v. Cusack 895
Notes and Questions 896
Hinds v. John Hancock Mutual Life Insurance Co. 898
Notes and Questions 903
Problem 15A: How Do Presumptions Really Work in Court? 905
§ 15.03 CRIMINAL PRESUMPTIONS 905
County Court of Ulster County v. Allen 905
Notes and Questions 909

Table of Cases TC-1

Table of Statutes TS-1

Index I-1

Chapter 1

BACKGROUND, THEORY, AND BASIC PROCEDURES

WHAT'S IT ALL ABOUT AND HOW DOES IT HAPPEN? EVIDENTIARY FRAMEWORK, ROLE OF THE PLAYERS, AND RULES OF THE ROAD (F.R.E. ARTICLE I)

§ 1.01 INTRODUCTION

[A] The Classroom and the Real World

During your study of evidence law, your teacher may purposely indulge in the perhaps artificial assumption that one day you will try cases. To train you on this assumption is one way to help ensure that evidence is taught and learned well.

It is a game worth playing. A thorough knowledge of evidence rules as practiced at trial is important whether or not you ever go to trial. What can be *proven* largely determines the result if any legal transaction you may be handling as a lawyer ultimately did have to go to trial. The result you *would* get *if* you went to trial is what people usually mean by legal rights and obligations. If parties know clearly in advance what each side could prove were litigation to become necessary, nine times out of ten, there will be no need for litigation.

A knowledge of evidence law therefore is important to most of the functions you will be performing as a lawyer. Negotiating or drafting a contract, tax planning, will drafting, handling a securities issue, planning a corporate merger, putting together a business or financial deal — whatever it is, you will be better off if you know what would be accepted as proof if push came to shove and litigation resulted. Rights without acceptable evidence to establish your version of the facts are not rights. If the other side has all the admissible evidence and you have none, they may not be deterred from trampling on your client as the arrangement you designed unfolds, despite what may have appeared to be strict written safeguards.

Isn't it useful to know in advance, for example, that failure to respond to a letter may be admissible evidence of acquiescence in the fact or position stated? That a note jotted on one's calendar contemporaneously with a meeting, conversation, or telephone call is admissible evidence thereof? Might this not influence your conduct during or following negotiations, exchanges, or planning sessions?

Although we may find it useful to assume you are a potential trial lawyer, the evidence course by itself will not equip you to go out and try a case. Other skills are needed as well. A trial practice course, a litigation clinic, and a substantial apprenticeship are all desirable. They will assume you have previously mastered evidence law. The body of principles in evidence is generally thought lengthy, distinctive, and complex enough, that they should be taught separately from these other courses.

The words of the rules are often determinative, but sometimes they leave room for interpretation. Admissible evidence is, in a very real sense, what the judge (often the trial judge, appellate courts being reluctant to interfere on many matters except at the extremes) *can be convinced* is admissible evidence.

American evidence law is in a sense "dominated" by the Federal Rules of Evidence ("Fed. R. Evid." or "F.R.E."), which have applied in federal proceedings since 1975 and are sometimes cited by state courts as a kind of advisory "restatement" informing their common-law process or aiding in interpretation of a similar written rule. *See generally* ROTHSTEIN, THE FEDERAL RULES OF EVIDENCE (3d ed. 2006, updated yearly). The Advisory Committee Notes (original drafters' comments) and legislative history of the Federal Rules of Evidence are important interpretive tools. Many states have their own codifications closely (but not always entirely) patterned on the Federal Rules of Evidence. In 1974, the prestigious Uniform Rules of Evidence (recommended to the states) were redrafted to largely conform to the Federal Rules of Evidence. Nevertheless, a few states stick to a mainly uncodified common-law system of Evidence. Some states, like California and New Jersey, adopted codifications somewhat different from and preceding the Federal Rules of Evidence. Whatever the sources of evidence law in a jurisdiction, however, and despite differences of detail, there is a remarkable commonality among them in major principles.[1]

[B] Development and Key Concepts of Evidence Law[2]

(1) *What is Evidence Law?* The course in evidence is the study of the rules regulating the proof of facts in the judicial trial of lawsuits. Only occasionally do the rules make distinctions between civil and criminal cases, and between jury trials and judge trials.

In a jury trial, the *judge* decides whether evidence is admissible, and for what purposes. The jury determines what admissible evidence to believe, what it weighs, and what inferences to draw, except where inferences may be limited by a rule or ruling conveyed to the jury by a judicial instruction. The jurors' task is to decide what the true facts of the case are and apply to them the tort law, contract law, criminal law, or other governing law, that the judge furnishes them by instruction. In a bench trial (judge trial), the judge performs both the judge and jury functions.

(2) *Categories of Proof.* There are three general categories of proof:

— *"testimonial"* (witnesses, documents, or recordings, reporting facts),

---

[1] Recent revisions of the Uniform Rules include a number of changes with the result that they no longer so precisely mirror the Federal Rules of Evidence, although in general outline they are still the same.

[2] Study Guide Reference: Evidence in a Nutshell, Chapter1:I. It is also a good idea at this point to read through the detailed table of contents (table of rules) of the Federal Rules of Evidence.

— *"real"* (the knife used in the crime; the contract or deed sued upon; the narcotics seized in the raid), and

— *"representational"* (charts, models, maps, demonstrations, computer simulations, experiments).

From the above, it can easily be seen that items of evidence are either:

(a) witnesses, or

(b) things (documents, weapons, narcotics, recordings, explanatory aids like models, etc.) (sometimes called "objects").

Exhibits: Things in category (b) are called "exhibits" by lawyers. Normally, an exhibit cannot be introduced without a knowledgeable witness to connect it to the case and render it admissible. As you can tell from the examples of exhibits just given, some exhibits have some real evidential value, and other exhibits, like maps, models, or charts, merely help illustrate or explain other evidence or argument or what a witness is saying. Hence, we have the terms "real" and "representational."

Except for certain distinctive mechanical requirements applicable only to exhibits (see, e.g., F.R.E. Articles IX and X, and F.R.E. Rule 106, all concerning writings and the like), the rules of evidence are the same for witnesses and exhibits. All the basic rules (hearsay, character, relevance, privilege, etc.) apply to both.

(3) *Main Form of Proof in Anglo-American Trials.* In the Anglo-American trial system, proof mainly consists of live witnesses presented in open court under oath before the jury, judge, and parties, and subject to perjury laws. Cross-examination of the witnesses in that setting is the principal (though not the only) form of testing their reliability. It is for these reasons that we have an evidentiary rule against hearsay (that is, against second-hand reporting in court of what someone has said outside of court).

(4) *Exclusionary Rules; Admissibility vs. Weight.* Determining the *admissibility* of evidence is the judge's domain; determining its *weight* is the jury's (including, normally, assessing the credibility or incredibility of witnesses, credibility being a matter upon which reasonable people can differ). The course in evidence is mainly the study of exclusionary rules — that is, rules rendering certain items of evidence inadmissible.

Frequently the judge will have discretion concerning which one of these two pigeonholes (weight or admissibility) is the right one in which to place a defect or weakness in a piece of evidence. The judge will need to be convinced by the lawyers where to place it. If the judge decides it is a matter of weight, he/she will tell the lawyer seeking exclusion: "The evidence is admissible. Your objection is really just a matter of weight for the jury to consider. Show it to the jury through cross-examination or other evidence. Argue it to the jurors in closing argument."

If one had to sum up all of evidence law in a phrase, one could say evidence law embodies a struggle to determine by rule (or frequently by an exercise of judicial discretion) when a jury's interpretation of the weight or effect of a particular piece of evidence will be within a reasonable range of rational interpretations, in which event the evidence should be received before the jury; and when it is likely to be outside that range — that is, a clearly unreasonable misinterpretation — in which case the evidence probably should be withheld from the jury. In other words, there can be reasonable disagreement about the force and effect of evidence, and this is tolerated, even encouraged. That is what we have a jury for. But some assessments of force or effect are beyond the range of the reasonable and are not permitted.

In many areas of Evidence (except where there is a categorical exclusion by a rule, as, e.g., under the hearsay rule or privilege), there is almost always a debate between the lawyers on the two sides of a case about whether something that is wrong with a particular piece of evidence impedes its admissibility or is merely a matter to be shown and argued to the jury as a matter depreciating or eliminating the piece's weight. This is especially so where the judge has discretion to exclude or not, as under F.R.E. Rule 403 (which asks the judge to balance the probative value of a piece of evidence against its potential to mislead, to prejudice, to confuse, or to consume more time than it is worth), F.R.E. Rule 701 (which asks the judge to determine whether a lay opinion would be "helpful"), and under several other rules.

Indeed, this may be thought of as the central issue in Evidence: When is something a matter merely of weight; and when is it a matter of admissibility? When does the judge tell an objector to evidence, "argue what is wrong with the evidence to the jury and they may decrease or eliminate altogether the weight they might be inclined to give it," and when is the matter fatal to admittance of the evidence? It is sometimes said — inexactly but somewhat helpfully — that defects/weaknesses in a piece of evidence that are deemed major result in inadmissibility whereas lesser ones are for the jury to take into account.

(5) *Evidence Rules as "Filters."* The rules of evidence are a series of individual "filters," filtering out evidence for different reasons. An item of evidence must survive all filters. Put another way, each evidence rule is a hurdle to be overcome, and all hurdles must be overcome.

EXAMPLE:

> Evidence about a particular conversation may survive the hearsay rule ("hearsay filter"), say because of an exception to the hearsay rule, yet it may still be inadmissible because the conversation expressly states that defendant "is a mean and vindictive person" (thus violating the character rule or "character filter"); or because its relevance is marginal or it would take too much time or inject too much prejudice considering its low worth (the "relevancy" or "prejudice" or "time" filters); or because it is a privileged conversation; etc.

(6) *The Four Pillars of Evidence.* Four reasons are found for filtering out evidence. Virtually all of the rules are variations or applications of them and are derived from them. The four are:[3]

— **Relevancy**, a fundamental logical as well as practical requirement. Relevance asks: Does this piece of evidence, assuming it is true, bear any logical connection to this case? Does it have any tendency to prove or

---

[3] The four pillars are in logical order. If listed to reflect the fundamental distinctiveness of the Anglo-American legal system, the third — the hearsay notion — would be first.

disprove or change the likelihood of anything legitimately provable? Even though relevance somewhat limits the pool of information, it is still too large to be manageable within a finite time. Hence the next pillar.

— The **Counterweights to Relevancy** (such as time, prejudice, misleadingness), balanced against degree of relevance (probative value). If all relevant evidence were receivable, trials would still be too long and easily sidetracked. There comes a point of diminishing returns in the reception of minimally relevant evidence.

The counterweights limit the reception of relevant evidence. They are necessary considerations of practicality. They are concessions to the shortness of life and the fallibility of human fact-finders.

— **Hearsay**, a notion of reliability: that witnesses should be present, displayed, cross-examined under oath — not reported in writing or second-hand. This is in fact the hallmark of the Anglo-American legal system.

The hearsay rule embodies values similar to the Constitutional Confrontation Clause but applies beyond merely protecting the criminal defendant.

— **Privilege**, mainly embodying solicitude for other concerns of society than that litigation be accurate, efficient, and expeditiously determined. The husband-wife, lawyer-client, and physician-patient privileges come to mind. The thought behind them is that certain overriding benefits to society accrue from fostering these communications and relationships and the services they perform, and that the benefits outweigh the loss of evidence. Though relatively infrequently invoked, privileges protect important social values.

(7) *Direct vs. Circumstantial Evidence.* Items of evidence divide into two broad categories based on how they persuade, *i.e.*, based on whether they require an inference or not:

(a) direct evidence (basically eyewitness accounts) and

(b) circumstantial evidence (virtually everything else, *e.g.* a photo of, or witness accounts of, animal tracks in the snow offered to prove a dog passed by; or traces of DNA left at the crime scene offered to prove guilt).

Circumstantial evidence requires inferences to reach the important conclusion. But circumstantial evidence, in isolation or combined with other circumstantial evidence, can sometimes be even stronger than eyewitness evidence.

EXAMPLE:

In a number of recent cases, DNA evidence (circumstantial evidence) has freed from death row people who had been convicted by seemingly unequivocal, very positive eyewitness identification. Not only can DNA evidence be extremely strong, but empirical studies show that eyewitnesses are not as reliable as they seem.

As a general proposition, both direct and circumstantial evidence are treated by all the same rules of evidence, including relevance and its counterweights. So do not make too big a thing of the distinction.

(8) *Easier to Apply Some Rules to Direct Evidence.* Despite what has just been said, however, it is easier to determine and weigh relevance and its counterweights in the case of direct evidence. The relevance of an eyewitness (direct evidence) will ordinarily be easy to determine.

EXAMPLE 1:

> If the witness says she saw the shooting, her account of what she saw is probably relevant in the shooting case arising from the shooting. At least this is so if she identifies the shooter (assuming she knows him) and identity is in dispute. And, normally, it will be clear that the dangers of unfair or undue prejudice (improper effect on the fact-finder), inordinate time consumption, or misleadingness, do not outweigh this powerful relevance or probative value. Any problems with this evidence will be problems of credibility for the jury to weigh.

Contrast with this direct evidence, the difficulty of assessing relevance and its counterweights regarding circumstantial evidence:

EXAMPLE 2:

> Same case. A witness says she saw this defendant commit another crime. This "other crime" evidence may or may not be relevant. If it *is* relevant, it is only *circumstantially* so: Its force in establishing that the defendant committed the crime currently charged depends on the inference that, all other things being equal, one who has committed such other crime is somewhat more likely to have committed the currently charged crime than another person. If it is relevant, the *degree* of relevance (probative value) is more doubtful than in Example 1. It may depend upon how similar the two crimes are and how separated in time. There also may be real dangers that the counterweights are present: that the jurors will indulge themselves in emotional prejudice against the defendant because of the other crime, feeling he should be punished for that, without careful consideration of whether he committed the charged crime.

EXAMPLE 3:

> Assume one must prove a dog passed by. Assume further that some *unidentifiable* animal tracks are seen in the snow. They might not necessarily belong to a dog, but they might. They are thus relevant. Circumstantially so. Are they worth the time and possible misleadingness? Because they are *unidentifiable,* this is a close question.

You will note that in the eyewitness evidence example (Example 1), all that needed to be assessed was witness credibility (a jury function, as previously noted). In the circumstantial evidence examples, there is in addition a question whether an inference could be drawn by a reasonable person (juror) and drawn strongly enough to outweigh any downside to the evidence. This is for the judge to determine in the relevance-and-its-counter-weights weighing. To avoid turning trial by jury into trial by judge, the judge is ***not*** to do it based only on what he or she thinks are the inferences and their strengths. Rather it must be done based upon what the judge thinks the ***range*** of ***reasonable people*** might think. If anyone in that range might think the inference follows fairly strongly, the judge should hesitate to keep it out whatever the judge himself or herself may think. Note that it is ***reasonable*** people, not just ***any*** people.

The judge must also recognize and weigh the fact that **exclusion** *of relevant evidence on these grounds can distort the case, too (because relevant means carrying us in some measure toward the truth), just as* **admission** *of the evidence into the trial may distort because of the prejudice or misleadingness. The judge's task is to weigh whether* **admission**, *or* **exclusion**, *will likely distort more.* ***In short, the judge must decide whether the trial will be better off with or without the evidence.*** *It is a judgment of "comparative distortion."*

During the evidence course, you will see that one of the judge's most difficult and subjective tasks is to make the computation we are speaking of, that is, to weigh the risk of prejudice, misleadingness, and time consumption, against the value of a piece of evidence that is being offered and has been objected to. Occasionally a rule of evidence might strike the balance automatically for the judge. But most often, the piece of evidence is not the subject of such a specific rule. Then, a generalized rule like F.R.E. 403 or its common-law analog applies. Such a rule expressly grants the judge power to do the balancing computation on her or his own, unconstrained by any more specific rule.

You will note that in the balancing, the judge is (at least in theory if not always in practice) confined to doing the weighing based on the assumption the facts related in the testimony are true, and is not to weigh the likelihood of the witness' credibility. Thus, the weighing contemplates only the strength of the inferences that flow from the facts (balanced against the potential for prejudice, etc.). This is because relevance (probative value) is to be determined on the assumption the evidence is true, and the jury is to decide credibility.

(9) *Historical Development and Structure of Codified Rules of Evidence: From Common Law to Federal Rules.* Evidence rules developed historically in a somewhat haphazard fashion, through a largely discretionary process of common-law case development, which still remains the process in a number of states today. Judges ruled on admissibility based on the individual facts of the case before them without too much concern that there be a cohesive body of evidence rules. But by approximately the middle of the twentieth century, rule-makers and commentators found it desirable to sort these haphazard rulings into some kind of coherent system. Thus, repeated rulings eventually became codified in codes like the Federal Rules of Evidence, which are of relatively recent vintage as legal developments go. The system adopted by the Federal Rules of Evidence, widely imitated among the states as well, can be described by the following taxonomy:

I. PROCEDURAL rules, which include (i) how-to-do-it "rules of the road," and (ii) evidentiary "shortcuts," i.e., rules rendering strict evidentiary proof unnecessary in isolated instances. The procedural rules are contained in:

Article I (offers, objections, and other "how-to" rules of the road);

Article II (judicial notice as an occasional "shortcut" or alternative to strict proof); and

Article III (legal presumptions as a "shortcut" or alternative to more direct proof of certain presumed facts).

II. RELEVANCY rules (including counterweights to relevancy). The relevancy rules are contained in:

Article IV (covering the general requirement of relevance; plus a general rule for the judge to use to balance relevance against certain counterweights; and then a series of specific rules pre-determining the balance for the judge for certain specific, foreseen, repetitive categories of evidence, such as character evidence, evidence of insurance, evidence of safety measures after an injury, evidence of settlement and compromise attempts, etc. In essence, each of these specific rules expresses a general ban on a specific category of evidence and certain limited exceptions to each ban).

III. SOCIAL POLICY rules. These are the evidentiary *privileges*, like Physician-Patient, Attorney-Client, Husband-Wife, etc. These rules say, "disregard the consequences to the particular litigation and to finding the truth — we have some social policies outside the courtroom to protect."

Article V contains these social policy (privilege) rules.

IV. RELIABILITY rules. Whereas the relevancy rules assume the testimony or document is true, and then ask whether what is related therein is relevant and not outweighed by other considerations, reliability rules are directed at insuring the reliability of what is reported by the witnesses or documents. The reliability rules are contained in:

Article VI (reliability of witnesses in general: competency; personal knowledge; direct and cross-exam; impeaching witness credibility);

Article VII (special rules to assure the reliability of experts and opinion testimony);

Article VIII (the hearsay rule and its exemptions and exceptions: second-hand evidence allowed where a category of repetition is assumed by the law to be necessary and reliable);

Article IX (authentication or genuineness of documents, recordings, and the like); and

Article X (the requirement of the original document or recording, if available, as the best evidence of its contents, rather than a copy).

[Like most legal categories, the four in our taxonomy are not always pure. E.g., some policy or procedural elements are found in some rules primarily in the relevancy or reliability areas. Nevertheless, the categories describe the primary functions of the rules in them and are conceptually useful.]

Most states now have codes similar to the Federal Rules of Evidence, using even the same rule numbers. Several other states are still in the common-law mode, but may find the Federal Rules persuasive because the Federal Rules in large measure codify the "best version" of the common law, and because the common-law process is malleable.

The Federal Rules themselves are broad enough to allow *some* continued common-law-process type development and to allow the use of common law decisions for interpretive guidance.

§ 1.02 COURTROOM SCENARIO AND SOME BASIC PROCEDURES[4]

[A] Offers and Objections

Read Federal Rule of Evidence 103, "Rulings on Evidence."

(1) *Making Objections.* Assume you wish to make a hearsay objection to a question by opposing counsel to a witness, "Mr. Witness, state what you heard said at that party about X [a relevant matter] on that occasion." Which of the following statements would be a proper way to raise the objection as soon as the question is asked?

(a) "I object, Your Honor."

(b) "I object, Your Honor, on grounds that the matter about to be elicited is incompetent, irrelevant, immaterial, and hearsay."

(c) "I object, Your Honor, on grounds that the matter about to be elicited is irrelevant."

(d) "I object, Your Honor, on grounds that the matter about to be elicited is incompetent."

(e) "I object, Your Honor, on grounds that the matter about to be elicited is hearsay."

(f) "[I object;] may we approach the bench, Your Honor?" At the bench: "Your Honor, the matter about to be elicited is hearsay."

What are the perils of using the wrong form? Are there any exceptions?

(2) *Establishing a Factual Prerequisite.* Fed. R. Evid. 104 entrusts admissibility decisions to the judge. Before the judge can rule on this objection, the attorney offering the evidence politely makes known to the judge that he has something to say concerning it. He then states that he believes the testimony will come within the excited utterance exception to the hearsay rule (don't worry if you do not understand the hearsay rule and any exceptions yet; that is not the point of this exercise):

OFFERING COUNSEL: "Your Honor, the testimony will come within the exception to the hearsay rule for excited utterances, because the witness will say he heard a Mr. John Miller loudly suddenly exclaim 'X' [a fact relevant to the lawsuit but not self-evidently a matter inspiring excitement] at the party.

[4] Study Guide Reference: Evidence in a Nutshell, Chapter 1:II–IV; Chapter 11:IV.

OPPOSING COUNSEL: "There is no evidence in this case that this Mr. John Miller was in a state of excitement when he said that, and such excitement is indispensable for the excited utterances exception to apply."

Assuming the lawyer we have called "opposing counsel" is correct on the law and that there is nothing yet in the record factually indicating excitement, identify which of the following you think are available to the judge as options:

(a) *Conditional Exclusion.* Exclude the testimony by Mr. Witness about what Mr. John Miller said at the party until evidence is introduced in the normal course of the case that Mr. John Miller was speaking in a state of excitement. (Whose responsibility would it be to raise the issue at that later point?)

(b) *Conditional Admission.* Let in Mr. Witness's testimony about what Mr. John Miller said at the party subject to later exclusion if it is not proved later in the normal course of the case that Mr. John Miller spoke while excited. (Whose responsibility would it be to raise the issue at that later point? How could the evidence be excluded then?)

(c) *Decide Now: Minihearing.* Hold a kind of minihearing now in which evidence could be taken to resolve the question whether Mr. John Miller spoke excitedly. (In connection with this choice, consider whether or when the jury should be privy to such a minihearing; what kind of evidence would be received in it; and who, judge or jury, should decide whether John Miller was excited. It is not necessary to definitively resolve these questions at this point in the course.)

(3) *How Should Counsel Respond to an Objection?* Suppose the sequence of the above trial transcript is as follows, rather than as above:

Q. "Mr. Witness, tell the jury what you heard Mr. John Miller say at that party."

COUNSEL: "Objection. Hearsay."

OFFERING COUNSEL: "The testimony will be within the exception for excited utterances."

COURT: "Objection sustained. The evidence is excluded."

Q. [By offering counsel]: "Mr. Witness, turning now to another matter, did there come a time later that evening when you returned home from the party?"

A. "Yes. About 1:00 a.m. I returned home and went to bed."

Assume that in fact, on the law, the judge's ruling is incorrect, and because of it, the offering attorney loses the case. Can he raise the error on appeal and obtain a reversal, or has he committed some fatal flaw as to form? Why might the law require you to proceed in such a way?

(4) *Can Counsel Wait to Hear the Evidence Before Objecting?* Suppose the sequence had been as follows:

Q. "Mr. Witness, tell the jury what you heard Mr. John Miller say at that party."

A. "He said 'X'."

OPPOSING COUNSEL: [Makes proper objection in proper form.]

How is this different from the previous sequences? Assume the testimony is indeed inadmissible on the grounds asserted by objecting counsel. Why might the trial judge still be within his rights to overrule the objection? Additionally, is there a preferable term than "objection, your Honor"?

(5) *Pretrial Rulings.* If a problem of admissibility of a piece of evidence can be foreseen in advance of its coming up at trial and the factors affecting admissibility can be sufficiently and conveniently shown, do you suppose a judge might rule on it *then*, at the time foreseen, if a motion is made? Such "motions *in limine*," as they are called, are permitted. Do you suppose that the factors affecting admissibility always will be able to be shown in advance?

Rule 103(a)(2) was amended in 1999 to resolve the question of whether *in limine* motions must be renewed at trial. The rule now provides that:

> Once the court makes a definitive ruling on the record admitting or excluding evidence, either at or before trial, a party need not renew an objection or offer of proof to preserve a claim of error for appeal.

Does it solve the problem? What is a "definitive" ruling?

(6) *Strategic Use of Objections.* Do you suppose trial attorneys make all valid objections to evidence that they know of and could make? Or are there sometimes tactical reasons to forgo objections? Can jury backlash to objections be minimized by phraseology?

Do you imagine lawyers sometimes have other reasons for making objections than that they really believe the material is legally objectionable? What might they be? Is that ethical?

[B] Making the Record: Admitted and Excluded Evidence[5]

(1) *Objections and Offers Must Be on the Record.* Normally, a trial-judge's erroneous ruling admitting evidence will likely not be reviewed by an appeals court if an objection does not appear in the written trial record (a contemporaneous transcription of the words spoken at trial which is usually the only thing appellate courts will look at to find out what happened at trial). So, too, if there is an erroneous trial-judge exclusion of evidence and proper procedures at trial to preserve the right to review have not been taken (such as an offer of proof) by the party complaining of the error. *See* F.R.E. 103. This is because only "plain error" (obvious egregious error) will be reviewed when proper "error-preserving" measures weren't taken by the party at trial. On what is plain error, see *United States v. Marcus*, 560 U.S. 258 (2010). The Supreme Court there found that the

---

[5] Study Guide Reference: Evidence in a Nutshell, Chapter 11:IV.

Court of Appeals improperly took account of trial judge error unraised below, to vacate convictions for sex trafficking and forced labor. The Supreme Court held that before cognizance can be taken of such error, the error must be "plain error," a long standing concept that limits when unobjected-to errors may be reviewed. Under the "plain error" concept, a high hurdle must be overcome, the Court says: not only must the error be "plain," but there must be a reasonable probability that the error affected defendant's substantial rights and seriously impacted the fairness, integrity, or public reputation of judicial proceedings. In *Henderson v. United States*, 133 S. Ct. 1121 (2013), the Supreme Court clarified that when the law has changed since trial, rendering something done there plainly erroneous, it is sufficient under the plain error doctrine that the error is plain (clear, obvious) at the time of the appellate review, not necessarily at the time of trial.

(2) *Forgetting to Offer the Evidence. Guetersloh v. C.I.T. Corp.*, 451 S.W.2d 759 (Tex. Civ. App. 1970), *writ ref'd n.r.e.*, was a suit on a promissory note by C.I.T. Corporation against M.F. and Herman Guetersloh, as makers of the note. The trial court granted judgment for the plaintiff. On appeal, the defendant's first point of error was that plaintiff C.I.T. Corporation failed to introduce the note into evidence. During the trial, plaintiff produced the original document; it was inspected by defendant's trial counsel; it was marked by the court reporter as "plaintiff's exhibit 1"; it was handed to the judge, and it was included by the court reporter among the exhibits that were part of the proceeding. However, *plaintiff never offered it into evidence, and the judge never made a ruling ordering that it be received or admitted.* Therefore, the defendant argued, neither it nor its contents could have been properly considered by the trial court. Without the note as an exhibit, the trial record would be inadequate to sustain a finding of the existence, possession, or terms of the note.

The appellate court nevertheless affirmed. There is a requirement that a party offer the exhibit and that the court rule on its admittance. But the court reasoned that the precise word, "offer," was not required, nor did the court's ruling have to take any particular form. Here, there was an *implied* offer and admittance:

> The defendant's trial counsel treated the note as though it were in evidence. In fact, during the testimony the defendant's counsel objected to a question on the ground that it would "vary the terms of the contract which is already in evidence." The circumstances here indicate that the note was introduced in evidence.

(3) *Desirability of a Clear Record of Evidence to Support a Favorable Judgment.* Although plaintiff prevailed in *Guetersloh* and the decision leaves a sense that justice was done, it would have been better if this appellate issue never had arisen. Plaintiff could not be certain of victory.

(4) *The Record as Including Both Admitted and Excluded Evidence.* The trial judge's ruling admitting an exhibit is necessary because the record includes both evidence that has been received for the jury's consideration and information that has been excluded (e.g., offers of proof received outside the jury's presence).

(5) *Necessary Steps for Admitting an Exhibit.* In federal courts, exhibits may be marked and admitted in a pretrial conference. But in courts in which pretrial

admittance is not customary, the following is a list of steps that may be necessary: (1) Have the exhibit marked by the court reporter or courtroom deputy. "May I have this photograph marked as Plaintiff's Exhibit 1 for identification?" (2) Have the sponsoring witness identify it. "It's a photograph of the accident scene." (3) Lay the predicate to authenticate and show relevancy. "And does Plaintiff's Exhibit 1 fairly and accurately depict the accident scene as you saw it?" "Yes." (4) Tender it to opposing counsel, who may object. (5) Formally offer it into evidence. "I offer Plaintiff's Exhibit 1 into evidence, your honor, after having tendered it to opposing counsel." (6) Be ready to argue its admissibility against an objection. (7) If the court does not explicitly rule, take affirmative steps to obtain a ruling. "Is Plaintiff's Exhibit 1 admitted, your honor?" "Yes." (8) Take steps to have the exhibit communicated to the jury. "May the bailiff pass Plaintiff's Exhibit 1 to the jurors, your honor?" [Note: Custom varies; for example, in some jurisdictions, such as California state courts, an exhibit should be shown to opposing counsel before the witness speaks about it.]

(6) *Evidence as Primarily Exclusionary Rules.* If the purpose of a trial is to reconstruct exactly what happened regarding the litigated event, would you say that the more evidence the fact-finder receives, the better? Then how do you explain that the study of evidence law is primarily the study of exclusionary rules?

PROBLEM 1A: PRESERVING ERROR FOR AN APPEAL WHEN YOUR EVIDENCE IS EXCLUDED: MAKING AN OFFER OF PROOF.

Imagine that you have called an expert witness to establish the standard of care in a medical malpractice case. After you elicit the expert's qualifications, your opponent objects: "He's unqualified under Rule 702." The trial judge promptly agrees: "That's sustained. His testimony is excluded." You think the judge is dead wrong, and you consider this expert's testimony crucial to your case. Although appellate reversal on evidence grounds is not easy to obtain, you want to preserve the ground here. Fed. R. Evid. 103 says that the "substance of the evidence [must be] made known to the court by offer." What should you do? If you were the opponent, seeking to exclude the evidence, what else might you do to support the judge's ruling and avoid reversal?

[C] How Evidence Rules Relate to the Totality of Events and Stages in Jury Trial

Evidence law mostly rears its head during the trial itself. But there is a relationship between evidence law and other stages of the process, too.

For example, the pleadings govern the evidence by defining the legal issues that are of consequence to the determination of the action. Discovery in civil cases extends to matters "reasonably calculated to lead to admissible evidence," and hence it ultimately is dependent on evidence rules. Further, discovery materials frequently are admissible evidence. Summary judgment depends on evidence substitutes, such as affidavits and discovery products, but the "summary judgment evidence" usually has to show that it would be admissible.

The trial itself may be regarded as consisting of the eighteen stages set forth under the next heading. In reading through them, bear in mind that evidence law plays some role at stages other than the obvious stages.

For example, during the voir dire (jury selection) stage, a lawyer, ostensibly seeking to find out if jurors will react "impartially" to certain trial evidence, may be allowed to refer to admissible evidence. She/he may really be seeking to tilt the jury in advance. Or plaintiff's attorney in a negligence action may, with some justification, seek to find out if jurors have a connection with the defendant's liability insurer, ostensibly to ferret out bias. But the lawyer also thereby implies to the jury the inadmissible fact that defendant has such insurance, which may be the lawyer's real purpose.

Similarly, at the motion for a new trial stage, the directed verdict stage, the judgment-notwithstanding-the-verdict stage, or other similar stage, the judge may need to review the record of both admitted and excluded evidence and the permissible and impermissible inferences from the evidence. This is all because at these stages the judge may be being asked to reconsider whether any of his/her evidentiary rulings were erroneous, or to decide whether the state of the evidence justifies submission to the jury or makes factual issues so clear that they can be decided as a matter of law without a jury verdict.

The Eighteen Stages of a Jury Trial

Although there are jurisdictional variations, a jury trial usually follows the sequence of eighteen stages set forth below. *In the material below, "plaintiffs" includes "prosecutors" except as noted.* "P" is the symbol for both.

(1) *Trial Date Setting; Final Pretrial Conference.* The trial date may have been set for years, or a few weeks, or months. Federal procedure rules contemplate a final pretrial conference of the parties' lawyers before the judge, near the trial date. The pretrial order issuing from the conference often specifies witnesses, testimony subjects, and documents that will be offered as evidence.

(2) *Motions on the Eve of Trial.* These may be requests for orders concerning jury selection (e.g., for individual rather than judicial examination of jurors), for evidence rulings, etc. A "motion *in limine*" (lim-in-ee) ("at the threshold") requests advance exclusion of prejudicial or inadmissible evidence or advance admission of evidence, or asks that the proponent of certain evidence raise admissibility outside the jury's presence before attempting introduction.

(3) *Voir Dire Examination of Jurors.* Just before trial, the judge, or the attorneys, or both, depending upon the jurisdiction and the court, question an assembled panel of potential jurors about their qualifications. The questions often include inquiry about jurors' preconceptions about the evidence. Sometimes the lawyers submit questions for the judge to ask.

(4) *Challenges to Potential Jurors.* During the examination of jurors, attorneys may "challenge" particular jurors — that is, have them disqualified for a good legal reason ("good cause"). Each side is also allowed to remove a certain number of potential jurors without giving reasons. The first twelve panel members who remain are impaneled and sworn. In some courts, for some kinds of cases, or by

agreement, a lesser number, such as six, may suffice.

(5) *Opening Statements.* First, the plaintiff's attorney (or prosecutor), then the defendant's attorney, gives an opening statement. In some jurisdictions, the defendant may choose to give his/hers after the plaintiff (or prosecutor) rests its evidentiary presentation, right before defendant's evidentiary presentation begins. The opening statement is confined to previewing the evidence of that side of the case and technically should not contain "argument."

(6) *"Invoking the Rule" (Sequestering Witnesses).* Either attorney may demand prospective witnesses be ordered not to sit in on the trial, listen to the evidence, nor discuss the case except with the attorneys. This is to assure independence of their stories.

(7) *The Right to Open and Close.* The party with the burden on the whole case (usually plaintiff/prosecutor) normally has the right to open and close the opening statements (and the evidence, and the summations, see *infra*).

(8) *Plaintiff's (Prosecutor's) Evidence ("Plaintiff's or Prosecutor's Case-in-Chief").* Plaintiff/Prosecutor calls her first witness. Plaintiff's/Prosecutor's evidence also may include documents, items, stipulations, discovery products, or facts judicially noticed by the court. *All evidence must be submitted in accordance with the rules of evidence. Each of plaintiff's/prosecutor's witnesses is put through a direct examination by plaintiff's/prosecutor's counsel, and, on its heels, a cross-examination by defense counsel (if defense counsel desires).* (The judge *may* then allow a re-direct examination responding to new points in the cross-examination, and possibly a re-cross to answer *that.* Further exams are rare.) The plaintiff/prosecutor ends this phase of trial by saying "plaintiff/prosecutor rests."

(9) *Motion for Judgment as a Matter of Law or "Directed Verdict."* After P rests, defendant may move to have the case taken from the jury and terminated by the judge on the ground that the plaintiff's (or prosecutor's) evidence cannot support a verdict. (Alternatively, particular unsupported issues may be removed from the case this way.)

(10) *Defendant's Evidence ("Defendant's Case-in-Chief").* After P rests, defendant may choose to submit evidence. The same evidentiary rules and kinds of exam (direct, cross, etc.) control. At the conclusion, the defendant rests.

(11) *Rebuttal and Surrebuttal Evidence.* A civil plaintiff now may move for judgment as a matter of law against defendant (on the whole case or on individual issues). If there is no such judgment, the plaintiff or prosecutor now may offer evidence in rebuttal to defendant's evidence. The defendant may then offer surrebuttal, to which plaintiff or prosecutor again may respond, etc. These later stages are discretionary with the judge.

(12) *Motion for Judgment as a Matter of Law (or "Directed Verdict") at the Close of the Evidence.* When everyone has finally rested (closed), either party in a civil case and the defendant in a criminal case may move for judgment as a matter of law (or directed verdict). [Often it is advisable for both parties to make the motion at this point since a motion during trial can be a prerequisite in federal

practice to a similar motion later, after trial.] Alternatively, particular issues may be removed from the case this way.

(13) *The Charge Conference: Requests and Rulings.* Attorneys must be given an opportunity to request jury charges (judge's instructions to the jury). In federal courts, requests relating to the substantive law usually must be made before trial; in some state courts they may be made at the close of the evidence. Typically, judges confer with the parties on charges. Federal procedural rules require that the court inform the parties of its rulings on requested charges before the attorneys give their jury arguments. Instructions concerning what uses the jury may and may not make of particular evidence may be requested and given immediately upon the introduction of the evidence, as well as at this later stage before the case is finally submitted to the jury. Sometimes both are done.

(14) *Jury Argument.* At the close of all the evidence, before the jury retires to finally deliberate, the attorneys at last get a chance to argue interpretations of the law and the evidence to the jury, giving their explanations of the way in which the jurors should resolve the issues; urging which of competing reasonable factual inferences jurors should draw from the evidence (theoretically limited to reasonable inferences); and how the law should be applied (within reasonable readings of the law and the judge's instructions). In short, the lawyers urge what the jury should find. The party with the burden of proof on the whole case (usually the plaintiff or prosecutor) normally opens this summation stage by giving his/her set of arguments in a lengthy speech. The defendant goes next. The plaintiff (prosecution) ordinarily then gets to answer, in a final rebuttal summation argument.

(15) *The Court's Charge and Submission of the Case to the Jury (Verdict Forms).* The judge then instructs the jury on applicable law. Often instructions are criticized as being full of jargon and not understandable to average jurors. Some states, like California, are redrafting their instructions to be juror friendly, since an unintelligible instruction is not likely to be followed.

The judge submits a question, or series of questions, to the jury, together with a form for its verdict. Sometimes the form asks only the bottom line question (guilty, not guilty; liable, not liable; amount of damages). Sometimes, however, there is a series of questions ultimately leading to a final verdict (leaving it to the judge to determine the verdict from the particular answers). This is known as a special interrogatory form of verdict or special verdict, as opposed to a general verdict.

In some jurisdictions, the court charges the jury before the attorneys give their jury arguments.

(16) *Objections to the Charge.* The attorneys must be given an opportunity to place their objections to the charge on the record. Most courts prohibit appellate review of errors in the charge unless objected to before the jury retired.

(17) *Jury Deliberations; Further Charges or Questions; Verdict.* The jury retires to deliberate. In certain circumstances, the jury after retiring may ask the judge via a written note for some kind of legal or factual clarification or to have certain

testimony read back. Judges sometimes comply. The judge may give some further charges.

The jury returns written answer(s) to the judge's verdict-form question(s) (described at 15 above). The jury's answer(s) are the verdict. The judge receives the verdict if it is in order. He/she may send the jury back to deliberate further if it is not in order, or when jurors communicate inability to agree on a verdict. At some point, to avoid coercion of jurors against their conscience, the judge must accepts a "hung" jury, that is, an inability to agree, which is counted as no verdict either way.

After receipt of the verdict, either side may demand that the jury be polled (that is, that each juror be asked individually whether the verdict reflects his or her verdict). The jurors then may be discharged. Some jurisdictions provide for verdicts that are not unanimous (or even for seating fewer than twelve jurors) in certain situations.

(18) *Post-Trial Motions and Judgment.* The loser in a civil case (and a criminal defendant who loses) may move for judgment as a matter of law (or "judgment notwithstanding the verdict") or for a new trial. In the absence of such interference with the jury's verdict, the judge has the responsibility for turning the jury's verdict into a legally binding judgment. Any judgment is usually embodied in an order granting or denying the requested relief.

PROBLEM 1B: INDIRECT IMPLICATION OF INSURANCE MATTERS IN VOIR DIRE AND FINAL ARGUMENT.

You are the defense lawyer for Don D. Fendant in a civil negligence case arising out of an automobile accident. Don is insured for up to $1 million by Acme Casualty Company, which also pays your fee. During the voir dire examination, your opponent — the lawyer for the plaintiff, Paul Payne — asks the jurors: "Have any of you ever worked for an insurance company, or have any of you had friends or relatives who did?" When two jurors hold up their hands, he questions them further, including asking: "Can you decide this case without regard to whether an insurance company may actually be the one to pay?" Later, at the end of the case, your opponent begins his final argument to the jury by saying: "Ladies and gentlemen, the great thing about the jury system is that poor Paul Payne doesn't have to submit his claim to some stingy guy sitting in a tall building in a city like Omaha, Nebraska, or Hartford, Connecticut." What if anything would you do to counteract each of these matters?

PROBLEM 1C: THE AFFIDAVIT BASED ON INADMISSIBLE HEARSAY — CAN IT PREVENT SUMMARY JUDGMENT?

Assume that the plaintiff has sued ten different firms for allegedly supplying plaintiff's employer with what are claimed to be defective asbestos products that plaintiff believes caused him to develop cancer. One defendant, Asbesco Inc., denies that it ever supplied plaintiff's employer with any products, and it files an affidavit of its sales manager stating: "I have been Asbesco's sales manager ever since Asbesco was founded, and I can and do state, on my personal knowledge, that

Asbesco never has supplied any product to plaintiff's employer." Asbesco moves for summary judgment on the strength of this affidavit. Plaintiff counters with an affidavit saying: "To the best of my knowledge, my employer purchased some of these asbestos products from Asbesco, because various of my fellow employees in the purchasing department, whose identities I cannot now recall, once informed me that Asbesco was a supplier to our employer." Fed. R. Civ. P. 56 requires that affidavits be on personal knowledge, and they must set forth "such facts as would be admissible in evidence." Should the summary judgment be granted or denied?

§ 1.03 LIMIT ON JUDGE'S CONDUCT OF TRIAL: IMPARTIALITY[6]

In connection with this section, look at the powers given the judge under Federal Rules of Evidence 611 (mode and order of interrogation and presentation), 614 (calling and interrogation of witnesses by the judge) (note specially its procedure for objections), and 706 (judge-appointed experts). These are only some of the powers the judge has. But the judge must exercise all of them impartially. Judicial impartiality is too big a subject to be handled here in its entirety. We will be content with just a few examples.

NOTES AND QUESTIONS

(1) *Federal Rules of Evidence Rejected Judicial Comment Rule.* The Supreme Court Draft (1972) of the Federal Rules of Evidence proposed a Fed. R. Evid. 105 entitled "Summing-up and Comment by Judge." It provided in its entirety:

> After the close of the evidence and arguments of counsel, the judge may fairly and impartially sum up the evidence and comment to the jury upon the weight of the evidence and the credibility of the witnesses, if he also instructs the jury that they are to determine for themselves the weight of the evidence and the credit to be given to the witnesses and that they are not bound by the judge's summation or comment.

The drafters' commentary (Advisory Committee Note) said:

> The rule states the present rule in the federal courts. *Capital Traction Co. v. Hof*, 174 U.S. 1 (1899). The judge must, of course, confine his remarks to what is disclosed by the evidence. He cannot convey to the jury his purely personal reaction to credibility or to the merits of the case; he can be neither argumentative nor an advocate. *Quercia v. United States*, 289 U.S. 466 (1933).

This rule was rejected by Congress for the expressed reason that, although the power embodied in the rule is not disapproved, the matter is considered more properly a subject of procedure than evidence. There did seem to be some feeling, however, that a written rule might overly encourage the use of this power.

---

[6] Study Guide Reference: Evidence in a Nutshell, Chapter 1:IV, at "Judicial Comment on Weight of Evidence" and "Argument by Attorneys to Jury."

(2) *Ways in which the Judge Exercises a De Facto Right to Comment.* The judge's power to comment is more cautiously formulated in a number of jurisdictions as only a power to "sum up" or "marshal" the evidence. In many jurisdictions, it is denied altogether. But there may be other devices that in part serve the same purpose. Can you name some? (E.g., presumptions; instructions on the proper purpose of evidence; and commonly found instructions on factors to consider in evaluating particular kinds of evidence such as eyewitness identifications, testimony by the criminal defendant, accomplice testimony, testimony by children or police officers, evidence of flight, absence of evidence, etc. Are there others?)

Indirect judicial comment may be conveyed by statements made by the judge while discussing a counsel's objection to evidence; questions from the bench to counsel; the judge's tone of voice; inflections; or nonverbal conduct. Particularly onerous is such nonverbal, unrecorded conduct as appearing highly attentive during one side's questioning or closing argument and distracted, bored, or disagreeable during the other's, or an approving attitude only when addressing one side. Alert counsel may be able to overcome or deal with open on-the-record direct judicial commentary, but generally is unable to deal effectively with "body language" and tone of voice that does not appear in the record.

(3) *Improper Judicial Comments Can Result in Reversible Error. United States v. Yates*, 553 F.2d 518 (6th Cir. 1977): Yates appealed from his jury conviction of bank robbery. He had signed a confession before the F.B.I. but maintained that he did not know what he was signing, did not rob the bank, thought he was under investigation for writing bad checks, and wanted to cooperate with the F.B.I. When the government attorney asked to have the confession read to the jury at the time it was introduced, the trial judge said in the jury's hearing that reading aloud would be unnecessary because the jury will have an opportunity to read it themselves later. The court also said "it is clear in the record from the testimony of [the F.B.I. Agents] that this defendant did admit his participation in the bank robbery, so call your next witness." Noting the traditional broad power of federal trial judges to comment on the evidence in civil and criminal cases, the Court of Appeals stated that the power is traditionally circumscribed by a requirement of fairness and impartiality, and that the comment here exceeded this limit by striking directly at the heart of Yates' central contentions. Although Yates had not yet testified, the trial court should have realized his position from an earlier suppression hearing. While the trial judge merely may have been observing that the document was self-explanatory, the jury may have understood otherwise.

When a judge makes an impermissible comment, what dilemma faces an attorney contemplating an objection? Should the need to object to preserve appellate review be abrogated here?

(4) *Judicial Instructions on the Court's Comments.* A typical jury instruction, entitled "Court's Comments on Evidence," reads as follows:

> The law of the United States permits the Judge to comment to the jury on the evidence in the case. Such comments, when made, are only expressions of the Judge's opinion as to the facts, and you are not bound by that opinion. If, during the course of this trial or this charge, I have made or make any comment on any evidence, or any comment which you

> interpret as an expression or intimation of opinion as to any fact, you are free to disregard it. You are the sole and exclusive judges of all issues of fact in this case.

Some instructions to the jury are mandatory and must be obeyed. Will it be easy for the jury to know which are and are not mandatory?

(5) *Judge Argues with Witness.* In *Crandell v. United States*, 703 F.2d 74 (4th Cir. 1983), a civil suit was brought by the Crandells for medical malpractice on the part of medical personnel at the Quantico Marine Base. The Crandells, who were Marines there, alleged that their 6-month-old daughter, Jennifer, was not diagnosed quickly enough as having spinal meningitis. As a result, they claimed, she became severely retarded. A part of the transcript in the trial court is reproduced below. It shows an exchange between the judge and plaintiff's expert witness:

Judge: [T]here was growth deficiency prior to the meningitis, isn't that what you just said?

Witness: No. [F]rom a review of the history.

Judge: (Interposing) Certainly, you couldn't exist without history, could you, Doctor?

Witness: No.

Judge: Well, I didn't think you could. You couldn't diagnose any thyroid without having a very complete history.

Witness: We could, yes.

Judge: You could? Could you tell me now if I have got a headache, Doctor?

Witness: A headache is a symptom, not a disease.

Judge: Could you tell me whether I have a thyroid deficiency without asking questions — my, my, my, Doctor, you are the first doctor in all my 80 years that ever told me substantive symptoms, which is history, didn't mean a thing to you.

William O. Snead (the Crandells' lawyer): He didn't say that.

Witness: I didn't say that.

Judge: I know what he said. I know what he means. He said he didn't need the history.

Witness: To make a diagnosis of hypothyroidism in an infant.

Judge: That's what he said. He didn't need the history.

Witness: Yes, sir. I can explain why.

Judge: Well, that's your opinion.

Snead: Could he explain it?

Judge: Let him explain it. I don't want you to testify. You brought him over here as an expert.

Witness: [I can make the diagnosis by merely looking at the patient without a word being spoken because it is so characteristic.]

Judge: Well, I am sure if I had my right arm cut off you can tell me I am missing my right arm. I am conscious of that.

The Court of Appeals, citing this as an example, reversed a judgment for defendants, because of unfair interference by the judge with the Crandell's expert witness. What dilemma is counsel in when deciding whether to object to this kind of questioning? Should the rules excuse failure to object and allow appellate review regardless?

(6) *Judge Takes Over Questioning of Witness.* In *State v. Perkins*, 45 S.E.2d 17 (W. Va. 1947), the defendant was convicted of the murder of her husband. She testified in her own behalf. Her counsel asked her one question on redirect examination, which she did not answer. The trial judge then of his own motion asked 41 questions of her, typified by the following:

Q. Mrs. Perkins, you have told the jury you had a blackout on the evening when you found your husband with this woman and you don't remember anything except what your husband did to you, is that right?

A. That is exactly right.

Q. You remember everything that happened from then on until this shooting?

A. Yes, sir.

Q. You remember your husband standing with a flashlight in his hand and his gun in his hand?

A. Yes, sir.

Q. You remember that?

A. Yes, sir.

Q. Then you testified to the jury that you had a blackout from that time on, is that right?

A. Yes, sir.

Q. You don't know what happened?

A. I don't remember anything that happened until later that evening in the hospital.

Q. When the blackout struck you where were you standing?

A. In the doorway. . . .

Q. Where was he?

A. In the hall.

Q. Facing each other?

A. Yes.

Q. And you don't know how that gun which has been exhibited in evidence got there in the hallway and found there after you were shot?

A. I don't remember ever having that gun in my hands.

Q. You didn't have a blackout except on those two occasions, is that right?

A. I don't understand what you mean.

Q. You told the jury your mind was a blank at the time of the trouble with this woman, and now you tell the jury your mind was a blank from the time your husband was standing there in the hall and you were in the room facing him.

A. I guess I was so mad I don't remember anything else.

Defendant (via counsel) thereupon objected and rested her case. The appellate court notes that neither the demeanor of the trial judge nor whether the questions were brusque appears in the record. Notwithstanding that no single question seems objectionable, 41 questions of this sort intimated to the jury the judge's opinion on central facts, the appellate court holds; the trial judge's belief in guilt can be very influential; he may ask questions to make necessary clarifications but he should not take over the duties of the prosecutor. (Query: Is it risky for the judge to exercise the limited power this opinion (and most others) gives him?) Conviction reversed.

The dissent, applying the same standard, feels that the prosecutor had not succeeded in developing certain necessary pertinent facts; the trial judge is not a mere umpire; a trial is not a game; the judge has the duty to direct and conduct the trial; and no particular opinion of the judge emerged from the questioning here.

(7) *Not All Judicial Participation Results in Reversal.* In *United States v. Robinson*, 635 F.2d 981 (2d Cir. 1980), in affirming a conviction for heroin smuggling, the court observed:

> [T]he trial judge is more than a moderator or umpire and has an active responsibility to see that a criminal trial is fairly conducted. His participation during trial — whether it takes the form of interrogating witnesses, addressing counsel, or some other conduct — must [however] never reach the point at which it appears clear to the jury that the court believes the accused is guilty. [T]he trial judge's conduct of this trial left much to be desired. However, the question is whether his behavior was so prejudicial that it denied a fair, as distinguished from a perfect, trial.

While finding this a difficult and close case, the court affirms the conviction owing to the following considerations: (1) Criticisms of counsel, though serious, were but a small part of the extensive trial record. (2) Most of the remarks were made outside the jury's presence. (3) Without proof, such as a videotape or sound recording, showing the alleged prejudicial gestures, tone of voice, and facial expressions of the judge, the remarks made before the jury do not on the record indicate hostility, belief or disbelief in witnesses or positions, or partiality. (4) At the end of the trial the judge expressed gratitude to defense counsel for work well done and told the jury that whether the judge or jury liked or disliked any lawyers in the case was irrelevant. (5) Many of the judge's objectionable remarks were provoked by defense counsel's own improper behavior (evidenced by statements of the judge in the record and statements by the government attorney on appeal). (6) The judge was evenhanded in the other rulings in the case, ruling for and against both defense and prosecution relatively equally. (7) The appellate court examined in detail the performance of defense counsel and enumerated many particulars in which defense counsel did a thorough and extensive job and in total effectively put the government to its proof, leaving no stone unturned. (8) The judge's questioning of witnesses did not indicate any belief or disbelief in any witness or position but was merely to clarify ambiguities. (9) The judge instructed the jury that the jury alone determines the credibility of witnesses.

(8) *Ability of Judge to Call Witnesses. United States v. Karnes*, 531 F.2d 214 (4th Cir. 1976):

> A trial judge has the authority, if not the duty, to call witnesses who possess relevant information when the parties decline to call them. But the due process clause requires that a court be impartial. This impartiality is destroyed when the court assumes the role of prosecutor and undertakes to produce evidence, essential to overcome the defendant's presumption of innocence, which the government has declined to present. Further, in this case the jury was never told why the witnesses were called as court witnesses and was not instructed that these witnesses were entitled to no greater credibility [than ordinary witnesses]. . . . [T]he same result could have been achieved by an accepted means: [A] judge may afford wide latitude to the government to lead, to cross-examine, and partially to impeach such witnesses.

(9) *Some Typical Instructions Related to the Role of Judge, Jury, and Counsel, Given By the Judge to the Jury Just Before Jury Retires For Final Deliberation*:

> **Jury Not To Take Cue From Judge.** You are not to be influenced by anything I may have said or done that suggested I am inclined to favor the position of either party. I have not intended to intimate any opinion as to what witnesses are worthy of belief or disbelief; what facts are or are not established; or what inferences should be drawn from the evidence. If I seemed to indicate an opinion on any of these matters, you must disregard that seeming indication.
>
> **Court's Questions to Witnesses.** I may have asked questions of a witness, in order to bring out some fact not fully developed by the testimony. Do not take my questions as any indication of my opinion as to how you should determine the issues of fact. You may disregard all comments of the Court in arriving at your own findings as to the facts.
>
> **Inadmissible and Stricken Evidence.** It is the duty of counsel to object when the other side offers testimony or other evidence that she believes is not properly admissible. If I sustained an objection you must disregard the question and not speculate as to what the answer would have been. If, after a question was asked and an answer given by the witness, I ruled that the answer should be stricken from the record, you are to disregard both the question and the answer in your deliberations. Likewise, exhibits to which I sustained an objection, or ordered stricken, are not evidence and you must not consider them.

Evidence in the Case. The statements of counsel should not be considered as evidence unless such statements were made as admissions or stipulations conceding the existence of a fact or facts.

Jury's Recollection Controls. If any reference by me or counsel to evidence does not coincide with your own recollection of the evidence, it is your recollection that should control during your deliberations

§ 1.04 PURPOSE-LIMITING INSTRUCTIONS TO THE JURY[7]

Read Federal Rule of Evidence 105, "Limiting Evidence That is Not Admissible Against Other Parties or for Other Purposes."

Sometimes a given piece of evidence tends to prove two different propositions, one of which is proper for the jury to consider, the other not. (In fact, this happens more frequently than one might expect.) As an example, usually it is improper for plaintiff to use evidence of the defendant's liability insurance in a negligence case. But there is an exception to this general rule when the evidence is used for a purpose other than to prove fault. Let us say that one of the principal witnesses for the defense is an investigator who is an employee of defendant's insurer; the plaintiff would consider this important evidence of bias, and a court might well allow it for that purpose. At the same time, however, the law recognizes that the evidence is prejudicial. The court probably would give a "limiting instruction" cautioning the jury that it could not consider insurance in connection with the negligence issue. A similar situation arises where evidence is admissible against one party but not another party, though it may appear to implicate both.

UNITED STATES v. WASHINGTON

United States Court of Appeals, Second Circuit
592 F.2d 680 (1979)

PER CURIAM.

Appellant was arrested on March 17, 1978, after he and a companion, a suspected bank robber, attempted to elude federal officers in a high-speed automobile chase through the Borough of Queens in New York City. When the car in which appellant was a passenger was forced to stop by a truck that was blocking the street, appellant emerged from the vehicle as if to surrender, then suddenly bolted into the crowd that had gathered. The officers gave chase and cornered appellant in an alley. When he brandished a gun at the approaching officers, he was shot.

Appellant subsequently was charged in a two-count indictment with one count of assaulting federal officers, 18 U.S.C. §§ 111, 1114, and one count of possession of a deadly weapon by a convicted felon, 18 U.S.C. App. § 1202(a)(1). After a jury convicted him on both counts, he was sentenced to eight years imprisonment on the

---

[7] Study Guide Reference: Evidence in a Nutshell, Chapter 1:II, at "Curative and Cautionary Instructions to the Jury: Common Law and F.R.E. 105."

first and given a suspended two-year sentence on the second.

To establish the elements of the section 1202(a)(1) offense, the Government introduced a stipulation between the parties that appellant had been convicted of a prior felony. After referring to the prior conviction in his charge, the district judge refused defense counsel's request to instruct the jury that the conviction could not be considered as evidence of a general propensity to commit crimes but could be considered only to establish the prior felony element of count two of the indictment.

Where evidence is admissible for one purpose but is inadmissible for another, the trial judge should, when requested, instruct the jury as to the limited purpose for which the evidence may be considered. Fed.R.Ev. 105. This circuit has consistently held that evidence of prior criminal conduct which is admissible for a limited purpose must, where the defendant requests, be accompanied by a limiting instruction.

Although the nature of appellant's prior felony was not revealed to the jury, we believe that the revelation that appellant previously had been convicted of a felony was sufficient to entitle him to the limiting instruction he requested.

Although there was substantial evidence of appellant's guilt, we cannot say it is highly probable that the failure to give a limiting instruction did not contribute to the verdict. Accordingly, we reverse and remand for a new trial.

NOTE

Obligation of Counsel to Ask for Limiting Instruction. See United States v. Gilmore, 730 F.2d 550 (8th Cir. 1984) (under Fed. R. Evid. 105, burden of requesting limiting instruction lies with party who desires instruction to be given; where no request was made for limiting instruction after evidence of prior drug dealings was admitted, review on appeal was precluded).

PROBLEM 1D: LIMITING INSTRUCTIONS FOR PRIOR CONVICTIONS OFFERED TO IMPEACH: PROBLEM BASED ON UNITED STATES v. LIPSCOMB, 702 F.2d 1049 (D.C. CIR. 1983) (EN BANC).

Defendant Lipscomb was convicted of possession of heroin with intent to distribute. The prosecution's case-in-chief consisted of testimony from the arresting officers. The defendant, at his first trial, testified in his own defense and denied knowledge of the heroin. Fed. R. Evid. 609 allows certain evidence of a witness's prior convictions to be admitted for the purpose of impeaching the witness, and in accordance with this rule, the Government offered evidence that Lipscomb had been convicted of armed robbery eight years earlier. Pursuant to Fed. R. Evid. 105, the trial judge instructed the jury that it could consider the conviction only for the purpose of assessing Lipscomb's credibility and not in connection with his propensity or guilt of this heroin offense. The first trial ended in a hung jury.

At the second trial, defendant did not testify, the prior conviction was not admitted either, and defendant was convicted. Questions: (1) Do you think the instruction in the first trial was likely to have been helpful to the defendant (could it instead have been inadvertently harmful)? (2) Should the giving of the instruction be a factor in favor of affirming on appeal? (The en banc court did consider it as such, and it upheld the admissibility of the conviction with the instruction.)

Chapter 2

RELEVANCY AND ITS COUNTERWEIGHTS

THE GENERAL CONCEPTS (F.R.E. ARTICLE IV, RULES 401–403)

§ 2.01 RELEVANCE[1]

Read Federal Rules of Evidence 401, "Test for Relevant Evidence," and 402, "General Admissibility of Relevant Evidence."

Basic Nature of Rules 401–402. The most fundamental propositions in the Federal Rules of Evidence, probably, are embodied in Fed. R. Evid. 401 and Fed. R. Evid. 402. Fed. R. Evid. 401 defines relevant evidence. Fed. R. Evid. 402 then provides that all relevant evidence is admissible unless there is some exclusionary principle that excludes it. These two Rules govern the vast bulk of admissible evidence, even though exclusionary rules (such as the hearsay rule) comprise a larger percentage of the text of the Federal Rules of Evidence.

Fed. R. Evid. 401 is nontechnical and, by its terms, is extremely permissive in admitting even evidence with low probative value. Consider the following:

David Crump, *On the Uses of Irrelevant Evidence*
34 HOUS. L. REV. 1 (1997)

The definition of relevant evidence in the Federal Rules was drafted to avoid the restrictiveness of some earlier applications of the concept. For example, the Rule avoids the alternative formulation of [original] Uniform Rule of Evidence 1(2), which requires that the probative value consist of "a tendency in reason" to prove the matter at issue. The Federal Rules thus avoid undue emphasis on the logical process at the expense of experience, and they support the use of general principles from jurors' past perceptions. Similarly, the Federal Rules eschew any requirement that the proposition at issue be "disputed" or "in controversy," so that even background information, of a kind that every party agrees is true, can be received. Another liberalizing aspect of the definition is that it requires only that the fact at issue be one that is "of consequence" to the determination of the action, rather than imposing a standard of "materiality." The language thus signals that the fact to be proved may be "ultimate, intermediate or evidentiary." And rather than a minimal measure of probative value, the rule requires only that the evidence make a legally significant fact "more probable than it would be without the evidence," thus allowing

---

[1] Study Guide Reference: Evidence in a Nutshell, Chapter 1:I, at "Evidentiary Policies in a Jury Trial System: The Common Law and F.R.E. 102"; Chapter 3:I, at "The Definition of Relevant Evidence: F.R.E. 401," and at "Relevant Evidence Is Admissible Unless There Is an Exclusionary Rule: F.R.E. 402."

information to be admitted based upon the slightest increment in likelihood. This language is a helpful communication to the court of Professor McCormick's aphorism that "[a] brick is not a wall," or as Professor McBaine put it, ". . . [I]t is not to be supposed that every witness can make a home run."

But it is in the words "*any* tendency" — which form the leading phrase in the definition — that the liberality of the standard is most apparent. Strangely, the Advisory Committee does not explain its choice of this formula, although the Committee's Note parses each of the other phrases considered above. "Any" is a word that connotes the broadest possible universality, including the minute or infinitesimal. The dictionary offers such alternate definitions as "in whatever quantity or number, great or small; some;" or "in whatever degree; to some extent; at all." Taken literally, the word "any" thus signifies that the definition includes evidence with the slightest degree of probative value, even that which is infinitesimally small.

This definition of relevancy has a venerable pedigree. It reflects a choice between competing concepts advanced by the two greatest evidence scholars in history. Specifically, the drafters selected the Thayerian view that a lesser standard of "logical" relevance should be required, so that "evidence having only the slightest probative force" is admissible. In so doing, they rejected the Wigmorean preference for a test of "legal" relevance, which would have demanded "more than a minimum of probative value," alternatively stated as a "plus value" over such a minimum.

Given Rule 401, it takes real ingenuity to come up with an example of evidence that seems truly irrelevant. One of my favorites comes from Dean Newell H. Blakely, who was a great classroom teacher. Imagine that the defendant is on trial in Chicago for theft. The indictment charges that he stole a television set from the owner's home. The prosecutor offers testimony of an eyewitness, along with other evidence that is "of consequence" to the elements of the crime. This evidence sounds relevant, and under the Federal Rules it undoubtedly is.

But after the prosecution rests, the defense lawyer — with great fanfare, let us suppose — calls a witness to offer testimony that it was raining in Utah on the day in question. Isn't this evidence "irrelevant"?

The paradoxical answer is, not by the definition in the Federal Rules. One can construct chains of experiential and logical propositions — long chains, admittedly — that connect [this] evidence to the issues in the case. Rainfall in Utah has at least some statistical correlation to weather in Chicago, the site of the alleged crime. We can prove this proposition, if it is doubted, by producing an expert who will testify that precipitation in the Rockies correlates with weather systems elsewhere so that, ever so slightly, it is more probable that the weather was bad in Chicago given this fact than if we did not know it. And this inference, in turn, affects the credibility of eyewitness testimony identifying the defendant, thereby influencing the probability of existence of a fact that is of consequence. [T]o some degree — admittedly infinitesimally, but still to *some* degree — this dubious inference advances the proposition that the defendant is misidentified.

NOTES AND QUESTIONS

(1) *Is this Interpretation of the Relevancy Definition Unrealistic?* The logical chain between rainfall-in-Utah evidence and the possibility that weather in Chicago caused misidentification of the thief is so long that intuitively we might tend to regard such evidence as "irrelevant" to the proposition. Consider whether its extremely low probative value can justify categorizing this evidence as irrelevant under the Federal Rules of Evidence, or whether the Fed. R. Evid. 401 definition prevents this conclusion whenever there is any amount of probative value, no matter how small. What do the drafters' choice of Thayer's view and their adoption of the "any tendency" language of Fed. R. Evid. 401 mean in this context?

(2) *A Conclusion that Evidence is "Relevant" Does Not Mean that it is "Admissible."* At this point in our reasoning about rainfall-in-Utah evidence, we have considered only whether it is "relevant." But remember Fed. R. Evid. 402: relevant evidence is admissible only if it is not excluded by another rule. Fed. R. Evid. 403, for example, excludes evidence that causes an excessive "waste of time," and even if rainfall-in-Utah evidence satisfies the bare relevancy standard, most judges would promptly exclude it under Rule 403!

(3) *What is Relevancy?* Courts have attempted to get at the notion of relevancy with different language. Are the following three expressions consistent with each other and with Fed. R. Evid. 401?:

(a) *United States v. Craft*, 407 F.2d 1065 (6th Cir. 1969): Relevancy describes the relationship between a proffered item of evidence and a proposition that is provable or material in a given case. There is no legal test of relevancy and reference must be made to logic or general experience to demonstrate the existence of a relationship and its proximity or remoteness. Justice Cooley wrote in *Stewart v. People*, 23 Mich. 63 (1871): "The proper test for the admissibility of evidence ought to be, we think, whether it has a tendency to affect belief in the mind of a reasonably cautious person, who should receive and weigh it with judicial fairness."

(b) *Engel v. United Traction Co.*, 203 N.Y. 321, 96 N.E. 731 (1911): A fact is admissible as the basis of an inference only when the desired inference is a probable or natural explanation of the fact and a more probable and natural one than the other explanations, if any.

(c) *McCandless v. United States*, 298 U.S. 342 (1936): An offer of proof cannot be denied as remote or speculative because it does not cover every fact necessary to prove the issue. If it be an appropriate link in the chain of proof, that is enough.

Relevancy in the sense used in Fed. R. Evid. 401 was sometimes called, in pre-Federal Rules days, "logical relevancy," which then was contrasted with "legal relevancy," a term that some courts employed to refer to evidence that survived the balancing process now incorporated in Fed. R. Evid. 403.

Engel, above, seems to articulate a standard higher than Fed. R. Evid. 401. Is *Engel* requiring something akin to "legal relevancy" which is something different than "logical relevancy"?

STEVENSON v. STEWART

Pennsylvania Supreme Court
11 Pa. 307 (1849)

[A]ction of debt on a bill [promissory note] dated 6th July, 1844. The defendant pleaded forgery.

[W]itnesses testified the signature [on the note looked like defendant's].

The defendant then introduced several witnesses to prove that he was not in the country.

The plaintiff then called [a witness who] state[d] he loaned defendant $40, and took his note in June, 1844 [the admissibility of this is contested on this appeal of a verdict for plaintiff].

[E]vidence offered must correspond with the allegations and be confined to the point in issue. The effect is to exclude merely collateral facts, having no connection with the subject litigated, and, therefore, incapable of shedding light upon the inquiry, or affording ground for reasonable presumption or inference. Thus, in covenant, the issue was whether the defendant, who was a tenant of the plaintiff, had committed waste, and evidence of bad husbandry, not amounting to waste, was rejected, for this could only have the effect of misleading the jury. But it by no means follows that all collateral facts, presenting at first view no direct connection with the principal fact, are irrelevant, and therefore inadmissible. On the contrary, great latitude is allowed to the reception of indirect, or, as it is sometimes called, circumstantial evidence, the aid of which is constantly required, and, therefore, where direct evidence of the fact is wanting, the more the jury can see of the surrounding facts and circumstances, the more correct their judgment is likely to be.

This indirect evidence is sometimes drawn from the experience which enables us to trace a connection between an ascertained collateral fact and the fact otherwise undetermined; and it is more or less cogent, as this connection is known to be more or less natural and frequent. Where antecedent experience shows this mutuality of relation to be constant or with a great degree of uniformity, the inference deducible, it is said, is properly termed a presumption. But this species of proof embraces a far wider scope than this. It in fact includes all evidence of an indirect nature, whether the inferences afforded by it be drawn from prior experience, or be a deduction of reason from the circumstances of the particular case, or of reason aided by experience. . . . It is enough if these may tend, even in a slight degree, to elucidate the inquiry, or to assist, though remotely, to a determination probably founded in truth. Indeed, to require a necessary relation between the fact known and the fact sought, would sweep away many sources of testimony to which men daily recur in the ordinary business of life, and that cannot be rejected by a judicial tribunal, without hazard of shutting out the light.

Merely foreign matter must be avoided; but, though in appearance foreign, if it bear at all on the main subject, it must be heard. As an illustration of this rule, we may take the ordinary case of an indictment for knowingly uttering counterfeited bank notes, in which proof of the possession or of the prior or subsequent utterance of other simulated notes, though of a different description, is constantly admitted as material to the question of guilty knowledge, touching the subject of the indictment. Another instance occurred in this court, in a case where the question was as to the date of a receipt given by the plaintiff to the defendant for money paid by the latter to the former; evidence that the defendant had, on a certain day, alleged by the plaintiff to be the date of the receipt in question, received from another source a sum of money, was held to be relevant. And yet there was, in these instances, no necessary or even intimate relation between the ascertained facts and the conclusion sought; but the former suggested reasons favouring the respective hypothesis of the prosecution and of the plaintiff and this was deemed enough to authorize their introduction to the jury.

[T]he question is forgery to a promissory note, averred to have been given for money loaned. Such investigations, founded in imputed fraud, naturally take a wide range. Among the most common topics of inquiry, is the pecuniary capacity of the supposed lender, and the necessitous condition of the alleged borrower. And these inquiries are legitimate. It is surely competent for the defendant to show that the plaintiff was, at the time of the alleged lending, a poor man, and probably unable to loan the sum in question; or that the defendant was himself possessed of money, and therefore not driven to the necessity of using his credit. If so, why should not the plaintiff be at liberty to prove that about the critical time the defendant was seeking to borrow? Standing unsupported, neither line of evidence would be sufficient to rebut the adverse allegation, but yet all must feel, that, in a doubtful case, the facts I have supposed to be made out by the defendant, would go far to determine in his favour. On the other hand, where the proofs were otherwise in equilibrio, the fact I have thought the plaintiff might show, would, questionless, furnish an argument of some weight in his scale. . . . [T]he convincing power of the inference is for the jury, when weighing the value of the fact proved; not for the judge, in determining the bare question of its relevancy. It is sufficient for the purposes of his inquiry, that it has some affinity with the principal inquiry, though this may be weak or remote. Such we think was the condition of the evidence received here; wherefore,

Judgment affirmed.

NOTES AND QUESTIONS

(1) *Assumptions of Continuing Conditions as Basis for Relevance.* As in the principal case, a human need or condition shown to have existed at one time in a person may increase the likelihood that it existed at another time. *See also United States v. Ives*, 609 F.2d 930 (9th Cir. 1979), *cert. denied*, 445 U.S. 919 (1980) (mental condition of defendant more than two years following killing is relevant to his sanity at time of killing, especially since disease was shown to be chronic).

(2) *But This Is Not Always the Case — It Depends on the Facts.* See, for example, *People v. Alksnis*, 682 N.E.2d 1112 (Ill. App. Ct. 1997), affirming the trial court's refusal to let the defendant display to the jury that his face had no acne or pock marks unless he was subjected to cross-examination. The judge said: "I don't believe it was relevant to have the jurors' view what his face appeared like two years

after the alleged incident." The assailant had been described as having acne immediately after the burglary.

CARTER v. HEWITT

United States Court of Appeals, Third Circuit
617 F.2d 961 (1980)

GIBBONS, CIRCUIT JUDGE.

[Carter, a state prison inmate, brought this civil rights action alleging that he was severely beaten by defendant prison guards. From a judgment against him he appeals.]

The incident giving rise to this appeal occurred during Carter's cross-examination. Carter was shown a letter written by one "Abdullah" to a fellow inmate at Huntingdon. Carter admitted that he had written the letter, and also admitted that he had denied writing this same letter when he had been questioned as to its authorship in an earlier prison disciplinary proceeding. Defense counsel asked Carter to read the letter. Carter objected on the grounds of relevance, claiming that the letter had been written six months after the alleged beating. The Magistrate then ordered Carter to read the letter but expressly reserved ruling on whether the letter was admissible. Complying with the Magistrate's direction, Carter read the letter aloud. The letter, which was undated, generally described to its unidentified recipient how to file a complaint charging prison guard brutality. In its most significant portion, the letter reads:

> This is a set up my brother — compile complaints to be use for bullshit courts, possibly news media, and a radio program in Pittsburg [sic] & W.D.A.S. down Philly. We want to establish a pattern of barbaric brutal harassment [sic] and turn it on these chumps to the max.

Defense counsel suggested that this letter was a direction to file a false brutality complaint. Carter claimed that he was only encouraging the filing of a legitimate complaint.

We believe, quite simply, that the letter is admissible, substantive evidence because it bears on the central factual issue in the case — whether Carter was beaten by prison guards on September 22, 1977. The standard of relevance established by the Federal Rules of Evidence is not high: evidence is relevant if it has "any tendency to make the existence of any fact that is of consequence to the determination of the action more probable or less probable than it would be without the evidence." F.R. Evid. 401 (emphasis added). A fact-finder could reasonably interpret this letter as reflecting a plan on Carter's part to promote the filing of false complaints. A fact-finder could further draw the inference that Carter's own complaint about being beaten on September 22, 1977 had been filed pursuant to that plan. Thus, the letter is relevant: it has some tendency to make Carter's assertion that he was beaten less likely to be true than it would be without the evidence. Since the letter is relevant, it is also admissible, unless its admission is otherwise restricted. F.R. Evid. 402. . . .

Assume Carter's letter had stated, instead of its actual content, "I think we can put these prison guards on the defensive by establishing a pattern of prison guard harassment. I intend doing so by encouraging prisoners to file numerous false complaints against the guards. Pursuant to this plan, I filed a false complaint of a beating by three guards on September 22, 1977."

If the hypothetical letter described above [is] admissible, as surely [it is], then so is Carter's; the differences [between] them go only to probative weight, not admissibility. While some inferences, no doubt, must be drawn from Carter's letter to reach the conclusion that he had a plan of filing false complaints and encouraging others to do so, and that the complaint about the incident of September 22, 1977 was part of this plan, these inferences only render the letter less probative, not less admissible.

Carter contends that the letter should have been excluded under F.R. Evid. 403.

This rule cannot help Carter. It does not offer protection against evidence that is merely prejudicial, in the sense of being detrimental to a party's case. Rather, the rule only protects against evidence that is unfairly prejudicial. Evidence is unfairly prejudicial only if it has "an undue tendency to suggest decision on an improper basis, commonly, though not necessarily, an emotional one." Advisory Committee's Note, F.R. Evid. 403. . . . A classic example of unfair prejudice is a jury's conclusion, after hearing a recitation of a defendant's prior criminal record, that, since the defendant committed so many other crimes, he must have committed this one too. This is an improper basis of decision, and the law accordingly prohibits introduction of prior convictions to demonstrate a propensity to commit crime. F.R. Evid. 404.

Carter's letter, while undoubtedly prejudicial to his case in that it resulted in the district court ruling against him, presents no danger of unfair prejudice. The letter was offered by the defendants to suggest that no beating occurred on September 22, 1977 and that Carter was lying when he testified to the contrary. This, of course, was the central issue at trial. . . . In a case such as the one here where the witnesses on each side take diametrically opposed positions, the fact finder's task is to determine which witnesses are more credible. If the Magistrate, after hearing the letter read, drew the inference that Carter was lying, it cannot be claimed that this was an improper basis of decision. . . . Thus, Carter . . . cannot demand exclusion of the letter under Rule 403.

NOTES AND QUESTIONS

(1) *Evidence that is Relevant to a Proposition that is Not itself of Consequence Under the Substantive Law or Pleadings is Not Relevant: "Of Consequenceness" is What Used to be Called "Materiality."* In *Williams v. Board of Regents of University System*, 629 F.2d 993 (5th Cir. 1980), *cert. denied*, 452 U.S. 926 (1981), a police lieutenant sued his superiors for wrongful discharge from the police force. (He was discharged allegedly for disclosing to the public a portion of a police accident report that he believed to have been altered by his superiors.) One of the defenses to the lawsuit was that the lieutenant breached a department policy of secrecy of such reports. The trial court excluded defendant's evidence, consisting of

witnesses and documents that would show the existence of such a policy. Such exclusion formed the basis of appeal. The Court of Appeals said:

> To be admissible evidence must be relevant, and the resolution of the question of relevance is in the province of the presiding judge. Relevant evidence is defined in Fed. R. Evidence § 401 as "evidence having any tendency to make the existence of any fact that is of consequence to the determination of the action more probable or less probable than it would be without the evidence.". . . With respect to the instant question, . . . the operative language of the definition of relevance is "of consequence to the determination": it must be shown that the evidence to be offered has a legal connection to the action. Here, the evidence would be of consequence to the action only if reliance on the policy would constitute a defense to the discharge.

The court found that such a policy would not be a defense because the policy contravened a state statute and regulations thereunder. Thus the trial judge's exclusion was sustained.

(2) *Flight as Evidence of Guilt*: *United States v. Jackson*, 405 F. Supp. 938 (E.D.N.Y. 1975). The common law admitted various kinds of avoidance-motivated behaviors, including flight, false alibi, and destruction of evidence, as circumstantial evidence of guilt. Cases decided under the Federal Rules of Evidence also follow this general principle. For example, in *Jackson*, the court admitted evidence that defendant was in Georgia shortly after the New York robbery for which he was on trial. Notice the long chain of inferences that is necessary for this evidence to be deemed relevant: presence in Georgia equals flight, flight equals consciousness of guilt, consciousness of guilt equals actual guilt, and actual guilt equals actual guilt not just for some offense, but for the very New York offense at issue. Consider whether this chain of inferences is excessively long. (Does the chain of reasoning, flight-to-guilt, begin to make even rainfall-in-Utah evidence sound good?)

(3) *Beer Cans in the Car in a Drunk Driving Case: Does it Matter if they are Unopened? or Warm? or so Old that they're Rusty?* Another result that shows the inclusiveness of the relevancy concept is the admissibility of liquor containers in drunk driving cases. Courts often admit such items into evidence even if there is no proof that they contributed to the defendant's alleged intoxication, and indeed, even when it is clear they could not possibly have contributed at all. *See, e.g.*, *Rodriguez v. State*, 282 S.W. 225 (Tex. Crim. App. 1926) (bottle of tequila found at place of collision); *Marshall v. State*, 262 S.W.2d 491 (Tex. Crim. App. 1953) (empty beer cans); *Talley v. State*, 399 S.W.2d 559 (Tex. Crim. App. 1966) (21 unopened beer cans). Try your hand at constructing the chain of propositions that must be inferred to make this evidence relevant.

(4) *The Exclusion of Relevant Evidence*. Remember, however, that concluding that flight in a robbery case and beer cans in a drunk driving case are "relevant" is not the same as concluding that they are "admissible." How could an attorney make credible arguments for exclusion in either of these cases?

(5) *Is "Irrelevant" Evidence Literally Impossible, Under the Rule 401 Definition?:* Crump, *On the Uses of Irrelevant Evidence*, *supra*. Consider the possibility

that there is no such thing as irrelevant evidence, in that the definition of relevant evidence encompasses every possibly arguable proposition:

> Professor McCormick told us that "[a] brick is not a wall." The Federal Rules stand for the analogous proposition that a single atom within a brick is not a wall, either, but if the test is "any" substance no matter how small, then the atom qualifies just as the brick does. A structure of bricks can make a wall, and by the same token, so can a conglomeration of atoms. . . . An atom — in fact, "any" atom that would, or could, or even *might* combine with others to build the wall — is admissible.
>
> In fact, the complete picture is even more universally inclusive than the rainfall-in-Utah example suggests. The definition of relevant evidence, I submit, is perfectly indiscriminate. It literally admits any arguable factual proposition, in any case. First, at some statistical level, observed instances of any given fact will show some degree of positive or negative correlation with any other fact. Second, in a limited universe, exhaustion of all facts distinct from the fact at issue may be "relevant." Imagine that we are attempting to prove that most emeralds on the crust of the Earth are green. Inductive proof of that fact is advanced by the finding of a green emerald, and each additional such discovery is an increment in the proof. But also, we can argue that the proposition is advanced by the finding of a brown stone, or any other not-green-object-that-is-not-an-emerald. As we exhaust the finite stuff that could disprove the questioned proposition, we increase the probability that the proposition is true. [T]he logical conclusion is that the brown stone is relevant in the Rule 401 sense to the green emeralds inquiry. It is proof by elimination. Paradoxically, it is relevant precisely because it is *irrelevant*!

Is this reasoning persuasive to you — or is it so excessively academic that it seems silly? Remember, once again, that relevancy is not the same as admissibility, and so even if Fed. R. Evid. 401 creates an indiscriminately inclusive definition, it still may not be unworkable. It merely forces the exclusionary rules to work harder.

(6) *The Exclusion in Rule 402 of "Evidence which is Not Relevant."* Notice, however, that Fed. R. Evid. 402 provides, "Evidence which is not relevant is not admissible." Does this sentence imply that some category of evidence that is "not relevant" *must* exist, or is it implicitly contradicted by the inclusiveness of the definition in Fed. R. Evid. 401? Judicial decisions, it should be added, usually do not analyze the language in this nitpicking fashion, and they often categorize evidence as "irrelevant" without defining the term. Perhaps this approach suggests that the problem does not really matter. But perhaps it does matter, and perhaps the courts' analyses of close questions of relevancy would be improved by better resolution of the concept of irrelevancy.

PROBLEM 2A: RONALD SHIPP'S OFFER OF "DREAM EVIDENCE" IN THE TRIAL OF O.J. SIMPSON: WAS IT RELEVANT?

At the trial of O.J. Simpson for the murders of his ex-wife (Nicole) and her friend, a longtime acquaintance named Ronald Shipp testified that Simpson had confided to him the night after the murders, "kind of jokingly," about his dreams of murder: "You know, to be honest, Shipp, I've had some dreams of killing her." Judge Lance Ito admitted this evidence over defense objection. *See* Freemantle, *"Dreams of Killing Her": Simpson Acquaintance Tells of Night After Killings*, HOUS. CHRONICLE, Feb. 2, 1995, § A, at 1, col. 1. A number of psychologists interviewed the next day for newspaper stories criticized this evidence on the ground that it "doesn't reflect anything about whether he in fact murdered her." As one psychologist put it, "If we all were tried for the dreams we had, we'd all be in jail." Talan, *Simpson Dreams Outside Reality, Psychologists Say*, HOUS. CHRONICLE, Feb. 2, 1995, § A, at 6, col. 1.

(1) Was this dream evidence "relevant" in the Fed. R. Evid. 401 sense? (Judge Ito actually applied the California Evidence Code, which contains a slightly different test of relevance, but one that is similar enough to Fed. R. Evid. 401 for these purposes.)

(2) Try to construct the chain of inferences that would be necessary to make Shipp's testimony relevant.

(3) Does it matter, in evaluating relevance, that most psychologists would have concluded that the necessary propositions were unscientific?

(4) Finally, remember that relevance does not equal admissibility, and consider how a defense attorney might argue that such dream evidence, even if relevant, should be excluded. For a discussion of a number of relevancy issues that arose during Simpson's trial see Raeder, *Irrelevancy: It's All in the Eyes of the Beholder*, 34 Hous. L. Rev. 103 (1997).

PROBLEM SET 2B: ILLUMINATING THE JUDGE'S TASK IN DECIDING RELEVANCE

(1) *The Missing Heel.* Is the shoe with the missing heel admissible in the following case?

Plaintiff's action is for damages for the wrongful death of her husband. [The allegation is that defendant's servant was negligent in having the decedent load material on top of defendant's elevator, which had a dangerous condition on it that caused decedent to fall to his death. The defendant answered that such was not the cause of the fall, and that decedent fell while loading atop the elevator for some other reason, such as a heart attack, for which defendant would not be liable.] Decedent, as an independent contractor in the moving and hauling business, was hired by one of defendant's tenants to move a bookcase from the sixth floor of the New York Life Building in Minneapolis to another building. Decedent, accompanied by his own helper, entered defendants' New York Life Building and obtained the use of the freight elevator. It was found that the bookcase was too large to be placed inside the elevator. The elevator operator, then stated that the bookcase should be placed on top of the elevator, but that to do so more help was needed. Since help could not be obtained for another 15 minutes, decedent and his helper stated that they could handle it alone.

The top of the elevator was of steel construction. It was flat and composed of three sections running horizontally with the front of the elevator. Each section had a reinforcing angle iron around its edge about one inch in height. The same type of angle iron, with one side projecting upward, also extended around the entire outer edge of the top. There were no safety guards or rails around the outer edge.

Decedent picked up one end of the bookcase and commenced backing onto the top of the elevator while his helper, who was then facing him, carried the other end. While in this position, the two men could not see each other because the bookcase was between them. Decedent crossed over the center beams and set his end of the bookcase down. The helper then pulled the bookcase out of the elevator shaft only to discover that decedent had disappeared. Decedent was found at the bottom of the adjoining elevator shaft. Five days later he died from his injuries.

One of decedent's shoes with its heel torn loose was [offered] into evidence on the theory that it provided a basis for an inference that decedent's heel had caught on the inch-high angle iron around the edge of the elevator, and that as a proximate result thereof he was caused to trip and plunge to his death.

(2) *Critique the Decision about the Heelless Shoe.* This problem is based on *Standafer v. First Nat'l Bank of Minneapolis*, 52 N.W.2d 718 (Minn. 1952). The evidence was admitted by the trial judge, and there was a verdict for the plaintiff. Defendant appealed the admission of the shoe. The Supreme Court of Minnesota held:

> One of decedent's shoes with its heel torn loose was admitted into evidence on the theory that it provided a basis for an inference that decedent's heel had caught on the inch-high angle iron around the edge of the elevator, and that as a proximate result thereof he was caused to trip and plunge to his death. Another theory which is at least equally persuasive is that the heel was torn loose by striking some structural object in the course of the fall of decedent's body to the bottom of the shaft. Circumstantial evidence which justifies not only an inference in support of the verdict but with equal consistency justifies a nonsupporting inference of equal persuasive weight is inadmissible, in that a jury may not base its conclusions upon mere conjecture. . . . Clearly, it was error to admit the shoe into evidence. . . . Although it was error to admit . . . the shoe . . . , it is difficult, in the light of the entire evidence, to perceive that any prejudice could have resulted.

Was the decision that the shoe should have been excluded (a) right for the right reasons, (b) right for the wrong reasons, or (c) wrong? Could the court's test serve as an accurate statement of the test for the sufficiency of evidence to make a question for the jury? Is this the same thing as admissibility?

(3) *Love Letters.* The prosecution, in a murder case, wishes to introduce, as its first piece of evidence, letters by the defendant to the victim's spouse proclaiming

defendant's love for the spouse. Under the test articulated by *Standafer* in the problem immediately *supra*, could this be done?

(4) *Attempted Suicide.* Defendant, charged with a crime, attempts to commit suicide while in jail awaiting trial. This fact is offered by the prosecution as evidence at trial. (a) Is it relevant? (b) Is it admissible? (c) Is it sufficient for conviction?

Can you answer problem (4) (a) or (b) without more facts? What facts would you like to know, and why would they make a difference? On attempted suicide as evidence of guilt, see, for example, *State v. Lawrence*, 146 S.E. 395 (N.C. 1929).

(5) *Statistics.* Assume you are living in the late 1940s. You must prove that a certain car that passed by a certain crossing at a certain moment was black. To do this, you wish to adduce proof that 60 percent of all cars are black. Is this proof relevant? Is it sufficient proof that the car was black? For a more detailed discussion of statistics, see § 6.07.

§ 2.02 FORMALISTIC LOGIC (UTILIZED BY SOME TO DETERMINE RELEVANCE)

(1) *Syllogism.* A syllogism is a logical construct consisting of a major premise, a minor premise, and a conclusion (in that order). "All emeralds are green; this object is an emerald; therefore, this object is green." Syllogism is a method of "deductive" logic (see below), and its argument is valid only if the premises are true and syllogistic in form. In particular, the major premise must be absolute rather than probabilistic (for example, the conclusion would not be valid if the premise were "*some* emeralds are green," as opposed to "all"), and the premises must be true (the argument would be fallacious if it were inaccurate to state that all emeralds are green, or that this object is an emerald).

(2) *Use of Syllogism in Legal Reasoning: The So-Called "IRAC" Method is Syllogistic.* A great deal of reasoning used in the law is syllogistic. For example, statements of legal principles, definitions of crimes or claims, statutes and rules typically are major premises in legal reasoning. Thus, in scrutinizing a criminal homicide under the Model Penal Code, one might set forth (1) a major premise: "the elements of murder under § 210 are present when a person causes the death of another human being recklessly under circumstances manifesting extreme indifference to the value of human life;" (2) a minor premise: "this defendant is a person who caused the death of another human being, the victim, by driving 100 miles per hour in a school zone and thus recklessly under circumstances manifesting extreme indifference to the value of human life;" and (3) a conclusion: "the elements of murder under the Model Penal Code are present."

(3) *Fallacy Arising from Defective Premises or Inaccurate Syllogism Form.* Such logic lends itself to numerous possibilities of fallacy. For example, if the homicide described above were subject to the defense of insanity, it would not be a Model Penal Code murder; the major premise really can be stated only as that "some" such incidents are murder. Further, the defendant can be convicted only if the minor premise is true; as stated above, the factual analysis omits requirements such as proof beyond a reasonable doubt and the use of properly admitted evidence.

Finally, it is possible to introduce fallacy by manipulation of the syllogistic form: "All fish can swim, John can swim, therefore, John is a fish." This last example has superficial resemblances to deductive logic, but it mixes unpersuasive analogy with a nonsyllogism.

(4) *Analogy.* Analogy is a form of reasoning in which one thing is inferred to be similar to another thing in a certain respect, on the basis of known similarities in other respects. In short, if the controlling or most important aspect of the thing is the same, the inference is that the characterization is the same. Whereas the syllogistic form produces uniformly valid deductive logic, analogy does not. It is "fuzzier." For example, an analogy is useful only if we pick out the correct aspects of the known subject on which to build the analogy. Thus, the argument that John is a fish because he is like a fish in that he can swim is a species of analogic argument, but not a persuasive one. On the other hand, analogy can be a powerful device: "If it has feathers like a duck, quacks like a duck, walks like a duck, and sports a bill like a duck, it must *be* a duck." The usefulness of such reasoning is offset by the need to avoid confusing it with the universal validity of syllogistic logic, and it is readily manipulated by the selection of characteristics on which to base the analogy.

(5) *Use of Analogy in Legal Reasoning.* Legal reasoning includes heavy use of analogy, just as it does of syllogism. "Newspapers are protected by the First Amendment; radio is like newspapers in the relevant aspects; therefore, radio is protected by the First Amendment exactly as are newspapers." This analogy might be valid for many propositions, such as the illegality of government censorship of truthful matters of public concern on the radio, *see CBS, Inc. v. Democratic Nat'l Comm.*, 412 U.S. 94 (1973), but it would falsely predict other propositions, such as the obligation to publish a reply to a personal attack, which exists in broadcast media but not print. *Compare Red Lion Broadcasting Co. v. FCC*, 395 U.S. 367 (1969) (broadcasters can be required to allow reply to personal attack), *with Miami Herald Pub. Co. v. Tornillo*, 418 U.S. 241 (1974) (newspaper may not be required to print such a reply). In fact, the entire process of applying, distinguishing, and evolving case law, the endeavor that consumes most of law school, is heavily reliant on analogy.

(6) *"Deductive" Logic as Contrasted with "Inductive" Reasoning.* "Deductive" logic is a process in which the conclusion follows necessarily from the premises presented. Thus a properly constructed syllogism, based on premises that are true, leads to a necessarily accurate conclusion. (One may hypothesize a dreamland or parallel universe in which syllogisms do not hold, but short of that assumption, the conclusion is due absolute confidence.) "Induction," on the other hand, refers to any form of reasoning in which the conclusion, though supported by the argument, does not follow from it as a matter of necessity. Thus, analogy is a form of induction. The term also applies to the use of observations about samples as evidence for a proposition about the whole class of things from which the sample is taken. "The average temperature in Michigan has been colder every year that we know of during December than in July. Therefore, inductive logic tells us that during this coming year, December in Michigan probably again will be colder than July."

(7) *Scientific Method as Inductive; Validity.* Sometimes inductive reasoning merits a high level of confidence. Our knowledge of the law of gravity, for example, is based on induction, but we are sure enough of it to know, at a high level of certainty, what will happen if someone jumps off the Empire State Building. The scientific method is dependent on induction. In fact, some definitions of science rely on verification by experiment, which is to say, on proof by induction.

(8) *The Problem of Inductive Reasoning: Bertrand Russell's Chicken.* But induction is only generalization from experience, and it is vulnerable to fallacy. Improper sampling techniques, mischaracterization of evidentiary facts, and the like can result in fallacious conclusions. One famous illustration, attributed to Bertrand Russell, hypothesizes a chicken who has been fed by a farmer every day of his life, and who confidently runs to greet the farmer with the expectation of food; but one day, instead, the farmer wrings the chicken's neck (which, after all, is the purpose of chickens). Russell's blunt conclusion: "It would have been better for the chicken if its inductive inferences had been less crude." Indeed, if the chicken had adopted a different sampling technique, it would have learned that a large percentage of its fellows have been killed by the humans who fed them, giving rise to the inductive insight that confidence in one's human guardian is unjustified if you are a chicken. More broadly, Russell's example shows why it is hazardous to repose excessive confidence in any method of inductive logic.

(9) *Mixing Inductive and Deductive Logic.* History has never disclosed an instance of two different individuals with identical fingerprints. As a matter of inductive logic, we therefore tend to infer that all occurrences of an individual's fingerprint demonstrate the presence of that identified individual. On the basis of this inductively created major premise, coupled with the minor premise that the defendant's fingerprint was found on the murder weapon, we infer as a matter of deductive logic that the defendant touched the murder weapon.

But this series of logical arguments, as in virtually all such complex chains, is vulnerable. What are the sources of error in the deduction of the major premise that all fingerprints show the presence of the person to whom they belong? What possibilities of error inhere in the minor premise, that this particular item of evidence is the defendant's fingerprint?

§ 2.03 THE COUNTERWEIGHTS[2]

Read Federal Rule of Evidence 403, "Excluding Relevant Evidence for Prejudice, Confusion, Waste of Time, or Other Reasons."

[A] The Structure and Operation of Rule 403

(1) *Rule 403 as "The Great Override."* Fed. R. Evid. 403 is the workhorse of the Federal Rules of Evidence. No matter how one reads them, Fed. R. Evid. 401 and 402 admit a massive amount of marginal evidence, a great deal of which ought to be excluded. Fed. R. Evid. 403, which has been called the "great override," is the most important tool that enables the trial judge to do this job.

---

[2] Study Guide Reference: Evidence in a Nutshell, Chapter 3:II.

(2) *An Unevenly Weighted Balancing Test, Loaded in Favor of Admissibility.* Notice, however, that even Fed. R. Evid. 403 is written in language that favors admissibility. Evidence is not excluded under Fed. R. Evid. 403 unless counterweights, such as prejudice or confusion, "substantially outweigh" the probative value. What happens if the prejudice and the probative value are equal? (The evidence is admissible.) What if the prejudice exceeds the probative value, but only by a small amount (rather than "substantially")? Under the literal terms of the Rule, the evidence still is admissible. It often is said that the Federal Rules of Evidence express a policy of liberal admissibility, and even Fed. R. Evid. 403 favors "letting it in."

(3) *Weighing Prejudice Against Probative Value. United States v. Robinson*, 560 F.2d 507 (2d Cir. 1977) (en banc), *cert. denied*, 435 U.S. 905 (1978), held that on a charge of armed robbery, evidence of the defendant's possession at the time of arrest of a weapon similar to that indicated by independent evidence to have been possessed by him at the time of his participation in the alleged crime may be introduced, and that the district court's admission of the evidence should not be disturbed for abuse of discretion in the absence of a showing that the trial judge acted arbitrarily or irrationally, which he did not, the court said. The dissent observed that:

> Without evidence that Robinson was in possession of a gun at the time of his arrest (because the trial judge in the exercise of his discretion excluded it), there was a hung jury in the first trial. With such evidence (admitted by another trial judge in the exercise of his discretion), it still took a second Allen charge [i.e., an instruction to a deadlocked jury urging them to come to a conclusion] and further deliberation to move the second jury to vote for conviction. One is led to infer that the testimony as to possession of the gun made a crucial difference (despite limiting instructions).
>
> Before the balancing process mandated by Fed. R. Evid. 403 can begin, the court must determine that the evidence in issue is "relevant," as that term is defined in Rule 401. The relevancy test of Rule 401 is an extremely modest one. Since the bank robbers had carried guns, evidence of appellant's later possession of a gun does meet the rule's test of having "any tendency" to make appellant's participation in the robbery "more probable". . . .
>
> Once evidence is deemed relevant, the trial court must then weigh carefully its probative value against the danger of unfair prejudice that evidence creates. . . .
>
> We recognized in *United States v. Ravich* that "[t]he length of the chain of inferences necessary to connect the evidence with the ultimate fact to be proved necessarily lessens the probative value of the evidence." Here the "chain of inferences" contained two tenuous links. First, from appellant's possession of a .38 ten weeks after the robbery, the jury would have had to infer that he possessed a .38 at the time of the robbery, when he might just as well have purchased the gun in the interval between the robbery and his arrest. Second, even assuming that appellant, along with thousands of other

> New Yorkers, possessed a .38 on the date of the robbery, and assuming that a .38 was actually used in the robbery, the jury would then have had somehow to infer that appellant's undistinctive .38 was the .38 used in the robbery. This inference was highly problematic on the facts of the case, since no evidence was introduced linking appellant's gun to the robbery. With two such difficult inferences to be overcome, the probative value of the testimony that appellant possessed a .38 ten weeks after the robbery must be characterized as slight.
>
> I believe that this slight probative value "is substantially outweighed by the danger of unfair prejudice." Fed. R. Evid. 403. The danger is that such inflammatory evidence may distract the jury from the question of guilt or innocence of a specific crime, leading it to return a conviction not because the defendant committed a particular robbery, but rather in order to punish him for carrying a gun or for being an unsavory character.
>
> The trial court's limiting instruction here was directed at dispelling this danger, but, in my view, was inadequate for this purpose. It mentioned the proper use of the gun evidence, the identification purpose, only once and did not mention any of the intermediate inferences necessary to connect the gun evidence to appellant's identity as a robber, e.g., whether appellant had the gun on the date of the robbery. Moreover, as Judge Mansfield has recently noted, certain types of evidence are likely to be used "improperly" by a jury, "notwithstanding instructions." [*Cf.*] *United States v. Puco*, (2d Cir. 1971). . . .

(4) *Further Example of Weighing Prejudice Against Probative Value: Admissibility of After-the-Fact Evidence in "Reasonable Appearances" Determinations.* In *Sherrod v. Berry*, 856 F.2d 802 (7th Cir. 1988), the court reversed a $1.6 million dollar verdict in a civil rights action because the trial judge admitted evidence that the shooting victim was found to be unarmed after he was shot and killed by a police officer, which evidence the appeals court deemed irrelevant to the determination of the objective reasonableness of the officer's conduct under the circumstances at the time of the officer's action:

> [W]e are convinced that the objective reasonableness standard requires that Officer Berry's liability be determined exclusively upon an examination and weighing of the information Officer Berry possessed immediately prior to and at the very moment he fired the fatal shot.

Is evidence that Sherrod was unarmed (information not available to Officer Berry) irrelevant? Or does it tend to induce the trier of fact to premise its ultimate determination of liability on an improper basis: namely, to infer from the fact that Sherrod was unarmed that Officer Berry's use of his weapon was unreasonable?

(5) *Further Example: Conclusory Opinions in Reports.* Regarding Fed. R. Evid. 403, *see also Pollard v. Metropolitan Life Ins. Co.*, 598 F.2d 1284 (3d Cir. 1979) (word "accidental" should be excluded from coroner's and other reports in life insurance suit where accidental nature of death is the issue; jury would be misled into thinking reports were based on complete investigation and that they dealt with precisely same issue as case and were legally binding.

(6) *Other Rule 403 Issues. See also United States v. Zipkin*, 729 F.2d 384 (6th Cir. 1984) (appellate review of trial court's decision under Fed. R. Evid. 403 is limited; appellate court "must look at the evidence in the light most favorable to its proponent, maximizing its probative value and minimizing its prejudicial effect"); *United States v. Petrov*, 747 F.2d 824 (2d Cir. 1984), *cert. denied*, 471 U.S. 1025 (1985) (in prosecution for mailing obscene material, trial court should have made basis for admission and exclusion of evidence clear on record; this is particularly so in Fed. R. Evid. 403 decisions); *United States v. Anderson*, 575 F. Supp. 31 (S.D.N.Y. 1983) (in criminal prosecution, where defendant claimed his tape-recorded statements were ambiguous and thus inadmissible, district court held these statements could be read to support "the inference of consciousness of guilt which in turn supports an inference of actual guilt;" that statements need not be unambiguous; that statements were just a factor to consider; also ambiguity is a matter of weight to be argued to jury).

As general authority for using Fed. R. Evid. 403 to exclude even probative evidence, see *United States v. Flenory*, 619 F.2d 301 (3d Cir. 1980), for the proposition that even eyewitness identification of a suspect, under certain circumstances, could be excluded under Fed. R. Evid. 403.

SPRINT/UNITED MANAGEMENT COMPANY v. MENDELSOHN

552 U.S. 379 (2008)

[Mendelsohn sued Sprint for age discrimination. Sprint filed a motion *in limine* to exclude the testimony of former employees, alleging discrimination by supervisors who had no role in the employment decision Mendelsohn challenged, on the ground that this evidence was irrelevant to the case's central issue, see Fed. Rules Evid. 401, 402, and unduly prejudicial, see Rule 403. The District Court granted the motion and excluded evidence of discrimination against those not "similarly situated" to Mendelsohn. The Tenth Circuit treated that order as applying a *per se* rule that evidence from employees of other supervisors is irrelevant in age discrimination cases, concluded that the District Court abused its discretion by relying on the Circuit's *Aramburu* case, determined that the evidence was relevant and not unduly prejudicial, and remanded for a new trial.]

[Here, the Supreme Court determines that the Tenth Circuit erred in concluding that the District Court applied a *per se* rule and thus improperly engaged in its own analysis of the relevant factors under Rules 401 and 403. The Court holds that the Tenth Circuit should have remanded the case for the District Court to clarify its ruling.]

. . . II

. . . A

In deference to a district court's familiarity with the details of the case and its greater experience in evidentiary matters, courts of appeals afford broad discretion to a district court's evidentiary rulings. This Court has acknowledged: "A district court is accorded a wide discretion in determining the admissibility of evidence under the Federal Rules. Assessing the probative value of [the proffered evidence], and weighing any factors counseling against admissibility is a matter first for the district court's sound judgment under Rules 401 and 403 . . . ." *United States v. Abel*, 469 U.S. 45, 54, 105 S.Ct. 465, 83 L.Ed.2d 450 (1984). This is particularly true with respect to Rule 403 since it requires an "on-the-spot balancing of probative value and prejudice, potentially to exclude as unduly prejudicial some evidence that already has been found to be factually relevant." *Old Chief v. United States*, 519 U.S. 172, 183, n. 7, 117 S.Ct. 644, 136 L.Ed.2d 574 (1997).

Here, however, the Court of Appeals did not accord the District Court the deference we have described as the "hallmark of abuse-of-discretion review." *General Elec. Co. v. Joiner*, 522 U.S. 136, 143, 118 S.Ct. 512, 139 L.Ed.2d 508 (1997). Instead, it reasoned that the District Court had "erroneous[ly] conclu[ded] that *Aramburu* controlled the fate of the evidence in this case." 466 F.3d, at 1230, n. 4. [In that decision, *Aramburu*, the Tenth Circuit had held that certain kinds of allegedly discriminatory acts by different supervisors were not relevant in a case alleging discrimination by a particular supervisor, but *Arambaru* had involved a different kind of alleged discrimination.]

. . . [T]he District Court's discussion of the evidence neither cited *Aramburu* nor gave any other indication that its decision relied on that case. The minute order included only two sentences discussing the admissibility of the evidence: "Plaintiff may offer evidence of discrimination against Sprint employees who are similarly situated to her. 'Similarly situated employees,' for the purpose of this ruling, requires proof that (1) Paul Ruddick *[sic]* was the decision-maker in any adverse employment action; and (2) temporal proximity." Contrary to the Court of Appeals' conclusion, these sentences include no analysis suggesting that the District Court applied a *per se* rule excluding this type of evidence. . . .

When a district court's language is ambiguous, as it was here, it is improper for the court of appeals to presume that the lower court reached an incorrect legal conclusion. A remand directing the district court to clarify its order is generally permissible and would have been the better approach in this case.

B

In the Court of Appeals' view, the District Court excluded the evidence as *per se* irrelevant, and so had no occasion to reach the question whether such evidence, if relevant, should be excluded under Rule 403. The Court of Appeals, upon concluding that such evidence was not *per se* irrelevant, decided that it was relevant in the circumstances of this case and undertook its own balancing under Rule 403. But questions of relevance and prejudice are for the District Court to determine in the first instance. *Abel, supra*, at 54, 105 S.Ct. 465 ("Assessing the probative value of [evidence], and weighing any factors counseling against admissibility is a matter first for the district court's sound judgment under Rules 401 and 403 . . ."). . . .

We note that, had the District Court applied a *per se* rule excluding the evidence, the Court of Appeals would have been correct to conclude that it had abused its discretion. Relevance and prejudice under Rules 401 and 403 are determined in the context of the facts and arguments in a particular case, and thus are generally not amenable to broad *per se* rules. See Advisory Committee's Notes on Fed. Rule Evid. 401, 28 U.S.C.App., p. 864 ("Relevancy is not an inherent characteristic of any item of evidence but exists only as a relation between an item of evidence and a matter properly provable in the case"). But, as we have discussed, there is no basis in the record for concluding that the District Court applied a blanket rule.

III

The question whether evidence of discrimination by other supervisors is relevant in an individual ADEA case is fact based and depends on many factors, including how closely related the evidence is to the plaintiff's circumstances and theory of the case. Applying Rule 403 to determine if evidence is prejudicial also requires a fact-intensive, context-specific inquiry. Because Rules 401 and 403 do not make such evidence *per se* admissible or *per se* inadmissible, and because the inquiry required by those Rules is within the province of the District Court in the first instance, we vacate the judgment of the Court of Appeals and remand the case with instructions to have the District Court clarify the basis for its evidentiary ruling under the applicable Rules. [Vacated and Remanded.]

[B] Rule 403 Provides Judicial Options other than Admissibility/Inadmissibility

UNITED STATES v. JACKSON

United States District Court, Eastern District of New York
405 F. Supp. 938 (1975)

WEINSTEIN, DISTRICT JUDGE.

Defendant, accused of robbing a bank at gunpoint, has made pretrial motions for advance rulings that evidence that he used a false name on being arrested in Georgia shortly after the robbery is inadmissible because its probative value is outweighed by the risk of unfair prejudice.

Rule 403 of the Federal Rules of Evidence grants discretion to exclude relevant evidence in the interest of preventing unfair prejudice to a party. . . .

Defendant's motion raises a complex Rule 403 question, rich in factual nuances. The bank robbery took place on August 28, 1971 [in New York]. Defendant was arrested in Georgia on November 7, 1971. Stopped for a traffic check, defendant had no license but did have false identification. The defendant was arrested for driving without a license. Guns were found in the car. Subsequently, defendant escaped from the local jail.

Presence in another jurisdiction is arguably proof of flight resulting from consciousness of guilt. Use of a false name increases the probative force of this circumstantial line of proof.

Because a person may leave a jurisdiction for any number of innocent reasons, courts are often reluctant to admit evidence of flight.

The probability the defendant left New York to escape arrest for the bank robbery is somewhat reduced by the fact that at the time of his departure he had been indicted by the state for assault. It seems improbable, however, that if he were fleeing it was from the earlier assault since the indictment had been handed up in July, 1971, and the evidence will apparently show that the defendant remained in New York until just after the bank robbery in August.

The probative value of defendant's conduct is heightened by the posture of the government's proof. It is apparent that the surveillance photographs and the eye-witness testimony are not likely to make out a completely positive identification of defendant. The government, therefore, has legitimate need for corroborative value.

The other side of the coin under Rule 403 is the possibility that defendant will be unfairly prejudiced. The Georgia patrolman's testimony will acquaint the jury with the fact of defendant's unrelated arrest and surrounding uncomplimentary circumstances. This revelation will necessarily impinge on the protective policy of Rule 404(b) of the Federal Rules of Evidence which excludes other crimes when their primary use is to show generalized propensity to violate the law. Even if the fact that defendant and his companions were heavily armed and subsequently escaped from the local Georgia jail were concealed, the jury might well infer from the Georgia events that defendant was engaged in a nation-wide crime spree. Beyond all this, the government's argument — flight, therefore guilty mind respecting the bank robbery, therefore guilt of the robbery — cannot be fairly evaluated without revelation of the [New York] state court indictment. This would acquaint the jury with the assault incident.

In sum, the government's offer of proof entails the risk that unrelated crimes will be brought to the attention of the jury. At the very least, the jury might well be confused if it is called upon to resolve conflicting interpretations of what is essentially a collateral event. The question of whether the risk of inaccurate fact-finding by the jury will be increased more by reception than by exclusion of the evidence is thus a close one.

Still other considerations must be accorded some weight in determining admissibility under Rule 403. Among these is the delay in the completion of the trial which will necessarily be occasioned by the calling of at least one additional witness, the patrolman, who may be subjected to extended cross-examination. . . .

With the evidentiary and pertinent policy considerations in such an ambiguous posture, it is apparent that a ruling that the government's proof is either wholly admissible or wholly inadmissible would not be completely satisfactory. Accordingly, we hold that the evidence relating to defendant's arrest in Georgia will be inadmissible at trial, provided that defendant enter into a stipulation to the effect that he was in Georgia shortly after the robbery and that while there he used a false name.

[A] conditional ruling of this sort is justified by Rule 102 of the Federal Rules of Evidence. Rule 403, read in the light of Rule 102, contemplates a flexible scheme of discretionary judgments by trial courts designed to minimize the evidentiary costs of protecting parties from unfair prejudice. Conditioning exclusion of proof of the arrest upon the entry of a stipulation is a practical solution to the problem here. Elimination of all references to the Georgia apprehension effectively removes the risk that the jury will perceive the defendant as a national crime figure. At the same time, the stipulation will afford the jury a concrete basis for the inference that defendant left New York to escape capture for the bank robbery.

NOTE

Creative Opportunities for Counsel. As it did for the judge in this case, Fed. R. Evid. 403 also provides some creative opportunities for counsel. *See, e.g., Old Chief v. United States*, 519 U.S. 172 (1997) (offer of defense counsel to stipulate in order to preclude prosecution from introducing evidence of nature of prior conviction; discussed in § 3.01[C]).

[C] Some Potential Limits on Rule 403

BALLOU v. HENRI STUDIOS, INC.

United States Court of Appeals, Fifth Circuit
656 F.2d 1147 (1981)

Williams, Circuit Judge.

On the afternoon of June 14, 1977, an automobile struck the rear of an eighteen-wheel tractor-trailer which was parked entirely on the right hand shoulder of a curved, divided highway in Beaumont, Texas. The driver of the car, Jesse Ballou, was killed instantly; Ballou's sole passenger, twelve-year-old Leonard Herman Clay, died two days later. The plaintiffs — Yolanda Ballou and Terrence Ballou, the children of Jesse Ballou, and Lula Mae LeBlanc, the mother of Leonard Herman Clay — filed this diversity suit [in federal district court] against Appellant Henri Studios, Inc., alleging that the deaths of Jesse Ballou and Leonard Herman Clay were proximately caused by the negligence of Henri Studios' employee, John Woelfel, the driver of the truck. Henri Studios, inter alia, denied that Woelfel's conduct was negligent and asserted that the collision was caused by the negligence of the deceased driver of the car, Jesse Ballou.

Prior to trial, the plaintiffs filed a motion in limine seeking to prevent the introduction at trial of any evidence that Jesse Ballou was intoxicated at the time of the collision. Specifically, the motion in limine sought to exclude the results of a blood alcohol test performed by the Beaumont Regional Crime Laboratory upon a blood sample allegedly taken from the body of Ballou which reflected that his blood contained 0.24% alcohol by weight at the time of his death. On the day the trial of the case began, the district court held a hearing outside the presence of the jury on the issue whether the results of the blood alcohol test should be excluded from evidence at trial. After hearing argument and testimony, the district court sustained the motion in limine and ruled the results of the blood test inadmissible.

[Henri Studios claims] that the district court erred in excluding the results of the blood alcohol test.

[T]he plaintiffs presented two basic arguments for exclusion of the results of the blood test. First, they contended that the results of the blood test were inadmissible because the defense had failed to establish an adequate "chain of custody" for Ballou's body and the blood sample, and had failed to show that adequate precautions had been taken to prevent the possibility of contamination of the blood sample. Second, the plaintiffs sought to refute the results of the blood test through proof that Ballou was not intoxicated at the time of the collision.

To support their claim that Ballou was not intoxicated, the plaintiffs first argued that the blood test was the only evidence of Ballou's intoxication at the time of the collision, noting that none of the persons who had come into contact with Ballou's body had noticed the presence of alcohol about his body. The plaintiffs then called to the stand Mrs. Eula Eisenhower, a registered nurse employed by Dr. Washburn, a Beaumont doctor whose office was located only a short distance from the site of the collision. Mrs. Eisenhower testified that on the afternoon of June 14, 1977, Jesse Ballou came to Dr. Washburn's office, accompanied by Leonard Herman Clay, to have some stitches removed from his hand. She testified that in removing the stitches she was eighteen inches from Ballou's face, and that Ballou did not have alcohol on his breath and did not act intoxicated, and that she was positive that he was not intoxicated. She also stated that due to experience with alcoholism in her family, she was familiar with the smell of alcohol. According to Mrs. Eisenhower, Ballou left Dr. Washburn's office at 2:30 p.m. The police report of the collision listed the time of the arrival of the officers at the scene of the wreck at 2:40 p.m.; by that time, Ballou's body had already been taken to the hospital. Finally, the plaintiffs introduced a portion of the deposition of Jim Middleton, the chemist who performed the blood alcohol test, in which Middleton testified that it would probably take at least one hour of steady consumption of alcohol in order for a person to reach a blood alcohol level of 0.24%.

In response to the plaintiffs' arguments, Henri Studios outlined the chain of events leading from the removal of Ballou's body from his automobile through the chemist's analysis of one of the samples of his blood, describing in some detail the chain of custody of Ballou's body and the blood samples. In addition, counsel outlined the procedures pursuant to which the blood samples were labeled and one of the samples analyzed by the chemist. Finally, the defendant noted the chemist's deposition testimony that the test results indicated Ballou was grossly intoxicated at the time of the collision and that such a level of intoxication would greatly impede Ballou's ability to drive his car safely.

After hearing the foregoing argument and testimony, the district judge sustained the motion in limine [and thereby excluded the evidence].

After Henri Studios objected to the court's ruling, the court granted it permission to supplement the record for purposes of appeal with additional testimony concerning the blood samples and the blood alcohol test.

During the trial, plaintiffs introduced the deposition testimony of the ambulance driver and the emergency medical technician (EMT) who transported Ballou's body to the hospital and from the hospital to the funeral home. The EMT testified that

Ballou had no perceptible vital signs by the time his body was placed in the ambulance. Both the ambulance driver and the EMT testified that Ballou had been given no drugs, injections, oxygen or anesthetics, and that his body had not been bathed in alcohol or any substance with an alcohol base. The plaintiffs then introduced the deposition testimony of the doctor who examined Ballou in the emergency room of the hospital. The doctor testified that Ballou was dead on arrival at the hospital at 3:00 p.m., and that he was given no drugs or medication at the hospital. The doctor did not know whether Ballou's body was cleaned or swabbed in any manner before it was transported to the funeral home, but he noted that Ballou's hospital records contained no indication that his body had been cleaned.

After the defendant rested its case and outside the presence of the jury, Henri Studios proffered the testimony of the police officer who supervised the taking of the blood samples, the chemist who performed the blood alcohol test, and the mortician who took the blood samples. Officer Frank Coffin, a detective with the Beaumont Police Department, testified that he personally observed the taking of the blood samples from Ballou's body. Coffin testified that before Ballou's blood was extracted, he visually inspected the blood sample vials and determined that the seal on the vials had not been broken. After the blood was extracted and placed in the vials, Coffin labeled the vials with Ballou's name. To insure that the blood in the vials was that of Jesse Ballou, Coffin photographed and took a fingerprint from the body from which the blood had been taken. Later, Coffin located Ballou's fingerprint card among those at the police station, compared it with the print taken from Ballou, and determined that the fingerprints taken from the body matched Ballou's file print. According to Coffin, the blood vials remained in his possession until he locked them in the evidence room at the police station for the evening. Coffin testified that the next morning he personally delivered the same vials of blood to either Bill McClain or Jim Middleton, both of whom were chemists in the crime laboratory, for analysis.

Jim Middleton testified that he was employed by the Beaumont Regional Crime Laboratory as a chemist, and that one of his duties was to perform analyses on various types of evidence brought into the laboratory for subsequent use in litigation. After testifying with respect to his qualifications as an expert, Middleton stated that officer Coffin had personally delivered two vials of blood to him at the crime laboratory on the morning of June 15, 1977. Middleton testified that a laboratory submission form was prepared for the vials, and that the vials were numbered pursuant to departmental procedures. He also stated that the seals on the vials had not been broken at the time they were received, and that the vials had been labeled by officer Coffin with Ballou's name. Middleton testified that he locked the vials in a refrigerated box until performing the chemical analysis on the blood on June 24, 1977. He stated that he checked the seals on the vials again before performing the blood alcohol test, and that they were not broken. According to Middleton, the ten-day period of refrigeration of the blood would not affect the results of the blood alcohol test since the vials contained anti-coagulant and preservative chemicals.

Middleton described in detail the procedures he used in analyzing the blood sample labeled and numbered as Ballou's. He stated that he was familiar with the chemicals and apparatus used, that the chemicals were properly mixed, and that the test was a scientifically accepted method for determining the level of ethyl alcohol in the bloodstream. He testified that in addition to the blood alcohol test, he ran a test to determine if there were any contaminants in the blood sample which could affect the test results, and that the test revealed that there were no such contaminants in the sample. Middleton testified that the results of the blood alcohol test showed that Ballou's blood contained 0.24% ethyl alcohol by weight, with a margin of error of plus or minus 0.01%. He also stated that a person with a blood alcohol content of 0.24% was grossly intoxicated, and that such a person could not safely operate a motor vehicle.

Finally, the defendant presented the deposition testimony of the mortician at the funeral home to which Ballou's body was taken from the hospital. The mortician testified that neither he nor the funeral home had kept any record of taking a blood sample from Ballou's body, and that he had no independent recollection of drawing blood from Ballou. Therefore, the mortician testified only as to the procedures he generally utilized in drawing blood samples. According to the mortician, he normally used a dry scalpel to make an incision in a vein from which to draw blood, and that the scalpel was usually cleaned with a solution of formaldehyde and water. The mortician also stated that before taking a blood sample, he generally did not swab the area from which the blood sample would be taken with alcohol or start the embalming process. Finally, the mortician testified that although the general practice was for a police officer to bring the sealed vials to the funeral home on the day the blood sample was to be taken, occasionally officers would leave empty, sealed vials at the funeral home and on such occasions funeral home employees would have access to the vials.

After the defendant proffered this additional evidence, the district court again ruled the results of the blood alcohol test inadmissible. . . .

Under Rule 403 of the Federal Rules of Evidence, a district court may exclude evidence, even if relevant, "if its probative value is substantially outweighed by the danger of unfair prejudice." A trial court's ruling on admissibility under Rule 403's balancing test will not be overturned on appeal absent a clear abuse of discretion.

Although the district court neither stated with precision the grounds for its decision to exclude the results of the blood alcohol test nor specifically invoked Rule 403, the record clearly reveals that the court excluded the evidence because it believed that its prejudicial potential substantially outweighed its probative value. The court's comments also reveal that the court believed that the results of the blood alcohol test lacked "credibility." According to the court, its primary reason for determining that the test results lacked credibility was the testimony of Mrs. Eisenhower that Ballou was not intoxicated just a few minutes before the collision and Jim Middleton's testimony that it would probably take at least one hour of alcohol consumption to reach a blood alcohol level of 0.24%. But the court's comments also indicate that the court may have characterized the results of the blood test as lacking credibility out of concern that breaks in the "chain of custody" of Ballou's body and the blood samples had occurred or because of the possibility that the samples had been contaminated.

In challenging the exclusion, Henri Studios argues, inter alia, (1) that the court's decision to believe Mrs. Eisenhower's testimony rather than the results of the blood alcohol test constituted a credibility choice which should properly have been reserved for the jury; and (2) that an adequate showing was made with respect to the chain of custody and lack of contamination of Ballou's body and blood samples, and that therefore any evidence concerning possible breaks in the chain of custody or contamination go to the weight and not the admissibility of the evidence. Because we agree with both of these contentions, and in addition conclude as a matter of law that the potential for unfair prejudice of the blood alcohol test did not substantially outweigh its probative value, we hold that the exclusion of the results of the test was an abuse of discretion requiring a reversal of the judgment and a new trial.

Henri Studios' argument that the district court made an impermissible credibility choice in deciding to believe Mrs. Eisenhower's testimony rather than the results of the blood alcohol test is well taken. . . . Of course, since the court found that the test results lacked credibility, they were assigned little or no probative value in the Rule 403 balancing test, which ultimately led to their exclusion from evidence.

. . . [W]e have recently held that "Rule 403 does not permit exclusion of evidence because the judge does not find it credible." *United States v. Thompson*, 615 F.2d 329, 333 (5th Cir. 1980). "Weighing probative value against unfair prejudice under [Rule] 403 means probative value with respect to a material fact *if the evidence is believed, not the degree the court finds it believable.*" *Bowden v. McKenna*, 600 F.2d 282, 284-85 (1st Cir. 1979), *cert. denied*, 444 U.S. 899 (1979) (footnote omitted and emphasis added). . . .

In our view, the district court also erred in declaring that the test results were not credible (and therefore assigning them little or no probative value) due to concerns regarding possible breaks in the "chain of custody" or contamination of Ballou's body or the blood samples. It is firmly established in this Circuit that the question whether the proponent of evidence has proved an adequate chain of custody goes to the weight rather than the admissibility of the evidence, and is thus reserved for the jury. Likewise, the issue of alteration, contamination or adulteration of the evidence is a question for the jury once the proponent of the evidence makes a threshold showing that reasonable precautions were taken against the risk of alteration, contamination or adulteration. The proponent of the evidence "need not rule out every conceivable chance that somehow the identity or character of the evidence underwent change. So long as the court is persuaded that as a matter of normal likelihood the evidence has been adequately safeguarded, the jury should be permitted to consider and assess it in light of the surrounding circumstances." *[United States v.] Lane* [591 F.2d 961 (D.C. Cir. 1979)]. . . . Under Fed. R. Evid 901, once the proponent of the evidence meets the threshold requirement of showing that "in reasonable probability the article has not been changed in any important respect from its original condition," *United States v. Albert*, 595 F.2d 283 (5th Cir. 1979), *cert. denied*, 444 U.S. 963, any doubts raised concerning the possibility of alteration or contamination of the evidence go to the weight and not the admissibility of the evidence.

[We] hold that Henri Studios made the necessary threshold showing that reasonable precautions were taken against the risk of alteration or contamination of Ballou's body and the blood samples. It necessarily follows that the court's doubts concerning an adequate "chain of custody" and possible contamination of the blood samples were not appropriate bases for its assignment of low probative value to the evidence.

The question remains whether the test results, when properly taken as true, have a potential for unfair prejudice that substantially outweighs their probative value. We hold as a matter of law that the potential for unfair prejudice of the test results does not substantially outweigh their probative value.

The results of the blood alcohol test indicate that Ballou was intoxicated at the time of the collision. Proof of Ballou's intoxication is, of course, highly relevant to and probative of one of the ultimate questions before the jury — Ballou's contributory negligence — and would doubtless have a major effect on the jury's apportionment of fault. On the other hand, in our view the potential prejudice of the test results is comparatively slight. As this court has consistently held, " 'unfair prejudice' as used in Rule 403 is not to be equated with testimony simply adverse to the opposing party. Virtually all evidence is prejudicial or it isn't material. The prejudice must be 'unfair.' ". . . Unfair prejudice within the context of Rule 403 "means an undue tendency to suggest [a] decision on an improper basis, commonly, though not necessarily, an emotional one." Notes of the Advisory Committee. . . . While there is a slight possibility that evidence of Ballou's intoxication might adversely affect the jury's deliberation on issues other than Ballou's contributory negligence, this slight potential for unfair prejudice is virtually insignificant when compared with the high relevance and probative value of the evidence. We therefore conclude that the district court committed reversible error in excluding the results of the blood test. . . .

NOTE

Should Credibility be Factored into Prejudice Analysis? Do you agree with the general proposition of this case that credibility considerations should not be part of the judge's determination of whether probativity outweighs prejudice, time consumption, misleadingness, etc.?

GULF STATES UTILITIES CO. v. ECODYNE CORP.

United States Court of Appeals, Fifth Circuit
577 F.2d 1031 (1978)

CHARLES CLARK, CIRCUIT JUDGE.

Gulf States brought suit against Ecodyne claiming that Ecodyne had negligently designed the [cooling] towers and had negligently selected the materials used in constructing the towers, which acts of negligence were claimed to have been the cause of the failure of Tower A. The district judge held that Gulf States had failed to carry its burden of proof regarding the cause of the structural failure. Judgment was accordingly rendered for Ecodyne.

During the course of [this] bench trial, Gulf States attempted to prove that similar towers built by Ecodyne had experienced similar structural failures. Gulf States also offered a copy of a complaint filed by Ecodyne in the Superior Court of

California, against the California Redwood Association, et al., Ecodyne's supplier of redwood. That complaint alleged that the redwood supplied to Ecodyne was inferior in quality and that misrepresentations were made to Ecodyne regarding the quality of the redwood. The allegations strongly implied that the cause of failures of several towers built by Ecodyne, including Tower A built for Gulf States, was the failure of the wood to meet specifications. Gulf States makes the same allegations against Ecodyne in the instant case. As the district judge recognized, this evidence was relevant under Fed. R. Evid. 401. The district judge refused to admit the proof of the other failures and the California complaint into evidence on the ground that, although relevant, the evidence was inadmissible under Fed. R. Evid. 403. The district judge reasoned that the evidence would be prejudicial to a jury and that since he would not let a jury hear the evidence, he should not hear it in a bench trial.

The exclusion of this evidence under Rule 403's weighing of probative value against prejudice was improper. This portion of Rule 403 has no logical application to bench trials. Excluding relevant evidence in a bench trial because it is cumulative or a waste of time is clearly a proper exercise of the judge's power, but excluding relevant evidence on the basis of "unfair prejudice" is a useless procedure. Rule 403 assumes a trial judge is able to discern and weigh the improper inferences that a jury might draw from certain evidence, and then balance those improprieties against probative value and necessity. Certainly, in a bench trial, the same judge can also exclude those improper inferences from his mind in reaching a decision. The significant question is whether the trial judge's action here produces an error or defect that affected substantial rights of Gulf States. The judge heard the offer of proof but said he would not consider this evidence in making his factual determinations. We have no choice but to believe him. He is trained to recognize and to exclude those matters which the rules of evidence require be discarded. Indeed, in this very case the trial judge acknowledged the possibility that this court might disagree with his ruling and direct him to consider this evidence. That possibility has now materialized. The major policy underlying the harmless error rule is to preserve judgments and avoid waste of time. Discarding a jury's verdict is extremely wasteful. Requiring a district judge to examine more evidence and reevaluate his decision is not nearly so prodigal.

We vacate the judgment of the district court and remand the case for further proceedings, leaving to the district court's discretion determination of what further hearings or proceedings are necessary upon remand.

UNITED STATES v. KNIGHT

United States Court of Appeals, Third Circuit
700 F.3d 59 (2012)

Roth, Circuit Judge:

. . . On May 12, 2008, Amon Thomas and Shadrock Frett engaged in a violent gun fight at Frett's apartment in St. Croix, United States Virgin Islands. Both men sustained gunshot wounds which resulted in their hospitalization at Juan Luis Hospital in St. Croix. Thomas, less severely injured than Frett, was discharged on May 16, 2008. Five days later, on May 21, 2008, at approximately 3:50 a.m., six masked gunmen entered the hospital, located Frett, and shot him to death.

A police investigation revealed that the gunmen entered the hospital through an employee entrance with the benefit of an employee "swipe card," proceeded directly to Frett's room, committed the murder, and left in under three minutes. Based on these circumstances, investigators suspected that a hospital employee may have been involved in the crime in some capacity. They examined the hospital's electronic patient records system, which showed that Knight, an admissions clerk, had accessed Frett's records at 7:24 p.m. on May 20, 2008, just hours before he was killed. Investigators subsequently obtained Knight's cell phone records, which indicated that she had telephone conversations with Thomas's brother, Halik Milligan, at 7 p.m. and 7:30 p.m. that same evening.

On January 26, 2009, Thomas Drummond, a special agent from the Federal Bureau of Investigation, and Dino Herbert, an officer of the Virgin Islands Police Department, jointly interviewed Knight about the hospital shooting. During her questioning, Knight stated to the investigators that she had no prior knowledge that someone would enter the hospital and kill Frett. She claimed that she did not know Frett's room number on May 20, 2008, and that she did not remember accessing the hospital's records system to ascertain it that night. She admitted that Milligan was her boyfriend but denied that she had any phone conversations with him on May 20th. She further stated that she never disclosed Frett's room number to anyone.

The following day, January 27, 2009, Herbert and Drummond obtained a warrant and arrested Knight for making false statements to a federal agent. . . . They again questioned her, but this time confronted her with her cell phone records . . . and with a printout from the hospital's records system. . . . Faced with this evidence, Knight admitted that, prior to May 20, 2008, Milligan had asked her whether she could obtain Frett's room number and that she informed him that she could. . . .

[Knight later claimed that these admissions were coerced, and she testified in a manner that resulted in three perjury charges. She also was charged with conspiracy to murder Frett but was acquitted of this charge.] She was convicted, however, on the three perjury charges and sentenced to 36 months imprisonment. Knight now appeals, arguing that the District Court erred in . . . admitting irrelevant and unfairly prejudicial evidence pertaining to the May 12th shooting at Frett's apartment and the May 21st shooting at the hospital. . . . We will review the District Court's decision regarding the admissibility of evidence for abuse of discretion. . . .

. . . *Admission of Evidence Related to the May 12th & May 21st Shootings*

Prior to trial, Knight moved *in limine* to exclude evidence regarding both the gun battle between Frett and Thomas on May 12, 2008, and the subsequent killing of Frett on May 21, 2008, at the hospital. The motion was denied, and the jury heard evidence of both of these events. Knight contends on appeal that this evidence was irrelevant to the perjury charges and therefore should have been excluded under Rule 401 of the Federal Rules of Evidence. She further argues that even assuming its relevancy, the evidence was unfairly prejudicial and thus should have been excluded on the basis of Rule 403.

We conclude, however, that the evidence was not irrelevant to the perjury charges because it put into context why Knight was accessing Frett's hospital records and the nature of her relationship with Milligan and through him with Thomas. This inclusion of evidence of both shootings helped to explain why Knight committed perjury by lying about her access to the electronic hospital records and the reasons for that access.

Moreover, Knight's argument overlooks the fact that she was concurrently on trial for conspiracy to murder Frett. In order to establish her guilt on this charge, the government had to prove that she and at least one other person (1) intentionally entered into an agreement (2) with the purpose of killing Frett (3) with malice aforethought. . . . Any evidence that has a tendency to make this account more probable than it otherwise would be is relevant. *See* Fed. R. Evid. 401. Evidence related to the May 12th shooting at Frett's apartment is also relevant because it suggests a motive for the conspiracy to kill Frett and provides a link between that conspiracy and Knight.

Finally, we reject Knight's contention that evidence of these shootings should have been excluded on account of unfair prejudice. "Unfair prejudice means an undue tendency to suggest decision on an improper basis, commonly, though not necessarily, an emotional one." Fed R. Evid. (advisory committee's note). Relevant evidence may be excluded for this reason only if its "probative value is *substantially outweighed* by a danger of unfair prejudice." Fed. R. Evid. 403 (emphasis added). In determining whether evidence must be excluded as unfairly prejudicial, we owe "considerable deference" to the judgment of the District Court and we will not disturb its ruling unless it was "arbitrary or irrational." *United States v. Universal Rehab. Servs. Inc.*, 205 F.3d 657, 665 (3d Cir. 2000) (en banc). As we have outlined, evidence of both shootings was relevant to all the charges against Knight in significant ways. Knight contends, however, that this relevance is trumped by the risk that the evidence might have led the jury to convict her in order to punish someone for the shootings rather than because of a conclusion that she was guilty of perjury. We find no merit in this argument. With respect to the May 12th [earlier] shooting at Frett's apartment, Knight makes no claim that the Government alleged or even implied that she had any involvement, and we therefore see no risk that the jury would have sought to punish her for that incident. Regarding the May 21st hospital shooting, evidence of that shooting is critical to explain the perjury. Moreover, to the extent that the jury was motivated to convict Knight in order to punish someone for that shooting, it could have found her guilty on the conspiracy charge. We see no logic in Knight's argument that the jury would acquit her on the conspiracy charge but punish her for the underlying events by convicting her of perjury.

PROBLEM 2C: ADAMSON v. CALIFORNIA, 332 U.S. 46, 58–59 (1947).

Adamson was convicted of murder. The evidence included his fingerprint inside the victim's residence near a point of forced entry, his effort to sell a diamond ring after the murder, together with the fact that two diamond rings that the victim customarily wore were missing, and other incriminating circumstances. One item of evidence since has proved to be particularly controversial, although the United States Supreme Court analyzed it only briefly:

> Finally, appellant contends that due process of law was denied him by the introduction as evidence of tops of women's stockings that were found in his room. The claim is made that such evidence inflamed the jury. The lower part of a woman's stocking was found under the victim's body. The top was not found. The corpse was barelegged. The tops from defendant's room did not match the lower part found under the dead body. The California court held that the tops were admissible as evidence because this "interest in women's stocking tops is a circumstance that tends to identify defendant" as the perpetrator of the crime. We do not think the introduction of this evidence violated any federal constitutional right.

This decision was based on the Constitution, and it reflected only a conclusion that the evidence did not violate due process. The lower court had applied California's then-existing law of evidence.

(1) What analysis would control the trial judge's resolution of the issues of relevance and admissibility today, if the same silk stocking evidence were offered in a federal case identical to *Adamson*?

(2) Particularly consider how the trial judge today would treat the claim that the evidence "inflamed the jury."

(3) In addition, consider an arguable fact that the Supreme Court did not mention (or know): Adamson worked as a stevedore, and it then was common for stevedores of his ethnicity to wear stocking tops as head coverings, to hold back their hair and keep out dust and refuse. Does this factor affect the analysis or alter the result?

PROBLEM 2D: TAPES OF LONG-PAST 911 CALLS IN THE TRIAL OF O.J. SIMPSON: APPLYING RULE 403.

The day after he admitted Ronald Shipp's dream evidence in O.J. Simpson's murder trial (see problem in § 2.01, *above*), Judge Ito admitted the tapes of two 911 calls placed by an obviously frightened Nicole Simpson roughly five years and two years before the murders; in the latter, she described Simpson as "ranting and raving" with anger toward her (and he could be heard dramatically in the background, doing just that). *See* Freemantle, *Simpson Jury Hears 911 Call: Ex-Wife Says He's "Ranting, Raving" in 1993 Tape*, HOUS. CHRONICLE, Feb. 3, 1995, § A, at 1, col. 1.

(1) What reasoning process would a judge need to follow to analyze this evidence and to rule as Judge Ito did, if Fed. R. Evid. 401–403 were controlling? (Judge Ito actually applied the California Evidence Code, which is differently phrased but similar to the Federal Rules for these purposes.)

(2) Would it have made sense for the judge to exercise discretion to exclude any of these items?

PROBLEM SET 2E: ILLUMINATING THE JUDGE'S TASK IN DECIDING RELEVANCE AND COUNTERWEIGHTS

(1) *Polygraph Results: Are they Relevant, and if so, are they Admissible?* Even the lay public knows there is a general rule excluding results of polygraph examinations (or what colloquially are called lie-detector tests). But given Fed. R. Evid. 401's liberal standard, it seems clear that a polygraph examiner's opinion normally would be relevant, because it would have a "tendency" to make issues of consequence that depended on credibility appear more likely or less likely to be true. Why, then, are polygraph results generally excluded? Might there be some cases in which they properly could be admitted? *See* § 6.02[B], polygraph problem.

(2) *Infidelity.* Plaintiff sues for personal injuries received in a collision between his car and defendant's truck. He adduces medical testimony that the collision resulted in an irritation of a nerve root, impairing his left arm. Defendant offers a psychiatric report of a neurological exam done on plaintiff, which states that plaintiff is actually suffering from a "conversion reaction" because of anxiety concerning his separation from his wife and children and his frustrated wish to marry his secretary with whom he had been living. The report states this is responsible for his arm problem. You represent plaintiff. What would you do at this point? Result?

This is the case of *Kilarjian v. Horvath*, 379 F.2d 547 (2d Cir. 1967). The plaintiff raised an objection on grounds similar to those in Fed. R. Evid. 403, and the trial judge excluded the portions of the report indicating plaintiff was living with the secretary and intended to marry her. On appeal, it was held that it was within the discretion of the trial judge to exclude relevant evidence that he believes presents a risk of prejudice outweighing probative value. His exclusion and a judgment for plaintiff were affirmed. Would admission also have been upheld?

(3) *Blowing Up the Statue of Liberty.* Defendant is charged with smuggling explosives in order to, and conspiring to, blow up the Statue of Liberty. Defendant defends on grounds of entrapment — that the New York City Police Department solicited him to do it (so they could arrest him). (Assume he holds beliefs that make him undesirable to the police.) The main witness for the prosecution is Wood, an undercover agent for the New York City Police Department. The defendant attempts to put on a witness, Teahan, a 19-year-old youth who was a member of the Congress of Racial Equality, who will testify that Wood solicited Teahan to blow up the Statue of Liberty. (Defendant makes an offer of proof that Teahan will so testify, upon the prosecution's objection to Teahan's testimony.) What ruling would you expect?

This problem is based on *United States v. Bowe*, 360 F.2d 1 (2d Cir.), *cert. denied*, 385 U.S. 961 (1966). The trial court excluded Teahan's testimony, and the Court of Appeals said:

> Appellant's strongest argument is that Teahan's testimony was relevant to the defense of entrapment on the theory that it tended to show a custom on Wood's part to urge persons to engage in acts of violence against government property, which would justify an inference that he made similar suggestions to appellants or, simply, that it showed his intention to

> induce appellants to engage in unlawful activity. There is little doubt that the testimony was relevant to the defense of entrapment. Thus the issue here is whether the exclusion of the admittedly relevant evidence constituted an abuse of discretion by the trial judge. We conclude that it did not.
>
> A trial judge has discretion to exclude evidence which is only slightly probative if its introduction would confuse and mislead the jury by focusing its attention on collateral issues and if it would unnecessarily delay the trial. . . . Here, Teahan's testimony was only slightly probative with respect to the extent of Wood's encouragement of the appellants since, at the time it was offered, there was substantial evidence in the record showing that Wood had encouraged and attempted to influence appellants in adopting a plan to destroy government property. Thus, Teahan's testimony was only cumulative as to whether Wood had encouraged appellants to act and had some bearing, but not much, on whether Wood had been the creative force behind the scheme, i.e., whether appellants were unwary innocents or unwary criminals. On the other hand, it is apparent, as the trial judge stated after hearing extensive argument, that the introduction of the proferred [sic] testimony would have opened up a trial within a trial. It would not only have been proper to call witnesses to the alleged conversation in July, 1964 between Teahan and Wood, . . . but other witnesses might have been called for impeachment purposes. The trial judge correctly concluded that the confusion and delay which would have resulted from the introduction of Teahan's testimony outweighed its slight probative value.

Is the evidence merely cumulative, when it tends to be repetitive of other testimony about Wood?

(4) *Would a Warning have Made a Difference?* Plaintiff was injured when a can of Drano (drain cleaner), placed by her on a shelf where it might come in contact with moisture, exploded upon becoming wet. She sued the manufacturer for not having a warning on the can about the danger of explosion upon contact of the can with water. One issue was whether the warning would have made any difference (i.e., a causation issue). The following was propounded at trial to plaintiff by her attorney, and the following answer given, over objection:

Q. I want to ask if she knew that day what she knew after the accident, that this would explode with water in it, would she have kept it on the shelf.

A. I would not.

Is this admissible?

This question has come up in a number of cases. Most often, but not universally, the evidence is excluded, but the courts are not agreed on rationale. In *Drackett Products v. Blue*, 152 So. 2d 463 (Fla. 1963), on which the problem is based, the court held:

> The law seems well established that testimony consisting of guesses, conjecture or speculation — suppositions without a premise of fact — are clearly inadmissible in the trial of causes in the courts of this country. A statement by a witness as to what action he would have taken if something

> had occurred which did not occur . . . or what course of action a person would have pursued under certain circumstances which the witness says did not exist will ordinarily be rejected as inadmissible and as proving nothing.

Relevance can fall down at either of two stages: (1) the tendency of the evidence to prove the proposition it is offered for; or (2) the pertinence of that proposition under the substantive law, pleadings, or other orders entered controlling the issues. An objection based on (2) usually is phrased "the evidence is immaterial" or "the proposition is not of consequence to the determination of the lawsuit," but "irrelevant" also usually does the trick.

(5) *Statements Made Before the Event.* Is the testimony of the acquaintance of Curtis admissible in the following murder prosecution of Curtis for the death of Bently?:

> On April 27, 1976 the body of Barbara Bently was discovered in Ahwanee Meadow of Yosemite National Park. During an interview with the victim's roommate, police officers learned that the victim had been with Curtis on the evening prior to the discovery of her body. The agents interviewed Curtis and learned that on the night of April 26, he and Bently had gone out to dinner and then returned to Curtis' room. He told them that the victim thereafter physically rejected Curtis' sexual advances which resulted in her scratching his face as she pushed him away. A significant amount of physical evidence was admitted which suggested that Curtis had killed Bently during the course of a rape or attempted rape. Curtis testified and denied this.
>
> At trial, the prosecutor elicited the following testimony from an acquaintance of Curtis:

Q. Referring you to about the last week in March, and the early part of April, can you state whether or not you had a conversation with [Curtis]?

A. Yeah.

Q. Can you tell us, the Court and the Jury, what conversation took place between the both of you?

A. We was talking about ladies in general.

Q. Talking about ladies?

A. Uh-huh.

Q. Did Mr. Curtis say anything about ladies?

A. Uh-huh. . . .

Q. What did he say?

A. Uh, well, we was talking about, you know, getting down with certain ladies, and he said that if he ever took a lady out and she didn't give him what he wanted, he'd kick their [expletive deleted] and take it.

Is this testimony of the acquaintance admissible if an objection in proper form is made?

This problem is based on *United States v. Curtis*, 568 F.2d 643 (9th Cir. 1978). Curtis was convicted and he appealed the trial court's admission of the testimony. The Court of Appeals held:

> Rule 403 of the Federal Rules of Evidence provides that "[a]lthough relevant, evidence may be excluded if its probative value is substantially outweighed by the danger of unfair prejudice." This evidentiary precept is couched in terms which unmistakenly indicate that the operation of this balancing formula is within the sound discretion of the trial judge. Our careful review of the record leads us to conclude that the district judge did not abuse his discretion in determining that the probative value of the challenged testimony outweighed its potentially prejudicial impact. Curtis' second attack on the admissibility of this testimony centers around its relevance. The core of this argument is that because the challenged statement was made approximately a month prior to the murder and was a vague bravado statement not referring to the victim or any other particular person, the statement is not relevant to this specific crime and, therefore, should have been excluded. We cannot agree.
>
> Rule 401 of the Federal Rules of Evidence contains a very expansive definition of relevant evidence. . . . [Curtis's] prior statement as to what he would do in such circumstances is plainly relevant. Although relevant evidence may be excluded in certain cases under Rule 403, the district judge did not abuse his discretion in declining to do so.

Is this what you expected?

(6) *A Shake of the Head.* Rule on the admissibility of the conversation between Mr. Bill and the Doctor in the following case:

> The plaintiffs are beneficiaries in a policy of insurance issued by the defendant upon the life of their son, LeRoy Leo Bill, who died on January 12, 1961. Liability being denied by the insurer, this action was brought by the plaintiffs. The defendant alleged that the death of the insured was the result of suicide, which raises the only substantial question in the case. [T]he policy was voided under its terms if death was brought about by suicide.
>
> The evidence disclosed that LeRoy, a 17 year old boy, had been employed as a farm hand by Howard Niedert since September 21, 1960. On the late afternoon of January 12, 1961, he [LeRoy] was engaged in doing the chores and, when Mrs. Niedert arrived home about five o'clock, she talked with him. She observed nothing unusual about him and he went on about his tasks. She later saw him riding a saddle horse driving the cattle from the pasture, and that was the last time anyone saw him alive. Apparently all the chores had been done except for the task of throwing down some hay or straw.

When Mr. Niedert arrived home about six o'clock that evening, LeRoy had not returned to the house for his evening meal. When the lad had not appeared by 6:30 o'clock, Niedert went to look for him and observed a light on in the barn. Upon entering the door he saw LeRoy's legs extending through a small opening 22 x 20 in the floor of the hay mow, used to lower bales of hay and straw for the stock. He thought LeRoy was sitting on the loft floor asleep, until he climbed the ladder in another chute to the floor above. Then "he could see the string to him" and went over to him. The "string" was a piece of binder twine tied to an overhead two by eight inch beam some five feet and eleven inches above the floor, and attached to LeRoy's neck by a noose. The authorities and LeRoy's parents were called. . . .

[The question here involves defendant's offer of] testimony of the medical examiner, Dr. Willis K. Dankle, as to a conversation he had with the plaintiff Ernest Bill, in the presence of the other plaintiff, Norma Bill. . . . [I]n chambers, Dr. Dankle was interrogated in this way:

Q. Doctor, did you have a conversation with Ernest Bill in the presence of Norma Bill at the Niedert farmhouse just before you left on the night of January 12th?

A. Yes.

Q. What did that conversation consist of on your part and on his?

A. I said to Mr. Bill, "Is there any doubt in your mind that your son committed suicide?" and if I might describe the situation, he and his wife were sitting at the table, mourning and tearful, and he just shook his head.

Q. In what direction, Doctor, if you will say it so that the record can pick it up?

A. A lateral motion of the head.

Q. That is commonly interpreted as a negative sign?

A. Which I interpreted as a negative sign.

Is this admissible?

This case is based on *Bill v. Farm Bureau Life Ins. Co.*, 119 N.W.2d 768 (Iowa 1963). The trial court ruled as follows:

Well, I will tell you, I am going to follow my judgment on this. I think that if the plaintiff had volunteered that there wasn't any doubt in his mind the boy committed suicide that would be perfectly admissible but here we have got an entirely negative approach; somebody puts this subject of suicide out there in the form of a question; he doesn't make any audible answer to it at all. I think there is too much ground for conjecture there on the part of the jury as to the implications they can draw from that. . . . I just don't believe that is enough that I dare let that go to the jury.

My ruling is going to be that it is not going to be admitted.

The Iowa Supreme Court, in reviewing the trial court's action, ruled as follows:

> There is no doubt that the matter inquired into was a proper one, and the doctor should have been permitted to answer all of the questions with the possible exception of the final one, which dealt with his interpretation of the negative sign, the head shake. That the plaintiff Ernest Bill had no doubt his son had committed suicide was an admission against interest; and the error of the court in excluding it was further compounded by the fact that both plaintiffs were permitted to testify, over objection, that they knew of no reason why their son should have intentionally taken his life. The excluded testimony would not only have shown an admission but would have tended to counter and contradict [that].
>
> [T]he point decided by the court seems to have been that the lateral motion of the head made by Ernest Bill was too uncertain in its meaning and so was so speculative the jury should not have been permitted to pass upon it. With this we do not agree. A nod of the head is universally understood to be an affirmative or "yes" answer; a shake of the head is equally well understood to mean a negative or "no" reply. It is true the lateral motion might in some circumstances mean merely bewilderment or confusion, and "I don't know" answer. But this was an interpretation to be made by the jury.

Who was right? Why does it matter what the father thought about the cause of his son's death? What if he was wrong, because there is an explanation for his son's behavior that would make it likely that the death was accidental?

(7) *Exclusion of Defense Evidence that Someone Else Committed the Murders.* In *United States v. MacDonald*, 688 F.2d 224 (4th Cir. 1982), *cert. denied*, 459 U.S. 1103 (1983), defendant (appellant) was charged with killing his family. His defense emerges in the following excerpt from the opinion:

> [A]ppellant lays fault to the District Court's exercise of discretion in excluding the testimony of seven witnesses, all of whom would have testified to various inculpatory comments or statements assertedly made by Helena Stoeckley. The exclusion of this evidence, charges MacDonald, was error in that it abridged appellant's Fifth Amendment right to call witnesses in his own defense, was admissible under Rule 804(b)(3) (hearsay exception for declarations against interest) and, in any event, constituted proper impeachment of Stoeckley's own testimony. Reviewing the evidence in question, we analyze these contentions in turn.
>
> Since the commission of the crimes in February 1970, MacDonald has maintained that he and his family all were victims of a bizarre cult attack. He claims that the perpetrators included three men and a woman wearing a floppy hat, having blond hair, and wearing boots. The woman, he says, was Helena Stoeckley.
>
> At trial, Stoeckley testified that although her hair was brown in color, she owned a blond wig at the time of the crimes. She further said that she owned a floppy hat and boots. Although her recollection of events on the evening of February 16 and during the early morning hours of February 17

was, at best, hazy, she recalls not wearing the blond wig. However, she admitted to burning the wig and discarding the boots two days later.

While Stoeckley offered this much evidence seeming to corroborate MacDonald's version of the killings, the remainder of her testimony either contradicted him or tended to undercut his narration of the events. For example, she testified that she had never seen MacDonald before trial, had never been in his Fayetteville apartment, and while she vaguely felt that she might have had some connection with the crimes, since she had no explanation of her whereabouts between midnight and 5:30 a.m., she insisted she was not present at their commission. In all, the evidence disclosed that Stoeckley's memory was exceedingly poor and that she was constantly under the influence of narcotic drugs.

Because of this faulty memory, appellant sought to introduce a series of inculpatory statements through other witnesses. In this proffer to the District Court, in the absence of the jury, it was shown that these witnesses would give evidence substantially as follows:

1) Robert A. Brisentine, an Army investigator assigned to the homicides, interviewed Stoeckley April 23 and 24, 1971, approximately 14 months after the crime. Stoeckley told him she was present during the murders, but did not think that she had taken part. . . .

2) James Gaddis, an officer of the Nashville Police Department, revealed that Stoeckley had confessed her belief that she was involved in the crimes in the fall of 1970. She also said that she knew others who were involved.

3) P.E. Beasley, a former detective with the Fayetteville Police Department, explained that Stoeckley had been a reliable drug informant for several years prior to the murders. On the morning of February 18, 1970, the day after the fateful events, she told Beasley, in response to his accusation that she matched MacDonald's description of the female intruder, "[i]n my mind, it seems I saw this thing happen. . . . I was heavy on mescaline.". . .

4) Jane Zillioux, a Nashville neighbor of Stoeckley throughout the fall of 1970, said that Stoeckley had confided to her that she could not return to Fayetteville because she was involved in murders there. She further confessed that the victims were a woman and two small children and that she had disposed of the clothes she had been wearing to sever her connection with the crimes.

5) Charles Underhill, another Nashville acquaintance, testified that Stoeckley told him "they killed her and the two children."

6) William Posey, a neighbor of Stoeckley in Fayetteville, testified that Stoeckley told him a few days after the slayings that she didn't kill anyone herself, but did hold a light while the crime was in progress. . . .

7) Wendy Rouder, one of MacDonald's lawyers, testified that two days after Stoeckley had testified she could not remember anything about the night of

> the crime, she told Rouder "I still think I could have been there that night.". . .

The court upheld the exclusion of all of this evidence under Fed. R. Evid. 403 (and other grounds). The court found that Stoeckley's extrajudicial statements were vague and unreliable, and she had testified that she had not been involved in the crimes. Is this constitutional? Should not the jury, rather than the judge, get a chance to appraise the credibility of the evidence offered by the defendant? On the constitutionality of requiring a threshold for proof of an alternative possible perpetrator, see note (4) § 2.04[B], *infra*.

(8) *Unexplained Money Found on the Defendant.* The defendant, Ball, was arrested for the robbery of a jewelry store that occurred three weeks earlier. Is the following evidence admissible?:

> When Ball was finally subdued and arrested the officers took from his person and impounded a brown felt hat, "a brownish" windbreaker type jacket, trousers, gray shirt and shoes — these were exhibits one and two. . . . [T]he prosecuting attorney inquired of Officer Powell, "Did you also seize his personal effects?" Defense counsel, evidently knowing and anticipating, objected "to any testimony relevant (sic) to any personal effects seized upon this Defendant at the time he was arrested by reason of the fact it is immaterial and irrelevant and tends to neither prove nor disprove any facts involved and ask that the jury be discharged and a mistrial be declared." The court overruled the objection and the officer said, "Ball's personal effects consisted of two hundred and fifty eight dollars and two cents in cash, with the denominations of the bill(s), two one hundred dollar bills, a twenty — two twenties, a ten, a five, three ones and two pennies." [T]he bills and pennies comprising the $258.02 [were made exhibit three.] According to the officer, [the victim] was unable to identify the money as having come from the jewelry store robbery.

This problem is based on *State v. Ball*, 339 S.W.2d 783 (Mo. 1960). The Missouri Supreme Court held:

> The proof of the money here was evidently on the theory that Ball did not have or was not likely to have such a sum of money on his person prior to the commission of the offense. . . . [H]e had been out of the penitentiary about eight months and the inference the state would draw is that he had no visible means of support and no employment and could not possibly have $258.02 except from robberies. Of course, there was no such proof and Ball claimed that he had worked intermittently for a custodian or janitor of an apartment house and that he had won the $258.02 in a series of crap games at a named place. . . . [T]he evidence was not in fact relevant and in the circumstances was obviously prejudicial for if it did not tend to prove the offense for which the appellant was on trial the jury may have inferred that he was guilty of another robbery.

Would you say that it is a proper objection to evidence (under the concept of relevancy) that the proposition for which the evidence is offered "does not necessarily follow"? Compare this to another ruling in the same decision that permitted evidence that the defendant fled when approached by police shortly after the crime. Is it required that it "necessarily" follow that the defendant committed the act before evidence is considered sufficient to get the prosecution's (or plaintiff's) case to the jury?

§ 2.04 "OVERRIDING" RULES 401–403 BY RE-CHARACTERIZING UNDERLYING COMPONENTS OF MATERIALITY OR PROBATIVE VALUE

[A] Review of the Concepts of Materiality and Probative Value

(1) *"Materiality" and "Probative Value" Components of Relevancy.* Fed. R. Evid. 401 does not use the term "materiality" in defining relevant evidence. Materiality, at common law, had to do with identifying the issue to which the evidence was connected and determining whether it was legally provable in the case. The drafters of Fed. R. Evid. 401 considered this term too technical and legalistic. The present "of consequence" language may be thought of as a liberalized embodiment of the older concept of materiality, and the term "materiality" still is useful today.

(2) *"Probative Value."* Fed. R. Evid. 401 similarly avoids defining any required degree of proof or threshold of relevancy, and it does not use the term "probative value." But Fed. R. Evid. 403 uses the term "probative value" in specifying the quantity of evidentiary force that is to be balanced against prejudice and other counterweights. The degree of "probative value" a piece of evidence has can be thought of as a measure of the degree of relevance of the evidence.

(3) *Materiality, Probative Value, and Rule 401.* Modern "materiality," then, refers to the way in which the target fact, to which the evidence is connected, is "of consequence" to the determination of the action. "Probative value" is the strength of its "tendency" to make this fact appear more or less probable. Viewed in this way, materiality and probative value can be seen as two components in the Fed. R. Evid. 401 definition of relevancy.

(4) *Montana v. Egelhoff: A Problem of Relevant Evidence.* Consider the following case. Does the Montana law mean that the questioned inference is unduly prejudicial? Or does it mean that the inference lacks relevancy, because the law defines it as not material or as having no probative value?

[B] Possible Re-Characterization

MONTANA v. EGELHOFF

United States Supreme Court
518 U.S. 37 (1996)

JUSTICE SCALIA announced the judgment of the Court and delivered an opinion, in which CHIEF JUSTICE REHNQUIST, JUSTICE KENNEDY, and JUSTICE THOMAS join.

[Egelhoff went on a drinking binge with Pavola and Christenson. Later he was discovered in the back seat of Christenson's car yelling obscenities, with a blood alcohol level that measured 0.36 percent an hour later. Pavola and Christenson were in the front seat, each dead from a single gunshot wound. The murder weapon, Egelhoff's .38, lay on the floor. Egelhoff had gunshot residue on his hands.

[Egelhoff was convicted of two counts of deliberate homicide, which under Montana law required proof that he had "purposefully" or "knowingly" killed his companions. These terms, in turn, required proof either that it was Egelhoff's "conscious object . . . to cause such a result" or that he was "aware [of] a high probability that his acts [would] cause [the] result." Egelhoff's defensive theory at trial was that (1) an unidentified fourth person must have committed both murders because his intoxication made him physically incapable of committing them, and (2) [his intoxication] also negated proof of the required mental state (although it accounted for his inability to remember any of the relevant events). The trial court permitted Egelhoff to use evidence of intoxication to negate physical capacity, as relevant to his fourth person defense, but not as to his mental state. Instead, the judge instructed the jury, in accordance with Montana Code § 45-2-203, that it was forbidden to consider Egelhoff's "intoxicated condition . . . in determining the existence of a mental state which is an element of the offense."

[The Montana Supreme Court reversed, holding these rulings denied Egelhoff due process. Here, the Supreme Court reverses the reversal.]

[T]he cornerstone of the Montana Supreme Court's judgment was the proposition that the Due Process Clause guarantees a defendant the right to present and have considered by the jury "*all relevant evidence* to rebut the State's evidence on all elements of the offense charged." Respondent does not defend this categorical rule; he acknowledges that the right to present relevant evidence "has not been viewed as absolute." That is a wise concession, since the proposition that the Due Process Clause guarantees the right to introduce all relevant evidence is simply indefensible. . . . Relevant evidence may, for example, be excluded on account of a defendant's failure to comply with procedural requirements. And any number of familiar and unquestionably constitutional evidentiary rules also authorize the exclusion of relevant evidence. [Fed. R. Evid. 403 cited.] Hearsay rules similarly prohibit the introduction of testimony which, though unquestionably relevant, is deemed insufficiently reliable. [The State's law] in this regard is not subject to proscription under the Due Process Clause unless it "offends some principle of justice so rooted in the traditions and conscience of our people as to be ranked as fundamental." *Patterson v. New York*, 432 U.S. 197, 201-202 (1977). . . .

Our primary guide in determining whether the principle in question is fundamental is, of course, historical practice. Here that gives respondent little support. By the laws of England, wrote Hale, the intoxicated defendant "shall have no privilege by this voluntarily contracted madness, but shall have the same judgment as if he were in his right senses." . . . The historical record does not leave room for the view that the common law's rejection of intoxication as an "excuse" or "justification" for crime would nonetheless permit the defendant to show that intoxication prevented the requisite *mens rea*. . . .

Against this extensive evidence of a lengthy common-law tradition decidedly against him, the best argument available to respondent is the one made by his *amicus* and conceded by the State: Over the course of the 19th century, courts carved out an exception to the common law's traditional across-the-board condemnation of the drunken offender, allowing a jury to consider a defendant's intoxication when assessing whether he possessed the mental state needed to commit the crime charged, where the crime was one requiring a "specific intent."

[T]he burden remains upon respondent to show that the "new common law" rule — that intoxication may be considered on the question of intent — was so deeply rooted at the time of the Fourteenth Amendment (or perhaps has become so deeply rooted since) as to be a fundamental principle which that Amendment enshrined. That showing has not been made.

It is not surprising that many States have held fast to or resurrected the common-law rule prohibiting consideration of voluntary intoxication in the determination of *mens rea*, because that rule has considerable justification — which alone casts doubt upon the proposition that the opposite rule is a "fundamental principle." A large number of crimes, especially violent crimes, are committed by intoxicated offenders; modern studies put the numbers as high as half of all homicides, for example. Disallowing consideration of voluntary intoxication has the effect of increasing the punishment for all unlawful acts committed in that state, and thereby deters drunkenness or irresponsible behavior while drunk.

There is, in modern times, even more justification for laws such as § 45-2-203 than there used to be. Some recent studies suggest that the connection between drunkenness and crime is as much cultural as pharmacological — that is, that drunks are violent not simply because alcohol makes them that way, but because they are behaving in accord with their learned belief that drunks are violent. This not only adds additional support to the traditional view that an intoxicated criminal is not deserving of exoneration, but it suggests that juries — who possess the same learned belief as the intoxicated offender — will be too quick to accept the claim that the defendant was biologically incapable of forming the requisite *mens rea*. Treating the matter as one of excluding misleading evidence therefore makes some sense.

We held in *Chambers* that "the exclusion of [certain] critical evidence, coupled with the State's refusal to permit [petitioner] to cross-examine McDonald, denied him a trial in accord with traditional and fundamental standards of due process." 410 U.S., at 302. We continued, however:

In reaching this judgment, we establish no new principles of constitutional law. Nor does our holding signal any diminution in the respect traditionally accorded to the States in the establishment and implementation of their own criminal trial rules and procedures. Rather, we hold quite simply that under the facts and circumstances of this case the rulings of the trial court deprived Chambers of a fair trial. . . .

[I]n re Winship, 397 U.S. 358, 364 (1970), announced the proposition that the Due Process Clause requires proof beyond a reasonable doubt of every fact necessary to constitute the charged crime, and *Sandstrom v. Montana*, 442 U.S. 510, 524 (1979), established a corollary, that a jury instruction which shifts to the defendant the burden of proof on a requisite element of mental state violates due process. These decisions simply are not implicated here because, as the Montana court itself recognized, "[t]he burden is not shifted" under § 45-2-203. [T]he State introduced considerable evidence from which the jury might have concluded that respondent acted "purposely" or "knowingly." [For example, that respondent] had to retrieve the gun from the glove compartment before he used it was strong evidence that it was his "conscious object" to commit the charged crimes, as was the execution-style manner in which a single shot was fired into the head of each victim. . . .

[T]he people of Montana have decided to resurrect the rule of an earlier era, disallowing consideration of voluntary intoxication when a defendant's state of mind is at issue. Nothing in the Due Process Clause prevents them from doing so, and the judgment of the Supreme Court of Montana to the contrary must be reversed.

JUSTICE GINSBURG, concurring in the judgment.

Beneath the labels (rule excluding evidence or redefinition of the offense) lies the essential question: Can a State, without offense to the Federal Constitution, make the judgment that two people are equally culpable where one commits an act stone sober, and the other engages in the same conduct after his voluntary intoxication has reduced his capacity for self-control? For the reasons that follow, I resist categorizing § 45-2-203 as merely an evidentiary prescription, but join the Court's judgment refusing to condemn the Montana statute as an unconstitutional enactment.

[T]o obtain a conviction, the prosecution must prove only that (1) the defendant caused the death of another with actual knowledge or purpose, *or* (2) that the defendant killed "under circumstances that would otherwise establish knowledge or purpose 'but for' [the defendant's] voluntary intoxication."

Comprehended as a measure redefining *mens rea*, § 45-2-203 encounters no constitutional shoal.

JUSTICE O'CONNOR, with whom JUSTICE STEVENS, JUSTICE SOUTER, and JUSTICE BREYER join, dissenting.

[H]ere, to impede the defendant's ability to throw doubt on the State's case, Montana has removed from the jury's consideration a category of evidence relevant to determination of mental state. . . . The justification for this disallowance is the

State's desire to increase the likelihood of conviction of a certain class of defendants who might otherwise be able to prove that they did not satisfy a requisite element of the offense. In my view, the statute's effect on the criminal proceeding violates due process.

Justice Ginsburg concurs in the Court's judgment based on her determination that § 45-2-203 amounts to a redefinition of the offense that renders evidence of voluntary intoxication irrelevant to proof of the requisite mental state.

A state legislature certainly possesses the authority to define the offenses it wishes to punish. . . . There is, however, no indication that such a "redefinition" occurred. The Montana Supreme Court held that evidence of voluntary intoxication *was* relevant to the requisite mental state.

NOTES AND QUESTIONS

(1) *Isn't Intoxication Evidence "Relevant" to Mental State under Rule 401 (But If So, Could It Be Excludable under Rule 403)?* Notwithstanding some contrary suggestions in these opinions, isn't it clear beyond question that intoxication is "relevant" to mental state (at least if one considers the Fed. R. Evid. 401 definition)? Justice Scalia suggests that intoxication evidence might be considered "misleading" — because in light of modern science, juries may be "too quick to accept the claim that the defendant was biologically incapable of forming the requisite mens rea." Consider whether this reasoning could have justified exclusion under Fed. R. Evid. 403, which allows exclusion if the counterweights "substantially outweigh" the probative value.

(2) *Is the Evidence Legally Not "Material" in the Common Law Sense (because Montana has Implicitly Redefined the Offense, or for Other Reasons)?* Perhaps what Montana has done is to make intoxication "immaterial" to mental state. Is this what Justice Ginsburg is saying? (Note Justice Ginsburg's analysis: the Montana statute resembles a substantive law defining intoxication as legally equivalent to the required mental state.)

§ 2.05 JUDGE'S ROLE UNDER F.R.E. 104[3]

Read Federal Rule of Evidence 104, "Preliminary Questions."

(1) *Rule 104(a) is for Questions Other than Relevancy: The Judge's Role is Determinative.* Fed. R. Evid. 104(a) is relatively simple and intuitive. The judge decides issues of admissibility under the Rules. Thus, the judge must resolve fact questions that determine whether a given item of hearsay is admissible under an exception to the hearsay rule, or whether a defendant's confession was voluntary. These are called "questions of preliminary fact." If the judge admits the evidence, the jury then must decide how much weight to give it. In *Bourjaily v. United States*, 483 U.S. 171 (1987), the Court clarified that the judge decides these so-called preliminary fact questions under Fed. R. Evid. 104(a) normally by a preponderance

[3] Study Guide Reference: Evidence in a Nutshell, Chapter 1:III.

of the evidence. In making this decision, the judge can consider inadmissible evidence that is not privileged.

(2) *Rule 104(b): "Conditional" Relevancy Preserves a Role for the Jury.* It sometimes happens, however, that the relevance of one fact is conditioned on proof of another fact. Fact B, for example, is relevant only if Fact A is established. But what if Fact A is hotly disputed? In this event, there is a strong argument that the judge alone should not determine the admissibility of Fact B by finding for or against Fact A, because then the parties would be deprived of a jury trial of Fact A. Therefore, Fed. R. Evid. 104(b) contains a special provision for "relevancy conditioned on fact." The trial judge's role is only to decide whether there is enough evidence of Fact A to warrant a jury finding. Prima facie proof, or minimally sufficient evidence, requires submission to the jury of a conditionally relevant fact. Rothstein, *Intellectual Coherence in an Evidence Code*, 28 Loy. L.A. L. Rev. 1259 (1995); Callen, *Conditional Relevancy and Constrained Resources*, 2003 Mich. St. L. Rev. 1243.

PROBLEM 2F: IMPEACHMENT OF MARK FUHRMAN IN THE O.J. SIMPSON TRIAL FOR BIAS, BUT NOT AS TO PLANTING EVIDENCE: WAS THE JUDGE'S RULING CORRECT?

In O.J. Simpson's double murder trial, one of the prosecution's witnesses was Officer Mark Fuhrman. Fuhrman testified to finding a bloody glove on the defendant's premises. On cross-examination, Fuhrman denied using racial slurs. The defense theory was that the bloody glove had been removed from the crime scene and planted at Simpson's home (although the defense offered no direct evidence of this fact) and that Fuhrman (a white man) had often used racial slurs (against African-Americans) and was biased against Simpson (an African-American). To support these theories, the defense offered tape recordings, made by a fiction writer for whom Fuhrman served as a consultant, in which Fuhrman's voice could be heard repeatedly using racial slurs and admitting to numerous instances of misconduct, including the planting of evidence.

Judge Lance Ito's ruling allowed into evidence only two recorded instances of racial slurs by Fuhrman, neither which involved official misconduct. The judge also permitted the defense to inform the jury of the total number of such slurs. But the judge excluded Fuhrman's descriptions of misconduct, including the planting of evidence, on the ground that there was no credible evidence that the bloody glove had been planted. Given this state of evidence, arguably, Fuhrman's statements about prior misconduct had little probative value in comparison to their prejudice. *See Simpson Jury Will Hear Two Racist Insults: To Blacks Boasts by Fuhrman*, Hous. Chronicle, Sept. 1, 1995, § A, at 1, col. 5. "The underlying assumption requires a leap in law and logic that is too broad," Judge Ito explained. The defense had not supplied "factual support" sufficient to reach "the minimal threshold necessary to find inquiry into the planting-of-evidence theory relevant." *Id.* The judge applied the California Evidence Code.

Question: Could Judge Ito's ruling be explained under Fed. R. Evid. 104 if the case had been in federal court? Could it be explained under Fed. R. Evid. 403?

§ 2.06 EMERGING PATTERNS OR QUASI-RULES IN APPLICATION OF RULE 403 FACTORS: PRETRIAL EXPERIMENTS AS CASE IN POINT

[A] Pretrial Experiments as Case in Point

(1) *Substantial Similarity.* In *American Nat'l Watermattress Corp. v. Manville*, 642 P.2d 1330 (Alaska 1982), plaintiff (Manville) sued for injury when, due to an intercompartmental leak, plaintiff's waterbed overturned. Alaska has rules like the Federal Rules of Evidence. A pretrial experiment of plaintiff was offered at trial:

> At trial, Manville presented a video tape of an experiment conducted out of court by [Manville's] expert. The tape shows a waterbed of the same make and model as Manville's, set on a pedestal of the same dimensions as Manville's. The waterbed was set up with the total amount of water recommended in the instructions; however, some of the water was put into the surrounding air frame to simulate the effect of a leak between the water and air compartments.
>
> During the experiment, Manville's expert periodically released air from the air frame and then walked around the mattress and lifted and pushed it to show the effect each release of air had on its stability. After several releases of air, the expert rolled into the air mattress and it flipped off the pedestal, ending up on top of the expert on the floor.
>
> The tape is technically well done. The photography is clear. The video tape is not overdramatized.
>
> At trial, the video tape was shown to the jury with the expert narrating it.
>
> ANWC objected to the admission of the video tape on the grounds that the test had not been developed under conditions substantially similar to those existing in Manville's bedroom on the night of the accident.
>
> ANWC raised four basic dissimilarities. First, the amount of air and water in the experimental mattress may have been different than Manville's. Second, the experimental mattress had no protective liner. Third, there did not appear to be air in the water part of the experimental mattress while there probably were bubbles in the Manville mattress. Fourth, ANWC claims the expert got into the bed differently than did Manville.
>
> The leading Alaska case on the admissibility of experimental evidence is *Love v. State*. . . . [The court there stated that the test is "substantial similarity"]:
>
>> The rule of substantial similarity does not require an identity of conditions but only that degree of similarity which will insure that the results of the experiment are probative. In some cases a high degree of similarity may not be attainable, yet the evidence nevertheless may be enlightening to the jury.

The court went on to note that the determination involves a balancing process:

> As with other forms of circumstantial evidence, the trial judge may, in his discretion, exclude the experimental evidence after a determination that the probative value of the experimental evidence is outweighed by the possibility of prejudice, confusion of the issues or undue consumption of time. . . .

The court listed two principles to be followed in applying the above tests:

> Are the dissimilarities likely to distort the results of the experiment to the degree that the evidence is not relevant? Can the dissimilarities be adjusted for or explained so that their [e]ffect on the results of the experiment can be understood by the jury?

In the present case, the experiment easily meets the standards of *Love* and its progeny. First, there was a substantial similarity of conditions. The same make and model of air mattress was tested on the same size pedestal. The expert testified that the waterbed had been set up according to the manufacturer's directions, except for allowing water into the air frame to simulate an intercompartmental leak. Second, Manville's expert satisfactorily explained the effect of the various dissimilarities. The expert testified that the lack of the plastic liner would have no effect on the results. He also testified that air added to the water compartment would have no effect. Finally, ANWC's claim that the way the expert rolled into the bed was different than the way Manville got into bed on the night of the accident was a fact question for the jury. They could themselves compare the video tape scene with Manville's testimony as to how she got into the bed that night.

(2) *Effect of Paucity of Other Evidence.* In *Bauman v. Volkswagenwerk Aktiengesellschaft*, 621 F.2d 230 (6th Cir. 1980), plaintiff's 1971 Volkswagen Karman Ghia was sideswiped by a Plymouth, then struck a telephone pole. Plaintiff was thrown out and badly hurt. Plaintiff contended the door opened prematurely from the relatively mild sideswipe, and Volkswagen countered that it opened upon hitting the pole (which would be an understandable and expectable opening):

> Volkswagen contends that the district court erred in admitting evidence of "hammer tests" conducted by plaintiffs' expert, Dr. Sissom. . . . The tests were intended to simulate the side-swipe collision where the door handle of the [Volkswagen] made contact with the Plymouth. During the tests Dr. Sissom remained inside the car, his back leaning against the driver's door and his feet pushing on the passenger door. At the same time his assistant hit the outside door handle with a rubber mallet. The results were that in 1971 and 1972 Volkswagens, an average of two blows were required to actuate the door latch and cause the door to open.
>
> . . . [T]his evidence was far from conclusive on the question of whether the door latch was defectively designed. But we believe it was admissible. . . .

In an uncertain situation such as this, where neither plaintiff remembers the accident and the jury must simply measure probabilities, expert testimony may be valuable. . . . Where the part is not patently defective, expert testimony is the only available method to establish defectiveness.

[B] Other Emerging Categories

As the pretrial experiment cases show, cases on relevance-and-its-counterweights sometimes can be grouped into more precise categories. In the case of pretrial experiments, a kind of flexible "quasi-rule" or "rule-of-thumb" has emerged to guide the Fed. R. Evid. 403-type calculus (the "substantial similarity" test, which must be applied with the Rule 403 factors firmly in mind). Below are some additional rough groupings of cases that are emerging pursuant to repeated application of naked balancing, but they are even less categorical than the pretrial experiment decisions. Perhaps the opinions in this entire section, including pretrial experiments, may be viewed as transitional cases in a current journey from Fed. R. Evid. 403 to more specific codifications of the kind treated in the other Rules of Article IV in our Chapter 3.

(1) *Categorizing the Cases: Financial Condition.* Evidence of "financial condition" of a party frequently comes up. *See, e.g., State v. Ball*, 339 S.W.2d 783 (Mo. 1960), cited in ***PROBLEM SET*** § 2.03[C]. *See also Stevenson* (the first principal case in § 2.01). In *United States v. Mangan*, 575 F.2d 32 (2d Cir.), *cert. denied*, 439 U.S. 931 (1978), the government was permitted to show unrelated securities purchases of $12,000 on the part of defendant IRS agent in a prosecution for a scheme to defraud the government by creating fictitious taxpayers entitled to refunds. The securities purchases were introduced to show it was unlikely that a person with a reported gross income of $20,000 and a taxable income of $10,000 could afford such purchases unless he had received the money from another source, the inference being that it was from the illegal scheme. Noting that the amount involved in the securities purchases was neither shown to be suddenly acquired nor large, and that there was no showing of defendant's net worth at the beginning of the period nor evidence that defendant did not have alternative legal sources for money, the Court of Appeals states that it would not have admitted the evidence and expresses wonderment at why the government would imperil an otherwise strong case with such doubtful evidence of such small probative force, involving such a small amount of money. Nevertheless, the Court of Appeals, emphasizing Fed. R. Evid. 401's liberal test and the discretionary nature of Fed. R. Evid. 403 as a counterbalance to Fed. R. Evid. 401, holds that the trial judge was within his discretion and that at any rate this evidence would not have had any effect on the verdict.

See also Berman Enterprises, Inc. v. Local 333, United Marine Div. International Longshoremen's Ass'n, 644 F.2d 930 (2d Cir.), *cert. denied*, 454 U.S. 965 (1981). Plaintiff Berman alleged that the Union Local committed antitrust and labor law violations that damaged Berman's business. High salaries of Berman's officers were allowed to be shown by the Local in order to refute the claim that the business was damaged. Since the Local made no special appeal to class prejudice or prejudice that would arise out of a disparity in financial standing, there was much other evidence, and this evidence was admitted for a limited purpose, prejudice under Fed. R. Evid. 403 did not outweigh the probative value of the evidence.

Plumb v. Curtis, 33 A. 998 (Conn. 1895), suggests that relative financial standing of putative agent and putative boss would be permitted to help show whether expensive goods (payment for which was being sought by means of a lawsuit) had been purchased by the agent for himself or for the boss's account, and that perhaps both need not necessarily be shown. The court recognized that financial standing normally is too prejudicial and its probativeness too low to be admitted. What are the dangers of "financial" evidence?

The introduction of evidence of the defendant's lavish lifestyle and gambling was affirmed in *United States v. Jackson-Randolph*, 282 F.3d 369 (6th Cir. 2002). Although the Sixth Circuit noted it had previously recognized that prosecutorial appeals to wealth and class biases can create prejudicial error, it found that the defendant's expenditure of nearly $4 million, some of which could not be accounted for from her legitimate income, showed her motive for committing mail fraud, embezzlement, and money laundering. The court also rejected any requirement that the lifestyle evidence must be directly connected to illegitimate sources. What factors should be considered to help determine when such evidence is too prejudicial?

(2) *Categorizing the Cases: Sexual Liaisons.* Another such category is evidence of sexual liaisons. *See, e.g., Kilarjian v. Horvath*, 379 F.2d 547 (2d Cir. 1967), noted in ***PROBLEM SET*** § 2.03[C], *above.* In *United States v. Kilbourne*, 559 F.2d 1263 (4th Cir.), *cert. denied*, 434 U.S. 873 (1977), despite the inevitable prejudice, the prosecution in a murder case was allowed to show that the defendant was having sexual relations with the deceased, in order to support the theory that the killing was done out of jealousy. What is the danger of this type of evidence?

In *United States v. McRae*, 593 F.2d 700 (5th Cir.), *cert. denied*, 444 U.S. 862 (1979), the court holds that Fed. R. Evid. 403 does not exclude evidence of the defendant's intimate relations with certain other women two months after his wife's death, in view of the fact that defendant in his testimony dwelt on his grief and intense devotion to his wife and introduced medical testimony of his hospitalization for grief after the death, all to support the contention of accidental discharge of the gun with which he was accused of killing his wife. However, the most prejudicial form of the evidence was excluded, evidence that included recounting his expressions of contempt for his dead wife.

(3) *Categorizing the Cases: Gruesome Photographs.* Courts have tended to permit photographs of crime scenes, even if gruesome, under both the common law and rules similar to the Federal Rules of Evidence. What are the dangers? The defendant in *Long v. State*, 823 S.W.2d 259 (Tex. Crim. App. 1991), *cert. denied*, 505 U.S. 1224 (1992), was convicted of murder and sentenced to death. Among other issues, he argued on appeal that numerous crime scene and autopsy photographs of three women whom the evidence indicated he had killed with a hatchet were improperly admitted. The court analyzed this contention under a state rule similar to Fed. R. Evid. 403:

> [T]he controlling factor is whether the probative value of the photographs was greatly outweighed by their prejudicial effect. The prejudicial effect may be determined by the number of exhibits offered, their gruesomeness, their detail, their size, whether they were black and white or color, whether they are naked or clothed, and by factors unique to each situation photographed.
>
> In the instant case, the medical examiner used the autopsy photographs to illustrate and explain his testimony to the jury. . . . Since verbal descriptions were admissible, the photographs were admissible unless their probative value was substantially outweighed by their prejudicial effect.

See also *United States v. Kilbourne*, 559 F.2d 1263 (4th Cir.), *cert. denied*, 434 U.S. 873 (1977), in which photographs of the decedent's body at the crime scene were permitted, despite the prejudice, to show the proximity of the body to certain items linked to the defendant, including a package of cigarettes and a gin bottle, and to support the prosecution's theory that the killer had acted deliberately and with premeditation.

In *United States v. Calvert*, 523 F.2d 895 (8th Cir. 1975), *cert. denied*, 424 U.S. 911 (1976), photographs of decedent's body at the homicide scene, lying face down in a pool of dried blood with his pockets pulled inside out and various objects scattered around the body, were held to be excludable under Fed. R. Evid. 401 and 403, since the fact of death and defendant's causing of the death were not issues in the case, which was a prosecution for wire and mail fraud, i.e., taking out insurance policies on the life of the decedent while intending to kill him. However, the Court of Appeals holds that admission of the photographs was harmless error, in the light of all the other evidence.

(4) *Categorizing the Cases: Motion Pictures and Jury Views. Johnson v. William C. Ellis & Sons Ironworks, Inc.*, 604 F.2d 950 (5th Cir. 1979), *modified*, 609 F.2d 820 (5th Cir. 1980), shows that the same framework applies with respect to motion pictures and jury views. In this case, a wrongful death suit where decedent's head had been caught in a cotton press, his surviving spouse sought to introduce a film showing the press in operation or, alternatively, to take the jury to view the press in operation. Both were held properly excludable on grounds that the operation of the machine was adequately described in testimony and that prejudice and misleadingness might result because only a small portion of the film portrayed the part of the press actually involved in the accident, and the film showed guards that had been installed on the press after the accident. Time also was cited. The jury view was considered infected with the same problems.

(5) *Categorizing the Cases: Real Evidence.* The same ad hoc approach under Fed. R. Evid. 403 is followed with respect to the introduction of real evidence (an item actually involved in the case, such as a gun or knife) and demonstrative evidence (something used as an explanatory aid at trial). The question usually is some variant of the following: Does this kind of evidence more help the jury understand than it tends to consume time, appeal to emotions, overinflate, unduly dramatize, and lead the jury to concentrate on only one issue? As above in these notes, much discretion in these ad hoc areas is allowed to the trial judge, and appellate courts rarely interfere. In *Smith v. Ohio Oil Co.*, 134 N.E.2d 526 (Ill. App. Ct. 1956), these

principles were utilized to uphold the use of a plastic model of a human pelvis skeleton as an explanatory aid during the testimony of plaintiff's medical witness in an automobile accident case. The court notes that the pelvis is the most difficult area to visualize and that the physician adverted to the model only in one small portion of his testimony. The doctor testified to the accuracy of the model and its need to assist his explanation.

PROBLEM 2G (END-OF-CHAPTER PROBLEM): "AMERICAN TALIBAN" AND AL QAEDA EVIDENCE.

John Walker Lindh, the "American Taliban," received a 20-year sentence when he pled guilty to serving as a soldier for the Taliban, and carrying a rifle and hand grenades while a soldier. He was originally charged with additional counts that linked him to al Qaeda, particularly: conspiring to provide material support and resources to al Qaeda, a foreign terrorist organization; providing material support and resources to al Qaeda; conspiring to contribute services to al Qaeda; and contributing services to al Qaeda. The allegations in the indictment traced his conversion to the Islamic faith, his religious studies in Yemen and Pakistan, his voluntary association with the Taliban, and his oath of allegiance to jihad.

The indictment alleged Lindh committed the following acts: He attended al Qaeda's al-Farooq camp for military training and participated fully in the camp's training activities, despite being told early in his stay that "Bin Laden had sent forth some fifty people to carry out twenty suicide terrorist operations against the United States and Israel." As part of his al Qaeda training, Lindh took "terrorist training courses in, among other things, weapons, orienteering, navigation, explosives and battlefield combat." This training included the use of "shoulder weapons, pistols and rocket-propelled grenades, and the construction of Molotov cocktails." During his stay at al-Farooq, Lindh met personally with Bin Laden, "who thanked him and other trainees for taking part in jihad." He also met with a senior al Qaeda official, Abu Mohammad al-Masri, who inquired whether Lindh was interested in traveling outside Afghanistan to conduct operations against the United States and Israel. Lindh declined this offer in favor of going to the front lines to fight. He was issued rifles and grenades after his training; traveling with others to the front line in Takhar, Afghanistan, where he opposed the Northern Alliance forces, remaining with his fighting group after the entry of the United States into the conflict and following the September 11, 2001 terrorist attacks, "despite having been told that Bin Laden had ordered the [September 11] attacks, that additional terrorist attacks were planned, and that additional al Qaeda personnel were being sent from the front lines to protect Bin Laden and defend against an anticipated military response from the United States." Lindh remained with his fighting group from October to December 2001, "after learning that United States military forces and United States nationals had become directly engaged in support of the Northern Alliance in its military conflict with Taliban and al Qaeda forces." His group surrendered at Konduz and some of the detainees staged a violent uprising at the Qala-i-Janghi (QIJ) prison that resulted in the death of an American intelligence agent. For a detailed factual recital of the indictment, see *United States v. Lindh*, 212 F. Supp. 2d 541 (E.D. Va. 2002).

If a trial had taken place on the al Qaeda counts, is the following evidence relevant under F.R.E. Rules 401–402, and if so, subject to exclusion under Rule 403?

(1) Evidence that Lindh had converted to the Islamic faith.

(2) A videotape taken after September 11, in which Osama Bin Laden admits his involvement in the attacks to his followers who praise Allah for the destruction. Lindh is not mentioned in the tape and is unlikely to have seen it before his capture.

(3) Pictures and videotapes showing two planes flying into the twin towers, the implosion of the buildings and the aftermath of the attacks.

(4) A list of everyone who was killed in the September 11 attacks, along with a small photograph of each victim.

Generally, in terrorism trials, do you suppose Rule 403 can preclude all prejudicial evidence? What about cases in which the prosecution must prove that the organization the defendant allegedly belongs to is a "terrorist organization"? Are there ways of lessening the prejudicial effect of terrorism evidence? *See generally* Vidmar, *When All of Us Are Victims: Juror Prejudice and "Terrorist" Trials*, 78 Chi.-Kent L. Rev. 1143 (2003).

Chapter 3

RELEVANCY AND ITS COUNTERWEIGHTS CONTINUED

SPECIFIC EXCLUSIONARY RULES BASED LARGELY ON RELEVANCY AND COUNTERWEIGHTS: CHARACTER, COMPROMISE, REMEDIAL MEASURES, INSURANCE (F.R.E. ARTICLE IV, RULES 404–415)

§ 3.01 CHARACTER EVIDENCE (OTHER THAN IMPEACHMENT): SPECIFIC INSTANCES

[A] Specific Acts Offered to Prove "Action in Conformity": Generally Inadmissible[1]

Read Federal Rule of Evidence 404(b), "Character Evidence: Crimes or Other Acts."

Fed. R. Evid. 404(b) is in actuality a separate, self-contained rule, in the sense that it need not be read together with any of the other portions of Fed. R. Evid. 404 or 405. It is the rule that governs specific-instance character evidence, including other crimes or wrongs.

Fed. R. Evid. 404(b) is studied before 404(a) or 405 here because specific-instance evidence presents the policy conflicts that are involved in all forms of evidence of character. To help you get oriented to the kind of evidence dealt with by F.R.E. 404(b), consider the following questions:

(1) *Prior Burglary in Assault Case.* Defendant is charged with assault and battery, committed for no particular reason except to be a bully. The prosecution wishes to introduce into evidence the fact that on a previous occasion he committed burglary on an unrelated, unoccupied house. Is this evidence relevant? Is it objectionable?

(2) *Prior Burglar as Babysitter.* You are going to take your two-year-old child to either Mr. A or Mr. B for child-sitting while you are at work. A and B are identical in every respect except A has a burglary conviction in his record. Whom would you choose?

(3) *Prior Assault in Assault Case.* In the same case as Question (1), the prosecution instead attempts to introduce evidence that defendant has, on a

[1] Study Guide Reference: Evidence in a Nutshell, Chapter 4:I.

previous occasion, committed another assault on someone else. Is this distinguishable from the evidence in Question (1)?

(4) *Prior Very Similar Assault in Assault Case.* In the same case as Question (3), assume the assault that is the subject of the present prosecution was committed by wrapping ice cubes in a sack and beating the victim over the head (the idea being that the weapon would melt and disappear). Assume the offered previous assault also was with ice cubes in a sack. Is this evidence distinguishable from the evidence in Question (3)? Would it help further if the victims were the same?

(5) *Should Such Evidence Be Admitted?* Assuming you found a relevance or policy distinction among Questions (1), (3), and (4), in which question *should* the evidence be admissible? If a line should be drawn, should it be between (1) and (3), or between (3) and (4)?

(6) *Rule 404(b).* Now look at Fed. R. Evid. 404(b). Assuming you found a distinction among questions (1), (3), and (4), does the Rule draw the line between admissibility and inadmissibility as you thought it should? Why does Fed. R. Evid. 404(b) draw a line based on the purpose or issue for which the evidence is offered, rather than based on degree of probative force or degree of prejudice?

UNITED STATES v. CALVERT

United States Court of Appeals, Eighth Circuit
523 F.2d 895 (1975), *cert. denied,* 424 U.S. 911 (1976)

The rule (against admitting evidence of crimes other than the one charged) is based on three dangers in the presentation of "other crimes" evidence. First, it is feared that

> . . . a jury might overestimate the probative value of such evidence by assuming that merely because the defendant has committed crimes before, he is likely to be guilty of the offense charged. . . .

Case Note, 87 Harv. L. Rev. 1074, 1076 (1974). Second, is

> . . . the recognized tendency of men to punish a bad man now that he has been caught, even though his guilt on this occasion has not been satisfactorily established. . . .

And finally, it is felt that it is unfair to require a defendant to defend against and disprove crimes for which he has never been charged or indicted.

NOTE ON THE NOTICE PROVISION

Notice Provision. Rule 404(b) contains a notice provision. The American Bar Association, Committee on Rules of Procedure and Evidence, Criminal Justice Section, had recommended a similar provision in a report at 120 F.R.D 299, 330 (1988) (P. Rothstein, chair). Does this provision take care of the problem last noted in the *Calvert* extract?

[B] Contours of Exclusion of Specific-Acts Evidence[2]

[1] Evidence Whose Probativity Depends on Human Tendency to Repeat: Must Not be Characterized as Character or Propensity Reasoning

JONES v. STATE
Texas Court of Criminal Appeals
376 S.W.2d 842 (1964)

WOODLEY, PRESIDING JUDGE.

The state relied upon circumstantial evidence to show appellant's guilt of theft of money from the person of Hause.

Hause testified that on December 13, 1962, the appellant [Ms. Jones] came to his auto parts place of business around 3 P.M., while he was working on a generator; she grabbed C. V. Wells, who later became a partner in the business, and propositioned him for sexual intercourse. She had her hands all over him. He pushed her away. She then said she had to urinate and was shown an outside rest room. On the way she fell, or claimed to have fallen, and Hause, thinking she was drunk, tried to get her up. She raised up her dress and grabbed him.

Before he could drag her out she turned around and rubbed "her rear end" on him. She then said she had to use the telephone. He did not see her again.

Some five minutes after the appellant left, Hause reached for his handkerchief and discovered that the $150 or more he had in his billfold was gone, but the billfold was in his pocket and the checks were still in it.

The state was permitted to prove that the appellant, on March 6, 1963, went to an automobile service shop or Transmission Shop in Austin during the noon hour and, after announcing that she wanted to use the bathroom, grabbed Mr. Grady, the proprietor, and propositioned him and he "pushed her back because she was drunk." She grabbed him again and then walked out. He discovered some 15 minutes later that the $125 he had in his billfold was gone.

The state was also permitted to introduce evidence to the effect that the appellant, on or about December 31, 1962, went to the place of business of an Orthopedic Brace Company where the proprietor, Mr. Hess, was at work at his bench, put her hand on him like she was trying to keep from falling and acting "as if she was trying to solicit a street job," and as though she was drugged or doped. She then left suddenly and the brace maker soon found that his billfold, in which he had $20 or more, was gone. The billfold was later recovered, its contents other than the money was intact. . . .

The evidence of the brace maker and the owner of the Transmission Shop was admitted over the objection that it was "irrelevant and immaterial, highly prejudi-

---

[2] Study Guide Reference: Evidence in a Nutshell, Chapter 4:III, V–VIII.

cial. It is at a time different and subsequent to the date alleged in the indictment."

The evidence was offered and was admitted only for the purpose of showing identity, intent, motive, malice or common plan or scheme. It was so limited in the court's charge. . . .

The intent of the appellant in making physical contact with Mr. Hause was material and was uncertain. Proof that the money was taken as well as the intent of the appellant rested upon the circumstances.

The two collateral offenses show more than a similarity in results. They show a common plan and systematic course of action. The peculiar way in which the other business men lost their money upon the same course of conduct by the appellant was a circumstance that was available to the state to prove the appellant's guilt of theft from the person of Hause. The evidence showed system, not merely systematic crime, and the court did not err in admitting it for the limited purposes stated.

[Affirmed.]

HUDDLESTON v. UNITED STATES

United States Supreme Court
485 U.S. 681 (1988)

CHIEF JUSTICE REHNQUIST delivered the opinion of the Court.

This case presents the question whether[,] before admitting evidence of an "other act" to prove intent, identity, plan, etc. under Fed. R. Evid. 404(b), the district court must itself make a preliminary finding that the Government has proved the "other act" by a preponderance of the evidence before it submits the evidence to the jury. We hold that it need not do so.

Petitioner, Guy Rufus Huddleston, was charged with one count of selling stolen goods in interstate commerce and one count of possessing stolen property in interstate commerce. The two counts related to two portions of a shipment of stolen Memorex videocassette tapes that petitioner was alleged to have possessed and sold, knowing that they were stolen.

The evidence at trial showed that a trailer containing over 32,000 blank Memorex videocassette tapes with a manufacturing cost of $4.53 per tape was stolen from the Overnight Express yard in South Holland, Illinois, sometime between April 11 and 15, 1985. On April 17, 1985, petitioner contacted Karen Curry, the manager of the Magic Rent-to-Own in Ypsilanti, Michigan, seeking her assistance in selling a large number of blank Memorex videocassette tapes. After assuring Curry that the tapes were not stolen, he told her he wished to sell them in lots of at least 500 at $2.75 to $3 per tape. Curry subsequently arranged for the sale of a total of 5,000 tapes, which petitioner delivered to the various purchasers — who apparently believed the sales were legitimate.

There was no dispute that the tapes which petitioner sold were stolen; the only material issue at trial was whether petitioner knew they were stolen. The District Court allowed the Government to introduce evidence of "similar acts" under Rule

404(b), concluding that such evidence had "clear relevance as to [petitioner's knowledge]." The first piece of similar act evidence offered by the Government was the testimony of Paul Toney, a record store owner. He testified that in February 1985, petitioner offered to sell new 12" black and white televisions for $28 apiece. According to Toney, petitioner indicated that he could obtain several thousand of these televisions. Petitioner and Toney eventually traveled to the Magic Rent-to-Own, where Toney purchased 20 of the televisions. Several days later, Toney purchased 18 more televisions.

The second piece of similar act evidence was the testimony of Robert Nelson, an undercover FBI agent posing as a buyer for an appliance store. Nelson testified that in May 1985, petitioner offered to sell him a large quantity of Amana appliances — 28 refrigerators, 2 ranges, and 40 icemakers. Nelson agreed to pay $8,000 for the appliances. Petitioner was arrested shortly after he arrived at the parking lot where he and Nelson had agreed to transfer the appliances. A truck containing the appliances was stopped a short distance from the parking lot, and Leroy Wesby, who was driving the truck, was also arrested. It was determined that the appliances had a value of approximately $20,000 and were part of a shipment that had been stolen.

Petitioner testified that the Memorex tapes, the televisions, and the appliances had all been provided by Leroy Wesby, who had represented that all of the merchandise was obtained legitimately. Petitioner stated that he had sold 6,500 Memorex tapes for Wesby on a commission basis. Petitioner maintained that all of the sales for Wesby had been on a commission basis and that he had no knowledge that any of the goods were stolen.

In closing, the prosecution explained that petitioner was not on trial for his dealings with the appliances or the televisions. The District Court instructed the jury that the similar acts evidence was to be used only to establish petitioner's knowledge, and not to prove his character. The jury convicted petitioner on the possession count only.

A divided panel of the United States Court of Appeals for the Sixth Circuit initially reversed the conviction, concluding that because the Government had failed to prove by clear and convincing evidence that the televisions were stolen, the District Court erred in admitting the testimony concerning the televisions. [O]n rehearing, the court affirmed the conviction. "Applying the preponderance of the evidence standard . . . , we cannot say that the district court abused its discretion in admitting evidence of the similar acts in question here." The court noted that the evidence concerning the televisions was admitted for a proper purpose and that the probative value of this evidence was not outweighed by its potential prejudicial effect. [For some reason the defendant has only appealed the admission of the evidence of the televisions, not the appliances. — Eds.]

[W]e conclude that such evidence should be admitted if there is sufficient evidence to support a finding by the jury that the defendant committed the similar act.

Federal Rule of Evidence 404(b) — which applies in both civil and criminal cases — generally prohibits the introduction of evidence of extrinsic acts that might adversely reflect on the actor's character, unless that evidence bears upon a relevant issue in the case such as motive, opportunity, or knowledge. Extrinsic acts evidence may be critical to the establishment of the truth as to a disputed issue, especially when that issue involves the actor's state of mind and the only means of ascertaining that mental state is by drawing inferences from conduct. The actor in the instant case was a criminal defendant, and the act in question was "similar" to the one with which he was charged. Our use of these terms is not meant to suggest that our analysis is limited to such circumstances.

Before this Court, petitioner argues that the District Court erred in admitting Toney's testimony as to petitioner's sale of the televisions. [Petitioner does not dispute that Nelson's testimony concerning the Amana appliances was properly admitted under Rule 404(b).] The threshold inquiry a court must make before admitting similar acts evidence under Rule 404(b) is whether that evidence is probative of a material issue other than character. [P]etitioner acknowledges that this evidence was admitted for the proper purpose of showing his knowledge that the Memorex tapes were stolen. He asserts, however, that the evidence should not have been admitted because the Government failed to prove to the District Court that the televisions were in fact stolen.

Petitioner argues from the premise that evidence of similar acts has a grave potential for causing improper prejudice. For instance, the jury may choose to punish the defendant for the similar rather than the charged act, or the jury may infer that the defendant is an evil person inclined to violate the law. Because of this danger, petitioner maintains, the jury ought not to be exposed to similar act evidence until the trial court has heard the evidence and made a determination under Federal Rule of Evidence 104(a) that the defendant committed the similar act. [A]ccording to petitioner, the trial court must make this preliminary finding by at least a preponderance of the evidence.

We reject petitioner's position, for it is inconsistent with the structure of the Rules of Evidence and with the plain language of Rule 404(b). [Following Fed. R. Evid. 401-403, which deal with broad principles,] [R]ules 404 through 412 address specific types of evidence that have generated problems. Generally, these latter Rules do not flatly prohibit the introduction of such evidence but instead limit the purpose for which it may be introduced. Rule 404(b), for example, protects against the introduction of extrinsic act evidence when that evidence is offered solely to prove character. The text contains no intimation, however, that any preliminary showing is necessary before such evidence may be introduced for a proper purpose. If offered for such a proper purpose, the evidence is subject only to general strictures limiting admissibility such as Rules 402 and 403.

Petitioner's reading of Rule 404(b) as mandating a preliminary finding by the trial court that the act in question occurred not only superimposes a level of judicial oversight that is nowhere apparent from the language of that provision, but it is simply inconsistent with the legislative history behind Rule 404(b). The Advisory Committee specifically declined to offer any "mechanical solution" to the admission of evidence under 404(b). Rather, the Committee indicated that the trial court should assess such evidence under the usual rules for admissibility: "The determination must be made whether the danger of undue prejudice outweighs the probative value of the evidence in view of the availability of other means of proof and other factors appropriate for making decisions of this kind under Rule 403.". . .

This is not to say, however, that the Government may parade past the jury a litany of potentially prejudicial similar acts that have been established or connected to the defendant only by unsubstantiated innuendo. Evidence is admissible under Rule 404(b) only if it is relevant. In the Rule 404(b) context, similar act evidence is relevant only if the jury can reasonably conclude that the act occurred and that the defendant was the actor. In the instant case, the evidence that petitioner was selling the televisions was relevant under the Government's theory only if the jury could reasonably find that the televisions were stolen.

Such questions of relevance conditioned on a fact are dealt with under Federal Rule of Evidence 104(b). Rule 104(b) provides:

> When the relevancy of evidence depends upon the fulfillment of a condition of fact, the court shall admit it upon, or subject to, the introduction of evidence sufficient to support a finding of the fulfillment of the condition.

In determining whether the Government has introduced sufficient evidence to meet Rule 104(b), the trial court neither weighs credibility nor makes a finding that the Government has proved the conditional fact by a preponderance of the evidence. The court simply examines all the evidence in the case and decides whether the jury could reasonably find the conditional fact — here, that the televisions were stolen — by a preponderance of the evidence.

. . . In assessing whether the evidence was sufficient to support a finding that the televisions were stolen, the court here was required to consider not only the direct evidence on that point — the low price of the televisions, the large quantity offered for sale, and petitioner's inability to produce a bill of sale — but also the evidence concerning petitioner's involvement in the sales of other stolen merchandise obtained from Wesby, such as the Memorex tapes and the Amana appliances. Given this evidence, the jury reasonably could have concluded that the televisions were stolen, and the trial court therefore properly allowed the evidence to go to the jury.

We share petitioner's concern that unduly prejudicial evidence might be introduced under Rule 404(b). We think, however, that the protection against such unfair prejudice emanates not from a requirement of a preliminary finding by the trial court, but rather from four other sources: first, from the requirement of Rule 404(b) that the evidence be offered for a proper purpose; second, from the relevancy requirement of Rule 402 — as enforced through Rule 104(b); third, from the assessment the trial court must make under Rule 403 to determine whether the probative value of the similar acts evidence is substantially outweighed by its potential for unfair prejudice; and fourth, from Federal Rule of Evidence 105, which provides that the trial court shall, upon request, instruct the jury that the similar acts evidence is to be considered only for the proper purpose for which it was admitted.

NOTES AND QUESTIONS

(1) *How Much Similarity is Needed to Show Intent?* In *United States v. Beechum*, 582 F.2d 898 (5th Cir. 1978), the defendant, a substitute letter carrier for the United States Postal Service, was convicted of unlawfully possessing an 1890 silver dollar that he knew to be stolen from the mails. To establish that Beechum intentionally and unlawfully possessed the silver dollar, the Government introduced into evidence two Sears, Roebuck & Co. credit cards found in Beechum's wallet when he was arrested. Neither card was issued to Beechum, and neither was signed. The Government also introduced evidence indicating that the cards had been mailed some ten months prior to Beechum's arrest to two different addresses on routes he had serviced. Beechum's defense was that he intended to return the coin, which had fallen out of the mail, but could not find his supervisor. The trial court erroneously prohibited the prosecutor's questioning about the credit cards. The Court of Appeals observed:

> Where the issue addressed is the defendant's intent to commit the offense charged, the relevancy of the extrinsic offense derives from the defendant's indulging himself in the same state of mind in the perpetration of both the extrinsic and charged offenses. The reasoning is that because the defendant had unlawful intent in the extrinsic offense, it is less likely that he had lawful intent in the present offense.
>
> Once it is determined that the extrinsic offense requires the same intent as the charged offense and that the jury could find that the defendant committed the extrinsic offense, the evidence satisfies the first step under rule 404(b). The extrinsic offense is relevant (assuming the jury finds the defendant to have committed it) to an issue other than propensity because it lessens the likelihood that the defendant committed the charged offense with innocent intent . . . Evidence is relevant once it appears "to alter the probabilities of a consequential fact." Weinstein & Berger, Weinstein's Evidence (1976). The probative value of the evidence is a matter to be weighed against its potential for undue prejudice [only at the second step of the analysis — that is, when the evidence is scrutinized under Rule 403, having satisfied the first step, which is that it qualifies under Rule 404(b)], and the similarity of the physical elements of the charged and extrinsic offenses figures in [only] at this [second] stage.
>
> The overall similarity of the extrinsic and charged offenses in this case generates sufficient probity to meet the rule 403 test that the probative value of the evidence not be substantially outweighed by its unfair prejudice. We think this to be true even if it could not be established that the credit cards were stolen from the mail. At the least, there was sufficient evidence for the jury to find that Beechum possessed property belonging to others, with the specific intent to deprive the owners of their rightful possession permanently. . . .
>
> The probity of the credit card evidence in this case is augmented by the lack of temporal remoteness. Although Beechum may have obtained the cards as much as ten months prior to his arrest for the possession of the silver dollar, he kept the cards in his wallet where they would constantly

> remind him of the wrongfulness of their possession. . . . He would have been forced to argue that his state of mind was schizoid — that he intended at the same time to relinquish the coin but to keep the cards. . . .

Would *Beechum* have allowed the prior crime if it had been breaking and entering a locked park? Assault? Murder? At which "step" of the analysis would such crimes have been eliminated, if at all? Does this render Fed. R. Evid. 404(b) a dead letter, leaving only Fed. R. Evid. 403? Does Fed. R. Evid. 403 give the trial judge any guidance?

(2) *Common Scheme or Plan.* In *People v. Tassell*, 679 P.2d 1 (Cal. 1984), defendant was convicted of kidnapping and forcible oral copulation. His defense was that the woman consented. The prosecution introduced as part of its case-in-chief evidence of two prior sex offenses against two other women who appeared as witnesses. They testified about sex offenses committed by the defendant in much the same way as he was alleged to have done on this occasion. Taking other courts to task for ruling differently, the court holds the evidence should not have been admitted, although the error was harmless. The evidence was presented to the jury under the "common plan or scheme" exception to the general rule against admission of other crimes evidence. But, the court says, there was no issue of either identity or intent. In such circumstances, the court says, "common plan or scheme" is just a euphemism for disposition, which may not be proved by prior crimes: "disposition" in this case merely translates into "indifference to consent." Note that *Tassell* was overruled by *People v. Ewoldt*, 867 P.2d 757 (Cal. 1994), which held that evidence that the defendant committed prior, uncharged lewd acts on the victim's older sister was admissible, even though the evidence was uncorroborated. *Ewoldt* concluded that *Tassell:*

> is based upon the erroneous premise that a common design or plan cannot be established by evidence reflecting that the defendant committed markedly similar acts of misconduct against similar victims under similar circumstances, unless all of these acts are part of a single, continuing conception or plot. As we have explained, evidence of a common design or plan is admitted not to prove the defendant's intent or identity, but to prove that the defendant engaged in the conduct alleged to constitute the charged offense. Such evidence, therefore, is not admitted to establish that the defendant has a criminal disposition or bad character, but to prove that he or she committed the charged offense pursuant to the same design or plan used in committing the uncharged criminal acts.

Which decision correctly interprets common design or plan? *See* Imwinkelried, *Using a Contextual Construction to Resolve the Dispute Over the Meaning of the Term "Plan" in Federal Rule of Evidence 404(b)*, 43 U. Kan. L. Rev. 1005 (1995) (discussing both cases). Is there really a difference between "plan" in the *Ewoldt* sense and disposition, propensity, or character?

Does "plan" in Fed. R. Evid. 404(b) mean that all the crimes that are part of the plan had to be planned at the same time? What if the intention to do the first one was formed, then the first one was executed, and after execution, an intention to do the second one was formed, and then the second one was executed; and so on? Is it enough that all the crimes proceeded according to a similar blueprint?

Is there reason to treat sex offense cases differently than others? *See* § 3.03[B], *below*; Bryden & Park, *Other Crimes Evidence in Sex Offense Cases*, 78 MINN. L. REV. 529 (1994). California Evidence Code § 1108 now permits evidence of prior sexual assaults so long as not unduly prejudicial.

(3) *Prior Crimes did Not Satisfy Rule 404(b).* In *United States v. Benedetto*, 571 F.2d 1246 (2d Cir. 1978), defendant (a meat inspector) was charged with taking bribes from meat packers in return for favorable inspections. The government introduced in its case-in-chief other instances of taking bribes from meat packers, not charged in the indictment, wherein, as in some of the charged offenses, $10-$15 was passed to defendant in a handshake. Defendant had let it be known that he intended to (and subsequently did) testify that he never took any bribes from anyone and that he intended to (and subsequently did) introduce testimony of other meat packers that he took no bribes from them (to show good character). His defense was that the complaining meat packers trumped up the charges because he was a strict inspector. The court held that the government's "other bribes" evidence could not come in under Fed. R. Evid. 404(b) to show "knowledge, intent, and a general plan or scheme" because defendant did not claim that he took the money innocently or mistakenly, but rather that he didn't take it — thus knowledge or intent were not in issue. On plan or scheme, the court said the "handshake" method was not so unusual or distinctive a method as to earmark the matters as the handiwork or signature of the accused and was nothing more than repeated commission of crimes of the same class, no more distinctive than using glassine bags to pack heroin. It might be different, the court holds, had the methods of the crimes been, for example, to leave money in a coffee can each Friday. The court finds some force to the "identity" argument: that the evidence shows a continuing plan to use defendant's position to get payoffs. But the court holds the evidence admissible primarily because of defendant's testimony that he never took bribes. Thus, the government's evidence came in to contradict or impeach. (The court holds it to be a mere technicality that the evidence came in before defendant's testimony.) A concurring judge emphasizes that defendant introduced his own proof of other instances, licensing the government here, but is troubled that since the evidence was not admitted on a limited theory of impeachment, no instruction was asked or given limiting the evidence to such use. (The majority holds the failure to instruct not to be plain error in light of the great strength of the other evidence against the defendant and the closeness of the Fed. R. Evid. 404(b) question.)

(4) *Subsequent Crimes to Show Lack of Duress.* In *United States v. Hearst*, 638 F.2d 1190 (9th Cir. 1980), *cert. denied*, 451 U.S. 938 (1981), one of the points made was that the other crimes subsequent to the charged offense helped to refute a claim that the charged offense was committed under duress (brought to bear by a group that originally had kidnapped the defendant). The other crimes, however, also were committed during the period of alleged captivity. Would the other crimes tend to rebut duress in such circumstances?

(5) *The Government may be Able to Use Evidence of a Similar Crime Under Rule 404(b) Even When Defendant has been Acquitted of that Crime: Dowling v. United States*, 493 U.S. 342 (1990). Dowling was convicted of bank robbery, committed by a man wearing a distinctive ski mask and carrying a small pistol. The Government offered evidence that a similarly masked and armed individual had

attempted to rob a victim named Henry. This witness, Henry, identified Dowling as the perpetrator. The Supreme Court upheld use of this other-crime evidence under Fed. R. Evid. 404(b) to prove Dowling's identity, notwithstanding the fact that Dowling had been acquitted of the Henry offense, and it rejected claims of double jeopardy and due process violations. "[T]he Government did not have to demonstrate that Dowling was the man who entered the [Henry] home beyond a reasonable doubt." Pursuant to *Huddleston*, all that was required was that "the jury [could] reasonably conclude that the act occurred and that the defendant was the actor." Acquittal on a reasonable-doubt standard did not negate the lesser proof thus required under Fed. R. Evid. 404(b).

(6) *Due Process is Not Offended by Other-Acts Evidence Even if There Is No Affirmative Proof that Defendant Committed the Other Acts, if They Are Admitted for a Proper Purpose, such as Disproof of Accident: Estelle v. McGuire*, 502 U.S. 62 (1991). McGuire was convicted in California state courts of the murder of his infant daughter, Tori. Two physicians testified that Tori was a victim of battered child syndrome. McGuire brought Tori to a hospital:

> The baby was bluish in color and was not breathing. The attending physician noticed a large and relatively recent bruise on Tori's chest with multiple bruises around it, as well as black and blue marks around her ears. Efforts to revive the child were unsuccessful; Tori died 45 minutes after being brought to the hospital. An autopsy revealed 17 contusions on the baby's chest, 29 contusions in her abdominal area, a split liver, a split pancreas, a lacerated large intestine, and damage to her heart and one of her lungs. The autopsy also uncovered evidence of rectal tearing, which was at least six weeks old, and evidence of partially healed rib fractures, which were approximately seven weeks old.

[M]cGuire stated his belief that Tori's injuries must have resulted from a fall off the family couch. [A]fter a police officer expressed skepticism at this explanation, McGuire replied that "[m]aybe some Mexicans came in" while he was upstairs. This evidence all was held admissible under the California Evidence Code and California battered child decisions. But on federal habeas corpus, the Ninth Circuit held that in the absence of affirmative proof that McGuire had caused Tori's injuries, the other injuries and battered-child evidence, together with jury instructions, denied McGuire due process.

The United States Supreme Court reversed the reversal. In doing so, it focused not on construing evidence rules, but on whether the California proceeding violated the Constitution:

> When offered to show that certain injuries are a product of child abuse, rather than accident, evidence of prior injuries is relevant even though it does not purport to prove the identity of the person who might have inflicted those injuries. [T]he evidence demonstrated that Tori's death was the result of an intentional act by someone, and not an accident.

(7) *Why is Rule 404(b) Focused on Purpose, Not Probative Force?* Why does Fed. R. Evid. 404(b) draw a line based on the purpose or issue for which the

evidence is offered, rather than based on degree of probative force or degree of prejudice?

(8) *Continuum of Similarity.* Because of the division into purposes, some jurisdictions seem to believe that there are different requirements for each purpose. For example, *Ewoldt*, discussed in note (2), *above*, states that the amount of similarity necessary to admit a prior crime depends on the purpose for which it is being introduced. It establishes a continuum on which the least degree of similarity is needed to prove intent and the most to prove identity, with plan falling in the middle. Should such a requirement depend more on the facts of the particular case than on the particular catchword being employed?

NOTE ON THE NARROW VIEW OF OTHER-ACTS EVIDENCE: APPLICATION OF FLORIDA'S WILLIAMS RULE TO THE TRIAL OF WILLIAM KENNEDY SMITH

Florida's Williams Rule: Williams v. State, 110 So. 2d 654 (Fla.), *cert. denied*, 361 U.S. 847 (1959). Florida, under a rule ostensibly somewhat similar to Fed. R. Evid. 404(b), tends to exclude other-acts evidence unless it is highly particularized. Among other requirements, the evidence must be like a signature; it is not enough that it is merely probative of an issue such as identity. Not only must it be similar, but highly unusual as well. In this regard, Florida's *Williams* rule, as it is called, may be more restrictive than many interpretations of Fed. R. Evid. 404(b), and it seems to be applied more restrictively than rules in many other states.

The William Kennedy Smith Trial: Exclusion of Defendant's Three Prior Sexual Assaults with Similarities to the Charged Offense. William Kennedy Smith's trial for rape made headlines, nationwide, in part because the defendant was a nephew of the late President John F. Kennedy, in part because of the extraneous-offense evidence, and in part because the charged offense allegedly occurred at the Palm Beach compound owned by the defendant's other uncle, Senator Edward Kennedy. Smith's defense was consent; the prosecution presented starkly different testimony by the victim, however, suggesting a Jekyll-and-Hyde change in the defendant's personality, whereby he suddenly and brutally overpowered the victim after inducing her to go where the two were alone. To rebut the defense of consent and to prove intent, the prosecutor offered evidence of three prior sexual assaults with certain similarities, including the same Jekyll-and-Hyde modus operandi as well as similarities in the appearances of the victims. But none of the offenses was so unusual that it could be compared to a signature. In addition, the identity of the assailant was not in question. The trial judge considered these prior assaults at a pretrial "*Williams* rule hearing," as Florida law provides.

See Mark Hansen, *Experts Expected Smith Verdict: Even a Perfect Prosecutor Can Lose Date Rape Cases, Pundits Say*, A.B.A. J., Feb. 1992, at 18. This article reports the outcome of the *Williams* rule hearing, as well as the result that it precipitated at trial:

> To a trained observer, the turning point in the rape trial of William Kennedy Smith occurred before the first witness had taken the stand.

> It came [with a pretrial ruling that] refused to allow the testimony of three women who claimed that Smith had also raped or assaulted them in the past.
>
> "A top prosecutor doing a perfect job would have a difficult time winning a case like this," said Bruce Rogow, a law school professor at Nova University. "Any hopes the prosecution had of winning this case probably evaporated when the judge excluded the *Williams* rule evidence.". . .
>
> Yet few found fault with the judge's decision. Experts say the rule allowing the introduction of such evidence has been narrowly construed by the Florida Supreme Court. In one often-cited case, the court threw out the murder conviction of a man accused of tying his victim's hands behind her back with her bra because his trial included evidence that the defendant had sexually assaulted two other women whose hands were tied, but . . . not with their bras.

The Hands-Tied-in-Back Case. The hands-tied-in-back case referred to above is *Drake v. State*, 400 So. 2d 1217 (Fla. 1981). In that case, defendant was convicted of a brutal murder. Both in the murder case and in two prior cases, Drake had tied the women's hands behind their backs in the process of assaulting them. The Florida court reversed, and its analysis of this evidence reflects that State's narrow approach:

> The "mode of operating" theory of proving identity is based on both similarity of and the unusual nature of the factual situations being compared. A mere general similarity will not render the similar facts legally relevant to show identity. [The] points of similarity must have some special character or be so unusual as to point to the defendant. The only similarity between the two incidents introduced at trial and Reeder's murder is the tying of the hands behind the victims' backs and that both had left a bar with the defendant. There are many dissimilarities, not the least of which is that the collateral incidents involved only sexual assaults while the instant case involved murder with little, if any, evidence of sexual abuse. Even assuming some similarity, the similar facts offered would still fail the unusual branch of the test. Binding of the hands occurs in many crimes involving many different criminal defendants. This binding is not sufficiently unusual to point to the defendant in this case, and it is, therefore, irrelevant to prove identity.

Is the Williams Rule Good or Bad? See Rodriguez v. State, 675 So. 2d 189 (Fla. Dist. Ct. App. 1996) (reversing robbery conviction because of evidence of another robbery six days earlier, which was similar but not uniquely so). In the wake of the William Kennedy Smith trial, NEWSWEEK editorialized in favor of "relaxing" the *Williams* rule and showing "faith in jurors." Kaplan, *Palm Beach Lessons: Should Date-Rape Law Be Reformed, Giving Extra Latitude to Prosecutors?* NEWSWEEK, Dec. 23, 1991, at 30, 31.

Florida has not shied away from *Williams*, and has handed down decisions that may make it even more stringent. For example, *Kulling v. State*, 827 So. 2d 311 (Fla. Dist. Ct. App. 2002), reversed a conviction of a male defendant for lewd or lascivious exhibition (masturbation) in the presence of a female child under sixteen. Evidence had been introduced at trial that the defendant exposed himself and masturbated on two other occasions in front of two nearby women neighbors in the same neighborhood, in public, from a similar distance. As in the case of the child, the defendant stared and made eye contact while in the act, apparently even though he knew he was known to and could be identified by the victims in all three cases. The appeals court held this course of proof was improper despite the similarities. The evidence contained, in the court's view, no characteristics that were so unusual or distinctive as to point to the defendant or constitute his "fingerprint" or signature. The court said the conduct was no different than that engaged in by other public masturbators, and held that therefore it was only introduced to show character or propensity, which are forbidden purposes.

Is Florida's approach appropriate to protect defendants from prejudice? Does it protect victims or potential victims sufficiently? Would you relax it only in the case of sex crimes? *See* § 3.03[B], *below.*

[2] Evidence Whose Probativity Does Not Depend on Human Tendency to Repeat (Not Character or Propensity Reasoning)

UNITED STATES v. PELTIER

United States Court of Appeals, Eighth Circuit
585 F.2d 314 (1978), *cert. denied*, 440 U.S. 945 (1979)

Ross, Circuit Judge.

On June 26, 1975, two Special Agents of the Federal Bureau of Investigation, Jack Coler and Ronald Williams, were murdered on the Pine Ridge Indian Reservation in South Dakota. Leonard Peltier, Robert Eugene Robideau, Darrell Dean Butler, and James Theodore Eagle were charged with first-degree murder. Peltier was tried by a jury, was convicted and was sentenced to life imprisonment. He appeals. In June of 1975, Special Agents Coler and Williams were engaged in felony criminal investigations on the Pine Ridge Indian Reservation. On June 25 and 26, they were attempting to locate and arrest four individuals, including James Theodore Eagle, who were charged with armed robbery and assault with a deadly weapon. [As they were engaged in the investigation, persons in a van fired on them. The killing shots, however, were apparently fired at close range by someone emerging from the van. Members of an Indian movement known as AIM were apparently involved.]

The evidence against Peltier was primarily circumstantial. At the trial, the parties stipulated to the following facts: On November 22, 1972, Peltier was charged with attempted murder in Milwaukee, Wisconsin. He was arrested, and was released on bond. On July 29, 1974, he failed to appear for trial and a bench warrant was issued for his arrest. Peltier was aware of the outstanding arrest warrant and knew he would be returned to Milwaukee to stand trial.

The defendant agreed to stipulate to these facts only after the district court rejected his argument that they were not relevant. The government argues that this evidence was admissible under Rule 404(b) to prove motive, because it tended to show why Peltier reacted with deadly force when followed by the F.B.I. agents. We agree. The key issue at trial was the identity of the murderer, and evidence tending to show motive was clearly relevant.

Moreover, the probative value of the evidence was not substantially outweighed by the danger of unfair prejudice [under Fed. R. Evid. 403]. The evidence was highly probative, especially when considered in conjunction with a statement Peltier made after his arrest in Canada to the effect that the two agents were shot when they came to serve him with a Wisconsin warrant. Furthermore, the government took steps to minimize the danger of unfair prejudice. The fact that the person Peltier allegedly assaulted in Wisconsin was an off-duty police officer was withheld from the jury. The stipulation was read to the jury at the end of the government's case. Finally, the following cautionary instruction was given:

> "Evidence has been admitted relating to other crimes, wrongs or actions alleged to have been committed by the defendant in this case. Such evidence is not to be considered to prove the character of the defendant in order to show that he acted in conformity therewith on June 26, 1975.". . . .

We hold that the district court did not abuse its discretion in admitting this evidence.

Affirmed.

UNITED STATES v. CUNNINGHAM

United States Court of Appeals, Seventh Circuit

103 F.3d 553 (7th Cir. 1996), *cert. denied*, 520 U.S. 1192 (1997)

Posner, Circuit Judge.

[Defendant, a nurse, was charged with tampering with syringes by removing Demerol, a painkiller, resulting in failure of pain medication for some patients. The trial court admitted evidence that she had stolen Demerol on a prior occasion (but excluded her conviction for that act). The court also allowed proof that her license had been suspended but was reinstated conditioned upon drug tests, some of which she falsified. The Court of Appeals upheld these rulings as consistent with Fed. R. Evid. 404(b) and 403, on the ground that the defendant's addiction to Demerol provided motive and the suspension provided context by which the jury could understand the other evidence.]

[Under Fed. R. Evid. 404(b),] the fact that Cunningham had stolen Demerol in the past could not be introduced to show that she is likely to have stolen Demerol in the present. But evidence of prior conduct may be introduced (subject to the judge's power to exclude it under Rule 403 as unduly prejudicial, confusing, or merely cumulative) for other purposes, for example to show the defendant's motive for committing the crime with which he is charged.

"Propensity" evidence and "motive" evidence need not overlap. They do not, for example, when past drug convictions are used to show that the defendant in a robbery case is an addict and his addiction is offered as the motive for the robbery. *See, e.g., People v. McConnell*, 124 Mich. App. 672, 335 N.W.2d 226, 230 (1983); *cf. People v. Moreno*, 61 Cal. App. 3d 688, 693-94, 132 Cal. Rptr. 569 (1976) (man's theft of a woman's underwear). They do overlap when the crime is motivated by a taste for engaging in that crime or a compulsion to engage in it (an "addiction"), rather than by a desire for pecuniary gain or for some other advantage to which the crime is instrumental in the sense that it would not be committed if the advantage could be obtained as easily by a lawful route. Sex crimes provide a particularly clear example. Most people do not have a taste for sexually molesting children. As between two suspected molesters, then, only one of whom has a history of such molestation, the history establishes a motive that enables the two suspects to be distinguished. A "firebug" — one who commits arson not for insurance proceeds or revenge or to eliminate a competitor, but for the sheer joy of watching a fire — is, like the sex criminal, a person whose motive to commit the crime with which he is charged is revealed by his past commission of the same crime. The greater the overlap between propensity and motive, the more careful the district judge must be about admitting under the rubric of motive evidence that the jury is likely to use instead as a basis for inferring the defendant's propensity, his habitual criminality, even if instructed not to. But the tool for preventing this abuse is Rule 403, not Rule 404(b).

Because Cunningham's addiction was not to *stealing* Demerol but to consuming it, this case is like *Moreno*, where the defendant's sexual fetish supplied the motive for his stealing women's underwear, and *McConnell*, where the defendant's drug addiction supplied the motive to rob — he needed money to buy drugs.

The evidence of Cunningham's suspension might seem to have been superfluous and equivocal, as being merely the civil equivalent of the criminal conviction that the judge properly excluded. But the suspension, unlike the conviction, did not merely duplicate the evidence of Cunningham's addiction or insinuate a propensity to steal; it also provided essential background to the evidence of her having falsified the results of tests required as a condition of regaining her license. That evidence furnished the basis for an inference that she had falsified the test results in order to enable her to continue to feed her addiction. Without knowing that she had been suspended, the jury would have wondered why she had been tested and had falsified the test results. The admission of bad-acts evidence to contextualize, and by contextualizing enable the jury to understand, other evidence is a recognized exception to the prohibition of bad-acts evidence.

NOTES AND QUESTIONS

Acts Integral to the Charged Crime. Often a court will find that Fed. R. Evid. 404(b) need not be complied with because the act in question is integral to the crime charged. *See United States v. Leichtman*, 742 F.2d 598 (11th Cir. 1984) (in prosecution for kidnapping conspiracy stemming from illegal drug transaction, drug transaction held not to be "other crime" within meaning of Rule 404(b) because evidence of drug transaction was inextricably intertwined with evidence necessary to prove crime charged). If a defendant is charged with robbery, and the getaway car was stolen shortly before the robbery, how close in time must the car theft be to the robbery to be considered integral? Is evidence that the defendant embarked on a crime spree integral, or precluded as showing bad character?

[3] Revisiting Evidence Whose Probativity Depends on Human Tendency to Repeat: Is it Necessarily Doomed if we Recognize that it is Propensity Evidence?

Reconsider the evidence in *Jones, Huddleston*, and *Beechum* in Subsection [B][1], *above*. The evidence admitted in those cases plainly seems to be admitted on the theory that the person had a certain tendency or propensity and therefore is more likely to have acted (or thought) in accord with it than someone who did not have it (all other things being equal between the two people). That theory, however, is called, in those cases, "plan" or some other permissive catchword of the kind found in Fed. R. Evid. 404(b)(2), rather than "character" or "propensity" and acting in accord therewith, which would sound like the prohibited purpose in Rule 404(b)(1).

But isn't that so-called "permitted" theory identical to the prohibited purpose? Isn't it proving "character" in order to prove an act in conformity therewith? Or is there some difference between "character" on the one hand and "tendency" or "propensity" on the other? Can one have a "character" (or even a "character trait") of rubbing bodies to distract while removing a wallet (see *Jones*)? Wouldn't it be helpful if the rule gave us a definition of this key term ("character")? Is there a definition suggested by these cases that is related to the purposes of the rule against character evidence? Was the propensity in the mentioned cases too specific to be banned? Is it only *general* propensity that is banned? See if this is borne out by the following materials.

HAMMANN v. HARTFORD ACCIDENT AND INDEMNITY CO.

United States Court of Appeals, Sixth Circuit
620 F.2d 588 (1980)

BOYCE F. MARTIN, JR., CIRCUIT JUDGE.

Bruce Hammann brought an action to recover under a fire insurance policy for damage to a barn. He appeals a jury verdict for the defendant.

The fire was first observed around 8:00 a.m. shortly after Hammann returned from the barn. He had been alone there for approximately thirty minutes before his wife spotted the fire and gave the alarm. The defendant, Hartford Accident and Indemnity Company, presented expert testimony as to the origin and nature of the fire. It had three places of origin in the upper loft, was incendiary in nature, and was started by use of an accelerant. Hammann suggested that the fire was started by lightning but offered no substantial proof.

The main thrust of Hammann's appeal concerns the admission into evidence of his previous fire experiences. Hammann contends that such evidence was irrelevant and prejudicial. At least six other fires had occurred on various tracts of property belonging to the plaintiff over the years. Four of them resulted in insurance recoveries. The trial judge excluded evidence of fires which did not result in any recovery. Also excluded was any evidence of the circumstances surrounding the four fires yielding insurance recoveries.

Defendant argues that evidence of other fires was properly admitted under Rule 404(b), Fed. R. Evid. The trial court entertains broad discretion in making a determination of admissibility under Rule 404(b). We must determine whether such discretion was abused in ruling that the probative value of such fires outweighed their potentially prejudicial effect.

Here, the evidence of prior fires was properly admitted for a number of reasons: Defendant attacked Hammann's credibility by establishing that he had willfully concealed several occurrences of fires from the defendant. Second, the trial court properly instructed the jury that the fires were to be considered as bearing only on Hammann's motive. Lastly, Hartford asserted the defense of incendiarism which included evidence of Hammann's intent or knowledge of the occurrence.

Affirmed.

NOTES AND QUESTIONS

(1) *Brides of the Bath.* When an act is committed repeatedly in a particular way, courts typically will permit evidence of that act regardless of whether the defendant planned them all together. In other words, there need not be a master plan created at one time so long as the blueprint or "modus operandi" of each unrelated act appears to be sufficiently similar. Thus, in *Rex v. Smith*, 114 L.T.R. 239 (Crim. App. 1915), generally referred to as the "Brides of the Bath" case, the fact that several other similarly property-endowed wives of the defendant were found drowned in a bathtub was admitted as evidence in his murder trial for the death of one particular wife by drowning in a bathtub.

We might view this as showing the defendant's "specific propensity." The trait of drowning one's wives in the bathtub is not meant to raise the specter of general bad propensity or character, i.e., that the defendant is a bad or violent person and likely acted in accord with this trait on this occasion, but rather to show that he has a specific propensity to intentionally drown his wives in the bathtub, and likely acted in accord with that specific propensity. We would not say a person has a "character" to drown his wives in the bathtub. Character refers to a very general propensity (badness, violence, lawlessness, etc.). But we *would* say he has a specific propensity to do so. Does this make sense in view of the purpose of the character rule? Does the "modus operandi" theory of admissibility, used to produce admissibility in a wide variety of Fed. R. Evid. 404(b) cases, always amount to specific propensity? In the actual case, a number of phrases like those in Rule 404(b)(2) were used to justify admissibility. (What ones come to mind? Motive? Plan? Intent? Absence of mistake? All seem to apply.)

A type of specific propensity reasoning was used in the O.J. Simpson case when the judge permitted evidence of the defendant's prior acts of domestic violence against his murdered wife on the theory that they had in common the same victim and the same defendant. *See* Raeder, *The Admissibility of Prior Acts of Domestic Violence: Simpson and Beyond*, 69 S. Cal. L. Rev. 1463 (1996). *Cf. State v. Pooler*, 696 So. 2d 22 (La. Ct. App. 1997) (reverse situation, wife kills allegedly violent husband; pattern of husband's domestic violence allowed to be proven to show his violence on this occasion and also as basis for expert testimony on victim's state of mind).

Of course, we still beg the question of how similar the events have to be to constitute specific propensity rather that general propensity. In other words, we still have the question, when does "character" become "pattern?" (2) *Is Specific Propensity Prohibited as Character Evidence?* Professor Rothstein has made the point in a series of writings and lectures over the last fifteen years that character is not synonymous with propensity, but simply one kind of propensity: one that is amorphous and morally tinged. As a result, he distinguishes the specific propensity to repeatedly do a certain thing in a certain way from the general character ban and concludes that specific tendencies addressed to the manner or means of carrying out the offense should not be viewed as prohibited by Fed. R. Evid. 404. See, most recently, Rothstein, *Intellectual Coherence in an Evidence Code*, 28 Loy. L.A. L. Rev. 1259 (1995). Similarly, Professors Park and Bryden have observed that:

> One could construe the concept of "character" as referring only to traits manifesting a general propensity, such as a propensity toward violence or dishonesty. Under this interpretation, a situationally specific propensity, such as a propensity to lurk in the back seats of empty cars in shopping centers as a prelude to sexual assaults on the owners, would be too specific to be called a trait of character.

"Other Crimes" Evidence in Sex Offense Cases, 78 Minn. L. Rev. 529, 565 (1994). Do you agree?

(3) *"Doctrine of Chances."* Professor Imwinkelried argues that the "doctrine of chances" is a concept that permits the admission of prior similar conduct of the defendant without invoking the ban on character evidence (or even invoking propensity) because the fact-finder evaluates the odds of an innocent person being repeatedly involved in similar suspicious circumstances, rather than focusing on the actor as a bad person. *See generally* Imwinkelried, Uncharged Misconduct Evidence § 4.01 (1998); and his article, *An Evidentiary Paradox: Defending the Character Evidence Prohibition by Upholding a Non-Character Theory of Logical Relevance, the Doctrine of Chances*, 40 U. Rich. L. Rev. 419 (2006).

United States v. Woods, 484 F.2d 127 (4th Cir. 1973), *cert. denied*, 415 U.S. 979 (1974), is the paradigm case applying the doctrine of chances. In *Woods*, the defendant was charged with the death of a child in her care. Evidence existed that a number of children previously in her care died mysteriously. The likelihood that the current death was accidental decreased with the existence of so many other unrelated deaths. Thus, the jury can infer that the probability of so many accidental deaths happening to one caretaker is slight without inferring that the defendant has bad character (or indeed, a propensity) and therefore committed the crimes.

In contrast, Professor Rothstein responds that what underlies the doctrine of chances is the propensity-based reasoning that innocent people act differently than guilty people. It is only because of a once-guilty person's propensity to repeat that the probability of present guilt is higher for that person. Otherwise, it would be equal to the probability of present guilt of a previously uninvolved person. Rothstein, *Intellectual Coherence, supra.* With which view do you agree?

PROBLEM 3A: IS THE SIMILARITY DISTINCTIVE ENOUGH TO ADMIT THE PRIOR CRIME?

The defendant was convicted of capital murder (of Bertha). He claimed that the admission of his confession to a prior murder (of Nancy) was error. The State argued that the "Nancy" confessions were relevant to identity because the Bertha and Nancy murders were extremely similar. To support its argument, the State offered a chart outlining the similarities between the two cases:

BERTHA MARTINEZ CASE	**NANCY SHOEMAKER CASE**
VICTIM PROFILE	VICTIM PROFILE
— One (1) Victim	— One (1) Victim
— Female Victim	— Female Victim
— Child Victim	— Child Victim
— Same Approx. Age (8 yrs old)	— Same Approx. Age (9 yrs old)
— Victim was "Unknown Stranger"	— Victim was "Unknown Stranger"
KIDNAPPING	KIDNAPPING
— Victim was Abducted	— Victim was Abducted
— Victim was Abducted/Public Area	— Victim was Abducted
	— Victim was Abducted/Public Area
— Victim was Abducted Near Victim's Home	— Victim was Abducted Near Victim's Home
— Victim was Physically Relocated (City Park/Comanche St. Residence)	— Victim was Physically Relocated (Bell Plaine, Kansas)
DEFENDANT HAD "NEXUS" TO LOCATION OF ABDUCTION	DEFENDANT HAD "NEXUS" TO LOCATION OF ABDUCTION
— Defendant was Resident of Nearby Brown School	— Defendant Delivered "Penny Power" Circulars in this area
VICTIM PHYSICALLY ASSAULTED	VICTIM PHYSICALLY ASSAULTED
VICTIM SEXUALLY ASSAULTED	VICTIM SEXUALLY ASSAULTED
VICTIM MURDERED	VICTIM MURDERED
— Defendant "strangled" victim	— Defendant "strangled" victim
VICTIM'S BODY "DUMPED"	VICTIM'S BODY "DUMPED"
DEFENDANT COMMITTED OFFENSE WITH CO-ACTOR	DEFENDANT COMMITTED OFFENSE WITH CO-ACTOR
— Woody and Murlene Broughton	— Donny Wacker

DEFENDANT INVOLVED WITH "SEARCH" DEFENDANT CLAIMED "TROPHY" FROM CRIME — Wore Bertha Martinez's Underwear	DEFENDANT INVOLVED WITH "SEARCH" DEFENDANT CLAIMED "TROPHY" FROM CRIME — Took Nancy Shoemaker's Underwear

The State argued that the extraneous offense was critical on the issue of identity because there was no physical evidence to connect appellant to the offense and some of the physical evidence arguably could indicate to the contrary. Should the evidence of the prior murder be admitted? Are the similarities distinctive enough or shared by a number of child murders? Does the fact that both murders were of children affect your analysis? Is modus operandi really specific propensity? This chart was used in *Lane v. State*, 933 S.W.2d 504 (Tex. Crim. App. 1996) (*en banc*), which affirmed the admission of the defendant's "Nancy" confessions. Do you agree with this result?

On the use of specific instances of other conduct in both the civil and the criminal context (both of which are embraced by Fed. R. Evid. 404(b)), including evidence of other failures in products liability cases (which may or may not be embraced by Fed. R. Evid. 404(b)), see IMWINKELRIED, UNCHARGED MISCONDUCT EVIDENCE (1998).

For additional very informative materials, see American Bar Association Criminal Justice Section, Committee on Rules of Criminal Procedure and Evidence, *Federal Rules of Evidence: A Fresh Review and Evaluation*, 120 F.R.D. 299, 322–30 (1988) (Rothstein, chair); Leonard, *The Use of Character to Prove Conduct: Rationality and Catharsis in the Law of Evidence*, 58 U. COLO. L. REV. 1 (1987); Uviller, *Evidence of Character to Prove Conduct: Illusion, Illogic and Injustice in the Courtroom*, 130 U. PA. L. REV. 845 (1982); Graham, *Evidence as to Character — Other Crimes, Wrongs or Acts*, 19 CRIM. L. BULL. 349 (1983).

[C] Other Bad Acts More Directly in Issue[3]

Read Federal Rule of Evidence 405, "Methods of Proving Character."

OLD CHIEF v. UNITED STATES
United States Supreme Court
519 U.S. 172 (1997)

JUSTICE SOUTER delivered the opinion of the Court.

Subject to certain limitations, 18 U.S.C. § 922(g)(1) prohibits possession of a firearm by anyone with a prior felony conviction, which the government can prove

---

[3] Study Guide Reference: Evidence in a Nutshell, Chapter 4:VIII; X at "Concessions, Offers to Stipulate"; III at "Intent or Knowledge."

by introducing a record of judgment or similar evidence identifying the previous offense. Fearing prejudice if the jury learns the nature of the earlier crime, defendants sometimes seek to avoid such an informative disclosure by offering to concede the fact of the prior conviction. The issue here is whether a district court abuses its discretion if it spurns such an offer and admits the full record of a prior judgment, when the name or nature of the prior offense raises the risk of a verdict tainted by improper considerations, and when the purpose of the evidence is solely to prove the element of prior conviction. We hold that it does.

In 1993, petitioner, Old Chief, was arrested after a fracas involving at least one gunshot. The ensuing federal charges included not only assault with a dangerous weapon and using a firearm in relation to a crime of violence but violation of 18 U.S.C. § 922(g)(1). This statute makes it unlawful for anyone "who has been convicted in any court of law, a crime punishable by imprisonment for a term exceeding one year" to "possess in or affecting commerce, any firearm." "[A] crime punishable by imprisonment for a term exceeding one year" is defined to exclude "any Federal or State offenses pertaining to antitrust violations, unfair trade practices, restraints of trade, or other similar offenses relating to the regulation of business practices" and "any State offense classified by the laws of the State as a misdemeanor and punishable by a term of imprisonment of two years or less." 18 U.S.C. § 921(a)(20).

The earlier crime charged in the indictment against Old Chief was assault causing serious bodily injury. Before trial, he moved for an order requiring the government "to refrain from mentioning — by reading the Indictment, during jury selection, in opening statement, or closing argument — and to refrain from offering into evidence or soliciting any testimony from any witness regarding the prior criminal convictions of the Defendant, *except* to state that the Defendant has been convicted of a crime punishable by imprisonment exceeding one (1) year." He offered to "solve the problem here by stipulating, agreeing and requesting the Court to instruct the jury that he has been convicted of a crime punishable by imprisonment exceeding one (1) year[]." He argued that the offer to stipulate to the fact of the prior conviction rendered evidence of the name and nature of the offense inadmissible under Rule 403 of the Federal Rules of Evidence, the danger being that unfair prejudice from that evidence would substantially outweigh its probative value.

The Assistant United States Attorney refused to join in a stipulation, insisting on his right to prove his case his own way, and the District Court agreed, ruling orally that, "If he doesn't want to stipulate, he doesn't have to." At trial, over renewed objection, the Government introduced the order of judgment and commitment for Old Chief's prior conviction. This document disclosed that on December 18, 1988, he "did knowingly and unlawfully assault Rory Dean Fenner, said assault resulting in serious bodily injury," for which Old Chief was sentenced to five years' imprisonment. The jury found Old Chief guilty on all counts, and he appealed. . . .

As a threshold matter, there is Old Chief's erroneous argument that the name of his prior offense as contained in the record of conviction is irrelevant to the prior-conviction element, and for that reason inadmissible under Rule 402 of the Federal Rules of Evidence. Rule 401 defines relevant evidence as [Rule quoted.]

[Evidence of the conviction] served to place Old Chief within a particular sub-class of offenders for whom firearms possession is outlawed by § 922(g)(1). A documentary record of the conviction for that named offense was thus relevant evidence in making Old Chief's § 922(g)(1) status more probable than it would have been without the evidence.

Nor was its evidentiary relevance under Rule 401 affected by the availability of alternative proofs of the element to which it went, such as an admission by Old Chief that he had been convicted of a crime "punishable by imprisonment for a term exceeding one year" within the meaning of the statute. The 1972 Advisory Committee Notes to Rule 401 make this point directly:

> The fact to which the evidence is directed need not be in dispute. While situations will arise which call for the exclusion of evidence offered to prove a point conceded by the opponent, the ruling should be made on the basis of such considerations as waste of time and undue prejudice (see Rule 403), rather than under any general requirement that evidence is admissible only if directed to matters in dispute.

If, then, relevant evidence is inadmissible in the presence of other evidence related to it, its exclusion must rest not on the ground that the other evidence has rendered it "irrelevant," but on its character as unfairly prejudicial, cumulative or the like, its relevance notwithstanding.

The term "unfair prejudice," as to a criminal defendant, speaks to the capacity of some concededly relevant evidence to lure the factfinder into declaring guilt on a ground different from proof specific to the offense charged. So, the Committee Notes to Rule 403 explain, " 'Unfair prejudice' within its context means an undue tendency to suggest decision on an improper basis, commonly, though not necessarily, an emotional one."

Such improper grounds certainly include the one that Old Chief points to here: generalizing a defendant's earlier bad act into bad character and taking that as raising the odds that he did the later bad act now charged (or, worse, as calling for preventive conviction even if he should happen to be innocent momentarily). . . .

Rule of Evidence 404(b) reflects [the] common law tradition by addressing propensity reasoning directly: "Evidence of other crimes, wrongs, or acts is not admissible to prove the character of a person in order to show action in conformity therewith." Fed. Rule Evid. 404(b). There is, accordingly, no question that propensity would be an "improper basis" for conviction and that evidence of a prior conviction is subject to analysis under Rule 403.

As for the analytical method to be used in Rule 403 balancing, two basic possibilities present themselves. An item of evidence might be viewed as an island, with estimates of its own probative value and unfairly prejudicial risk the sole reference points in deciding whether the danger substantially outweighs the value. . . . Or the question of admissibility might be seen as . . . [taking] account of the full evidentiary context of the case as the court understands it when the ruling must be made. . . . If an alternative were found to have substantially the same or greater probative value but a lower danger of unfair prejudice, sound judicial discretion would discount the value of the item first offered and exclude it if its discounted probative value were substantially outweighed by unfairly prejudicial risk. Even under this second approach, as we explain below, a defendant's Rule 403 objection offering to concede a point generally cannot prevail over the Government's choice to offer evidence showing guilt and all the circumstances surrounding the offense.[7]

The first understanding of the rule is open to a very telling objection. That reading would leave the party offering evidence with the option to structure a trial in whatever way would produce the maximum unfair prejudice consistent with relevance. It would be very odd for the law of evidence to recognize the danger of unfair prejudice only to confer such a degree of autonomy on the party subject to temptation, and the Rules of Evidence are not so odd.

Rather, a reading of the companions to Rule 403, and of the commentaries that went with them to Congress, makes it clear that what counts as the Rule 403 "probative value" of an item of evidence, as distinct from its Rule 401 "relevance," may be calculated by comparing evidentiary alternatives. The Committee Notes to Rule 401 explicitly say that a party's concession is pertinent to the court's discretion to exclude evidence on the point conceded. Such a concession, according to the Notes, will sometimes "call for the exclusion of evidence offered to prove [the] point conceded by the opponent."

In dealing with the specific problem raised by § 922(g)(1) and its prior-conviction element, there can be no question that evidence of the name or nature of the prior offense generally carries a risk of unfair prejudice to the defendant. Where a prior conviction was for a gun crime or one similar to other charges in a pending case the risk of unfair prejudice would be especially obvious. . . .

Old Chief's proffered admission would, in fact, have been not merely relevant but seemingly conclusive evidence of the element. Old Chief clearly meant to admit that his felony did qualify, by stipulating "that the Government has proven one of the essential elements of the offense." As a consequence, although the name of the prior offense may have been technically relevant, it addressed no detail in the definition of the prior-conviction element that would not have been covered by the stipulation or admission. Logic, then, seems to side with Old Chief.

There is, however, one more question to be considered. . . . [T]he Government invokes the familiar, standard rule that the prosecution is entitled to prove its case by evidence of its own choice, or, more exactly, that a criminal defendant may not stipulate or admit his way out of the full evidentiary force of the case as the government chooses to present it. The authority usually cited for this rule is *Parr v. United States*, 255 F.2d 86 (CA5), *cert. denied*, 358 U.S. 824 (1958), in which the Fifth Circuit explained that the "reason for the rule is to permit a party 'to present to the jury a picture of the events relied upon. To substitute for such a picture a naked admission might have the effect to rob the evidence of much of its fair and legitimate weight.' "

This is unquestionably true as a general matter. The "fair and legitimate weight"

---

[7] While our discussion has been general because of the general wording of Rule 403, our holding is limited to cases involving proof of felon status. On appellate review of a Rule 403 decision, a defendant must establish abuse of discretion, a standard that is not satisfied by a mere showing of some alternative means of proof that the prosecution in its broad discretion chose not to rely upon.

of conventional evidence . . . reflects the fact that making a case with testimony and tangible things not only satisfies the formal definition of an offense, but tells a colorful story with descriptive richness. Unlike an abstract premise, . . . a piece of evidence may address any number of separate elements, striking hard just because it shows so much at once; the account of a shooting that establishes capacity and causation may tell just as much about the triggerman's motive and intent. Evidence thus has force beyond any linear scheme of reasoning, and as its pieces come together a narrative gains momentum, with power not only to support conclusions but to sustain the willingness of jurors to draw the inferences, whatever they may be, necessary to reach an honest verdict. This persuasive power of the concrete and particular is often essential to the capacity of jurors to satisfy the obligations that the law places on them. Jury duty is usually unsought and sometimes resisted, and it may be as difficult for one juror suddenly to face the findings that can send another human being to prison, as it is for another to hold out conscientiously for acquittal. When a juror's duty does seem hard, the evidentiary account of what a defendant has thought and done can accomplish what no set of abstract statements ever could, not just to prove a fact but to establish its human significance, and so to implicate the law's moral underpinnings and a juror's obligation to sit in judgment. Thus, the prosecution may fairly seek to place its evidence before the jurors, as much to tell a story of guiltiness as to support an inference of guilt, to convince the jurors that a guilty verdict would be morally reasonable as much as to point to the discrete elements of a defendant's legal fault.

But there is something even more to the prosecution's interest[, in that there is] the need for evidence in all its particularity to satisfy the jurors' expectations about what proper proof should be. Some such demands they bring with them to the courthouse, assuming, for example, that a charge of using a firearm to commit an offense will be proven by introducing a gun in evidence. . . . "If [jurors'] expectations are not satisfied, triers of fact may penalize the party who disappoints them by drawing a negative inference against that party." Expectations may also arise in jurors' minds simply from the experience of a trial itself. The use of witnesses to describe a train of events naturally related can raise the prospect of learning about every ingredient of that natural sequence the same way. If suddenly the prosecution presents some occurrence in the series differently, as by announcing a stipulation or admission, the effect may be like saying, "never mind what's behind the door," and jurors may well wonder what they are being kept from knowing. A party seemingly responsible for cloaking something has reason for apprehension, and the prosecution with its burden of proof may prudently demur at a defense request to interrupt the flow of evidence telling the story in the usual way.

In sum, the accepted rule that the prosecution is entitled to prove its case free from any defendant's option to stipulate the evidence away rests on good sense. A syllogism is not a story, and a naked proposition in a courtroom may be no match for the robust evidence that would be used to prove it.

This recognition that the prosecution with its burden of persuasion needs evidentiary depth to tell a continuous story has, however, virtually no application when the point at issue is a defendant's legal status, dependent on some judgment rendered wholly independently of the concrete events of later criminal behavior charged against him. As in this case, the choice of evidence for such an element is usually not between eventful narrative and abstract proposition, but between propositions of slightly varying abstraction, either a record saying that conviction for some crime occurred at a certain time or a statement admitting the same thing without naming the particular offense. . . . Nor can it be argued that the events behind the prior conviction are proper nourishment for the jurors' sense of obligation to vindicate the public interest. Congress has made it plain that distinctions among generic felonies do not count for this purpose; the fact of the qualifying conviction is alone what matters under the statute. The most the jury needs to know is that the conviction admitted by the defendant falls within the class of crimes that Congress thought should bar a convict from possessing a gun, and this point may be made readily in a defendant's admission and underscored in the court's jury instructions. Finally, . . . proof of the defendant's status goes to an element entirely outside the natural sequence of what the defendant is charged with thinking and doing to commit the current offense. Proving status without telling exactly why that status was imposed leaves no gap in the story.

Given these peculiarities of the element of felony-convict status there is no cognizable difference between the evidentiary significance of an admission and of the legitimately probative component of the official record the prosecution would prefer to place in evidence. In this case, as in any other in which the prior conviction is for an offense likely to support conviction on some improper ground, the only reasonable conclusion was that the risk of unfair prejudice did substantially outweigh the discounted probative value of the record of conviction, and it was an abuse of discretion to admit the record when an admission was available. What we have said shows why this will be the general rule when proof of convict status is at issue, just as the prosecutor's choice will generally survive a Rule 403 analysis when a defendant seeks to force the substitution of an admission for evidence creating a coherent narrative of his thoughts and actions in perpetrating the offense for which he is being tried. *[Reversed and remanded.]*

JUSTICE O'CONNOR, with whom CHIEF JUSTICE BEHNQUIST, JUSTICE SCALIA, and JUSTICE THOMAS join, dissenting:

The Court today announces a rule that misapplies Federal Rule of Evidence 403 and upsets, without explanation, longstanding precedent regarding criminal prosecutions.

As a threshold matter, evidence is excludable only if it is "unfairly" prejudicial, in that it has "an undue tendency to suggest decision on an improper basis." The evidence tendered by the Government in this case — the order reflecting petitioner's prior conviction and sentence for assault resulting in serious bodily injury — directly proved a necessary element of the § 922(g)(1) offense, that is, that petitioner had committed a crime covered by § 921(a)(20). Perhaps petitioner's case was damaged when the jury discovered that he previously had committed a felony and heard the name of his crime. But I cannot agree with the Court that it was *unfairly* prejudicial for the Government to establish an essential element of its case against petitioner with direct proof of his prior conviction.

The structure of § 922(g)(1) itself shows that Congress envisioned jurors' learning the name and basic nature of the defendant's prior offense. [T]he statute excludes from § 922(g)(1)'s coverage certain business crimes and state misdemeanors punishable by imprisonment of two years or less. Within the meaning of § 922(g)(1), then, "a crime" is not an abstract or metaphysical concept. Rather, the Government must prove that the defendant committed a *particular* crime. In short, under § 922(g)(1), a defendant's prior felony conviction connotes not only that he is a prior felon, but also that he has engaged in specific past criminal conduct.

Even more fundamentally, in our system of justice, a person is not simply convicted of "a crime" or "a felony." Rather, he is found guilty of a specified offense, almost always because he violated a specific statutory prohibition. For example, in the words of the order that the Government offered to prove petitioner's prior conviction in this case, petitioner "did knowingly and unlawfully assault Rory Dean Fenner, said assault resulting in serious bodily injury, in violation of Title 18 U.S.C. §§ 1153 and 113(f)."

The principle is illustrated by the evidence that was admitted at petitioner's trial to prove the other element of the § 922(g)(1) offense — possession of a "firearm." The Government submitted evidence showing that petitioner possessed a 9mm semiautomatic pistol. Although petitioner's possession of any number of weapons would have satisfied the requirements of § 922(g)(1), obviously the Government was entitled to prove with specific evidence that petitioner possessed the weapon he did. In the same vein, consider a murder case. Surely the Government can submit proof establishing the victim's identity, even though, strictly speaking, the jury has no "need" to know the victim's name, and even though the victim might be a particularly well loved public figure. The same logic should govern proof of the prior conviction element of the § 922(g)(1) offense. That is, the Government ought to be able to prove, with specific evidence, that petitioner committed a crime that came within § 922(g)(1)'s coverage. . . .

[Fed. R. Evid. 404(b)] expressly contemplates the admission of evidence of prior crimes for other purposes, "such as proof of motive, opportunity, intent, preparation, plan, knowledge, identity, or absence of mistake or accident." The list is plainly not exhaustive, and where, as here, a prior conviction is an element of the charged offense, neither Rule 404(b) nor Rule 403 can bar its admission. The reason is simple: In a prosecution brought under § 922(g)(1), the Government does not submit evidence of a past crime to prove the defendant's bad character or to "show action in conformity therewith." It tenders the evidence as direct proof of a necessary element of the offense with which it has charged the defendant.

Any incremental harm resulting from proving the name or basic nature of the prior felony can be properly mitigated by limiting jury instructions. . . . Indeed, on petitioner's own motion in this case, the District Court instructed the jury that it was not to "consider a prior conviction as evidence of guilt of the crime for which the defendant is now on trial."

The Court also holds that, if a defendant charged with violating § 922(g)(1) concedes his prior felony conviction, a district court abuses its discretion if it admits evidence of the defendant's prior crime that raises the risk of a verdict "tainted by improper considerations."

Why, precisely, does the Court think that this item of evidence raises the risk of a verdict "tainted by improper considerations"? Is it because the jury might learn that petitioner assaulted someone and caused serious bodily injury? If this is what the Court means, would evidence that petitioner had committed some other felony be admissible, and if so, what sort of crime might that be? Or does the Court object to the order because it gave a few specifics about the assault, such as the date, the location, and the victim's name? Or perhaps the Court finds that introducing the order risks a verdict "tainted by improper considerations" simply because the § 922(g)(1) charge was joined with counts charging petitioner with using a firearm in relation to a crime of violence, in violation of 18 U.S.C. § 924(c), and with committing an assault with a dangerous weapon, in violation of 18 U.S.C. § 1153 and 18 U.S.C. § 113(c) (1988 ed.)? Under the Court's nebulous standard for admission of prior felony evidence in a § 922(g)(1) prosecution, these are open questions.

More troubling still is the Court's retreat from the fundamental principle that in a criminal prosecution the Government may prove its case as it sees fit. The Court reasons that, in general, a defendant may not stipulate away an element of a charged offense because, in the usual case, "the prosecution with its burden of persuasion needs evidentiary depth to tell a continuous story." The rule has, however, "virtually no application when the point at issue is a defendant's legal status, dependent on some judgment rendered wholly independently of the concrete events of later criminal behavior charged against him."

On its own terms, the argument does not hold together. A jury is as likely to be puzzled by the "missing chapter" resulting from a defendant's stipulation to his prior felony conviction as it would be by the defendant's conceding any other element of the crime. The jury may wonder why it has not been told the name of the crime, or it may question why the defendant's firearm possession was illegal, given the tradition of lawful gun ownership in this country.

The Constitution requires a criminal conviction to rest upon a jury determination that the defendant is guilty of every element of the crime of which he is charged beyond a reasonable doubt. . . . At trial, a defendant may thus choose to contest the Government's proof on every element; or he may concede some elements and contest others; or he may do nothing at all. Whatever his choice, the Government still carries the burden of proof beyond a reasonable doubt on each element.

It follows from these principles that a defendant's stipulation to an element of an offense does not remove that element from the jury's consideration. The usual instruction regarding stipulations in a criminal case reflects as much: "When the attorneys on both sides stipulate or agree as to the existence of a fact, you may accept the stipulation as evidence and regard that fact as proved. You are not required to do so, however, since you are the sole judge of the facts.". . . Does the Court think a different rule applies when the defendant attempts to stipulate, over the Government's objection, to an element of the charged offense? If so, that runs counter to the Constitution. . . .

Also overlooked by the Court is the fact that, in "conceding" that he has a prior felony conviction, a defendant may be trying to take the issue from the jury altogether by effectively entering a partial plea of guilty, something we have never before endorsed. Federal Rule of Criminal Procedure 23(a) does not permit a defendant to waive a jury trial unless the Government consents, and we have upheld the provision as constitutional. A defendant who concedes the prior conviction element of the § 922(g)(1) offense may be effectively trying to waive his right to a jury trial on that element.

. . . I respectfully dissent.

NOTES AND QUESTIONS

(1) *No Discretion in Judge to Refuse to Tell Jury there is a Felony Conviction Element to the Offense when Defendant in an Old Chief Situation Stipulates he has a Prior Felony Conviction.* In a recent decision on a variant of *Old Chief*, trial Judge Weinstein ruled that the jury would be precluded from learning that the charged statutory offense (the same one charged in *Old Chief*) required a prior felony conviction, if defendant stipulated prior to trial that he had one. The jury would then be asked only whether they find he possessed a firearm. The Second Circuit reversed in *United States v. Chevere*, 368 F.3d 120 (2d Cir. 2004), holding that while it was discretionary to withhold the nature or underlying facts of the conviction, the judge could not prevent the jury from learning of the requirement of and existence of the prior felony conviction altogether, since it was a "crucial element" of the offense. The court noted that where the prior conviction is essential to proving the crime, "it is by definition, not prejudicial." Is this realistic? Is a limiting instruction sufficient? Is there a value served by the appeal court's approach?

What about bifurcation? The appeals court left open the possibility of bifurcation in some "extraordinarily unusual case." How would bifurcation work here? What would be bifurcated from what? What element would be tried first? While *Chevere* did not announce a per se ban on bifurcation in this context, it rejected the defendant's argument that because his credibility was central to the case, bifurcation was necessary.

(2) *Stipulations as Tactical Possibilities. Old Chief* should suggest to you that there may be some tactical reason or advantage for some counsel in some cases to offer to concede certain issues, especially where a rule indicates there are certain permitted and certain unpermitted purposes for evidence. What considerations should counsel weigh in deciding whether to make such an offer?

(3) *Dangers in Accepting Stipulations.* In *Dawson v. Delaware*, 503 U.S. 159 (1992), a death penalty case, the Court held it was constitutional error under the First and Fourteenth Amendments (Right of Association) to admit (at the punishment phase) a stipulation the prosecution entered into with defendant (to avoid prejudice to defendant) about the defendant's membership in the "Aryan Brotherhood," a white racist prison gang. It was so sanitized of "prejudice" that it was not relevant to any issue being decided at the punishment phase. Although the Court said it would have been different if the evidence showed that the gang was associated with drugs and violent escape attempts from prisons and advocated the murder of other inmates, the brief stipulation only indicated that a gang in the defendant's prison called itself the "Aryan Brotherhood"; when and where the gang originated; and that it entertained white racist beliefs. "[T]he narrowness of the stipulation left the Aryan Brotherhood evidence totally without relevance to Dawson's sentencing proceeding."

As a prosecutor, what is your incentive to enter into any stipulation offered by the defendant? Are any ethical obligations implicated?

PROBLEM 3B: THE FALLOUT FROM OLD CHIEF — DOES ITS PRINCIPLE EXTEND BEYOND ISSUES OF "STATUS" TO AFFECT PROOF ABOUT OTHER ELEMENTS, SUCH AS INTENT, ETC.?

United States v. Crowder, 87 F.3d 1405 (D.C. Cir. 1996) (en banc), *vacated without op., remanded*, 519 U.S. 1087 (1997): Defendants were convicted of possession of drugs with intent to distribute. They appealed on the ground that, although they offered to stipulate that anyone who possessed the quantities at issue must have had knowledge and intent to distribute, the trial court allowed into evidence other bad acts, including other acts of drug sales, on the theory that they showed intent or knowledge under Fed. R. Evid. 404(b). Defendants' theory was that the offered stipulation eliminated any issue of intent or knowledge and left only the issue of possession to be decided: one defendant claimed mistaken identity and the other, arrested after a chase, simply denied possession. Defendants argued that the need for further evidence of intent and knowledge was removed. Before the decision in *Old Chief*, the en banc Court of Appeals, over a dissent, agreed and reversed:

> Where a defendant offers unequivocally to concede elements of a crime — intent and knowledge in these prosecutions under 21 U.S.C. § 841(a)(1) — and agrees to a jury instruction that the Government need not prove those elements, we hold that bad acts evidence offered solely to prove those elements is inadmissible because the defendant's concession of intent and knowledge deprives the evidence of any value other than what Rule 404(b)'s first sentence unambiguously prohibits: "to prove the character of a person in order to show action in conformity therewith.". . .
>
> [T]he dissent argues that our holding will undermine prosecutors' "legitimate trial strategy" of presenting "live testimony and documentary evidence" rather than accepting a concession and a "cold" jury instruction. The dissent does not articulate exactly how the Government's inability to introduce extrinsic bad acts evidence to prove knowledge or intent could affect its case, and with good reason — it will not.

The Supreme Court vacated this decision and remanded it for reconsideration in light of *Old Chief v. United States*, 519 U.S. 172 (1997), reproduced *above*. How does the Supreme Court's recognition in *Old Chief* of the usual need for "evidentiary depth" regarding nonstatus elements of the offense affect the issues on reconsideration in *Crowder*? On remand, the en banc D.C. Circuit in *Crowder* affirmed the convictions. *United States v. Crowder*, 141 F.3d 1202 (D.C. Cir. 1998), *cert. denied*, 525 U.S. 1149 (1999).

PROBLEM SET 3C: WHAT IS A "STATUS" ELEMENT OF AN OFFENSE WITHIN THE RULE OF OLD CHIEF?

The Supreme Court's reasoning seems to hinge on the conclusion that "status" is a peculiar offense element, and that "evidentiary depth" is not necessary when status is stipulated. What other kinds of offense elements fall within this principle? Consider the following:

(1) *Sexual Activity with a Child ("Statutory Rape").* "Statutory rape" is the term used for having sex with a consenting but underage person, because of special statutory provisions fashioned for such encounters. Often, however, even forcible sexual assaults are charged as "statutory rape" when the alleged victim is underage, to avoid the need for proof of force and intent. Defendant Des Picable, who is 25, is on trial for the sexual assault of Ima Minor, who is only twelve years old, although Des claims she has the appearance of being much older. Defendant's defense is mistaken identity. He denies the act of intercourse. He offers to stipulate that the alleged victim, Ima, is less than seventeen years of age (which is the statutory element), and on this basis, he argues that proof of her actual age (twelve), as well as of the force the evidence shows he used, are precluded, and that the only issue is whether he had sexual relations with Ima. What result?

(2) *Unlicensed Medical Practice.* Dr. X is on trial for the unlicensed practice of medicine. He denies that his activities, which he says consisted of advice and the furnishing of nutrition, are the practice of medicine, whereas the Government says he diagnosed, considered drug interactions, and dispensed substances in a way that does constitute the practice of medicine. Dr. X offers to stipulate to his status, i.e., that he is not licensed to practice medicine. He argues that this stipulation removes any need that the Government might otherwise have to offer evidence of the underlying facts, namely that he once held a medical license, which was revoked by the Board of Medical Examiners. Might a potential juror feel a legitimate need for "evidentiary depth" on this issue?

PROBLEM SET 3D: CONCLUDING THOUGHTS ON EVIDENCE OF OTHER ACTS

(1) *Serial Murders.* In a high profile case in Atlanta, prosecutors introduced evidence linking Wayne B. Williams to the slayings of ten young African Americans, in addition to the two murders with which he had been charged. Fibers and bloodstain evidence seemed to connect Williams to the 10 killings (after the verdict, a number of commentators questioned the validity of the fiber evidence), as did witnesses who may have seen him with three of the victims. The twelve victims ranged in age from 11 to 27 (all described as young people), and the methods of death ranged from strangulation to drowning (all described as "asphyxiation"). Dr. Feegel, an assistant county medical examiner, told jurors that no similar killings had occurred since Williams' arrest. Is this case consistent with the William Kennedy Smith case, § 3.01[B][1], *supra*? Different jurisdictions interpret superficially similar rules with different degrees of strictness.

Should the uncharged murders have been admissible? In cases of this kind, why doesn't the prosecution charge the defendant in the indictment with the other crimes and prosecute for all of them at the trial? Is it because of weakness in the evidence that he committed the other crimes? (I.e., introducing them under the principle of Fed. R. Evid. 404(b), second sentence, relieves the prosecution of the necessity of proving them beyond a reasonable doubt.) Or because there has not been time to work up a sufficient case on the other crimes, and the public is anxious to have a trial? Or because it makes the case simpler, easier to grasp, shorter, and perhaps more dramatic or direct? Or because the statute of limitations has run on the others? Or because the evidence linking defendant with the other crimes has only just been discovered? Might all of these be possible justifications in one case or another? Should the prosecution be able to use in evidence crimes that it could not successfully prosecute (owing to factors such as those mentioned above)? Is this course justified by considerations of public expense?

Should the evidence that the crimes stopped when the defendant was caught be allowed to be called to the jury's attention? Since probably not all murders in the area ceased, how can you be sure that the relevant series stopped? Is there any character or "other crimes" (or "lack of other crimes") problem here? See *People v. Hernandez*, 55 Cal. App. 4th 225 (Cal. Ct. App. 1997), holding that the witness's testimony regarding her search of "Sherlock," a computerized police-report databank, to be reversible error where the witness testified to the fact that no similar crimes occurred before the defendant moved into the area and after he was arrested. The court treated the error as a hearsay problem.

Suppose it were sought to be brought out, instead of the above, that the series of crimes did *not* stop. Would that present a problem of character or other crimes of a third person? Should it be admissible? Could you constitutionally bar this evidence?

(2) *Can Specific Acts Supporting a Self-Defense Claim be Introduced?* In a prosecution for murder, defendant pleads self-defense. Can he, under Fed. R. Evid. 404–405, introduce specific instances of aggressive or violent conduct (not amounting to habit) on the part of the deceased (other than on the particular occasion in issue)?:

(a) to show deceased was likely the first aggressor against defendant (in the incident that led to decedent's death); and/or

(b) to show that defendant, knowing of these other incidents, was reasonable in interpreting decedent's reach for a handkerchief in decedent's pocket (in the incident that led to decedent's death) as an attack on him (i.e., as a reach for a gun or knife). (Incidentally, this theory, if permissible, in contradistinction to the other theory, would require showing defendant's knowledge of the other incidents.)

Or are the defendants in these two cases confined to introducing opinion and reputation evidence concerning decedent to establish these two theories (as is permitted under Rule 404(a) as conditioned by 405(a))? In answering these questions, consider the entirety of Rules 404 and 405.

§ 3.02 OTHER WAYS OF PROVING CHARACTER: OPINION AND REPUTATION EVIDENCE[5]

Read Federal Rules of Evidence 404(a), "Character Evidence: Crimes and Other Acts," and Rule 405(a), "Methods of Proving Character."

[A] Opinion and Reputation Character Evidence That Is NOT Related to Action In Conformity: Allowed

CARBO v. UNITED STATES
United States Court of Appeals, Ninth Circuit
314 F.2d 718 (1963), *cert. denied*, 377 U.S. 953 (1964)

MERRILL, CIRCUIT JUDGE.

[One of the defendants named] Sica moved to dismiss the indictment against him (Counts 1 and 5) for the reason that he was unduly prejudiced by the charge in Paragraph 3(c) that the conspiracy contemplated the use of "persons known to said victim to have underworld reputations and to possess the necessary power to execute the conspirators' demands by force and violence" and the enlistment of Sica for this purpose. The motion was denied. Sica also objected to the introduction of testimony by Leonard and Nesseth to the effect that by reputation they knew of Sica as an "underworld" man and a "strong-arm" man. The objection was overruled. Sica assigns error in these respects.

In discussing the admissibility of evidence of bad moral character the Supreme Court in *Michelson v. United States*, 1948, 335 U.S. 469, 475, states:

> Courts that follow the common-law tradition almost unanimously have come to disallow resort by the prosecution to any kind of evidence of a defendant's evil character to establish a probability of his guilt . . . The state may not show defendant's prior trouble with the law, specific criminal acts, or ill name among his neighbors, even though such facts might logically be persuasive that he is by propensity a probable perpetrator of the crime. The inquiry is not rejected because character is irrelevant; on the contrary, it is said to weigh too much with the jury. . . .

[But the] nature of Sica's reputation was not introduced into the case for the purpose of characterizing him as a bad man likely to resort to the conduct with which he is charged. This was not the source of its relevance.

Instead the prosecution relied on the reputation of Sica as a probative fact enabling the jury to infer that Sica had intervened with Leonard and Nesseth knowing that his presence would instill fear in them and intending to manipulate this fear for the benefit of Carbo and Palermo; and further, to conclude that Carbo and Palermo had secured Sica's participation with full realization that his effectiveness was based upon the fear his reputation could inspire in the victims.

---

[5] Study Guide Reference: Evidence in a Nutshell, Chapter 4:II, X.

. . . To prove a substantive act of extortion it is essential to show the generation of fear in the victim. To prove a substantive act of attempted extortion it is necessary to prove an attempt to instill fear. To prove a conspiracy to extort it is necessary to show a plan to instill fear.

Here Sica stood in the position of a dangerous weapon to be used to strike fear into the hearts of Leonard and Nesseth. It was part of the prosecution's case to charge and to prove that the conspirators considered Sica to occupy this position. That Leonard and Nesseth considered him to be dangerous and that fear reasonably resulted from his appearance because of his reputation constituted relevant facts upon this part of the prosecution's case.

It is true that (despite the precautionary steps taken by the judge as later discussed) the jury may have permitted this evidence to bear upon the probability of Sica's guilt. The question is whether this possibility renders such evidence unduly prejudicial and inadmissible. If so, the United States is precluded from establishing a material part of its case.

The question then is not whether the United States may use Sica's reputation as a sword against him, but whether he may himself make use of it as a shield to immunize himself from proof of the means by which the conspirators planned to frighten their victims into submission. If he may, then all who are known to live by violence are free to extort by the tacit threat of violence conveyed by their reputations; for the reasonableness of the resulting fear, as determined by its cause, may not be presented to the jury.

We cannot accept this result as a sound balance of the conflicting interests involved.

This, in our judgment (with such safeguards as were taken by the trial judge), is a proper case for application of what has been termed the "multiple admissibility doctrine." As stated in WIGMORE, EVIDENCE (3d ed. 1940) § 13, page 300:

> When an evidentiary fact is offered for one purpose, and becomes admissible by satisfying all the rules applicable to it in that capacity, it is not inadmissible because it does not satisfy the rules applicable to it in some other capacity, and because the jury might improperly consider it in the latter capacity. This doctrine, although involving certain risks, is indispensable as a practical rule.

In *State v. Belisle*, 1920, 19 N.H. 444, 111 A. 316, 317, defendant Lyman was charged with assault upon a policeman. The victim, Fox, had sought to defend himself by drawing a gun. To justify this defense he was permitted to testify that Lyman was, Fox believed, a man who would resort to force. The court stated:

> The argument that the disposition, character, and reputation of Lyman are not evidence that he assaulted Fox is sound. The difficulty with the defendant's case is that, while the evidence was not admissible for that purpose, it was clearly admissible to prove the reasonableness of the mode of defense from threatened attack adopted by Fox. . . .

To avoid confusion of issues and to foreclose the jury from using the reputation evidence to convict defendants on the "bad man" theory, the court below, upon admitting the testimony in question, instructed the jury as to the limited consideration which might be given. The subject was again dealt with in the court's charge to the jury. We have no doubt but that to the maximum extent possible, prejudice flowing from any confusion of issues by the jury was eliminated. . . .

We conclude that the district court did not err in denying Sica's motion to dismiss the indictment or in admitting the evidence of Sica's reputation.

NOTE

Comparison Between Specific Instance and Reputation/Opinion Testimony. What would have been the result in *Carbo* if the form of the evidence had been specific instances of particular violent acts Sica had committed in the past, offered for the same purpose as the reputation evidence in *Carbo*? *See State v. Hinchliffe*, 987 A.2d 988 (Vt. 2009) (affirming admission under 404(b) of evidence of defendant's prior assault of his girlfriend, as relevant to whether a reasonable person in her position would fear bodily injury, an element of stalking).

[B] Opinion and Reputation Character Evidence Allowed (in Exceptional Situations) to Show Action in Conformity

A PREVIEW OF THE CONFUSING LAW HERE

(1) *The Law in This Area Is a "Grotesque Structure," Made of "Misshapen Stones."* In *Michelson v. United States*, 335 U.S. 469 (1948), the Supreme Court was asked to prohibit prosecution responses to certain character testimony offered by the defendant. The Court said, "We concur in the general opinion of courts, textwriters and the profession that much of this law is archaic, paradoxical and full of compromises and compensations by which an irrational advantage to one side is offset by a poorly reasoned counter-privilege to the other." The Court's conclusion tells why this material will be confusing: "But somehow it has proved a workable even if clumsy system. . . . To pull one misshapen stone out of the grotesque structure is more likely simply to upset its present balance between adverse interests than to establish a rational edifice."

(2) *How It Starts: Under Rule 404(a)(2)(A): The Criminal Defendant Defends with Character Evidence.* The criminal defendant, under this Rule, is permitted to call character witnesses to a "pertinent trait" of his good character, to show that he is unlikely to have committed the crime. Many writers have recognized that this evidence is not very strong. But one can imagine a defendant in a close case saying, "it would be unfair not to let me show by this evidence that I would never have committed this crime!" In fairness to the criminal defendant, the law permits character evidence.

(3) *The Limited Forms of Character Evidence: "Reputation" or "Opinion."* In keeping with the weakness of the evidence, Rule 405 says that the evidence may only be offered "as to reputation" or "in the form of an opinion." The Rules are not intended to lengthen the trial with the defendant's life story: just, "What is his reputation?" or "What is your opinion of his character?" Although it does not always

happen, the essentials could be conveyed by one question and one answer. Furthermore, the question must be limited to a "pertinent trait," says Rule 404; for example, a defendant tried for assault can offer evidence that he is "peaceable and non-violent," but not that he is "honest."

(4) *The Prosecution's Three Possible Responses to the Defendant's Character Evidence.* Now comes the more complicated structure. If the defendant offers good character evidence, the prosecution may have evidence or information to the contrary, and it would be strange to allow the defendant's evidence but not the prosecution's counter to it. Therefore, the law provides the prosecutor three methods of response.

(a) *First, Cross Examining the Defendant's Character Witnesses about Specific Acts: "Have You Heard" Questions.* The first method of response is in Rule 405(a), last sentence, which says that the prosecution can cross-examine the defendant's character witnesses, and inquiry is allowable into "relevant specific instances of [defendant's] conduct." What does this mean? Imagine that the defendant's character witnesses do not know what they are talking about. They say, for example, that the defendant is "peaceful and law-abiding," but the prosecutor is holding a report showing that the defendant has repeatedly committed acts of violence. This part of Rule 405 allows the prosecutor to make "inquiry" into these "specific acts" of violence, to show, in essence, that the defendant's character witnesses are poorly informed. Historically, this kind of inquiry has involved what are called "have you heard" questions. "Have you heard that he was arrested on July 1 of last year for murder?" "No, I never heard that." "Have you heard that he committed the crime of assault in January of this year?" "No, I haven't." Cases under the Federal Rules also sometimes allow "Did you know," treating it as the equivalent.

The prosecutor is not permitted to prove the bad acts, just to inquire about them. The theory is that the questions test the knowledge of the witness, or, if the witness says she knows of the acts and still gives the good character endorsement, then the implication is she has bad judgment. The jury will be instructed, at least if a request is made, that the bad acts are not to be credited as true or as indicating defendant has a character or propensity or proclivity that suggests in any way that he would commit the crime he is charged with. Of course, the lawyers are aware that a suggestion of the reality of the bad acts gets across to the jury, and the Rules do not really effectively counteract this impression, although they do not condone it. Another counterintuitive principle is that the bad acts do not have to be crimes, and the prosecutor does not have to have proof of them. Just a good-faith belief that they occurred is enough.

(b) *Second, Impeaching the Defendant's Character Witnesses in any Other Way Permitted by the Rules of Impeachment of Witnesses Generally.* See, e.g., Rules 607-609 and the general subject of impeachment of credibility, taken up elsewhere in this book.

(c) *Third, Rebuttal With "Bad" Character Evidence.* Rule 404(a) allows the prosecutor to "rebut" the defendant's evidence by calling (when it is the government's turn to put on its case) its own character witnesses. (See Rule 404(a)(2)(A)(last clause)). In other words, the government can call bad-character witnesses. This is the only one of the three that allows the jury to draw an inference that the defendant has a character or propensity or proclivity suggesting that he committed the crime he is charged with (i.e., the reverse of the inference from defendant's character witnesses).

The Supreme Court is right: the structure is grotesque, or at least counterintuitive. But if we are to admit character evidence, the stones that make up the structure are likely to be misshapen, and if we pull any one of the out, the Rules might not work properly.

(5) *How Can the Criminal Defendant Avoid These Prosecution Responses? Don't Call Character Witnesses!* That's easy. The defendant can just decide not to call character witnesses in the first place. Rule 404 allows the defendant to initiate the calling of character witnesses, but it allows the prosecution only "to rebut the same." Thus, if the defendant has a long criminal record and is well known to many police officers who have handled him, his best course is to avoid character witnesses altogether.

NOTE ON THE HISTORICAL DEVELOPMENT OF CHARACTER RULES [THE FEDERAL RULES COMPARED WITH THE COMMON LAW]

(1) *"Reputation" or "Opinion"? For What Kind of Character? And What about Defendant's Use of "Specific Incidents"?: People v. Van Gaasbeck*, 82 N.E. 718 (N.Y. 1907). While this case may contain in part a conclusion or two that is not current law (except in some states that are still in the common-law mode), it sets out well the main issues and adopts a number of conclusions that are still very good law most places today, including under the Federal Rules of Evidence. Defendant was convicted of manslaughter, and he appealed the exclusion of two witnesses to his good character for being "peaceable" and "quiet." One witness would have testified that the defendant's "reputation" for these pertinent traits was good; the other would have testified that he "knew [the defendant's] character" in these respects and that it was good. The New York high court held that the evidence of the first witness, testifying about *reputation*, was admissible, but that of the second, about the witness's own *opinion* of the defendant, was not. [Important Note: the current Federal Rules of Evidence would admit both reputation *and opinion*, today — Eds.] Along the way, the court held that *specific instances* manifesting good character offered by a defendant were not admissible, that evidence should be about a pertinent trait, and that "negative" evidence (consisting of evidence that a witness had not heard anything bad) was proper reputation evidence [Note: all of these propositions are also current law today under the Federal Rules of Evidence as well]:

> The evidence . . . should not be [about] the *general* good reputation of the defendant, but may be [only about] his reputation in respect to the particular traits involved in the accusation [here, "peacefulness and quiet"

or the equivalent, and not just general "good reputation"]. [This is still good law even under the Federal Rules.]

. . . [W]hile the community reputation as to particular traits is admissible upon the question of character, the personal knowledge and belief of the witness must be excluded. Thus, in *Hirschman v. People*, 101 Ill. 568, where the defendant was tried on an indictment for manslaughter, it was held that he was properly permitted to give evidence of his general reputation in regard to peace and quiet, but that no error was committed in excluding all particular transactions . . . tending to prove a quiet and peaceable disposition [which is still the position of the Federal Rules, i.e., specific instances are banned — Eds.]. . . . "The reputation which is the subject of proof in courts . . . means the estimate in which the individual is held by the community, and not the private opinion entertained of him by the witnesses. . . ." [Note: Remember, the Federal Rules do allow opinion, as well, today.] . . .

Three conclusions are involved in our review of this case: First, that upon a criminal prosecution evidence is receivable in behalf of the accused that he has enjoyed a good reputation in respect to the traits involved in the charge against him; second, that evidence is not receivable . . . when such evidence consists solely of the personal knowledge and observation of his conduct by witnesses [But remember that the Federal Rules allow opinion today but not specific acts — Eds.] . . . ; and, third, that negative evidence is receivable to establish a good reputation [i.e., evidence that the witness has "heard nothing bad" about the pertinent trait — still receivable under the Federal Rules today — Eds.].

(2) *The Prosecutor's Inquiry on Cross-Examination into "Specific Instances of Conduct": Awkard v. United States*, 352 F.2d 641 (D.C. Cir. 1965). This case suggests that even today under the Federal Rules, which generally permit the "Have you heard" question, the use of the question may be limited by a judge under the Rule 403 probative-prejudice-time calculus in circumstances where the question is not particularly probative of the character witness's lack of veracity. The defendant was convicted of assault. She introduced evidence from two character witnesses (one a minister) who testified to her reputation for peace and good order, but both witnesses were from a different community and had known about the defendant "when she was just a kid," many years before the present offense. The prosecutor, of course, pointed out to the jury that the testimony concerned a wholly different time in the defendant's life. The prosecutor also asked whether the witnesses had heard of defendant's arrests and convictions for assault, which were more recent than the character witnesses' knowledge. The Court of Appeals reversed, even though it recognized that have-you-heard questions about specific instances could be admissible. The character evidence being attacked was already shown to be "weak," was impeached by its lack of timeliness, and could have been stricken as inadmissible. Therefore the court regarded the have-you-heard questions as prejudicial. The character evidence being attacked had already been shown to be not worth much, and anyway the have-you-heard question was not addressed to the time the witnesses purported to know the defendant, they already having in essence admitted they did not know him during the period covered by the question.

Thus the question "could not be thought to test the accuracy, reliability, or credibility" of the character testimony:

> This jurisdiction . . . has endorsed the general rule that the prosecutor can . . . inquire on cross-examination whether a defendant's character witness "has heard" of defendant's prior arrests or convictions. . . . Nevertheless, the risks of undue prejudice to the defendant are great. . . .

(3) *What, Then, Are the Issues Today?* Here are some of the questions raised by the cases in this section:

(a) *Inadmissible Character Evidence.* When can the trial judge exclude defensive character evidence as insufficiently relevant or otherwise inconsistent with the Rules?

(b) *The Degree of Latitude for the Prosecutor's Attacks on Character Witnesses.* How far may the prosecutor go in using "have you heard" or "did you know" questions about the defendant's bad acts, to challenge the defendant's character witnesses?

(c) *The Form of the Character Evidence.* How broadly (if at all) can the defendant make use of character evidence (outside pertinent traits, or by documentary evidence)?

(d) *The Relationship of Rule 404(a) to Rule 404(b).* Character evidence used by the defense for propensity (meaning, "I have good character, so you can believe I didn't commit this crime") is easily confused with the use of similar-act evidence under Rule 404(b) (to prove patterns of conduct showing intent, identity, and similar matters).

(e) *Attacking or Supporting the Alleged Victim with Character Evidence.* Rule 404(a)(2) allows character evidence about the alleged victim. When can the defendant use this kind of evidence to show that the alleged victim was really the one at fault, and how may the prosecutor use character to defend against claims that the alleged victim was the first aggressor?

UNITED STATES v. YARBROUGH

United States Court of Appeals, Tenth Circuit
527 F.3d 1092 (2008)

MURPHY, CIRCUIT JUDGE.

[A jury convicted Yarbrough, who was a state police officer, of obstructing an official federal proceeding, of conspiracy, and of providing unlawful notice of a search warrant. The issues centered on an FBI investigation of a friend of Yarbrough's named Daniels for drug, money laundering, and gambling offenses. Yarbrough was included in the FBI's investigation as part of a joint operation. On his own account, he notified Daniels that Daniels was under investigation. Later, when a search warrant issued, Yarbrough called a mutual friend and asked him to warn Daniels about the impending search (an action that presumably resulted in a less-than-successful search). Yarbrough declined to participate in the search, explaining that he knew Daniels.]

[During his trial,] Yarbrough testified he warned Daniels about the execution of the warrant because he was a close friend, he knew Daniels was not involved in illegal conduct, and he thought [FBI] Agent Lotspeich was engaged in a fishing expedition. [Thus, the issues did not concern whether Yarbrough had committed the actions charged, but whether he did them with a wrongful mens rea.]

. . . Although the district court correctly [decided other appellate issues when it] admitted [certain] disputed wiretap evidence and properly refused to instruct the jury on the issue of entrapment, it committed reversible error when it excluded Yarbrough's proffered character evidence. . . . [T]his court reverses Yarbrough's conviction and remands to the district court for further proceedings consistent with this opinion. . . .

. . . Character Evidence

Yarbrough sought to introduce at trial character evidence of his integrity and status as a law-abiding, trusted police officer, pursuant to Federal Rule of Evidence 404(a)(1) and 405. He asserted evidence of his law-abiding nature was directly relevant to the charges at issue, which alleged he corruptly impeded and conspired to corruptly impede an investigation, as well as unlawfully and willfully provided notice of the existence of a search and seizure warrant to prevent the execution of such warrant. The district court excluded Yarbrough's character witnesses on the ground the proffered evidence went to Yarbrough's "state of mind at a particular incident," rather than to the existence of "operative facts." Yarbrough asserts on appeal that the district court erred in excluding his proffered character witnesses on this basis. The district court's decision to exclude evidence is reviewed for abuse of discretion and will be reversed only if the decision is "arbitrary, capricious, whimsical, or manifestly unreasonable." . . . "A district court by definition abuses its discretion when it makes an error of law."

[The court added in a footnote, "To be more precise, a review of the trial transcript reveals the district court drew a distinction, for purposes of Rule 404(a)(1), between cases where a defendant sought to introduce character evidence to dispute the existence of a historical fact (i.e., defendant is generally of peaceful character and thus would not have struck the victim) and Yarbrough's situation (i.e., it is undisputed Yarbrough undertook certain actions and all that is disputed is whether he did so with a prohibited mens rea). The district court incorrectly ruled character evidence was admissible in the former situation but not in the latter."]

The Federal Rules of Evidence specifically provide that at trial a defendant may adduce "evidence of a pertinent trait of character." Fed. R. Evid. 404(a). The Rules further provide that "proof [of character] may be made by testimony as to reputation or by testimony in the form of an opinion." Fed. R. Evid. 405(a). Taken together, these rules make clear that although propensity evidence is generally not allowed, "when . . . the defendant in a criminal case seeks to offer evidence of his good character to imply that he is unlikely to have committed a crime, the general rule against propensity evidence is not applied." . . .

[In a footnote, the court added: "The government's briefing on this issue is somewhat puzzling. The government simply cites to Federal Rule of Evidence

608(a) and asserts that because Yarbrough's character for truthfulness had not been attacked he was not entitled to adduce character evidence at trial. Rule 608 certainly does limit the admission of character evidence *of a witness* to those situations where the *witness's* character has been attacked. ("[E]vidence of truthful character is admissible only after the character of the witness for truthfulness has been attacked by opinion or reputation evidence or otherwise."). It does not, however, deal in any way with the issue of the admissibility of evidence *of a defendant's* good character. That issue is covered byRule 404(a), which specifically provides that evidence of a pertinent character trait of a criminal defendant is generally relevant and admissible at trial.]

Despite the plain language set out above, the district court excluded character evidence because the underlying facts were not in dispute and the only issue for the jury was whether Yarbrough acted with a prohibited mind set at the time he undertook those undisputed actions. We cannot discern in Rule 404(a) the distinction announced by the district court. Instead, in a remarkably similar situation, this court has recognized that such evidence is not only relevant, but also vitally important. In *Peterson v. United States*, the defendant was tried and convicted on two counts of tax evasion. At trial he admitted the underpayment of taxes but denied any wrongful intent. When the defendant indicated his intent to adduce three character witnesses, the district court belittled the use of character witnesses and limited the defendant to one such witness. On appeal, this court noted as follows:

> The rule is well established that "a defendant may offer his good character to evidence the improbability of his doing the act charged." As said in *Michelson v. United States*, 335 U.S. 469, 476 (1948), "character is relevant in resolving probabilities of guilt." In a case such as this where the defendant admits understatement of income and defends solely on the lack of wilful intent, the character of the defendant is an important element. In the exercise of a sound judicial discretion a court may limit the number of witnesses permitted to testify to a single fact and the extent to which cumulative testimony may be received. It may be that in some instances, particularly where a fact is not contested, a limitation to one witness is proper. However, to restrict a defendant to one character witness is a harsh limitation in a case such as this where the sole defense is lack of wilful intent.

Thus, contrary to the conclusion of the district court, *Petersen* makes clear that character evidence is admissible in cases, such as this one, where the sole issue before the jury is whether a defendant undertook his undisputed acts with a prohibited state of mind. Because its decision to exclude Yarbrough's character witnesses was based on a legally erroneous reading of Rule 404(a), the district court abused its discretion in excluding the proffered evidence.

This court's inquiry does not, however, end with that conclusion. Pursuant to the Federal Rules of Criminal Procedure, we must disregard the district court's error unless it affected Yarbrough's substantial rights . . . The government has not argued, however, that if the district court erred in excluding Yarbrough's proffered character witnesses, the error was harmless. Accordingly, it has failed to carry its burden of demonstrating Yarbrough's substantial rights were not affected by the district court's error. Even if this court were to exercise its discretion to initiate harmless error review sua sponte, we would still conclude the error here affected Yarbrough's substantial rights. A review of the entire trial transcript reveals that although Yarbrough's actions were uncontested, his state of mind was highly controverted. In *Petersen*, this court concluded that in such situations, "the character of the defendant is an important element." . . . Yarbrough's substantial rights were affected and he is entitled to a new trial.

UNITED STATES v. BAH

United States Court of Appeals, Second Circuit
574 F.3d 106 (2009)

JACOBS, CHIEF JUDGE:

Defendant-Appellant Boubacar Bah appeals from a judgment of conviction . . . on one count of operating an unlicensed money transmitting business in New York in violation of 18 U.S.C. section 1960.

[Bah defended at trial, in part, by calling character witnesses. The character evidence asserted that Bah's character for "truthfulness" was good, and presumably, the trial judge allowed this character evidence on the theory that "truthfulness" was a "pertinent trait" in response to an accusation of illegal operation of a business. The issue on appeal concerns the fact that the trial court also permitted the prosecution to cross-examine one witness pursuant to Rule 405(a), which allows inquiry about "relevant specific instances of conduct." Unlike many such questions, the cross examination here did not concern arrest, convictions, or crimes, as is often permitted; instead, the cross-examination, here, involved a customer's accusation of fraud. In this part of the opinion, the court upholds the allowance of the cross-examination:]

Bah contends that the district court improperly permitted the government to cross-examine one of his character witnesses about a letter from a former customer accusing him of fraud.

Federal Rule of Evidence 404(a) permits a defendant to offer character evidence. If a defendant chooses to introduce such evidence, the government may question the defendant's witnesses regarding "relevant specific instances of conduct." Fed. R. Evid. 405(a). "We review the district court's decision to allow the question[ing] for abuse of discretion, bearing in mind that once a defendant offers character testimony, the prosecution is afforded substantial latitude [to cross-examine]." *United States v. Reich*.

Bah called three character witnesses. One of them, Amadou Diallo, testified that Bah had a reputation for truthfulness in the community, and cited an instance in which Bah helped resolve a situation between Diallo and Bah's brother. On cross-examination, the district court permitted the government — over Bah's objection — to question Diallo about a letter in which a former customer accused Bah of fraud. Diallo testified that he was unaware of the accusation and that it did not impact his view of Bah or his reputation in the community.

Bah cites the Eighth Circuit's decision in *United States v. Monteleone*, for the proposition that a prosecutor may only cross-examine a character witness based on events "likely to have become a matter of general knowledge, currency or reputation in the community." In *Monteleone*, the character witness was cross-examined about the defendant's alleged perjury before a grand jury investigating a drug crime. Because grand jury proceedings are required by law to be kept secret, *Monteleone* ruled that the government lacked a good faith basis for believing that the defendant's alleged perjury was likely to have been known in the witness's community.

Monteleone, of course, is not binding in our circuit, but even if it were, this case is distinguishable for three reasons. First, the evidence presented on cross-examination did not derive from a secret proceeding; to the contrary, the author of the letter expressed a desire that Bah's actions be widely publicized to other customers and the Better Business Bureau. Second, the challenged evidence did not involve criminal conduct, but dishonesty in Bah's business dealings — information closely related to the subject of Diallo's direct testimony, and far less inflammatory (and [less] potentially prejudicial) than the evidence at issue in *Monteleone*. Third, we have previously observed that the Eighth Circuit has limited *Monteleone* to cases involving reputation evidence and that it has been more permissive in admitting evidence to impeach opinion testimony. *See Reich*. In this case, Diallo testified as to his personal opinion of Bah [as well as Bah's reputation]. For these reasons, *Monteleone* is unpersuasive. [The court nevertheless vacated the conviction on other grounds, having thus addressed the character evidence issue for retrial.]

In light of the "substantial latitude" afforded the government [to impeach] character witness testimony offered by the defense, the district court did not abuse its discretion in permitting the government to question Diallo about the complaint against Bah.

NOTE ON HOW TO READ THE CASE OF *UNITED STATES v. DRAPEAU*

(1) *The Following Case, Drapeau, Differs from Those Involving Defendant's Character; the Issue Instead Is the Alleged Victim's Character.* Rule 404(a)(2)(A) says that the defendant can call character witnesses in his own defense, to show *his own* good character. But that is not all that the character evidence Rule does. Rule 404(a)(2)(B) allows the defendant (and sometimes, the prosecutor) to call character witnesses about the *alleged victim* of a crime. This kind of evidence, from the defendant, usually is used to show the alleged victim's bad character for violence, in support of a self-defense claim. (The Rule is reciprocal. The prosecutor can use good character evidence about the victim to negate the charge that the victim was the first aggressor.)

(2) *But Character Evidence about the Victim under 404(a)(2)(B) Must Be Witness Testimony, about Reputation or Opinion.* The defendant in *Drapeau*, below, offered two kinds of evidence. First, he offered *documentary* evidence allegedly showing that the victim was violent, in the form of tribal resolutions and a memorandum. Second, he offered character *witnesses*. Rule 405(a), which imposes

a limit on all 404(a)'s permitted showings of character, says that all 404(a)'s character evidence may be offered only in the form of reputation or opinion by character *witnesses*. (In spite of some initial confusion, the trial court allowed the character *witnesses* — a correct ruling — but the defendant then declined to call them before the jury.) The trial judge excluded the *documentary* evidence, and this exclusion is the source of this appeal.

(3) *Confusion Between Rule 404(a) and Rule 404(b) in the Drapeau Case.* The case is confusing, because the trial judge was confused. And the trial judge's confusion was understandable, because the defense attorney's offer of the evidence created a problem about the difference between Rule 404(a) and Rule 404(b). Rule 404(b), covered earlier in this chapter, allows "pattern"-type evidence or other evidence to show motive, intent, identity, and similar issues. The documentary evidence in *Drapeau* might — conceivably — have been relevant and admissible under 404(b) to show that Drapeau feared the alleged victim (and that therefore his defensive conduct was reasonable), but only if Drapeau knew about the documentary evidence, in advance. (There was no evidence in the case of such advance knowledge.) Character evidence permitted under 404(a) does not require this advance knowledge, but 404(a) does not seem to allow documentary evidence. You may conclude that the trial judge's rulings ultimately avoided error in spite of the confusion (and the appellate court affirms), but you will have to sort out the Rules to make your conclusion.

UNITED STATES v. DRAPEAU

United States Court of Appeal, Eighth Circuit
644 F.3d 646 (2011)

WOLLMAN, CIRCUIT JUDGE.

Harold Drapeau, Jr., was convicted of assaulting, resisting, or impeding a federal officer resulting in bodily injury, in violation of 18 U.S.C. section 111(a)(1) and (b), and was sentenced to twenty-seven months' imprisonment and three years of supervised release. Drapeau appeals his conviction and sentence, arguing that the district court erred by . . . improperly excluding character evidence of the alleged victim [under Rule 404(a)(2), and by committing other alleged errors]. . . . We affirm. . . .

[Robert Mousseau, a Bureau of Indian Affairs, pursued Defendant Drapeau in a police chase after receiving a dispatch about Drapeau's potential involvement in a disturbance and a radio message from a fellow officer informing him that Drapeau had been stopped, but had fled. Eventually, Mosseau located Drapeau at Drapeau's residence. Mousseau's vehicle was equipped with a camera, and he wore a remote microphone. He attempted to gain entry into the residence. He did not yet have reason to arrest Drapeau, but he wanted to speak to him about the possible disturbance and check on a child he heard crying in the home. The following incident occurred after Mousseau had made numerous attempts to enter:]

After Mousseau failed to gain entrance through the front door, he broke the screen off the front window. As Mousseau put his right arm through the window,

Drapeau pressed the window downward against Mousseau's arm, injuring it. Using his left arm, Mousseau pushed the window up and released his right arm. He then deployed his taser into the home. Drapeau ceased pressing down on the window and ran towards the back of the home.

Mousseau ran around outside to the backyard, where he met Drapeau exiting through the back door. Mousseau arrested Drapeau [and] placed him in the BIA vehicle. . . .

Drapeau . . . pleaded not guilty [of assaulting an officer] and requested a jury trial. Drapeau sought to present evidence of Mousseau's character pursuant to Federal Rule of Evidence 404(a)(2), by filing a pretrial notice and during the pretrial conference. [Remember, 404(a)(2) allows character evidence of an alleged victim for violence, as relevant to a claim that the alleged victim was in fact the first aggressor, in support of a defense of self-defense — Eds.] The evidence consisted of seven tribal resolutions and an unsigned memo to United States Senator John Thune. The first resolution was written by the Nebraska Winnebago Tribe in 2005, describing Mousseau's misconduct and requesting his permanent removal as a police officer from the Winnebago Law Enforcement Services Department. Thereafter, Mousseau transferred to the Crow Creek BIA duty station, whereupon the Crow Creek Sioux Tribal Council adopted the other six resolutions and memo in response to numerous complaints against Mousseau and requested his removal from the Crow Creek Sioux Indian Reservation. In the memo to Senator Thune, a Crow Creek Sioux Tribe civil rights group requested an internal investigation of Mousseau and the police department. During the pretrial conference, the district court preliminarily [ruled that at least some of the resolutions] might become admissible if Drapeau testified that he was aware of them.

Drapeau [through counsel of course] sought to use the character evidence to prove his intent to defend himself and his family and to prove his state of mind. [This sounds like an offer under 404(b), intent. motive, etc., to show justifiable fear. — Eds.] He asserted that the evidence would demonstrate Mousseau's reputation for violence, aggressiveness, and excessive use of his taser. Drapeau also sought to inquire of character witnesses as to Mousseau's reputation in the community. During the pretrial conference, the government objected to the evidence, arguing that the resolutions and reputation testimony were irrelevant to demonstrate Drapeau's state of mind unless he was aware of them before the incident. Drapeau responded that the offered evidence did not constitute Rule 404(b) evidence [i.e., it was not being offered to show what his counsel originally seemed to say, his reasonable fear of Mousseau — Ed.], but instead was admissible pursuant to Rule 404(a)(2) [involving first-aggressor character evidence]. The district court preliminarily denied Drapeau's motion to present the tribal resolutions and reputation testimony evidence. . . .

Following the denial of the motion, Drapeau made an offer of proof of the tribal resolutions and urged their admission as character evidence pursuant to Rule 404(a)(2). Drapeau also proffered four character witnesses who would have testified as to Mousseau's reputation for violence and unlawfulness. The district court excluded the proffered evidence and reiterated its view that the character evidence was inadmissible because Drapeau had not offered any evidence regarding his awareness of the resolutions or Mousseau's reputation. [In preliminary proceedings, a witness] testified that before the incident she and Drapeau were aware of Mousseau's reputation for being "mean, short-tempered," and untruthful, including a willingness to make "up stories to cover his wrongs." She also testified that they were unaware of the tribal resolutions until after the incident. After her testimony, the district court renewed its exclusion of the resolutions and memo but reversed its preliminary denial of Drapeau's reputation witnesses, stating that Drapeau could call whatever witnesses he wished. [In other words, reputation and opinion evidence about the victim, Mousseau, from bad-character witnesses, would be admissible, but not the documents, in accordance with 404(a)(2) as conditioned by 405. — Eds.] The district court then recalled the jury. [But] Drapeau rested without presenting any evidence, and the jury found him guilty. . . .

Drapeau contends that the district court improperly excluded the proposed [documentary] evidence of [victim] Mousseau's reputation for aggression and unlawfulness. "Evidence of a person's character or a trait of character is not admissible for the purpose of proving action in conformity therewith on a particular occasion," except in criminal cases when it is "evidence of a pertinent trait of character of the alleged victim of the crime offered by an accused." Fed.R.Evid. 404(a)(2). "When a defendant raises a self-defense claim, reputation evidence of the victim's violent character is relevant to show the victim as the proposed aggressor." [Case citation.] "In all cases in which evidence of character or a trait of character of a person is admissible, proof may be made by testimony as to reputation or by testimony in the form of an opinion." Fed.R.Evid. 405(a).

Drapeau now asserts on appeal that he offered the tribal resolutions and memo to demonstrate that Mousseau was the first aggressor. In Drapeau's pretrial notice of intent to present evidence and during the pretrial conference, he cited Rule 404(a)(2) but stated that he was offering the tribal resolutions and memo for the purpose of proving his state of mind, which is not one of the purposes encompassed within Rule 404(a)(2). *See United States v. Keiser*, 57 F.3d 847, 854 (9th Cir. 1995). Assuming for the purposes of argument that Drapeau in fact presented the tribal resolutions and memo for the purpose of showing Mousseau was the first aggressor, his failure to present evidence of his prior awareness would not have been grounds for excluding that evidence. *See Id.* at 854. ("Thus, whether the defendant knew of the victim's character at the time of the crime has no bearing on whether victim character evidence should come in under [Rule] 404(a)(2).") The [documentary] evidence would still have been inadmissible under Rules 404(a)(2) [as limited by] 405(a), however, because it was not in the proper form of *witness* testimony. [Recall that the district court allowed the proposed character-witness testimony, as opposed to the documents in question, and thus the character-witness testimony would have been admitted if Drapeau had offered it, but he did not. — Eds.] Accordingly, any error in requiring evidence of Drapeau's pre-incident knowledge would not have affected Drapeau's substantial rights because the tribal resolutions and memo would have been excludable [in any event] pursuant to Rule 405(a) [because not in the proper form, i.e., not witness testimony]. [The court here is only considering the particular rule, 404(a)(2) (as necessarily limited by 405(a)), that defendant's counsel says he was invoking, not 404(b). 405(a), limiting the form of the evidence, conditions only 404(a)(2), not 404(b). — Eds.]

In light of Drapeau's stated purpose, it was understandable why the district court was under the impression that Drapeau was actually seeking to present the evidence pursuant to Rule 404(b), not Rule 404(a)(2), as he had recited. The fact that the tribal resolutions and memo were not in the form of witness testimony would not have prevented Drapeau from offering the evidence under Rule 404(b). [In a footnote, the court pointed out that Rule 404(b) provides, "Evidence of other crimes, wrongs, or acts is not admissible to prove the character of a person in order to show action in conformity therewith. It may, however, be admissible for other purposes, such as proof of motive, opportunity, intent, preparation, plan, knowledge, identity, absence of mistake or accident. . . . — Eds.] But, as the district court stated, Drapeau would have been required to present evidence that he had pre-incident knowledge of the evidence. *See United States v. Bordeaux*, 570 U.S. 1041, 1049 (8th Cir. 2009)("[E]vidence of prior bad acts of the victim are admissible under Rule 404(b) to establish the defendant's state of mind and the reasonableness of the defendant's use of force," citing . . . *United States v. Scout*, 112 F.3d 955, 962 n.7 (8th Cir. 1997) ("[The defendant] testified that he did not know the identity of the police officers pursuing him. Because [the officer's] alleged reputation for violence could therefore not have affected [the defendant's] state of mind when assaulting [the officer], [the officer's] reputation — and how it was derived — was irrelevant."). . . . During the hearing outside the presence of the jury, [Drapeau's wife] testified that Drapeau had not known of the resolutions before the incident. Drapeau failed to present any evidence to the contrary, and he does not pursue this theory on appeal. Accordingly, we need not further address whether the district court erred in excluding the tribal resolutions and memo under Rule 404(b). [Affirmed.]

NOTES AND QUESTIONS

(1) *Pertinent Traits.* What is a "pertinent" character trait under the Federal Rules of Evidence that a criminal defendant may show under the special dispensation that allows him to show his good character (Fed. R. Evid. 404(a)(2)(A)) via reputation and opinion? *See United States v. Jackson*, 588 F.2d 1046 (5th Cir.), *cert. denied*, 442 U.S. 941 (1979):

> Jackson contends that he should have been allowed to introduce testimony supporting his reputation for "truth and veracity." The trial court [correctly] excluded this evidence on the ground that Jackson's reputation for truth and veracity was not pertinent to the crime with which he was charged [conspiracy to distribute, and possession of, heroin]. In asserting that "an accused can always prove the existence of the trait of veracity in his character as a method of supporting his credibility," Jackson assumes that a defendant's credibility is in issue in any criminal prosecution. However[,] not all criminal indictments impugn the defendant's truthfulness and veracity. Since evidence of the trait of truthfulness is not pertinent to the criminal charges of conspiracy to distribute heroin or possession of heroin, Rule 404 forbids its introduction as circumstantial evidence of innocence of those crimes.
>
> Furthermore, when Jackson elected to take the stand at his trial he did not automatically acquire the right to bolster his credibility. Where an

accused takes the stand as witness he places his credibility in issue as does any other witness. If the prosecution chooses to attack his credibility, he may then introduce evidence of his good character for truthfulness and veracity [but]:

> *Evidence of truthful character is admissible only after the character of the witness for truthfulness has been attacked* by opinion or reputation evidence or otherwise.

Fed. R. Evid. 608 (emphasis added).

Compare *Sahin v. Maryland*, 653 A.2d 452 (Md. 1995) (truthfulness not admissible as circumstantial evidence that defendant did not commit crime of drug distribution, but once defendant testified, evidence that he committed crime of drug distribution with which he was charged was an attack on his character for truthfulness sufficient to permit evidence of good character for truthfulness).

(2) *Counsel Must Request Limiting Instruction. Government of the Virgin Islands v. Roldan*, 612 F.2d 775 (3d Cir. 1979), *cert. denied*, 446 U.S. 920 (1980), was an appeal of a conviction for first-degree murder. Defendant Roldan appealed the admission of evidence of his prior conviction elicited by the government from Luz Maria Cruz, a relative of the defendant. Defendant's good character had been elicited earlier by defendant's counsel from the same witness, as follows:

Q. Would you [Mrs. Cruz] say that he [Roldan] is a lonely unsociable fellow?

A. He is a man that never bother (sic) anybody.

After this exchange, no further character evidence was introduced by defendant. Cruz was subsequently asked by the Government:

Q. Mrs. Cruz, you are aware, are you not, that the Defendant was convicted previously of murder in the first degree?

It is this line of questioning of which defendant complained on appeal. At the trial stage, Roldan did not request a limiting jury instruction, merely objecting to the question. The Court of Appeals stated:

> It is clear that the sole purpose for which evidence of Roldan's prior conviction was admissible was to impeach Cruz' credibility and impair her assessment of Roldan's good character. Even though Roldan "opened the door," evidence of his *prior conviction* [i.e., a specific instance of a bad act] is not made admissible by Rule 405(a) *to show his bad character.* In this respect the Federal Rules of Evidence do not purport to alter the prior common law. Whenever an exception under Fed. R. Evid. 405 allows introduction of prior bad acts, the defendant is entitled to a limiting jury instruction to the effect that the prior bad act testimony does not bear on the defendant's propensity to commit such crimes again. In this case, no such cautionary instruction was given.
>
> Roldan's counsel, however, never submitted an oral or written request to so charge and affirmatively stated that he had agreed with the court's instructions. Under such circumstances, failure to give a cautionary

instruction is not plain error and therefore does not require reversal of Roldan's conviction. *United States v. Cooper*, 577 F.2d 1079, 1088-89 (6th Cir.), *cert. denied*, 439 U.S. 868 (1978) (citing cases and concluding that almost every Circuit that has considered the issue has refused to find plain error).

PROBLEM SET 3E: REVIEWING AND EXTENDING CHARACTER CATEGORIES; AND SOME BASIC TACTICS.

(1) *Can a Perjury Defendant's Character Witness Be Impeached by Inquiring About Defendant's Assault Conviction?* A criminal defendant, in a perjury prosecution, puts on a good-character witness within the rules you have learned concerning what is proper evidence in this regard. The prosecution on cross-examination asks the good-character witness whether the witness has heard that the defendant was convicted of assault and battery during the period the witness professes to know about. Admissible?

(2) *How Should Prosecution Respond?* A criminal defendant in a perjury prosecution puts on a good-character witness who testifies to the defendant's reputation for peacefulness. Should you as prosecutor:

(a) Object?

(b) Wait until cross-examination of the witness, at which point you will ask him if he has heard of defendant's previous conviction for assault and battery (handed down during the period testified to) of which you happen to have proof?

(c) Do both?

§ 3.03 CHARACTER IN CASES OF SEXUAL CRIMES AND RELATED OFFENSES

[A] Complainant's Sexual Character, Conduct, or Propensity: Restricted Admissibility Under F.R.E. 412's "Rape Shield" and Similar State Rules[6]

Read Federal Rule of Evidence 412, "Sex Offense Cases: The Victim's Sexual Behavior or Predisposition."

Historical Perspective: From Whence We Have Come. The state law even as late as the 1970s was quite receptive to evidence of the sexual complainant's sexual past. In *State ex rel. Pope v. Superior Court*, 545 P.2d 946 (Ariz. 1976), the court said:

> Almost every jurisdiction permits the substantive use of evidence [of] unchastity where the defense of consent is raised in forcible rape. A majority limit [it] to a showing of the general reputation for unchastity, while a minority in addition allow specific prior acts of unchastity.

---

[6] Study Guide Reference: Evidence in a Nutshell, Chapter 4:IV at "The 'Rape Shield.' "

The court indicates that as late as 1973, Arizona cases customarily admitted both, on the theory that "the woman who has once departed from the paths of virtue is far more apt to consent to another lapse." The decision covers many interesting points, including an instruction to the jury in many jurisdictions that rape is easily charged and difficult to disprove (see discussion and citations in *United States v. Vik*, 655 F.2d 878 (8th Cir. 1981)), the special corroboration of the victim's word required in many jurisdictions, the requirement in some jurisdictions that rape must be shown to have been resisted with utmost force, and empirical data bearing on the incidence of unwarranted claims of rape, a matter that is at the heart of the so-called "necessity" behind some of these rulings. Today, all states but one have some form of "rape shield," like Rule 412, whether by rule, statute, or judicial decision. *See* Rothstein, *Federal Evidence Rule 412 on Sex Victim's Character*, 15 CRIM. L. BULL. 353 (1979) (suggesting alterations of Fed. R. Evid. 412, which in part were subsequently adopted into the federal rule and which a number of states subsequently picked up in one form or another in their rape shield laws).

OLDEN v. KENTUCKY

United States Supreme Court
488 U.S. 227 (1988)

PER CURIAM.

[Olden was convicted of forcible sodomy on Starla Matthews. Olden's defense was consent, and he claimed that Matthews had concocted her version of events to explain to her live-in boyfriend, Russell, why she was seen emerging from Olden's car. The trial judge excluded evidence of Matthews' living arrangements with Russell. The Kentucky Court of Appeals affirmed. The United States Supreme Court, per curiam, reversed.]

The [Kentucky] court specifically held that evidence that Matthews and Russell were living together was not barred by the State's rape shield law. Ky. Rev. Stat. Ann. § 510.145. Moreover, it acknowledged that the evidence in question was relevant to petitioner's theory of the case. But it held, nonetheless, that the evidence was properly excluded as "its probative value [was] outweighed by its possibility for prejudice." By way of explanation, the court stated: "[T]here were the undisputed facts of race; Matthews was white and Russell was black. [T]estimony that Matthews and Russell were living together at the time of trial may have created extreme prejudice against Matthews."

The Kentucky Court of Appeals failed to accord proper weight to [Olden's] Sixth Amendment right "to be confronted with the witnesses against him." That right includes the right to conduct reasonable cross-examination. [S]ubject to "the broad discretion of a trial judge to preclude repetitive and unduly harassing interrogation, the cross-examiner has traditionally been allowed to impeach, i.e. discredit, the witness." "[T]he exposure of a witness's motivation in testifying is a proper and important function of the constitutionally protected right of cross-examination."

While a trial court may, of course, impose reasonable limits to take account of such factors as "harassment, prejudice, confusion of the issues, the witness's safety, or interrogation that would be repetitive or marginally relevant," the limitation here was beyond reason.

NOTES AND QUESTIONS

(1) *Is there Any Constitutional Guarantee that would Apply if the Evidence were Other than Cross-Examination?* Suppose Matthews refuses on retrial to admit to her relationship with Russell. Does *Olden* mean "other" evidence of the relationship must be admissible?

(2) *Sexual Orientation as Excluded by Rape Shield.* In *State v. Murphy*, 919 P.2d 191 (Colo. 1996), Murphy sought to prove that his alleged victim was homosexual, as relevant to his defense of consent to the charge of forcible sexual assault committed by means of handcuffs and sadomasochism. The Colorado shield excludes past sexual conduct; the Colorado Supreme Court, however, construed this phrase to cover the "closely related" matter of sexual orientation and excluded it also. What result under Fed. R. Evid. 412, which generally excludes sexual "predisposition"?

(3) *Claim of Mistaken Belief: Effect on Rape Shield.* It is not always clear under the substantive law of rape whether defendant's reasonable belief in consent negates the *mens rea* (the required state of mind of defendant) for rape. If it does negate the *mens rea*, the sex victim's sexual reputation (or even other sexual acts) or the opinion of the defendant or others, or both, may be relevant to the *mens rea* of the crime. The claim of mistaken belief in consent from appearances, reputation, or other acts often is made in cases where defendant was intoxicated. But the claim of mistaken belief is not confined to cases of intoxication. It can come up in any case where an argument can be made that the victim seemed willing in the eyes of the defendant but in the victim's own eyes she was not willing (at least not willing to have intercourse). The defendant may offer evidence of sex acts by the victim with several others (for example, at the same "party," termed an "orgy" by one court) or evidence of her bad reputation to bolster his claim of reasonable belief in consent. Would this evidence be relevant? Admissible? Under Fed. R. Evid. 412?

For an extensive analysis of the myriad of issues concerning Rule 412, see Myrna S. Raeder, *Litigating Sex Crimes in the United States: Has the Last Decade Made Any Difference?*, 6 Int'l Comm. on Evid. Issue 2, Art. 6 (2008), available at http://www.bepress.com/ice/vol.6/iss.2/art.6.

(4) *Constitutional Implications of Specific Rape Shield Applications.* The Oregon rape shield survived a constitutional challenge (at least as to the particular application) in *Anderson v. Morrow*, 371 F.3d 1027 (9th Cir. 2004). The defendant was convicted of having sexual intercourse with a person (identified as "JH") incapable of consent by reason of mental defect. The complainant was a 28-year-old moderately retarded woman with the emotional maturity of a six- to eight-year-old and the communication skills of a five- to seven-year-old child. She also had a number of other impairments. The defendant attempted to introduce evidence describing her sexual history, purported promiscuity, and public displays of sexual acts to rebut her being incapable of consent. The trial judge allowed some of the evidence, specifically her sexual activity with two former boyfriends, her previous

encounter with the defendant, and testimony describing her public acts of seductive behavior. However, the trial judge excluded "testimony that JH was a 'cat in heat'; reports from a counselor who worked with JH 'to try to resolve problems with her sexuality'; testimony from her former boyfriend who described her sexual drive as 'excessive'; testimony from two community members recounting how they witnessed JH rubbing her body against men, grabbing their crotches, and picking up men on street corners." This exclusion of what the appeals court described as "the more defamatory evidence," which the appeals court felt portrayed JH in a demeaning way as a "wanton and promiscuous woman," was held by the appeals court to be a proper and constitutional exercise of the trial judge's discretion granted under the rape shield. Was the correct balance reached?

(5) *Procedural Considerations.* Most rape shields have some type of notice provision (e.g., 10 or 14 days in advance), which must be followed before any evidence arguably within an exception to the shield is offered. In *Michigan v. Lucas*, 500 U.S. 145 (1991), the Michigan shield law required notice within 10 days following arraignment, of proposed evidence, here evidence that the victim and defendant had a past sexual relationship, offered on the issue of consent. The Supreme Court held that a failure to comply with such a provision could justify exclusion of the defendant's evidence, despite the defendant's claim that such exclusion automatically violates the Sixth Amendment right of confrontation.

(6) *Legitimate Defenses Precluded by Rape Shield?* In one celebrated case, the victim of a rape recanted (after the defendant had been imprisoned for six years) and stated the rape had not occurred, and that the story had been fabricated because she mistakenly thought she was pregnant by her boyfriend (not the defendant) and did not wish to lose the love and affection of the sexually strict foster home in which she was living. *See* THE WASHINGTON POST, May 9, 1985, p. C1. Had defendant suspected this at the time, would he have been able to put on the facts necessary to suggest this to the jury with strength? Consider the effect of the rape shield laws studied in this section, including Fed. R. Evid. 412.

(7) *Sexual Misconduct Includes Sexual Harassment.* In *Wolak v. Spucci*, 217 F.3d 157 (2d Cir. 2000), Rule 412's provisions regarding civil cases was interpreted to include sexual harassment suits. As a result, where the complaint contained allegations of being demeaned with pornography in the workplace, questions about parties at which pornographic videos were shown while the plaintiff was present were improperly permitted. Why were the questions regarded as inadmissible under the standard set forth in Rule 412(b)(2)?

[B] Broader Admissibility of Defendant's Other Conduct or Propensity in Sexual Cases: F.R.E. 413–415[7]

Read Federal Rules of Evidence 413, "Similar Crimes in Sexual-Assault Cases"; 414, "Similar Crimes in Child Molestation Cases"; and 415, "Similar Acts in Civil Cases Involving Sexual Assault or Child Molestation."

---

[7] Study Guide Reference: Evidence in a Nutshell, Chapter 4:IV at "The Wide-Open Admissibility of Sexual Misconduct Against Sexual Offense Defendants: F.R.E. 413–415."

Historical Perspective: From Whence We Have Come. For a historical perspective, see *Hodge v. United States*, 126 F.2d 849 (D.C. Cir. 1942) ("In prosecutions for sexual offenses, however, there is a well established exception [to the ban on other wrongs], which [exception] is that as the mental disposition of the defendant at the time of the act charged is relevant, evidence that at some prior time he was similarly disposed is also relevant"); *State v. Spreigl*, 272 Minn. 488, 139 N.W.2d 167 (1965) (adopting *Hodge* principle subject to giving advance written notice to defendant of intent to use offenses). This type of exception to the character ban has been called either "lustful disposition" or "depraved sexual instinct." While such exceptions were fairly common, states that adopted rules patterned on Fed. R. Evid. 404 and 405 sometimes have viewed them as inconsistent with these rules, although the belief that sexual depravity is a compulsion has been cited to justify continuation of the former practice even under the new rules. On what rationale might this be justified under the language of the rules?

The adoption in 1994 of Rules 413–415 was quite controversial, and opposed by many evidence commentators, the American Bar Association, and the Judicial Conference. *See, e.g.*, Raeder, *American Bar Association Criminal Justice Section Report to the House of Delegates*, reprinted in 22 Fordham Urb. L.J. 343 (1995). The rules were passed in what has widely been reported as a political compromise, in which Congresswoman Molinari provided the final vote needed to pass President Clinton's Crime Bill in exchange for the inclusion of Rules 413–415 in the legislation. For a detailed discussion of this history see Scallen, *Analyzing "The Politics of [Evidence] Rulemaking,"* 53 Hastings L.J. 843 (2002).

[1] Rules 413-415: The General Principle

UNITED STATES v. ROBERTS

United States Court of Appeals, Tenth Circuit
88 F.3d 872 (1996)

Per Curiam.

[Defendant Roberts, who was Chief of the Choctaw Nation of Oklahoma, was indicted for sexual abuse offenses against three women. He sought to exclude evidence from nine additional women who alleged that he had abused them over the past twenty years. The District Court granted his motion *in limine*. In the Court of Appeals, the Government relied on Fed. R. Evid. 413, but the Court of Appeals here rejects this contention and holds that the new Rule is "inapplicable here" because the indictment against Roberts already was pending when it was adopted. The Court believed that Congress intended Fed. R. Evid. 413 to apply only to those criminal cases not already pending when the Rule became effective.

[The Government therefore was relegated to arguing that the evidence from the nine previously abused women was admissible under Fed. R. Evid. 404(b). The Court of Appeals here remands this issue to the District Court for a hearing "to determine whether the government has established that Mr. Roberts engaged in a common scheme to abuse sexually women subject to his authority and whether each woman's testimony fits this pattern." The court outlines the government's theory that must be proved on remand as follows:]

In particular, the government noted, "such evidence will be introduced to show a pattern of verbal and physical conduct and behavior by the defendant, directed toward the victims during a time when said victims were employed by the Choctaw Nation of Oklahoma." Moreover, in response to Mr. Roberts' motion in limine, the government stated the evidence would be used to show "the defendant's knowledge that young female employees are easy to victimize without fear of reprisal," and to establish the "defendant's opportunity, in that he used his position as Chief" to take advantage of women subject to his authority. The district court did not analyze the individual evidence concerning each of the nine women to determine whether the government had presented sufficient facts to demonstrate Mr. Roberts engaged in a common scheme to abuse sexually women working under his authority. Instead, the court focused exclusively on whether the evidence demonstrated the defendant's intent to abuse sexually the three women named in the indictment.

[The Court of Appeals sharply distinguishes Fed. R. Evid. 404(b) from newer Fed. R. Evid. 413. The court in the following passages implies that admissibility would be probable under Fed. R. Evid. 413 even without the "common scheme" or "pattern" necessary to trigger Fed. R. Evid. 404(b)]:

As is evident from the text of the Rule, Fed. R. Evid. 413 was designed to create a "general rule [ ] of admissibility in sexual assault cases for evidence that the defendant has committed offenses of the same type on other occasions." Fed. R. Evid. 413 historical notes (statement of Rep. Molinari). Rule 413 provides a specific admissibility standard in sexual assault cases, replacing Fed. R. Evid. 404(b)'s general criteria.

The new rules will supersede in sex offense cases the restrictive aspects of Federal Rule of Evidence 404(b). In contrast to Rule 404(b)'s general prohibition of evidence of character or propensity, the new rules for sex offense cases authorize admission and consideration of evidence of an uncharged offense for its bearing "on any matter to which it is relevant."

[2] Interplay of this Sexual Misconduct Evidence, F.R.E Rule 403, and the Constitution

(1) *Is Rule 403 Applicable to Evidence Offered Under Rules 413–415? Is that Necessary to Save Constitutionality?* Fed. R. Evid. 413 provided (before restyling in Dec. 2011) that sexual assault evidence "is admissible" and "may be considered" as to any matter "to which it is relevant." That language could be interpreted as suggesting that automatic admissibility follows from minimal relevance, even if there are substantial counterweights such as prejudice, confusion, or delay. In other words, the language could be read as dispensing with Fed. R. Evid. 403. On the other hand, textual interpretation could have also supported the opposite conclusion, since Fed. R. Evid. 413 used the phrase "*may* be considered," did not say the evidence "shall" be admitted, and did not expressly override Fed. R. Evid. 403, a result that one might infer Congress would state explicitly had it intended it. Arguments about the purposes of Rules 413–415 also can be structured to support

either result, as can arguments about legislative history. Look closely at the current version of the rule (as restyled in 2011). Does/can the restyled language change things? Was it intended to? Both *United States v. Sumner*, 119 F.3d 658 (8th Cir. 1997) and *United States v. Larson*, 112 F.3d 600 (2d Cir. 1997) hold that Fed. R. Evid. 403 applies.

In *Sumner*, the defendant denied committing the specific acts of sexual abuse with the complainant, a child. The prosecution introduced evidence of two prior incidents with other children on the issue of intent. (Was it a mistake for the prosecution to so confine the purpose of the offer under the Rule? Especially in light of what follows here?) Sumner had offered to stipulate to the intent element (i.e., I did not commit the abuse, but anyone who did would have had the requisite intent). The court reversed his conviction. If Fed. R. Evid. 403 was found not to be applicable, would the application of Fed. R. Evid. 414 have been unconstitutional? *See, e.g., State v. Burns*, 978 S.W.2d 759 (Mo. 1998) (en banc), holding that a statute mandating admission of propensity evidence violated defendant's constitutional right to be tried only on the offense charged.

On the question of constitutionality consider also the following dissent from denial of rehearing and hearing en banc in *United States v. Mound*, 157 F.3d 1153 (8th Cir. 1998). The original decision, found at 149 F.3d 799 (8th Cir. 1998), upheld the constitutionality of Rules 413 and 414, against a challenge on due process and equal protection grounds, by applying Rule 403. Certiorari was denied at 525 U.S. 1089 (1999). The dissent from denial of rehearing reads as follows:

> Morris Sheppard Arnold, Circuit Judge, dissenting, joined by McMillian, Wollman, and Beam, Circuit Judges.
>
> Because this case seems to me to involve "a question of exceptional importance," see Fed. R. App. P. 35(a)(2), I dissent from the order denying the suggestion for rehearing en banc. Fed. R. Evid. 413 runs counter to a centuries-old legal tradition that views propensity evidence with a particularly skeptical eye. The common law, of course, is not embodied in the Constitution, but the fact that a rule has recommended itself to generations of lawyers and judges is at least some indication that it embodies " 'fundamental conceptions of justice," *Dowling v. United States*, 493 U.S. 342, 352 (1990), quoting *Mooney v. Holohan*, 294 U.S. 103 (1935) (per curiam). It also cannot be irrelevant that the members of two committees, consisting of 40 persons in all, and appointed by the Judicial Conference of the United States to examine Fed. R. Evid. 413 before its passage, all but unanimously urged that Congress not adopt the rule because of deep concerns about its fundamental fairness. . . .
>
> It seems to me that the en banc court ought to consider, as one commentator has put it, whether Fed. R. Evid. 413 "presents [so] great a risk that the jury will convict a defendant for his past conduct or unsavory character" that it violates due process. We might well conclude that the common-law rule against propensity evidence has as distinguished a legal pedigree as, say, the rule that guilt must be proved beyond a reasonable doubt. . . . .

Compare *People v. Donoho*, 788 N.E.2d 707 (Ill. 2003), holding that a state statutory provision permitting the admission of evidence of other sex crimes to show a defendant's propensity to commit sex offenses did not violate either the state or federal constitutional equal protection clauses. In doing so it noted that besides the federal rules, courts in 25 additional states have broadened the exceptions to the ban on other-crimes evidence in sexual offense cases. While the exceptions vary, they indicate a continuing trend towards flexibility in admitting evidence of sexual offenses.

(2) *The California Approach.* Cal. Evid. Code § 1108 is California's analogue to Fed. R. Evid. 413–415. In the trial of a sexual offense case, it provides that "evidence of another sexual offense is not made inadmissible" by the character rules "if the evidence is not inadmissible pursuant to [Cal. Evid. Code] Section 352" (which is California's analogue to Fed. R. Evid. 403). California thus explicitly subjects this evidence to the equivalent of a Fed. R. Evid. 403 analysis. The California Supreme Court upheld the provision in *People v. Falsetta*, 986 P.2d 182 (Cal. 1999), *cert. denied*, 529 U.S. 1089 (2000).

UNITED STATES v. GUARDIA

United States District Court, District of New Mexico
955 F. Supp. 115 (1997)

Black, District Judge.

The case began as a result of a complaint made by Carla G., a patient at the Kirtland Air Force Base Hospital, where Defendant, Dr. Guardia, worked as a gynecologist on contract through his employer, the UNM Hospital. After several visits, Ms. G. complained about the way Defendant performed medical procedures and the things he said during and after examinations. As a result of Ms. G.'s complaint, the FBI began contacting Defendant's prior Kirtland patients. One of the many patients that Defendant had treated, Francesca L., indicated to the FBI inquiry that she also thought Defendant's behavior during her examination was sexual and inappropriate. Based on the complaints of these two women, the Grand Jury returned a six-count Indictment against Defendant for criminal sexual penetration and simple battery.

During discovery, the Government indicated it had learned of other women who felt Defendant's examinations were inappropriate and that the Government would subpoena these women to testify regarding Defendant's behavior during his examinations of each of them. Counsel for Defendant indicated that since a chaperone was present during the examination of at least two of these women, the chaperones would be called to testify for the defense. Moreover, both counsel indicated that substantial expert testimony would be offered as to the medical justification for the specific medical procedures and/or techniques to which each of these women objected and how the ethical rules of various medical associations would apply. Defense counsel also indicated areas of cross examination she would raise regarding some of the non-prosecuting witnesses' gynecological and pharmacological histories, in an attempt to explain why they might be uncomfortable with, or misperceive, the actions of a male gynecologist.

. . . [T]hese Rules arose out of congressional debate on the Violent Crime Control and Law Enforcement Act of 1994. There was initially some debate on whether and how these Rules would be construed in conjunction with Rules 403 and 404. A common sense reading of Rule 403, however, indicates that since it applies only to evidence otherwise admissible, it applies to evidence otherwise admissible under Rule 413. This also appears to be the developing consensus of judges, lawyers, and legal scholars. *See, e.g.*, MANUAL OF MODEL CRIMINAL JURY INSTRUCTIONS FOR THE DISTRICT COURTS OF THE EIGHTH CIRCUIT § 2.08, Committee Comments (1996). . . .

This Court, however, has been unable to find any congressional history or legal authority to support the premise that Rule 413 is intended to substantially lengthen trials or require additional expert testimony. [T]his Court is persuaded that the additional four witnesses the Government proposes to call under Rule 413 add little probative value to the testimony of the two prosecuting witnesses but have the definite potential to confuse the jury and unnecessarily extend the trial.

The two complaining witnesses whose testimony was presented to the Grand Jury, Carla G. and Francesca L., described Defendant's alleged inappropriate conduct in massaging the clitoris during his examinations. The Government further proffers Francesca L.'s testimony that while smiling, Defendant told her, "I love my job."

Initially, the Court notes that the tendered Rule 413 witnesses will interject confusingly similar, but potentially distinguishable, legal issues into the trial. For example, one of the Rule 413 witnesses, Patricia N., reported that Defendant fondled her breasts without a chaperone present and subsequently informed her that he had "enjoyed" the experience. Another Rule 413 witness, Michelle A., reported that Defendant fondled her breasts, hips, and buttocks without gloves, asking Michelle A. if she was "having fun." Neither of the original complaining witnesses reported anything related to fondling of the breasts or buttocks. In the ordinary trial, if the jury believed a defendant touched a victim in these private places, an assault would be established. In the context of an ostensible medical examination, however, additional prosecution or defense expert testimony would be required on these collateral matters to establish the appropriate procedure for breast and rectal examinations by a gynecologist. . . .

Another Rule 413 witness, Renee C., while also alleging inappropriate clitoral touching, was seen for a pap smear following laser treatment. Again, different expert testimony relating to appropriate follow-up to laser surgery will be required. The fourth witness, Juli H., also had a biopsy. This is an issue which is the focal point of her complaint, and again will necessitate expert testimony. Moreover, in the case of at least two of the Rule 413 witnesses, chaperones were present, so the events at issue were likely witnessed. As such, a swearing match between at least three persons may be required to establish the factual predicate for such expert testimony. This would essentially create a trial within a trial with regard to allegations by non-prosecuting witnesses, related to actions for which Defendant is not charged.

Most significantly, however, this case involves a highly limited and unusual form of "sexual assault." Indeed, unlike virtually every other form of such conduct, the jury will be unable to determine the propriety, much less the legality, of most of the conduct which forms the basis of the charges without the aid of expert testimony. Since each such situation is different, then, multiplying complaining witnesses will multiply conflicting expert testimony. Moreover, since much of the expert testimony regarding the Rule 413 witnesses will of necessity overlap the expert testimony regarding the two complaining witnesses, the potential for confusion is magnified.

At oral argument, the Assistant United States Attorney argued that by adopting Rule 413, Congress has already determined that repeated instances of similar conduct will not confuse the jury so long as the incidents are relatively close in time. The Court finds nothing in the congressional debate to support this conclusion, and thinks the Wright & Miller treatise more accurately portrays the difficulty in a case like this, where the criminal nature of the prior acts is not obvious:

> Because the jury must first find that the defendant committed the uncharged crimes before it can use them as evidence of the charged crime, the trial of a single offense can be converted into two, three, four, or more trials if the defendant does not concede the commission of the uncharged crimes. . . .

A trial court has the authority, if not the duty, to exclude evidence which will likely confuse the jury on peripheral issues. In the present context, however, the Government argues it has an absolute right to present a stream of witnesses "to show that the defendant has an on-going disposition to commit sexual assaults against his female patients." This Court is aware of debate over the constitutionality of Rule 413, but does not believe it necessary to confront that debate here. Rather, the Court believes it is more appropriate to interpret Rule 413, like the other Rules of Evidence, to "secure fairness in administration, elimination of unjustifiable expense and delay, and promotion of growth and development of the law of evidence to the end that the truth may be ascertained and proceedings justly determined." Fed. R. Evid. 102. These goals would not be served by allowing six rather than two witnesses to testify as to how they believe Defendant sexually assaulted them and, more importantly, subjecting the jury to the expert testimony necessary for it to determine the legal significance of such testimony by each Rule 413 witness.

NOTES AND QUESTIONS

(1) *Should this Evidence Properly have been Admissible Not Only Under Rule 413, but even Under Rule 404(b), as Showing Motive, Common Scheme, Etc.?* Perhaps an argument can be constructed that the other misconduct evidence here shows that defendant employed a common plan or scheme, consisting of his touchings of sexual body parts during gynecological examinations coupled with similar kinds of statements. Perhaps it also demonstrates motive, particularly in light of defendant's contemporaneous remarks. Is there, thus, a credible argument that this evidence should be admitted even under the more restrictive test of Rule 404(b)?

(2) *Did the District Judge Faithfully Follow Rule 413?* Perhaps one can argue that an inherently ambiguous offense that requires expertise to detect presents precisely the situation in which other misconduct evidence would be most valuable,

rather than most unnecessary. Is the District Judge's concern that evidence about multiple accusations will constitute an unmanageable "trial within a trial" undercut by Congress's evident awareness that Rule 413 always would result in admittance of evidence of multiple accusations, which necessarily would require a trial within a trial every time? Is the court's reasoning about jury confusion sound?

(3) *The District Judge's Rule 403 Analysis.* The District Judge's decision to apply Fed. R. Evid. 403, as the citations indicate, is in accord with the conclusions of most commentators that Fed. R. Evid. 403 does apply. But is the court's discretionary exclusion of the questioned evidence supportable under the balancing test of Fed. R. Evid. 403 — in other words, is the relevance "substantially outweighed" by counterweights? Does Fed. R. Evid. 413 appear to change the analysis of the prejudice factor, in that it omits the concerns of Fed. R. Evid. 404(b) against propensity evidence?

[C] Extending Admissibility of Propensity Evidence Beyond Sexual Offenses

(1) *California Allows Domestic Violence Evidence Subject to Exclusion for Prejudice, Etc.* California Evidence Code Section 1109 provides, in relevant part, "(a)(1) [I]n a criminal action in which the defendant is accused of an offense involving domestic violence, evidence of the defendant's commission of other domestic violence is not made inadmissible [by the character rule] if the evidence is not inadmissible pursuant to Section 352." Section 352 is the California equivalent of F.R.E. 403. Thus, prior acts of domestic violence may be admitted under Section 1109 to prove disposition to commit such acts. This provision survived a constitutional challenge based on due process grounds in *People v. Escobar*, 82 Cal. App. 4th 1085 (Cal. Ct. App. 2000). And the state's basis for the classification (i.e., for confining this admissibility provision to these kinds of cases), which basis included the special difficulty of proving these cases, satisfies the rational basis test under the constitution's equal protection clause, according to *Smith v. Roe*, 232 F. Supp. 2d 1073 (C.D. Cal. 2002). Evidence Code § 1109(a)(2) permits evidence of prior abuse to an elder or dependent adult.

The statute has been amended to require notice, and a hearing at which corroboration and remoteness are factors. To the extent a prior act is more than ten years old, it is only admissible if necessary in the interests of justice.

(2) *The Policy Issues.* What are the policy justifications for permitting such propensity evidence? Is it the same for domestic violence as elder abuse? As sex offenses? Do you agree with these exceptions to the general ban on character evidence? For a discussion of some of these issues written prior to the enactment of § 1109, see Raeder, *The Admissibility of Prior Acts of Domestic Violence: Simpson and Beyond*, 69 S. Cal. L. Rev. 1463 (1996).

§ 3.04 CHARACTER VERSUS HABIT[8]

Read Federal Rule of Evidence 406, "Habit; Routine Practice."

REYES v. MISSOURI PACIFIC RAILROAD COMPANY

United States Court of Appeals, Fifth Circuit
589 F.2d 791 (1979)

JAMES C. HILL, CIRCUIT JUDGE.

Shortly after midnight on June 17, 1974, appellant Reyes was run over by appellee-railroad's train as he lay on the railroad tracks near a crossing in Brownsville, Texas. Reyes brought this diversity suit against the railroad, alleging negligence on the part of the railroad's employees in failing to discover the plaintiff as he lay on the tracks and stop the train in time to avoid the accident. The railroad answered by claiming that Reyes, dressed in dark clothing that night, was not visible from the approaching train until it was too late for its employees to avert the accident. Moreover, the railroad alleged that Reyes was contributorily negligent because he was intoxicated on the night of the accident and passed out on the tracks before the train arrived. Reyes explained his presence on the railroad tracks by claiming that he was knocked unconscious by an unknown assailant as he walked along the tracks.

Reyes made a motion *in limine* to exclude the evidence relating to his prior misdemeanor convictions for public intoxication. The railroad opposed this motion, arguing that the convictions were admissible to show that Reyes was intoxicated on the night of the accident. The district court agreed and refused to grant Reyes' motion.

The record in this case makes clear that the railroad intended for Reyes' prior convictions to show that he was intoxicated on the night of the accident. Indeed, that purpose was the only possible one for which the evidence could be offered. Moreover, the trial judge specifically noted in the motion *in limine* hearing that evidence of the prior convictions would be relevant to the issue of whether Reyes was intoxicated on the night of the accident. Because the evidence of Reyes' prior convictions was admitted for the sole purpose of showing that he had a character trait of drinking to excess and that he acted in conformity with his character on the night of the accident by becoming intoxicated, we conclude that the prior convictions were inadmissible character evidence under Rule 404.

The suggestion that the prior convictions constituted evidence of Reyes' "habit" of excessive drinking is equally unpersuasive. Rule 406 allows the introduction of evidence of the habit of a person for the purpose of proving that the person acted in conformity with his habit on a particular occasion. Habit evidence is considered to be highly probative and therefore superior to character evidence because "the uniformity of one's response to habit is far greater than the consistency with which one's conduct conforms to character or disposition." MCCORMICK ON EVIDENCE § 195 at 463 (2d ed. 1972).

---

[8] Study Guide Reference: Evidence in a Nutshell, Chapter 4:VII.

Perhaps the chief difficulty in deciding questions of admissibility under Rule 406 arises in trying to draw the line between inadmissible character evidence and admissible habit evidence. Quite often the line between the two may become blurred:

> Character and habit are close akin. Character is a generalized description of one's disposition, or one's disposition in respect to a general trait, such as honesty, temperance, or peacefulness. "Habit," in modern usage, both lay and psychological, is more specific. It describes one's regular response to a repeated specific situation. If we speak of character for care, we think of the person's tendency to act prudently in all the varying situations of life, in business, family life, in handling automobiles and in walking across the street. A habit, on the other hand, is the person's regular practice of meeting a particular kind of situation with a specific type of conduct, such as the habit of going down a particular stairway two stairs at a time, or of giving the hand-signal for a left turn, or of alighting from railway cars while they are moving. The doing of the habitual acts may become semi-automatic. [*Id.*]

Although a precise formula cannot be proposed for determining when the behavior may become so consistent as to rise to the level of habit, "adequacy of sampling and uniformity of response" are controlling considerations. Notes of Advisory Committee on Fed. R. Evid. 406. Thus, the probative force of habit evidence to prove intoxication on a given occasion depends on the "degree of regularity of the practice and its coincidence with the occasion." McCormick on Evidence § 195 n. 16 (2d ed. 1972).

We do not undertake here to prescribe the precise quantum of proof necessary to transform a general disposition for excessive drinking into a "habit" of intemperance; we simply find that four prior convictions for public intoxication spanning a three and one-half year period are of insufficient regularity to rise to the level of "habit" evidence. Consequently, we hold the evidence to be inadmissible under Rule 406 as well.

NOTES AND QUESTIONS

(1) *Character or Habit?: Habit as Very Specific Conduct.* On character or habit of negligence, see *Greenwood v. Boston & M. R.R.*, 88 A. 217 (N.H. 1913) (testimony of coworkers — that decedent was "careful about his work and always attended to his work" as railroad yard man and that he was a "careful man" — was not habit evidence but rather inadmissible character evidence to show that he was not contributorily negligent, i.e., to show that he did not fail to keep a proper lookout when he was hit by train cars while clearing snow from the switch; evidence would have to be more specifically addressed to repetitive conduct concerning that particular operation, i.e., snow removal from the switch and keeping lookout; evidence also would need to be somewhat involuntary).

(2) *Character or Habit?: Habit as Relatively Nonvolitional.* In *Levin v. United States*, 338 F.2d 265 (D.C. Cir. 1964), *cert. denied*, 379 U.S. 999 (1965), the defendant, Levin, was accused of taking money on a particular day and time at a

particular locale. That time was the commencement of the Sabbath. After his rabbi testified as a character witness, the following tender was made by counsel for defendant:

> I wish to go into the subject matter with this witness concerning Mr. Levin's habit of being home on the Sabbath and using him as an expert to testify when the Sabbath commenced and what Orthodox ritual requires.

This testimony was ruled inadmissible. The court found no error:

> It seems apparent to us that an individual's religious practices would not be the type of activities which would lend themselves to the characterization of "invariable regularity." Certainly the very volitional basis of the activity raises serious questions as to its invariable nature, and hence its probative value. As Chamberlayne has observed:
>
> > The probative force of habit, whether the question arises in a civil or criminal case, is based principally upon the fact that habitual conduct is largely free from the complicating and confusing element of volition which makes the relevancy of moral conduct merely deliberative, but, on the contrary, brings such conduct in line with the activities of the body which are under the control of the subliminal mind, i.e., are of the automatic nature, practically under the uniformity of natural law. In fact, the probative strength of habit is in proportion to the extent to which it assumes this automatic character.
>
> Needless to say, the observance of the Sabbath in a particular manner involves a volitional assent, however guided or instructively urged.

(3) *Character or Habit?: Habit as Numerous, Regular Responses to Same Set of Stimuli.* On the general subject of what constitutes habit, see *Wilson v. Volkswagen of America, Inc.*, 561 F.2d 494 (4th Cir. 1977), *cert. denied*, 434 U.S. 1020 (1978):

> It has been repeatedly stated that habit or pattern of conduct is never to be lightly established, and evidence of examples, for purpose of establishing such habit, is to be carefully scrutinized before admission.
>
> The reason for such an attitude toward evidence of habit is the obvious danger of abuse in such evidence resulting from "the confusion of issues, collateral inquiry, prejudice and the like," or, as one court has phrased it, "the collateral nature of [such] proof, the danger that it may afford a basis for improper inferences, the likelihood that it may cause confusion or operate to unfairly prejudice the party against whom it is directed." It is only when the examples offered to establish such pattern of conduct or habit are "numerous enough to base an inference of systematic conduct" and to establish "one's regular response to a repeated specific situation" or, to use the language of a leading text, where they are "sufficiently regular or the circumstances sufficiently similar to outweigh the danger, if any, of prejudice and confusion," that they are admissible to establish pattern or habit. In determining whether the examples are "numerous enough" and "sufficiently regular," the key criteria are "adequacy of sampling and

uniformity of response," or, as an article cited with approval in the Note to Rule 406 puts it, on the "adequacy of sampling" and the "ratio of reactions to situations." These criteria and this method of balancing naturally follow from the definition of habit itself as stated in the Model Code of Evidence: "Habit means a course of behavior of a person regularly repeated in like circumstances."

While precise standards for measuring the "extent to which instances must be multiplied and consistency of behavior maintained in order to support an inference of habit and pattern of conduct, cannot be formulated," it is obvious that no finding is supportable under Rule 406, Federal Rules of Evidence, which fails to examine critically the "ratio of reactions to situations."

(4) *Rule 406 Continues Common Law for the Most Part. See also Meyer v. United States*, 464 F. Supp. 317 (D. Colo. 1979), *aff'd*, 638 F.2d 155 (10th Cir. 1980) (dentist's habit of informing patients in other cases of risks from extraction of third molar, as established by testimony of dental assistants, accepted as evidence leading to finding it was probably done in this case, as against claim of malpractice for failure to inform of risks):

Rule 406 is, of course, merely a codification of the common law rule of evidence which existed prior to the adoption of the Federal Rules of Evidence in 1975. Thus, cases dealing with habit are illustrative even if decided prior to the formal enactment of the rules.

In the context of Rule 406, habit is a person's or organization's practice of handling a particular kind of situation with a specific type of conduct. Habit is one's regular response to a repeated specific situation. In similar fashion, an organization's regularity of action is within the purview of Rule 406.

Habit in modern usage is described as "a tendency to act in a certain way or to do a certain thing; usual way of acting; custom; practice. . . ." WORLD BOOK DICTIONARY (1971 ed.).

(5) *Habit of Organizations: Common-Law Corroboration Requirement Abolished.* On the analogue of habit for organizations, which is called "routine practice," see *Envirex, Inc. v. Ecological Recovery Assocs.*, 454 F. Supp. 1329 (M.D. Pa. 1978):

ERA first contends that the Court erred in admitting page 18 of the Contract entered into between Envirex and ERA into evidence. At the trial, it was ERA's contention that it was not bound by the conditions on page 18 because that page was not attached to the contract when it was sent from Envirex to ERA for approval. Mr. Schibelka, an officer of Envirex, testified at the trial that as part of its routine business practice, Envirex would have sent a complete proposal, including page 18 to all general contractors with which it contracted. ERA, citing Pennsylvania case law, contends that custom or usage of an organization is not admissible to establish a fact in its favor but may be received as corroborative of facts already proved.

> Rule 406 states that evidence of the routine practice of an organization, whether corroborated or not, is relevant to prove that the conduct of the organization on a particular occasion was in conformity with the routine practice. Therefore, the Court did not err in admitting page 18 into evidence.
>
> The copy of the agreement between the parties introduced by ERA did not contain page 18. Special verdict question No. 1 submitted to the jury read as follows: "Was page 18 attached to the Envirex proposal of August 22, 1973 when the proposal was sent to Ecological Recovery Associates?" The jury responded in the affirmative.

In *C. F. W. Constr. Co. v. Travelers Ins. Co.*, 363 F.2d 557 (6th Cir. 1966), similar evidence to that in *Envirex* was not admitted because the company manager laying the foundation did not say it was done in every or most instances.

PROBLEM SET 3F: PRACTICE IN IDENTIFYING HABIT OR ROUTINE PRACTICE AS OPPOSED TO CHARACTER.

(1)(a) *The Line Between Character and Habit.* Assume that it is alleged in a personal injury lawsuit that the defendant was driving in excess of the posted speed limit to try to make a light ahead when the collision occurred. Assume further that the collision took place at Twelfth and Main Streets, while defendant was on the way to work on the particular morning. At what point in the progression below (if at all) does the evidence cross over from character evidence to habit evidence? (Assume that the form of the evidence — i.e., opinion evidence, reputation evidence, or specific-instance evidence — tending to establish the point indicated by each number is acceptable.)

i. Evidence that defendant is a careless person (i.e., bumps into people when he is walking, drops pots in the kitchen, etc.).

ii. Evidence he is a careless driver.

iii. Evidence he speeds when driving. (By "speeds," assume we mean going in excess of the posted speed.)

iv. Evidence he speeds when driving to work in the mornings.

v. Evidence he speeds at Twelfth and Main to make the light while on the way to work in the mornings.

Is there anything else we would need to know to answer this question? Assume all such facts are constant or equal as between the numbered items of evidence and are such as to maximize the chance of admissibility. Which of the numbered items stand the best chance of getting in? Where does the line come?

(b) Suppose it is alleged the accident was due to taking his eyes off the road at Twelfth and Main. Would any of the above (all relating to speed) qualify?

(2) *Habit and Rule 404(b).* In problem (1)(a) in this set, *the Line Between Character and Habit*, assuming the form of proof in each of the numbered items is specific instances, do any of the numbered items qualify as evidence admissible pursuant to Fed. R. Evid. 404(b), second sentence?

Does habit differ from what would be allowed pursuant to the second sentence of Fed. R. Evid. 404(b)? Could that Rule be used as an alternative ground for admissibility in each of the instances the courts in this section say is admissible as habit?

(3) *Accident-Proneness.* In problem (1)(a), if item i showed such a severe condition that it justified the term "accident proneness," would the evidence be admissible? Would an expert have to so diagnose it? How would you articulate the argument for admissibility in terms of the Federal Rules of Evidence?

(4) *Who was the Pilot?* In a wrongful death lawsuit between the surviving families, it becomes important to find out who was piloting a private airplane at the time of its crash that killed both its occupants, because pilot error seems to have been the cause. The two, who were business partners, used the plane on business trips, as the present trip was. There is no direct evidence concerning which one of them was piloting. It could be piloted from either of the chairs, which were side-by-side. Both men were experienced pilots. Their remains and the remains of the plane are completely destroyed. There is, however, testimony that, on these business trips, Mr. A customarily piloted and Mr. B customarily copiloted (with the same degree of regularity or invariability as in *Levin*, cited in Note (2) preceding the problem set, *above*, in this section). All other things being equal, how could the two cases (*Levin* and this one) be distinguished so as to admit the evidence here? Clue: In *Levin*, would the evidence have been admitted to show that the charred body at Levin's home found after a Sabbath-time fire was Levin's? (Assume that Levin has disappeared and the family makes a claim on his death-by-fire insurance policy.)

(5) *Are Similar Acts of Discrimination Admissible?* In a lawsuit charging statutory racial or sex discrimination in hiring, firing, renting, or refusing to rent to a particular person, can previous or subsequent acts of similar discrimination against others by the defendant (perhaps even prestatute or barred by the time-for-filing limitations in the statute) be introduced? If so, under what conditions? Would it be habit, or character, or other acts or wrongs under the second sentence of Fed. R. Evid. 404(b)? Or is there another theory? *See Hazelwood School District v. United States*, 433 U.S. 299, 309–10 n.15 (1977); *Williams v. Anderson*, 562 F.2d 1081 (8th Cir. 1977); *Miller v. Poretsky*, 595 F.2d 780 (D.C. Cir. 1978).

§ 3.05 OTHER TRANSACTIONS, SIMILAR OCCURRENCES, AND PROFILES: CHARACTER, HABIT, OR SOMETHING ELSE?

LINTHICUM v. RICHARDSON

Court of Appeals of Texas
245 S.W. 713 (1922)

O'QUINN, J.

Appellee sued appellant for the title and possession of 27 acres of land, alleging that he was the legal owner thereof, but that he had borrowed $176.22 in money from appellant, and, in order to secure the payment of same, had executed a deed to said land to appellant, which was intended only as a mortgage to secure said debt, and that at the time of the execution of said deed appellant agreed with appellee to reconvey said land to appellant whenever appellee paid to appellant said sum of money, and that he had tendered said money.

Was the deed from appellee to appellant intended by the parties and understood by them to be a mortgage? The plaintiff, appellee here, testified positively that such was the case, while the defendant, appellant here, just as positively testified that he bought the land outright, and that no such understanding as that the conveyance was a mortgage was had or considered.

Appellant complains that evidence was admitted that shortly before the transaction between appellant and appellee, Sam Richardson, brother of appellee, borrowed $350 from appellant and deeded to appellant his 27-acre interest in the same estate, with the understanding that appellant was to deed it back to him for $400, which was done.

The objections to the testimony should have been sustained. The similarity of the terms of the transaction with Sam Richardson and that of appellee is very marked; the loaning of money, receiving a general warranty deed, promise to later reconvey the land, all agree with the contention of appellee as to what the terms of his contract with appellant were. [T]he jury might have been induced to believe, from the fact that appellant had made such an agreement with Sam Richardson, that he had made a similar one with appellee, as was claimed by him.

"Persons capable of contracting have the right to make such contracts as they see proper, and the fact that a defendant has made a particular contract with a third person does not tend to show that he has made a similar contract with the plaintiff."

[T]he judgment is reversed.

JOHNSON v. GULICK

Nebraska Supreme Court
46 Neb. 817, 65 N.W. 883 (1896)

NORVAL, J.

Plaintiff brought suit upon a promissory note for $1,296, purporting to be made by the defendants. The defendants admit the execution and delivery of the note, but aver that it was consideration [for] three-fifths of the corporate stock in the Commercial Publishing Company of Ogden, Utah; that plaintiff, in order to induce the defendants to make said purchase, knowingly and falsely represented to them that said corporation was the owner of a franchise in the Western Associated Press of the value of $4,000; that the defendants relied upon said representations; that the same were false and untrue.

The defendants, in making out their case, produced and read the deposition of one J. S. Painter, who, after testifying that he and one Murphy, prior to the sale of the stock to the defendants, purchased of the plaintiff, Johnson, six-tenths interest in the Ogden Daily Commercial, deposed, in answer to questions, as follows: [He stated Johnson told him before the purchase, on several occasions, that Commercial owned the Western Associated Press Franchise and that it was worth $10,000.]

[Plaintiff appeals admission of this evidence, arguing that] proof of representations made by the plaintiff to persons other than the defendants does not tend to establish that the representations charged were made. We think this position sound. The evidence was clearly inadmissible, and had the effect to mislead the jury. From the fact that the plaintiff made the representations to Painter testified to by him, the inference cannot be properly drawn that the same or similar representations were made by plaintiff to the defendants. "It is not competent to a party imputing fraud to another to offer evidence to prove that the other has dealt fraudulently at other times, and in transactions wholly disconnected with that which is on trial." Evidence of other transactions than those under investigation is admissible, but only for the purpose of proving the scienter or intent, when that is in issue in the case.

Possibly, it was offered and admitted upon the ground that it was essential for the defendants to establish scienter; that is, that the plaintiff, at the time of making the representations, knew them to be false. The better rule, and the one adopted by this court, is that the intent or good faith of the person making false statements is not in issue in such [a case as this.] And the trial court so instructed the jury in the case at bar. It follows that the evidence was incompetent and immaterial. [T]he judgment is reversed. [This is a fairly typical ruling — Eds.]

KARSUN v. KELLEY

Oregon Supreme Court
258 Or. 155, 482 P.2d 533 (1971)

TONGUE, JUSTICE.

[This is an action by the purchaser of stock to recover the amount of the purchase price from the sellers of the stock. Plaintiff appeals.]

The sole issue on appeal is whether the admission of evidence of other false representations, similar to those alleged to have been made to defendant, but made to two other purchasers of stock at about the same time, was error.

Plaintiff testified that [defendant broker] Mr. Kelley told him about the operations of Diagnostic Centers, Inc. and represented to him that the prospectus for the corporation was not only out of date, but should be disregarded because the company "had turned the corner and was operating in the black," contrary to the prospectus. Kelley represented that plaintiff was very fortunate to be able to get the stock because the offering of the stock was "definitely being closed" that weekend. In reliance plaintiff said that he purchased 600 shares. Plaintiff also testified that five days later, Kelley told him that there was still a limited amount of the stock available and that the company was then in the process of negotiations with a "big chain" to install its products. In reliance plaintiff purchased 900 additional shares.

[T]hese representations were not true. Later the price of the stock [fell drastically.]

[P]laintiff offered the testimony of two witnesses that at about the same time defendant Kelley made substantially the same representations to them. Defendants objected [that] knowledge by defendants that representations made by them were false [is not a requisite of this cause of action]. [D]efendants simply denied that they made the alleged representations and contended that all statements made to plaintiff were true. As a result, [they argue,] "scienter," or knowledge, was not an issue in the case, so as to make such evidence admissible.

[P]laintiff contended that such testimony was admissible: (1) As evidence that the representations were made by defendants with knowledge that they were false, for the reason that even if the "real issue" was whether the representations were made and whether they were false, the jury was "entitled to know" whether defendants knew that they were false; (2) As evidence that such statements were made as a part of a plan, design or scheme to promote the sale of the stock; and (3) As evidence that the alleged statements were representations of material facts, as alleged by plaintiff, but denied by defendants.

[T]he trial judge overruled defendants' objections, but twice cautioned the jury that the testimony was not to be considered as proof that any representations made by Kelley to plaintiff were untrue, but only upon the limited question, whether, if false representations were made to plaintiff, they were made by Kelley with knowledge of their falsity.

[E]vidence that a person performed a certain act at a particular time is not ordinarily admissible to prove that he performed a similar act at some other time. Thus, it is generally held that in an action for fraud evidence of misrepresentations made by defendant to other persons is not ordinarily admissible as evidence that misrepresentations were made by defendant to plaintiff.

It has been held by this court, however, that in an action for fraud, similar fraudulent representations to other persons may be admissible upon the issue of defendants' intent, motive or "scienter"; i.e., knowledge that the representations were false. This brings us to the question whether "scienter," or knowledge, is a proper issue in an action [of this kind] and, if so, whether it was an issue in this case.

[K]nowledge that a misrepresentation was or was not false may [normally] be an issue [in a case like the present case] and evidence of false statements by the defendants to other persons may be admissible on that issue. In this case, however, defendants not only did not plead lack of such knowledge as an affirmative defense, but before evidence of similar misrepresentations to the two other witnesses was offered in evidence, defendants made it clear upon the record that they made no contention that if any misrepresentations were made by defendant Kelley he did not know of their falsity, but that defendants' sole contention was that they made no false representations to plaintiff.

This, in our view, completely removed from the case the possible issue of "scienter" or knowledge of the falsity of the alleged misrepresentations and, as a result, also removed that ground as a basis for the admissibility of the testimony of these two witnesses.

Defendants acknowledge that evidence of other acts or representations may be admissible to show a continuing plan or scheme, as an exception to the general rule excluding such evidence. Defendants contend, however, that this exception "is applicable only to cases of fraud" in which "the pleadings allege a plan or scheme to defraud." Defendant also contends that, in any event, this exception "does not permit the introduction of evidence of similar representations for the purpose of showing that other representations were in fact made," but only to show intent, motive or knowledge, which was not in issue in this case.

Union Central Life Insurance Co. v. Kerron did not limit evidence of other fraudulent acts in fraud cases to the issue of motive, intent or knowledge, as distinguished from evidence offered to establish the performance of the fraudulent act. Also, that decision did not limit such evidence to cases in which a plan or design to defraud had been pleaded. [N]o such design or plan was pleaded in that case.

[T]he exception relating to evidence of other representations to show knowledge or intent is treated as one which is separate and distinct from the offer of such testimony as probative evidence that the representations in issue were in fact made. Thus, it is stated by McCormick:

> If the actual making of the misrepresentations charged in the suit is at issue, then to show the party's conduct in making the representations or committing the other acts of fraud as alleged, it is competent to prove other representations closely similar in purport or other fraudulent acts, when they may be found to be parts of a larger or continuing plan or design, of

which the acts or misrepresentations in suit may also be found to be an intended part or object. Courts often seem to overlook the availability of this theory of admissibility.

The rationale for such a rule is stated as follows in Wigmore:

> When the very doing of the act charged is still to be proved, one of the evidential facts receivable is the person's Design or Plan to do it. This in turn may be evidenced by conduct of sundry sorts as well as by direct assertions of the design. But where the conduct offered consists merely in the doing of other similar acts, it is obvious that something more is required than that (of) mere similarity. The added element, then, must be, not merely a similarity in the results, but such a concurrence of common features that the various acts are naturally to be explained as caused by a general plan of which they are the individual manifestations.

It was held in *Kelty v. Fisher*, a malpractice case, that evidence of another almost identical act by defendant on another patient with the same illness and in the same hospital room was relevant and admissible for the reason that such evidence had probative value on the question whether the act of malpractice involving plaintiff's decedent was done, as alleged.

[A]s held by the foregoing authorities, even in cases in which there is no issue of "scienter," but in which the issue is one of "conduct," as in this case, evidence of other similar conduct may be admissible on that issue if there is "such a concurrence of common features that the various acts are naturally explained as caused by a general plan of which they are the individual manifestations." Thus, it remains to consider whether the evidence of other representations, as offered in this case, satisfies this test.

In this case, aside from the testimony of representations that the prospectus was out of date and to be disregarded, plaintiff testified that defendant Kelley represented to him that the direct sale of the stock was "definitely being closed"; that there was only a limited amount of the stock still available and that plaintiff would be "fortunate" to be able to get some of it.

The representations by Kelley to the two witnesses offered by plaintiff, as testified by them, were strikingly similar. Thus, they both testified that at "about the same time in June of 1968" Kelley also represented to them that "the issues were almost sold out and he had a few left"; that "if we wanted some we should talk to him that night"; that "if there was a possibility that it wasn't sold out at that time that we could get in on it," and that "we were pretty lucky in getting in on it."

In our judgment, such representations, as made to these two witnesses, according to their testimony, when compared with those testified to by plaintiff, also on two separate occasions, demonstrates "such a concurrence of common features" so as to lead to the conclusion that "the various acts are naturally explained as caused by a general plan of which they are the individual manifestations," within the meaning of the test.

NOTES AND QUESTIONS

Which Case is Correct? The last two cases, *Johnson* and *Karsun*, appear to be opposite holdings to one another as to proof of the making of the representation. Which is correct? In *Johnson*, which did the evidence tend to prove more reliably, in your view: the act, or knowledge of falsity (if that were an issue)? Did the court get hung up on meaningless formalism? Both cases say that *scienter* could be proved by the evidence if it were in issue. But wouldn't a *lack* of *scienter* account for saying the same falsity to purchasers on several occasions? Would the "plan" theory of *Karsun* work if both sides conceded the innocence of the representation (assuming this were a suit for rescission, not requiring *scienter*)? Should it?

CLARK v. STEWART

Ohio Supreme Court

126 Ohio St. 263, 185 N.E. 71 (1933)

STEPHENSON, JUDGE.

[Stewart (senior) was sued in the trial court by Clark. The Court of Appeals, an intermediate appellate court, reversed a judgment for plaintiff, and plaintiff appeals here. Personal injuries were alleged to have been inflicted by the negligent driving of defendant's son, Walter, while acting within the scope of employment as agent for defendant. The complaint invoked two theories: respondeat superior, and the negligence of the father in entrusting his vehicle to a seventeen-year-old son known by the father to be an incompetent, inexperienced, and careless driver.]

[I]t was admitted by counsel for the defendant that at the time of the collision in question the son was the agent of the father [and acting within the scope of the agency]. This brought the case within the theory of respondeat superior. It will be noted that this admission falls short of admitting liability, but counsel seem to think that by this admission the charge that the father was negligent in intrusting his car to his son, who was an incompetent driver, was taken out of the case entirely. This court cannot subscribe to that contention.

It is claimed that error was infused into the case when counsel for plaintiff called the defendant for cross-examination under the statute and propounded the following questions:

Q. Before January 5, 1931, how many automobile accidents had Walter Stewart had? (Defendant objects.)

And thereupon court recessed for a few minutes, the court first admonishing the jury. And thereupon after the jury returned to the court room the objection was sustained. To all of which the plaintiff excepted.

Q. Had you ridden with Walter when he drove the car?

A. Yes, sir.

Q. You have ridden with him when he drove the car sixty miles an hour, haven't you?

A. No, sir.

Q. Ever ride with him when he ran into another car?

A. No, sir.

Q. You make the statement he never ran into any one, how do you know?

A. If he broke the machine or damaged the machine I would know it, wouldn't I?

Q. [Now you say you ought to know if Walter ever had the car broken up, let's see if you know. Didn't he run into somebody at Matson's Corner and have the car broken up?] (Defendant objects.)

Court: He may answer if he knows. (Defendant excepts.)

Q. (Stenographer reads question.)

A. Not as I know of.

Q. Not that you know of?

A. Not my car.

Q. Well, whose car was it?

A. I don't know.

Q. Sir?

A. He was driving the milk route for his brother and was coming out of the road and somebody ran into him, that is all.

Q. Was Walter driving your car and ran into another car, just outside of Monroe? (Defendant objects; overruled; defendant excepts.)

Q. Don't you know Walter had the reputation of driving fifty or sixty miles an hour? (Defendant objects.)

Court: He may answer yes or no, as to whether he knows. (Defendant excepts.)

A. He did not have that reputation.

Q. Do you have any personal knowledge of his running into other automobiles? (Defendant objects; overruled; defendant excepts.)

A. Well, I know he never ran into any other automobiles.

It is insisted that specific instances are incompetent as bearing upon the question of a reckless, negligent course of conduct. The authorities are without number that such questions are germane.

We will admit that if this issue [the incompetence of the driver] had not been in the case, and this seems to have been the view taken by the Court of Appeals, it would have constituted misconduct of the grossest character. But such issue was in the case by force of the pleadings, and it was not taken out by reason of the admission of agency.

[The Court of Appeals' order of reversal was affirmed on other grounds.]

NOTES AND QUESTIONS

(1) *Proving Negligent Entrustment.* What instruction should be given the jury in *Clark*? Will it be easy to follow? Can you analyze *Clark* under Fed. R. Evid. 404–405? After the stipulation or admission of agency referred to in the case, why would plaintiff want to keep the negligent entrustment count in the case, under which he would have to prove (1) that the father acted unreasonably, and (2) that the son drove negligently (otherwise the father's unreasonableness in turning over the car to a careless driver had nothing to do with what caused the accident, under well-known proximate cause principles); whereas under the respondeat superior count, all he has to prove is that the son drove negligently. Does plaintiff want to preserve the entrustment count so that he can introduce the evidence of the son's bad driving record? Why does he want to introduce *that*? So he can prove that the father acted unreasonably? But then what this means is plaintiff wants to have an additional item to prove so that he can prove it. Or are his reasons for wanting to preserve the count and introduce the evidence more nefarious?

(2) *Striking the Negligent Entrustment Count: Patterson v. East Texas Motor Freight Lines*, 349 S.W.2d 634 (Tex. Civ. App. 1961):

> Appellants plead several grounds of negligence against the driver of the truck, and in addition plead the truck company was guilty of negligence on the theory of "negligent entrustment." Appellants alleged the driver was an employee of the truck company and acting within the scope of his employment at the time of the collision. The appellees stipulated and agreed that this was true and that the doctrine of respondeat superior would apply. Appellees then moved the trial court to strike the allegation as to negligent entrustment which motion was granted and the appellants contend this was error. We are unable to agree with appellants. Evidence as to prior accidents, or prior acts of negligence on the part of the driver, would be admissible only to prove the driver was unsafe or incompetent, and not to prove he was negligent on the occasion in question. The theory of negligent entrustment in order to bind the truck company became immaterial as soon as the stipulation as to course of employment was made. There was no issue left to submit to the jury upon which this testimony as to negligent entrustment would be admissible.

Why does the court in *Patterson* strike the negligent entrustment count? What does the court hope to accomplish? Have the plaintiff's rights been hurt by this? Does he have any valid objection to the striking? In what way is he harmed by it? Has his job been made any harder? Refer to the questions in Note (1) immediately *supra* in answering these questions. Notice that the court in *Patterson* does what the court was requested to do by the defendant (but refused to do) in *Clark*. Notice that the stipulation was the same in both. Which approach (both of them found in various jurisdictions) is the best? As to the effect of stipulations, see *Old Chief, supra*.

(3) *Stipulations as Tactical Possibilities.* Does all of this (including *Old Chief, supra* § 3.01[C]) suggest there may be some tactical reason or advantage for some counsel in some cases, to offer to concede certain issues, where a rule indicates there are certain permitted and certain unpermitted purposes for evidence? What

considerations should counsel weigh in deciding whether to make such an offer?

SAN ANTONIO TRACTION COMPANY v. COX

Court of Civil Appeals of Texas
184 S.W. 722 (1916)

MOURSUND J.

George Cox sued the San Antonio Traction Company for personal injuries, which he claimed to have received in alighting from a street car on or about July 23, 1914. He alleged that while he was undertaking to get off of the car at the crossing of the San Antonio & Aransas Pass Railway on the west end car line, the car was carelessly and negligently started too suddenly and without notice or warning before plaintiff had sufficient time to alight, and in so starting the car it was jerked, with the result that plaintiff was thrown or fell from the car and received the injuries described.

Defendant denied the happening of the accident and the negligence alleged, and further alleged that Cox and some 10 or 11 members of his family have continuously "worked together, conspired, assisted, and abetted each other in propounding false and fraudulent claims against this defendant," and "that this suit and the claim propounded herein is a part and parcel of said co-operation, conspiracy, and abetting of the above-named parties for the purpose of obtaining money from this defendant." Defendant also alleged that if plaintiff was suffering from any injury or disability, "such injury or disability is the result, not of any accident alleged in plaintiff's petition, but of another and prior accident for which this defendant is not liable."

The trial resulted in a verdict and judgment in favor of plaintiff.

Appellant complains of the exclusion of certain testimony which, as shown by the bill of exceptions, would have been given by the witness, Fred J. Johnston, in answer to questions propounded, viz.:

> Mrs. Lula Brown Cox, the mother of plaintiff, has had two claims against the company, one very recently, and the other in March 18, 1914. Phillip Cox, plaintiff's brother, and Phoebe Cox Villareal, plaintiff's sister, each have had a claim against the company, respectively, on February 25, 1914, and March 4, 1914, and George Cox has had two claims against the company, one involved in this suit, and one on March 4, 1914, in all of which the claimants claimed that the accident involved occurred while they were getting off of the street car of the defendant and claiming injuries thereby. Also plaintiff's aunt, Minnie Brown Leak, has had two claims for herself, one on March 16, 1914, and one on March 29, 1915, in which she claims to have received injuries while getting off one of the company's cars, and Mrs. Leak propounded a claim for her daughter, Rosa, supposed to have occurred on January 30, 1915, while Rosa was getting off of one of the company's cars. Another aunt of the plaintiff, Mary Brown Callaghan, propounded a claim against the defendant for an accident which she claims to have occurred on March 23, 1914, while getting off of one of the street cars of the defendant. R.G. Brown, plaintiff's uncle, also has recently

> propounded a claim against the traction company for injuries supposed to have been received while getting off of one of the cars of the defendant, and in addition to this plaintiff's cousin, Lacy Brown, has had two claims against the company, one on January 29, 1914, and one on March 4, 1914, in one of which he claims to have received injuries while a passenger on one of defendant's street cars, and his (Lacy's) wife has also made a claim for injuries supposed to have been received on March 4, 1914, the same day as Lacy's second accident. Mrs. Lizzie Webb, Lacy Brown's mother-in-law, claimed to have had an accident on May 24, 1914, while she was getting off of one of the company's street cars.

Defendant also sought to introduce various releases signed by relatives of Cox upon payment being made them for injuries claimed to have been sustained, and separately sought to introduce a release signed by Lacy, a cousin of plaintiff, which was witnessed by plaintiff.

It is contended that all of this evidence should have been admitted as bearing upon the answer of defendant alleging that plaintiff and certain members of his family had conspired against defendant to procure unmerited damages by means of false and fraudulent claims. In this connection appellant quotes portions of the testimony of plaintiff which show that he has no definite recollection of any details concerning the operatives of the car or the car itself, and show a recklessness in testifying concerning his witness, Saunders, calculated to cast great doubt upon his entire testimony. It is also pointed out that every one of the motormen and conductors on that car line testified positively that no such accident occurred on that day with reference to his car.

The testimony excluded shows a remarkable condition of affairs. About 17 claims were propounded by Cox and his relatives, all of which, except 2, were for injuries alleged to have been sustained in alighting from cars. To get off of a street car is a simple thing, and it is inconceivable that all of these people could have been caused to fall by reason of negligence of the operatives of the cars. Surely the company had no desire to willfully inflict injuries upon the members of this family, and surely these people were not all suffering from infirmities such as to prevent them from getting off of a street car without assistance. In spite, however, of the warnings furnished by similar accidents to members of the family, they appear not to have learned caution, but continued taking the risk, a terrible one as to them, of getting off of street cars, with the result that every now and then one of them would be injured just like the others were. We think it is so highly improbable that all of these claims could be honest ones, that a jury would be justified in inferring that fraud had been practiced with regard to some of them. The testimony indicates a bad state of affairs, but we do not think, had it been admitted, it would, with the other testimony, have justified a charge on conspiracy. The evidence fails to connect plaintiff with the other claims, except in one instance in which he was with a cousin when he had his fall, and also witnessed the release executed by him to the company. We fail to find in the testimony given or excluded that evidence of concerted action such as is required to constitute a conspiracy. It is just as probable, if not more so, that each incident stood alone as that a conspiracy existed, and it is mere guesswork to say that any of the parties conspired together. If some of the claims were fraudulent, they may have been propounded upon the initiative of the complainant alone, without consulting with or being aided or abetted by any one, being induced thereto by the apparent ease with which claims could be collected, as shown by experiences of other members of the family.

The issue in this case was whether plaintiff was injured by reason of the negligence of the company as alleged by him, or whether, as is contended by defendant, no such incident as testified to by plaintiff occurred, or if it did, that it was willfully brought about by him, and not caused by negligence of the company. Proof of a conspiracy and of his connection therewith would undoubtedly tend strongly to corroborate the testimony of the employees of defendant that no such incident occurred, or might lead the jury to believe that he willfully permitted himself to be thrown from the steps. But as above pointed out the evidence admitted fails to show any conspiracy between any of the members of the family who propounded claims, and the evidence excluded, considered alone or with that admitted, would not justify a charge on conspiracy, for it merely shows transactions of a similar nature, not connected with each other and not constituting a necessary element in a plan to reach an ulterior object. We conclude the court did not err in regard to the matters complained of in the first four assignments of error, and they are overruled.

NOTES AND QUESTIONS

(1) *Relation to Rule 404(b).* Can *San Antonio Traction* be analyzed under Fed. R. Evid. 404(b)? Does the court seem to be having reference to Fed. R. Evid. 404(b) principles? Is this appropriate?

(2) *Common Sense.* If a lawsuit is not about what is most probable, what is it about?

(3) *Role of Pleadings.* Was there perhaps a tactical mistake in the defendant's pleadings (answer) or argument? Should the court have felt bound by this?

(4) *Previous Claims Admitted. Cf. Evans v. Greyhound Corp.*, 200 A.2d 194 (D.C. 1964):

> Cross-examination of appellant brought out the fact that she had a history of two previous claims for which she had received payments in settlement. [A]n instruction was properly given directing the jury to take into consideration that it is unusual for a person not engaged in hazardous activities to suffer negligent injuries repeatedly within a short period and at the hands of different persons. It was the function of the jury to decide from all the evidence and from its observation of appellant on the stand whether she was merely unfortunate or was 'claim-minded.' The appellant's answers respecting two prior injury claims were properly admitted.

Is *Greyhound* analyzable in terms of Fed. R. Evid. 404(b)? In which case (*San Antonio Traction* or *Greyhound*) is the evidence more reliable? Has the court (in either of the cases or both) been led astray by meaningless formalism? In which case is the ruling most likely to lead the jury into an incorrect result?

JOHN DEERE COMPANY v. MAY

Court of Appeals of Texas, Waco
773 S.W.2d 369 (1989)

[Plaintiff obtained judgment in a product liability action against Deere, whose bulldozer ran over and killed plaintiffs' decedent. No one had observed the fatal accident. Plaintiffs offered evidence of 34 other incidents in which Deere bulldozers allegedly had shifted into gear while in neutral with the engine running. The trial judge admitted a videotaped demonstration of a Deere bulldozer shifting into gear, allowed limited questioning about the 34 other incidents, and let in testimony from another suit about another similar incident. Deere argued on appeal that these events were not established as "substantially similar" because there was no demonstration that they involved the same model, the same adjustments, or the same degree of wear and tear as the bulldozer involved in the suit; thus, Deere argued that the general Rule 403 requirement of probative value not "substantially outweighed" by prejudice required exclusion. The Court of Appeals here rejects these arguments and affirms.]

What constitutes reasonably similar circumstances under the facts presented? [Deere's] argument, that the dozers had to be reasonably similar before there could be a reasonable similarity of circumstances, is rejected. Identical circumstances are not required. May's death and the other incidents occurred under reasonably similar circumstances if they involved the same type of occurrence, i.e., the circumstances would be similar if the dozers moved after being left in neutral with the engine running.

Determining that the extraneous occurrences were relevant does not automatically guarantee their admissibility. [Rule 403] requires the trial court to apply a "balancing test."

Lacking direct evidence, the plaintiffs were forced to rely on circumstantial evidence to prove that John Deere dozers had a propensity to self-shift from neutral into reverse and that this dangerous propensity had caused May's death. One cannot prove a propensity by proving a single occurrence. The extent and adequacy of the warning would be affected by the degree of danger to May: a greater propensity to self-shift [w]ould require a more imperative and urgent warning. Furthermore, [plaintiffs] could recover exemplary damages if they proved that John Deere knew of the greater danger but acted with conscious indifference.

Extraneous incidents [c]an be extremely harmful to the defendant. However, evidence cannot be excluded just because it may prejudice the opposing party before the fact finder. [S]uch danger must substantially outweigh its relevance before it can be excluded.

HAAKANSON v. ALASKA
Court of Appeals of Alaska
760 P.2d 1030 (1988)

SINGLETON, JUDGE.

[Haakanson was convicted of sexual abuse of a minor. The Alaska Court here reverses the conviction because the trial judge had admitted evidence that Haakanson fit a "Child Sexual Abuser Profile."]

Alaska State Trooper Rodney Guinn was the state's first witness. He testified that there are certain characteristics which are common to child sexual abusers. Some of the characteristics he mentioned were an unusual interest in children, using treats to attract children, allowing children to do things they may not be allowed to do at home, and paying extra attention to them. He testified that child sexual abusers may own particular items, including sexual aids, sexually explicit photographs, and photos or films of children that are not necessarily sexually explicit.

The court subsequently admitted photographs of the three victims, fully clothed, which were found in Haakanson's trailer. Also admitted were a sexually explicit magazine and photo, cut out of the magazine, with the names of M.D.C. and Arthur written above the partially-clad woman and nude man in the photo. The court further admitted bags of candy found in Haakanson's home as well as a game, "Searching for Gold." [There also was other evidence that defendant fit the profile.]

There is a strong argument that such profile evidence is inadmissible as character evidence under Alaska Evidence Rule 404(a), which reads in part: "Evidence of a person's character or a trait of his character is not admissible for the purpose of proving that he acted in conformity therewith on a particular occasion."

Several jurisdictions have addressed the related issue of a "battering parent" or "child batterer" profile, and have held that evidence of such profiles is inadmissible character evidence.

At least one jurisdiction has allowed expert testimony explaining pedophilia to the jury. *State v. Swallow*, 350 N.W.2d 606, 609 (S.D. 1984). The expert in *Swallow*, however, testified that certain adults are sexually gratified by fondling children or looking at photographs of nude children. This was the same conduct that Swallow was charged with in the indictment. Thus, the prosecution could show that Swallow fit the description of a pedophile by proving that he committed the offenses with which he was charged. The pedophile testimony [w]as substantially different than Trooper Guinn's testimony, which listed otherwise innocent characteristics, such as giving candy to children, as evidence of guilt.

We have recently addressed the related issue of the admissibility of expert testimony regarding behavioral characteristics common to child victims of sexual abuse. [These cases,] read together, permit expert testimony that responds to a defense claim that a complaining witness' conduct is inconsistent with being sexually abused by showing that similar conduct is exhibited by those who are sexually abused. These decisions do not permit testimony offered to prove that the complaining witness is sexually abused by showing that the complaining witness exhibits behavior similar to that exhibited by sexually abused children.

[The Alaska court also reasoned that the profile evidence did not meet the State's standards for expert testimony. This issue is raised in Chapter 6 of this book.]

NOTES AND QUESTIONS

(1) *Variations in Analysis of Defendant-Profile Evidence.* Note the Alaska court's distinguishing of the South Dakota Supreme Court's decision to admit a pedophilia-related profile: the Alaska court says the defendant in the South Dakota case was linked to the profile by evidence about the offense at trial, whereas Haakanson was linked to it by innocent acts "such as giving candy to children." But if the basis for decision is Fed. R. Evid. 404(a), excluding "character" evidence, is this distinction unpersuasive? Instead, the difference in outcomes may reflect a difference in the way the two courts interpret Fed. R. Evid. 404(a) — some courts feeling that psychological proclivities established by some recognized discipline are different from character. There are variations in the way that different courts evaluate syndrome and profile evidence, and the issue still is evolving.

(2) *Gang and Drug Profiles.* Courts vary as to the admissibility of expert testimony profiling the modus operandi of various types of criminals, such as drug dealers. *See People v. Hernandez*, 55 Cal. App. 4th 225 (Cal. Ct. App. 1997) (discussing inadmissibility of drug courier and auto theft ring profiles); *Headley v. Tilghman*, 53 F.3d 472 (2d Cir. 1995). Can gang membership and behavior be introduced? Under what circumstance? *See State v. Stone*, 802 P.2d 668 (Or. Ct. App. 1990) (reversing conviction for unauthorized use of vehicle because evidence was introduced as to general pattern of gang activity concerning use of stolen or borrowed vehicles for drive-by shootings in order to establish that presence of shotguns in car indicated gang activities were planned, and therefore defendant should have known vehicle was stolen.)

(3) *Victim Behavioral Syndromes — Do they Present a Different Issue from Defendant Profiles?: United States v. Dorian*, 803 F.2d 1439 (8th Cir. 1986). Consider whether victim-syndrome evidence is different from defendant-related syndromes. For example, rape trauma syndrome sometimes is offered to corroborate evidence of sexual assault by demonstrating that behavior that intuitively might appear inconsistent or ambiguous actually is a predictable effect of such an assault. Or, as another example, child abuse accommodation syndrome may explain why a child alleged to have been sexually abused by a relative may cooperate with the offender, keep the secret, and initially deny the abuse. Thus, in *Dorian, supra*, evidence of this kind was used to explain the child witness's behavior and to support reception of her hearsay statements under the residual exception in Fed. R. Evid. 803(24) (now Fed. R. Evid. 807).

Arguably, victim syndrome evidence is different from a profile of a defendant because it is not offered as circumstantial evidence of the victim's probable behavior, that is, it is not directed toward demonstrating that the victim "acted in conformity with" the syndrome. Instead, the alleged victim's behavior is known, and it is proved by other evidence. The syndrome evidence then is used to explain why the behavior occurred and to relate it to more direct evidence of the offense. Arguably, the evidence thus does not violate Fed. R. Evid. 404's exclusion of character evidence offered to prove conduct. (Is this distinction persuasive?)

(4) *Injury Syndromes, such as Battered Child Syndrome.* In *Estelle v. McGuire*, 502 U.S. 62 (1991) (cited in Note (6) under § 3.01[B][1], *above*), the state offered evidence of numerous injuries to the child victim, together with two physicians' diagnoses of battered child syndrome. The state courts upheld the admissibility of this evidence under applicable rules, and the United States Supreme Court upheld it against a due process attack. How should this kind of syndrome evidence be evaluated under Fed. R. Evid. 404? (A suggestion: it seems unlikely that a syndrome explaining broken bones, lacerations and other physical injuries is properly to be excluded by calling it "character" evidence, and in any event, battered child evidence usually is not offered to show any "action in conformity" with it by the child.)

PROBLEM 3G: MUNCHAUSEN SYNDROME BY PROXY EVIDENCE AS PROOF OF IDENTITY AND INTENT TO INJURE: WOULD IT VIOLATE RULE 404(a) OR (b)?

"Munchausen-by-proxy" is an unusual syndrome whereby one person (usually a parent) covertly injures another (usually a child) to obtain psychological rewards such as attention, sympathy, or admiration. A profile of such offenders would show that most are mothers of children too young to communicate, who are more attentive than average, and who are unusually interested in and knowledgeable about health care and medicine. Direct evidence is difficult to obtain, and often the most persuasive indicator is frequent ambiguous injuries, too repetitive to be coincidental, occurring while the mother is present. Can the prosecution, consistent with Fed. R. Evid. 404, ask a properly qualified expert witness to explain Munchausen-by-proxy in such a case, as a means of demonstrating identity, rebutting accident, and showing motive? (If not, won't it be impossible to prove the true nature of such a crime?) *See People v. Phillips*, 122 Cal. App. 3d 69 (Cal. Ct. App. 1981) (affirming admission). Do you agree?

§ 3.06 SUBSEQUENT REMEDIAL MEASURES[9]

Read Federal Rule of Evidence 407, "Subsequent Remedial Measures."

The evidence rules treated in this section and the next section, relating to subsequent remedial measures and settlements, rest not only on considerations of relevancy and its counterweights, but also on social policy considerations akin to privileges, that is, to encourage certain conduct regardless of whether the excluded evidence is "good" evidence or not.

---

[9] Study Guide Reference: Evidence in a Nutshell, Chapter 3:III at "Subsequent Remedial Measures: F.R.E. 407."

ADAMS v. CHEVRON USA, INC.

United States Court of Appeals, Fifth Circuit
2010 U.S. App. LEXIS 14088 (June 23, 2010) (unpublished decision)

JERRY E. SMITH, CIRCUIT JUDGE:

Louis and Michelle Adams appeal a judgment following a jury trial awarding them damages for an injury Louis sustained. They challenge the allocation of fault, the award of general damages, [and] the exclusion of evidence [by the trial court, under Rule 407]. . . . We affirm in all respects.

Louis, an employee of Fluor/Plant Performance Services ("P2S"), was injured while working on an offshore platform owned by Chevron. He was required to run tubing though an overhead space in the standby generator room, but he was unable to use a ladder to access that space, because a two-tier battery stand was in the way. He decided to climb onto the battery stand to reach the overhead space, but as he climbed down, the bottom tier gave way, and he twisted his knee, requiring several surgeries.

Louis and his wife, Michelle, sued Chevron under the Outer Continental Shelf Lands Act, which directs that Louisiana tort law applies. [The Act says that although an offshore platform is within the federal jurisdiction, the substantive law of the upland state applies.] The jury apportioned fault [according to the Louisiana law of comparative negligence] as follows: Chevron 10%; Louis 60%; and P2S 30%. It awarded Louis $ 591,000 in damages, including $ 85,000 in general damages for pain and suffering, and awarded Michelle $ 20,000 for loss of consortium, but reduced those awards by 90% in accordance with Louisiana's comparative fault scheme. [P2S was protected by workers compensation laws because it was plaintiff's employer, and it therefore was not liable for its comparative share of the damages. The Adamses can recover, here, only for the relatively small amount of Chevron's comparative fault.]

The Adamses filed a post-verdict motion for judgment as a matter of law and alternative motion for new trial. . . . [The motion for new trial was based upon a decision of the trial court to exclude certain work orders showing that Chevron had redesigned the battery stand after the accident to convert it to a step, by which Plaintiff Adams could have accessed the generator room in greater safety. The Adamses argue that this evidence would have shown a lesser percentage of fault on Louis's part and a higher percentage on Chevron's part.] The district court denied both motions and entered judgment in accordance with the verdict. . . .

First, trial testimony supported a finding that Louis was 60% at fault. . . . Louis's use of the battery stand as a step ladder violated several of P2S's safety rules. [Louis also failed to inspect the battery stand, which was "rotten"] . . .

The evidence also supported a finding that P2S was 30% at fault for Louis's injury. . . .

Finally, contrary to the Adamses' contention, the evidence did not overwhelmingly show that Chevron's fault was the primary cause of the accident. Although the jury found that Chevron was negligent in maintaining the platform, it reasonably concluded that Louis's and P2S's carelessness, including various safety-rule violations, accounted for the lion's share of fault. . . .

[With respect to the issue about Rule 407, t]he Adamses argue that copies of Chevron's work order slips for converting the battery stand into a step should not have been excluded as evidence of subsequent remedial measures. [W]e find no error.

The admissibility of evidence of subsequent remedial measures is governed by Federal Rule of Evidence 407. [Rule quoted.]

The Advisory Committee Notes explain that the primary justification for rule 407 is the "social policy of encouraging people to take, or at least not discouraging them from taking, steps in furtherance of added safety." Fed.R.Evid. 407, Advisory Committee Note (1972). The rule also seeks to ensure that negligence is properly determined "according to what the defendant knew or should have known *prior to the accident*, not what the defendant knew as a result of the accident."

The Adamses claim that the purpose of seeking to introduce the slips was not to prove negligence, but to establish that (1) Chevron owned the battery stand; (2) Chevron had control over the maintenance of the stand; and (3) it was feasible to replace the wooden inserts with a more sturdy type of material. Although those claims track rule 407's list of permissible purposes for introducing evidence of subsequent measures, none of those issues was "controverted" at trial. Chevron never maintained that it did not own the battery stand, that it did not have control over the maintenance of the stand, or that it was not feasible to replace the wooden inserts in the stand with a more durable material. Therefore, the district court properly excluded the work order slips. . . . [Affirmed.]

NOTES AND QUESTIONS

(1) *Should Rule 407 Even Apply Here? Arguably, Showing Percentages of Negligence Is Not "Prov[ing] Negligence"!* The Adamses did not need to use the remedial measure evidence to "prove negligence" on Chevron's part, because the jury found Chevron negligent without that evidence. Actually, the Adamses wanted to use the remedial measure evidence to prove the *percentages* of fault, including reducing their own share of the causative fault — and this is a different issue. But consider whether the purposes of the rule (avoiding discouragement to improve safety and avoiding hindsight) would be affected by introduction of this evidence. Should Rule 407 apply here?

(2) *Remedial Measures Often Are Very Persuasive Evidence.* The evidence of the remedial measure, here, might well have influenced the jury to attribute more fault to Chevron. Remedial measure evidence can be powerful. Does this aspect of the issue help to support exclusion under Rule 407? Or does it mean that the jury ought to hear evidence of this kind, since it is important evidence?

(3) *Instructions.* Can erroneous injection into a trial of a subsequent remedial measure be cured by an instruction? What should be considered in determining whether an instruction will cure it? When a remedial measure is admissible for one purpose but not another, is an instruction sufficient to guard against the impermis-

sible use? What should be considered in determining whether an instruction will be a sufficient safeguard?

(4) *Ethical Considerations.* Is it ethical for an attorney to rely on an admissible purpose to get in evidence of a subsequent remedial measure when his real purpose is an impermissible purpose? Does it depend on particular circumstances? What circumstances?

(5) *Product Liability Actions.* Fed. R. Evid. 407 has been amended to clarify that subsequent remedial measures also are barred when offered to prove "a defect in a product, a defect in a product's design, or a need for a warning or instruction." While this resolves the issue definitively in federal courts, the states still are split about whether to apply their own versions of Fed. R. Evid. 407 to strict product liability actions. One influential case holding remedial measures are admissible in such cases is *Ault v. International Harvester Co.*, 528 P.2d 1148 (Cal. 1975):

> [W]e are not persuaded that the rationale which impelled the Legislature to adopt the section for cases involving negligence is applicable to strict liability.
>
> When the context is transformed from a typical negligence setting to the modern products liability field, the "public policy" assumptions justifying this evidentiary rule are no longer valid. The contemporary corporate mass producer of goods, the normal products liability defendant, manufactures tens of thousands of units of goods; it is manifestly unrealistic to suggest that such a producer will forgo making improvements in its product, and risk innumerable additional lawsuits and the attendant adverse effect upon its public image, simply because evidence of adoption of such improvement may be admitted in an action found on strict liability for recovery on an injury that preceded the improvement.

(6) *When is an Act Subsequent?* On whether a corrective measure is truly subsequent, see *Ramos v. Liberty Mutual Ins. Co.*, 615 F.2d 334 (5th Cir. 1980), *cert. denied*, 449 U.S. 1112 (1981). In *Ramos*, a safer redesigned product was put into manufacture before the allegedly unsafe product failed (although possibly after another similar product of the manufacturer failed — the court expressly refuses to consider this, though, because it was not argued). The court states Fed. R. Evid. 407, as then written, would be inapplicable. (What would Fed. R. Evid. 407's policy dictate? Was there another means for the court to effectuate it?) As to Fed. R. Evid. 401 and Fed. R. Evid. 403, the court states the evidence would be relevant to the cause of the accident, knowledge by defendant of a problem, and feasibility of alternatives. *Ramos* illustrates that remedial measures seldom come up in isolation from other evidentiary issues. The other issue (frequent in product liability cases) was failure of other similar (perhaps not identical) products in similar (perhaps not identical) circumstances. In the decision there also is an example of the special interrogatory form of verdict.

Fed. R. Evid. 407 was amended to relate the timing to "after an injury or harm allegedly caused by an event." This would seem to permit evidence of a subsequent remedial measure that occurred after a different accident, but before the accident at issue in the current litigation. The intent was the opposite. Which way makes the most sense? Does the current language in the Rule (as restyled without intended change of meaning) clarify things?

§ 3.07 SETTLEMENT MATTERS (COMPROMISE, OFFERS TO COMPROMISE, WITHDRAWN PLEAS, AND RELATED MATTERS)

[A] Civil Cases[10]

Read Federal Rules of Evidence 408, "Compromise Offers and Negotiations," and 409, "Offers to Pay Medical and Similar Expenses."

RAMADA DEVELOPMENT CO. v. RAUCH

United States Court of Appeals, Fifth Circuit
644 F.2d 1097 (1981)

TUTTLE, CIRCUIT JUDGE.

On December 13, 1972, Martin Rauch signed a contract in which the Ramada Development Company ["Ramada"] agreed to design, furnish, and construct [for him] a 160-unit Ramada Inn Motor Hotel and Restaurant in Venice, FL. [Rauch refused to make payments or accept the hotel, because of alleged defects in it. Ramada sued him, and won. Rauch appeals.]

Rauch's final assertion of error in the jury proceeding concerns the district court's exclusion of a document referred to as the Goldsmith Report. Goldsmith was an architect employed by Ramada in 1974 to study the defects that Rauch had alleged at that time. Rauch claims that he sought to introduce this report as "a part of his case in chief," because it confirmed the majority of the alleged defects. The district court heard testimony regarding the origins of the report and concluded that it was inadmissible under Federal Rule of Evidence 408 because the report was a tool used in an unsuccessful settlement attempt. Rauch contends that this ruling was in error because Rule 408 does not exclude all evidence presented in settlement attempts and there was the lack of any pre-trial understanding that the report could not be used in evidence.

This rule is designed to encourage settlements by fostering free and full discussion of the issues. The previous common law rule held that admissions of fact [or opinion that would otherwise comply with rules of evidence] made in negotiations were admissible "unless hypothetical, stated to be 'without prejudice,' or so connected with the offer as to be inseparable from it." Advisory Committee Notes, 28 USCA Federal Rules of Evidence, Rule 408. After the House Committee rejected a proposed deviation from the common law rule, the Senate Committee amended the [House's] proposed rule, because:

The real impact of this [House] amendment however, is to deprive the rule of

---

[10] Study Guide Reference: Evidence in a Nutshell, Chapter 3:III at "Compromises, Settlement Negotiations, and Medical Payments: F.R.E. 408–409."

much of its salutary effect. The exception for factual [and opinion] admissions was believed by the Advisory Committee to hamper free communication between parties and thus to constitute an unjustifiable restraint upon efforts to negotiate settlements — the encouragement of which is the purpose of the rule. Further, by protecting hypothetically phrased statements, it constituted a preference for the sophisticated, and a trap for the unwary. S Rep No. 1277, 93d Cong, 2d Sess, reprinted in [1974] US Code Cong & Ad News 7051, 7057.

The Goldsmith Report thus appears to fit squarely within the exclusionary scope of Rule 408. The only indication given by the parties of the report's origins, is the testimony of Leonard Gilbert whose testimony can only be construed as supporting the position that Goldsmith was commissioned by Ramada to prepare a report that would function as a basis of settlement negotiations regarding the alleged defects in the motel. The report was to identify arguable defects that could then be discussed in monetary terms in the negotiations. The Goldsmith Report, as described by Mr. Gilbert, thus represents a collection of statements made in the course of an effort to compromise, and the district court properly held it inadmissible under the main provision of Rule 408.

[B] Criminal Cases: Guilty Pleas and Plea Negotiations[11]

Read Federal Rule of Evidence 410, "Pleas, Plea Discussions, and Related Statements."

UNITED STATES v. MEZZANATTO

United States Supreme Court
513 U.S. 196 (1995)

Justice Thomas.

[Mezzanatto was arrested after proposing to deliver methamphetamine to an undercover officer. He and his attorney asked to meet with the prosecutor to discuss the possibility of cooperating with the Government. At the beginning of the meeting, the prosecutor informed Mezzanatto that he had no obligation to talk, but if he wanted to cooperate he would have to be completely truthful. Further, as a condition to proceeding with discussions, the prosecutor stated that Mezzanatto would have to agree that any statements he made could be used to impeach any contradictory testimony he might give at trial. Mezzanatto conferred with his attorney and then agreed to proceed on these terms. He admitted the present offense, including knowledge of the methamphetamine. However, he made several statements that the prosecutor believed were untruthful — for example, he denied visiting the methamphetamine laboratory for at least a week before the arrest, when surveillance evidence showed his car on the property the day before — and the Government terminated the discussions for this reason.]

[At trial, Mezzanatto maintained that he did not know the delivery package

[11] Study Guide Reference: Evidence in a Nutshell, Chapter 3:III "Withdrawn Guilty Pleas and Plea Negotiations: F.R.E. 410."

contained methamphetamine, and he testified that he believed the laboratory made plastic explosives for the CIA. The trial judge permitted the Government, over defense objection, to impeach Mezzanatto with his prior inconsistent statements during the plea negotiations. The Ninth Circuit reversed, concluding that Mezzanatto could not lawfully waive the rules, including Fed. R. Evid. 410, that excluded his plea-negotiation statements. The Supreme Court reversed the reversal and upheld the waiver.]

The Ninth Circuit's analysis is directly contrary to the approach we have taken in the context of a broad array of constitutional and statutory provisions. Rather than deeming waiver presumptively unavailable absent some sort of express enabling clause, we instead have adhered to the opposite presumption. A criminal defendant may knowingly and voluntarily waive many of the must fundamental protections afforded by the Constitution.

Indeed, evidentiary stipulations are a valuable and integral part of everyday trial practice.

Respondent suggests that the plea-statement Rules establish a "guarantee [to] fair procedure" that cannot be waived. [T]here may be some evidentiary provisions that are so fundamental to the reliability of the fact-finding process that they may never be waived without irreparably "discredit[ing] the federal courts." But enforcement of agreements like respondent's plainly will not have that effect. The admission of plea statements for impeachment purposes enhances the truth-seeking function.

[R]ule[] 410 [and the related Rule of Criminal Procedure] "create, in effect, a privilege of the defendant." [They] leave open the possibility that a defendant may offer such statements into evidence for his own tactical advantage. Thus, the plea-statement rules expressly contemplate a degree of party control that is consonant with the background presumption of waivability.

[T]here is no basis for concluding that waiver will interfere with the Rules' goal of encouraging plea bargaining. [A]lthough the availability of waiver may discourage some defendants from negotiating, it is also true that prosecutors may be unwilling to proceed without it.

[I]f prosecutors decide that certain crucial information will be gained only by preserving the inadmissibility of plea statements, they will agree to leave intact the exclusionary provisions of the plea-statement Rules.

Finally, respondent contends that waiver agreements should be forbidden because they invite prosecutorial overreaching and abuse.

[T]his possibility "does not justify invalidating all such agreements." Instead, the appropriate response to respondent's predictions of abuse is to permit case-by-case inquiries into whether waiver agreements are the product of fraud or coercion. We hold that absent some affirmative indication that the agreement was entered into unknowingly or involuntarily, an agreement to waive the exclusionary provisions of the plea-statement Rules is valid and enforceable.

[Justice Ginsburg, joined by Justices O'Connor and Breyer, concurred but argued that waivers for use in the Government's case-in-chief would present a different question. Justice Souter, joined by Justice Stevens, dissented, arguing that the legislative history showed that Congress meant to encourage pleas and therefore to protect "unrestrained candor." The Rules "are thus meant to create something more than a personal right shielding an individual from his imprudence. Rather, [they] are meant to serve the federal judicial system by creating the conditions understood by Congress to be effective in promoting reasonable plea agreements."]

NOTES AND QUESTIONS

(1) *Broader Waiver.* A few Justices in *Mezzanatto* indicated that a waiver allowing use of Rule 410 evidence in the prosecutor's "case-in-chief" would present a different question. This view of these Justices presumably would uphold a waiver licensing any use *after* the prosecutor's case-in-chief: that is, not only *impeachment of defendant* (where the defendant himself testifies in the defense case to facts contrary to those he asserted in the Rule 410 evidence) as in *Mezzanatto* itself, but also *refutation of other defense evidence* the defendant puts on in his own case that is contrary to the facts he asserted in the Rule 410 material, even if the defendant himself does not testify. For example, *United States v. Velez*, 354 F.3d 190 (2d Cir. 2004), in the course of rejecting an ineffective-assistance-of-counsel claim concerning a lawyer who let his defendant/client sign such a waiver, said that an express waiver is valid even though it broadly waived defendant's right to exclude Rule 410 material in all circumstances in which the defense presents contradictory testimony, evidence, or arguments — whether or not defendant himself testifies.

United States v. Burch, 156 F.3d 1315 (D.C. Cir. 1998), interpreting the logic of the majority in *Mezzanatto*, indicates a broader waiver rule: that Rule 410 can be expressly waived for purposes even beyond impeachment and that a broad waiver can expressly license the evidence to be used even in the prosecutor's case-in-chief.

(2) *A Contrary Holding.* But see *United States v. Rebbe*, 314 F.3d 402 (9th Cir. 2002), which affirmed the use of plea negotiations in the particular case, by expressly relying on the fact that the negotiations were not introduced in the prosecutor's case-in-chief, which the court indicated would have raised questions both under the express terms of the waiver and under the views expressed by some of the Justices in Mezzanatto.

(3) *Policy.* From the standpoint of society, what are the pros and cons of allowing Rule 410 waivers? What are the consequences to defendant from engaging in them? What are the consequences for the prosecution? Will waivers always be demanded? And given?

§ 3.08 EVIDENCE INDICATING OR SUGGESTING INSURANCE[12]

Read Federal Rule of Evidence 411, "Liability Insurance."

---

[12] Study Guide Reference: Evidence in a Nutshell, Chapter 3:III, at "Liability Insurance: F.R.E. 411."

CHARTER v. CHLEBORAD

United States Court of Appeals, Eighth Circuit
551 F.2d 246, *cert. denied*, 434 U.S. 856 (1977)

PER CURIAM.

This is a diversity action to recover damages for alleged medical malpractice. In June of 1973, plaintiff was struck by a truck while working as a highway flagman. The accident caused extensive injuries to both of plaintiff's legs. Plaintiff was hospitalized and placed under the care of a general practitioner and defendant, a surgeon. Surgery was performed on both legs. As a result of severe complications plaintiff was transferred to another hospital where both legs were amputated above the knee.

The trial of the matter resulted in a jury verdict for defendant and the district court denied plaintiff's motion for a new trial. Plaintiff presents two issues on appeal. [P]laintiff argues that the district court erred in limiting the cross-examination of a rebuttal witness for the defense.

Plaintiff offered the testimony of Dr. Joseph Lichtor, M.D., a Kansas City, Missouri orthopedic surgeon. Dr. Lichtor testified as to his opinion of the requisite standard of care defendant should have used when treating plaintiff. He compared the treatment given and concluded that defendant had been negligent. Finally, Dr. Lichtor testified that the cause of the complications and subsequent amputations was defendant's negligence.

As a part of his rebuttal case, defendant offered the testimony of John J. Alder, an attorney from the Kansas City area. Mr. Alder testified that Dr. Lichtor's reputation for truth and veracity in the Kansas City area was bad. On cross-examination Mr. Alder testified that he did some defense work in medical malpractice cases. He also stated that some of his clients in those cases were insurance companies.

Plaintiff's counsel then asked him to name some of those companies and defendant objected to the relevancy of the matter. After a conference at the Bench the district court refused to allow further questioning on the subject of insurance. As plaintiff stated in his motion for a new trial, Mr. Alder was employed by the same liability carrier who represents defendant in this action.

It is well established that the existence of a liability insurance policy is not admissible to show one's negligence or other wrongful conduct. Fed. R. Evid. 411 (1975). This rule has its basis in the belief that such evidence is of questionable probative value or relevance and is often prejudicial. Advisory Committee's Note, Fed. R. Evid. 411 (1975). Evidence of the existence of insurance may be offered for other purposes, however. Rule 411 of the Federal Rules of Evidence provides several examples: [quoted].

In this case the fact that defendant's insurer employed Mr. Alder was clearly admissible to show possible bias of that witness. Defendant does not dispute this obvious import of Rule 411 but urges that for several reasons the district court's exclusion of the evidence was not reversible error.

First defendant argues that plaintiff was required to make a formal offer of proof. Rule 103(a)(2) of the Federal Rules of Evidence provides that error may not be predicated upon a ruling excluding evidence unless:

> . . . the substance of the evidence was made known to the court by offer or was apparent from the context within which questions were asked.

However, it is clear from the transcript, particularly the conversation between counsel out of the hearing of the jury, that the court was aware of the general nature of the evidence to be offered.

Based upon Rule 403 of the Federal Rules of Evidence defendant also argues that the trial court acted within its discretion in excluding evidence of insurance. This argument is without merit. In our opinion the probative value of the evidence far outweighs any danger of unfair prejudice. Also, there is no indication in the record or briefs of the parties that any particular prejudice was threatened in this case. Rule 403 was not designed to allow the blanket exclusion of evidence of insurance absent some indicia of prejudice. Such a result would defeat the obvious purpose of Rule 411.

Defendant's final argument against reversal is that any error was harmless and did not affect a substantial right of the plaintiff. To pass on this argument we must view the total circumstances of the case. Plaintiff's claim rested for the most part on the credibility of his expert witness. When defendant undertook to impeach that witness plaintiff was entitled to attempt to show possible bias of Mr. Alder as surrebuttal. Considering the importance of expert testimony in this case we cannot conclude that the trial court's exclusionary ruling was mere harmless error.

Accordingly, the judgment of the district court is reversed and the action is remanded with directions to grant the plaintiff a new trial.

NOTES AND QUESTIONS

(1) *Tactical Considerations.* Should defense counsel have foreseen what would happen if she used Mr. Alder as a witness? Did putting Mr. Alder on the stand prove to be a tactical mistake? Was the prospect of upside gain worth the downside risk?

(2) *Difficult Determinations and Motions in Limine.* Often the party wishing to exclude evidence of insurance will bring an *in limine* motion to avoid any question or inadvertent reference to insurance at trial. But, as noted in *Weiss v. La Suisse Societe D'Assurances Sur La Vie*, 293 F. Supp. 2d 397 (S.D.N.Y. 2003), Rule 411 is not a bar to the introduction of evidence regarding liability insurance in all cases, and it may not be clear at the time of the *in limine* motion whether the evidence is offered for the prohibited purpose, or whether one of the "exceptions" to the rule may apply, and whether Rule 403 may nonetheless bar the evidence. The problem is exacerbated by the "open-ended" nature of the rule: What may be recognized as permitted "other purposes" other than those specifically listed in the rule?

In *Weiss*, an action was brought by thirty members of New York's Chassidic communities claiming discrimination by a Swiss company for strictly interpreting a contract and denying pay-outs under it to them. The company claimed it was not doing this because of discriminatory motives, but rather was concerned it would suffer major financial losses if it made the payments. The plaintiffs wished to show the company was insured (called "reinsurance" in the opinion) against such losses. On a motion *in limine* by the company to exclude the evidence under Rule 411 in advance of trial, the trial judge noted that rebutting "poor mouthing" or the like may be an acceptable purpose for insurance evidence under Rule 411. The judge then continued as follows:

> [T]he success of Plaintiffs' claims will turn on the reasonableness of Defendant's claim that its actions were motivated by financial concerns rather than discriminatory considerations. Evidence that Defendant had insurance to cover the losses may well be directly relevant to whether or not Defendant's proffered defense to claims that they discriminated against Jewish policy holders was a pretext or not. I will rule on this motion at the close of Defendant's case. If I do allow [this] evidence of reinsurance, I will give the jury an appropriate limiting instruction.

What sorts of things does the judge need to know to rule? Can it ever be an abuse of discretion for the judge to refuse to rule prior to trial?

PROBLEM SET 3H: EXPLORING PERMISSIBLE PURPOSES, INSTRUCTIONS, AND REMEDIES.

(1) *Distinguishing the Cases.* Concerning (i) weight, and (ii) admissibility, can you distinguish among the following cases (each in which plaintiff's counsel attempts to offer evidence directly or indirectly suggesting the defendant is insured against the kind of liability being pressed in the case) (a) under the Federal Rules, and (b) under a common-law system? (Assume that the common-law system does a naked balance of probativity versus prejudice. In each case also consider the possibility of partial admissibility or of redaction):

> I. Plaintiff's counsel in an automobile negligence personal injury action wishes to ask defendant car-owner-driver if he has automobile liability insurance. His only reason for so asking is that people who have such insurance may be expected to relax their care when driving or can afford to pay a judgment or both.
>
> II. Auto negligence personal injury case. Defendant was driving on the wrong side of the road. When warned by his passenger immediately prior to the collision (caused by driving on the wrong side), defendant said:
>
> **A.** "I have insurance, so I don't care."
>
> Or
>
> **B.** "Don't worry: I have insurance."
>
> Or
>
> **C.** "Why should I worry: I have insurance."
>
> Plaintiff wishes to offer evidence that defendant said this. (Distinguish among the lettered cases and from I. Also consider admissibility of part of the statements.)

III. Same case as II above, except the defendant's statement is made sometime after the collision, and takes the following form:

A. "I wasn't careful; I had insurance."

Or

B. "Don't worry: My insurance company will take care of it." (Does it matter whether defendant may be presumed to know insurance pays only if he is at fault, as where he is a business man sued for a business wrong and has business insurance?)

Or

C. "Why should I worry: I have insurance." (Distinguish among the lettered cases, and distinguish each from each of the previous numbered and lettered pieces of evidence. Consider also admissibility of discrete parts of the statements.) (See, regarding III, *Takoma Park Bank v. Abbott*, 179 Md. 249, 19 A.2d 169 (1941), *cert. denied*, 314 U.S. 672 (1941).)

IV. Auto negligence personal injury case. Plaintiff sues the young driver and his parents. Plaintiff wishes to offer evidence that the mother said, at some time prior to the collision, "My boy is careless: We have taken out insurance on him." (Consider this aside from the hearsay and character evidence problem, confining yourself to the insurance problem. Consider the possibility of admissibility of part.)

(2) *Opening the Door.* Automobile negligence personal injury case. Defendant has somehow suggested (improperly) to the jury that he may not be covered by insurance for this occurrence. Can plaintiff now attempt to show that defendant probably is covered? Instead of objecting? In addition to objecting?

Are the facts of this case distinguishable from Problem (1) I, *above*, with respect to admissibility? How (in terms of policy and rule language in the Federal Rules of Evidence and common law)? (By "policy" we mean factors mentioned in Fed. R. Evid. 403 or the common-law analogue.)

(3) *Adverse Statement in Insurance Report.* Automobile negligence personal injury case. Plaintiff wishes to show that defendant has stated a fact adverse to defendant's case in a report defendant has made in writing to defendant's automobile liability insurer. (Put aside any privilege problems.) Does this stand a better chance of admissibility than the evidence in Problem (1) I, *above*? Why (in terms of policy and rule language)? What would be the advantages and disadvantages of admitting only the fact that defendant made a statement to such-and-such effect (the damaging fact) but suppressing the fact that the statement was in a report to the insurance company?

(4) *Insurance on the Issue of Ownership of Car.* Automobile negligence personal injury case. Defendant, who was not the driver, but may be the owner of the vehicle driven negligently, is sued under a commonly found statute making the owner of a car liable or presumptively liable, under certain conditions. Ownership for these purposes is not determined by registered title ownership alone, but by counting up incidents and indicia that usually go along with ownership, possession, and control.

The question of ownership, possession, and control is hotly contested and very close in this case because the driver was the defendant's daughter, who was attending law school in defendant's town and drove and cared for the car a substantial amount of the time. Plaintiff wishes to show that the car's automobile liability insurance policy names the defendant as the primary person. How does this compare admissibility-wise with Problem (1) I, *above*, from the standpoint of policy, Fed. R. Evid. 411, and the common-law system? Should it matter how many other incidents of ownership, possession, and control are available as proof? Should it matter whether or not the issue of ownership, possession, and control is hotly contested and very close? Contested at all? Are all of the situations we have discovered as possible exceptions to the absolute ban on insurance-suggestive evidence (epitomized by Problem (1) I, *above*) merely candidates for admission, subject to the probative-prejudice-time-etc. balancing on the particular facts of the case (in some measure in the judge's discretion) (*see* Fed. R. Evid. 403)? In this Problem (4), would redaction be a good idea?

(5) *Witness Who is Employee of Opponent's Insurer.* Automobile personal injury negligence case. A witness for the defendant testifies he saw plaintiff speeding. Plaintiff wishes to impeach the witness by showing he is an employee of the automobile liability insurance company with whom defendant has a policy. Insofar as admissibility is concerned, is this distinguishable from Problem (1) I? Would it make any difference if the affiliation by the witness was with a different automobile liability insurance company than the defendant's?

(6) *Inconsistency in Statement Given to Insurance Agent.* Automobile personal injury negligence case. Plaintiff as witness is impeached by defendant's revelation that plaintiff made a contrary statement (in writing) on a previous occasion. Plaintiff is prepared to show that this statement came about in the following way:

An agent of defendant's automobile liability insurer visited plaintiff to take a statement. He then went away, typed it up, and returned to plaintiff's house and asked him to sign it, which plaintiff did.

Does defendant, by impeaching this way, run the risk plaintiff will be allowed to show the circumstances of the making of the statement, which would reveal that defendant was insured? How does plaintiff's evidence compare with Problem (1) I, *above*? Is there any way the legitimate force of this evidence might be obtained without the prejudice, i.e., without revealing that the agent of defendant that took the statement was from an insurance company? Would that do the trick?

(7) *Motives for Introducing Evidence of Insurance.* In all of the above Problems, excluding (1) I, plaintiff will have an "official" purpose for admission of the evidence, and an "unofficial," "real," or "secret" purpose. What will be the latter, even though the former may prevail in the eyes of the law? Is this ethical?

(8) *Remedies for Impermissible Insurance Evidence Being Heard by the Jury.* What should be the remedy if impermissible liability insurance evidence gets into the record before defendant can object? What factors should the trial judge consider in fashioning the remedy? Is a mistrial (new trial) in order more often here than in the case of other inadmissible evidence? How is the appropriateness of ordering a mistrial (new trial) affected by the fact that, at least in the case of

automobile liability insurance, the jury already knew, before the suggestion of insurance was made, that the defendant probably (or even mandatorily) was insured?

Should this somewhat automatic assumption by the jury license the defendant to show his lack of insurance coverage, if that is indeed the fact? (The usual rule has been, at least in the past, that lack of coverage normally cannot be shown unless there has been something affirmative in the case suggesting coverage.) Should the jury's assumption affect the question whether erroneous admission of insurance evidence is harmless error on appeal? Should it affect the willingness of courts to let in insurance evidence where there is some legitimate purpose for it alongside the illegitimate purpose?

(9) *Voir Dire About Insurance.* In personal injury cases and also other types of cases, plaintiffs often argue that, in selecting a jury, questions to prospective jurors should be allowed on the subject of whether jurors are affiliated with (or whether anyone connected with a juror is affiliated with) defendant's liability insurer, if any, or, more broadly, with any liability insurer (on grounds such affiliation with any liability insurer might make the juror defense-minded and therefore biased against plaintiff). It is argued by plaintiffs that this makes sense, in order to protect the plaintiff against biased jurors, and that such questions stand on a par with other questioning that goes on of jurors to uncover other biases. (The questions may be asked by either the judge or the lawyers. Practice varies.) Defendants argue that such questions obviously plant the suggestion that defendant is insured and prejudices him along the lines of Problem (1) I, *above*. But of course here it has more justification than in Problem (1) I. Is there any way you can think of to get the main part of the benefit for the judicial system, without the disadvantages? Or at least minimizing or somewhat safeguarding against the disadvantages? E.g., would you allow the inquiry only if the defendant (or a codefendant) is in fact insured? Allow inquiry only into affiliation with defendant's insurer, not other insurers? Prohibit inquiry unless there is some concrete reason to believe some juror has an insurance affiliation? Limit questions to direct affiliations on the part of the juror, not on the part of his family? Ask whatever questions are allowed about insurance, on a form that goes to every juror long before any smaller group is sent to the place where selections will be made for a particular case? Ask it orally of all prospective jurors before that narrowing?

Chapter 4

COMPETENCY, EXAMINATION, AND CREDIBILITY OF WITNESSES

THE "CENTER STAGE" OF THE TRIAL (F.R.E. ARTICLE VI)

§ 4.01 INTRODUCTION: PRESENTING WITNESS TESTIMONY AT TRIAL

In considering the matters in this chapter, it will be helpful to recall the normal order of presentation of evidence at trial. Ordinarily the plaintiff (or prosecutor) first presents his or her evidence (witnesses, documents, etc.). After the plaintiff (prosecutor) indicates he or she has no more evidence to present in his or her case, the defendant then presents the defendant's case (witnesses, documents, etc.). During the plaintiff's (prosecution's) case, however, the defendant has an opportunity to cross-examine each of the plaintiff's (prosecution's) witnesses as each witness's direct examination (i.e., the examination by the party who called the witness to the stand, here the plaintiff or prosecution) is concluded. A redirect examination may be in order after the cross-examination, and, possibly, a recross after a redirect, etc. (After the cross-examination stage, the judge makes a determination as to whether new points have rendered these subsequent examinations necessary.)

Similarly, the plaintiff (prosecution) is given an opportunity to cross-examine defense witnesses during the defense case as the defendant's direct examination of each is concluded, with similar possibilities of redirect, recross, etc.

After the defense case, the plaintiff (prosecution) may be allowed to again present evidence in the form of witnesses, documents, etc. (called a "rebuttal case") with the same opportunities for cross-examination, redirect, etc., as before; and following this "rebuttal case," the defense again may get a chance to put on witnesses, documents, etc., in "surrebuttal" (also called "rejoinder"), again subject to possible cross-examination, redirect, etc. (Rebuttal and surrebuttal, etc., depend on whether the judge feels they have been rendered necessary by what has gone before.)

Argument of counsel to the fact-finder is confined to opening and closing statements at the beginning and end of the presentation of evidence stage and may not take place during the presentation of evidence stage. (Counsel in practice frequently use voir dire, objections, responses thereto, and extended phraseology of questions as an opportunity to argue to the jury; is this ethical?) The judge's instructions to the jury come at the end of the case, principally, although instructions about evidence also may be given during the presentation of evidence stage. Practice varies as to whether the instructions that come after all the evidence is in are to come before or after the closing arguments of counsel. (Can you think of pros and cons for each method?)

In presenting evidence, counsel always must consider ethical obligations. Ethical problems can be particularly acute in presenting witnesses, especially one's own client as a witness. For example, in *Nix v. Whiteside*, 475 U.S. 157 (1986), the court held that the Sixth Amendment right of a criminal defendant to assistance of counsel is not violated when an attorney refuses to cooperate with the defendant in presenting perjured testimony at his trial. Counsel had advised the defendant that if he testified falsely, it would be counsel's duty to advise the court that he felt defendant was committing perjury, and that counsel probably would be allowed to impeach that testimony and would seek to withdraw from representation if defendant insisted on committing perjury. The defendant ultimately testified truthfully, but after conviction claimed that he had been deprived of a fair trial by counsel's admonitions not to lie.

§ 4.02 PREREQUISITES FOR WITNESS TESTIMONY: COMPETENCY AND PERSONAL KNOWLEDGE[1]

[A] General Competency Rules

Read Federal Rules of Evidence 601, "Competency to Testify in General"; 603, "Oath or Affirmation to Testify Truthfully"; and 610, "Religious Beliefs or Opinions."

UNITED STATES v. ROACH

United States Court of Appeals, Fifth Circuit
590 F.2d 181 (1979)

GEE, CIRCUIT JUDGE.

Roach and Stewart, wearing masks and carrying guns, robbed a bank in Dallas, Georgia [a federal crime. They stole various items, including] a security package containing a dye bomb designed to emit a red, tear gas-like substance within minutes after removal.

Brenda Jackson, Stewart's girlfriend, testified that Roach and Stewart had robbed the bank and that she was driving the getaway car when the dye bomb exploded, making it difficult for them to see. Roach switched places with Jackson and began driving. Stewart threw the shotgun out of the car and, after a bit, fled with the stolen money.

Stewart was apprehended a month later in Baton Rouge, Louisiana.

About three months before trial, Brenda Jackson received a psychiatric examination and was judged competent to stand trial. She was also found to have used drugs intermittently. Questioning Jackson's competence to be a witness against his

---

[1] Study Guide Reference: Evidence in a Nutshell, Chapter 6:I; and Chapter 7:I.

client, Roach's attorney was given access to the psychiatric report, and the court granted his request for a preliminary examination into Jackson's current mental state. Though Jackson had been emotionally troubled during the previous three months and admitted using drugs on two occasions in that time, her answers to questions by government and defense attorneys were lucid and discriminating. The trial judge asked no questions, nor were expert witnesses employed. At the end of the hearing, the judge declared Jackson competent to testify.

Roach complains that these procedures were insufficient guarantees of a fair trial: another psychiatric examination should have been ordered; experts should have testified; the judge should have personally questioned Jackson since Rule 104 of the Federal Rules of Evidence requires him to decide preliminary questions regarding the "qualification of a person to be a witness or the admissibility of evidence."

As to the necessity of a psychiatric examination, we have held that the district court has broad discretion in determining whether to order such examinations. Given the earlier examination and the further preliminary hearing, there can be no serious claim of abuse of discretion. Moreover, under the Federal Rules of Evidence it is doubtful that mental incompetence would even be grounds for disqualification of a prospective witness. Rule 601 provides that "[e]very person is competent to be a witness except as otherwise provided in these rules," and nowhere is mental competence mentioned as a possible exception. The Notes of the House Committee on the Judiciary state that one effect of Rule 601 is to abolish mental capacity as a ground for rendering a person incompetent as a witness. The Advisory Committee in their Notes on the Rules took a similar view, observing that the question of capacity was one "particularly suited to the jury as one of weight and credibility subject to judicial authority to review the sufficiency of the evidence."

If these views are to be rigorously adhered to, there seems no longer to be any occasion for judicially ordered psychiatric examinations or competency hearings of witnesses — none, at least, on the theory that a preliminary determination of competency must be made by the district court. If the court finds the witness otherwise properly qualified, the witness should be allowed to testify and the defendant given ample opportunity to impeach his or her perceptions and recollections. That the court here went further and allowed the preliminary hearing into Jackson's competence is an added ground for affirming the jury's verdict rather than a reason to set it aside.

UNITED STATES v. ALLEN

United States Air Force Court of Military Review
13 M.J. 597 (1982)

MILLER, J.

[Allen was a driver for the Air Force who transported preschool children. He was convicted of sexual offenses against several of the children in his care. On appeal, he argued that the children should not have been deemed competent to testify. The court rejected this contention, focusing on the responses of a four-year-old girl designated as "R" to questions exploring her qualification.]

During direct preliminary examination these questions included repeated references to Jesus and the Devil. R was asked where each lived, if they were good or bad, if Jesus loved her and if Jesus would want her to tell the truth today. When asked what happens when she doesn't tell the truth, R responded that her mother puts hot sauce on her tongue, an occurrence which she emphatically indicated she didn't like. When initially asked if telling the truth and lying were good or bad, R's answer indicated a proper understanding of the terms. [Later,] [t]he child, who, at this time had been testifying for an extended period of time, answered by saying telling the truth was bad and lying was good. R concluded both cross and re-direct preliminary examination by declaring that she would tell the truth in court.

Rule 601 reads, "Every person is competent to be a witness except as otherwise provided in these rules." This language clearly creates more than a mere presumption of competence. In fact, it actually re-defines the term "competent witness" so as to include any person who, when called to provide non-privileged testimony: (1) declares, pursuant to an oath or affirmation as prescribed in Rule 603 that he or she will testify truthfully, and (2) is not sitting as military judge or court panel member [the equivalent of a juror] on the very court panel before which he or she is about to testify.

Other preliminary questions, apparently designed to demonstrate R's knowledge, understanding, and intelligence, were also asked. They added to the effectiveness of the Rule 603 questions [set out above]. These questions related principally to the weight and credibility the court could give to R's testimony. We conclude that the accused was not prejudiced by the military judge's ruling.

The questions asked to demonstrate the children's knowledge, understanding and intelligence were probably designed to establish proof that the children were competent to testify as witnesses. Such proof was formerly required by the "old" rules of evidence. Such proof was not required, however, under F.R.E. 601.

Affirmed.

NOTES AND QUESTIONS

(1) *Child Witnesses.* Congress has enacted 18 U.S.C. § 3509 to regulate child testimony in federal court. The statutory scheme includes a presumption that children are competent and permits exclusion of child testimony only for "compelling reason," not simply due to the age of the child. In addition, it provides for the manner of presenting child testimony in order to facilitate a child-friendly courtroom. A few states even have eliminated competency determinations *and the need for an oath* in criminal cases when children testify to their own physical or sexual abuse. Does this raise any constitutional concerns?

In *Kentucky v. Stincer*, 482 U.S. 730 (1987), the Supreme Court held that the defendant's rights under the Constitution's Due Process Clause and Confrontation Clause were not violated by his exclusion from a hearing held to determine the competency of two child witnesses, where the questioning was limited to competency issues, neither girl was asked about the substantive testimony she would give at trial, and the competency objection was renewable in open court at trial. *See generally* Lyon, *Child Witnesses and the Oath: Empirical Evidence*, 73 S. Cal. L. Rev. 1017 (2000), suggesting that a developmentally sensitive form of oath has a positive effect on child competency. For a discussion of child victims as witnesses, see Myrna S. Raeder, *Enhancing the Legal Profession's Response to Victims of Child Abuse*, 24 Crim. Just. 12 (Spring 2009).

Section 3509(c)(9) prohibits psychological evaluations of children without a showing of compelling need. Thus, in *United States v. Snyder*, 189 F.3d 640 (7th Cir. 1999), *cert. denied*, 528 U.S. 1097 (2000), it was not error to deny a psychological examination of an eleven year old complaining witness ("Doe"), where the motion asserted that "Doe's prior statements demonstrated that he could not differentiate between truth and fantasy, and that '[u]pon information and belief,' Doe was being treated with anti-depressants that 'can have extreme side effects on individuals which could make the witness incompetent to testify at trial.' " What type of showing would justify an examination? *In re Michael H*, 2002 S.C. LEXIS 198 (Oct. 9, 2002), a case not governed by the federal statute, noted that jurisdictions split over what circumstances, if any, permit a judge to order a psychological evaluation of a victim.

(2) *Cautionary Instructions.* Even if a particular infirmity of a witness is not considered proper grounds for incompetency, it nevertheless may result in a cautionary instruction to the jury (in addition to counsels' arguments and showings on weight and credibility). Such an instruction typically is given when a child testifies.

(3) *Using Rule 403 to Exclude Marginal Testimony.* It also should be remembered that while some factor about a witness, such as infancy, drugs, alcohol, mental deficiency, insanity, etc., may not technically be grounds for incompetency under the federal branch of Fed. R. Evid. 601, it may on particular facts result in exclusion under Fed. R. Evid. 403. Might it also result in an incompetency of sorts under Fed. R. Evid. 603? Also, remember that a judge may declare evidence insufficient for a jury to convict. Finally, competency to stand trial should not be confused with competency to testify. The standard for the former is whether the defendant is unable to understand the nature and consequences of the proceedings against him or to assist properly in his defense. *See, e.g.*, *United States v. Nickels*, 324 F.3d 1250 (11th Cir. 2003). Similarly, in *Andrews v. Neer*, 253 F.3d 1052 (8th Cir. 2001), the involuntary commitment of a witness for schizophrenia did not render the patient incompetent to testify.

(4) *Oaths and Affirmations.* Sometimes witnesses will have religious or cultural beliefs that result in their objecting to taking the traditional oath. Affirmations are permitted as well as oaths. In *United States v. Ward*, 989 F.2d 1015 (9th Cir. 1993), it was held reversible error not to permit the defendant to take his own oath in addition to the traditional oath where the court's refusal resulted in his being excluded as a witness.

Arrangements should be made to have the witness take any alternate oath or affirmation out of the presence of the jury if the witness's beliefs might arouse prejudice. *See* McCormick, Evidence § 48 (1954) ("the disclosure of atheism or agnosticism, or of affiliation with some strange or unpopular sect, will often in many communities be fraught with intense prejudice"). Can an atheist ever be sworn as a witness? *See United States v. Saget*, 991 F.2d 702 (11th Cir.) (affirming refusal of trial judge to strike testimony of atheist who testified he was telling truth "to the best of my ability"), *cert. denied*, 510 U.S. 950 (1993).

Fed. R. Evid. 610 prohibits a witness's religious beliefs from being inquired into to impeach or enhance credibility. Are they relevant to determining competency? See *United States v. Sampol*, 636 F.2d 621 (D.C. Cir. 1980), affirming the trial court's refusal to permit counsel for Ignacio Novo to cross-examine Canete about his devotion to the Luceme religion in a case that did not involve that religion. On voir dire, Canete testified he faithfully adhered to the teachings of that sect and consulted with spirits of his religion before taking certain actions. He had no religious beliefs that would cause him to violate his oath to testify truthfully. The trial judge cut off further inquiry into Canete's religious practices at that point.

[B] Dead Man's Statutes or Rules

REINKE v. STEWART

United States District Court, Middle District of North Carolina
8 Fed. Evid. Rep. 217 (1981)

GORDON, CHIEF JUDGE

This action is brought [in federal court] under 42 U.S.C. § 1983 [deprivation of rights provided by law] by J.C. Reinke, administrator of the estate of his son, John Reinke, Jr. The defendants are two Southern Pines policemen, Stewart and McNeill, and the City of Southern Pines. The plaintiff alleges that the Fourteenth Amendment rights of his intestate son were violated by the failure of the policemen to take John Reinke, Jr. before a judicial official, or to take other steps required by law, after arresting him and taking him into custody. Stewart and McNeill found the plaintiff's intestate sleeping on the side of the street. [T]he policemen took [him] to the city limits and let him out on U.S. Highway No. 1. Tragically, he was struck and killed by a motorist shortly thereafter. The toxicology report reveals that his blood alcohol content was .17% at the time of death.

Stewart and McNeill have moved for summary judgment and have filed affidavits in support. The plaintiff has moved to strike those portions of the affidavits which relate the "transaction" the defendants had with plaintiff's decedent after they found him lying beside the street and until he was left on the highway outside city limits. The plaintiff asserts that these parts of the affidavits violate the North Carolina "Dead Man's Statute." Fortunately, it is unnecessary for the court to plunge into the murky waters which constitute the body of decisional law concerning this statute. Plaintiff's reliance on Fed. R. Evid. 601 is misplaced. Rule 601 provides that "with respect to an element of a claim or defense as to which State law supplies the rule of decision, the competency of a witness shall be determined in accordance with state law." By its own terms, the Rule applies only to diversity actions. The rule of decision regarding the policemen's liability under § 1983 is clearly one of federal law; the North Carolina Dead Man's Statute does not apply.

NOTES AND QUESTIONS

(1) *Variations Among Dead Man's Statutes.* Dead Man's Statutes vary significantly. Usually they prohibit the testimony of a party or interested witness concerning any contract, transaction, or communication with the decedent. Some extend to tort actions. Others permit the testimony if corroborated. Many provide for waiver in a variety of circumstances. Some statutes related to the subject are not incompetencies at all, but are a special hearsay exception allowing hearsay reports of what the dead person said. Local law must be consulted. What do you suppose is the policy behind these provisions? Why is there no such provision in the Federal Rules of Evidence? For a discussion of how such statutes still pose problems in some jurisdictions, see Dibley, *The Deadman's Statutes — Who is an Interested Party in Wisconsin?* 87 Marq. L. Rev. 1025 (2004).

(2) *Why Doesn't Rule 601 Apply One Standard of Competency to All Cases?* Considering each of the possible kinds of witness incompetency that exist, what justification, with respect to each, is there for providing, in Fed. R. Evid. 601, that in certain state-law cases, the state law of competency shall govern? Why is this one of the few places where the Rules apply local law?

[C] Hypnotically Refreshed Testimony

ROCK v. ARKANSAS

United States Supreme Court
483 U.S. 44 (1987)

BLACKMUN, JUSTICE.

The issue presented in this case is whether Arkansas' evidentiary rule prohibiting the admission of hypnotically refreshed testimony violated petitioner's constitutional right to testify on her own behalf as a defendant in a criminal case.

[Vickie Lorene Rock was convicted of manslaughter for shooting her husband. She testified that, because she could not remember the precise details of the event, she twice underwent hypnosis by a trained neuropsychologist. These sessions were tape-recorded. The trial judge, however, followed Arkansas' categorical rule that no hypnotically refreshed testimony could be admitted and limited Rock's testimony to a repetition of her statements to the doctor before hypnosis, as reported in the doctor's notes. The Arkansas Supreme Court affirmed, holding that the limits on her testimony did not violate Rock's constitutional right to testify and that hypnotically refreshed testimony was inadmissible per se as unreliable. The United States Supreme Court here reverses.]

Petitioner's claim that her testimony was impermissibly excluded is bottomed on her constitutional right to testify in her own defense. At this point in the development of our adversary system, it cannot be doubted that a defendant in a criminal case has the right to take the witness stand and to testify in his or her own defense. This, of course, is a change from the historic common-law view, which was that all parties to litigation, including criminal defendants, were disqualified from testifying because of their interest in the outcome of the trial.

The question now before the Court is whether a criminal defendant's right to testify may be restricted by a state rule that excludes her post-hypnosis testimony. This is not the first time this Court has faced a constitutional challenge to a state rule, designed to ensure trustworthy evidence, that interfered with the ability of a defendant to offer testimony. In *Washington v. Texas*, 388 U.S. 14 (1967), the Court was confronted with a state statute that prevented persons charged as principals, accomplices, or accessories in the same crime from being introduced as witnesses for one another. The statute, like the original common-law prohibition on testimony by the accused, was grounded in a concern for the reliability of evidence presented by an interested party. [The Court held the statute unconstitutional under the Sixth Amendment, particularly the Compulsory Process Clause.]

Just as a State may not apply an arbitrary rule of competence to exclude a material defense witness from taking the stand, it also may not apply a rule of evidence that permits a witness to take the stand, but arbitrarily excludes material portions of his testimony. In *Chambers v. Mississippi*, 410 U.S. 284 (1973), the Court invalidated a [particular application of a] State's hearsay rule on the ground that it abridged the defendant's right to "present witnesses in his own defense."

Of course, the right to present relevant testimony is not without limitation. [B]ut restrictions of a defendant's right to testify may not be arbitrary or disproportionate to the purposes they are designed to serve.

In establishing its per se rule, the Arkansas Supreme Court simply followed the approach taken by a number of States that have decided that hypnotically enhanced testimony should be excluded at trial on the ground that it tends to be unreliable.[14] Other States that have adopted an exclusionary rule, however, have done so for the testimony of witnesses, not for the testimony of a defendant. The Arkansas Supreme Court failed to perform the constitutional analysis that is necessary when a defendant's right to testify is at stake.[15]

[M]any courts have eschewed a per se rule and permit the admission of hypnotically refreshed testimony.[16] Hypnosis by trained physicians or psychologists has been recognized as a valid therapeutic technique since 1958, although there is no generally accepted theory to explain the phenomenon, or even a consensus on a single definition of hypnosis. The use of hypnosis in criminal investigations,

---

[14] [The court's footnote cites decisions from seventeen states, alphabetically from Alaska to Washington, excluding hypnotically affected evidence as unreliable.]

[15] [T]his case does not involve the admissibility of testimony of previously hypnotized witnesses other than criminal defendants and we express no opinion on that issue.

[16] Some jurisdictions have adopted a rule that hypnosis affects the credibility, but not the admissibility, of testimony. *See, e.g., Beck v. Norris*, 801 F.2d 242, 244-245 (CA6 1986).

Other courts conduct an individualized inquiry in each case. *See, e.g., McQueen v. Garrison*, 814 F.2d 951, 958 (CA4 1987) (reliability evaluation); *Wicker v. McCotter*, 783 F.2d 487, 492-493 (CA5 1986) (probative value of the testimony weighed against its prejudicial effect); *State v. Iwakiri*, 106 Idaho 618, 625, 682 P.2d 571, 578 (1984) (weigh "totality of circumstances").

In some jurisdictions, courts have established procedural prerequisites for admissibility in order to reduce the risks associated with hypnosis. Perhaps the leading case in this line is *State v. Hurd*, 86 N.J. 525, 432 A.2d 86 (1981).

however, is controversial, and the current medical and legal view of its appropriate role is unsettled.

Responses of individuals to hypnosis vary greatly. The popular belief that hypnosis guarantees the accuracy of recall is as yet without established foundation and, in fact, hypnosis often has no effect at all on memory. The most common response to hypnosis, however, appears to be an increase in both correct and incorrect recollections. Three general characteristics of hypnosis may lead to the introduction of inaccurate memories: the subject becomes "suggestible" and may try to please the hypnotist with answers the subject thinks will be met with approval; the subject is likely to "confabulate," that is, to fill in details from the imagination in order to make an answer more coherent and complete; and, the subject experiences "memory hardening," which gives him great confidence in both true and false memories, making effective cross-examination more difficult. Despite the unreliability that hypnosis concededly may introduce, however, the procedure has been credited as instrumental in obtaining investigative leads or identifications that were later confirmed by independent evidence.

The inaccuracies the process introduces can be reduced, although perhaps not eliminated, by the use of procedural safeguards. One set of suggested guidelines calls for hypnosis to be performed only by a psychologist or psychiatrist with special training in its use and who is independent of the investigation.

Suggestion will be less likely also if the hypnosis is conducted in a neutral setting with no one present but the hypnotist and the subject. Tape or video recording of all interrogations, before, during, and after hypnosis, can help reveal if leading questions were asked.

The more traditional means of assessing accuracy of testimony also remain applicable in the case of a previously hypnotized defendant. Certain information recalled as a result of hypnosis may be verified as highly accurate by corroborating evidence. Cross-examination, even in the face of a confident defendant, is an effective tool for revealing inconsistencies. Moreover, a jury can be educated to the risks of hypnosis through expert testimony and cautionary instructions.

We are not now prepared to endorse without qualifications the use of hypnosis as an investigative tool; scientific understanding of the phenomenon and of the means to control the effects of hypnosis is still in its infancy. Arkansas, however, has not justified the exclusion of all of a defendant's testimony that the defendant is unable to prove to be the product of pre-hypnosis memory.

[The] circumstances present an argument for admissibility of petitioner's testimony in this particular case, an argument that must be considered by the trial court.

Reversed and remanded.

CHIEF JUSTICE REHNQUIST, with whom JUSTICE WHITE, JUSTICE O'CONNOR, and JUSTICE SCALIA join, dissenting:

In deciding that petitioner Rock's testimony was properly limited at her trial, the Arkansas Supreme Court cited several factors that undermine the reliability of hypnotically induced testimony.

[This] Court candidly admits that the increased confidence inspired by hypnotism makes "cross-examination more difficult," thereby diminishing an adverse party's ability to test the truthfulness of defendants such as Rock. Nevertheless, we are told, the exclusion of a defendant's testimony cannot be sanctioned because the defendant "above all others may be in a position to meet the prosecution's case." In relying on such reasoning, the Court apparently forgets that the issue before us arises only by virtue of Rock's memory loss, which rendered her less able "to meet the prosecution's case."

In conjunction with its reliance on broad principles that have little relevance here, the Court barely concerns itself with the recognition, present throughout our decisions, that an individual's right to present evidence is subject always to reasonable restrictions. Surely a rule designed to exclude testimony whose trustworthiness is inherently suspect cannot be said to fall outside this description.

NOTE

Can the Testimony of Witnesses other than Criminal Defendants Be Barred if They Have Been Hypnotized? The holding in *Rock* is applicable only to criminal defendants. Can other witnesses be prohibited from testifying if their memories are refreshed through hypnosis? A number of states have statutes regulating hypnotic refreshment, some of which bar testimony of witnesses other than a criminal defendant. *Compare Borawick v. Shay*, 68 F.3d 597 (2d Cir. 1995), *cert. denied*, 517 U.S. 1229 (1996), affirming summary judgment for the defense after the plaintiff was prohibited from testifying to her alleged sexual abuse by her aunt and uncle based on hypnotically induced or refreshed recollections. The court reviewed the literature and case law, holding that admissibility should be determined on a case-by-case basis using a totality of circumstances approach and listing factors for the trial judge to consider. *See generally* Webert, *Are the Courts in a Trance? Approaches to the Admissibility of Hypnotically Enhanced Witness Testimony in Light of Empirical Evidence*, 40 Am. Crim. L. Rev. 1301 (2003) (surveying three approaches to hypnotically enhanced evidence and arguing for exclusion). Does *Rock* have implications for *Scheffer*, *infra*, § 11.06 and 6.02 [C]?

[D] Judges and Jurors

Read Federal Rules of Evidence 605, "Judge's Competency as Witness" and 606, "Juror's Competency as Witness."

TANNER v. UNITED STATES

United States Supreme Court
483 U.S. 107 (1987)

O'Connor, Justice

[After his conviction for mail fraud, Tanner moved for leave to interview the jurors. The trial judge denied leave. Nevertheless, several jurors apparently contacted Tanner's lawyer on their own. One of them, Hardy, said he "felt like the jury was on one big party" during the trial. This and other contacts led to affidavits and other written evidence that four jurors, including Hardy, consumed between them "a pitcher to three pitchers" of beer during various recesses, that they additionally had mixed drinks, that several smoked marijuana regularly during the trial, two ingested cocaine, and the foreperson repeatedly consumed a liter of wine at lunch. One juror sold another a quarter pound of marijuana during the trial, several fell asleep, and one described himself to Hardy as "flying." As Hardy saw it, "Mr. Tanner should have a better opportunity to get someone who would review the facts right."]

[The trial judge refused to conduct an evidentiary hearing into these apparent facts and denied a new trial. The Eleventh Circuit and the Supreme Court, per Justice O'Connor, upheld this ruling. The Supreme Court relied on Fed. R. Evid. 606(b) and its exclusion of impeachment of verdicts by jurors by testimony not involving "extraneous prejudicial information" or "outside influence".]

Lower courts [under the common law] used this internal/external distinction to identify those instances in which juror testimony impeaching a verdict would be permissible. The distinction was not based on whether the juror was literally inside or outside the jury room when the alleged irregularity took place; rather, the distinction was based on the nature of the allegation. For example, under a distinction based on location a juror could not testify concerning a newspaper read inside the jury room. Instead, of course, this has been considered an external influence about which a juror may testify. Similarly, under a rigid locational distinction jurors could regularly be required to testify after the verdict as to whether they heard and comprehended the court's instructions, since the charge to the jury takes place outside the jury room. Courts wisely have treated allegations of a juror's inability to hear or comprehend at trial as an internal matter.

Most significant for the present case, however, is the fact that lower federal courts treated allegations of the physical or mental incompetence of a juror as "internal" rather than "external" matters.

Substantial policy considerations support the common-law rule. "[Otherwise,] [j]urors would be harassed and beset by the defeated party. [T]he result would be to make what was intended to be a private deliberation, the constant subject of public investigation — to the destruction of all frankness and freedom of discussion and conference."

Petitioners have presented no argument that Rule 606(b) is inapplicable to the juror affidavits and the further inquiry they sought in this case, and, in fact, there appears to be virtually no support for such a proposition.

NOTES AND QUESTIONS

(1) *Juror Conduct.* In *United States v. Kimberlin*, 527 F. Supp. 1010 (S.D. Ind.), *aff'd without op.*, 673 F.2d 1335 (7th Cir. 1981), *cert. denied*, 456 U.S. 964 (1982), a juror's remarks concerning the defendant that "[t]hey ought to hang him now, so that we can go home" was not found to require reversal under Fed. R. Evid. 606(b). Even juror deliberation discussions making it clear that the jury concentrated

exclusively on the fact that the defendant did not take the stand, despite the judge's instructions not to consider that, have not been considered extraneous information. *See State v. Rodriquez*, 116 F.3d 1225 (8th Cir. 1997). In some states, *e.g.*, Cal. Evid. Code § 1150, the judge can consider conduct occurring during deliberations, but not any testimony concerning how such conduct actually affected the jurors. Would the result in *Tanner* or the cases in this note have been different in such a jurisdiction?

(2) *Impeaching the Verdict.* Under the Federal Rule, could jurors testify to show there was a clerical error in transmitting or recording their verdict? Could any of the following conduct be used to impeach a jury verdict pursuant to Fed. R. Evid. 606(b)? If not, should it be?

(a) Violent coercion by other jurors of the jurors who were holding out against conviction.

(b) Rampant racial remarks against defendant by most jurors during their deliberations.

(c) Experiments done in the jury room by the jurors with a gun introduced in evidence, which show that the trigger could not have been triggered accidentally in a scuffle the way defendant contended at trial.

(3) *Distinctions in the Rule Regarding Time and Form of Evidence.* Does Rule 606(b) make a distinction based upon when the misconduct takes place: during the trial vs. during the deliberations (the period after both sides rest and the jury retires to consider what verdict to bring in; usually the only time jurors are allowed to discuss the case)? Does it make a distinction concerning whether a juror statement is the evidence of the misconduct vs. other evidence of the misconduct (such as testimony of a bailiff who witnessed it)?

(4) *Tanner Erroneous?* Based on the technical terms of the Rule 606(b) itself, can you make an argument that the decision in *Tanner* is incorrect? Can you, based on policy?

[E] Personal Knowledge

Read Federal Rule of Evidence 602, "Need for Personal Knowledge."

(1) *What is Personal or Firsthand Knowledge?* The requirement of personal knowledge, or firsthand knowledge as it is sometimes called, means that the witness must have personally observed any fact he or she testifies to. In other words, a witness may not state as fact something he or she was told, or only infers. (The latter may have an exception for certain well-based inferences, in liberalized modern evidence law, if the inference is itself soundly based on sufficient firsthand observations of the witness. *See* note (5) below.)

(2) *Proof of Personal Knowledge.* Typically, personal knowledge is established by the testifying witness herself. The degree of proof of personal knowledge that must be made before the judge lets the witness testify, is quite low. It is, as the Rule says, merely "proof sufficient to support a finding" of personal knowledge. This means that even if the judge does not believe the witness had personal knowledge, if a juror might disagree with the judge and still be thought reasonable by the

judge, the burden is satisfied. You will note that this is the standard provided by Rule 104(b), as well.

(3) *Varieties of Fact Testimony Where as a Practical Matter Personal Knowledge Becomes an Issue: Where Witness Could Not Have Observed; or Where Witness Reports as Fact What He Only Heard from Another; Relationship to Hearsay Rule.* Other than cases in which it is clear that the witness could not have seen what he or she testifies about, lack of personal knowledge can become an issue when the witness relates as fact what someone else said. For example, the witness testifies "The Ford went through the red light" but cross examination or some earlier questioning reveals the witness did not see the incident, but only heard this from someone else, who did see it. The witness lacks personal knowledge of the fact he is testifying to: a Ford going through a red light. If the statement of the other person, who saw the accident, is admissible through an exception to the hearsay rule (dealt with in other chapters herein), then our witness (who heard that statement of that other person) could testify to the statement, but must do so in the form of "X said the Ford went through the red light" rather than just "The Ford went through the red light", for, in the latter case, there would still be a violation of the personal knowledge rule, since the witness is testifying to a fact (Ford going through red light) of which he was not personally percipient.

(4) *Personal Knowledge Requirement Normally Applies Only to Lay Witnesses.* Unlike purportedly percipient lay witnesses, experts, to the extent they are testifying to their expert opinions on matters to be established through other evidence, are exempted from the personal knowledge requirement. *See* Rule 703, Chapter 5.

(5) *Insufficient Basis for Personal Knowledge.* In *State v. Ranieri*, 586 A.2d 1094 (R.I. 1991), a conviction was reversed where the victim "had no personal knowledge of her assailant's identity because she had an insufficient opportunity to view the assailant." The perpetrator had grabbed her from behind and she did not identify the defendant until shortly before trial 18 months later. The victim had made previous allegations against the defendant. Her reason for the delay was that she was scared of the defendant. It also was error to permit the other eyewitness to identify the defendant, where he saw only the assailant's "upper lip" area; there was nothing distinctive about his lips and he testified that the other faces in the photo array had similar lips.

(6) *Lack of Certainty does Not Negate Personal Knowledge.* The witness need not be certain, and can testify "I believe" or "I think," so long as this connotes only that the witness is cautious and not that he has insufficient personal knowledge to testify to the facts or conclusions in his testimony. It may take some early cross-examination (sometimes known as *"voir dire,"* a term with many different meanings in the law of evidence), interrupting the direct examination, to clarify what exactly is signified by the tenuous nature of the witness's phrasing, and what his personal firsthand observations actually were. *See, e.g., M.B.A.F.B. Federal Credit Union v. Cumis Ins. Soc.*, 681 F.2d 930 (4th Cir. 1982), and *State v. Thorp*, the first case in our next chapter. In *Strickland Transp. Co. v. Ingram*, 403 S.W.2d 192 (Tex. Civ. App. 1966), the court states that when an ordinary witness testifies he "learned" something, the court must decide whether he means he was *told* it, inferred it from

other facts, or personally observed it. Only in the latter instance would the testimony be admissible. The court seemed peculiarly willing to assume that personal observation was meant by the witness, unless it is shown that is not what was meant.

§ 4.03 FORM OF QUESTIONS IN DIRECT AND CROSS-EXAMINATION[5]

Read Federal Rule of Evidence 611, "Mode and Order of Examining Witnesses and Presenting Evidence."

(1) *Narratives and Other Procedural Matters are Discretionary Under Rule 611(a).* Fed. R. Evid. 611(a) gives the judge discretion concerning narrative versus specific questions and answers in federal courts. The same discretionary provision also covers many, many other matters, such as when redirect, recross, etc., are allowed (subject to the concept of at least some "right" to develop and attack material and the concept of abuse of discretion); when rebuttals and surrebuttals are allowed (also subject to the same concepts), and more. Within its scope also are questions concerning what may be taken to the jury room, whether transcripts of a tape recording and the playing of the tape recording both are to be received (clarity and undue emphasis are the factors to be balanced), and whether both summaries and the material underlying the summaries are to be received (the same factors are to be balanced; see also Fed. R. Evid. 1006). And there are others. There seems to be considerable overlap with Fed. R. Evid. 403. Notice that Fed. R. Evid. 611(a) specifically allows the judge to control harassment or embarrassment of witnesses (often perpetrated in the name of attack on credibility). Obviously this may not be used to prevent legitimate attacks on credibility, and for the most part courts resolve doubts in favor of allowing the attack. But this can give rise to some nice questions.

Discretion under Fed. R. Evid. 611(a), while broad, is not unlimited. *See, e.g., United States v. Zarintash*, 736 F.2d 66 (3d Cir. 1984) (trial court in drug prosecution committed abuse of discretion warranting new trial in refusing to read certain testimony of defense witness to deliberating jury at its request; testimony was not lengthy and went to heart of jury's determination of guilt or innocence; reading of testimony would not have delayed deliberations significantly or caused jury to focus undue attention on insignificant portion of record).

For the interesting proposition that Fed. R. Evid. 611(a) and Fed. R. Evid. 102 license a trial judge to require direct examination in written form, with the witness being submitted for cross-examination, see U.S. District Judge Charles Richey's article, *A Modern Management Technique for Trial Courts to Improve the Quality of Justice: Requiring Direct Testimony to be Submitted in Written Form Prior to Trial*, 72 Geo. L.J. 73 (1983).

(2) *Dangers Associated with Leading Questions: Basis for Possible Relaxations of Ban. Audibert v. Michaud*, 111 A. 305 (Me. 1920):

---

[5] Study Guide Reference: Evidence in a Nutshell, Chapter 6:X at "Method of Examination of Witnesses: Leading and Non-Leading Questions and Related Matters: F.R.E. 611."

> The legitimate object of all examination is the eliciting of the truth, and the danger which arises from so-called leading questions is that untruth may be stated by a witness who is either indifferent to his oath or overzealous in the cause and eager to adopt any suggestion made by the attorney although not in accordance with the fact. It is not the mere leading, but the leading into temptation that is to be avoided. The end is to obtain the actual recollections of the witness and not the allegations of another person, adopted by the witness and falsely delivered as his. [S]uggestive interrogation [may lead] to the dispatch of business, and sometimes it may be absolutely necessary to recall the attention of the witness to facts which had passed from his memory. This is objectionable mainly when [the interrogator has] a disposition to afford information [to] elicit a false answer, and the witness to make use of it for such sinister purpose.

(3) *Leading Questions to Develop the Testimony of Children.* In *United States v. Littlewind*, 551 F.2d 244 (8th Cir. 1977), the defendant was convicted of forcible rape of one of two girls of 13 and 14 years old. (He was jointly tried for both. The rapes were two hours apart.) The two victims were called to the stand by the government and examined in direct examination by leading questions. On appeal, he argued that this was "forcing" them to testify and unduly influenced them to conform to their prior statements to police rather than to their best recollection. The Court of Appeals holds that although Fed. R. Evid. 611(c) provides that leading questions should not normally be used on direct examination, there is an express exception when leading questions are necessary to develop the testimony. The Advisory Committee Note states:

> Numerous exceptions have [traditionally] achieved recognition [and are codified by the rule]: The witness who is hostile, unwilling, or biased; the child witness or the adult with communication problems, [etc.]. The matter clearly falls within the area of control by the judge over the mode and order of interrogation and presentation, and accordingly is phrased in words of suggestion rather than command.

Both young girls had shown themselves during the testimony to be extremely hesitant and reticent, as is understandable concerning such a traumatic occurrence. The trial judge's reassurances to them helped only mildly. In these circumstances he did not abuse his discretion to permit leading questions in the direct examination.

(4) *Other Types of Objectionable Questions.* There are other kinds of questions that also are frequently objectionable: compound questions ("Did you go to the spot and see the murder?"); misleading questions; questions that assume certain premises ("When did you stop beating your spouse?"); vague or difficult-to-understand questions; questions that are not clear as to time or place; etc. Basically, the factors at work in judging the form of questions are those involved in Fed. R. Evid. 403 and Fed. R. Evid. 611(a). Chief Justice Bell, in *Steer v. Little*, 44 N.H. 613 (1863), condemned, among others, questions "where the question assumes any fact that is in controversy, so that the answer may really or apparently admit the fact. Such are the forked questions habitually put by some counsel, if unchecked; as,

What was the plaintiff doing when the defendant struck him?, the controversy being whether the defendant did strike. A dull or forward witness may answer the first part of the question and neglect the last."

§ 4.04 CROSS-EXAMINATION: OTHER ASPECTS

[A] Right to Cross-Examine Witnesses[6]

The Right to Cross-Examine. A number of evidentiary doctrines would seem to allow considerable restriction of cross-examination. And yet deep in our legal system is the notion that a fair trial requires a certain degree of latitude for the cross-examiner. In *United States v. Caudle*, 606 F.2d 451 (4th Cir. 1979), the defendant was convicted of defrauding the federal government. The issue at trial was how much of a report was the work of Dr. Levy and how much was that of the defendant. At trial, Dr. Levy was called by the prosecution. On recross-examination, defendant's counsel sought to take Dr. Levy through a page-by-page examination of the report, just as the government had done on redirect. The trial judge denied this request on grounds that the questions already had been asked and answered on redirect examination. Defense counsel said that he wished to establish "not whether the words where the same [as had been questioned about on redirect], but whether the sense is the same." The Court of Appeals orders a new trial because this ruling denied defendant's Sixth Amendment right in a criminal case to cross-examine the witnesses against him, as well as his common-law right. Citing general language establishing a right (within limits) to cross-examination in *Davis v. Alaska*, 415 U.S. 308 (1974), *Alford v. United States*, 282 U.S. 687 (1931), and *Pointer v. Texas*, 380 U.S. 400 (1965), the court states:

> It is properly within the trial judge's discretion to prevent one party from repeating a question already asked by that party. Where there is more than one defendant or defense attorney it may also be proper to prevent one defense attorney from repeating a question already asked by another defense attorney. It is quite a different thing, however, to prevent the defense from asking a question on the grounds that it has already been asked by the prosecution. The fact [that on direct examination the questions] had been asked and answered is a reason to permit cross-examination, not a reason to deny it.
>
> The Supreme Court and other courts have been nearly unanimous that the right of confrontation in cross-examination is an essential and fundamental requirement. [C]ross-examination "is beyond any doubt the greatest legal engine ever invented for the discovery of truth." [Wigmore.] [I]ts efficacy in testing the accuracy and [completeness] of testimony is well understood. [Witness testimony] is subject not only to the possible infirmities of falsification or bias; it is also subject to the inaccuracies which inevitably flow from the fallibility of human powers of observation, memory

[6] Study Guide Reference: Evidence in a Nutshell, Chapter 8:V, at "Beyond Hearsay: Other Implications of the Confrontation Clause: (2) The Criminal Defendant's Right to Cross-Examine Without Undue Restriction of the Questions." Also review F.R.E. 611, assigned at the head of § 4.03, *supra*.

and description. "The annals are filled with instances in which testimony, plausible when supplied on examination in chief, has by cross-examination been shown to be, for one or more of the reasons mentioned, faulty or worthless."

The second major function of cross-examination (which is not involved in the instant case) is to show that the witness is biased, prejudiced, or untrustworthy for any reason. The facts which diminish the personal trustworthiness or credibility of the witness will also, in every likelihood, have remained undisclosed under direct examination. For these reasons, cross-examination is guarded against legislative and judicial action by the Constitution of the United States and the States.

[T]he reasons that we have given apply with equal strength to recross-examination where new matter is brought out on redirect examination. Examining counsel is normally expected to elicit everything from a witness, so far as possible, at the first opportunity. Where, as here, new matter is brought out on redirect examination, the defendant's first opportunity to test the truthfulness, accuracy, and completeness of that testimony is on recross-examination. To deny recross-examination on matter first drawn out on redirect is to deny the defendant the right of any cross examination as to that new matter.

[T]he trial judge has broad discretion to control the scope and extent of cross-examination. However, entirely consistent with that rule, "it is only after the right of cross-examination has been substantially and thoroughly exercised that the allowance of further cross-examination becomes discretionary with the trial court." In concrete terms, then, the trial judge's discretion insulates only his decision that an *area* of cross-examination has been *sufficiently explored* and that further inquiry would be pointless. A considerably stricter standard applies when an appellate court is called upon to review a ruling which *foreclosed altogether* a valid area of cross-examination.

See also *Nulf v. International Paper Co.*, 656 F.2d 553 (10th Cir. 1981), recognizing a right to cross-examine in civil cases.

[B] Scope of Cross-Examination[7]

(1) *The "Wide Open" Rule Versus the Restrictive Rule of Cross-Examination.* In *Boller v. Cofrances*, 166 N.W.2d 129 (Wis. 1969), the court rejected the rule (adopted in many jurisdictions, and in essence codified by Fed. R. Evid. 611(b)) against questioning any witness "beyond the scope of direct examination [except for impeachment]" as having "no intrinsic merit and does not demonstrably assist in the search for the truth. Rather, by encouraging pettifogging objections that go to form and not substance, the rule is likely to be disruptive of trial procedure and results in appeals that basically have no merit." It downplayed the importance of

[7] Study Guide Reference: Evidence in a Nutshell, Chapter 6:X, at "The Scope of Cross-Examination: Common Law and F.R.E. 611." Also review F.R.E. 611(b), assigned at the head of § 4.03, *supra*.

ensuring the orderly presentation of evidence, adopting instead the "wide open" rule that permits any relevant and otherwise admissible cross-examination, subject to the sound discretion of the trial judge to determine whether to exclude any questions. The court cites Wigmore: "Cross-examination is the greatest engine for getting at the truth; and a rule which needlessly hampers its exercise as this one does cannot be a sound one." Then it continues:

> McCormick also emphasizes the deleterious effect of the [restrictive] rule [especially] in the prosecution of criminals:
>
> > [T]he accused may limit his direct examination to some single aspect of the case, such as age, sanity or alibi, and then invoke the court's ruling that the cross-examination be limited to the matter thus opened. Surely the according of a privilege to the accused to select out a favorable fact and testify to that alone, and thus get credit for testifying but escape a searching inquiry on the whole charge, is a travesty on criminal administration. In jurisdictions following the wide-open practice there is of course no obstacle to cross-examining the accused upon any matters relevant to any issue in the entire case.

Does the fact that the privilege against self-incrimination would not allow the prosecution to call defendant to the stand suggest a countervailing argument to McCormick's view? Also, compare the next note, *below*.

(2) *How Does the Fifth Amendment Affect the Operation of Rule 611(b)?* On the relationship of the Fifth Amendment to Fed. R. Evid. 611(b), see *United States v. Beechum*, 582 F.2d 898 (5th Cir. 1978) (Fed. R. Evid. 611(b) may give judge discretion to allow cross-examination into matters outside scope of direct examination, insofar as general rules pertaining to scope of cross-examination are concerned; but it does not purport to say whether testifying criminal defendant waives Fifth Amendment privilege against self-incrimination as to such matters, a question not yet definitively decided), *cert. denied*, 440 U.S. 920 (1979).

See also *Hankins v. Civiletti*, 614 F.2d 953 (5th Cir. 1980), where the court upheld a civil contempt citation:

> Clearly, Hankins has waived his Fifth Amendment privilege with regard to matters relevant to his direct testimony. He argues on appeal, however, that his statements on direct exposed him only to cross-examination within the meager bounds of possession, custody, and control of the records, and not to inquiry regarding the whereabouts or fate of the records. We cannot agree that Hankins' direct testimony opened only so narrow an inquiry. Although we do not speculate as to the extent of permissible cross-examination, we do find that the questions propounded to Hankins were proper cross-examination within the subject matter of his direct testimony.

(3) *Impeachment Not Restricted by Rule Limiting Questions to Scope of the Direct.* The restrictive rule of cross-examination does not restrict matters going to impeachment. Those are governed by the separate rules relating to impeachment, considered elsewhere in this book. Either impeachment that is within those other rules is always considered to be "opened up" by, and thus "within the scope" of, the direct examination under the restrictive rule, or (what amounts to the same thing),

the restrictive rule restricts only substantive, as opposed to impeachment, matters. *See Nulf v. International Paper Co.*, 656 F.2d 553 (10th Cir. 1981). A number of decisions emphasize that impeachment questions ordinarily should have a good faith basis — for example, you should not ask whether a witness has been convicted of perjury, or made a previous statement contrary to his current testimony, unless there is at least some (perhaps scanty) reason to believe there may have been such an event, that you can allege to the judge at the bench, if called on it. *See, e.g., United States v. Zaccaria*, 240 F.3d 75 (1st Cir. 2001).

§ 4.05 IMPEACHMENT: SOME GENERAL PRECEPTS[8]

Read Federal Rule of Evidence 607, "Who May Impeach a Witness."

(1) *Some Pertinent Definitions.* Evidence may be relevant to "credibility" of a witness, or to the "substantive issues" in a case, or both. In either case, it is subject to the same relevancy and counterweights analysis and to the other rules of evidence (although sometimes the credibility purpose of evidence may remove it from the prohibited purpose named by a rule of evidence). Credibility evidence may be subject to some additional rules as well, as the following sections make clear. (In theory, these additional rules probably derive from concepts of relevancy and its counterweights.)

"Credibility evidence" may be divided into "impeachment" and "support" of credibility. "Extrinsic evidence" is a term used to describe evidence, usually impeachment evidence, offered through a different route than a witness's own words during cross-examination.

"Impeachment" and "cross-examination" are not coextensive terms. Can you say why?

"Contradiction" is "technically" not impeachment, although it may incidentally have some impeachment effect. It is substantive evidence that is relevant to the main issues in the case, but is contrary to some other testimony in the case.

"Collateral matters" are statements made by a witness that a court feels are not important enough to allow impeachment or contradiction on, usually only when extrinsic evidence is offered. *See* the seminal early English case of *Attorney-General v. Hitchcock*, 1 Exch. 90 (1847). The opinion of Baron Rolfe discusses a hypothetical in which a witness is asked whether he has received a bribe and answers no. The next question is whether he had ever said he received a bribe. While the former answer can be contradicted, the latter cannot.

(2) *The Role of the Jury in Assessing Credibility: Some Common Jury Instructions.* In many jurisdictions, bar associations or commentators have put together books of "pattern" or standardized jury instructions on various subjects, based on the cases. These are frequently given, although they sometimes are modified by the particular judge. The lawyers also may submit their own versions for the judge's consideration, and may argue over exact words and object to certain instructions.

---

[8] Study Guide Reference: Evidence in a Nutshell, Chapter 6:II, IV–V.

In the area of witness credibility, after the close of all the evidence but before deliberations, typically the jury may be instructed as follows:

— Witnesses are rebuttably "presumed to speak the truth," but "contradictory evidence, the manner and character of the testimony, demonstrated bias, prejudice, or hostility of a witness, evidence of motivation," etc., can overcome that presumption.

— In case of "conflict in testimony, you must judge credibility and determine which version is true."

— "You are the sole judge of a witness' credibility and the weight to be accorded his or her testimony and must consider and weigh all the testimony carefully."

— Factors bearing on credibility and weight are: "demeanor and behavior of the witness on the stand," "manner of testifying," "whether the witness seems a truthful individual and to possess an accurate memory and recollection," "motive," "opportunity and ability to observe," "interest in outcome," "friendship or animosity toward or relationship to other persons in the case," "reasonableness and probability of the testimony," "other contradiction or corroboration," "conscious or unconscious bias or prejudice," "intelligence," "state of mind," and the like.

— "Inconsistencies and discrepancies between or within testimony may or may not cause the jury to discredit such testimony."

— "Two or more persons may see or hear the same event differently."

— "Innocent misrecollection and failure of recollection do occur."

— "Consider whether the discrepancy pertains to a matter of importance, and whether it is intentional."

— "If you believe testimony to be willfully false on a material matter about which reasonable mistake is unlikely, you may, if you wish, disregard all or any part of that witness's testimony or credit any part you find worthy of belief."

— "The weight of evidence does not necessarily depend on the number of witnesses testifying on either side; you should consider all the facts and circumstances and may decide credibility lies with the side having the smaller number."

— "You are not required to accept even uncontradicted testimony of unimpeached witnesses, but may decide that it is unworthy of belief."

— "The government is not required to meet its burden to prove elements of the offense by any particular number of witnesses; a single witness may constitute proof beyond a reasonable doubt, if you so find."

— "A party need not call or put on all witnesses, documents or other evidence that may bear on the case or be mentioned; however, if it is available to the party, it may be a factor to consider, if you wish, in deciding weight and credibility of the other evidence; however, the law never imposes a duty on a criminal defendant to call any witness or put on any evidence and no adverse inference may be drawn from his failure to do so."

In individual cases, the instructions on these points, if given, may or may not be made more specific or tailored to address particular pieces of evidence. Instructions (either the same or different ones) also may be given during the course of the trial, e.g., upon receipt of or rejection of particular pieces of evidence.

The instructions given in this note relate to the jury's role regarding credibility generally. Jury instructions relating to specific kinds of impeachment evidence are discussed as we come to those specific kinds of evidence *infra*.

(3) *The Common-Law Rule Prohibiting You from Impeaching Witnesses that You Yourself Have Called: The Voucher Rule.* The common-law view was that a party could not impeach a witness whom the same party has called to the stand. The party "vouched for" any witness he or she called. There were exceptions to this rule, however, and one exception was that a party could both ask leading questions and impeach when calling an "adverse" witness, defined to be the adverse party himself or (if the adverse party is an organization) an officer, director, or managing agent thereof. In such a situation, the rationale behind the general rule did not apply.

Another common-law exception to the traditional rule against counsel impeaching his or her own witness is made when the witness genuinely surprises counsel (through no lack of diligence on counsel's part) with a change of story that affirmatively damages counsel's case. In *Bushaw v. United States*, 353 F.2d 477 (9th Cir. 1965), *cert. denied*, 384 U.S. 921 (1966), a prosecution witness in a bank robbery case told the FBI in a signed statement that defendant had come to her (shortly after the robbery) and asked if she would marry him if he came into lots of money, and that he then talked of remodeling her carpet shop. Before trial, she repudiated the statement and told the prosecutor she would do so at trial as well. Nevertheless, the government called her at trial, and when she said defendant did not say those things to her, attempted to impeach her with the prior inconsistent statement. The court expressed doubt that this was surprise, but was certain that this was not affirmative damage (as it would be if she had testified, for example, that he professed to having no money), since she merely failed to supply expected favorable testimony but did not supply unfavorable testimony. A party "is not permitted to get before the jury, under the guise of impeachment, an [inadmissible, out-of-court, hearsay] statement of [a] witness, by calling [her] to the stand when there is good reason to believe [she] will decline to testify as desired, and when in fact [she] only so declines."

The voucher rule was rejected by Fed. R. Evid. 607. The voucher rule's specific application in *Chambers v. Mississippi*, 410 U.S. 284 (1973), violated a criminal defendant's constitutional guarantee to due process. In *Chambers*, the voucher rule together with the hearsay rule operated to exclude reliable defense evidence of a third person's (the witness') confession to the crime with which the defendant was charged. *Chambers* held that to be unconstitutional.

(4) *Impeaching with Constitutionally Defective Evidence.* Evidence obtained in violation of a criminal defendant's constitutional rights, such as those found in the Fourth and Fifth Amendments, cannot be used directly against that defendant by the prosecution in its case-in-chief. However, the Court has recognized that the Constitution should not be applied in a way that gives the defendant a right to commit perjury. Thus, in *Harris v. New York*, 401 U.S. 222 (1971), and *United States*

v. Havens, 446 U.S. 620 (1980), the Court permitted impeachment of a criminal defendant by constitutionally deficient evidence. In *Harris*, it was a statement obtained in violation of the defendant's *Miranda* rights; in *Havens*, physical evidence seized in violation of the Fourth Amendment that contradicted the defendant's testimony. However, *Doyle v. Ohio*, 426 U.S. 610 (1976), holds that a defendant cannot be impeached with his or her silence following a *Miranda* warning; and *James v. Illinois*, 493 U.S. 307 (1990), bans the use of evidence illegally seized from a defendant to impeach a defense *witness*.

Note that the Supreme Court has not found any due process violation when a defendant is impeached by prearrest silence not involving any custodial interrogation. *See Jenkins v. Anderson*, 447 U.S. 231 (1980). In *Kansas v. Ventris*, 556 U.S. 586 (2009), the Court held that the defendant's statement to an informant taken in violation of the Sixth Amendment right to counsel was admissible to impeach his inconsistent testimony at trial.

(5) *Common Lines of Attack on Credibility*. The following sections treat some of the more common forms of impeachment evidence or "lines of attack" on credibility of witnesses: (1) evidence that the witness has made a prior inconsistent statement; (2) evidence that the witness is biased (for any number of reasons); (3) the witness's propensity for falsehood shown by (a) evidence that the witness has committed misconduct for which he or she has not been convicted, (b) evidence that he or she has been convicted of a crime, and (c) reputation or opinion evidence concerning the witness; and (4) expert evidence of the unreliability of eyewitness identifications. There are others. For example, it is common to attack defects in perception, which can range from the use of alcohol or drugs at the time of the incident to bad eyesight and faulty memory.

§ 4.06 PRIOR INCONSISTENT STATEMENTS[9]

Read Federal Rules of Evidence 613, "Witness's Prior Statement."

(1) *The Traditional Rule: The Queen's Case*. The rule requiring that a foundation be laid for impeachment by a prior inconsistent statement had its genesis in *The Queen's Case*, 2 Br. & B. 284, 129 Eng. Rep. 976 (1820), requiring that a detailed foundation be laid before evidence of a contrary out-of-court statement could be admitted. A witness had to be asked whether or not on a specific date, at a specific place and in the presence of specific persons, he or she made a particular statement: "If it be intended to bring the credit of a witness into question by proof of anything he may have said or declared touching the cause, the witness is first asked, upon cross-examination, whether or not he has said or declared that which is intended to be proved." The purposes of these foundational requirements are "(1) to avoid unfair surprise to the adversary, (2) to save time, as an admission by the witness may make extrinsic proof unnecessary, and (3) to give the witness in fairness a chance to explain the discrepancy." 1 STRONG, MCCORMICK ON EVIDENCE § 37, at 120 (4th ed. 1992).

---

[9] Study Guide Reference: Evidence in a Nutshell, Chapter 6:III.

(2) *What is the Foundational Requirement for Extrinsic Evidence Pursuant to Rule 613?* In *United States v. Hudson*, 970 F.2d 948 (1st Cir. 1992), the court discussed the foundation for admitting extrinsic evidence pursuant to Fed. R. Evid. 613:

> Next, the government contends that the foundation for admitting extrinsic evidence through Benson about James Hudson's prior statement was never properly laid pursuant to Fed. R. Evid. 613(b), since James Hudson was never "afforded an opportunity to explain or deny [his earlier statement]." The government urges us to reconsider our ruling in *Barrett* in which we explained that the foundation requirements of 613(b) do not require that the witness be confronted with the statement while on the witness stand, but rather, only that the witness be available to be recalled in order to explain the statement during the course of the trial. *Barrett*, 539 F.2d at 254–56. The government properly notes that the Fifth, Ninth, and Tenth Circuits have upheld the refusal to admit proof through extrinsic evidence of prior inconsistent statements unless the witness has first been afforded the opportunity to deny or explain those statements. *See e.g., United States v. Greer*, 806 F.2d 556, 559 (5th Cir. 1986); *United States v. Cutler*, 676 F.2d 1245, 1249 (9th Cir. 1982); *United States v. Bonnett*, 877 F.2d 1450, 1462 (10th Cir. 1989). The Eighth Circuit has followed suit, at least in circumstances in which there are considerable logistical difficulties in arranging for the recall of inmate witnesses sought to be impeached through extrinsic evidence of prior inconsistent statements. *United States v. Lynch*, 800 F.2d 765, 770 (8th Cir. 1986), *cert. denied*, 481 U.S. 1022 (1987). We decline the invitation. Assuming without deciding that James Hudson's expression of bias against appellant constituted a prior inconsistent statement with respect to his trial testimony, we reaffirm our earlier analysis as set forth in *Barrett*. The approach there taken is wholly consistent with the requirements of Fed. R. Evid. 613(b), as explained by the notes of the Advisory Committee: "the traditional insistence that the attention of the witness be directed to the statement on cross examination is relaxed in favor of simply providing the witness an opportunity to explain and the opposite party an opportunity to examine the statement, with no specification of any particular time or sequence," and is supported by the great weight of authority.
>
> Here, as in *Barrett*, we have no basis for assuming that James Hudson, a federal prisoner, was not available for recall or that the government would have been prejudiced by admission of the statement without the opportunity for adequate rebuttal and examination. Even though the district court possesses a substantial measure of discretion under Fed. R. Evid. 613(b), it would resurrect the now-discredited procedure laid down in *Queen Caroline's Case*, 2 Brod. & Bing. 284, 313, 129 Eng.Rep. 976 (1820), if we excluded James Hudson's statement on the ground of an inadequate evidentiary foundation when the district court acted without any evaluation of the availability of the witness sought to be impeached or, alternatively, without any expressed consideration of whatever delay or inconvenience might have been caused by defense counsel's failure to confront James

Hudson, on cross-examination, with his allegedly inconsistent statement.

We think it is important to note that the trial court's fundamental error lay not in a mistaken interpretation of Rule 613(b) but in its failure to exercise its discretion. Even if a proponent is not always required to lay a prior foundation under Rule 613(b), a trial court is free to use its informed discretion to exclude extrinsic evidence of prior inconsistent statements on grounds of unwarranted prejudice, confusion, waste of time, or the like. *See, e.g., Nachtsheim v. Beech Aircraft Corp.*, 847 F.2d 1261, 1276-77 (7th Cir. 1988) (suggesting that trial court has discretion under Fed. R. Evid. 403 to exclude evidence not excluded by Fed. R. Evid. 613[b]). Moreover, Fed. R. Evid. 611(a) allows the trial judge to control the mode and order of interrogation and presentation of evidence, giving him or her the discretion to impose the common-law "prior foundation" requirement when such an approach seems fitting. Here, however, there is no sign that the trial judge sought to exercise these powers.

What are the advantages and disadvantages of the Rule in *The Queen's Case*? Is it really dead? In *United States v. Schnapp*, 322 F.3d 564 (8th Cir. 2003), the refusal of a trial judge to permit testimony about a prior inconsistent statement, on grounds quite similar to *The Queen's Case*, was upheld, even though the witness-to-be-impeached was available to be recalled by the government to respond to the impeachment later in the trial. How do you suppose this was justified under the Federal Rules of Evidence?

(3) *Can Extrinsic Evidence be Shown when the Witness Admits the Inconsistency?* In *State v. Woods*, 687 P.2d 1201 (Ariz. 1984), the court states that under Arizona Rule 613, the substantial equivalent of Fed. R. Evid. 613, it is within the trial judge's discretion pursuant to Fed. R. Evid. 403 to decide whether a prior inconsistent statement that can be used substantively (e.g., pursuant to Fed. R. Evid. 801(d)(1)(A)) can be proved up through extrinsic proof when the witness has admitted it during cross-examination. The court feels in that situation it may well be important for the jury to hear the tone of voice on the tape of the inconsistent statement, or see the handwriting on the inconsistent document, or look at the film and judge the demeanor of the witness if the inconsistent statement is on film. Would the court have ruled differently if the statement was not substantively admissible? Does Fed. R. Evid. 613 apply to both? Does Fed. R. Evid. 613 alone settle the matter?

UNITED STATES v. MEZA

United States Court of Appeals, Fifth Circuit
701 F.3d 411 (2012)

HIGGINSON, CIRCUIT JUDGE:

. . . [T]hree shotguns and a rifle were stolen from a pawn shop in Wichita Falls, Texas. The police determined that an individual named Chris Sanchez ("Sanchez") had committed the robbery and they found one of the guns at his house. After his arrest, Sanchez told police where he had sold another of the guns, a Mossberg 12 gauge shotgun. Police searched the property of defendant-appellant Cristobal Meza, III ("Meza"), a convicted felon, and found the shotgun in a shed. They then searched Meza's house and found two boxes of ammunition (12 gauge Winchester shotgun shells). . . . Meza was arrested a few blocks away from the residence.

. . . Meza was charged in a two-count indictment. Count 1 charged Meza with being a felon in possession of a firearm and Count 2 charged Meza with being a felon in possession of ammunition, both in violation of [federal law]. Meza reached a plea agreement with the government, whereby he agreed to plead guilty to Count 1 in exchange for dismissal of Count 2, thereby capping his maximum sentence at 120 months. . . . [B]ut because Meza used cocaine while he was released on bond, his guideline range rose to 235–293 months. Because this guideline range was more than the 120 month sentence contemplated under the plea agreement, the district court found that the agreement "undermine[d] the sentencing guidelines and statutory purposes of sentencing," and rejected the plea agreement. The case proceeded to trial.

The district court held a one day trial. . . . The government called five witnesses, consisting of four law enforcement officers and Sanchez. The government began by calling Detective Gerald Schulte of the Wichita Falls Police Department. Schulte testified that he investigated the pawn shop break-in, and that Sanchez's tip led the police to search Meza's house. Schulte also testified that, prior to execution of the search warrant, the police conducted surveillance of the property, and observed Meza leaving the house. Schulte testified that the shotgun was found in a shed on top of a washing machine and that ammunition was found inside the house. On cross-examination, Schulte explained that the police verified that Meza owned the property after they found his name on the property's water bills.

The government then called Sanchez to the stand. A week before trial, Sanchez had told investigating agents that he had sold one of the stolen guns to Meza. At trial, Sanchez admitted that he had stolen the guns from the pawn shop, and had hidden one of the guns at Meza's house, a so-called "trap house [i.e., a location for illegal drug dealing, occupied by many transient people]." Sanchez then, however, recanted his earlier statements to investigators:

Q. So when you were arrested for the pawn shop break-in, did you talk to some police officers?

A. Yes, ma'am.

Q. And did you tell them what you did with the guns?

A. Yes, ma'am. I lied and said I sold them to this man [Meza]. . . .

Q. And what about when you talked to Agent Benavides last week? What about that?

A. I lied again.

Q. Why did you lie?

A. Because I was scared. I already told them I sold them to this man, and I never sold them to this man. This man didn't have nothing to do with it. . . .

Q. Did you know that they found one of the guns you stole in his — at his house?

A. That's the trap house. Everybody goes in there. That's where I had my guns hidden. I don't even know if they knew that they were there or not. That's where everybody goes and chills.

Q. So you're saying he doesn't live there?

A. I don't — everybody lives there. If you need a place to go, that's where you go.

Q. . . . [D]o you recall going in the car with the police officers and pointing out the house where Meza lived?

A. Yeah, I lied. I knew where he lived before. . . .

Q. Okay. So you're saying that when you told the police officers back in July that you sold the gun to him and showed them where he lived — the gun was found there?

A. Yeah, I put it there.

Q. Oh, you put it there?

A. Yes, ma'am. . . .

Q. Okay. And then what about when you spoke to Agent Benavides this past week and you told him that you sold the gun to him?

A. I lied. I know I made a mistake. It's just I didn't want to dig myself into a deeper hole than what I'm already in. I thought because of putting it off on somebody else, I would get away with it, but I didn't. . . .

On cross-examination, Sanchez stated that "[a] lot" of other people besides Meza had access to the house, . . . Sanchez also denied that he was lying on the stand because he had been intimidated by Meza.

After Sanchez, the government called FBI Special Agent Fernando Benavides. Benavides testified about his interviews with Sanchez. According to Benavides, Sanchez stated that he was fearful of Meza, and did not want to give his name for the police reports. The government then sought to introduce an audio recording of Benavides's interrogation of Sanchez. Meza objected on hearsay grounds, and at first suggested that it could be offered as impeachment evidence with a proper limiting instruction. The government responded as follows:

> Mr. Sanchez's testimony was extremely relevant to certain elements, namely, Mr. Meza's knowing possession of the firearm, the fact that firearm was found at Fillmore street, which Sanchez knew to be Meza's residence.
>
> After the Government called him, he has changed his story and became, essentially, a hostile witness. So we are offering it, one, to impeach Mr. Sanchez's testimony; but two, the evidence is relevant regarding the essential elements.

After further discussion with the district court, the government argued that the statement was admissible under Federal Rule of Evidence 613(b) for impeachment purposes. When asked whether Rule 613(b) applied, defense counsel clarified:

> [I]f [the witness] den[ies] that statement — if he denied that he had made an inconsistent statement, then I think you're able to offer extrinsic evidence to prove that he has, in the past, made a prior inconsistent statement. Here, I don't think it applies to the extent that he admitted he made a prior inconsistent statement.

The district court overruled the hearsay objection, found the tape admissible under Rule 613(b), and stated that it would give the jury a cautionary instruction. Meza then objected on Rule 403 grounds. The district court also overruled this objection.

The district court then played for the jury the audio recording of Sanchez's conversation with Benavides. When it did so, it provided a limiting instruction, informing the jury that it could not consider the recording for the truth of the matters asserted, but only to consider Sanchez's credibility. . . . On the recording, Benavides asked Sanchez about his sale of the stolen firearms. Sanchez at first stated that he did not remember to whom he had sold the firearms, and asked to see his earlier statement to police. When asked a second time, Sanchez said, "I sold one [firearm] to Chris Meza." When asked where the transaction occurred, Sanchez again said that he could not remember, but eventually stated, "I guess I went to his house," which he identified as being on Fillmore Street (Meza's street). . . . After the recording was played, Benavides confirmed that Sanchez's testimony at trial contradicted what he had previously told investigators.

[The government then called other witnesses who independently testified so as to prove Meza's guilt. The jury found Meza guilty, and the judge sentenced him to 240 months' confinement.]

A. Standard of Review

This court "review[s] a district court's evidentiary rulings for abuse of discretion, subject to harmless-error analysis." *Girod*, 646 F.3d at 318. . . .

B. The district court did not abuse its discretion in allowing the government to impeach its witness, Chris Sanchez, with a prior inconsistent statement pursuant to Federal Rule of Evidence 613(b).

. . . When confronted with the prior inconsistent statements, Sanchez did not deny making them, but rather on direct, cross, redirect and recross examination, explained that he had lied because he had been scared and did not know what to do. When the government offered audio recording of Sanchez's original statements to law enforcement incriminating Meza, Meza's counsel objected on hearsay and Rule 403 grounds. The district court . . . overruled the objections. . . .

On appeal, Meza argues that Sanchez's prior statements to Benavides were inadmissible because Sanchez did not deny making those statements. . . . In response, the government argues that the extrinsic audio recording was admissible because Sanchez "attempted to explain [his prior inconsistent statement] by claiming that he was afraid of being caught in a lie by the authorities," whereas in fact he had told authorities that he was scared of Meza. The government argues that the jury was entitled to consider Sanchez's prior statement to judge his credibility. The government also argues that any error was harmless.

We hold that the district court did not err in admitting, along with explicit limiting instructions for impeachment use only, Sanchez's prior statements under Rule 613(b), which provides, "[e]xtrinsic evidence of a witness's prior inconsistent statement is admissible only if the witness is given an opportunity to explain or deny the statement and an adverse party is given an opportunity to examine the witness about it, or if justice so requires."

The plain language of the Rule [seems to license prior inconsistent statements for impeachment and] makes no exception for prior inconsistent statements that are explained instead of denied. What the Rule does require is a foundation requirement that a witness have the chance either to explain or to deny the inconsistent statement before extrinsic proof is allowed. . . . Here, Meza contends that Sanchez spoke truthfully at trial when he explained his earlier statement incriminating Meza as a frightened but false effort to blame-shift; the government, contrastingly, contends that Sanchez's denial of the correctness of his earlier statement is an evasion, an attempt to exculpate Meza, whom Sanchez fears. Either purpose is plausible but neither is determinative for admissibility. . . .

. . . In *Greer* [another, earlier, case], a cooperating co-defendant testified for the government and implicated defendant Greer in an obstruction of justice scheme, but "admitted on cross-examination that he made [a] previous inconsistent [tape-recorded] statement" when he denied the obstruction. That admission, we stated, made the recording "excludable." [That was probably because it was] an unequivocal admission making any inconsistency negligible, so warranting exclusion [rather than an explanation which Rule 613(b) suggests warrants admission of the extrinsic evidence]. . . .

Regardless, we find that any evidentiary error would have been harmless for several reasons. First, . . . there was more than sufficient evidence to convict Meza under Count 1 and Count 2, without Sanchez's statement. Second, . . . the recording reiterates statements that Sanchez admitted to making when he was questioned by the prosecutor[, so the contents of the recording were already before the jury]. . . .

As emphasized above, the district court gave limiting instructions on three separate occasions. This court has relied upon proper limiting instructions to support a finding of harmlessness.

C. The district court did not abuse its discretion under Federal Rule of Evidence 403 in admitting Sanchez's prior inconsistent statement.

Meza also objected to the admission of Sanchez's statement on Rule 403 grounds, an objection he re-urged after his Rule 613 objection was overruled. The district court overruled this objection.

Under Rule 403, a district court may "exclude relevant evidence if its probative value is substantially outweighed by a danger of . . . unfair prejudice." The standard of review for an alleged Rule 403 violation is " 'especially high' and requires 'a clear abuse of discretion' for reversal." *United States v. Setser*, 568 F.3d 482, 495 (5th Cir.2009). . . .

Meza argues that the probative value of Sanchez's prior statements was minimal, as Sanchez had acknowledged his recantation on the stand. Meza maintains that the potential for undue prejudice was great because it allowed the government to "improperly focus the jury on an inculpatory (but unsworn) prior version of Sanchez's statement rather than the exculpatory trial testimony made under oath." Meza further argues . . . the government intended to use Sanchez's statements as more than impeachment evidence. The government contends that the probative value of Sanchez's prior statement was high because Sanchez's credibility was a critical issue at trial, whereas any prejudicial effect was minimal because the district court issued limiting instructions regarding the recording and the statement was cumulative of Sanchez's admission on the stand. The government also argues that admission of the statement, even if erroneous, was harmless.

We hold that the district court did not commit a clear abuse of discretion in admitting the statements. . . . Although the statements prejudiced Meza, this prejudice was not unfair and did not substantially outweigh the statements' probative value. [Conviction affirmed.]

NOTES AND QUESTIONS

(1) *Was the Evidence Here Really Admissible under Rule 613?* Rule 613 appears not to be a rule that prescribes that inconsistent statements are admissible, but merely says that *if* they are admissible under other law, here are the procedures to be used. The allowance of inconsistent statements to impeach is merely a product of the relevancy rules (and a long standing practice at common law). It is unquestionable here that the prior statement would be admissible under the relevancy rules for the purpose of impeachment, and the only questions would be (a) whether the evidence was sufficiently made known to the jury by the witness' admission on the stand of having made it, so that the extrinsic evidence of it would be redundant or a waste of time, or would unduly emphasize it, which are Rule 403 concerns; or (b) whether the danger of hearsay use could be adequately safeguarded against by a Rule 105 limiting instruction to the jury, also a Rule 403 concern. The answer to the latter is usually yes (except in the special *Morlang* situation, treated in the note two notes hence).

(2) *California's Different Solution: Prior Inconsistent Statements Are Generally Admissible as Nonhearsay.* California avoids problem (b) altogether by exempting prior inconsistent statements from the hearsay rule. Cal. Evid. Code §§ 769, 770, 1201, 1235 (as long as the witness had an "opportunity to explain or deny the statement"). Under Federal Rule of Evidence 801(d)(1), some, but not all, prior statements of witnesses are exempted from the hearsay rule, so the problem still exists as to the others.

(3) *United States v. Morlang*, 531 F.2d 183 (4th Cir. 1975). Defendant Morlang was convicted of bribery. The government called to the stand a witness named Wilmoth and asked him about a fact he allegedly knew that incriminated Morlang,

but the government knew that Wilmoth was going to deny the fact. After Wilmoth's direct testimony denying the fact, the government called another witness, Crist, who testified that on the contrary, Wilmoth had made a statement to him indicating the Morlang-incriminating fact. This testimony was offered as a prior inconsistent statement of Wilmoth, purportedly to impeach Wilmoth. If offered as other than impeachment of credibility, the testimony would have been inadmissible under the hearsay rule.

The court reversed the conviction and remanded for a new trial, explaining that "[t]he real purpose for calling Wilmoth was apparently to elicit from him" the denial that he in fact offered, as a subterfuge for offering the alleged prior inconsistent statement. If this kind of evidence were allowed, said the court, it would "permit the government, in the name of impeachment, to present testimony to the jury by indirection which would otherwise be inadmissible [because of the hearsay rule]."

Morlang does not stand for the proposition that if a prior statement is susceptible of both an impermissible hearsay use as well as a permissible impeachment use, the evidence is inadmissible. Nor does it mean such evidence is inadmissible if the offering party is aware of the possibility — and indeed hopes — that the jury will use it for the impermissible purpose despite a limiting instruction. *Morlang* does not deny that normally admission with a limiting instruction would be proper. But the reason the prior statement was inadmissible in *Morlang* was that the government *knew* the witness would deny the incriminating fact and called him to the stand anyway, just to get the impermissible evidential inference before the jury. If the purpose for the evidence was really only to impeach the witness's denial and remove that denial from the case, a much more effective way to do that would have been to *refrain from introducing the direct-exam testimony of the witness in the first place.* So it was an obvious ruse.

(4) *Limits on Refreshing Memory or Impeaching by Inconsistency.* In *United States v. Shoupe*, 548 F.2d 636 (6th Cir. 1977), the appellate court found the trial court committed reversible error by permitting the prosecutor, in the presence of the jury, to recite to a recalcitrant government witness a litany of leading questions that incorporated the entire substance of his unsworn, oral statements inculpating the appellants. The court rejected the contentions that this was an appropriate mechanism to refresh the witness's present recollection or that it served the legitimate purpose of impeaching a hostile witness's credibility. The witness claimed that he had neither present recollection nor past awareness of who his accomplices were. He attempted to rationalize this aberration by stating he had been "shooting a lot of dope at the time [and] was strung up." The court said:

> The tenor of Hall's initial testimony convinces us that the trial court would have been justified in permitting limited impeachment of him, using the substance of Agent Cleary's memorandum, under Rule 613(a) of the Federal Rules of Evidence. . . .
>
> [But we] hold that the recitation by the prosecutor of the entire substance of a witness's disavowed, unsworn prior statements, which, if credited by the jury, would be sufficient to sustain a conviction, abridged defendants' right to a fair trial in violation of the Due Process Clause of the 5th Amendment.

Our holding should not be interpreted as a blanket rejection of impeachment by prior inconsistent statements in situations similar to this. [Courts can protect the rights of the accused by limiting the scope of impeachment or determining in advance, through independent evidence, that the statements are reliable.]

(5) *Jury Instruction for Impeachment by Prior Inconsistent Statements.* Unless the prior inconsistent statement also qualifies as substantive evidence under a hearsay exemption or exception, an instruction something like the following often is given:

> The testimony of a witness may be discredited or impeached by showing that he has previously made statements which are inconsistent with his present testimony. The prior statement is admitted into evidence solely for your consideration in evaluating the credibility of the witness. You may consider the prior statement only in connection with your evaluation of the credence to be given to the witness' present testimony in court. You must not consider the prior statement as establishing the truth of any fact contained in that statement.
>
> If you believe that any witness has been thus impeached and discredited, it is your exclusive province to give his testimony such weight, if any, as in your judgment it is fairly entitled to receive.

§ 4.07 BIAS[10]

UNITED STATES v. ABEL
United States Supreme Court
469 U.S. 45 (1984)

JUSTICE REHNQUIST delivered the opinion [for a unanimous] Court.

Respondent John Abel and two cohorts were indicted for robbing a savings and loan in Bellflower, Ca., in violation of 18 U.S.C. §§ 2113(a) and (d). The cohorts elected to plead guilty, but respondent went to trial. One of the cohorts, Kurt Ehle, agreed to testify against respondent and identify him as a participant in the robbery.

Respondent informed the District Court at a pretrial conference that he would seek to counter Ehle's testimony with that of Robert Mills. Mills was not a participant in the robbery but was friendly with respondent and with Ehle, and had spent time with both in prison. Mills planned to testify that after the robbery Ehle had admitted to Mills that Ehle intended to implicate respondent falsely, in order to receive favorable treatment from the government. The prosecutor in turn disclosed that he intended to discredit Mills' testimony by calling Ehle back to the stand and eliciting from Ehle the fact that respondent, Mills, and Ehle were all

---

[10] Study Guide Reference: Evidence in a Nutshell, Chapter 6:VI. Review Federal Rules of Evidence 403 and 610.

members of the "Aryan Brotherhood," a secret prison gang that required its members always to deny the existence of the organization and to commit perjury, theft, and murder on each member's behalf.

Defense counsel objected to Ehle's proffered rebuttal testimony as too prejudicial to respondent. After a lengthy discussion in chambers the District Court decided to permit the prosecutor to cross-examine Mills about the gang, and if Mills denied knowledge of the gang, to introduce Ehle's rebuttal testimony concerning the tenets of the gang and Mills' and respondent's membership in it. The District Court held that the probative value of Ehle's rebuttal testimony outweighed its prejudicial effect, but that respondent might be entitled to a limiting instruction if his counsel would submit one to the court.

At trial Ehle implicated respondent as a participant in the robbery. Mills, called by respondent, testified that Ehle told him in prison that Ehle planned to implicate respondent falsely. When the prosecutor sought to cross-examine Mills concerning membership in the prison gang, the District Court conferred again with counsel outside of the jury's presence, and ordered the prosecutor not to use the term "Aryan Brotherhood" because it was unduly prejudicial. Accordingly, the prosecutor asked Mills if he and respondent were members of a "secret type of prison organization" which had a creed requiring members to deny its existence and lie for each other. When Mills denied knowledge of such an organization the prosecutor recalled Ehle.

Ehle testified that respondent, Mills, and he were indeed members of a secret prison organization whose tenets required its members to deny its existence and "lie, cheat, steal [and] kill" to protect each other. Respondent's counsel did not request a limiting instruction and none was given.

The jury convicted respondent. On his appeal a divided panel of the Court of Appeals reversed. The Court of Appeals held that Ehle's rebuttal testimony was admitted not just to show that respondent's and Mills' membership in the same group might cause Mills to color his testimony; the court held that the contested evidence was also admitted to show that because Mills belonged to a perjurious organization, he must be lying on the stand. This suggestion of perjury, based upon a group tenet, was impermissible. The court reasoned:

> It is settled law that the government may not convict an individual merely for belonging to an organization that advocates illegal activity. Neither should the government be allowed to impeach on the grounds of mere membership, since membership, without more, has no probative value. It establishes nothing about the individual's own actions, beliefs, or veracity. [707 F.2d 1013, 1016 (1983).]

The court concluded that Ehle's testimony implicated respondent as a member of the gang; but since respondent did not take the stand, the testimony could not have been offered to impeach him and it prejudiced him "by mere association." *Id.*, at 1017.

Both parties correctly assume, as did the District Court and the Court of Appeals, that the question is governed by the Federal Rules of Evidence. But the Rules do not by their terms deal with impeachment for "bias," although they do expressly treat impeachment by character evidence and conduct, Rule 608, by evidence of conviction of a crime, Rule 609, and by showing of religious beliefs or opinion, Rule 610. Neither party has suggested what significance we should attribute to this fact. Although we are nominally the promulgators of the Rules, and should in theory need only to consult our collective memories to analyze the situation properly, we are in truth merely a conduit when we deal with an undertaking as substantial as the preparation of the Federal Rules of Evidence. In the case of these Rules, too, it must be remembered that Congress extensively reviewed our submission, and considerably revised it.

Before the present Rules were promulgated, the admissibility of evidence in the federal courts was governed in part by statutes or rules, and in part by case law. This Court had held in *Alford v. United States*, 282 U.S. 687 (1931) that a trial court must allow some cross-examination of a witness to show bias. This holding was in accord with the overwhelming weight of authority in the state courts as reflected in Wigmore's classic treatise on the law of evidence. Our decision in *Davis v. Alaska*, 415 U.S. 308 (1974) holds that the Confrontation Clause of the Sixth Amendment requires a defendant to have some opportunity to show bias on the part of a prosecution witness.

With this state of unanimity confronting the drafters of the Federal Rules of Evidence, we think it unlikely that they intended to scuttle entirely the evidentiary availability of cross-examination for bias. One commentator, recognizing the omission of any express treatment of impeachment for bias, prejudice, or corruption, observes that the Rules "clearly contemplate the use of the above-mentioned grounds of impeachment." E. Cleary, McCormick on Evidence, § 40 p. 85 (3d ed. 1984).

We think this conclusion is obviously correct. Rule 401 defines as "relevant evidence" evidence having any tendency to make the existence of any fact that is of consequence to the determination of the action more probable or less probable than it would be without the evidence. Rule 402 provides that all relevant evidence is admissible, except as otherwise provided by the United States Constitution, Act of Congress, or by applicable rule. A successful showing of bias on the part of a witness would have a tendency to make the facts to which he testified less probable in the eyes of the jury than it would be without such testimony.

The correctness of the conclusion that the Rules contemplate impeachment by showing of bias is confirmed by the references to bias in the Advisory Committee Notes to Rules 608 and 610, and by the provisions allowing any party to attack credibility in Rule 607, and allowing cross-examination on "matters affecting the credibility of the witness" in Rule 611(b). The Courts of Appeals have upheld use of extrinsic evidence to show bias before and after the adoption of the Federal Rules of Evidence.

Ehle's testimony about the prison gang certainly made the existence of Mills' bias towards respondent more probable. Thus it was relevant to support that inference. Bias is a term used in the "common law of evidence" to describe the relationship between a party and a witness which might lead the witness to slant, unconsciously or otherwise, his testimony in favor or against a party. Bias may be induced by a witness' like, dislike, or fear of a party, or by the witness' self-interest. Proof of bias is almost always relevant because the jury, as finder of fact and weigher of credibility, has historically been entitled to assess all evidence which might bear on the accuracy and truth of a witness' testimony. The "common law of evidence" allowed the showing of bias by extrinsic evidence, while requiring the cross-examiner to "take the answer of the witness" with respect to less favored forms of impeachment.

Mills' and respondent's membership in the Aryan Brotherhood supported the inference that Mills' testimony was slanted or perhaps fabricated in respondent's favor. A witness' and a party's common membership in an organization, even without proof that the witness or party has personally adopted its tenets, is certainly probative of bias. Mills' and respondent's membership in the Aryan Brotherhood was not offered to convict either of a crime, but to impeach Mills' testimony. Mills was subject to no sanction other than that he might be disbelieved. For purposes of the law of evidence the jury may be permitted to draw an inference of subscription to the tenets of the organization from membership alone, even though such an inference would not be sufficient to convict beyond a reasonable doubt in a criminal prosecution under the Smith Act [criminalizing membership in a subversive organization].

Respondent argues that even if the evidence of membership in the prison gang were relevant to show bias, the District Court erred in permitting a full description of the gang and its odious tenets. Respondent contends that the District Court abused its discretion under Federal Rules of Evidence 403, because the prejudicial effect of the contested evidence outweighed its probative value. In other words, testimony about the gang inflamed the jury against respondent, and the chance that he would be convicted by his mere association with the organization outweighed any probative value the testimony may have had on Mills' bias.

Respondent specifically contends that the District Court should not have permitted Ehle's precise description of the gang as a lying and murderous group. Respondent suggests that the District Court should have cut off the testimony after the prosecutor had elicited that Mills knew respondent and both may have belonged to an organization together. This argument ignores the fact that the *type* of organization in which a witness and a party share membership may be relevant to show bias. If the organization is a loosely knit group having nothing to do with the subject matter of the litigation, the inference of bias arising from common membership may be small or nonexistent. If the prosecutor had elicited that both respondent and Mills belonged to the Book of the Month Club, the jury probably would not have inferred bias even if the District Court had admitted the testimony. The attributes of the Aryan Brotherhood — a secret prison sect sworn to perjury and self-protection — bore directly not only on the *fact* of bias but also on the *source* and *strength* of Mills' bias. The tenets of this group showed that Mills had a powerful motive to slant his testimony towards respondent, or even commit perjury outright.

A district court is accorded a wide discretion in determining the admissibility of evidence under the Federal Rules. Assessing the probative value of common membership in any particular group, and weighing any factors counseling against admissibility is a matter first for the district court's sound judgment under Rules 401 and 403 and ultimately, if the evidence is admitted, for the trier of fact.

[The] precautions [employed by the trial judge] did not prevent *all* prejudice to respondent from Ehle's testimony, but they did in our opinion ensure that the admission of this highly probative evidence did not *unduly* prejudice respondent.

The judgment of the Court of Appeals is reversed.

NOTES AND QUESTIONS

(1) *Is Evidence of Bias Permitted if it Violates Rule 610?* As a general proposition, evidence of religious beliefs of a witness is not admissible to credit or discredit a witness. *See* Fed. R. Evid. 610; *Government of Virgin Islands v. Petersen*, 553 F.2d 324 (3d Cir. 1977) (also raising relationship between defendant's religious beliefs in nonviolence, in this murder case, and good character testimony allowed by Fed. R. Evid. 404(a)(1) and Fed. R. Evid. 405(a)). What if the "Aryan Brotherhood" in *Abel* were a religious cult and the pledge made amongst its members were an article of faith. Would Fed. R. Evid. 610 affect this case? What would it take to show that the Brotherhood was a religious cult and the pledge an article of faith? *Compare State v. Heinz*, 485 A.2d 1321 (Conn. App. Ct. 1984), in which the court held defendant should have been allowed to cross-examine concerning religious beliefs of a witness whom the state called as an expert on community standards in defendant's pornography prosecution. The witness belonged to an antipornography organization called Connecticut Citizens for Decency and an antismut group called the Blue Berets, who believed they received messages from the Virgin Mary through polaroid photographs and through trances of a housewife in Bayside, New York, where the group conducted vigils before a styrofoam statue. The right to confrontation was implicated, the court said. Would such cross-examination be permissible under Fed. R. Evid. 610?

(2) *Bias Versus Propensity.* Did the Court make a mistake in not deeming the showing in *Abel* to be a variety of propensity reasoning, and thus prohibited except as allowed by Fed. R. Evid. 608 and Fed. R. Evid. 609?

(3) *Is a Witness from Another Country Biased by the Tenets of its Legal System? Williams v. United States*, 696 A.2d 1085 (D.C. 1997), held that defendant was not entitled to cross-examine the complaining witness, who was visiting the United States from Austria, a country in which a person accused of crime allegedly is guilty until proven innocent, regarding her attitudes as to presumption of innocence. Did it make a difference that her identification of the defendant in a photo array occurred before the defendant was accused of the crime?

(4) *What Foundation is Necessary Before Admitting Extrinsic Evidence of Bias?* In *United States v. Harvey*, 547 F.2d 720 (2d Cir. 1976), the sole identification witness at the defendant's trial for bank robbery was a Priscilla Martin, who testified that on the afternoon of April 22, while passing by on a bus, she observed a man she identified as appellant (defendant) at the bank. Mrs. Martin had been acquainted with appellant for a number of years and had lived in the same house with him. On cross-examination, defense counsel questioned Mrs. Martin as to whether she ever accused appellant of fathering her child and then failing to support this child. Mrs. Martin denied these charges and further denied that appellant visited her in the hospital after the birth of the child. Mrs. Martin also

denied that she confided in appellant's mother, Mrs. Catherine Harvey, that appellant was the father of the child or that she stated that she would "take revenge" on appellant for not "owning up" to this child.

Following Mrs. Martin's testimony, appellant sought to introduce testimony of Mrs. Harvey that Mrs. Martin accused appellant of fathering her child and refusing to support it and that Mrs. Martin further explained that when her husband learned of this he beat her and broke her leg, necessitating the hospital treatment. The trial judge refused this proffer of testimony, considering it "collateral" and inadmissible under Fed. R. Evid. 613(b). The Appeals Court disagreed:

> This Circuit follows the rule, applicable in a number of other circuits, that a proper foundation must be laid before extrinsic evidence of bias may be introduced. Prior to the proffer of extrinsic evidence, a witness must be provided an opportunity to explain the circumstances suggesting bias. In cross-examination of Mrs. Martin, defense counsel clearly asked her whether she had ever accused defendant of fathering her child, whether she had ever stated she would "take revenge" on the defendant and whether she had confided in Mrs. Harvey that defendant was the father of her child. To each of the questions, Mrs. Martin answered no. Thus, on at least three occasions, the witness was afforded an opportunity to explain or deny circumstances suggesting prejudice. Since Mrs. Harvey would have testified that all statements heard by her were made at the same identifiable time and identified place, the reference to Mrs. Harvey as the other party to the conversation should have obviated any surprise to the government as to the when and where of the proffered testimony.
>
> Although the scope of a defendant's right to introduce evidence of bias is not limitless, and may be restricted as the trial court in its sound discretion deems proper, it is rarely proper to cut off completely a probative inquiry that bears on a feasible defense.
>
> The right to "place the witness in his proper setting and put the weight of his testimony and his credibility to a test" is an essential safeguard to a fair trial. *Alford v. United States*, 282 U.S. 687 (1931).

Does this decision mean that the court feels that a *Queen's Case* type of foundation applies to impeachment by means of showing bias? Some variety of that kind of impeachment? What variety? What does the fact the Federal Rules of Evidence are silent about foundation in the case of bias, but not in the case of prior inconsistent statement, mean? Federal courts differ on whether and when a foundation of this type is required for showings of bias.

(5) *Instructions on Bias.* A variety of jury instructions commonly are given covering various kinds of witnesses who might have a bias: instructions that the criminal defendant or other party who testifies is to be judged like any other witness, but the jury may consider his interest in the case; that special scrutiny should be given to the testimony of accomplices and caution exercised in accepting or convicting on such if it is uncorroborated; that certain factors should be considered in evaluating testimony of immunized witnesses, informers, or addicts; and that police officers should not be given any more or less credence than others.

As with the more general instructions, and indeed all instructions, the exact wording the judge will adopt is of great concern to the lawyers in a particular case, because it can emphasize and de-emphasize certain factors and can be more fact-specific or less. The wording (as well as whether or not an instruction will be given at all) varies from case to case, and as in the case of all instructions, these matters are fought out between the lawyers and the judge in chambers, with the lawyers submitting written requests for particular instructions. The judge rules on them, and objections are taken for appellate review.

(6) *Evidence of Bias may be Constitutionally Required to be Admitted Even if it Violates Other Rules. Davis v. Alaska*, 415 U.S. 308 (1974), is a key case concerning a criminal defendant's right of confrontation concerning bias, even where it conflicts with prohibitions such as that on the impeachment of a witness by juvenile convictions. Chief Justice Burger wrote the opinion reversing the defendant's conviction:

> We granted certiorari in this case [involving robbery of the "Polar Bar" and stealing of its safe] to consider whether the Confrontation Clause requires that a defendant in a criminal case be allowed to impeach the credibility of a prosecution witness by cross-examination directed at possible bias deriving from the witness' probationary status as a juvenile delinquent when such an impeachment would conflict with a State's asserted interest in preserving the confidentiality of juvenile adjudications of delinquency.
>
> Richard Green was a crucial witness for the prosecution. At the time of the trial and at the time of the events Green testified to, Green was on probation by order of a juvenile court after having been adjudicated a delinquent for burglarizing two cabins. Green was 16 years of age at the time of the Polar Bar burglary, but had turned 17 prior to trial.
>
> [P]etitioner's counsel made it clear that he would not introduce Green's juvenile adjudication as a general impeachment of Green's character as a truthful person but, rather, to show specifically that at the same time Green was assisting the police in identifying petitioner he was on probation for burglary. From this petitioner would seek to show — or at least argue — that Green acted out of fear or concern of possible jeopardy to his probation. Not only might Green have made a hasty and faulty identification of petitioner to shift suspicion away from himself as one who robbed the Polar Bar, but Green might have been subject to undue pressure from the police and made his identifications under fear of possible probation revocation.
>
> The trial court granted the motion for a protective order.
>
> Although prevented from revealing that Green had been on probation, counsel for petitioner did his best to expose Green's state of mind. Green denied that he was upset or uncomfortable about the discovery of the safe. He claimed not to have been worried about any suspicions the police might have been expected to harbor against him, though Green did admit that it

crossed his mind that the police might have thought he had something to do with the crime.

[As to his being questioned by police about the safe found near his home, Green was asked by defense counsel if he'd ever been questioned like that before, and denied it. Objection was sustained to going further.]

The Sixth Amendment to the Constitution guarantees the right of an accused in a criminal prosecution "to be confronted with the witnesses against him."

Cross-examination is the principal means by which the believability of a witness and the truth of his testimony are tested. Subject always to the broad discretion of a trial judge to preclude repetitive and unduly harassing interrogation, the cross-examiner is not only permitted to delve into the witness' story to test the witness' perceptions and memory, but the cross-examiner has traditionally been allowed to impeach, i.e., discredit, the witness. One way of discrediting the witness is to introduce evidence of a prior criminal conviction of that witness. By so doing the cross-examiner intends to afford the jury a basis to infer that the witness' character is such that he would be less likely than the average trustworthy citizen to be truthful in his testimony. The introduction of evidence of a prior crime is thus a general attack on the credibility of the witness. A more particular attack on the witness' credibility is affected by means of cross-examination directed toward revealing possible biases, prejudices, or ulterior motives of the witness as they may relate directly to issues or personalities in the case at hand. We have recognized that the exposure of a witness' motivation in testifying is a proper and important function of the constitutionally protected right of cross-examination.

We cannot speculate as to whether the jury, as sole judge of the credibility of a witness, would have accepted [defense counsel's] line of reasoning. But we do conclude that the jurors were entitled to have the benefit of the defense theory before them so that they could make an informed judgment as to the weight [of] "a crucial link in the proof of petitioner's act." [Counsel should have been allowed to show] a basis for an inference of undue pressure because of Green's vulnerable status as a probationer, as well as of Green's possible concern that he might be a suspect in the investigation.

We cannot accept the Alaska Supreme Court's conclusion that the cross-examination that was permitted defense counsel was adequate to develop the issue of bias properly to the jury.

The State argues that exposure of a juvenile's record of delinquency would likely cause impairment of rehabilitative goals of the juvenile correctional procedures. [Indeed, the request for the protective order and its granting was based on an Alaska statute granting such protection.]

In this setting we conclude that the right of confrontation is paramount to the State's policy of protecting a juvenile offender. Whatever temporary embarrassment might result to Green or his family by disclosure of his

> juvenile record — if the prosecution insisted on using him to make its case — is outweighed by petitioner's right to probe into the influence of possible bias in the testimony of a crucial identification witness.

Note: Fed. R. Evid. 609(d) contains a restriction on using juvenile adjudications somewhat similar to that overridden by the Court in *Davis*. Would it also have been overridden? Does 609 apply to bias, or to another type of impeachment?

(7) *Possible Limits on Davis*. Would *Davis* have ruled the same if the testimony being impeached had not been such a "crucial link"? If Green had no conceivable involvement in the crime? If the State's jurisdiction over him had ended? If the evidence was offered other than on cross-examination? Are there implications in the case suggesting a right to introduce important defense evidence *other* than impeachment?

§ 4.08 MISCONDUCT NOT RESULTING IN CONVICTION[11]

Read Federal Rule of Evidence 608(b), "A Witness's Character for Truthfulness or Untruthfulness": "Specific Instances of Conduct"

CARTER v. HEWITT

United States Court of Appeals, Third Circuit
617 F.2d 961 (1980)

[The detailed facts of this case appear in the portion of the opinion excerpted in § 2.01 *supra*. The defendant offered a letter purportedly written by the plaintiff that could be used to infer that the plaintiff had fabricated the claim that he had been beaten. This portion of the opinion deals with the admissibility of the letter, set forth there, for impeachment of the letter writer's testimony under Fed. R. Evid. 608.]

The Magistrate and the district court found the letter admissible in part because it bore on Carter's credibility in testifying that he had suffered a beating at the hands of the defendants. Carter claims this use of the letter violates the limitations on [extrinsic evidence of] impeachment set forth in Fed. R. Evid. 608(b). We disagree.

The principal concern of the rule is to prohibit impeachment of a witness through extrinsic evidence of his bad acts when this evidence is to be introduced by calling other witnesses to testify. Thus, Weinstein and Berger describe the extrinsic evidence ban as follows:

> Courts often summarize the no extrinsic evidence rule by stating that "the examiner must take his [the witness's] answer." This phrase is descriptive of federal practice in the sense that the cross-examiner cannot call other witnesses to prove the misconduct after the witness' denial; it is misleading insofar as it suggests that the cross-examiner cannot continue pressing for an admission — a procedure specifically authorized by the

---

[11] Study Guide Reference: Evidence in a Nutshell, Chapter 4:IX, at "Impeachment by Non-Convicted for Misconduct 'Probative of Untruthfulness': F.R.E. 608(b)," and at "Character or Propensity for Incredibility of Victim and Perpetrator in Sex Cases."

second sentence of Rule 608(b). J. Weinstein & M. Berger, Weinstein's Evidence ¶ 608[05], at 608-22 (1978) (footnote omitted).

Similarly, McCormick writes:

> In jurisdictions which permit character-impeachment by proof of misconduct for which no conviction has been had, an important curb is the accepted rule that proof is limited to what can be brought out on cross-examination. Thus, if the witness stands his ground and denies the alleged misconduct, the examiner must "take his answer," not that he may not further cross-examine to extract an admission, but in the sense that he may not call other witnesses to prove the discrediting acts. E. Cleary, McCormick on Evidence § 42, at 84 (2d ed. 1972) (footnotes omitted).

Thus, the great majority of the decisions finding violations of rule 608(b) do so when the extrinsic evidence that is challenged is obtained from a witness other than the one whose credibility is under attack. When, however, the extrinsic evidence is obtained from and through examination of the very witness whose credibility is under attack, as is the case here, we must recognize that the rule's core concerns are not implicated. There is, however, an even more significant reason for finding no violation of the extrinsic evidence rule here: Carter did not deny having written the letter; rather, he conceded his authorship but claimed that the letter was not an effort to encourage the filing of false complaints.

Carter's adoption of the letter, and thus his admission of the act used to impeach him, distinguishes this case from every case where the witness, whose credibility is under attack, has denied the evidence which had been obtained from or through him, thus leading to a holding that the extrinsic evidence rule has been violated. In those cases, the witness has denied, rather than admitted, the acts used to impeach him. The impeachment process thus would have required the examiner to produce additional evidence to refute the witness's denial of the acts charged. Such a process makes apparent the basis for the rule against extrinsic evidence: if refutation of a witness's denial were permitted through extrinsic evidence, these collateral matters would assume a prominence at trial out of proportion to their significance. In such cases, then, extrinsic evidence may not be used to refute the denial, even if this evidence might be obtained from the very witness sought to be impeached. But, as we have observed, Carter's case does not present such a situation.

The impeaching letter with which Carter was confronted was not met by a denial of his authorship. Carter's admission that he wrote the letter distinguishes this case from all cases relied on by him. Carter relies especially heavily on *United States v. Herzberg*, 558 F.2d 1219 (5th Cir.), *cert. denied*, 434 U.S. 930 (1977). In *Herzberg*, two defendants were convicted of using the mails in a scheme to defraud. On cross-examination, the prosecutor asked one of the defendants, Barnes, if any fraud litigation had arisen out of a business relationship he had had with a Mrs. Vosack. In response to Barnes's denial, the prosecutor showed Barnes the opinion of the Arizona Supreme Court in a suit brought by Mrs. Vosack against him and others, and asked him to read aloud the last sentence of the opinion. This sentence revealed that the court was affirming a decision below that Barnes had defrauded Vosack. The court held that this line of questioning violated the extrinsic evidence ban of rule 608(b). 558 F.2d at 1222-23.

Thus, the *Herzberg* court found rule 608(b) violated only when the evidence was introduced after Barnes denied his bad act. Every other case in which the extrinsic evidence ban has been found violated by evidence brought forth during cross-examination of the witness under attack likewise fits this pattern. In each case, the extrinsic evidence was employed after a denial by the witness under attack of the specific instances of conduct. *See, e.g., United States v. Turquitt*, 557 F.2d 464 (5th Cir. 1977); *United States v. Dinitz*, 538 F.2d 1214 (5th Cir. 1976), *cert. denied*, 429 U.S. 1104 (1977); *Carlsen v. Javurek*, 526 F.2d 202 (8th Cir. 1975).

The sole case analogous to this one, i.e., in which the challenged witness did not clearly deny the alleged instances of conduct, found no violation of rule 608(b) when documentary proof of those instances was introduced during questioning of the witness. In *United States v. Senak*, 527 F.2d 129 (7th Cir. 1975), *cert. denied*, 425 U.S. 907 (1976), an attorney was charged with unlawfully soliciting payment from clients whom he had been assigned to represent in his position of public defender. On cross-examination, the prosecution asked Senak whether he had reported a certain fee on his income tax return. He responded that, if his return did not disclose the fee, then it was solely through neglect rather than intentional wrongdoing. The prosecution then introduced into evidence Senak's IRS records, which revealed that the fee had not been reported.

Senak claimed that this cross-examination violated rule 608(b), but his contention was rejected. While the court's reasoning is not perfectly clear, it concludes that the introduction of the records did not constitute proof of specific instances of conduct through extrinsic evidence, but merely inquiry into such conduct on cross-examination, which is permitted by the rule. *See* 527 F.2d at 145. Thus, no violation of rule 608(b) was found even though the IRS records were utilized and admitted as extrinsic evidence.

The distinction noted here between our case and those cases in which the extrinsic evidence ban was found to be violated by evidence brought forth during cross-examination of the witness under attack — that Carter admitted the conduct charged while all other witnesses denied it — provides a sound basis for allowing admission of Carter's letter. The purpose of rule 608(b)'s extrinsic evidence ban, as noted, is "to avoid minitrials on wholly collateral matters which tend to distract and confuse the jury." *United States v. Simmons*, 444 F. Supp. 500, 507 (E.D.Pa. 1978) [*aff'd on other grounds*, 591 F.2d 206 (3d Cir. 1979)]. Wigmore similarly describes the rationale behind the common law ban on extrinsic evidence: to prevent confusion of issues through proliferation of testimony on minor matters; and to prevent unfair surprise arising from false allegations of improper conduct. 3A Wigmore on Evidence § 979, at 826-27 (Chadbourn rev. ed. 1970). These reasons for barring extrinsic evidence lose their force when the witness whose credibility is challenged concedes the alleged acts. No issues are confused or time wasted through a trial of a collateral matter: no trial is needed since the matter is conceded. The trial judge may exercise control over the degree to which the conceded matters are explored through his power to bar irrelevant or cumulative evidence. Fed. R. Evid. 402, 403. Nor is there any danger of unfair surprise through false charges of bad conduct. If the witness concedes the matter, we may be confident that the charges were not false.

Thus, there is no need in such a case to invoke rule 608(b)'s ban on extrinsic evidence, particularly where, as here, credibility is the critical issue.**[11]** We conclude, then, that the use of Carter's letter for impeachment purposes on cross-examination, and its admission, did not offend rule 608(b). [The court also held that Fed. R. Evid. 403, though applicable to evidence allowed under Fed. R. Evid. 608(b), should not, on the particular facts, keep this evidence out. Fed. R. Evid. 404 also was rejected as a grounds for its exclusion.]

[Judgment against Carter affirmed.]

NOTES AND QUESTIONS

(1) *Contradiction is Not a Way Around the Extrinsic Evidence Ban. United States v. Perez-Perez*, 72 F.3d 224 (1st Cir. 1995): The defense claimed it had been erroneously prohibited from offering testimony to impeach the credibility of a government witness, officer Ricardo Nieves Lopez. During cross-examination, Nieves conceded that fellow police officers had accused him of various incidents of misconduct. Nieves maintained that these allegations were baseless and had been made only to retaliate for his testimony in Perez's previous trial. The defense called an officer Hernandez to elicit testimony that Nieves had engaged in the alleged misconduct. In affirming the exclusion, the court explained:

> The notion underlying [Fed. R. Evid. 608(b)] is that while certain prior good or bad acts of a witness may constitute character evidence bearing on veracity, they are not evidence of enough force to justify the detour of extrinsic proof. Thus, Rule 608(b) barred Hernandez' testimony insofar as it was offered to show that Nieves had a propensity to lie. Of course, Hernandez' testimony would not only have suggested that Nieves was of bad character but would also have contradicted Nieves' own denials on the witness stand. Impeachment by contradiction is a recognized mode of impeachment not governed by Rule 608(b), but by common-law principles. But, again largely for reasons of efficiency, extrinsic evidence to impeach is only admissible for contradiction where the prior testimony being contradicted was itself material to the case at hand. Here, Nieves' alleged misconduct was not material to Perez' guilt or innocence.

(2) *Which Rule Applies — Bias or Rule 608(b)?* In *United States v. Calvert*, 523 F.2d 895 (8th Cir. 1975), *cert. denied*, 424 U.S. 911 (1976), appellant complained he was cut short in cross-examining the government's chief witness (the alleged front man of defendant) as to the witness's previous (apparently not prosecuted) violation of the Mann Act (interstate transportation of women for immoral purposes) and as to his separate arrest for child molestation. Appellant's theory was that these were relevant to the possibility of inducements to the witness and to whether it was likely that defendant would use such a person as a front man. The appellate court felt the matters had been adequately explored, because the trial court had allowed the defense to ask the witness whether there had been any inducements, such as immunity, and to ask the witness and defendant whether defendant was told of the witness's record of such offenses and whether the witness had a reputation for them, and therefore the appellate court upheld the trial court on all scores.

Query: Would Fed. R. Evid. 608(b) (with its limitations concerning the nature of the crime and extrinsic evidence) cover this? Or is this in the category of bias? Does it, in this case, make any difference? Would it if defendant had attempted to introduce extrinsic evidence of the derelictions and the court felt that the other questioning did not adequately cover the matter?

(3) *If the Evidence is Otherwise Admissible to Show Bias, it Doesn't Matter that it would be Inadmissible Under Rule 608(b).* See the Supreme Court's decision in *United States v. Abel*, excerpted in § 4.07. In a portion of the decision omitted from the excerpt in § 4.07, the Court dealt with the defendant's claim that the impeachment in the case should not be classed as bias, but rather as misconduct of the kind dealt with by Fed. R. Evid. 608(b), and thus should have been restricted as provided in that Rule. That portion of the decision follows:

> Respondent makes an additional argument based on Rule 608(b). That Rule allows a cross-examiner to impeach a witness by asking him about specific instances of past conduct, other than crimes covered by Rule 609, which are probative of his veracity or "character for truthfulness or untruthfulness." The Rule limits the inquiry to cross-examination of the witness, however, and prohibits the cross-examiner from introducing extrinsic evidence of the witness' past conduct.
>
> Respondent claims that the prosecutor cross-examined Mills about the gang not to show bias but to offer Mills' membership in the gang as past conduct bearing on his veracity. This was error under Rule 608(b), respondent contends, because the mere fact of Mills' membership, without more, was not sufficiently probative of Mills' character for truthfulness. Respondent cites a second error under the same Rule, contending that Ehle's rebuttal testimony concerning the gang was extrinsic evidence offered to impugn Mills' veracity, and extrinsic evidence is barred by Rule 608(b).
>
> The Court of Appeals appears to have accepted respondent's argument to this effect, at least in part. It said:
>
> > Ehle's testimony was not simply a matter of showing that Abel's and Mills' membership in the same organization might "cause [Mills], consciously or otherwise, to color his testimony." Rather it was to show as well that because Mills and Abel were members of a gang whose members "will lie to protect the members," Mills must be lying on the stand.
>
> It seems clear to us that the proffered testimony with respect to Mills' membership in the Aryan Brotherhood sufficed to show potential bias in favor of respondent; because of the tenets of the organization described, it might also impeach his veracity directly. But there is no rule of evidence which provides that testimony admissible for one purpose and inadmissible for another purpose is thereby rendered inadmissible; quite the contrary is the case. It would be a strange rule of law which held that relevant, competent evidence which tended to show bias on the part of a witness was

> nonetheless inadmissible because it also tended to show that the witness was a liar.
>
> We intimate no view as to whether the evidence of Mills' membership in an organization having the tenets ascribed to the Aryan Brotherhood would be a specific instance of Mills' conduct which could not be proved against him by extrinsic evidence except as otherwise provided in Rule 608(b). It was enough that such evidence could properly be found admissible to show bias.

(4) *Liberal Interpretation of Bias.* See also *United States v. Ray*, 731 F.2d 1361 (9th Cir. 1984), holding that Fed. R. Evid. 608(b) does not bar introduction of evidence to show a witness is biased; instead it regulates only the admissibility of evidence offered to prove the truthful or untruthful character of a witness. Thus, the rule should not have been used to prevent a narcotics defendant from showing the bias of a former codefendant, who turned government witness pursuant to a plea agreement, by cross-examining him on his post-plea drug dealings. On what theory would they be relevant to bias?

(5) *Evidence of Bias that Involves Wrongdoing Sometimes can be Barred by Rule 403.* In *State v. Lovato*, 580 P.2d 138 (N.M. Ct. App.), *cert. denied*, 580 P.2d 972 (1978), the defendant was convicted of second degree murder. His appeal involved evidence of the motive of a witness, Patricia Duran, who lived with defendant from March 1974 until July 1976. The killing occurred in June 1975. In October 1976, Duran informed the Crime Stoppers Program in Albuquerque that defendant did the killing. The defendant was permitted to cross-examine Duran concerning specific instances of conduct for the purpose of attacking her credibility and sought, but was not permitted, to cross-examine her concerning some additional conduct and to introduce the testimony of two witnesses concerning it. In affirming the conviction, the court observed:

> Defendant was correct in urging that he could cross-examine the witness as to a motive to testify falsely and could introduce extrinsic evidence which showed such a motive. Yet, if the asserted motive evidence was in fact no more than evidence of character and conduct attacking the credibility of the witness, its admissibility would be governed by Evidence Rule 608. The distinction between evidence which shows motive and evidence which shows no more than character and conduct will often be difficult to draw. Our holding is based on the assumption that defendant's proffered evidence was in fact evidence of Duran's motive to testify falsely.
>
> Defendant's tendered cross-examination of Duran was that she had been addicted to heroin in July, 1976, that she returned to New Mexico in early September, 1976, and that she denied using heroin from the time of her return through January, 1977. The tendered extrinsic evidence was that Duran sought to purchase heroin four times — in September, 1976, in the fall of 1976 and twice in January, 1977. Defendant asserts this tendered testimony would show that Duran was a heroin user who needed money to support her habit and turned defendant in for money.

[Duran had testified that she was paid $1000 by the Crime Stoppers Program for her signed written statement and grand jury testimony and expected to receive an additional $1000 if, after testifying at the trial, a conviction resulted.]

Assuming, but not deciding, that defendant's contention had a sufficient factual basis in the tendered testimony, it was not error to exclude it. There was other evidence before the jury showing that money motivated Duran's report and testimony that defendant committed the crime. The killing was in July, 1975. Duran did not report the killing until seeing a newspaper article in October, 1976 which informed the reader that Crime Stoppers was offering a monetary reward in connection with the killing. Two to four days after the newspaper article appeared, Duran contacted Crime Stoppers. Duran testified that she telephoned because she wanted to "get into the Crime Stoppers program." Duran testified as to the monetary reward received and expected. Testimony as to Duran's purported heroin use would not have added to the testimony, already before the jury, that Duran was motivated by money.

The trial court, in its discretion, could properly exclude the tendered testimony which was cumulative. Evidence Rule 403.

PROBLEM 4A BASED ON NONCONVICTION MISCONDUCT IN UNITED STATES v. AMAECHI, 991 F.2d 374 (7th Cir. 1993).

Defendant appealed his conviction for importing heroin by attacking the admission of evidence under Fed. R. Evid. 608(b). The court affirmed:

[T]he district judge permitted the United States to impeach Amaechi with misrepresentations he made on various immigration forms and tax returns. Federal Rule of Evidence 608(b) permits a litigant to bring out specific instances of the conduct of a witness to attack his credibility. [D]efendant put his own credibility in issue by taking the stand, offering a series of character witnesses, and mounting a defense that he was framed. Having put his character in issue, a defendant may be cross-examined about instances of untruthfulness. In this case, the government introduced no extrinsic evidence of Amaechi's false or fraudulent immigration or tax forms. The prosecutor accepted Amaechi's answers without introducing extrinsic evidence; indeed the prosecutor did not need such evidence because defendant admitted that the forms were false.

Questions: (1) How well does the court of appeals' opinion follow Fed. R. Evid. 608(b)? (2) What circumstances enable a party, under the Rule, to impeach a witness with misconduct not resulting in a conviction? The court says specific instances of untruthfulness can be used to impeach credibility when defendant has "put his character in issue"; is this analysis accurate? (3) The court implies that the defendant may invite misconduct not resulting in a conviction by raising any of a broad array of defensive issues, including "mounting a defense that he was framed." Under the Rule, is this accurate? (4) The court recognizes that the prosecutor could not have offered extrinsic evidence of the misconduct but points out that defendant admitted it. What could have been done under the Rule if he had denied it? (5)

Overall, however, the court's affirmance may be consistent with the Rule, even if one critiques its reasoning. Why?

§ 4.09 CONVICTIONS[12]

Read Federal Rule of Evidence 609, "Impeachment by Evidence of a Criminal Conviction."

HISTORICAL NOTE

(1) *Historic Note Concerning Luck Case.* In *Luck v. United States*, 348 F.2d 763 (D.C. Cir. 1965), the defendant, who was on trial for housebreaking and larceny, and testified in his own behalf, was impeached by questions regarding a prior plea of guilty to grand larceny. The court next to the District of Columbia code provision governing impeachment use of ordinary convictions and, by a process of construction centering on the words "may be admitted" rather than "shall," found that it permitted, as a discretionary matter, the admission of such evidence, upon a weighing of probative value against prejudice (including the impermissible tendency of the jury to believe that because he committed the earlier crime, he probably committed, or should be punished for, the present one). The court further stated:

> In exercising discretion in this respect, a number of factors might be relevant, such as the nature of the prior crimes, the length of the criminal record, the age and circumstances of the defendant, and, above all, the extent to which it is more important to the search for truth in a particular case for the jury to hear the defendant's story than to know of a prior conviction. . . . The possibility of a rehearsal of the defendant's criminal record in a given case, especially if it means that [the defendant may then invoke his self-incrimination privilege and opt not to testify, and thus that] the jury will be left without one version of the truth, may or may not contribute to that objective. The experienced trial judge has a sensitivity in this regard which normally can be relied upon to strike a reasonable balance between the interests of the defendant and of the public. We think Congress has left room for that discretion to operate.

Compare the *Luck* rule (whose equivalent still applies in some states and was incorporated in part in Fed. R. Evid. 609) *with* Fed. R. Evid. 609.

The issue posed by *Luck* and its overruling (concerning judicial discretion) in the 1970 congressional amendment of the D.C. code was the most hotly contested issue in the congressional debates in 1973-74 over whether to adopt the Federal Rules of Evidence and what they should provide. (It also has been a burning issue in state evidence codification.) The final outcome, current Fed. R. Evid. 609, is an evident compromise.

A number of positions were considered by Congress, including a position that

---

[12] Study Guide Reference: Evidence in a Nutshell, Chapter 4:IX at "Character Impeachment by Criminal Convictions: F.R.E. 609" (including subsections).

admits the two classes of convictions recognized in Fed. R. Evid. 609 but with a weighing and balancing provision applicable to both categories; permitting *only* crimes of dishonesty and false statement (either (a) absolutely, or (b) subject to a weighing power); permitting only crimes of dishonesty or false statement that also are punishable by a year or more imprisonment (with or without the balancing power); etc. In California and Texas, convictions must be for crimes of moral turpitude.

(2) *Jury Instructions.* At least in criminal cases where the defendant-as-witness is being impeached under Fed. R. Evid. 609, a limiting jury instruction normally should be sought by the defense because of the potential misuse by the jury of this type of impeachment evidence as propensity evidence indicating that the defendant was more likely to commit the current crime. The jury is generally told that:

> Evidence of a defendant's previous conviction of a felony is to be considered by the jury only insofar as it may affect the credibility of the defendant as a witness, and must never be considered as evidence of guilt of the crime for which the defendant is on trial.

UNITED STATES v. SMITH

United States Court of Appeals, D.C. Circuit
551 F.2d 348 (1976)

McGowan, Circuit Judge

[This was one of the first decisions to be required to distinguish between the *Luck* standard and the then newly enacted Fed. R. Evid. 609. Smith appealed from a conviction for armed bank robbery, trial of which began 17 days after the Rules became effective. The trial judge ruled that if defendant Gartrell chose to testify, his prior attempted robbery conviction could be used by the government to impeach him. The Court of Appeals judge who had previously written *Luck* here remands this case as to Gartrell.]

Gartrell's claim in this regard presents difficulty, because the controlling relevance of Rule 609 was unrecognized at trial. In the colloquy of record about admissibility, the Rule was never mentioned by the prosecution, the defense, or the court. The district judge seems to have decided to permit use of Gartrell's prior conviction by reference to earlier law in this Circuit. *See Luck v. United States*, 348 F.2d 763 (1965). This was error.

Despite substantial surface similarity, the inquiry to be conducted by the trial court under Rule 609(a) differs significantly from that mandated by *Luck* and its progeny. Adherence to the proper standard by the District Court might have produced a different ruling on the impeachment question. Rule 609 has been designed to work important changes in the approach of federal courts to the problems of impeachment by prior conviction:

> (i) Evidence of some prior convictions (i.e., convictions for crimes involving dishonesty or false statement) is now automatically admissible for the

> purpose of attacking the credibility of a witness. With respect to these convictions, trial courts are no longer free to exercise the discretion they enjoyed under *Luck*. Congress has substituted its judgment that evidence of such crimes is always sufficiently related to credibility to justify its admission, regardless of possible prejudice to the defendant.
>
> * * *
>
> (iii) Crucial for present purposes, the language of Rule 609(a)(1), as enacted, manifests an intent to shift the burden of persuasion with respect to admission of prior conviction evidence for impeachment [of the criminal defendant]. *Luck* held that such evidence could be excluded "where the trial judge believes the prejudicial effect of impeachment far outweighs the probative relevance of the prior conviction to the issue of credibility." *Gordon* reiterated this test, and emphasized that "[t]he burden of persuasion in this regard is on the accused. . . . The underlying assumption [of *Luck*] was that prior convictions would ordinarily be admissible unless this burden is met." 383 F.2d at 939. The prosecution now must bear the burden of establishing that prior conviction evidence should be admitted.

The Government has contended that Gartrell's earlier crime, attempted robbery, involved "dishonesty or false statement," as that phrase is used in the Federal Rules of Evidence. If this contention were accurate, the Government would be correct in its conclusion that Rule 609(a)(2) provides for the automatic admissibility of evidence of Gartrell's prior conviction. The District Court's decision could be upheld, even though rendered without reference to the newly-applicable Rules. However, the Government has misconstrued the language in question, partially through a misplaced reliance on comments of this court in cases decided under *Luck*. Attempted robbery is not a crime involving "dishonesty or false statement" within the meaning of Rule 609(a)(2). If Gartrell's prior conviction is to be admitted at all, it must be admitted only after the court makes the determination prescribed in Rule 609(a)(1).

The Conference Committee Report fully supports this position:

> By the phrase "dishonesty and false statement" the Conference means crimes such as perjury or subornation of perjury, false statement, criminal fraud, embezzlement, or false pretense, or any other offense in the nature of crimen falsi, the commission of which involves some element of deceit, untruthfulness, or falsification bearing on the accused's propensity to testify truthfully. H.R. Conf. Rep. No. 93-1597 93d Cong. 2d Sess. 9, reprinted in [1974] U.S. Code Cong. & Admin. News, pp. 7098, 7103.

Congress clearly intended the phrase to denote a fairly narrow subset of criminal activity. Moreover, research into the derivation of the term "crimen falsi" indicates that Congress's restrictive construction comports with historical practice. While commentators have uncovered some divergence between civil and common law usage, the expression has never been thought to comprehend robbery or other crimes involving force. Even in its broadest sense, the term "crimen falsi" has encompassed only those crimes characterized by an element of deceit or deliberate interference with a court's ascertainment of truth.

[The court cites some cases under Fed. R. Evid. 609(a)(2) holding that larceny, assault, possession of an unlicensed gun, and narcotics offenses do not qualify; but also citing a case to the contrary regarding larceny; one that was uncertain about robbery; and one that suggests the facts need to be looked to.]

The issue under Rule 609(a)(2) is entirely different from that confronted by this court in cases descendant from *Luck*. The new Rule provides that a prior conviction for a crime involving dishonesty or false statement is automatically admissible for impeachment purposes. With respect to such evidence, the trial court enjoys no discretion. In its Conference Committee Report, Congress has spelled out the meaning of the phrase "dishonesty or false statement" as it is used in Rule 609(a)(2). The Report plainly shows that the set of crimes involving dishonesty or false statement under the Rule is not coterminous with the set of crimes bearing on credibility in the *Luck-Gordon* analysis.

[Remanded.]

UNITED STATES v. ESTES

United States Court of Appeals, Fifth Circuit
994 F.2d 147 (1993)

PER CURIAM.

[Estes was convicted of being a felon in possession of a firearm. The only witness to his possession was Officer Yeager, who had discovered the firearm after he stopped Estes in traffic. Ironically, Yeager, who now was a legitimate public official, had a 12-year-old conviction for impersonating a public official, a misdemeanor under state law. The Government filed a motion *in limine*, which the trial court granted, to prevent defense counsel from mentioning this conviction.]

[Estes] contends that the district court failed to perform the balancing test required by Fed. R. Evid. 609(b) and relied only on the age of the conviction as a basis for excluding the evidence. He contends that this conviction was probative of Yeager's credibility and was critical evidence because the evidence against him came exclusively from Yeager. He argues that the Government has failed to show any danger of prejudice from admission of this evidence. Fed. R. Evid. 609(b) provides that evidence of convictions is not admissible if the conviction is more than ten years old, unless the court determines that the probative value of the conviction substantially outweighs its prejudicial effect.

[T]he district court has broad discretion in its application of this rule; and when made, the weighing of probative value and prejudicial effect must be made on the record [in this Circuit].

We do not know exactly why the court granted the Government's motion *in limine* to exclude Yeager's conviction because it is not a part of the record. Estes asserts that the district court did not apply the required balancing test [on the record,] which would require a remand.

We read Rule 609(b) to say that the probative value of a conviction over ten years old is outweighed by its prejudicial effect. The general rule is inadmissibility. It is only when the court *admits* evidence of a conviction over ten years old that the court must engage in a balancing test on the record.

Finally, we have serious doubt that the conviction was admissible anyway, because it was not the type of conviction allowed to be used for impeachment under Fed. R. Evid. 609. The crime of impersonating a public servant under [applicable state law] is a Class A misdemeanor punishable by no more than one year.

NOTES AND QUESTIONS

(1) *Preserving Error for Appellate Review.* Courts frequently are requested to and do rule on the admissibility of evidence proffered under Fed. R. Evid. 609 before the witness (say the criminal defendant) takes the stand. The request, which may be made by either counsel, and even may be made and ruled on before trial, may be called a motion *in limine* (at the threshold). The criminal defendant, who has a constitutional right not to testify, may need to know in advance in order to make an intelligent decision whether to take the stand. Suppose the advance ruling goes against the criminal defendant, who believes (quite correctly, let us suppose), that the trial judge is wrong. Must the defendant testify in order to preserve the impeachment issue for appeal? In *Luce v. United States*, 469 U.S. 38 (1984), a unanimous Supreme Court held that a defendant must take the stand and suffer the Fed. R. Evid. 609 impeachment in order to raise any issue on appeal concerning the court's ruling. *Luce* viewed the issue as entirely speculative if the defendant did not testify. Many circuits had previously considered it sufficient for the defense to make an offer of proof concerning the testimony so that the court could apply the Fed. R. Evid. 609 balancing test. Query: What could be said in favor of the view of those circuits that would have permitted review?

The Eleventh Circuit has adopted the *Luce* approach for impeachment under Fed. R. Evid. 608(b) as well as Fed. R. Evid. 609. *United States v. DiMatteo*, 759 F.2d 831 (11th Cir.), *cert. denied*, 474 U.S. 860 (1985). Is the problem dealt with in *Luce* a more generalized problem than merely Rule 608 and 609 impeachment? Should it be resolved by a generalized answer?

In *Ohler v. U.S.*, 529 U.S. 753 (2000), the Supreme Court held that a defendant who preemptively introduces evidence of a prior conviction on direct examination (in order to "take the wind out of the sails" of the prosecution, who defendant knows, from an advance ruling by the court, will be allowed to use it), may not claim on appeal that the ruling allowing the admission of such evidence was error. What impact does this have on what defendants will do and the way the jury views the defendant's testimony?

(2) *Does Estes Neglect the "Automatic Admit" Provision at the End of Rule 609(a)?* Fed. R. Evid. 609(a)(2) contains what sometimes is referred to as an "automatic admit" provision: If the crime involved "dishonesty or false statement," it is admissible regardless of punishment. Does the conviction here, for impersonating a public servant, fit this category, and if so, is the court's reasoning undermined? Courts vary as to what crimes fit this category. For example, even willful failure to file a federal income tax return has generated conflicting case law on whether it qualifies. *Compare Cree v. Hatcher*, 969 F.2d 34 (3d Cir. 1992) (no), *with United States v. Wilson*, 985 F.2d 348 (7th Cir. 1993) (yes).

(3) *What is Included in the "Automatic Admit" Provision for Crimes of Dishonesty or False Statement — Not Shoplifting: United States v. Amaechi*, 991 F.2d 374 (7th Cir.), *cert. denied*, 508 U.S. 979 (1993). In this case, the trial court excluded defendant's offer of a shoplifting conviction to impeach a prosecution witness. The court of appeals upheld the exclusion, following the apparently general rule that shoplifting does not involve dishonesty or false statement: "[W]e agree with nine other circuits that to include shoplifting as a crime of dishonesty would swallow the rule and allow any past crime to be used for impeachment purposes." Given that shoplifting is a form of theft, and, in particular, one involving some deceptive conduct, does this holding make sense (is theft "dishonest" within the (narrow) meaning of the Rule)?

(4) *Courtroom Example. United States v. Seamster*, 568 F.2d 188 (10th Cir. 1978), provides an example (not necessarily a model) of Fed. R. Evid. 609 impeachment in an actual trial setting. Defendant was charged with burglary. He testified, denying his involvement. He then was cross-examined as follows:

Q. (By Mr. Price) Are you a convicted felon?

MR. BOURK: Your Honor, we will object to that, [Rule] 609A.

THE COURT: It only goes to the credibility of the witness. Overruled. And I say to the jury, if he has had, it has nothing to do with this, the charge in this case, but it only serves as to the credibility of this witness. You may answer.

A. (The Witness) Yes, sir.

Q. (By Mr. Price) Were you not convicted of the felony of burglary in the second degree by a jury in Lawton, Oklahoma, in which you were represented by counsel on January 15, 1975?

MR. BOURK: Your Honor, we object to this question on the same grounds.

THE COURT: Yes, sustained. You need not go into detail.

Q. (By Mr. Price) Were you not convicted of burglary in the second degree?

THE COURT: Yes, he has answered that; and it only goes, ladies and gentlemen of the jury, to the credibility of this witness' testimony. It has nothing whatsoever to do and you cannot consider it in any way with reference to the charge in this court.

Q. (By Mr. Price) Were you not also convicted in Frederick, Oklahoma on March 4, 1975 of burglary second degree?

MR. BOURK: Your Honor, we object to the question and ask that the answer not be given under 609A.

THE COURT: Overruled.

A. (The Witness) Yes.

MR. PRICE: No further questions.

PROBLEM 4B: IMPEACHING THE CAREER CRIMINAL UNDER RULE 609.

Your client, Darcy Jones, is on trial for armed robbery. Darcy wishes to testify and present an alibi. Darcy has the following record of prior convictions: assault with intent to commit murder, for which the conviction was fifteen years ago and the release date twelve years ago; vehicular homicide, eleven years ago, release nine years ago; theft, eight years ago, release seven years ago; perjury, six years ago, sentence of probation; armed robbery, five years ago, release two years ago; and burglary, conviction and release simultaneous with the armed robbery conviction. Darcy also wants to corroborate his alibi with the testimony of a friend, Leslie Smith, who has a five-year-old conviction for manslaughter. For each of these convictions, analyze your odds of persuading the judge to exclude it under Fed. R. Evid. 609.

§ 4.10 REPUTATION AND OPINION EVIDENCE OF CHARACTER FOR LACK OF VERACITY[13]

Read Federal Rule of Evidence 608(a), "A Witness's Character for Truthfulness or Untruthfulness.": "Reputation or Opinion Evidence"

OSBORNE v. UNITED STATES

United States Court of Appeals, Eighth Circuit
542 F.2d 1015 (1976)

MARKEY, JUDGE.

Parker and Osborne appeal from their joint conviction by jury of bank robbery.

The government's key witness, Douglas, testified that the defendants discussed with him the possibility of robbing the bank. [Douglas participated in one attempt on the bank, but not the charged robbery.]

Appellants' joint contention centers around the trial court's refusal to allow a defense witness to testify regarding Douglas' reputation for truth and veracity in the community. Appellants argue that Douglas' testimony was crucial to the government's case and that his credibility was open to question. The proffered testimony, according to appellants, would have indicated that Douglas' reputation in the community for truth and veracity was not good.

We, of course, agree with appellants that Fed.R.Evid. 608(a) specifically provides that the credibility of a witness may be attacked by evidence of reputation. We have long recognized that testimony relating to the reputation for truth and veracity in the community of a witness is relevant and therefore admissible. In the broad, general sense of the Rule, therefore, the trial court erred in excluding appellants' proffered testimony. The question remains, however, whether that error was of such

---

[13] Study Guide Reference: Evidence in a Nutshell, Chapter 4:IX at "Character Impeachment by Opinion or Reputation Evidence: F.R.E. 608(a)."

prejudicial nature as to warrant a new trial.

We are convinced that the exclusion was not prejudicial. Douglas himself testified to his implication in the first robbery attempt, to his experimentation with drugs, and to his undesirable discharge from the Army. He further admitted that the United States Attorney's Office would recommend dropping the charge against him for testifying at the trial. Parker effectively corroborated Douglas' testimony regarding his implication in the prior attempt. Thus the excluded testimony could only have been cumulative at best.

During direct examination, Douglas was questioned regarding his whereabouts directly prior to and during the crime. He testified that he picked up his girl friend from work at 1:00 for lunch and returned her to work at 2:00 thereafter picking up his sister from work at 2:20. The robbery occurred at 1:15. Defense counsel characterizes this testimony as a "bolstering" of Douglas' testimony before his credibility had been put into issue.

We have recognized the general rule to be that "until the reputation of a witness for truth and veracity has been assailed by evidence in relation to it, it is not in issue, and that there accordingly exists in such a situation no right to introduce testimony in support of it." The basis for the rule is a legal presumption that witnesses are of good moral character and that, absent evidence to the contrary, no purpose is served in denying evidence of bad character. Fed.R.Evid. 608(a). [T]he Notes of the Advisory Committee on the Proposed Rules are in accord:

> Character evidence in support of credibility is admissible under the rule only after the witness' character has first been attacked, as has been the case at common law.

This rule is inapplicable to the testimony challenged here, however. Establishing the whereabouts of Douglas preceding, during, and after the crime was background evidence relating to the actual robbery. This testimony was relevant to show that while Douglas was initially involved in planning the robbery, he withdrew from the venture and established his complete withdrawal by detailing his activities during the period in which the offense was committed. We hold that it was not error for the trial court to admit testimony which, in this case, detailed Douglas' movements or whereabouts during the robbery.

Affirmed.

§ 4.11 EYEWITNESS TESTIMONY

As reported in *"We're Sorry" A Case of Mistaken Identity*, Time Magazine, Oct. 4, 1982, p. 45, police officers in Columbus responded to a call of someone loitering suspiciously. Inside, police discovered a man wearing a ski mask carrying burglary tools. In the intruder's car, police discovered a list of rape victims. The culprit, surprisingly, was Dr. Edward Jackson. The list of rape victims led police to suspect that they had found the "Grandville Rapist," allegedly responsible for nearly 100 assaults in the area. A grand jury indicted Jackson on a total of 94 separate counts, including multiple rape and burglary charges.

But there was a twist: two of the rapes charged to Dr. Jackson were already "solved." Another man, William Jackson, was in prison serving long sentences for two of the same rapes now attributed to Dr. Jackson. William Jackson had been convicted after two victims picked him out of a photo array. Time reported, "The resemblance between the two men, who are not related, is indeed striking: both are tall, slender blacks with short Afros, sparse beards, mustaches and similar facial features." [Editors' Note: In photos accompanying the Time article, the two look nothing alike.]

William Jackson was released. According to Time, he said of the victims that identified him: "It ain't their fault." He retains bitter feelings about the system that mistakenly imprisoned him. According to the article, he said, "They took away part of my life, part of my youth. I spent five years down there, and all they said was 'We're sorry.'"

NOTES AND QUESTIONS

(1) *DNA Sometimes Contrary to Eyewitness Identification.* In recent years, a growing number of persons convicted on the basis of unequivocal eyewitness identification testimony, some on death row, have been freed by later-conducted DNA tests (or other scientific or powerful evidence or third-party confessions) that relatively conclusively establish under the circumstances, that the person could not have committed the crime. Some of these people have been imprisoned for a major portion of their lives before the discovery. The discovery, testing, and presentation of such exculpatory evidence often gets done only because of the persistence of an unusually devoted lawyer working without pay for years. Not every convicted criminal gets such devotion, nor is DNA or other evidence that would exculpate often available even if the person is innocent. It is thus to be expected that there are more cases than come to light, wherein innocent impecunious people languish in prison because of faulty eyewitness identification (or other causes such as sloppy or corrupt police or prosecution work, as rare as that may be — but a number of these cases have come to light as well). When such exculpatory evidence does come forward, not all jurisdictions have a regular procedure to consider release from prison, and the person must rely on the erratic and chancy institution of discretionary executive clemency, which often has a political component as well.

What do you suppose are the causes of faulty eyewitness identification testimony?

(2) *Impeaching Eyewitnesses by Expert Testimony.* In *United States v. Downing*, 753 F.2d 1224 (3d Cir. 1985), Judge Becker reviewed the admissibility of expert testimony concerning the reliability of identifications made by eyewitnesses:

> [W]e find persuasive more recent cases in which courts have found that, under certain circumstances, this type of expert testimony can satisfy the helpfulness test of Rule 702. For example, in *State v. Chapple*, 135 Ariz. 281, 660 P.2d 1208 (1983) (applying Arizona's version of the Federal Rules of Evidence), the Supreme Court of Arizona set aside a jury's guilty verdict and ordered a new trial on the ground that the trial court had erroneously excluded an expert on eyewitness identification offered by the defendant. In

addressing the question whether the expert's testimony would have been "helpful" to the jury in reaching an *informed* decision, the court noted several specific factual "variables" that were present in that case which, the defendant's expert was prepared to testify, reduced the eywitnesses' ability to perceive and remember accurately.

The proffer stated that the expert would testify concerning: (1) the "forgetting curve," i.e., the fact that memory does not diminish at a uniform rate; (2) the fact that, contrary to common understanding, stress causes inaccuracy of perception and distorts one's subsequent recall; (3) the "assimilation factor," which indicates that witnesses frequently incorporate into their identifications inaccurate information gathered after the event and confused with the event; (4) the "feedback factor," which indicates that when identification witnesses discuss the case with each other they can unconsciously reinforce their individual identifications; and (5) the fact that studies demonstrate the absence of a relationship between the confidence a witness has in his or her identification and the actual accuracy of that identification. Each of these "variables" goes beyond what an average juror might know as a matter of common knowledge, and indeed some of them directly contradict "common sense." For this reason, the Arizona Supreme Court concluded that the expert's testimony would have assisted the jury in reaching a correct decision.

In another case, *United States v. Smith*, 736 F.2d 1103 (6th Cir. 1984) (per curiam), the Sixth Circuit held that expert testimony on the reliability of eyewitness identification met the "helpfulness" test of Fed. R. Evid. 702 and therefore had been improperly excluded. The excluded testimony would have focused on "a hypothetical factual situation identical" to the facts of the case and would have explained (1) that a witness who does not identify the defendant in a first line-up may "unconsciously transfer" his visualization of the defendant to a second line-up and thereby incorrectly identify the defendant the second time; (2) that studies demonstrate the inherent unreliability of cross-racial identifications; and (3) that an encounter during a stressful situation decreases the eyewitness' ability to perceive and remember and decreases the probability of an accurate identification. In concluding that this evidence would have assisted the jury in reaching an accurate decision, the court emphasized that the expert's proffered testimony was based upon "the exact *facts* before the court and not only might have assisted the jury, but might have refuted their otherwise common assumptions about the reliability of eyewitness identification." The California Supreme Court has adopted this view. In *People v. McDonald*, 690 P.2d 709 (Cal. 1984) the Court held that, under certain narrow circumstances, it will be error for trial courts to exclude qualified expert testimony on eyewitness perception and memory.

The literature concerning the psychology of eyewitness testimony is voluminous. *See generally* Loftus & Doyle, Eyewitness Testimony: Civil and Criminal (3d ed. 1997); Wells & Olson, *Eyewitness Identification*, 54 Ann. Rev. Psychol. 277 (2003); *cf.* Zaragoza, et al., Memory and Testimony in the Child Witness (1995).

(3) *Instructions Cautioning Jurors About Reliance on Eyewitness Testimony.* In *United States v. Telfaire*, 469 F.2d 552 (D.C. Cir. 1972), the court suggested, in

an appendix, the instruction appearing below. Appellate courts have generally not required (although some have recommended or upheld the giving of) an instruction on eyewitness identification, entrusting the matter to the discretion of the trial judge, even when the sole eyewitness' identification is the central, and a hotly contested, issue. Corroborating evidence of guilt often is given as a reason for not requiring it. The propounded model instruction reads as follows:

> One of the most important issues in this case is the identification of the defendant as the perpetrator of the crime. The Government has the burden of proving identity, beyond a reasonable doubt. It is not essential that the witness himself be free from doubt as to the correctness of his statement. However, you, the jury, must be satisfied beyond a reasonable doubt of the accuracy of the identification of the defendant before you may convict him. If you are not convinced beyond a reasonable doubt that the defendant was the person who committed the crime, you must find the defendant not guilty.
>
> Identification testimony is an expression of belief or impression by the witness. Its value depends on the opportunity the witness had to observe the offender at the time of the offense and to make a reliable identification later.
>
> In appraising the identification testimony of a witness, you should consider the following:
>
> (i) Are you convinced that the witness had the capacity and an adequate opportunity to observe the offender?
>
> Whether the witness had an adequate opportunity to observe the offender at the time of the offense will be affected by such matters as how long or short a time was available, how far or close the witness was, how good were lighting conditions, whether the witness had had occasion to see or know the person in the past.
>
> [In general, a witness bases any identification he makes on his perception through the use of his senses. Usually the witness identifies an offender by the sense of sight — but this is not necessarily so, and he may use other senses]. (Sentences in brackets to be used only if appropriate. Instructions to be inserted or modified as appropriate to the proof and contentions.)
>
> (ii) Are you satisfied that the identification made by the witness subsequent to the offense was the product of his own recollection? You may take into account both the strength of the identification, and the circumstances under which the identification was made.
>
> If the identification by the witness may have been influenced by the circumstances under which the defendant was presented to him for identification, you should scrutinize the identification with great care. You may also consider the length of time that lapsed between the occurrence of the crime and the next opportunity of the witness to see defendant, as a factor bearing on the reliability of the identification.

> [You may also take into account that an identification made by picking the defendant out of a group of similar individuals is generally more reliable than one which results from the presentation of the defendant alone to the witness].
>
> [(iii) You may take into account any occasion in which the witness failed to make an identification of defendant, or made an identification that was inconsistent with his identification at trial].
>
> (iv) Finally, you must consider the credibility of each identification witness in the same way as any other witness, consider whether he is truthful, and consider whether he had the capacity and opportunity to make a reliable observation on the matter covered in his testimony.
>
> I again emphasize that the burden of proof on the prosecutor extends to every element of the crime charged, and this specifically includes the burden of proving beyond a reasonable doubt the identity of the defendant as the perpetrator of the crime with which he stands charged. If after examining the testimony, you have a reasonable doubt as to the accuracy of the identification, you must find the defendant not guilty.

Somewhat atypically of courts around the country, the Supreme Court of New Jersey made *mandatory* the giving of a jury instruction expressly allowing the jury to consider, if they think appropriate, that cross-racial identifications may be subject to special problems concerning accuracy, in cases where the sole witness' identification is critical and uncorroborated by other evidence. In the case at issue, the victim, who eventually identified the defendant, had been unable to do so for 7-8 months after the crime, originally had been unable to identify the photograph of the defendant and no forensic evidence linked the defendant to the crime. There is a good discussion of the whole area, citing studies and the law around the country. The case is *State v. Cromedy*, 158 N.J. 112, 727 A.2d 457 (1999). Curiously, the court refused, however, to authorize expert testimony regarding cross-racial identification, saying the area was not scientifically certain enough for that.

§ 4.12 MISCELLANEOUS CREDIBILITY ISSUES

(1) *Psychological Examinations of Complaining Witnesses.* See *Murphy v. Superior Court*, 689 P.2d 532 (Ariz. 1984), holding that a complainant in a rape case may be ordered to undergo a psychological examination only when her mental condition has been placed in issue and there is little or no corroboration of her allegations; and *Commonwealth v. Widrick*, 467 N.E.2d 1353 (Mass. 1984), holding that a trial judge may have statutory power to order a psychiatric examination to determine a witness's competency; such a matter is totally within the judge's discretion; but he or she has no statutory or inherent authority to order a complaining or corroborating witness in a sexual offense case to undergo psychiatric examination, the results of which would be available to impeach the witness at trial. The court cites a policy against possible harassment and the privacy policy underlying the state's Rape Shield law. The majority rule among the states permits a judge to compel such an examination, the court notes, but such a rule is tied to the corroboration requirement in sex offense cases, which Massachusetts does not have.

See also *United States v. Vik*, 655 F.2d 878 (8th Cir. 1981) (transportation of minor girls (who became government witnesses) for prostitution; appellate court upheld trial court's refusal to allow clinical psychologist, who had examined them for two hours, to testify for defense as to their personality type and veracity; matter was within court's discretion).

(2) *Immunizing Witnesses to Obtain their Testimony.* Throughout this chapter, a recurring fact pattern has been the appearance of government witnesses who might be receiving favorable treatment of some kind by the government in connection with possible criminal charges against them and the effect this may have on their credibility.

A related consideration is that the government may have granted some of its witnesses immunity from use of what they say (or even from prosecution, except for perjury) to get around the problem of them invoking the Fifth Amendment. Can the defense require a similar grant in order to induce or require defense witnesses to testify? *See United States v. Thevis*, 665 F.2d 616, 638–41 (5th Cir.) (judge may not grant immunity to defense witness simply because he has essential exculpatory information unavailable from other sources), *cert. denied*, 459 U.S. 825 (1982). *Thevis* also deals with the delicate problem of whether the prosecution may reveal that one of its witnesses is in a witness protection program. The potential for prejudice to the defendant under Fed. R. Evid. 403 is great, because it looks like the witness needs protection from the defendant. But there might be countervailing considerations, also under Fed. R. Evid. 403. One might be that defendant might show it as impeachment if the prosecution does not reveal it.

(3) *Rehabilitating a Witness's Credibility.* Not much has been said in this chapter about support of credibility, as opposed to impeachment of credibility. The rubric is often voiced that credibility may not be supported unless first attacked (because witnesses are presumed credible until shown otherwise), and that even then the support is restricted so as to limit it to more-or-less direct meeting of the attack. This has resulted in a few special rules in a number of jurisdictions (e.g., a limitation like that found for prior consistent statements used substantively in Fed. R. Evid. 801(d)(1)(B) often is found for such statements used on credibility), but they are administered with a large measure of discretion. *See also* Fed. R. Evid. 608(a). Courts do not like to waste too much time on this sort of thing (i.e., support) if it is not particularly meaningful. Obviously, policies like those in Fed. R. Evid. 403 are at work. In addition to the few other instances we have encountered along the way, see particularly *Blackwell v. Franzen*, 688 F.2d 496 (7th Cir. 1982) (typical use of prior consistent statement), *cert. denied*, 460 U.S. 1072 (1983); *United States v. Brown*, 547 F.2d 438 (8th Cir.) (repair or rehabilitation of credibility largely within discretion of trial judge), *cert. denied*, 430 U.S. 937 (1977); *United States v. Jackson*, 588 F.2d 1046 (5th Cir.), *cert. denied*, 442 U.S. 941 (1979) (Is being made a defendant in a criminal case a sufficient attack on credibility character to license support of credibility under Fed. R. Evid. 608?).

For a case upholding discretion to prevent defendant from introducing evidence of his truthful character under Fed. R. Evid. 608(a), even though the prosecution (after defendant testified in his own behalf) had been allowed to call two rebuttal witnesses who testified about defendant's reputation for untruthfulness and their opinion about his untruthfulness, see *United States v. Haimowitz*, 706 F.2d 1549 (11th Cir. 1983), *cert. denied*, 464 U.S. 1069 (1984). Compare *State v. Grecinger*, 569 N.W.2d 189 (Minn. 1997), an attempted murder case, holding that the credibility of the complaining witness could be rehabilitated by expert opinion testimony concerning Battered Womans' Syndrome (BWS) in the prosecution's case-in-chief when it was offered after the victim's credibility had been attacked by the defense during opening statement and cross-examination. A concurring opinion cites Raeder, *Proving the Case: Battered Woman and Batterer Syndrome: The Double-Edged Sword: Admissibility of Battered Woman Syndrome by and Against Batterers in Cases Implicating Domestic Violence*, 67 U. Colo. L. Rev. 789 (1996), concerning potential prejudicial effect of social science evidence when offered by the prosecution. See § 6.05[A], *infra*, for a discussion of battered woman syndrome.

(4) *Improper Vouching for Witness's Credibility by Closing Argument and Elicited Testimony.* In *United States v. Rudberg*, 122 F.3d 1199 (9th Cir. 1997), a conviction for various drug crimes was reversed because the government vouched for the credibility of its witnesses, thereby putting its own prestige behind them, where the vouched witnesses were the only ones connecting the defendant to the conspiracy. The court cited the testimony of an FBI agent explaining the significance of a "Rule 35" motion to reduce the sentence of another government witness as inferring that the witnesses' stories were independently confirmed by experienced FBI agents. The witnesses who were given sentence reductions also testified about them. In addition, the prosecutor explained to the jury in closing argument that Rule 35 lets witnesses who give the government substantial assistance obtain lesser sentences "to tell you the truth" about their knowledge of the conspiracy. The court reversed despite the lack of objection at trial and the giving of a standard instruction warning that testimony of witnesses who had received benefits from the government should be considered more cautiously than that of other witnesses.

What do you think of this opinion?

(5) *Prosecutor's Credibility Argument Against Defendant did Not Violate the Constitutional Rights of the Defendant.* In *Portuondo v. Agard*, 529 U.S. 61 (2000), the Supreme Court held that a prosecutor's comments during summation, calling the jury's attention to the fact that the defendant had an opportunity to hear other witnesses testify and to tailor his testimony, did not unlawfully burden his right to be present at trial, to be confronted with witnesses, or to testify on his own behalf and did not violate his right to due process. If the defense expects such a summation, are there still valid reasons to call the defendant as the last witness?

§ 4.13 SEQUESTRATION OF WITNESSES[15]

Read Federal Rule of Evidence 615, "Excluding Witnesses."

(1) *Definition and Purpose of Sequestration.* "Sequestration" (barring witnesses from hearing one another) is meant to guard against witnesses influencing each other in the sense of either lining up their stories or refuting the other's story.

---

[15] Study Guide Reference: Evidence in a Nutshell, Chapter 6:XI, at "Witness Preparation and Sequestration: F.R.E. 615."

(2) *Who is Exempted from Sequestration?* In *Varlack v. S.W.C. Caribbean, Inc.*, 550 F.2d 171 (3d Cir. 1977), the court sequestered all witnesses. On appeal, the court observed that a corporation is not a natural person and thus cannot make use of the exception to sequestration provided for in Fed. R. Evid. 615(1). As to the exception in Fed. R. Evid. 615(2), the characterization of a witness as "a former owner of the corporation" did not designate him with sufficient clarity as the corporate representative. Nor was his presence demonstrated to be "essential to the presentation of [the company's] case" within the meaning of Fed. R. Evid. 615(3). For the same reasons the company's due process claim was held groundless. However, as to the individual who later became a party, his rights under Fed. R. Evid. 615(1) were violated by the combination of the court's exclusion of him until he became a party and the court's delay in ruling on the motion to add him as a party until after the plaintiff and another eyewitness had testified. He was sequestered during some very important testimony. The court did not consider whether this also violated due process. In *Roberts ex rel. Johnson v. Galen of Virginia, Inc.*, 325 F.3d 776 (6th Cir. 2003), the court upheld the exemption from sequestration of a former employee, as a designated officer, where the corporation had no current employees.

(3) *Federal Agents can be the Government's Representative. In re United States*, 584 F.2d 666 (5th Cir. 1978): In this criminal trial for conspiracy defendants invoked Fed. R. Evid. 615 requiring the exclusion of witnesses from the courtroom. Pursuant to the exception embodied in Fed. R. Evid. 615(2), the government designated a federal agent who had been involved in the preparation of the case as its representative to be present at trial. The trial court rejected the government's request, holding that the agent's testimony appeared (from an earlier motion to suppress) to be of prime importance to the case. However, the Court of Appeals holds that Fed. R. Evid. 615(2) comprehends just such federal agents, i.e., those responsible for the preparation of the case, if that is who the government wishes to designate, citing the congressional history of the rule, in particular the Senate Report, and the Advisory Committee Notes to the Federal Rules of Evidence. The Court of Appeals suggests that the trial court could guard against undue influence on the agent's testimony by ordering that he testify first, under Fed. R. Evid. 611(a). The trial court cannot, however, bar his subsequent testimony. A separate opinion by another judge in the same case quarrels with the majority suggestion that the right of an organization (such as a government agency, a corporation, a partnership, a trust, etc.) to designate a representative at trial under Fed. R. Evid. 615(2) can be conditioned, restricted, or burdened by requiring that representative to testify at a particular time. Fed. R. Evid. 615(2) was intended to put an organization on a par with individual parties covered by Fed. R. Evid. 615(1). (Query: Could an individual's right be so conditioned?) This judge sees nothing in Fed. R. Evid. 615 or Fed. R. Evid. 611 that authorizes such restriction.

(4) *No Prejudice Letting Witness Stay when he was Later Designated Exempt from Sequestration Rule. United States v. Cueto*, 611 F.2d 1056 (5th Cir. 1980): In this attempted bank robbery case, the defense invoked sequestration of all witnesses pursuant to Fed. R. Evid. 615 at the beginning of trial. The government did not request at that time that one Cavanaugh, its agent on the case, be exempted pursuant to Fed. R. Evid. 615(2). However, Cavanaugh remained in the courtroom while the first two witnesses, called by the government, testified. Then the

government called Cavanaugh to testify. Defendant objected on the grounds of Fed. R. Evid. 615. The Court of Appeals holds that Cavanaugh qualified under Fed. R. Evid. 615(2) for exemption from sequestration and that the delay in invoking the 615(2) exemption for him until he was called to the stand made no difference unless defendant could show prejudice thereby. Since the first two witnesses testified about events occurring before Cavanaugh came onto the scene, about which Cavanaugh gave no testimony, there was no prejudice, and Cavanaugh was properly allowed to testify.

(5) *More than One Government Representative may be Exempt from Sequestration Rule. United States v. Alvarado*, 647 F.2d 537 (5th Cir. 1981): Nonjury conviction of conspiracy to possess marijuana. Two Drug Enforcement Administration agents (one the case agent and another an ordinary agent) were allowed to remain at counsel's table throughout the trial despite invocation of Fed. R. Evid. 615. One of them testified only at the end of the trial. Both of them were alleged to have tailored their testimony to earlier witnesses and to have signaled other lay witnesses while the latter were on the stand. The Court of Appeals states that the second and third exceptions to Fed. R. Evid. 615 justified the trial judge in permitting both to be present. It is within the trial judge's discretion to determine how many witnesses will be excused from sequestration (absent abuse of discretion), and whether to require such excused witnesses to testify early in the course of the trial. While unusual, in *United States v. Green*, 293 F.3d 886 (5th Cir. 2002), *cert. denied*, 538 U.S. 981 (2003), the court affirmed the exemption of three investigators from sequestration due to the complexity of this drug conspiracy case.

(6) *Litigants Must Argue to the Trial Judge Reasons Justifying Exemption: Application of Rule to Expert Witnesses who will Give Opinions. Morvant v. Construction Aggregates Corp.*, 570 F.2d 626 (6th Cir. 1978): The family of a tugboat skipper, who perished when the tugboat sank, sued the tugboat owner. The trial court excluded from the courtroom plaintiff's expert on marine surveying, despite Fed. R. Evid. 615(3) and despite plaintiff's argument thereunder that it was essential to the expert's forthcoming testimony on causation that the expert hear the facts as reported by the other witnesses as his basis, so that a hypothetical need not be given. This streamlined method of expert testimony is contemplated and encouraged by Fed. R. Evid. 703, it was argued; in such a situation the danger guarded against by Fed. R. Evid. 615 is not present because one witness's version of the facts will not influence covertly another's, and presence in the courtroom may lead to more, rather than less, accuracy. On appeal, a different or additional ground was urged by plaintiff, also under Fed. R. Evid. 615(3): that the complicated facts, unusual circumstances, and highly technical nature of the unseaworthiness issue made the advice of an expert, on the spot, essential to the presentation of plaintiff's case. The Court of Appeals states that under Fed. R. Evid. 615(3), the party has the burden of showing that the witness's presence is essential. While plaintiff's argument in the Court of Appeals would, if factually supported, have compelled the trial court to exempt the witness from sequestration under Fed. R. Evid. 615(3), it was not advanced at trial and therefore must be disregarded. As to the other arguments made below, the Court of Appeals cites commentators supporting them but holds that exemption from sequestration on these grounds is almost totally within the discretion of the trial judge. *See also United States v. Seschillie*, 310 F.3d

1208 (9th Cir. 2002), *cert. denied*, 538 U.S. 953 (2003). The court finds error in an expert's exclusion to be harmless where the party did not argue why the witness was essential. Even aside from this, the court expressly declines to conclude that an expert will always meet the criteria of rule 615(3).

(7) *Sanctions for Violation of Sequestration Rule.* Violation of a sequestration order can result in drastic remedies. *See, e.g., United States v. McClure*, 734 F.2d 484 (10th Cir. 1984) (trial judge did not abuse discretion in refusing to allow defense witness to testify; witness was expected to testify that he was owner of gun that had been found in automobile of accused; refusal was based on witness's presence in courtroom in violation of sequestration order). *See also* Markon, "Moussaoui Prosecutors Get a Break," WASHINGTON POST, Mar. 18, 2006 (911 conspirator's death penalty almost ruled out by judge because government lawyer gave witnesses a partial trial transcript). But see next notes.

(8) *Mistrial Based on Violation of Sequestration did Not Prohibit Retrial.* In *United States v. Pollack*, 640 F.2d 1152 (10th Cir. 1981), defendants were charged with borrowing money from the bank to buy cocaine. On cross-examination of one of two bank officials who were government witnesses, it became apparent that the two had discussed their testimony with each other (to "clear up" conflicts, as one put it). When it became apparent that the two bank officials had violated the court's sequestration order, the trial court excused the jury and explored the matter, by questioning both counsel and both witnesses. This revealed that the two witnesses had not been present when the exclusionary order was entered. The prosecuting attorney failed to advise one of them at all about the order and had told the other only in very general terms three weeks prior to trial that he should not discuss the case with others. Defense counsel specifically agreed with the trial court's conclusion that this was mere inadvertence and not bad faith. Ultimately defense counsel moved for a mistrial. The trial judge expressed his understanding that when a defendant moves for a mistrial defendant cannot later assert former jeopardy. Defense counsel agreed. The trial judge then declared a mistrial. When the case was retried, defense counsel moved to bar a new trial on grounds of double jeopardy, declaring that he had done more research, and that the prosecutor was guilty of more than mere inadvertence. The trial judge refused to reopen the matter and proceeded with the new trial, at which defendant was convicted. The appellate court affirms the conviction. Is there a lesson here for counsel? Is this why some counsel are reluctant to seem agreeable on anything?

(9) *Legislation Concerning Presence of Victims at Trial.* In the Oklahoma City bombing case, the judge originally ordered that family members who would be "victim impact" witnesses in any penalty phase of the capital case could not attend the guilt phase of the trial. He later reconsidered this ruling in light of a Congressional statute (*see* 18 U.S.C. §§ 3510, 3593) that was passed specifically to overrule his decision. The statutory scheme provides that a "court shall not order any victim of an offense excluded from the trial because that person later testifies to a victim impact statement during the sentencing hearing," and that "the victim's attendance at the trial shall not be construed to pose a danger of creating unfair prejudice." Is this constitutional? The judge ultimately let such victims and their families attend the trial, but told the defense it could raise specific objections at the sentencing hearing to testimony that it claimed had been influenced in some way by

what was observed during trial. Does this comport with the statute? The legislation has now in effect been incorporated into Rule 615, by the addition of subsection (4). See the Rule as assigned above.

SELECTED CHAPTER REVIEW PROBLEMS 4C.

(1) *How do Inconsistent Statements Affect the Sufficiency of Evidence Needed to Get to the Jury?* Personal injury automobile negligence action. Bus runs into a Ford. Driver of Ford sues. A witness on the stand testifies that the Ford went through a red light. (He testifies for the bus company.) Plaintiff puts another witness on the stand who overheard the first witness say, on an earlier occasion that does not qualify for an exemption from or exception to the hearsay rule, that the bus went through the red light. (Can the plaintiff put on this testimony? Assume that he can and that he has used the proper procedure.) Assume that without the evidence of this second witness, the judge thinks that the plaintiff has insufficient evidence of the bus driver's negligence to get to the jury. But the judge thinks that plaintiff would have sufficient evidence to get to the jury if plaintiff had some evidence that the bus went through the red light. Does plaintiff get to the jury?

(2) *What Use can the Jury Make of Inconsistent Statements in Rendering Verdict?* Same case. But this time the judge thinks the plaintiff has sufficient evidence of the bus driver's negligence to get to the jury even without the second witness's testimony. (The second witness does testify.) Assume that without the second witness's testimony, the jury is not convinced of the bus's negligence. But they believe that the former statement reported by the second witness is true and this convinces them of the bus's negligence. What verdict do they bring in if they obey the instructions?

(3) *Can You Contradict a Witness About his Earlier Statement on the Color of the Light?* Automobile negligence personal injury action involving a collision between a Ford and a bus. A witness (W-1) for the driver of the Ford testifies that your client (the driver of the bus) went through the red light. You have independent eyewitnesses who will testify that the bus had a green light. You also have a witness who will testify that he heard W-1 make an earlier statement off the stand (not qualifying for any exception to or exemption from the hearsay rule) that the bus had a green light, whom you want to put on if you cannot get W-1 to admit that he said that. Assuming everything is done correctly procedurally, can you introduce this evidence?

(4) *Can You Contradict Witness About the Color of his Clothing?* Same as problem (3), except that W-1 testified (which will be the subject of your attack) not that the bus went through a red light, but rather that "I was all dressed up in my navy blue pin-striped suit when I spotted this bus and this Ford." (Assume that at another point in the testimony he provided some fairly strong evidence against you about either speed or the color of the light.) You did not object to the "blue suit" statement. Assuming everything is done correctly procedurally, can you introduce testimony from your witness that he saw W-1 and W-1 was not wearing a blue suit but rather was wearing a brown one? Can you try to elicit from W-1 during cross-examination that he had previously said he was wearing a brown suit? If he won't admit making that statement, can you put on a witness (always assuming

everything is done correctly procedurally) who will say he heard W-1 make that former statement?

(5) *Can You Contradict a Witness About the Presence of a Crowd at the Scene?* In problem (4), suppose W-1 testified not that he was wearing a blue suit, but rather that there was an enormous crowd at the scene. Your offered evidence is directed at establishing there was no one else at the scene or that he had previously said there was no one else at the scene. Does this change of facts make any difference?

(6) *Can You Contradict a Witness About the Color of his Suit if that is Why he Remembers Date and Time of Accident?* Same case as problem (4), with the addition that W-1 adds that the day and time is indelibly fixed in his memory because he had just gone to pick up his new blue pin-striped suit and had put it on to wear to an interview. Precise day and time is important in the lawsuit because there had been another accident between a similar car and bus on another day near in time to this one and the witness has said that he does not know makes of cars. Does this make any difference to your ability to attack his statement about what color suit he was wearing in the fashions described in Problem (4)?

(7) *When Can You Use Extrinsic Evidence without Foundation?* Defendant puts on a witness (W-2) to testify that he has seen a witness who has testified for the prosecution (W-1) at the home of the prosecuting attorney on a number of social occasions, such as birthdays, dinner parties, cocktail parties, etc. None of this was brought up on cross-examination of W-1. Can W-2 testify?

Chapter 5

RELIABILITY OF OPINION TESTIMONY

LAY AND EXPERT OPINION: BASIC DOCTRINE AND PROCEDURAL CONSIDERATIONS (F.R.E. ARTICLE VII)

§ 5.01 LAY OPINION[1]

[A] Common-Law Restrictions

STATE v. THORP
North Carolina Supreme Court
72 N.C. 186 (1875)

READE, J.

The prisoner was charged with drowning her child in a river. A witness saw her going towards the river with a child in her arms. The witness said he knew the prisoner and identified her, he knew the child also, but he was one hundred yards off and was not sure who the child in her arms was. He was then asked "Is it your best impression that the child she had in her arms, was her son Robert Thorp?" The witness said it was. This question was objected to but was admitted. [This] question was leading, but there is a more substantial objection to it.

[If] in this case the witness had been asked "Did you know the deceased child? Yes. Did you see it in the person's arms? Yes. Did you recognize it as the deceased? Yes, I think it was, that is my best impression." All that would have been proper. But we think the case presented to us will bear the interpretation that the witness said, "I saw the prisoner have a child in her arms. I was so far off that I could not tell what child it was, but I knew that she had a child of her own, and I suppose she would not have been carrying any other child than her own, therefore I think it was her own child. That is my best impression." And this was clearly improper. This was but his inference from what he saw and knew. A witness must speak of facts within his knowledge. He knew that the prisoner had a child of her own, and he knew that she had a child in her arms, and these facts it was proper for him to state, but he could not go further and say, "from these facts which I know I infer that the child was her own, I am not sure but that is my best impression." Evidently at that distance he could not recognize one child from another in the arms of the prisoner. It was probably but little more distinct than a bundle and he just took it to be her

---

[1] Study Guide Reference: Evidence in a Nutshell, Chapter 7:I.

child because she had it in her arms. Probably this was all he meant by his "best impression." And it was error to allow it.

NOTES

(1) *Collective Facts Rule.* In *Virginia Ry. & Power Co. v. Burr*, 133 S.E. 776 (Va. 1926), the court discussed whether a witness (not an expert) could testify that an object lying in a cabin covered by an overcoat "looked to him very much like a man." Such statements are within the "collective facts rule," the court said, which holds that:

> Impressions which are based upon a great variety of circumstances and a combination of appearances, which because either of the witness' infirmity or the infirmity of our language cannot be adequately or better expressed, may be testified to by those who have personally observed the facts.

More recently, the collective facts rule was relied on by the Kentucky Supreme court in *Clifford v. Commonwealth*, 7 S.W.3d 371 (Ky. 1999), as justifying testimony by an undercover police officer who monitored a conversation between a suspected defendant and another police officer, that one suspect's voice sounded like that of a black male. The officer's "inability to more specifically describe or to demonstrate 'how a black man sounds' merely proves the reason for the collective facts rule, i.e., that it would be difficult or impossible for the witness to give such a description or demonstration." The Court indicated the collective facts or collective opinion rule is a corollary to Rule 701's rational basis test.

(2) *Other Common-Law Exceptions to Traditional Rule. Baltimore & Ohio R.R. v. Schultz*, 1 N.E. 324 (Ohio 1885), considered the exceptions to the general rule that witnesses must testify to facts and not opinions. It stated:

> [O]pinions of non-experts, who state, so far as is practicable, the facts on which their opinions are grounded, will be received on questions of identity as applied to persons, things, animals, or handwriting; and of the size, color, and weight of objects; of time and distance; of the mental state or condition of another; of insanity and intoxication; of the affection of one for another; of the physical condition of another as to health or sickness (in which latter case, however, the opinion of a non-expert will not be heard upon the particular disease, or cause thereof); of values; [and] of the soundness of animals. [F]or a witness to undertake to place before a jury all the facts and symptoms from which he had formed the opinion that a person was angry, drunk, sick, in love, or insane, would be to abandon himself to a hopeless attempt at mimicry and undignified descriptions and limitations, as ludicrous as they would be vain and unprofitable.
>
> A few general propositions reflect the current of authority: (1) That witnesses shall testify to facts and not opinions is the general rule. (2) Exceptions to this rule have been found to be, in some cases, necessary to the due administration of justice. (3) Witnesses shown to be learned, skilled, or experienced in a particular art, science, trade, or business may, in a proper case, give their opinions upon a given state of facts. This exception is limited to experts. (4) In matters more within the common observation

and experience of men, nonexperts may, in cases where it is not practicable to place before the jury all the primary facts upon which they are founded, state their opinions from such facts, where such opinions involve conclusions material to the subject of inquiry. (5) In such cases the witnesses are required, so far as may be, to state the primary facts which support their opinions. (6) Where it is practicable to place palpably before the jury the facts supporting their opinions, the witnesses should be restricted, in their testimony, to such facts, and the jurors left to form their opinions from these facts, unaided by the mere opinions of the witnesses. (7) [W]here it does not appear upon the whole record but that the jury was equally capable with the witnesses of forming an opinion from the facts stated, it is error to admit in evidence the opinion of witnesses.

[B] Lay Opinions Under Federal Rules of Evidence

Read Federal Rule of Evidence 701, "Opinion Testimony by Lay Witnesses." Section (c) of the rule was added in the year 2000 to clear up some confusion and conflict in the cases.

BOHANNON v. PEGELOW

United States Court of Appeals, Seventh Circuit
652 F.2d 729 (1981)

Campbell, Senior District Judge.

On April 7, 1978, the plaintiff, J.B. Bohannon, was arrested by a Milwaukee Vice Squad detective and charged with pandering. After the charge was dismissed, he filed this action against the arresting officer, Howard Pegelow, claiming that he was arrested without probable cause and in violation of his civil rights. The cause was tried before a jury which awarded plaintiff $10,000 in compensatory damages and $15,000 in punitive damages. The defendant appeals.

On the night of April 7, 1978, [defendant was conducting] an investigation of prostitution at the Ambassador Hotel. The Ambassador was operating as a commercial hotel but was also providing housing for Marquette University students. That evening, the plaintiff, a student at Marquette, was visiting a fellow student, Julene Leatherman, who lived at the hotel. Bohannon and his friend were sitting in the lobby and observed the defendant as he was attempting to contact certain alleged prostitutes. Eventually, Pegelow went upstairs and arrested a woman and her male companion. As the defendant was escorting that couple through the lobby to an awaiting police vehicle, he stopped and arrested Bohannon as well.

The defendant alleged that earlier in the evening Bohannon had initiated a conversation with him in which he offered to sell the sexual favors of his girlfriend for thirty-five dollars. The plaintiff claimed that all he ever said to the detective was a brief "How you doing?" However, based on the defendant's accusation, Bohannon was charged with pandering.

The plaintiff asserted his innocence throughout the proceedings and refused to plea bargain with the District Attorney's Office. The charge was dismissed without prejudice on April 25, 1978, and the District Attorney's Office informed Pegelow that the charge would not be reissued. Despite that knowledge, the defendant continued to investigate the plaintiff and pressed for his prosecution. There was evidence that in his zeal, the defendant manufactured and tampered with certain evidence in the case.

The plaintiff argued that Pegelow's special concern with this case arose as a result of an investigation of [Pegelow] by the District Attorney's Office. That probe was initiated approximately one week after plaintiff's arrest and involved that incident as well as other arrests made by the defendant. However, at the conclusion of that investigation, no criminal charges were filed against Pegelow.

Utilizing a special verdict form, the jury found that the defendant was not acting in good faith when he arrested the plaintiff and that his actions deprived the plaintiff of liberty without due process of law. Additionally, the jury concluded that the defendant had acted wantonly and maliciously, thereby justifying punitive damages.

The defendant argues that the trial court erred by admitting the lay opinion testimony of Julene Leatherman in which she suggested that the arrest was motivated by racial prejudice. The appellant claims that the testimony was merely a personal opinion regarding the mental state of another and was therefore incompetent evidence. However, Federal Rule of Evidence 701 permits lay opinion testimony and does not limit the subject matter to which it can relate. Initially, it should be noted that all of the cases [cited by appellant for exclusion] were decided prior to the promulgation of Rule 701.

Appellant has cited no case decided under Rule 701 which has excluded lay opinion testimony as to the mental state of another. However, there are cases which have specifically permitted such testimony.

An analysis of Rule 701 supports those decisions. If Congress had intended to limit the competency of lay opinion testimony it could have so stated as it did in other Rules of Evidence, *see* Rules 404, 608(b), 609(a). However, Congress did not do so and appellate courts should not graft exceptions and limitations upon the Rules of Evidence.

This does not mean that lay opinion testimony as to another person's mental state must be admitted by the trial court. The Rule states that the testimony must be "helpful to a clear understanding of his [the witness'] testimony or the determination of a fact in issue." Additionally, the considerations outlined in Rule 403 apply. Thus, the decision as to admissibility is within the sound discretion of the trial judge and the issues involved are peculiarly suited to his determination. An appellate court is hardly in a position to reevaluate, based on a cold record, the helpfulness of certain testimony or the subtle balancing of factors contained in Rule 403. The trial judge's decision on such issues must be a clear abuse of discretion to justify reversal and a new trial.

The appellant claims that the trial court abused its discretion in admitting Leatherman's opinion because the rest of her testimony did not contain any facts indicating racial prejudice. Therefore, appellant argues, the opinion could not have been "rationally based on the perception of the witness," as required by Rule 701.

However, it is undisputed that the witness observed the arrest. In a similar situation, the Fifth Circuit stated:

> When, as here, the witness observes first hand the altercation in question, her opinions on the feelings of the parties are based on her personal knowledge and rational perceptions and are helpful to the jury. The Rules require nothing more for admission of the testimony.

John Hancock, 585 F.2d at 1294. Appellant's argument relates to the weight to which the evidence is entitled and not to its admissibility. Rule 701 contemplates that such weaknesses in the testimony be elicited and emphasized through cross-examination. (See Notes of Advisory Committee.)

Appellant also argues that Leatherman's opinion testimony should not have been admitted because it related to a key issue in the case, i.e., the motivation of the defendant. Rule 704, however, permits opinion testimony on ultimate issues, so exclusion was not required. Additionally, the special verdict form utilized in this case did not require a finding that the defendant's actions were motivated by racial prejudice, but merely that they were wanton and malicious. As noted in the district judge's post-trial order, there was ample evidence from which the jury could have found malice.

NOTES AND QUESTIONS

(1) *Reversal Based on Lack of Personal Knowledge in Similar Case.* Contrast *Hester v. BIC Corp.*, 225 F.3d 178 (2d Cir. 2000), which reversed an award in a Title VII discrimination action where a lay witness who was a co-worker testified that the supervisor's treatment of the employee was race-based, without having personal knowledge of the facts that formed the basis of the employer's adverse action. Are the decisions irreconcilable? If so, which is correct?

(2) *Lay Opinions in Criminal Cases: Not Much Difference.* In the criminal context, see *United States v. Smith*, 550 F.2d 277 (5th Cir.), *cert. denied*, 434 U.S. 841 (1977), a case in which the defendants were found by a jury to be guilty of misapplication of federal funds concerning the Comprehensive Employment and Training Act of 1973 (CETA), and claimed reversible error in admitting into evidence the following exchange:

The Court: Do you have any appreciation of whether or not Mr. Wallace knew and understood the requirements [of CETA]?

A. [Mrs. Walker]: As I understood, he understood them.

The court said:

> The testimony in question was given by a Mrs. Letha Walker. At the time of the trial Mrs. Walker was Youth Coordinator of CETA and had known Wallace since his employment by CETA. Mrs. Walker had ample opportunity to observe Wallace in his position of Assistant Director and her testimony complied with the first requirement of Rule 701, that the opinion be based on personal observations. The requirement that the testimony facilitate an understanding of a factual issue is also satisfied since Wallace's

knowledge of the CETA rules and regulations was a critical issue to be determined at trial. . . . Wallace further contends that the admission of Walker's opinion on this matter was improper since his knowledge related to an ultimate issue of fact. This argument has no merit under Rule 704 of the Federal Rules of Evidence.

(3) *Inferences in Fact or Opinion.* In *Lubbock Feed Lots, Inc. v. Iowa Beef Processors, Inc.*, 630 F.2d 250 (5th Cir. 1980), the question was whether the relationship between a commodities broker, Heller, and a meat packer (IBP) was one of agency or of a dealer and purchaser. Although Guss, Heller's business partner, stated in his deposition that he knew nothing of Heller's cattle business, his deposition was read to the jury. The deposition showed that he was not involved with Heller's cattle-buying transactions and knew little about them beyond the identity of the feedlots from which Heller bought cattle. Guss testified that Heller had not introduced him to the operators of the various feedlots, that he did not travel with Heller on cattle-buying trips, that Heller had not described the cattle-buying activities to him, and that he did not know the specific details of Heller's cattle-buying business. Nevertheless, he said, he knew "in general" how Heller operated. Over IBP's objections, the reading of the deposition continued, and Guss's testimony revealed that he was aware of some details of Heller's cattle business from telephone conversations he had overheard. Guss stated that his "understanding" was that Heller bought cattle for IBP. He testified that he had formed this understanding from the fact that Heller spoke to IBP's Russ Walker four or five times a day, rather than from any direct statements by Heller to that effect. In affirming the admission of the deposition, the court stated:

> The role of judicial discretion in the application of Rule 701 is obvious:
>
> > [T]he terms "fact" and "opinion" denote merely a difference of degree of concreteness of description or a difference in nearness or remoteness of inference. The opinion rule operates to prefer the more concrete description to the less concrete, the direct form of statement to the inferential. McCormick on Evidence § 12, at 26 (2d ed. 1972).
>
> To the extent that the objections raise the issue of admissibility under the lay opinion rule we conclude that the court determined in its discretion that the testimony met the requirements of that rule — "tenuous" as that evidence may have been. Guss's inference was predicated upon conduct observed personally, the inference is one that a normal person might draw from those observations, and it is an inference that the district court could, in its discretion, consider helpful in the determination of a disputed fact — the nature of Heller's relationship to IBP.

(4) *More on Lack of Sufficient Basis for Lay Opinion.* In *Gorby v. Schneider Tank Lines, Inc.*, 741 F.2d 1015 (7th Cir. 1984), the court properly excluded testimony of an eyewitness to the effect that one driver could have avoided the accident and the other "did everything he could":

> Highlan was prepared to state two opinions. In our view, Judge Sharp properly excluded the two opinions because neither was based upon first-hand knowledge or observation. First, Highlan was prepared to state

that Welsch did "everything he could to avoid [the] accident." Highlan, however, was not present in the truck's cab with Welsch. Highlan could only observe the semi-tanker truck from a car in the opposite lane of traffic and thus could not know the exact measures Welsch took to avoid the accident. More significantly, Highlan could not know when Welsch perceived Gorby's truck. Furthermore, even if Highlan had been present in the cab with Welsch, we would still find that the opinion was not based upon first-hand knowledge or observation. Appellant never established that Highlan was familiar with the Schneider semi-tanker truck. In particular, appellant never established that Highlan was familiar with the safety equipment semi-tanker trucks carry, the distances over which trucks may safely stop, the load the Schneider truck carried, or the brake and steering equipment of such trucks. The mere fact that Highlan was a motorist with twenty-nine years of experience did not give him the personal knowledge necessary to formulate an admissible lay opinion, and Judge Sharp properly exercised his discretion to exclude Highlan's first opinion.

Highlan was also prepared to state that Gorby could have avoided the accident. The exclusion of this opinion presents a closer question than does the exclusion of the first opinion because a pick-up truck more closely resembles an ordinary car than it does a semi-tanker truck. Our review, however, is limited to identifying an abuse of discretion, and we conclude there was no abuse. There is nothing in the record to indicate that Highlan was familiar with the type of pick-up truck Gorby drove, its safety features, its acceleration and stopping times, or the load it was carrying on the night of the accident. The record fails to disclose that Highlan ever set foot in a pick-up truck, and the district court could well find that Highlan's testimony was based upon speculation rather than upon first-hand knowledge.

(5) *Lay Opinion on Sanity.* People familiar with a person whose sanity is in issue always have been permitted to testify on this issue. The amount of familiarity necessary to support such an opinion varies. For example, Cal. Evid. Code § 870 permits testimony when the "witness is an intimate acquaintance."

(6) *Lay Opinion on Identity.* Lay opinion is permitted that the person in a photograph taken at the scene is the same individual as the defendant, particularly in cases where the defendant's appearance has changed since the incident. *See United States v. Borrelli*, 621 F.2d 1092 (10th Cir.), *cert. denied*, 449 U.S. 956 (1980); *see also United States v. Miranda*, 986 F.2d 1283 (9th Cir.) (such testimony is particularly valuable where witnesses are able to make identification based on familiarity with characteristics of defendant not immediately observable by jury at trial), *cert. denied*, 508 U.S. 929 (1993).

ASPLUNDH MANUFACTURING DIVISION v. BENTON HARBOR ENGINEERING

United States Court of Appeals, Third Circuit
57 F.3d 1190 (1995)

BECKER, JUDGE.

[Jeffrey Sackerson's estate brought a wrongful death action against Asplundh, which manufactured an aerial lift mounted onto a truck chassis and used in tree trimming operations that Sackerson, an employee of the City of Portland, was operating at the time of his death. Asplundh and its insurer, National Union, brought a third-party action seeking contribution and indemnity from Benton Harbor, the manufacturer of the lower boom cylinder containing the piston rod which allegedly fractured and caused the accident. The district court entered judgment for Asplundh and National Union in the amount of $185,881.60, twenty percent of the Sackerson settlement. The version of rule 701 in effect at the time did not contain section (c).]

Jones, the witness whose testimony is at issue, had been fleet maintenance supervisor for the City of Portland for more than ten years at the time of the accident and was responsible for all city equipment, including the Asplundh aerial lift. After the accident, Jones and his employees took apart and inspected the aerial lift's boom assembly and observed the rod from a distance of about fifteen inches. In his deposition, Jones stated his opinion that a component of the lower boom assembly — the rod end — had fractured. Jones expressed the opinion that the fracture was caused by metal fatigue and was attributable to the design of the rod end. Specifically, he stated that there was a "problem" because Benton Harbor's design called for a hole to be drilled through the rod end at a point where it was threaded. Moreover, Jones noted that the cylinder rod had oxidized around a portion of the break which was a different, duller color than the rod's fresh break. From this, Jones concluded that the break occurred in stages. Jones also related that the break was in a threaded area where a hole had been drilled through the rod. Jones concluded that the rod fatigued inside the rod eye, causing the accident, stating that the stop block on the lower boom cylinder rods did not contribute to the accident.

The question we are presented with is whether it was permissible for Jones to express the opinion that the rod end had broken due to metal fatigue and that the design of the rod end was a "problem." In our view these opinions are not ones that an average lay person would be equipped to draw, absent sufficient specialized knowledge or experience. We disagree with the dissent's assertion that "[f]atigue failure of metal is not unfamiliar" to persons "such" as Jones, and simply do not believe that the average lay person, absent sufficient knowledge or experience with metals, is qualified to offer a meaningful opinion on questions of metal fatigue of this nature. Metal fatigue is a technical concept.

While the average lay person — examining the rod end and seeing that it had broken in a spot where the rod end was threaded and a hole had been drilled through it — might well properly conclude under Rule 701 that the rod end had broken at what appeared to be its weakest point, such a person could not reasonably go further and conclude that the rod end was defectively weak at this point. We simply do not believe that the realm of common knowledge extends to such issues as the presence and cause of metal failure and the proper design of hydraulic cylinders. Given the requirements of Rule 701, Asplundh needed to demonstrate that Jones possessed relevant experience or specialized knowledge germane to his opinion in order to satisfy the rationally derived and helpfulness standards of the rule. While a lay witness may acquire this additional insight either by formal education or practical experience, it appears Jones simply possessed neither.

Asplundh suggests that it is enough that Jones observed the rod end firsthand, that his opinion testimony helped the jury to determine the cause of the lift's failure and the role played in it by the rod manufactured by Benton Harbor, and that Jones was subject to cross-examination. As we have stated, under Rule 701 the trial judge must play some gatekeeping role so as to ensure that the rationally derived and helpfulness requirements of the rule are met.

To use a simple yet illustrative example, if an issue in a case was whether the sun revolved around the earth, and the proponents of the Ptolemaic system proposed to prove their case by lay opinion testimony, such testimony could satisfy Asplundh's requirement of "firsthand" observation ("I have observed the sun firsthand for many years, and I have seen that each day it moves across the sky from the east to the west."). Such testimony would also be helpful to the jury to the extent that it would tend to suggest a result that the jury should reach. And such testimony could be subjected to cross-examination by a proponent of the Copernican system. But it does not follow that this lay opinion testimony meets the rational basis or helpfulness requirements as they are contemplated by Rule 701 or that it would be admissible. Yet nothing in the district court's analysis would have excluded such testimony.

We are convinced that the court's admission of Jones's opinion testimony was not harmless and therefore represents reversible error, since we cannot conclude that "it is highly probable that the error did not contribute to the judgment."

NOTES AND QUESTIONS

(1) *What is the Judge's Gatekeeping Role Concerning Lay Opinion?* Do you agree with Judge Becker's restrictions on lay opinion under the Federal Rules of Evidence? Is this a category of testimony that falls between lay and expert opinion? See also *United States v. Figueroa-Lopez*, 125 F.3d 1241 (9th Cir. 1997), a case in which the prosecution forgot to qualify its witness as an expert. The Ninth Circuit held it was error (albeit harmless) to admit testimony by a DEA agent that the defendant's behavior was consistent with that of an experienced drug trafficker:

> Here, the agents testified that the following behaviors were consistent with an experienced drug trafficker: 1) countersurveillance driving; 2) use of code words to refer to drug quantities and prices; 3) use of a third-person lookout when attending a narcotics meeting; 4) use of a rental car to make the drug delivery; 5) hiding the cocaine in the door panels of a car; and 6) dealing in large amounts of very pure cocaine. These "observations"

require demonstrable expertise; in fact, several times, the Government instructed the witness to answer questions "based upon your training and experience." Additionally, one agent testified that his familiarity with the fact that narcotics traffickers sometimes speak in code is based upon the training that he had at the DEA Academy.

The Government blurs the distinction between Federal Rules of Evidence 701 and 702. Lay witness testimony is governed by Rule 701, which limits opinions to those "rationally based on the perception of the witness." Rule 702, on the other hand, governs admission of expert opinion testimony concerning "specialized knowledge." The testimony in this case is precisely the type of "specialized knowledge" governed by Rule 702. A holding to the contrary would encourage the Government to offer all kinds of specialized opinions without pausing first properly to establish the required qualifications of their witnesses. In addition, the Government's argument subverts the requirements of Federal Rule of Criminal Procedure 16(a)(1)(E) that requires the Government to "disclose to the defendant a written summary of [expert] testimony the government intends to use . . . during its case in chief."

In sum, rather than testimony "based on the perceptions of the witness" — as the district court described it when overruling Lopez's objections — the bulk of the above opinion testimony is properly characterized as testimony based on the perceptions, education, training, and experience of the witness. It requires precisely the type of "specialized knowledge" of law enforcement governed by Rule 702. Trial courts must ensure that experts are qualified to render their opinions and that the opinions will assist the trier of fact.

(2) *Amendment Clarifies Who is Lay Witness.* Rule 701(c) was added to the rule to clarify that an ostensible lay person testifying on the basis of special experience may be subject to the rules concerning expert witnesses. The Advisory Committee note accompanying this amendment specifically states that Rule 701:

> has been amended to eliminate the risk that the reliability requirements set forth in [amended] Rule 702 will be evaded through the simple expedient of proffering an expert in lay witness clothing. Under the amendment, a witness' testimony must be scrutinized under the rules regulating expert opinion to the extent that the witness is providing testimony based on scientific, technical, or other specialized knowledge within the scope of Rule 702. *See generally Asplundh Mfg. Div. v. Benton Harbor Eng'g.* . . . By channeling testimony that is actually expert testimony to Rule 702, the amendment also ensures that a party will not evade the expert witness disclosure requirements set forth in Fed.R.Civ.P. 26 and Fed.R.Crim.P.16 by simply calling an expert witness in the guise of a layperson.

(3) *Post Amendment Cases.* There is still some tension as to the limits of Rule 701. In *Bank of China, New York Branch v. NBM LLC*, 359 F.3d 171 (2d Cir. 2004), the Court reversed a conviction under the Racketeer Influenced and Corrupt Organizations (RICO) Act because a bank employee was allowed to testify as a lay witness that certain transactions between defendants did not comport with the

business community's understanding of normal, true, trade transactions between a buyer and seller. The Court would not have barred all opinion testimony by the witness, noting that "[t]he fact that Huang has specialized knowledge, or that he carried out the investigation because of that knowledge, does not preclude him from testifying pursuant to Rule 701, so long as the testimony was based on the investigation and reflected his investigatory findings and conclusions, and was not rooted exclusively in his expertise in international banking." However, some of his testimony was not based on his personal investigation, but on his banking experience.

In contrast, *United States v. Colon Osorio*, 360 F.3d 48 (1st Cir. 2004), affirmed a defendant's conviction of possession of a firearm by a felon, where the prosecution witness testified that the weapon moved in interstate commerce. The defendant objected that the witness was not designated as expert in the prosecution's pretrial disclosures. The court held this testimony was lay, rather than expert opinion, because it was based on the witness's personal visit to a Massachusetts plant where the weapon was manufactured, and because the witness's conclusions were derived "from a process of reasoning familiar in everyday life — the firearm was manufactured outside of Puerto Rico [where the defendant was caught with it] and thus must have moved in interstate commerce." Is this a fair reading of Rule 701?

See also *Tampa Bay Shipbuilding & Repair Co. v. Cedar Shipping Co., Ltd.*, 320 F.3d 1213 (11th Cir. 2003), a civil case, where the admission of testimony offered by a ship repairer's employees and/or officers as to whether certain charges relating to ship repair were fair and reasonable or in line with similar services provided by similar operations was affirmed as lay opinion under Rule 701. Can this decision be explained by the long history of courts permitting owners and officers of businesses to testify about matters related to their business, often without qualifying as an expert?

Does the amendment provide sufficient guidance to distinguishing lay from expert opinion?

§ 5.02 EXPERTS: THE COMMON-LAW TRADITION[2]

DEAVER v. HICKOX

Illinois Appellate Court
81 Ill. App. 2d 79, 224 N.E.2d 468 (1967)

Trapp, J.

[This is an appeal from judgments against the defendant. The actions for wrongful death of Deaver followed a collision of two automobiles. There were no competent eyewitnesses to the accident.]

---

[2] Study Guide Reference: Evidence in a Nutshell, Chapter 7:II, at "Introduction: Experts: Special Latitude Under Both Common Law and F.R.E.," and "Regulation of Experts Under the Common Law: Mainly Procedural: A Necessary Step to Understanding the F.R.E."

The sole basis of the appeal is the action of the trial court in admitting, over objection, the expression of an opinion by a state highway police officer, Joe McCombs, as to the speed of the vehicles prior to the collision.

The witness had been a state police officer for about eight years. He had six weeks recruit training at the State Police Academy in Springfield, a two-week course on traffic control and accident investigation at Northwestern University, a two-week refresher course conducted by Northwestern University, and a one-month course in basic police work at the University of Illinois Police Institute in Champaign, Illinois. In the accident investigation course many aspects were studied, including taking care of the injured, measurement of skid marks, estimating damage to vehicles and accident reports. As expressed in ambiguous language, determination of speed in reference to skid marks and damage to vehicles was studied. The officer has investigated between 450 and 500 automobile accidents.

The witness was asked the following question to which objection was made:

Q. Officer, based upon your schooling, your training, and your experience, and based upon your personal observation of the length of the skid marks left by the defendant's car, the type and condition of the oiled surface roadway that you observed there at that time, and the type and extent of damage to the defendant's car, the damage to the left side of the plaintiff's — pardon me — of the doctor's car, the damage to the right side of the doctor's car, the fact that the doctor's car had damage to the top, the fact that the doctor's car had rolled over on its top, the size of each of the automobiles that you observed there, and the general construction of the Buick, and the respective location and distance of each car from the intersection, as you observed them there, now, based upon those observations do you have an opinion as to the speed of the defendant's Falcon when it struck the doctor's automobile?

After objection, the court interrogated the witness out of the presence of the jury as follows:

The Court: Let me ask you, Officer, do you feel that you have sufficient background to express an opinion on the matter?

A. Yes, I have an opinion. I can't say exactly, naturally. I don't think anyone can. I think I [rely on] past experience more than education.

The jury was then returned to the courtroom. The witness was then asked:

Q. Now, officer, based on the observations which you have made and which we placed in our question to you do you have an opinion as to the speed of the defendant's Falcon when it struck the doctor's Buick?

A. I do.

Q. And what is that opinion?

A. My opinion is that the speed at the time of impact would be between sixty and sixty-five miles an hour.

It is to be noted that in the colloquy with the court, the witness largely abandoned the use of any training and education but expressed reliance upon his investigation of accidents over the eight years of police service. The record is bare upon whether such investigations referred to included any tests or computations or other such determinations of speed of vehicles based upon physical damage. The witness had never previously qualified as an expert upon the subject.

From American Jurisprudence Proof of Facts, Vol. 10, we find several statements regarding the qualifications necessary in making computations of this nature. Included are a knowledge of physics and the study of mechanics, i.e., the characteristics of motion and energy and the formulas using the characteristics of momentum, inertia, velocity and friction. It is further said that where there is a substantial weight or design difference between the colliding vehicles, the calculations should be made by technical experts with formulas which consider several aspects of force of impact other than damage.

First, no statement was elicited from the witness, or from others, that there exists a science requiring special skills beyond the ken of the average juror from which a judgment of speed with reference to the vehicles involved could be made with any degree of certainty. Second, no statement was elicited from the witness that he was possessed of the skills necessary to make a determination of speed with relative certainty from the facts presented to him. Third, no discussion was elicited with reference to the factors involved in making a determination of speed either from skid marks, or damage to the vehicles, or from a combination of the two. Fourth, assuming that special skills exist from which a determination of speed may be made with relative certainty, no inquiry was made as to whether such special skills beyond the ken of the average juror were in fact employed by the witness, or anyone else in this case. Fifth, if particular factors were employed to make the determination of speed, those factors were not analyzed in any manner sufficient to enable the jury to determine whether all factors used in arriving at the judgment were, in fact, present. Sixth, as to the degree of certainty of the officer's opinion, an entirely different impression is gained from the testimony presented to the jury, and that presented to the court out of the presence of the jury. Seventh, it appears that if it may be assumed that there is a science involving special skills for determining speeds of vehicles from physical facts which skills are beyond the ken of the average juror, it affirmatively appears that the officer did not use those skills but relied rather upon a generalization of his own experience, which the officer himself described as a speculation.

We approve as a minimum, the statement in WIGMORE ON EVIDENCE, 3rd edition sec. 1927 as follows:

> Where an expert witness, testifying from personal observations gives his opinion as testimony, it is usually necessary to predicate in express terms *hypothetically*, the data upon which the opinion is based. The reason is that otherwise the jury would be unable to tell whether his opinion was meant by him to be applied to the facts ultimately found by the jury.

Even with an expert the court and jury are entitled to know the basis of the opinion.

It is not an answer to say that the matters herein discussed all go to the weight of the evidence. The court should, at a minimum, determine that the witness possesses special skills necessary to cope with the factors of determination involved, and second, that he actually employed those factors prior to permitting the opinion to be given to the jury. Thereafter, even though the matter be beyond the ken of the ordinary juror, the expert's actual analysis of facts which can be known to the juror must be given to make the testimony a matter which can be weighed. A mere statement by an expert without basis or analysis is simply authority by assertion.

Reversed and remanded.

NOTES AND QUESTIONS

(1) *How Far "Beyond the Ken" of Jurors?* See *McClure v. Koch*, 433 S.W.2d 589 (Mo. 1968), excluding an engineer's opinion that a certain degree of slope to a ramp caused the plaintiff's fall, because the court felt the jurors could evaluate the evidence based on their own experiences. The thrust of the opinion is that the matter must be totally beyond lay ken before an expert will be allowed to testify.

(2) *Better Able to Reach the Conclusion.* In *Manney v. Housing Authority*, 79 Cal. App. 2d 453 (Cal. Ct. App. 1947), the issue was the admissibility of a fire chief's opinion as to the cause of a dormitory fire, which he said was caused by a heating duct. He was permitted to testify as an expert. The court, after discussing various rulings in various fact situations, concluded that the ultimate question to be determined in every case in which expert testimony is tendered is whether the matter to be testified to is "outside of the common [human] experience, [and whether the expert,] by reason of his superior knowledge, is *better able* [than the fact-finder] to reach a conclusion from the facts." [Emphasis supplied.] "If this case is one for expert testimony, this is so not because the expert has witnessed the facts, but because he is qualified by reason of his special knowledge to form an opinion on the facts while the ordinary juror is not." The italicized language shows that this is a slightly more liberal test than in *McClure*, Note (1), *supra*. Is it as liberal as Fed. R. Evid. 702? The court notes that other jurisdictions would have excluded because of strict application of the "beyond lay ken" test. The court places stress on the fact that a heating duct as a cause is not likely to be well known to a jury and holds the testimony admissible.

(3) *Restrictions on Hypothethicals.* For a detailed example of a plaintiff's lengthy (six closely printed pages) hypothetical question to a physician in a personal injury case, and a court's searching analysis of the question, see *Ingram v. McCuiston*, 134 S.E.2d 705 (N.C. 1964). The objections made were that the hypothetical assumed facts not supported by the evidence, was in part based on opinions by other doctors, included unnecessary facts, was argumentative, and colored the facts in plaintiff's favor. The court finds each of these to be a proper objection. In the course of the decision, the court says:

> Under our system the jury finds the facts and draws the inferences therefrom. The use of hypothetical questions is required if it is to have the benefit of expert opinions upon factual situations of which the experts have no personal knowledge. However, the hypothetical question has been so

abused that criticism of it is noted by every authority on evidence. The most meritorious of the criticisms are that the questions are often slanted for partisan advantage and are often so long and involved as to confuse rather than assist the jury, and, like some appellate court opinions, contain detailed recitals of factual surplusage not essential to support the conclusions reached. . . . To be competent a hypothetical question may include only facts which are already in evidence or those which the jury might logically infer therefrom. After a careful examination of the record, we find no evidence to support [certain specified] facts which were assumed in the hypothetical question involved on this appeal.

POINTER v. KLAMATH FALLS LAND & TRANSPORTATION CO.

Oregon Supreme Court
59 Or. 438, 117 P. 605 (1911)

McBride, J.

[Action by H. E. Pointer against the Klamath Falls Land & Transportation Company. Judgment for plaintiff. Defendant appeals.]

The defendant had constructed a street railway in Klamath Falls, and plaintiff, while driving a wagon heavily loaded with lumber along one of the streets, found it necessary to make a turn, and in doing so ran against a rail that projected above the surface of the street, and he was thrown from his wagon and seriously injured. Plaintiff claims that the injury resulted from the careless and negligent manner in which the rails were left projecting above the surface of the street. Defendant pleaded contributory negligence [in] that plaintiff was standing on the load. [Defendant] called several witnesses, who claimed to be experienced drivers to show that under the circumstances the usual, correct, and customary position while driving was to sit on the load. Plaintiff called several witnesses, and over the objection of defendant, propounded substantially the following question: "In handling four horses would you consider it careless to stand on a load of lumber and drive them in, coming upon an incline and making a turn?" And also this question: "Would you consider it careless, reckless, or negligent to stand upon a wagon loaded with lumber, upon which there is no seat, driving four horses up a street with an incline and making a turn?" Both these questions were answered in the negative.

We are inclined to think that the testimony of skilled drivers, as to the proper and customary position of a driver, under the circumstances detailed, is admissible; but the question went further than that, and practically required the witness to give an opinion upon the ultimate fact to be decided by the jury, namely, the fact of plaintiff's negligence. This was a usurpation of the functions of the jury, and was reversible error. We think it reasonably well settled that, where either negligence, recklessness, or carelessness constitute the ultimate fact for the jury to decide, it is not competent for an expert witness to express an opinion upon that ultimate fact, but he can only go so far as to state the usual customary method of doing an act or state from his experience the dangers, if any, attendant upon doing it in a manner suggested by the question put to him.

The judgment of the circuit court is reversed, and a new trial ordered.

SIRICO v. COTTO

New York City Civil Court
67 Misc. 2d 636, 324 N.Y.S.2d 483 (1971)

YOUNGER, JUDGE.

To support her [personal injury] case on damages, plaintiff called as a witness Dr. Stanley Wolfson, a specialist in radiology. Dr. Wolfson testified that plaintiff had been sent to him by the treating physician and that, in due course, Dr. Wolfson had taken a number of X-ray photographs of plaintiff's spine. After studying them, he wrote a report setting forth his conclusions and sent it, together with the X-ray plates, directly to the treating physician. All that Dr. Wolfson had with him as he sat on the witness stand was a copy of his report. Having refreshed his recollection from it, he was asked to describe what he had found in the X-rays and to state his opinion with respect to plaintiff's physical condition. At this point, defense counsel objected. In order to afford plaintiff an opportunity to make her record, the jury was excused, and Dr. Wolfson completed his testimony in its absence. He said that the X-rays showed a flattening of plaintiff's lumbar lordosis and a scoliosis of her mid-lumbar spine with convexity towards the left, from which he would conclude that plaintiff was suffering from the consequences of a lumbar-sacral sprain. As to the whereabouts of the X-ray plates, Dr. Wolfson knew only that he had sent them to the treating physician. That gentleman did not testify. Plaintiff's counsel did not have the plates in his possession, nor did he explain his failure to produce them. I sustained defendants' objection and, upon the jury's return to the courtroom, excused Dr. Wolfson.

The problem, then, is whether Dr. Wolfson, without the X-ray plates, might describe what he had seen in them and state the significance he ascribed to his observations. Two lines of analysis are available, each of which leads to the same conclusion — that Dr. Wolfson's testimony is inadmissible.

[Discussion of applicability of the best evidence rule; held to bar Dr. Wolfson's recounting of what the X-ray showed, because X-ray was not in evidence.]

Second, Dr. Wolfson's opinion. An expert's opinion must be based upon the record. Dr. Wolfson's opinion to the effect that plaintiff was suffering from the consequences of a lumbar-sacral sprain was based upon information not in evidence. It was based wholly upon the X-ray plates, and those plates were strangers to the record of this trial.

NOTE

Other Restrictions on Experts at Common Law. An additional decision worth reading on the subject of expert testimony under the traditional pre-Federal Rules of Evidence system that still exists in a number of states is *Sheptur v. Procter & Gamble Distributing Co.*, 261 F.2d 221 (6th Cir. 1958) (testimony of expert that it was reasonably medically *possible* (rather than probable) that defendant caused plaintiff's skin condition with its detergent is not sufficient), *cert. denied*, 359 U.S. 1003 (1959). What, if anything, does Fed. R. Evid. 702 do to this rule, which often is said to apply at both the admissibility and the sufficiency-of-evidence stage — would Rule 702 affect the requirement of "reasonable medical certainty" (or "reasonable medical probability") at both stages? Compare with *Sheptur, Ideal Food Products Co. v. Rupe*, 261 P.2d 992 (Ariz. 1953).

§ 5.03 EXPERTS: FIRST WAVE OF REFORM OF THE COMMON LAW: THE ADVENT OF THE FEDERAL RULES OF EVIDENCE: EXPANSION OF WHO ARE EXPERTS? TO WHAT MAY THEY TESTIFY?[3]

Read Federal Rule of Evidence 702, "Testimony by Expert Witnesses." Acquaint yourself with all the expert rules, Rules 703-706. Note Rule 704, generally abolishing (with a narrow exception) the common-law rule against testimony on ultimate issues.

In this "First Wave of Reform," treated in this section, that came in 1975 with the Federal Rules of Evidence, subsections (b), (c), and (d) of Rule 702 were not in the rule. They were added in the year 2000. Subsections (b), (c), and (d), and the cases it attempts to codify (*Daubert* and *Kumho*) are the "Second Wave of Reform," treated *infra* in Chapter 6. They require a somewhat detailed consideration by the judge of the merits of what is actually being said in the testimony, to provide greater assurances of reliability, rather than merely looking only at the expert's qualifications for what he/she is saying and the testimony's apparent helpfulness on its face to the fact-finder.

Section (b) of Rule 704, reinstating the common-law prohibition on ultimate opinions in a narrow class of cases (i.e., expert witnesses testifying on mental issues in criminal cases) was added in 1984 as a result of the acquittal (but subsequent indefinite civil confinement) on insanity grounds, of the attempted assassin of President Reagan, John Hinckley.

UNITED STATES v. JOHNSON

United States Court of Appeals, Fifth Circuit
575 F.2d 1347 (1978), *cert. denied*, 440 U.S. 907 (1979)

Charles Clark, Circuit Judge.

[Lipper was found guilty of crimes of importing marijuana.]

He first argues that it was improper to permit de Pianelli to testify as an expert concerning the origin of the marijuana. Appellants concede that the substance with which they were dealing was marijuana. They contend, however, that there was no objective evidence showing that the marijuana was imported from outside the

---

[3] Study Guide Reference: Evidence in a Nutshell, Chapter 7:IIA, at "Liberalized Procedural Treatment of Experts Under the F.R.E.: Rules 702-705 as Initially Enacted (and Still Largely in Place Today)."

customs territory of the United States. Since no marijuana was ever seized, the only nonhearsay evidence concerning the origin of this marijuana came from de Pianelli. When de Pianelli was first asked to state whether the marijuana had come from Colombia, counsel for defendants objected. The jury was then excused and de Pianelli was examined on voir dire and cross-examined by defense counsel. During voir dire, he admitted that he had smoked marijuana over a thousand times and that he had dealt in marijuana as many as twenty times. He also said that he had been asked to identify marijuana over a hundred times and had done so without making a mistake. He based his identification upon the plant's appearance, its leaf, buds, stems, and other physical characteristics, as well as upon the smell and the effect of smoking it. On cross-examination he stated that he had been called upon to identify the source of various types of marijuana. He explained that characteristics such as the packaging, the physical appearance, the smell, the taste, and the effect could all be used in identifying the source of the marijuana. It was stipulated that he had no special training or education for such identification. Instead, his qualifications came entirely from "the experience of being around a great deal and smoking it." He also said that he had compared Colombian marijuana with marijuana from other places as many as twenty times. Moreover, he had seen Colombian marijuana that had been grown in the United States and had found that it was different from marijuana grown in Colombia. Before the jury he related his experiences with marijuana and explained that he had tested a sample of marijuana from each importation and had verified that it came from Colombia.

Lipper contends that the source of marijuana is not a matter requiring expert opinion and that there was no foundation for de Pianelli's testimony. Lipper further contends that it was an error to qualify de Pianelli as an expert because he had never been to South America and, of course, had never smoked marijuana there or seen it growing in South America. Finally, Lipper contends that de Pianelli's testimony was conclusively rebutted by an associate professor of biological science at Florida State University, Loren C. Anderson.

In *Crawford v. Worth*, 447 F.2d 738, 740-41 (5th Cir. 1971), we stated the principle which guides appellate review of trial court determinations concerning expert testimony:

> The federal rule . . . is ". . . the trial judge has broad discretion in the matter of the admission or exclusion of the expert evidence, and his action is to be sustained unless manifestly erroneous." . . . In this Circuit: "The expert qualification of a witness is a question for the trial judge, whose discretion is conclusive unless clearly erroneous as a matter of law." . . .

Here the subject of the inference, the source of the marijuana, is related to the occupation of selling illegal drugs and to the science of botany, neither of which is likely to be within the knowledge of an average juror. For the government to obtain a conviction it was necessary that it prove that the marijuana came from outside the customs territory of the United States. Testimony which would identify the source of the marijuana would be of obvious assistance to the jury. It was therefore proper for the trial court to consider whether de Pianelli was qualified to provide such testimony.

Rule 702 of the Federal Rules of Evidence provides that expertise may be obtained by experience as well as from formal training or education. [D]e Pianelli's testimony during voir dire revealed that his substantial experience in dealing with marijuana included identification of Colombian marijuana. In light of that testimony, the trial court was within its discretion in deciding to admit the testimony for the jury's consideration.

The introduction of testimony from an expert witness does not foreclose the issue from consideration by the jury, which need not accept the expert's testimony. A defendant is free to introduce his own expert to challenge the prosecution's witness. Here the defense introduced the testimony of Professor Anderson, who said that it was impossible to determine the origin of a particular sample of marijuana by examining its physical characteristics. The trial court instructed the jury in general terms concerning the weight it should give to testimony. In addition, it specifically instructed the jury regarding expert witnesses and concluded with this admonition: "You should consider such expert opinion received in this case and give it such weight as you think it deserves." Thus the conflict between the experts was correctly presented to the jury for resolution.

The only remaining challenge to de Pianelli's status as an expert is the argument that no one can acquire the skill which he professed to have. That objection may be rephrased in the words of this court in *International Paper Company v. United States*, 227 F.2d 201, 205 (5th Cir. 1955): "an opinion is no better than the hypothesis or the assumption upon which it is based." If the hypothesis is proved to be flawed, the witness should not be allowed to testify. This type of objection would be directed at, for example, the testimony of someone purporting to tell the color of a person's hair from fingerprints or the use of a testing device that had not been generally accepted by the scientific community.

Neither at trial nor on appeal have the appellants directly argued that no one can distinguish marijuana that has been grown in Colombia from other marijuana. They have, however, done so implicitly, and we believe that they tried to do so through the testimony of Professor Anderson. We shall therefore briefly consider that objection.

On the record before us we cannot say that the claim of an ability to identify Colombian marijuana is so inherently implausible that, as a matter of law, a jury should not be permitted to hear testimony on the identification. [D]e Pianelli claimed that he could identify Colombian marijuana. Professor Anderson disputed that claim. But Professor Anderson admitted that climatological differences could produce differences in the marijuana plants. Professor Anderson's testimony was based upon the lack of scientific tests which would demonstrate that marijuana grown in Colombia differed from that grown elsewhere. Tests had shown, however, that marijuana grown in Canada differed from marijuana grown in other locations. Thus, there was some ambiguity in Professor Anderson's testimony. The issue was one that could have been resolved by the jury. In allowing the jury to consider the question and to hear the same arguments counsel now make to us, the trial court did not err.

Affirmed in part.

NOTES AND QUESTIONS

(1) *Lay or Expert Opinion?* Is there any difference in the type of testimony given by the "experts" in either of the above cases than what was treated as lay opinion testimony in *Asplundh, supra* § 5.01[B]?

(2) *Law Enforcement Officials as Experts.* In criminal cases, it has become common for the prosecutor to offer testimony of police and Drug Enforcement Agents on a variety of topics. Results are not always consistent. A sampling includes: (a) testimony on crime families; *compare United States v. Pungitore*, 910 F.2d 1084 (3d Cir. 1990) (affirmed), *cert. denied*, 500 U.S. 915 (1991), *with United States v. Long*, 917 F.2d 691 (2d Cir. 1990) (reversed as not relevant); (b) testimony about types of drug transactions; *compare United States v. Rivera*, 971 F.2d 876 (2d Cir. 1992) (affirmed), *with United States v. Cruz*, 981 F.2d 659 (2d Cir. 1992) (reversed; testimony that drug wholesalers use intermediaries to avoid arrest), *and United States v. Castillo*, 924 F.2d 1227 (2d Cir. 1991) (reversed; testimony regarding practice of making customers sniff cocaine); (c) testimony about drug courier profiles; *compare United States v. Foster*, 939 F.2d 445 (7th Cir. 1991) (affirmed; testimony given by drug agent who was eyewitness) *with United States v. Lui*, 941 F.2d 844 (9th Cir. 1991) (reversed; drug courier profile was not relevant to proving guilt at trial); and (d) testimony about narcotics jargon; *see United States v. Simmons*, 923 F.2d 934 (2d Cir.), *cert. denied*, 500 U.S. 919 (1991). Expert evidence on the practices of drug trafficking organizations has also been held to be inadmissible (at least on the particular facts) when the defendant was charged with possession with intent to distribute, but not conspiracy. *See United States v. Pineda-Torres*, 287 F.3d 860 (9th Cir.), *cert denied*, 537 U.S. 1066 (2002).

Do some of these cases also implicate the ban on character testimony? See *Castillo*, finding error because the testimony about typical Washington Heights drug dealers was used to "propound the impermissible theory that appellants' guilt could be inferred from the behavior of unrelated persons," and *Cruz*, finding error where drug defendant was referred to as the "Dominican" and the witness implied that drug dealers in the neighborhood often shared that ethnic background. In contrast, reference to "Jamaican" drug dealers was not error where used to explain hidden meaning of a Jamaican caller's coded questions, not to suggest guilt by national origin. *See Headley v. Tilghman*, 53 F.3d 472 (2d Cir.), *cert. denied*, 516 U.S. 877 (1995).

(Some of the testimony by law enforcement officials, as well as others, may also raise issues that will be considered in Chapter 6, concerning ratcheted-up standards for reliability of the opinion. *See, e.g., United States v. Harris*, 192 F.3d 580 (6th Cir. 1999) (methods and operations of street level drug dealers post-*Kumho*).)

(3) *Expert Opinion "Not Helpful".* The Minnesota Supreme Court rejected expert testimony concerning gang activity and gang affiliation in *State v. DeShay*, 669 N.W.2d 878 (Minn. 2003), a prosecution for conspiracy to commit first-degree controlled-substance crime for the benefit of a gang. The Court held that to the extent the evidence was relevant in this non-complex drug conspiracy case, it was largely duplicative of testimony of witnesses with first-hand knowledge; it was also not helpful or relevant to have expert testimony that crimes committed by criminal gangs in general run the gamut from "murder for hire" to property crimes, that

defendant's gang engaged in drive-by shootings, or that certain individuals associated with defendant's gang and involved in the case had prior convictions for criminal sexual conduct and crimes committed for the benefit of a gang. The testimony strongly suggested to the jury that a law enforcement specialist believed the State's witnesses and therefore the jury should find the defendant guilty. However, the admission of the testimony was found to be harmless.

(4) *Expert Qualifications. See Fox v. Dannenberg*, 906 F.2d 1253 (8th Cir. 1990):

> It is important also to note that Rule 702 does not rank academic training over demonstrated practical experience. . . . [A]n individual can qualify as an expert where he possesses sufficient knowledge gained from practical experience, even though he may lack academic qualifications in the particular field of expertise. See, e.g., *Davis* . . . (witness with relevant practical experience but no medical training competent to testify as to the probabilities of transmitting gonorrhea); *Loudermill* . . . (witness who was not a medical doctor but who had other substantial scientific training held competent to testify as to the cause of plaintiff's cirrhosis of the liver); *Circle J Dairy* . . . (witness who was not a veterinarian and had no advanced degrees qualified to testify as an expert as to damage to cattle because he had significant practical experience with health problems in dairy cattle).
>
> The threshold question of whether a witness is competent as an expert is solely for the trial judge. Once the trial court has determined that a witness is competent to testify as an expert, challenges to the expert's skill or knowledge go to the weight to be accorded the expert testimony rather than to its admissibility. The question of the expert's credibility and the weight to be accorded the expert testimony are ultimately for the trier of fact to determine.
>
> Fox sought to introduce the testimony of two engineers who would have testified that Todd Dannenberg was driving the car at the time of the accident. The first expert was Jay Pfeiffer, who is a licensed engineer with a firm that specializes in transportation and accident investigation and analysis. Pfeiffer holds a bachelor's degree in engineering with additional course work toward a graduate degree. He claims to have specialized in investigating and analyzing traffic accidents for approximately nine years; he has investigated over 1,000 accidents. The second expert was Dr. Thomas E. Mullinazzi, who is the Associate Dean of the School of Engineering at the University of Kansas. He has a doctorate in civil engineering and specializes in transportation engineering. He is a member of several professional engineering organizations and has published papers in his field. He claims that he has 12 years of experience in the investigation and analysis of traffic accidents. Both experts would have based their opinion that Dannenberg was driving the car on the following factors: the physical forces operating on the car at the time of the accident, the location of the two boys immediately following the accident, the pattern of the boys' injuries, and the damage to the interior of the car.

> The district court did not allow either engineer to testify. The district court reasoned that because one of the factors that Pfeiffer and Mullinazzi would have considered in reaching their opinions was the victims' injury patterns, they were not qualified because neither one had training or education in medical science.
>
> We believe that this finding was an abuse of discretion. The question of who was driving is primarily a question of physical science rather than of medical science. . . . In their combined 20-plus years of experience in accident reconstruction they undoubtedly have acquired some knowledge of the medical aspects of traffic injury patterns.
>
> The shortcomings in their qualifications are not so serious as to render their opinions so fundamentally unsupported that [they] cannot help the factfinder. . . . Rather, it is . . . for the jury, with the assistance of vigorous cross-examination, to measure the worth of the opinion[s].

(5) *Can't Require Too Much Expertise.* In *Stagl v. Delta Airlines, Inc.*, 117 F.3d 76 (2d Cir. 1997), judgment was reversed where the judge excluded an expert as not being qualified because his experience was too general to render an opinion that Delta was negligent in supervising the interaction between passengers and the baggage carousel. The court found that, according to the judge's requirements, expertise was required in airport management or design or baggage claims, which would have required working for the industry:

> Accordingly, to require the degree of specificity the court imposed came close to letting that industry indirectly set its own standards. At times this cannot be avoided. But where, as here, well-trained people with somewhat more general qualifications are available, it is error to exclude them. For this reason, the court should have allowed Fischer, an undoubted expert in human-machine interactions, to testify.

(6) *Experts Who Lie About Qualifications.* But what about experts who lie about their qualifications? *See* Giannelli, *False Credentials*, 16 CRIM. JUST. 40 (Fall 2001). See *Chein v. Shumsky*, 373 F.3d 978 (9th Cir. 2004), holding a medical doctor's perjury conviction did not materially affect the outcome of a personal injury case, but admitting that his stated qualifications were misleading,

(7) *Experts Cannot Offer Opinions Beyond Their Qualifications.* In *Wilson v. State*, 803 A.2d 1034 (Md. 2002), the trial court did not abuse its discretion in prohibiting the defense pathologist from testifying as to retail practices in the life insurance industry. The defendant was charged with killing his child, and had taken out an insurance policy on the child's life. His defense was that the child died naturally from Sudden Infant Death Syndrome ("SIDS"). Defense counsel had proffered at the bench that Dr. Jones, the defense expert, knew of a study from a company in Connecticut, which apparently found that 22 or 23% of parents purchased infant life insurance. Who would have been qualified to offer this opinion?

(8) *Experts Who Fabricate their Testimony, as Opposed to their Credentials.* In the past several years a small number of forensic experts have been exposed as simply making up their testimony. In several of these cases, the number of convictions potentially affected has been substantial. *See, e.g.*, Giannelli, *Fabricated*

Reports, 16 Crim. Just. 49 (Winter 2002). Misstatement can also become an issue in high profile cases. For example, Secret Service laboratory director Larry Stewart has been charged with perjuring himself during his testimony in the famous Martha Stewart trial. In particular, he is accused of testifying falsely that he participated in an ink-test for a contested notation, when in fact he allegedly did not participate in the test. Would this render the testimony inadmissible? What are the safeguards against such testimony?

§ 5.04 MORE FIRST-WAVE REFORM OF THE COMMON LAW BY THE FEDERAL RULES OF EVIDENCE: EXPANSION OF ADMISSIBILITY OF (OTHERWISE INADMISSIBLE) FACTS AND DATA CONSIDERED BY EXPERT, AND OPINION BASED THEREON[4]

Read Federal Rules of Evidence 703, "Bases of an Expert's Opinion Testimony," and 705, "Disclosing the Facts or Data Underlying an Expert's Opinion."

Rule 703 originally stopped after the words "need not be admissible". The remainder was added in the year 2000, to remedy uncertainty reflected in conflicting decisions about whether the rule licensed only testifying to the *opinion* that was based on the reasonably-relied-upon inadmissible basis, or also licensed testifying to the inadmissible *basis itself* as well.

WILSON v. CLARK

Illinois Supreme Court

84 Ill. 2d 186, 417 N.E.2d 1322, *cert. denied*, 454 U.S. 836 (1981)

Moran, Justice.

Plaintiff, John Wilson, brought an action against defendant, Dr. David Clark, following the alleged negligent medical treatment of the plaintiff which resulted in the amputation of his right leg below the knee. Following a jury trial, a verdict was returned for the defendant. . . .

We next consider plaintiff's argument that the trial court erred in allowing his hospital records to be admitted into evidence without proper foundation, and in permitting a hypothetical question based on those records.

After the hospital records were placed in evidence, defense counsel was permitted to tell defendant's expert witness, Dr. Nyman, to assume the facts stated in the hospital records to be true and to further assume additional facts regarding plaintiff's treatment. Upon this foundation, defense counsel was then allowed to ask Dr. Nyman to give his opinion of whether the "hypothetical" Dr. Clark exercised the degree of knowledge and expertise expected of a board-certified orthopedic surgeon in Kane County.

---

[4] Study Guide Reference: Evidence in a Nutshell, Chapter 7:IIA, at "Liberalized Procedural Treatment of Experts Under the F.R.E.: Rules 702-705 as Initially Enacted (and Still Largely in Place Today)" (procedural liberalizations 3 to 5 only).

The hospital records in this case were admitted into evidence without a proper foundation. However, we believe it is unnecessary for hospital records to be admitted in order to elicit an expert medical opinion. This court in *People v. Ward* (1975) held that medical records may be used by an expert witness in forming an opinion as to an accused's sanity even though the reports are not admitted into evidence. Although *Ward* involved a treating doctor giving an opinion we believe that Federal Rule of Evidence 703, upon whose rationale the case relied, makes no distinction between the opinions of treating and non-treating doctors.

Both Federal and State courts have interpreted Federal Rule 703 to allow opinions based on facts not in evidence. None of these cases makes a distinction between treating and nontreating experts. According to these cases, the key element in applying Federal Rule 703 is whether the information upon which the expert bases his opinion is of a type that is reliable.

In addition, the advisory committee's note to Federal Rule 703 makes it clear that the rule applies to expert opinions based on firsthand observation, hypothetical questions, or presentation of data outside the court. The note provides:

> Facts or data upon which expert opinions are based may, under the rule, be derived from three possible sources. The first is the firsthand observation of the witness, with opinions based thereon traditionally allowed. A treating physician affords an example. The second source, presentation at the trial, also reflects existing practice. The technique may be the familiar hypothetical question or having the expert attend the trial and hear the testimony establishing the facts. The third source contemplated by the rule consists of presentation of data to the expert outside of court and other than by his own perception.

According to the note, allowing expert opinions based on facts not in evidence dispenses with "the expenditure of substantial time in producing and examining various authenticating witnesses. [The physician's] validation, expertly performed and subject to cross-examination, ought to suffice for judicial purposes."

Generally it is extremely time consuming to call into court every person who made an entry in the hospital records. We hold that, in the future, as later stated, due to the high degree of reliability of hospital records, an expert may give his response to a hypothetical question based on facts contained in those records, even if the hospital records themselves are not in evidence.

Further, in following the modern trend under Federal Rule 705, an expert may give an opinion without disclosing the facts underlying that opinion.

Under Rule 705 the burden is placed upon the adverse party during cross-examination to elicit the facts underlying the expert opinion. The advisory committee's note to Rule 705 allows an expert opinion without disclosure of underlying facts whether the opinion is based on firsthand or second-hand information. In light of Illinois' extensive pretrial discovery procedures, this does not place an undue burden on the cross-examining party.

This court's following of Federal Rules 703 and 705 comports with the modern trend liberalizing certain trial procedures. Eighteen states have adopted Federal

Rule 703 verbatim or with minor changes. In addition, California, Kansas, and New Jersey have adopted similar provisions. Adoption of these two rules eliminates the time consuming process of posing long hypothetical questions that afford an opportunity to sum up or reiterate the evidence in the middle of the case.

[B]ecause this opinion represents a change in Illinois law, we hold that, except as to the parties herein, to which this change shall apply in the retrial, the law of this case shall apply only to cases in which the initial complaints are filed on and after the date of this opinion, or in which the trial commences on or after September 1, 1981.

AMERICAN UNIVERSAL INSURANCE CO. v. FALZONE

United States Court of Appeals, First Circuit
644 F.2d 65 (1981)

Per Curiam.

Appellant's house burned in 1976. Appellee insurance companies brought this diversity action claiming arson and seeking a declaration that they were not liable for the loss. The jury made a special finding of arson. Appellant cites as error the district court's ruling on an evidentiary point.

The evidentiary ruling was made at the close of plaintiffs' case. Appellant moved to strike the opinion testimony of a state fire marshal, Ricker, that the fire was of human origin, because part of Ricker's opinion had been based on information from other fire marshals on the inspection team that the furnace or heating system was not the cause of the fire. It appears that Ricker had made his own observations of a lawnmower on which burned fragments of wood had fallen from above, suggesting that the fire had not started in the basement, this tending to rule out the furnace as the source; he had also observed in the basement oil tanks two-thirds or three-quarters full; he had eliminated other possible causes — the sun's rays, lightning, spontaneous combustion, electrical wiring; one complete candle had been found, as well as a wrapper devised for two candles, and other items of circumstantial evidence. Ricker also relied on the statements from his team members, who were more experienced in inspecting oil burners.

The district court's refusal to strike Ricker's testimony was fully justified by Federal Rule of Evidence 703. Even more illuminating, in the light of the facts of this case, are the accompanying advisory notes, which read in part:

> Facts or data upon which expert opinions are based may, under the rule, be derived from . . . presentation of data to the expert outside of court and other than by his own perception. In this respect the rule is designed to broaden the basis for expert opinions beyond that current in many jurisdictions and to bring the judicial practice into line with the practice of the experts themselves when not in court. Thus a physician in his own practice bases his diagnosis on information from numerous sources and of considerable variety, including statements by patients and relatives, reports and *opinions* from nurses, technicians and other doctors, hospital records and X rays. Most of them are admissible in evidence, but only with

> the expenditure of substantial time in producing and examining various authenticating witnesses. The physician makes life-and-death decisions in reliance upon them. His validation, expertly performed and subject to cross-examination, ought to suffice for judicial purposes. (Emphasis added.)

Appellant conceded Ricker's expert qualifications. Ricker testified that his conclusions were based upon his own investigation of the ruins together with reports from his coinvestigators Bissett and Rollins with whom he said he worked as a "team." Since it is reasonable for one state fire marshal to rely on the contemporaneous and on-the-scene opinions of other investigators on his team as to the portion of the investigation that they carried out within their competence, Ricker's testimony was properly admitted. Fed. R. Ev. 703. The important requirement that reliance be reasonable — a matter requiring the district court's careful consideration — was amply satisfied in this case.

Affirmed.

NOTES AND QUESTIONS

(1) See also *United States v. Marler*, 614 F.2d 47 (5th Cir. 1980), where a deputy fire marshal was allowed to testify that a fire was the result of arson.

(2) *The Expert as a Conduit for Hearsay.* In *Village of Ponca v. Crawford*, 26 N.W. 365 (Neb. 1886), plaintiff fell on a sidewalk and sued the village. His son, a physician, testified for him that he had examined the father but was puzzled by what might be the cause of plaintiff's enlarged breast, so he called in three other physicians, who decided the condition was due to a tumor resulting from injury, and thus that was the opinion of all of them, including the witness. Plaintiff's counsel tried in vain to get the witness to emphasize any role the son himself and the son's medical learning and experience might have played in or contributed to the joint decision. The admission of the son's testimony was held to be reversible error. It is unclear whether merely the recounting of the other physicians' opinions was inadmissible, or whether the whole testimony (including the son's opinion) was inadmissible. The court's brief rationale is that the testimony was "simply hearsay." Was the court necessarily adopting the older view prospectively rejected in *Wilson v. Clark*? Or was it adopting the Federal Rules of Evidence view? Or something in between? Did plaintiff's lawyer make any error in preparation of this case?

Compare *United States v. Smith*, 869 F.2d 348 (7th Cir. 1989), which observed that an expert cannot simply summarize out-of-court statements, but found that the expert was not just an "understudy." Compare *United States v. Tran Trong Cuong*, 18 F.3d 1132 (4th Cir. 1994), finding it was error for an expert to testify that a well-respected physician agreed with him. Compare *Pelster v. Ray*, 987 F.2d 514 (8th Cir. 1993), reversing a civil fraud judgment where a "criminal investigator" based his testimony on odometer readings that any lay person could have compared.

(3) *Typical Jury Instructions.* Most courts have pattern jury instructions telling the jury to consider the expert's qualifications and bases for his or her opinion in weighing the testimony. California Jury Instruction 2.40 (BAJI) states, in part, that "[a]n opinion is only as good as the facts and reasons on which it is based."

The jury is instructed further in BAJI 2.41 that in cases of conflicting expert testimony it may choose to believe the expert testimony it finds more credible.

PROBLEM 5A: MULTIPLE EXPERTS FOR THE PRICE OF ONE, AND INSULATION OF THE OTHERS FROM CROSS — OR, IS INTRODUCTION OF THE HEARSAY "FACTS AND DATA," CONSIDERED BY THE EXPERT UNDER RULE 703, NECESSARY FOR THE JURY TO EVALUATE THE OPINION?

Defendant's medical expert, Dr. Bluster, opines that the cause of the rupture of plaintiff's fundibulum was not any act of malpractice by the defendant doctor, but rather that plaintiff contracted a serious disease called coreopsis in a manner unrelated to the operation that the defendant performed. After eliciting this opinion, defendant's counsel offers into evidence the documentary basis of the "facts and data" that Dr. Bluster considered — which consists of several hearsay summaries of the operation prepared for this purpose by defendant's colleagues, plus numerous articles about coreopsis-caused fundibulum ruptures. "This evidence is necessary for the jury to see that Dr. Bluster's opinion rests on a sound basis, your honor," says defense counsel. "The expert is entitled to consider these 'facts and data' under Rule 703." But plaintiff's counsel vehemently objects: "It's nothing but a pile of hearsay from so-called experts I can't cross-examine!"

How should the court rule? Does Rule 703 compel only one possible outcome? What possible choices are available to the judge?

Chapter 6

SCIENTIFIC AND PROBABILISTIC EVIDENCE

Special Instances of Expert Evidence (F.R.E. Article VII)

§ 6.01 TRADITIONAL *FRYE* STANDARD[1]

UNITED STATES v. BROWN

United States Court of Appeals, Sixth Circuit
557 F.2d 541 (1977)

Celebrezze, Circuit Judge.

[The Planned Parenthood Association located near the campus of Wayne State University was firebombed.] Suspects fleeing the scene fired upon university police. Brown was apprehended in the vicinity by Detroit police officers responding to a radio call. At the time of the arrest, Appellant [i.e., Brown] and two others were subjects of a massive manhunt because of their suspected involvement in gun battles which had left one officer dead and several wounded. In the back seat of the patrol car on the way to police headquarters, Appellant confessed to the firebombing. Appellant was convicted by a jury.

Appellant contests the admission of expert testimony comparing a sample of his hair with three hairs of unknown origin found on a bottleneck discovered at the site of the firebombing. The controversy surrounds tests on the hair samples conducted by Mr. Bayard and Dr. Muggli using a technique known as ion microprobic analysis. Ion microprobic analysis is a technique for measuring the trace element content of a sample matrix. Both ion microprobic analysis and neutron activation analysis proceed from the theory that matrices from a common source will have similar trace element contents and that matrices from different sources will exhibit dissimilar trace element contents. In neutron activation analysis the sample matrix is irradiated by neutrons. The trace element content is determined by measuring gamma rays emitted from the now-radioactive sample. . . . In ion microprobic analysis the trace element content of a sample matrix is measured by the number and mass of the ions it releases when pierced by an ion beam. The device for conducting ion microprobic analysis essentially consists of two mass spectrometers.

---

[1] Study Guide Reference: Evidence in a Nutshell, Chapter 7:II B, at "Introduction," and at "What is 'Scientific Evidence'? An Amorphous Category of Expert Evidence Singled Out for Special Rigorous Treatment," and at "Scientific Evidence: The Tests for Admissibility," and "The Common Law Frye Test: 'General Acceptence' ".

The first mass spectrometer generates a magnetic field which separates ions according to their mass. A beam composed of one type of ion is then projected toward the sample matrix. The ion beam's striking the matrix causes it to cast off ions of varying mass and numbers which are collected and measured by a second mass spectrometer. The data collected by the ion microprobe mass analyzer indicates the concentration of trace elements in the matrix. Although the initial use of ion microprobic analysis was to test metals and inorganic materials, experiments have been conducted using organic matrices as well. At the McCrone Institute, Mr. Bayard and Dr. Muggli have been experimenting with human hair as a matrix. In the course of their experiments they have used the ion microprobe mass analyzer to trace the element content of approximately 130 samples of human hair. Each sample was tested for 25 to 40 elements. Comparisons of the samples were made by charting the data supplied by the mass analyzer and visually comparing the charts of elements for each sample against charts of other samples tested.

[In the present case] based on a comparison of charts prepared on the hair samples supplied by the prosecution and the samples they had previously tested, Bayard and Muggli [concluded] that the hairs were of common origin. After holding a special evidentiary hearing, the District Court ruled that the technique of ion microprobic analysis was well accepted in the field and that expert testimony based thereon was admissible. The Court allowed the witnesses to testify on the findings of their experiments on human hair and the results of the tests conducted on the hair samples in this case, but would not permit the prosecution's experts to state their ultimate conclusion that the unknown hairs belonged to Appellant. Appellant contends that it was error to admit any testimony based on ion microprobic analysis of human hair.

A necessary predicate to the admission of scientific evidence is that the principle upon which it is based "must be sufficiently established to have gained general acceptance in the particular field to which it belongs." *Frye v. United States*, 293 F. 1013, 1014, 54 App. D.C. 46 (1923). In *United States v. Franks* . . . we equated general acceptance in the scientific community with a showing that the scientific principles and procedures on which expert testimony is based are reliable and sufficiently accurate. However, [a]bsolute certainty of result or unanimity of scientific opinion is not required for admissibility. Conflicting testimony concerning the conclusions drawn by experts, so long as they are based on a generally accepted and reliable scientific principle, ordinarily go to the weight of the testimony rather than to its admissibility. . . .

Appellant admits that ion microprobic analysis is not a new technique and has attained a sufficient degree of acceptance in the field of mass spectrometry. However, Appellant contends that ion microprobic analysis when used to make hair comparisons is a new technique which has yet to be accepted by the scientific community. He also criticizes the procedures followed by the prosecution's experts in conducting their hair experiments and he claims that certain theories on the properties of human hair propounded by the witnesses during their testimony are novel and unsupported.

[W]e are inclined to agree with Appellant that the Government failed to fulfill the threshold requirement of demonstrating that ion microprobic analysis is a generally accepted procedure for comparing samples of human hair and that the experiments conducted by their experts carry sufficient indicia of reliability and accuracy to be said to cross "the line between the experimental and demonstrable stages." *Frye*. Research has failed to disclose a single reported case where testimony based on microprobic analysis of hair has been admitted into evidence. . . . [N]o attempt was made to match the test samples against a statistically valid test group. There is a clear danger of misidentification where a test compares the hair of a black defendant from Detroit with hairs taken from a predominantly white test group collected primarily in Chicago. . . . .

[*Reversed.*]

NOTES AND QUESTIONS

(1) *Frye Controlled the Admission of Scientific Evidence. Frye* was the dominant test in this country until the advent of *Daubert v. Merrell Dow Pharmaceuticals, Inc.*, 509 U.S. 579 (1993), *infra.* Although *Frye* concerned the admissibility of a machine that was a precursor to the modern polygraph, its criteria were applied to all manner of scientific evidence. Even today, a significant number of states still follow its requirements. The heart of *Frye* is contained in the following paragraph (emphasis added):

> Just when a scientific principle or discovery crosses the line between the experimental and demonstrable stages is difficult to define. Somewhere in this twilight zone the evidential force of the principle must be recognized, and while courts will go a long way in admitting expert testimony deduced from a well-recognized scientific principle or discovery, *the thing from which the deduction is made must be sufficiently established to have gained general acceptance in the particular field in which it belongs.*

There has always been considerable disagreement as to whether Frye applies only to criminal cases and whether it applies only to "novel" scientific evidence.

(2) *Problems in Applying Frye.* A number of questions arise when applying *Frye*. What is general acceptance — is a simple majority sufficient? How broadly or narrowly should the relevant scientific community be defined? Can the testimony of the inventor of the technique establish its foundation, or are disinterested scientists necessary? As the present case shows, there is an almost infinite continuum from very basic principles (e.g., that bombarding materials with ions releases other ions) through less basic principles (e.g., that these other ions reveal component elements related to their mass) to specific principles (e.g., that this technique can be applied to organic materials) to even more specific principles (that the technique can be applied to hair). The same continuum can be applied to questions concerning the uniqueness of an individual's hair. To which "principle(s)" does the requirement of general acceptance apply? And acceptance of what? — that it is 100% reliable? Some of these questions persist under *Daubert.* Courts vary in their responses to all of these queries.

(3) *"Conservative" Nature of Frye Test. Frye* often is referred to as a "conservative" test, meaning that it delays or prevents the admission of valid

scientific evidence. In fact, the California Supreme Court observed in *People v. Kelly*, 549 P.2d 1240 (Cal. 1976):

> *Frye* was deliberately intended to interpose a substantial obstacle to the unrestrained admission of evidence based upon new scientific principles. Several reasons founded in logic and common sense support a posture of judicial caution in this area. Lay jurors tend to give considerable weight to "scientific" evidence when presented by "experts" with impressive credentials. We have acknowledged the existence of a "misleading aura of certainty which often envelops a new scientific process, obscuring its currently experimental nature."

After *Daubert*, the California Supreme Court reaffirmed its allegiance to *Frye* in *People v. Leahy*, 882 P.2d 321 (Cal. 1994), quoting from *Kelly* that "there is ample justification for the exercise of considerable judicial caution in the acceptance of evidence developed by new scientific techniques," and finding that "[n]othing occurring in the years since *Kelly* was decided requires us to reconsider that conclusion."

Are there other reasons that support the use of *Frye*? Should *Frye* be limited to criminal cases where indigent defendants typically do not have the resources to challenge new science? What types of "junk science" are problematic in civil cases?

(4) *Frye Is Not Dead.* A few years ago a count revealed that approximately 15 states still applied *Frye*. These include many of the most populous states, such as California, Florida, Illinois, Michigan, New York, and Pennsylvania. Moreover, even in federal court, both *Daubert* and *Kumho*, discussed later in this chapter, permit at least partial reliance on peer review and general acceptance. Some believe that rather than *Frye* being dead, the *Daubert/Kumho* standard has expanded *Frye's* applicability to all expert testimony, rather than just scientific expertise, criminal cases, or novel scientific evidence.

§ 6.02 CURRENT TEST UNDER RULE 702: *DAUBERT* AND ITS FALLOUT[2]

Read Federal Rules of Evidence 702, "Testimony by Expert Witnesses." Focus on (b), (c), and (d) of the rule, which were added after the *Daubert* and *Kumho* decisions, reproduced below. Those subsections of the rule were intended to codify those decisions.

[2] Study Guide Reference: Evidence in a Nutshell, Chapter 7:IIB & C from "Tests Based on the F.R.E. in the Immediately Pre-Daubert Era" through "Categories of Expert and Scientific Evidence."

[A] *Daubert* Decision

DAUBERT v. MERRELL DOW PHARMACEUTICALS, INC.

United States Supreme Court
509 U.S. 579 (1993)

JUSTICE BLACKMUN delivered the opinion of the Court.

In this case we are called upon to determine the standard for admitting expert scientific testimony in a federal trial.

Petitioners Jason Daubert and Eric Schuller are minor children born with serious birth defects. They and their parents sued respondent [a]lleging that the birth defects had been caused by the mothers' ingestion of Bendectin, a prescription anti-nausea drug marketed by respondent.

After extensive discovery, respondent moved for summary judgment, contending that Bendectin does not cause birth defects in humans and that petitioners would be unable to come forward with any admissible evidence that it does. In support of its motion, respondent submitted an affidavit of Steven H. Lamm, physician and epidemiologist, who is a well-credentialed expert on the risks from exposure to various chemical substances. Doctor Lamm stated that he had reviewed all the literature on Bendectin and human birth defects — more than 30 published studies involving over 130,000 patients. No study had found Bendectin to be a human teratogen (*i.e.*, a substance capable of causing malformations in fetuses).

Petitioners did not (and do not) contest this characterization of the published record regarding Bendectin. Instead, they responded to respondent's motion with the testimony of eight experts of their own, each of whom also possessed impressive credentials. These experts had concluded that Bendectin can cause birth defects. Their conclusions were based upon [1] "in vitro" (test tube) and [2] "in vivo" (live) animal studies that found a link between Bendectin and malformations; [3] pharmacological studies of the chemical structure of Bendectin that purported to show similarities between the structure of the drug and that of other substances known to cause birth defects; and [4] the "reanalysis" of previously published epidemiological (human statistical) studies.

The District Court granted respondent's motion for summary judgment. The court stated that scientific evidence is admissible only if the principle upon which it is based is " 'sufficiently established to have general acceptance in the field to which it belongs.' "

The United States Court of Appeals for the Ninth Circuit affirmed. Citing *Frye v. United States*, 293 F. 1013, 1014, 54 App.D.C. 46, 47 (1923), the court stated that expert opinion based on a scientific technique is inadmissible unless the technique is "generally accepted" as reliable in the relevant scientific community.

The court emphasized that other Courts of Appeals considering the risks of Bendectin had refused to admit reanalyses of epidemiological studies that had been neither published nor subjected to peer review. [C]ontending that reanalysis is generally accepted by the scientific community only when it is subjected to verification and scrutiny by others in the field, the Court of Appeals rejected petitioners' reanalyses as "unpublished, not subjected to the normal peer review process and generated solely for use in litigation."

In the 70 years since its formulation in the *Frye* case, the "general acceptance" test has been the dominant standard for determining the admissibility of novel scientific evidence at trial. The *Frye* test has its origin in a short and citation-free 1923 decision concerning the admissibility of evidence derived from a systolic blood pressure deception test, a crude precursor to the polygraph machine. In what has become a famous (perhaps infamous) passage, the then Court of Appeals for the District of Columbia described the device and its operation and declared (emphasis added):

> Just when a scientific principle or discovery crosses the line between the experimental and demonstrable stages is difficult to define. Somewhere in this twilight zone the evidential force of the principle must be recognized, and while courts will go a long way in admitting expert testimony deduced from a well-recognized scientific principle or discovery, *the thing from which the deduction is made must be sufficiently established to have gained general acceptance in the particular field in which it belongs.*

The merits of the *Frye* test have been much debated, and scholarship on its proper scope and application is legion. Petitioners contend that the *Frye* test was superseded by the adoption of the Federal Rules of Evidence. We agree. . . .

Here there is a specific Rule that speaks to the contested issue. Rule 702, governing expert testimony, provides:

> If scientific, technical, or other specialized knowledge will assist the trier of fact to understand the evidence or to determine a fact in issue, a witness qualified as an expert by knowledge, skill, experience, training, or education, may testify thereto in the form of an opinion or otherwise.

Nothing in the text of this Rule establishes "general acceptance" as an absolute prerequisite to admissibility. The drafting history makes no mention of *Frye*, and a rigid "general acceptance" requirement would be at odds with the "liberal thrust" of the Federal Rules and their "general approach of relaxing the traditional barriers to 'opinion' testimony."

That the *Frye* test was displaced by the Rules of Evidence does not mean, however, that the Rules themselves place no limits on the admissibility of purportedly scientific evidence. [U]nder the Rules the trial judge must ensure that any and all scientific testimony or evidence admitted is not only relevant, but reliable.

The primary locus of this obligation is Rule 702, which clearly contemplates some degree of regulation of the subjects and theories about which an expert may testify. [T]he subject of an expert's testimony must be "scientific . . . knowledge."[8] The adjective "scientific" implies a grounding in the methods and procedures of science.

---

[8] Rule 702 also applies to "technical, or other specialized knowledge." Our discussion is limited to the scientific context because that is the nature of the expertise offered here.

Similarly, the word "knowledge" connotes more than subjective belief or unsupported speculation. The term "applies to any body of known facts or to any body of ideas inferred from such facts or accepted as truths on good grounds." Webster's Third New International Dictionary 1252 (1986). Of course, it would be unreasonable to conclude that the subject of scientific testimony must be "known" to a certainty; arguably, there are no certainties in science. . . . But, in order to qualify as "scientific knowledge," an inference or assertion must be derived by the scientific method. Proposed testimony must be supported by appropriate validation — *i.e.*, "good grounds," based on what is known.

Rule 702 further requires that the evidence or testimony "assist the trier of fact to understand the evidence or to determine a fact in issue." This condition goes primarily to relevance. "Expert testimony which does not relate to any issue in the case is not relevant and, ergo, non-helpful." The consideration has been aptly described [a]s one of "fit." "Fit" is not always obvious, and scientific validity for one purpose is not necessarily scientific validity for other, unrelated purposes. The study of the phases of the moon, for example, may provide valid scientific "knowledge" about whether a certain night was dark, and if darkness is a fact in issue, the knowledge will assist the trier of fact. However (absent creditable grounds supporting such a link), evidence that the moon was full on a certain night will not assist the trier of fact in determining whether an individual was unusually likely to have behaved irrationally on that night. Rule 702's "helpfulness" standard requires a valid scientific connection to the pertinent inquiry as a precondition to admissibility. . . .

Faced with a proffer of expert scientific testimony, then, the trial judge must determine at the outset, pursuant to Rule 104(a), whether the expert is proposing to testify to (1) scientific knowledge that (2) will assist the trier of fact to understand or determine a fact in issue.[11] This entails a preliminary assessment of whether the reasoning or methodology underlying the testimony is scientifically valid and of whether that reasoning or methodology properly can be applied to the facts in issue.

Ordinarily, a key question to be answered in determining whether a theory or technique is scientific knowledge that will assist the trier of fact will be whether it can be (and has been) tested. "Scientific methodology today is based on generating hypotheses and testing them to see if they can be falsified; indeed, this methodology is what distinguishes science from other fields of human inquiry." Popper, Conjectures and Refutations: The Growth of Scientific Knowledge 37 (5th ed. 1989) ("[T]he criterion of the scientific status of a theory is its falsifiability, or refutability, or testability").

Another pertinent consideration is whether the theory or technique has been subjected to peer review and publication. Publication (which is but one element of peer review) is not a *sine qua non* of admissibility; it does not necessarily correlate

---

[11] Although the *Frye* decision itself focused exclusively on "novel" scientific techniques, we do not read the requirements of Rule 702 to apply specially or exclusively to unconventional evidence. Of course, well-established propositions are less likely to be challenged than those that are novel, and they are more handily defended. Indeed, theories that are so firmly established as to have attained the status of scientific law, such as the laws of thermodynamics, properly are subject to judicial notice under Fed. Rule Evid. 201.

with reliability, and in some instances well-grounded but innovative theories will not have been published. Some propositions, moreover, are too particular, too new, or of too limited interest to be published. But submission to the scrutiny of the scientific community is a component of "good science," in part because it increases the likelihood that substantive flaws in methodology will be detected. The fact of publication (or lack thereof) in a peer-reviewed journal thus will be a relevant, though not dispositive, consideration in assessing the scientific validity of a particular technique or methodology on which an opinion is premised.

Additionally, in the case of a particular scientific technique, the court ordinarily should consider the known or potential rate of error, see, e.g., *United States v. Smith*, 869 F.2d 348, 353-354 (CA7 1989) (surveying studies of the error rate of spectrographic voice identification technique), and the existence and maintenance of standards controlling the technique's operation. See *United States v. Williams*, 583 F.2d 1194, 1198 (CA2 1978) (noting professional organization's standard governing spectrographic analysis).

Finally, "general acceptance" can yet have a bearing on the inquiry. A "reliability assessment does not require, although it does permit, explicit identification of a relevant scientific community and an express determination of a particular degree of acceptance within that community." Widespread acceptance can be an important factor in ruling particular evidence admissible, and "a known technique that has been able to attract only minimal support within the community," may properly be viewed with skepticism.

The inquiry envisioned by Rule 702 is, we emphasize, a flexible one. [The list is not "definitive," and there can be other factors.] . . . The focus, of course, must be solely on principles and methodology, not on the conclusions that they generate. . . .

Respondent expresses apprehension that abandonment of "general acceptance" as the exclusive requirement for admission will result in a "free-for-all" in which befuddled juries are confounded by absurd and irrational pseudoscientific assertions. In this regard respondent seems to us to be overly pessimistic about the capabilities of the jury, and of the adversary system generally. Vigorous cross-examination, presentation of contrary evidence, and careful instruction on the burden of proof are the traditional and appropriate means of attacking shaky but admissible evidence. Additionally, in the event the trial court concludes that the scintilla of evidence presented supporting a position is insufficient to allow a reasonable juror to conclude that the position more likely than not is true, the court remains free to direct a judgment and likewise to grant summary judgment.

Petitioners and, to a greater extent, their *amici* exhibit a different concern. They suggest that recognition of a screening role for the judge that allows for the exclusion of "invalid" evidence will sanction a stifling and repressive scientific orthodoxy and will be inimical to the search for truth. [Y]et there are important differences between the quest for truth in the courtroom and the quest for truth in the laboratory. Scientific conclusions are subject to perpetual revision. Law, on the other hand, must resolve disputes finally and quickly. [W]e recognize that in practice, a gatekeeping role for the judge, no matter how flexible, inevitably on occasion will prevent the jury from learning of authentic insights and innovations.

That, nevertheless, is the balance that is struck by Rules of Evidence designed not for the exhaustive search for cosmic understanding but for the particularized resolution of legal disputes.

To summarize: "general acceptance" is not a necessary precondition to the admissibility of scientific evidence under the Federal Rules of Evidence, but the Rules of Evidence — especially Rule 702 — do assign to the trial judge the task of ensuring that an expert's testimony both rests on a reliable foundation and is relevant to the task at hand.

[Vacated and remanded.]

Chief Justice Rehnqist, with whom Justice Stevens joins, concurring in part and dissenting in part.

[T]he Court concludes, correctly in my view, that the *Frye* rule did not survive the enactment of the Federal Rules of Evidence, and I therefore join [the first parts] of its opinion. The second question presented in the petition for certiorari [of what standard does apply] necessarily is mooted by this holding, but the Court nonetheless proceeds to construe Rules 702 and 703 very much in the abstract, and then offers some [vague and abstract] "general observations."

But even if it were desirable to make "general observations" not necessary to decide the questions presented, . . . the Court decides that "[i]n a case involving scientific evidence, *evidentiary reliability* will be based upon *scientific validity*.". . .

I am at a loss to know what is meant when it is said that the scientific status of a theory depends on its "falsifiability," and I suspect [lower court judges] will be, too.

I do not doubt that Rule 702 confides to the judge some gatekeeping responsibility in deciding questions of the admissibility of proffered expert testimony. But I do not think it imposes on them either the obligation or the authority to become amateur scientists in order to perform that role. I think the Court would be far better advised in this case to decide only the questions presented, and to leave the further development of this important area of the law to future cases.

NOTES AND QUESTIONS

(1) *Two Issues Presented by a Daubert Question: First, is the Testimony "Reliable" Enough to Qualify as Scientific Knowledge? Second, will it "Assist" the Jury in Deciding the Case?* The *Daubert* opinion breaks Fed. R. Evid. 702 into two component parts. First, there is the question whether the testimony satisfies a standard of "reliability." This issue apparently does not concern whether the ultimate conclusions are true, but rather it asks whether the principles used by the expert rest on a reliable methodology. The second question is one of (the Court says) relevance: Can the principles "assist" the jury in this case?

(2) *Analyzing the "Relevance," "Assistance," or "Fit" Issue: The "Werewolf Inquiry."* If the scientific principle addressed by the expert is to assist the jury, it must have some relation to the issues presented in the case. This, as the Court puts it, is a "question of 'fit.'" In other words, a given scientific principle may be extremely reliable, but if it is unrelated to the issues in the case, it cannot "assist" the jury in deciding the case, as Fed. R. Evid. 702 requires. For example, Boyle's Law describes the relationship between volume, pressure, and temperature of an ideal gas: V(1) X P(1)/T(1) = V(2) X P(2)/T(2). This is an (approximately) reliable principle within its bounds of application, but if an automobile-accident reconstruction expert were to attempt to use Boyle's Law in some way to determine the momentum of a vehicle after a collision, this reasoning would lack relevance. Boyle's Law simply does not "assist" in the determination of momentum.

The Court gives a different but analogous example: Phases of the moon may be relevant if the issue is darkness, but they are unlikely to assist the jury to determine whether human beings were prone at a given time to irrational behavior, i.e., "scientific" testimony based on werewolf or "lunacy" legends is not admissible under Fed. R. Evid. 702. This example has led some lawyers to suggest that *Daubert* requires the trial judge to conduct a "werewolf inquiry": Rule 702 requires the court to determine whether the scientific principle has a better relationship to the case than phases of the moon have to inferences about werewolf-like human behavior. Is this prong any different than the relevancy decision required in determining the admissibility of other types of evidence? If not, why did the Court separately identify it? Is the Court's "werewolf" principle any different from its "scientific reliability" criterion?

(3) *Analyzing the "Reliability" or "Scientific Knowledge" Prong: A Flexible Inquiry, Including but Not Limited to the Four Named Factors of "Falsifiability," "Peer Review," "Error Rates," and "General Acceptance."* The other question is whether the evidence is sufficiently "scientific" to qualify under Fed. R. Evid. 702. This inquiry, says the Court, is about whether the "principles" and "methodology" are "reliable," not whether the "conclusions" are true. The Court identifies four factors. First, a "key question" is whether the principle is "falsifiable": can it be derived from experimentation or comparison of data; is it capable of replication? For example, Boyle's law is reliable and scientific because experimentation produces repeatable results; but the "Golden Rule" ("Do unto others . . .") is not. Second, peer review (or examination by others with similar knowledge) is relevant. Third, error rates (including professional standards to control error rates), and fourth, general acceptance (the old *Frye* determinant) are relevant but not determinative. The trial judge is supposed to conduct a "flexible" inquiry, using these factors to the extent that they are useful, with none automatically determinative, and with the possibility of other factors.

(4) *Specific Application of Fit and Reliability: General Electric Co. v. Joiner, 522 U.S. 136 (1997).* In *Joiner*, the Supreme Court held it was not an abuse of discretion for the trial judge to exclude expert opinion based on animal studies on which respondent's experts relied to support his contention that exposure to PCBs had contributed to his cancer. The studies involved infant mice that had developed cancer after being exposed to massive doses of PCBs. Joiner was an adult human being whose alleged exposure to PCBs was far less than the exposure in the animal

studies. The cancer that these mice developed was alveologenic adenomas; Joiner had developed small-cell carcinomas. No study demonstrated that adult mice developed cancer after being exposed to PCBs. One of the experts admitted that no study had demonstrated that PCBs lead to cancer in any other species. The Supreme Court observed:

> The issue was whether these experts' opinions were sufficiently supported by the animal studies on which they purported to rely. The studies were so dissimilar to the facts presented in this litigation that [in the absence of explanation of how these seemingly far-removed animal studies could be extrapolated to humans] it was not an abuse of discretion for the District Court to have rejected the experts' reliance on them.
>
> Respondent points to *Daubert's* language that the "focus, of course, must be solely on principles and methodology, not on the conclusions that they generate." He claims that because the District Court's disagreement was with the conclusion that the experts drew from the studies, the District Court committed legal error and was properly reversed by the Court of Appeals. But conclusions and methodology are not entirely distinct from one another. Trained experts commonly extrapolate from existing data. But nothing in either *Daubert* or the Federal Rules of Evidence requires a district court to admit opinion evidence which is connected to existing data only by the ipse dixit of the expert. A court may conclude that there is simply too great an analytical gap between the data and the opinion proffered.

(5) *Codification of Daubert Principles.* Rule 702 was amended to reflect *Daubert's* focus on reliability. Subsection (b), (c), and (d) were added to the rule. Is the current standard actually more difficult to meet than *Daubert* requires?

(6) *U.S. Supreme Court Upholds Ban on Polygraph Testimony Offered by an Accused.* In *United States v. Scheffer*, 523 U.S. 303 (1998), an accused was charged with uttering bad checks, wrongfully using methamphetamine, failing to go to his appointed place of duty, and absenting himself from his unit without authority. His polygraph examination indicated that in the opinion of the Air Force examiner administering the test there was "no deception" in the respondent's denial that he had used drugs since enlisting. However, urinalysis revealed the presence of methamphetamine. In denying his motion to introduce the polygraph evidence to support his testimony that he did not knowingly use drugs, the military judge relied on Military Rule of Evidence 707, which makes polygraph evidence inadmissible in court-martial proceedings. The Supreme Court held that Military Rule of Evidence 707 did not unconstitutionally abridge the right of accused members of the military to present a defense. The Court found that Rule 707 serves the legitimate interest of ensuring that only reliable evidence is introduced. Not only is there no consensus that polygraph evidence is reliable, but the scientific community and the state and federal courts are extremely polarized on the matter.

(7) *Scheffer Rejects Government's Non-Court Use of Polygraphs as Admission of Reliability.* The Court gave short shrift to the argument that because the Government — and in particular the Department of Defense — uses polygraph testing, the Government must consider polygraphs reliable. "Governmental use of

polygraph tests, however, is primarily in the field of personnel screening, and to a lesser extent as a tool in criminal and intelligence investigations, but not as evidence at trials. Such limited, out of court uses of polygraph techniques obviously differ in character from, and carry less severe consequences than, the use of polygraphs as evidence in a criminal trial. They do not establish the reliability of polygraphs as trial evidence." Do you agree?

(8) *Fallout of National Academy of Science (NAS) Report.* In 2009, the NAS published a report entitled *Strengthening Forensic Science in the United States: A Path Forward,* which criticized the state of forensic science in the United States. The report was referenced in *Melendez-Diaz, infra* Chapter 11, as a reason why cross-examination is necessary to evaluate expert testimony. Defendants are making more *Daubert* motions relying on the report, and at least one judge (Judge Nancy Gertner) has issued a standing order that provides in part: "At or prior to the pretrial conference, parties are ORDERED to: . . . state whether or not either party seeks a *Daubert/Kumho* hearing prior to trial; and . . . state the witnesses required for the *Daubert/Kumho* hearing and the exhibits that the parties seek to admit."

The order notes that the NAS report raised profound questions that need to be carefully examined in every forensic case prior to trial such as "(1) the extent to which a particular forensic discipline is founded on a reliable scientific methodology that gives it the capacity to accurately analyze evidence and report findings and (2) the extent to which practitioners in a particular forensic discipline rely on human interpretation that could be tainted by error, the threat of bias, or the absence of sound operational procedures and robust performance standards."

[B] *Daubert* Applies to All Experts, Not Just "Scientific" Ones

KUMHO TIRE COMPANY, LTD. v. CARMICHAEL

United States Supreme Court
526 U.S. 137 (1999)

JUSTICE BREYER delivered the opinion of the Court.

In *Daubert* this Court focused upon the admissibility of scientific expert testimony. It pointed out that such testimony is admissible only if it is both relevant and reliable. And it held that the Federal Rules of Evidence "assign to the trial judge the task of ensuring that an expert's testimony both rests on a reliable foundation and is relevant to the task at hand." The Court also discussed certain more specific factors, such as testing, peer review, error rates, and "acceptability" in the relevant scientific community.

This case requires us to decide how *Daubert* applies to the testimony of engineers and other experts who are not scientists. We conclude that *Daubert's* general holding — setting forth the trial judge's general "gatekeeping" obligation — applies not only to testimony based on "scientific" knowledge, but also to testimony based on "technical" and "other specialized" knowledge. *See* Fed. Rule

Evid. 702. We also conclude that a trial court may consider one or more of the more specific factors that *Daubert* mentioned when doing so will help determine that testimony's reliability. But, as the Court stated in Daubert, the test of reliability is "flexible," and *Daubert's* list of specific factors neither necessarily nor exclusively applies to all experts or in every case. . . . Applying these standards, we determine that the District Court's decision in this case — not to admit certain expert testimony — was within its discretion and therefore lawful.

On July 6, 1993, the right rear tire of a minivan driven by Patrick Carmichael blew out. In the accident that followed, one of the passengers died, and others were severely injured. In October 1993, the Carmichaels brought this diversity suit against the tire's maker and its distributor, whom we refer to collectively as Kumho Tire, claiming that the tire was defective. The plaintiffs rested their case in significant part upon deposition testimony provided by an expert in tire failure analysis, Dennis Carlson, Jr., who intended to testify in support of their conclusion. Carlson's depositions relied upon certain features of tire technology that are not in dispute.

Carlson's testimony also accepted certain background facts about the tire in question. He assumed that before the blowout the tire had traveled far. (The tire was made in 1988 and had been installed some time before the Carmichaels bought the used minivan in March 1993; the Carmichaels had driven the van approximately 7,000 additional miles in the two months they had owned it.) Carlson noted that the tire's tread depth, which was 11/32 of an inch when new, had been worn down to depths that ranged from 3/32 of an inch along some parts of the tire, to nothing at all along others. He conceded that the tire tread had at least two punctures which had been inadequately repaired.

Despite the tire's age and history, Carlson concluded that a defect in its manufacture or design caused the blow-out. He rested this conclusion in part upon three premises which, for present purposes, we must assume are not in dispute: First, a tire's carcass should stay bound to the inner side of the tread for a significant period of time after its tread depth has worn away. Second, the tread of the tire at issue had separated from its inner steel-belted carcass prior to the accident. Third, this "separation" caused the blowout.

Carlson's conclusion that a defect caused the separation, however, rested upon certain other propositions, several of which the defendants strongly dispute. First, Carlson said that if a separation is *not* caused by a certain kind of tire misuse called "overdeflection" (which consists of underinflating the tire or causing it to carry too much weight, thereby generating heat that can undo the chemical tread/carcass bond), then, ordinarily, its cause is a tire defect. Second, he said that if a tire has been subject to sufficient overdeflection to cause a separation, it should reveal certain physical symptoms. Third, Carlson said that where he does not find at least two of the four physical signs (and presumably where there is no reason to suspect a less common cause of separation), he concludes that a manufacturing or design defect caused the separation. Carlson added that he had inspected the tire in question. He conceded that the tire to a limited degree [demonstrated the physical signs indicative of overdeflection]. But, in each instance, he testified that the symptoms were not significant, and he explained why he believed that they did not reveal overdeflection. For example, the extra shoulder wear, he said, appeared primarily on one shoulder, whereas an overdeflected tire would reveal equally abnormal wear on both shoulders. Carlson concluded that the tire did not bear at least two of the four overdeflection symptoms, nor was there any less obvious cause of separation; and since neither overdeflection nor the punctures caused the blowout, a defect must have done so.

The court agreed with Kumho that it should act as a *Daubert*-type reliability "gatekeeper," even though one might consider Carlson's testimony as "technical," rather than "scientific." The court then examined Carlson's methodology in light of the reliability-related factors that *Daubert* mentioned, such as a theory's testability, whether it "has been a subject of peer review or publication," the "known or potential rate of error," and the "degree of acceptance . . . within the relevant scientific community." After reconsidering the matter, the court agreed with the plaintiffs that Daubert should be applied flexibly, that its fourt factors were simply illustrative, and that other factors could argue in favor of admissibility. It conceded that there may be widespread acceptance of a "visual-inspection method" for some relevant purposes. But the court found insufficient indications of the reliability of "the component of Carlson's tire failure analysis which more concerned the Court, namely the methodology employed by the expert in analysis." It consequently affirmed its earlier order declaring Carlson's testimony inadmissible and granting the defendant's motion for summary judgment. The Eleventh Circuit reversed. We granted certiorari in light of uncertainty among the lower courts about whether, or how, Daubert applies to expert testimony that might be characterized as based not upon "scientific" knowledge, but rather upon "technical" or "other specialized" knowledge.

We believe that it applies to all expert testimony.

For one thing, Rule 702 itself says:

> If scientific, technical, or other specialized knowledge will assist the trier of fact to understand the evidence or to determine a fact in issue, a witness qualified as an expert by knowledge, skill, experience, training, or education, may testify thereto in the form of an opinion or otherwise.

This language makes no relevant distinction between "scientific" knowledge and "technical" or "other specialized" knowledge. It makes clear that any such knowledge might become the subject of expert testimony. . . .

Neither is the evidentiary rationale that underlay the Court's basic *Daubert* "gatekeeping" determination limited to "scientific" knowledge. *Daubert* pointed out that Federal Rules 702 and 703 grant expert witnesses testimonial latitude unavailable to other witnesses on the "assumption that the expert's opinion will have a reliable basis in the knowledge and experience of his discipline." . . .

Finally, it would prove difficult, if not impossible, for judges to administer evidentiary rules under which a gatekeeping obligation depended upon a distinction between "scientific" knowledge and "technical" or "other specialized" knowledge. There is no clear line that divides the one from the others. Disciplines such as engineering rest upon scientific knowledge. Pure scientific theory itself may depend for its development upon observation and properly engineered machinery. . . .

We conclude that *Daubert*'s general principles apply to the expert matters described in Rule 702. [W]here such testimony's factual basis, data, principles, methods, or their application are called sufficiently into question, the trial judge must determine whether the testimony has "a reliable basis in the knowledge and experience of [the relevant] discipline."

The petitioners ask more specifically whether a trial judge determining the "admissibility of an engineering expert's testimony" *may* consider several more specific factors that *Daubert* said might "bear on" a judge's gate-keeping determination. These factors include:

— Whether a "theory or technique . . . can be (and has been) tested";

— Whether it "has been subjected to peer review and publication";

— Whether, in respect to a particular technique, there is a high "known or potential rate of error" and whether there are "standards controlling the technique's operation"; and

— Whether the theory or technique enjoys "general acceptance" within a "relevant scientific community." 509 U.S. at 592-594.

Emphasizing the word "may" in the question, we answer that question yes.

Engineering testimony rests upon scientific foundations, the reliability of which will be at issue in some cases. In other cases, the relevant reliability concerns may focus upon personal knowledge or experience. [T]here are many different kinds of experts, and many different kinds of expertise. *See* Brief for United States as *Amicus Curiae* 18-19, and n. 5 (citing cases involving experts in drug terms, handwriting analysis, criminal *modus operandi*, land valuation, agricultural practices, railroad procedures, attorney's fee valuation, and others). Our emphasis on the word "may" thus reflects *Daubert*'s description of the Rule 702 inquiry as "a flexible one." *Daubert* makes clear that the factors it mentions do not constitute a "definitive checklist or test.". . .

Indeed, those factors do not all necessarily apply even in every instance in which the reliability of scientific testimony is challenged. It might not be surprising in a particular case, for example, that a claim made by a scientific witness has never been the subject of peer review, for the particular application at issue may never previously have interested any scientist. Nor, on the other hand, does the presence of *Daubert*'s general acceptance factor help show that an expert's testimony is reliable where the discipline itself lacks reliability, as, for example, do theories grounded in any so-called generally accepted principles of astrology or necromancy.

Daubert's questions can help to evaluate the reliability even of experience-based testimony. In certain cases, it will be appropriate for the trial judge to ask, for example, how often an engineering expert's experience-based methodology has produced erroneous results, or whether such a method is generally accepted in the relevant engineering community. Likewise, it will at times be useful to ask even of a witness whose expertise is based purely on experience, say, a perfume tester able to distinguish among 140 odors at a sniff, whether his preparation is of a kind that others in the field would recognize as acceptable.

. . . To say this is not to deny the importance of *Daubert*'s gatekeeping requirement. . . . Rather, we conclude that the trial judge must have considerable leeway in deciding in a particular case how to go about determining whether particular expert testimony is reliable. That is to say, a trial court should consider the specific factors identified in *Daubert* where they are reasonable measures of the reliability of expert testimony.

The trial court must have the same kind of latitude in deciding *how* to test an expert's reliability, and to decide whether or when special briefing or other proceedings are needed to investigate reliability, as it enjoys when it decides whether or not that expert's relevant testimony is reliable. . . . Thus, whether *Daubert*'s specific factors are, or are not, reasonable measures of reliability in a particular case is a matter that the law grants the trial judge broad latitude to determine.

We further explain the way in which a trial judge "may" consider *Daubert*'s factors by applying these considerations to the case at hand. The District Court did not doubt Carlson's qualifications, which included a masters degree in mechanical engineering, 10 years' work at Michelin America, Inc., and testimony as a tire failure consultant in other tort cases. Rather, it excluded the testimony because, despite those qualifications, it initially doubted, and then found unreliable, "the methodology employed by the expert in analyzing the data obtained in the visual inspection, and the scientific basis, if any, for such an analysis." [T]he District Court determined that Carlson's testimony was not reliable. *It fell outside the range where experts might reasonably differ, and where the jury must decide among the conflicting views of different experts, even though the evidence is "shaky."* [Emphasis supplied — Eds.] In our view, the doubts that triggered the District Court's initial inquiry here were reasonable, as was the court's ultimate conclusion.

For one thing, and contrary to respondents' suggestion, the specific issue before the court was not the reasonableness in general of a tire expert's use of a visual and tactile inspection to determine whether overdeflection had caused the tire's tread to separate from its steel-belted carcass. Rather, it was the reasonableness of using such an approach, along with Carlson's particular method of analyzing the data thereby obtained, to draw a conclusion regarding the particular matter to which the expert testimony was directly relevant. That matter concerned the likelihood that a defect in the tire at issue caused its tread to separate from its carcass. The tire in question, the expert conceded, had traveled far enough so that some of the tread had been worn bald; it should have been taken out of service; it had been repaired (inadequately) for punctures; and it bore some of the very marks that the expert said indicated, not a defect, but abuse through overdeflection. The relevant issue was whether the expert could reliably determine the cause of *this* tire's separation.

Nor was the basis for Carlson's conclusion simply the general theory that, in the absence of evidence of abuse, a defect will normally have caused a tire's separation. Rather, the expert employed a more specific theory to establish the existence (or absence) of such abuse. Carlson testified precisely that in the absence of *at least two* of four signs of abuse he concludes that a defect caused the separation. And his analysis depended upon acceptance of a further implicit proposition, namely, that his visual and tactile inspection could determine that the tire before him had not been abused despite some evidence of the presence of the very signs for which he looked. For another thing, the transcripts of Carlson's depositions support both the trial court's initial uncertainty and its final conclusion. Those transcripts cast considerable doubt upon the reliability of both the explicit theory (about the need for two signs of abuse) and the implicit proposition (about the significance of visual inspection in this case). Among other things, the expert could not say whether the tire had traveled more than 10, or 20, or 30, or 40, or 50 thousand miles, adding that 6,000 miles was "about how far" he could "say with any certainty." The court could reasonably have wondered about the reliability of a method of visual and tactile inspection sufficiently precise to ascertain with some certainty the abuse-related significance of minute shoulder/center relative tread wear differences, but insufficiently precise to tell "with any certainty" from the tread wear whether a tire had traveled less than 10,000 or more than 50,000 miles. And these concerns might have been augmented by Carlson's repeated reliance on the "subjectiveness" of his mode of analysis in response to questions seeking specific information regarding how he could differentiate between a tire that actually had been overdeflected and a tire that merely looked as though it had been. They would have been further augmented by the fact that Carlson said he had inspected the tire itself for the first time the morning of his first deposition, and then only for a few hours. (His initial conclusions were based on photographs.)

Finally, the court, after looking for a defense of Carlson's methodology as applied in these circumstances, found no convincing defense. Rather, it found (1) that "none" of the *Daubert* factors, including that of "general acceptance" in the relevant expert community, indicated that Carlson's testimony was reliable; (2) that its own analysis "revealed no countervailing factors operating in favor of admissibility which could outweigh those identified in *Daubert*;" and (3) that the "parties identified no such factors in their briefs.". . . .

Respondents argue to us that a method of tire failure analysis that employs a visual/tactile inspection is a reliable method, and they point both to its use by other experts and to Carlson's long experience working for Michelin as sufficient indication that that is so. But no one denies that an expert might draw a conclusion from a set of observations based on extensive and specialized experience. Nor does anyone deny that, as a general matter, tire abuse may often be identified by qualified experts through visual or tactile inspection of the tire. [T]he question before the trial court was specific, not general. The trial court had to decide whether this particular expert had sufficient specialized knowledge to assist the jurors "in deciding the particular issues in the case."

The particular issue in this case concerned the use of Carlson's two-factor test and his related use of visual/tactile inspection to draw conclusions on the basis of what seemed small observational differences. We have found no indication in the record that other experts in the industry use Carlson's two-factor test or that tire experts such as Carlson normally make the very fine distinctions about, say, the symmetry of comparatively greater shoulder tread wear that were necessary, on Carlson's own theory, to support his conclusions. Nor, despite the prevalence of tire testing, does anyone refer to any articles or papers that validate Carlson's approach. Indeed, no one has argued that Carlson himself, were he still working for Michelin, would have concluded in a report to his employer that a similar tire was similarly defective on grounds identical to those upon which he rested his conclusion here. Of course, Carlson himself claimed that his method was accurate, but, as we pointed out in *Joiner*, "nothing in either *Daubert* or the Federal Rules of Evidence requires a district court to admit opinion evidence that is connected to existing data only by the *ipse dixit* of the expert."

Respondents additionally argue that the District Court too rigidly applied *Daubert's* criteria. They read its opinion to hold that a failure to satisfy any one of those criteria automatically renders expert testimony inadmissible. The District Court's initial opinion might have been vulnerable to a form of this argument. There, the court, after rejecting respondents' claim that Carlson's testimony was "exempted from *Daubert*-style scrutiny" because it was "technical analysis" rather than "scientific evidence," simply added that "none of the four admissibility criteria outlined by the *Daubert* court are satisfied." Subsequently, however, the court granted respondents' motion for reconsideration. It then explicitly recognized that the relevant reliability inquiry "should be 'flexible,' " that its " 'overarching subject [should be] . . . validity' and reliability," and that "*Daubert* was intended neither to be exhaustive nor to apply in every case." And the court ultimately based its decision upon Carlson's failure to satisfy either *Daubert's* factors *or any other* set of reasonable reliability criteria. In light of the record as developed by the parties, that conclusion was within the District Court's lawful discretion. . . .

[Reversed.]

NOTES AND QUESTIONS

(1) *Amendment Codifying Daubert/Kumho Principles.* In an attempt to codify *Daubert* and *Kumho*, Fed. R. Evid. 702 was amended in 2000 by the addition of subsections (b), (c), and (d) to the rule. This amendment and the two cases it codifies finally respond to criticisms that the rule as originally adopted opens the door too wide and uncritically to experts, and gives judges little guidance. These criticisms go back as far as the writing by Prof. Rothstein of the first book ever published on the Federal Rules of Evidence, and writings of his subsequently, and in his urgings as an advisor to Congress on the Rules even before the Rules were finally adopted. Some of this material is referenced in "Federal Rules of Evidence: A Fresh Review and Evaluation," Report of the American Bar Association, Committee on Rules of Procedure and Evidence, Criminal Justice Section, 120 F.R.D. 299 (1988), under Article VII.

The Advisory Committee Note to the amendment reads in part as follows:

> Rule 702 has been amended in response to *Daubert* and *Kumho*. . . . Consistently with *Kumho*, the Rule as amended provides that all types of expert testimony present questions of admissibility for the trial court in deciding whether the evidence is reliable and helpful. . . .
>
> No attempt has been made to "codify" [the] specific factors [mentioned in *Daubert*]. *Daubert* itself emphasized that the factors were neither exclusive nor dispositive. Other cases have recognized that not all the specific *Daubert* factors can apply to every type of expert testimony. In addition to *Kumho, see Tyus v. Urban Search Management*, 102 F.3d 256

(7th Cir. 1996) (noting that the factors mentioned by the Court in *Daubert* do not neatly apply to expert testimony from a sociologist). *See also Kannankeril v. Terminix Int'l, Inc.*, 128 F.3d 802, 809 (3d Cir. 1997) (holding that lack of peer review or publication was not dispositive where the expert's opinion was supported by "widely accepted scientific knowledge"). The standards set forth in the amendment are broad enough to require consideration of any or all of the specific *Daubert* factors where appropriate.

Courts both before and after *Daubert* have found other factors [pertinent], for example:

(1) Whether experts are "proposing to testify about matters growing naturally and directly out of research they have conducted independent of the litigation, or whether they have developed their opinions expressly for the purposes of testifying."

(2) Whether the expert has unjustifiably extrapolated from an accepted premise to an unfounded conclusion. *Joiner* (noting that in some cases a trial court "may conclude that there is imply too great an analytical gap between the data and the opinion proffered").

(3) Whether the expert has adequately accounted for obvious alternative explanations. *Claar* (testimony excluded where the expert failed to consider other obvious causes for the plaintiff's condition). *Compare Ambrosini* (the possibility of some uneliminated causes presents a question of weight, so long as the most obvious causes have been considered and reasonably ruled out by the expert).

(4) Whether the expert "is being as careful as he would be in his regular professional work outside his paid litigation consulting." *Sheehan. See also Kumho* (*Daubert* requires the trial court to assure itself that the expert "employs in the courtroom the same level of intellectual rigor that characterizes the practice of an expert in the relevant field").

(5) Whether the field of expertise claimed by the expert is known to reach reliable results for the type of opinion the expert would give. *See Kumho* (*Daubert's* general acceptance factor does not "help show that an expert's testimony is reliable where the discipline itself lacks reliability, as, for example, do theories grounded in any so-called generally accepted principles of astrology or necromancy"); *Moore* (clinical doctor was properly precluded from testifying to the toxicological cause of the plaintiff's respiratory problem, where the opinion was not sufficiently grounded in scientific methodology); *Sterling v. Velsicol Chem. Corp.* (rejecting testimony based on "clinical ecology" as unfounded and unreliable).

Other factors may also be relevant. Yet no single factor is necessarily dispositive. *See, e.g., Heller v. Shaw Industries, Inc.*, 167 F.3d 146, 155 (3d Cir. 1999) ("not only must each stage of the expert's testimony be reliable, but each stage must be evaluated practically and flexibly without bright-line exclusionary (or inclusionary) rules."); *Daubert v. Merrell Dow Pharmaceuticals, Inc.*, 43 F.3d 1311, 1317, n.5 (9th Cir. 1995) (noting that some expert disciplines "have the courtroom as a principal theater of operations" and as to these disciplines "the fact that the expert has developed an expertise principally for purposes of litigation will obviously not be a substantial consideration.").

The trial court's role as gatekeeper is not intended to serve as a replacement for the adversary system. "Vigorous cross-examination, presentation of contrary evidence, and careful instruction on the burden of proof are the traditional and appropriate means of attacking shaky by admissible evidence." [*Daubert.*] Likewise, this amendment is not intended to provide an excuse for an automatic challenge to the testimony of every expert. *See Kumho* (noting that the trial judge has the discretion "both to avoid unnecessary 'reliability' proceedings in ordinary cases where the reliability of an expert's methods is properly taken for granted, and to require appropriate proceedings in the less usual or more complex cases where the cause for questioning the expert's reliability arises").

When a trial court, applying this amendment, rules that an expert's testimony is reliable, this does not necessarily mean that contradictory expert testimony is unreliable. The amendment is broad enough to permit testimony that is the product of competing principles or methods in the same field of expertise. *See, e.g., Heller v. Shaw Industries, Inc.*, 167 F.3d 146, 160 (3d Cir. 1999) (expert testimony cannot be excluded simply because the expert uses one test rather than another, when both tests are accepted in the field and both reach reliable results). [P]roponents "do not have to demonstrate to the judge by a preponderance of the evidence that the assessments of their experts are correct, they only have to demonstrate by a preponderance of evidence that their opinions are reliable. . . . The evidentiary requirement of reliability is lower than the merits standard of correctness." [Cite.] *See also Daubert v. Merrell Dow Pharmaceuticals, Inc.*, 43 F.3d 1311, 1318 (9th Cir. 1995) (scientific experts might be permitted to testify if they could show that the methods they used were also employed by "a recognized minority of scientists in their field."); *Ruiz-Troche v. Pepsi Cola*, 161 F.3d 77, 85 (1 Cir. 1998) ("*Daubert* neither requires nor empowers trial courts to determine which of several competing scientific theories had the best provenance.").

The Court in *Daubert* declared that the "focus, of course, must be solely on principles and methodology, not on the conclusions they generate." Yet as the Court later recognized, "conclusions and methodology are not entirely distinct from one another." *Joiner.* Under the amendment, as under *Daubert*, when an expert purports to apply principles and methods in accordance with professional standards, and yet reaches a conclusion that other experts in the field would not reach, the trial court may fairly suspect that the principles and methods have not been faithfully applied. The amendment specifically provides that the trial court must scrutinize not only the principles and methods used by the expert, but also whether those principles and methods have been properly applied to the facts of the case. "[A]ny step that renders the analysis unreliable . . . renders the expert's testimony inadmissible. *This is true whether the step completely changes a reliable methodology or merely misapplies that methodology.*" [Cite.]

If the expert purports to apply principles and methods to the facts of the case, it is important that this application be conducted reliably. Yet it might also be important in some cases for an expert to educate the fact-finder about general principles, without ever attempting to apply these principles to the specific facts of the case. For example, experts might instruct the fact-finder on the principles of thermodynamics, or blood clotting, or on how financial markets respond to corporate reports, without ever knowing about or trying to tie their testimony into the facts of the case. The amendment does not alter the venerable practice of using expert testimony to educate the fact-finder on general principles. For this kind of generalized testimony, Rule 702 simply requires that: (1) the expert be qualified; (2) the testimony address a subject matter on which the fact-finder can be assisted by an expert; (3) the testimony be reliable; and (4) the testimony "fit" the facts of the case.

. . . While the relevant factors for determining reliability will vary from expertise to expertise, the amendment rejects the premise that an expert's testimony should be treated more permissibly simply because it is outside the realm of science. *See Watkins v. Telsmith, Inc.*, 121 F.3d 984, 991 (5th Cir. 1997) ("[I]t seems exactly backwards that experts who purport to rely on general engineering principles and practical experience might escape screening by the district court simply by stating that their conclusions were not reached by any particular method or technique."). Some types of expert testimony will be more objectively verifiable, and subject to the expectations of falsifiability, peer review, and publication, than others. Some types of expert testimony will not rely on anything like a scientific method, and so will have to be evaluated by reference to other standard principles attendant to the particular area of expertise. The trial judge in all cases of proffered expert testimony must find that it is properly grounded, well-reasoned, and not speculative before it can be admitted. The expert's testimony must be grounded in an accepted body of learning or experience in the expert's field, and the expert must explain how the conclusion is so grounded. "[W]hether the testimony concerns economic principles, accounting standards, property valuations, or other non-scientific subjects, it should be evaluated by reference to the 'knowledge and experience' of that particular field." [Cite].

The amendment requires that the testimony must be the product of reliable principles and methods that are reliably applied to the facts of the case. While the terms "principles" and "methods" [seem to connote "science", they also apply to] testimony based on technical or other specialized knowledge. For example, when a law enforcement agent testifies regarding the use of code words in a drug transaction, the principle used by the agent is that participants in such transactions regularly use code words to conceal the nature of their activities. The method used by the agent is the application of extensive experience to analyze the meaning of the conversations.

Nothing in this amendment is intended to suggest that experience alone — or experience in conjunction with other knowledge, skill, training, or education — may not provide a sufficient foundation. In certain fields, experience is the predominant, if not sole, basis for a great deal of reliable expert testimony. *See, e.g., United States v. Jones*, 107 F.3d 1147 (6th Cir. 1997) (no abuse of discretion in admitted the testimony of a handwriting examiner who had years of practical experience and extensive training, and who explained his methodology in detail); *Tassin v. Sears Roebuck*, 946 F. Supp. 1241, 1248 (M.S. La. 1996) (design engineer's testimony can be admissible when the expert's opinions "are based on facts, a reasonable investigation, and traditional technical/mechanical expertise, and he provides a reasonable link between the information and procedures he sues and the conclusions he reaches"). *See also Kumho* (stating that "no one denies that an expert might draw a conclusion from a set of observations based on extensive and specialized experience").

If the witness is relying solely or primarily on experience, then the witness must explain how that experience leads to the conclusion reached, why that experience is a sufficient basis for the opinion, and how that experience is reliably applied to the facts. The trial court's gatekeeping function requires more than simply "taking the expert's word for it." *See Daubert v. Merrell Dow Pharmaceuticals, Inc.*, 43 F.3d 1311 (9th Cir. 1995) ("We've been presented with only the expert's qualifications, their conclusions and their assurances of reliability, Under Daubert, that's not enough."). The more subjective and controversial the expert's inquiry, the more likely the testimony should be excluded as unreliable. *See O'Conner v. Commonwealth Edison Co.*, 13 F.3d 1090 (7th Cir. 1994) (expert testimony based on a completely subjective methodology held properly excluded). *See also Kumho* ("[I]t will at times be useful to ask even of a witness whose expertise is based purely on experience, say, a perfume tester able to distinguish among 140 odors as a sniff, whether his preparation is of a kind that others in the field would recognize as acceptable.").

[Subpart (b)] of Rule 702 calls for a quantitative rather than qualitative analysis [when it] requires that expert testimony be based on sufficient underlying "facts or data." The term "data" is intended to encompass the reliable opinions of other experts. "[F]acts or data" is broad enough to [encompass] hypothetical facts that are supported by the evidence.

[E]xperts sometimes reach different conclusions. . . . The emphasis in the amendment on "sufficient facts or data" is not intended to authorize a trial court to exclude an expert's testimony on the ground that the court believes one version of the facts and not the other.

There has been some confusion over the relationship between Rules 702 and 703. The amendment makes clear that the sufficiency of the basis of an expert's testimony is to be decided under Rule 702. In contrast, the "reasonable reliance" requirement of Rule 703 is a relatively narrow inquiry. When an expert relies on inadmissible information, Rule 703 requires the trial court to determine whether that information is of a *type* reasonably relied on by other experts in the field. If so, the expert can rely on the information in reaching an opinion. However, the question whether the expert is relying on a *sufficient* basis of information — whether admissible information or not — is governed by the requirements of Rule 702.

[A] jury [does not necessarily have to be] informed that a qualified witness is testifying as an "expert." Indeed, there is much to be said for a practice that prohibits the use of the term "expert" by both parties and the court at trial. Such a practice "ensures that trial courts do not inadvertently put their stamp of authority" on a witness' opinion, and protects the jury's being "overwhelmed by the so-called 'experts'." [Cite.] [Judges permissibly differ in their practice on this.]

(2) *A Critique of the Rule Amendment.* One of the authors of this casebook, Professor Crump, believes that the amendment to Rule 702 is harmful rather than helpful. First, he believes that the *Daubert-Kumho* reasoning is "flawed," because he believes it reflects an excessively narrow conception of what science is, rejecting the kinds of creative non-conforming leaps made by people like Sigmund Freud and Isaac Newton. The Court might be more free to adjust its concept without the amendment. Second, he doubts the wisdom of the Court's extension of scientific criteria to "technical or other specialized knowledge," because, for example, a garage mechanic may have valuable expertise, say, in diagnosing what is wrong with a car, but would be at a loss to try to give reasons that would satisfy the *Daubert* factors or anything like them. Third, he believes that the amendment does not adequately "codify" *Kumho.* That decision suggested that experience-based experts might be differently evaluated, a nuance that the amendment omits. Is there anything to these views? Does the Advisory Committee Note take care of these problems? *See* Crump, *The Trouble with Daubert-Kumho: Reconsidering the Supreme Court's Philosophy of Science*, 68 Mo. L. Rev. 1 (2003). See also Professor Raeder's view that the requirement of "sufficient facts or data" will result in more exclusions of otherwise admissible expert testimony. *Beyond Kumho*, 2 A.B.A. Tort Source 4 (Spring 2000).

(3) *Compare Amendment to F.R.E. with Amendment to Uniform Rules of Evidence.* An amendment to the Uniform Rules of Evidence ("U.R.E.") takes a different approach than Fed. R. Evid. 702. Rule 702 creates a rebuttable presumption of reliability based on *Frye*'s general acceptance test. However, the losing party can challenge the presumption based on a number of reliability factors. In other words, regardless of whether the testimony is presumed reliable or unreliable, there is an opportunity to contest admissibility based on reliability. Several of the factors are specifically directed toward nonscientific experts. Which approach do you think is better? Why? Does the Uniform Rule address any of Processor Crump's concerns stated just above? The Uniform Rule provides, in pertinent part:

(a) [This section is quite like the amended Federal Rule 702.]

(b) **Reliability deemed to exist.** A principle or method is reasonably reliable if its reliability has been established by controlling legislation or judicial decision.

(c) **Presumption of reliability.** A principle or method is presumed to be reasonably reliable if it has substantial acceptance within the relevant scientific, technical, or specialized community. A party may rebut the presumption by proving that it is more probable than not that the principle or method is not reasonably reliable.

(d) **Presumption of unreliability.** A principle or method is presumed not to be reasonably reliable is it does not have substantial acceptance within the relevant scientific, technical, or specialized community. A party may rebut the presumption by proving that it is more probable than not that the principle is reasonably reliable.

(e) **Other reliability factors.** In determining the reliability of a principle or method, the court shall consider all relevant additional factors, which may include:

(1) the extent to which the principle or method has been tested;

(2) the adequacy of research methods employed in [such] testing . . .

(3) the extent to which the principle or method has been published and subjected to peer review;

(4) the rate of error in the application of the principle or method;

(5) the experience of the witness in the application of the principle or method;

(6) the extent to which the principle or method has gained acceptance within the relevant scientific, technical, or specialized community; and

(7) the extent to which the witness' specialized field of knowledge has gained acceptance within the general scientific, technical, or specialized community.

Professor Raeder succeeded Prof. Rothstein as the American Bar Association's advisor to the Uniform Rules of Evidence drafting committee and participated in the drafting of this provision.

(4) *Is Kumho Really Frye in Disguise?* Does the Court (and Advisory Note) appear to rely heavily on "general acceptance" of experts in the particular field in its examples of what *Daubert* factors are likely to apply to nonscientific experts? Will courts in both scientific and nonscientific areas tend to do this more and more under *Daubert/Kumho* and the Rules amendments? What forces might incline judges to do this? Would courts, then, be essentially doing what the Uniform Rule recommends?

Can you envision fields in which experts generally agree to theories that may not be reliable? What about psychiatric testimony on issues such as dangerousness?

(5) *What Type of Validation is Applicable to "Social Science" Expertise?* Is social science evidence capable of validation? Would some of the likely empirical testing raise ethical questions, particularly in the area of syndrome evidence offered in rape, battering and child abuse cases? *See also* Section 6.05.

(6) *When can the Court Refuse a Reliability Hearing?* What categories of expertise will courts "grandfather" in under the rubric of avoiding "unnecessary" reliability proceedings in "ordinary" cases, as *Kumho* expressly says it permits? A number of fields have never been subjected to rigorous review, including fingerprinting, handwriting analysis, and psychiatric testimony. When is it an abuse of discretion not to hold a hearing? Conversely, is it ever an abuse of discretion to require a hearing? So far, challenges to lack of *Daubert* hearings have not proved very successful in criminal cases. In *United States v. Charley*, 189 F.3d 1251 (10th Cir. 1999), *cert. denied*, 528 U.S. 1098 (2000), the court held it was harmless error in a sexual abuse trial to permit, against the accused, without a reliability determination, a pediatrician's unconditional opinion of sexual abuse. Nor, in another case, was a failure to require a *Daubert* hearing deemed ineffective assistance of counsel. *Miller v. Mullin*, 354 F.3d 1288 (10th Cir. 2004). In contrast, absence of a reliability determination with respect to an expert's testimony as to why he thought race influenced the tenure decision in a Title VII action, resulted in a reversal in *Mukhtar v. California State University, Hayward*, 299 F.3d 1053 (9th Cir. 2002). Eleven judges dissented from a denial of rehearing *en banc*, 319 F.3d 1073 (9th Cir. 2003) (13 were needed to grant the petition). The eleven deplored that a new trial had been ordered for the procedural failing, without consideration of whether the evidence was admissible. Do you agree with the dissenting judges that this result is "arbitrary" and "unfair"? Even if the evidence of reliability in the record was not sufficient for the appellate court to decide the issue, was a retrial the only appropriate remedy?

(7) *Degree of Reliability: The Fudge Factor.* With regard to *Daubert/Kumho* and Rule 702, how reliable is "reliable"? When exactly is unreliability so severe that it is (in *Kumho's* words) "outside the range where experts might reasonably differ, and where the jury must decide among the conflicting views of different experts, even though the evidence is 'shaky?' " Is the reason this was not a problem in *Kumho* that the expert's testimony was very obviously far "off the wall" in an area where the judges (even as lay people) could clearly see that the reasoning and conclusions flew in the face of common sense, no other experts seemed to share the methodology, and the witness even seemed to contradict the very principles he said he employed?

(8) *Manipulation of the Test.* Do portions of the last six paragraphs of *Kumho* that urge particularity rather than generality show that the result is dependent upon what level of abstraction the court's microscope is focused on? Can something wrong be found with any expert testimony this way? Conversely, could any testimony, even that in *Kumho*, be approved by manipulating this focus? Is the court clear as to where focus should be?

(9) *Advice to Experts.* Can experts, with careful articulation, insulate themselves from *Kumho* rejection? What particular pieces of advice would you give your expert witness?

(10) *Effects of the Daubert Trilogy on the System.* The expert trilogy *Daubert/Joiner/Kumho* seems to require federal judges to be reliability and "fit" gatekeepers in nearly every case in which an expert is called, but subjects their decisions to the abuse of discretion standard. Compared to previous federal practice, will the trilogy result in more experts being excluded? Remember, the bottom line in each of the three Supreme Court cases was to affirm the exclusion of an expert. What are the advantages and disadvantages of a more skeptical judicial view toward experts?

Bear in mind that some federal courts were not applying *Frye* to some large category of cases, frequently civil cases, or cases where the expert was not involved in a scientific endeavor, or where the science was not novel. Those courts tended to read the Rules very liberally, requiring little more than qualifications of the expert, and exerting no regulation of the substance of what was testified to, believing that was for the adversary process and the jury. As to those courts, in those kinds of cases, *Daubert* could be expected to make the courts more stringent, even though where *Frye* had applied, *Daubert* might be expected to be a loosening of the standards, at least as to evidence with little or no track record that was nevertheless scientifically rigorous.

The Rand Civil Justice Institute has rigorously investigated and reported on the effect of *Daubert* on federal civil cases in a statistical study to which Prof. Rothstein was an advisor. See "Changes in the Standards for Admitting Expert Evidence in Federal Civil Cases Since the *Daubert* Decision" (2001) (Pub. No. MR-1439-ICJ, Rand Institute for Civil Justice, Santa Monica, California).

(11) *Do Courts Interpret Reliability Differently in Criminal than Civil Cases?* An August, 1999 study of nearly 1600 citations to *Daubert* in federal and state court concluded that civil defendants win their reliability challenges to plaintiffs' proffers most of the time, and that criminal defendants virtually always lose their reliability challenges to government proffers. *See* Risinger, *Navigating Expert Reliability: Are Criminal Standards of Certainty Being Left on the Dock?* 64 Alb. L. Rev. 99 (2000). What reasons might justify or at least explain such a difference in outcome? For a general discussion of *Kumho's* effect in criminal cases, see Giannelli & Imwinkelried, *Scientific Evidence: The Fallout from Supreme Court's Decision in Kumho Tires*, 14 Crim. Just. 12 (Winter 2000). *See also* Raeder, *The Judge as Gatekeeper*, in National Conference on Science and the Law Conference Proceedings (National Institute of Justice Research Forum, July 2000 NCJ 179630). For a more detailed analysis of whether evidence rules generally are applied similarly in civil and criminal cases, see Raeder, *Cost-Benefit Analysis, Unintended Consequences, and Evidentiary Policy: A Critique and a Rethinking of the Application of a Single Set of Evidence Rules to Civil and Criminal Cases*, 19 Cardozo L. Rev. 1585 (1998).

(12) *Daubert/Kumho Approach Gets Mixed Reviews in the States.* A survey of state practice revealed that state law concerning expert testimony is unsettled. *See* Bernstein & Jackson, *The Daubert Trilogy in the States*, 44 Jurimetrics J. 351 (2004). The variations are manifold. A number of states have not adopted *Daubert*. Few states have adopted *Daubert, Joiner*, and *Kumho*. Some have adopted *Daubert*, but not *Kumho*. Others have adapted parts of the trilogy to their own previous standards. The article concludes that "contrary to the prevailing impres-

sion, the *Daubert* trilogy is not yet the majority standard even among the states that have rejected *Frye*." Does this lack of uniformity pose difficulties for experts? For lawyers? For actual and potential litigants? More generally, does it have an impact on the substantive development of the law? On society?

HO v. MICHELIN NORTH AMERICA, INC.

United States Court of Appeals, Tenth Circuit
2013 U.S. App. LEXIS 6318 (Mar. 29, 2013)

Carlos F. Lucero, Circuit Judge.

Melinda Ho appeals a district court order excluding proposed tire expert testimony and granting summary judgment in favor of Michelin North America, Inc. ("Michelin"). . . . [W]e affirm.

I

In 2007, Ho was injured in a car accident. A third party, Linda Lange, was driving on the highway when her front left tire suffered a belt and tread detachment. Lange's vehicle veered left, crossed into oncoming traffic, and struck Ho's vehicle head on. Ho filed a products liability action against Michelin, the manufacturer of Lange's tire, alleging defective design and manufacturing, failure to warn, breach of warranty, and negligence.

Ho designated two experts to testify regarding the cause of the tire failure. Patrick Cassidy, a Ph.D. chemist, testified that age is a "major issue" in tire failures and that age "ha[d] an effect in this case as to the cause of failure." However, Cassidy admitted that there were several potential causes of tire failure, and that he "would not testify that this tire failed because of age." Cassidy also stated that, based on his investigation, there was "no scientific evidence" that the tire at issue had a manufacturing defect. With respect to design defect, Cassidy testified that a tire without a nylon cap ply would be defectively designed, but conceded that he could not say whether a nylon cap ply would have made a difference in this particular detachment. Finally, Cassidy stated that he was not a warning expert and could offer no expert insights into warning claims.

Ho also offered William Woehrle as an expert. Woehrle has a B.S. in Physics and has worked in the tire industry for nearly forty years. He also has thirty years of experience teaching accident investigation courses. Woehrle physically examined the tire at issue and opined that the failure was the result of "insufficient fatigue endurance performance," which was due primarily to two root causes: improper belt step-offs and a severe offset, or "dog ear," on the tire. Inadequate adhesion, excessive age, and the absence of a nylon cap ply were also "contributing factors" according to Woehrle. Woehrle rejected the suggestion that over-deflection (caused by overloading or under-inflation) or impact damage caused the tire failure.

In his deposition, Woehrle admitted that there is a tolerance for some step-off variation. Woehrle did not know if the tire's belt placement issues fell within Michelin's specifications. He also conceded that the peer-reviewed literature suggests that step-offs and dog ears do not cause belt separations, and he was unable to cite any peer-reviewed literature supporting his contrary theory. With respect to his belief that the tire had inadequate adhesion, Woehrle rested his conclusion on the presence of brassy colored wires. However, Woehrle admitted that the presence of brassy wires does not necessarily suggest a defect. He also relied on a single publication to draw this causal connection, issued by a tire expert with significant reputation issues following the entry of sanctions in another tire case.

Woehrle also acknowledged that his positions on over-deflection and road impacts — that they do not cause belt detachments — were contrary to the prevailing view in the scientific community. For example, Cassidy, the plaintiff's witness, testified that both issues could cause belt detachment. After being deposed, Woehrle conducted "drop testing" on a single tire to support his theory that impact does not cause tread detachment. A background document describing the development of this test states that a different type of test provides more consistent results.

With respect to design defect, Woehrle stated that the absence of a nylon cap ply was the only design defect he claimed. He admitted that he had never designed a tire that was produced, and was not qualified to act as a tire designer. Woehrle later clarified that he did not claim that the absence of a nylon cap ply was a defect, but rather that this feature would have been beneficial. He noted that nylon cap plies were one of several methods to alleviate stress at belt edges, but that nylon cap plies had some disadvantages. Finally, as to warning defect, Woehrle admitted that he was not a warning expert and that he did not think age was an "applicable" issue in this case.

The district court granted [Michelin's motion to exclude both witnesses and granted summary judgment for Michelin]. . . . After unsuccessfully seeking reconsideration, Ho filed a timely notice of appeal.

II

[Here, the court cites *Daubert* and summarizes it holding. Expert testimony must be "not only relevant, but reliable." The four non-exhaustive *Daubert* factors are [1] testability and testing, [2] peer review and publication, [3] error rate, and [4] degree of acceptance.] . . .

A

Ho argues that the district court committed several legal or procedural errors in conducting the *Daubert* analysis. We reject each of these assertions.

First, Ho contends that the district court impermissibly treated the four *Daubert* factors as exclusive in concluding that Woehrle's experience could not qualify him as an expert. It is true that the four *Daubert* factors "do *not* constitute a definitive checklist or test." *Kumho*. . . .

We disagree with Ho's characterization of the district court's order. The court explicitly noted that the *Daubert* factors are non-exhaustive, and that "experience may qualify an expert to render an opinion under Rule 702." However, the court concluded that Ho failed to tie Woehrle's specific, testable opinions to anything other than "generalized experience," holding that "proper fulfillment of the court's gatekeeping duty requires more than passing along the opinion of a generally qualified expert merely because of his credentials." The district court appropriately considered experience along with the other *Daubert* factors, but held that Ho did not explain how Woehrle's experience rendered his particular opinions in this case reliable. As in *Kumho*, the district court "ultimately based its decision upon [an expert's] failure to satisfy either *Daubert's* factors *or any other* set of reasonable reliability criteria." The district court properly applied Rule 702 in so doing.

Second, Ho argues that the district court impermissibly focused on the reliability of Woehrle's conclusions rather than his methods. "[A] trial court's focus generally should not be upon the precise conclusions reached by the expert, but on the methodology employed in reaching those conclusions." [*Daubert* and *Kumho.*] However, we read the district court's order as holding Woehrle's conclusions were not reliable because they were not supported by reliable methodology. "Although it is not always a straightforward exercise to disaggregate method and conclusion, when the conclusion simply does not follow from the data, a district court is free to determine that an impermissible analytical gap exists between premises and conclusion." *Norris v. Baxter Healthcare Corp.*, 397 F.3d 878, 886 (10th Cir.2005).

Third, Ho claims that the district court failed to make detailed findings regarding Woehrle's methodology. We have held that a district court must create "a sufficiently developed record in order to allow a determination of whether the district court properly applied the relevant law." . . . As noted *supra*, the district court permissibly held that Woehrle did not tie his general experience in the tire industry to the specific opinions he advanced in this case. It did so in a thorough and well-reasoned memorandum and order. We have no trouble conducting appellate review of the court's holding.

Fourth, Ho contends the district court erred by issuing its *Daubert* ruling without conducting a hearing. She relies on our statement in *United States v. Nacchio*, 555 F.3d 1234 (10th Cir.2009) (en banc), that "it would be an abuse of discretion for the district court to unreasonably limit the evidence upon which it based its *Daubert* decision." *Id.* at 1250. From this statement, Ho claims that a *Daubert* hearing is required whenever requested. . . . [O]ur precedent is clear that "a district court has discretion to limit the information upon which it will decide the *Daubert* issue." . . .

B

In addition to her procedural arguments, Ho claims that the district court abused its discretion in various and sundry manners by excluding Woehrle's testimony. We hold that the district court's decision fell within the bounds of permissible choice.

Ho first claims that the district court abused its discretion by holding that Woehrle could not establish reliability based on his experience. As discussed *supra*, we reject this characterization of the district court's order. . . .

We agree with the district court's characterization of Woehrle's testimony. For example, when asked why he believed that a dog ear of at least a tenth of an inch is significant, Woehrle responded: "My experience at Uniroyal together with other cases that I'd worked on where indeed I've been able to — I've been able to derive a cause-effect relationship between dog-ears and root causes of belt separation failures." Similarly, when asked to support his claim that step-offs can cause belt separation, Woehrle responded that he was "not aware of any publicly published information that supports my claim. I only base it on my experience at Uniroyal and what we dealt with." These responses are typical of the ipse dixit nature of Woehrle's testimony.

We have no quarrel with the proposition that experience may qualify an expert. However, the district court was correct to hold that credentials alone do not suffice. The expert at issue in *Kumho Tire*, for example, was subject to exclusion despite his impeccable qualifications because his methodology was not reliable. Further, as Woehrle acknowledged, the peer-reviewed literature suggests the opposite of his opinions. . . . Given the yawning "analytical gap . . . between premises and conclusion," we conclude that the district court permissibly rejected Woehrle's reliance on generalized experience.

Second, Ho argues that the district court improperly rejected Woehrle's design defect testimony on the ground that Woehrle was not a tire designer. "[A]s long as an expert stays within the reasonable confines of his subject area, . . . a lack of specialization does not affect the admissibility of [the expert] opinion, but only its weight." . . . However, we once again reject Ho's characterization of the district court order.

Although the district court noted Woehrle's concession that he was not qualified to design a tire, this was not the sole basis of its ruling. It further relied in part on the fact that Woehrle's design theory has been ruled inadmissible in other cases. [Cites.] *But see* [contrary case] (holding defect theory regarding nylon cap plies admissible). The court also held that "Ho provides no rejoinder to Michelin's specific challenges as to Woehrle's expertise as to her claims of . . . design defect." It ultimately concluded that Woehrle's opinion did not "rest on any attempt to rationally balance" the advantages and disadvantages of a nylon cap ply.

Ho bore the burden of establishing that Woehrle's design defect opinion would be admissible under Rule 702.. . . . Ho simply points to Woehrle's lengthy experience in the tire industry without explaining how that experience supports his opinion that the lack of a nylon cap ply constituted a design defect. Experience is not necessarily a password to admissibility, and neither the district court nor this court will connect the dots on behalf of a litigant. . . .

Third, Ho contends the district court erred in ruling that Woehrle was not qualified to provide opinion testimony regarding defective warning. Ho appears to argue that Woehrle's testimony should have been admitted to bolster her contention that Michelin was liable for a complete failure to warn consumers of the connection between tire age and structural integrity. . . . However, Woehrle also testified that he did not consider "age to be applicable" to the tire failure at issue, and that he was "not offering opinions in this case concerning warnings or the effectiveness of warnings." We conclude that any claimed error would be harmless under these circumstances.

In Ho's fourth substantive attack on the district court's decision, she argues that the court erred in excluding the results of Woehrle's impact testing of a single tire. The district court provided several reasons for rejecting this evidence: drop tests are less reliable than pendulum tests according to the document upon which Woehrle relied; the test lacked a measured error rate; Woehrle's opinion was not supported by peer-reviewed evidence or even extensive testing; and Woerhle's claim that impacts do not cause belt detachment is contrary to the generally accepted engineering literature. Each of these factors was permissibly considered. . . .

Finally, Ho argues that the district court's ruling was flawed because tactile and visual inspection is an acceptable methodology. She relies on *Kumho Tire*, in which the Court stated that this methodology is well-recognized among tire experts. [But t]he district court did not hold that tactile and visual inspection was problematic. Instead, it concluded that "too great an analytical gap" existed between Woehrle's unsupported theories regarding potential causes of belt separation and his underlying data. We affirm that conclusion.

[Summary judgment in favor of Michelin AFFIRMED.]

[C] How Should "Fit" and "Reliability" Factors Under *Daubert-Kumho* Be Evaluated?

(1) *How Close Must the "Fit" Be?* In *In re Joint E. & S. Dist. Asbestos Litig.*, 52 F.3d 1124 (2d Cir. 1995), the background evidence strongly supported a principle that exposure to asbestos was associated with particular kinds of cancer, although not with the particular type of cancer that plaintiff contracted. The plaintiff's expert physician, however, concluded that plaintiff's cancer was caused by asbestos, apparently from an extension of the well-established principle and the elimination of other causes. The court of appeals upheld this use of expert testimony: the "fit" need not be perfect; it merely must be relevant in the sense of assisting the jury. The court also expressed the notion that the gatekeeping role should not be highly technical and restrictive, like "St. Peter at the gates of heaven."

(2) *How do the Various Factors of Falsifiability, Peer Review, etc., Weigh Against Each Other in Defining the Gatekeeper Role?* In *United States v. Bonds*, 12 F.3d 540 (6th Cir. 1993), the government offered DNA evidence, including FBI testimony that declared a "match" with the defendant. The defendant offered a post-trial report by a committee of the National Academy of Sciences (the "NAS Report") criticizing part of the FBI's methodology. The court nevertheless found that the DNA evidence was relevant (a sufficiently close fit to be "helpful"), and also found that it was sufficiently reliable. The court considered ten factors, including, in addition to the relevance inquiry, such other considerations as testability of the FBI theory, actual testing, peer review, error rates, general acceptance of principles, general acceptance of methods, use of data reasonably relied on by similar experts, use by the trial-level magistrate of a court-appointed expert, and balance of relevance versus counterweights under Fed. R. Evid. 403.

The *Bonds* court upheld the trial court's admittance of the testimony in spite of the NAS Report. It acknowledged the flaws in the FBI methodology, but held that the flaws did not negate peer review, and concluded that, although the error rates were troublingly significant, they were not alone determinative. In short, much science is "subject to reasonable dispute," and the existence of a better, more accurate approach — if the NAS could be said to provide this — does not destroy the admissibility of the one that is offered. The shortcomings of the evidence could be shown as a matter of weight for the jury to consider.

(3) *What Other Factors can be Considered in Addition to the Four Described by the Supreme Court?: Bonds, supra, and In re Paoli R.R. Yard PCB Litig., 35 F.3d 717 (3d Cir. 1994), cert. denied, 513 U.S. 1190 (1995).* In *Bonds, supra,* the Court expanded the list of factors. In *Paoli,* the court did likewise. In addition to the Supreme Court's four factors of testability (falsifiability), peer review, error rates, and general acceptance, the court added: (5) the existence and maintenance of standards controlling the technique (probably already included in the concept of error rate in *Daubert*); (6) the degree to which the expert is qualified; (7) the relationship of the technique to "more established modes of scientific analysis;" (8) the "non-judicial uses to which the scientific techniques are put"; and (9) any other relevant factors. The ultimate inquiry is whether the testimony is "based on the 'methods and procedures of science' rather than on 'subjective belief or unsupported speculation.' "

PROBLEM 6A: THE FIFTH CIRCUIT ALLOWS FOR SOME ADMISSIBILITY OF POLYGRAPH EVIDENCE AFTER DAUBERT: UNITED STATES v. POSADO, 57 F.3d 428 (5th Cir. 1995).

Posado and others were charged with cocaine offenses. They filed a motion to suppress the seized cocaine. The Government relied on consent and produced consent forms signed by all defendants. Defendants claimed, however, that the consent had been obtained only after arrest, search, and seizure, rendering it invalid, a version that the arresting officers denied. The court describes the polygraph evidence as follows:

> Perceiving that the suppression hearing would amount to a "swearing match" (that the defendants would be likely to lose), the defendants arranged to submit to polygraphs to establish the truth of the assertions in their affidavits. Well before the tests were given, counsel for the defendants contacted the prosecution and extended the opportunity to participate in the tests. The defendants also offered to stipulate that the results would be admissible in any way the government wanted to use them, at trial or otherwise. The prosecution declined this opportunity.
>
> Subsequently, the defendants were examined by polygraph experts Paul K. Minor and Ernie Hulsey. Both Minor and Hulsey concluded that in each case "deception was not indicated." Thereafter, the defendants moved for an order allowing Minor and Hulsey to testify regarding the results of the three tests at the pretrial suppression hearing or, in the alternative, for a hearing on the admissibility of polygraph results as expert evidence. . . . In support of their request for a *Daubert* hearing on the issue, defendants submitted the affidavit of another polygraph expert, Dr. Stan Abrams, Ph.D., to establish that polygraph technique possesses sufficient scientific validity to be admissible.

> [T]he district court summarily refused to consider the polygraph testimony and also refused to consider whether the testimony was reliable and relevant under the Federal Rules of Evidence.

The Court of Appeals then remanded for a redetermination of admissibility:

> There can be no doubt that tremendous advances have been made in polygraph instrumentation and technique in the years since *Frye*. The test at issue in *Frye* measured only changes in the subject's systolic blood pressure in response to test questions. Modern instrumentation detects changes in the subject's blood pressure, pulse, thoracic and abdominal respiration, and galvanic skin response. Current research indicates that, when given under controlled conditions, the polygraph technique accurately predicts truth or deception between seventy and ninety percent of the time. Remaining controversy about test accuracy is almost unanimously attributed to variations in the integrity of the testing environment and the qualifications of the examiner. Such variation also exists in many of the disciplines and for much of the scientific evidence we routinely find admissible under Rule 702. Further, there is good indication that polygraph technique and the requirements for professional polygraphists are becoming progressively more standardized. In addition, polygraph technique has been and continues to be subjected to extensive study and publication. Finally, polygraphy is now widely used by employers and government agencies alike.

The court next considered the Fed. R. Evid. 403 analysis required by *Daubert*. It concluded that certain factors lessened the potential prejudice, including the defendants' offer to allow the prosecution to participate, the pretrial nature of the proceedings (entailing "relaxed" evidence rules), and the judge's better ability than a jury's to resist intimidation by the evidence. . . .

> It is with a high degree of caution that we have today opened the door to the possibility of polygraph evidence in certain circumstances. We may indeed be opening a legal Pandora's box.

Questions:

(1) Is this opinion a correct application of *Daubert*?

(2) If so, what factors or conditions should suffice to satisfy the fit and reliability requirements for polygraph evidence offered in a hearing before a judge?

(3) What about a trial before a jury?

(4) Is the court's Fed. R. Evid. 403 analysis persuasive?

(5) Is the per se rule of exclusion, which this opinion rejects, a better resolution of the basic issues?

(6) Is the court's ruling limited to defense evidence?

The Supreme Court rejected a constitutional challenge to a jurisdiction's per se ban on polygraph evidence (the ban was applied here against the criminal defendant) in *United States v. Scheffer*, 523 U.S. 303 (1998). . . .

[D] Procedures for Deciding *Daubert/Kumho* Issues[5]

Read Federal Rule of Evidence 706, "Court Appointed Expert Witnesses."

(1) *The (Deferential) Standard of Review on Appeal — Abuse of Discretion.* In *General Electric Co. v. Joiner*, 522 U.S. 136 (1997), the Court of Appeals held that a "particularly stringent standard of review" was to be applied to the exclusion of expert testimony on *Daubert* grounds. The Supreme Court reversed:

> [W]hile the Federal Rules of Evidence allow district courts to admit a somewhat broader range of scientific testimony than would have been admissible under *Frye*, they leave in place the "gatekeeper" role of the trial judge in screening such evidence. A court of appeals applying "abuse of discretion" review to such rulings may not categorically distinguish between rulings allowing expert testimony and rulings which disallow it. We likewise reject respondent's argument that because the granting of summary judgment in this case was "outcome determinative," it should have been subjected to a more searching standard of review. On a motion for summary judgment, disputed issues of fact are resolved against the moving party — here, petitioners. But the question of admissibility of expert testimony is not such an issue of fact, and is reviewable under the abuse of discretion standard.
>
> We hold that the Court of Appeals erred in its review of the exclusion of Joiner's experts' testimony. In applying an overly "stringent" review to that ruling, it failed to give the trial court the deference that is the hallmark of abuse of discretion review.

(2) *The Trial Judge Applies a Preponderance Standard.* In a footnote in *Daubert*, the Supreme Court held that a preponderance standard governs the trial judge's consideration of the factors involved in *Daubert* testing. This apparently is so irrespective of the ultimate standard of persuasion applicable to the fact-finder on the merits. But how does the trial judge apply a "preponderance" standard to a multi-factor balancing test if some of the factors (e.g., testability) favor admissibility and others (e.g., lack of peer review, high error rates) oppose it?

(3) *The Daubert/Kumho Inquiry is Not Bound by the Rules of Evidence.* The Court's citation in *Daubert* to Fed. R. Evid. 104(a) is accompanied by a footnote quoting its language, including the provision that, "In making [the] determination, [the trial judge] is not bound by the rules of evidence except those as to privileges." Thus the trial judge can consider hearsay and opinion from an indefinite variety of sources. Would it be appropriate in a toxic tort case for the judge to consider a high school chemistry text? An article from the Journal of the American Medical Association? A newspaper clipping reporting a similar injury? The opinions of attorneys?

(4) *Ways to Help Judges Make Appropriate Daubert/Kumho Rulings.* Is an adversarial system of justice suited to the judge's task in determining the validity

---

[5] Study Guide Reference: Evidence in a Nutshell, Chapter 7:II B, at "Scientific Evidence After *Daubert*."

of scientific principles or techniques? In *Joiner, supra* note (1), Justice Breyer's concurring opinion suggested ways to help judges meet their "*Daubert* gatekeeping function":

> Among these techniques are an increased use of Rule 16's pretrial conference authority to narrow the scientific issues in dispute, pretrial hearings where potential experts are subject to examination by the court, and the appointment of special masters and specially trained law clerks.
>
> In the present case, the New England Journal of Medicine has filed an amici brief "in support of neither petitioners nor respondents" in which the Journal writes:
>
> > [A] judge could better fulfill this gatekeeper function if he or she had help from scientists. Judges should be strongly encouraged to make greater use of their inherent authority . . . to appoint experts. . . . Reputable experts could be recommended to courts by established scientific organizations, such as the National Academy of Sciences or the American Association for the Advancement of Science.
>
> Brief for The New England Journal of Medicine 18-19; *cf.* Fed. Rule Evid. 706 (court may "on its own motion or on the motion of any party" appoint an expert to serve on behalf of the court, and this expert may be selected as "agreed upon by the parties" or chosen by the court). . . .

§ 6.03 MINOR PREMISE — WAS TEST PROPERLY CONDUCTED?[6]

Introductory Note: The Minor Premise. Scientific evidence may be conceived of as having the following sequence of reasoning: (1) "If x then y" (the "major premise," i.e., the scientific principle or theory, to which *Daubert* and *Frye* would seem to be principally addressed); (2) We have here an "x" (the minor premise, usually dependent on proper procedures having been followed during, e.g., collection, preservation, transfer, and testing of any sample that may be involved); (3) "Therefore y follows."

PRUITT v. STATE

Tennessee Supreme Court
216 Tenn. 686, 393 S.W.2d 747 (1965)

White, Justice.

Pruitt was tried and convicted for second degree murder growing out of an automobile accident in which two pedestrians were killed.

Pruitt testified that [after the accident] he then went into his house and drank half of a half pint of whiskey. About an hour later he was arrested and taken to

[6] Study Guide Reference: Evidence in a Nutshell, Chapter 7:II, at "Introduction: Experts: Special Latitude Under Both Common Law and F.R.E."

Police Headquarters. The arresting officer and another officer who observed Pruitt at that time testified that in their opinion he was intoxicated.

[A]t Police Headquarters, plaintiff in error [Pruitt] was given a Breathalyzer test for intoxication. The test was administered by Police Officer Ingle. The results of the test showed .18 per cent alcohol in plaintiff in error's blood. By statute, T.C.A. § 59-1033 (1955), a concentration of at least .15 per cent alcohol by weight creates a rebuttable presumption of intoxication. [Note: Today, the intoxication standard would be much lower, perhaps .08%. — Eds.]

[Pruitt contends the] evidence of the results of the Breathalyzer test was improperly admitted because the officer who performed the test was not competent as an expert to either administer the test or to testify as to its results, and, in addition, he did not follow the necessary precautions.

[T]he Borkenstein Breathalyzer operates on the principle that vapor alcohol from the lungs will oxidize in a solution of potassium dichromate and 50% sulfuric acid. The solution then loses some of its original yellow color and the color change is recorded by a photoelectric cell in comparison with an identical yellow solution which has not been exposed to the alcohol.

First, the subject blows a certain volume of alveolar (deep lung) air into a cylinder-piston chamber, the cylinder measuring exactly 52.5 cubic centimeters. This volume of air, heated at about 40 to 55 degrees Centigrade, is bubbled through the test ampule of potassium dichromate and sulfuric acid. The test ampule should be at a temperature of about 65 degrees Centigrade (approximately 150 degrees Fahrenheit). From the degree of oxidation measured by the photoelectric cell, the weight of alveolar air alcohol that causes that much color change is measured.

This alveolar air alcohol percentage is then converted by a calibrated scale to indicate the blood alcohol content. The principle behind this conversion is the fact that the same amount of alcohol, by weight, found in 52.5 cc. of alveolar air is that to be found in 1/40 cc. of the subject's blood, a ratio of 1:2100. Also, this formula is based on the fact that in the average normal individual, the carbon dioxide (CO2) content of alveolar air is 5.5 per cent.

The Breathalyzer is considered a reliable device for measuring intoxication. [Scientific study of use under experimental and police department conditions cited, finding close correlation to blood alcohol.]

Whatever the device used, this Court has held that qualified experts must operate the machine, and they, or someone else qualified, must interpret these test results in evidence before a trial court. But this does not mean that this Court must accept without question the discretion of the trial judge, especially where no foundation or predicate has been laid for qualification of the expert.

The State is required to show that the measuring device is scientifically acceptable and accurate for the purpose for which it is used, and that the witness who presents the test results is qualified to interpret them. If such testimony is admitted without proper predicate and qualification, it can be shown on cross-examination that such witness is not qualified, and it is then proper to strike his testimony. If the witness were properly qualified in advance, cross-examination would only test his credibility as an expert.

There is no settled formula for determining proper qualifications for an operator of an intoxication testing device. The cases vary from one that holds two days' training sufficient to qualify a witness, to our own decision which held that a witness who operated the device should be able to understand [the mathematical calculations relating] alveolar air alcohol content to blood alcohol content. [Citations.]

In *People v. Morgan*, 236 N.Y.S.2d 1014 (Misc. 1962), a witness who was "not [a] medical doctor, pathologist, biologist, hematologist, physiologist, biochemist or toxicologist," but who had six months' training as a practical nurse and "on-the-job training" under a police lab director in urine analysis was held not a competent expert to testify as to transposition or interpolation from urine alcohol content to blood alcohol content. [Here, the court offers additional authorities.] . . .

There is a practical limitation on the facilities of police administration to provide trained toxicologists or pathologists. It is not beyond practical limits, however, to provide expert technicians with an understanding of the theoretical and operative functions of a single device for testing intoxication. He must at least be able to understand why a breath test can be translated into a certain percentage of alcohol in the blood. . . .

Police Officer Ingle was not shown to have been qualified to present adequately the results of the Breathalyzer test. He had about one week's training from two superior police officers in how to operate the machine, but there is nothing in the record to indicate his knowledge of the theory behind the machine and the principle of conversion from alveolar air alcohol content to blood alcohol content.

There is also undisputed proof that Officer Ingle did not conduct the test properly and thus did not take precautions against the possibility of inaccurate results. It is a recognized requirement by experts in the operation of a Breathalyzer that before beginning the test, the operator must observe the person tested for at least fifteen (15) minutes before [he] blows into the instrument.

The purpose of this waiting period is to make sure that the person tested has no foreign matter in his mouth, that he doesn't hiccough, vomit, belch, smoke, or take another drink — all of which could produce a false reading. Also, this period is used to keep the subject quiet, as violent physical activity may produce an abnormally high carbon dioxide content which would make the reading inaccurate. If there is suspected recent drinking or foreign matter in the mouth, a duplicate sample of breath should be taken in another 15 minutes for comparison with the first test. [Scientific treatise on subject cited.]

For these reasons we are compelled to hold that the evidence of the Breathalyzer test results was improperly admitted and should have been stricken from the record.

Reversed and remanded.

NOTES AND QUESTIONS

(1) *The Instrument Must be Properly Calibrated and Tested.* For admissibility, a number of decisions also require, in addition to some minimum qualifications as in the principle case, a certain quantum of evidence that the device was properly and timely calibrated and tested reasonably close in time to its use on the defendant. All of these requirements are related to what we have called "the minor premise."

(2) *Chain of Custody.* Much scientific evidence involves taking a specimen and having it tested. There must be some proof that the specimen tested was the specimen taken from the relevant person, thing, or place, and that it is unlikely to have become adulterated or altered in any relevant respect, but the proof need not be absolutely "airtight." (What should be the standard? What should be the result of contrary evidence?)

§ 6.04 DNA[7]

STATE v. WHITTEY

Supreme Court of New Hampshire
149 N.H. 463, 821 A.2d 1086 (2003)

DALIANIS, J.

[D]efendant Whittey was convicted following a jury trial of first-degree murder in the course of rape. On appeal, he argues that the Superior Court erred by finding that the results of polymerase chain reaction based short tandem repeat DNA testing were admissible scientific evidence. We affirm.

Yvonne Fine was found dead in her home. Following an autopsy, the examiner concluded that Fine's death was caused by strangulation, and that she had bruises on her body that could have been caused by sexual assault and penetration.

A serologist confirmed that there was still a usable semen sample in the victim's pajama pants and stored them in a freezer. [T]he State sent the pajama pants, a slipper, and the defendant's underwear, as well as fingernail scrapings, to Cellmark Diagnostics (Cellmark) for DNA analysis. Cellmark used a form of DNA testing known as polymerase chain reaction (PCR) based short tandem repeat (STR) DNA profiling and concluded that DNA in the semen sample on the pajama pants matched the defendant's DNA profile. The examiner also concluded that the DNA in a semen stain on the slipper matched the defendant's DNA profile.

[T]he defendant moved to exclude the use of DNA evidence at trial because the PCR-based STR analysis was not admissible under the standard set forth in *Frye*. Following a four-day evidentiary hearing at which the trial court heard detailed expert testimony and received exhibits, the court concluded that PCR-based STR DNA testing was scientifically reliable and, therefore, admissible for purposes of the *Frye* standard.

---

[7] Study Guide Reference: Evidence in a Nutshell, Chapter 7:II C, at "Other Standard Tests on Bodily Substances: Paternity, Rape, Assault, and Homicide Cases: Identifying the Culprit."

Scientific Reliability of PCR-Based STR DNA testing

Although we have [subsequently] adopted the test set forth in *Daubert* for determining the admissibility of scientific evidence, both parties stipulated that, for the purposes of this case, the proper standard for determining the scientific admissibility of PCR-based STR DNA testing is that set forth in *Frye.* To be admissible under *Frye*, we require: 1) general acceptance in the relevant scientific community of the scientific theory or principle; and 2) general acceptance in the relevant scientific community of the techniques, experiments, or procedures applying that theory or principle. We review the trial court's rulings on evidentiary matters, including those regarding the reliability of novel scientific evidence, with considerable deference. When the reliability or general acceptance of novel scientific evidence is not likely to vary according to the circumstances of a particular case, however, we review that evidence independently.

Because we have previously discussed the general theory underlying DNA profiling [in *Vandebogart*] we begin our discussion with a brief overview of PCR-based STR DNA testing. As with other forms of DNA testing, the PCR-based STR method begins with the extraction of DNA from a sample. The strands of DNA are then split in half using heat application and small segments are duplicated using the PCR technique. The PCR method refers to the amplification of DNA material where a chemical reaction takes place in which polymerase, an enzyme, is used to copy a specific DNA location so that the particular DNA region can be typed and compared to DNA of a known sample. The PCR procedure duplicates the DNA segments to the point where they are numerous enough to be measured by a process that involves: 1) tagging the relevant DNA segments with fluorescent dye; 2) scanning the sample containing the tagged DNA segments with a laser; and 3) recording the results of the laser scan by computer. The PCR method allows an analyst to obtain a DNA profile from a smaller amount of DNA than previously [possible under the DNA technique known as] restriction fragment length polymorphism (RFLP) testing, the profiling technique examined in *Vandebogart.*

STR testing, which involves the testing of DNA at three or more genetic markers, is a subtype of the PCR method. The PCR-based STR testing in this case involved the use of thirteen segments, or loci, of DNA. These thirteen loci are the same ones that are used in the federal DNA database known as the combined DNA index system. At each locus, an individual's genetic code contains a combination of chemical markers organized into a pattern. These chemical patterns repeat themselves and these repeats can be chemically cut apart from one another. At any particular chromosomal locus, an individual will have a characteristic inherited from each of his or her parents, known as an allele. Further, at any given locus, a person will have DNA with a specific number of repeats of these alleles from each parent. Thus, for example, a person's PCR-based STR DNA profile for a particular DNA locus could contain a ten-repeat allele from his or her mother and a twelve-repeat allele from his or her father. STR testing involves the examination of short repeats and distinguishes between individuals by comparing the number of repeats at certain loci.

In performing the PCR-based STR testing, Cellmark used commercial test kits manufactured by Perkin-Elmer/Applied Biosystems known as the "Profiler Plus" and "Cofiler." These test kits contain synthetic primers and enzymes that facilitate DNA amplification and DNA typing at the thirteen loci. Cellmark also used a machine called the ABI Prism 310 Genetic Analyzer, which marks the DNA using fluorescent dyes and separates the copied DNA by length. The results from this procedure are then printed in the form of peaks on a graph known as an electropherogram, which is interpreted by a DNA analyst. If the pattern of repeats in the known DNA strand matches the pattern in the questioned strand, the analyst reports that the donor of the known sample cannot be conclusively eliminated as the source of the questioned sample. Similar to RFLP testing, the analyst performs a statistical calculation to quantify the significance of the similarity between the known and questioned samples.

[D]efendant does not challenge the admissibility of the PCR method of DNA analysis, which "has received widespread acceptance in courts." Rather, he argues that: 1) Cellmark's techniques and methodology in interpreting PCR-based STR DNA tests, as well as the commercial test kits used in this case, have not undergone sufficient validation studies; and 2) the STR technology cannot adequately distinguish stutter and other artifacts from sample-specific peaks, which affects the system's ability to identify components of mixed DNA samples.

While we have previously examined the general theory of DNA profiling and the methods and techniques involved in RFLP testing, we have yet to address the reliability of PCR-based STR DNA testing. While decisions concerning this form of DNA testing are not widespread, the majority of jurisdictions that have addressed the admissibility of PCR-based STR DNA testing have held that the techniques and procedures used in such testing are scientifically reliable. In 1996, the National Research Council issued a report stating that "one of the most promising of the newer PCR techniques involves amplification of loci containing Short Tandem Repeats (STRs), that STR testing is coming into wide use, [and] that STR loci appear to be particularly appropriate for forensic use." Numerous articles published in both scientific and forensic journals acknowledge the widespread acceptance of PCR-based STR DNA testing in the forensic setting. Moreover, PCR-based STR DNA testing is recognized and used in virtually every State and by the Federal Bureau of Investigation.

At the *Frye* hearing, one of the State's expert witnesses, Doctor Robin Cotton, a forensic scientist and molecular biologist who works as a forensic laboratory director for Cellmark, testified that the PCR method of STR DNA testing, as well as the methods and techniques underlying the use of the Profiler Plus and Cofiler kits with the 310 Genetic Analyzer, are generally accepted in the relevant scientific communities of forensic science and molecular biology. *Cf. Jackson* (stating that general acceptance in scientific community may be established by testimony of director or supervisor of DNA forensic laboratory). She also stated that "over a hundred forensic laboratories [are] doing DNA testing across the country," and that "virtually all of the labs that intend to continue DNA testing are either in the process of validating or have completed validation of the 13 loci." In addition, she stated that all laboratories utilizing the fluorescent STR method are testing samples at least thirteen loci. Finally, the trial court noted that Doctor Cotton testified that PCR-based STR testing has largely replaced RFLP testing as the standard DNA test in the forensic field.

The defendant attempts to discredit the (state's experts) on the ground that they are biased. It is well settled that the trier of fact is in the best position to measure the persuasiveness of evidence and the credibility of witnesses. [T]he proper way to expose a witness's bias is through vigorous cross-examination during the hearing.

The defendant next argues that the PCR-based STR DNA test is not admissible under *Frye* because the commercial testing kits used in this case and Cellmark's internal laboratory procedures have not undergone sufficient validation testing. The State argues, and the trial court ruled, that these validation concerns are not relevant to the *Frye* analysis. We agree. First, "the Cofiler and Profiler materials kits do not represent a separate part of the [DNA] typing process, but rather, simply contain materials for beginning the PCR process." Thus, questions as to the reliability of these commercial testing kits go to the weight of the evidence, not their admissibility.

Similarly, questions relating to the internal validation procedures of an individual testing laboratory go to either the admissibility or the weight to be given the evidence in a particular case, not admissibility under *Frye. See Vandebogart* (challenges to laboratory's testing protocols and procedures are questions of foundation or weight to be dealt with at trial). In *Vandebogart* we rejected the argument that RFLP DNA testing was not generally accepted in the scientific community because, among other reasons, certain FBI internal validation studies were insufficient. For this reason, we also agree with the trial court that the defendant's argument, that Cellmark failed to conduct sufficient validation studies before raising the minimum relative fluorescence unit (RFU) level at which it would consider a peak on the electropherogram an allele from forty RFUs to sixty, goes to the weight of the evidence rather than its admissibility under *Frye*.

Nevertheless, the testimony at the *Frye* hearing supports the trial court's findings that both Cellmark's testing procedures and the Profiler Plus and Cofiler testing kits are validated and scientifically reliable. Doctor Cotton testified regarding the validation studies Cellmark conducted with respect to PCR-based STR DNA testing. She explained that her laboratory performed numerous studies and experiments addressing various issues such as the limits of the instrument's detection and the ability of analysts to interpret mixed samples. She further testified that the majority of laboratories in the United States use the same methods and instruments as Cellmark. The State also introduced a summary of Cellmark's internal validation studies.

In addition, there was evidence introduced that Perkin-Elmer conducted validation studies of its test kits. This evidence included articles that were submitted for publication addressing the design of the kits and the procedures for performing experiments. Doctor Chakraborty testified that his laboratory was involved in testing the Profiler Plus and Cofiler test kits during their developmental stages. Finally, we note that other courts have found the Profiler Plus and Cofiler test kits to be scientifically reliable. *See, e.g., Owens*, (recognizing that courts throughout the country have found that STR DNA profiling using the Profiler Plus and Cofiler test kits is reliable and generally accepted by scientific community). . . .

While the defendant's expert witnesses were critical of the sufficiency of both Cellmark's and Perkin-Elmer's validation studies, scientific unanimity is not required to render such theory or technique admissible under *Frye*. The isolated criticisms of the defendant do not defeat the existence of a general consensus in the scientific community that PCR-based STR DNA testing is reliable.

The defendant also argues that PCR-based STR testing is not admissible under *Frye* because the technology cannot adequately distinguish stutter and other artifacts from sample-specific peaks on an electropherogram, which affects the ability to analyze mixed samples. Specifically, he asserts that the problems of stutter and other artifacts have not been sufficiently studied by Cellmark, Perkin-Elmer, or the scientific community to render STR testing admissible under *Frye*.

An "artifact" is a result that does not come from the things one actually intends to test. One form of artifact is called a "stutter," which occurs in STR testing when a small sample of production of a fragment is one base pair shorter than the true allele. Artifacts are not unique to STR tests, but rather are present in many forms of DNA testing. Doctor Cotton testified that the scientific community understands artifacts and can work around them.

Testimony at the *Frye* hearing established that mixed samples, which involve DNA of two or more people, are one of the most common things that scientists encounter in forensic science. Doctor Peter D'Eustacio, a defense expert, testified that mixture interpretation has been examined extensively and is not a new concept in forensic science. The State introduced various articles at the *Frye* hearing addressing specifically the testing and interpretation of mixtures in the forensic DNA setting. Cellmark has also conducted various internal validation studies to address the problems of mixtures. Finally, Doctor Cotton stated that Cellmark follows the DNA Advisory Board guidelines, which cover such areas as validation testing and internal operating procedures to ensure testing accuracy.

While the presence of artifacts could affect an analyst's interpretation of an electropherogram, this fact does not undermine the general acceptance of the techniques, methods, or procedures by which the data is produced.

[W]e hold that interpretive issues raised by the defendant are properly the subject of cross-examination and affect the weight to be given such evidence in a particular case. *See Trala* (defendant's challenges to FBI laboratory's testing methodology involving stutters, allelic dropout and the ability to analyze mixed samples are directed to the weight of the evidence and not its admissibility).

Lastly, the defendant asserted that Cellmark's method of interpreting electropherograms to calculate a DNA match constitutes an improper application of the product rule. "The product rule is one technique used to determine the probability of finding a match between a DNA sample from a suspect and DNA material found in a body fluid sample recovered from a crime scene.". . . . "Under the product rule, the frequency in the population base of each allele disclosed in the DNA test is multiplied to produce the frequency of the combination of all the alleles found." Use of the product rule has been found generally accepted in the scientific community.

. . .

Even assuming without deciding that Cellmark did misapply the product rule, we disagree with the defendant that this renders the results of PCR-based STR DNA testing inadmissible under *Frye*. The contention that Cellmark failed to follow generally accepted techniques when analyzing DNA under the product rule is an issue that goes to the weight that evidence should be given in a particular case, not the general admissibility under Frye. *See Vandebogart*; *see also Smith* (argument that laboratory's techniques rendered its frequency calculations scientifically unreliable was a question of weight, not admissibility); *Kinder* (criticism of particular methods used to apply product rule pertain to the weight to be given the DNA evidence at trial).

As a result, based upon the evidence presented during the *Frye* hearings and the overwhelming acceptance of PCR-based STR DNA testing in other cases, we affirm the trial court's ruling that the methods and techniques used in PCR-based STR DNA testing are generally accepted in the scientific community.

Affirmed.

NOTES AND QUESTIONS

(1) *Difference Under Daubert? Whittey* did not apply *Daubert* because New Hampshire shifted to *Daubert* after the *Whittey* trial, though before the *Whittey* appeal. Would application of the *Daubert* standard have made a difference in *Whittey*? Would application of present Fed. R. Evid. 702 (as amended in 2000)? Pay particular attention to the things the court in *Whittey* says are matters of weight, for the lawyers to thrash out before the trier-of-fact. Would they be matters of admissibility under *Daubert?* (See *Beasley*, *supra*, for at least one view of what *Daubert* would say on this. *See also Jakobetz*, *supra*. Are those cases necessarily what *Daubert* means?) Would such matters be matters of admissibility under current Fed. R. Evid. 702 (as amended in 2000)? Are *Daubert* (and *Kumho*) different from current Fed. R. Evid. 702 (as amended in 2000), on this question? Did the 2000 amendments faithfully codify *Daubert/Kumho* on this? Are there other respects in which the amendments are arguably not a faithful codification of *Daubert/Kumho?*

(2) *A View on the Difference Between Frye and Rule 702 (and Daubert?)* As *Whittey* shows, courts struggle with defining in some objective way what part of a scientific process is policed by the jurisdiction's test for scientific evidence (*Frye* or *Daubert*) and what part is left to other rules of evidence and/or weight. The Washington State Supreme Court sized up the problem (and the solution), in the following way, as summarized by Prof. Nathan Schachtman in his legal blog:

> [T]he Washington Supreme Court decided a nuisance case against a local utility for fear of future illnesses from exposure to electro-magnetic frequency radiation (EMF). *Lakey v. Puget Sound Energy, Inc.* (Mar. 6, 2013). The defendant moved for the exclusion of plaintiff's expert (under *Frye* and Rule 702), Dr. Carpenter, [who] was Director of the Institute for Health and the Environment at the University at Albany and Professor of Environmental Health Sciences [at the University's] School of Public Health. He also [was] Dean of [that] School and Director of the Wadsworth Center for Laboratories and Research of the New York State Department of Health, [and was] active in testifying about EMF. The trial court

conducted a three-day *Frye* hearing, at which both sides offered expert witness testimony. Plaintiffs called Carpenter, and the defendants called an epidemiologist, and a professor at Dartmouth's Geisel School of Medicine [who was] a specialist in the molecular and cellular biology of brain tumors. [Defense experts] testified [at the hearing] that Carpenter had failed to follow generally accepted epidemiologic methodology of considering all pertinent data: Carpenter had "cherry picked" [and] selectively ignored studies that contradicted his conclusions. Even among the studies that Carpenter had relied upon, he ignored data that undermined or contradicted his conclusion. Furthermore, Carpenter ignored the toxicologic data and studies available. Among the studies ignored by Carpenter were the most recent, and most carefully conducted, studies. The trial court excluded Carpenter.

The Supreme Court reversed the trial court's *Frye* [exclusion because] the plaintiffs' witnesses sufficiently deployed a generally accepted method when they waded into the field of epidemiology [since] epidemiology is generally accepted. *Frye* does not require that expert witnesses apply the established methodology well, reliably, or soundly. [E]xpert witnesses are immunized from exclusion by relying upon studies from a generally accepted discipline, no matter how poorly or selectively they have analyzed and interpreted these studies. An expert witness's errors in engaging with a particular scientific discipline that is in general considered generally accepted "go to the weight, not the admissibility, of the evidence unless the error renders the evidence unreliable," the Court said.

[However,] Carpenter was properly excluded under Rule 702. Carpenter's cherry-picking vitiated the reliability of his opinion,

> . . . seriously tainting his conclusions because epidemiology is an iteractive science relying on later studies to refine earlier studies in order to reach better and more accurate conclusions. [He] refused to account for the data from the toxicological studies, which epidemiological methodology requires unless the evidence for the link between exposure and disease is unequivocal and strong, which is not the case here. [He] also selectively sampled data within one of the studies he used, taking data indicating an EMF-illness link and ignoring the larger pool of data within the study that showed no such link. [His] treatment of this data created a false impression about what the study actually showed.

Can you link this ruling to subdivisions (b), (c), and/or (d) in current Federal Rule 702? Is the court actually relying on a principle like that in Federal Rule 702(d)? Although those subdivisions were not in the Washington rule, it could be argued that the courted acted as though they (or at least (d)) effectively were. Would the courts also apply to *Daubert* as it did to *Frye*? If so, is it arguable that Federal Rule 702 is not a faithful codification of Daubert?

(3) *Does Proper Performance of Protocols Go to Weight or Admissibility?* This is a specific form of the issue treated in notes (1) and (2) above, and part of the issue in *Whittey*. In *United States v. Martinez*, 3 F.3d 1191 (8th Cir. 1993), *cert. denied*,

510 U.S. 1062 (1994), the court discussed the conflicting case law on the issue of whether the "minor premise" — the expert's use of the technology — goes to weight or admissibility when the technology in question is DNA profiling:

> The fact that we have taken judicial notice of the reliability of the technique of DNA profiling does not mean that expert testimony concerning DNA profiling is automatically admissible under *Daubert*. A number of courts have required that the trial court further inquire into whether the expert properly performed the techniques involved in creating the DNA profiles. We must consider whether such a requirement exists after *Daubert*.
>
> We believe that the reliability inquiry set forth in *Daubert* mandates that there be a preliminary showing that the expert properly performed a reliable methodology in arriving at his opinion. The *Daubert* Court stated that "under the Rules, the trial judge must ensure that any and all scientific testimony or evidence admitted is not only relevant, but reliable." This suggests that the inquiry extends beyond simply the reliability of the principles or methodologies in the abstract. In order to determine whether scientific testimony is reliable, the court must conclude that the testimony was derived from the application of a reliable methodology or principle in the particular case.
>
> At the same time, the Court specifically counseled courts to respect the differing functions of judge and jury. It stated that the focus of the foundational inquiry "must be upon the principles and methodology, not on the conclusions that they generate." Thus, we conclude that the court should make an initial inquiry into the particular expert's application of the scientific principle or methodology in question. The court should require the testifying expert to provide affidavits attesting that he properly performed the protocols involved in DNA profiling.
>
> If the opponent of the evidence challenges the application of the protocols in a particular case, the district court must determine whether the expert erred in applying the protocols, and if so, whether such error so infected the procedure as to make the results unreliable. We emphasize, however, that this inquiry is of necessity a flexible one. Not every error in the application of a particular methodology should warrant exclusion. An alleged error in the application of a reliable methodology should provide the basis for exclusion of the opinion only if that error negates the basis for the reliability of the principle itself. We agree with the Third Circuit that an allegation of failure to properly apply a scientific principle should provide the basis for exclusion of an expert opinion only if "a reliable methodology was so altered [by a particular expert] as to skew the methodology itself." [Cite.]

Similarly, the court in *Armstead v. State*, 673 A.2d 221 (Md. 1996), observed that while DNA evidence ordinarily will be admissible:

> [T]he trial judge retains the discretion to exclude DNA evidence if errors in the laboratory procedures render it so unreliable that it would not be

> helpful to the trier of fact. We recognize that courts in other jurisdictions have adopted differing views regarding whether challenges to the laboratory procedures used in a specific case go to the admissibility of DNA evidence or merely to its weight. We believe the better approach is generally to treat individualized errors in application of the DNA technique as matters of weight, but to permit trial judges discretion to exclude DNA evidence if such errors were made in the course of testing that the evidence would not be helpful to the fact-finder.

Does the revision to Fed. R. Evid. 702, which requires that the expert "apply the principles and methods reliably to the facts of the case," transform into a challenge to admissibility rather than credibility or weight, the proper application of protocols? Some analysts call this "prong two" of the analysis, "prong one" being the reliability (or acceptability) of the scientific technique itself. In your view, does the revision of 702 track *Daubert/Kumho* on which prong is a matter of admissibility and which (if any) a matter of weight? Could an argument be made that it doesn't?

As used by most analysts, "prong two" is, as you can see, addressed to "the minor premise." *See* § 6.03, *supra*. Is the *Pruitt* case in that section, and the position described in note (1) following *Pruitt*, in conflict with what the cases in the current section say is only a matter of weight?

Other challenges to the minor premise may focus on collection, preservation, and contamination of specimens before they reach the laboratory. This was a major part of the defense presentation in the O.J. Simpson case.

(4) *Technology as a Moving Target.* Technology is a moving target behind which the courts always lag. For example, RFLP technology is not only fully accepted, but as the testimony in *Whittey* indicates, it may now have taken second place to newer forms of DNA analysis. Even the older versions of PCR are gradually becoming surpassed, with STR being the current gold standard, in part because of its use in DNA data bank systems throughout the United States. Even here, beginning the PCR/STR protocol with an unusually low amount of DNA, known as "low copy number" ("LCN") or "low template" ("LT"), makes DNA analysis controversial, though it survived a challenge in *United States v. Grinnage*, 2012 U.S. App. LEXIS 13337 (3d Cir. June 29, 2012).

(5) *Mitochondrial DNA. See State v. Scott*, 33 S.W.3d 746 (Tenn. 2000) concerning this variant of DNA. Mitochodrial DNA (mtDNA) is DNA taken from a different part of the cell, and is sometimes available in usable amounts or usable form form when other DNA is not. Since mtDNA is only inherited from the mother, all maternal relatives will share the same mtDNA profile. Mitochondrial DNA testing is performed by extracting the DNA from the mitochondria (an area of the cell outside the nucleus). The DNA is then amplified and examined to determine its sequences of A's, G's, T's, and C's. The sequence is then compared to another sequence donated by a known person. If the sequences are identical, the examiner compares the sequence to the available database of mtDNA sequences to determine if he has ever seen that same sequence. The statistic will be based upon the frequency of similar DNA patterns occurring within the database and within each group in the database. The final result simply either excludes the tested individual as the sample donor or confirms that such individual is within a certain percentage

of the population, which could have donated the sample. The advantage of mtDNA is that it can be obtained from some sources that nuclear DNA cannot, such as from bone, teeth, or hair shafts. Moreover, mtDNA can be obtained from small amounts of material, from degraded material, or even from dead cells. However, because of the extreme sensitivity of the material, it is particularly susceptible to contamination.

Note that the experts who establish the validity or general acceptance of a scientific technology such as DNA (or other matching technology) may not be the same as those who validate the statistical computations. In the case of DNA, the former are typically molecular biologists, while the latter may be population geneticists.

(6) *Is the Statistical Evidence More or Less Prejudicial than having the Expert Testify that the Defendant's DNA Matched the Samples Found on the Victim?* In *United States v. Martinez*, 3 F.3d 1191 (8th Cir. 1993), *cert. denied*, 510 U.S. 1062 (1994), in note (3) *above*, the court deferred consideration of whether the expert's testimony that there was a "match" is more prejudicial than the actual statistics concerning the match:

> The district court barred the expert from testifying about his conclusion that as a matter of probability, one Native American in 2600 could have provided DNA that matched the samples found on the victim in this case, concluding that such evidence was substantially more prejudicial than probative. Martinez contends that the exclusion of [this statistical] evidence prejudiced him because the jury would conclude that he was the only possible source of the DNA found on the victim.
>
> After the district court decided to admit the DNA match evidence, the court invited counsel to comment on the propriety of admitting statistical evidence of the likelihood of a match. In response to this invitation, Martinez' counsel suggested that the court exclude the probability evidence, citing a Georgia case in which the court allowed evidence of a DNA match but excluded statistical evidence on the probability of a match. Having specifically requested that the district court exclude the statistical evidence, Martinez may not now complain about its exclusion.

What should juries be told about the significance of a match? Is there some way of explaining the significance of a match without requiring a specific probability estimate? Testimony that a defendant could not be excluded as the source of the DNA has also been permitted without explaining the statistical relevance of the nonexclusion result, such as the percentage of the population that could be excluded. *See Rodriguez v. State*, 273 P.3d 845 (Nev. 2012).

(7) *Computing Statistics Concerning a Random Match.* The question of statistics has been quite controversial and produced what many called the "DNA Wars" lasting until approximately 1996. For a succinct recounting of the history, see Kaye, *DNA, NAS, NRC, DAB, RFLP, PCR, and More: An Introduction to the Symposium on the 1996 NRC Report on Forensic DNA Evidence*, 37 JURIMETRICS J. 395 (1997).

The main area of contention was whether subgroupings within the general population skew the assumptions underlying the computation of frequency of a random match. In 1992, the National Research Council, associated with the National Academy of Science, published a Report, now known as NRC I, that contained a number of recommendations concerning the use of DNA technology. Its most controversial proposal was the adoption of a "ceiling principle" for estimating the probability of finding a particular DNA profile in a random population. The results obtained by applying this "principle" significantly weakened the prosecution's statistics. For example, if a prosecution expert would estimate a 1-in-100,000 chance of a random match based on his data, the "ceiling principle" might result in an estimate of 1-in-10,000 chance of a random match.

Prosecutors and others who viewed the "ceiling principle" as a political compromise, rather than a scientific truth, fought against its adoption by courts. Ironically, this sometimes resulted in the DNA evidence being completely excluded because lack of agreement about the statistics meant that the evidence did not meet *Frye*, which required general acceptance. In other words, the fact that the technology is generally accepted was only half the battle; the explanation of what a "match" meant in terms of population genetics also has to be generally accepted. Thus, in excluding such evidence, courts would quote from the NRC I report that "[t]o say that two patterns match, without providing any scientifically valid estimate (or, at least, an upper bound) of the frequency with which such matches might occur by chance, is meaningless." Ultimately the NRC undertook a new study and in 1996 issued another report, NRC II, concluding that no "ceiling principle" is necessary to deal with questions of population substructure. In the interim, the FBI had completed an extensive worldwide population study, which found that substructure was not a significant problem and that the product rule was generally reliable. Also, it is now common to estimate probabilities based on particular databases comparing individuals of the same racial backgrounds, but even here the question arises whether this is legitimate unless other evidence in the case indicates the race of the assailant. The FBI announced that it will declare an absolute identification when the figures reach a magnitude approaching the population of the United States. It remains to be seen whether courts will accept such testimony.

See generally Symposium: The Evaluation of Forensic DNA Evidence, 37 JURIMETRICS J. 395, 395–506 (1997).

(8) *Laboratory Error Rate.* Another issue that has become quite controversial is whether or to what extent laboratory error rate should be incorporated into the statistics concerning a random match. The defense argument boils down to the following question: what does it matter if the probability of a random match is one in one million if the probability of an error by the lab is one in 200? In other words, the latter statistic is the only one the jury should be told, because we do not know if this is the time the lab was wrong. *See* Scheck, *DNA and Daubert*, 15 CARDOZO L. REV. 1959 (1994). This position has not been viewed favorably by the courts, which generally consider the argument as going to the weight of the random match statistical evidence, not its admissibility. Some suggest that, at a minimum, the lab error rate should be factored into the statistics indicating the probability of a random match; this would increase the probability of finding a random match. The entire question of laboratory testing and whether precautions should be taken to

ensure that a laboratory does not know when it is being tested also has proved controversial. *See generally* Koehler, *On Conveying the Probative Value of DNA Evidence: Frequencies, Likelihood Ratios, and Error Rates*, 67 U. Colo. L. Rev. 859 (1996).

(9) *Legislating the Admissibility of DNA Evidence. Armstead v. State*, 673 A.2d 221 (Md. 1996) held that a statute declaring that DNA evidence "is admissible" to prove identity eliminates not only traditional *Frye* hearings to prove that the technique has gained general acceptance in the relevant scientific community, but also "inverse *Frye* hearings" to rebut the presumption of acceptance. The statute also was held to have eliminated the discretion of the trial court to weigh probative value against prejudicial effect. However, the court said that while the statute precluded generalized challenges to admissibility of DNA evidence, except for constitutional challenges, it permitted case-specific challenges to the manner in which the particular test was conducted. The statute also rendered admissible not just the "raw" evidence of a DNA match but the necessary contextual statistics. Because the statute does not specify a method, either the "product rule" or the "ceiling principle" may be applied and presented in evidence. As a result, neither the use of the product rule nor the failure of the prosecution experts to change the statistics to reflect the laboratory error rate resulted in fundamental unfairness so as to deny the defendant due process. The case-specific challenges to the evidence did not show that the evidence was so unreliable on its face that defendant's due process rights were violated. Remember that matters held not to affect admissibility may affect the weight of the evidence.

Do you suppose the statute applies regardless of what method of DNA analysis is applied? Even brand-new forms?

Note that the holding leaves open the possibility that a statute's admission of "scientific" evidence could be unconstitutional.

(10) *How can Indigent Defendants Effectively Challenge the Admission of DNA Under Daubert?* Challenging new science never is easy. Under *Frye*, new science is presumptively inadmissible until generally accepted, so criminal defendants do not face new technology until the scientific community is comfortable with it. This rule helps to ensure that the public will not consider it unjust for defendants to lose their liberty as a result of such evidence. *Daubert* offers more opportunity for prosecutors to argue for the admission of reliable new science, not yet generally accepted. Under either standard, the defendant can argue that the particular tests at issue were improperly conducted. But how is an indigent defendant able to effectively challenge the admission or weight of DNA? *Ake v. Oklahoma*, 470 U.S. 68 (1985), held that due process required an indigent defendant to have access to a psychiatrist to present an insanity defense in a capital case. However, most courts require a specific showing of need for an expert, and it is not at all clear that a DNA expert is considered the type of expert to which a defendant is automatically entitled. *Compare People v. Leonard*, 569 N.W.2d 663 (Mich. Ct. App. 1997) (affirming denial of DNA expert), *with Dubose v. State*, 662 So. 2d 1189 (Ala. 1995) (defendant against whom DNA evidence will be offered must have access to DNA expert).

(11) *DNA Exonerations.* In the last few years, DNA has been responsible for exonerating more than 300 individuals who were convicted of serious crimes, some of which carried the death penalty. Ironically, studies of what went wrong in those cases indicate that one of the major causes of erroneous convictions is faulty scientific evidence. In other words, the experts were either mistaken, overreaching, or in a few well publicized cases, simply fabricating the results. Microscopic hair analysis has been a common problem. Indeed, many labs are now confirming hair analysis with mtDNA testing. Is strict adherence to *Daubert* or *Frye* sufficient in the scientific arena or are additional controls needed? Discovery and competence of counsel issues are often implicated. Accreditation of laboratories, and certification of forensic personnel is typically not required. Professor Raeder co-chaired a committee of the Criminal Justice Section of the American Bar Association that was charged with creating policy recommendations for dealing with these issues. *See* ACHIEVING JUSTICE, FREEING THE INNOCENT, CONVICTING THE GUILTY, REPORT OF THE ABA CRIMINAL JUSTICE SECTION'S AD HOC INNOCENCE COMMITTEE TO INSURE THE INTEGRITY OF THE CRIMINAL PROCESS (Ganelli & Raeder, eds., 2006). *See also* Raeder, *What Does Innocence Have To Do With It?: A Commentary On Wrongful Convictions and Rationality*, 2003 MICH. ST. L. REV. 1315.

(12) *No Constitutional Right to Post-trial Access to DNA.* Despite many DNA exonerations, the Supreme Court held in *District Attorney's Office for the Third Judicial District v. Osborne*, 557 U.S. 52 (2009), that there is no freestanding constitutional right to obtain post-conviction access to prosecution evidence for DNA testing under the Due Process clause. Moreover, the standard to obtain post-conviction relief on habeas corpus is exceedingly high. *See* Myrna S. Raeder, *Postconviction Claims of Innocence*, 24 CRIM. JUST. 14 (Fall, 2009). Is finality of judgment as important a reason to deny relief as it was prior to DNA?

(13) *Are the Witnesses Who Lay the Foundation for Admissibility, Interested Practitioners of the Technique, Whose Best Customers are the Prosecution?* What witnesses, organizations, and studies are likely sources of the evidence upon which general acceptability or reliability is determined? Whose customary and accepted use of the technique — whose endorsement — seems to carry the day? Is the fox being put in charge of the chicken house? Is there a difference between *Frye* and *Daubert* (or current Fed. R. Evid. 702) on this?

§ 6.05 PSYCHOLOGY, MENTAL HEALTH, SOCIAL SCIENCES, AND RELATED FIELDS

[A] The Relevance and Reliability of the Expert Opinion

POOSHS v. PHILLIP MORRIS USA, INC.

United States District Court, Northern District of California
287 F.R.D. 543 (2012)

PHYLLIS J. HAMILTON, District Judge.

[In this products liability case against a tobacco products manufacturer and others, the defendants moved to exclude four of the plaintiff's experts. One of them was a licensed mental health counselor, who also was a physician, and who worked as a university faculty member at a tobacco research facility. She would have testified to the addictive nature of defendant's tobacco products, the defendants' longstanding knowledge of their effects, the defendant's efforts to downplay these facts, and related opinions. The court excluded the testimony of this witness, as follows:]

A. Legal Standard

A witness who has been qualified as an expert by knowledge, skill, experience, training, or education may give an opinion on scientific, technical, or otherwise specialized topics if (1) the expert's scientific, technical, or other special knowledge will help the trier of fact understand the evidence or determine a fact in issue, (2) the testimony is based upon sufficient facts or data, (3) the testimony is the product of reliable principles and methods, and (4) the witness has applied the principles and methods reliably to the facts of the case. Fed.R.Evid. 702; *see also Daubert.*

The proponent of expert testimony bears the burden of establishing by a preponderance of the evidence that the admissibility requirements are met. *See* Fed.R.Evid. 702, Advisory Committee Notes. Although there is a presumption of admissibility, the trial court is obliged to act as a "gatekeeper" with regard to the admission of expert scientific testimony under 702. *Kumho Tire Co., Ltd.*

Thus, *Daubert* requires a two-part analysis. The court first determines whether an expert's testimony reflects "scientific knowledge," whether the findings are "derived by the scientific method," and whether the work product is "good science" — that is, whether the testimony is reliable and trustworthy. The court then determines whether the testimony is "relevant to the task at hand." [Here, the court lists the four nonexclusive *Daubert* factors.]

Nevertheless, depending on the type of expert testimony offered, these factors may not be appropriate to assess reliability. *Kumho.* Other factors that might be considered include whether an expert has unjustifiably extrapolated from an accepted premise to an unfounded conclusion or whether an expert has adequately accounted for obvious alternative explanations. [Cite.] The trial court should also be mindful that reliability is not determined based on the "correctness of the expert's conclusions but the soundness of his methodology." In addition, a court may exclude expert testimony on the ground that an expert's purported methodology fails to explain his final conclusion. *Joiner* ("[N]othing in either *Daubert* or the Federal Rules of Evidence requires a district court to admit opinion evidence that is connected to existing data only by the *ipse dixit* of the expert. A court may conclude that there is simply too great an analytical gap between the data and the opinion proffered."). . . . The court should also consider whether an expert prepared his methodology for purposes of litigation, or articulated the methodology before litigation and without any incentive to reach a particular outcome.

Rule 702's second prong concerns relevancy, or "fit." *See Daubert.* Expert opinion testimony is relevant if the knowledge underlying it has a "valid . . . connection to the pertinent inquiry," and it is reliable if the knowledge underlying it "has a reliable basis in the knowledge and experience of [the relevant] discipline."

B. Defendants' Motion [to Exclude] . . . Dr. Valerie B. Yerger

Dr. Yerger was trained as a naturopathic physician, although she does not currently practice in that field. She also has a certificate in [mental health] counseling, but is not licensed as a psychologist or psychiatrist. Dr. Yerger is currently an Assistant Adjunct Professor of Social and Behavioral Sciences in the School of Nursing at the University of California, San Francisco ("UCSF"). As an Assistant Adjunct, she has given approximately one lecture per year for the past eight years, on the subject of menthol. She is also on the faculty of the UCSF Center for Tobacco Control Research and Education.

. . . UCSF holds a large archive of millions of digitally-stored historical documents relating in some way to tobacco or tobacco research. The document database maintained by UCSF is available on the Internet to anyone who wishes to search it. Dr. Yerger claims to specialize in searching those documents and "interpreting" what she finds in the documents. She . . . asserts that she has analyzed tobacco documents "related to attempts by the tobacco industry to engage in various manufacturing and marketing practices over multiple decades."

In her report, Dr. Yerger offers opinions on the following, apparently based on her review of these tobacco documents — (1) that cigarettes are addictive and hazardous when used as intended; (2) that tobacco companies have long known that nicotine is addictive and that smoke delivers carcinogens; (3) that the intention of the "Frank Statement" was to influence public sentiment regarding the tobacco industry; (4) that cigarette companies deliberately "engineered cigarettes" to be an effective "nicotine delivery device," while at the same time marketing cigarettes as "low tar," "light," or "mild" to create the illusion that such cigarettes were "safer;" or adding menthol, which affected the "impact" or "grab" of the cigarettes; (5) that while openly challenging the link between second-hand smoke and lung cancer, PM simultaneously secretly conducted tests of second-hand smoke.

Defendants argue that Dr. Yerger's opinions should be excluded in their entirety. Defendants contend that Dr. Yerger is not qualified to testify as to any of the opinions in her report, and because her opinions are not based on a reliable methodology.

The court finds that the motion must be GRANTED. Dr. Yerger is not qualified as an expert in researching document archives. She holds no degree in history or social science, has not studied or received a degree in library science, and has never received formal training under a formal curriculum on archival database research. Nor has she explained how she conducted her searches. While she claims that there are "well-developed protocols" for searching documents based on the "snowball technique," she does not explain what those protocols are, and has conceded that the search involves a human element in refining search terms used in the technique that may lead to bias in the document collection process.

Moreover, even were Dr. Yerger qualified as an expert in archival research, that would not qualify her to opine on the subject matter of the documents she finds. Dr. Yerger is not an expert on cigarette design, as she herself admitted in her deposition, and has not conducted any studies to determine, *e.g.*, how tar and nicotine levels can influence smoke inhalation in nicotine delivery, and how additives can facilitate smoke inhalation in nicotine delivery.

Dr. Yerger is not qualified in any scientific discipline that would enable her to render reliable opinions regarding addiction, the addictive qualities of cigarettes, the "adulteration" of cigarettes, the action of nicotine on the human body, the effect on the human body of secondhand smoke, or any of the other topics listed in her report. She does not hold any appointments in UCSF's graduate programs in biochemistry and molecular biology, chemistry and chemical biology, epidemiology and translational science, or the history of health sciences, and has no degree in toxicology, pharmacology, psychiatry, or psychology. There is no evidence that she is familiar with the diagnostic methods used by health professionals to diagnose addiction, and she has conducted no independent scientific investigation regarding the effects of nicotine, has no scientific expertise in nicotine's effects on the human body, and has no opinion on what level of nicotine would not be addictive.

Moreover, testimony "interpreting" cigarette company documents would not assist the jury because those documents speak for themselves.

[At this point, the court proceeded to exclude one other witness (an epidemiologist with background in effects of arsenic who offered to testify about the cause of the plaintiff's lung cancer), but it refused to exclude still two other witnesses (an economist who would testify about damages and an epidemiologist who focused on public health who would testify about tobacco manufacturers' alleged attempt to belittle known health risks of smoking).]

NOTES AND QUESTIONS

(1) *A Case Featuring Analogous Internet Research Issues but with the Opposite Result: Walden v. City of Chicago*, 755 F. Supp. 2d 942 (N.D. Ill. 2010). In this case, the plaintiff sued the city and others on the claim that he had been falsely convicted because of a coerced confession. The original conviction occurred in 1952, and he was sentenced to 75 years but ultimately was pardoned on a finding of innocence. In order to successfully sue the city on account of the conduct of its police officers, the law required him to prove that the conduct resulted from an "official policy or custom" of the city. To demonstrate this official policy or custom, the

plaintiff proposed to call as a witness an academic historian, who would state, based upon historical research into relevant documents, that the city did indeed have a policy or custom of coercing confessions at the time in question, and that it particularly targeted black men who were accused of raping white women, like the plaintiff. The court refused to exclude the testimony:

> Defendant's argument that Lipari's research could have been done by "anyone" with access to the university computer system is . . . unavailing. Contrary to Defendant's suggestion, while internet search engines have made researching on the internet accessible to people of all educational and professional backgrounds, historical research, like legal research, requires far more than simply running a Google search. In focusing on the accessibility of the databases that Lipari used, Defendant ignores the other aspects of historical research that require training and education, including knowing where to search for sources, formulating searches based on an understanding of the history of the period in question, and evaluating the reliability of sources. . . .
>
> Defendant also claims that Lipari is not qualified because he offers opinions on matters in which he has no expertise. Defendant finds fault with Lipari's statement that certain interrogation methods were illegal despite not knowing the law of interrogation and his conclusion that there was a "psychological aspect" to the interrogations despite not being a psychologist. This argument, however, overlooks the nature of Lipari's work; he is an academic historian who uses historical sources to draw conclusions about the time period in question. If the sources upon which his conclusions were based are reliable, which Defendant does not question, he need not also be a lawyer and psychologist to rely upon the expertise of those who authored the reports. The Court thus finds that based on Lipari's educational background, training, and his experience in researching and writing about the relationship between the African — American community and the Chicago Police Department in the 20th Century, he is qualified to testify as an expert in this case.

In the course of reaching its conclusions, the court emphasized that the authorities governing admissibility were "liberal" and that the standard was "low."

(2) *What Makes the Difference between These Two Cases?* Possibly, the difference lies in the predispositions of the two judges! The *Pooshs* court, which excluded the evidence, emphasized that the "burden" of proving admissibility fell upon the proponent. The *Walden* court, on the other hand, emphasized that the standard was "low." Both of these propositions can be justified by authority. But they seem show a difference in predisposition. The *Walden* opinion relies upon the training and experience of the witness in evaluating the reliability of sources, and it cites the witness's study of the subject at hand. But in response to this argument, it could be pointed out that the witness in *Pooshs* apparently also had deep experience with the databases in which she specialized, and she had mental health and medical training that could have been relevant. Are decisions in these kinds of cases really just arbitrary, depending mainly on the predilections of the judges?

[B] The Inadmissibility of Opinions on Mental Elements of a Charged Crime: Rule 704(b)

Read Federal Rule of Evidence 704, "Opinion on an Ultimate Issue."

UNITED STATES v. VALLE

United States District Court, Southern District of New York
2013 U.S. Dist. LEXIS 14864 (Feb. 2, 2013)

[The defendant was charged with conspiracy to commit kidnapping. The Government contended that he and his co-conspirator — in e-mails, internet chat rooms, and specialty social networking sites — discussed "in graphic detail, plans to kidnap, torture, kill and cannibalize specific and identified women." His defense was that these were on sexual fetish web sites "that cater to violent sexual fantasy, sadomasochism, and bondage, as well as rape, genital mutilation, dismemberment, and cannibalism," but that he "had no criminal intent, and that his 'chats' over the internet reflect[ed] nothing more than sexual fantasies." He claimed to suffer from a psychological condition called "paraphilia," which allegedly causes sexual excitement from these kinds of violent fantasies. The Government, among other evidence, offered the defendant's e-mail exchanges with the co-conspirator and electronic messages to the websites, and images and videos that the defendant downloaded to his computer showing acts of violence, including staged torture and staged videos of women being hunted in the woods. Defendant and his e-mail co-conspirators used names and pictures of real women, whom they had followed to get the pictures. The wife of one of the co-conspirators became afraid and exposed the men and helped police get access to her spouse's computer. The wife of the other was not concerned with what the men were doing, saying she thought it was just play.]

[As part of his defense, defendant proposed to call two expert witnesses, Drs. Herriot and Deitz, whom the Government sought to exclude in an *in limine* motion. The trial judge's summary of the proposed testimony and his ruling on that motion follows. The judge uses the summary of proposed testimony prepared by defendant's counsel in defendant's proffer.]

Dr. Herriot is an expert on sexual communications and behavior on the internet. He has extensive background in computer sciences, with 30 years of experience as an internet professional. He is also learned in human sexuality. [He is] Professor of Clinical Sexuality at the Institute for the Advanced Study of Human Sexuality . . . and a certified clinical sexologist. Combining his two fields, his Ph.D. thesis [was] on sexual communication on the internet . . . [He] has conducted additional research, given lectures, and testified on the subject matter of sexual behaviors on the internet. [He] has conducted a large number of interviews and studied internet communications initiated in websites devoted to sexual deviancies and fetishes. [He] testified as an expert on sexual communications on the internet in federal, state, and military courts. [He] has a B.S. in computer science from Stanford and a Ph.D. in human sexuality from the Institute for the Advance Study of Human Sexuality. [He] will explain to the jury how the internet works and how people communicate and socialize on the internet via social media websites, like Facebook, "fetish" websites, emails, and instant messages. [He] will testify about a distinct culture which exists on the internet in sexual "fetish" and similar websites. People who participate often adopt the personas of a fantasy character . . . . [He] will explain that many people who engage in internet communications, especially in sexually explicit websites, alter their real personas [as] to identity, age, gender, physical appearance, station in life, profession, [etc.] Typically, [they] weave a bit of truth about themselves with a great deal of imagination and exaggeration. . . . They "play" out scenarios and encourage the individuals with whom they are communicating to do the same and build on or add to the scenario. [It's like] improvisational theatre, intended to allow [expression of] imaginations freely . . . . [He] will also discuss the entertainment value of the horror movie-like imagery used in dark "fetish" websites. [S]exually explicit websites, specifically, encourage people to engage in fantastical role play and chat about matters which they otherwise would not discuss in face-to-face conversations. The anonymity and lack of verification of the internet encourages imaginative play acting. [He] will testify to cues that indicate whether internet communications are consistent with the participants engaging in fantasy role play . . . [including] whether [they] used screen names, the nature of the public profiles created, the nature of the website, whether the chats appear to compress time in an unrealistic manner, are implausible and provocative, their tempo, whether they are consistent with factual details provided, and how the chats conclude.

[The trial judge concludes that Dr. Herriot's testimony is admissible. The judge's reasoning here is omitted because it is similar to his reasoning concerning the testimony of Dr. Dietz, which is set forth below. But in addition, as to Dr. Herriot, the trial judge notes that at trial several matters, including the nature of the "studies" and "cues" referred to above, will have to be fleshed out in Herriot's testimony or the testimony will be excludable as not being based on "sufficient facts or data" as required by Rule 702.]

Dr. Dietz, [the other defense expert, a well-credentialed and well-known forensic psychiatrist, M.D., and Ph.D.,] will address a number of subjects that are highly relevant to this case, including the likelihood of violent conduct by men who are sexually aroused by sexually sadistic images; the coping mechanisms such men often develop, including role play over the internet; and the psychological condition [Paraphilia] that Valle allegedly suffers from, and how that condition has manifested itself in his actions. All of these topics are beyond the ken of the average juror, and Dr. Dietz is well situated by his education, training, research, and academic study and writings to address these issues. The Court [therefore] concludes that Dr. Dietz's proposed testimony is . . . [relevant under Rules 401-402] and likely to be helpful to the jury under Fed. R. Evid. 702.

In arguing that Dr. Dietz's testimony will not be helpful to the jury, the Government relies primarily on *United States v. DiDomenico*, 985 F.2d 1159 (2d Cir.1993), affirming exclusion of expert testimony regarding defendant's supposed "dependent personality disorder." In excluding the proposed expert testimony as unnecessary and not helpful to the jury, then District Judge Cabranes noted that it was offered to show the defendant's "asserted vulnerability and susceptibility to being duped by her boyfriend. Expert testimony on this relatively commonplace experience is simply inappropriate." The Second Circuit agreed, finding that the defendant's claim that she acted under the influence of her boyfriend "was not hard to assimilate and . . . addressed a subject matter within the experience of the jury."

The proffered expert testimony here is of an entirely different nature. Dr. Dietz will not be addressing any matters that can fairly be described as "commonplace experience[s]." The subject matter at issue is likely to be entirely foreign to the jury, and Dr. Dietz's testimony is likely to be helpful to the jury in assessing Valle's state of mind.

The Government also contends that Dr. Dietz's proposed testimony should be excluded as violative of Fed.R.Evid. 704(b). [Rule quoted.]

Defendant argues that Dr. Dietz's testimony will not violate Rule 704(b), because "[h]e will not state an opinion about whether Mr. Valle did or did not have the criminal intent to conspire or kidnap. He will not even opine about whether Mr. Valle had the *capacity* to form criminal intent."

Instead, Defendant argues, Dr. Dietz will offer testimony designed to assist the jury in understanding Valle's highly unusual psychiatric condition, which causes him to experience sexual arousal from discussing, or viewing scenes of, imagined psychological or physical suffering of women, particularly in a sexual context. Dr. Dietz will further testify that "Mr. Valle's internet communications and related actions in this case are consistent with the *modus operandi* of fantasy role-play and storytelling engaged in by people who have Paraphilia." None of this proposed testimony addresses the ultimate issue of criminal intent, however, nor does it improperly usurp the jury's role. The jury could accept Dr. Dietz's testimony *in toto* and still conclude that Valle had criminal intent — *i.e.*, that he agreed with another individual to kidnap a female victim.

The cases cited by the Government are not to the contrary, because they involve proposed expert testimony indicating that the defendant lacked the mental capacity to commit the charged offense, or had a belief system that prevented the defendant from forming the requisite intent for the charged crime.

In *DiDomenico* above, the defendant was charged with wire fraud and interstate transportation of stolen property. The Government alleged that the defendant had assisted her boyfriend in selling stolen computer equipment. The defendant proffered a psychiatrist's opinion that she suffered from "dependent personality disorder with narcissistic features." DiDomenico's counsel argued that the proposed testimony "would assist the jury to determine DiDomenico's state of mind during the relevant time period," but denied that the psychiatrist "would testify on the ultimate issue of whether DiDomenico knew that the computer equipment was stolen." The district court excluded the proffered expert testimony and the Second Circuit affirmed . . . . The court concluded that the psychiatrist's proposed testimony was properly excluded under Rule 704(b) because it amounted to an opinion about whether the defendant had the mental capacity to commit the crime: "While DiDomenico proclaims that she did not offer [the psychiatrist] to testify as to the ultimate issue of whether she knew the computer equipment was stolen, this is semantic camouflage. We read [the psychiatrist's] proffered testimony as stating the bottom-line inference, and leaving it to the jury merely to murmur, 'Amen.'"

The nature of Dr. Dietz's proposed testimony is entirely different. While evidence of "passive-dependent personality disorder" was offered in *DiDomenico* and *Bright* to demonstrate that defendants lacked the mental capacity to accept that the property at issue was stolen, Dr. Dietz will not opine as to Valle's mental capacity or whether he had criminal intent. The possibility that the jury may infer from Dr. Dietz's testimony that Valle did not intend to kidnap anyone — and that his chats were mere sexual fantasy — does not require exclusion of Dr. Dietz's testimony. See *DiDomenico* . . . ("Clearly, Rule 704(b) does not prohibit all expert testimony that gives rise to an inference concerning a defendant's mental state. Rule 704(b) does not prevent the expert from testifying to facts or opinions from which the jury could conclude or infer the defendant had the requisite mental state"); see also *United States v. Dunn* . . . ("It is only as to the last step in the inferential process — a conclusion as to the defendant's actual mental state — that Rule 704(b) commands the expert to be silent.")

United States v. Dupre is also inapposite. In *Dupre*, a wire fraud case, the Second Circuit affirmed the district court's exclusion of a psychologist's opinion that the defendant's intense, pervasive religious beliefs significantly interfere with her ability to see her involvement in the "investment project" in a realistic manner and significantly contribute to her ongoing conviction that she has been involved in a legitimate enterprise with benevolent intentions. The court ruled that the proffered opinion was properly excluded under Fed. R. Evid. 403, and also commented that "the proffered evidence might have constituted an impermissible opinion about the 'ultimate issue' of whether Dupre possessed the mental state constituting an element of wire fraud." Again, Dr. Dietz will not testify as to Valle's mental capacity and whether he acted with criminal intent, and his opinions are not incompatible with a finding that Valle had the requisite criminal intent . . . .

[On the government's argument that the two Drs. will be "cumulative" of each other under Rule 403, the court holds that they will not be, because Dr. Herriot will testify about people in general who use these websites, whereas Dr. Deitz will testify specifically about the defendant. Further, Dr. Dietz will address a particular disease, Parafilia, which Dr. Herriot will not. The judge states he will be vigilant at trial to prevent them giving cumulative testimony.]

[Thus, the court denied the Government's motion to exclude these two defense expert witnesses. But even though the witnesses were allowed to and did testify, the defendant was nevertheless convicted at trial of this very serious crime, which carries a lengthy sentence. — Eds.]

NOTES AND QUESTIONS

(1) *Experts Prohibited from Testifying to Ultimate Opinion Regarding Sanity.* This rule (704(b)) arose out of dissatisfaction with the acquittal on grounds of insanity of John Hinckley, who attempted to assassinate President Reagan. The defense psychiatrists gave ultimate opinions that Hinckley had a mental illness that made him unable to conform his conduct to the dictates of the law and to appreciate the wrongfulness of his acts, the legal tests for insanity at that time.

704(b) does not always favor the prosecution, though. For example, *United States v. Boyd*, 55 F.3d 667 (D.C. Cir. 1995), held that Rule 704(b) barred an officer's expert testimony opining that "hypothetical" facts exactly mirroring alleged facts surrounding defendant's arrest showed "possession with intent to distribute," rather than possession for personal use. The testimony violated Rule 704(b)'s ban on expert witnesses stating their opinion as to whether the defendant had the mental state constituting an element of the crime charged. (Other decisions, however, have allowed this attempted end run around the rule, holding that this kind of hypothetical testimony is acceptable.)

Query: How does Fed. R. Evid. 704(b) affect the psychiatric expert who testifies about the "future dangerousness" of a defendant, typically in the death penalty phase of a trial? The admission of such testimony survived a Constitutional challenge in *Barefoot v. Estelle*, 463 U.S. 880 (1983), but that case did not involve any type of Rule 704(b) restriction.

(2) *Does Rule 704(b) Reach Beyond Psychiatrists and Other Mental Health Experts? United States v. Watson*, 260 F.3d 301 (3d Cir. 2001), reversed a conviction for violation of 704(b) where a narcotics agent (not a psychiatrist or mental health expert) testified that the defendant who was intercepted on a bus with 100 plastic bags of crack cocaine and marijuana possessed the drugs with the intent to distribute to someone else. See also *Boyd* in note (1) above. But a few circuits rely on 704(b)'s legislative history as intending to reach only psychiatrists and other mental health experts. *See, e.g., United States v. Gastiaburo*, 16 F.3d 582 (4th Cir.), *cert. denied*, 513 U.S. 829 (1994). However, *United States v. Morales*, 108 F.3d 1031 (9th Cir. 1997), explains that this result is foreclosed by the plain language of the rule. *Morales* held that Rule 704(b) would apply to testimony of a defense accountant if he testified to an innocent mental state of defendant in the financial wrongdoing charged in the case. But it reversed the conviction excluding the evidence because it found that the proposed testimony — indicating that the defendant had a weak grasp of bookkeeping — would not have stated an opinion that would necessarily compel the conclusion that Morales did not make the false entries willfully. So it was not directly testimony as to the defendant's mental state that is an element of the crime such as would be barred by the rule.

[C] Post-Traumatic Stress Disorder, Related Syndromes, and Related Evidence[8]

NEW MEXICO v. ALBERICO

Supreme Court of New Mexico
116 N.M. 156, 861 P.2d 192 (1993)

FROST, JUSTICE.

[Two cases were consolidated to decide the admissibility of post-traumatic stress disorder (PTSD). The New Mexico Supreme Court here holds that expert opinion testimony regarding PTSD is admissible for establishing whether the alleged victim exhibits symptoms of PTSD that are consistent with rape or sexual abuse.]

---

[8] Study Guide Reference: Evidence in a Nutshell, Chapter 7:II C, at "Syndrome Evidence: from Child Abuse Accommodation Syndrome to Rape Trauma Syndrome" through "Evidentiary Issues in Syndrome Evidence: F.R.E. 404 and 702."

Several other jurisdictions have considered the admissibility of expert testimony regarding PTSD or RTS [Rape Trauma Syndrome]. [Both syndromes describe a number of reactions that can occur when a person is subjected to a traumatic event. PTSD is the more general term, since it does not specify the exact nature of the stressful event that is alleged to be the cause of the symptoms — Eds.] Almost every court that has addressed this issue has concluded that PTSD evidence is admissible to explain a victim behavior that is apparently inconsistent with having been raped if the defense has made it an issue. In addition, the jurisdictions are virtually unanimous in disallowing expert testimony that comments directly on the credibility of the rape victim.

As to the issue of whether such evidence is admissible to prove sexual abuse or nonconsensual intercourse, the courts are about evenly split. Some jurisdictions allow PTSD testimony to show that the victim was sexually abused or to rebut the defense of consent. Other jurisdictions forbid PTSD testimony for the purpose of proving that sexual abuse in fact occurred. At least one court has upheld the introduction of PTSD testimony for the incongruous purpose to show lack of consent but not to prove rape. Some courts specifically prohibit an expert from testifying that the alleged victim suffers from "rape trauma syndrome" while allowing PTSD testimony because of the former term's latent assumption that the only cause of the syndrome is rape. "The concern with unfair prejudice is largely reduced when the terminology does not equate the syndrome exclusively with rape." . . . In holding that PTSD testimony was inadmissible, however, at least one court found no meaningful semantic distinction between RTS and PTSD.

Other courts have concluded that PTSD evidence is a scientifically reliable or generally accepted means of determining whether sexual abuse occurred, but have excluded it on Rule 403 grounds. In addition, many courts recognize that PTSD is founded upon good science, but even some of those jurisdictions that found PTSD to be "generally accepted" conclude that it will not assist the trier of fact to determine whether a rape occurred because it is a therapeutic method that was not intended to be used as a forensic tool.

In both [of the cases currently before us] the prosecution sought the introduction of expert testimony to show that a crime had been committed: that is, in Alberico to show that the alleged victim did not consent to intercourse; and in Marquez to show that sexual abuse had taken place.

The issue is not, however, as the Court of Appeals stated, "whether a diagnosis of PTSD or RTS is a valid means of determining whether a rape occurred;" rather, it is whether PTSD evidence is probative of whether a rape occurred. In other words, the issue is whether the evidence has "any tendency to make the existence of [a material issue] more probable or less probable than it would be without the evidence." There is no requirement that a scientific technique or method prove conclusively what it purports to prove.

We hold that PTSD testimony is grounded in valid scientific principle. DSM III-R [This is the diagnostic manual used by the psychiatric community — Eds.] is specialized literature that specifically catalogues the symptoms of mental disorders and prescribes the method by which the psychological evaluation should take place. DSM III-R, according to the State's experts, is widely used in courtrooms, not only for issues of sex abuse, but for issues concerning sanity and competency as well. PTSD is generally accepted by psychologists and psychiatrists as a valid technique for evaluating patients with mental disorders. The existence of DSM III-R and its general acceptance in psychology indicate that PTSD has been exposed to objective scientific scrutiny and empirical verification.

Furthermore, the PTSD diagnosis appears to be grounded in basic behavioral psychology. DSM III-R accumulated the symptoms of mental disorders by examining human reactions to certain events or stimuli. The theory behind PTSD is that a severe traumatic experience impacts upon the human psyche and exhibits itself in certain identifiable symptoms that are linked to a specific stressor or cause. In evaluating an alleged victim of sexual abuse, the psychologist compares her symptoms with known reactions to sexual abuse and attempts to correlate the victim's symptoms with the known causes of behavioral patterns that have been categorized. In that way, the PTSD diagnosis is no different from any other method or technique in behavioral psychology.

In addition, several jurisdictions that have disallowed PTSD testimony on the issue of whether sexual abuse occurred emphasized that psychologists could not pinpoint the cause of the PTSD although they could diagnose the symptoms. In the present cases, however, the experts testified that psychologists can isolate the cause of the symptoms because different stressors manifest themselves in different symptoms. We are more persuaded by evidence as to the current state of the technique than by judicial determinations of validity based on evidence that is many years old.

All of the expert testimony in these two cases establishes that victims of sexual abuse may exhibit identifiable symptoms that have been catalogued in DSM III-R. If a complainant suffers from PTSD symptoms, it indicates that she might have been sexually abused. Thus, testimony regarding a complainant's PTSD symptoms has the tendency to show that she might have been sexually abused.

From our perusal of all of the pertinent case law concerning PTSD, we perceive two flaws. First, of the courts that have held PTSD or RTS testimony to be inadmissible to show the cause of the symptoms, several have predicated that ruling, at least in part, upon the assumption that jurors will be awed by the "aura of infallibility" of expert opinion testimony. [W]e are not persuaded that jurors are as enthralled by experts as many appellate courts assume they are. In any event, the jury has the discretion to believe or disbelieve any testimony that it hears.

The [lower Alberico Appeals] Court claimed that while it is generally accepted that rape victims exhibit identifiable symptoms, PTSD does not allow a psychologist to "predict back" to the cause of the symptoms. Of course, the Court of Appeals and some of the other courts listed earlier would allow PTSD testimony to rebut the defense of inconsistent behavior only when the defense has made it an issue. The issue, however, is whether PTSD testimony is grounded in scientific knowledge, and the scientific validity of PTSD is not dependent on whether the defense has made it an issue in the case.

Allowing an expert to testify that PTSD symptoms are a common reaction to sexual assault for the purpose of rebutting the defense that the victim's reactions to the alleged incident are inconsistent with sexual assault is no different from allowing the expert to testify that the alleged victim's symptoms are consistent with sexual abuse. Both of these purposes for which PTSD evidence is offered rest on the valid scientific premise that victims of sexual abuse exhibit identifiable symptoms. Either the PTSD diagnosis is a valid scientific technique for identifying certain symptoms of sexual abuse or it is not.

Allowing PTSD testimony to explain a complainant's apparent inconsistent behavior after the alleged incident is no less prejudicial than allowing an expert to testify that the complainant's symptoms are consistent with sexual abuse. In the first instance, the jury can just as easily infer from the explanatory testimony that the complainant was raped because the expert is testifying that rape victims act a certain way and the complainant acted that way.

We perceive two drawbacks in allowing PTSD testimony. The first is that the diagnosis relies in large part upon what the alleged victim reports to the examining psychologist. Any prejudice that might result from self-reporting, however, can be cured by cross-examination addressing the point that the diagnosis is based upon what the complainant says, not upon an independent evaluation of her truthfulness. The other consideration is the cautionary note in DSM III-R pertaining to the different meanings of the same terms in a clinical setting and in a legal setting. For example, credibility in psychology is not the same as credibility in the courtroom. As we discuss below, this concern is allayed by avoiding testimony regarding the complainant's credibility altogether. Thus, PTSD testimony is not unduly prejudicial.

While PTSD testimony may be offered to show that the victim suffers from symptoms that are consistent with sexual abuse, it may not be offered to establish that the alleged victim is telling the truth; that is for the jury to decide. We have held before that expert testimony is admissible even if it touches upon an ultimate issue to be decided by the trier of fact. Rule 704, however, does not sanction the practice in all cases of calling an expert witness to tell the jury that a witness is telling the truth.

Each of the experts in both of these cases testified that while they try to determine if the victim's story is inherently consistent, that does not translate into a determination of whether the victim is telling the truth. One of the experts characterized psychology as having no "truth-telling machine." The experts testified that it was not their function to pass on the credibility of complainants in the legal sense. Accordingly, we expressly prohibit direct testimony regarding the credibility or truthfulness of the alleged victim of sexual abuse. See Townsend v. State, 103 Nev. 113, 734 P.2d 705, 709 (1987) (holding that it is improper to directly characterize alleged victim's testimony as either truthful or false).

Both of the State's experts in Marquez testified that it was not their function to determine if the complainant was telling the truth, but then both testified in effect that the complainant was telling the truth and that she said she was abused by her father. What they meant, no doubt, was that the complainant's story was highly consistent within the psychological meaning of that term. Being "highly consistent," however, was incorrectly translated into the legal conclusion that the complainant was not fabricating her story.

In addition to prohibiting expert testimony as to the alleged victim's credibility, the expert may not testify as to the identity of the alleged perpetrator of the crime. Allowing such testimony encroaches too far upon the jury's function as arbiter of the witnesses' credibility. Although a psychologist can independently evaluate the victim's allegations of sexual abuse by cross-checking her symptoms with those recognized in DSM III-R, there appears to be no similar verification for identifying the alleged abuser. The psychologist must rely in large part upon the victim's story, and allowing the psychologist to testify as to the identity of the accused serves only to repeat what the complainant told the examining expert and thus bolster her credibility. Incidental verification of a victim's story or indirect bolstering of her credibility, however, is not by itself improper. All testimony in the prosecution's case will tend to corroborate and bolster the victim's story to some extent. Direct comments on the victim's credibility, however, like those by the State's experts in Marquez, are beyond the scope of permissible expert opinion testimony.

We hold that expert testimony concerning RTS is inadmissible mainly because it is not part of the specialized manual DSM III-R like PTSD is, even though there is evidence in the record that RTS is generally accepted by psychologists just like PTSD is. We do not pass on the question of whether the diagnosis itself, "rape trauma syndrome," is too suggestive or so emotionally charged as to be unduly prejudicial.

It almost goes without saying that the expert will not be allowed to state an opinion in terms of causality; in other words, the expert may not testify that the victim's PTSD symptoms were in fact caused by sexual abuse. This again vouches too much for the credibility of the victim and encroaches too far upon the province of the jury to determine the truthfulness of the witnesses.

Allowing an expert to couch his or her testimony in terms of causality may also breach a cardinal rule of science. In other words, allowing an expert to testify that a complainant was in fact raped would allow the expert to give testimony that is not grounded in scientific principle and which does not tend to show what the testimony is offered to prove.

NOTES AND QUESTIONS

(1) *Syndromes Based on Post-Traumatic Stress Disorder (PTSD).* Several syndromes are based on PTSD, such as Rape Trauma Syndrome (RTS), Battered Woman Syndrome (BWS), and Vietnam Veteran's Syndrome. Yet not all syndromes have been equally accepted in the courtroom. For example, BWS evidence has been viewed by some as an attempt to change the substantive law of self-defense. Its primary use is to demonstrate that a woman who killed her spouse or intimate partner after years of battering had a heightened sense of awareness of danger due to the syndrome and to explain why the woman stayed with her batterer. Initially, BWS testimony often was excluded from the courtroom, but today BWS evidence has been permitted even by jurisdictions that require syndrome testimony to meet the *Frye* standard. Ironically, while the existence of BWS now is generally accepted by the courts, academics and psychologists are challenging some of its basic tenets and attempting to reconfigure its dimensions.

BWS evidence also has been used by victims to argue their duress in committing crimes not directed against their batterers, as, e.g., where the allegation is the batterer made them rob others, or injure a child. *See* Dore, *Downward Adjustment and the Slippery Slope: The Use of Duress in Defense of Battered Offenders*, 56 OHIO ST. L.J. 665 (1995) (listing articles and cases focusing on duress). Its exclusion when offered to show that the defendant did not have the requisite intent to place her child in a dangerous situation even resulted in reversal of the defendant's conviction in *Barrett v. State*, 675 N.E.2d 1112 (Ind. Ct. App. 1996). But see *United States v. Dixon*, 413 F.3d 520 (5th Cir. 2005) (rejecting the testimony, on the defense of duress, because defense requires objectively reasonable perception of danger), *cert. granted* on burden of proof of duress, 546 U.S. 1135 (2006). BWS evidence has also been introduced by the prosecution to explain why a battered woman who is the victim of such crimes as battery, rape, or kidnapping may recant her initial accusation or delay in reporting. *United States v. Young*, 316 F.3d 649 (7th Cir. 2002), affirmed the admission of testimony for the prosecution by a psychiatric mental health nurse who explained why the victim has recanted her story about being kidnapped and abused. The trial judge had admitted the testimony after holding a *Daubert* hearing. *See, in addition Arcoren v. United States*, 929 F.2d 1235 (8th Cir.), *cert. denied*, 502 U.S. 913 (1991). *See also State v. Grecinger*, 569 N.W.2d 189 (Minn. 1997), an attempted murder case, holding that BWS evidence was admissible in the prosecution's case-in-chief against an alleged batterer when it was offered after the victim's credibility was attacked by the defense during opening statement and cross-examination. A concurring opinion cites Raeder, *The Double-Edged Sword: Admissibility of Battered Woman Syndrome by and Against Batterers in Cases Implicating Domestic Violence*, 67 U. Colo. L. Rev. 789 (1996), concerning the potential prejudicial effect of social science evidence when offered by the prosecution.

In contrast to BWS, Rape Trauma Syndrome (RTS) has met with much less courtroom success. *See* Frazier & Borgida, *Rape Trauma Syndrome: A Review of Case Law and Psychological Research*, 16 LAW & HUM. BEHAV. 293 (1992). *Alberico* does not permit RTS evidence, while admitting more general PTSD testimony. Yet, if RTS is simply an aspect of PTSD, does this make sense? Should it matter in determining admissibility if the testimony is being offered by the defense or by the prosecution? Does the debate about syndrome testimony have political as well as scientific overtones? *See* Mosteller, *Syndromes and Politics in Criminal Trials and Evidence Law*, 46 DUKE L.J. 461 (1996).

See generally McCord, *Syndromes, Profiles and Other Mental Exotica: A New Approach to the Admissibility of Nontraditional Psychological Evidence in Criminal Cases*, 66 OR. L. REV. 19 (1987).

(2) *Social Science Framework Evidence.* Often the real impetus for introducing syndrome evidence is to provide a social science framework in which to analyze the evidence. In most cases the jury has a shared understanding of background information, such as the fact that drivers need to be more careful when it rains. Those advocating that the jury be given social science context argue that the general public has a variety of misconceptions about such topics as rape, child abuse, and domestic violence; therefore they need to be given a framework that dispels myths and describes the shared characteristics of individuals who experi-

ence such abuse. *See, e.g.*, Bowman, *A Matter of Justice: Overcoming Juror Bias in Prosecutions of Batterers Through Expert Witness Testimony of the Common Experiences of Battered Women*, 2 S. CAL. REV. L. & WOMEN'S STUD. 219 (1992). Thus, now BWS evidence often is introduced (on behalf of the woman) in settings where it is not clear that the woman suffered from the syndrome, because it is the only avenue of admissibility for explaining to the jury information about domestic violence that may be necessary to dispel commonly held, but incorrect, assumptions about the nature of battering relationships. Such use may have the unintended consequence of instigating efforts to impeach the woman as not fitting the syndrome, and thus not being a "real" victim.

When social science evidence is used by prosecutors, the question arises whether it is really character evidence in disguise. When it is used by the defense, the question is whether it results in unwarranted acquittals based on sympathy. *See generally* Mosteller, *Is the Jury Competent? Legal Doctrines Governing the Admissibility of Expert Testimony Concerning Social Framework Evidence*, 52 LAW & CONTEMP. PROBS. 85 (1989); Raeder, *The Better Way: The Role of Batterers' Profiles and Expert "Social Framework" Background in Cases Implicating Domestic Violence*, 68 U. COLO. L. REV. 147 (1997); Vidmar & Schuller, *Juries and Expert Evidence: Social Framework Testimony*, 52 LAW & CONTEMP. PROBS. 133 (1989).

Some profile evidence clearly is viewed as inadmissible character evidence. *See, e.g.*, *United States v. Gillespie*, 852 F.2d 475 (9th Cir. 1988) (child molester's profile).

Compare *Estelle v. McGuire*, 502 U.S. 62 (1991), finding no due process violation where evidence of battered child (shaken baby) syndrome was introduced by the prosecution to show the intentional nature of the abuse. Unlike the other syndromes, which are psychological in nature, shaken baby syndrome is based on the child's physical condition.

(3) *Should Syndrome and Social Science Evidence be Subject to Frye?* After *Kumho*, syndrome and social science evidence is subject to a challenge on the basis of its reliability. Jurisdictions vary as to whether syndrome and social science evidence fall within the ambit of *Frye* and strict *Daubert*. Even within a jurisdiction, courts may vary as to what, if any, type of psychological testimony should be required to pass through a rigorous judicial gatekeeper. Here, and under a Rule 403 type analysis, something depends on a court's notion of juror gullibility. In *People v. Stoll*, 783 P.2d 698 (Cal. 1989), the court rejected the philosophy "that juries are incapable of evaluating properly presented references" by experts to this type of evidence. A California court had earlier permitted expert testimony concerning a diagnosis of Munchausen Syndrome by Proxy in the prosecutor's case-in-chief where the defendant had not put her mental state into issue. That syndrome explains how a mother who is outwardly devoted to her young child fabricates or creates physical illness in her child to obtain attention and sympathy. See *People v. Phillips*, 122 Cal. App. 3d 69 (Cal. Ct. App. 1981), stating that the "rules of evidence do not preclude innovation." *Phillips* found *Frye* not to be applicable because this was not scientific evidence.

Many states apply *Frye* or strict *Daubert* and thus are less likely to admit. *See generally* 1 GIANNELLI & IMWINKELRIED, SCIENTIFIC EVIDENCE §§ 9-3 to 9-5 (3d ed.

1999). See also Showalter, *Distinguishing Science from Pseudo-Science in Psychiatry: Expert Testimony in the Post-Daubert Era*, 2 VA. J. SOC. POL'Y & L. 211 (1995), arguing that *Daubert* provides little guidance for evaluating psychiatric testimony.

(4) *Psychiatrists and Psychologists After Kumho.* Imagine a psychiatrist who testifies that she has been practicing for twenty years, has diagnosed hundreds of persons with chronic undifferentiated schizophrenia, and knows from that experience alone that such persons respond poorly to conventional psychoanalysis. Is this sort of opinion excludable if the expert cannot identify extrinsic testing, peer review, error rates, and general acceptance? Perhaps the expert's own repeated experience establishes falsifiability and replication, and therefore reliability. What factors can be used to assess reliability? Professor Christopher Slobogin has found that most traditional psychiatric evidence is being admitted regardless of its reliability. *See* Slobogin, *Psychiatric Evidence in Criminal Trials: To Junk or Not to Junk?* 40 WM. & MARY L. REV. 1 (1998).

Note that in a pre-*Daubert* decision, the Supreme Court affirmed (as constitutional) the admission of expert psychiatric testimony on a defendant's future dangerousness against the defendant in a capital sentencing hearing, even though the American Psychiatric Association had argued that two out of three such predictions were wrong. *Barefoot v. Estelle*, 463 U.S. 880 (1983). Dangerousness testimony is still common. However, its reliability remains open to question. *See, e.g.*, Beecher-Monas, *The Epistemology of Prediction: Future Dangerousness Testimony and Intellectual Due Process*, 60 WASH. & LEE L. REV. 353 (2003). One study found that in sentencing decisions, it was virtually impossible to negate evidence of dangerousness even in otherwise weak cases. Diamond et al., *Juror Reactions to Attorneys at Trial*, 87 J. CRIM. L. & CRIMINOLOGY 17 (1996). In 2004, the Texas Defender Service published a report, *Deadly Speculation: Misleading Texas Capital Juries with False Predictions of Future Dangerousness*, that casts doubt on expert predictions of future dangerousness in capital cases. The study followed 155 inmates labeled dangerous by prosecution experts during the sentencing phase of their trials. Only 8 of them, or about 5%, were subsequently involved in serious assaults. What are the likely critiques of such a study? Is it the burden of the defense to prove testimony about dangerousness is unreliable, or must the prosecution prove it is reliable? What type of evidence would support testimony about dangerousness?

(5) *Social Science Evidence in Civil Cases.* Not all cases in which social science evidence is offered are criminal. Should that affect the admissibility decision? In *Tyus v. Urban Search Management*, 102 F.3d 256 (7th Cir. 1996), *cert. denied*, 520 U.S. 1251 (1997), the court reiterated its adherence to *Daubert* in assessing the admissibility of social science testimony. The case was remanded for a hearing on whether a psychologist should be permitted to testify about how an advertising campaign works and the effect of all-white campaigns on African-Americans (the expert had been excluded below), noting that "[s]ocial scientists in particular may be able to show that commonly accepted explanations for behavior are, when studied more closely, inaccurate. These results sometimes fly in the face of conventional wisdom."

[D] Psychological Testimony in Child Abuse Cases

(1) *Child Sexual Abuse Accommodation Syndrome (CSAAS).* In many cases involving children, the prosecution offers Child Sexual Abuse Accommodation Syndrome (CSAAS). The work of Summit, *The Child Sexual Abuse Accommodation Syndrome*, 7 Child Abuse & Neglect 177 (1983), identified the syndrome, which "represents a common denominator of the most frequently observed victim behaviors." It describes five categories of behavior, including two preconditions to the abuse: secrecy and helplessness, followed by feelings of entrapment and accommodation of the abuse, delay in reporting it, and later retraction of the accusation. The symptoms do not invariably prove abuse and similar ones can occur in unabused as well as abused children. In *State v. J.Q.*, 617 A.2d 1196 (N.J. 1993), the Court held that because CSAAS "has a limited, therapeutic purpose and not a predictive one," it could not be used as affirmative evidence that molestation had occurred, but could be used only for the limited purpose of explaining why a child's reactions "are not inconsistent with having been molested."

In *State v. W.L.*, 650 A.2d 1035 (N.J. Super. Ct. App. Div. 1995), the role of CSAAS evidence was explained as "the other side of the coin of fresh complaint evidence (in rape cases) and fulfills the same function, namely, to respond to preconceived but not necessarily valid ideas jurors may have regarding the consistency of the post-assault conduct of a victim who claims to have been sexually abused with the fact of an actual act of abuse." However, not all courts agree. See *Newkirk v. Kentucky*, 937 S.W.2d 690 (Ky. 1996), holding that not only is evidence about CSAAS generally inadmissible, but testimony that it is generally common for children to report sexual abuse and then retract such allegations also is inadmissible to explain why a ten-year-old child recanted her allegations. The court observed that:

> We recognize that some will regard this opinion as regressive and unenlightened. Some will wrongly conclude that we fail to recognize the extent of child sexual abuse or even that we elevate the rights of criminals over defenseless children. We remind those who hold such views that every person accused of committing a crime is entitled to the presumption of innocence and to have such presumption continue until guilt is proven beyond a reasonable doubt. The admission of theoretical expert evidence which presumes guilt from the very fact of the accusation is contrary to our most fundamental rights. Moreover, if we should embark upon the path toward freely admitting expert testimony of this nature, it would be difficult to turn back. For instance, if an expert can testify that children who accuse adult family members of sexual abuse are probably telling the truth despite a subsequent recantation, it would follow that a step-parent so accused could introduce expert opinion that children often fabricate accusations against step-parents. Likewise, if symptomatic evidence of CSAAS is admissible to prove abuse, the absence of such symptoms would necessarily be admissible to prove that abuse had not occurred. Such a result would be most undesirable as even Dr. Sullivan testified that not all children who have been sexually abused exhibit symptoms commonly associated with

CSAAS. We join with the Pennsylvania Supreme Court in *Commonwealth v. Dunkle*, 529 Pa. 168, 602 A.2d 830 (1992), as follows:

> We are all aware that child abuse is a plague in our society and one of the saddest aspects of growing up in today's America. Nevertheless, we do not think it befits this Court to simply disregard long-standing principles concerning the presumption of innocence and the proper admission of evidence in order to gain a greater number of convictions. A conviction must be obtained through the proper and lawful admission of evidence in order to maintain the integrity and fairness that is the bedrock of our jurisprudence. *Id.* at 838.

In final analysis, the more that courts permit experts to advise the jury based on probability, classifications, syndromes and traits, the more we remove the jury from its historic function of assessing credibility. While a criminal may be facile with his denials and explanations and a child may be timid and halting, we entrust to the wisdom of the twelve men and women who comprise the jury the responsibility to sort between the conflicting versions of events and arrive at a proper verdict.

See also Hadden v. State, 690 So. 2d 573 (Fla. 1997), holding that CSAAS must satisfy *Frye* to be admitted, and that it was not presently generally accepted by a majority of experts in psychology.

Do you think that testimony aimed at explaining how children react to child abuse is more likely to be admitted if the expert simply discusses the distinctive conduct and does not mention CSAAS at all?

See generally MYERS ON EVIDENCE IN CHILD, DOMESTIC, AND ELDER ABUSE CASES (2005); *see also* Raeder, *Navigating Between Scylla and Charybdis: Ohio's Efforts to Protect Children Without Eviscerating the Rights of Criminal Defendants — Evidentiary Considerations and the Rebirth of Confrontation Clause Analysis in Child Abuse Cases*, 25 TOL. L. REV. 43 (1994) (discussing expert testimony in child abuse cases, including CSAAS).

(2) *Expert Testimony on Implanted Memory. United States v. Rouse*, 111 F.3d 561 (8th Cir.), *cert. denied*, 522 U.S. 905 (1997), concerns expert testimony on implanted memory in child witnesses. Four Native American defendants were convicted of aggravated sexual abuse of five young girls, aged 20 months to seven years. The majority held that the exclusion of certain defense expert testimony by a Dr. Underwager was harmless error, after an earlier panel decision reversing the convictions was vacated. The majority observes that:

> Dr. Underwager testified [to the jury] at length concerning his own research into the ways in which the reliability of children's allegations of physical or sexual abuse may be tainted by adult questioning practices that suggest false answers or even implant false memories. [He] identified for the jury practices of "suggestibility" that produce unreliable child testimony — use of leading or coercive questions; communicating adult assumptions that cause the child to give what is perceived as the desired answer; repetitive questioning; play therapy, which Dr. Underwager opined has "no scientific support"; adult use of rewards or negative reinforcement

that motivate children to lie; and "cross germination" among a group of children who pick up stories from each other. Dr. Underwager opined that "a memory can be created . . . by questioning someone." Moreover, "[t]he younger the child, the greater the suggestibility, the more vulnerable they are to the influences."

When the prosecution successfully objected to some questions put to Dr. Underwager, defendants made an offer of proof at the end of his direct examination. In a three-page narrative answer to the question whether "there's been a practice of suggestibility employed" with the child victims, Dr. Underwager opined (i) that therapist Kelson had exerted "massive social influence" on the victims; (ii) that Kelson engaged in "highly suggestive and highly contaminating" practices; (iii) that the prosecutor used leading questions at trial and the children "were comfortable doing the yes/no bit," showing "they'd learned" to answer yes; (iv) that Van Roe's use of diagrams was "very suggestive and very leading"; (v) that the children "were kidnapped . . . taken from their families, taken to this strange place where all of the people are concerned that they talk about sex abuse"; and (vi) that the "total environment [was] one of the most powerful and coercive influences upon children that I've seen." The district court excluded these opinions as not proper subjects of expert opinion.

A qualified expert may explain to the jury the dangers of implanted memory and suggestive practices when interviewing or questioning child witnesses, but may not opine as to a child witness's credibility. That leaves a troublesome line for the trial judge to draw — as the expert applies his or her general opinions and experiences to the case at hand, at what point does this more specific opinion testimony become an undisguised, impermissible comment on a child victim's veracity?

In a vigorous dissent that incorporates his previous majority decision in the vacated opinion, Judge Bright details how common interviewing practices can produce an altered memory. Relying heavily on an article by Ceci & Bruck, *Suggestibility of Child Witnesses: A Historical Review and Synthesis*, 113 Psychol. Bull. 403–39 (1993), which reviewed the research and writing on the subject, Judge Bright argues that it "supports the view that the very matters observed and testified to by Dr. Underwager can produce biased, untrue or false memories in children, and more particularly young children."

His dissent cites the article as documenting adequate research indicating the following:

1. A subject's, particularly a child's, original verbal answers are better remembered than the actual events themselves, yes-no questioning leads to more error, and young children are particularly vulnerable to coaching and leading questions.

2. Children desire to comply or cooperate with the respected authority figure interviewer and will attempt to make answers consistent with what they see as the intent of the questioner, rather than consistent with their knowledge of the event, even if the question is bizarre. Interviewer bias can

skew results, as a child often will attempt to reflect the interviewer's interpretation of events, particularly when more than one interviewer shares the same presuppositions. If the interviewer's original perception is incorrect, this can lead to high levels of inaccurate recall.

3. Repeated questions can produce a change of answers, since the child may interpret the question as "I must not have given the correct response the first time," and the child's answers may well become less accurate over time.

4. Younger children are more susceptible to suggestibility than older children, especially in the context of stereotyping. Stereotypes organize memory, sometimes distorting what is perceived by adding thematically congruent information that was not perceived, and stereotype formation interacts with suggestive questioning to a greater extent for younger rather than older children. Studies have shown children are particularly susceptible to an interviewer's "bad man" stereotype, and when repeatedly told the actor is a bad man, they may construct a false account of an event, often embellished with perceptual details in keeping with the stereotype.

5. The use of anatomical dolls or sexually explicit materials will not necessarily provide reliable evidence, as children may be encouraged to engage in sexual play with dolls, etc., even if the child has not been sexually abused, and further no normative data exists on unabused children's use of dolls.

6. "[A] major conclusion is that contrary to the claims of some, children sometimes lie when the motivational structure is tilted toward lying." Patterns of bribes for disclosures, implied threats in nondisclosures, or insinuations that peers already have told investigators of suspects' abusive behavior are highly suggestive. Children will lie for personal gain, and material and psychological rewards need not be of a large magnitude to be effective.

7. Dr. Underwager testified regarding the concept of "cross-germination" among the children. Children in studies and in actual cases have shown that peer pressure or interaction with other children has effects on the accuracy of their reporting: they will provide an inaccurate response when other children "already have told" in order to go along with a peer group or be part of the crowd. In several cases where convictions have been overturned, children were shown to have talked with one another about the abuse; sometimes even siblings questioned siblings to get them to "open up" or provide incriminating evidence.

The Ceci-Bruck article's summary relating to interviewing of children stated: "Our review of the literature indicates that children can indeed be led to make false or inaccurate reports about very crucial, personally experienced, central events."

Query: Do you think that any guidelines or procedural safeguards should be established to ensure that interviewers do not contaminate the testimony of children? If so, what might they include? Is this an issue for the courts or for the professions (e.g., law enforcement, social workers, psychologists, and psychiatrists)? The stakes are very high. Even when a child is completely reliable, attacks based on implanted memory due to suggestive interviewing techniques can make it difficult for the prosecution to obtain a conviction or to have the conviction affirmed on appeal. As a result, children, our most vulnerable population, cannot be adequately protected from abusers. However, suggestive interviewing also can result in unjust convictions caused by children who do not recognize that they have been manipulated by the adults whom they trust. *See* MacFarlane, *Diagnostic Evaluations and the Use of Videotapes in Child Sexual Abuse Cases*, 40 U. MIAMI L. REV. 135 (1985).

PROBLEM 6B: PROFILE EVIDENCE AND BEHAVIORAL SYNDROMES AFTER DAUBERT — WHAT STANDARD GOVERNS EXPERT TESTIMONY ABOUT THE CHARACTERISTICS OF SEXUAL ABUSERS AND BATTERED CHILDREN?

In § 3.05 of this book, relating to character, a portion of the *Haakanson* case is presented to raise the question whether profiles and syndromes are excludable as character evidence under Rule 404. In *Haakanson* the Alaska Court of Appeals excluded evidence that defendant Haakanson fit an alleged "Child Sexual Abuser Profile." But some courts admit similar evidence, at least in some circumstances, holding that it does not violate the character rules. That same section and the present sections, reveal the admittance of evidence about pedophilia characteristics in South Dakota, child sexual abuse accommodation syndrome in the Eighth Circuit, and battered child syndrome in California, as well as other instances of admittance of syndromes, profiles or related evidence in other jurisdictions. Some uses of syndromes are closer to character evidence than others.

These syndrome cases also raise issues about expert testimony under Rule 702. Thus, for example, the Alaska court went beyond Rule 404 and also held the profile evidence against Haakanson inadmissible under Alaska's standards for experts, applying the then-controlling *Frye* rule. The expert was a state trooper experienced in investigating child sexual abuse cases:

> [I]n cases such as this, [the standard] should be virtually the equivalent of compliance with the *Frye* rule.
>
> The state did not establish that [its expert's] assumptions were shared by a consensus of experts in the mental health field nor that [he] was a member of the relevant group of experts. Even if the profile evidence did not offend [R]ule 404(a), it would not be admissible under the standard [governing expert testimony].

Questions:

(1) How should *Daubert/Kumho* be applied if the expert has gained all of his specialized knowledge from on-the-job training — or "experience," as Fed. R. Evid. 702 permits? (In such a situation, mightn't the expert be qualified under the terms of Rule 702 even if he or she hasn't studied peer-reviewed publications or formal error rates?)

(2) Under *Daubert/Kumho*, how do we measure the relevance or "fit" issue? (Does an opinion based on soft sciences or behavioral syndromes allow a looser "closeness of fit" between the profile and the defendant or victim characteristics to which it is applied than would be required for hard sciences?)

(3) Under *Daubert/Kumho*, how do we evaluate the other issue, that is the reliability issue, for behavioral evidence — do we still consider falsifiability (or testability), peer review, error rates, and acceptance, all in the same way?

[E] Perception and Memory in Adults

(1) *Eyewitness Experts*. Another type of expert evidence that has met with great hostility by the courts is the eyewitness expert, who testifies as to problems with perception, memory, and cross-racial identification that weigh against the accuracy of witness identifications, no matter how confidently made (especially when the original incident was stressful). *See* § 4.11. Obviously, some of the concern is the belief that such information will make jurors overly question eyewitness identifications, thereby reaching unwarranted not-guilty verdicts. Numerous cases find no error when the judge decides to exclude the eyewitness expert. *See, e.g., United States v. Hicks*, 103 F.3d 837 (9th Cir. 1996) (upholding exclusion of defense eyewitness expert, while affirming admission of PCR evidence); *United States v. Smith*, 122 F.3d 1355 (11th Cir. 1997) (affirming exclusion and noting that it had found only one case in which exclusion of eyewitness expert had been reversed). In *United States v. Welch*, 368 F.3d 970 (7th Cir. 2004), the exclusion of eyewitness/expert testimony was affirmed, the court saying such testimony would not assist the jury because it was common knowledge that one may mistake a person for someone else who is similarly dressed, and it did not require an expert witness to point out that memory decreases over time since the eyewitnesses in this case knew the defendant very well prior to the crime. While the decision emphasized that expert testimony regarding eyewitness identification, memory, and perception is not *per se* unhelpful, it suggested generally that the district court's decision on this topic should be given great deference. However, in some situations exclusion can result in reversal, such as in California when the victim is the only eyewitness or the eyewitness identifications are questionable and the defendant claims mistaken identity. *See People v. McDonald*, 690 P.2d 709 (Cal. 1984). The question of whether such expert eyewitness testimony must meet *Daubert* also has been raised. *See United States v. Kime*, 99 F.3d 870 (8th Cir. 1996) (eyewitness expertise fails *Daubert*), *cert. denied*, 519 U.S. 1141 (1997); *United States v. Amador-Galvan*, 9 F.3d 1414 (9th Cir. 1993) (remanding for *Daubert* hearing.). *Newsome v. McCabe*, 319 F.3d 301 (7th Cir.), *cert. denied*, 539 U.S. 943 (2003), posed an atypical use of eyewitness testimony. A pardoned prisoner brought a civil rights action alleging that police officers had manipulated lineup results to achieve identification of him and then covered up their manipulation. *Newsome* affirmed the introduction by plaintiff of testimony about plaintiff's eyewitness expert's experiment, employing panels of persons who viewed photos of both the probably real perpetrator and the plaintiff. The testimony was found to comport with standards of reliability in the field of eyewitness testimony (showing a very low numerical chance of the several eyewitnesses at trial mistakenly identifying plaintiff without manipulation) and was found helpful to the

jury in determining the possibility that misidentification had occurred by chance. Was it a factor that the pardoned prisoner was wrongfully convicted? Unlike most eyewitness testimony cases, there was no doubt here about the person's innocence. As indicated above, one unspoken issue regarding eyewitness experts is the concern that jurors will be distracted from convicting the guilty. In other words, jurors will typically find doubt based on an eyewitness expert's testimony, regardless of whether it is warranted. *Cf. United States v. Dorsey*, 45 F.3d 809 (4th Cir.) (affirming exclusion of forensic anthropologist's testimony that defendant was not person depicted in surveillance photographs as failing *Daubert* criteria), *cert. denied*, 515 U.S. 1168 (1995).

Somewhat atypically of courts around the country, the Supreme Court of New Jersey made *mandatory* the giving of a jury instruction expressly allowing the jury to consider, if they think appropriate, that cross-racial sole witness' identifications may be subject to special problems concerning accuracy, in cases where the sole witness identification is critical and uncorroborated by other evidence. In the case at issue, the victim, who eventually identified the defendant, had been unable to do so for 7-8 months after the crime, originally had been unable to identify a photograph of the defendant, and no forensic evidence linked the defendant to the crime. There is a good discussion of the whole area, citing studies and the law around the country. The case is *State v. Cromedy*, 158 N.J. 112, 727 A.2d 457 (1999). Curiously, the court refused, however, to authorize expert testimony regarding cross-racial identifications, saying the area was not scientifically certain enough for that.

(2) *Repressed Memory.* The question of whether a witness can testify to a previously "repressed memory" also has generated controversy. Typically, the memory is one of abuse during childhood, which may lead to a criminal prosecution. The memory often emerges in therapeutic sessions with a psychologist or psychiatrist. Is such retrieval of memories subject to a screening under *Daubert* or *Frye* to determine if the memories are reliable? In *State v. Hungerford*, 697 A.2d 916 (N.H. 1997), the court found that a memory that previously had been completely absent from a witness's conscious recollection could not be separated from the process, if any, that facilitated its recovery, and remanded for a pretrial reliability determination to be made on a case-by-case basis. *See also* § 4.02[C].

§ 6.06 CRIMINAL CASES: FORENSIC EVIDENCE OTHER THAN DNA

[A] Handwriting

UNITED STATES v. CRISP

United States Court of Appeals, Fourth Circuit
324 F.3d 261 (2003)

King, Circuit Judge.

Patrick Leroy Crisp appeals multiple convictions arising from an armed bank robbery in North Carolina. Crisp maintains that his trial was tainted by the Government's presentation of inadmissible expert testimony. As explained below, the prosecution's handwriting evidence was properly admitted, and we affirm the convictions. [At trial, a handwriting expert, Special Agent Thomas Currin, a "questioned document analyst" for twenty-four years with the State of North Carolina Bureau of Investigation ("SBI"), testified that Crisp had authored a handwritten incriminatory Note.]

Crisp challenges the admissibility of the opinions of Currin. Crisp contends that the basic premise behind handwriting analysis is that no two persons write alike, and thus that forensic document examiners can reliably determine authorship of a particular document by comparing it with known samples. He maintains that these basic premises have not been tested, nor has an error rate been established. In addition, he asserts that handwriting experts have no numerical standards to govern their analyses and that they have not subjected themselves and their science to critical self-examination and study.

While the admissibility of handwriting evidence in the post-*Daubert* world appears to be a matter of first impression for our Court, every circuit to have addressed the issue has concluded, as on the fingerprint issue, that such evidence is properly admissible [citing cases from four different circuits admitting the evidence]. Certain district courts, however, have recently determined that handwriting analysis does not meet the *Daubert* standards.

On voir dire, and then on direct examination, [Currin] explained that all questioned documents that come into the SBI are analyzed first by a "questioned document examiner"; and that the initial analysis is then reviewed by another examiner. Currin discussed several studies showing the ability of qualified document examiners to identify questioned handwriting. In addition, he had passed numerous proficiency tests, consistently receiving perfect scores. Currin testified to a consistent methodology of handwriting examination and identification, and he stated that the methodology "has been used not only at the level of state crime laboratories, but [also in] federal and international crime laboratories around the world." When he was questioned regarding the standards employed in questioned document examination, Currin explained that every determination of authorship "is based on the uniqueness of [certain] similarities, and it's based on the quality and the skill and the training of the document examiner."

At trial, Currin drew the jury's attention to similarities between Crisp's known handwriting exemplars and the writing on the Note. Among the similarities that he pointed out were the overall size and spacing of the letters and words in the documents; the unique shaping of the capital letter "L" in the name "Lamont"; the spacing between the capital letter "L" and the rest of the word; a peculiar shaping to the letters "o" and "n" when used in conjunction with one another; the v-like formation of the letter "u" in the word "you"; and the shape of the letter "t," including the horizontal stroke. Currin also noted that the word "tomorrow" was misspelled in the same manner on both the known exemplar and the Note. He went on to testify that, in his opinion, Crisp had authored the Note.

[L]ike fingerprint analysis, handwriting comparison testimony has a long history of admissibility in the courts of this country. *See, e.g., Robinson v. Mandell*, 20 F. Cas. 1027 (D. Mass. 1868). The fact that handwriting comparison analysis has achieved widespread and lasting acceptance in the expert community gives us the assurance of reliability that *Daubert* requires. Furthermore, as with expert testimony on fingerprints, the role of the handwriting expert is primarily to draw the jury's attention to similarities between a known exemplar and a contested sample. Here, Currin merely pointed out certain unique characteristics shared by the two writings. Though he opined that Crisp authored the Note in question, the jury was nonetheless left to examine the Note and decide for itself whether it agreed with the expert.

To the extent that a given handwriting analysis is flawed or flimsy, an able defense lawyer will bring that fact to the jury's attention, both through skillful cross-examination and by presenting expert testimony of his own. But in light of Crisp's failure to offer us any reason today to doubt the reliability of handwriting analysis evidence in general, we must decline to deny our courts and juries such insights as it can offer.

Affirmed.

MICHAEL, CIRCUIT JUDGE, dissenting.

The majority believes that expert testimony about handwriting identification is reliable because the techniques in these fields have been accepted and tested in our adversarial system over time. This belief leads the majority to excuse fingerprint and handwriting analysis from the more careful scrutiny that scientific expert testimony must now withstand under *Daubert* before it can be admitted. In Patrick Leroy Crisp's case the government did not prove that its expert identification evidence satisfied the *Daubert* factors or that it was otherwise reliable. I respectfully dissent for that reason. In dissenting, I am not suggesting that handwriting evidence cannot be shown to satisfy *Daubert.* I am only making the point that the government did not establish in Crisp's case that this evidence is reliable. The government has had ten years to comply with *Daubert.* It should not be given a pass in this case.

NOTES AND QUESTIONS

(1) *Is Adversarial Testing Enough? Crisp* involved a challenge to fingerprint evidence as well as to handwriting. The Court viewed both of these disciplines as long established. The Ninth Circuit reached the same conclusion when affirming the admission of ultimate opinion about authorship in *United States v. Prime*, 363 F.3d 1028 (9th Cir. 2004), finding handwriting similarity evidence had been generally accepted in the courts for decades. Is adversarial testing the same as scientific testing for purposes of satisfying *Daubert?*

(2) *Limiting Testimony of Handwriting Examiners.* The majority notes several district courts that have found handwriting indentification wanting under *Daubert.* There have also been a number of district court judges who have limited handwriting examiners to explanations about factors used to compare handwriting, and perhaps to pointing out similar features in the proven exemplar and the questioned handwriting, but not allowing them to testify to the ultimate conclusion that the two are written by the same person or that the defendant authored the questioned document. *See, e.g., United States v. Starzecpyzel*, 880 F. Supp. 1027 (S.D.N.Y. 1995).

When Judge Matsch, presiding over the notorious Oklahoma City Bombing trial of Timothy McVeigh, tentatively ruled against a handwriting expert giving an ultimate opinion, the government withdrew the expert.

If handwriting comparison techniques flunk *Daubert/Kumho*, can examiners testify at all? What would be the result if handwriting experts were prohibited? Since jurors can perform their own comparisons could this result in less informed decisions? Is this why judges might permit explanatory testimony, or pointing out similarities, while barring ultimate opinions as to authorship?

(3) *Ultimate Opinion Permitted by Expert with "Exceptionally Impressive Credentials." United States v. Rutland*, 372 F.3d 543 (3d Cir. 2004), affirmed a conviction where an expert testified to the ultimate issue, the authorship of a key document, in the trial of a financial advisor charged with conspiracy to obtain money and property through a fraudulent scheme. The court posed the narrow issue of whether expert opinion testimony should reach the ultimate issue when the expert has exceptionally impressive credentials. The defendant argued that in light of the expert's credentials and experience in high-profile cases, "the probative value of his opinion on authorship was substantially outweighed by the danger that the jury would accept his opinion based on his extraordinary experience rather than on his underlying analysis." The court noted that the defendant's "suggestion of limiting an expert from testifying to the ultimate issue if the expert has stellar qualifications leads to an absurd result. Parties would be forced to determine if their proposed experts were overly qualified, and find less qualified experts." Do you agree with this analysis of prejudice?

(4) *How Should Handwriting Experts be Evaluated for Admissibility?* The application of *Kumho* (or *Daubert)* to questioned document examiners has been controversial. A variety of approaches to this question are possible. First, one might consider the analyst in the same light as a baseball player who, through repeated practice, has learned to hit a pitched ball. In this view, the analyst is not so much a

scientist as a practitioner, whose repeated experiences have led to an ability to identify genuine documents based on trial and error techniques, incorporation of successful methods, and reinforcement. (But can one ever know for sure if the identifications were correct, so that trial-and-error and reinforcement can work? Is a trial that convicts a person who has been identified in testimony by the expert a sort of self-fulfilling prophecy rather than validation of the identification?) Another view is that the analyst is like an alert layperson who uses faculties shared by everyone in the public but who knows what to look for. By this reasoning, one would conclude that anyone can draw the relevant conclusions about a graphic sample, but the analyst, like a guide, is useful to point out which characteristics to look for. Finally, one might view the analyst as applying cognizable, refinable principles to repeatable events. This description fits the handwriting expert who, for example, relies on a rule that a given characteristic, such as a lift or curve, is more readily imitated or disguised than another characteristic, such as the slant of one's letters.

(5) *Graphologists.* There are no set qualifications for questioned document examiners. Membership in the American Board of Forensic Document Examiners is not required. Courts have even permitted graphologists to testify as to who authored a questioned document. Graphology is the study of handwriting to determine personality. However, recent decisions are fairly uniform in affirming exclusion of graphologists. *See* Giannelli, *Expert Qualifications: Who are these Guys?* 19 CRIM. JUST. 70 (Spring, 2004). Should handwriting analysts be certified before they can testify?

(6) *Forensic Stylistics. United States v. Van Wyk,* 83 F. Supp. 2d 515 (D.N.J. 2000), a prosecution for making threatening communications, addressed the question whether an agent of the FBI could testify as a forensic stylistics expert and whether forensic stylistics is a reliable technique to allow the expert to identify the defendant as the author of the otherwise unidentified threatening letters. Forensic stylistics and text analysis both involve the examination of text or writing style — the manner of expressing oneself, rather than characteristics of the handwriting or of the particular typewriter, printer, pen, ink, paper, or other thing used. The expert, sometimes a kind of linguist, analyzes and describes the style of writing of a document of questioned authorship and compares or contrasts its language to that of documents known to be written by a given author.

The Court concluded that the expert, Agent Fitzgerald, was qualified to testify for the prosecution, even though he did not have a degree in linguistics, forensic stylistics, or text analysis. He had, however, among other things, in the course of his five years at the FBI's Center for the Analysis of Violent Crimes, attended threat assessment, psychotherapy assessment, and risk assessment seminars that involved matters related to the analysis of text, and, while there, had taught and conducted research in text analysis, analyzed text on a weekly or even daily basis for the five years, and worked on text analysis in a number of high profile matters including the notorious Unabomber case (where the textual identification of the Unabomber apparently proved to be correct).

The judge then determined that the agent should not be permitted to testify to his conclusion as to the identity of the author of the unknown writings, the judge adopting the approach to general handwriting testimony taken in such cases as

Starzecpyzel and *McVeigh*, mentioned in note (2) *supra:*

> The reliability of text analysis, much like handwriting analysis, is questionable because, as discussed supra, there is no known rate of error, no recognized standard, no meaningful peer review, and no system of accrediting an individual as an expert in the field. [The literature on any such field is quite limited.] Consequently, the existing data for forensic stylistics cannot definitively establish, as can DNA data, that a particular person is "the" author of a particular writing. . . .
>
> [T]he Court is satisfied that Fitzgerald's testimony as to the specific similarities and idiosyncrasies between the known writings and questioned writings, as well as testimony regarding, for example, how frequently or infrequently in his experience, he has seen a particular idiosyncrasy, will aid the jury in determining the authorship of the unknown writings. The internal evidence related to the "four corners" of the writings is admissible.

The case was affirmed on appeal, without too much discussion, at 262 F.3d 405 (3d Cir. 2001).

[B] Fingerprinting

UNITED STATES v. LLERA PLAZA

United States District Court, Eastern District of Pennsylvania
188 F. Supp. 2d 549 (2002)

POLLAK, DISTRICT JUDGE.

In the government's list of witnesses expected to be called at the upcoming trial, on drug and murder charges, of defendants, there are four Federal Bureau of Investigation (FBI) fingerprint examiners and one FBI fingerprint specialist. To bar the testimony of these anticipated witnesses, the defendants filed a Motion. The principal question posed was whether fingerprint identification evidence is sufficiently reliable to meet the standards for expert testimony set by Rule 702 of the Federal Rules of Evidence as explicated by the Supreme Court in *Daubert v. Merrell Dow Pharmaceuticals, Inc.* and reaffirmed in *Kumho Tire Co., Ltd. v. Carmichael.* . . . Resolution of these linked questions required consideration of evidence as to (1) the theoretical basis of fingerprint identification and (2) the procedures by which someone familiar with fingerprints arrives at a judgment that a fingerprint impressed on some surface (a so-called "latent" print) by an unknown person and thereafter found by and "lifted" from that surface by law enforcement technicians is — or is not — a print which "matches" a known person's "known exemplar" fingerprint (a so-called "rolled" print), thereby signifying that the person who made the latent print is — or is not — the person who made the rolled print.

. . .

On January 7, 2002, I filed an opinion and order addressed to the defendants' motion and the government's counter-motion [179 F. Supp. 2d 492. This earlier decision is often referred to as *Llera Plaza I*, the current decision being known as *Llera Plaza II* — Eds.]

First, I concluded that, as the government had contended, it was beyond reasonable dispute that the fingerprints of each person (a) are unique to that person and (b) are (barring some serious and deeply penetrating wound to the hand that substantially alters or defaces the surface of one or more of the fingers or of the palm) permanent from birth to death. I therefore ruled that, pursuant to Rule 201, I would take judicial notice of the uniqueness and permanence of fingerprints. I was in effect, accepting the theoretical basis of fingerprint identification — namely, that a showing that a latent print replicates (is a "match" of) a rolled print constitutes a showing that the latent and rolled prints are fingerprints of the same person.

Second, I considered whether the ACE-V fingerprint identification system employed by the FBI sufficiently conforms to the *Daubert* standards of reliability under Rule 702. I described the four fingerprint examination procedures — "analysis," "comparison," "evaluation," and "verification," — for which "ACE-V" is an acronym: "analysis" by an initial fingerprint examiner of the observably distinctive patterns of a latent print; "comparison" by the examiner of the latent print patterns with those of a rolled print; "evaluation" by the examiner of these compared patterns with a view to determining whether the prints are, or are not, impressions made by the same finger or palm; and "verification" by a second examiner who repeats the analysis, comparison and evaluation steps in order to verify, or not, the initial examiner's finding. Based on the *Mitchell* record, I came to the following conclusions with respect to ACE-V's conformity to the *Daubert* factors:

> The one *Daubert* factor that ACE-V satisfies in significant fashion is the fourth factor: ACE-V has attained general acceptance within the American fingerprint examiner community. However, the court finds that ACE-V does not adequately satisfy the "scientific" criterion of testing (the first *Daubert* factor) or the "scientific" criterion of "peer review" (the second *Daubert* factor). Further, the court finds that the information of record is unpersuasive, one way or another, as to ACE-V's "scientific" rate of error (the first aspect of *Daubert's* third factor), and that, at the critical evaluation stage, ACE-V does not operate under uniformly accepted "scientific" standards (the second aspect of *Daubert*'s third factor).

These conclusions did not, however, lead to a determination that fingerprint identification testimony could play no role whatsoever. The substance of my ruling was as follows:

> The *Daubert* difficulty with the ACE-V process is by no means total. The difficulty comes into play at the stage at which, as experienced specialists Ashbaugh [of the Royal Canadian Mounted Police] and Meagher [of the FBI] themselves acknowledge, the ACE-V process becomes "subjective" — namely, the evaluation stage. By contrast, the antecedent analysis and comparison stages are, according to the testimony, "objective" analysis of the rolled and latent prints and comparison of what the examiner has observed in the two prints. Up to the evaluation stage, the ACE-V fingerprint examiner's testimony is descriptive, not judgmental. . . . Accordingly, this court will permit the government to present testimony by fingerprint examiners who, suitably qualified as "expert" examiners by

virtue of training and experience, may (1) describe how the rolled and latent fingerprints at issue in this case were obtained, (2) identify and place before the jury the fingerprints and such magnifications thereof as may be required to show minute details, and (3) point out observed similarities (and differences) between any latent print and any rolled print the government contends are attributable to the same person. What such expert witnesses will not be permitted to do is to present "evaluation" testimony as to their "opinion" (Rule 702) that a particular latent print is in fact the print of a particular person. The defendants will be permitted to present their own fingerprint experts to counter the government's fingerprint testimony, but defense experts will also be precluded from presenting "evaluation" testimony. Government counsel and defense counsel will, in closing arguments, be free to argue to the jury that, on the basis of the jury's observation of a particular latent print and a particular rolled print, the jury may find the existence, or the non-existence, of a match between the prints.

I.

The government moved for reconsideration of the ruling. . . . Accordingly, I agreed to reconsider the January 7 ruling. [In the following discussion of new evidence since Jan. 7, the court reverses itself.]

II. . . .

A. The Testimony of the Government Witnesses

Stephen Meagher:

The first portion of Mr. Meagher's testimony was a run-through of the ACE-V process, visually illustrated by overhead projections of fingerprints whose distinctive patterns of "friction ridges" are frequently given further distinctive character by markings commonly termed "loops," "whorls," "arches," and "deltas" [known as "Galton points"].

Although the observation of Galton points that are common to the latent print and the rolled print has traditionally been one of the mainstays of the "comparison" and "evaluation" stages of ACE-V, Mr. Meagher emphasized in his testimony that no minimum number of Galton points is required in order to achieve a reliable identification. . . . Mr. Meagher's testimony on this point is of some significance, because in my January 7 opinion, in concluding that the ACE-V process appeared to lack uniformly controlling standards, I noted that, on the basis of what I had gleaned from the *Mitchell* record, here and abroad there appeared to be a lack of uniformly controlling identification standards.

The bulk of Mr. Meagher's testimony was a description and assessment of the proficiency tests administered annually to certified FBI fingerprint personnel (as I understand it, only certified examiners are presented by the government as fingerprint identification witnesses in court) in the years 1995-2001. Each person tested received a packet containing copies of a number of latent prints (whose source, although unknown to the test-taker, was known to the test-makers) and copies of a smaller number of known exemplars; the test-taker would then undertake to determine identities, or non-identities, between the latent prints and the known exemplars. . . .

Mr. Meagher presented a tabulation of the proficiency test results for the seven years 1995-2001. Sixteen of the 447 test takers were supervisory personnel who, having administered the internal test, took the external test. In the course of the seven years, one error was recorded on an external test: one person mistakenly identified a latent print as matching one of the known exemplars — a "false positive." All errors on the FBI fingerprint proficiency tests are inquired into; but a false positive — being mistakenly inculpatory — is thought by the FBI to call for particularly demanding scrutiny. The inquiry conducted with respect to the error led Mr. Meagher to conclude that the error was not one of faulty evaluation but of faulty recording of the evaluation — i.e., a clerical rather than a technical error.

The *internal* tests taken over the seven years numbered 431. These tests generated three errors. Each of the three errors was a missed identification — i.e., a failure by the test taker to find a match between a latent print and a known exemplar which in fact existed; such an error is a "false negative" which, being mistakenly exculpatory, is regarded by the FBI as considerably less serious than a false positive.

In sum, the 447 proficiency tests administered in the seven years from 1995 through 2001 yielded four errors — a proficiency error rate of just under 1%.

I asked Mr. Meagher whether he was aware of instances in which "identification testimony turned out to be mistaken" in instances of "criminal prosecutions in the United States not involving FBI fingerprint identification testimony." Mr. Meagher [responded] ". . . Yes . . . I don't want to imply that there's many, but I am aware of a few.". . .

Kenneth O. Smith:

Mr. Smith's testimony addressed the preparation and content of the external fingerprint identification proficiency tests distributed to and graded by CTS for numerous forensic laboratories including the FBI Laboratory. . . . Mr. Smith was of the view that the difficulty of the CTS tests corresponds reasonably closely to the difficulty presented to fingerprint examiners by their day-to-day work.

B. The Testimony of the Defense Witnesses

Allan Bayle:

Mr. Bayle is "a fingerprint examiner and a forensic scene examiner." He served at New Scotland Yard for twenty-five years until June of last year when he moved to the private sector as a consultant. Mr. Bayle is a Fellow of the (UK) Fingerprint Society and, like Mr. Meagher, a member of the International Association for

Identification. He has testified in English courts as a fingerprint expert "[h]undreds of times." Mr. Bayle had reviewed copies of the internal FBI proficiency tests before taking the stand. He found the latent prints utilized in those tests to be markedly unrepresentative of the latent prints that would be lifted at a crime scene. Mr. Bayle found the test latent prints to be far clearer than the prints an examiner would routinely deal with. The prints were too clear — lacking in the "background noise" and "distortion" one would expect in latent prints lifted at a crime scene. Further, Mr. Bayle testified, the test materials were deficient in that there were too few latent prints that were not identifiable: at a typical crime scene only about ten per cent of the lifted latent prints will turn out to be matched. In Mr. Bayle's view the paucity of non-identifiable latent prints "makes the test too easy. It's not testing their ability. It doesn't test their expertise. [I]f I gave my experts these tests, they'd fall about laughing." On cross-examination, Mr. Bayle was shown a latent print the government expects to introduce at the upcoming trial. "[I]sn't it correct," government counsel asked, "that what you're looking at right there is much easier than the latents that are in the test?" "Yes" [Bayle answered]. . . .

Janine Arvizu and Ralph Norman Haber:

Ms. Arvizu's expertise is in the area of laboratory quality assessment. Dr. Haber is a psychometrician. Neither one professed any familiarity with fingerprint identification. But both appeared to be quite knowledgeable about the principles of effective skills testing. They were highly critical of the FBI proficiency tests. The test materials and uninformative attendant literature, taken together with the ambiguity as to the conditions governing the taking of the tests (e.g., may the test takers consult with one another? To what extent is taking the test perceived to be competitive with, or subordinated to, the performance of concurrent work assignments?), gave few clues as to what the test makers intended to measure. For both Ms. Arvizu and Dr. Haber, the stratospheric test success rate was hardly reassuring; to the contrary, it raised "red flags." As to ACE-V itself, Dr. Haber offered the thought that "verification" was a misnomer for the final stage: a procedure in which a second fingerprint examiner knows the result arrived at by a previous examiner, and is asked to go over the same ground, would be better described as "ratification.". . .

III.

Is ACE-V a "Scientific" Technique?

The opinion of January 7 undertook to respond to the parties' competing arguments as to whether ACE-V meets *Daubert's* requirements. Characterizing ACE-V as "scientific" in the Rule 702 and *Daubert* sense, the government argued that the *Mitchell* record established that ACE-V met all four of the *Daubert* guidelines. The defendants, reading the *Mitchell* record and *Daubert* differently, argued otherwise. In the January 7 opinion I accepted the battleground as the parties had defined it, and on that basis I concluded that [under *Daubert* factors] (1) and (2), ACE-V was not supported by "testing" or by "peer review" in the "scientific" sense contemplated by *Daubert*; (3) the rate of error was "in limbo" and consensus on controlling standards was lacking; and (4) while there was "general acceptance" of ACE-V in the fingerprint identification community, that community was not a " 'scientific community' " in *Daubert's* use of the term.

ACE-V . . . is not, in my judgment, itself a science. But its claim on the attention of courts derives from the fact that it is rooted in science — that fingerprints are unique and are permanent. . . .

ACE-V as a "Technical" Discipline: Daubert Through the Prism of Kumho

In adjusting the focus of inquiry from ACE-V's status as a "scientific" discipline to its status as a "technical" discipline, one modifies the angle of doctrinal vision [of the *Daubert* factors].

The *Kumho Tire* Court's injunction that the gatekeeping requirement is designed to insure "that an expert . . . employs in the courtroom the same level of intellectual rigor that characterizes the practice of an expert in the relevant field" serves as a reminder that fingerprint identification is not a discipline that is confined to courtroom use. It is a discipline relied on in other settings — e.g., in identifying the dead in mass disasters. . . . In this reexamination there are two points to be addressed. One is the extent to which the several *Daubert* factors "are reasonable measures of the reliability of [this 'technical'] expert testimony." The other is whether the recent enlargement of the record — the three days of hearings on the motion for reconsideration — alters in some significant way the pertinent facts drawn from the *Mitchell* record.

(a) "peer review" and "general acceptance":

The fact that fingerprint specialists are not "scientists," and hence that the forensic journals in which their writings on fingerprint identification appear are not "scientific" journals in *Daubert's* peer review sense, does not seem to me to militate against the utility of the identification procedures employed by fingerprint specialists. I conclude that the fingerprint community's "general acceptance" of ACE-V should not be discounted because fingerprint specialists — like accountants, vocational experts, accident-reconstruction experts, appraisers of land or of art, experts in tire failure analysis, or others — have "technical, or other specialized knowledge" rather than "scientific knowledge," and hence are not members of what *Daubert* termed a "scientific community."

(b) "testing":

The key to the admissibility of expert testimony under *Daubert* and *Kumho Tire* is reliability, and this, of course, derives directly from the text of Rule 702, which contemplates that "(1) the testimony is based upon sufficient facts or data, (2) the testimony is the product of reliable principles and methods, and (3) the witness has applied the principles and methods reliably to the facts of the case." Bearing this in mind, "testing" in the *Daubert* sense [is] a criterion of reliability. Disagreeing with contentions that the "verification" phase of ACE-V constitutes *Daubert* "testing," or, in the alternative, that a century of litigation has been a form of "adversarial" testing that meets *Daubert's* criteria, I concluded in the January 7 opinion that

Daubert's testing factor was not met, and I have found no reason to depart from that conclusion.

(c) "rate of error" and "standards controlling the technique's operation":

In the January 7 opinion I found no persuasive information with respect to rate of error. And I found [concerning standards] (1) "whether a minimum number of Galton points must be identified before a match can be declared, varies from jurisdiction to jurisdiction. [T]he United Kingdom employs a sixteen-point minimum, Australia mandates that twelve points be found in common, and Canada uses no minimum point standard. In the United States, state jurisdictions set their own minimum point standards, while the FBI has no minimum number that must be identified to declare an 'absolutely him' match"; (2) there appeared to be no uniformly accepted qualifying standards for fingerprint examiners; and (3) the identification judgments made by fingerprint examiners at ACE-V's "evaluation" stage — i.e., in determining whether there is a "match"—are "subjective." [We now address] what new light — if any — is shed upon rate of error, or upon controlling standards, by the recent three days of hearings?

(i) "rate of error":

The factual case presented by the government was chiefly devoted to demonstrating, through the testimony of Mr. Meagher, that certified FBI fingerprint examiners have scored spectacularly well on the in-house annual proficiency tests-that, in the absence of actual data on rate of error, proficiency test scores of those who would be expert witnesses should be taken as a surrogate form of proof: if certified examiners rarely make a mistake on ACE-V proficiency tests, it stands to reason (so the theory would have it) that they rarely make a mistake when presenting ACE-V testimony in court. To rebut the government's proof, the defense witnesses undertook to demonstrate that the proficiency tests were inadequate. . . . On the record made before me, the FBI examiners got very high proficiency grades, but the tests they took did not.

[O]n the present record I conclude that the proficiency tests are less demanding than they should be. [They are] of little assistance in providing a measure of the relative competence of the test takers. But the defense witnesses offered not a syllable to suggest that certified FBI fingerprint examiners as a group, or any individual examiners among them, have not achieved at least an acceptable level of competence. The record shows that over the years there have been at least a few instances in which fingerprint examiners, here and abroad, have made identifications that have turned out to be erroneous. But Mr. Meagher knew of no erroneous identifications attributable to FBI examiners. . . . It has been open to defense counsel to present examples of erroneous identifications attributable to FBI examiners, and no such examples have been forthcoming. I conclude, therefore, on the basis of the limited information in the record as expanded, that there is no evidence that the error rate of certified FBI fingerprint examiners is unacceptably high.

(ii) "standards controlling the technique's operation":

The January 7 opinion found that three aspects of ACE-V manifested an absence of generally accepted controlling standards: (a) there appeared to be no agreed qualification standards for fingerprint examiners; (b) jurisdictions varied widely with respect to the minimum number of Galton points required for finding a "match"; (c) the ultimate "evaluation" judgment was termed "subjective." . . . On reviewing these issues on the basis of the expanded record I reach the following conclusions:

(a) Whatever may be the case for other law enforcement agencies, the standards prescribed for qualification as an FBI fingerprint examiner are clear: To be hired by the FBI as a fingerprint trainee, one must be a college graduate, preferably with some training in one of the physical sciences; to become a certified fingerprint examiner, the trainee must complete the FBI's two-year in-house training program which winds up with a three-day certifying examination. The uniformity and rigor of these FBI requirements provide substantial assurance that properly controlling qualification standards are in place and are in force.

(b) The absence of a Galton minimum under FBI auspices, as against maintenance of a high Galton threshold in the United Kingdom, the jurisdiction whose police first systematized fingerprint identification for law enforcement purposes, could be perceived as troublesome — i.e., connoting a lack of rigor in FBI standards. However, it appears that the July 7, 1999 *Mitchell* testimony with respect to the United Kingdom did not accurately reflect the then state of United Kingdom law and is now entirely out of date. The *Mitchell* testimony failed to take account of a leading case decided some two months earlier — *Regina v. Buckley*, 143 SJ LB 159 (April 30, 1999), in which the Court of Appeal (Criminal Division) stated that "[i]f there are fewer than eight similar ridge characteristics, it is highly unlikely that a judge will exercise his discretion to admit such evidence and, save in wholly exceptional circumstances, the prosecution should not seek to adduce such evidence," whereas "[i]f there are eight or more similar ridge characteristics, a judge may or may not exercise his or her discretion in favour of admitting the evidence." The Court of Appeal then proceeded to list elements that should inform the trial judge's exercise of discretion: How the discretion is exercised will depend on all the circumstances of the case, including in particular: (i) the experience and expertise of the witness; (ii) the number of similar ridge characteristics; (iii) whether there are dissimilar characteristics; (iv) the size of the print relied on, in that the same number of similar ridge characteristics may be more compelling in a fragment of print than in an entire print; and (v) the quality and clarity of the print on the item relied on, which may involve, for example, consideration of possible injury to the person who left the print, as well as factors such as smearing or contamination.

. . . [T]he fact that England has, after many years of close study, moved to the position which prevails in Canada and which the FBI has long subscribed to, leads me to conclude that there is sufficient uniformity within the principal common law jurisdictions to satisfy *Daubert*.

In the January 7 opinion, the aspect of the *Daubert* inquiry into "the existence and maintenance of standards controlling the technique's operation," that was of greatest concern was the acknowledged subjectivity of the fingerprint examiner's stated opinion that a latent print and a known exemplar are both attributable to the same person. Government witnesses Meagher and Ashbaugh both described the "match" opinion as "subjective," and defense witness Dr. David Stoney agreed. . . . There are, to be sure, situations in which the subjectiveness of an opinion properly gives rise to reservations about the opinion's reliability. But there are many situations in which an expert's manifestly subjective opinion (based on "one's personal knowledge, ability and experience") is regarded as admissible evidence in an American courtroom: a forensic engineer's testimony that a bottom-fire nailer's defective design caused an unintended "double-fire," resulting in injury to the plaintiff, *Lauzon v. Senco Products*, 270 F.3d 681 (8th Cir. 2001); an electrical engineer's testimony that fire in a clothes drier was caused by a thermostat malfunction, *Maryland Casualty Co. v. Therm-O-Disc*, 137 F.3d 780 (4th Cir. 1998); a marketing researcher's testimony as to consumer interpretations of advertising claims, the testimony being based on a market survey of consumers, *Southland Sod Farms v. Stover Seed Co.*, 108 F.3d 1134 (9th Cir. 1997). In each instance the expert is operating within a vocational framework that may have numerous objective components, but the expert's ultimate opining is likely to depend in some measure on experiential factors that transcend precise measurement and quantification. As compared with the degree of subjectiveness inherent in one or more of the foregoing examples of expert opinion testimony, the subjective ingredients of opinion testimony presented by a competent fingerprint examiner appear to be of substantially more restricted compass.

In sum, contrary to the view expressed in my January 7 opinion, I am now persuaded that the standards which control the opining of a competent fingerprint examiner are sufficiently widely agreed upon to satisfy *Daubert's* requirements [in this regard].

(3) Completing the Daubert/Kumho Assessment

Having re-reviewed the applicability of the *Daubert* factors through the prism of *Kumho*, I conclude that the one *Daubert* factor which is both pertinent and unsatisfied is the first factor — "testing.". . . Scientific tests of ACE-V — i.e., tests in the *Daubert* sense — would clearly aid in measuring ACE-V's reliability. But, as of today, no such tests are in hand. . . .

[But] I have found, on the record before me, that there is no evidence that certified FBI fingerprint examiners present erroneous identification testimony, and, as a corollary, that there is no evidence that the rate of error of certified FBI fingerprint examiners is unacceptably high. I am not persuaded that courts should defer admission of testimony with respect to fingerprinting — which Professors Neufeld and Scheck term "[t]he bedrock forensic identifier of the 20th century"— until academic investigators financed by the National Institute of Justice have made substantial headway on a "verification and validation" research agenda. . . .

Conclusion

[The court changes its mind from its earlier ruling and determines that the previously excluded evaluative fingerprint identification evidence is admissible.]

At the upcoming trial, the presentation of expert fingerprint testimony by the government, and the presentation of countering expert fingerprint testimony by any of the defendants, will be subject to the court's oversight prior to presentation of such testimony before the jury, with a view to insuring that any proposed expert witness possesses the appropriate expert qualifications and that fingerprints offered in evidence will be of a quality arguably susceptible of responsible analysis, comparison and evaluation.

NOTES AND QUESTIONS

(1) *More Controversy about Fingerprint Testimony.* A report by the National Academy of Sciences in 2009 cautioned about fingerprinting, particularly noting that "merely following the steps of ACE-V does not imply that one is proceeding in a scientific manner or producing reliable results." This report has led to a number of defense challenges, so far mostly unsuccessful. *See, e.g., United States v. Stone,* 848 F. Supp. 2d 714 (E.D. Mich. 2012). The exclusion of defense testimony by a professor who had extensively studied the reliability of fingerprinting techniques, but was not a fingerprint analyst, has been upheld. *See People v. Gonzalez,* 2012 Cal. App. Unpub. LEXIS 1294 (Feb. 22, 2012) (unreported decision). A few judges have limited the types of opinions that experts can testify to, particularly claims of "no error rate" and identifying the defendant "to the exclusion of all others." Both of these claims were debunked in the NAS report, and more recently the fingerprint community has proposed related limitations for analyst testimony in a report by the National Institute of Standards and Technology, National Institute of Justice. *See* Latent Print Examination and Human Factors: Improving the Practice Through a Systems Approach (Feb. 2012). In addition, the admission into evidence of a fingerprint examiner's testimony that a second fingerprint examiner confirmed his identification of defendant's fingerprint was found not to be harmless in *Potts v. Florida,* 57 So. 3d 292 (Fla. Dist. Ct. App. 2011).

(2) *FBI Admits Fingerprint Mistake.* On the strength of a sworn affidavit by an FBI fingerprint analyst who claimed "100 percent positive identification," federal agents obtained a material witness warrant to arrest Oregon lawyer Brandon Mayfield on suspicion of involvement in the March 2004 Spanish train bombings. The FBI discovered his fingerprint on a bag of detonators recovered after the Madrid bombing that killed 191 people. Mayfield had represented a defendant in a child custody case who was linked to terrorism and is Muslim. Two weeks later, Mayfield was released after the FBI admitted it wasn't his fingerprint after all. Does such a mistake implicate the reliability of the technique, or simply the reliability of the expert in the particular case? Is the technique itself subjective? The Mayfield debacle has caused some internal reforms in FBI fingerprint procedures. *See* McCall, *"Report Says Fingerprint Misidentification 'Watershed' for FBI,"* Assoc. Press (Mar. 11, 2006). What, if anything, does this do to the reasoning in *Llera Plaza*?

UNITED STATES v. SCOTT

United States Court of Appeals, Eleventh Circuit
2010 U.S. App. LEXIS 23720 (Nov. 16, 2010)

PER CURIAM:

Varian Scott appeals his convictions and sentences for conspiracy to commit health care fraud and 20 counts of health care fraud. . . . He . . . asserts that he was deprived of a fair trial because the district court admitted unreliable expert testimony concerning fingerprint examination. . . . For the reasons set forth below, we affirm Scott's convictions and sentences. . . .

During Scott's trial, the district court held a *Daubert* hearing concerning the government's expert fingerprint evidence. The fingerprint examiner, LeCroy, explained that she analyzed fingerprints using the ACE–V method, which consists of four steps: analysis, comparison, evaluation, and verification. Under the analysis step, the examiner determines if a partial, or latent, print has sufficient unique features, known as "minutia," to be compared to another fingerprint. At the comparison step, the examiner compares the latent fingerprints to a known set of fingerprints. Under the evaluation step, the examiner reaches one of three conclusions: (1) identification or individualization, meaning that both the latent prints and the inked prints were made by the same individual; (2) exclusion, meaning that the known individual did not make the latent prints; or (3) an inconclusive result. After the examiner makes an evaluation, her work is reviewed by a second examiner in the verification step. If both examiners come to the same conclusion, the results are officially reported. During her five years as a fingerprint examiner, LeCroy had made 1 technical error and 20 to 30 administrative errors.

On cross-examination, LeCroy acknowledged that there were no studies showing that latent fingerprints are unique. In certain cases, fingerprint evidence has produced incorrect identifications. Although fingerprint examiners describe their conclusions in absolute terms, there are no scientific studies as to how complete a latent print needs to be in order to be unique. Unlike DNA evidence, there is no known percentage error rate for fingerprint examination. Fingerprint examination is based on published methodologies, but it is subjective in that the comparison is being made by a human. No two prints are exactly identical. The examiner must determine whether any differences between the prints are caused by factors such as pressure or distortion or whether the two prints are actually unique. Although the ACE–V method has been in use for 15 to 20 years, it is not based on scientific or statistical studies.

The district court ruled that LeCroy's testimony was admissible under *Daubert*. . . .

In her trial testimony, LeCroy explained the ACE–V process to the jury. She stated that she detected a number of latent prints on prescription pads seized by the government, and had matched five of those latent prints to Scott's known fingerprints. Scott cross-examined LeCroy concerning the possible flaws and drawbacks of fingerprint examination. . . .

The Supreme Court has provided a non-exclusive list of factors for the district court to consider: (1) whether the expert's theory can be and has been tested; (2) whether the theory has been subjected to peer review and publication; (3) the known or potential rate of error of the particular scientific technique; and (4) whether the technique is generally accepted in the scientific community. These factors are only general guidelines, and the trial judge has "considerable leeway in deciding in a particular case how to go about determining whether particular expert testimony is reliable." *Kumho Tire.*

In this case, the district court did not abuse its discretion by admitting expert testimony concerning fingerprint examination. At the *Daubert* hearing, the government established that fingerprint testing follows a formal, established methodology. Although there is no scientifically determined error rate, the examiner's conclusions must be verified by a second examiner, which reduces, even if it does not eliminate, the potential for incorrect matches. The ACE–V method has been in use for over 20 years, and is generally accepted within the community of fingerprint experts. Based on this information, the district court did not commit an abuse of discretion by concluding that fingerprint examination is a reliable technique.

More generally, federal courts routinely have upheld the admissibility of fingerprint evidence under *Daubert*. . . . Finally, we note that Scott was able to cross-examine the government's expert at trial concerning the possible flaws in her methodology. The district court's decision to admit the fingerprint expert's testimony, subject to a searching cross-examination, did not fall outside the permissible "range of choice" in this case.

[C] Miscellaneous Evidentiary Challenges in Criminal Cases

(1) *Ballistics Evidence.* While ballistics evidence has long been permitted, there are still a number of issues that raise *Daubert* concerns, not all of which can be treated here. There are several different kinds of comparisons embraced by the term "ballistics evidence." The one in longest use has been the comparison of marks on a bullet (the head and/or casing) that was found at a crime scene or in a human body, to features of the gun and barrel from which the bullet allegedly was fired, normally belonging to the criminal defendant, in an assault or murder case. Another variety compares the mixture of metals in the head and/or casing of a bullet used in a crime with the mixture of metals in a supply of bullets (perhaps unspent) in the possession of the defendant. (The assumption is that bullets bought together share certain characteristics in this regard, perhaps having been manufactured at the same time from the same molten batch of metal.) This latter kind of ballistics analysis does not require that the actual criminal gun be found.

The Committee On Scientific Assessment Of Bullet Lead Elemental Composition Comparison, of the National Research Council of the National Academy of Sciences, issued a report in February, 2004 concerning analysis when no gun is found or bullets are too mangled to view rifling marks, but unused bullets belonging to a suspect are discovered — basically, our second variety of ballistics evidence. The FBI, which has used this technique since the 1960s, asked the Research Council for advice on how to analyze bullet lead and present the findings in court in a sound, scientific manner. The report concluded:

> Because of variations in the bullet manufacturing process, there is inadequate data to support statements that a crime scene bullet came from a particular box of ammunition or that it was manufactured on a given date. And because very limited information exists on where bullets are distributed, FBI examiners should not testify as to the probability that a crime scene bullet came from a defendant.

In view of the 40 year long use of the technique, how does this conclusion comport with the argument that testing by actual forensic practice is sufficient?

United States v. Foster, 300 F. Supp. 2d 375, 376 (D. Md. 2004), recently held, applying *Daubert*, that ballistics evidence of both varieties, including comparisons of spent cartridge casings where there was no "known" weapon recovered, was sufficiently reliable to be admissible. The microscopic analysis in question was made by one examiner and immediately confirmed by another. Does experience and this kind of confirmation ensure reliability under *Daubert/Kumho*?

(2) *Cultural Stereotyping.* The Ninth Circuit has upheld the exclusion of expert evidence from a sociologist, offered to support a criminal defendant's contention that he was smuggling drugs under duress. The sociologist would have testified that the defendant's reluctance to approach the Mexican police for help was consistent with general Mexican attitudes toward law enforcement, in view of widespread government corruption and the reach and power of Mexican drug cartels. *United States v. Verduzco*, 373 F.3d 1022 (9th Cir. 2004), agreed with the trial judge that the expert's cultural testimony was more prejudicial than probative, particularly where the defendant was an American citizen who had been educated in the United States.

Cultural evidence also fared poorly in a civil case. *Jinro America Inc. v. Secure Investments, Inc.*, 266 F.3d 993 (9th Cir. 2001), reversed a conviction that rested on cultural testimony by an investigator based in South Korea who had no education or training as a cultural expert generally, or as an expert on Korean culture specifically. Rather, he offered his impressionistic generalizations about Korean businesses based on his personal investigative experiences, his "hobby" of studying Korean business practices, unspecified input from his office staff and his marriage to a Korean woman — hardly an adequate foundation, the court felt, for the type of expert opinion he offered the jury about the alleged propensity of Korean businessmen to engage in fraudulent activity, including the avoidance of Korean currency laws. How can the reliability of cultural evidence be evaluated?

Is the evidence in these cases character evidence?

Does the evidence in this note have anything in common with any of the syndrome evidence above in Section 6:05 [C]?

(3) *Bitemarks.* Despite strong evidence of his innocence presented at trial, Krone was convicted of a capital offense based on weak circumstantial evidence bolstered by bite mark evidence on the murder victim's breast, identifying Krone as the assailant, by comparison with a cast of Krone's teeth. When bite marks are in soft tissue, as here, there is some controversy about whether such comparisons are reliable. In *State v. Krone*, 182 Ariz. 319, 897 P.2d 621 (1995), the Arizona Supreme Court's *en banc* decision ordering a retrial (for failure to disclose a videotape of the bitemark evidence to the defendant in advance) said that the physical evidence

could neither exclude nor include Krone as the perpetrator, and without the bite mark evidence the State had no case. Krone was eventually cleared by DNA analysis. Though the reliability of soft-tissue bitemark evidence is controversial, courts differ as to its admissibility. See also, on bitemarks, *State v. Swinton*, Section 12.01 [E] infra.

Lip prints and ear marks have also met with mixed reviews.

When does the presentation of this type of evidence raise ethical issues for prosecutors?

(4) *Drug Cases.* Expert testimony on a variety of issues is frequently offered by the prosecutor in these cases. *See* § 5.03, note (2). Since *Kumho*, such testimony may be challenged for lack of reliability. Most such testimony survives, typically based on the experience of the testifying officer. *See, e.g., United States v. Hankey*, 203 F.3d 1160 (9th Cir. 2000) (police gang expert testifying about gang's code of silence). However, a few of the more subjective expert opinions have failed *Daubert.* For example, *United States v. Hermanek*, 289 F.3d 1076 (9th Cir. 2002), *cert. denied*, 537 U.S. 1223 (2003), held it was error (albeit harmless) for an agent to offer interpretations of words and phrases he encountered for the first time in this case as referring to cocaine. The offer of proof described only the method for interpreting words "commonly used" in the drug trade — i.e., words with which he was "familiar." It therefore offered no basis for assessing the reliability of his interpretation of words and phrases encountered for the first time in this case.

Similarly, in *United States v. Cruz*, 363 F.3d 187 (2d Cir. 2004), expert testimony by a Drug Enforcement Administration agent, stating that the defendant's explanation that he had been asked to "watch [a drug dealer's] back while he did business" meant that he was participating in countersurveillance for the dealer with knowledge of the nature of the deal, constituted overreaching and therefore was inadmissible under *Daubert.* The interpreted phrase was ambiguous and thus outside the ambit of the agent's "drug jargon" expertise, and the government had also failed to identify him as expert. *Cruz* also held that even with the disputed testimony, the evidence was insufficient. Are courts more likely to find *Daubert* violations when they do not affect the outcome of the case?

It has been widely noted that civil litigants fare better on *Daubert* challenges than do criminal defendants. What are some of the possible reasons for this difference?

(5) *Knife Mark Identification.* In *Ramirez v. State*, 810 So. 2d 836 (Fla. 2001), the Supreme Court of Florida held that an expert's procedure for identifying knife marks left on the victim's body from microscopic examination was not generally accepted by scientists active in the field and that the knife mark identification evidence was thus inadmissible to establish the particular knife as the murder weapon. In addition, the court said, disinterested and impartial testimony is needed to establish general scientific recognition under the *Frye* test. While Florida still adheres to the *Frye* test of "general acceptance," it measured this particular technique at least in part by how well the toolmark expert's technique did on the *Daubert* factors — a practice that many *Frye* states now follow.

§ 6.07 MATHEMATICAL PROBABILITY EVIDENCE[9]

PEOPLE v. COLLINS

California Supreme Court
68 Cal. 2d 319, 438 P.2d 33 (1968)

SULLIVAN, JUSTICE.

A jury found defendant Malcolm Ricardo Collins and his wife, defendant Janet Louise Collins, guilty of second degree robbery. Malcolm appeals from the judgment of conviction.

About 11:30 a.m. Mrs. Juanita Brooks, who had been shopping, was walking home along an alley in the San Pedro area of the City of Los Angeles. As she stooped down to pick up an empty carton, she was suddenly pushed to the ground by a person whom she neither saw nor heard approach. She was stunned by the fall and felt some pain. She managed to look up and saw a young woman running from the scene. According to Mrs. Brooks the latter appeared to weigh about 145 pounds, was wearing "something dark," and had hair "between a dark blond and a light blond," but lighter than the color of defendant Janet Collins' hair as it appeared at trial. Immediately after the incident, Mrs. Brooks discovered that her purse, containing between $35 and $40, was missing.

About the same time as the robbery, John Bass, who lived on the street at the end of the alley, was in front of his house watering his lawn. As he looked in that direction, he saw a woman run out of the alley and enter a yellow automobile parked across the street from him. Bass then saw that it was being driven by a male Negro, wearing a mustache and beard. At the trial Bass identified defendant as the driver of the yellow automobile. However, an attempt was made to impeach his identification by his admission that at the preliminary hearing he testified to an uncertain identification at the police lineup when defendant was beardless.

In his testimony Bass described the woman who ran from the alley as a Caucasian, slightly over five feet tall, of ordinary build, with her hair in a dark blond ponytail, and wearing dark clothing. He further testified that her ponytail was "just like" one which Janet had in a police photograph.

Janet was employed as a housemaid in San Pedro. Her employer testified that she had arrived for work at 8:50 a.m. and that defendant had picked her up in a light yellow car about 11:30 a.m. Janet was wearing her hair in a blonde ponytail but lighter in color than it appeared at trial.

There was evidence from which it could be inferred that defendants had ample time to drive from Janet's place of employment and participate in the robbery.

Officer Kinsey, who was investigating the robbery, went to defendants' home. Janet, whose hair appeared to be a dark blonde, was wearing it in a ponytail. Malcolm did not have a beard.

---

[9] Study Guide Reference: Evidence in a Nutshell, Chapter 3:I, at "Statistical Probabilities: A Particular Problem of Relevancy."

According to the officer, Malcolm stated that he sometimes wore a beard but that he did not wear a beard on June 18 (the day of the robbery), having shaved it off on June 2.

The victim could not identify Janet and had never seen defendant. The identification by the witness Bass, who observed the girl run out of the alley and get into the automobile, was incomplete as to Janet and may have been weakened as to defendant. There was also evidence, introduced by the defense, that Janet had worn light-colored clothing on the day in question, but both the victim and Bass testified that the girl they observed had worn dark clothing.

[T]he prosecutor called an instructor of mathematics at a state college. Through this witness he sought to establish that, assuming the robbery was committed by a Caucasian woman with a blond ponytail who left the scene accompanied by a Negro with a beard and mustache, there was an overwhelming probability that the crime was committed by any couple answering such distinctive characteristics. The witness testified, in substance, to the "product rule," which states that the probability of the joint occurrence of a number of *mutually independent* events is equal to the product of the individual probabilities that each of the events will occur. *Without presenting any statistical evidence whatsoever in support of the probabilities for the factors selected*, the prosecutor then proceeded to have the witness *assume* probability factors for the various characteristics which he deemed to be shared by the guilty couple and all other couples answering to such distinctive characteristics.[10]

Applying the product rule to his own factors the prosecutor arrived at a probability that there was but one chance in 12 million that any couple possessed the distinctive characteristics of the defendants. Accordingly, under this theory, it was to be inferred that there could be but one chance in 12 million that defendants

---

[10] Although the prosecutor insisted that the factors [i.e., numbers — Eds.] he used were only for illustrative purposes — to demonstrate how the probability of the occurrence of mutually independent factors affected the probability that they would occur together — he nevertheless attempted to use factors which he personally related to the distinctive characteristics of defendants. In his argument to the jury he invited the jurors to apply their own factors, and asked defense counsel to suggest what the latter would deem as reasonable. The prosecutor himself proposed the individual probabilities set out in the table below. Although the transcript of the examination of the mathematics instructor and the information volunteered by the prosecutor at that time create some uncertainty as to precisely which of the characteristics the prosecutor assigned to the individual probabilities, he restated in his argument to the jury that they should be as follows:

Individual Probability	Characteristic
1/10	A. Partly yellow automobile
1/4	B. Man with mustache
1/10	C. Girl with ponytail
1/3	D. Girl with blond hair
1/10	E. Negro man with beard
1/1000	F. Interracial couple in car

In his brief on appeal defendant agrees that the foregoing appeared on a table presented in the trial court.

were innocent and that another equally distinctive couple actually committed the robbery. Expanding on what he had thus purported to suggest as a hypothesis, the prosecutor offered the completely unfounded and improper testimonial assertion that, in his opinion, the factors he had assigned were "conservative estimates" and that, in reality "the chances of anyone else besides these defendants being there, having every similarity, is somewhat like one in a billion."

Both defendants took the stand in their own behalf. They denied any knowledge of or participation in the crime and stated that after Malcolm called for Janet at her employer's house they went directly to a friend's house in Los Angeles where they remained for some time. According to this testimony defendants were not near the scene of the robbery when it occurred. Defendants' friend testified to a visit by them "in the middle of June" although she could not recall the precise date.

[T]he specific technique presented through the mathematician's testimony and advanced by the prosecutor to measure the probabilities in question suffered from two basic and pervasive defects — an inadequate evidentiary foundation and an inadequate proof of statistical independence. First, as to the foundation requirement, we find the record devoid of any evidence relating to any of the six individual probability factors used by the prosecutor and ascribed by him to the six characteristics as we have set them out in footnote 10, *ante*. To put it another way, the prosecution produced no evidence whatsoever showing, or from which it could be in any way inferred, that only one out of every ten cars which might have been at the scene of the robbery was partly yellow, that only one out of every four men who might have been there wore a mustache, that only one out of every ten girls who might have been there wore a ponytail, or that any of the other individual probability factors listed were even roughly accurate.

The bare, inescapable fact is that the prosecution made no attempt to offer any such evidence. Instead, through leading questions having perfunctorily elicited from the witness the response that the latter could not assign a probability factor for the characteristics involved, the prosecutor himself suggested what the various probabilities should be and these became the basis of the witness' testimony. It is a curious circumstance of this adventure in proof that the prosecutor not only made his own assertions of these factors in the hope that they were "conservative" but also in later argument to the jury invited the jurors to substitute their "estimates" should they wish to do so. We can hardly conceive of a more fatal gap in the prosecution's scheme of proof. A foundation for the admissibility of the witness' testimony was never even attempted to be laid, let alone established. His testimony was neither made to rest on his own testimonial knowledge nor presented by proper hypothetical questions based upon valid data in the record. [See] *Evidence: Admission of Mathematical Probability Statistics Held Erroneous for Want of Demonstration of Validity* (1967) DUKE L.J. 665, 675-678. In [*State v. Sneed*, 414 P.2d 858 (N.M. 1966)], the court reversed a conviction based on probabilistic evidence, stating: "We hold that mathematical odds are not admissible as evidence to identify a defendant in a criminal proceeding *so long as the odds are based on estimates, the validity of which have* [*sic*] *not been demonstrated.*" (Italics added.)

But, as we have indicated, there was another glaring defect in the prosecution's technique, namely an inadequate proof of the statistical independence of the six factors. No proof was presented that the characteristics selected were mutually independent, even though the witness himself acknowledged that such condition was essential to the proper application of the "product rule" or "multiplication rule." (See Note, *supra*, DUKE L.J. 665, 669-670, fn. 25.) To the extent that the traits or characteristics were not mutually independent (e.g. Negroes with beards and men with mustaches obviously represent overlapping categories, the "product rule" would inevitably yield a wholly erroneous and exaggerated result even if all of the individual components had been determined with precision. (Siegel, Nonparametric Statistics for the Behavioral Sciences (1956) 19; see generally Harmon, Modern Factor Analysis (1960).)

In the instant case, therefore, because of the aforementioned two defects — the inadequate evidentiary foundation and the inadequate proof of statistical independence — the technique employed by the prosecutor could only lead to wild conjecture without demonstrated relevancy to the issues presented. It acquired no redeeming quality from the prosecutor's statement that it was being used only "for illustrative purposes" since, as we shall point out, the prosecutor's subsequent utilization of the mathematical testimony was not confined within such limits.

We now turn to the [next] fundamental error caused by the probability testimony. Quite apart from our foregoing objections to the specific technique employed by the prosecution to estimate the probability in question, we think that the entire enterprise upon which the prosecution embarked, and which was directed to the objective of measuring the likelihood of a random couple possessing the characteristics allegedly distinguishing the robbers, was gravely misguided. At best, it might yield an estimate as to how infrequently bearded Negroes drive yellow cars in the company of blonde females with ponytails.

The prosecution's approach, however, could furnish the jury with absolutely no guidance on the crucial issue. *Of the admittedly few such couples, which one, if any, was guilty of committing this robbery?* Probability theory necessarily remains silent on that question, since no mathematical equation can prove beyond a reasonable doubt (1) that the guilty couple *in fact* possessed the characteristics described by the People's witnesses, or even (2) that only *one* couple possessing those distinctive characteristics could be found in the entire Los Angeles area.

[W]e observe that the prosecution's theory of probability rested on the assumption that the witnesses called by the People had conclusively established that the guilty couple possessed the precise characteristics relied upon by the prosecution. But no mathematical formula could ever establish beyond a reasonable doubt that the prosecution's witnesses correctly observed and accurately described the distinctive features which were employed to link defendants to the crime. Conceivably, for example, the guilty couple might have included a light-skinned Negress with bleached hair rather than a Caucasian blonde; or the driver of the car might have been wearing a false beard as a disguise; or the prosecution's witnesses might simply have been unreliable.

The foregoing risks of error permeate the prosecution's circumstantial case. Traditionally, the jury weighs such risks in evaluating the credibility and probative value of trial testimony, but the likelihood of human error or of falsification obviously cannot be quantified; that likelihood must therefore be excluded from any effort to assign a *number* to the probability of guilt or innocence. Confronted with an equation which purports to yield a numerical index of probable guilt, few juries could resist the temptation to accord disproportionate weight to that index; only an exceptional juror, and indeed only a defense attorney schooled in mathematics, could successfully keep in mind the fact that the probability computed by the prosecution can represent, *at best*, the likelihood that a random couple would share the characteristics testified to by the People's witnesses — *not necessarily the characteristics of the actually guilty couple.*

[E]ven assuming that failing could be discounted, the most a mathematical computation could ever yield would be a measure of the probability that a random couple would possess the distinctive features in question. In the present case, for example, the prosecution attempted to compute the probability that a random couple would include a bearded Negro, a blonde girl with a ponytail, and a partly yellow car; the prosecution urged that this probability was no more than one in 12 million. Even accepting this conclusion as arithmetically accurate, however, one still could not conclude that the Collinses were probably the guilty couple. On the contrary, as we explain in the Appendix, the prosecution's figures actually imply a likelihood of over 40 percent that the Collinses could be "duplicated" by at least one other couple who might equally have committed the San Pedro robbery. Urging that the Collinses be convicted on the basis of evidence which logically establishes no more than this seems as indefensible as arguing for the conviction of X on the ground that a witness saw either X or X's twin commit the crime.

Again, few defense attorneys, and certainly few jurors, could be expected to comprehend this basic flaw in the prosecution's analysis. Conceivably even the prosecutor erroneously believed that his equation established a high probability that no other bearded Negro in the Los Angeles area drove a yellow car accompanied by a ponytailed blonde. In any event, although his technique could demonstrate no such thing, he solemnly told the jury that he had supplied mathematical proof of guilt.

Sensing the novelty of that notion, the prosecutor told the jurors that the traditional idea of proof beyond a reasonable doubt represented "the most hackneyed, stereotyped, trite, misunderstood concept in criminal law." He sought to reconcile the jury to the risk that, under his "new math" approach to criminal jurisprudence, "on some rare occasion . . . an innocent person may be convicted." "Without taking that risk," the prosecution continued, "life would be intolerable . . . because . . . there would be immunity for the Collinses, for people who chose not to be employed to go down and push old ladies down and take their money and be immune because how could we ever be sure they are the ones who did it?"

In essence, this argument of the prosecutor was calculated to persuade the jury to convict defendants whether or not they were convinced of their guilt to a moral certainty and beyond a reasonable doubt. Undoubtedly the jurors were unduly impressed by the mystique of the mathematical demonstration but were unable to assess its relevancy or value. Although we make no appraisal of the proper applications of mathematical techniques in the proof of facts, we have strong feelings that such applications, particularly in a criminal case, must be critically examined in view of the substantial unfairness to a defendant which may result from ill conceived techniques with which the trier of fact is not technically equipped to cope.

In the light of the closeness of the case [the jury took a long time and cast many ballots], which as we have said was a circumstantial one, there is a reasonable likelihood that the result would have been more favorable to defendant. [T]he "trial by mathematics" so distorted the role of the jury and so disadvantaged counsel for the defense, as to constitute in itself a miscarriage of justice. The judgment against defendant must therefore be reversed.

NOTES AND QUESTIONS

(1) *How Far does Collins Extend?* Does *Collins, supra,* mean that any evidence that is based on the improbability or unlikelihood (but not impossibility) of someone other than defendant having committed the crime is inadmissible? That any evidence that only narrows the class of persons to which the criminal belongs to a class to which the defendant belongs is inadmissible? That any evidence based on the improbability or unlikelihood of several factors coalescing in more than one individual is inadmissible? That any evidence based on the fact that only a small number of individuals would display a combination of features displayed by the defendant is inadmissible?

(2) *Comparison with Other Forensic Evidence Relying on Probability.* How does the evidence in *Collins* differ from the population statistics probability evidence in the DNA cases above? Indeed, how does it differ from the population frequencies, or the probabilities, involved in standard serology (A, B, O etc. blood-type) evidence, handwriting evidence, fingerprint evidence, tool mark evidence, bite mark evidence, typewriter identification evidence, or any other forensic evidence that relies on the unlikelihood or coincidentality of another person than the defendant being possessed of a rather unique combination of factors found to belong to him or in his possession? Could a person be convicted of a bombing on the basis of his possession (in his workshop) of the exact combination of materials found (in an after-the-explosion investigation) to have been in the bomb that caused the explosion? Would the evidence that those materials were found in both the bomb and the workshop be inadmissible because the strength of the inference of guilt depends upon the degree of rarity of people possessing such a combination of materials in their workshop? Does almost all reasoning about any evidence whatsoever, involve probabilities? For example, even if it is conceded that a particular threatening letter to the murder victim came from a particular typewriter, aren't there going to have to be probability estimates based on how many people may have had access to the typewriter, and the likelihoods of a threatener carrying out the threat?

(3) *What will Jurors do Without Probability Estimates?* In *Collins, supra,* even if the expert evidence in question there is excluded, won't the jury inevitably have to form some estimate of the probabilities of more than one couple displaying the characteristics displayed by the defendant couple? Is the jury's undisciplined guess as to the probabilities better than the expert's? Does *Collins* mean that explicit giving, in testimony, of probability figures is what is forbidden?

(6) *Are Statistics Permissible in Prosecution for Multiple SIDS Deaths in Same Family Where the Dead Children are Genetically Related?* When one child dies of Sudden Infant Death Syndrome (SIDS) it is a tragedy. When two children in a family die of SIDS, particularly when the father has a life insurance policy for each, and they die the first time he takes care of them alone, the question is whether it is murder, despite an initial SIDS diagnosis. In *Wilson v. State*, 370 Md. 191, 803 A.2d 1034 (2002), the trial judge permitted the State to use statistical data and a product rule computation to prove the improbability of two Sudden Infant Death Syndrome ("SIDS") deaths in a single family to bolster the state's otherwise weak case. Judge Raker, writing for Maryland's highest court reversed the conviction. The following evidence (according to the opinion) was offered at trial:

Dr. Kokes testified that "[t]he death rate from Sudden Infant Death Syndrome back in 1987 was somewhere between 1 to 2 deaths for every 1,000 live births." He also noted that Garret had cerebral swelling, a condition that effects less than one percent of children who die from SIDS. Employing the product rule, Dr. Kokes multiplied the probability of a child's dying of SIDS and the probability of a SIDS death involving cerebral swelling. He concluded that "the mathematical possibility of having a SIDS death occurring with cerebral swelling would be 1 in 100,000 live births." Dr. Kokes then took into account the fact that Garrett was the second child in the family to die of SIDS. He multiplied the probability of Garrett's dying from SIDS, 1 in 100,000, by the probability of Brandi's dying of SIDS, 1 in 1,000. He concluded that the probability that Garrett died from SIDS was 1 in 100,000,000.

Dr. Norton also testified as to the probability that Garrett died of SIDS. Dr. Norton relied on different statistics that indicated that SIDS occurs in 1 infant out of every 2,000 live births. Dr. Norton employed the product rule and concluded that the probability of two SIDS deaths occurring in one family is 1 in 2,000 multiplied by 1 in 2,000, or 1 in 4,000,000.

During rebuttal closing argument, the State's Attorney referred to the statistics that the experts relied on in forming their opinion that Garrett's death was criminal homicide, and argued the probability of petitioner's innocence. The State's Attorney did not merely argue that there was a low probability that two SIDS deaths would occur in one family; he argued that there was a low probability that petitioner was innocent. He told the jury, "[i]f you multiply his numbers, instead of 1 in 4 million, you get 1 in 10 million that the man sitting here is innocent."

In reversing the conviction, the court said:

> In light of the widespread disagreement as to the causes of SIDS, we are unable to find general acceptance of the notion that there is no genetic component to SIDS. Unanimity is not required for general acceptance, but it is clear to us that a genuine controversy exists within the relevant scientific community. In sum, there was inadequate proof of the statistical independence of SIDS deaths within a single family. Therefore the product rule should not be employed in calculating the likelihood of multiple SIDS deaths within a single family. See *People v. Collins.* The curative instruction was found not to solve the prejudice caused by the prosecutor's misuse of the statistics.The courts that have considered this issue have concluded that

it is impermissible to assign a number to the probability of guilt or innocence. [As *Collins* said:]

> Confronted with an equation which purports to yield a numerical index of probable guilt, few juries could resist the temptation to accord disproportionate weight to that index; only an exceptional juror, and indeed only a defense attorney schooled in mathematics, could successfully keep in mind the fact that the probability computed by the prosecution can represent, at best, the likelihood that a random couple would share the characteristics testified to by the People's witnesses — not necessarily the characteristics of the actually guilty couple.'

In *State v. Harbold* (Ill. 1984), the court stated:

> Testimony expressing opinions or conclusions in terms of statistical probabilities can make the uncertain seem all but proven, and suggest, by quantification, satisfaction of the requirement that guilt be established 'beyond a reasonable doubt.' We believe that testimony to statistical probabilities encouraged the jury to disregard evidential risks traditionally weighed in determining guilt or innocence, and focused unfairly upon a numerical conclusion. As such, we find that the testimony violated one of the primary requirements of expert opinion, that the opinion be an aid to the jury. In light of the closeness of this circumstantial case, we cannot say that this improper testimony, which gave a false impression of precision in the measurement of guilt, did not affect the jury's deliberations.

(7) *Overseas Experience.* Several cases have been reversed in England based on similar unreliable statistics introduced in cases where more than one SIDS death occurred in a family. SIDS is called "cot death" there. In one case, the prosecution's expert squared 8,500, the chance of a single cot death to arrive at a one in 73 million chance that two of the defendants' babies could have died naturally. More than 5000 cases of newborn babies taken away from their parents merely because previous babies had died have been attempted to be reviewed. *See The Probability of Injustice*, The Economist 13 (Jan. 24, 2004).

Chapter 7

THE HEARSAY RULE

BASIC HEARSAY (F.R.E. ARTICLE VIII, RULE 801(a)–(c))

§ 7.01 CONCEPT OF HEARSAY AND ITS RATIONALE[1]

Read Federal Rules of Evidence 801(a), (b), and (c), "Definitions (Hearsay)" and 802, "Hearsay Rule."

[A] Introduction

For the derivation of the ban against hearsay, see generally 1 J. STEPHEN, A HISTORY OF THE CRIMINAL LAW OF ENGLAND 326 (1883). A famous example is provided by the trial of Sir Walter Raleigh for treason in 1603. A crucial element of the evidence against him consisted of the out-of-court statements of one Cobham, implicating Raleigh in a plot to seize the throne. Raleigh had since received a written retraction from Cobham, and believed that Cobham would now testify in his favor. After a lengthy dispute over Raleigh's right to have Cobham called as a witness, Cobham was not called, and Raleigh was convicted. At least one author traces the Confrontation Clause to the reaction of the common law to these abuses at the Raleigh trial.

When a witness testifies to a statement made by someone else (D, the declarant), the hearsay concerns revolve around our inability to probe the declarant's perception, memory, sincerity and narration. In other words, we do not know if D was mistaken, lying, joking, had a faulty memory, misspoke, misunderstood something, or made an ambiguous reference. Our distrust of hearsay is centered on the absence of cross-examination in a courtroom setting where D must testify under oath and in the presence of jurors who can evaluate D's demeanor in assessing the weight to give the statement.

For more on the basic concept of hearsay, see Garland, *An Overview of Relevance and Hearsay: A Nine Step Analytical Guide*, 22 Sw. U. L. Rev. 1039 (1993); Graham, *"Stickperson Hearsay": A Simplified Approach to Understanding the Rule Against Hearsay*, 1982 U. ILL. L. REV. 887 (1982); Park, *McCormick on Evidence and the Concept of Hearsay: A Critical Analysis Followed by Suggestions to Law Teachers*, 65 MINN. L. REV. 423 (1981); Tribe, *Triangulating Hearsay*, 87 HARV. L. REV. 957 (1974); Younger, *Reflections on the Rule Against Hearsay*, 32 S.C. L. REV. 281 (1980).

---

[1] Study Guide Reference: Evidence in a Nutshell, Chapter 8:I & II.

[B] Elements of Basic Hearsay: Statement, Other than by Witness Now Testifying, Offered to Prove Truth of Matter Asserted

LEAKE v. HAGERT

North Dakota Supreme Court
175 N.W.2d 675 (1970)

PAULSON, JUDGE.

[Plaintiff Leake appealed from a verdict dismissing his complaint, based on personal injury and property damage allegations that defendant Hagert negligently drove her automobile into the rear of a plow being towed by a tractor that Leake was operating. Hagert counterclaimed, maintaining that the sole and proximate cause of the collision was Leake's negligence in operating his vehicle "upon a public highway after sunset, without proper lights, reflectors, or other warnings." Leake argues that the trial court erred in admitting, over his objection, testimony of an adjuster (Gross) who investigated the accident.]

Gross testified that Allen Leake's son told him, with reference to the small rear light on the tractor, that the red lens had been out for some time. Edward Gross's testimony concerning the statement of Allen Leake's son was hearsay.

The hearsay rule prohibits use of a person's assertion as equivalent to testimony of the fact asserted, unless the assertor is brought to testify in court on the stand, where he may be probed and cross-examined as to the grounds of his assertion and his qualifications to make it.

Leake's son did not testify in the present action; he was not a party to the action; his statement was not made under oath; his statement was not subject to cross-examination; and he was not available as a witness because he was overseas. We find that it was error for the trial court to admit into evidence the testimony concerning what Leake's son said to Edward Gross; the son's statement was hearsay and should have been excluded.

NOTE

Query on Nature of the Out-of-Court Statement: Would it matter if the statement had been written or sworn?

CREAGHE v. IOWA HOME MUTUAL CASUALTY CO.

United States Court of Appeals, Tenth Circuit
323 F.2d 981 (1963)

SETH, CIRCUIT JUDGE.

The plaintiff-appellant has an unsatisfied judgment against Muril J. Osborn obtained in a damage action which arose from a collision between the plaintiff's car and Osborn's truck. In the case at bar, appellant alleges that the appellee insurance company was the insurer of Osborn's truck at the time of the accident, and seeks to collect this judgment from it. The appellee admits that at one time it issued a liability policy to Osborn, but asserts that he cancelled it shortly before the accident. Osborn was not a party to this suit and did not appear as a witness.

When one of appellee's agents wrote the policy, Osborn sent the agent a check for a part of the balance due [on the premium] after the initial payment, but it was returned by the bank marked insufficient funds. The agent testified that he called Osborn about the check, and was told by Osborn that he was going to cancel the insurance and would come by to pick up the returned check. Osborn did come to the agent's office and, in the presence of the agent, stated he wanted the insurance cancelled immediately. The check was returned to Osborn.

Appellant challenges the [admission of the agent's testimony] as to what was said by the insured, on the occasion when he came to the agent's office to receive back the check[, as] hearsay.

The hearsay rule does not exclude relevant testimony as to what the contracting parties said with respect to the making or the terms of an oral agreement. The presence or absence of such words and statements of themselves are part of the issues in the case. This use of such testimony does not require a reliance by the jury or the judge upon the competency of the person who originally made the statements for the truth of their content. Neither the truth of the statements nor their accuracy are then involved. [W]e are not concerned with whether the insured was truthful or not when he told the agent he wanted the policy cancelled and that he did not need it any more. It is enough for the issues here presented to determine only whether or not he made such statements to the agent. The fact that these statements were made was testified to by the agent, and his competency and truthfulness as to this testimony was subject to testing through cross-examination by counsel for appellant. [A]n oral termination of a written contract [is like] the formation of an oral agreement. The reasons for the rule permitting such testimony are the same.

Courts have uniformly held that conversations as to the making and the terms of oral agreements may be testified to by any person who heard them. For example, in *Young v. State Farm Mutual Automobile Insurance Co.*, 244 F.2d 333 (4th Cir. 1957), the action was against an insurer on an automobile policy. The questioned testimony was by insurer's agent as to a conversation between the insured and a person driving insured's car. The court held the testimony was not hearsay and was admissible to prove the understanding as to the permitted use of the car by the driver. [T]his issue could only be proved by the statements of the parties to the transaction. Thus, as in the case at bar, testimony of a party present was offered to prove an oral agreement by relating the conversation of the contracting parties.

Affirmed.

NOTES AND QUESTIONS

(1) *Solicitation as Nonhearsay: Not for "Truth."* In *Los Robles Motor Lodge, Inc. v. Department of Alcoholic Beverage Control*, 54 Cal. Rptr. 547 (Cal. Ct. App. 1966), the rationale explained in *Creaghe* was utilized to admit the testimony of two

state investigators as to conversations they had with two females at the Motor Lodge in which the females solicited the agents for sexual acts. The solicitation was grounds for revocation of the Lodge's license.

(2) *False Impersonation as Nonhearsay: Not for "Truth."* In *United States v. Bankston*, 603 F.2d 528 (5th Cir. 1979), a case involving charges of conspiracy to kidnap and sell into prostitution, a statement (to police investigating the case) by one of the alleged conspirators (a woman) — that she was Patricia Krauss (the kidnapped woman) and that the little girl with her (also kidnapped) was her daughter — was held admissible. The statement was admitted not for its truth, but as an act constituting execution of the conspiracy and also showing guilty knowledge or concealment.

(3) *Statement Showing Knowledge or Warning as Nonhearsay: Not for "Truth."* In *Morgan v. Consolidated Rail Corp.*, 509 F. Supp. 281 (S.D.N.Y. 1980), statements made in Senate hearings that there was a problem across the country with items being thrown by passengers out of windows of moving trains were admitted in a suit against a railroad for an injury from a bottle so thrown. The theory was that the statements, whether true or false, should have been known to the defendant and that the defendant thereby should have been alerted to the problem. *See also Safeway Stores, Inc. v. Combs*, 273 F.2d 295 (5th Cir. 1960) (woman fell in spilled ketchup; manager's wife heard husband say immediately prior to the incident, "Lady, please don't step in that ketchup"; words were admissible as warning).

FERRARA v. GALLUCHIO

New York Court of Appeals
5 N.Y.2d 16, 176 N.Y.S.2d 996, 152 N.E.2d 249 (1958)

CONWAY, CHIEF JUDGE.

Plaintiff wife, who was suffering from bursitis in the right shoulder, received a series of X-ray treatments from defendants, doctors specializing in X-ray therapy. After the third treatment she experienced a nauseous feeling. [Despite her continued complaints, defendants continued the treatments.] Subsequent thereto, the shoulder began to itch, turned pink, then red, and blisters formed. These blisters ruptured and the skin peeled, leaving the raw flesh of the shoulder exposed. Scabs formed leaving the shoulder with a permanently marginated area of skin. This condition was diagnosed as chronic radiodermatitis which was caused by the X-ray therapy.

[Approximately] two years after the treatments, the plaintiff was referred by her attorney to a dermatologist for examination. [He] advised the plaintiff to have her shoulder checked every six months inasmuch as the area of the burn might become cancerous.

The instant action is for malpractice. Plaintiff introduced, on the issue of mental anguish, the testimony of a neuro-psychiatrist to the effect that she was suffering from a severe cancerophobia [sic] is, the phobic apprehension that she would ultimately develop cancer in the site of the radiation burn. The witness further testified that she might have permanent symptoms of anxiety.

The jury rendered a verdict in favor of plaintiffs.

The plaintiff's statement that the dermatologist told her she should have the shoulder checked every six months because there was a possibility that cancer might develop was not adduced to establish the fact that the site of the burn might become cancerous. As her attorney said at the trial, "we are not making any claim that this person is going to sustain a cancer. We are going on a neurosis." Since the statement of the dermatologist was introduced not for the purpose of proving that plaintiff would develop cancer but merely for the purpose of establishing that there was a basis for her mental anxiety, such testimony was not objectionable hearsay.

[*Affirmed.*]

NOTES AND QUESTIONS

(1) *Offering the Diagnostic Statement in Ferrara to Prove Not Just Fear of Cancer but also the Likelihood of Cancer.* Would the challenged evidence in *Ferrara* have been inadmissible had the plaintiff, *in addition* to the cancerophobia claim, alleged that she would sustain a cancer as a result of the radiation burn?

(2) *Background and "Truth of the Matter Asserted."* Is testimony of a police radio call, describing an assailant, hearsay when admitted as "background" for the officers' actions? *See United States v. Sallins*, 993 F.2d 344 (3d Cir. 1993) (reversible error); compare *United States v. Inadi*, 475 U.S. 387, n.11 (1986), where Justice Powell refers to a telephone conversation between co-conspirators as "not introduced in order to prove the truth of the matters asserted, but as background for the conspiracy, or to explain the significance of certain events."

(3) *Rule 403 Balancing (Because These Cases Involve Both Permissible Non-Hearsay and Prohibited Hearsay).* Fed. R. Evid. 403 can play any role in the judge's decision to admit background facts. For example, in *United States v. Williams*, 358 F.3d 956 (D.C. Cir. 2004), the court rejected evidence offered as background because of the considerable prejudicial effect of the police officers' testimony that they apprehended the defendant on the basis of information provided by non-testifying complaining witnesses who claimed that they had been robbed at gunpoint. The defendant was charged with being a felon in possession of a firearm. Aside from an officer's observation of the defendant tossing an unidentified object as the officer pursued him, there was no evidence connecting defendant to the handgun in question, and the prosecution easily could have explained the context of the events in question without referring to the robbery suspects as armed. In *Williams*, the failure of counsel to object to the evidence resulted in a remand to determine whether the defendant had been given ineffective assistance of counsel.

MAHONE v. LEHMAN

United States Court of Appeals, Ninth Circuit
347 F.3d 1170 (2003)

ALARCÓN, CIRCUIT JUDGE.

Mr. Mahone, [the plaintiff in this civil rights action,] seeks reversal of the judgment entered in favor of each of the [defendants] following a trial by jury. In his pro se complaint, Mr. Mahone alleged that, while an inmate at Washington State's Clallam Bay Correctional Center prison, [because he had torn up his cell in what he says was a fit of temporary insanity], he was placed [naked] in solitary confinement in a bare strip cell, [for 10 days, at a temperature of 50-55 degrees], without clothing, property, [toilet paper, shower, sink, or other way to wash himself, and without any blanket or mattress for sleeping on the stone slab bed,] or regular access to running [or drinking] water, in violation of the Eighth Amendment. Mr. Mahone contends that the district court committed prejudicial error in admitting hearsay evidence.

During the cross-examination of [Plaintiff] Mahone, defense counsel asked the following question: "Mr. Mahone, have you received any diagnosis from any mental health provider or therapist regarding mental and emotional suffering [concerning the stay in the bare cell]?" Mr. Mahone replied: "Yes. . . ." [Defense] counsel than posed the following question: "Can you tell the jury what you've been diagnosed as?" Mr. Mahone's counsel objected on the ground that the question called for hearsay. Before defense counsel could respond, the court stated: "he knows what he's been seeing a doctor for, so he can say." Mr. Mahone responded to defense counsel's question as follows:

> Well, I was interviewed by some Western State Hospital staff. . . . The Western State Hospital psychiatrist — it was about three and one student — came to diagnose me, and they said that they believed that I was faking it, and then they [said] I was an anti-sociopathic, something, something. In other words, in the beginning they said that my symptoms that I was experiencing was a fake, that I was lying. And then the last part of their diagnosis, they diagnosed some type of mental illness actually, and it was something to the effect of anti-sociopathic behavior, something, something, big collegiate words, psychiatric collegiate words. I can't say them all.

Mr. Mahone's counsel renewed his hearsay objection to the question, moved to strike the answer, and requested that the jury be admonished to disregard it. The court did not expressly rule on the renewed objection or the motions. Instead, the court stated: "Well, he doesn't have to go into any hearsay. He can just answer why he went to see the doctor." In light of the fact that Mr. Mahone's response was already before the jury, the court's failure to grant the motion to strike the answer because it contained inadmissible hearsay is incomprehensible.

We are persuaded that the district court erred as a matter of law in concluding that the therapist's diagnosis of Mr. Mahone's mental state was not hearsay. In defending the district court's ruling on admissibility, [defendants] argue that the extra-judicial diagnosis was admissible "to establish whether or not Mr. Mahone was justified in claiming significant mental trauma" resulting from the conditions of his confinement in the strip cell.

[A]n extra-judicial statement is hearsay and inadmissible when the immediate inference the proponent wants to draw is the truth of an assertion on the statement's face. . . . The [offering attorney in *Orr*, an earlier case relied on by the appeals court here,] argued that the out-of-court statements made by a third party were solicited [i.e. put into evidence] by the [offering attorney] so that the jury could [ultimately] draw a particular inference [different from anything actually said by the third party]. We held in *Orr* that, "[a]lthough [the evidence] was not offered [ultimately] to prove the truth of the matter asserted [by the third party], it [was] nonetheless hearsay" because the inference the [offering attorney] sought to draw, "depend[ed] on the truth of [the third party's] statement. . . ." [citing Fed.R.Evid. 801(c) and cases].

[Defendants] have conceded that the extra-judicial statement was offered to prove that Mr. Mahone "was not justified in claiming significant mental trauma." The jury could only draw this inference, however, if it believed the therapist's opinion that Mr. Mahone was lying. . . . [W]e conclude that the district court erred in admitting the therapist's opinion [and that it was prejudicial error because of its likely effect on the jury's assessment of Mr. Mahone's credibility].

[Reversed.]

NOTES AND QUESTIONS

(1) *Limits to Counsel's Manipulation: "Thin" or "Ruse" Purposes and Analyzing the Offered Chain of Inference.* As you can see from the cases in this section, the name of the game is for offering counsel to come up with some relevant purpose that is not "for the truth of the matter asserted by the declarant." But, as this case (*Mahone*) and our two-claim variant of *Ferrara*, above, suggest, there are limits to what counsel can do in this regard, some of which follow.

(2) *Occasional Rejection of Independent Relevant Purpose. Ferrara* itself, above (preceding *Mahone*), involving the *single* claim of cancerphobia from the X-ray burn, suggests that courts normally let the evidence in if *any* non-hearsay purpose that is relevant (and independent of any hearsay purpose) can be dredged up by offering counsel — despite other more obvious hearsay uses that might be made of the evidence, which the court will instruct the jury against (see F.R.E. 105). The *two-claim variant* of *Ferrara* that we have put in after *Ferrara* should suggest to you that sometimes (though rarely, in the hearsay area) the offered proper, non-hearsay, independent purpose, though relevant, may be regarded as too thin or pretextual in comparison with another, more obvious use or purpose, also relevant, but which constitutes an improper hearsay use or purpose; and an instruction against the improper use will be deemed an insufficient safeguard. In this eventuality, the evidence will be entirely excluded, for any of the purposes. Basically, this is a question of Rule 403 balancing: when does the danger (prejudice) of the improper use outweigh the proper use? In the hearsay area, it rarely does.

(3) *Attempts to Too Finely Parse the Inference.* The present case, *Mahone*, limits counsel's ingenuity in coming up with non-hearsay purposes in another way. It makes clear that if *any* intermediate proposition that is a necessary step along the way to what offering counsel says he hopes the jury will conclude from the evidence, corresponds with what the declarant asserted, the evidence is offered for the prohibited "truth-of-the-matter-asserted-by-the-declarant" purpose, regardless of what offering counsel says is his ultimate purpose. There does not have to be a correspondence with counsel's *ultimate* purpose for the evidence to be excluded as being "offered [by counsel] for the truth of the matter asserted by the declarant." (It may help you visualize this, to think about it this way: the ultimate proposition is not truly an independent purpose.)

TOMA PROBLEM SET 7A: ARE THE FOLLOWING STATEMENTS OFFERED FOR THE "TRUTH OF THE MATTER ASSERTED" (TOMA)?

In each of the following problems you should consider all three elements of basic hearsay: a statement, other than by the declarant while now testifying, offered to prove the "truth of the matter" asserted. The last element, TOMA, however, is determinative for most of these problems.

(1) *The Allegedly Slanderous Statement.* You represent plaintiff in a slander action. You put on the stand a witness who heard the defendant slander the plaintiff and you question her as follows:

Q: "Ms. Witness, tell the ladies and gentlemen of the jury what you heard the defendant say on that occasion."

OPPOSING COUNSEL: "Your Honor, this calls for hearsay. It was an out-of-court statement."

Assume the witness would have answered "He said plaintiff stole his watch." What will you answer opposing counsel? Aside from any exception or exemption for party admissions (which we have not yet studied), is this a hearsay usage of this out-of-court statement? Who is correct?

(2) *"I'll Pay You if You Mow My Lawn."* In an action to compel payment for a lawn-mowing job that was done, Martin, the plaintiff, puts a witness (W) on the stand, who testifies that W overheard Frank, the defendant, state to Martin "I agree to pay you ten dollars if you mow my lawn." Aside from any exception or exemption for party admissions (which we have not yet studied), is this a hearsay usage of this out-of-court statement?

(3) *The Legally Operative Delivery: "Here is Your Corn."* You represent plaintiff, Hanson, in a case in which plaintiff owned and leased a farm to one Schrik under a written lease, the terms of which gave plaintiff two-fifths of the corn to be grown. The tenant (Schrik) subsequently gave a mortgage to defendant bank on the tenant's share of the crops before any corn was yet planted. The mortgaged property was later sold at auction by the bank with his permission. At this sale, a crib of corn containing 393 bushels was sold by the bank to defendant Johnson. If plaintiff owned the corn, it was converted by defendants.

In an effort to prove that the corn was owned by plaintiff, and that it was a part of his share, can plaintiff testify, over the objections of hearsay and self-serving, that when the tenant was about through husking corn, after the mortgage but before the sale, plaintiff was on the farm and the tenant pointed and said: "Mr. Hanson, here is your corn for this year, this double crib here and this single crib here is your share for this year's corn; this belongs to you, Mr. Hanson." (One of these was the crib sold to Johnson.)

Could a bystander be called and against the same objection testify to having heard the talk in substantially the same language? Assume in each case that the jurisdiction's property law recognizes no title to property (at least, no title that would be superior to a purchaser who took the property in good faith ignorance of the claim) in someone when all that person has is a contractual right to an undifferentiated share, with no actual or constructive possession. *See Hanson v. Johnson*, 201 N.W. 322 (Minn. 1924) (statements are admissible). Why?

(4) *The Man Who Said, "I Work for the Gas Pipeline Corporation."* You represent McAfee in a lawsuit for personal injuries from an explosion in a gas pipeline against the Travis Gas Corporation, the owner of the pipeline. On the day McAfee was injured, one Joe Woods of the Federal Petroleum Company appeared (apparently dressed in a Travis uniform and driving what appeared to be a Travis truck) on the premises where McAfee was employed and said something to him. McAfee then went with Woods to where the pipeline was leaking and was in the act of pointing out such leaks to Woods when Woods struck a match on the sole of his shoe to light a cigarette. The blaze from the match ignited the escaping gas, causing an explosion.

At the trial, McAfee proposes to prove that on the occasion in question, Woods said that he was an employee of the people who owned the pipeline and asked McAfee to show him the place where the leaks were.

Can he? Assume that the evidence is offered for either of two purposes: (1) to rebut contributory negligence by showing that McAfee acted reasonably in approaching the leak with Woods, or (2) to prove that Woods was acting as an actual or apparent agent of Travis Gas so as to hold the company liable. *See McAfee v. Travis Gas Corp.*, 153 S.W.2d 442 (Tex. 1941) (exclusion was error where there was independent evidence of agency). Why?

(5) *The Manufacturer's Instructions.* You represent an assembler of truck bodies charged with negligence in having welded the bodies to the chassis rather than bolting them. Can the assembler introduce a brochure he had received from the manufacturer stating that the safest practice is to weld rather than bolt them? *See McGinty v. Motor Truck Equipment Corp.*, 397 S.W.2d 263 (Tex. Civ. App. 1965) (upholding admission). Why?

Note: Consider whether it makes a difference if the evidence is offered to prove (1) that welding is in fact safer, or (2) the assembler's reasonableness in choosing to weld.

(6) *The "Precious Cargo" Letter.* Consider *United States v. Mazyak*, 650 F.2d 788 (5th Cir. 1981), *cert. denied*, 455 U.S. 922 (1982):

Appellants were each convicted of conspiracy to import marijuana and conspiracy to possess marijuana. The operations allegedly were carried on by means of a ship. Appellants challenged the admission of what was called the "precious cargo" letter at trial, contending that the letter was hearsay.

The letter was addressed to all four defendants by name. It read in full: "Dear Grand Banks Lady. I say to you farewell your journey for you carry my greatest treasure. On precious cargo my thoughts are with you. I bid you farewell. Love Julie." The letter was discovered in the wheelhouse of the ship.

The Court held: "The government offered the letter for the limited purpose of linking the appellants with the vessel and with one another. The use of the letter for this limited purpose was not hearsay. The letter was not introduced to prove the truth of the matter asserted; rather, it was introduced as circumstantial proof that the appellants were associated with each other and the boat."

Do you agree?

(7) *"I am King Tut."* In order to establish the mental incompetence of the testator, and hence the invalidity of his will, certain of his relatives introduce evidence that he was heard declaring, at around the time of making his will, "I am King Tut." Is this a hearsay usage of this out-of-court statement?

(8) *Clocks, Phone Books, Investment Advice, and the Babysitter's Reputation.* Are we relying on hearsay when we (a) look at a clock to find out what time it is, (b) use a telephone directory to find a person's telephone number or address, (c) rely on written financial statements or oral and written recommendations in making an investment, or (d) hire a babysitter on recommendations from our neighbors?

§ 7.02 STATEMENTS IMPLIED FROM WORDS OR CONDUCT[2]

WRIGHT v. TATHAM

Exchequer Chamber, 1837
7 Ad. & E1. 313

PARKE, BARON.

[Tatham, as heir to Marsden, deceased, sues to obtain property formerly belonging to the latter. Wright, who was Marsden's servant while Marsden was alive, claimed the property under Marsden's will. Tatham challenged the will by alleging that Marsden was not competent when he made it. The trial judge excluded three letters written to Marsden offered as evidence of Marsden's soundness of mind. One of the letters, from the Rev. Oliver Marton, Vicar of Lancaster, requested Marsden to instruct his attorney to negotiate a settlement of a dispute pending between Marsden and the parish, stating that without a settlement much trouble and expense would result to both sides and to the community, although the Vicar

[2] Study Guide Reference: Evidence in a Nutshell, Chapter 8:II.

himself was not directly involved. The other two letters were primarily social.]

First, then, were all or any of these letters admissible on the issue in the cause as acts done by the writers, assuming, for the sake of argument, that there was no proof of any act done by the testator upon or relating to these letters or any of them — that is, would such letters or any of them be evidence of the testator's competence at the time of writing them?

[T]he writing and sending the letters by their respective writers were acts done by them towards the testator. It is argued that the letters would be admissible because they are evidence of the *treatment* of the testator *as* a competent person by individuals acquainted with his habits and personal character; that they are more than mere statements to a third party indicating an opinion of his competence by those persons; they are acts done towards the testator by them, which would not have been done if he had been incompetent, and from which, therefore, a legitimate inference may, it is argued, be derived that he was so.

Each of the three letters, no doubt, indicates that in the opinion of the writer the testator was a rational person. He is spoken of in respectful terms in all. Mr. *Ellershaw* describes him as possessing hospitality and benevolent politeness; and Mr. *Marton* addresses him as competent to do business to the limited extent to which his letter calls upon him to act; and there is no question but that, if any one of those writers had been living, his testimony founded on personal observation, that the testator possessed the qualities would be admissible on this issue. But the point to be determined is, whether *these letters* are admissible as proof that *he did possess these qualities*?

I am of opinion that, according to the established principles of the law of evidence, the letters are all inadmissible for such a purpose. One great principle in this law is, that all facts which are relevant to the issue may be proved; another is, that all such facts as have not been admitted by the party against whom they are offered, or some one under whom he claims, ought to be proved under the sanction of an oath (or its equivalent introduced by statute, a solemn affirmation), either on the trial of the issue or some other issue involving the same question between the same parties or those to whom they are privy.

[T]he question is, whether the contents of these letters are evidence of the *fact to be proved upon this issue* — that is, the actual existence of the qualities which the testator is, in those letters, by implication, stated to possess; and those letters may be considered in this respect to be on the same footing as if they had contained a direct and positive statement that he was competent. *For this purpose* they are mere hearsay evidence, statements of the writers, not on oath, of the truth of the matter in question, with this addition, that they have acted upon the statements on the faith of their being true, by their sending the letters to the testator. That the so acting cannot give a sufficient sanction for the truth of the statement is perfectly plain; for it is clear that, if the same statements had been made by parol or in writing to a third person, that would have been insufficient; and this is conceded by the learned counsel for the plaintiff in error. Yet in both cases there has been an acting on the belief of the truth, by making the statement, or writing and sending a letter to a third person; and what difference can it possibly make that this is an acting of the same nature by writing and sending the letter to the testator? It is admitted, and most properly, that you have no right to use in evidence the fact of writing and sending a letter to a third person containing a statement of competence, on the ground that it affords an inference that such an act would not have been done unless the statement was true, or believed to be true, although such an inference no doubt would be raised in the conduct of the ordinary affairs of life, if the statement were made by a man of veracity. But it cannot be raised in a judicial inquiry; and, if such an argument were admissible, it would lead to the indiscriminate admission of hearsay evidence of all manner of facts.

Further, it is clear that an acting to a much greater extent and degree upon such statements to a third person would not make the statements admissible. For example, if a wager to a large amount had been made as to the matter in issue by two third persons, the payment of that wager, however large the sum, would not be admissible to prove the truth of the matter in issue. You would not have had any right to present it to the jury as raising an inference of the truth of the fact, on the ground that otherwise the bet would not have been paid. It is, after all, nothing but the *mere statement* of that fact, with strong evidence of the belief of it by the party making it. Could it make any difference that the wager was between the third person and one of the parties to the suit? Certainly not. The payment by other underwriters on the same policy to the plaintiff could not be given in evidence to prove that the subject insured has been lost. Yet there is an act done, a payment strongly attesting the truth of the statement, which it implies, that there had been a loss. To illustrate this point still further, let us suppose a third person had betted a wager with Mr. *Marsden* that he could not solve some mathematical problem, the solution of which required a high degree of capacity; would payment of that wager to Mr. Marsden's banker be admissible evidence that he possessed that capacity? The answer is certain; it would not. It would be evidence of the fact of competence given by a third party not upon oath.

Let us suppose the parties who wrote these letters to have stated the matter therein contained, that is, their knowledge of his personal qualities and capacity for business, on oath before a magistrate, or in some judicial proceeding to which the plaintiff and defendant were not parties. No one could contend that such statement would be admissible on this issue; and yet there would have been an act done on the faith of the statement being true, and a very solemn one, which would raise in the ordinary conduct of affairs a strong belief in the truth of the statement, if the writers were faith-worthy. The acting in this case is of much less importance, and certainly is not equal to the sanction of an extra-judicial oath.

Many other instances of a similar nature, by way of illustration, were suggested by the learned counsel for the defendant in error, which, on the most cursory consideration, any one would at once declare to be inadmissible in evidence. Others were supposed on the part of the plaintiff in error, which, at first sight, have the appearance of being mere facts, and therefore admissible, though on further consideration they are open to precisely the same objection. Of the first description are the supposed cases of a letter by a third person to any one demanding a debt, which may be said to be a treatment of him *as a debtor*, being offered as proof that the debt was really due; a note, congratulating him on his high state of bodily vigour, being proposed as evidence of his being in good health; both of which are manifestly at first sight objectionable. To the latter class belong the supposed conduct of the family or relations of a testator, taking the same precautions in his absence as if he were a lunatic; his election, in his absence, to some high and responsible office; the conduct of a physician who permitted a will to be executed by a sick testator; the conduct of a deceased captain on a question of seaworthiness, who, after examining every part of the vessel, embarked in it with his family; all these, when deliberately considered, are, with reference to the matter in issue in each case, mere instances of hearsay evidence, mere statements, not on oath, but implied in or vouched by the actual conduct of persons by whose acts the litigant parties are not to be bound.

The conclusion at which I have arrived is, that proof of a particular fact, which is not of itself a matter in issue, but which is relevant only as implying a statement or opinion of a third person on the matter in issue, is inadmissible in all cases where such a statement or opinion not on oath would be of itself inadmissible; and, therefore, in this case the letters which are offered only to prove the competence of the testator, that is the truth of the implied statements therein contained, were properly rejected, as the mere statement or opinion of the writer would certainly have been inadmissible.

[The letters were held inadmissible by this court, as well as by the House of Lords in an appeal reported at 5 Clark & Finnelly 670.]

NOTES AND QUESTIONS

(1) *The Statement of an Unknown Bettor, Used Against an Accused Bookmaker.* In *State v. Tolisano*, 70 A.2d 118 (Conn. 1949), police, raiding an apartment of the defendant (Charles Clayton), where they suspected an illegal horse-race betting operation was being conducted, answered the telephone when it rang and heard this: "This is Al, Charlie. Doc wants a $10.00 number hitch on eight races at Saratoga." The court admitted this in the betting prosecution on the theory it was not offered for the truth of the statement but as an *operative fact*: to prove that bets were being placed. Query: Is there an implied statement here that may be being offered for its truth? *See United States v. Zenni*, 492 F. Supp. 464 (E.D. Ky. 1980) (similar facts; Fed. R. Evid. 801(a)(2)'s "declarant's intention" test applies to words as well as "nonverbal conduct"; thus not hearsay; changes *Tatham* test of "intention of offeror to use as implied statement").

(2) *"I Didn't Tell About You" as Hearsay. Cf. United States v. Reynolds*, 715 F.2d 99 (3d Cir. 1983) (statement "I didn't tell them anything about you" made while in custody is a hearsay statement that "you are involved" under Fed. R. Evid., regardless of declarant's intent to so assert, since offered as meaning the latter). This decision arguably is inconsistent with the bookmaker case cited above. Can you explain why? *See* Kirgis, *Meaning, Intention, and the Hearsay Rule*, 43 Wm. & Mary L. Rev. 275 (2001); *Park, "I Didn't Tell Them About You": Implied Assertions as Hearsay Under the Federal Rules of Evidence*, 74 Minn. L. Rev. 783 (1990).

UNITED STATES v. JACKSON

United States Court of Appeals, Tenth Circuit
88 F.3d 845 (1996)

McKay, Circuit Judge.

Defendant Kenneth Cody Jackson appeals from his conviction for carjacking and related firearm offenses. He argues that the district court impermissibly allowed the introduction of hearsay evidence used to identify him. We affirm.

The carjacking victim was talking on a pay phone at a Circle K convenience store when a man came up behind him with a chrome-colored snub-nose revolver and demanded the keys to his car. The carjacker was wearing an open-face ski mask and a blue jacket. While the carjacker was holding the revolver to the victim's head, a nearby eyewitness yelled out, "Kenny, don't do it!" After taking money from the victim, the carjacker sped away in his newly acquired automobile.

The police were soon notified and quickly spotted the stolen car. Police officers gave chase. The carjacker jumped from the car and fled on foot. Although the officers pursued him, they were unable to apprehend him at that time. Nevertheless, three officers had gotten a good look at the carjacker's face and later were able to identify him as the defendant in this case. The police recovered from the car a snub-nose revolver and a ski mask. They also recovered a blue jacket which had been discarded by the carjacker during the foot chase. Inside the jacket the officers found a pager. The pager went off and displayed a telephone number. The officer called the number and heard a female voice say, "Is this Kenny?" This statement as well as the statement, "Kenny, don't do it!" were admitted against Mr. Jackson over his objection.

[The court first holds that the victim's testimony repeating the bystander's statement, "Kenny, don't do it!" was admissible as an "excited utterance" under the hearsay exception provided by Fed. R. Evid. 803(2).]

Finally, Mr. Jackson argues that the district court impermissibly allowed the introduction at trial of the declaration, "Is this Kenny?" The district court admitted the declaration as nonhearsay pursuant to Fed. R. Evid. 801(d)(1)(C) [a testifying witness's prior statement of identification] or as an exception to the hearsay rule under Fed. R. Evid. 803(24) [the "catchall" exception now in Rule 807]. On appeal, the government does not contest Mr. Jackson's argument that neither rule applies. Rather, the government argues that the declaration was non-hearsay because it was not a statement within the meaning of Rule 801(a)(1) and (c).

As an initial matter, we point out that evidence does not become inadmissible simply because the district court relied on an erroneous reason for admitting it. So long as the evidence is admissible under some legally correct theory, no error occurred.

In this case, the evidence was admissible because it was non-hearsay under Rule 801(a)(1) and (c). Rule 801(c) provides that " 'Hearsay' is a statement . . . offered in evidence to prove the truth of the matter asserted." A "statement" is defined in Rule 801(a)(1) as "an oral or written assertion." Although "assertion" is not defined in

Rule 801, the advisory committee notes state that "nothing is an assertion unless intended to be one." Fed. R. Evid. 801 advisory committee's note. The question, "Is this Kenny?" cannot reasonably be construed to be an intended assertion, either express or implied. Were we to construe this question completely in Mr. Jackson's favor, it might be possible to imply that the declarant believed Mr. Jackson was in possession of the pager and therefore he was the person responding by telephone to the declarant's message. The mere fact, however, that the declarant conveyed a message with her question does not make the question hearsay. "[I]t is difficult to imagine any question . . . that does not in some way convey an implicit message." Rather, the important question is whether an assertion was intended. We find it hard to believe in this case that the declarant intended to assert that Mr. Jackson was in possession of the pager and that he was responding to her call. If any doubt remains, we believe it is resolved by the fact that Rule 801 places "the burden upon the party claiming that the intention [to make an assertion] existed; ambiguous and doubtful cases will be resolved against him and in favor of admissibility." Fed. R. Evid. 801 advisory committee's note. Mr. Jackson has not met this burden.

NOTES AND QUESTIONS

(1) *Questions as Assertions.* Do you agree that questions are not assertions? *See Lexington Ins. Co. v. Western Pa. Hosp.*, 423 F.3d 318 (3d Cir. 2005) (question was not an assertion; per Becker, J.). Or should "assertions" be interpreted more broadly? Is the real issue determining what the question is offered to prove? Do we do that for other implied assertions? Is there a reason for doing so with questions? If a declarant's statement or question has several intended implications, can we then look to what the statement or question is offered to prove, and still remain faithful to the "declarant's intention" test of the Federal Rules of Evidence?

(2) *Inscriptions.* In *United States v. Hensel*, 699 F.2d 18 (1st Cir.), *cert. denied*, 461 U.S. 958 (1983), a glass inscribed "Dink" was not considered an assertion, although it linked the defendant to the charged conspiracy.

(3) *A Case to Compare to Jackson: A Request for Drugs.* Garner was convicted of possession of cocaine with intent to distribute and related offenses. After a traffic stop, the police found drugs in his car, and arrested him. When they answered his cell phone, an unidentified caller said "can I get a 40," slang for $40 worth of cocaine. He hung up when asked his name. That statement supplied the evidence of intent to distribute. Was it hearsay? *Garner v. State*, 995 A.2d 694 (Md. 2010), affirmed its admission as "a verbal act that established the consequential fact that defendant was in possession of a telephone called by a person who requested to purchase cocaine." Do you agree?

ALTKRUG v. WILLIAM WHITMAN CO.

New York Supreme Court, Appellate Division
185 A.D. 744, 173 N.Y.S. 669 (1919)

SMITH, JUDGE.

The plaintiff is a jobber in woolens, and the defendant is a commission house, agent for the Arlington Mills. The complaint sets forth for the delivery of 300 pieces of what was called 759. The complaint seeks to recover, first, for the difference in value of the pieces delivered and the value that they would have had, if they had been according to sample — in other words, for a breach of warranty; second, for the failure to deliver the balance of the goods contracted for.

The judgment must be reversed for the admission of improper evidence. The court allowed the defendant to show that these goods which the plaintiff rejected were afterwards sold to other customers [under identical terms and circumstances], who made no complaint in reference thereto. This was clearly hearsay evidence as to the opinions of other customers upon these goods. This evidence was most mischievous evidence, and might well have been a controlling factor in the minds of the jury in determining that the goods in question were up to sample.

NOTE

Federal Rules of Evidence Change Result in Altkrug. In *De Marines v. KLM Royal Dutch Airlines*, 580 F.2d 1193 (3d Cir. 1978), plaintiff sued the airlines for an alleged sudden drop in pressurization (on the plane in which he and many others were passengers) that allegedly caused a permanent loss in his equilibrium. The court held admissible testimony from the airline that no other claims had been made against the airline. The court said such evidence was relevant because it affected the probability that there was a pressurization accident. Any weakness in so indicating was a matter of weight for the jury, the court said, and suggested that if it had been a more severe weakness it might be a matter to be handled by Fed. R. Evid. 403. Why did the court not find an implied statement here, that was being offered for its truth, with the result that the evidence would be hearsay, as in *Altkrug*? What implied statements, offered for their truth, made by whom as declarants, would *Altkrug* have found here? *Altkrug* is of course the natural outcome of the common law position expressed by *Wright v. Tatum, supra.*

IMPLIED STATEMENT PROBLEM SET 7B: IS THERE A "STATEMENT"? IF SO, WHAT IS THE "MATTER ASSERTED" (DOES IT INCLUDE IMPLIED MATTERS)?

In the following problems, evaluate all elements of basic hearsay: a statement, other than by the declarant while now testifying, offered to prove the truth of the matter asserted. These problems, however, depend heavily on deciding whether there is a statement, and if so, what it asserts. (Just how far is it appropriate to go in inferring implied assertions?)

(1) *Analyzing Wright v. Tatham Under the Federal Rules of Evidence: A Different Result?* Would the Federal Rules of Evidence produce the same result as the common-law position expressed in *Wright* if the Federal Rules were applied to the facts of *Wright*? The Federal Rules of Evidence depend on whether the statement is offered for the "truth of the matter asserted."

(2) *The Student Who Holds Up a Hand.* Student Jones testifies on the stand that Professor Kingsfield asked the class if any of them drove to school that day and that student Martin raised his hand. This testimony is offered to prove that Martin did drive that day. Is this hearsay under the Federal Rules? Under the common-law position expressed in *Wright*?

(3) *The Student Who Raises a Hand Because There's a Fly Nearby.* Under Problem (2) above, if the judge is convinced that Martin was raising his hand only to catch a fly at that moment, what should be the result under the Federal Rules of Evidence regarding whether the evidence is hearsay? Do we wind up with a situation where the evidence is most likely to be admissible when it is weakest (i.e., intended to catch a fly rather than intended as an assertion)? How can that be justified?

(4) *"He Ran when the Alarm Went Off."* You represent a defendant charged with burglary. You wish to introduce evidence that immediately after the burglary, as the alarm system went off, Evans, not the defendant, was seen running from the scene. Would this be hearsay under the Federal Rules of Evidence? Under *Wright, supra*?

(5) *Definitions.* Apply each of the following definitions of hearsay to *Leake* (*see* § 7.01[B]) and to each of the cases in this section. Do they make a difference to the outcome?

> (a) Hearsay evidence is testimony in court, or written evidence, of a statement made out of court, which statement is offered to show the truth of the matter stated therein. A "statement" as used herein can be either express or implied, and the words or conduct from which it is implied need not necessarily be intended as a substitute for the statement.
>
> (b) [First sentence the same as in (a) above.] A "statement" as used herein is a verbal or written assertion and may not be implied except from something intended at the time as a substitute for the statement.
>
> (c) Hearsay evidence is evidence in court of something said or done out of court that depends for its value in the case on the accuracy and [or?] sincerity of that out-of-court person, in the same fashion as does the testimony of witnesses on the stand in ordinary nonhearsay cases.
>
> (d) Hearsay evidence is evidence in court of something said or done out of court, concerning which cross-examination, the oath, the solemnity and importance of the courtroom proceedings, exposure of demeanor to the fact-finder or opponent, or the possibility of penalty for falsehood would have been substantially helpful in regard to reliability, in the same fashion that they normally help with witnesses on the stand, had the out-of-court person been subject to them at the time.

(e) Hearsay evidence is evidence offered to show a belief held by someone not presently testifying, which belief is offered to show the truth of the matter believed.

(6) *Decedent's Criticism of Widow; Offered to Reduce Damages.* In a wrongful death action brought by the wife of the deceased, defendant offers a statement of decedent, "My wife is a witch," to reduce the probable amounts decedent would have given his wife had he lived, hence reducing her damages. Is this offered "for the truth of the matter asserted"? Can it be viewed as the implied declaration "I think my wife is a witch" or "I hate my wife," with the result that it is offered "for the truth of the matter asserted" (in the implied statement)?

(7) *The Papermate Pen Survey: "[I Think] It's a Papermate."* In a lawsuit charging a competitor with selling pens with a deceptive similarity in appearance to Papermate pens, thereby misleading customers, the Papermate Company wishes to introduce the results of oral surveys it took in which men and women on the street, when shown the non-Papermate pen, thought it was a Papermate. Under the various definitions of hearsay, does it make any difference whether they said "It's a Papermate" or "I think it's a Papermate"? Does such a distinction make practical sense? Can the exact words be reconstructed? Would placing a premium on exact wording lead to fraud in the reporting of what they said?

Under the Federal Rules of Evidence, would "It's a Papermate" be considered the implied statement "I think it's a Papermate"? Under the Federal Rules of Evidence, would "I think it's a Papermate" be considered the implied statement "It's a Papermate"? If, under the Federal Rules of Evidence, or under other law, each statement can be implied from the other, does this get you anywhere?

§ 7.03 OUT-OF-COURT WORDS (OR CONDUCT) STATING OR REVEALING DECLARANT'S STATE OF MIND[3]

LOETSCH v. NEW YORK CITY OMNIBUS CORP.

New York Court of Appeals
291 N.Y. 308, 52 N.E.2d 448 (1943)

THACHER, JUDGE.

Appeal by defendant from judgment in favor of plaintiff in a wrongful death action.

[D]efendants-appellants offered in evidence [which was excluded] the will of the decedent [which stated:]

---

[3] Study Guide Reference: Evidence in a Nutshell, Chapter 8:IV. If certain conditions are met, out-of-court statements of, or demonstrating, a state of mind of declarant are treated by some decisions as "not hearsay" and by some as hearsay that falls within a "state-of-mind exception" to the hearsay rule. The result is the same. Both arguments should be made wherever possible. At this point we examine arguments that they are not hearsay.

> Whereas I have been a faithful, dutiful, and loving wife to my husband, Dean Yankovich, and whereas he reciprocated my tender affections for him with acts of cruelty and indifference, and whereas he has failed to support and maintain me in that station of life which would have been possible and proper for him, I hereby limit my bequest to him to one dollar.

The will, executed within four months prior to decedent's death, was relevant to an understanding of the relations which existed between the decedent and her husband. It is always proper to make proof of the relations of the decedent to the person for whose benefit the action is maintained, because such proof has a bearing upon the pecuniary loss suffered by the person entitled to the recovery.

The measure of loss is to be determined solely from the standpoint of the surviving spouse and is strictly limited to compensation for pecuniary loss. Accordingly, the amount recoverable in any particular case must be very largely influenced by the nature of the relationship between the beneficiary and the deceased. [Her] disposition voluntarily to [provide non-obligatory sums to the beneficiary during her life] is of essential importance to the jury in determining pecuniary loss.

Such declarations are evidence of the decedent's state of mind and are probative of a disposition on the part of the declarant which has a very vital bearing upon the reasonable expectancy, or lack of it, of future assistance or support if life continues. No testimonial effect need be given to the declaration, but the fact that such a declaration was made by the decedent, whether true or false, is compelling evidence of her feelings toward, and relations to, her husband. As such it is not excluded under the hearsay rule but is admissible as a verbal act.

[*Reversed.*]

BRIDGES v. STATE

Supreme Court of Wisconsin

247 Wis. 350, 19 N.W.2d 529 (1945)

FRITZ, JUSTICE.

[Appeal from conviction for indecent liberties with 7-year-old Sharon Schunk. Was defendant the culprit? That depended on whether the place Sharon was taken during the crime was the house and room at 125 East Johnson Street, where defendant lived.]

Defendant contends the court erred in admitting testimony by police officers as to matters stated by Sharon in defendant's absence. He claims these statements were hearsay evidence and therefore were not admissible.

There is testimony by police officers and also Mrs. Schunk as to statements which were made to them by Sharon during the course of their investigations. In those statements she spoke of various matters and features which she remembered and which were descriptive of the exterior and surroundings of the house; and of the room and various articles and the location thereof therein. It is true that testimony as to such statements was hearsay and, as such, inadmissible if the purpose for which it was received had been to establish thereby that there were in fact the stated articles in the room, or that they were located as stated, or that the exterior features or surroundings of the house were as Sharon stated. That, however, was not in this case the purpose for which the evidence as to those statements was admitted. It was admissible in so far as the fact that she had made the statements can be deemed to tend to show that at the time those statements were made — which was a month prior to the subsequent discovery of the room and house at 125 East Johnson Street — she had knowledge as to articles and descriptive features which, as was proven by other evidence, were in fact in or about that room and house. If in relation thereto Sharon made the statements as to which the officers and her mother testified, then those statements, although they were extra-judicial utterances, constituted at least circumstantial evidence that she then had such knowledge; and that such state of mind on her part was acquired by reason of her having been in that room and house prior to making the statements.

[A]ffirmed.[4]]

NOTES AND QUESTIONS

(1) *Is the Court Correct in Its Technical Hearsay Analysis?* Ask yourself the following:

(a) Does the establishing of the actual features of defendant's premises depend on the little girl's credibility? (To make it easier, assume the "other evidence" of the features of the premises were a series of photographs.)

(b) Isn't her statement really or impliedly "I was molested at an apartment having features X, Y, and Z" or "I was at an apartment with those features"? Aren't these offered for their truth?

(c) Is her statement impliedly "I have a picture in my mind of a house and room with such-and-such features"? If so, doesn't that make it offered to prove the truth of the fact it states (that her mind indeed contained a picture of . . .)? Would that necessarily make it hearsay, or is it still not hearsay because the fact stated (the existence of a mental picture) is an internal, subjective fact, rather than an external, objective fact?

(d) Would the prosecution's theory work as well, if she had said "I have no awareness of a house and room with such-and-such features (naming the features of defendant's house and room)"? Does the prosecution's offered inference really depend upon the truth of her statement?

(2) *Is the Court Correct as a Matter of Policy?* Are there problems of the little girl's credibility, akin to those that normally inhere in on-the-stand testimony in nonhearsay cases, that you as defense counsel would like to explore by cross-

---

[4] [Do you suppose the jury was instructed "You must find that the house and room had such-and-such features *from the other evidence*. Then and only then can you consider her statements, and only as showing her awareness of those features"? — Eds.]

examining the declarant — e.g., how she obtained the knowledge (from her mother, or the police, or from selling girl scout cookies at the apartment); is this a frame-up to solve a difficult crime, or a mistake; was she lying; etc.?

(3) *Constitutional Issues.* Are there any constitutional concerns you have about the use of the challenged evidence in *Bridges*? Are they different from hearsay concerns?

PROBLEM SET 7C: IMPLIED STATEMENT THEORY COMBINED WITH STATE-OF-MIND THEORY.

Consider the hearsay analysis issues raised by the following:

(1) *"[I Think] It's a Zippo."* In *Zippo Mfg. Co. v. Rogers Imports, Inc.*, 216 F. Supp. 670 (S.D.N.Y. 1963), Zippo, a manufacturer of cigarette lighters, sued Rogers for producing a lighter that by its appearance suggested it was a Zippo. To prove that the Rogers' lighters were being mistaken for Zippo's, Zippo introduced the results of a survey, in which people out-of-court were shown Rogers' lighters and when asked what kind of lighter it was, responded "It is a Zippo" or "I think it is a Zippo." The court admitted the evidence, stating that some courts would do so because the statements were not hearsay, since they were not offered for the truth of the matter asserted, and others would do so because of the "state of mind" principle. The court also said the circumstances under which the survey was conducted were proper (indicating accuracy) and the evidence was necessary, there being little other practical way to prove the point. In finding that the survey had been properly conducted, the court noted that the interviewees had no interest in the matter, that the questions were fairly worded so as not to suggest an answer, that the sampling involved large numbers and was fairly done, and that the respondents did not know in advance the purpose of the survey. Do the considerations mentioned in the last two sentences have anything to do with hearsay analysis, or with other evidentiary concepts? Specifically, what other concepts?

(2) *Adding "I Think" or "I Believe" to the Declaration: Any Difference?* Under a "truth of the matter asserted" analysis, does it make any difference whether the declarants in *Loetsch* and *Zippo*, *supra*, prefaced their declaration by the words "I think" (or "I believe") or not? In *Leake*, § 7.01, the "taillight's out" case, would it have made any difference if the declarant had prefaced his declaration that the taillight was out by "I think" (or "I believe")? Would he then come within the principle that declarant's statement of his state of mind is not hearsay, espoused by the cases in this section?

(3) *Distinguishing Bridges (the Molested Child Case) from Other Cases.* If *Leake* (§ 7.01) could not be brought within the state of mind principle by the addition of the words "I think" or "I believe," how is it that *Bridges*, the molested child case, qualifies for the state of mind principle?

(4) *Your "Rudder" Amidst Complexity.* Liberal use of the concept of implied statements combined with the state-of-mind-of-declarant concept can provide an attorney with considerable "flexibility," as perhaps best illustrated by the notes following the *Bridges* case, *supra* this section. But as a judge — if you become one — in situations where there are a number of ways to cut the cake, perhaps your

rudder should be to ask: (1) what is the offered statement relevant to; (2) is it relevant to the lawsuit for these purposes; and (3) are there credibility issues of the kind that the hearsay rule is meant to address?

Chapter 8

EXEMPTIONS FROM THE HEARSAY RULE

SPECIALLY DEFINED NON-HEARSAY (F.R.E. ARTICLE VIII, RULE 801(D))

§ 8.01 FORMER STATEMENTS OF PRESENTLY TESTIFYING WITNESSES[1]

Read Federal Rules of Evidence 801(d)(1), "Definitions (Hearsay): Statements That are Not Hearsay: Declarant-Witness's Prior Statement," and 613, "Witness's Prior Statements [Procedures]."

[A] Introduction

The question presented here usually is treated as a question of whether these former statements are hearsay in the first place, although conceptually it is just as possible to treat them as hearsay and ask whether there should be an exception for them. It doesn't make any difference in practical effect which of these two routes is chosen — the outcome will be the same.

Although some of the following cases and materials preceded the Federal Rules of Evidence, they were considered by the drafters of the Rules and influenced the shape of the Rules, and they still are the law in some places. As you read the following materials, consider how each of the evidentiary positions reported (or mentioned within a case) differs from the Federal Rules of Evidence. Although they may differ from the Rules, they are respectable positions in other jurisdictions. In addition, there are periodic movements to change the Federal Rules of Evidence.

CALIFORNIA EVIDENCE CODE

Prior Statements of Witnesses

§ 1235. Inconsistent statement. Evidence of a statement made by a witness is not made inadmissible by the hearsay rule if the statement is inconsistent with his testimony at the hearing and is offered in compliance with Section 770.

[**§ 770. Evidence of inconsistent statement of witness.** Unless the interests of justice otherwise require, extrinsic evidence of a statement

---

[1] Study Guide Reference: Evidence in a Nutshell, Chapter 9:I; II.

made by a witness that is inconsistent with any part of his testimony at the hearing shall be excluded unless:

(a) The witness was so examined while testifying as to give him an opportunity to explain or to deny the statement; or

(b) The witness has not been excused from giving further testimony in the action.]

§ 1236. Prior consistent statement. Evidence of a statement previously made by a witness is not made inadmissible by the hearsay rule if the statement is consistent with his testimony at the hearing and is offered in compliance with Section 791.

[**§ 791. Prior consistent statement of witness.** Evidence of a statement previously made by a witness that is consistent with his testimony at the hearing is inadmissible to support his credibility unless it is offered after:

(a) Evidence of a statement made by him that is inconsistent with any part of his testimony at the hearing has been admitted for the purpose of attacking his credibility, and the statement was made before the alleged inconsistent statement; or

(b) An express or implied charge has been made that his testimony at the hearing is recently fabricated or is influenced by bias or other improper motive, and the statement was made before the bias, motive for fabrication, or other improper motive is alleged to have arisen.]

§ 1238. Prior identification. Evidence of a statement previously made by a witness is not made inadmissible by the hearsay rule if the statement would have been admissible if made by him while testifying and:

(a) The statement is an identification of a party or another as a person who participated in a crime or other occurrence;

(b) The statement was made at a time when the crime or other occurrence was fresh in the witness' memory; and

(c) The evidence of the statement is offered after the witness testifies that he made the identification and that it was a true reflection of his opinion at that time.

[B] Inconsistent Statements as Non-Hearsay

UNITED STATES v. TRUMAN

United States Court of Appeals, Second Circuit
688 F.3d 129 (2012)

LOHIER, CIRCUIT JUDGE:

The Government appeals from a judgment issued by the United States District Court for the Northern District of New York granting Defendant — Appellee Jeffrey E. Truman, Sr.'s ("Truman") motion for a judgment of acquittal and conditionally granting Truman's motion for a new trial . . . , after a jury trial in which Truman was convicted of various arson-related charges in connection with the destruction by fire of a vacant building that he jointly owned. A principal witness against Truman at trial, his son, Jeffrey Truman, Jr. ("Truman, Jr."), had been convicted in New York state court of setting fire to the building and had thereafter cooperated with the federal Government.

Contrary to the District Court's analysis, we conclude that Truman, Jr.'s refusal to answer certain questions at trial did not render his testimony for the Government "incredible as a matter of law," and that Truman, Jr.'s prior testimony against Truman in a separate state court trial was properly admitted as nonhearsay under Federal Rule of Evidence 801(d)(1)(A). . . . Accordingly, we vacate the District Court's judgment of acquittal and its order conditionally granting a new trial, and we remand for entry of a judgment consistent with the jury's guilty verdict and for sentencing.

[The defendant, Truman Senior, was a partner in JMM Properties, LLC, which purchased a vacant commercial building. The building was insured for more than $ 4 million. Later, his broker told Truman Sr. that the land alone, without the building, "was worth as much or more than it was worth with the building on it." JMM was financially strapped, and the building was without tenants and losing money. Truman Sr. paid large amounts of his own money to keep JMM solvent and was near insolvency himself. On a fall evening in November, the building burned down. Investigators determined that the cause was arson.

[Truman Jr., the defendant's son, was arrested by New York state authorities and confessed to having committed the crime. Apparently unaware of his son's confession, Truman Sr. joined his partners in filing an insurance claim. Ultimately, both Truman Sr. and Truman Jr. were arrested by New York authorities. Truman Jr., the son, pleaded guilty in state court in exchange for a sentence of two years. In accordance with his plea agreement, Truman Jr. then cooperated with New York authorities and testified against his father at a state-court trial of Truman Sr. But the New York prosecutors were unable to produce a witness to corroborate Truman Jr.'s testimony, and since New York, like many states, requires corroboration of an accomplice witness, they dismissed the New York case against Truman Sr. But retrial in a federal court after a state-court acquittal has been repeatedly held not to violate the double jeopardy clause of the Constitution, and a federal prosecution of Truman Sr. therefore was still permissible.]

After the state charges against Truman were dismissed, the United States began its own investigation. In January 2010 Truman, Jr. entered into a cooperation agreement with the United States Attorney's Office pursuant to which he agreed to give "complete, truthful, and accurate information during . . . statements [to the Government] and subsequent testimony before a federal grand jury and during subsequent proceedings". . . .

At Truman's federal trial, the Government called Truman, Jr. as a witness. He first testified about his criminal history. . . . He then testified that he burned down the . . . building. [He stated that he used cardboard boxes and wooden pallets soaked with gasoline and kerosene that his father had left in the building.] While acknowledging that he had discussed the building with his father the day before the arson, Truman, Jr. declined to disclose what his father had told him.

When the Government asked Truman, Jr. why he set the fire and about the content of his conversations with his father, he refused to answer. The District Court confirmed that Truman, Jr. would not answer and warned him that his refusal would constitute a breach of the cooperation agreement with the Government. He still refused, saying, "I can't," and, "I can't do this." In response, and over Truman's objection, the Government read portions of Truman, Jr.'s testimony from Truman's state court trial, in which Truman, Jr. confirmed that his father had asked him to start the fire:

Question [asked earlier in the state court trial]: Jeffrey, did you have any information about the gasoline and kerosene before going over to the [building] that morning?

Answer: Yes.

Question: And from whom did you receive that information?

Answer: My father.

Question: And when did you receive that information?

Answer: The night before. . . .

Question: And what did your dad tell you about the gasoline and kerosene? . . .

Answer: Told me what room they were in and where in the room. . . .

Question: And did he tell you anything with regards for the purpose for those being there?

Answer: For burning the building down. . . .

Question: And you said a week before [the fire] you had a discussion with your dad as well. What did he say to you at that time?

Answer: He asked me if I would do it.

After the testimony was read, Truman, Jr. confirmed that he had so testified during the state court trial.

. . . [On cross-examination, Truman Jr.] proceeded to answer defense counsel's questions about peripheral matters relating to his state court testimony, and he maintained that his state court testimony had been truthful. He also acknowledged giving to the police [a] written statement explicitly implicating his father in the arson, which was admitted into evidence, and he testified that the confession was true. . . .

Several Government witnesses corroborated Truman, Jr.'s testimony regarding his father's involvement in the arson. . . . Telephone and toll records further corroborated Truman, Jr.'s account of traveling to [another city] with his father to dispose of [evidence]. . . .

Testifying in his defense, Truman denied any role in the arson or the related fraud. . . .

The jury deliberated for less than a day before convicting Truman. . . . [But t]he District Court granted [Truman's Motion for Acquittal] after concluding that Truman, Jr.'s federal and state court trial testimony was "incredible as a matter of law" [because of Truman Jr.'s refusal to answer questions in the federal trial].

The District Court also conditionally granted Truman's motion for a new trial . . . [partly on the ground] that it had erroneously admitted Truman, Jr.'s prior state court testimony because it was hearsay, irrelevant, unfairly prejudicial and misleading. . . .

[Here, the Court of Appeals disagrees, first, with the trial judge's conclusion that Truman Jr.'s testimony was "incredible as a matter of law." Although the son's failure to testify fully, as required under his cooperation agreement with the government, his criminal record and history of alcohol and drug abuse, his perjury in the state proceedings, and the inconsistencies in his testimony all impaired his credibility, assessing his credibility was the province of the jury, which was properly instructed. The Court of Appeals holds that the grant of the Motion for Acquittal was error, and it reinstates the conviction. It then considers the Motion for New Trial, which was based on the admitting of Truman Jr.'s state-court testimony, as follows.]

The District Court also concluded that a new trial was warranted because Truman, Jr.'s state court testimony was inadmissible hearsay. We disagree. A statement is nonhearsay if "[t]he declarant [(1)] testifies" at trial, "[(2)] is subject to cross-examination about a prior statement, and [(3)] the statement is inconsistent with the declarant's testimony and [(4)] was given under penalty of perjury at a trial, hearing, or other proceeding or in a deposition." Fed.R.Evid. 801(d)(1)(A).

Truman, Jr. answered every question posed to him in cross-examination about his prior state court testimony, and therefore he was "subject to cross-examination" within the meaning of Rule 801(d)(1)(A). His prior testimony was also "inconsistent" with his refusal to answer questions about that testimony on direct examination at trial. In *United States v. Marchand*, we held that "if a witness has testified to . . . facts before a grand jury and forgets or denies them at trial, his grand jury testimony . . . falls squarely within Rule 801(d)(1)(A)." Our holding in *Marchand* naturally extends to a trial witness's refusal to answer questions posed and answered in prior sworn state court testimony. To the extent *Marchand* did not specifically address this issue, however, we now join all of our sister courts that have addressed the question in holding that where, as here, a witness who testifies under oath and is subject to cross-examination in a prior state court proceeding explicitly refuses to answer the same questions at trial, the refusal to answer is inconsistent with his prior testimony and the prior testimony is admissible under Rule 801(d)(1)(A). *See, e.g., United States v. Iglesias*, . . . (refusal to testify with more than "one word admissions, evasive and rambling responses, and equivocations" inconsistent with "clear and straightforward" prior testimony). . . . Our holding also coheres with a principal purpose of Rule 801(d)(1)(A), which is to protect against the "turncoat witness who changes his story on the stand and deprives the party calling him of evidence essential to his case." Notes of Advisory Committee [to the Rule].

Besides Rule 801(d)(1)(A), the District Court pointed to two alternative reasons for concluding that it had improperly admitted Truman, Jr.'s state court testimony. First, it explained that the Government failed to lay a "proper foundation" establishing that Truman, Jr.'s "refusal to answer was firm and unchangeable," as appears to be required under Federal Rule of Evidence 804(a)(2) as a precondition to considering a declarant unavailable for the purpose of admitting the declarant's hearsay statement under Federal Rule of Evidence 804(b). [That Rule applies only if the witness is "unavailable," but it is not the rule at issue here. This unavailability requirement is raised in a later chapter — Eds.]. The District Court erred in reaching this conclusion, however, because the requirements of Rule 804 are irrelevant to determining whether testimony is admissible as nonhearsay pursuant to Rule 801, which was the basis for admitting Truman, Jr.'s prior testimony at trial [and which does not require unavailability, but in fact actually requires the witness to testify at trial]. Second, the District Court determined that Truman, Jr.'s testimony was inadmissible because it could not "properly be credited" and therefore was irrelevant under Federal Rule of Evidence 402 and unfairly prejudicial or misleading under Federal Rule of Evidence 403. The court's conclusion, however, rested on the determination that Truman, Jr.'s testimony was incredible as a matter of law — a determination that we have already concluded was reached in error. The District Court therefore exceeded its discretion in granting a new trial on these bases as well.

[Acquittal and New Trial vacated; conviction reinstated.]

NOTES AND QUESTIONS

(1) *Do Each of the Prior Statements Admitted Here Really Qualify, under Rule 801(d)(1)(A)?* The court admits the witness's prior state court testimony because it holds that the earlier, affirmative testimony is inconsistent with the witness's refusal to testify at the current trial. But is a later refusal to answer really "inconsistent" with an earlier affirmative statement? Notice the Advisory Committee's explanation that Rule 801(d)(1)(A) is intended to protect against the "turncoat witness who . . . deprives the party calling him of evidence," and consider whether this policy supports the appellate court's holding. In *United States v. Matlock*, 109 F.3d 1313 (8th Cir.), *cert. denied*, 522 U.S. 872 (1997), a government witness who was part of the alleged drug conspiracy minimized the role of the defendant at trial. The trial judge permitted the witness' plea hearing testimony as a prior inconsistent statement. On appeal, *Matlock* held that "inconsistency is not limited to diametrically opposed answers but may be found in evasive answers, inability to recall, silence, or changes of position."

(2) *Truman Jr.'s Statement to Police.* The court in *Truman* also says that the witness's written statement to police officers, implicating his father, was in evidence, but it does not analyze the admissibility of this confession. Consider whether this written statement was itself really admissible, given the requirement that the prior inconsistent statement must have been "given under penalty of perjury at a trial, hearing, or other proceeding or in a deposition."

(3) *Should the Statements Have Been Considered to Meet the Basic Hearsay Definition in the First Place?* Notice that the witness testified that the prior

statements were true, even though he refused to testify to the subjects they addressed. Should this mean that the prior statements did not meet the definition of basic hearsay in the first place, and that Rule 801(d)(1)(A) was not needed? On the one hand, the definition of hearsay literally applies even to a witness's repetition of the witness's own earlier statement. But on the other hand, it is common for lawyers to give a witness an exhibit and ask the witness whether the exhibit is "true and accurate," and in that situation, the exhibit usually is not considered hearsay. Can it be said that the exhibits containing the written statement and the state-court testimony were not offered for the truth of the matters asserted, and that the relevant statements "offered for their truth" are the witness's confirmation that the exhibits are true? (This theory seems to stretch the concept, but it may not be easy to explain definitively why it is wrong.)

(4) *Modern Codes: Sufficiency: What if the Inconsistent Statement is Crucial — Or is Unsworn?* Under the more modern codes, can a conviction be upheld when the key evidence implicating the defendant is a prior inconsistent statement of a testifying witness? *Compare United States v. Orrico*, 599 F.2d 113 (6th Cir. 1979) (reversing conviction where statement barely met minimal requirements for admissibility), *with State v. Newsome*, 682 A.2d 972 (Conn. 1996) (affirming conviction and rejecting any per se rule requiring corroboration). Should it matter if the jurisdiction only requires the statement to be inconsistent, not under oath? Does this have constitutional dimensions? *See California v. Green*, 399 U.S. 149 (1970) (impliedly upholding state conviction based in part on unsworn inconsistent statement); *cf. United States v. Owens*, 484 U.S. 554 (1988) (upholding federal conviction based primarily on unsworn prior identification, which unlike inconsistent statements are not required by Federal Rules of Evidence to be sworn).

(5) *What is a "Proceeding" Under* F.R.E. *801(d)(1)(A) — Can it Include Anything that Produces a Sworn Statement?* Would an affidavit sworn to before a notary public be a statement made at an "other proceeding" within Rule 801(d)(1)(A)? *See United States v. Castro-Ayon*, 537 F.2d 1055 (9th Cir.) (upholding admissibility of statement made under oath during interrogation by INS border patrol agent because of relatively formal nature of interrogation and other factors), *cert. denied*, 429 U.S. 983 (1976).

[C] Consistent Statements as Non-Hearsay

TOME v. UNITED STATES

United States Supreme Court
513 U.S. 150 (1995)

KENNEDY, JUSTICE.

[Tome was charged with sexually abusing his own four-year-old daughter, A.T. He shared joint custody of A.T. with his ex-wife, but had primary physical custody of the child. The mother had unsuccessfully petitioned to change this arrangement, but was awarded custody during the summer. The prosecution alleged that the crime was committed while the child was in Tome's custody and later was disclosed while she was with her mother. Tome's defensive theory was that the allegations were concocted to avoid the return of A.T. to her father's custody. At trial, A.T., then six and one-half-years old, testified to the offense, giving one-word and two-word answers to leading questions on direct examination, and appearing reluctant to answer many points on cross-examination. The judge expressed his concerns about her lapses of as much as 40-55 seconds before answering questions, and her apparent loss of concentration, concluding "We have a very difficult situation here." The Government also presented six witnesses (A.T.'s mother, babysitter, social worker, and three pediatricians) to rebut the charge that she was improperly motivated by a desire to live with her mother. These witnesses repeated out-of-court statements about the offense that A.T. had made while in her mother's custody. The district court admitted these purported prior consistent statements under Federal Rule 801(d)(1)(B), and Tome was convicted. The Tenth Circuit adopted the Government's argument that the statements were admissible even though they were uttered after the time that the alleged motive to fabricate was asserted to have arisen. The Tenth Circuit recognized that some Courts of Appeals had interpreted the Rule to apply only to pre-motive statements, but it reasoned that any such "pre-motive requirement is a function of the relevancy rules, not the hearsay rules," and that automatic exclusion of post-motive statements was "clearly too broad . . . because it is simply not true that an individual with a motive to lie always will do so." Rather, the court considered motive, circumstances, and other factors to evaluate the relevance of the statements to the credibility issue. Here, the Supreme Court reverses and holds that the statements were not admissible under Rule 801(d)(1)(B).]

At issue is the interpretation of a provision in the Federal Rules of Evidence bearing upon the admissibility of statements, made by a declarant who testifies as a witness, that are consistent with the testimony and are offered to rebut a charge of a "recent fabrication or improper influence or motive." Fed. Rule Evid. 801(d)(1)(B). The question is whether out-of-court consistent statements made after the alleged fabrication, or after the alleged improper influence or motive arose, are admissible under the Rule.

II

The prevailing common-law rule for more than a century before adoption of the Federal Rules of Evidence was that a prior consistent statement introduced to rebut a charge of recent fabrication or improper influence or motive was admissible if the statement had been made before the alleged fabrication, influence, or motive came into being, but it was inadmissible if made afterwards.

The question is whether Rule 801(d)(1)(B) embodies this temporal requirement. We hold that it does.

A

Rule 801 defines prior consistent statements as nonhearsay only if they are offered to rebut a charge of "recent fabrication or improper influence or motive." Fed. R. Evid. 801(d)(1)(B). Noting the "troublesome" logic of treating a witness' prior consistent statements as hearsay at all (because the declarant is present in court and subject to cross-examination), the Advisory Committee decided to treat those consistent statements, once the preconditions of the Rule were satisfied, as nonhearsay and admissible as substantive evidence, not just to rebut an attack on the witness' credibility. A consistent statement meeting the requirements of the Rule is thus placed in the same category as a declarant's inconsistent statement made under oath in another proceeding, or prior identification testimony, or admissions by a party opponent.

The Rules do not accord this weighty, nonhearsay status to all prior consistent statements. To the contrary, admissibility under the Rules is confined to those statements offered to rebut a charge of "recent fabrication or improper influence or motive," the same phrase used by the Advisory Committee in its description of the "traditiona[l]" common law of evidence, which was the background against which the Rules were drafted. Prior consistent statements may not be admitted to counter all forms of impeachment or to bolster the witness merely because she has been discredited. In the present context, the question is whether A.T.'s out-of-court statements rebutted the alleged link between her desire to be with her mother and her testimony, not whether they suggested that A.T.'s in-court testimony was true. The Rule speaks of a party rebutting an alleged motive, not bolstering the veracity of the story told.

This limitation is instructive, not only to establish the preconditions of admissibility but also to reinforce the significance of the requirement that the consistent statements must have been made before the alleged influence, or motive to fabricate arose. That is to say, the forms of impeachment within the Rule's coverage are the ones in which the temporal requirement makes the most sense. Impeachment by charging that the testimony is a recent fabrication or results from an improper influence or motive is, as a general matter, capable of direct and forceful refutation through introduction of out-of-court consistent statements that predate the alleged fabrication, influence or motive. A consistent statement that predates the motive is a square rebuttal of the charge that the testimony was contrived as a consequence of that motive. By contrast, prior consistent statements carry little rebuttal force when most other types of impeachment are involved. McCormick § 49, p. 105 ("When the attack takes the form of impeachment of character, by showing misconduct, convictions or bad reputation, it is generally agreed that there is no color for sustaining by consistent statements. The defense does not meet the assault.").

There may arise instances when out-of-court statements that postdate the alleged fabrication have some probative force in rebutting a charge of fabrication or improper influence or motive, but those statements refute the charged fabrication in a less direct and forceful way. Evidence that a witness made consistent statements after the alleged motive to fabricate arose may suggest in some degree that the in-court testimony is truthful, and thus suggest in some degree that the testimony did not result from some improper influence; but if the drafters of Rule 801(d)(1)(B) intended to countenance rebuttal along that indirect inferential chain, the purpose for confining the types of impeachment that open the door to rebuttal by introducing consistent statements becomes unclear. If consistent statements are admissible without reference to the time frame we find imbedded in the Rule, there appears no sound reason not to admit consistent statements to rebut other forms of impeachment as well. Whatever objections can be leveled against limiting the Rule to this designated form of impeachment and confining the rebuttal to those statements made before the fabrication or improper influence or motive arose, it is clear to us that the drafters of Rule 801(d)(1)(B) were relying upon the common-law temporal requirement.

The underlying theory of the Government's position is that an out-of-court consistent statement, whenever it was made, tends to bolster the testimony of a witness and so tends also to rebut an express or implied charge that the testimony has been the product of an improper influence. Congress could have adopted that rule with ease, providing, for instance, that "a witness' prior consistent statements are admissible whenever relevant to assess the witness's truthfulness or accuracy." The narrow Rule enacted by Congress, however, cannot be understood to incorporate the Government's theory.

B

[Section II B was not joined by a majority of the Court. Justice Kennedy found support for the conclusion that Rule 801(d)(1)(B) embodies the common-law pre-motive requirement by examining the Advisory Committee Notes to the Federal Rules of Evidence, which rely on Wigmore and McCormick as authority for the common-law approach and state an "unwillingness to countenance the general use of prior prepared statements as substantive evidence." Rule 801(d), which "enumerates three situations in which the statement is excepted from the category of hearsay," was expressly contrasted by the Committee with Uniform Rule of Evidence 63(1) (1953), "which allows *any* out-of-court statement of a declarant who is present at the trial and available for cross-examination." When a witness presents important testimony damaging to a party, the party will often counter with at least an implicit charge that the witness has been under some influence or motive to fabricate. If Rule 801 were read so that the charge opened the floodgates to any prior consistent statement that satisfied Rule 403, as the Tenth Circuit concluded, the distinction between rejected Uniform Rule 63(1) and Rule 801(d)(1)(B) would all but disappear.]

C

The Government's final argument in favor of affirmance is that the common-law premotive rule advocated by petitioner is inconsistent with the Federal Rules' liberal approach to relevancy and with strong academic criticism, beginning in the 1940's, directed at the exclusion of out-of-court statements made by a declarant who is present in court and subject to cross-examination. This argument misconceives the design of the Rules' hearsay provisions.

Hearsay evidence is often relevant. That does not resolve the matter, however. Relevance is not the sole criterion of admissibility. Otherwise, it would be difficult to account for the Rules' general proscription of hearsay testimony (absent a specific exception), let alone the traditional analysis of hearsay that the Rules, for the most part, reflect. That certain out-of-court statements may be relevant does not dispose of the question whether they are admissible.

The Government's reliance on academic commentators critical of excluding out-of-court statements by a witness is subject to like criticism. Given the Advisory Committee's rejection of both the general balancing approach to hearsay, and of Uniform Rule 63(1), the Government's reliance on the views of those who advocated these positions is misplaced.

The statement-by-statement balancing approach advocated by the Government and adopted by the Tenth Circuit creates the precise dangers the Advisory Committee noted and sought to avoid: It involves considerable judicial discretion; it reduces predictability; and it enhances the difficulties of trial preparation because parties will have difficulty knowing in advance whether or not particular out-of-court statements will be admitted.

D

The case before us illustrates some of the important considerations supporting the Rule as we interpret it, especially in criminal cases. If the Rule were to permit the introduction of prior statements as substantive evidence to rebut every implicit charge that a witness' in-court testimony results from recent fabrication or improper influence or motive, the whole emphasis of the trial could shift to the out-of-court statements, not the in-court ones. The present case illustrates the point. In response to a rather weak charge that A.T.'s testimony was a fabrication created so the child could remain with her mother, the Government was permitted to present a parade of sympathetic and credible witnesses who did no more than recount A.T.'s detailed out-of-court statements to them. Although those statements might have been probative on the question whether the alleged conduct had occurred, they shed but minimal light on whether A.T. had the charged motive to fabricate. At closing argument before the jury, the Government placed great reliance on the prior statements for substantive purposes but did not once seek to use them to rebut the impact of the alleged motive.

We are aware that in some cases it may be difficult to ascertain when a particular fabrication, influence, or motive arose. Yet, as the Government concedes, a majority of common-law courts were performing this task for well over a century, and the Government has presented us with no evidence that those courts, or the judicial circuits that adhere to the rule today, have been unable to make the determination.

III

Courts must be sensitive to the difficulties attendant upon the prosecution of alleged child abusers. In almost all cases a youth is the prosecution's only eye witness. But "[t]his Court cannot alter evidentiary rules merely because litigants might prefer different rules in a particular class of cases." When a party seeks to introduce out-of-court statements that contain strong circumstantial indicia of reliability, that are highly probative on the material questions at trial, and that are better than other evidence otherwise available, there is no need to distort the requirements of Rule 801(d)(1)(B). If its requirements are met, Rule 803(24) exists for that eventuality. We intimate no view, however, concerning the admissibility of any of A.T.'s out-of-court statements under that section, or any other evidentiary principle. These matters, and others, are for the Court of Appeals to decide in the first instance.

The judgment of the Court of Appeals for the Tenth Circuit is reversed, and the case is remanded for further proceedings consistent with this opinion.

[The concurring opinion of JUSTICE SCALIA is omitted.] JUSTICE BREYER, with whom THE CHIEF JUSTICE, JUSTICE O'CONNOR and JUSTICE THOMAS join, dissenting:

The basic issue in this case concerns not hearsay, but relevance. As the majority points out, the common law permitted a lawyer to rehabilitate a witness (after a charge of improper motive) by pointing to the fact that the witness had said the same thing earlier — but only if the witness made the earlier statement *before* the motive to lie arose. The reason for the time limitation was that, otherwise, the prior consistent statement had no *relevance* to rebut the charge that the in-court testimony was the product of the motive to lie.

The majority believes that a hearsay-related rule, Federal Rule of Evidence 801(d)(1)(B), codifies this absolute timing requirement. I do not. Rule 801(d)(1)(B) has nothing to do with relevance. Rather, that Rule carves out a subset of prior consistent statements that were formerly admissible only to rehabilitate a witness (a nonhearsay use that relies upon the fact that the statement was made). It then says that members of that subset are "not hearsay." This means that, *if* such a statement is admissible for a particular rehabilitative purpose (to rebut a charge of recent fabrication, improper influence or motive), its proponent now may use it substantively, for a hearsay purpose (i.e., as evidence of its truth), as well.

The majority is correct in saying that there are different kinds of categories of prior consistent statements that can rehabilitate a witness in different ways, including statements (a) placing a claimed inconsistent statement in context; (b) showing that an inconsistent statement was not made; (c) indicating that the witness' memory is not as faulty as a cross-examiner has claimed; and (d) showing that the witness did not recently fabricate his testimony as a result of an improper influence or motive. But, I do not see where, in the existence of several categories, the majority can find the premise, which it seems to think is important, that the reason the drafters singled out one category (category (d)) was that category's special probative force in respect to rehabilitating a witness. Nor, in any event, do I understand how that premise can help the majority reach its conclusion about the common-law timing rule.

More important, the majority's conclusion about timing seems not to follow from its "especially probative force" premise. That is because probative force has little to do with the concerns underlying hearsay law. Hearsay law basically turns on an out-of-court declarant's reliability, as tested through cross-examination; it does not normally turn on the probative force (if true) of that declarant's statement. The "timing" circumstance (the fact that a prior consistent statement was made after a motive to lie arose) may diminish probative force, but it does not diminish reliability. Thus, from a hearsay perspective, the timing of a prior consistent statement is basically beside the point.

At the same time, one can find a *hearsay*-related reason why the drafters might have decided to restrict the Rule to a particular category of prior consistent statements. Juries have trouble distinguishing between the rehabilitative and substantive use of the kind of prior consistent statements listed in Rule 801(d)(1)(B). Judges may give instructions limiting the use of such prior consistent statements to a rehabilitative purpose, but, in practice, juries nonetheless tend to consider them for their substantive value. On this rationale, however, there is no basis for distinguishing between *pre* and *post* motive statements, for the confusion with respect to each would very likely be the same.

Assuming Rule 801(d)(1)(B) does not codify the absolute timing requirement, I must still answer the question whether, as a *relevance* matter, the common-law statement of the premotive rule stands as an absolute bar to a trial court's admission of a postmotive prior consistent statement for the purpose of rebutting a charge of recent fabrication or improper influence or motive. The majority points to statements of the timing rule that do suggest that, for reasons of relevance, the law of evidence *never* permits their admission. Yet, absolute-sounding rules often allow exceptions. And, there are sound reasons here for permitting an exception to the timing rule where circumstances warrant.

For one thing, one can find examples where the timing rule's claim of "no relevancy" is simply untrue. A postmotive statement is relevant to rebut, for example, a charge of recent fabrication based on improper motive, say, when the speaker made the prior statement while affected by a far more powerful motive to tell the truth. A speaker might be moved to lie to help an acquaintance. But, suppose the circumstances *also* make clear to the speaker that only the truth will save his child's life. Hence, postmotive statements can, *in appropriate circumstances*, directly refute the charge of fabrication based on improper motive, not because they bolster in a general way the witness' trial testimony, but because the circumstances indicate that the statements are not causally connected to the alleged motive to lie.

For another thing, the common law premotive rule was not as uniform as the majority suggests. A minority of courts recognized that postmotive statements could be relevant to rebut a charge of recent fabrication, improper influence or motive under the right circumstances.

This Court has acknowledged that the Federal Rules of Evidence worked a change in common-law relevancy rules in the direction of flexibility. The codification, as a general matter, relies upon the trial judge's administration of Rules 401, 402, and 403 to keep the barely relevant, the time wasting, and the prejudicial from the jury.

Irrespective of these arguments, one might claim that, nonetheless, the drafters, in writing Rule 801(d)(1)(B), relied on the continued existence of the common-law relevancy rule, and that Rule 801(d)(1)(B) therefore reflects a belief that the common-law relevancy rule would survive. But, I would reject that argument. For one thing, if the drafters had wanted to insulate the common-law rule from the Rules' liberalizing effect, this would have been a remarkably indirect (and therefore odd) way of doing so — both because Rule 801(d)(1)(B) is utterly silent about the premotive rule and because Rule 801(d)(1)(B) is a rule of hearsay, not relevancy. For another thing, there is an equally plausible reason why the drafters might have wanted to write Rule 801(d)(1)(B) the way they did — namely, to allow substantive use of a particular category of prior consistent statements that, when admitted as rehabilitative evidence, was especially impervious to a limiting instruction.

In this case, the Court of Appeals, applying an approach consistent with what I have described above, decided that A.T.'s prior consistent statements were probative on the question of whether her story as a witness reflected a motive to lie. There is no reason to reevaluate this factbound conclusion. Accordingly, I would affirm the judgment of the Court of Appeals.

NOTES AND QUESTIONS

(1) Offering Post-Motive Prior Statements with a Limiting Instruction Confining them to Credibility Issues: Is this a Proper Alternative, after Tome? Consider the possibility that, in *Tome*, the prosecution (on retrial, if any) were to offer the same prior statements — but the court were to give a limiting instruction telling the jury that the statements could be considered only for the purpose of assessing the child's credibility. The statements would not be hearsay if confined to this purpose (do you see why?). Thus, the literal holding of *Tome*, as well as most of its reasoning, arguably would be inapplicable. This approach might be supported by the broad relevancy rules of Fed. R. Evid. 401–402, as well as Fed. R. Evid. 613(a), which implies the admissibility of "prior statements" affecting credibility. The trial judge still would face a difficult balancing question under Fed. R. Evid. 403 (why?). Question: Is this alternative theory of admissibility a viable one after *Tome*, or is it implicitly foreclosed by the opinion in *Tome*?

(2) The "Catchall" as an Alternative in Tome. The majority expressly reserves the question whether, on remand, admissibility might be upheld pursuant to former Fed. R. Evid. 803(24) — the "catchall" exception for "good" hearsay evidence that doesn't fit any other exception. The Court sets out the requirements for the catchall near the end of its opinion. Does it seem to fit here (and if it does, does this conclusion indirectly support the arguments of the dissenters)? On remand, the catchall was rejected because the statement lacked trustworthiness for the same reason that it could not meet the criteria of Fed. R. Evid. 801(d)(1)(B), i.e., the motive to fabricate preceded its making. (Note that Fed. R. Evid. 803(24) now is Fed. R. Evid. 807).

[D] Statements of Identification

UNITED STATES v. OWENS

United States Supreme Court
484 U.S. 554 (1988)

Scalia, Justice.

[John Foster's memory was severely impaired by an assault. Afterward, in a hospital, Foster described the assault and identified Owens from a photo spread. At Owens' trial for assault with intent to commit murder, Foster could not remember seeing his assailant, or seeing any hospital visitors except the FBI agent who interviewed him, or whether any visitor had suggested that Owens was the assailant. He did, however, remember identifying Owens's photo. The trial judge admitted testimony about Foster's prior identification pursuant to Fed. R. Evid. 801(d)(1)(C). The Court of Appeals reversed, citing the hearsay rule in Fed. R. Evid. 802 and the Confrontation Clause. The Supreme Court reversed the reversal and upheld the admissibility of the evidence.]

II

Respondent has argued that this Court's jurisprudence concerning suggestive identification procedures shows the special dangers of identification testimony, and the special importance of cross-examination when such hearsay is proffered. Respondent has not, however, argued that the identification procedure used here was in any way suggestive. There does not appear in our opinions, and we decline to adopt today, the principle that, because of the mere possibility of suggestive procedures, out-of-court statements of identification are inherently less reliable than other out-of-court statements.

III

Respondent urges as an alternative basis for affirmance a violation of Federal Rule of Evidence 802, which generally excludes hearsay. Rule 801(d)(1)(C) defines as not hearsay a prior statement "of identification of a person made after perceiving the person," if the declarant "testifies at the trial or hearing and is subject to cross-examination concerning the statement." The Court of Appeals found that Foster's identification statement did not come within this exclusion because his memory loss prevented his being "subject to cross-examination concerning the statement."

It seems to us that the more natural reading of "subject to cross-examination concerning the statement" includes what was available here. Ordinarily a witness is regarded as "subject to cross-examination" when he is placed on the stand, under oath, and responds willingly to questions. Just as with the constitutional prohibition, limitations on the scope of examination by the trial court or assertions of privilege by the witness may undermine the process to such a degree that meaningful cross-examination within the intent of the Rule no longer exists. But that effect is not produced by the witness' assertion of memory loss — which, as discussed earlier, is often the very result sought to be produced by cross-examination, and can be effective in destroying the force of the prior statement.

This reading seems even more compelling when the Rule is compared with Rule 804(a)(3), which defines "[u]navailability as a witness" to include situations in which a declarant "testifies to a lack of memory of the subject matter of the declarant's statement." Congress plainly was aware of the recurrent evidentiary problem at issue here — witness forgetfulness of an underlying event — but chose not to make it an exception to Rule 801(d)(1)(C).

The premise for Rule 801(d)(1)(C) was that, given adequate safeguards against suggestiveness, out-of-court identifications were generally preferable to courtroom identifications. Thus, despite the traditional view that such statements were hearsay, the Advisory Committee believed that their use was to be fostered rather than discouraged. Similarly, the House Report on the Rule noted that since, "[a]s time goes by, a witness' memory will fade and his identification will become less reliable," minimizing the barriers to admission of more contemporaneous identification is fairer to defendants and prevents "cases falling through because the witness can no longer recall the identity of the person he saw commit the crime."

Respondent argues that this reading is impermissible because it creates an internal inconsistency in the Rules, since the forgetful witness who is deemed "subject to cross-examination" under 801(d)(1)(C) is simultaneously deemed "unavailable" under 804(a)(3). This is the position espoused by a prominent commentary on the Rules, *see* 4 J. Weinstein & M. Berger, Weinstein's Evidence 801-120 to 801-121, 801-178 (1987). It seems to us, however, that this is not a substantive inconsistency, but only a semantic oddity resulting from the fact that Rule 804(a) has for convenience of reference in Rule 804(b) chosen to describe the circumstances necessary in order to admit certain categories of hearsay testimony under the rubric "Unavailability as a witness." These circumstances include not only absence from the hearing, but also claims of privilege, refusals to obey a court's order to testify, and inability to testify based on physical or mental illness or memory loss. Had the rubric instead been "unavailability as a witness, memory loss, and other special circumstances" there would be no apparent inconsistency with Rule 801, which is a definition section excluding certain statements entirely from the category of "hearsay." The semantic inconsistency exists not only with respect to Rule 801(d)(1)(C), but also with respect to the other subparagraphs of Rule 801(d)(1). It would seem strange, for example, to assert that a witness can avoid introduction of testimony from a prior proceeding that is inconsistent with his trial testimony, *see* Rule 801(d)(1)(A), by simply asserting lack of memory of the facts to which the prior testimony related. But that situation, like this one, presents the verbal curiosity that the witness is "subject to cross-examination" under Rule 801 while at the same time "unavailable" under Rule 804(a)(3). Quite obviously, the two characterizations are made for two entirely different purposes and there is no requirement or expectation that they should coincide.

For the reasons stated, we hold that Federal Rule of Evidence 802 is [not] violated by admission of an identification statement of a witness who is unable, because of a memory loss, to testify concerning the basis for the identification. The decision of the Court of Appeals is reversed, and the case is remanded for proceedings consistent with this opinion.

NOTES AND QUESTIONS

(1) *What Kinds of "Identifications" Fit this Rule?* A few decisions at common law held that former statements of witnesses who are now testifying should be exempt from the hearsay rule if and only if they deal with identification of a culprit, as where the witness had identified the offender on the scene, or in an interview, or in a lineup or from photographs. Some of these seemed to confine this rule to the situation where the witness himself relates his earlier statement, as opposed to someone else relating the witness's earlier statement. More recently courts have permitted identifications even when the witness recants at trial. *See United States*

v. O'Malley, 796 F.2d 891 (7th Cir. 1986). On occasion, a statement naming the person who committed the crime has not been permitted. *See* discussion in *State v. Turvey*, 618 N.E.2d 214 (Ohio Ct. App. 1992), disapproving child abuse cases that admit statements made by children to mothers or doctors naming close relatives as their assailants under the rubric of prior identifications. *Turvey* viewed such statements as addressing the fact that a crime had been committed, not identifying an unknown molester.

(2) *Constitutional Aspects of Criminal Identification: The (Post-Indictment) Right to Counsel at Lineup — United States v. Wade, 388 U.S. 218 (1967).* Wade was tried for robbery and conspiracy to rob a bank. The evidence identifying Wade consisted of an at-trial identification of him by two eyewitnesses. Thus, no hearsay problem was presented by the facts of *Wade*. However, the witnesses had previously identified Wade in a pretrial, post-indictment police lineup. The majority opinion in *Wade* states that pretrial identification proceedings are often staged in a manner that would cast considerable doubt on the validity of the at-trial identification too, and that, unless represented by counsel at the time, a defendant would have difficulty at trial in re-creating the identification procedures so as to show their unfair features. The Court held that an accused's rights of confrontation and assistance of counsel are violated unless defense counsel is given notice of the pendency of the pretrial, post-indictment identification proceeding and afforded the opportunity to be present. The at-trial identification testimony still might be admissible if, on remand, the court determined that it had an "independent origin," i.e., it resulted from the actual event and not from the lineup. *See also Gilbert v. California*, 388 U.S. 263 (1967).

(3) *The Due Process Right Against an "Unduly Suggestive" Lineup*: *Stovall v. Denno, 388 U.S. 293 (1967)*. In this case it was held that the *Wade-Gilbert* rule was not retroactive, but that there is a general due process right (that applies even in situations not covered by the *Wade-Gilbert* rule) to have the out-of-court identification conducted under circumstances that are not "unduly suggestive" to the witness in the light of the exigencies of the circumstances; and if an in-court identification is tainted by or is the product of an unduly suggestive out-of-court identification, the in-court one is also bad. Facts (from the opinion):

> Dr. Behrendt was stabbed to death in the kitchen of his home about midnight August 23. Dr. Behrendt's wife, also a physician, had followed her husband to the kitchen and jumped at the assailant. He knocked her to the floor and stabbed her 11 times. The police found a shirt on the kitchen floor and keys in a pocket which they traced to petitioner. They arrested him on the afternoon of August 24.
>
> Mrs. Behrendt was hospitalized for major surgery to save her life. The police, without affording petitioner time to retain counsel, arranged with her surgeon to permit them to bring petitioner to her hospital room about noon of August 25, the day after the surgery. Petitioner was handcuffed to one of five police officers who, with two members of the staff of the District Attorney, brought him to the hospital room. Petitioner was the only Negro in the room. Mrs. Behrendt identified him from her hospital bed.

The Court held that there was no error in this process. The right to counsel did not apply retroactively (and it does not constitutionally attach before indictment anyway). As for whether the "one-person lineup" conducted in the hospital was unduly suggestive, the key word is "unduly," which depends on the exigencies of the circumstances.

(4) *What Constitutes "Undue Suggestion?"* For a case shedding further light on what may be considered suggestive, see *Palmer v. Peyton*, 359 F.2d 199 (4th Cir. 1966). Palmer involved the admissibility of an identification of defendant's voice in the station-house by the victim of an attack. In making the identification, the victim did not actually confront the defendant and had no opportunity to compare his voice with other voices. Moreover, police had exhibited a shirt to her similar in color to that worn by her attacker and told her it was defendant's shirt. The Court held that these events violated defendant's due process rights.

See also Biggers v. Tennessee, 390 U.S. 404 (1968). In this case, a rape victim was shown photos by police over a period of months; one of the photos was of a person who looked like the defendant. Subsequently, police allowed the victim to view the defendant alone. During this encounter the victim was told that the defendant was a suspect. The defendant was ordered to speak the words spoken by the rapist. The victim then identified him as the rapist, an identification she repeated at trial, saying her identification was based on defendant's voice. The Court held that the circumstances in this case were not unduly suggestive under due process, although undue suggestivity was recognized as an independent principle for exclusion apart from *Wade* and *Gilbert*.

(5) *What Effect does the 1968 Omnibus Crime Control Act have on these Cases?* See the following provision in the Omnibus Crime Control and Safe Streets Act of 1968, 18 U.S.C. § 3502:

> Admissibility in evidence of eyewitness testimony:
>
> The testimony of a witness that he saw the accused commit or participate in the commission of the crime for which the accused is being tried shall be admissible in evidence in a criminal prosecution in any trial court ordained and established under Article III of the Constitution of the United States.

What does this do to *Wade, Gilbert*, and *Stovall*, or what do they do to it? What does it do to other rules of evidence that might affect admissibility in a given case? *Dickerson v. United States*, 530 U.S. 428 (2000), held that the requirement of *Miranda* warnings is constitutionally based, though imposed by case law, and therefore it cannot be overruled by a Congressional act that attempted to do so. Would the Court hold similarly with respect to the legislative provision set forth here, and the constitutional rulings it seems to affect?

§ 8.02 ADMISSIONS OF PARTY[2]

Read Federal Rule of Evidence 801(d)(2), "Definitions (Hearsay): Statements That are Not Hearsay: An Opposing Party's Statement [i.e., a Party Admission]."

---

[2] Study Guide Reference: Evidence in a Nutshell, Chapter 9:III.

[A] Introduction

The Federal Rules of Evidence treat admissions as exempted from the definition of hearsay. The Advisory Notes explain that their admissibility "is the result of the adversary system rather than satisfaction of the conditions of the hearsay rule. No guarantee of trustworthiness is required." The common law considered admissions to be hearsay, and many lawyers find it more convenient in thinking about the subject of hearsay to go along with the more traditional classification that party admissions are hearsay, but that there is an exception to the hearsay rule for them. As a practical matter, it makes no difference which of the two approaches is used — the practical result is the same.

Admissions fall into a number of categories, the most important of which are the party's own statements, adopted statements, authorized statements, statements by agents and employees, and statements by co-conspirators.

[B] Basic Doctrine

SUSEMIEHL v. RED RIVER LUMBER CO.

Illinois Appellate Court 306 Ill. App.
430, 28 N.E.2d 743 (1940)

WOLFE, PRESIDING JUSTICE.

[A wrongful death action was filed by plaintiff, the administrator of the estate of Walter Susemiehl, who was killed in an automobile accident, against Red River Lumber and Walter Gehrke, a salesman for Red River and operator/owner of the car that collided with decedent's car. Red River's defense was that at the moment of the accident Gehrke was not acting within the course and scope of his employment but was either an independent contractor or on a frolic of his own. Red River argues on appeal that the trial court erred in admitting the workers' compensation accident report made by J.P. Rinn and mailed to Red River's insurer.]

[T]he report made out by Mr. J.P. Rinn, the Managing Officer of the Red River Lumber Company, [stated] that their employee, Walter Gehrke, had been injured [on the job] and the report was made for the purpose of claiming compensation for such injuries.

This exhibit was admitted on the theory that it was an admission by the defendant company and that such is competent evidence, for the jury to consider.

It is seriously contended that it was error for the Court to admit this exhibit because the same was made out not on the personal knowledge of Mr. Rinn, but on hearsay, and therefore not binding as an admission of the defendant, the Red River Lumber Company.

In the [Oklahoma] case of *Little Fay Oil Co. v. Stanley* [217 P. 377], the plaintiff, Stanley, claimed he was injured in the course of employment and brought suit under the Compensation Act. An award was allowed, and the case came before the Supreme Court. The respondent claim[ed] that there was no evidence to support the award, the company claiming that Stanley was not its employee, but that of one Miller, an individual contractor. Upon the hearing the plaintiff offered in evidence a report filed with the Industrial Commission by the Oil Company ten days after the accident, in which report it was stated, that the plaintiff was an employee on the day he was injured, in the course of employment, and that he had been employed by them one day as a time-worker at $14 per day. The Oil Company claimed this report was made through a misapprehension of fact by an officer of the Company at Tulsa who acted upon the information received over the telephone, and this office was under a misapprehension of the facts and therefore the admission should not have been admitted as an admission. The Court, in their opinion, uses this language:

> The fact that the statements contained in the report of the employer were made by a person who did not have personal knowledge of the facts did not render the admission made in the report incompetent as evidence, but simply went to the weight to be given the admission as evidence.

Sparr & Green v. Wellman, 11 Mo. 230 [quotes authority which states]:

> An admission is the statement of a fact against the interest of a party making it — but it is not essential to constitute it an admission, that the fact should have come under the personal observation of the declarant. Undoubtedly admissions of the latter kind are much stronger than where the declaration is of a fact, of which the party could have no personal knowledge. But where a party believes a fact upon evidence sufficient to convince him of its existence, his declaration of the existence of that fact, if against his interest, is evidence against him.

In *Kitchen v. Robbins*, 29 Ga. 713, it is stated:

> Are no admissions good against a party, unless founded on his personal knowledge? The admissions would not be made except on evidence which satisfies the party who is making them against his own interest, that they are true, and that is evidence to the jury that they are true. Admissions do not come in, on the ground that the party making them, is speaking from his personal knowledge, but upon the ground that a party will not make admissions against himself unless they are true. The fact that he makes them against his interest, can be reasonably explained only on the supposition that he is constrained to do so by the force of the evidence. The source from which a knowledge of the facts is derived, is a circumstance for the jury to consider in estimating the value of the evidence, but that is all.

[The Court properly admitted plaintiff's exhibit against Red River.] This was an admission that Gehrke, at the time of the accident was an employee and agent of the defendant company, and was driving his car on regular company business.

NOTES AND QUESTIONS

(1) *Firsthand or Personal Knowledge Rule, and Opinion Rule: Do they Apply to Party Admissions Made Out-of-Court?* In *Janus v. Akstin*, 20 A.2d 552 (N.H. 1941), defendant told the victim's husband that defendant's dog "jumped" the victim, although defendant did not see the accident. (A witness on the stand saying

the same thing would be held to violate the personal knowledge rule.) The victim's husband was allowed to testify to this statement as a party admission in the personal injury action on the basis that defendant would not "make statements of fact contrary to his interest unless he is satisfied [they] are true." Thus, defendant did not need to have personal knowledge but could infer from "clues" or what others said. Is there reason to distinguish from *Akstin* the present case, or any other case, where the admission is made by an agent, or where the statement is not realized to be against self-interest at the time made? Would the same rationale of "contrary to self interest" apply? *See Mahlandt v. Wild Canid Survival & Research Center, Inc.*, 588 F.2d 626 (8th Cir. 1978), an action for damages arising out of an alleged attack by a wolf (Sophie) on a child. The court held it was reversible error to exclude a note from an agent of the defendant that "Sophie bit a child," even though the agent was not present when the child was bitten. The statement would be admissible against the corporate defendant, as well as the individual agent who signed it. The decision extensively discusses the matter of lack of personal knowledge in the context of both personal party admissions, and admissions by an agent, under the Federal Rules of Evidence, noting the disparate views of leading treatises and the Federal Rules Advisory Committee (which favored admissibility), and holding that a statement lacking personal knowledge, which it seems to distinguish from a statement incorporating hearsay, is admissible against both the agent, and the principal.

Are other hearsay exceptions (than party admissions) distinguishable? Suppose the rationale of *Akstin* had been (as is sometimes said) that to enforce a rule requiring personal knowledge would not merely result in rephrasing of the answer (as when it is enforced against a witness rather than a declarant) but would probably result in a loss of the evidence (or a distortion of the evidence because the party's statement at trial will be colored by litigation motivation). Would that rationale change any of your answers to the questions above in this note?

Is there reason to treat a statement about employment, as in the principal case, more leniently as respects secondhand knowledge, than other statements?

Would *Akstin* have applied the same rule it applied if the defendant had said "the dog jumped the victim" on the witness stand instead of off it?

In *Strickland v. Davis*, 128 So. 233 (Ala. 1930), in accord with the usual result in cases like *Strickland* and *Akstin*, plaintiff in an auto collision case was allowed to testify that defendant had said, some time after the accident, that defendant was "at fault" for the accident, on rationales similar to the two mentioned above in this note (although it was said a live witness could not indulge in such conclusory statements or opinions in an ordinary case). The court said that the fact that there was opinion or conclusion in the statement, the vagaries of what was meant, and the possibly different standard of what the law means by "fault" could be taken into account by the jury in assessing weight. Does *Susemiehl*, the principal case, present a problem of this sort? Ask yourself all the questions in the present note about this rule as well, under each of the two rationales.

There is considerable agreement on relaxation of the personal knowledge and opinion rules as respects out-of-court personal or agent-made party admissions, but not as much agreement respecting other hearsay exemptions and exceptions.

(2) *Bribing Witnesses.* One recurring type of admission is the attempt by a party to bribe someone to perjure himself so as to support the party's version of the facts. *Moriarty v. London, Chatham & Dover Railway Co.*, 5 L.R. Q.B. 314 (1870), is an English case in which a husband and wife sued a railroad for her injuries. One defense witness, Whymark, testified that the husband stated he would give one-third of any award he received if Whymark would testify that he (Whymark) saw the accident and it occurred in an agreed-upon manner. The admission of the testimony was affirmed on the theory that it indicated the plaintiff "knew perfectly well his cause was an unrighteous one."

PROBLEM 8A: "IT WAS ALL MY FAULT . . ." OFFERED AGAINST THE PLAINTIFF IN (1) A SURVIVAL ACTION; (2) A WRONGFUL DEATH CASE.

Plaintiff, who is the administrator and surviving wife of deceased, killed by the allegedly negligent driving of defendant, sues defendant (1) in the wife's capacity as administrator, for the pain and suffering of the deceased and (2) on her own behalf for damages accruing to the wife from the loss of the husband, all joined in one lawsuit, but in two separate counts. Defendant wishes to introduce the testimony of someone to whom the decedent had said "It was all my fault; I am solely to blame." Is this "admission" admissible? Should any limitations on its use be imposed by instructions to be given to the jury? Do they make sense? *See Eldredge v. Barton*, 122 N.E. 272 (Mass. 1919) (holding evidence admissible in survival claim, where estate is successor in interest, but not in wife's action in her own right). The two "conflicting admissibilities" may require balancing of relevance versus prejudice similar to modern Rule 403. Beware, the facts here are slightly different than in *Eldredge*. Does the doctrine of that case exist under the Federal Rules of Evidence?

[C] Adoptive Admissions

UNITED STATES v. FLECHA

United States Court of Appeals, Second Circuit
539 F.2d 874 (1976)

FRIENDLY, CIRCUIT JUDGE.

Appellant [Flecha] was tried before a jury. The indictment charged the importation of 287 pounds of marijuana and related charges. The jury returned guilty verdicts.

As a result of information received from the Customs Service at Galveston, Texas, customs agents set up a surveillance of [a] vessel.

Not satisfied with this compelling case, the prosecutor elicited from Agent Cabrera that, as all five defendants were standing in line [upon arrest on board the ship] he heard Gonzalez say in Spanish, apparently to Flecha: "Why so much excitement? If we are caught, we are caught." The three lawyers who represented defendants Banguera, Suarez and Pineda-Marin immediately sought an instruction that this was "not binding" on their clients; the court said "Granted." Counsel for Flecha then joined in the application. Judge Weinstein asked Agent Cabrera how far away Flecha was from Gonzalez; Cabrera answered that Flecha was right next to Gonzalez, only six to twelve inches away. The judge then denied Flecha's application.

Although the judge did not articulate his reasons for granting the applications of Banguera, Suarez and Pineda-Marin but denying Flecha's, it is not difficult to reconstruct what his thought process must have been. To state the matter in terms of the later-enacted Federal Rules of Evidence, which in respects here relevant do not differ from the common law, the judge properly concluded that Gonzalez' declaration was not admissible as "a statement by a co-conspirator of a party during the course and in furtherance of the conspiracy," Rule 801(d)(2)(E), since the conspiracy was over and the statement was not in furtherance of it. He must also have concluded that the declaration was not admissible under Rule 803(2), the hearsay exception for "[a] statement relating to a startling event or condition made while the declarant was under the stress of excitement caused by the event or condition." This was probably right since Gonzalez' plea by its own terms indicated a lack of excitement. His allowing Gonzalez' statement to stand against Flecha although not against the three other objectors must thus have rested on a belief that as to Flecha the case fell within Rule 801(d)(2)(B), allowing receipt, as an admission of the party against whom it is offered, of "a statement of which he has manifested his adoption or belief in its truth."

The brief voir dire demonstrates that the judge fell into the error of jumping from the correct proposition that hearing the statement of a third person is a necessary condition for adoption by silence, to the incorrect conclusion that it is a sufficient one. After quoting the maxim "silence gives consent," Wigmore explains "that the inference of assent may safely be made only when no other explanation is equally consistent with silence; and there is always another possible explanation — namely, ignorance or dissent — *unless the circumstances are such that a dissent would in ordinary experience have been expressed if the communication had not been correct.*" However, "the force of the brief maxim has always been such that in practice a sort of working rule grew up that *whatever was said in a party's presence* was receivable against him as an admission, because presumably assented to." Before receiving an admission by silence the court must determine, inter alia "whether he [the party] is in such a situation that he is at liberty to make any reply" and "whether the statement is made under such circumstances, and by such persons, as naturally to call for a reply, if he did not intend to admit it."

We find it hard to think of a case where response would have been less expectable than this one. Flecha was under arrest, and although the Government emphasizes that he was not being questioned by the agents, and had not been given Miranda warnings, it is clear that many arrested persons know, without benefit of warnings, that silence is usually golden. Beyond that, what was Flecha to say? If the Spanish verb used by Gonzalez has the same vagueness as "caught," it would have been somewhat risible for Flecha, surrounded by customs agents, to have denied that he had been. Of course, Flecha could have said "Speak for yourself" or something like it, but it was far more natural to say nothing.

There is no force in the Government's argument that Gonzalez' statement "was not admitted for its truth, but rather for what it showed about Gonzalez' and Flecha's state of mind," and thus was not hearsay. Of course, it was not hearsay as to Gonzalez but in order to be relevant against Flecha, it would have to be at least a description by Gonzalez of Flecha's state of mind ("You know you are guilty") and that would be hearsay unless Flecha adopted it by silence.

We have thought it desirable to write on this in order to prevent future reliance on the "working rule" so rightly condemned by Wigmore and other eminent jurists, rather than because of the effect of the ruling in this case. For we agree with the Government that the error was harmless on the particular facts.

NOTES AND QUESTIONS

(1) *Even if it isn't an Adoptive Admission by Flecha, can You Argue that Gonzales' Statement or Flecha's Response isn't Hearsay?* In *Flecha*, under the Federal Rules of Evidence would the evidence be hearsay in the first place, under Fed. R. Evid. 801(a) and (c), before you even get to Fed. R. Evid. 801(d)(2)? *See generally* Schaitkin, *"Negative Hearsay" — The Sounds of Silence*, 84 DICK. L. REV. 605 (1980).

(2) *Adoption of an Accusation of Crime by Silence: A Negative View.* See *Commonwealth v. Dravecz*, 424 Pa. 582, 227 A.2d 904 (1967), for the view, persuasively and eloquently put, that it is always beneath one's dignity to dignify an accusation by responding, and thus responsive silence should never be admissible as an admission. The argument for inadmissibility is perhaps more persuasive on the facts of the case than as a general proposition: defendant was confronted by police with his superior, a shop foreman. The police read him the foreman's statement that defendant had appeared at the foreman's residence with some of the merchandise that had been stolen from their employer. (The court also states that using the silence would be inconsistent with our rules that a person may be silent to even the most damning evidence at trial and that before trial he need not respond to accusations by police. The court notes that using the silence is essentially compelling self-incrimination.)

(3) *But Adoptions by Silence Often are Admitted. Dravecz* is a minority view, at least if it is meant to apply outside the police situation. Admissions by silence/adoption are commonly admitted in both civil and criminal cases. The test (although variously phrased) is essentially whether a reasonable person would make a denial if the statement were untrue. Why is that the test? Is there a second test that also must be met, stemming from the Constitution, in the police situation?

In *United States v. Hoosier*, 542 F.2d 687 (6th Cir. 1976), the court held admissible the fact that a statement incriminating defendant (reference to a large sum of money in defendant's room) was made by defendant's girlfriend to a third person, in defendant's presence. (Police were not involved.) The fact that defendant met it by silence was admissible as an admission by silence (or adoption).

Is this kind of evidence "binding," or may the opponent of the evidence still argue to the jury that the silence or failure to respond is meaningless, despite the fact it may be admitted into evidence?

Why might a situation where police are involved be distinguishable from one where they are not? Should it make any difference if *Miranda* warnings have been given? (Consider, on these two questions, both the Constitution and the evidentiary "reasonable person" test.)

(4) *Can Adoption of Accusations be Inferred from Post-Arrest Silence in Response to Miranda Warnings? The Problem of Doyle v. Ohio.* A related question governed by the same considerations is whether silence about an alibi or other excuse (or the like), in circumstances where one might naturally have protested innocence and asserted it well before trial can be used to impeach a story of innocence at trial. This frequently comes up in the context that the silence was to the police, which presents both evidentiary and constitutional considerations. *See United States v. Hale*, 422 U.S. 171 (1975), and *Doyle v. Ohio*, 426 U.S. 610 (1976) (excluding evidence of post-arrest silence after *Miranda* warnings, partly on the ground that it would be anomalous to infer admission by silence when defendant has been told he has a right to remain silent). But these cases were distinguished in *Jenkins v. Anderson*, 447 U.S. 231 (1980), addressing prearrest silence, without warnings, which involves different issues. An inference of adoption by silence may be permitted in certain circumstances and not others.

In addition, the mere asking at trial of a question violating *Doyle* is not error if the judge has not permitted a response and instructs the jury to disregard any improper questions. *Greer v. Miller*, 483 U.S. 756 (1987). Similarly, examination about a defendant's inconsistent statement does not implicate *Doyle* even though the inconsistent descriptions of events may be said to involve "silence" insofar as it omits facts included in the other version. *Anderson v. Charles*, 447 U.S. 404 (1980). The presence or absence of *Miranda* warnings by police at the time of the silence by the accused or the failure to tell the story later told by him at trial is a factor to consider. *Cf. United States v. Moore*, 104 F.3d 377 (D.C. Cir. 1997) (custody, not interrogation, is the triggering mechanism for the right of pretrial silence under *Miranda*; finding error where defendant's post-arrest silence was introduced by prosecution, even though it was prior to *Miranda* warning).

See, for a state case, *State v. Hunt*, 323 S.E.2d 490 (N.C. Ct. App. 1984). In this case, defendant, without *Miranda* warnings, remained silent while he was arrested for murdering his wife on the basis of accusations by his stepson. At trial defendant claimed he saw his stepson commit the crime. The court allows the impeachment, saying that it strains credibility that a reasonable person would remain silent and let the real murderer go free when he learned of his wife's death and his stepson's accusation. The court states there is nothing ambiguous about his silence. (Are there other considerations?) *Compare Wainwright v. Greenfield*, 474 U.S. 284 (1986), holding that defendant's post-arrest silence following a recital of *Miranda* warnings is inadmissible to prove his sanity at the time of the offense. In *Wainwright*, the defendant did not testify in his own behalf.

(5) *Adoptive Admissions in Civil Cases.* In *Sea-Land Service, Inc. v. Lozen Int'l, LLC*, 285 F.3d 808 (9th Cir. 2002), the exclusion of an e-mail was reversible error in part because:

> Jacques' original e-mail was forwarded to Lozen Int'l by Laurie Martinez, a . . . Sea-Land employee. She copied the entire body of Jacques'

memorandum into her e-mail and prefaced it with the statement, "Yikes, Pls note the rail screwed us up. . . ." Martinez thereby incorporated and adopted the contents of Jacques' original message, because her remark "manifested an adoption or belief in [the] truth" of the information contained in the original e-mail.

PROBLEM 8B: "YOU WENT THROUGH A RED LIGHT!"

Jones is involved in an auto collision. He is somewhat shaken up, and is looking for a telephone to call his wife, when a bystander calls to him from the curb: "You went through a red light." Jones does not respond. In the distance a policeman is approaching on foot to see what happened. In the litigation arising out of this collision, a witness is offered against Jones to testify to having witnessed this "exchange" between the bystander and Jones. Rule on the admissibility, or state what factors you would consider or need to know more about and why they would make a difference. Who (judge or jury) decides whether the "reasonable person" test is met?

[D] Admissions by Agents Authorized to Speak for Principals

CONTRACTOR UTILITY SALES CO., INC. v. CERTAIN-TEED PRODUCTS CORP.

United States Court of Appeals, Seventh Circuit
638 F.2d 1061 (1981)

SPRECHER, CIRCUIT JUDGE.

The final argument we must confront is [defendant] Certain-teed's contention that the district court improperly excluded from evidence portions of [plaintiff] Cusco's original complaint [in this suit, which complaint was amended after filing] which are relevant to both the breach of contract and fraud claims. Certain-teed attempted, at three points during the trial, to introduce into evidence a portion of Cusco's original complaint which stated that:

> [T]he Defendant, in order to establish a market with the sales territory dominated by Plaintiff, induced Plaintiff to enter into an exclusive Sales Agency Agreement with the Defendant by fraudulently misrepresenting to the Plaintiff that the Defendant would grant to the Plaintiff an exclusive sales territory and maintain the plaintiff on the same status as other agents and distributors of the Defendant regarding price, availability of materials, etc.

Certain-teed claims that this portion of the original, but superseded, complaint should have been admitted as relevant evidence. Certain-teed argues that, if admitted, this evidence would have enabled Certain-teed to refute Cusco's claim, stated in its final complaint, that Certain-teed induced Cusco to execute the Sales Agents Agreement by fraudulently representing that Certain-teed would keep Cusco "competitive with his contractor-customers in the rural water market."

Certain-teed also contends that this evidence is relevant to contest Lance's interpretation of the alleged "keep competitive" representation.

[I]t appears the district court concluded that, despite the inconsistencies between the pleadings, superseded pleadings are inadmissible. This is incorrect as a matter of law, and, for the reasons explained below, constitutes reversible error.

Although prior pleadings cease to be conclusive judicial admissions, they are admissible in a civil action as evidentiary admissions. As noted in *Raulie v. United States*, 400 F.2d 487, 526 (10th Cir., 1968):

> When a pleading is amended or withdrawn, the superseded portion ceases to be a conclusive judicial admission; but it still remains as a statement once seriously made by an authorized agent, and as such it is competent evidence of the facts stated, though controvertible, like any other extrajudicial admission made by a party or his agent.

Perhaps Cusco can explain away the inconsistency; but that is a matter for trial, not a reason to exclude the evidence. Similarly, the fact that the original complaint is unverified [i.e., not sworn to] goes to the weight rather than the admissibility of the original complaint.

Introduction of the prior complaint is an understandable and legitimate means of [establishing facts contrary to the party's present position.] Cusco may well be able to explain why the alleged representations were characterized in such different terms. But, Certain-teed should be permitted to introduce this portion of the prior pleading and put Cusco to the task of explaining the inconsistency.

The district court's refusal to allow introduction of this portion of the original complaint cannot be characterized as harmless error under Rule 103 of the Federal Rules of Evidence. The true characterization of Certain-teed's representations was critical to Cusco's fraud claim. The apparent conflict in Cusco's complaints is material and significant. The exclusion was prejudicial and reversible error.

NOTES AND QUESTIONS

(1) *The Principal's Participation in an Alleged Admission by an Agent: Does it Matter?* Should it make any difference whether the pleading has been verified by the client? What about other filings, e.g., answers to interrogatories — are they admissions, regardless of whether verified by the client? To what extent might the lawyer drafting a pleading risk liability to her client in a case like the one above?

(2) *Lawyers Statements as Admissions of Client.* Is an opening statement by an attorney for a criminal defendant made in a prior trial in the same case an admission that can be used against the defendant in the later trial under Fed. R. Evid. 801(d)(2) when it is inconsistent with the opening statement at the later trial? *See United States v. McKeon*, 738 F.2d 26 (2d Cir. 1984). The Second Circuit extended such a principle to the prosecution in *United States v. GAF Corp.*, 928 F.2d 1253 (2d Cir. 1991), in a case involving the defense's attempt to introduce the government's bill of particulars offered in a previous trial of the same matter.

[E] Admissions by Unauthorized Agents or Employees about Matters within their Scope

RUDZINSKI v. WARNER THEATRES, INC.

Wisconsin Supreme Court
16 Wis. 2d 241, 114 N.W.2d 466 (1962)

CURRIE, JUSTICE.

Action to recover damages [for] injuries sustained when Mrs. Rudzinski fell in defendant's movie theater.

In attempting to leave the theater, Mrs. Rudzinski entered the middle lobby and walked a few steps towards the center pair of doors, and fell.

Upon examination at the trial, she was asked if she knew what caused her fall. She responded: "Well, there were slippery and wet spots all around, scattered."

[Plaintiff must prove] actual or constructive notice to defendant of the existence of these spots prior to the accident. [V]erdict was directed against plaintiffs on the ground that there was no evidence which would sustain a finding of notice.

On this appeal plaintiffs [contend that the] court excluded evidence of a post accident conversation, between an usher and a janitor, which constituted an admission of actual notice on the part of the usher which would be binding upon defendant.

Mrs. Rudzinski testified that she was rendered semi-conscious and dazed by the fall and that afterwards, two men, presumably ushers, picked her up. Mrs. Rudzinski then noticed a janitor mopping up the floor.

Plaintiffs' counsel sought to question her about a statement [usher] Kuntz allegedly made to this janitor, but the court sustained an objection thereto. An offer of proof as to this statement was then made in the form of questions put to Mrs. Rudzinski and her answers thereto. In this offer of proof, she testified that Kuntz stated to the janitor: "Now you come when it's too late, after someone falls. Why didn't you come a half hour ago when I called you?" and that the janitor made no response. If this excluded testimony had been admitted it would have given rise to the inference that Kuntz had actual notice of the wet spots on the center lobby floor approximately one-half hour before the accident. Kuntz later denied having had any conversation with a janitor.

Plaintiffs maintain that the excluded statement was admissible as an admission of an agent, binding his principal, the defendant.

In order for an agent's statement to be admissible against his principal, it must have been spoken within the scope of the authority of the agent to speak for the principal. Professor Edmund M. Morgan, in 2 Basic Problems of Evidence, page 236, states: is necessary to distinguish sharply between authority to do an act or to deal with a specified matter and authority to talk about it. The latter is usually a requisite of admissibility of statements made by the agent."

The authority to speak for the principal may, of course, be implied, and usually the implications of the relationship furnish the basis for the authority. However, in the instant case no foundation of agency was laid from which such an implication could be drawn. Also, the evidence is undisputed that it was not part of the duties of Kuntz to direct the work of the janitors in the theater. Therefore, there was neither express nor implied authority on his part to speak for defendant in the matter.

There is a further compelling reason why the excluded statement is not admissible as an admission binding the defendant. This is because it was a statement made by one employee to a fellow employee. [S]tatements made by an agent to his principal, or to another agent of the principal, are not admissible as admissions. Comment [a] accompanying [Restatement, Agency, Second, § 287] states that:

> Statements of agents which the principal has authorized to be made to third persons are admissible against him under the same circumstances as those made by himself, since if the principal is willing to give them to the world it is not unfair that they should be subsequently used against him. On the other hand, statements made by the agent to the principal or to other agents are statements which the principal does not intend to be given to the world or to be considered as his statements. He does not in any way vouch for their truth. The historical fiction of the identity of principal and agent is not operative in transactions between them.

[*Judgment reversed on other grounds.*]

Gordon, Justice (concurring).

I believe that the excluded testimony should have been received into evidence as an admission. In my opinion, this was an admission made by an agent on a *topic* which was within the scope of his duties.

We exclude hearsay as evidence because we doubt its inherent trustworthiness, but we make an exception when such hearsay is in the nature of an admission. The *raison d'etre* for this exception to the hearsay rule is that trustworthiness surrounds admissions. The same considerations which give credibility to the [admission] of a principal should apply to his employee. Loyalty to an employer's interests is the rule, rather than the exception.

The test of admissibility should not rest on whether the principal gave the agent authority to make declarations. No sensible employer would authorize his employee to make damaging statements. The right to speak on a given topic must arise out of the nature of the employee's duties. The errand boy should not be able to bind the corporation with a statement about the issuance of treasury stock, but a truck driver should be able to bind his employer with an admission regarding his careless driving. Similarly, an usher should be able to commit his employer with an observation about a slippery spot on the lobby floor.

It is enough to show the existence of the employment and the general nature of the employee's work. There may be cases where a further foundation will be needed to develop that the utterances are fairly within the employee's scope of authority. Surely there can be little doubt that a theater usher's range of discussion properly includes the clean-up of a wet lobby floor.

The scope of an agent's actions is not controlled by the exact terms of his employment contract. Is it realistic that any contract of employment between the theater and the usher would provide that the usher could or could not direct the work of the janitors? Furthermore, it is immaterial whether or not the usher could call upon the janitor, because the statement contains an admission of knowledge of an unsafe condition in the theater lobby and should have been received to reflect that knowledge.

That this usher was entitled to heed the state of the lobby floor is inherent in the majority's opinion; they have reversed because the wet spots were "in plain view of this usher and the jury would be warranted in concluding that he should have seen them." In other words, the jury could infer the corporation's knowledge from the mere presence of the usher, but the jury must be denied those oral statements of the usher which would prove the knowledge.

I am mindful of the Restatement's view as set forth in 2 Agency 2d:

> 286. In an action between the principal and a third person statements by an agent to a third person are admissible in evidence against the principal to prove the truth of facts asserted in them as though made by the principal, if the agent was authorized to make the statement or was authorized to make, on the principal's behalf, any statements concerning the subject matter.
>
> 287. Statements by an agent to the principal or to another agent of the principal are not admissible against the principal as admissions; such statements may be admissible in evidence under other rules of evidence.

I would reject the Restatement's position [in § 286]. I recognize that there are expressions in previous decisions of this court which support the majority's position. I respectfully submit that they should be overruled.

The Restatement's [other] rule excluding admissions made by an agent to a fellow agent is especially confounding. These admissions are said to be barred because they are statements which "the principal does not intend to be given to the world or to be considered as his statements." In my opinion, the test is one of trustworthiness, and it is even less likely that an agent would misrepresent his employer's interests to a fellow agent than he would to an outsider. If the declaration be an admission against interest it should be received when asserted to a stranger, and, a fortiori, when asserted to a co-employee in the presence of a stranger.

Professor Wigmore is quite caustic about the judicial exclusion of an agent's admissions. For example, he discusses *Rankin v. Brockton Public Market* [153 N.E. 97 (Mass. 1926)] in which a customer in a store was hit on the head; the court excluded the saleslady's admission that it was she who had tossed the item of store equipment which had struck the plaintiff because the saleslady "had no authority to bind the defendant." Wigmore commented as follows [IV Wigmore, Evidence, § 1078, p. 121 (1940)]:

> Yet she had authority to sell goods and make a profit for defendant; then why not an authority to say how she sold them? Such quibbles bring the law justly into contempt with laymen.

Rule 63(9) of the [1953] Uniform Rules of Evidence would likewise appear to contemplate the receipt of admissions by an agent:

> As against a party a statement that would be admissible if made by the declarant is admissible if (a) the statement concerned a matter within the scope of an agency or employment of the declarant for the party and was made before the determination of such relationship . . . or (c) one of the issues between the party and the proponent of the evidence of the statement is a legal liability of the declarant and the statement tends to establish that liability.

McCormick [Hornbook Treatise On Evidence, § 244, p. 519 (1954)] states:

> The evidence should be tested by its trustworthiness . . . The agent is well informed about acts in the course of the business, his statements offered against the employer are normally against the employer's interest, and while the employment continues, the employee is not likely to make such statements unless they are true. Accordingly, the commentators have advocated a widening of the common law [to let] in the agent's statement, if "the declaration concerned a matter within the scope" of the declarant's employment, "and was made before the termination of the agency or employment." Some of the recent cases, in result if not in theory, support this wider test. Its acceptance by courts generally seems expedient.

In *Slifka v. Johnson* (2d Cir., 1947), 161 F.2d 462, 469, Judge Augustus Hand said:

> It would be strange to have a rule of agency binding a principal to unauthorized acts of an agent, when done within the apparent scope of his authority, and yet to adopt a rule of evidence which would exclude statements naturally made in the course of the agency. Such a rigid view does not accord with the current broadening of the rules of evidence or with the spirit of contemporary remedial statutes.

In *Myrick v. Lloyd* (1946), 158 Fla. 47, 27 So.2d 615, the defendant's agent, while driving the defendant's car, struck a boy. As the agent was going to the hospital with the parents of the injured boy, he told them that the accident was his fault and not the fault of their son. The court held the statement of the agent admissible because it was made within the scope of his authority:

> We recognize a conflict of authority on this question; however we have chosen the above as the more practical and liberal rule. The statement had reference to matters occurring within the scope of his employment. When so acting the agent was acting for the principal who might have made such an admission himself against his own interest.

In *Arenson v. Skouras Theatres Corp.* (1944), 131 N.J. L. 303, 36 A.2d 761, the plaintiff sued to recover for injuries incurred when he sat on a theater seat that was wet with a liquid containing a chemical that burned him. Testimony was offered at the trial with respect to admissions concerning the substance on the seat made by an usherette to the manager in the presence of the plaintiff. In holding that the testimony was admissible under the admissions exception to the hearsay rule, the court stated:

> Were the statements in question made by the agents of the defendant in the execution of their agency? There seems no room for doubt that they were so made. The manager was clearly charged with the duty of operation and to see that acts of employees were not negligent. It is clear that the manager was conducting a transaction for the principal, an inquiry into an immediate occurrence that was in the execution of his duty, and that the answers of the girl to such queries of the manager form part of the act — the inquiry — which was being conducted for the benefit of the principal by its agent. The answers of the girl were as much part of the act as if the principal had propounded the same inquiry to the manager. Here each was an agent of the principal for certain duties and each was acting within the scope of the agency in asking and answering questions.

In *Whitaker v. Keuogh* (1944), 144 Neb. 790, 14 N.W.2d 596, the plaintiff offered to show that after the collision the defendant's driver said, "Lady, I am sorry. I just saw you the instant I collided with you." The court ruled that "the evidence was properly receivable as an admission."

In *Robinson v. Fort Dodge Limestone Co.* (1960, Iowa), 106 N.W.2d 579, 584, the agent, one Underberg, testified that some frozen chunks had fallen off a pile and caused the injury. Over objection that the statement was inadmissible because the agent had no authority to make it, the court ruled that:

> Knowledge on the part of Underberg is knowledge of defendant. The statement of Underberg was admissible to show his knowledge of the condition of the limestone at or before the time of the injury.

The testimony received in each of the above cases would have to be rejected if the Restatement rule were applied. I consider the Restatement rule especially unsound in that it would bind a principal with the statements of his employee to third persons only in the unrealistic situation in which the agent was authorized to make statements.

In conclusion, I would exclude the admissions of an agent when:

a) He purports to speak on a subject beyond the scope of his duties or personal knowledge, or

b) He is shown to have an animus against his principal which negatives the trustworthiness of his declaration, or

c) His admission is made after his employment has been terminated.

There was no showing that the usher had any hostility towards his employer or had ceased to be an employee at the time of the admission. Because the topic of conversation was patently within an usher's range of responsibilities, I would favor admission of Mrs. Rudzinski's proffered testimony. Its weight and credibility should be left to the jury.

NOTES AND QUESTIONS

(1) *Scope of Employment.* What would be the result under Federal Rule 801(d)(2)(D)? How broad is that rule? Does it extend to e-mails written by an employee about matters within the scope of his employment? *See, e.g., Sea-Land Service, Inc. v. Lozen Int'l, LLC*, 285 F.3d 808 (9th Cir. 2002) (yes). (In that case, the e-mail was signed with an electronic signature by the employee. Is that necessary?)

The Federal Rule is limited to statements made during the existence of the relationship. What about statements in a resignation letter? *See Young v. James Green Management, Inc.*, 327 F.3d 616 (7th Cir. 2003) (it was not error to exclude the letter, but even if trial court abused its discretion, the error was harmless).

(2) *Are Statements Made or Adopted by Someone in Government Properly Admissible Against the Government as Admissions?* Is a statement made by an informer in a sworn affidavit that the prosecution has submitted to a magistrate in support of a search warrant an admission when offered by the defense? See *United States v. Morgan*, 581 F.2d 933 (1978), accepting this position. The Federal Rules specifically provide that in certain circumstances statements made by government agents are admissible against the government as substantive evidence. *See* Fed. R. Evid. 803(8).

However, in a number of pre-Federal Rules of Evidence decisions, several circuits adopted a public policy argument that the government should not be bound by in-court statements of its agents. The court in one of these cases, *United States v. Santos*, 372 F.2d 177 (2d Cir. 1967), seemed to be distinguishing government agents from agents in corporate cases (whose statements regarding matters within the scope of the agency may be attributed to their principals) on the rationale that government agents are "supposedly uninterested personally in the outcome of the trial." The court did not explain the significance of this premise. We are not told whether it follows that (a) it would be unfair to impute to the government responsibility for the statements of its agents, or (b) such statements lack the special assurances of trustworthiness that attend the out-of-court statements of nongovernment agents.

Most courts currently seem to reject the notion that out-of-court statements of government agents or informants can be admitted against the prosecution as admissions. See *Lippay v. Christos*, 996 F.2d 1490 (3d Cir. 1993), for a more recent case finding no error in excluding an informant's statements when offered by the defense. *See also United States v. Yildiz*, 355 F.3d 80 (2d Cir. 2004), reaffirming what it sees as a common law exclusion of such statements, saying that a change was not intended by the drafters of the Federal Rules of Evidence. Is such exclusion appropriate in light of the absence of any exception for governmental agents in the rule? Do you see an acceptable rationale for this distinction?

Cf. United States v. American Tel. & Tel. Co., 498 F. Supp. 353 (D.C. 1980) (in antitrust action brought by Department of Justice, admitting statements by various Executive Branch agencies; rejecting notion that agencies should be considered distinct entities from Department of Justice).

(3) *Admissions by Employees of the Bankrupt Company as Inadmissible Against the Bankruptcy Trustee.* On another type of agency admission, see *Calhoun v. Baylor*, 646 F.2d 1158 (6th Cir. 1981):

> [Defendants] argue that the adversary principle embedded in Rule 801(d)(2) means that the trustee in bankruptcy, as successor in interest, is bound by the statements of the agents [non-defendants Bell and Pollack] of Stax [the bankrupt company.] We disagree. In a suit alleging fraud by Bell and other Stax employees against Stax's creditors, those creditors should not be bound by the agents' statements. Rule 802(d)(2) does not include statements by predecessors-in-interest among the types of statements that the rule makes admissible. . . . Under the common law rule declarations by a predecessor in title offered against a successor were often admitted.

PROBLEM 8C: "I AM TO BLAME: I DROPPED THE THING."

An employee of the telephone company is up a pole repairing a telephone line, when a piece of equipment falls from where he is and injures someone below. The following day he states to a member of the family of the injured person, "I am to blame: I dropped the thing." In addition, later the company's claims agent speaks with the family and says, "Our employee was to blame: he dropped the thing." Rule on the admissibility of these two statements, as testified to by family members who heard them, in a lawsuit based on the accident. (Be aware the answer may be different under the common law than under the Federal Rules of Evidence).

[F] Co-Conspirator Statements

BOURJAILY v. UNITED STATES

United States Supreme Court
483 U.S. 171 (1987)

REHNQUIST, CHIEF JUSTICE.

Federal Rule of Evidence 801(d)(2)(E) provides: "A statement is not hearsay if . . . [t]he statement is offered against a party and is . . . a statement by a coconspirator of a party during the course and in furtherance of the conspiracy." We granted certiorari to answer three questions regarding the admission of statements under Rule 801(d)(2)(E): (1) whether the court must determine by independent evidence that the conspiracy existed and that the defendant and the declarant were members of this conspiracy; (2) the quantum of proof on which such determinations must be based; and (3) whether a court must in each case examine the circumstances of such a statement to determine its reliability.

In May 1984, Clarence Greathouse, an informant working for the Federal Bureau of Investigation (FBI), arranged to sell a kilogram of cocaine to Angelo Lonardo. Lonardo agreed that he would find individuals to distribute the drug. When the sale became imminent, Lonardo stated in a tape-recorded telephone conversation that he had a "gentleman friend" who had some questions to ask about the cocaine. In a subsequent telephone call, Greathouse spoke to the "friend" about the quality of the drug and the price. Greathouse then spoke again with Lonardo, and the two arranged the details of the purchase. They agreed that the sale would take place in a designated hotel parking lot, and Lonardo would transfer the drug from Greathouse's car to the "friend," who would be waiting in the parking lot in his own car. Greathouse proceeded with the transaction as planned, and FBI agents arrested Lonardo and petitioner immediately after Lonardo placed a kilogram of cocaine into petitioner's car in the hotel parking lot. In petitioner's car, the agents found over $20,000 in cash.

Petitioner was charged with conspiring to distribute cocaine [a]nd possession of cocaine with intent to distribute. The Government introduced, over petitioner's objection, Angelo Lonardo's telephone statements regarding the participation of the "friend" in the transaction. [T]he trial court held that Lonardo's out-of-court statements satisfied Rule 801(d)(2)(E) and were not hearsay. Petitioner was convicted on both counts and sentenced to 15 years. The United States Court of Appeals for the Sixth Circuit affirmed. [W]e affirm.

Before admitting a co-conspirator's statement over an objection that it does not qualify under Rule 801(d)(2)(E), a court must be satisfied that the statement actually falls within the definition of the Rule. There must be evidence that there was a conspiracy involving the declarant and the nonoffering party, and that the statement was made "during the course and in furtherance of the conspiracy." Federal Rule of Evidence 104(a) provides: "Preliminary questions concerning . . . the admissibility of evidence shall be determined by the court." [T]he Federal Rules, however, nowhere define the standard of proof the court must observe in resolving these questions.

We are therefore guided by our prior decisions regarding admissibility determinations that hinge on preliminary factual questions. We have traditionally required that these matters be established by a preponderance of proof. Evidence is placed before the jury when it satisfies the technical requirements of the evidentiary Rules, which embody certain legal and policy determinations. The inquiry made by a court concerned with these matters is not whether the proponent of the evidence wins or loses his case on the merits, but whether the evidentiary Rules have been satisfied. Thus, the evidentiary standard is unrelated to the burden of proof on the substantive issues, be it a criminal case or a civil case. The preponderance standard ensures that before admitting evidence, the court will have found it more likely than not that the technical issues and policy concerns addressed by the Federal Rules of Evidence have been afforded due consideration. As in *Lego v. Twomey*, 404 U.S. 477, 488 (1972), we find "nothing to suggest that admissibility rulings have been unreliable or otherwise wanting in quality because not based on some higher standard." We think that our previous decisions in this area resolve the matter. *See, e.g.*, *Colorado v. Connelly*, [479 U.S. 157 (1986)] (preliminary fact that custodial confessant waived rights must be proved by preponderance of the evidence); *Nix v. Williams*, 467 U.S. 431, 444, n. 5 (1984) (inevitable discovery of illegally seized evidence must be shown to have been more likely than not); *United States v. Matlock*, 415 U.S. 164 (1974) (voluntariness of consent to search must be shown by preponderance of the evidence); *Lego v. Twomey*, *supra* (voluntariness of confession must be demonstrated by a preponderance of the evidence). Therefore, we hold that when the preliminary facts relevant to Rule 801(d)(2)(E) are disputed, the offering party must prove them by a preponderance of the evidence.

[Petitioner] nevertheless challenges the admission of Lonardo's statements. Petitioner argues that in determining whether a conspiracy exists and whether the defendant was a member of it, the court must look only to independent evidence — that is, evidence other than the statements sought to be admitted. Petitioner relies on *Glasser v. United States*, 315 U.S. 60 (1942), in which this Court first mentioned the so-called "bootstrapping rule." The relevant issue in *Glasser* was whether Glasser's counsel, who also represented another defendant, faced such a conflict of interest that Glasser received ineffective assistance. Glasser contended that conflicting loyalties led his lawyer not to object to statements made by one of Glasser's co-conspirators. The Government argued that any objection would have been fruitless because the statements were admissible. The Court rejected this proposition:

> "[S]uch declarations are admissible over the objection of an alleged co-conspirator, who was not present when they were made, only if there is proof *aliunde* that he is connected with the conspiracy. Otherwise, hearsay would lift itself by its own bootstraps to the level of competent evidence."

The Court revisited the bootstrapping rule in *United States v. Nixon*, 418 U.S. 683 (1974), where again, in passing, the Court stated: "Declarations by one defendant may also be admissible against other defendants upon a sufficient showing, by independent evidence, of a conspiracy among one or more other defendants and the declarant and if the declarations at issue were in furtherance of that conspiracy." Read in the light most favorable to petitioner, *Glasser* could mean that a court should not consider hearsay statements at all in determining preliminary facts under Rule 801(d)(2)(E).

Both *Glasser* and *Nixon*, however, were decided before Congress enacted the Federal Rules of Evidence in 1975. [R]ule 104(a) provides: "Preliminary questions concerning . . . the admissibility of evidence shall be determined by the court. . . . In making its determination it is not bound by the rules of evidence except those with respect to privileges." Similarly, Rule 1101(d)(1) states that the Rules of Evidence (other than with respect to privileges) shall not apply to "[t]he determination of questions of fact preliminary to admissibility of evidence when the issue is to be determined by the court under Rule 104." The question thus presented is whether any aspect of *Glasser*'s bootstrapping rule remains viable after the enactment of the Federal Rules of Evidence.

Petitioner concedes that Rule 104, on its face, appears to allow the court to make the preliminary factual determinations relevant to Rule 801(d)(2)(E) by considering any evidence it wishes, unhindered by considerations of admissibility. That would seem to many to be the end of the matter. Congress has decided that courts may consider hearsay in making these factual determinations. Out-of-court statements made by anyone, including putative co-conspirators, are often hearsay. Even if they are, they may be considered, *Glasser* and the bootstrapping rule notwithstanding. But petitioner nevertheless argues that the bootstrapping rule, as most Courts of Appeals have construed it, survived this apparently unequivocal change in the law unscathed and that Rule 104, as applied to the admission of co-conspirator's statements, does not mean what it says. We disagree.

Petitioner claims that Congress evidenced no intent to disturb the bootstrapping rule, which was embedded in the previous approach, and we should not find that Congress altered the rule without affirmative evidence so indicating. [W]e think that the Rule is sufficiently clear that to the extent that it is inconsistent with petitioner's interpretation of *Glasser* and *Nixon*, the Rule prevails.

Nor do we agree with petitioner that this construction of Rule 104(a) will allow courts to admit hearsay statements without any credible proof of the conspiracy, thus fundamentally changing the nature of the co-conspirator exception. Petitioner starts with the proposition that co-conspirators' out-of-court statements are deemed unreliable and are inadmissible, at least until a conspiracy is shown.

Petitioner's theory ignores two simple facts of evidentiary life. First, out-of-court statements are only *presumed* unreliable. The presumption may be rebutted by appropriate proof. Second, individual pieces of evidence, insufficient in themselves to prove a point, may in cumulation prove it. [A] *per se* rule barring consideration of these hearsay statements during preliminary factfinding is not therefore required. Even if out-of-court declarations by co-conspirators are presumptively unreliable, trial courts must be permitted to evaluate these statements for their evidentiary worth as revealed by the particular circumstances of the case. [I]f the opposing party is unsuccessful in keeping the evidence from the fact-finder, he still has the opportunity to attack the probative value of the evidence as it relates to the substantive issue in the case. *See, e.g.*, Fed. Rule Evid. 806 (allowing attack on credibility of out-of-court declarant).

We think that there is little doubt that a co-conspirator's statements could themselves be probative of the existence of a conspiracy and the participation of both the defendant and the declarant in the conspiracy. Petitioner's case presents a paradigm. [E]ach one of Lonardo's statements may itself be unreliable, but taken as a whole, the entire conversation between Lonardo and Greathouse was corroborated by independent evidence. The friend, who turned out to be petitioner, showed up at the prearranged spot at the prearranged time. He picked up the cocaine, and a significant sum of money was found in his car. On these facts, the trial court concluded, in our view correctly, that the Government had established the existence of a conspiracy and petitioner's participation in it.

We need not decide in this case whether the courts below could have relied solely upon Lonardo's hearsay statements to determine that a conspiracy had been established by a preponderance of the evidence. [I]t is sufficient for today to hold that a court, in making a preliminary factual determination under Rule 801(d)(2)(E), may examine the hearsay statements sought to be admitted.

We also reject any suggestion that admission of these statements against petitioner violated his rights under the Confrontation Clause of the Sixth Amendment. [The Court's analysis of the Confrontation Clause issue is omitted here.]

The judgment of the Court of Appeals is *Affirmed*.

NOTES AND QUESTIONS

(1) *Should the Judge Decide Conspiracy Foundation Questions, or Leave Minimally Sufficient Evidence to the Jury? Bourjaily* left no doubt that under the Federal Rules of Evidence the foundational issue is governed by Fed. R. Evid. 104(a), meaning that the court admits the co-conspirator statement and allows the jury to assess its significance, if the court finds the predicate for its admissibility by a preponderance. In contrast, some states treat this as a Rule 104(b) issue (*i.e.*, a conditional relevancy question for which the judge need not even conclude that the facts make the statement admissible, but only that some reasonable person might so conclude). This is a low threshold. *See, e.g.*, Cal. Evid. Code § 403, Comment of Assembly Committee on Judiciary. *See generally* Garland & Schmitz, *Of Judges and Juries: A Proposed Revision of Federal Rule of Evidence 104*, 23 U.C. DAVIS L. REV. 77 (1989). What are the policy reasons for and consequences of treating this as a conditional relevancy problem?

(2) *The Separate Issue of Sufficiency of the Statement Alone, as Sole Foundation. Bourjaily* left open whether the statement was sufficient to establish the co-conspirator foundation (alternatively called the "predicate") in the absence of any other evidence. A subsequent modification of Fed. R. Evid. 801(d)(2) makes clear that the statement alone will not satisfy the criteria. *Qualley v. Clo-Tex Int'l, Inc.*, 212 F.3d 1123 (8th Cir. 2000), reversed a conviction because of the lack of sufficient evidence other than the statement supporting the existence of the defendant's knowledge of and participation in the alleged conspiracy. How often do you think this problem arises?

(3) *The Order of Proof of the Co-Conspirator Statement Predicate in a Case where at Least One Charge is Criminal Conspiracy.* An important issue lies concealed in the proof requirements for co-conspirator statements. Should the Government have to demonstrate that the particular defendant in fact conspired with the declarant *before* any statement of an alleged co-conspirator can be introduced into evidence? The marginal defendant, whose alleged participation in the conspiracy is doubtful, especially would want the Government to be required to offer rigorous proof of her participation before introducing any statements by people the defendant claims are not her co-conspirators.

On the other hand, a rigorous insistence on the order of proof may be unworkable. The Government may have a dozen or more witnesses from whom bits and pieces of the conspiracy will emerge. If the Government must first prove each defendant's participation in the conspiracy in a hearing before the judge alone, the Government may have to offer each witness twice. Jury trials already are protracted enough, and most trial judges will be reluctant to conduct this double procedure, preferring not to stop the trial and hold an inquiry out of the jury's presence. The evidence will be jumbled and difficult for the jury to follow. Furthermore, the *Bourjaily* case indicates that the statement is actually part of the predicate, so that arguably it is illogical to exclude it until the proof of which it is a part is complete. Where do these arguments leave the issue? Most courts have yielded to the pragmatic concerns and relaxed the order of proof, allowing the jury to hear the statements before full proof of the predicate emerges. Then, in cases in which the whole of the evidence before the jury does not later support the inference of the conspiracy predicate as to a given defendant, the court faces the choice of an instruction to disregard (knowing that it will be difficult for the jury to follow), or declaring a mistrial.

PROBLEM 8D: "HE ASKED ME FOR A BRIBE!"

Decide the following case:

The defendant, Harry D. Iaconetti, a federal government contract inspector, was found guilty by a jury of soliciting a bribe and attempting to extort money from two government suppliers.

The government's chief witness against the defendant was Mr. Lioi, an officer in a corporation seeking a government contract. Mr. Lioi testified that on February 10, the defendant told him that it would be "hard to justify" a favorable pre-award survey, a prerequisite to the awarding of a contract, unless one percent of the contract price were paid to the defendant. After the defendant requested the bribe, Mr. Lioi discussed it with his partners and counsel for the corporation, contacted the FBI, and arranged for future conversations with the defendant to be secretly recorded.

To rebut the government's case, the defendant relied primarily on his own testimony. He denied each government witness' version of their unrecorded conversations with him. Furthermore, he testified that instead of requesting a bribe from Mr. Lioi on February 10, he was offered an unsolicited bribe of $1,000 by Mr. Lioi despite his repeated assurances that the contract would be awarded to the firm. He explained the tapes as recordings of conversations in which he was "leading on" Mr. Lioi in order to "gather evidence."

Immediately after his arrest, with the money in his possession, the defendant had told the FBI that the bribery discussions with Mr. Lioi had been a joke.

Because of the conflicting interpretations that could be given portions of the tapes, because understanding the taped discussions depends in part on what happened at the February 10th meeting, and because the defendant flatly contradicted Mr. Lioi's version of the meeting on the 10th, the government presented two rebuttal witnesses. The witnesses related Mr. Lioi's reports to them on the 10th of the defendant's statements earlier that day. These reports were substantially the same as Mr. Lioi's testimony that the defendant had solicited a bribe. The witnesses were Mr. Goldman, a business partner of Mr. Lioi, and Mr. Stern, the attorney for the firm.

Defendant made a timely objection to the testimony of these two witnesses; the ground stated was that the testimony was prejudicial inadmissible hearsay.

Analyze this contention and give your reasons. This problem is based on *United States v. Iaconetti*, 406 F. Supp. 554 (E.D.N.Y.), *aff'd*, 540 F.2d 574 (2d Cir. 1976). Your analysis should include (1) whether the witness' testimony about Lioi's reports of Iaconetti's bribe solicitation meets the basic hearsay definition (you probably will conclude that they do, but explain why); (2) whether the co-conspirator statement exemption applies (including the duration and furtherance requirements); and (3) whether the exemption for prior consistent statements might apply (see the preceding section). *Are any other exemptions applicable?*

REVIEW PROBLEMS FOR CHAPTERS 7 AND 8: HEARSAY QUIZ: IS IT HEARSAY AFTER CONSIDERING THE GENERAL DEFINITION AND THE EXEMPTIONS (NOT THE EXCEPTIONS)?

For each of the following problems, decide whether the evidence is hearsay or non-hearsay and explain why. Use the definitions in Fed. R. Evid. 801, including the general definition set forth in 801 (a) through (c) and the exemptions set forth in 801(d). If the evidence satisfies the provisions of (a) through (c), and also any of the provisions of (d), it is normally permissible to say it is hearsay but within an exemption. However, for purposes of this quiz, call such evidence non-hearsay (as you also would if it was (a) through (c) that it did not satisfy). We ask you to do this for this quiz to emphasize that technically, the entire Rule 801 is definitional.

Do not decide the separate question of admissibility (i.e., do not worry about relevance or prejudice, and do not try to guess about the possible hearsay exceptions that will be covered in the next chapters). The only questions are whether the item is hearsay or non-hearsay — and why.

(1) In a slip-and-fall case, plaintiff proposes to testify that "an unknown bystander warned me as I walked into defendant's store that the floor was slippery." (Offered to prove defendant's negligence in maintaining its floor.)

(2) Same as (1), except that other evidence identifies the bystander as the defendant's store manager on duty.

(3) Same as (2), except offered by defendant to show plaintiff's advance knowledge that the floor was slippery, as relevant to a defense of contributory negligence.

(4) As evidence that the substance possessed by defendant was heroin, the prosecution offers a written report of the chemist who analyzed it, identifying the substance as heroin.

(5) Same as (4), except that the report is offered after the completion of the chemist's testimony, during which he stated under oath that the substance was heroin and was extensively cross-examined about alleged deficiencies in his laboratory.

(6) Same as (5), except that defense counsel also impeached the chemist by suggesting he conformed his testimony to a prosecutor's request, immediately before the chemist took the stand, that he identify the substance as heroin; and the report is offered solely to repair the chemist's credibility.

(7) Same as (6), except that the report is offered to prove that the substance is heroin.

(8) After the chemist in the last several questions has testified, has been impeached, and has been rehabilitated by his report, defense counsel calls a bartender as a witness to prove that the chemist, while at the bar, confided to the bartender that the substance was only powdered sugar. Can the bartender's testimony be introduced? (Offered only to impeach the chemist.)

(9) Same as (8), but offered to prove that the substance in fact was powdered sugar.

(10) The prosecutor offers a police officer's testimony that when she arrived at the scene of a robbery and asked where the robber was, the robbery victim wordlessly pointed to the defendant. The victim since has died from unrelated causes and does not testify. The police officer's testimony is offered to prove the robber's identity.

(11) Same as (10), except that the victim has testified and identified the defendant and is capable of being cross-examined.

(12) As evidence that John lacked testamentary capacity, will contestants offer evidence that the State had confined John in a facility for the criminally insane during the time he made his will.

(13) As evidence that John lacked testamentary capacity, will contestants offer evidence that John said, "I am insane."

(14) As evidence that John lacked testamentary capacity, will contestants offer evidence that he claimed to own properties that other evidence shows he did not own.

(15) As evidence that Alice was talking on the phone to Richard, the proponent offered Janet's testimony that Alice said, "Goodbye, Richard," into the phone before hanging up.

(16) As evidence that Widgco's widgets are not defective, defendant Widgco offers testimony from Widgco's consumer relations manager that in his decade in this job, he has never heard a single complaint of defect.

(17) As evidence that its salesman lacked actual authority (i.e., lacked actual permission from the employer) to accept an order from the plaintiff without a credit check, defendant offers proof that its manager previously had given the salesman a written notice stating, "You are not authorized to accept any order without a credit check."

(18) As (contrary) proof that the salesman *did* have actual authority to accept the order without a credit check, plaintiff offers evidence that the salesman (whom defendant admits was then its salesman) said to plaintiff, "I have actual authority to accept this order without a credit check."

(19) As evidence that Sandra conspired to distribute heroin, confidential informant Betty proposes to testify that Miriam gave her a package and said, "Get $ 1,000 from Sandra at the corner of Fifteenth and Green for this heroin, because I've arranged with Sandra to move it on the street," coupled with the fact that when Betty got to Fifteenth and Green, Sandra furtively grabbed the package and surreptitiously handed her $1,000 in cash.

(20) Same as (19), except that Sandra never appeared at Fifteenth and Green and no other conduct of Sandra is in evidence.

(21) As evidence in a murder trial, to prove the act of murder, the prosecutor offers a written statement of the defendant's stepson that the defendant killed the

stepson's sister (the victim).

(22) Same as (21), except the trial is to determine whether the defendant should get custody of his stepson, and the evidence is offered to demonstrate that the stepson has a poor relationship with the defendant.

(23) In a hit-run case, the prosecutor offers a photograph of a car showing its license plate, which admissible evidence shows has the number corresponding to a car registered to the defendant.

(24) As evidence of provocation in a murder trial, the defendant offers a statement of a family friend to the defendant shortly before the homicide, telling her that the victim molested the defendant's child.

(25) Same facts as (24), but the statement is offered in a trial of the alleged molester to prove the criminal act.

(26) Same facts as above, but the statement is offered in a commercial case between the family friend and the molester to show that the family friend did not like the alleged molester.

(27) As evidence of defendant's drug possession in a drug possession case, the prosecutor offers testimony that a trained canine sniffed the defendant's luggage and barked, signifying that drugs were in the luggage.

(28) As evidence in a suit arising from an automobile accident, the plaintiff offers testimony of a bystander that the traffic light facing the defendant was red when the defendant entered the intersection.

Chapter 9

THE "STRONG" HEARSAY EXCEPTIONS

HEARSAY EXCEPTIONS NOT REQUIRING SHOWING OF UNAVAILABILITY (F.R.E. ARTICLE VIII, RULE 803)

§ 9.01 INTRODUCTION[1]

The Twin Policies of Necessity and Trustworthiness. The two concepts underlying all hearsay exceptions are (1) need and (2) reliability. For the most part, however, the hearsay exceptions in Fed. R. Evid. 803 have been created because of the trustworthy nature of the information. Often something about the way in which a statement was made gives it greater supposed reliability, such as stress negating the ability to compose a lie. Ask yourself what policy justifications support each of the exceptions as you study them. Also ask if the assumptions made always result in accurate information.

Contrasting Rule 803 Exceptions, which do Not Require Unavailability, with Rule 804 Exceptions, which do. In contrast to the exceptions found in Fed. R. Evid. 803, the Fed. R. Evid. 804 exceptions (in Chapter 10) are based more explicitly on need. The decision has been made that we would rather have the declarant testify, but if that is not possible because the declarant is unavailable, then we would rather have the hearsay than nothing at all. Because 803 exceptions operate regardless of availability, we call them the "strong" exceptions, in contrast to the 804 exceptions, which we call "weak" because they are deemed second-best to the live testimony. You might wish to refer to a provocative article about influences on the formation and application of exceptions: Bein, *Substantive Influences on the Use of Exceptions to the Hearsay Rule*, 23 B.C. L. REV. 855 (1982).

As you study the hearsay exceptions, also keep in mind the following related issues, which appear throughout these chapters:

(1) *Multiple-Level Hearsay.* Fed. R. Evid. 805 provides that multiple hearsay is admissible so long as each layer fits an exception or exemption. In addition, in some cases, a particular layer may not be offered for a hearsay purpose. Thus, you must determine how many statements actually are imbedded in the testimony or document, how each statement is being used, and whether it fits into one or more of the exceptions or exemptions or is not otherwise defined as hearsay.

(2) *Completeness Doctrine.* Fed. R. Evid. 106 establishes a "rule of completeness," which permits parts of a writing or recorded statement to be admitted that in fairness should be considered contemporaneously with another part being

---

[1] Study Guide Reference: Evidence in a Nutshell, Chapter 9:I.

offered into evidence. *See Beech Aircraft Corp. v. Rainey*, 488 U.S. 153 (1988). Courts vary about the extent to which otherwise inadmissible hearsay is permitted under this doctrine.

(3) *Impeachment of the Declarant.* Fed. R. Evid. 806 provides for impeachment of hearsay declarants in the same manner as if they had testified at trial. *See United States v. Lechoco*, 542 F.2d 84 (D.C. Cir. 1976). However, courts divide over whether Rule 608(b)'s ban on extrinsic evidence of prior bad acts applies in the context of hearsay declarants. *See United States v. Saada*, 212 F.3d 210 (3d Cir. 2000) (discussing case law). Upholding the ban may require the party against whom the statement is admitted to call the declarant to testify. What countervailing arguments justify the ban? *See generally* Hornstein, *On the Horns of an Evidentiary Dilemma: The Intersection of Federal Rules of Evidence 806 and 608(b)*, 56 Ark. L. Rev. 543 (2003). Similarly, strict application of Rule 613(b) might not make sense.

(4) *The Applicability to Hearsay of Nonhearsay Rules, Particularly Fed. R. Evid. 403.* Even if the Hearsay Rule has been satisfied, is there some other rule that would prohibit the evidence? For example, the evidence may be too prejudicial, and therefore excludable under Fed. R. Evid. 403, or may violate the character evidence rules.

§ 9.02 EXCITED UTTERANCES AND PRESENT SENSE IMPRESSIONS[2]

Read Federal Rule of Evidence 803(1) and (2) "Hearsay Exceptions; Availability of Declarant Immaterial: Present Sense Impression and Excited Utterance."

UNITED STATES v. FROST

United States Court of Appeals, Tenth Circuit
684 F.3d 963 (2012)

Tymkovich, Circuit Judge.

Adam Frost was tried and convicted for the rape of a 17–year–old girl and was sentenced to 200 months' imprisonment. In this appeal, Frost challenges his conviction on the grounds that the trial court plainly erred in admitting the hearsay testimony of several witnesses, including the victim's sister, a nurse, and law enforcement officers . . . . Although some of the challenged testimony was admitted in error, none was so obvious or prejudicial as to warrant reversal under the plain-error standard [which applies, instead of usual standards, because there was no objection to this testimony at trial] . . . . Accordingly, we AFFIRM the judgment of the district court . . . .

---

[2] Study Guide Reference: Evidence in a Nutshell, Chapter 10:II at "Present Sense Impressions and Excited Utterances: F.R.E. 803(1) and (2)."

A. Background
1. Undisputed Facts

. . . [D]efendant Adam Frost, a 28–year–old, and the 17–year old victim, A.W., both lived near Ignacio, Colorado . . . . Frost lived with his mother, Bernice Harris. A.W. was friends with 12–year–old K.A., a girl related to Frost.

On the evening of November 27, . . . A.W. and K.A. met at a casino on the Southern Ute Indian Reservation. Their plan was to meet up with Frost so that he could purchase alcohol for them. They met up with Frost at his residence, walked to the Thriftway, a nearby convenience store, to buy alcohol, and returned to Frost's room, where they drank and watched television. At some point, K.A. left the room and Frost had sex with A.W. Soon thereafter, A.W. left the house, used her cellphone to call her sister, and told her she had been raped. Her sister met her back at the Thriftway and took her home.

When A.W. got home, she repeated her account of the rape to her parents, who called the police. When the police arrived, she again repeated her story. Then she went to the hospital, received a rape-kit examination, and repeated her story a fourth time to the examining nurse. Finally, she was interviewed by an FBI agent. [Most of these statements of A.W. were relayed to the jury through the various witnesses].

2. Frost's Theory of the Case

Frost did not testify at trial. But Frost's counsel admitted in her opening statement that Frost had a sexual encounter with A.W., and claimed it was consensual . . . .

3. A.W.'s [The Victim's] Testimony

On direct examination, A.W. testified she had known K.A. "[a]bout a couple of days" prior to her encounter with Frost . . . .The two girls met Frost at his residence and went to the Thriftway, where Frost purchased alcohol. They returned to Frost's residence; Frost entered through the front door and, because Harris was home, he let A.W. and K.A. in through his bedroom window. A.W. and K.A. sat on Frost's bed and drank while Frost played video games . . . .

At some point, K.A. left the room to go to the bathroom. While she was gone, Frost placed his hand in A.W.'s hand. When K.A. returned, A.W. told her she needed to use the bathroom herself. K.A. had to help her to the bathroom because she was too drunk to get up by herself. In the bathroom, A.W. told K.A. she should not have left her alone with Frost and that she wanted to leave . . . .

Later, Harris, Frost's mother, entered the room. She saw K.A. and ordered her to leave the room. Frost and K.A. had hidden A.W. under a blanket on Frost's bed and told her to be quiet; apparently Harris did not see her.

After Harris left, Frost climbed into the bed with A.W. He touched her [in inappropriate places removing her clothing] . . . . A.W. told him to stop and unsuccessfully tried to push him away. Frost removed his shorts and penetrated A.W . . . which caused A.W. to cry out.

. . . Harris reentered Frost's room and told A.W. to get out of the house. A.W. put on her shoes and jacket, and Harris showed her out the front door.

As soon as she left the house, at approximately 3:00 AM, A.W. used her cellphone to call her sister, Bridget W., and told her Frost had raped her. Bridget then met A.W. back at the Thriftway. Bridget brought A.W. home, where she told her mother and stepfather she had been raped. Her parents called the police.

Officers Monica Medina and Jacob Steinhage arrived and questioned A.W. about the incident. A.W. was then driven to a nearby hospital, where she was interviewed and examined by Lynne Murison, a nurse practitioner and certified rape examiner. [The examination showed, among other things, that A.W. had injuries to her vagina and anus.] Finally, A.W. was interviewed at the hospital by John Wallace, an FBI agent . . . .

4. Alleged Hearsay Testimony

After A.W. testified, the government put on several witnesses with whom A.W. had spoken in the hours following her encounter with Frost: Bridget W., Medina, Steinhage, Murison, and Wallace. These witnesses repeated what A.W. told them about the rape. Frost did not object to these statements as hearsay.

a. Bridget W.'s [the Sister's] Testimony

A.W.'s older sister Bridget W. testified about the phone call she received from A.W. at approximately 3:00 AM on November 28, shortly after A.W. left Frost's residence. According to Bridget, A.W. "was crying, and she sounded really scared." A.W. told Bridget she had been raped by K.A.'s relative. Bridget asked her if she was referring to "Eli," a different relative of K.A.'s, and A.W. corrected her: "No, it was Adam." Bridget told A.W. to meet her at the Thriftway, down the hill from Frost's residence.

Bridget got a friend to drive her to the Thriftway, where she met A.W. A.W. had "[t]ears coming down her face," and was "shaking." From there, Bridget and A.W. traveled to A.W.'s home . . . . Their mother called the police, and two police officers soon arrived. A.W.'s father also arrived. Bridget sat on a recliner in the living room, holding A.W. and "just crying together."

The police officers "start[ed] asking [A.W.] what happened." A.W. identified Adam Frost as her assailant. A.W. "tells them a little bit, but she doesn't really tell everything until we get to the hospital.". . .

Bridget traveled with A.W. to the hospital . . . . At the hospital, A.W. asked Bridget to accompany her during her medical examination; "she seemed really scared and nervous." During the exam, "she was shaking" and looked uncomfortable.

b. Officer Medina's and Officer Steinhage's Testimony

[A.W. made similar statements to the officers before being taken to the hospital, although not as complete as those to her sister. She also made statements to the hospital nurse who examined her and still later, to the FBI agent. All of these witnesses testified and described A.W.'s demeanor, including her having a hard time talking, shaking, and crying. They also repeated her statements about the rape. Their testimony is attacked as inadmissible and plain error on appeal.]

B. Discussion . . . .

We conclude the district court did not plainly err in admitting any of this testimony. First, the admission of Bridget W.'s testimony was not error because of the excited utterance exception to the hearsay rule. *See* Fed.R.Evid. 803(2). Second, even if in error, the admission of the testimony of Officers Medina and Steinhage under the excited utterance exception was not plain error . . . . [Finally,] even if the admission of Agent Wallace's testimony was error, the error did not affect the fairness of the proceedings [and therefore it was not plain error] . . . .

1. Standard of Review: Plain Error

Because Frost did not object to the admission of the challenged testimony at trial, we review the district court's decision only for plain error. "Plain error occurs when there is (1) error, (2) that is plain, which (3) affects substantial rights, and which (4) seriously affects the fairness, integrity, or public reputation of judicial proceedings." . . . An error is "plain" if it is "clear or obvious at the time of the appeal." *United States v. Cordery*, 656 F.3d 1103, 1106 (10th Cir.2011) . . . .

2. Bridget W.'s [the Sister's] Testimony

. . . The Federal Rules of Evidence allow the admission of hearsay testimony if the declarant's statement is the result of a startling or stressful event: [Rule 803(2) quoted.]

Rule 803's advisory notes explain the rationale for this exception and offer some guidance regarding how we should apply it:

> The theory of Exception (2) is simply that circumstances may produce a condition of excitement which temporarily stills the capacity of reflection and produces utterances free of conscious fabrication. Spontaneity is the key factor . . . .
>
> With respect to the time element . . . the standard of measurement is the duration of the state of excitement. How long can excitement prevail? Obviously there are no pat answers and the character of the transaction or event will largely determine the significance of the time factor.
>
> Permissible subject matter of the statement is [not] limited . . . to description or explanation of the event or condition . . . the statement need

> only relate to the startling event or condition, thus affording a broader scope of subject matter coverage.

Recently, in *United States v. Smith* . . . (10th Cir.2010), we summarized our approach to Rule 803(2):

> The so-called excited-utterance exception has three requirements: (1) a startling event; (2) the statement was made while the declarant was under the stress of the event's excitement; and (3) a nexus between the content of the statement and the event. [T]here is no precise amount of time between the event and the statement beyond which the statement cannot qualify as an excited utterance. Admissibility hinges on a statement's contemporaneousness with the excitement a startling event causes, not the event itself. There is no hard time limit that must be met under Rule 803; what is relevant is whether the declarant is still under the excitement of the startling event.

A.W.'s statements to Bridget W. satisfy all three requirements of the excited utterance exception. First, A.W. called Bridget W. directly after experiencing two startling events: being raped, and being kicked out by Harris in the middle of the night. Second, the facts indicate A.W. was under the stress of the events when she called Bridget; she was crying, and was still crying and visibly upset when Bridget arrived to pick her up several minutes later. Third, the statement related directly to the startling event: A.W. told Bridget she had been raped by Frost. Thus, Bridget W.'s hearsay testimony was covered by the excited utterance exception and therefore was admissible.

3. Officer Medina's and Officer Steinhage's Testimony

The government argues the testimony of Officers Medina and Steinhage was also admissible under the excited utterance exception. A.W.'s hearsay statements to the officers clearly satisfy the first and third requirements of the exception: the statements were made after startling events and related to those events. It is less than clear, however, whether these statements satisfy the requirement that "the statement[s] w[ere] made while the declarant was under the stress of the event's excitement." A.W.'s statements were a product of police questioning approximately an hour after the encounter, and the exception does not encompass every statement made in response to police interrogation while the declarant is upset. At the same time, there is no categorical rule that statements made to police are per se inadmissible under the excited utterance exception.

In determining whether statements to police are admissible as excited utterances, courts have looked to two primary factors. First, they have looked to the spontaneity of the statement . . . . *Compare, e.g., United States v. Arnold* (admitting victim's exclamation to police that the defendant had threatened her with a gun), with *Paxton v. Ward* (finding statement inadmissible because, among other reasons, it "was not spontaneously volunteered, but rather was offered in response to questioning").

But even if prompted by questioning, a statement may be admissible if the questions are somewhat open-ended. *See, e.g., United States v. Phelps* (district court did not abuse its discretion by admitting statements to officer where "[e]ach time [victim] began to talk to [officer] about the shooting, she began to cry, despite [officer's] attempts to calm her down," and victim's "statements to [officer] were not made in response to suggestive questioning").

Second, courts have looked to the level of excitement experienced by the declarant. If the declarant's excitement level is severe, then even statements made in response to questioning may be admitted. *See, e.g., United States v. Belfast* (statement made four to five hours after victim tortured and threatened with death admissible) . . . . Not only life-threatening violence, but also sexual assault, are encounters that may produce the requisite level of emotional excitement in some victims . . . .

Conversely, statements made after a clear opportunity for reflection, even if entirely voluntary, may be inadmissible. *See, e.g., Winzer v. Hall* ("If [declarant] was able to calmly and coolly call 911 several hours after the threat and discuss both the threat and other circumstances, she must have weighed the costs of intrusion against the benefit of obtaining help from the police.").

Reviewing the facts here places this case somewhere in the middle. Although A.W. was no longer in danger, she had just been through an ordeal that anyone would find traumatic — let alone a seventeen-year-old girl with no prior sexual experience. The officers questioned A.W. within a short time after the alleged rape . . . . There are other facts, however, that cut against finding A.W.'s statements were spontaneous. Most significantly, the officers' testimony shows that they questioned A.W. in a detailed fashion . . . . A general question like "what happened?" may serve as a nudge that elicits an excited utterance, whereas responses to detailed questioning lack the characteristic spontaneity of an excited utterance.

Had Frost objected to the officers' testimony at trial, a strong case against admissibility could have been made. But Frost must show the error was plain — that it was "clear or obvious at the time of the appeal.". . . This he cannot do. A.W.'s statements to the officers came when she was still visibly upset . . . . Therefore, we find the court did not commit plain error in admitting the testimony of Officers Medina and Steinhage . . . .

4. Nurse Murison's Testimony

[The nurse's testimony repeating declarations by the victim to her were offered under a different exception, for medical-purpose statements — not under the excited utterance exception. Therefore, this part of the court's opinion is omitted. The medical exception is covered in a later section of this chapter. It is sufficient to note here that the statement to the nurse might be partly motivated by seeking medical treatment and in part to aid the legal investigation, presenting a possible problem under that exception.]

5. Agent Wallace's Testimony

Finally, Frost argues the admission of Agent Wallace's testimony was plain error. We find, however, that the admission of Agent Wallace's testimony neither prejudiced Frost, nor seriously affected the fairness, integrity, or public reputation of the proceedings. Thus, Frost cannot overcome the third and fourth prongs of plain-error review. [The court points out that the FBI agent's testimony was cumulative of many other witnesses who repeated A.W.'s statements and that it may even have been helpful to Frost because it conflicted in some details with A.W.'s testimony. The court does not analyze whether the FBI agent's testimony was properly admissible, concluding only that admitting it was not plain error.] . . .

[Affirmed.]

NOTES AND QUESTIONS

(1) *What Parts of the Questioned Evidence, if Any, Were Improperly Admitted?* The court suggests, in its introduction, that "some of the challenged testimony was admitted in error." Which parts? The court says, for example, that "a strong case against admissibility [of the police officers' testimony] could have been made" if there had been an objection. But it is clear that the victim was still under heavy stress much later, at the hospital, and the officers' questioning began without specifics, by "asking [A.W.] what happened." Was all or part of the officers' evidence admissible?

(2) *The Statement Must "Relate to" the Startling Event.* In *United States v. Vargas*, 689 F.3d 867 (7th Cir. 2012), the defendant was convicted of attempted possession of cocaine. The evidence included long, coded discussions and negotiations about buying cocaine, and the defendant was arrested at the appointed distribution place, a parking lot, with $45,000 in cash inside a shoe box. The questioned evidence was the defendant's own statement of protest immediately upon arrest: "I was here buying a truck, Man!" The trial court admitted a videotape of the defendant's appearance and arrest, but the tape was edited to exclude this exculpatory statement, and the court of appeals upheld the exclusion. The statement was (1) excited and spontaneous, (2) in response to the declarant's arrest, but the court of appeals held that it did not (3) "relate[] to [the] startling event," because "[i]nstead, . . . the statement related to Vargas's arrival at the [parking lot], a 'prior' event." Does this holding make sense? Consider the Advisory Committee's Note, which is quoted in the principal case, *Frost, supra:* " Permissible subject matter of the statement is [not] limited . . . to description or explanation of the event or condition . . . the statement need only relate to the startling event or condition, thus affording a broader scope of subject matter coverage."

(3) *Dissipation of the Excitement.* See *Hamilton v. Huebner*, 19 N.W.2d 552 (Neb. 1945), in which the court refused to accept as an excited utterance, to show cause of death, testimony of members of a family that their deceased father told them after coming home from work that he had been injured while working on a motor. (Why was this rejected, do you suppose?)

(4) *A Statement too "Reflective" to be an Excited Utterance.* In *United States v. Smith*, 520 F.2d 1245 (8th Cir. 1975), a wife's statement immediately upon being searched and drugs being found on her, that her husband planted them on her, was held to be too reflective and self-serving to qualify as an excited utterance. (It was

also held not to be a co-conspirator statement usable against the husband. Why?)

(5) *Can an Answer to a Question be an Excited Utterance?* Does questioning defeat the spontaneity required of an excited utterance, or does it depend on the circumstances? *See United States v. Joy*, 192 F.3d 761 (7th Cir. 1999), *cert. denied*, 530 U.S. 1250 (2000), affirming admission of a 911 recording in which the declarant responded to the dispatcher's questions such as "what happened" and "who did it?'

(6) *Personal Knowledge*. Compare *Bemis v. Edwards*, 45 F.3d 1369 (9th Cir. 1995), which held that a 911 call by a person who reports events about which he lacks personal knowledge is not within Fed. R. Evid. 803(1) or Fed. R. Evid. 803(2).

PEOPLE v. LOVETT

Michigan Court of Appeals
85 Mich. App. 534, 272 N.W.2d 126 (1978)

J.H. Gillis, Presiding Judge

Defendant was convicted of felony murder.

The penultimate issue which this Court will address concerns the admissibility of statements made by Ms. Guster's 3-year-old child, Gretchen, who witnessed the crime but refused to testify in open court. [The victim of this rape-murder was babysitting for the Gusters at the time of the crime.]

It appears that the child made several statements to her mother and her new babysitter concerning how the victim was raped and killed. These statements were made approximately one week after the crime.

The trial court allowed Ms. Guster and the babysitter to testify as to these statements concluding that they fell within the "excited utterance" exception to the hearsay rule.

The precise question presented appears to be of first impression in this state.

In dealing with children of tender years, hearsay statements made by children who are victims of sexually related offenses are admissible under certain circumstances.

In sex offenses, hearsay statements made by a victim of tender years to a witness who subsequently testifies to the content of these declarations are admissible as part of the "res gestae" of the crime if the delay from the time of the incident to the time of the conversation is adequately explained.

The Michigan Rules of Evidence provide the following exception to the hearsay rule: [MRE 803(2), identical to Fed. R. Evid. 803(2), quoted].

The statements made and the actions taken by the child in the instant case were clearly the product of a startling event, the rape and murder of a young woman. The statements were spontaneous, *i.e.*, not prompted by any questioning.

In addition, the delay in the instant case was adequately explained. First, Gretchen had stayed with her grandparents for the week immediately following the crime. The week Gretchen returned, she made the statements to her new babysitter, and shortly thereafter began to talk about the crime to her mother when she got "in certain moods."

The circumstances presented in this matter lead us to the conclusion that the rule should be extended to this case even though the child was not the victim of the crime. The indicia of reliability is strong in the instant matter.

The court cautioned the jurors as to the hearsay nature of the child's testimony, and told them to give it careful scrutiny.

The result reached herein is in conformity with MRE 102: [Rule quoted; identical to Fed. R. Evid. 102].

Accordingly, the trial court did not err in admitting the child's testimony.

[Affirmed.]

NOTES AND QUESTIONS

(1) *Child Hearsay and Public Policy.* Is not the court making its decision on public policy, rather than legal, grounds, and justifying the policy with legalese? Is there anything wrong with this? Do we see a tendency of the courts to bend the hearsay rule to admit statements of children? If so, why? Be aware that most courts do not require a showing of competency (understanding of duty to tell the truth) of the child declarant for excited utterances because reliability is based on the declarant's reaction to stress, not on the declarant's understanding of the duty to tell the truth.

(2) *"Rekindled" Excitement, Long After the Event.* In *United States v. Napier*, 518 F.2d 316 (9th Cir.), *cert. denied*, 423 U.S. 895 (1975), a week after a woman returned from the hospital after a brutal assault that resulted in brain damage, she saw a photograph in a newspaper, to which she responded in "great distress and horror and upset," saying "He killed me, he killed me." The admission of this statement at the trial of the defendant who was the person in the picture was affirmed. Where the victim "having never discussed the assault with her family, was suddenly and unexpectedly confronted with a photograph of her alleged assailant there can be no doubt that the event was sufficiently 'startling' to provide adequate safeguards against reflection and fabrication." Some refer to this type of phenomenon as rekindling the startling event. Does this also meet the "relating to" requirement of the Federal Rule? Would it fit a requirement found in some states and in part in Fed. R. Evid. 803(1), that it describe the event?

(3) *Unknown Declarants.* In *Canton v. Kmart Corp.*, 2012 U.S. App. LEXIS 6372 (3d Cir. Mar. 29, 2012) (unpublished opinion), Canton slipped and fell in a Kmart store, and there was a nearby open bottle of liquid soap on a shelf that had created a slippery condition. "While standing in the area immediately after Canton fell, [a bystander] noted that she heard a Kmart employee admit that someone told her about the spill but that she [the employee] failed to respond to the spill right away." The bystander could have testified to this utterance, but no one could identify the alleged employee, and the court excluded the evidence on the ground that

"utterance[s] of [an] unidentified declarant [are] not admissible under Rule 803(2)." When the declarant is unidentified, the court explained, "it becomes more difficult to satisfy the established case law requirements for admission of a statement under" 803(2). Without this evidence, Canton was unable to prove negligence, because a slippery condition is not enough; there has to be evidence of the defendant's notice and failure to timely remedy it. Kmart therefore obtained a summary judgment of nonliability. Consider whether this holding is consistent with the Rule — which does not require identification of the declarant.

In *Jackson v. United States*, 359 F.2d 260 (D.C. Cir.), *cert. denied*, 385 U.S. 877 (1966), on colorful facts, the court held that the victim of a purse-snatching could testify to the yells of unidentified bystanders that defendant had done it, even though the victim did not know who did it (or who yelled). This was said to be an excited utterance. Coupled with finding the exact denominations of money stolen on defendant, and alternate threats and excuses made by defendant to pursuers, the evidence was sufficient to convict. Can *Jackson* and *Canton* be reconciled?

(4) *Res Gestae. Lovett* uses the term *res gestae*. While this does not appear in the Federal Rules or modern codes, it is often mentioned in the case-law. *State v. Hansen*, 989 P.2d 338 (Mont. 1999), notes that: "For the most part, *res gestae* refers to statements made immediately before, during, or immediately after the commission of a crime, by the accused, victim, or a bystander, as a spontaneous reaction or utterance stimulated by the excitement of the occasion, and made under such circumstances as to preclude contrivance or fabrication." *Hansen* finds the term unhelpful, since it includes present sense impressions, excited utterances, statements of bodily condition and mental states, each of which has its own hearsay exception. *Res gestae* can also reach evidence that is not introduced for a hearsay purpose. *Hansen* mentions that some states had very broad interpretations of evidence falling within the doctrine. What types of hearsay does *res gestae* not cover? Given its imprecision, this term should not be used, and its precise meaning should be questioned when relied upon by an opponent (or the judge).

HOUSTON OXYGEN CO. v. DAVIS

Texas Supreme Court
139 Tex. 1, 161 S.W.2d 474 (1942)

TAYLOR, J.

Pearl Davis [and] her husband [sued] Houston Oxygen Co. for injuries sustained by her minor son, Charles, in a collision between the company's truck and a Plymouth in which Charles was a passenger. [A verdict] for Pearl Davis and the boy were affirmed and the defendant [further] appeals [to this court].

Defendants contend that the courts below erred in holding inadmissible a statement offered by them, made by Mrs. Sally Cooper shortly before the accident occurred. Mrs. Cooper testified that on the date of the accident a Plymouth car headed north on State highway No. 35 passed her about four or five miles from the scene of the accident; that she at the time was driving a car in the same direction on the highway and that Jack Sanders and E. C. Cooper, her brother-in-law, were passengers with her. Sanders testified the Plymouth passed them on a curve of the highway, rough and uneven at that point, traveling "sixty or sixty-five miles" an hour, about four miles from the scene of the accident and that as it went out of sight it was "bouncing up and down in the back and zig zagging." When Sanders was asked if any one in the car made any statement as the Plymouth went by, plaintiffs objected. Defendants' bill of exception discloses that the excluded statement of Mrs. Cooper, made just after the Plymouth passed by, was, as testified to by Sanders for inclusion in the bill "they must have been drunk, that we would find them somewhere on the road wrecked if they kept that rate of speed up."

We have concluded, though the question is not free from difficulty, that the statement of Mrs. Cooper was admissible; that the trial court erred in not admitting the proffered testimony of Cooper and Sanders that Mrs. Cooper made it, and in not permitting Mrs. Cooper herself to testify she made the statement. It is sufficiently spontaneous to save it from the suspicion of being manufactured evidence. There was no time for a calculated statement. McCormick & Ray [Texas Evidence book] says:

> In one class of cases the requirement of spontaneity is somewhat attenuated. If a person observes some situation or happening which is not at all startling or shocking in its nature, nor actually producing excitement in the observer, the observer may yet have occasion to comment on what he sees (or learns from other senses) at the very time that he is receiving the impression. Such a comment, as to a situation then before the declarant, does not have the safeguard of impulse, emotion, or excitement, but there are other safeguards. In the first place, the report at the moment of the thing then seen, heard, etc., is safe from any error from defect of memory of the declarant. Secondly, there is little or no time for calculated misstatement, and thirdly, the statement will usually be made to another (the witness who reports it) who would have equal opportunities to observe and hence to check a misstatement. Consequently, it is believed that such comments, strictly limited to reports of present sense-impressions, have such exceptional reliability as to warrant their inclusion within the hearsay exception for Spontaneous Declarations.

The statement of Mrs. Cooper is not one the evidential value of which is purely cumulative, nor is it such as to relegate the determination of its admissibility to the trial court's discretion. Rather it was one in which the witness was alluding to an occurrence within her own knowledge in language calculated to make her "meaning clearer to the jury" than would a mere expression of opinion as to the speed at which the passing car was moving.

We find neither in the statement nor in the circumstances under which it was made (if it was) any basis upon which to invoke the discretion of the trial court as to its admissibility. It is competent evidence the consideration of which, since it is relevant and not merely cumulative, is determinable as a matter of law under an established rule of evidence.

The inference to be drawn as to whether the statement was made, and the inferences flowing from it (if made) are solely for the jury, and the trial court erred in excluding the testimony from its consideration.

Defendants contend the making of the statement was too remote in point of time. Had it been made under the stress of emotion, or if the party seeking the benefit of its admission were the one who made it, a different question would be presented.

Certainly the statement in the present case (made, if it was, about four miles before the witness reached the scene of collision) was not so remote in point of time as to be without relevance to its cause. The Court of Civil Appeals erred in affirming the action of the trial court in excluding the testimony.

[Reversed and Remanded.]

NOTES AND QUESTIONS

(1) *Hearsay that Contains Speculative Opinion.* What about the rule against opinion? Wasn't Mrs. Cooper's statement in *Houston Oxygen* an opinion? Note that the Federal Rules of Evidence do not exclude opinion if it is "rationally based on perception" and "helpful" to the jury. Fed. R. Evid. 701. Consider whether this statement qualifies and, if so, whether its speculative nature should have influenced the hearsay exception issue.

(2) *The Differences between 803(1) and 803(2), Including the Time Factor.* The case of *Hilyer v. Howat Concrete Co.*, 578 F.2d 422 (D.C. Cir. 1978), graphically illustrates the difference between Fed. R. Evid. 803(1) and Fed. R. Evid. 803(2), and discusses the time elapsing between event and declaration. Fifteen to 45 minutes was considered too long a time after a construction accident for Fed. R. Evid. 803(1) but not necessarily for Fed. R. Evid. 803(2), depending on other factors that also bear on excitement. The evidence was held admissible for its truth as an excited utterance. The evidence also was admissible to impeach declarant, who testified and who shortly after the declaration changed his story.

(3) *Time Delay and Lack of Excitement Lead to Exclusion.* In *United States v. Cain*, 587 F.2d 678 (5th Cir. 1979), the trial court admitted testimony by a state trooper regarding information he had received (that two males had left a truck) via CB radio transmission from an unidentified citizen. The CB broadcaster was said to be stating a "present sense impression" under Fed. R. Evid. 803(1). The Court of Appeals held the transmission was not admissible on this ground, nor was it an excited utterance under Fed. R. Evid. 803(2), because it appeared that two minutes after the broadcast, defendant (one of the males) was five miles away from the truck. Thus the broadcast could not have been contemporaneous with the sighting or "immediately thereafter." Moreover, there were no factors showing the broadcaster was excited when he transmitted; he was responding to a general request for information put out by police over the CB. *Cf. United States v. Santos*, 201 F.3d 953 (7th Cir. 2000), holding that handwritten complaints included in a business record were improperly admitted as present sense impressions because of lack of contemporaneousness.

(4) *Statement with Double Admissibility. United States v. Jackson*, 124 F.3d 607 (4th Cir. 1997), *cert. denied*, 522 U.S. 1066 (1998), held that a statement by the defendant's mother to a police officer that her son was threatening to kill members of her family fit within Rule 803(1) and Rule 803(2), because the event was both

ongoing and startling. Does it matter which rule applies?

(5) *Domestic Violence Cases.* The use of present sense impressions and excited utterances has become quite common in domestic violence trials, particularly when the complaining spouse recants or refuses to testify. Recordings from a 911 emergency call-in are a frequent form of such evidence in such cases. This evidence was criticized in Friedman & McCormack, *Dial-In Testimony*, 150 U. Pa. L. Rev. 1171 (2002), as violating the constitutional confrontation clause when the witness does not testify. The confrontation issue now must be evaluated under the new *Crawford* "testimonial" approach, which will be discussed in § 11.03[B].

PROBLEM SET 9A: PRESENT SENSE IMPRESSIONS, EXCITED UTTERANCES AND BEYOND.

The following problems require you to consider these two exceptions, but they also require you to consider other exceptions, exemptions, and the hearsay definition:

(1) *"I Was Just Running an Errand for My Employer."* Would a statement by a driver who has just hit someone with his car, "I was just running an errand for my employer," be admissible to prove scope of employment under either of the two Federal Rules of Evidence exceptions presently under study? What requirement (other than the "stress of excitement" requirement) in the federal "Excited Utterances" rule at least arguably might stand in the way, at least on some interpretations? Would it make it more, or less, difficult to admit the evidence if it were offered under the federal "Present Sense Impressions" rule? Alternatively, would the statement qualify as a party admission of the employer?

(2) *The Declarant Who Now Has Amnesia: "The Headlights Closed."* Plaintiff sues the manufacturer of his automobile, alleging that his crash at night was due to the fact that his headlights (the type that close flush with the car body) closed unexpectedly while he was on the highway, owing to a defect of manufacture. Since the car is totally demolished and there were no witnesses, and the plaintiff now has amnesia as to what happened (owing to injuries received in the crash), his only evidence that the lights closed is the testimony of his doctor that plaintiff was taken immediately to the hospital, in a coma that lasted for twenty hours, and upon regaining consciousness the plaintiff immediately told the doctor, "The headlights closed," lapsing again into unconsciousness. The plaintiff's amnesia also makes it impossible to remember this statement. Based on all the exceptions to the hearsay rule you have been studying in this and other sections, is this statement admissible? What arguments could be made? (*Chestnut v. Ford Motor Co.*, 445 F.2d 967 (4th Cir. 1971).)

(3) *Should We Adopt a "Recent Perception" Rule?* We have seen that the excited utterances exception became expanded so that declarations of present sense impressions also would be received (in certain jurisdictions), and that, in return for forgoing the requirement of excitement, the "present sense impression" rule tightens the time requirement. The next step in the evolution would be a "recent sense impressions" rule, embracing declarations of things recently (rather than immediately previously) perceived, but imposing certain additional safeguards to try to partly compensate for the relaxation of the time requirement. For example,

an earlier draft of the Federal Rules of Evidence had the following provision in Rule 804 (in addition to the two provisions of Fed. R. Evid. 803 presently under discussion):

> **Statement of recent perception.** A statement, not in response to the instigation of a person engaged in investigating, litigating, or settling a claim, which narrates, describes, or explains an event or condition recently perceived by the declarant, made in good faith, not in contemplation of pending or anticipated litigation in which he was interested, and while his recollection was clear [is not excluded by the hearsay rule if the declarant is unavailable as a witness].

What are the additional compensating requirements under this proposed rule that at least arguably help to make up for the relaxation of the time requirement? Do you think this is a wise rule?

(4) *What Factors Define an Excited Utterance?* Regarding something offered as an "excited utterance," are the following factors to be considered in arguing the issue of admissibility? Are they to be considered in arguing the issue of weight?

(a) The period of time between the startling event and the declaration.

(b) How exciting the event was.

(c) Whether the declarant was a bystander or a participant in the event.

(d) How directly the declaration relates to the immediate facts and circumstances of the event.

(e) The fact that the declarant had a motive to falsify.

(f) The fact that the declaration was in response to a question rather than blurted.

(g) The fact that expert psychologists agree that excited declarants are likely to be flustered and not very accurate or careful in regard to perception, memory, and reporting.

(h) The fact that the declarant is available. (If this is a matter of weight and not admissibility, what is the special necessity for this evidence?)

(i) The fact that declarant would be mentally incompetent as a witness.

(5) *Are 803(1) and 803(2) Redundant?* Why do we need Fed. R. Evid. 803(2), when we have Fed. R. Evid. 803(1)? Why do we need 803(1), when we have 803(2)?

§ 9.03 DECLARATIONS OF PRESENT MENTAL, EMOTIONAL, OR PHYSICAL CONDITION[3]

Read Federal Rule of Evidence 803(3), "Hearsay Exceptions — Regardless of Whether the Declarant is Available as a Witness: Then-Existing Mental, Emotional, or Physical Condition."

NOTES AND QUESTIONS

(1) *What is Included in the Present Mental-Etc. Condition Rule (803(3)) and How it Differs from the Medical Statement Rule (803(4)).* Fed. R. Evid. 803(3) combines what a number of cases at common law considered to be two distinct exceptions to the hearsay rule: declarations of present bodily feeling or condition, and declarations of present state of mind or emotion.

Statements of a relevant bodily feeling or condition may be made to anyone if the feeling or condition is contemporaneous with the statement of it. In other words, it does not have to be made to a physician or for purposes of medical diagnosis or treatment (a separate exception; see below). The underlying "guarantees" of trustworthiness here are different than for medically motivated statements: here it is the contemporaneousness and close proximity of declarant to the thing reported; there it is the motive of obtaining good medical services.

(2) *Statements About Contemporaneous Physical Condition.* In *House Moving, etc. v. Workmen's Compensation Appeal Bd.*, 391 A.2d 1105 (Pa. Commw. Ct. 1978), over a period of months after a workplace injury, decedent complained to his wife about nausea, vomiting, shortness of breath, exhaustion, numbness, cyanosis, and various pains (without which there would be insufficient evidence to attribute his death to the injury). The wife was allowed to testify to these complaints under the exception for present physical condition. The remainder of this section will treat questions regarding what is typically called "state of mind" of the declarant.

(3) *Children's Statements that they do Not Wish to Live with their Mother.* In *Melton v. Dallas County Child Welfare Unit*, 602 S.W.2d 119 (Tex. Civ. App. 1980), the court upheld admission of statements made by two children, 7 and 9 years old, to a caseworker regarding whether they wished to live with their mother or be adopted, as declarations of state of mind, even though offered "for the truth of the matter stated" (in that they were express statements of their wishes, offered to show their true wishes, which were relevant to the issue of whether the mother's conduct had endangered the children's well-being, and to the issue of where they would be happiest). The "matter stated" was their state of mind at the time of their statement of it. The state of mind was directly in issue, the court said. Thus, the evidence was within the present state of mind exception. (Query: Could you fashion an implied statement the children really are making, which would not fit this exception?)

(4) *Statements in an Alienation of Affections Case.* In *Adkins v. Brett*, 193 P.

---

[3] Study Guide Reference: Evidence in a Nutshell, Chapter 10:II at "Declarations of Declarant's Current State of Mind and the Like: F.R.E. 803(3)" (including its sub-divisions).

251 (Cal. 1920), plaintiff sued defendant for alienating the affections of plaintiff's wife. The court held that the plaintiff could testify to the wife's statement to him that, since the defendant had taken her riding, taken her to dinner, and bought her flowers, she now loved defendant and not plaintiff. The court held this admissible to prove the change of affections but not admissible to prove whether defendant did anything to produce the change. Explain why this ruling arguably is correct (note that the exception is for statements about present condition, not for statements of memory of past events).

(5) *Workers' Statements of Reasons for Leaving Employment.* In *Elmer v. Fessenden*, 24 N.E. 208 (Mass. 1889), a defamation action, plaintiff alleged that workers were leaving his factory *because defendant had said that the factory was unsafe*. Plaintiff's shop foreman was allowed to testify that the workers who were quitting gave that (the italicized matter) as their reason. The court held that this was admissible to show the workers' reason for leaving (which was relevant to causation of the damage of loss of workers) but not to show that the defendant said anything (i.e., actually uttered the allegedly defamatory words).

(6) *Multiple Admissibility Problems.* In both of the last two cases the court indicates that the general rule when hearsay evidence presents a "multiple admissibility" problem, i.e., is admissible for one but not for another purpose in a case, is to admit with a cautionary instruction, rather than exclude; but that in an extraordinary or exaggerated case that rule might be departed from and the evidence totally excluded. What factors might be considered to decide whether any particular case is an extraordinary case? What rule or rules in the Federal Rules of Evidence govern this determination?

(7) *Are Instructions or Redaction Useful Solutions to Multiple-Admissibility Hearsay Problems?* In both of the last two cases, exactly how would you instruct the jury? Tactically, would any party want the instruction? (What happens if I tell you not to think of elephants?) Also consider the possibility of redacting the out-of-court statement in each case (i.e., severing it into parts and admitting only part.) Would that be a more satisfactory solution than an instruction in each of these cases? What about the possibility of paraphrasing what the declarant said in each case?

UNITED STATES v. SAMANIEGO & BAEZ

United States Court of Appeals, Eleventh Circuit
345 F.3d 1280 (2003)

CARNES, CIRCUIT JUDGE

Like the brute Mongo in Mel Brooks's 1974 comedy classic Blazing Saddles, Roberto Duran [whose surname, Samaniego, he does not use professionally] once knocked out a horse with a single punch.[1]

---

[1] As Duran told the story in 1998:

> I was 14 or 15 . . . in my mother's home town of Guarare . . . . There was a fiesta. I had $150 in my pocket, which was a lot of money for me, and we were all drinking whiskey. There was a girl sitting next to me, teasing me, and I felt like a big shot. But I was running out of money

That horse, as well as countless human opponents who suffered the same fate in the streets and back alleys of Panama where Duran grew up, are not included in his career total of 104 officially sanctioned boxing wins — 69 of them by knockout — against only 16 losses.

Born into poverty, Roberto Duran grew up fighting on the streets where he earned the nickname "Manos de Piedra" — Hands of Stone. He started his professional boxing career at the age of 15 or 16. In 1972, when only 21 years old, Duran won the lightweight championship of the world by knocking out Ken Buchanan in the thirteenth round. As a lightweight, he achieved a near perfect record of 62 wins in 63 contests, which explains why Duran is widely regarded as one of the greatest boxers in that weight category in the history of the sport. He held the lightweight title from 1972 to 1979, when he put it down in order to fight as a welterweight.

Duran captured the welterweight championship in 1980 with a fifteen-round decision over Sugar Ray Leonard. Five months later Leonard took that title back from Duran, who conceded the fight in the eighth round by muttering what would become two of the most infamous words in boxing history: "no mas." Like a true champ, however, Duran got up off the mat of that embarrassing defeat to win championships in two more weight classes, defeating Davey Moore in 1983 for the junior middleweight title and then, at age 37, defeating Iran Barkley for the middleweight title in 1989. He was the first boxer to win championships in four different weight classes.

Even hands of stone don't last forever, and no one can out box time. The damage done by the pounding Duran had taken in the ring over the years was exacerbated in 2001 by a car crash in Argentina in which he suffered broken ribs and a punctured lung. In February of 2002, at the age of 50, Duran finally hung up his gloves after 34 years of professional boxing. He left the ring with his memories and his championship belts, and it is those belts that are at the center of this case. Duran claims that his championship belts were stolen from his house in Panama by his brother-in-law, Bolivar Iglesias, in September of 1993. Ever the fighter, Duran has waged a ten-year battle to regain his belts, which are the physical embodiment of his life's work and a reminder of the glory that once was his. It is late in the last round of that legal fight, which began when Duran filed a criminal complaint against Iglesias in Panama and convinced the FBI to investigate the disappearance of his belts.

It is undisputed that Duran's championship belts ultimately came into the hands of Luis Gonzalez Baez, a Miami businessman, and that Baez attempted to sell the belts to undercover FBI agents (who had set up a sting operation) for $200,000. Baez was arrested, but he claimed that the belts had not been stolen. The

---

to buy alcohol when someone said, "You call yourself Manos de Piedra (Hands of Stone), I betcha a bottle of whiskey and $50 you can't knock out that horse." . . . My uncle, Socrates Garcia was his name, pulled me aside. "I got a secret," he said. He told me to punch the horse behind the ear and "that horse will go down." He did. But I ripped my hand open. You could see right through to the bone. But I didn't feel any pain. I didn't go to the hospital. I stayed with the girl all night and didn't get one kiss.

Michael Katz, *Duran is Still Horsing Around*, N.Y. DAILY NEWS, June 2, 1998, at 75.

government confiscated the belts and filed an interpleader action in federal district court to determine whether Duran or Baez is the rightful owner of the belts. The case was tried to a jury, which returned a verdict in favor of Duran. This is Baez's appeal from the judgment the district court entered in accordance with that verdict.

Baez's principal contention on appeal is that the district court should not have admitted testimony about a purported apology from Bolivar Iglesias. Over Baez's objection, the district court permitted a number of witnesses, including Duran and some of his family members, to testify that Iglesias apologized in their presence for stealing the belts. Baez contends that testimony is inadmissible hearsay. The district court allowed it on the theory that the out-of-court statement described an existing state of mind or emotion, and for that reason fit within the hearsay exception set out in Federal Rule of Evidence 803(3). [Rule quoted.]

The question, as Baez's argument frames it, is whether Iglesias's apology falls within the exclusion from Rule 803(3) admissibility because it is a "statement of memory or belief to prove the fact remembered or believed" [in the words of the penultimate clause of the rule].

An apology is evidence of a then-existing state of mind or emotion: remorse. Iglesias's apology is admissible to prove the truth of the matter asserted — that Iglesias felt remorse at the time he made the apologetic statement. That is not the problem. The problem is, as we have observed, that "the state-of-mind exception does not permit the witness to relate any of the declarant's statements as to why he held the particular state of mind, or what he might have believed that would have induced the state of mind." [Case citation.] Consistent with that position, we have explained that the purpose of the exclusion from Rule 803(3) admissibility is "to narrowly limit those admissible statements to declarations of condition — 'I'm scared' — and not belief — 'I'm scared because [someone] threatened me.' " *Id.*

The testimony admitted in this case was not limited to the fact that Iglesias had expressed remorse, but also included the fact that he said he apologized for and asked forgiveness for having stolen the belts. The testimony most often came in response to questions from Duran's counsel about how the witness knew Iglesias had stolen the belts. What Iglesias said was offered to show not only that he was remorseful, but also that he had stolen the belts. Rule 803(3) expressly prohibits the use of a statement of then-existing state of mind in this way. That prohibition, the committee note explains, is necessary "to avoid the virtual destruction of the hearsay rule which would otherwise result from allowing state of mind, provable by a hearsay statement, to serve as the basis for an inference of the happening of the event which produced the state of mind." Fed. R. Evid. 803(3) advisory committee's note.

[The remainder of the opinion considers another hearsay exception for the same evidence, declarations against interest, Fed. R. Evid. 804(b)(3). See § 10.01, *infra*, where that portion of the opinion is reproduced in connection with a general discussion of unavailability of the declarant, required for the declarations against interest exception.]

NOTES AND QUESTIONS

(1) *Relevance of State of Mind.* As held in the principal case, statements introduced under 803(3) cannot be used to prove the acts causing the state of mind. Thus, the declarant's state of mind must be relevant for some other reason than for the facts it indicates that may have generated the state of mind.

In *United States v. Sesay*, 313 F.3d 591 (D.C. Cir. 2002) (a gun and drug possession case), the court excluded an out-of-court police statement offered by the defense to show the state of mind of the officers who arrested the defendants. The statement was essentially that the police understood that (i.e., had the state of mind that) there were "witnesses who saw the victim with the gun immediately after the shooting." The only issue at trial was who possessed the gun and drugs. Thus, the statement was only relevant if the police "understanding" (i.e., their state of mind) was an accurate reflection of underlying facts. But, as the principal case shows, it is not admissible for that purpose because it is hearsay and not within the state of mind principle. (Can you come up with another possible theory of relevance of the evidence that might make the evidence admissible?)

In *Sesay*, the *defense* offered the statement, *incriminating another*. Often, similar evidence of police belief in facts *incriminating the defendant*, is offered by the *prosecution* (evidence that, for example, police believed the *defendant* possessed a weapon or drugs or at least believed there were witnesses who would say that). The same analysis would suggest that this, too, is inadmissible. If you had to, could you come up with another theory of relevance of such evidence, perhaps a bit strained, that might qualify for admissibility under state of mind? For example, as background evidence or evidence lending narrative color, explaining why the police came, or acted in a certain way? Would Rule 403 then step in, on balance of the good and the bad from the evidence, to bar the evidence altogether, or could it be safely admitted with a jury instruction cautioning against the bad use? Alternatively, would such evidence be admissible in a probable cause hearing, as opposed to a determination at trial concerning guilt or innocence?

(2) *Statement of Fear.* A similar issue often arises in criminal prosecutions for an act of violence, where the victim has previously or subsequently (to the charged act) expressed fear of the defendant, in an out-of-court statement. The fear is based on and indicates violent action the defendant committed. The expression of fear may even explicitly mention that such violent action of defendant is the cause of the fear. Normally, the declarant's state of mind (fear) would not be *relevant* except insofar as it suggests or reflects there was a violent act by defendant. But it cannot be used for that purpose under the hearsay exception, as we learn from the principal case. The judge should instruct the jury not to consider the statement as proof of those acts, and should redact (excise) anything that suggests those acts. But then the state of mind (fear) usually will have no relevance left at all, because its only relevance is that it suggests the violent acts of the defendant. In a rare case, the state of mind may have some other minimal relevance left (for example, to show background about why a victim acted in a certain way), but Rule 403 may be a possible basis for excluding it altogether, even for that purpose, because of an overriding likelihood the jury will infer the acts giving rise to the fear, despite instructions not to.

The problem often arises when the victim has died from a violent wound allegedly inflicted by defendant. In the homicide prosecution, or wrongful death civil lawsuit, a witness may testify that the deceased said he/she fears the defendant because the defendant had previously threatened him/her. Frequently these are domestic violence cases, but not always. As indicated above, the question is, would this evidence be within 803(3)? *See Bains v. Cambra*, 204 F.3d 964 (9th Cir.), *cert. denied*, 531 U.S. 1037 (2000) (holding statements inadmissible under 803(3) and violative of the constitutional confrontation clause, but harmless error; for some new law on constitutional confrontation, see *Crawford* in § 11.03[B]). How do relevance and undue prejudice factor into the analysis? Does it matter for what purpose the evidence is introduced? E.g., to establish identity of the killer, or to rebut testimony that the decedent and defendant had a good relationship, or to rebut that the death was accidental, or to rebut that it was a suicide?

A few jurisdictions have or are considering a special hearsay exception for such victim statements especially in domestic violence situations. Are such statements especially trustworthy and necessary? More so than other excludable hearsay? On a par with the usual hearsay exceptions?

UNITED STATES v. PHEASTER

United States Court of Appeals, Ninth Circuit
544 F.2d 353 (1976), *cert. denied*, 429 U.S. 1099 (1977)

RENFREW, DISTRICT JUDGE.

[Appellants Pheaster and Angelo Inciso were tried before a jury and were convicted of conspiracy to kidnap and hold Larry Adell for ransom.]

Appellant Inciso argues that the district court erred in admitting hearsay testimony by two teenaged friends of Larry Adell concerning statements made by Larry on June 1, 1974, the day that he disappeared. Timely objections were made to the questions which elicited the testimony on the ground that the questions called for hearsay. In response, the Government attorney stated that the testimony was offered for the limited purpose of showing the "state of mind of Larry." After instructing the jury that it could only consider the testimony for that limited purpose and not for "the truth or falsity of what [Larry] said," the district court allowed the witnesses to answer the questions. Francine Gomes, Larry's date on the evening that he disappeared, testified that when Larry picked her up that evening, he told her that he was going to meet Angelo at Sambo's North at 9:30 P.M. to "pick up a pound of marijuana which Angelo had promised him for free."

She also testified that she had been with Larry on another occasion when he met a man named Angelo, and she identified the defendant as that man. Miss Gomes stated that it was approximately 9:15 P.M. when Larry went into the parking lot. Doug Sendejas, one of Larry's friends who was with him at Sambo's North just prior to his disappearance, testified that Larry had made similar statements to him in the afternoon and early evening of June 1st regarding a meeting that evening with Angelo. Mr. Sendejas also testified that when Larry left the table at Sambo's North to go into the parking lot, Larry stated that "he was going to meet Angelo and he'd be right back."

Inciso's contention that the district court erred in admitting the hearsay testimony of Larry's friends is premised on the view that the statements could not properly be used by the jury to conclude that Larry did in fact meet Inciso in the parking lot of Sambo's North at approximately 9:30 P.M. on June 1, 1974. The correctness of that assumption is, in our view, the key to the analysis of this contention of error. The Government argues that Larry's statements were relevant to two issues in the case. First the statements are said to be relevant to an issue created by the defense when Inciso's attorney attempted to show that Larry had not been kidnapped but had disappeared voluntarily as part of a simulated kidnapping designed to extort money from his wealthy father from whom he was allegedly estranged. In his brief on appeal, Inciso concedes the relevance and, presumably, the admissibility of the statements to "show that Larry did not voluntarily disappear." However, Inciso argues that for this limited purpose, there was no need to name the person with whom Larry intended to meet, and that the district court's limiting instruction was insufficient to overcome the prejudice to which he was exposed by the testimony.[12] Second, the Government argues that the statements are relevant and admissible to show that, as intended, Larry did meet Inciso in the parking lot at Sambo's North on the evening of June 1, 1974. If the Government's second theory of admissibility is successful, Inciso's arguments regarding the excision of his name from the statements admitted under the first theory is obviously mooted.

The Government's position that Larry Adell's statements can be used to prove that the meeting with Inciso did occur raises a difficult and important question concerning the scope of the so-called "*Hillmon* doctrine," a particular species of the "state of mind" exception to the general rule that hearsay evidence is inadmissible. [Note: The court discusses the facts and holding of *Mutual Life Ins. Co. v. Hillmon*, 145 U.S. 285 (1892), later in this opinion.] That the *Hillmon* doctrine should create controversy and confusion is not surprising, for it is an extraordinary doctrine. Under the state of mind exception, hearsay evidence is admissible if it bears on the state of mind of the declarant and if that state of mind is an issue in the case. For example, statements by a testator which demonstrate that he had the necessary testamentary intent are admissible to show that intent when it is in issue. The exception embodied in the *Hillmon* doctrine is fundamentally different, because it does not require that the state of mind of the declarant be an actual issue in the case. Instead, under the *Hillmon* doctrine the state of mind of the declarant is used inferentially to prove other matters which are in issue. Stated simply, the doctrine provides that when the performance of a particular act by an individual is an issue in a case, his intention (state of mind) to perform that act may be shown. From that intention, the trier of fact may draw the inference that the person carried out his intention and performed the act. Within this conceptual framework, hearsay evidence of statements by the person which tend to show his intention is deemed admissible under the state of mind exception. Inciso's objection to the doctrine

---

[12] Were this the only theory under which the testimony could come in, we would tend to agree with Inciso. In such a context, the potential prejudice would far outweigh the potential relevance of the testimony, and a limiting instruction would not sufficiently safeguard the defendant.

concerns its application in situations in which the declarant has stated his intention to do something with another person, and the issue is whether he did so. There can be no doubt that the theory of the *Hillmon* doctrine is different when the declarant's statement of intention necessarily requires the action of one or more others if it is to be fulfilled.

When hearsay evidence concerns the declarant's statement of his intention to do something with another person, the *Hillmon* doctrine requires that the trier of fact infer from the state of mind of the declarant the probability of a particular act not only by the declarant but also by the other person. Several objections can be raised against a doctrine that would allow such an inference to be made. One such objection is based on the unreliability of the inference but is not, in our view, compelling.[14] A much more significant and troubling objection is based on the inconsistency of such an inference with the state of mind exception. This problem is more easily perceived when one divides what is really a compound statement into its component parts. In the instant case, the statement by Larry Adell, "I am going to meet Angelo in the parking lot to get a pound of grass," is really two statements. The first is the obvious statement of Larry's intention. The second is an implicit statement of Angelo's intention. Surely, if the meeting is to take place in a location which Angelo does not habitually frequent, one must assume that Angelo intended to meet Larry there if one is to make the inference that Angelo was in the parking lot and the meeting occurred. The important point is that the second, implicit statement has nothing to do with Larry's state of mind. For example, if Larry's friends had testified that Larry had said, "Angelo is going to be in the parking lot of Sambo's North tonight with a pound of grass," no state of mind exception or any other exception to the hearsay rule would be available. Yet, this is in effect at least half of what the testimony did attribute to Larry.

Despite the theoretical awkwardness associated with the application of the *Hillmon* doctrine to facts such as those now before us, the authority in favor of such an application is impressive, beginning with the seminal *Hillmon* decision itself. *Hillmon, supra*, 145 U.S. 285 was a civil case involving a colorful dispute over certain life insurance claims. The factual issue in the case was whether Hillmon, who had purchased a number of life insurance policies naming his wife as beneficiary, had been killed by the accidental discharge of a gun in a campsite near Crooked Creek, Kansas. If he had been so killed, his wife was entitled to the benefits under the insurance policies. The defendant insurance companies contended, however, that Hillmon was not dead but was in hiding, and that the claims were part of a conspiracy to defraud the companies. While it was undisputed that someone had been killed in the campsite at Crooked Creek, there was complete disagreement as to who the victim was. The defendants in *Hillmon* introduced evidence which

---

[14] The inference from a statement of present intention that the act intended was in fact performed is nothing more than an inference. Even where no actions by other parties are necessary in order for the intended act to be performed, a myriad of contingencies could intervene to frustrate the fulfillment of the intention. The fact that the cooperation of another party is necessary if the intended act is to be performed adds another important contingency, but the difference is one of degree rather than kind. The possible unreliability of the inference to be drawn from the present intention is a matter going to the weight of the evidence which might be argued to the trier of fact, but it should not be a ground for completely excluding the admittedly relevant evidence.

tended to show that the body at Crooked Creek was not that of Hillmon, but was that of another man, Frederick Adoph Walters. As part of this attempt to show that it was Walters who was killed at Crooked Creek, the defendants attempted to introduce two letters written by Walters from Wichita, Kansas, shortly before he disappeared, never to be heard from again. In the letters, one written to his sister and the other to his fiancee, Walters stated that he intended to leave Wichita in the near future and to travel with a man named Hillmon. In the letter to his fiancee, Walters explained that Hillmon was making the expedition to search for a suitable site for a sheep ranch, and that Hillmon had promised him employment at the ranch on very favorable terms. Plaintiff's objection to the introduction of the letters on the ground that they were incompetent, irrelevant, and hearsay was sustained by the trial court.

The Supreme Court summarily rejected the argument that the letters were admissible "as memoranda made in the ordinary course of business," 145 U.S. at 295, but then held that they were admissible as evidence of Walters' intention:

> The letters in question were competent, not as narratives of facts communicated to the writer by others, nor yet as proof that he actually went away from Wichita, but *as evidence that*, shortly before the time when other evidence tended to show that he went away, *he had the intention of going, and of going with Hillmon, which made it more probable both that he did go and that he went with Hillmon, than if there had been no proof of such intention*. In view of the mass of conflicting testimony introduced upon the question of whether it was the body of Walters that was found in Hillmon's camp, this evidence might properly influence the jury in determining that question. 145 U.S. at 295–296 (emphasis added).

Although *Hillmon* was a civil case, the Supreme Court cited with approval a number of criminal cases in support of its decision. One of them, *Hunter v. State*, 11 Vroom (40 N.J.L.) 495, involved facts remarkably similar to those before us here. The Court summarized the facts and the holding of that case as follows:

> Upon an indictment of one Hunter for the murder of one Armstrong at Camden, the Court of Errors and Appeals of New Jersey unanimously held that Armstrong's oral declarations to his son at Philadelphia, on the afternoon before the night of the murder, as well as a letter written by him at the same time and place to his wife, each stating that he was going with Hunter to Camden on business, were rightly admitted in evidence. 145 U.S. at 299.

The Court then quoted a long passage from the opinion of Chief Justice Beasley in *Hunter*. The primary concern expressed in that passage was whether there was anything unnatural about the victim's statements that might suggest an ulterior purpose and, hence, unreliability. Having found no indicia of unreliability, Chief Justice Beasley brushed aside the suggestion that the specific reference to the defendant should have been omitted. Speaking rhetorically, Chief Justice Beasley asked:

> If it is legitimate to show by a man's own declarations that he left his home to be gone a week, or for a certain destination, which seems incontestable,

> why may it not be proved in the same way that a designated person was to bear him company?

The Chief Justice then concluded:

> If it was in the ordinary train of events for this man to leave word or to state where he was going, it seems to me it was equally so for him to say with whom he was going. *Hunter v. State* [11 Vroom], 40 N.J.L. 495, 534, 536, 538. 145 U.S. at 299.

The *Hillmon* doctrine has been applied by the California Supreme Court in *People v. Alcalde*, 148 P.2d 627 ([Cal.] 1944), a criminal case with facts which closely parallel those in *Hunter*. In *Alcalde* the defendant was tried and convicted of first degree murder for the brutal slaying of a woman whom he had been seeing socially. One of the issues before the California Supreme Court was the asserted error by the trial court in allowing the introduction of certain hearsay testimony concerning statements made by the victim on the day of her murder. As in the instant case, the testimony was highly incriminating, because the victim reportedly said that she was going out with Frank, the defendant, on the evening she was murdered. On appeal, a majority of the California Supreme Court affirmed the defendant's conviction, holding that *Hillmon* was "the leading case on the admissibility of declarations of intent to do an act as proof that the act thereafter was accomplished." 148 P.2d at 631. Without purporting to "define or summarize all the limitations or restrictions upon the admissibility of" such evidence, *id.* at 632, the court did mention several prudential considerations not unlike those mentioned by Chief Justice Beasley in *Hunter*. Thus, the declarant should be dead or otherwise unavailable, and the testimony concerning his statements should be relevant and possess a high degree of trustworthiness. *Id.* at 631. The court also noted that there was other evidence from which the defendant's guilt could be inferred. Applying these standards, the court found no error in the trial court's admission of the disputed hearsay testimony. "Unquestionably the deceased's statement of her intent and the logical inference to be drawn therefrom, namely, that she was with the defendant that night, were relevant to the issue of the guilt of the defendant." *Id.* at 632.

In addition to the decisions in *Hillmon* and *Alcalde*, support for the Government's position can be found in the California Evidence Code and the new Federal Rules of Evidence, although in each instance resort must be made to the comments to the relevant provisions.

Section 1250 of the California Evidence Code carves out an exception to the general hearsay rule for statements of a declarant's "then existing mental or physical state." The *Hillmon* doctrine is codified in Section 1250(2) which allows the use of such hearsay evidence when it "is offered to prove or explain acts or conduct of the declarant." The comment to Section 1250(2) states that, "Thus, a statement of the declarant's intent to do certain acts is admissible to prove that he did those acts." Although neither the language of the statute nor that of the comment specifically addresses the particular issue now before us, the comment does cite the *Alcalde* decision and, therefore, indirectly rejects the limitation urged by Inciso.

Although the new Federal Rules of Evidence were not in force at the time of the trial below, we refer to them for any light that they might shed on the status of the common law at the time of the trial. The codification of the state of mind exception in Rule 803(3) does not provide a direct statement of the *Hillmon* doctrine. Rule 803(3) provides an exemption from the hearsay rule for the following evidence: [Rule quoted]. Although Rule 803(3) is silent regarding the *Hillmon* doctrine, both the Advisory Committee on the Proposed Rules and the House Committee on the Judiciary specifically addressed the doctrine. After noting that Rule 803(3) would not allow the admission of statements of memory, the Advisory Committee stated broadly that

> The rule of *Mutual Life Ins. Co. v. Hillmon* [citation omitted] allowing evidence of intention as tending to prove the doing of the act intended, is, of course, left undisturbed. Note to Paragraph (3), 28 U.S.C.A. at 585.

Significantly, the Notes of the House Committee on the Judiciary regarding Rule 803(3) are far more specific and revealing:

> However, the Committee intends that the Rule be construed to limit the doctrine of *Mutual Life Insurance Co. v. Hillmon* [citation omitted] so as to render statements of intent by a declarant admissible *only to prove his future conduct, not the future conduct of another person*. House Report No. 93-650, Note to Paragraph (3), 28 U.S.C.A. at 579 (emphasis added).

Although the matter is certainly not free from doubt, we read the note of the Advisory Committee as presuming that the *Hillmon* doctrine would be incorporated in full force, including necessarily the application in *Hillmon* itself. The language suggests that the Advisory Committee presumed that such a broad interpretation was the prevailing common law position. The notes of the House Committee on the Judiciary are significantly different. The language used there suggests a legislative intention to cut back on what that body also perceived to be the prevailing common law view, namely, that the Hillmon doctrine could be applied to facts such as those now before us.

Although we recognize the force of the objection to the application of the *Hillmon* doctrine in the instant case,[18] we cannot conclude that the district court

---

[18] Criticism of the *Hillmon* doctrine has come from very distinguished quarters, both judicial and academic. However, the position of the judicial critics is definitely the minority position, stated primarily in dicta and dissent.

In his opinion for the Court in *Shepard v. United States*, 290 U.S. 96 (1933), Justice Cardozo indicated in dicta an apparent hostility to the *Hillmon* doctrine. Shepard involved hearsay testimony of a dramatically different character from that in the instant case. The Court reviewed the conviction of an army medical officer for the murder of his wife by poison. The asserted error by the trial court was its admission, over defense objection, of certain hearsay testimony by Mrs. Shepard's nurse concerning statements that Mrs. Shepard had made during her final illness. The nurse's testimony was that, after asking whether there was enough whiskey left in the bottle from which she had drunk just prior to her collapse to make a test for poison, Mrs. Shepard stated,"Dr. Shepard has poisoned me." One theory advanced by the Government on appeal was that the testimony was admissible to show that Mrs. Shepard did not have suicidal tendencies and, thus, to refute the defense argument that she took her own life. The Court rejected that theory, holding that the testimony had not been admitted for the limited purpose suggested by the Government and that, even if it had been admitted for that purpose, its relevance was far outweighed by the extreme prejudice it would create for the defendant. In rejecting the Government's theory, the Court refused to extend the state of mind exception to statements of memory. In his survey of the state of mind exception, Justice Cardozo appeared to suggest that the

erred in allowing the testimony concerning Larry Adell's statements to be introduced.

[Affirmed.]

NOTES AND QUESTIONS

(1) *The Two Branches of the Hillmon Doctrine.* From what appears of *Hillmon* in the principal case, it is apparent that *Hillmon* has two branches: (a) the authorization to use the statement to indicate the doing of the intended act by the declarant, and (b) the authorization to use it to indicate action by the other person. (All agree that (a) is a proper use.) Were both branches essential to the holding in *Hillmon*, do you suppose, or might it be argued that (b) was unnecessary, gratuitous dictum?

Does the reference to *Hillmon* in the Advisory Committee Note quoted in the principal case necessarily mean to embrace both branches of *Hillmon*? Does the text of the Rule itself?

(2) *Comparing Alcalde, Hillmon and Pheaster: "I Am Going Out with Frank."* Concerning the statement in *Alcalde*, as described in the principal case ("I am going out with Frank"), is it distinguishable from the statement in *Hillmon* or *Pheaster* in any pertinent respect? Is it severable into parts?

Hillmon doctrine is limited to "suits upon insurance policies," *id.* at 105, although the cases cited by the Court in *Hillmon* refute that suggestion.

The decision in *Shepard* was relied upon by Justice Traynor of the California Supreme Court in his vigorous dissent from the decision reached by the majority in *People v. Alcalde, supra*, 148 P.2d 627. Justice Traynor argued that the victim's declarations regarding her meeting with Frank could not be used to "induce the belief that the defendant went out with the deceased, took her to the scene of the crime and there murdered her without setting aside the rule against hearsay." *Id.* at 633. Any other legitimate use of the declaration, in his opinion, was so insignificant that it was outweighed by the enormous prejudice to the defendant in allowing the jury to hear it.

Finally, the exhaustive analysis of a different, but related, hearsay issue by the Court of Appeals for the District of Columbia in *United States v. Brown*, 490 F.2d 758, 160 U.S.App. D.C. 190 (1973), provides inferential support for the position urged by Inciso. The issue in that case was the admissibility of hearsay testimony concerning a victim's extrajudicial declarations that he was "[f]rightened that he may be killed" by the defendant. *Id.* at 762. After surveying the relevant cases, the court stated a "synthesis" of the governing principles. One of the cases which was criticized by the court was the decision of the California Supreme Court in *People v. Merkouris*, 52 Cal.2d 672, 344 P.2d 1 (1959), a case relied upon by the Government in the instant case. The court in *Merkouris* held that hearsay testimony showing the victim's fear of the defendant could properly be admitted to show the probable identity of the killer. The court in Brown expressed the following criticism of that holding, a criticism which might also apply to the application of the *Hillmon* doctrine in the instant case:

> Such an approach violates the fundamental safeguards necessary to the use of such testimony [citation omitted]. Through a circuitous series of inferences, the court reverses the effect of the statement so as to reflect on defendant's intent and actions rather than the state of mind of the declarant (victim). This is the very result that it is hoped the limiting instruction will prevent.
> 490 P.2d at 771 (emphasis in original).

For a frequently cited academic critique of the *Hillmon* doctrine, see Maguire, *The Hillmon Case — Thirty-Three Years* After, 38 Harv. L. Rev. 709 (1925).

(3) *Some Courts Impose Special Corroboration and/or Other Requirements Before Admitting the Evidence to Prove Conduct of the Non-Declarant. People v. James*, 717 N.E.2d 1052 (N.Y. 1999) adopted the view that statements of intent can be used to prove the conduct of another individual (who is usually the criminal defendant, as here). In doing so, it noted that some other courts require the following foundation for this use of state of mind evidence: (1) the declarant is unavailable; (2) the statement of the declarant's intent unambiguously contemplates some future action by the declarant, either jointly with the nondeclarant defendant or which requires the defendant's cooperation for its accomplishment; (3) to the extent that the declaration expressly or impliedly refers to a prior understanding or arrangement with the nondeclarant defendant, it must be inferable under the circumstances that the understanding or arrangement occurred in the recent past and that the declarant was a party to it or had competent knowledge of it; and (4) there is independent evidence of reliability, i.e., a showing of circumstances which all but rule out a motive to falsify, and evidence that the intended future acts were at least likely to have actually taken place. (Some jurisdictions apply a pared-down version of these requirements, simply requiring what they call "corroboration" before the evidence is admitted for this purpose.) Does such a foundation eliminate the concerns of those jurisdictions that ban such use of this type of evidence?

In *James*, the taped statement concerned a planned meeting involving the declarant, the defendant, and other police officers at which information about an upcoming police promotion examination was improperly disclosed. It was introduced in the defendant's perjury trial to contradict the defendant's grand jury testimony that such a meeting did not occur.

(4) *Forward-Looking Versus Backward-Looking Statements.* In *Shepard*, discussed in the footnote in *Pheaster*, the Court draws a bright line between statements that are forward-looking and statements that are backward-looking, disapproving the latter as potentially eradicating the hearsay ban. At trial, the Government had offered the alleged murder victim's statement that blamed her husband for poisoning her. On appeal, the Government argued that, even if inadmissible to prove that he poisoned her, it was admissible to prove the victim's state of mind, that she did not intend to commit suicide, in rebuttal to a defensive theory of suicide. The Court said:

> [The government] did not use the declarations by Mrs. Shepard [i.e., "Dr. Shepard has poisoned me"] to prove her present thoughts and feelings, or even her thoughts and feelings in times past. It used the declarations as proof of an act committed by some one else, as evidence that she was dying of poison given by her husband. This fact, if fact it was, the government was free to prove, but not by hearsay declarations. It will not do to say that the jury might accept the declarations for any light that they cast upon [rebutting the defensive theory of suicide] and reject them to the extent that they charged the death to some one else. Discrimination so subtle is a feat beyond the compass of ordinary minds. The reverberating clang of those accusatory words would drown all weaker sounds. It is for ordinary minds, and not for psychoanalysts, that our rules of evidence are framed. They have their source very often in considerations of administrative convenience, of practical expediency, and not in rules of logic. When the risk

of confusion is so great as to upset the balance of advantage, the evidence goes out.

There are times when a state of mind, if relevant, may be proved by contemporaneous declarations of feeling or intent. *Mutual Life Ins. Co. v. Hillmon*. The ruling in that case marks the high-water line beyond which courts have been unwilling to go. It has developed a substantial body of criticism and commentary. Declarations of intention, casting light upon the future, have been sharply distinguished from declarations of memory, pointing backwards to the past. There would be an end, or nearly that, to the rule against hearsay if the distinction were ignored.

The testimony now questioned faced backward and not forward. This at least it did in its most obvious implications. What is even more important, it spoke to a past act, and, more than that, to an act by someone not the speaker. Other tendency, if it had any, was a filament too fine to be disentangled by a jury.

PROBLEM 9B: "I AM KING TUT": NONHEARSAY, OR HEARSAY SUBJECT TO AN EXCEPTION?

In an earlier problem dealing with hearsay definition, we considered a declaration by a testator at the time of making his will, "I am King Tut," offered (via an overhearer) to reflect on his mental competence, and hence on the validity of his will.

We saw that, at least superficially, this is not hearsay because it was not offered for the truth of the matter stated (i.e., to show that he is indeed King Tut). We also saw, however, that some courts (at least under some rules or rulings) might be willing to take a deeper look. They might, for example, hold that this is an implied statement, "I believe I am King Tut," and since this is offered to show that he indeed believed he was King Tut (i.e., was telling the truth), this is offered for the truth of the matter (impliedly) stated and is hearsay. Still other courts might say, however, that even if we are willing to say for these purposes it is the implied statement "I believe I am King Tut," the truth of a statement about one's state of mind is not what we mean by "truth of the matter stated." Assuming, however, that the court is literal about the meaning of "truth of the matter stated," and thus holds that this implied statement ("I believe I am King Tut") is hearsay, would the present exception to the hearsay rule (the state of mind exception) cover the implied statement and make it admissible?

PROBLEM 9C: STATEMENTS OF INTENT OR MEMORY ABOUT THE PAST, PRESENT AND FUTURE.

Consider the following declarations of mental state. In some, the mental state declared about is directly in issue. In some, it is less directly in issue, in varying degrees. Which are encompassed within the state-of-mind hearsay exception? Which are not?

(1) *Contemporaneous Statement: "I Intend to Kill You."* X shoots and kills Y. Y's estate sues Y's life insurance company for the proceeds of the insurance on Y's life.

The company defends on grounds that the policy expressly provides that it pays off only if the death is accidental. The company denies the estate's claim that the gun was discharged accidentally. By way of proof, the company offers a witness who heard X declare to Y at the time of the shooting, "I intend to kill you."

(2) *Statement that I Intended to Kill Y in the Past.* Same as Problem (1), except the declaration by X was made some time after the shooting and states "I intended to kill Y."

(3) *"I Intend to Kill You" in the Future, Offered to Prove Both Intent and Act.* Same as (1), except the declarant's declaration "I intend to kill you" was not made at the time of the shooting but a week before. (a) Offered to show that the allegedly accidental discharge of the gun by X (declarant) was intentional. (b) Offered to show that it was X (the declarant) who discharged the gun at Y, in response to an allegation that someone else did.

(4) *"My Mind Contains a [Present] Picture . . ." of a Remembered Past Event.* The declaration is "My mind contains a picture that the Ford went through the red light." The declarant is conceded to have seen the Ford and the light at the relevant time. His declaration is offered in court via an overhearer of it. (Assume the case is an automobile collision case where the question is who went through the red light).

(5) *"I'm Going there Tomorrow with Bob."* Declarant states, "I'm going to Henley's Corner tomorrow, and Bob Jones is going with me." Three days later, declarant is found dead in a field somewhere removed from Henley's Corner. Bob Jones is prosecuted for declarant's murder. Can the prosecution put on a witness who heard the declaration, to testify to it?

(6) *The "Will Exception" in Fed. R. Evid. 803(4): Does it Allow Proof of Acts as well as Intent?* Declarant says "My mind contains a picture (memory, recollection) that last week I wrote (tore up) (altered) my will to my son Charles." This is offered in a will contest case, via one who overheard it. The declarant, the testator, has died. The dispute is as to whether he did the physical act referred to (which act is necessary to accomplish the making, revocation, or alteration of the will). Assume there is no dispute as to his intention to revoke, alter, or make the will.

(7) *"These Goods Are Perfectly Legitimate."* Defendant is charged with the crime of selling goods known by him to have been stolen by a third party (which were given to him by the third party). When approached by the police after his sale of the goods, defendant says, "What's the big deal? These goods are perfectly legitimate." At trial, defendant proffers that he said this, as evidence that he did not know the goods were stolen at the time he was caught, and therefore did not know they were stolen when he received and sold the goods. Is his evidence admissible for these purposes? *See* P. Rothstein, *Comments on Swift and Slobogin: Mental State Evidence*, 38 SETON HALL L. REV. 1395 (2008) (suggesting that courts would be likely to exclude this statement and that authorities support that result, but that it should be made admissible).

§ 9.04 STATEMENTS FOR PURPOSES OF MEDICAL DIAGNOSIS OR TREATMENT[8]

Read Federal Rule of Evidence 803(4), "Hearsay Exceptions — Regardless of Whether Dclarant is Available as a Witness: Statement Made for Medical Diagnosis or Treatment."

UNITED STATES v. IRON SHELL

United States Court of Appeals, Eighth Circuit
633 F.2d 77 (1980), *cert. denied*, 450 U.S. 1001 (1981)

STEPHENSON, CIRCUIT JUDGE

Defendant, John Louis Iron Shell, appeals from a jury conviction of assault with intent to commit rape.

The indictment in this case arose out of the defendant's acts [in] Antelope, within the Rosebud Indian Reservation [in] South Dakota. The defense conceded at trial that Iron Shell had assaulted Lucy, a nine-year-old Indian girl. The key questions at trial concerned the nature of the assault and the defendant's intent.

The defendant reached the Dillon house about 5:45 or 6:00 p.m. He talked and roughhoused briefly with Mike and Steve [Dillon children], and asked one of them to cook a hamburger. He then abruptly asked where his girlfriend Jeanne Brave was. When Mike said she was in St. Francis, the defendant was angered and said you can tell her to go to hell and kicked the door open and left.

Steve watched the defendant cross the highway in front of the Dillon house and enter the trail leading to [defendant's] mother's house. The defendant staggered somewhat and retraced his steps several times. Because of his strange behavior, Steve called Mike to the window. Both Mike and Steve testified that they saw the defendant approach Lucy who was near some cherry bushes just off the trail. Both saw the defendant grab Lucy and pull her down into some tall bushes. Steve testified he heard Lucy scream. Mike [and Steve] rode bicycle[s] to the spot. Mike testified that the defendant had his arm around Lucy and was trying to make her put her arm around him. The two boys alerted the neighbors.

Mae Small Bear was told by her granddaughter at about the same time that Lucy was "crying and hollering" in the bushes behind Small Bear's house. Small Bear walked to the bushes and saw Lucy lying on her back with the defendant lying beside her on his side.

At about this point Pam Lunderman arrived. She testified that she saw Lucy come out of the bushes pulling up her pants and crying. Lucy told Lunderman, "that guy tried to take my pants off."

Officer Marshall conducted an interview with Lucy [that evening] in the magistrate's home. Officer Marshall asked Lucy, "What happened?" In response

[8] Study Guide Reference: Evidence in a Nutshell, Chapter 10:II, at "Statements for Medical Diagnosis and Treatment: F.R.E. 803(4)."

Lucy related the following. Lucy said her assailant grabbed her and held her around the neck and told her to be quiet or he would choke her. He told her to take her pants down and when she refused, he pulled them partially off. Lucy told Officer Marshall, "he tried to what you call it me." Lucy also said that he had his hands between her legs. Officer Marshall recounted Lucy's statement in full at trial.[5]

Officer Marshall also testified that Lucy was not hysterical nor was she crying, but that her hair was messed and had leaves in it, that she appeared nervous and scared, and that her eyes were red.

Dr. Mark Hopkins, a physician with the Indian Health Service, [subsequently that night] examined Lucy. Dr. Hopkins was only aware that Lucy was allegedly a rape victim and was not told of the details surrounding the assault. During the examination, in response to questions posed by the doctor, Lucy told Dr. Hopkins she had been drug into the bushes, that her clothes, jeans and underwear, were removed and that the man had tried to force something into her vagina which hurt. She said she tried to scream but was unable because the man put his hand over her mouth and neck.[6] The doctor, over objection, repeated Lucy's statement at trial.

Dr. Hopkins' examination also revealed that there was a small amount of sand and grass in the perineal area but not in the vagina. He also found superficial abrasions on both sides of Lucy's neck and testified that they were consistent with someone grabbing her but qualified his statement by adding that he could not absolutely determine that they were so caused. Dr. Hopkins also testified that there was no physical evidence of penetration, the hymen was intact and no sperm was located.

[At trial] Lucy, a nine-year-old, was able to answer a number of preliminary questions demonstrating her ability to understand and respond to counsel but was unable to detail what happened after she was assaulted by the defendant. She did testify that she remembered something happening near the bushes and that a man had pushed her down. Lucy also said at trial that the man told her if she "didn't shut up he would choke me." In response to a series of leading questions she confirmed that the man had put his hand over her neck, hit her on the side of the face, held her down, taken her clothes off and that Mae Small Bear had scared the man, making him leave.[7] On cross-examination defense counsel did not explore any of the substantive issues, nor did he examine Lucy concerning the statement she made to

---

[5] Officer Marshall testified that Lucy did not spontaneously start to describe the incident but, in a halting manner, conveyed the facts as detailed above.

[6] Out of the presence of the jury, the doctor testified that he first asked Lucy "what happened" and she didn't answer. He asked whether she was in any pain and she pointed to her vaginal area. He asked if she hurt anywhere else and she didn't answer. Dr. Hopkins again asked "what happened" and Lucy said she had been drug into the bushes. The doctor then asked if the man "had taken her clothes off." She said yes, and then related the facts set out above. Dr. Hopkins testified that he was not "badgering" the patient, nor "dragging information out," but was asking "simple questions."

[7] The following is a representative sample of the prosecutor's direct examination of Lucy:

Q. What did the man do when he pushed you down, Lucy?

A. (Long hesitation)

Q. What did he do?

A. (Long hesitation)

Dr. Hopkins and Officer Marshall, although he had the opportunity.

Defendant challenges the admission of statements made by Lucy to Dr. Hopkins during his examination. The prosecution offered this testimony admittedly as hearsay but within the exception expressed in [Federal] Rule 803(4). The defendant argues that the questions asked by Dr. Hopkins and the information received in response to those questions were not "reasonably pertinent" to diagnosis or treatment. The defense stresses Dr. Hopkins' question in which he asked Lucy whether the man had taken her clothes off and suggests that this was asked by one in the role of an investigator, seeking to solve the crime, rather than a doctor treating or diagnosing a patient. The defendant also asserts that the doctor's examination would have been the same whether or not this extra information had been received. The defense argues that this point supports his claim that the questions were not pertinent to treatment or diagnosis because they had no effect on the doctor's examination. Lastly, the defendant urges that the doctor was employed for the specific purpose of qualifying as an expert witness and as such his testimony should be more suspect.

It is clear that Rule 803(4) significantly liberalized prior practice concerning admissibility of statements made for purposes of medical diagnosis or treatment. Rule 803(4) admits three types of statements: (1) medical history, (2) past or present sensations, and (3) inception or general cause of the disease or injury. All three types are admissible where they are "reasonably pertinent to diagnosis or treatment." The rule changed prior law in two main points. First, the rule adopted an expansive approach by allowing statements concerning past symptoms and those

---

Q. Did he hurt you any place?

A. (Long hesitation)

Q. Do you remember that?

A. (Long hesitation)

Q. Where did he put his hand, did he put his hand on your neck?

A. Yes.

Q. Did you get hit on the side of the face?

A. Yes.

Q. When he pushed you down, did he hold you down?

A. Yes.

Q. Did you start crying?

A. Yes.

The Court: As much as you can, phrase your questions in a way to avoid any unnecessary leading..

Q. What else happened when he had you down, Lucy; did he say anything to you, do you remember?

A. (Long hesitation)

Q. What did he say to you, can you tell me? Tell me what he said?

A. (Long hesitation)

Q. Could you do that for me?

A. Yes.

Q. Okay, tell me what he said?.

A. If I didn't shut up he would choke me.

which related to the cause of the injury. Second, the rule abolished the distinction between the doctor who is consulted for the purpose of treatment and an examination for the purpose of diagnosis only; the latter usually refers to a doctor who is consulted only in order to testify as a witness.

Lucy's statements fall primarily within the third category listed by 803(4).[9] The key question is whether these statements were reasonably pertinent to diagnosis or treatment. The rationale behind the rule has often been stated. It focuses upon the patient and relies upon the patient's strong motive to tell the truth because diagnosis or treatment will depend in part upon what the patient says. It is thought that the declarant's motive guarantees trustworthiness sufficiently to allow an exception to the hearsay rule. Judge Weinstein suggests another policy ground. He writes that "a fact reliable enough to serve as the basis for a diagnosis is also reliable enough to escape hearsay proscription." [4 Weinstein's EVIDENCE 803-129 (1979).] This principle recognizes that life and death decisions are made by physicians in reliance on such facts and as such should have sufficient trustworthiness to be admissible in a court of law. This rationale closely parallels that underlying rule 703 and suggests a similar test should apply, namely — is this fact of a type reasonably relied upon by experts in a particular field in forming opinions. Thus, two independent rationales support the rule and are helpful in its application. A two-part test flows naturally from this dual rationale: first, is the declarant's motive consistent with the purpose of the rule; and second, is it reasonable for the physician to rely on the information in diagnosis or treatment.

We find no facts in the record to indicate that Lucy's motive in making these statements was other than as a patient seeking treatment. Dr. Hopkins testified that the purpose of his examination was two-fold. He was to treat Lucy and to preserve any evidence that was available. There is nothing in the content of the statements to suggest that Lucy was responding to the doctor's questions for any reason other than promoting treatment. It is important to note that the statements concern what happened rather than who assaulted her. The former in most cases is pertinent to diagnosis and treatment while the latter would seldom, if ever, be sufficiently related. All of Lucy's statements were within the scope of the rule because they were related to her physical condition and were consistent with a motive to promote treatment. The age of the patient also mitigates against a finding that Lucy's statements were not within the traditional rationale of the rule.

During an extensive examination outside the presence of the jury, Dr. Hopkins explained in detail the relevancy of his questions to the task of diagnosis and treatment. He testified that a discussion of the cause of the injury was important to provide guidelines for his examination by pinpointing areas of the body to be examined more closely and by narrowing his examination by eliminating other areas. It is not dispositive that Dr. Hopkins' examination would have been identical to the one he performed if Lucy had been unable to utter a word. The doctor

---

[9] Dr. Hopkins testified that Lucy said she was experiencing pain in her vaginal area. This expression of a present symptom falls within the second category of 803(4) and would also be excepted from the hearsay rule under rule 803(3) covering a then existing physical condition. The remainder of Lucy's statement concerns the general character and nature of the cause of the injury. Because of the result we reach in this case, it is not necessary to discuss this distinction at length.

testified that his examination would have been more lengthy had he been unable to elicit a description of the general cause, although he stated the exam would have been basically the same. The fact that in this case the discussion of the cause of the injury did not lead to a fundamentally different exam does not mean that the discussion was not pertinent to diagnosis. It is enough that the information eliminated potential physical problems from the doctor's examination in order to meet the test of 803(4). Discovering what is not injured is equally as pertinent to treatment and diagnosis as finding what is injured. Dr. Hopkins also testified, in response to specific questions from the court, that most doctors would have sought such a history and that he relied upon Lucy's statements in deciding upon a course of treatment.

In light of this analysis we hold that it was not an abuse of discretion to admit the doctor's testimony. A recent Ninth Circuit case supports this. In *United States v. Nick* [604 F.2d 1199 (9th Cir. 1979)] a three-year-old boy was sexually assaulted by the defendant. At trial the examining physician was allowed under rule 803(4) to repeat the child's description of the assault including the victim's statements concerning the cause of the injury while omitting any comments about the identity of the assailant. *See also O'Gee v. Dobbs Houses, Inc.*, 570 F.2d 1084, 1089 (2d Cir. 1978) (Rule 803(4) clearly permits the admission into evidence of what the plaintiff told the physician about her condition and its origin so long as it was relied upon by the physician in formulating his opinion).

The defendant also asserts that it was prejudicial error to admit the hearsay testimony of Officer Marshall pursuant to 803(2). The rule allows admission of hearsay, otherwise competent, that is a "statement relating to a startling event or condition made while the declarant was under the stress of excitement caused by the event or condition." Fed R. Evid 803(2). Officer Marshall interviewed Lucy at 7:15 p.m.; somewhere between forty-five minutes and one hour [and] fifteen minutes after the assault. The defense argues that Lucy was no longer "under the stress of excitement caused by the event" when she talked to Officer Marshall. The defendant emphasizes that Lucy was described as quiet and not crying, and that she had not made any spontaneous statements since immediately following the assault. He also asserts that Lucy's statements were not spontaneous because they were in response to an inquiry and were the product of reasoned reflection fostered by conversations between herself and her companions following the assault. The government, in response, stresses that Officer Marshall described Lucy as scared and nervous with her eyes still red from crying and her hair was still messed from the assault.

The lapse of time between the startling event and the out-of-court statement although relevant is not dispositive in the application of rule 803(2). Nor is it controlling that Lucy's statement was made in response to an inquiry. Rather, these are factors which the trial court must weigh in determining whether the offered testimony is within the 803(2) exception. Other factors to consider include the age of the declarant, the physical and mental condition of the declarant, the characteristics of the event and the subject matter of the statements. In order to find that 803(2) applies, it must appear that the declarant's condition at the time was such that the statement was spontaneous, excited or impulsive rather than the product of reflection and deliberation.

Determination of this issue is a close question. There is testimony that the declarant was calm and unexcited. In contrast the same witness described Lucy as nervous and scared. Testimony from other sources suggested that Lucy had struggled with the defendant, that he had threatened her with serious harm and that he had unsnapped and pulled down her jeans. The stress and fear that such an occurrence would impose upon a young girl cannot be discounted. Officer Marshall testified that Lucy did not give a detailed narrative but spoke in short bursts about the incident. The officer emphasized at trial that she did not ask Lucy suggestive questions but merely reported what Lucy said. The officer only asked Lucy [one question:] "what happened?"

[W]e cannot say that the district court abused its discretion [whatever we personally might think should have been the resolution.] The single question "what happened" has been held not to destroy the excitement necessary to qualify under this exception to the hearsay rule. A lapse of about one hour has also been held not to remove the evidence from the 803(2) exception, especially where the declarant is a young child. It also has been noted that the lack of recall may indicate that the declarant was under stress at the time of the statement. It is a truism to state that each of these cases must be decided on its own circumstances. We find that in these circumstances considering the surprise of the assault, its shocking nature and the age of the declarant, it was not an abuse of discretion for the trial court to find that Lucy was still under the stress of the attack when she spoke to Officer Marshall. It was not unreasonable, in this case, to find that Lucy was in a state of continuous excitement from the time of the assault.

The defense also suggests that the admission of the two hearsay statements violates the confrontation clause. US Const Amend VI. This case differs from the usual confrontation-hearsay case in that the declarant was a witness at trial and was subject to cross-examination. It has been recognized, however, that even though a declarant is available to testify, the confrontation clause protection may be called into question because the declarant is too young to be subjected to a thorough cross-examination as envisaged by the constitution. *United States v. Nick, supra*, 604 F2d at 1202 (a two-year-old victim's hearsay statements to a doctor and his grandmother). This principle was also recognized in *California v. Green* where the Court remanded the case for a determination of whether "the nature of the opportunity to cross-examine" was dispositive of the confrontation issue. *California v. Green*, 399 US 149, 168–170. These cases recognize a special type of "unavailability" for purposes of the confrontation clause.

At trial Lucy was unable to repeat the statements she had made to Officer Marshall and Dr. Hopkins although she was able to provide some facts to support her earlier statements. Defense counsel cross-examined Lucy but did not ask about the assault or her statements shortly thereafter. It is difficult to conclude on this record that a more thorough cross-examination would not have provided the protections inherent in the confrontation clause. Nevertheless, assuming arguendo that Lucy was unavailable in the sense suggested by the *Nick* court, we conclude that the confrontation clause was not violated because the admitted hearsay statements, particularly those given to Dr. Hopkins, had sufficient indicia of reliability in order to afford the trier of fact a satisfactory basis for evaluating the truth of the prior statements. See *Ohio v. Roberts* [448 U.S. 56 (1980).]

[Portions of the opinion concerning harmless error have been deleted.]

Affirmed.

NOTES AND QUESTIONS

(1) *Distinguishing Other Grounds of Admissibility, such as Declarations of Present Condition or Basis of Expert Testimony.* Would any of the hearsay in *Iron Shell* be admissible on other grounds, e.g., Fed. R. Evid. 803(3)? Or as the basis of expert testimony? Would they be broader?

(2) *The Relevance of the Doctor's Motivation for Investigating.* Was the doctor concerned with Lucy's physical condition, mental condition, or something else? Would this make a difference as to scope of things admitted under Fed. R. Evid. 803(4)? What if he was concerned only with gathering information to see if there was a case? Is the inquiry under Fed. R. Evid. 803(4) what the doctor thought germane to treatment, or what the girl thought? Is the decision in *Iron Shell* influenced by what the judge believes at the inception about the likelihood that a little girl would trump up a charge and whether most such charges in court are true?

(3) *Statements to a Physician Employed Only to Testify: Admissible as "Diagnosis" Under 803(4)?* In *O'Gee v. Dobbs Houses, Inc.*, 570 F.2d 1084 (2d Cir. 1978), a stewardess (O'Gee) sued her employer for personal injury and was allowed to prove her consequent medical condition through the testimony of Dr. Koven. This was alleged to be error. On appeal the court said:

> That the trial court erred in permitting Dr. Koven to testify about other doctors' opinions raises questions of magnitude. Of the doctors O'Gee had consulted in the period immediately following the incident, a number were present right in New York, where the trial was held. Yet instead of calling any of these doctors, who had had a chance to examine her when both the nature of her injuries and the probability of their being sequelae of the incident would have been most apparent, she called only Dr. Koven, a doctor retained for the purposes of the litigation, and who first saw O'Gee in December of 1976, more than four years after the [incident].
>
> Prior to the adoption of the Federal Rules of Evidence, a non-treating doctor such as Dr. Koven would have been permitted to recite his patient's statements to him, not as proof of the facts stated, but only to show the basis of his opinion. The Federal Rules, however, rejected this distinction as being too esoteric for a jury to recognize. Rule 803(4) clearly permits the admission into evidence of what O'Gee told Dr. Koven about her condition, so long as it was relied on by Dr. Koven in formulating his opinion — a foundation that was properly laid. [Citing the Advisory Committee Note on the Rule.]
>
> Nowhere does the commentary on Rule 803(4) indicate, however, whether the Rule was intended to go so far as to permit a doctor to testify to his patient's version of other doctors' opinions, particularly when no

showing is made of those other doctors' unavailability. We need not reach the furthest extent of this issue, however, because Dr. Koven clearly stated that he was not relying solely on O'Gee's recollection of the other doctors' opinions, but actually had before him the reports of at least two of those doctors, and of the hospital where O'Gee's laminectomy was performed. Under the circumstances of this case, we do not think it was an abuse of discretion for Judge Weinstein to permit Dr. Koven to testify as he did. We observe, however, that while expert witnesses are to be permitted to explain the basis of their opinions, we do not here decide that that leeway extends to the kind of multiple hearsay that would have been present here in the absence of the doctors' reports.

Consider whether admitting the plaintiff's statements to a non-treating, testifying doctor is supported by the policies underlying the Rule.

(4) *What about a Statement by Someone Other than the Patient, such as the Mother of an Injured Child?* In *Lovejoy v. United States*, 92 F.3d 628 (8th Cir. 1996), the court in upholding admissibility said:

Pursuant to Federal Rule of Evidence 803(4), the District Court admitted statements made by Christine Lovejoy (victim's mother) to a nurse. Although Ms. Lovejoy testified at trial and recanted her allegations, she told the nurse examining the victim a few days after the incident that she was awakened by sounds coming from the bed in which Lovejoy and the victim were sleeping, that she saw Lovejoy standing by the victim with an erection and that the victim's underwear was down and her tee shirt was up.

Ms. Lovejoy made the statements while her daughter, who could not communicate orally or in writing on her own, was being examined by a medical professional in connection with allegations of sexual abuse. This information would aid the medical professionals examining the victim by "pinpointing areas of the body to be examined more closely and by narrowing [the] examination by eliminating other areas." A nurse often assists a physician in taking the history. The District Court did not abuse its discretion in deciding it was reasonably pertinent to the victim's diagnosis and treatment to know the details surrounding the incident for which the victim was being examined.

(5) *Given the Wording of Fed. R. Evid. 803(4), May a Statement by the Physician to the Patient Qualify?* In *Bombard v. Ft. Wayne Newspapers, Inc.*, 92 F.3d 560 (7th Cir. 1996), the court held that the statement of a physician to the patient was properly rejected:

The only evidence Bombard offers in support of the fact that he is a "qualified individual with a disability" is his testimony in his deposition, repeated later in his affidavit: "[W]hen I went to the doctor, before I knew I was terminated, that [sic] she said, 'Well, why don't we try and work just part time, half the day and gradually ease into it.' "

Rule 803(4) does not purport to except, nor can it reasonably be interpreted as excepting, statements by the person providing the medical attention to the patient. Bombard's testimony regarding his doctor's

> statement, submitted for the purpose of establishing his ability to perform the essential functions of his job with accommodation, is therefore inadmissible and incompetent evidence to oppose summary judgment.

Compare United States v. Rendini, 738 F.2d 530 (1st Cir. 1984) (notes taken by physician, who was chairman of panel that found city employee permanently disabled, were properly admitted in subsequent mail fraud action under Fed. R. Evid. 803(4) as reasonably pertinent to diagnosis).

PROBLEM SET 9D: STATEMENTS RELATING TO MEDICAL DIAGNOSIS OR TREATMENT.

In answering the following problems, answer not only with respect to the present hearsay exception, but also with respect to the exception for declarations of bodily feeling to lay persons.

(1) *The Patient's Narrative About the Scratch on His Arm.* Patient goes to a physician for treatment and has the following conversation, all of which is sought to be testified to (by a nurse who overheard it) on behalf of plaintiff (the patient) in his personal injury lawsuit against Martin Stevens for the incident reported. How much is properly admissible?

PATIENT: Ouch! My arm, my arm!

DOCTOR: Does your arm hurt here, as well [indicating the elbow]?

PATIENT: Well, actually, it does, you know. There is kind of a tingling sensation that runs down through the elbow area, then running the length of the lower arm, on the interior aspect, to the wrist, and into each of the five fingers, with the little finger hurting least. It didn't hurt that much when Martin Stevens scratched me with that nail five days ago on the 2500 block of Green Street near his house. But later that evening it got pretty bad. I'm worried because of the unsanitary conditions on that block on Green Street, which you know more about than I do — it might have gotten infected. When I was a child, I had a disease that at least at that time made me extra susceptible to things like this.

DOCTOR: Well, forget about the conditions on Green Street. They don't matter. There's no sign of infection. Your symptoms could not have come from infection. They're nerve damage.

(2) *Can the Nurse Testify to Statements Made to the Doctor for Nontreatment Purposes?* In Problem (1), suppose the patient went to this particular doctor not for treatment, but for purposes of securing his services for the litigation, or to obtain clearance for insurance or employment purposes. How much, if any, of the above conversation could the *nurse* testify to? Insofar as the nurse's testimony is concerned, does it make any difference what those nontreatment purposes were?

(3) *Offering the Patient's Statements Alternatively to Explain the Basis for Expert Testimony: Rules 703–705.* Can the doctor in Problem (1) testify to his medical opinion that is based on the conversation? Can he also, in the same testimony, recount germane portions of the conversation of the patient? *See* Fed. R.

Evid. 703–705. (If the statements are admitted on this basis, you should be aware that there is another issue, namely whether the jury could consider the statements for the truth or only as showing the basis of the opinion. We consider this issue in § 5.04, *supra*).

(4) *Statements to Medical Personnel Who are Not Physicians.* Suppose, in Problem (1), the conversation had not taken place between the doctor and the patient, but between the doctor's clerk, not medically trained, and the patient. Would that make a difference to admissibility (via one who overheard the conversation)?

(5) *Statements About Medical Condition to Nonmedical Persons.* Suppose the identical conversation had taken place between the patient and the patient's wife, instead of the patient and the doctor. Assume the wife was going to go to the doctor in connection with an ailment of her own. (No litigation was yet in the picture.) Could an overhearer of either the husband's statements to the wife, or of the wife's statements to the doctor relaying this material, testify in the subsequent lawsuit against Martin Stevens?

NOTE ON COURTS' WILLINGNESS TO EXPAND HEARSAY EXCEPTIONS IN CHILD ABUSE CASES

Iron Shell is elaborated on in *United States v. Renville*, 779 F.2d 430 (8th Cir. 1985), in which the court upheld admission of a physician's testimony recounting a child's identification of her stepfather as her abuser. The court reasoned that this information is pertinent to physicians treating emotional trauma.

Iron Shell appears to be an example of a group of cases in which hearsay exceptions are expanded to embrace statements of child victims in cases of sexual and other abuse. *See* Mosteller, *The Maturation and Disintegration of the Hearsay Exception for Statements for Medical Examination in Child Sexual Abuse Cases*, 65 LAW & CONTEMP. PROBS. 47 (2002). Sometimes this is done to spare the child the ordeal of testifying at trial. Sometimes there are other reasons. (What might they be?) While some decisions have refused to do so, in the years since *Iron Shell*, the use of statements by children identifying their assailants has continued to grow. *See generally* Raeder, *Remember the Ladies and the Children Too: Crawford's Impact on Domestic Violence and Child Abuse Cases*, 71 BROOK. L. REV. 311 (2005).

Contrast with *Iron Shell* the case of *W.C.L., Jr. v. People*, 685 P.2d 176 (Colo. 1984): Upon seeing a four-year-old child perform a suggestive action, the child's aunt spoke sharply to the child, who became startled and a few moments later, under questioning from the aunt, revealed that defendant, a 16-year-old relative living in the house, had tickled her genitals. The child was taken to a pediatrician — an expert in the diagnosis and treatment of child abuse — who found evidence of repeated penetrations. The child identified the defendant to the doctor. The child was found to be incompetent to testify against the defendant because she did not know what "to tell the truth" meant. The statements to the aunt and doctor were offered for admission under state rules identical to the Federal Rules of Evidence excited utterance and medical diagnosis exceptions to the hearsay rule. The court held that on the totality of the circumstances, the child's statement to the aunt was not uttered in excitement. Even if the aunt's sharp speaking to the child, rather than the assault, could be considered an exciting occurrence, time elapsed before the child's statement to the aunt, and the statement was in response to questioning.

Since the child did not know what "to tell the truth" meant, the child did not understand that accuracy was important in order to obtain proper medical treatment, and therefore the statement to the physician did not qualify for the exception for statements pursuant to medical diagnosis. However, the child's statements were not necessarily unreliable. If the state had adopted a catchall exception to the hearsay rule, such as Fed. R. Evid. 807, the court says, it would have found the evidence sufficiently trustworthy to qualify. The court notes in this respect the doctor's experience in sexual abuse and his opinion that testimony from young children about sexual activity is reliable. The physical evidence corroborated the child, and the child knew the defendant well and was not likely to have mistaken her assailant. The defendant had the opportunity to commit the crime. The child was not likely to intellectually contrive. Although the court may have power to create a rule of evidence, the court says, when one has been specifically considered and rejected by the legislature, as had the catchall exception, which had been well known under the federal rule, the court is not free to manufacture such an exception. The court notes that it would be desirable for the legislature to adopt such an exception to avoid pressure to torture the meaning of the listed exceptions and because of the difficulty of conceiving in advance of every situation in which there should be a hearsay exception.

While many cases admit under 803(4) a child's hearsay statement describing sexual abuse and identity of the abuser, some take a more restrictive view. For example, *United States v. Gabe*, 237 F.3d 954 (8th Cir. 2001), focusing on the "selfish treatment motivation" rationale of the rule, admits the victim's identification of the abuser only if the doctor has warned the child victim about the importance of the information for diagnosis and treatment. In *Gabe*, where the victim (a fifteen-year-old girl) was taken to the physician by the police, the identity of the abuser was deemed not important nor perceived by the victim to be important to the physician's medical examination, given that the physician, who had never seen the victim before, did not prescribe any medical treatment, did not evaluate whether she needed psychological counseling (another doctor had already prescribed counseling), and there was no evidence the victim repeated her accusation for purposes of medical diagnosis or treatment at all. For a state case holding, under a rule almost identical to Fed. R. Evid. 803(4), that a child abuse victim's designation of her mother as the abuser to a physician qualifies for the hearsay exception for statements for medical diagnosis or treatment (despite the usual exclusion under the exception of statements of identity or fault), see *Goldade v. Wyoming*, 674 P.2d 721 (Wyo. 1983), *cert. denied*, 467 U.S. 1253 (1984). The court cites the statutory and medical duty of the doctor (1) to determine whether there is imminent danger to the child's life or safety justifying protective custody, (2) to determine if the injuries were accidental or deliberate, and (3) to determine whether child abuse syndrome was present. The court holds that the "medical diagnosis" language in the rule covers the situation.

This rationale has been adopted by many cases that posit that the child's treatment will differ if the abuser is a family member, rather than a stranger. Is this what is usually thought of as medical treatment? Information concerning the identity of an assailant probably is useful to a psychologist attempting to help a victim, regardless of the victim's age.

Was this result foreseeable by the drafters of Fed. R. Evid. 803(4)? The advisory committee notes on Fed. R. Evid. 803(4) provide that statements as to fault ordinarily would not qualify. The notes use this example: "A patient's statement that he was struck by an automobile would qualify but not his statement that the car was driven through a red light." Another example concludes that a statement by a patient that he was shot would be admissible, but a statement that he was shot by a white man would not. And the fact that a patient strained himself while operating a machine may be significant to treatment, but the fact that the patient said the machine was defective may not. Is identity the same as fault?

The student should consider how the new Constitutional Confrontation Clause jurisprudence, treated infra in Chapter 11, would apply to these child statements, regardless of whether they are found to be within a hearsay exception.

A relatively new way to avoid the risk of damaging the child by putting him or her on the stand in open court in child sex abuse cases, has been the regulation of in-court testimony by the use of screens or various types of camera setups that keep the child from seeing (or even being in the same room as) the defendant, but permit contemporaneous cross-examination. See *Coy* and *Craig*, *infra*, § 11.03[A], which require (as a matter of constitutional confrontation) a particularized showing of necessity before such courtroom regulation is allowed. Query: do these cases apply to videotaped depositions as well, or must the prosecutor demonstrate that the child is unavailable? If so, is the possibility of trauma a sufficient showing?

§ 9.05 PAST RECOLLECTION RECORDED; "PRESENT MEMORY REFRESHED" DISTINGUISHED[13]

Read Federal Rules of Evidence 803(5), "Hearsay Exceptions — Regardless of Whether the Declarant is Available as a Witness: Recorded Recollection," and 612 "Writing Used to Refresh a Witness's Memory.

---

[13] Study Guide Reference: Evidence in a Nutshell, Chapter 5:III at "Refreshing Recollection with Privileged Information: The Potential for Waiver"; and Chapter 6:XI and Chapter 10:II at "Past Recollection Recorded: F.R.E 803(5)."

[A] Hearsay Exception: Recorded Recollection

HODAS v. DAVIS

New York Supreme Court, Appellate Division
203 A.D. 297, 196 N.Y.S. 801 (1922)

H.T. Kellogg, Acting P.J.

This action was for personal injuries sustained by the plaintiff through a collision at a railroad crossing between an automobile which he was driving, and a locomotive of the defendant. The plaintiff charged negligence in that no sufficient warning of the approach of the locomotive was given. The jury found in favor of the defendant. [T]his appeal was taken.

A witness named William Meddaugh was called by the defendant. His recollection of the accident was limited to the following: There had been an accident; he had been playing ball at the site of the accident; there was a demolished car near the railroad crossing and a man lying nearby; a train stood still at the crossing; the body of the man was taken on board the train. He testified that, about six months after the plaintiff's accident, he had sustained an accidental injury which had so impaired his memory that he could remember no facts concerning the accident other than as stated. A written statement setting forth some of the material facts in relation to the accident was exhibited to him. He recognized the signature at the foot of the statement as his own, but did not recall having signed his name thereto, or having made the statement. Neither did he recall any of the facts recited therein. He declined to testify that at the time he made the statement he knew the facts to be true which were therein stated. He was then asked:

> Now, I ask you whether or not, prior to the time of the happening of this accident to you, did you ever affix your signature to any paper which did not contain the true facts within your own knowledge?

His answer was, "No." The statement was then offered in evidence, under objection. The appellant contends that the admission of the statement constituted reversible error.

Memoranda of past recollection, contemporaneously made with the facts therein recited, although not constituting regular entries in the usual course of business, in the absence of independent present recollection, are receivable in evidence, provided their correctness is guaranteed by the persons making them. The question presented is whether or not the correctness of the statement subscribed by Meddaugh was sufficiently verified by him. Chamberlayne states that a memorandum is receivable "provided the maker of the memorandum is able to testify, not only that he made it under proper conditions of contemporaneousness and the like, but also that he knows now that at the time he made the memorandum he knew the facts and that the memorandum states them correctly." Judged by this test, the witness Meddaugh, who made no present assertion of previous knowledge of the truth of the facts recited, gave no proper guarantee of the correctness of the statement. Wigmore says:

> If the witness can say, "I distinctly remember that when I made or saw this memorandum, about the time of the events, I was then conscious of its correctness," his verification is satisfactory. But if he relies, not on a present recollection of his past state of mind, but on other indications, such as a habit, a course of business, a check mark on the margin, or merely the genuineness of his handwriting, the certainty is of a lower quality, though still satisfactory for most practical purposes. In general, it is conceded that when the witness' certainty rests on his usual habit or course of business in making memoranda or records, it is sufficient.

The witness Meddaugh, who recognized his handwriting, but failed to assert either a previous recollection or a present conviction of the correctness of the statement, failed to supply either guaranty of accuracy regarded by Wigmore as sufficient.

Memoranda of past recollection have been stated [in separate cases] by the Court of Appeals of this state to be sufficiently verified in the following instances: [1] When the author testifies "that he knew they would not have been made if he had not done the acts"; [2] when he testifies "that he had no doubt of the correctness" of the memoranda; [3] when he testifies "that he is confident that he knew the memorandum to be correct when it was made"; [4] when he testifies that "he has no doubt that it was accurate"; [5] when he testifies "that it was made correctly"; [6] when he testifies that the memorandum was one "which he intended to make correctly, and which he believes to be correct"; [7] when he says "that it was a true statement of the transactions, known to him at the time"; [8] when "he verifies their correctness"; [9] when he is "able to say in substance that" the writings "were undoubtedly true at the time they were written." It will be observed that in the cases the verification approved of consisted of positive testimony of correctness. Obviously no one can testify from memory to the correctness of unremembered facts. Such testimony, therefore, could not express knowledge; it could but express belief in correctness. When the cases cited are analyzed, therefore, it will be found that the verifications therein approved consist of statements of present "belief," "confidence," or lack of "doubt" in correctness, or assertions of present recollection of a previous knowledge of the truth of the memoranda. We are aware of no authorities in this state which authorize the introduction of memoranda of past recollection without such guaranties of correctness.

Meddaugh testified that he never affixed his signature "to any paper which did not contain the true facts" within his own knowledge. This was not equivalent to a statement that the memorandum in question contained the true facts for the reason that Meddaugh, who denied any recollection of making the statement, was incapable of so testifying. Nor do we think it was the equivalent of an assertion of present belief in the correctness of the statement. The witness may have stated a sufficient premise for entertaining that belief, but the conclusion that he so believed was not asserted. Belief in the correctness of a subscribed statement arises in the mind of a subscriber from a variety of causes known and unknown. It is an instinctive conviction, and therein lies its value. Such a belief cannot be supplied by any other than its maker upon any theory that what might justly have been believed was believed. Therefore we consider that error was committed in receiving the statement. [However, the court held the error to be harmless.]

[Affirmed.]

NOTES AND QUESTIONS

(1) *Three Positions Requiring Total, Partial, or No Lack of Present Memory.* Three different positions exist on the amount of memory that must be lacking before the exception for past recollection may be invoked: (a) A total lack of present recollection is required. (b) A partial lack of present recollection will do. (c) It is immaterial whether the witness remembers or not. What position do the Federal Rules take? Can a partial lack of present recollection be argued to be a total lack as to some details? Where does that get you?

(2) *Drunken Recollection. United States v. Edwards*, 539 F.2d 689 (9th Cir.), *cert. denied*, 429 U.S. 984 (1976), a decision written by then Circuit Judge Anthony M. Kennedy, upheld the admission of a statement given by a witness who registered a .25 blood alcohol level at the time of the interview. Although the fact that the witness was drunk "bears heavily on the weight the testimony is to be given" by a jury, it did not prevent the witness from being "capable of performing the relatively sophisticated mental functions necessary to recall past events." At trial, the witness stated that although he had no memory of the underlying facts, he believed the statement accurately reflected his recollection at the time it was made. The statement was signed and also contained the following inscription in the witness' handwriting: "I have read this statement of two pages and it is true and correct to the best of my knowledge." Would the result have been the same if there was testimony that the witness was rational during parts of the interview and hallucinating during the remainder?

(3) *Selective Memory. United States v. Williams*, 571 F.2d 344 (6th Cir.), *cert. denied*, 439 U.S. 841 (1978), illustrates a not infrequent problem: whether the statement really is being used to contradict the witness's current testimony, rather than as providing forgotten information. The statement in *Williams* resulted from a conversation with a Secret Service agent six months after the events it recited. It was written in the words of the agent, but signed under oath by the witness, Ball, who agreed it was generally correct. At trial, Ball testified, but claimed lack of memory concerning parts of the statements that were key to proving that the defendant, Glenn Williams, intentionally cashed government checks knowing they had forged endorsements. Ball was a friend of Williams, who operated a junkyard next door to the bar where the four forged checks were cashed. Ball claimed that he made the statement because he wanted to cooperate with the agent, who had frightened Ball by accusing him of passing bad checks. The judge admitted the statement pursuant to Fed. R. Evid. 803(5), stating that the witness was exercising "selective memory." In upholding the admission of the statement, the Court noted:

> There was no doubt that Ball had sufficient recollection to testify generally about his conversations with Williams. However, the critical question about those conversations was whether Williams had told him how the checks came into his possession. This was the very aspect of the conversations which Ball testified he could not recall.

(4) *How Fresh Must Memory Be When the Recordation is Made?* In *Williams, above*, the statement, made six months after the event in question, was considered to be fresh in memory. See also *United States v. Senak*, 527 F.2d 129 (7th Cir. 1975), *cert. denied*, 425 U.S. 907 (1976), which upholds admission of a statement made three years after the conversation in issue. Do either or both of these cases unduly expand the appropriate timing of such statements?

(5) *Is Personal Knowledge Required at the Time of Recordation?* In *People v. Zalimas*, 149 N.E. 759 (Ill. 1925), a drugstore owner made a memo at the time he sold arsenic to a woman, which identified her as "Mrs. Zalimas," the defendant, and contained the amount of the arsenic and the purpose for which it was sold (to kill rats). At the defendant's trial for poisoning her husband, the statement was admitted when the drugstore owner had no recollection of the woman to whom he sold the arsenic. On appeal, the conviction was reversed because the witness could not testify that the facts were correctly stated in the memo at the time it was made. The court found that "[h]e did not know the name of the purchaser, but inserted in the memorandum the name which the unknown purchaser chose to give him."

[B] "Present Memory Refreshed" Distinguished

IN RE THOMAS

Illinois Appellate Court, First District
65 Ill. App. 3d 136, 382 N.E.2d 556 (1978)

SULLIVAN, PRESIDING JUSTICE.

After a bench trial, respondent was found to be in violation of his probation.

Respondent was found delinquent based upon the commission of the offense of theft and was placed on probation for a period of 10 months. As a condition of his probation and pursuant to Unified Delinquency Intervention Service placement, he was required to reside in Lawrence Hall (the Hall), an institution where boys live under the care and direction of social workers.

Charles Sanders, program director of the Hall, testified that respondent was a resident there and that during this period he was personally aware of respondent's unauthorized absences from the Hall, as it was his practice to take roll call whenever a runaway was reported to him by one of the social workers. He could not, however, recall the exact dates of such absences and, over defense objection, he was permitted to refresh his recollection of the dates in question by consulting a memorandum which had been prepared at his direction from the attendance records by his secretary.

Respondent first contends that the trial court erred by admitting hearsay testimony over his objection. It is his position that the testimony of Sanders regarding the dates of respondent's absences was inadmissible because (1) Sanders' recollection could not be properly refreshed as he had no independent knowledge of the facts to which he testified, and (2) he was improperly permitted to refresh his recollection from a document which was not an original record.

A witness may testify only to facts within his knowledge and recollection, and to refresh and assist his memory, he may be afforded the use of a written instrument, memorandum or entry in a book. Here, it appears clear that Sanders testified he was personally aware of respondent's absences but did not remember the specific dates thereof until the memorandum in question was submitted to him. Respondent's objection to the witness reading from the document was sustained, and Sanders was instructed to "look at the document, refresh your recollection as to it and then put the document aside." The record discloses that after this instruction was given to him Sanders followed this procedure in testifying to the dates of respondent's absences, and no objection was made that he was not testifying from a refreshed recollection. Neither did respondent develop during cross-examination that he was not so testifying. In view thereof, we reject respondent's first contention that Sanders' recollection could not be properly refreshed, because he had no independent knowledge of the facts.

We also see no merit in respondent's second position that the memorandum was improperly used to refresh, because it was not an original record. As stated in *People v. Van Dyk* (1976), 40 Ill. App. 3d 275, 352 N.E.2d 327:

> [U]nlike those instances where through past recollection recorded the memorandum itself will be the evidence, the memorandum need not have been made by the witness nor be independently admissible into evidence, provided that, after inspecting it, the witness can speak to the facts from his own recollection.
>
> [In that case there were] multiple references to the refreshing report. [W]e noted:
>
> Where facts related in the testimony are detailed, the witness need not speak independent of the writing throughout his entire testimony, but may refer to it [periodically] for the purpose of further jogging his memory.

The State agrees that the memorandum would not have been admissible as a business record had it attempted to offer it as such into evidence, but it argues that it did not do so and that the document was properly used to refresh the recollection of one with personal knowledge, but an exhausted memory of its contents.

Sanders was instructed not to testify by reading from the document, and he looked at the memorandum prior to testifying to each set of dates. [W]e see no abuse of discretion in allowing Sanders to use the memorandum from time to time during his testimony to jog his memory as to the dates of respondent's absences.

Finally, respondent contends that the trial court, by allowing the use of the memorandum, deprived him of his constitutional right to confront and cross-examine witnesses, namely, the secretary who typed the memorandum and the person responsible for keeping the official record from which the memorandum was prepared. Again, we see no merit in this contention.

The cases cited by respondent do not support his position, as they were not concerned with the use of documents to refresh recollection, but rather involved situations where witnesses having no personal knowledge testified to the contents of the documents. Here, Sanders testified that he was personally aware of respondent's absences and, as stated above, the record discloses that he used the memorandum only to refresh his recollection concerning dates and then testified from a refreshed recollection. When a witness uses a document in such a manner, it is not necessary that the author be present. It matters only that the document refreshes recollection. Because Sanders was available and, in fact, was cross-examined, respondent was not deprived of any right of confrontation.

Affirmed.

NOTES AND QUESTIONS

(1) *Waiver of Privileges through Use of Documents to Refresh Memory.* If a document is used to prepare a witness to testify (a common practice), are any privileges, such as attorney-client or work-product privilege, lost under Fed. R. Evid. 612, so that the document will have to be disclosed to the other side if called for? If so, this well may impact how lawyers prepare witnesses. *See* Rothstein, *Attorney's Privileges Endangered by Three Recent Judicial Rulings*, LEGAL TIMES OF WASH., Jan. 22, 1979, at 22; Proposed N.Y. Evidence Rule 612. Compare *Bogosian v. Gulf Oil Corp.*, 738 F.2d 587 (3d Cir. 1984), and *Sporck v. Peil*, 759 F.2d 312 (3d Cir.), *cert. denied*, 474 U.S. 903 (1985), which are hostile to waivers, with *Berkey Photo, Inc. v. Eastman Kodak Co.*, 74 F.R.D. 613 (S.D.N.Y. 1977), a case that has been influential with trial courts, warning that waiver will be found when such refreshing of witnesses frustrates cross-examination. For a more detailed discussion of the relationship of refreshing memory or preparing witnesses and waiver of privilege in a civil context, see RAEDER, FEDERAL PRETRIAL PRACTICE, § 18 (3d ed. 2000). *See generally* ROTHSTEIN, FEDERAL RULES OF EVIDENCE (3d ed. 2006) at Rules 612 and 501. How does counsel find out that his opponent's witness has used a document to refresh before taking the stand at trial or deposition?

(2) *Disclosure in Criminal Cases Under the Jencks Act and Rule 26.2.* On the relationship between Fed. R. Evid. 612 and the Jencks Act (reenacted and broadened to cover both prosecution and defense in Fed. R. Crim. P. 26.2), which requires disclosure (of any previous relatively verbatim written statements of one's witnesses) to the other side, but expressly limits disclosure to after the witness has testified, see Foster, *The Jencks Act and Rule 26.2-Rule 612 Interface — "Confusion Worse Confounded,"* 34 OKLA. L. REV. 679 (1981).

PROBLEM SET 9E: CONCERNING REFRESHING RECOLLECTION AND RECORDED RECOLLECTION.

(1) *Proving the Antique Dealer's Losses by Memory, Refreshed Memory, and Recorded Recollection.* Plaintiff sues the gas company for an explosion in the gas lines that totally demolished his antique shop and all its contents. As a demonstration problem for class, prepare for the teacher to ask you to play the role of plaintiff's counsel and to conduct a direct examination of plaintiff to adduce exactly what items were in the antique shop. Plaintiff had gone through his store several days before the explosion and had personally compiled an inventory list of all the items in the store, which he has with him in court. Some of the items he remembers

without looking at the list. Some he remembers only if he now (at trial) looks at the list. Some he cannot remember at all. He may have consulted the list prior to trial as well. Be prepared to conduct the examination if called on by the teacher. (The teacher might play the role of plaintiff.) Also be prepared to play the role of objecting counsel in case the teacher asks the other members of the class to play that role.

(2) *The Dictated-but-Unread Memorandum.* Smith witnesses an automobile collision on the way to work. When he arrives at work, he asks his secretary to step in when she finishes her coffee break. She does so. He dictates a memorandum of what he saw and tells her to type it up and put it in the files (she is such a good secretary that he does not need to proofread it). He forgets all about it. A year later, he is subpoenaed to testify at the trial concerning the collision and to bring with him the memo (he had disclosed to an attorney on the case that he had such a memo). He remembers the collision, but not as sharply as the memo relates it. What use can be made of the memo? Any problems?

(3) *Multiple Recorders.* A saleswoman makes a sale of a flanged widget for $300.00 on February 2, 2006. As per company policy, she tells this to the company's bookkeeper, who writes it down in the ledger (i.e., records the sale, price, and date). That portion of the ledger is offered at trial to prove the sale, the price, and the date, since the time elapsed since the sale is such that it would be unrealistic to expect the salesperson to remember the particular sale even upon refreshing her memory. Could this document be admitted as recorded recollection? How? Who would have to testify to what? Note: the cumbersomeness of qualifying such documents as recorded recollection (and the frequent impossibility of doing so in modern businesses) is the reason for the next exception we will study, the business records rule.

§ 9.06 BUSINESS RECORDS[14]

Read Federal Rules of Evidence 803(6), "Hearsay Exceptions — Regardless of Whether the Declarant is Available as a Witness: Records of a Regularly Conducted Activity," and (7), "Absence of a Record of Regularly Conducted Activity," and 902(11) and (12), "Requirement of Authetication: Evidence That is Self-Autheticating: Certified Records of a Regularly Conducted Activity."

UNITED STATES v. HEDMAN

United States Court of Appeals, Seventh Circuit
630 F.2d 1184 (1980)

Bauer, Circuit Judge.

Defendants, John Hedman, Michael Jercich, Thomas Karnick and Henry Larsen [where charged] with various violations of federal statutes arising from the acceptance of monies allegedly extorted by them in their capacities as Building

[14] Study Guide Reference: Evidence in a Nutshell, Chapter 10:II at "Business Records: F.R.E. 803(6) ('Records of Regularly Conducted Activity')."

Inspection Supervisors assigned to the Construction and Technical Inspection Bureau of the City of Chicago. Defendants Hedman, Jercich and Larsen [were also charged] with the failure to report the income received from these extortionate activities on their federal income tax returns. Defendants-appellants appeal from the judgments of conviction entered upon the jury verdicts finding them guilty of conspiracy to commit extortion and extortion under color of official right [and] for filing fraudulent tax returns in violation of the federal income tax laws. We affirm . . . .

Between 1959 and the mid-1960's Bentley Weitzman, the President of Danley [Co.], would pay $25 to the building inspector for the district in which [a] non-conforming garage was being erected [by Danley]. The money for these payoffs was obtained from the receipts for construction work that was performed but not recorded on Danley's books. Weitzman testified that these receipts were also not reported on Danley's tax returns. From the mid-1960's until 1976, the task of making payoffs on construction that violated the Chicago Building Code was handled by Bentley Weitzman's father, Harry Weitzman. When a job did not violate the building code, Harry Weitzman would file a permit application and pay the required fee to the City of Chicago.

A routine procedure was established at Danley for processing non-conforming garages. When a job violated the Building Code, the employee at Danley who processed that job order would give Harry Weitzman a slip of paper indicating the address of the job and a notation that a violation existed. Weitzman would then write the name of the area supervisor for that job on the slip, and return the slip to the job file. At the same time, Weitzman would make an entry on a list he maintained of all non-conforming jobs. When the garage was being built, the slip would be returned to Weitzman. He accumulated slips for several days and then gave them to Irving Lazarus, Vice President of Danley. Lazarus would obtain cash from a walk-in safe located in Danley's offices, place $25 per slip in an envelope with the slips, and give the money and slips to Weitzman. Bentley Weitzman testified that, on occasion, he also provided the cash to his father.

When Harry Weitzman received the cash and slips from Lazarus, he would delete the job addresses from his list. He would then write the name of the supervisors on separate envelopes, place the appropriate amount of money in each envelope, and personally deliver them to all four defendants at either their offices in City Hall or their homes. On occasion, Weitzman would give to one supervisor an envelope to be delivered to another supervisor.

From 1968 or 1969 until 1976, Harry Weitzman kept a diary of these payoffs. At the top of each page of the notebook, Weitzman wrote the first name of a supervisor, e. g., "Mike," "Tom," "Hank," and "John." Also listed on these pages were the addresses of the non-conforming job sites, as well as the amounts, the dates, and the places of the payments made to each supervisor for those jobs. The diary detailed payments that were made to all four defendants individually, as well as payments that were made to one supervisor for delivery to another.

. . . When All State [another company] commenced a job that violated the Building Code, either the garage superintendent or the remodeling superintendent would telephone the appropriate supervisor and give him the address of the non-conforming job site. The All State employee would then give a slip of paper to the assistant bookkeeper, indicating the job name, the address, the supervisor and the amount of money to be paid to the supervisor. The bookkeeper would then write the name and address of the job on a separate piece of paper and place it, along with $25, into an envelope bearing the supervisor's name. The envelope often contained several job slips and amounts of money ranging from $25 to $100. The supervisors would then stop by the All State office and pick up the envelopes bearing their names. Three of the defendants, John Hedman, Michael Jercich, and Henry Larsen, received payoffs in this fashion from All State . . . .

[Other counts of the indictment] related to payoffs allegedly made to defendants Hedman and Jercich by the Ashland Building and Improvement Company . . . . [Other counts] involved payoffs allegedly made to defendants Hedman and Jercich by Airoom, Inc. Airoom is a construction company that specializes in building room additions in Chicago and its suburbs. Airoom purchased lumber for its construction projects from Rubenstein Lumber, which in turn purchased all of its lumber from suppliers outside of Illinois . . . . [Other counts of the indictment relate] to payoffs allegedly made to John Hedman by Solar Construction Company . . . .

[Other] counts charged defendants Hedman, Jercich and Larsen with the failure to report the [all the above] payoffs received from the above contractors on their federal income tax returns . . . .

In presenting its evidence related to the counts involving the Danley Lumber Company, the government offered into evidence a diary kept by Harry Weitzman, the Danley employee responsible for making payoffs to Chicago Building Inspection Supervisors. Over the vigorous objections of the appellants, the trial court admitted the diary as a business record under Rule 803(6) of the Federal Rules of Evidence. [Rule quoted.] Appellants have renewed their objection on appeal. We conclude that the trial court did not abuse its discretion in admitting the diary into evidence.

Harry Weitzman testified that after several years of making payoffs on behalf of Danley to Building Inspection Supervisors, he began recording these payoffs in a small notebook. The notebook contained an entry for every payoff he had made from 1968 or 1969 until 1976. An entry would be recorded in the office after a payment had been made. Harry Weitzman kept the diary in his desk at work and did not make the diary available to other employees at Danley. Weitzman further testified that the reason for maintaining the diary was to provide documentation if Irving Lazarus, the Vice President of Danley, ever demanded an accounting of the payments made to the supervisors. Despite objections by defense counsel that the diary was inadmissible under Rule 803(6) because it was not used or relied on by other Danley employees, nor required to be kept by Weitzman, and contained inaccuracies, Judge Bua admitted the diary on the basis of the foundation testimony, stating:

> The Court: I have heard enough. Mr. Newman, I think the key here in deciding this matter is whether the books record a regularly conducted business activity as opposed to some personal matter that the scrivener or the one who keeps the record is recording, and while it is a close case, I think it comes within the purview of 803(6). The court takes the position that really this goes all of your arguments of the defense go, good

arguments, go to the weight rather than to the admissibility, and the diary may be introduced into the record pursuant to the provisions of 803(6) of the Federal Rules of Evidence.

We agree with the district court that the diary was admissible. In that connection, our decision in *United States v. McPartlin*, 595 F.2d 1321 (7th Cir. 1979), is especially pertinent. In *McPartlin*, the government sought to admit into evidence desk calendar-appointment dairies authored by and containing records of the daily business activities of a witness. The diaries were kept strictly for the use of the witness and the entries therein were recorded at or near the time of the activity. The defendants in *McPartlin* objected to the admissibility of the diaries as business records because the entries were not made in sequence and because the diaries were relied on only by the witness. We upheld the admissibility of the diaries under Rule 803(6) on the grounds that they were records kept as part of a business activity and the entries were made with regularity at or near the time of the described event, and that verification by persons other than the one making the entry was unnecessary to establish verification. Moreover, we noted that since the witness had to rely on the entries made, there would be little reason for him to distort or falsify the entries. Finally, we observed that the degree of reliability necessary for the admission of diaries under the business record exception to the hearsay rule was greatly reduced because the declarant testified and was available for cross-examination.

The ratio decidendi of *McPartlin* is equally applicable to the contested admissibility of the diary in this case. Harry Weitzman testified that he kept the diary as part of a business activity. The entries were recorded with regularity at or near the date of the payoffs. Since Weitzman believed that he would be required to account to Lazarus for the payments, it was unlikely that he would have made false entries. Similarly, the fact that Weitzman was not told to keep the diary and did not make it available to others at Danley does not affect its admissibility under Rule 803(6). Finally, in this case, as in *McPartlin*, that the diaries recorded illicit business dealings is of no consequence; the illegal nature of those activities were nevertheless part of the normal business of Danley. *McPartlin*, *supra* at 1349.

[Affirmed]

NOTES AND QUESTIONS

(1) *Computer Records Admissible Under the Business Records Foundation.* Courts currently differ, even under similarly worded rules, as to how much of the computer process must be shown by way of foundation to admit computerized business records. Some require detailed information from the computer programmer and/or technical witness about the program, while some require no technical information at all, but merely require some nontechnical testimony from a lay person in the business that certain information is customarily put in and certain information customarily comes out. Banks and other institutions worry about the former view, which presents a security risk when the technical information is given in open court or spread on the public record, or even when it is merely disclosed to the parties. *See United States v. Young Brothers, Inc.*, 728 F.2d 682 (5th Cir.) (no

merit to defendant's contention that government was required to produce computer programmer to testify software was accurate), *cert. denied*, 469 U.S. 881 (1984).

When introduction of computer records was fairly new, courts, not surprisingly, demanded quite rigorous foundations, *see, e.g., Monarch Fed. Sav. & Loan Ass'n v. Genser*, 383 A.2d 475 (N.J. Super. Ct. Ch. Div. 1977). As courts became more familiar with computerized records, liberalized admissibility standards became common. *See United States v. Sanders*, 749 F.2d 195 (5th Cir. 1984), holding that computer printouts of medical claims received, processed, and paid by the state to a pharmacist were admissible under Fed. R. Evid. 803(6) as business records against the pharmacist on trial for Medicaid fraud, despite the fact that the printouts were generated in preparation for litigation. The pharmacist submitted Medicaid claims to an intermediate organization that keypunched the information onto magnetic tape for submission to the government. On receipt of the information, the government would load the data into computers that would verify certain information. When a check was mailed to the pharmacist, payment also was indicated on the computer records. Although the printouts themselves may have been made in preparation for litigation, the data contained therein already had been routinely entered into the computer at or near the time of the events recorded, the court notes, holding that it is not necessary that the printout itself be ordered in the ordinary course of business, at least when the program that calls forth the data only orders it out rather than sorting, compiling, or summarizing the information. Selective compilation might call for a different result, the decision indicates. Expressing similar receptive sentiments as *Sanders* is *Sea-Land Service, Inc. v. Lozen Int'l, LLC.* 285 F.3d 808 (9th Cir. 2002), which admitted a printout of a bill of lading, noting "it is immaterial that the business record is maintained in a computer rather than in company books." *See also Capital Marine Supply, Inc. v. M/V Roland Thomas II*, 719 F.2d 104 (5th Cir. 1983). *Compare United States v. Blackburn*, 992 F.2d 666 (7th Cir.) (computer printouts (of lensometer readings for eyeglasses) created at FBI's request were not kept in regular course of business, but admitted under "catchall" provision; see *infra*, § 10.05, in Chapter 10), *cert. denied*, 510 U.S. 949 (1993).

It is clear that, given a proper foundation, computer printouts will be received as business records, and there often will be a relaxation of some of the business records requirements. One of the relations, at least in some jurisdictions, is that the record may be printed out especially for the litigation, years after the event.

On the whole subject of the admissibility of computerized business records, see Bain & King, *Guidelines for the Admissibility of Evidence Generated by Computers for Purposes of Litigation*, 15 U.C.D. L. Rev. 951 (1982); Peritz, *Computer Data and Reliability: A Call for Authentication of Business Records Under the Federal Rules of Evidence*, 80 Nw. U. L. Rev. 956 (1986).

(3) *When is E-Mail a Business Record? See, e.g., Monotype Corp. PLC v. Int'l Typeface Corp.*, 43 F.3d 443 (9th Cir. 1994) (e-mail report prepared by employee of customer was not admissible as "business record," since document was not type of report that customer was in practice of making in regular course of its business). *See generally* Dreyer, Note: *When the Postman Beeps Twice: The Admissibility of Electronic Mail Under the Business Records Exception of the Federal Rules of*

Evidence, 64 FORDHAM L. REV. 2285 (1996).

(4) *Mere Printout from a Computer of Recorded Information Doesn't Make a Business Record.* Merely printing out information from a computer does not make the underlying information admissible. *See People v. Hernandez*, 55 Cal. App. 4th 225 (Cal. Ct. App. 1997). In *Hernandez*, police reports were culled for information on sex crimes, which were then fed into a computer, familiarly called "Sherlock." Do you agree with the following reasoning from the case?:

> We simply cannot find that the police department's daily internal procedure of having an employee take "facts" from police reports of sex crimes, put those "facts" into a sex crimes log, and in turn input those "facts" into Sherlock converts those facts contained in the police officer's sex crimes reports into competent, reliable, trustworthy evidence that is admissible at trial. In other words, the fact that hearsay evidence is put into a log and then again into a computer in the normal course of business does not render such evidence nonhearsay, when it is retrieved from the computer even when most of the [business record] requirements are met.

(5) *Requirement of Recording Near the Time of the Event.* What is it that must be nearly contemporaneous in a business record made from several internal transfers from document to document: the event sought to be proved and the final document produced at trial? Or the reception of each document and the transfer of its contents to the succeeding document? Is there a difference between computerized and other business records on this?

LORRAINE v. MARKEL AMERICAN INSURANCE COMPANY

United States District Court, District of Maryland
241 F.R.D. 534 (2007)

GRIMM, Chief United States Magistrate Judge.

Plaintiffs/Counter-Defendants Jack Lorraine and Beverly Mack bring this action to enforce a private arbitrator's award finding that certain damage to their yacht, *Chessie*, was caused by a lightning strike that occurred while *Chessie* was anchored in the Chesapeake Bay. Defendant/Counter-Plaintiff Markel American Insurance Company ("Markel") likewise has counterclaimed to enforce the arbitrator's award, which, in addition to concluding that certain damage to *Chessie*'s hull was caused by lightning, also concluded that the damage incurred was limited to an amount of $14,100, plus incidental costs. Following discovery, Plaintiffs moved for summary judgment, and Defendants filed a response in opposition and cross motion for summary judgment. I denied without prejudice both motions for the reasons discussed more fully below.

BACKGROUND

It is difficult for the Court to provide the appropriate background to the underlying arbitration in this case because, as will be discussed in greater detail below, neither party has proffered any admissible evidence to support the facts set forth in their respective motions. The scope of the arbitration agreement is the basis of this litigation. The final agreement states, in relevant part,

> "The parties to this dispute . . . have agreed that an arbitrator shall determine whether certain bottom damage in the amount of $36,000, to the Yacht CHESSIE was caused by the lightning strike occurring on May 17, 2004, or osmosis, as claimed by [Markel]."

The arbitrator issued his award . . . In it, he held that some, but not all, of *Chessie*'s hull damage was caused by lightning. This award forms the basis for the present litigation.

SUMMARY JUDGMENT STANDARD

Summary judgment is appropriate when there exists no genuine issue as to any material fact and a decision may be rendered as a matter of law.

If the party seeking summary judgment demonstrates that there is no evidence to support the nonmoving party's case, the burden shifts to the nonmoving party to identify specific facts showing that there is a genuine issue for trial. [T]he evidentiary materials submitted must show facts from which the finder of fact reasonably could find for the party opposing summary judgment. Moreover, to be entitled to consideration on summary judgment, the evidence supporting the facts set forth by the parties must be such as would be admissible in evidence. Unsworn, unauthenticated documents cannot be considered on a motion for summary judgment.

THE FEDERAL ARBITRATION ACT

. . . The question before the Court is whether the arbitrator exceeded his authority under the arbitration agreement by assigning a value to the damages attributable to the lightning strike that was less than the $36,000 claimed by Plaintiffs. If the answer is yes, then the court can vacate, remand, or modify the award. If the answer is no, then the court must grant Defendant's motion to confirm the award. . . .

I find that the language of the arbitration agreement is ambiguous; it could be read either to permit the arbitrator to determine the amount of damage to *Chessie*, or to limit his authority to determining only whether the claimed damages were caused by the lightning strike. Under normal circumstances, the Court would look to the documentary evidence provided by the parties, which in this case includes the arbitration agreement, award, and copies of e-mail correspondence between counsel, ostensibly supplied as extrinsic evidence of the parties' intent with regard to the scope of the arbitration agreement. In this case, however, the admissibility problems with the evidence presented are manifest. First, none of the documentary evidence presented is authenticated by affidavit or otherwise. Next, most of the facts relevant to the contract negotiations at issue have been provided by counsel ipse dixit, without supporting affidavits or deposition testimony. The evidentiary problems associated with the copies of e-mail offered as parol evidence likewise are substantial because they were not authenticated, but instead were simply attached to the parties' motions as exhibits.

Because neither party to this dispute complied with the requirement that they support their motions with admissible evidence, I dismissed both motions without prejudice to allow resubmission with proper evidentiary support. I further observed that the unauthenticated e-mails are a form of computer generated evidence that pose evidentiary issues that are highlighted by their electronic medium. Given the pervasiveness today of electronically prepared and stored records, as opposed to the manually prepared records of the past, counsel must be prepared to recognize and appropriately deal with the evidentiary issues associated with the admissibility of electronically generated and stored evidence. Research has failed to locate a comprehensive analysis of the many interrelated evidentiary issues associated with electronic evidence. Because there is a need for guidance to the bar regarding this subject, this opinion undertakes a broader and more detailed analysis of these issues than would be required simply to resolve the specific issues presented in this case. It is my hope that it will provide a helpful starting place for understanding the challenges associated with the admissibility of electronic evidence.

ADMISSIBILITY OF ELECTRONICALLY STORED INFORMATION

It has been noted that "[t]he Federal Rules of Evidence . . . do not separately address the admissibility of electronic data. . . . However, the Federal Rules of Evidence apply to computerized data as they do to other types of evidence. Fed.R.Evid. 102 contemplates that the rules of evidence are flexible enough to accommodate future "growth and development" to address technical changes not in existence as of the codification of the rules themselves. Further, courts have had little difficulty using the existing rules of evidence to determine the admissibility of ESI, despite the technical challenges that sometimes must be overcome to do so. *See, e.g., In re F.P.* ("Essentially, appellant would have us create a whole new body of law just to deal with e-mails or instant messages. . . . We believe that e-mail messages and similar forms of electronic communications can be properly authenticated within the existing framework of [the state rules of evidence].").

The process is complicated by the fact that ESI [i.e., electronically stored information] comes in multiple evidentiary "flavors," including e-mail, website ESI, internet postings, digital photographs, and computer-generated documents and data files.

Whether ESI is admissible into evidence is determined by a collection of evidence rules that present themselves like a series of hurdles to be cleared by the proponent of the evidence. Failure to clear any of these evidentiary hurdles means that the evidence will not be admissible. Whenever ESI is offered as evidence, either at trial or in summary judgment, the following evidence rules must be considered: (1) is the ESI **relevant** as determined by Rule 401 (does it have any tendency to make some fact that is of consequence to the litigation more or less probable than it otherwise would be); (2) if relevant under 401, is it **authentic** as required by Rule 901(a) (can the proponent show that the ESI is what it purports to be); (3) if the ESI is offered for its substantive truth, is it **hearsay** as defined by Rule 801, and if so, is it covered by an applicable exception (Rules 803, 804 and 807); (4) is the form of the ESI that is being offered as evidence an **original** or **duplicate** under the original writing rule, of if not, is there admissible secondary evidence to prove the content of the ESI (Rules 1001-1008); and (5) is the probative value of the ESI substantially outweighed by the danger of **unfair prejudice** or one of the other factors identified by Rule 403, such that it should be excluded despite its relevance. Preliminarily, the process by which the admissibility of ESI is determined is governed by Rule 104, which addresses the relationship between the judge and the jury with regard to preliminary fact finding associated with the admissibility of evidence. Because Rule 104 governs the very process of determining admissibility of ESI, it must be considered first.

Preliminary Rulings on Admissibility (Rule 104)

[This portion of the opinion dealing with how Federal Rules of Evidence 104(a) and (b) apply to all the evidentiary questions in an ESI case is reproduced *infra*, at the end of Section 12:01[A].]

Relevance (Rules 401, 402, and 105)

[This portion of the opinion dealing with relevance questions in an ESI case is reproduced *infra*, at the end of Section 12:01[A].]

Authenticity (Rules 901-902)

[This portion of the opinion dealing with authetication of ESI is reproduced *infra*, at the end of Section 12:01[A].]

Hearsay (Rules 801-807)

The fourth "hurdle" that must be overcome when introducing electronic evidence is the potential application of the hearsay rule. Hearsay issues are pervasive when electronically stored and generated evidence is introduced. To properly analyze hearsay issues there are five separate questions that must be answered: (1) does the evidence constitute a **statement**, as defined by Rule 801(a); (2) was the statement made by a "**declarant**," as defined by Rule 801(b); (3) is the statement being offered to prove the **truth of its contents**, as provided by Rule 801(c); (4) is the statement **excluded from the definition of hearsay by rule 801(d)**; and (5) if the statement is hearsay, is it covered by one of the exceptions identified at Rules 803, 804 or 807.

The requirements of a "Statement," Rule 801(a), made by a "Person", Rule 801(b).

The key to understanding the hearsay rule is to appreciate that it only applies to intentionally assertive verbal or non-verbal conduct, and its goal is to guard against the risks associated with testimonial evidence: perception, memory, sincerity and narration.

A writing or spoken utterance cannot be a "statement" under the hearsay rule unless it is made by a "declarant," as required by Rule 801(b), which provides "[a] 'declarant' is a *person* who makes a statement." (emphasis added). When an electronically generated record is entirely the product of the functioning of a computerized system or process, such as the "report" generated when a fax is sent showing the number to which the fax was sent and the time it was received, there is no "person" involved in the creation of the record, and no "assertion" being made. For that reason, the record is not a statement and cannot be hearsay.

Cases involving electronic evidence often raise the issue of whether electronic writings constitute "statements" under Rule 801(a). Where the writings are non-assertive, or not made by a "person," courts have held that they do not constitute hearsay, as they are not "statements." *United States v. Khorozian* ("[N]either the header nor the text of the fax was hearsay. As to the header, '[u]nder FRE 801(a), a statement is something uttered by "a person," so nothing "said" by a machine . . . is hearsay' " (second alteration in original)); *Safavian* (holding that portions of e-mail communications that make imperative statements instructing defendant what to do, or asking questions are nonassertive verbal conduct that does not fit within the definition of hearsay); *Telewizja Polska USA* (finding that images and text posted on website offered to show what the website looked like on a particular day were not "statements" and therefore fell outside the reach of the hearsay rule); *Perfect 10* (finding that images and text taken from website of defendant not hearsay, "to the extent these images and text are being introduced to show the images and text found on the websites, they are not statements at all-and thus fall outside the ambit of the hearsay rule."); *United States v. Rollins* ("Computer generated records are not hearsay: the role that the hearsay rule plays in limiting the fact finder's consideration to reliable evidence received from witnesses who are under oath and subject to cross-examination has no application to the computer generated record in this case. Instead, the admissibility of the computer tracing system record should be measured by the reliability of the system itself, relative to its proper functioning and accuracy."); *State v. Dunn* ("Because records of this type [computer generated telephone records] are not the counterpart of a statement by a human declarant, which should ideally be tested by cross-examination of that declarant, they should not be treated as hearsay, but rather their admissibility should be determined on the reliability and accuracy of the process involved."); *State v. Hall* (reviewing the admissibility of computer generated records and holding "[t]he role that the hearsay rule plays in limiting the fact finder's consideration to reliable evidence received from witnesses who are under oath and subject to cross-examination has no application to the computer generated record in this case. Instead, the admissibility of the computer tracing system record should be measured by the reliability of the system, itself, relative to its proper functioning and accuracy.").

The requirement that the statement be offered to prove its substantive truth.

The [next] question that must be answered in determining if evidence is hearsay is whether the statement is offered to prove its substantive truth, or for some other purpose. [E]ven if the evidence is an assertion, made by a declarant, it still is not hearsay unless offered to prove the truth of what is asserted. The advisory committee's note to Rule 801(c) underscores this: "If the significance of an offered statement lies solely in the fact that it was made, no issue is raised as to the truth of anything asserted, and the statement is not hearsay. The effect is to exclude from hearsay the entire category of 'verbal acts' and 'verbal parts of an act,' in which the statement itself affects the legal rights of the parties or is a circumstance bearing on conduct affecting their rights." Commentators have identified many instances in which assertive statements are not hearsay because they are not offered to prove the truth of the assertions: (1) statements offered to prove a claim that the statement was false or misleading, as in a fraud or misrepresentation case; (2) statements offered to "prove that because they were made, listeners had notice or knowledge of the information related in the statements," or to show the effect on the listener of the statement; (3) statements "offered to prove an association between two or more persons;" (4) statements offered as circumstantial evidence of the declarant's state of mind, or motive; (5) statements that have relevance simply because they were made, regardless of their literal truth or falsity-the so called "verbal acts or parts of acts," also referred to as "legally operative facts"; and (6) statements that are questions or imperative commands, such as "what time is it" or "close the door."

When analyzing the admissibility of electronically generated evidence, courts also have held that statements contained within such evidence fall outside the hearsay definition if offered for a purpose other than their substantive truth. *Siddiqui* (e-mail between defendant and co-worker not hearsay because not offered to prove truth of substantive content, but instead to show that a relationship existed between defendant and co-worker, and that it was customary for them to communicate by e-mail); *Safavian* (e-mail from lobbyist to defendant not hearsay because they were not offered to prove their truth, but to illustrate the nature of the lobbyist's work on behalf of clients to provide context for other admissible e-mail; and as evidence of the defendant's intent, motive and state of mind); . . . *Perfect 10*, 213 F.Supp.2d at 1155 (exhibits of defendant's website on a particular date were not "statements" for purposes of hearsay rule because they were offered to show trademark and copyright infringement, therefore they were relevant for a purpose other than their literal truth); *State v. Braidic* (e-mail sent by defendant to victim not hearsay because they were not offered to prove the truth of the statements.).

Finally, of particular relevance to this suit are the cases that have held that communications between the parties to a contract that define the terms of a contract, or prove its content, are not hearsay, as they are verbal acts or legally operative facts. . . . Because the e-mails that the parties to this suit attached as unauthenticated exhibits to their summary judgment papers were introduced for the purpose of proving the making of the agreement to arbitrate the dispute regarding the damage caused by the lightning strike, and the terms of this agreement, they are not hearsay if offered for this purpose because they are verbal acts, or legally operative facts. What the parties did not do, however, was articulate the non-hearsay purpose for which the e-mails were offered. . . . Evidence may be offered for more than one purpose, it may be relevant for its substantive truth, and potentially hearsay, or relevant for some other purpose, and non-hearsay. For this reason it is important for a party offering an exhibit into evidence to clearly explain each purpose for which it is offered, and address any hearsay issues associated with each purpose for which it is offered.

Is the evidence excluded from the definition of hearsay by Rule 801(d)(1) or 801(d)(2).

Once it has been determined whether evidence falls into the definition of hearsay because it is a statement, uttered by a declarant, and offered for its substantive truth, the final step in assessing whether it is hearsay is to see if it is excluded from the definition of hearsay by two rules: 801(d)(1), which identifies three types of prior statements by witnesses who actually testify and are subject to cross examination, which are excluded from the definition of hearsay, and 801(d)(2), which identifies five types of admissions by a party opponent that are excluded from the definition of hearsay. . . .

As can be seen from reading Rule 801(d)(1) and (2), there are specific foundational facts that must be established before the statement or admission can be accepted into evidence. These determinations are made by the trial judge under Rule 104(a), and therefore the rules of evidence, except for privilege, are inapplicable.

Given the near universal use of electronic means of communication, it is not surprising that statements contained in electronically made or stored evidence often have been found to qualify as admissions by a party opponent if offered against that party. *Siddiqui* (ruling that e-mail authored by defendant was not hearsay because it was an admission under Rule 801(d)(2)(A)); *Safavian* (holding that e-mail sent by defendant himself was admissible as non-hearsay because it constituted an admission by the defendant, 801(d)(2)(A), and as an "adoptive admission" under Rule 801(d)(2)(B)); *Telewizja Polska USA* (holding exhibits showing defendant's website as it appeared on a certain day were admissible as admissions against defendant); *Perfect 10* (admitting e-mail sent by employees of defendant against the defendant as admissions under 801(d)(2)(D)).

If, after applying the foregoing four-step analysis, it is determined that the electronic evidence constitutes a statement by a person that is offered for its substantive truth and is not excluded from the definition of hearsay by Rule 801(d)(1) or (2), then the evidence is hearsay, and is inadmissible unless it qualifies as one of many hearsay exceptions . . . [A] handful of hearsay exceptions repeatedly are used in connection with electronically generated or stored evidence. . . .

Given the widely accepted fact that most writings today are created and stored in electronic format, it is easy to see that the many types of documents and writings covered in Rule 803 will implicate electronic writings. Similarly, given the ubiquity of communications in electronic media (e-mail, text messages, chat rooms, internet postings on servers like "myspace" ["facebook"] or "youtube" or on blogs, voice mail, etc.), it is not surprising that many statements involving observations of events surrounding us, statements regarding how we feel, our plans and motives, and our feelings (emotional and physical) will be communicated in electronic medium.

Rule 803(1) Present Sense Impression.

Rule 803(1) creates an exception . . . [that is frequently used in electronic evidence cases]. . . .

Rule 803(2) Excited Utterance.

Closely related to Rule 803(1) is Rule 803(2), the excited utterance exception to the hearsay rule. . . .

The prevalence of electronic communication devices, and the fact that many are portable and small, means that people always seem to have their laptops, PDA's, and cell phones with them, and available for use to send e-mails or text messages describing events as they are happening. Further, it is a common experience these days to talk to someone on the phone and hear them typing notes of the conversation on a computer as you are talking to them. For these reasons, Rules 803(1) and (2) may provide hearsay exceptions for electronically stored communications containing either present sense impressions or excited utterances. *See, e.g., United States v. Ferber* (holding that e-mail from employee to boss about substance of telephone call with defendant in mail/wire fraud case did qualify as a present sense expression under Rule 803(1), but did not qualify as an excited utterance under Rule 803(2), despite the language at the end of the e-mail "my mind is mush."); *State of New York v. Microsoft* (analyzing the admissibility of series of exhibits including e-mail and e-mail "chains" under various hearsay exceptions, and ruling that an e-mail prepared several days after a telephone call that described the call did not qualify as a present sense impression under Rule 803(1) because the requirement of "contemporaneity" was not met).

Rule 803(3) Then Existing State of Mind or Condition.

This rule permits the statement of the declarant's state of mind, sensation, mental, emotional, or physical condition, as well as statements of motive, intent, plan or design, but excludes statements of memory or belief if offered to prove the truth of the fact remembered. Rule 803(3) has been used to prove a wide variety of matters, including the reason why the declarant would not deal with a supplier or dealer, motive, competency, ill-will, motive, lack of intent to defraud, willingness to engage in criminal conduct, the victim's state of mind in an extortion case, and confusion or secondary meaning in a trademark infringement case.

Rule 803(3) is particularly useful when trying to admit e-mail, a medium of communication that seems particularly prone to candid, perhaps too-candid, statements of the declarant's state of mind, feelings, emotions, and motives. In *New York v. Microsoft*, the court analyzed admissibility of e-mail and e-mail chains under a variety of hearsay rules, including 803(3). It concluded that an e-mail made several days following a telephone conversation did not qualify under Rule 803(3) because it contained more than just the declarant's state of mind, but also included the maker's memory or belief about the events that affected his state of mind, which is specifically excluded by Rule 803(3). *See also Safavian* (admitting e-mail that contained statements of defendant's state of mind under Rule 803(3)).

Rule 803(6) Business Records.

Rule 803(6) recognizes an exception to the hearsay rule for: [quoted]

It is essential for the exception to apply that it was made in furtherance of the business' needs, and not for the personal purposes of the person who made it. Given the fact that many employees use the computers where they work for personal as well as business reasons, some care must be taken to analyze whether the business record exception is applicable, especially to e-mail.

Rule 902(11) also is helpful in establishing the foundation elements for a business record without the need to call a sponsoring witness to authenticate the document and establish the elements of the hearsay exception. Rule 902(11) permits the self-authentication of a business record by showing the following: [quoted]

Because the elements for both rules are essentially identical, they frequently are analyzed together when Rule 902(11) is the proffered means by which a party seek to admit a business record. *See Rambus* (holding that analysis of Rule 803(6) and 902(11) go "hand in hand," and identifying the following requirements for authentication under Rule 902(11): (1) a qualified custodian or other person having personal knowledge makes the authenticating declaration, who must have "sufficient knowledge of the record-keeping system and the creation of the contested record to establish their trustworthiness;" (2) the declaration must establish that the record was made at or near the time of the occurrence or matters set forth in the document by someone with personal knowledge of these matters or from information provided by someone with personal knowledge thereof; (3) the declaration must show that the record is kept in the course of the regularly conducted activity of the business, and the "mere presence of a document . . . in the retained file of a business entity do[es] not by itself qualify as a record of a regularly conducted activity"; and (4) the declaration must establish that it is the regular practice of the business to keep records of a regularly conducted activity of the business, and "it is not enough if it is the regular practice of an employee to maintain the record of the regularly conducted activity . . . it must be the regular practice of the business entity to do so" — i.e. it is at the direction of the company that the employee maintain the record).

The business record exception is one of the hearsay exceptions most discussed by courts when ruling on the admissibility of electronic evidence. The decisions demonstrate a continuum running from cases where the court was very lenient in admitting electronic business records, without demanding analysis, to those in which the court took a very demanding approach and scrupulously analyzed every element of the exception, and excluded evidence when all were not met. For example, in *State of New York v. Microsoft*, the court analyzed the admissibility of "e-mail chains." The court held that an e-mail prepared by an employee did not qualify as a business record because, while it may have been the regular practice of the employee to send an e-mail following the receipt of a phone call that summarized the call, there had been no showing that it was the regular practice of the employer to require that the employee make and maintain such e-mails. The court was particularly careful in analyzing the hearsay issues associated with e-mail chains involving multiple employees of the same employer. It held that to establish a proper foundation, the proponent would have to show that when the source of the information related in the e-mail is someone other than the maker of the e-mail, that the source, the maker, "as well as every other participant in the chain producing the record, are [all] acting in the regular course of [the] business." If this showing is made, the court ruled, then the multiple levels of hearsay in the e-mail chain are covered by Rule 803(6). However, "[i]f the source of the information is an outsider, Rule 803(6) does not, by itself, permit the admission of the business record. The outsider's statement must fall within another hearsay exception to be admissible because it does not have the presumption of accuracy that statements made during the regular course of business have." The court also excluded another e-mail chain for failure of the proponent to establish a proper foundation, saying "[p]laintiffs have not established the requisite foundation that the multiple authors of these e-mails each composed their portion of the document in the course of regularly conducted business activity and that it was the regular practice of RealNetworks to compose such e-mail correspondence. Moreover, the multiple authors and forwarded nature of the e-mails undercuts the reliability of the information contained therein."

Similarly, in Rambus Inc. v. Infineon Tech. AG, . . . [c]ertain exhibits objected to by the defendant were e-mail chains prepared at least in part by persons outside of the business entity that maintained the e-mail as part of its records, and which was seeking their admissibility as business records. The court noted that there was "not a requirement that the records have been prepared by the entity that has custody of them, as long as they were created in the regular course of some [other] entity's business." The court added "[h]owever, it also is true that to satisfy Rule 803(6) each participant in the chain which created the record — from the initial observer-reporter to the final entrant — must generally be acting in the course of the regularly conduct[ed] business. If some participant is not so engaged, some other hearsay exception must apply to that link of the chain."

In contrast to the demanding approach taken in *Rambus* and *New York v. Microsoft*, the court in *United States v. Safavian* took a more flexible approach to the admissibility of e-mail chains. The defendant objected to the admissibility of e-mail chains, arguing that they were not trustworthy because they contained e-mails embedded within e-mails. The court overruled this objection, stating:

> "[t]he defendant's argument is more appropriately directed to the weight the jury should give the evidence, not its authenticity. While the defendant is correct that earlier e-mails that are included in a chain-either as ones that have been forwarded or to which another has replied-may be altered, this trait is not specific to e-mail evidence. It can be true of any piece of documentary evidence, such as a letter, a contract or an invoice. . . . The possibility of alteration does not and cannot be the basis for excluding e-mails as unidentified or unauthenticated as a matter of course. . . . We live in an age of technology and computer use where e-mail communication now is a normal and frequent fact for the majority of the nation's population and is of particular importance in the professional world. . . . Absent specific evidence showing alteration, however, the Court will not exclude any embedded e-mails because of the mere possibility that it can be done."

Notably, the court did not engage in the demanding business records exception analysis that was done by the courts in *Rambus* and *New York v. Microsoft*.

Perhaps the most demanding analysis regarding the admissibility of electronic evidence under the business record exception to the hearsay rule appears in *In re Vee Vinhnee*. In this case the appellate bankruptcy panel upheld the trial bankruptcy judge's exclusion of electronic business records, observing that "early versions of computer foundations [accepted by courts] were too cursory, even though the basic elements [of the business records exception] covered the ground." The court held that the proponent of an electronic business record was required to show that the paperless electronic record retrieved from its computer files was the same one as originally had been entered into its computer, noting that the "focus is not on the circumstances of the creation of the record, but rather on the circumstances of the preservation of the record during the time it is in the file so as to assure that the document being proffered is the same as the document that originally was created." It added:

> "[T]he logical questions extend beyond the identification of the particular computer equipment and programs used. The entity's policies and procedures for the use of the equipment, database, and programs are important. How access to the pertinent database is controlled and, separately, how access to the specific program is controlled are important questions. How changes in the database are logged or recorded, as well as the structure and implementation of backup systems and audit procedures for assuring the continuing integrity of the database, are pertinent to the questions of whether records have been changed since their creation."

The court reasoned that the "complexity of ever-developing computer technology necessitates more precise focus," because "digital technology makes it easier to alter text of documents that have been scanned into a database, thereby increasing the importance of audit procedures designed to assure the continuing integrity of the records."

In contrast to the demanding approach taken in *In re Vee Vinhnee*, many other courts have admitted electronic business records under a much more relaxed standard. *See, e.g.*, *United States v. Kassimu* (Establishing the foundation for a computer generated business record did not require the maker of the record, or even a custodian, but only a witness qualified to explain the record keeping system of organization); *United States v. Fujii* (holding that computerized check-in and reservation records were admissible as business records on a showing that the data reflected in the printouts was kept in the ordinary course of the business); *Sea-Land* (holding that copy of electronic bill of lading had been properly admitted as a business record because it had been produced from the same electronic information that had been contemporaneously generated when the parties entered into their contract. The court noted that "it is immaterial that the business record is maintained in a computer rather than in company books"); *Wapnick v. Commissioner of Internal Revenue* (computerized accounting records were admissible as business records because foundation was established by IRS agents who compared the data in the computer records with information in the company's tax returns, bank statements, and by contacting clients of the company to verify information in the computerized records).

The lesson to be taken from these cases is that some courts will require the proponent of electronic business records or e-mail evidence to make an enhanced showing in addition to meeting each element of the business records exception. These courts are concerned that the information generated for use in litigation may have been altered, changed or manipulated after its initial input, or that the programs and procedures used to create and maintain the records are not reliable or accurate. Others will be content to view electronic business records in the same light as traditional "hard copy" records, and require only a rudimentary foundation. . . . The cases further suggest that during pretrial discovery counsel should determine whether opposing counsel will object to admissibility of critical documents. This can be done by requesting a stipulation, or by propounding requests for admission of fact and genuineness of records under Fed.R.Civ.P. 36. If it is known that opposing counsel will object, or refuses to stipulate, or denies a Rule 36 request to admit genuineness, then the lawyer intending to introduce the electronic business record should be prepared to establish the business record exception under the most demanding standard required, to avoid exclusion of the evidence.

Rule 803(8) Public Records.

In addition to the above described hearsay exceptions, courts have found that electronic records also met the requirements of the public records exception under Rule 803(8) [quoted].

"[J]ustification for the exception is the assumption that a public official will perform his duty properly, and the unlikelihood that he will remember details independently of the record." Fed.R.Evid. 803(8) advisory committee's note. Moreover, "[s]ince the assurances of accuracy are generally greater for public records than for regular business records, the proponent is usually not required to establish their admissibility through foundation testimony. . . . The burden of proof concerning the admissibility of public records is on the party opposing their introduction." Weinstein. . . . Courts have applied this deferential standard of admissibility for electronic public records. *See, e.g., EEOC v. E.I. DuPont de Nemours and Co.* (holding that table of information compiled by U.S. Census Bureau was admissible as an exception to the hearsay rule as a public record under Rule 803(8), and rejecting claims that the posting of data on the Census Bureau's website rendered it untrustworthy); *Lester v. Natsios* (admitting e-mail of public agency, and noting that "[r]ecords of public agencies such as those challenged by plaintiff are generally admissible . . . under Fed.R.Evid. 803(8)"); *United States v. Oceguerra-Aguirre* (Court held that trial court properly admitted computerized records of Treasury Enforcement Communications System as public records under Rule 803(8) because documents falling under the public records exception are presumed to be trustworthy, and the burden is on the party challenging the records to establish untrustworthiness).

Rule 803(17) Market Reports, Commercial Publications.

Rule 803(17) recognizes as an exception to the hearsay rule: [quoted]

This exception covers "lists, etc., prepared for the use of a trade or profession . . . newspaper market reports, telephone directories, and city directories. The basis of trustworthiness is general reliance by the public or by a particular segment of it, and the motivation of the compiler to foster reliance by being accurate." Fed.R.Evid. 803(17) advisory committee's note. . . . At least one court has admitted electronically stored compilations and directories under Rule 803(17). *Elliott Assoc. L.P. v. Banco de la Nacion* (finding that plaintiff's expert report properly relied on prime rates of interest obtained from Federal Reserve Board website because they were reliable under Rule 803(17)).

A final observation needs to be made regarding hearsay exceptions and electronic evidence. Rule 802 generally prohibits the admission of hearsay unless one of the exceptions in Rules 803, 804 or 807 apply. What, then, is the effect of hearsay evidence that is admitted without objection by the party against whom it is offered? The general rule is that despite Rule 802, if hearsay is admitted without objection it may be afforded its "natural probative effect, as if it were in law admissible." *New York v. Microsoft*. This underscores the need to pay attention to exhibits offered by an opponent, as much as to those records that you need to introduce. A failure to raise a hearsay objection means that the evidence may be considered for whatever probative value the finder of fact chooses to give it.

In summary, when analyzing the admissibility of ESI for hearsay issues, counsel should address each step of the inquiry in order: does the evidence contain a statement, made by a person, which is offered for its substantive truth, but which does not fall into the two categories of statements identified in 801(d)(1) and 801(d)(2). If, as a result of this analysis, a determination is made that the evidence is hearsay, then it is inadmissible unless it covered by one of the exceptions found in Rules 803, 804 and 807.

If ESI has cleared the first three hurdles by being shown to be relevant, authentic, and admissible under the hearsay rule or an exception thereto, it must also be admissible under the original writing rule before it can be admitted into evidence or considered at summary judgment.

[The portions of the opinion dealing with relevance, authentication, the original writings rule, and potential prejudice, as applied to ESI is reproduced *infra*, at the end of Section 12.01[A] of this book.]

Conclusion

In this case the failure of counsel collectively to establish the authenticity of their exhibits, resolve potential hearsay issues, comply with the original writing rule, and demonstrate the absence of unfair prejudice rendered their exhibits inadmissible, resulting in the dismissal, without prejudice, of their cross motions for summary judgment. The discussion above highlights the fact that there are five distinct but interrelated evidentiary issues that govern whether electronic evidence will be admitted into evidence at trial or accepted as an exhibit in summary judgment practice. Although each of these rules may not apply to every exhibit offered, as was the case here, each still must be considered in evaluating how to secure the admissibility of electronic evidence to support claims and defenses. Because it can be expected that electronic evidence will constitute much of the evidence used in future motions practice or at trial, counsel should know how to get it right on the first try. The Court hopes that the explanation provided in this memorandum order will assist in that endeavor.

STATE v. BLAKE

Court of Appeals of Ohio, Twelfth District, Butler County
974 N.E.2d 730 (2012)

RINGLAND, J.

Defendant-appellant, Anthony Dion Blake, appeals from his conviction in the Butler County Court of Common Pleas for murder with a firearm . . . .

In his second assignment of error, Blake argues that Exhibit 40, which contained over 50 pages of [incriminating] text messages [from before and after the murder], was improperly admitted. Specifically, Blake contends: (1) the exhibit was not properly authenticated pursuant to Evid.R. 901(B)(6); (2) the exhibit did not qualify as a business record under Evid.R. 803(6); and (3) the exhibit should have been excluded pursuant to Evid.R. 403. . . .

Generally, hearsay is inadmissible, unless it falls within one of the numerous exceptions found in the Rules of Evidence . . . .One such exception is the business records exception under Evid.R. 803(6). This court has found on more than one occasion that a cellular telephone record may fall within the business records exception.

To qualify for admission under Rule 803(6), a business record must manifest four essential elements: (i) the record must be one regularly recorded in a regularly conducted activity; (ii) it must have been entered by a person with knowledge of the act, event or condition; (iii) it must have been recorded at or near the time of the transaction; and (iv) a foundation must be laid by the "custodian" of the record or by some "other qualified witness."

Even if these elements are established, a business record may be excluded if the "source of information or the method or circumstances of preparation indicate lack of trustworthiness." However, before a business record is admitted pursuant to Evid.R. 803(6), the record must be properly identified or authenticated.

The requirement of authentication or identification as a condition precedent to admissibility is satisfied by introducing "evidence sufficient to support a finding that the matter in question is what its proponent claims." Evid.R. 901(A). . . This threshold requirement for authentication of evidence is low and does not require conclusive proof of authenticity. Instead, the state only needs to demonstrate a "reasonable likelihood" that the evidence is authentic. Blake argues that the text messages should have been authenticated pursuant to Evid.R. 901(B)(6) and compared the messages to a telephone conversation. However, we find these records are more analogous to a business record and could have been authenticated as such.

In order to properly authenticate business records, a witness, such as an employee of the company, must testify as to the regularity and reliability of the business activity involved in the creation of the record. While firsthand knowledge of the business transaction is not required by the witness providing the foundation, the witness must be familiar with the operation of the business and the circumstances of the record's preparation, maintenance and retrieval, such that he can reasonably testify on the basis of this knowledge that the record is what it purports to be, and that it was made in the ordinary course of business consistent with the elements of Evid.R. 803(6).

With these principles in mind, we now turn to the record to determine whether Exhibit 40 was properly authenticated and admitted pursuant to Evid.R. 803(6). In support of admission, the state presented the testimony of Paula Papke, a manager with Cincinnati Bell Corporate Security and the custodian of the records. Papke identified Exhibit 40 as the content of text messages sent from and received by Blake's cellular telephone number December 29, 2010, through January 5, 2011. Papke testified that a limited amount of text message records are stored on the company's network and kept in the usual course of business. She explained that Cincinnati Bell retains these records for about seven days. Papke explained that these records show the telephone number of both the cellular telephone receiving the text and the number for the cellular telephone that sent the text. The record also includes the content of the actual text message and the arrival date and time. Papke did not testify as to the identity of the person who sent or received any of the text messages reflected in Exhibit 40.

Papke's testimony provided adequate foundation for the records pursuant to both Evid.R. 901(A) and 803(6). As a witness with knowledge of the business operations of Cincinnati Bell, Papke's testimony presented sufficient evidence to support a finding that the matter in question is what the proponent claims, namely the cellular telephone records, including text messages, belonging to a number separately identified as Blake's. She identified Exhibit 40 as the records she retrieved from the company's network in response to the subpoena for that specific number. In addition, because Papke was able to testify that these records were recorded during regularly conducted activity, and the messages were stored and kept in the ordinary course of business, the records were properly admitted under the business records exception to the hearsay rule.

Blake argues Exhibit 40 was not properly authenticated because there was no testimony from Papke or any other witness as to who actually prepared, sent, or received the text messages such that the records indicate a lack of trustworthiness. However, this argument goes to the weight of the evidence rather than its admissibility. As the cellular telephone records were properly authenticated and admitted, the jury was then free to believe or disbelieve Blake's defense that he was not the one sending the text messages. The jury heard and rejected this defense. Accordingly, there was no error, plain or otherwise, in the admission and authentication of Exhibit 40.

Blake also argues that the admission of Exhibit 40 should have been excluded pursuant to Evid.R. 403 . . . arguing that the records as a whole were unduly prejudicial and inflammatory as there were several text messages that were not relevant to any material fact of the case and could encourage the jury to convict merely based on improper character evidence . . . .[W]e review the trial court's admission of Exhibit 40 based on Evid.R. 403 for an abuse of discretion.

Under Evid.R. 403(A), exclusion of relevant evidence is mandatory where the "probative value [of the evidence] is substantially outweighed by the danger of unfair prejudice, of confusion of the issues, or of misleading the jury." Evid.R.

403(A). For the evidence to be excluded on this basis, the probative value must be minimal and the prejudice great.

It is clear from the record that the authorship of the text messages detailed in Exhibit 40 was an issue in the case. Albert Givens and Detective Bush provided testimony connecting Blake to the cellular telephone number from which these records came. Both testified that Blake's number was the same as that in Exhibit 40. The text messages sent from that number were highly relevant as these messages showed a continuous sequence of events that occurred just prior to the shooting and in the days following the shooting. The text messages sent to this number from other persons were still relevant, not for the truth of the matter asserted, but rather in establishing authorship and showing Blake's response to these messages. Several of the text messages sent to this number referred to Blake by name or by his nickname, "Face." Such text messages made it more likely that all of the text messages came from Blake. Finally, any possible prejudice presented by Exhibit 40 is diminished as Blake had an opportunity and did in fact cross-examine both Papke and Detective Bush regarding the fact that they could not state who in fact sent the text messages contained in Exhibit 40. Accordingly, we find the trial court did not err in admitting Exhibit 40 as the danger of unfair prejudice was minimal and did not substantially outweigh the probative value of the evidence. Blake's second assignment of error is overruled . . . .

[Affirmed.]

YATES v. BAIR TRANSPORT, INC.

United States District Court, Southern District of New York
249 F. Supp. 681 (1965)

TENNEY, DISTRICT JUDGE.

The respective parties herein request of the Court a ruling prior to trial on the admissibility of two proffered items of evidence: firstly, a police blotter report concerning the instant accident, and, secondly, medical reports of various doctors who examined plaintiff in connection with a prior Workmen's Compensation claim arising out of the accident.

The parties have stipulated that if the reporting officer were called he would testify that the police blotter was prepared by him in the regular course of his duties and filed with the Police Department in accordance with his and their regular practice and procedure. If the officer were called, it is further agreed that he would also testify that the photostatic copy was authentic. Plaintiff accordingly argues that a sufficient foundation has been laid for the admissibility of the report without the necessity of calling the police officer.

The Federal Business Records Act [28 U.S.C.] provides:

> § 1732. Record made in regular course of business: photographic copies.
>
> (a) In any court of the United States and in any court established by Act of Congress, any writing or record, whether in the form of an entry in a

> book or otherwise, made as a memorandum or record of any act, transaction, occurrence, or event, shall be admissible as evidence of such act, transaction, occurrence, or event, if made in the regular course of any business, and if it was the regular course of such business to make such memorandum or record at the time of such act, transaction, occurrence, or event or within a reasonable time thereafter.

It further provides that "[a]ll other circumstances of the making of such writing or record [i.e., a record kept in the ordinary course of business] including lack of personal knowledge by the entrant or maker, may be shown to affect its weight, but such circumstances shall not affect its admissibility." An identical provision with respect to the contents of the record and the personal knowledge of the maker or entrant is contained in Section 4518 of the New York Civil Practice Law & Rules. [The Federal Business Records Act is now superseded by Fed. R. Evid. 803(6), but its language still exists in a number of states — Eds.]

A copy of the police blotter report has been supplied to the Court. Therein the ownership of the vehicle in question is set forth.

In addition, the details of the accident are enumerated. The officer, as stated in the report, was not an eyewitness to the accident; in addition, under the heading of names and addresses of witnesses there appears the entry "none." Accordingly, it may be assumed that the information set forth in the report was supplied either by the driver of the truck, a helper, or the plaintiff.

Professor McCormick has summed up the state of the law as follows: "Thus the statements of by-standers recorded in a policeman's report of an accident would be denied admission as business records to show the facts reported."

It is clear that *Johnson v. Lutz*, 253 N.Y. 124, 170 N.E. 517 (1930), would preclude the admissibility of statements by bystanders given to a police officer at the scene of the accident:

> Where, however, the informant to the entrant of the record is under no duty to anyone to make a truthful account of the facts thus recorded, the record will not be admissible as proof of such facts. Aside from Wigmore, no competent authority in the field and few courts have dissented from this qualification obviously basic to the rationale of the business entry exception.

A case seemingly in point and holding such a report with statements of bystanders admissible is *McKee v. Jamestown Bakery Co.*, 198 F.2d 551 (3d Cir. 1952):

> The police report consists of a summary of statements made by witnesses to the accident and some photographs taken immediately after the accident. The refusal to admit the statements was error on the part of the court below. The report was made by Chief of Police Goetz in his official capacity and was therefore made in the 'regular course' of his business.

The majority of courts have followed the rule of *Johnson v. Lutz* in excluding records, even though the entrant was acting pursuant to business duty, where the informants were not. This limitation has elicited severe criticism from Professor

Wigmore and other commentators. They have argued that since the statute expressly rejects the necessity for personal knowledge on the part of the entrant, the only requirements for admissibility are that the entrant be acting in the regular course of his business and that the record be made at or near the time of the event. Some courts have seemingly adopted this view, admitting records regularly made although the information contained was derived ultimately from volunteers.

Despite criticism of the *Johnson* case, the limitation it imposes seems sound and in accord with the basic philosophy of the business entry statutes. These acts were intended to make admissible records which, because made pursuant to a regular business duty, are presumed to be reliable. The mere fact that recordation of third party statements is routine, taken apart from the source of the information recorded, imports no guaranty of the truth of the statements themselves. So to construe these statutes would make of them almost limitless dragnets for the introduction of random, irresponsible testimony beyond the reach of the usual tests for accuracy. *Johnson v. Lutz* did not ignore the statutory language making personal knowledge unnecessary, but merely emphasized that the presumption of reliability attaches only to statements made entirely in the course of business.

A record which contains the hearsay statements of volunteers [whether bystanders or participants, under no duty to supply information] then, does not by operation of the business record statutes become admissible to prove the truth of those statements.

The following reconciliation [by Professor McCormick] between the statutory language and the clear weight of authority appears correct:

> This [the statutory language stating that lack of personal knowledge of the maker or entrant goes to weight rather than admissibility] could be interpreted as abolishing the requirement of firsthand knowledge by one whose job is to know the facts. The more reasonable interpretation, however, is to read "entrant or maker" as meaning the recorder only and thus merely making clear that one who makes the record on reports of others need not know the facts, without broadening (beyond the probable intent of the drafters) the content of this hearsay exception to embrace records founded on reports by one who has no business duty to know the facts.

Or, as stated in *Standard Oil Co. of California v. Moore*, 251 F.2d 188 (9th Cir. 1957):

> But where the entrant or maker records information supplied by others, it must appear that "it was part of their regular course of business to report to him what the declarants themselves knew, as it was part of his business to record what they said." Where the information comes to the entrant or maker from unauthorized persons, the memorandum or record is therefore inadmissible, not because it contains hearsay, but because it was not made in the regular course of business.

Moreover, if the policeman testified in court, his testimony that a bystander told him that the accident occurred thusly would be hearsay and if not within one of the exceptions, inadmissible. Why a different result should be reached where the policeman writes what the bystander said instead of testifying to it, is not readily apparent.

In analyzing the cases, however, it must be borne in mind that there are numerous exceptions to the hearsay rule and that an utterance, while not properly admitted under one exception, may very well be admitted under another.

> It should be recognized, of course, that apart from the business entry statutes there are numerous exceptions to the hearsay rule — e.g., those covering statements regarding present mental or physical conditions, admissions, declarations against interest, spontaneous declarations, or dying declarations. A record of volunteer hearsay may be admissible as proof of the facts stated where such an exception exists. Many cases which have loosely applied the business entry statutes to admit records to prove the truth of volunteer statements may well have reached a correct result on this ground. They have failed, however, to recognize explicitly that the statutes are applicable only in admitting the first step of hearsay, while the second step is admitted because a further exception wholly independent of business records rules is appropriate. 48 COLUM. L. REV. at 928-29.

[I]n *Chemical Leaman Tank Lines, Inc. v. Stevens*, 21 App. Div. 2d 556, 251 N.Y.S.2d 240 (3d Dept. 1964), an under-sheriff, acting in the regular course of his duties, made a report of an accident, quoting in the report what the defendant had said to him concerning her behavior just prior to the accident, which was at variance with her later testimony at trial. Though the statement in the report, made by the defendant, was that of a volunteer under no duty to impart the information, the trial court held the report admissible and the ruling was affirmed on appeal. To hold the entire record admissible to prove the truth of all the matters set forth therein, including the defendant's "volunteered" remarks, without an analysis of the contents and character of the declarant, is to undermine the decision in *Johnson v. Lutz, supra*, and to remove the very sound policy considerations lying behind the "duty of the declarant" requirement engrafted onto the statute by that case. The end result of admissibility, however, is the correct one, better placed on different and more solid ground.

Since the report was made in the ordinary course of the under-sheriff's business, and it was his business to record the defendant's statements, the report with the statements was admissible under [the business record rule] only to show that these statements were in fact made by the defendant if that is relevant. Once it is established that the defendant made the statement (a statement inconsistent with her position at trial), the substantive contents of the statement are admissible, not under [the business record rule] but rather under the admission exception to the hearsay rule.

It appears that the Business Records Act overcomes the initial hurdle to the admissibility of evidence, but goes no further. Thus the hearsay statement (of a volunteer) contained in the police officer's report is no more admissible than the testimony of the police officer on the stand as to the hearsay statement made at the scene of the accident. If the making of the statement itself is relevant, it can be proved both by the report, which is a record kept in the ordinary course of business, as well as by the in-Court testimony of the officer. However, if the report is offered to prove the truth of the statement contained therein, the statement must either have been made in the regular course of business of the person making it, or must have an independent ground of admissibility such as an admission, etc., the same as the in-Court testimony of the officer as to the statements made, offered to prove the truth of what was said, must have an independent ground of admissibility, since all that can be shown under the Business Records Act is that in the regular course of business of the officer he wrote that X made the following statement to prove the truth of the fact that X made the statement, not the truth of the facts contained in the statement.

Accordingly, without knowing who made the statements and under what circumstances they were made, an insufficient foundation has presently been laid upon which to admit the proffered report over objection. [On the question whether business records is the applicable rule for police reports under the Federal Rules of Evidence, or whether the public records rule trumps, see § 9.07, Notes, *infra* — Eds.]

We next proceed to the second class of proffered documents — the reports of various doctors who examined plaintiff.

As appears in the pre-trial order filed herein the plaintiff, who was injured in the course of his employment, made a claim in workmen's compensation for the same injuries arising from the same occurrence as is the subject of this suit. The Liberty Mutual Insurance Company was the insurance carrier for Charles Noeding Trucking Co. Inc., in connection with that claim and was and is the insurance carrier for defendant Knickerbocker Dispatch, Inc.

In accordance with the regular procedure under the Workmen's Compensation Law, reports were submitted by certain physicians to the Insurance Company as well as to the Workmen's Compensation Board. Plaintiff wishes to introduce the reports of Doctors Youmans, Guthrie, Lewis, Fleck and Richman into evidence in lieu of calling them as witnesses, and has requested a pre-trial ruling as to their admissibility.

[A]ll the parties agreed as to the authenticity of the medical reports which are now being proffered. It further appears from the reports themselves, and it can very easily be verified, that Doctors Guthrie and Youmans examined plaintiff on behalf of Liberty Mutual Insurance Company, that Doctor Richman examined plaintiff on behalf of Interboro Mutual Indemnity Insurance Company, and that Doctors Fleck and Lewis were plaintiff's treating physicians. Accordingly, the reports have been sufficiently authenticated.

That the [reports were] prepared in the ordinary course of the business of [the] doctors is indicated by *White v. Zutell*, 263 F.2d 613 (2d Cir. 1959), which involved a medical report made by a specialist who had examined the plaintiff on behalf of the defendant's insurance carrier.

In sustaining the admissibility of the report, the Court stated:

> The making of this report was clearly a part of this specialist's "business"; indeed that is what he was commissioned to do. And it bears its own inherent guaranty of being what it purports to be — a detailed report

> of what he found medically upon examining the subject. That it might come up in the course of litigation does not affect this guaranty, unless to enhance it; what would be the use of such a report except to aid in fixing legal damage?

As stated in McCormick, "[W]ell reasoned modern decisions have admitted in accident cases the written reports of doctors of their findings from an examination of the injured party when it appears that is the doctor's professional routine or duty to make such report." But, it is argued, all the doctors' reports were prepared specifically for litigation (whether before the Workmen's Compensation Board, or in this suit) and at a time when the motive to misrepresent was present and the reports thus lack the trustworthiness necessary to permit their introduction. *Palmer v. Hoffman*, 318 U.S. 109 (1943) is cited in support of this argument.

In *Palmer v. Hoffman, supra*, the Court was concerned with the likely untrustworthiness of materials prepared specifically by a prospective litigant for courtroom use and thus held that the mere fact of regularity of preparation would not in itself be enough to justify the use of the evidence. The Business Records Act was interpreted in *Palmer* as facilitating the "admission of records which experience has shown to be quite trustworthy."

Accordingly, what must be found in the case at bar is an added element of trustworthiness which will counterbalance the fact that these reports were prepared in clear anticipation of litigation. With respect to the reports of Doctors Guthrie and Youmans, this added element is present.

> In *Pekelis v. Transcontinental & W. Air Inc.*, 187 F.2d 122 (2d Cir. 1951), we held that the district court was erroneous in refusing to admit the plaintiff's offer of certain accident reports prepared by boards set up by the defendant airline to investigate the crash of one of defendant's airplanes. We interpreted the decision in *Palmer v. Hoffman* to exclude accident reports only when they were prepared for use in litigation or when there was other indicia of their untrustworthiness. The *Pekelis* reports, the court pointed out, were against the interest of the entrant when made, were clearly not part of a story cooked up in advance of litigation in the disguise of business records and were offered as evidence by the party opposing the one which had had the reports prepared.
>
> In *Korte v. New York, N.H. & H.R.R.*, 191 F.2d 86 (2d Cir.), *cert. denied*, 342 U.S. 867, 72 S. Ct. 109, 96 L.Ed. 652 (1951), another accident case, the district court had admitted certain doctors' reports, offered by the plaintiff, which had been prepared at the request of the defendant railroad. We affirmed the district court. Again, we pointed out that the decision in *Palmer v. Hoffman* was directed against the admission of hearsay evidence prepared for a litigious or other self-serving purpose. The court in *Korte* doubted whether the *Palmer v. Hoffman* rationale extended to reports made by independent doctors. Regardless of this, the *Korte* court stated that its holding could rest on *Pekelis*, where it had been held that reports offered by the party adverse to the party for whom the reports were prepared were admissible. *United States v. New York Foreign Trade Zone Operators*, 304 F.2d 792, 798 (2d Cir. 1962).

Thus the thrust of [these] opinions supports the admissibility of a doctor's report made in the regular course of business (when litigation was on the horizon) "when offered by one other than the entrant or one for whom the entrant is then working, i.e., the carrier." . . .

That other courts have refused to follow *Korte* . . . is not binding on this Court.

[The court adverts to three of the offered documents, written by the doctors, Youmans and Guthrie, who were employed by Liberty Mutual, the defendant's insurer, but which documents were favorable to plaintiff.] Thus in the case at bar the fact that litigation involving Liberty Mutual was pending when these three reports were made, if anything, enhances the trustworthiness of the documents, since it is the plaintiff, not the defendant, who seeks their introduction (i.e., the party whose interest is adverse to that of the party on whose behalf the reports were made).

In *White v. Zutell*, 263 F.2d 613 (2d Cir. 1959), the plaintiff was asked whether he had ever been examined by a Doctor Gilshannon, and the defendants conceded that Doctor Gilshannon "a doctor of [their] choosing" had examined the plaintiff and made a report to the defendants. The report was turned over to plaintiff, and based on the foregoing foundation, was offered [by plaintiff] into evidence "as an admission against interest" as well as "a document kept by them [the insurance carrier] in the regular course of business." [T]he report was admitted into evidence.

Defendants' doctors

Accordingly, I am inclined to overrule the objection to the reports of Doctors Youmans and Guthrie.

No case, however, has been found or cited wherein a plaintiff was permitted to introduce self-serving reports made by doctors of his own choosing, in anticipation of litigation, to shore up his own case. [Drs. Lewis and Fleck who wrote reports favorable to plaintiff were employed by plaintiff in the present case.]

The fact that the record is self-serving is, of course, not determinative if made in the ordinary course of business without a view toward litigation. As stated in the recent case of *Taylor v. Baltimore and Ohio R.R.*, 344 F.2d 281, 286 (2d Cir. 1965):

> The report here was made when, so far as the record shows, no one thought Taylor had suffered any serious injury . . . .

Thus the situation with respect to the reports of the doctors employed by plaintiff is different than that of defendant's doctors (Doctors Guthrie and Youmans) and warrants a different result, since statements by [plaintiff's doctors] would (if statements by defendant's doctors can be deemed admissions) be self-serving with no added degree of trustworthiness. They are thus statements made on behalf of a party by persons more inclined to favor that party's position, and the fact that they were made for the purposes of litigation causes me sufficient concern to refuse to admit them at this time . . . .

Accordingly, where, as here, there is no counterbalancing force to the desire to promote the self-interest of the party on whose behalf the report was made, discretion dictates that the objection at this time be sustained [to the reports of Drs. Lewis and Fleck offered by plaintiff] and plaintiff be required to call [to the witness stand for live testimony] Doctors Lewis and Fleck. Insofar as Doctor Richman is concerned, his status is not clear with respect to the parties involved in the litigation, and with respect to his report there may not be present this added element of trustworthiness. Therefore, I will place him in the group of doctors employed by plaintiff and hold his report at this time inadmissible as well.

NOTES AND QUESTIONS

(1) *Who Can Authenticate Business Records*? The rules do not require the testimony of the custodian or maker, so long as the witness is qualified. Some courts are strict in requiring actual knowledge of the business at issue. Some courts are quite liberal. *See United States v. Bueno-Sierra*, 99 F.3d 375 (11th Cir. 1996) (Asst. Chief of Port Operations permitted to establish foundation for berth requests that were filled out by shipping company), *cert. denied*, 520 U.S. 1161 (1997). Even though the witness need not know the details of the individual record or even of the entire process, the witness must have some personal knowledge of the predicate. For example, a business records foundation could not be established by a government agent with no knowledge of a bank's recordkeeping procedures. This absence of foundation also prohibited introduction of the records under the catchall exception or as summaries. *United States v. Pelullo*, 964 F.2d 193 (3d Cir. 1992). Similarly, the foundation for a urinalysis report of the National Health Laboratories could not be established by a probation officer. *See Chavous v. State*, 597 So. 2d 943 (Fla. Dist. Ct. App. 1992).

See also *United States v. Riley*, 236 F.3d 982 (8th Cir. 2001), holding that a police officer could not establish the foundation for a state crime lab report where he did not have personal knowledge of how the records were prepared or maintained.

(2) *Certification, Without a Witness.* If the person is qualified to lay the foundation for the business record, it can be laid by him either in person or by certification. See Fed. R. Evid. 902(11) and (12) and the reference thereto in Fed. R. Evid. 803(6). In either case (live testimony or certification) the information about the record supplied by the person will be the same. He will usually mirror (either orally on the stand, or in the certificate) the exact language that is in the authentication-by-certificate provisions, Rules 902(11) or (12). *See United States v. Wittig*, *infra*, § 11.03[B]. (Do you think these Rule 902 provisions should be limited to civil cases? Might they exacerbate any constitutional confrontation problem?) *See*, for a more thorough discussion of the provisions, note (3) following the *Trotter* case in § 12.01[C], *infra*.

(3) *Widespread Public Use: Does This Broaden the Category of Qualified Witnesses?* When the record is relied upon by the public or individuals in a particular occupation, Rule 803(17) may provide an alternative route to admissibility. For example, in *United States v. Woods*, 321 F.3d 361 (3d Cir. 2003), a federal carjacking trial, the evidence that a car was transported in interstate commerce (which is a required jurisdictional element), came from an FBI special agent who relied on the National Insurance Crime Bureau's (NICB) national database to determine that the car's unique VIN number came from a manufacturing plant in another state. Although the court noted that the witness was not a custodian of the records with personal knowledge of how the NICB compiles and maintains its database, the testimony was admissible under Rule 803(17), because there was evidence that the database is relied upon by those in the industry and by law

enforcement agencies. Could the problem have been sidestepped altogether by realizing the FBI agent was an expert? Or would the requirements have been the same?

(4) *Absence of an Entry as Showing an Event Did Not Occur.* For an interesting factual illustration of the operation of Fed. R. Evid. 803(7) (absence of business records), see *United States v. Zeidman*, 540 F.2d 314 (7th Cir. 1976) (failure to find checks defendant allegedly sent).

PROBLEM 9F: COMPARING THE RULE TO THE SUPREME COURT DRAFT.

The "Supreme Court" draft of Federal Rule of Evidence 803(6) that went to Congress and was modified by Congress into the present rule provided:

> **Records of regularly conducted activity.** A memorandum, report, record, or data compilation, in any form, of acts, events, conditions, opinions or diagnoses, made at or near the time by, or from information transmitted by, a person with knowledge, all in the course of a regularly conducted activity, as shown by the testimony of the custodian or other qualified witness, unless the sources of information or other circumstances indicate lack of trustworthiness.

Can you spot at least four significant changes that the present rule makes from this, affecting four important problems? Do you suppose they all were intentional? Was there a change that, perhaps unintentionally, affects the solution to the problem concerning the police report in *Yates v. Bair Transport, supra,* this section? Is the change from "regularly conducted activity" to "business" significant, in view of the expansive definition of business in the final enactment? (The change was in the body of the rule, not the title. Is that of any significance?)

PROBLEM SET 9G: HIGHLIGHTING VARIOUS ASPECTS OF BUSINESS RECORDS.

Each of the following problems concerns one or more aspects of the business record predicate.

(1) *Records of the Poker Club.* You wish to object to the records of a neighborhood poker club being introduced into evidence as business records under the Federal Rules of Evidence, to establish that Mr. X won such-and-such amount on such-and-such date, a fact concededly relevant to the lawsuit. The club does keep such records, and this is one. A member of the club who knows the club's recordkeeping will lay a foundation. You wish to object that the club is not a business. Will you succeed? What is a better way to put your objection?

(2) *The "One-Shot" Accident Report, Offered by the Company that Prepared It.* Suppose a company has an accident on its premises and institutes an accident investigation, which issues in a report. Assume there never has been an accident before, and therefore never has been an accident investigation report before. Thus, this report does not have the "routineness" or regularity (in the sense of repetitiveness) of sales reports. Under the common law, the requirement under the

business records rule often is phrased "done in the regular course of business" or the equivalent. Is there some significant variation in the phraseology of the Federal Rule that either would facilitate or hinder admission of the accident report?

(3) *Doctors' Reports to Lawyers or Insurers for Litigation or Insurance Purposes: "Business" Records?* In an auto collision personal injury case, the injured plaintiff's treating doctor has written a report for plaintiff's lawyer as to the cause, severity, and duration of plaintiff's injuries. The plaintiff also has visited another doctor, at the request of the defendant's insurance company. This other doctor also has written a report, for the insurance company. The former report strongly favors plaintiff. The latter report is strongly against plaintiff's position. Be prepared to argue the question of admissibility of each of these reports as business records. If there are additional facts you need to know, be prepared to say what they are and why they make a difference.

(4) *"Patient States He Twisted Ankle . . ."* Is the evidence in the following case (*Watts v. Delaware Coach Co.*, 58 A.2d 689 (Del. 1948)) admissible as a business record? Be prepared to argue both sides in the case if called on by the teacher to represent one or the other of the sides:

On the night of August 31, 1946, Plaintiff testified that he attempted to board a bus operated by Defendant which was standing at a regularly designated bus stop to receive passengers, and that, as he placed his foot upon the step, the door was closed on his ankle and the bus started, throwing him to the ground with a sharp twist to his ankle. There were no witnesses to the accident. Defendant, who did not deny the injury, defended upon the ground that Plaintiff was hurt, not in attempting to board its bus, but because he twisted his ankle while walking at or near the bus stop. In support of this contention, Defendant produced all six drivers who operated its buses along the particular route on the evening in question. All testified that no accident occurred as related by Plaintiff. Defendant then offered in evidence the records of the hospital where Plaintiff was treated which contained a statement purportedly made by Plaintiff that he had broken his ankle by twisting it while walking along the sidewalk. The hospital intern who treated Plaintiff for his injuries on the night in question was called to the stand to qualify the hospital report for admission.

Plaintiff's counsel strenuously objected to the admission of that part of the hospital record, containing the words "Patient states he twisted ankle while walking along street."

(5) *Critique the Court's Opinion.* The actual court decision in the problem above held the evidence admissible as a business record on the following grounds. Critique the opinion (*Watts v. Delaware Coach Co.*, 58 A.2d 689 (Del. 1948)):

> The rule running through the above cases seems clearly to be this — that admissions by patients regularly entered in hospital records (all other requirements of the Business Records Act having been met) may be received in evidence at a trial only if so related to the complaint or injury involved as to facilitate prompt and intelligent diagnosis and treatment.
>
> After careful thought I have decided that Plaintiff's statement appearing in the record in the case at Bar to the effect that he twisted his ankle while

> walking along the street was "pathologically germane," to borrow an apt expression of Mr. Justice Drew's, to the injury which necessitated his attendance at the hospital. It is reasonable to suppose that the words "while walking along the street" were sufficiently descriptive of the injury to aid the attending physician to some extent in diagnosing and treating the fracture. The knowledge that the injury had occurred from a twist while walking ruled out the possibility of the ankle having been crushed. Though aware that the proposition is debatable, I am now inclined to the view that the statement was properly recorded *within the scope of hospital business.* [Emphasis added.]

(6) *Business Record that Originates from Persons Outside the Business.* Defendant is charged with mailing obscene matter through the U.S. mails on a number of occasions. The government attempts to introduce the records of the Post Office to establish the dates, that the mailings occurred, and the general nature of the mailings. Some of the records consist of envelopes sent to the Post Office (on which private citizens had jotted down what came in the envelope, and the dates received, pursuant to Post Office policy to request citizens who make complaints of this nature to do so; the envelopes then are put in a special file by the Post Office). Some of the other records consist of Post Office forms filled in by Post Office employees while talking on the telephone to customers making complaints, recording the date the mailing was received and the nature of the material. This also is Post Office policy. In addition, similar forms occasionally are filled in by customers of the Post Office who dropped in to post offices to make their complaints. Post Office policy also permits this. May all these records be introduced as business records? (Or as government records; see Fed. R. Evid. 803(8)? What is the relationship between the two rules?) *See United States v. Pent-R-Books, Inc.*, 538 F.2d 519 (2d Cir. 1976), *cert. denied*, 430 U.S. 906 (1977); *cf. United States v. Cestnik*, 36 F.3d 904 (10th Cir. 1994) (computerized money transfers were admissible, where Western Union verified identity of transfer recipients, but motel records of guest names were not admissible because no evidence motel verified identity of guests), *cert. denied*, 513 U.S. 1175 (1995).

(7) *Opinions or Diagnoses.* To establish the nature and cause of plaintiff's injury in a personal injury action, the plaintiff offers a portion of what is admitted to be a properly prepared and maintained hospital record concerning his case when he was hospitalized with the injury. There is no dispute that the particular entry was made in the regular course of hospitalization by authorized hospital personnel and was germane to his treatment. There is no claim that the portion is out of context. The portion reads:

> The patient suffered a papilledema of the left optic disc of about two diopters. Dr. Hutchings believes that the condition resulted from a fracture of the base of the skull, and some left optic nerve pressure. There is considerable dispute among the doctors, including some who treated him, as to whether plaintiff suffered a skull fracture, and it is not agreed that a fracture produces this condition.

Is the evidence admissible under a business records rule that provides that a business record may report: (a) only "acts, transactions, occurrences, events, or conditions"; or (b) "opinions and diagnoses [as well as the other things]"? Is the business records rule the only concern?

This problem is based on *Loper v. Andrews*, 404 S.W.2d 300 (Tex. 1966) (excluding evidence, based on since-superseded rule that omitted opinions and diagnoses, which the current Texas Rule and the Fed. R. Evid. both admit, contrary to some state rules). The decision divides opinions into a range, with those that are relatively certain, like a diagnosis of a broken bone, at the "admissible" end, and those that are more subject to debate, like whether trauma causes cancer, at the "inadmissible" end. The general problem dealt with by *Loper*, i.e., expert opinion in hearsay form, comes up under many hearsay exceptions (Fed. R. Evid. 803(6) (business records), Fed. R. Evid. 803(8)(C) (government records and reports), and Fed. R. Evid. 803(18) (learned articles and treatises), to name just a few).

§ 9.07 PUBLIC RECORDS[15]

Read Federal Rules of Evidence 803(8), "Hearsay Exceptions — Regardless of Whether the Declarant is Available as a Witness: Public Records" and (10), "Absence of a Public Record."

BEECH AIRCRAFT CORP. v. RAINEY

United States Supreme Court
488 U.S. 153 (1988)

JUSTICE BRENNAN DELIVERED THE OPINION OF THE COURT.

In this action we address a longstanding conflict among the Federal Courts of Appeals over whether Federal Rule of Evidence 803(8)(C), which provides an exception to the hearsay rule for public investigatory reports containing "factual findings," extends to conclusions and opinions contained in such reports.

I

[Respondents' spouses were killed when their Navy aircraft banked sharply to avoid another plane, lost altitude, and crashed. Respondents brought a product liability suit against Beech and others. The principal issue at trial was whether the crash resulted from a stall due to pilot error, as defendants contended, or whether it was caused by a "rollback" (or loss of engine power) due to a defect in the fuel control system, as plaintiffs claimed.

The trial judge admitted into evidence, after finding it to be sufficiently trustworthy, a Navy investigative report done by the office of the Judge Advocate General (the "JAG Report") pursuant to the JAG's legal duty. The Report was organized into sections labeled "finding[s] of fact," "opinions," and "recommendations," with some 60 attachments. Although the Report stated that it was "almost

---

[15] Study Guide Reference: Evidence in a Nutshell, Chapter 10:II at "Government Records and Reports: F.R.E. 803(8) ('Public Records and Reports')" (including all subdivisions) and at "Absence of an Entry in a Record: F.R.E. 803(7) and (10)."

impossible to determine exactly what happened" because of the destruction of the craft and death of the pilots, the principal investigator, Commander Morgan, set out a detailed possible reconstruction of the events leading to the crash. The admitted evidence, over Respondents' objection, contained most of the Report's evaluative conclusions, including a statement in the "opinion" section suggesting that the most probable cause of the accident was pilot error: "The most probable cause . . . was the pilot[s'] failure to maintain proper interval." The "opinions" also contained the caveat that there remained "the possibility that a 'rollback' did occur." As for Captain Morgan's detailed reconstruction, however, the trial judge excluded most of it as "nothing but a possible scenario."

The Eleventh Circuit reversed. Following its earlier decision in *Smith v. Ithaca Corp.*, 612 F.2d 215 (1980), it held that the reference to "factual findings" in Rule 803(C) did not encompass mere evaluative conclusions or opinions. The Supreme Court here reverses the reversal and holds that the opinions in the JAG Report were properly admitted (although it upholds the requirement of a new trial based on an unrelated issue).]

II

Controversy over what "public records and reports" are made not excludable by Rule 803(8)(C) has divided the federal courts from the beginning. In the present litigation, the Court of Appeals followed the "narrow" interpretation [w]hich held that the term "factual findings" did not encompass "opinions" or "conclusions." Courts of Appeals other than those of the Fifth and Eleventh Circuits, however, have generally adopted a broader interpretation. For example, the Court of Appeals for the Sixth Circuit, in *Baker v. Elcona Homes Corp.*, 588 F.2d 551, 557-558 (1978), held that "factual findings admissible under Rule 803(8)(C) may be those which are made by the preparer of the report from disputed evidence . . . ." [W]e agree and hold that factually based conclusions or opinions are not on that account excluded from the scope of Rule 803(8)(C).

Because the Federal Rules of Evidence are a legislative enactment, we turn to the "traditional tools of statutory construction" in order to construe their provisions. We begin with the language of the Rule itself. Proponents of the narrow view have generally relied heavily on a perceived dichotomy between "fact" and "opinion" in arguing for the limited scope of the phrase "factual findings." *Smith v. Ithaca Corp.* contrasted the term "factual findings" in Rule 803(8)(C) with the language of Rule 803(6) (records of regularly conducted activity), which expressly refers to "opinions" and "diagnoses." "Factual findings," the court opined, must be something other than opinions.

For several reasons, we do not agree. In the first place, it is not apparent that the term "factual findings" should be read to mean simply "facts" (as opposed to "opinions" or "conclusions"). A common definition of "finding of fact" is, for example, "[a] conclusion by way of reasonable inference from the evidence." Blacks Law Dictionary 569 (5th ed. 1979). [S]econd, we note that, contrary to what is often assumed, the language of the Rule does not state that "factual findings" are admissible, but that "*reports* . . . setting forth . . . factual findings" (emphasis added) are admissible. On this reading, the language of the Rule does not create a distinction between "fact" and "opinion" contained in such reports.

Turning next to the legislative history of Rule 803(8)(C), we find no clear answer to the question of how the Rule's language should be interpreted. [R]ather than the more usual situation where a court must attempt to glean meaning from ambiguous comments of legislators who did not focus directly on the problem at hand, here the Committees in both Houses of Congress clearly recognized and expressed their opinions on the precise question at issue. Unfortunately, however, they took diametrically opposite positions.

The House Judiciary Committee, which dealt first with the proposed rules after they had been transmitted to Congress by this Court, included in its Report but one brief paragraph on Rule 803(8):

> The Committee approved Rule 803(8) without substantive change from the form in which it was submitted by the Court. The Committee intends that the phrase 'factual findings' be strictly construed and that evaluations or opinions contained in public reports shall not be admissible under this Rule.

The Senate Committee responded at somewhat greater length, but equally emphatically:

> The House Judiciary Committee report contained a statement of intent that 'the phrase "factual findings" in subdivision (c) be strictly construed and that evaluations or opinions contained in public reports shall not be admissible under this rule.' The committee takes strong exception to this limiting understanding of the application of the rule. We do not think it reflects an understanding of the intended operation of the rule as explained in the Advisory Committee notes to this subsection . . . . We think the restrictive interpretation of the House overlooks the fact that while the Advisory Committee assumes admissibility in the first instance of evaluative reports, they are not admissible if, as the rule states, 'the sources of information or other circumstances indicate lack of trustworthiness.'
>
> The committee concludes that the language of the rule together with the explanation provided by the Advisory Committee furnish sufficient guidance on the admissibility of evaluative reports.

[I]t seems clear however that the Senate understanding is more in accord with the wording of the Rule and with the comments of the Advisory Committee.

The Advisory Committee's comments are notable, first, in that they contain no mention of any dichotomy between statements of "fact" and "opinions" or "conclusions." What was on the Committee's mind was simply whether what it called "evaluative reports" should be admissible. Illustrating the previous division among the courts on this subject, the Committee cited numerous cases [and statutes] in which the admissibility of such reports had been both sustained and denied. [W]hat is striking about all of these examples is that these were *reports that stated conclusions. E.g., Moran v. Pittsburgh-Des Moines Steel Co.*, 183 F.2d 467, 472–473 (CA3 1950) (report of Bureau of Mines concerning the cause of a gas tank explosion admissible); *Franklin v. Skelly Oil Co.*, 141 F.2d 568, 571-572 (CA10 1944) (report of state fire marshal on the cause of a gas explosion inadmissible); 42 U.S.C. § 269(b) (bill of health by appropriate official admissible as prima facie evidence of vessel's sanitary history and condition). [N]owhere in its comments is there the slightest indication that [the Committee] even considered the solution of admitting only "factual" statements from such reports. [W]hat the Committee referred to in the Rule's language as "reports . . . setting forth . . . factual findings" is surely nothing more or less than what in its commentary it called "evaluative reports." Its solution as to their admissibility is clearly stated in the final paragraph of its report on this Rule. That solution consists of two principles: First, "the rule . . . assumes admissibility in the first instance . . . ." Second, it provides "ample provision for escape if sufficient negative factors are present."

That "provision for escape" is contained in the final clause of the Rule: evaluative reports are admissible "unless the sources of information or other circumstances indicate lack of trustworthiness." This trustworthiness inquiry — and not an arbitrary distinction between "fact" and "opinion" — was the Committee's primary safeguard against the admission of unreliable evidence, and it is important to note that it applies to all elements of the report. Thus, a trial judge has the discretion, and indeed the obligation, to exclude an entire report or portions thereof — whether narrow "factual" statements or broader "conclusions" — that she determines to be untrustworthy.[11] Moreover, safeguards built into other portions of the Federal Rules, such as those dealing with relevance and prejudice, provide the court with additional means of scrutinizing and, where appropriate, excluding evaluative reports or portions of them. And of course it goes without saying that the admission of a report containing "conclusions" is subject to the ultimate safeguard — the opponent's right to present evidence tending to contradict or diminish the weight of those conclusions.

Our conclusion that neither the language of the Rule nor the intent of its framers calls for a distinction between "fact" and "opinion" is strengthened by the analytical difficulty of drawing such a line. It has frequently been remarked that the distinction between statements of fact and opinion is, at best, one of degree:

> All statements in language are statements of opinion, i.e., statements of mental processes or perceptions. So-called 'statements of fact' are only more specific statements of opinion. What the judge means to say, when he asks the witness to state the facts, is: 'The nature of this case requires that you be more specific, if you can, in your description of what you saw.'

In the present action, the trial court had no difficulty in admitting as a factual

---

[11] The Advisory Committee proposed a nonexclusive list of four factors it thought would be helpful in passing on this question: (1) the timeliness of the investigation; (2) the investigator's skill or experience; (3) whether a hearing was held; and (4) possible bias when reports are prepared with a view to possible litigation.

In a case similar in many respects to these, the trial court applied the trustworthiness requirement to hold inadmissible a JAG Report on the causes of a Navy airplane accident; it found the report untrustworthy because it "was prepared by an inexperienced investigator in a highly complex field of investigation." *Fraley v. Rockwell Int'l Corp.*, 470 F.Supp. 1264, 1267 (S.D. Ohio 1979). In the present litigation, the District Court found the JAG Report to be trustworthy. As no party has challenged that finding, we have no occasion to express an opinion on it.

finding the statement in the JAG Report that "[a]t the time of impact, the engine of 3E955 was operating but was operating at reduced power." Surely this "factual finding" could also be characterized as an opinion, which the investigator presumably arrived at on the basis of clues contained in the airplane wreckage. Rather than requiring that we draw some inevitably arbitrary line between the various shades of fact/opinion that invariably will be present in investigatory reports, we believe the Rule instructs us — as its plain language states — to admit "reports . . . setting forth . . . factual findings." The Rule's limitations and safeguards lie elsewhere: First, the requirement that reports contain factual findings bars the admission of statements not based on factual investigation. Second, the trustworthiness provision requires the court to make a determination as to whether the report, or any portion thereof, is sufficiently trustworthy to be admitted.

A broad approach to admissibility under Rule 803(8)(C), as we have outlined it, is also consistent with the Federal Rules' general approach of relaxing the traditional barriers to "opinion" testimony. [W]e see no reason to strain to reach an interpretation of Rule 803(8)(C) that is contrary to the liberal thrust of the Federal Rules.

III

[The Court holds, however, that after Beech had offered defensive portions of a particular letter written by Rainey, the trial judge erred in disallowing Rainey from introducing and explaining other parts of the same letter, pursuant to the completeness doctrine in Rule 106.]

NOTES AND QUESTIONS

(1) *Police and Other Reports Prepared "With an Eye Toward Litigation:" To What Extent Are They Admissible, for the Prosecution or for the Defense? United States v. Smith*, 521 F.2d 957 (D.C. Cir. 1975), concerned police department reports containing an identification of the assailant by the victim that was inconsistent with the victim's testimony. The trial judge refused to admit the document, but allowed the defense to use it to refresh recollection. On appeal, the Court agreed that exclusion was error:

> We hasten to specify the limits of our decision. We do not hold that a police record is admissible in a criminal proceeding as a business record, either as substantive evidence or for impeachment purposes, whenever the record meets the test of trustworthiness. We hold only that such a record is so admissible when offered by a criminal defendant to support his defense. We do not believe that such records may properly be so employed by the prosecution. While confrontation clause values figure in our reasoning, the primary basis for the distinction is the "litigation records" doctrine of *Palmer v. Hoffman*, 318 U.S. 109 (1943). In *Palmer* the Supreme Court affirmed a ruling by the Second Circuit that an accident report prepared by a since-deceased railroad engineer and offered by the railroad in its defense in a grade-crossing collision case did not qualify as a business record since the report was "dripping with motivations to misrepresent." 2 Cir., 129 F.2d

976, 991 (1942). The doctrine has since been applied to deny the business records exception to any document prepared with an eye toward litigation when offered by the party responsible for making the record.

In many cases where police records are offered, the litigation is civil in nature and between private parties. Thus the record has not been prepared at the behest of either party, the *Palmer* problem does not arise, and the records are routinely admitted. Where the police records are offered by the prosecution in criminal cases, there are two independent lines of cases. In one series of cases police records have been treated as admissible business records and the *Palmer* issue has not been raised. The second line of cases excludes under the *Palmer* doctrine the use of police records when offered by the prosecution, apparently without recognizing that police records may qualify as business records.

"Police reports are ordinarily excluded when offered by the party at whose instance they were made," but may still be admitted as business records when, as here, they are offered against that party, the prosecution, or any other party. Thus despite the limitations *Palmer* imposes on the business records doctrine, we have no doubt that the police records offered by appellant were admissible against the prosecution as business records.

How does this square with the exclusion in Fed. R. Evid. 803(8)(B) in criminal cases for matters observed by police officers? Does the language of the rule distinguish between use by prosecutors and defendants? *Smith* mentions the Federal Rules but applies previous law, under which police reports were treated under business records doctrine.

(2) *Can Police Reports Be Used Against Defendant as Business Records Under 803(6), Instead of Government Records Under 803(8)?* The excerpt from *Smith* in (1) would prohibit the prosecutor's use of Fed. R. Evid. 803(6) to admit police reports because they are litigation documents. *United States v. Oates*, 560 F.2d 45 (2d Cir. 1977), relied on the legislative history of the law enforcement exclusion in Fed. R. Evid. 803(8)(B) to reach the same result:

As already mentioned, Representative William Hungate, in presenting the report of the Committee of Conference to the House of Representatives, left no doubt that it was the belief of the Committee of Conference that under the new Federal Rules of Evidence the effect of FRE 803(8)(B) and (C) was to render law enforcement reports and evaluative reports inadmissible against defendants in criminal cases. It is thus clear that the only way to construe FRE 803(6) [the business record rule] so that it is reconcilable with this intended effect is to interpret FRE 803(6) and the other hearsay exceptions in such a way that police and evaluative reports not satisfying the standards of FRE 803(8)(B) and (C) may not qualify for admission under FRE 803(6) or any of the other exceptions to the hearsay rule.

Even if the remarks of Representatives Hungate and Dennis were not as clear as they are, we could still reach the same conclusion that, in view of the articulated purpose behind the narrow drafting of FRE 803 in general

> and FRE 803(8) in particular, FRE 803(6) must be read in conjunction with FRE 803(8)(B) and (C). Specifically, the pervasive fear of the draftsmen and of Congress that interference with an accused's right to confrontation would occur was the reason why in criminal cases evaluative reports of government agencies and law enforcement reports were expressly denied the benefit to which they might otherwise be entitled under FRE 803(8). It follows that this explanation of the reason for the special treatment of evaluative and law enforcement reports under FRE 803(8) applies with equal force to the treatment of such reports under any of the other exceptions to the hearsay rule. The prosecution's utilization of any hearsay exception to achieve admission of evaluative and law enforcement reports would serve to deprive the accused of the opportunity to confront his accusers as effectively as would reliance on a "public records" exception. Thus, there being no apparent reason why Congress would tolerate the admission of evaluative and law enforcement reports by use of some other exception to the hearsay rule (for example, the "business records" exception of FRE 803(6) or the "open-ended" exceptions of FRE 803(24) or 804(b)(5) [now 807]), it simply makes no sense to surmise that Congress ever intended that these records could be admissible against a defendant in a criminal case under any of the Federal Rules of Evidence's exceptions to the hearsay rule.

The *Oates* position that no end run can be made around the law enforcement exclusion has met with considerable resistance. *See, e.g.*, *United States v. Hayes*, 861 F.2d 1225 (10th Cir. 1988) (admitting hearsay seemingly barred by Fed. R. Evid. 803(8)(B) under Fed. R. Evid. 803(6)). Use of police reports as recorded recollection (Fed. R. Evid. 803(5)) has been well received because the officer is testifying, thereby alleviating Confrontation Clause concerns. *See United States v. Sawyer*, 607 F.2d 1190 (7th Cir. 1979), *cert. denied*, 445 U.S. 943 (1980). Is the *Oates* doctrine contrary to the usual notion that hearsay exceptions are cumulative? Does the cumulative notion apply to Fed. R. Evid. 807 when evidence fails the test of some other hearsay exception?

(3) *What is a "Law Enforcement" Report; Is a Chemist's Lab Report Included?* Another question is how broadly to interpret "law enforcement" in applying the Fed. R. Evid. 803(8)(B) exclusion. *Oates* barred the use of a chemist's report. Other decisions have viewed law enforcement more narrowly, allowing such reports. In addition, a number of courts have interpreted the exclusion as not applying to routine non-adversarial reports regardless of whether made by law enforcement personnel or whether they provide critical evidence against a criminal defendant. For example, *United States v. Grady*, 544 F.2d 598 (2d Cir. 1976), creates an unwritten exception for "routine lists" kept by police of the serial numbers of weapons found in Northern Ireland, which were admitted to prove defendant had illegally exported some of them from the U.S. and made false entries about them in federal firearms records. *See also United States v. Brown*, 9 F.3d 907 (11th Cir. 1993) (police department's receipt for gun), *cert. denied*, 513 U.S. 852 (1994); *United States v. Orozco*, 590 F.2d 789 (9th Cir. 1979) (computer cards of license plates observed passing border); *United States v. Quezada*, 754 F.2d 1190 (5th Cir. 1985) (INS form showing defendant was arrested and deported). Confrontation Clause

concerns raised by admission of such records will be considered in Chapter 11, where we will learn that the new "testimonial" approach to the Confrontation Clause seems to raise significant questions about the prosecutorial use of records that are created by law enforcement. *See particularly* § 11.03[B].

(4) *The Trustworthiness Proviso: What Kinds of Reports Does It Cover?* Does the trustworthiness requirement appearing at the end of Fed. R. Evid. 803(8) apply to all three classes of records embraced by the rule or just the last? *See Melville v. American Home Assur. Co.*, 443 F. Supp. 1064 (E.D. Pa. 1977), *rev'd on other grounds*, 584 F.2d 1306 (3d Cir. 1978) (trustworthiness requirement applies only to the last category, but if hearsay arguably fits it and another category, it should be classified as requiring trustworthiness). Rule 803(8) of the Uniform Rules of Evidence specifically requires trustworthiness for each category of public records and reports. Whether or not trustworthiness is a stated criterion, does Fed. R. Evid. 403 impose such a condition on all three classes of documents? *See, e.g., Distaff, Inc. v. Springfield Contracting Corp.*, 984 F.2d 108 (4th Cir. 1993) (noting report could be excluded based on Fed. R. Evid. 403); *Coleman v. Home Depot, Inc.*, 306 F.3d 1333 (3d Cir. 2002) (Becker J., affirms exclusion of an Equal Opportunity Commission letter of determination, pursuant to 403). *Cf. In the Matter of Oil Spill by the Amoco Cadiz off the Coast of France*, 954 F.2d 1279 (7th Cir. 1992) (admitting report made for litigation).

(5) *Is Exclusion for Untrustworthiness an Exception that Places the Burden of Proof on the Opponent?* Which party has the burden on the trustworthiness issue? *See In re Air Disaster at Lockerbie Scotland*, 37 F.3d 804 (2d Cir. 1994) (plain language of rule establishes general admissibility, unless report is deemed untrustworthy), *cert. denied*, 513 U.S. 1126 (1995). Thus, a court cannot cursorily reject a report as untrustworthy. *See Montiel v. City of Los Angeles*, 2 F.3d 335 (9th Cir. 1993) (remanding for review of Christopher Commission Report concerning Los Angeles riot).

(6) *Does the Government Records Exception Require a Source with Personal Knowledge?* Does Fed. R. Evid. 803(8) permit multiple hearsay regardless of the source, unlike Fed. R. Evid. 803(6)? *Amoco Cadiz*, referenced in (4), would answer affirmatively, but this is still an open question in other circuits or other applications.

(7) *Is There any Law Enforcement Exclusion in Rule 803(10)?* Does Fed. R. Evid. 803(10) contain any implied restriction for records of police or other law enforcement personnel? Even the Second Circuit, which is bound by *Oates*, refused to extend this ban. *See United States v. Yakobov*, 712 F.2d 20 (2d Cir. 1983). Can this raise any Confrontation Clause concerns when it is used in criminal cases to establish such key facts as the absence of any registration for a gun in a prosecution for illegal possession of a weapon? *See United States v. Hale*, 978 F.2d 1016 (8th Cir. 1992) (answering this question in the negative). *But consider* § 11.03[B], *infra*.

PROBLEM SET 9H: POLICE OFFICERS' OR INSURANCE REGULATORS' REPORTS IN DIFFERENT CASE SETTINGS.

In a negligence action for wrongful death, the plaintiff offers portions of a report by Officer Lauren Norder, who arrived at the scene within 15 minutes and has extensive training and experience in accident investigation, to the effect that (1) her activities included taking measurements of all skid marks, (2) she observed that the weather was clear, and (3) she concluded that "the most likely cause of the accident was that [defendant's] Buick entered the intersection against a red light."

(a) *Civil Suit Admissibility.* What is the likelihood that Officer Norder's report properly can be admitted in this civil suit?

(b) *Civil Suit Admissibility with Trustworthiness Issues.* Now, assume that Officer Norder is a probationary officer with some but not extensive training, and the victim was a police officer with whom she was acquainted. The trial judge has announced his intention to admit items (1) and (2), and possibly item (3), before the jury. What is the likelihood that this ruling is reversible error?

(c) *Criminal Prosecution.* Now, assume that Officer Norder is experienced and unbiased, but the report is offered by the prosecution in a criminal trial for negligent homicide. Does this criminal-case setting change the likelihood of error if the trial judge admits the three items?

(d) *Criminal Case; Separate Investigative Agency.* Would your answer change in the criminal setting if the report were made by a different governmental agency — e.g., by investigators of the State Department of Insurance, whose purpose is to determine whether defendant should be placed in the assigned risk pool (implying higher insurance rates) or to forfeit his driver's license?

PROBLEM SET 9I: SEC REPORT, OFFERED LATER IN A PRIVATE SECURITIES SUIT.

After an investigation, the SEC renders a decision that Lance Lawyer, an attorney, wrongfully participated in his client's decision to omit a material fact from a registration statement. On appeal, the finding is sustained, and the Supreme Court denies certiorari.

In a subsequent private suit against Lance Lawyer by investors for damages under the Securities and Exchange laws, may a shareholder introduce the SEC decision into evidence in support of his case against Lance to show (a) that a material fact was omitted, and (b) that Lance was among those responsible for the omission? [We do not treat here the very real possibility that Lawyer violated the Code of Professional Responsibility and the role, if any, that might play in this litigation.]

§ 9.08 MISCELLANEOUS OTHER HEARSAY EXCEPTIONS[17]

Fed. R. Evid. 803 includes a number of minor hearsay exceptions. Several concern family, religious, and property records. You should read through all the hearsay exceptions in Rule 803, even those we have not covered. The following exceptions should be specially noted:

---

[17] Study Guide Reference: Evidence in a Nutshell, Chapter 10:II at "Miscellaneous Rule 803 Hearsay Exceptions."

Fed. R. Evid. 803(16), Statements in ancient documents. The rule lowered the common-law requirement that documents be in existence for 30 years, to 20 years. A separate Fed. R. Evid. 901(b)(8) provides for authentication of ancient documents. *See* § 12.01, *infra.*

Fed. R. Evid. 803(17), Market reports, commercial publications. This rule often is used in business litigation and provides for introduction of all types of published compilations generally used and relied upon by the public or persons in particular occupations. *See also United States v. Woods*, 321 F.3d 361 (3d Cir. 2003), where the information used to ascertain that a car was transported in interstate commerce (a required jurisdictional element for the crime charged) came from a National Insurance Crime Bureau's (NICB's) national database that maintained lists of vehicle identification numbers correlated with place of manufacture of the vehicles. The NICB database was shown to be widely relied upon by various organizations and thus was held to be within 803(17).

Fed. R. Evid. 803(18), Learned treatises. This hearsay exception is considered in the concluding notes to § 5.06 *supra* because of its relationship to the older rule that treatises and articles could be used to impeach experts (and only for that purpose).

Fed. R. Evid. 803(21), Reputation as to character. This hearsay exception provides for the admission of character evidence, which is permitted by Fed. R. Evid. 404(a), Fed. R. Evid. 405(a), and Fed. R. Evid. 608(a). See the sections in other chapters, *supra*, that related to those rules.

Fed. R. Evid. 803(22), Judgment of previous conviction. *See United States v. Sutton*, 732 F.2d 1483 (10th Cir. 1984) (no hearsay exception for judgments of acquittal), *cert. denied*, 469 U.S. 1157 (1985); *United States v. Diaz*, 936 F.2d 786 (5th Cir. 1991) (misdemeanor convictions of nonparties could not establish their status as illegal aliens). *Cf. Hancock v. Dodson*, 958 F.2d 1367 (6th Cir. 1992).

Chapter 10

THE "WEAK" HEARSAY EXCEPTIONS

HEARSAY EXCEPTIONS THAT DEPEND ON UNAVAILABILITY OF DECLARANT (F.R.E. ARTICLE VIII, RULE 804)

§ 10.01 DEFINING UNAVAILABILITY OF DECLARANT[1]

Read Federal Rule of Evidence 804(a), "Hearsay Exceptions — Declarant Unavailable: Criteria for Being Unavailable."

WARREN v. UNITED STATES

District of Columbia Court of Appeals
436 A.2d 821 (1981)

KELLY, ASSOCIATE JUDGE.

[Appellant Warren was convicted of kidnapping, rape while armed, armed robbery, assault with intent to commit sodomy, and assault with a dangerous weapon.]

Over a period of eight months, a dozen women reported that they were kidnapped by persons riding in a green Chevrolet Vega or similar car and that they were sexually assaulted by their abductors. The jury found appellant guilty. [A]ppellant's convictions were reversed.

Before his retrial the government moved to introduce the transcripts of the prior trial testimony of complaining witnesses Sharon Williams, Debra Waters, Marilyn Reed and Linda Jenkins.

[The judge] rule[d] admissible the prior testimony of all of the complainants except Linda Jenkins, determining that Sharon Williams had died in an unrelated incident since the first trial, that Debra Waters could not be found, and that Marilyn Reed was "psychologically unavailable."

The government presented the prior testimony of the three female complainants by having secretaries from the United States Attorney's office play the role of the complainants. The prosecutor read the questions asked by the government at the first trial and the secretary responded by reading the complainant's answers. The secretaries also read the questions asked by the attorneys for appellant and his codefendant, and the witnesses' answers upon cross-examination. Portions of

---

[1] Study Guide Reference: Evidence in a Nutshell, Chapter 10:III at "The Definition of Unavailability: F.R.E. 804(a)."

testimony from a pretrial hearing on a motion to suppress identifications were read in a similar manner to the jury.

Appellant was convicted.

First, appellant contends that it was error to allow the prior trial testimony of complainants Marilyn Reed and Debra Waters to be read to the jury at his retrial.

The common law of this jurisdiction recognizes that prior recorded testimony is admitted into evidence as an exception to the hearsay rule when

> (1) the direct testimony of the declarant is unavailable, (2) the former testimony was given under oath or affirmation in a legal proceeding, (3) the issues in the two proceedings were substantially the same, and (4) the party against whom the testimony now is offered had the opportunity to cross-examine the declarant at the former proceedings.

Professor McCormick lists the following recognized categories of witness unavailability: death, absence, physical disability, mental incapacity (insanity), failure of memory, exercise of a privilege, refusal to testify and supervening disqualification, McCormick, Evidence § 253, at 609-12 (1972).

We are here asked to recognize a type of witness unavailability which, to our knowledge, has been expressly sanctioned in only two cases, one from California, and the other from New York. The courts in both cases have done so by interpreting codified rules of evidence defining medical unavailability to include, in California, a "then-existing physical or mental illness or infirmity," and in New York, inability to attend "by reason of insanity, sickness or infirmity."

In *People v. Gomez*, 103 Cal. Rptr. 80, 83-84 (Cal. App. 1972), the California statute was interpreted to require a showing that "the illness or infirmity must be of comparative severity; it must exist to such a degree as to render the witness' attendance, or his testifying, relatively impossible and not merely inconvenient." In *Gomez*, the witness' unavailability under this standard was established by two psychiatrists who testified that she was "very vulnerable to stress; she had a tendency to psychomotor seizures which were difficult to diagnose and treat" and that her present and future mental health might well be injured by testifying before the court.

The decision in *People v. Lombardi*, 39 App. Div. 2d 700, 701, 332 N.Y.S.2d 749, 750-51 (1972), *aff'd*, 303 N.E.2d 705 (1973), upheld a lower court finding that it would endanger the witness' health to testify again, where testimony by the witness' husband and her psychiatrist could reasonably have satisfied the court that had the witness "been required to appear and testify in person her mental and physical health would have been seriously jeopardized" and would have resulted in a "further and perhaps successful attempt at suicide." The witnesses in both the California and New York cases were rape victims.

Contrary to appellant's contentions it is our duty, as judges, to adapt the common law to reflect evolving norms and new circumstances, including new scientific and medical understanding, [thus] it is wise to look to other considered legislative and judicial judgments.

It is also useful to note Fed. R. Evid. 804(a)(4), and the corresponding Uniform Rule of Evidence, one or the other of which has been adopted by nineteen states, and which provide that a declarant is unavailable if he "is unable to be present or to testify at the hearing because of death, or then existing physical or mental illness or infirmity." (Emphasis added.) The only case of which we are aware applying the mental infirmity part of this definition is *United States v. Benfield*, 593 F.2d 815 (8th Cir. 1979), where appellant's conviction was reversed because of a violation of his Sixth Amendment right to confront the government's witness face-to-face. On testimony by a psychiatrist that the witness should not be required to endure a trial situation or to face her kidnapper because of her mental condition, the lower court agreed to allow the witness to testify at a videotaped deposition instead, later to be introduced at trial, at which defendant's counsel, but not the defendant, would be present. The defendant was allowed to observe the proceedings on a monitor and interrupt them to summon his lawyer. The witness, however, was kept unaware of the defendant's presence. The Court of Appeals in *Benfield* did not object to the finding of unavailability, but reversed on the basis of reliability. It found that the purpose of face-to-face encounter is to assure proper cross-examination by reinforcing the witness' recollection, veracity and communication. In the present case, unlike in *Benfield*, appellant's physical presence at the first trial when Marilyn Reed testified against him, satisfied this function.

In ruling as he did, [the trial judge in our case] cautiously extended the traditional definition of witness unavailability to include psychological unavailability of the type demonstrated in the case of Marilyn Reed, but to exclude the lesser degree of psychological infirmity demonstrated by Linda Jenkins. After evaluating the testimony of two psychiatrists, one of whom he personally appointed to obtain an independent, second opinion, he excused Reed from testifying because the experts agreed that she "would undergo far greater mental anguish than normally accompanies court appearances of the victims of rapes (and presumably other such crimes as kidnapping, terrorism, and hijacking) and that her appearance in court would be likely to lead to severe psychosis, even possible suicide."

We reject appellant's claim that the evidence does not support this finding. At the [first pretrial hearing on the matter], Dr. Leon Yochelson testified that Reed was suffering from a severe mixed psychoneurosis with particular emphasis on depressive mood, phobic reaction and anxiety. He found that the depth of her depression had reached suicidal levels and that suicidal tendencies were still present. Dr. Yochelson's testimony was based on two interviews as well as police reports and testimony from Marilyn Reed's prior court appearance.

Dr. Gray diagnosed Reed as suffering from a narcissistic personality disorder substantial enough to be considered a mental defect, and as vulnerable to transient psychosis as a result of stress. She informed Dr. Gray that she would rather be jailed for contempt than testify again. Dr. Gray found "there would be a small but very real risk that she would become temporarily psychotic as a result of testifying."

Dr. Gray did state that the risk of damage would be minimized if Reed's religious group were to actively support her in testifying against the defendant. The court was apparently not reassured. In disallowing introduction of the prior trial testimony of Linda Jenkins, the judge noted the experts' disagreement regarding the relative harm likely to be suffered by that witness in relation to the burden carried by the average victim-witness.

The ruling below was not only supported by the evidence, but was also a reasonable construction of the witness unavailability rule. We do not intend to sanction a new category of medical unavailability in all cases where witnesses are likely to suffer adverse emotional or psychological effects as a result of testifying against their assailants. But in the extreme circumstances presented here [as respects Reed, in contradistinction to Jenkins,] we agree that the grave risks to the witness' psychological health justify excusing her live in-court testimony.

The trial court's failure to request, sua sponte, an updated report of psychological health is supported by a reasonable presumption of continuing mental condition and by the necessity to both parties of obtaining a ruling on the admissibility of the prior testimony sufficiently in advance so that both sides might prepare for trial accordingly.

Appellant's challenge to the admission of Debra Waters' prior trial testimony also rests on a claim of improper timing. Since what must be established is the witness' unavailability at the time of trial, appellant contends that the court should have made a renewed finding of Waters' unavailability at the opening of his retrial, which was almost one year after testimony by Detective Virgil Hopkins about his unsuccessful attempts at locating the witness. The trial judge reasonably relied on a presumption that the status quo would remain unchanged, unless one of the parties suggested otherwise. Neither appellant, nor the government, whose good faith efforts to locate the witness must continue till the trial date, informed the court of a change in the status quo. The government had met its burden of showing Waters' unavailability and the evidence it presented left no hope that the witness might yet be located with the passage of time or by some other avenue of discovery.

[*Reversed on other grounds.*]

UNITED STATES v. SAMANIEGO & BAEZ

United States Court of Appeals, Eleventh Circuit
345 F.3d 1280 (2003)

CARNES, CIRCUIT JUDGE.

[The reader is referred to § 9.03, *supra*, for the facts of this case, involving the famous boxer Roberto Duran (Samaniego), and for disposition of the other hearsay exception involved in the case (Fed. R. Evid. 803(3), state of mind).]

Our conclusion that Iglesias's apology was not properly admitted under Rule 803(3) does not end the matter. Although the district court admitted the statement under Rule 803(3), Duran offered the testimony concerning the apology as a statement against interest by a declarant unavailable at trial, which is admissible under Rule 804(b)(3). The district court did not reach that alternative ground for admissibility, but we do because we will not hold that the district court abused its discretion where it reached the correct result even if it did so for the wrong reason.

Close v. United States, 336 F.3d 1283, 1285 n.1 (11th Cir. 2003) ("'We may not reverse a judgment of the district court if it can be affirmed on any ground, regardless of whether those grounds were used by the district court.'"). . . . The part of Iglesias's apology in which he admitted having stolen Duran's belts is a statement against interest, because it would "subject the declarant to civil or criminal liability" within the meaning of Rule 804(b)(3). For a statement against interest to be admissible under Rule 804, however, the declarant must have been unavailable at the time of the trial within the meaning of Rule 804(a).

Iglesias was not present at the trial, but that does not mean he was unavailable for Rule 804 purposes. Subsection (a) of that rule tells us a witness should be considered unavailable in five separate circumstances, only one of which is relevant in this case: The declarant is unavailable if he "is absent from the hearing and the proponent of a statement has been unable to procure the declarant's attendance (or in the case of a hearsay exception under subdivision (b)(2), (3), or (4), the declarant's attendance or testimony) by process or other reasonable means." Fed. R. Evid. 804(a)(5).

Duran could not procure Iglesias's attendance or testimony by process because Iglesias, a citizen of Panama, apparently was living in that country at the time of the trial, and "foreign nationals located outside the United States . . . are beyond the subpoena power of the district court." *United States v. Drogoul*, 1 F.3d 1546, 1553 (11th Cir. 1993). Duran did enlist the help of Iglesias's immediate family in an attempt to locate him and persuade him to return to the United States and testify. Iglesias's sister, who is Duran's wife, testified that she and her mother had tried to locate Iglesias on five different occasions, but finding him had proven impossible. Iglesias's mother testified that she had tried to contact him in order to get him to come back and testify but was unable to get Iglesias.

Using the efforts of Iglesias's sister and mother, as Duran did, is a reasonable means of attempting to locate Iglesias in Panama and persuade him to travel to the United States to testify. It follows that Duran did establish Iglesias was unavailable to testify under Rule 804(a)(5), so the out-of-court statement Iglesias made was admissible under Rule 804(b)(3) as a statement against interest. The district court did not abuse its discretion in admitting the statement, albeit on the wrong ground.

Affirmed.

PERRICONE v. KANSAS CITY S. R. CO.

United States Court of Appeals, Fifth Circuit
630 F.2d 317 (1980)

[Plaintiff driver brought action against defendant railroad in the Federal District Court in Beaumont, Texas for personal injuries and property loss sustained when plaintiff drove over defendant's railroad tracks. Plaintiff claimed defendant failed to keep the crossing in proper condition for public use and failed to warn drivers of the hazardous condition. A jury granted judgment to plaintiff and awarded substantial damages. The trial court denied defendant's motion for a new trial. On appeal, defendant contended that the testimony of a witness in a prior trial should not have been read into the record.]

. . . . When the defense rested its case, counsel for the plaintiff moved the Court to allow him to read into evidence the testimony given by H. J. Fontenot in a state court trial in another case against the railroad for damages allegedly incurred at the same crossing.

Plaintiff's counsel said to the Court:

> "I can't find the man. If I could have found him, I would have, but I can't find the man — Mr. Fontenot — anywhere and we have made a search to try to locate him and haven't been able to."

Counsel for the railroad objected on the ground that plaintiff had made an inadequate showing of the nonavailability of the witness. The District Judge said, "I feel almost certain that you are heading for error in this case . . . ."

Since it was late in the day counsel was allowed to consider the matter overnight. The next morning, counsel insisted on his motion, again reiterating that, "we have made a diligent effort to locate Mr. Fontenot, and have been unable to do so. We don't know where this man is at all."

The Court then allowed plaintiff's counsel to read to the jury the recorded testimony of H. J. Fontenot, as given in a state court trial some eighteen months earlier, attached as Appendix A hereto.

It must be noted that although, for weeks, Fontenot's name had, at the instance of plaintiff's counsel, been on the witness list, no witness subpoena had been issued for him.

Right after the jury returned its verdict, the railroad claim agent went to work to see if he could find the missing witness. In about two hours Fontenot was found, at work, about a mile from the courthouse.

The transcript in the hands of counsel, admitted in evidence, showed that when Fontenot testified in the other trial he lived in China, Texas — near Beaumont. The record, developed after Fontenot had been found, shows that he had a telephone in China, listed to H. J. Fontenot. He had just recently moved to Beaumont but upon dialing the China number a recording would state his new Beaumont number.

We do not question the good faith of counsel's belief that he had made, or caused to be made, a diligent search for Fontenot. The record demonstrates, however, that he was clearly mistaken.

Fontenot was not an agent or an employee of the railroad. He was not a defendant in the case. The railroad had not "manifested its adoption or belief in the truth of his statement;" although it had called him as a witness in the previous trial. Obviously, this recorded testimony, even if otherwise admissible had Fontenot been present, could have been admissible only under Rule 804(a)(5) [as it applies to Rule 804(b)(1)] and then only if the plaintiff had been unable to procure his presence by process or other reasonable means, as Rule 804(a)(5) requires.

Fontenot's statement concerned the crucial issue in the case. In the status of this record we cannot say that it was harmless. It necessarily follows that the presentation of the statement to the trial jury, as the trial judge anticipated, was reversible error. A new trial cannot be avoided.

[Reversed and Remanded.]

APPENDIX A

Recorded Testimony of H. J. Fontenot as Read to the Perricone Jury:

QUESTION: "Mr. Fontenot, for the record will you state your full name, please?"

ANSWER: "Harland James Fontenot."

QUESTION: "Okay. Where do you presently live, Mr. Fontenot?"

ANSWER: "China, Texas."

QUESTION: "By whom are you presently employed?"

ANSWER: "By Bethlehem Steel."

QUESTION: "What sort of work do you do for Bethlehem?"

ANSWER: "Pipefitter."

QUESTION: "Okay. Let me ask you about this crossing. This is about the Archie Street Crossing. Did you go across that crossing to and from work yourself?"

ANSWER: "Yes, sir."

QUESTION: "How would you characterize that crossing when you crossed it?"

ANSWER: "Well I'd characterize it going slow, because anything, I believe over five miles an hour, it ain't safe."

QUESTION: "You're going to have some trouble, right?"

ANSWER: "Yes, sir."

QUESTION: "All right. Now, let me ask you this: What about a car going over the crossing at, say five, six or seven miles an hour, should it have made it over there with no trouble from your experience in crossing that crossing?

ANSWER: "Well, I've always crossed it slower. I mean, I would almost stop and go across it, and I'd say it depends on the shocks, or the car, and all that, how tough the car would be, I guess."

QUESTION: "But you do cross it, and you have crossed it every day coming to work?"

ANSWER: "Right."

QUESTION: "And you had crossed it and you hadn't hung up on any high rails at the crossing?"

ANSWER: "No. I went real slow, though, there. I crossed it, I guess at two miles an hour. I just rolled across it. Because you can go over that track once fast and you won't do it no more, or you hit your head on the ceiling."

QUESTION: "All right. What do you think the fastest a man could cross that track at?"

ANSWER: "I'd say safely at five miles an hour without maybe messing up your front end."

NOTES AND QUESTIONS

(1) *The Constitutional as well as Evidentiary Relevance of Unavailability.* In criminal cases, a showing of unavailability may have constitutional as well as hearsay dimensions. See (under the Confrontation Clause) discussion of *Crawford* case, § 11.03[B] *infra*, and *Barber v. Page*, 390 U.S. 719 (1968), which reversed a state conviction where the principal evidence at trial was preliminary hearing testimony of a witness who at the time of trial was incarcerated in a federal prison and the state made "absolutely no effort" to obtain his presence. *Barber* describes the various means by which prisoners and other individuals can be brought to court, regardless of their location.

(2) *Loss of Memory.* See *United States v. Amaya*, 533 F.2d 188 (5th Cir. 1976), *cert. denied*, 429 U.S. 1101 (1977), which discusses unavailability grounded on a witness's loss of memory regarding the subject matter underlying the prior testimony due to an intervening accident.

(3) *Government's Refusal to Grant Immunity.* Does the government's failure to grant a witness immunity prohibit it (pursuant to the last sentence in Rule 804(a)) from introducing hearsay under an exception that requires unavailability? See *United States v. Lang*, 589 F.2d 92 (2d Cir. 1978), answering no. Compare *United States v. Morrison*, 535 F.2d 223 (3d Cir. 1976), where the court found prosecutorial misconduct in denial of immunity.

(4) *Use of Depositions Under Fed. R. Civ. P. 32.* Fed. R. Civ. P. 32(a)(3) provides in part:

> The deposition of a witness, whether or not a party, may be used by any party for any purpose if the court finds: (A) that the witness is dead; or (B) that the witness is at a greater distance than 100 miles from the place of trial or hearing, or is out of the United States, unless it appears that the absence of the witness was procured by the party offering the deposition; or (C) that the witness is unable to attend or testify because of age, illness, infirmity, or imprisonment; or (D) that the party offering the deposition has been unable to procure the attendance of the witness by subpoena; or (E) upon application and notice, that such exceptional circumstances exist as to make it desirable, in the interest of justice and with due regard to the importance of presenting the testimony of witnesses orally in open court, to allow the deposition to be used.

In what respects is this definition of unavailability different from that found in the Federal Rules of Evidence? Is Fed. R. Civ. P. 32 an additional exception to the hearsay rule? *Cf.* Comment, *Admissibility of Prior-Action*

Depositions and Former Testimony Under Fed. R. Civ. P. 32(a) and Fed. R. Evid. 804(b)(1): Courts' Differing Interpretations, 41 WASH. & LEE L. REV. 155 (1984).

PROBLEM SET 10A: VARIOUS WAYS IN WHICH WITNESSES MAY BE UNAVAILABLE AND HOW TO ESTABLISH THEIR UNAVAILABILITY

(1) *The Procedure for Lack of Memory or Refusal to Testify.* Under Fed. R. Evid. 804(a)(3), must the judge take the witness's word that the witness has forgotten, or must she make a finding of fact about the loss of memory? That is, suppose she thinks the witness is lying. If she so believes, may she order that the hearsay exception proffered under Fed. R. Evid. 804(b) be disallowed? Before disallowance, must the court go so far as to order the witness to testify under Fed. R. Evid. 804(a)(2), and allow the exception only if the witness persists in refusing to testify on grounds that he cannot remember? Can the judge make a finding of lack of memory (without the declarant ever being presented for questioning by the judge or counsel concerning his memory) on independent evidence (say, perhaps, a deposition or other evidence)?

(2) *The Witness Whom You Know will Claim Privilege and Refuse to Testify Even if Ordered.* You wish to use a Fed. R. Evid. 804(b) hearsay exception. You have inquired of declarant and his attorney (both of whom reside in the district) as to whether declarant will testify, since it is a situation of obvious self-incrimination for him. Both of them state emphatically that he will refuse to testify on grounds of the privilege against self-incrimination, whatever the judge may rule about his right to so refuse. Considering Fed. R. Evid. 804(a)(1) and (2), if you relate this conversation to the judge and she accepts it as true, have you made out a case of unavailability such that you can use the hearsay exception? Or does the witness need to be put to the test by being subpoenaed and called to the court to testify?

(3) *The Waived Privilege that Nonetheless is Claimed.* In Problem (2), suppose the hearsay exception is Fed. R. Evid. 804(b)(1) (former testimony). There is a persuasive argument that the declarant has waived the privilege by testifying in the earlier proceeding. If you call him and he insists on refusing to testify, despite the fact that the judge orders him to, is he nevertheless unavailable?

(4) *What Constitutes "Unavailability" for a Witness Who Does Not Appear?* Fed. R. Evid. 804(a) unified the definition of unavailability for all the hearsay exceptions that utilize the concept of unavailability (i.e., those in Fed. R. Evid. 804(b)), and broadened it beyond the death or insanity required by some of the older cases dealing with some of the hearsay exceptions. However, mere absence beyond the subpoena reach of the jurisdiction no longer suffices, as it did under some of the exceptions under some previous cases. Under the Federal Rules of Evidence, in which of the following cases is the allegation of unavailability sufficient (if proved) to license use of a portion of the transcript of a former trial?

(a) "Your Honor, I would like to use this transcript. As you can see, the declarant is not present at this trial."

(b) [Identical to above, but offeror adds:] "And, Your Honor, I have no idea where he can be found."

(c) "Your Honor, I have found declarant within the district. I have repeatedly requested him to come to this trial, and he has repeatedly refused."

(d) "Your Honor, I have found declarant within the district. I asked him if he would come to the trial and testify, and he emphatically assured me that he would love to come and testify, so I did not subpoena him, but rather relied on him to come voluntarily. But as you can see, he has not shown up."

(e) "Your Honor, I have found declarant in the district and subpoenaed him, but he has not come."

(f) "Your Honor, the declarant, who is not here, is beyond the subpoena reach of this court, and always has been since the inception of this suit."

(g) "Your Honor, the declarant, who is not here, is beyond the subpoena reach of this court, and always has been since the inception of suit; nevertheless I have repeatedly sought to persuade him to come, but to no avail."

(h) [Federal prosecutor offers transcript, and says:] "Your Honor, the declarant is not here because he is in federal prison in another state 3000 miles from here."

(i) [State prosecutor, offering the transcript, in a state having rules identical to the Federal Rules of Evidence:] "Your Honor, he is in a state prison in another state 3000 miles from here."

(5) *Duty to Depose in CERTAIN CASES.* Fed. R. Evid. 804(a)(5)(B) says something that was not widely found in previous law: that *if you are relying on (a)(5)-type unavailability* (that is, absence despite diligent efforts to procure presence, *not* unavailability under the other subdivisions of (a) like death, illness, privilege, failure to remember, or refusal to testify) AND you are hoping to use *certain* hearsay exceptions under 804(b) (i.e., statements under belief in impending death, which is subdivision (b)(2), or statements against interest, which is subdivision (b)(3), or statements of personal or family history, which is subdivision (b)(4), but not former testimony, which is subdivision (b)(1), nor forfeiture by wrongdoing, which is subdivision (b)(6)), then you cannot establish unavailability (despite diligent but fruitless efforts to procure attendance) if you either (1) have on hand the declarant's deposition on the matter, or (2) passed up a *reasonable* opportunity to get his deposition testimony on the matter either because you (a) unreasonably failed to take his deposition at all, or (b) unreasonably failed to ask him to address the matter when you did have him in a deposition under questioning. Based on this, see if you can give arguments for both sides in the following situation (each side may make some additional assumptions consistent with the given facts if necessary for its argument):

> You are involved as a defendant in federal civil litigation filed over a year ago. Shortly after the filing of the suit, you took the deposition of one Mr. Jones, who is not a party, but had certain relevant knowledge concerning

matter "A" involved in the lawsuit. After that deposition, and unrelated to it, the complaint was amended so that matter "B" also became involved in the lawsuit (which you had hoped would not happen). "B" is a matter about which Jones also had knowledge but about which you did not ask him at the time of the deposition, confining yourself to asking about matter "A." Some time after the complaint was amended in this way, you considered deposing Jones again but decided against it because of the distance and expense involved now that Jones had moved to another state; because the stakes in the lawsuit are not extremely large; because you already had a witness who heard Jones make a statement, favorable to you, on matter "B" (a statement which, if correct on "B," is quite adverse to Jones' own interests in another unrelated transaction); and because you figured you could subpoena Jones to testify at the trial if necessary. Shortly before trial, however, Jones disappears completely, despite great efforts on your part to find him (you have decided that his testimony on "B" will be very important to you). Can you offer the overheard statement of Jones on "B" as a declaration against interest?

§ 10.02 FORMER TESTIMONY[2]

Read Federal Rule of Evidence 804(b)(1), "Hearsay Exceptions — Declarant Unavailable: Former Testimony."

LLOYD v. AMERICAN EXPORT LINES, INC.

United States Court of Appeals, Third Circuit
580 F.2d 1179 (1978)

ALDISERT, CIRCUIT JUDGE.

I.

This lawsuit emanates from a violent altercation between Alvarez and a fellow crew member, electrician Frank Lloyd, that occurred when their ship was in the port of Yokohama, Japan. Lloyd filed an action against Export [the ship's owner] in the District Court seeking redress for injuries sustained in the fight. Export joined Alvarez as a third-party defendant and Alvarez in turn counter-claimed against Export. Lloyd did not proceed in his case as plaintiff, failing to appear. The jury returned a verdict in favor of Alvarez against Export.

It was Alvarez' theory that Export negligently failed to use reasonable precautions to safeguard him from Lloyd after Export had knowledge of Lloyd's dangerous propensities.

The jury was not permitted to hear any version of the fight other than that of Alvarez; it was denied the opportunity of hearing the account rendered by Lloyd,

---

[2] Study Guide Reference: Evidence in a Nutshell, Chapter 10:III at "Former Testimony: F.R.E. 804(b)(1)" (including its subdivision).

who was the other participant in the affray and its only other eyewitness. It is the refusal of the district court to admit a public record of a prior proceeding and excerpts of Lloyd's testimony therein that constitutes the major thrust of Export's appeal. Export contends that this evidence was admissible in the form of transcripts and a final report from a Coast Guard hearing [regarding] charges of misconduct brought against [Lloyd] for the fight with Alvarez. At that hearing, both Lloyd and Alvarez were represented by counsel and testified under oath.

II.

The admissibility of the Decision and Order of the Coast Guard hearing examiner, and excerpts from the transcript of that proceeding are governed, respectively, by Federal Rules of Evidence 803(8)(C) and 804(b)(1).

A.

The Coast Guard proceeding was a rather elaborate hearing conducted before a professional hearing examiner. In addition to documentary evidence, testimony was received under oath, subject to direct and cross examination, on two charges leveled against Lloyd: that he "did wrongfully assault and batter ROLANDO ALVAREZ, a fellow crew member, with his fists," and that he "did wrongfully fail to perform his duties due to intoxication." The hearing examiner found that the first specification, or charge, was "not proved by substantial evidence" and that the second "was dismissed at the end of the investigating officer's case for the failure to make out a prima facie case."

As required by Fed. R. Evid. 803(8)(C), the Coast Guard Decision and Order is a report of a public office or agency — a hearing examiner of the Coast Guard's parent agency, the United States Department of Transportation — which sets forth "factual findings resulting from an investigation made pursuant to authority granted by law" and which is offered in a civil action.

We reject appellee's contention that the Coast Guard Decision and Order consists in large part of the opinions of the hearing examiner and thus fails to meet the "factual findings" requirement of the Rule. Our reading of the portion of the document to which Alvarez objects indicates that the hearing examiner did no more than summarize the evidence and point out inconsistencies therein. Finally, whatever uncertainties may have existed at common law regarding the admissibility of reports such as the one before us, we are persuaded that, with the adoption of the Federal Rules of Evidence, the matter is resolved and the Decision and Order is admissible.

C.

Alvarez objects to the admission of Lloyd's testimony on two grounds: first, there was insufficient proof that Lloyd was unavailable to testify at trial as contemplated in Rule 804(a)(5), and, second, the Coast Guard proceeding did not qualify under Rule 804(b)(1).

[N]umerous attempts were made by Export to depose Lloyd, but he repeatedly failed to appear. Finally, on the day set for trial, Export learned that Lloyd would not appear. Lloyd's counsel represented to the court that extensive efforts had been made to obtain his appearance, but they had failed, due at least in part to his seafaring occupation. Export and Lloyd's own counsel were unable to obtain his appearance in an action in which he had a formidable interest as a plaintiff. [Rule 804(a)(5) is satisfied.]

D.

We turn now to the more difficult question: did Alvarez or a "predecessor in interest" have the "opportunity and similar motive to develop the testimony by direct, cross or redirect examination" as required by Rule 804(b)(1)? In rejecting the proffered evidence, the district court took a strict view.

We note at the outset that inasmuch as Congress did not define "predecessor in interest," that interpretive task is left to the courts. We find no definitive guidance in the reports accompanying language changes made as the Rules were considered, in turn, by the Supreme Court and the houses of Congress. As originally submitted by the Supreme Court, Rule 804(b)(1) would have allowed prior testimony of an unavailable witness to be received in evidence if the party against whom it was offered, or a person with "motive and interest similar," had an opportunity to examine the witness. The House of Representatives adopted the present language [adding to the above quoted requirement the "predecessor in interest" requirement as well], the Committee on the Judiciary offering this rationale:

> The Committee considered that it is generally unfair to impose upon the party against whom the hearsay evidence is being offered responsibility for the manner in which the witness was previously handled by another party. The sole exception to this, in the Committee's view, is when a party's predecessor in interest in a civil action or proceeding had an opportunity and similar motive to examine the witness.

The Senate Committee on the Judiciary viewed the import of this change as follows:

> Although the committee recognizes considerable merit to the rule submitted by the Supreme Court, a position which has been advocated by many scholars and judges, we have concluded that the difference between the two versions is not great and we accept the House amendment.

We, too, fail to see a compelling difference between the two approaches.

In our analysis of this language change, we are aware of the basic thrust of subdivision (b) of Rule 804. It was originally designed by the Advisory Committee on Rules of Evidence of the Judicial Conference of the United States to strike a proper balance between the recognized risk of introducing testimony of one not physically present on a witness stand and the equally recognized risk of denying to the fact-finder important relevant evidence. Even in its slightly amended form as enacted by Congress, Rule 804 still serves the original intention of its drafters: "The rule expresses preferences: testimony given on the stand in person is preferred over hearsay, and hearsay, if of the specified quality, is preferred over complete loss of the evidence of the declarant."

Although Congress did not furnish us with a definition of "predecessor in interest," our analysis of the concept of interests satisfies us that there was a sufficient community of interest shared by the Coast Guard in its hearing and Alvarez in the subsequent civil trial to satisfy Rule 804(b)(1).

Alvarez sought to vindicate his individual interest in recovering for his injuries; the Coast Guard sought to vindicate the public interest in safe and unimpeded merchant marine service. Irrespective of whether the interests be considered from the individual or public viewpoints, however, the nucleus of operative facts was the same — the conduct of Lloyd and Alvarez. And although the results sought in the two proceedings differed — the Coast Guard contemplated sanctions involving Lloyd's mariner's license, while Alvarez sought private substituted redress, *i.e.*, monetary damages — the basic interest advanced by both was that of determining culpability and, if appropriate, exacting a penalty for the same condemned behavior thought to have occurred. The Coast Guard investigating officer not only preferred charges against Lloyd but functioned as a prosecutor at the subsequent proceeding as well. Thus, he attempted to establish at the Coast Guard hearing what Alvarez attempted to establish at the later trial: Lloyd's intoxication, his role as the aggressor, and his prior hostility toward Alvarez.

We strive to avoid interpretations that are wooden or mechanical, like obsolete common law pleadings, and to favor those that facilitate the presentation of a complete picture to the fact-finder. With this approach in mind, we are satisfied that there existed, in the language of Rule 804(b)(1), sufficient "opportunity and similar motive [for the Coast Guard investigating officer] to develop [Lloyd's] testimony" at the former hearing to justify its admission against Alvarez at the later trial.

While we do not endorse an extravagant interpretation of who or what constitutes a "predecessor in interest," we prefer one that is realistically generous over one that is formalistically grudging. We believe that what has been described as "the practical and expedient view" expresses the congressional intention: "if it appears that in the former suit a party having a like motive to cross-examine about the same matters as the present party would have was accorded an adequate opportunity for such examination, the testimony may be received against the present party." Under these circumstances, the previous party having like motive to develop the testimony about the same material facts is, in the final analysis, a predecessor in interest to the present party.

The judgment of the district court will be reversed and the cause remanded for a new trial.

STERN, CONCURRING:

I join in the majority opinion, except insofar as it construes the "predecessor in interest" language of Rule 804(b)(1). The majority here holds that because the Coast Guard investigating officer shared a community of interest with Alvarez he was Alvarez's predecessor in interest. I believe that this analysis is contrary to the Rule's clear language and is foreclosed by its legislative history.

I would hold that it is admissible, not under 804(b)(1), but rather under the catch-all exception to the hearsay rule, 804(b)(5) [now Fed. R. Evid. 807 — Eds].

804(b)(1), as originally submitted by the Supreme Court, would have permitted the introduction of former testimony if the party against whom it was offered, or a person "with motive and interest similar" to the party, had an opportunity to examine the witness. But Congress rejected this approach. [It required that such a similarly motivated and interested person also be a "predecessor in interest."]

The Senate accepted the House change, although it may not have fully appreciated its significance.

It is true that Congress nowhere defined "predecessor in interest," but it seems clear that this phrase, a term of art, was used in its narrow, substantive law sense. Although the commentators have expressed disapproval of this traditional and restrictive rule, they recognize that a "predecessor in interest" is defined in terms of a privity relationship.

"The term 'privity' denotes mutual or successive relationships to the same rights of property. Thus, there are privies in estate, as donor and donee." *Metropolitan St. Ry. v. Gumby*, 99 F. 192 (2d Cir. 1900).

The majority rejects the view that the Rule's wording signals a return to the common law approach requiring privity or a common property interest between the parties, and finds it sufficient that the Coast Guard investigator shared a community of interest with Alvarez. But community of interest seems to mean only that the investigating officer sought to establish the same facts as Alvarez attempted to prove in the instant suit. Used in this sense, community of interest means nothing more than similarity of interest or similarity of motive. But similar motive is a separate prerequisite to admissibility under 804(b)(1) and thus the majority's analysis which reads "predecessor in interest" to mean nothing more than person with "similar motive" eliminates the predecessor in interest requirement entirely.

Moreover, while I appreciate the fact that the Coast Guard investigator sought to establish Lloyd's wrongdoing and that Alvarez sought to do the same, I do not believe that this establishes the kind of "common motive" sufficient to satisfy 804(b)(1).

A prosecutor or an investigating officer represents no ordinary party. He shoulders a peculiar kind of duty, even to his very adversary, a duty which is foreign to the adversarial process among ordinary litigants. The prosecutor, it is true, must seek to vindicate the rights of the alleged victim, but his interests go far beyond that. His interest in a prosecution is not that he shall win a case, but that justice shall be done.

The investigating officer was under no duty to advance every arguable issue against Lloyd in the vindication of Alvarez's interests, as Alvarez's own counsel would have been.

The majority's holding makes admissible against Alvarez the testimony of all witnesses who appeared at the Coast Guard hearing — not just Lloyd — and this without any showing of necessity by the proponent of such evidence. Indeed, under the majority view, all kinds of testimony adduced at all kinds of administrative hearings — hearings before the Civil Aeronautics Board on airplane disasters; hearings before the Federal Communications Commission on misuse of broadcast licenses; hearings before the Securities and Exchange Commission on securities fraud, just by way of example — would be admissible in subsequent civil suits, albeit that the parties were entirely different. The net result would be charging the party against whom the hearsay evidence is being offered with all flaws in the manner in which the witness was previously handled by another, and all flaws in another's choice of witnesses.

NOTE

(1) *Does the Lloyd Court's Reasoning Equate the "Opportunity and Motive" Requirement with "Predecessor in Interest," Nullifying the Latter?* Two illuminating decisions involving the issue of "predecessor-in-interest" for the purpose of Fed. R. Evid. 804(b)(1): *In re Master Key Antitrust Litig.*, 72 F.R.D. 108 (D. Conn. 1976), where the issue was whether the United States government would be deemed a predecessor-in-interest to a private party when both were making antitrust claims against the same defendant; the court gave a broad interpretation to "predecessor-in-interest"; and *In re IBM Peripheral EDP Devices Antitrust Litig.*, 444 F. Supp. 110 (N.D. Cal. 1978), in which the court took a more restrictive view, stating that *Master Key* was limited to a situation where the relationship is like that between the antitrust division of the Justice Department and private plaintiffs (the antitrust policy indicating a Congressional intention that there be deemed to be a commonality of interest), as in *Master Key* itself. Thus, in *IBM*, two different private antitrust plaintiffs (against the same defendant) were not considered in such a relationship. *IBM* states that equating "predecessor-in-interest" with "opportunity and similar motive to develop the testimony," which language also appears in the rule, renders nugatory Congress's express addition to the draft of the Federal Rules of Evidence of the predecessor-in-interest requirement. *Lloyd* and *Master Key* seem to equate the two phrases. See also *Clay v. Johns-Manville Sales Corp.*, 722 F.2d 1289 (6th Cir. 1983), *cert. denied*, 467 U.S. 1253 (1984), substantially equating the two phrases.

(2) *Limits Even on Generous Views of Predecessor-in-Interest.* Even Courts that approve of *Lloyd's* generous interpretation of predecessor-in-interest sometimes balk when the individuals in question have no clearly established common interest or relationship relevant to the case. *See New England Mut. Life Ins. Co. v. Anderson*, 888 F.2d 646 (10th Cir. 1989). The insurance company, claiming that a widow had fraudulently procured a policy, offered testimony of a witness from the criminal trial of the widow's paramour for solicitation of murder of her husband. Admission would have required the paramour, Reverend Bird, to have been a predecessor-in-interest of the widow, who was not tried with the Reverend. The Tenth Circuit affirmed the exclusion of the testimony. Do you suppose this was based on possible dissimilar motive?

UNITED STATES v. SALERNO

United States Supreme Court
505 U.S. 317, 112 S. Ct. 2503 (1992)

THOMAS, JUSTICE.

[*Salerno* concerned the question whether the Rule permits a criminal defendant to introduce the grand jury testimony of a witness who asserts the Fifth Amendment privilege at trial. Respondent (defendant) Salerno and others, alleged members of the Genovese Family of La Costa Nostra, were convicted of racketeering in connection with a bid-rigging scheme by which construction contracts were allocated to a so-called "Club" of six conspiring companies. DeMatteis and Bruno, who were owners of Cedar Park Construction Company, testified before the grand jury under a grant of immunity and denied that they or Cedar Park had participated. At trial, however, the Government offered evidence that Cedar Park was a member of the Club. Respondents subpoenaed DeMatteis and Bruno, but they invoked the Fifth Amendment and refused to testify.

Respondents (defendants) then offered transcripts of DeMatteis's and Bruno's grand jury testimony pursuant to the former testimony exception in Fed. R. Evid. 804(b)(1). The district court excluded the transcripts for lack of a "similar motive" on the part of the prosecution to develop the testimony before the grand jury. The Second Circuit reversed, reasoning that although "the government may have had no motive . . . to impeach" the witnesses before the grand jury, this factor was "irrelevant," and the testimony should have been admitted to maintain "adversarial fairness." The Supreme Court, per Justice Thomas, here reverses the reversal and remands to the Second Circuit for it to examine the "similar motive" issue.]

Nothing in the language of Rule 804(b)(1) suggests that a court may admit former testimony absent satisfaction of each of the Rule's elements. [T]he respondents [u]rge us not to read Rule 804(b)(1) in a "slavishly literal fashion." They contend that "adversarial fairness" prevents the United States from relying on the similar motive requirement in this case.

When Congress enacted the prohibition against admission of hearsay in Rule 802, it placed 24 exceptions in Rule 803 and 5 additional exceptions in Rule 804. [T]o respect its determination, we must enforce the words that it enacted. The respondents, as a result, had no right to introduce DeMatteis' and Bruno's former testimony under Rule 804(b)(1) without showing a "similar motive." This Court cannot alter evidentiary rules merely because litigants might prefer different rules in a particular class of cases.

The respondents finally argue that adversarial fairness may prohibit suppression of exculpatory evidence produced in grand jury proceedings. They note that, when this Court required disclosure of a grand jury transcript in *Dennis v. United States*, 384 U.S. 855 (1966), it stated that "it is rarely justifiable for the prosecution to have exclusive access" to relevant facts.

We again fail to see how we may create an exception to Rule 804(b)(1). The *Dennis* case, unlike this one, did not involve a question about the admissibility of evidence. Rather, it concerned only the need to disclose a transcript to the defendants. Moreover, in *Dennis*, we did not hold that adversarial fairness required the United States to make the grand jury transcript available. Instead, we ordered disclosure under the specific language of Federal Rule of Criminal Procedure 6(e). In this case, the language of Rule 804(b)(1) does not support the respondents. [N]either *Dennis* nor anything else that the respondents have cited provides us with this authority.

The question remains whether the United States had a "similar motive" in this case. [The United States] argues that a prosecutor generally will not have the same motive to develop testimony in grand jury proceedings as he does at trial. A prosecutor, it explains, must maintain secrecy during the investigatory stages of the criminal process and therefore may not desire to confront grand jury witnesses with contradictory evidence. It further states that a prosecutor may not know, prior to indictment, which issues will have importance at trial and accordingly may fail to develop grand jury testimony effectively.

The Court of Appeals, as noted, erroneously concluded that the respondents did not have to demonstrate a similar motive in this case to make use of Rule 804(b)(1). It therefore declined to consider fully the arguments now presented. Rather than to address this issue here in the first instance, we think it prudent to remand the case for further consideration.

[Justice Blackmun's concurrence emphasizes that "similar motive" does not mean "identical motive" and that the similar-motive inquiry depends on the facts of each case. Justice Stevens dissented, arguing that the participation of Cedar Park was so essential to the Government's case that the Government had a clear motive, even before the grand jury, to challenge the witnesses' testimony immediately: "[T]hus, when the prosecutors doubted Bruno's and DeMatteis' veracity before the grand jury — as they most assuredly did — they unquestionably had an 'opportunity and similar motive to develop the testimony by direct, cross, or redirect examination' within the meaning of Rule 804(b)(1)."]

NOTES AND QUESTIONS

(1) *Is it Anomalous that Unavailability is Required Here?* Why is unavailability required for this particularly reliable form of hearsay, as compared with the hearsay admitted under certain other exceptions that do not require unavailability? (Note that preparation of a document for litigation purposes, such as an affidavit, is one of the historical concerns of the hearsay rule.)

(2) *Is Salerno Inconsistent with Prior Decisions?* Can defense counsel now argue that the assumption in *California v. Green* discussed and apparently adopted in *Ohio v. Roberts* (*see* § 11.03[A], *infra*) — that the motive to cross-examine in preliminary hearings always is similar to that at trial — is inconsistent with the reasoning in *Salerno*, which requires case-by-case analysis?

(3) *Videotaping: Could it Change Results?* Does the possibility of videotaping testimony solve any of the problems connected with the hearsay exception? Does it create any? See, for example, 18 U.S.C. § 3509 for provisions concerning child witnesses.

PROBLEM SET 10B: IS THERE STILL A REQUIREMENT OF IDENTITY OF PARTIES AND ISSUES?

(1) *A Criminal Case Followed by a Civil Case.* In Case X, Jones is prosecuted for homicide of Smith. Some time later, in Case Y, Jones is sued civilly for the wrongful death of Smith. The alleged killing is the same event in both. A witness who testified against Jones in Case X has died by the time of Case Y. The plaintiff in Case Y wishes to use against Jones a transcript of the testimony the witness gave in Case X recounting the killing, to which the witness was an eyewitness. What would be the result under the various permutations of the common law about which you may have read? Under the Federal Rules of Evidence? Are there additional facts you need to know to answer any of these questions? Would you want to know what kind or degree of homicide, what penalty was risked, or what the civil stakes were?

(2) *Different Parties.* Consider the following sets of judicial cases:

SET 1: 1st proceeding: J vs. A
2nd proceeding: X vs. A

SET 2: 1st proceeding: A vs. B
2nd proceeding: A vs. Q

SET 3: 1st proceeding: A vs. B
2nd proceeding: A plus X vs. B

In each of these sets, under the common law, and under the Federal Rules of Evidence, can a transcript of a witness's testimony given in the first proceeding be used in the second, assuming the issue is the same and the witness is dead by the time of the second proceeding? Under at least some of the positions, do you need to know more facts? What do you need to know, and why? Which position is most in accord with the policy of the exception?

§ 10.03 DYING DECLARATIONS[3]

Read Federal Rule of Evidence 804(a)(2), "Hearsay Exceptions — Declarant Unavailable: Statement Under Belief of Imminent Death."

[3] Study Guide Reference: Evidence in a Nutshell, Chapter 10:III at "Statements Under Belief of Impending Death (Known as 'Dying Declarations'): F.R.E. 804(b)(2)."

PLESSY v. STATE

Court of Appeals of Arkansas
388 S.W.3d 509 (2012)

WAYMOND M. BROWN, JUDGE.

This is an appeal from a Sebastian County jury trial finding the appellant, Quincy Jay Plessy, guilty of first-degree murder and committing a felony with a firearm . . . . He . . . contends that the trial court erred . . . by finding that statements by the victim were admissible as a dying declaration and by [other rulings]. We affirm on all points.

Factual Background

. . . Thomas Xavier Clayton was found by witnesses at an intersection in Fort Smith with multiple gunshot wounds after falling or being thrown from the back seat of a maroon four-door vehicle. Clayton was transported to St. Edward's Hospital, where he died less than an hour later. Appellant Quincy Jay Plessy was arrested . . . . [A] jury convicted Plessy of first-degree murder and sentenced him to 360 months in the Arkansas Department of Correction with a consecutive five-year firearm enhancement, for a total sentence of 420 months . . . . Plessy timely filed a notice of appeal . . . .

Trial Court Did Not Err in Admitting Statement as a Dying Declaration

Arkansas Rule of Evidence 802 prohibits the admission of hearsay except as provided by law or by the rules of evidence. Under the hearsay exception found in Rule 804(b)(2), however, hearsay from an unavailable declarant, such as a deceased declarant, is not excluded if it is "[a] statement made by a declarant while believing that his death was imminent, concerning the cause or circumstances of what he believed to be his impending death." [This language is functionally identical to language in the Federal Rule. — Eds.] The trial court determines whether a statement is admissible as a dying declaration, and we will not reverse that determination absent an abuse of discretion.

Dying declarations are deemed inherently trustworthy. The principal consideration upon which such statements are admitted is that a person who realizes that death is inevitable as a result of the injury inflicted speaks with solemnity and will not resort to fabrication in order to unjustly punish another. A sense of imminent death need not be shown by the declarant's express words alone; it can be supplied by inferences fairly drawn from his condition. *Boone v. State*. . .(holding that, based on the obvious severity of the wound, combined with the victim's almost immediate collapse and inability to breathe, trial court did not abuse its discretion in admitting testimony about victim's statement).

Plessy filed a pretrial motion to exclude Thomas Clayton's response, "Q," when first responder Roy Smith asked who shot him, arguing that the testimony would show that Clayton gave different responses to the two witnesses who discovered him before Smith arrived. At a hearing on the motion, the trial court heard Smith's testimony on this matter and on Clayton's condition when he was discovered. Smith testified that Clayton had multiple wounds, was in distress and had no feeling in his legs, and began to go in and out of consciousness shortly after he identified "Q" as the person who shot him. Smith also testified that when he heard Clayton say "Q," he immediately confirmed what Clayton had said with Brad Turner. The trial court denied Plessy's motion and ruled that the statement was admissible as a dying declaration even if Clayton made differing statements to other witnesses. At trial, Roy Smith gave the same testimony, and Brad Turner testified that he too heard Clayton say "Q." The medical examiner, Dr. Daniel Konzelmann, testified that Clayton had sustained eight gunshot wounds, including one that penetrated his aorta, and that four bullets were inside his body at the time of the autopsy. Witness testimony at trial also indicated that Clayton died less than an hour after the shooting occurred.

Plessy argues that the trial court should have excluded Clayton's "Q" statement to Smith and Turner because Clayton gave conflicting statements to witnesses, thus rendering the statement inherently untrustworthy. This argument is without merit. At trial, one witness, Ty Adams, testified that he saw Clayton fall out of the car and went to assist him. When he asked Clayton who threw him out of the car, Clayton said he did not know. Adams then asked if he knew who he had been with in the car, but Clayton replied only that he had been shot. Adams testified that Clayton appeared to be in shock and not able to communicate. Another eyewitness, Brian Johnson, testified that when he asked Clayton who shot him, Clayton just moaned. Subsequently, when firefighters Roy Smith and Brad Turner arrived, Clayton managed to say "Q" when Smith asked who had shot him. The record does not show inconsistency or contradiction in his responses to questions; rather, it indicates that Clayton was mortally injured and struggling to communicate. Moreover, it is the province of the jury to determine the reliability of identification testimony and to weigh any inconsistencies in evidence; neither of those concerns affect the threshold question of whether the testimony is admissible.

Plessy argues that Clayton's one-word statement, "Q," should have been ruled inadmissible because it did not specifically describe the cause and circumstances of his death. However, it is sufficient for a dying declaration to concern or refer to the cause or circumstances of what the declarant believed to be his impending death. Clayton's statement was made in response to the question of who shot him. As such, it clearly referred to and concerned the circumstances and cause of his impending death, and qualifies as a dying declaration . . . . [Affirmed.]

NOTES AND QUESTIONS

(1) *Unlike Verdi or Wagner, the Courts Do Not Expect Dying Declarants to Express Themselves Eloquently: Moore v. State*, 81 So. 3d 1147 (Miss. Ct. App. 2011). It would be preferable if dying declarations were specific, consistent, and detailed, but unlike the dying protagonist in an opera, dying declarants in real life do not usually sing arias, and the courts seem to recognize that their statements will require context, explanation, and judgments by the jury. In the *Moore* case, the deceased told a witness after a robbery, "[o]ne of those boys shot me." Defense counsel argued that admitting this statement was error because, since there were

two robbers, "he could not cross-examine the victim to determine which 'boy' " had shot the victim. The court rejected this argument, just as the court in the principal case, *Plessy, supra*, rejected a similar argument about the indeterminacy of the one-word declaration, "Q." In light of the nature of dying declarations, do these kinds of rulings seem appropriate, or is non-specificity, coupled with the inability to cross-examine, more important?

(2) *Cases Excluding Proposed Dying Declarations: Trascher v. Territo*, 89 So. 3d 357 (La. 2012). Among other issues, this case emphasizes the point that dying declarations can be admitted in civil cases, although the court excluded the statement here. Decedent's survivors sued asbestos providers after he died of asbestosis. The alleged dying declaration was his deposition, which had to be interrupted repeatedly because of his weak condition and finally was recessed, after which he soon died. The statement was not admissible as a deposition because it had not been completed. The statement also did not suffice as having been made under a "belief in impending death," said this court, because it was given in response to questions rather than spontaneous, the parties contemplated resuming the deposition, and the deceased expected to die within six months. The court explained, "there must be a 'settled hopeless expectation' that death is near at hand, and what is said must be spoken in the hush of its impending presence." The rule does not expressly require either "hopelessness" or a "hush." Does the ruling make sense?

In *State v. Matthews*, 938 N.E.2d 1099 (Ohio Ct. App. 2010), the court noted that the alleged murder victim had been treated earlier by emergency personnel, and it held that statements given during questioning by police officers later that night and the following day were not admissible. The deceased died soon after, and her injury was critical. "However, beyond the horrific nature of Tomlinson's injury, there is no evidence that she believed she was dying. A grievous wound and the victim's being in critical condition alone are not enough to establish the deceased's sense of impending death."

(3) *Won't These Kinds of Statements Almost Always Qualify as Excited Utterances, Anyway, if They Really Are Dying Declarations?* Remember, the failure of a statement to qualify under one particular exception doesn't mean that it can't qualify under another exception. In *Moore, supra*, the court upheld the admissibility of numerous statements made by the victim under the excited utterance and medical-purposes exceptions, although they perhaps could have been dying declarations too.

(4) *Trustworthiness.* What is argued to be the special guarantee of trustworthiness under this hearsay exception? Do you believe it makes the evidence trustworthy? Are these declarants likely to be more, or less, reliable than other declarants, considering that they are injured, sick, at death's door, and probably befuddled? Is that only a matter of weight to be argued to the jury?

(5) *The Religious Origins of the Exception.* Does the rationale of the exception indicate that the exception should not apply to atheists? Would that be a matter of weight?

(6) *Necessity: Does it Justify the Federal Rule?* Can you justify confining the rule to criminal homicide cases, as at common law? Or to the kinds of cases named

in the Federal Rule? Is necessity a justification for using questionable evidence in the most critical cases — those having the greatest punishment (and the worst consequences if we get the wrong person), i.e., homicide cases, as at common law? Should we be *more*, or *less*, careful about the evidence allowed in such cases? Is necessity a sound justification for the Federal Rules' position that these declarations are admissible in the most serious (criminal homicide) and the least serious (civil) cases, but not in the cases in the middle (criminal cases that are not homicide cases)?

PROBLEM SET 10C: VARIOUS ASPECTS OF DYING DECLARATIONS.

(1) *"It was No Accident."* Would the declarations in the following case, a prosecution for murder, be admissible under the present exception? (*See Connor v. State*, 171 A.2d 699 (Md.), *cert. denied*, 368 U.S. 906 (1961)):

> After the defendant [Mr. Connor] had opened the door of his automobile, parked in front of the house, and had started the motor and turned on the parking lights, he saw his former wife standing at the left hand door. She demanded the $25 he had promised her and when he responded that he had no intention of giving it to her then or later, an altercation ensued as he attempted to drive slowly off while she followed alongside of the automobile and got in front of it. At this point he idled the motor long enough to tell her that he would give her the money on the next day and then, putting the automobile in gear, he again "started to move slowly" while she "insisted on staying in the same spot," but he continued to move forward about ten feet with her moving backward and still yelling for the money until there came a time when he did not "see her any more." Then he "gave it [the automobile] the gas" and moved away rapidly for about a hundred feet. In so doing — though he claimed he was not aware of it — the defendant drove over his former wife, crushed her chest and pelvis and dragged her body for at least a part of the distance he had traveled. She died at 5:40 p.m. on the same day. The evidence in question here is the following direct examination of the police officer who came to the scene:

Q. What, if anything, did Mrs. Connor, the person lying in the street say to you or to anyone in your presence?

A. I asked Mrs. Connor certain questions at that time.

Q. Was she conscious at the time?

A. Yes, sir. [But she was almost in shock.]

Q. What did you ask her and what did she answer?

A. I asked Mrs. Connor: "Did your husband do this to you?"

Q. What did she answer?

(The Witness). She answered yes. I asked her at that time "Was this an accident?" I asked: "Was this an accident or was it deliberate?" She answered: "It was no accident." [She also said "He did it; he has beaten me up in the past. There is $20,000 in my savings account. Give it to my children."]

There is an allegation that at least part of the husband's motivation was that he was afraid she would discover the previous removal by him of money from her savings account; no money and no savings account could be found.

Prior to this testimony there had been testimony by another witness that he had heard the injured woman say "get a priest." There was also prior testimony by another officer to the effect that the woman kept saying "take care of my baby."

Consider each declaration separately. (In *Connor v. State, above*, which we have somewhat altered, the court upheld admission as dying declarations.)

(2) *The Declarant Who Does Not Die.* Suppose that in Problem (1) Mrs. Connor did not in fact die of that injury but became unavailable for trial in some other way: death due to another cause or disappearance despite diligent efforts to find her. (The case then might be a prosecution for assault with intent to kill, rather than murder.) Unbeknownst to her, all she had were a few broken ribs. Would the "guarantee of accuracy" be any less? What would be the result under the common law? Under the Federal Rules of Evidence?

(3) *The Declarant Who is Unaware of the Danger.* Suppose in Problem (1) Mrs. Connor had been unaware of how desperate her physical condition obviously and actually was and expected to recover. Could her declaration qualify under the present exception?

(4) *Procedures for Admitting the Statement: Fed. R. Evid. 104(a) or (b)?* In the case in Problem (1), who decides whether the declarant knew she was about to die? Judge or jury? For what purpose? To what degree must it be proven? *See* Fed. R. Evid. 104(a), (b). Even if the judge decides the issue, should the evidence on it be adduced before the jury? Is *Chaplin* different from the Federal Rules procedures on these matters?

§ 10.04 DECLARATIONS AGAINST INTEREST[4]

Read Federal Rule of Evidence 804(a)(3), "Hearsay Exceptions — Declarant Unavailable: Statements Against Interest."

[A] Declarations Against Pecuniary and Proprietary Interests

(1) *The Limited Common-Law View: Money or Property.* At common law, declarations against interest were limited to those against pecuniary or proprietary interests. Strict common law required the statement to clearly and directly implicate a property or money interest on its face, but later cases broadened the exception to statements that inferentially were against such an interest. *See Gichner v. Antonio Troiano Tile & Marble Co.*, 410 F.2d 238 (D.C. Cir.

---

[4] Study Guide Reference: Evidence in a Nutshell, Chapter 10:III at "Declarations Against Interest: F.R.E. 804(b)(3)" (including all subdivisions).

1969). The exception applies when the statement "threatens the loss of employment, or reduces the chances for future employment, or entails possible civil liability." *Gichner.* The current Federal Rule goes even further, broadening the recognized interests.

(2) *Lack of Awareness that the Statement is Against Interest.* In *Filesi v. United States*, 352 F.2d 339 (4th Cir. 1965), the IRS asserted that Alfred Filesi, a tavern owner, owed cabaret excise taxes (plus penalties and interest) for certain past years because the tavern permitted dancing, making it a "cabaret." Filesi denied there was dancing. An IRS agent testified for the government that Henry Muller (who was, during the years for which the tax was claimed to be due, a partner of Filesi in the tavern, but no longer was a partner at the time of the interview) told him, in an interview, that there was dancing at the tavern during the relevant years. The court held that this statement was inadmissible as a declaration against interest because there was no proof indicating Muller was aware that dancing triggered the cabaret tax, although Muller did know that both partners would be liable for any tax found to be due during the years in issue. Thus, Muller was not aware the statement was against his pecuniary interest.

(3) *Mixed Motive Cases: Statements that Both Favor and Hurt the Declarant.* In *Demasi v. Whitney Trust & Sav. Bank*, 176 So. 703 (La. Ct. App. 1937), Casimo Demasi sued the bank to recover a $650 deposit made by him and his wife. The bank defended that the Demasis' daughter, Carrie Arena, withdrew the money (except for $70) with the consent of Mrs. Demasi. A first trial resulted in judgment for the bank. Mrs. Demasi immediately applied to the bank for the remaining $70, and in order to get it Mrs. Demasi executed an affidavit for the bank, to the effect that Carrie had withdrawn the money with Mrs. Demasi's permission. An appeal of the first trial was pending. It eventually resulted in a new trial being ordered. At the second trial (by which time Mrs. Demasi had died), the affidavit was admitted as a declaration against interest. (Her former trial testimony also was admitted.)

On appeal by Mr. Demasi, the court held that as respects the affidavit, in Mrs. Demasi's mind, her self-interest motivation (to get the $70) preponderated over the against-interest aspect (harm to the Demasi's lawsuit), especially since (1) she was a simple woman, (2) the gain of $70 was immediate, (3) winning the lawsuit seemed remote (a trial had already been lost and winning both an appeal and the next trial would seem remote to her), and (4) she may not have been fully aware of how damaging the statement was. Thus, the statement was not "against interest."

(4) *Is a Tax Return a "Statement Against Interest" Because it Reflects Taxes Due?* In *Veach's Adm'r v. Louisville & I. Ry. Co.*, 228 S.W. 35 (Ky. Ct. App. 1921), suit was brought against the streetcar company for negligently running into and killing Katherine Veach. The damages claimed were her loss of future earnings. To help prove her earnings, the administrator offered a copy of Katherine's income tax return made out shortly before she died and submitted to the IRS. The court held that the income tax return was not a declaration against interest. Do you agree?

[B] Declarations Against Penal Interest

WILLIAMSON v. UNITED STATES

United States Supreme Court
512 U.S. 594 (1994)

JUSTICE O'CONNOR delivered the opinion of the Court, except as to Part II-C.

In this case we clarify the scope of the hearsay exception for statements against penal interest. Fed. Rule Evid. 804(b)(3).

I

A deputy sheriff stopped the rental car driven by Reginald Harris for weaving on the highway. Harris consented to a search of the car, which revealed 19 kilograms of cocaine in two suitcases in the trunk. Harris was promptly arrested.

Shortly after Harris' arrest, Special Agent Donald Walton of the Drug Enforcement Administration (DEA) interviewed him by telephone. During that conversation, Harris said that he got the cocaine from an unidentified Cuban in Fort Lauderdale; that the cocaine belonged to petitioner Williamson; and that it was to be delivered that night to a particular dumpster. Williamson was also connected to Harris by physical evidence: The luggage bore the initials of Williamson's sister, Williamson was listed as an additional driver on the car rental agreement, and an envelope addressed to Williamson and a receipt with Williamson's girlfriend's address were found in the glove compartment.

Several hours later, Agent Walton spoke to Harris in person. During that interview, Harris said he had rented the car a few days earlier and had driven it to Fort Lauderdale to meet Williamson. According to Harris, he had gotten the cocaine from a Cuban who was Williamson's acquaintance, and the Cuban had put the cocaine in the car with a note telling Harris how to deliver the drugs.

Agent Walton then took steps to arrange a controlled delivery of the cocaine. But as Walton was preparing to leave the interview room, Harris "got out of [his] chair . . . and . . . took a half step toward [Walton] . . . and . . . said, . . . 'I can't let you do that,' threw his hands up and said 'that's not true, I can't let you go up there for no reason.' " Harris told Walton he had lied about the Cuban, the note, and the dumpster. The real story, Harris said, was that he was transporting the cocaine to Atlanta for Williamson, and that Williamson was traveling in front of him in another rental car. Harris added that after his car was stopped, Williamson turned around and drove past the location of the stop, where he could see Harris' car with its trunk open.

Because Williamson had apparently seen the police searching the car, Harris explained that it would be impossible to make a controlled delivery.

Harris told Walton that he had lied about the source of the drugs because he was afraid of Williamson. Though Harris freely implicated himself, he did not want his story to be recorded, and he refused to sign a written version of the statement.

Walton testified that he had promised to report any cooperation by Harris to the Assistant United States Attorney. Walton said Harris was not promised any reward or other benefit for cooperating.

Williamson was eventually convicted of possessing cocaine with intent to distribute, conspiring to possess cocaine with intent to distribute, and traveling interstate to promote the distribution of cocaine. When called to testify at Williamson's trial, Harris refused, even though the prosecution gave him use immunity and the court ordered him to testify and eventually held him in contempt. The District Court then ruled that, under Rule 804(b)(3), Agent Walton could relate what Harris had said to him.

The Court of Appeals for the Eleventh Circuit affirmed without opinion. [The Supreme Court here reverses.]

II

A

To decide whether Harris' confession is made admissible by Rule 804(b)(3), we must first determine what the Rule means by "statement," which Federal Rule of Evidence 801(a)(1) defines as "an oral or written assertion." One possible meaning, "a report or narrative," Webster's Third New International Dictionary 2229, defn. 2(a) (1961), connotes an extended declaration. Under this reading, Harris' entire confession — even if it contains both self-inculpatory and non-self-inculpatory parts — would be admissible so long as in the aggregate the confession sufficiently inculpates him. Another meaning of "statement," "a single declaration or remark," *ibid.*, defn. 2(b), would make Rule 804(b)(3) cover only those declarations or remarks within the confession that are individually self-inculpatory.

Although the text of the Rule does not directly resolve the matter, the principle behind the Rule, so far as it is discernible from the text, points clearly to the narrower reading. Rule 804(b)(3) is founded on the commonsense notion that reasonable people, even reasonable people who are not especially honest, tend not to make self-inculpatory statements unless they believe them to be true. This notion simply does not extend to the broader definition of "statement." [O]ne of the most effective ways to lie is to mix falsehood with truth, especially truth that seems particularly persuasive because of its self-inculpatory nature.

In this respect, it is telling that the non-self-inculpatory things Harris said in his first statement actually proved to be false, as Harris himself admitted during the second interrogation. And when part of the confession is actually self-exculpatory, the generalization on which Rule 804(b)(3) is founded becomes even less applicable. [M]ere proximity to other, self-inculpatory, statements does not increase the plausibility of the self-exculpatory statements.

We therefore cannot agree with Justice Kennedy's suggestion that the Rule can be read as expressing a policy that collateral statements — even ones that are not in any way against the declarant's interest — are admissible. Nothing in the text of Rule 804(b)(3) or the general theory of the hearsay Rules suggests that admissibility should turn on whether a statement is collateral to a self-inculpatory statement. [W]e see no reason why collateral statements, even ones that are neutral as to interest, should be treated any differently from other hearsay statements that are generally excluded.

Congress certainly could, subject to the constraints of the Confrontation Clause, make statements admissible based on their proximity to self-inculpatory statements. But we will not lightly assume that the ambiguous language means anything so inconsistent with the Rule's underlying theory. In our view, the most faithful reading of Rule 804(b)(3) is that it does not allow admission of non-self-inculpatory statements, even if they are made within a broader narrative that is generally self-inculpatory. The district court may not just assume for purposes of Rule 804(b)(3) that a statement is self-inculpatory because it is part of a fuller confession, and this is especially true when the statement implicates someone else.

Justice Kennedy suggests that the Advisory Committee Notes to Rule 804(b)(3) should be read as endorsing the position we reject — that an entire narrative, including non-self-inculpatory parts (but excluding the clearly self-serving parts), may be admissible if it is in the aggregate self-inculpatory. The Notes read, in relevant part:

> [T]he third-party confession . . . may include statements implicating [the accused], and under the general theory of declarations against interest they would be admissible as related statements . . . . Whether a statement is in fact against interest must be determined from the circumstances of each case. Thus a statement admitting guilt and implicating another person, made while in custody, may well be motivated by a desire to curry favor with the authorities and hence fail to qualify as against interest . . . . On the other hand, the same words spoken under different circumstances, *e.g.*, to an acquaintance, would have no difficulty in qualifying . . . .

This language, however, is not particularly clear, and some of it — especially the Advisory Committee's endorsement of the position taken by Dean McCormick's treatise — points the other way:

> A certain latitude as to contextual statements, neutral as to interest, giving meaning to the declaration against interest seems defensible, but bringing in self-serving statements contextually seems questionable . . . . [A]dmit[ting] the disserving parts of the declaration, and exclud[ing] the self-serving parts . . . seems the most realistic method of adjusting admissibility to trustworthiness, where the serving and disserving parts can be severed.

Without deciding exactly how much weight to give the Notes in this particular situation, we conclude that the policy expressed in the statutory text points clearly enough in one direction that it outweighs whatever force the Notes may have. And though Justice Kennedy believes that the text can fairly be read as expressing a policy of admitting collateral statements, for the reasons given above we disagree.

B

We also do not share Justice Kennedy's fears that our reading of the Rule "eviscerate[s] the against penal interest exception," or makes it lack "meaningful effect." There are many circumstances in which Rule 804(b)(3) does allow the admission of statements that inculpate a criminal defendant. Even the confessions of arrested accomplices may be admissible if they are truly self-inculpatory, rather than merely attempts to shift blame or curry favor.

For instance, a declarant's squarely self-inculpatory confession — "yes, I killed X" — will likely be admissible under Rule 804(b)(3) against accomplices of his who are being tried under a co-conspirator liability theory. Likewise, by showing that the declarant knew something, a self-inculpatory statement can in some situations help the jury infer that his confederates knew it as well. And when seen with other evidence, an accomplice's self-inculpatory statement can inculpate the defendant directly: "I was robbing the bank on Friday morning," coupled with someone's testimony that the declarant and the defendant drove off together Friday morning, is evidence that the defendant also participated in the robbery.

Moreover, whether a statement is self-inculpatory or not can only be determined by viewing it in context. Even statements that are on their face neutral may actually be against the declarant's interest. "I hid the gun in Joe's apartment" may not be a confession of a crime; but if it is likely to help the police find the murder weapon, then it is certainly self-inculpatory. [T]he question under Rule 804(b)(3) is always whether the statement was sufficiently against the declarant's penal interest "that a reasonable person in the declarant's position would not have made the statement unless believing it to be true," and this question can only be answered in light of all the surrounding circumstances.

C

In this case, however, we cannot conclude that all that Harris said was properly admitted. Some of Harris' confession would clearly have been admissible under Rule 804(b)(3); for instance, when he said he knew there was cocaine in the suitcase, he essentially forfeited his only possible defense to a charge of cocaine possession, lack of knowledge. But other parts of his confession, especially the parts that implicated Williamson, did little to subject Harris himself to criminal liability. A reasonable person in Harris' position might even think that implicating someone else would decrease his practical exposure to criminal liability, at least so far as sentencing goes. Small fish in a big conspiracy often get shorter sentences than people who are running the whole show, especially if the small fish are willing to help the authorities catch the big ones.

Nothing in the record shows that the District Court or the Court of Appeals inquired whether each of the statements in Harris' confession was truly self-inculpatory. As we explained above, this can be a fact-intensive inquiry, which would require careful examination of all the circumstances surrounding the criminal activity involved; *we therefore remand to the Court of Appeals to conduct this inquiry in the first instance.*

JUSTICE SCALIA, concurring:

I join the Court's opinion, which I do not understand to require the simplistic view of statements against penal interest that Justice Kennedy attributes to it.

[A] declarant's statement is not magically transformed from a statement against penal interest into one that is inadmissible merely because the declarant names another person or implicates a possible codefendant. For example, if a lieutenant in an organized crime operation described the inner workings of an extortion and protection racket, naming some of the other actors and thereby inculpating himself on racketeering and/or conspiracy charges, I have no doubt that some of those remarks could be admitted as statements against penal interest. Of course, naming another person, if done, for example, in a context where the declarant is minimizing culpability or criminal exposure, can bear on whether the statement meets the Rule 804(b)(3) standard. The relevant inquiry, however — and one that is not furthered by clouding the waters with manufactured categories such as "collateral neutral" and "collateral self-serving," — must always be whether the particular remark at issue (and not the extended narrative) meets the standard set forth in the Rule.

JUSTICE GINSBURG, with whom JUSTICE BLACKMUN, JUSTICE STEVENS, and JUSTICE SOUTER join, concurring in part and concurring in the judgment:

I join Parts I, II-A, and II-B of the Court's opinion.

Unlike Justice O'Connor, [I] conclude that Reginald Harris' statements [d]o not fit, even in part, within the exception described in Rule 804(b)(3), for Harris' arguably inculpatory statements are too closely intertwined with his self-serving declarations to be ranked as trustworthy. Harris was caught red-handed with 19 kilos of cocaine — enough to subject even a first-time offender to a minimum of 12 1/2 years' imprisonment. He could have denied knowing the drugs were in the car's trunk, but that strategy would have brought little prospect of thwarting a criminal prosecution. He therefore admitted involvement, but did so in a way that minimized his own role and shifted blame to petitioner Fredel Williamson (and a Cuban man named Shawn).

To the extent some of these statements tended to incriminate Harris, they provided only marginal or cumulative evidence of his guilt. They project an image of a person acting not against his penal interest, but striving mightily to shift principal responsibility to someone else.

[I] concur in the Court's decision to vacate the Court of Appeals' judgment, however, because I have not examined the entire trial court record; I therefore cannot say the Government should be denied an opportunity to argue that the erroneous admission of the hearsay statements [c]onstituted harmless error.

JUSTICE KENNEDY, with whom THE CHIEF JUSTICE and JUSTICE THOMAS join, concurring in the judgment:

I

There has been a long-running debate among commentators over the admissibility of collateral statements. Dean Wigmore took the strongest position in favor of admissibility, arguing that "the statement may be accepted, not merely as to the specific fact against interest, but also as to every fact contained in the same statement." [D]ean McCormick's approach regarding collateral statements was more guarded. He argued for the admissibility of collateral statements of a neutral character; and for the exclusion of collateral statements of a self-serving character. For example, in the statement "John and I robbed the bank," the words "John and" are neutral (save for the possibility of conspiracy charges). On the other hand, the statement "John, not I, shot the bank teller" is to some extent self-serving and therefore might be inadmissible. Professor Jefferson took the narrowest approach, arguing that the reliability of a statement against interest stems only from the disserving fact stated and so should be confined "to the proof of the fact which is against interest."

II

Because the text of Rule 804(b)(3) expresses no position regarding the admissibility of collateral statements, we must determine whether there are other authoritative guides on the question. In my view, three sources demonstrate that Rule 804(b)(3) allows the admission of some collateral statements: the Advisory Committee Note, the common law of the hearsay exception for statements against interest, and the general presumption that Congress does not enact statutes that have almost no effect.

First, the Advisory Committee Note establishes that some collateral statements are admissible. In fact, it refers in specific terms to the issue we here confront: "[o]rdinarily the third-party confession is thought of in terms of exculpating the accused, but this is by no means always or necessarily the case: it may include statements implicating him, and under the general theory of declarations against interest they would be admissible as related statements."

[Second,] [a]bsent contrary indications, we can presume that Congress intended the principles and terms used in the Federal Rules of Evidence to be applied as they were at common law. "From the very beginning of this exception, it has been held that a declaration against interest is admissible, not only to prove the disserving fact stated, but also to prove other facts contained in collateral statements connected with the disserving statement."

There is yet a third reason weighing against the Court's interpretation, one specific to statements against penal interest that inculpate the accused. [A]bsent a textual direction to the contrary, [w]e should assume that Congress intended the penal interest exception for inculpatory statements to have some meaningful effect. That counsels against adopting a rule excluding collateral statements. [I]ndeed, as one commentator indicated, the conclusion that no collateral statements are admissible — the conclusion reached by the Court today — would "eviscerate the against penal interest exception."

To be sure, under the approach adopted by the Court, there are some situations where the Rule would still apply. For example, if the declarant said that he stole certain goods, the statement could be admitted in a prosecution of the accused for receipt of stolen goods in order to show that the goods were stolen. But as the commentators have recognized, it is likely to be the rare case where the precise self-inculpatory words of the declarant, without more, also inculpate the defendant. I would not presume that Congress intended the penal interest exception to the Rule to have so little effect with respect to statements that inculpate the accused.

I note finally that the Court's decision applies to statements against penal interest that exculpate the accused as well as to those that inculpate the accused. Thus, if the declarant said, "I robbed the store alone," only the portion of the statement in which the declarant said "I robbed the store" could be introduced by a criminal defendant on trial for the robbery. [T]he Court gives no justification for such a rule and no explanation that Congress intended the exception for exculpatory statements to have this limited effect.

III

Though I would conclude that Rule 804(b)(3) allows admission of statements collateral to the precise words against interest, that conclusion of course does not answer the remaining question whether all collateral statements related to the statement against interest are admissible; and if not, what limiting principles should apply.

[It] [a]ppears that the Advisory Committee Note, by its reference to (and apparent incorporation of) McCormick, contemplates exclusion of a collateral self-serving statement, but admission of a collateral neutral statement.

In the criminal context, a self-serving statement is one that tends to reduce the charges or mitigate the punishment for which the declarant might be liable. For example, if two masked gunmen robbed a bank and one of them shot and killed the bank teller, a statement by one robber that the other robber was the triggerman may be the kind of self-serving statement that should be inadmissible. By contrast, when two or more people are capable of committing a crime and the declarant simply names the involved parties, that statement often is considered neutral, not self-serving.

In sum, I would adhere to the following approach with respect to statements against penal interest that inculpate the accused. A court first should determine whether the declarant made a statement that contained a fact against penal interest. If so, the court should admit all statements related to the precise statement against penal interest, subject to two limits. Consistent with the Advisory Committee Note, the court should exclude a collateral statement that is so self-serving as to render it unreliable (if, for example, it shifts blame to someone else for a crime the defendant could have committed). In addition, in cases where the statement was made under circumstances where it is likely that the declarant had a significant motivation to obtain favorable treatment, [t]he entire statement should be inadmissible.

NOTES AND QUESTIONS

(1) *Would Williamson have Treated the Statement the Same if it were Made in a Non-Custodial Setting?* In *United States v. Boone*, 229 F.3d 1231 (9th Cir. 2000), *cert. denied*, 532 U.S. 1013 (2001), the court, interpreting *Williamson*, affirmed admission against defendant of statements of a non-testifying accomplice tape-recorded by his girlfriend without his knowledge, that implicated accomplice and defendant in an armed robbery. The court noted that at the time the statements were made, the accomplice was confiding in his girlfriend and had no motive to shift the blame to someone else or minimize his own culpability. (Is this really true? Or does he think he will get less disapproval from his girlfriend if the crime was a shared endeavor?)

On what theory does the statement in *Boone* disadvantage the declarant, as required by the rule? Or, quite the contrary, does he think he gets "points" from his girlfriend for looking like a "big man," so the statement is to his advantage?

(2) *What Does Williamson Mean? Should It be Strictly or Narrowly Interpreted?* Strict interpretation of *Williamson* will narrow the usefulness of this exception. See, e.g., *Ciccarelli v. Gichner Sys. Group, Inc.*, 862 F. Supp. 1293 (M.D. 1994), which noted that if a declarant says "John and I robbed the bank," *Williamson* would appear to admit only the statement "I robbed the bank." Is this really what *Williamson* means? Standing alone, the relevance of this statement in a prosecution against John is negligible, if there are no other circumstantial links to the defendant. Or it is misleading, suggesting the declarant and not the defendant did it?

(3) *Self-Inculpatory or Self-Serving?* It is often difficult to determine whether one of these in-custody mixed statements, insofar as it implicates the defendant with the declarant, is truly self-inclupatory or simply made to curry favor with the authorities. See *United States v. Riley*, 657 F.2d 1377 (8th Cir. 1981), reversing a conviction where declarant implicated herself in a crime that was less serious than that of the defendant. In *United States v. Mendoza*, 85 F.3d 1347 (8th Cir. 1996), a statement that identified the defendant as a source of drugs was held not to be sufficiently against the declarant's interest where it was made after she was caught red-handed with $16,000 and was told that the defendant had been caught near the drug drop-off point.

(4) *Williamson was an Interpretation of a Federal Evidentiary Rule, Not the Constitution.* The precise problem of *Williamson* and the above notes after the *Williamson* case may be rendered moot in some measure because the constitutional confrontation clause has, subsequent to *Williamson* and those note cases, been interpreted to ban statements like these when offered against a criminal defendant, at least when they are knowingly made by third parties to law enforcement authorities, in the awareness that they may have evidentiary value — and this constitutional prohibition applies, of course, whatever a rule of evidence may say. *See* Chapter 11, and in particular, the *Crawford* case. Nevertheless, *Williamson's*

approach to the rule (examining each part or implication of the statement for its against-interest quality) has important implications for the applicability of Fed. R. Evid. 804(b)(3) in other contexts than those within the constitutional ban. Such other contexts may include statements made *without* knowledge or awareness of government involvement or potential evidentiary value; statements made to *private* parties; statements offered *by* the criminal defense; and statements offered in *civil* cases. It is also worth remembering that not only are declarations against *penal* interest affected — by both *Williamson* and the new confrontation approach — but so also are declarations against other interests.

Would the statement in *Boone*, *supra*, note (1), preceding the new confrontation clause jurisprudence, now be *constitutionally* banned? Would police have to be involved in some way in the girlfriend's taping, to trigger the ban? Would it be sufficient if she did it alone, with intent to give it to the police? Do police have to be involved in advance? Did declarant have to know of police involvement? Of potential evidentiary use? Against who? *See* Chapter 11, § 11.03[B], discussion of *Crawford.*

(5) *The Uniform Rule.* The Federal Rule differs significantly from Rule 804(b)(3) of the Uniform Rules, recommended to the states by their drafters, which says in pertinent part: "A statement or confession offered against the accused in a criminal case, made by a codefendant or other individual implicating both the codefendant or other individual and the accused, is not within this exception." Does this reject more than *Williamson* rejects? More than the Constitution says must be rejected? Would this approach have negated the need for *Williamson*, or does that case reach other types of declarations as well? *See generally* Raeder, *Finding the Proper Balance in Hearsay Policy: The Uniform Rules Attempt to Stem the Hearsay Tide in Criminal Cases Without Prohibiting All Nontraditional Hearsay*, 54 OKLA. L. REV. 631 (2001).

(6) *Are Plea Allocutions Declarations Against Penal Interest?* Presently courts vary about the admissibility of statements made by co-defendants who plead guilty when introduced at the defendant's trial as a declaration against penal interest. The co-defendant may be unavailable because of a refusal to testify. In the circumstances of the case he may even retain a valid Fifth Amendment privilege. *Compare United States v. Moskowitz*, 215 F.3d 265 (2d Cir.), *cert. denied*, 531 U.S. 1014 (2000) (affirming admission), *with United States v. Vega*, 221 F.3d 789 (5th Cir. 2000), *cert. denied*, 531 U.S. 1155 (2001) (no abuse of discretion in refusing to admit plea colloquy that exculpated defendant). Should there be a difference depending upon whether it inculpates or exculpates the defendant? Constitutionally, can such statements be admitted *against* the defendant after *Crawford*? See Note (5), immediately *supra. Crawford* is not entirely clear about whether, when statements are made to law enforcement, to courts, or to other official governmental operations, they will be deemed "testimonial" even without awareness that the statement may make evidence in some other proceeding or investigation. But the case suggests they will be. See discussion in § 11.03[B]. *Crawford* specifically alludes to allocutions as untested testimonial statements.

UNITED STATES v. THOMAS

United States Court of Appeals, Fifth Circuit
571 F.2d 285 (1978)

GODBOLD, CIRCUIT JUDGE.

This case requires us to consider Federal Rule of Evidence 804(b)(3). The appellant, Thomas, was tried for bank robbery jointly with Weeks. At trial Thomas sought to place a U.S. Magistrate on the stand to testify that Weeks, at the close of the preliminary hearing for all those indicted in the robbery, made statements exculpating Thomas. The trial judge ruled the evidence inadmissible, and both Thomas and Weeks were convicted. Only Thomas has appealed.

[The] government was willing to stipulate, that after the [preliminary] hearing but before leaving the courtroom Weeks had stated "they ought to let Rowland Thomas go, he didn't have anything to do with it." Weeks made the statement not only within the hearing of the Magistrate but also in the presence of the attorneys for the prosecution and for the defendants and a newspaperman.

To be admissible under 804(b)(3), a statement [against penal interest] must meet three tests: the declarant's testimony must be unavailable; the statement must so far tend to subject the declarant to criminal liability that a reasonable man in his position would not have made the statement unless he believed it to be true'; and the statement, if offered [in a criminal case] must be corroborated by circumstances clearly indicating its trustworthiness.

Weeks' testimony was clearly unavailable. Weeks did not take the stand, obviously relying on the privilege against self-incrimination. Rule 804(a)(1) requires an express assertion of the privilege and a ruling by the court that the privilege constitutes unavailability, but here the existence of the privilege and Weeks' right to assert it and Weeks' unavailability as a witness are patent.

The statement offered by Thomas satisfies the requirement that it be against Weeks' penal interest. The government argues that Weeks' statement was not against his penal interest because he did not expressly confess to the crime involved. We do not read Rule 804(b)(3) to be limited to direct confessions of guilt. Rather, by referring to statements that "tend" to subject the declarant to criminal liability, the Rule encompasses disserving statements by a declarant that would have probative value in a trial against the declarant. Thus, we held to be against penal interest a statement that the declarant had given the accused a package of heroin instead of a package of Valium. Although the statement did not confess to the crime charged against the accused (possession with intent to distribute heroin), the statement implied the declarant's guilt of a felony, knowing possession of heroin.

In circumstances even more analogous to the present case, the First Circuit held a statement to be against penal interest. In *U.S. v. Barrett*. . . the deceased declarant Tilley had discussed the crime being tried. The accused presented a witness to testify that Tilley had stated during this conversation "Bucky [the accused] wasn't involved. It was Buzzy." The Court held the statement admissible under 804(b)(3) because

> [W]e think that Tilley's [the declarant's] alleged remarks sufficiently tended to subject him to criminal liability that a reasonable man in his position would not have made the statement unless he believed it to be true. Although the remarks did not amount to a clear confession to a crime we do not understand the hearsay exception to be limited to direct confessions. A reasonable person would have realized that remarks of the sort attributed to Tilley strongly implied his personal participation in the crimes and hence would tend to subject him to criminal liability. Though by no means conclusive, the statement would be important evidence against Tilley were he himself on trial for the crimes.
>
> Nor do we overlook the fact that exculpating Barrett [the accused] was not in itself against Tilley's interest. The district court seemed to suggest that in order for exculpatory remarks such as Tilley's to be admissible as against interest, the innocence of the accused must itself be prejudicial to the declarant. [We read 804(b)(3) more broadly. Such of Tilley's remarks as exculpated "Bucky" and inculpated "Buzzy" should here be considered as part of the statement against Tilley's interest.]

We conclude that Weeks' statement would not have been made by a reasonable man in his position unless he believed it to be true. Weeks made the statement exculpating Thomas at the close of the preliminary hearing at which Weeks had entered a plea of not guilty. The statement was not elicited by questioning, was facially spontaneous, and was made in the presence of [many]. Moreover, the statement, which implies that the declarant has knowledge of the crime, was inconsistent with Weeks' plea of not guilty and would have probative value in the government's case against him. All these circumstances lend credibility. We conclude that the statement falls within the letter and rationale of the exception provided in Rule 804(b)(3).

The statement was thus admissible under Rule 804(b)(3) if "corroborating circumstances clearly indicate the trustworthiness of the statement."

The record clearly indicates the trustworthiness of the statement. Even according to government witness Echols, Thomas was only marginally involved in the robbery; he did not assist in the planning, and the details of the robbery were never discussed in front of him. Echols received money from Weeks, but Thomas did not. Weeks gave his clothes to Echols and told Echols to burn them and his [Echols'] also. Thomas' clothes were not included in these instructions. No one other than Echols was able to tie Thomas to the robbery. The only evidence to contradict Thomas' seemingly marginal connection with the robbery was Echols' testimony that Weeks told him on the morning of the robbery that Thomas would drive and Echols' statement that Thomas suggested circling the bank until the customers inside left. Echols, however, testified that Weeks planned the robbery and secured Thomas' participation. Thus, Weeks' statement exculpating Thomas is given credibility because of Echols' characterization of Weeks as the mastermind and conduit to Thomas.

The statement has additional credibility because the possibility of fabrication, which is the rationale of the corroboration requirement, is slight. Weeks made the statement spontaneously in front of a number of people, and the witness to the statement, a U.S. Magistrate, is entitled to credibility. Weeks had no motive to falsify (unlike Echols, who had pleaded guilty to a lesser count of the indictment) and, indeed, incurred personal risk in making the statement. Under these facts, we hold that corroborating circumstances clearly indicate the trustworthiness of the statement.

The conviction is reversed.

NOTES AND QUESTIONS

(1) *What Corroboration is Sufficient?* Statements under Fed. R. Evid. 804(b)(3) must, in these cases, be attended by "corroborating circumstances clearly indicating trustworthiness." Does this comport with a right to defend, under Due Process? *See Chambers v. Miss.*, § 11.06, *infra*. For more on what constitutes sufficient corroboration under the Rule, and whether the statement must directly exculpate in order to be subject to this requirement, see *Lowery v. Maryland*, 401 F. Supp. 604 (D. Md. 1975), *aff'd without opinion*, 532 F.2d 750 (4th Cir.), *cert. denied*, 429 U.S. 919 (1976) (discussing whether factors impugning credibility may be considered under the corroboration requirement). *See also United States v. Worley*, 88 F.3d 644 (8th Cir. 1996) (affirming exclusion of testimony due to lack of corroboration). In *Worley*, an inmate who had been in jail with the defendant would have testified that the main prosecution witness had admitted she had planted a gun in the defendant's briefcase.

United States v. Amerson, 185 F.3d 676 (7th Cir.), *cert. denied*, 528 U.S. 1029 (1999), affirmed the exclusion of a defendant-exculpating affidavit by a person who claimed he had thrown the drugs that the defendant allegedly abandoned when the defendant knocked on the door of the apartment being searched. The affiant took the Fifth Amendment at trial, and the judge excluded the statement for lack of corroborated trustworthiness. The case includes a lengthy dissent by Judge Posner. The decision clearly raises the issue of whether police denials of an affiant's statement can negate corroboration.

(2) *Statements Against "Social Interest."* A few states include statements made against social interest, i.e., statements that would subject the declarant to "hatred, ridicule, or disgrace." *See* Cal. Evid. Code 1230; Tex. R. Evid. 803(24). What are the policy arguments pro and con for this expanded definition? Are these arguably already covered by other interests? Would a declaration of illegitimacy qualify? What about a person admitting to being a snitch in prison? Is there any safeguard in such a rule that would guard against statements that are only mildly embarrassing?

PROBLEM 10D: A STATEMENT ALLEGEDLY ADMITTING HEROIN USE.

In a state prosecution for murder against a physician accused of giving his wealthy wife fatal amounts of a medication she was on for her heart, the defense wishes to have a friend of the wife testify that the wife told the friend she was a frequent heroin user as well, unbeknownst to the husband. (Heroin would make the wife much more susceptible to the bad effects of the heart medication.) Is the testimony admissible?

NOTE

Note on Skipped Hearsay Exceptions. You will note at this point we are skipping two hearsay exceptions in Fed. R. Evid. 804(b): subdivision (4) (statement of personal or family history), and subdivision (6) (forfeiture by wrongdoing). We leave the former, a rarely used and conceptually uncomplicated exception, for you to read preferably immediately on your own, since you now have considerable experience in analyzing hearsay exceptions. The latter we treat in Chapter 11, under our examination of the constitutional Confrontation Clause foreiture doctrine. The "forfeiture" hearsay exception originated as and is probably reasonably coterminous with the analogous concept of waiver of confrontation rights by wrongdoing. However, the student is advised to quickly read through the "forfeiture" hearsay exception now, as well.

§ 10.05 "CATCHALL" OR RESIDUAL EXCEPTION[5]

Read Federal Rule of Evidence 807, "Residual Exception."

HUFF v. WHITE MOTOR CORP.

United States Court of Appeals, Seventh Circuit
609 F.2d 286 (1979)

TONE, CIRCUIT JUDGE.

In the trial of this diversity action for wrongful death, the court excluded a statement of the plaintiff's decedent, made while he was hospitalized for treatment of the injuries from which he later died. We hold that unless the declarant was not mentally competent when he made the statement, it should have been admitted under the so-called residual exception to the hearsay rule established by Rules 803(24) and 804(b)(5) of the Federal Rules of Evidence. We remand for a determination by the district court of the preliminary question of competence and for a new trial if the declarant is found to have been competent.

In a previous appeal in this case we held that under Indiana law a manufacturer has a duty to design a motor vehicle so that it will not be unreasonably dangerous if it is involved in a collision, and therefore we reversed a summary judgment for defendant based on a contrary view of Indiana law. In the opinion in that case the essential facts were summarized as follows:

> On September 4, 1970 Jessee Huff was driving a truck-tractor manufactured by the defendant White Motor Corporation near Terre Haute, Indiana when it jackknifed on the highway, sideswiped a guardrail, and collided with an overpass support. Aside from the structural damage to the

[5] Study Guide Reference: Evidence in a Nutshell, Chapter 10:IV–V.

> tractor, the fuel tank ruptured and caught fire. The flames engulfed the cab area occupied by Huff. The severe burns he received in the fire caused his death nine days later. Helen L. Huff filed this action seeking damages for wrongful death of her husband based on the theory that the defective design of the fuel system caused the fire that took Huff's life.

Defendant offered and the trial court excluded the testimony of Melvin Myles, who was the husband of Mrs. Huff's cousin and a friend and neighbor of the Huffs for many years. Myles' testimony, presented out of the presence of the jury, was that, when he and one Richard King visited Huff in his hospital room two or three days after the accident, Huff gave the following description of how the accident occurred:

> [H]e told us first more or less what happened and this U.S. 41 there has a bad curve there and he told us as he was approaching the curve or starting into it his pant leg was on fire and he was trying to put his pant leg out and lost control and hit the bridge abutment and then the truck was on fire.

The district court excluded this testimony as hearsay, rejecting defendant's argument that Huff's statement was an admission under Rule 801(d)(2) or admissible under the residual exception, Rules 803(24) and 804(b)(5). On appeal, defendant argues that the evidence was admissible on both theories the district court rejected and also as a statement against interest under Rule 804(b)(3). We do not consider the latter argument, because Rule 804(b)(3) was not mentioned to the district court as a basis for admitting the evidence.

Defendant first argues that Huff's statement is admissible as an admission because privity exists between Huff and his widow, who brings this wrongful death action. At common law, privity-based admissions have been generally accepted by the courts.

Plaintiff argues that privity is lacking here because under Indiana law a wrongful death action is not derivative. [T]his should not be controlling, and the exclusion by "some courts" of statements of the deceased in wrongful death cases because the action is not "derivative" is based on "a hypertechnical concept of privity."

The admissibility of privity-based admissions in the federal courts is now controlled, of course, by the Federal Rules of Evidence. A reading of Article VIII of those rules, the article on hearsay, leads us to conclude that privity-based admissions are to be tested for admissibility under the residual exception provided for in Rules 803(24) and 804(b)(5) rather than under the admissions provision, Rule 801(d)(2). Although neither the rules themselves nor the Advisory Committee Notes refer to privity-based admissions, and Congress added nothing on the subject in its consideration of the rules, the language of Rule 801(d)(2) and the general scheme of the hearsay article support our conclusion. Privity-based admissions are within the definition of hearsay, Rule 801(c), an extra-judicial statement offered "to prove the truth of the matter asserted," and are not among the specifically defined kinds of admissions that despite Rule 801(c) are declared not to be hearsay in Rule 801(d)(2). Nor are they covered by any of the specific exceptions to the hearsay rule listed in Rules 803 and 804. Thus privity-based admissions are not admissible as such, if the rules are to be read literally. Moreover, the very explicitness of Rule 801(d)(2) suggests that the draftsmen did not intend to authorize the courts to add new categories of admissions to those stated in the rule. No standards for judicial improvisation or discretion are provided in Rule 801(d)(2), as they are in Rules 803(24) and 804(b)(5).

The admissibility of Huff's statement depends, therefore, upon the residual exception, which is stated in Rules 803(24) and 804(b)(5).

We recognize at the outset that in applying this exception the district court has a considerable measure of discretion. If, however, we arrive at "a definite and firm conviction that the court below committed a clear error of judgment in the conclusion it reached based upon a weighing of the relevant factors," and that the error was prejudicial, we must reverse. We also recognize that Congress "intended that the residual hearsay exceptions will be used very rarely, and only in exceptional circumstances." Committee on the Judiciary, S Rep No. 93-1277, Note to Paragraph (24); *see also United States v. Kim*, 595 F.2d 755 (D.C. Cir. 1979); *United States v. Bailey*, 581 F.2d 341 (3d Cir. 1978). We think such circumstances are present here.

In reviewing a ruling made in the exercise of the trial court's discretion, we are greatly aided when the record contains a statement of the reasons for the ruling and any findings made under Rule 104(a) on preliminary questions of fact relevant to admissibility. Here nothing of this sort is available. Although the defendant relied on the residual exception, it was not mentioned in the court's explanation of its ruling excluding the evidence. Under these circumstances, we have little choice except to attempt to replicate the exercise of discretion that would be made by a trial judge in making the ruling.

Hearsay evidence must fulfill five requirements to be admissible under the residual exception. We apply them to resolve the issue before us.

1. Trustworthiness

The circumstantial guarantees of trustworthiness on which the various specific exceptions to the hearsay rule are based are those that existed at the time the statement was made and do not include those that may be added by using hindsight. Evidence admissible under the residual exception must have "*equivalent* circumstantial guarantees of trustworthiness." Rules 803(24) and 804(b)(5) (emphasis added). Therefore, the guarantees to be considered in applying that exception are those that existed when the statement was made. In contrast, the probative value of an admission of a party-opponent, classified as non-hearsay by Rule 801(d)(2), is based on its inconsistency with the position asserted in court, and that probative value does not depend on whether the party knew when making it that it would be against his interest in a later lawsuit. Accordingly, in evaluating the circumstantial guarantees of trustworthiness with respect to Huff's statement, we may not consider its probative value as an admission of one who would be bringing the action if he had survived.

Turning to the circumstances we may properly consider for the present purposes, we note that Huff's statement was an unambiguous and explicit report of the events he had experienced two or three days earlier; it contained neither opinion nor speculation. He was not being interrogated, so there was no reason to give any explanation of how the accident happened unless he wanted to do so. There was no reason for him to invent the story of the preexisting fire in the cab. The story was contrary to his pecuniary interest, *cf.* Rule 804(b)(3), whether or not he was aware of a possible claim against the manufacturer of the vehicle. A fire of unexplained cause on Huff's clothing would tend to indicate driver error and to fix the responsibility for the accident, with attendant adverse pecuniary consequences, on him.

Plaintiff also argues that it is unlikely that Huff made the statement, because Mrs. Huff testified that he was not physically able to carry on a conversation. Even if we were to consider facts bearing on the reliability of Myles' reporting of the incident in determining its admissibility, we would not be persuaded that it should have been excluded for this reason. Mrs. Huff was an interested witness and, moreover, was assisted by her counsel's leading questions in giving the testimony relied on. No reason is suggested why Myles, a friend and relative by marriage, would have manufactured the story. Although the trial judge did not address the residual exception and made no credibility finding, it appears from his remarks that he credited Myles' testimony.

In our view, however, the reliability of the witness' testimony that the hearsay statement was in fact made is not a factor to be considered in deciding its admissibility. We recognize that the Third Circuit said otherwise in the *Bailey* case. But, as we have already noted, the circumstantial guarantees of trustworthiness necessary under the residual exception are to be "equivalent" to the guarantees that justify the specific exceptions. Those guarantees relate solely to the trustworthiness of the hearsay statement itself. The specific exceptions to the hearsay rule are not justified by any circumstantial guarantee that the witness who reports the statement will do so accurately and truthfully. That witness can be cross-examined and his credibility thus tested in the same way as that of any other witness. It is the hearsay declarant, not the witness who reports the hearsay, who cannot be cross-examined. Therefore, although we do not think Myles' testimony would fail a reliability test, that test is not to be applied by the court but by the jury, as with any other witness.

For the same reason, the probability that the statement is true, as shown by corroborative evidence, is not, we think, a consideration relevant to its admissibility under the residual exception to the hearsay rule. Because the presence or absence of corroborative evidence is irrelevant in the case of a specific exception, it is irrelevant here, where the guarantees of trustworthiness must be equivalent to those supporting specific exceptions. Accordingly, in reaching our decision we do not rely upon the evidence to which defendant has pointed as corroborating Huff's story of the fire in the cab.

All that we have said in explaining why the statement possesses circumstantial guarantees of trustworthiness presupposes that Huff was mentally competent to make a responsible statement. If he was not, the circumstantial guarantees of trustworthiness stated above melt away. Although it can be argued plausibly that the question of mental competence should be left to the jury, we believe the judge should decide this question as a preliminary question of fact under Rule 104(a). It is true that if Huff were the witness the question would be left to the jury. *See* Rule 601.

But he is a hearsay declarant, not a witness, and the circumstantial guarantees of trustworthiness on which the admissibility of the hearsay depends all presuppose the mental capacity of a reasonable man in the position Huff was in. If that mental capacity was lacking, so are the guarantees of trustworthiness. Since it is the judge who must determine whether the requisite guarantees exist, he must determine whether Huff possessed the requisite capacity. The burden is on the proponent of the evidence to prove capacity by a preponderance of the evidence.

The case will be remanded for a determination of whether Huff possessed the mental capacity of a reasonable man. If Huff possessed the capacity, the evidence is admissible and a new trial will be necessary. If the judge decides otherwise, a new trial will be unnecessary, since the exclusion [was correct].

2. Materiality

Rules 803(24) and 804(b)(5) require that the statement be offered as evidence of a material fact, which we take to be a requirement of relevance. Defendant argues that the existence of a fire in the cab before the crash would be relevant to the issue of what caused the fuel to ignite after the crash, plaintiff having pleaded, offered proof, and argued that the location of the battery and battery mechanism as a result of a design error was a likely cause of ignition. Plaintiff responds that there were several possible sources of ignition. Assuming this to be true, the evidence was nevertheless relevant. The "fact that is of consequence" for purposes of the application of Rule 401 is that, as defendant contended, the fuel was ignited by a fire in the cab that was not due to a defect in the vehicle. If proved, that fact would be "of consequence to the determination of the action." The evidence in issue would tend "to make the existence of [that] fact more probable or less probable than it would be without the evidence." Accordingly, the evidence is plainly relevant.

3. Probative Importance of the Evidence

To be admissible under the residual exception, the statement must be "more probative on the point for which it is offered than any other evidence [the defendant] can procure through reasonable efforts." Huff's statement satisfies this requirement. The other evidence is expert opinion and Hicks' circumstantial testimony about what he saw when he arrived at the scene after the crash. Only Huff was in the cab immediately before the crash and knew whether there was a fire in the cab at that time. Unless the hearsay is admitted, there will be no direct evidence on that question. Moreover, the unique probative quality that would lie in Huff's admission if he had survived to bring this action is not lost when the action is brought by his widow for his wrongful death.

4. The Interests of Justice

The hearsay statement is to be admitted only if doing so will best serve the general purposes of the Federal Rules of Evidence and the interests of justice. As we have already said, the circumstantial guarantees of trustworthiness and the probative value of the statement are strong. The need for the only available direct evidence on the issue of whether there was a fire in the cab, which, if it existed, would have been a likely source of ignition of the fuel, is obvious. There is no reason to believe the jury will not be equipped to evaluate the evidence. Admission of the evidence will best serve the interests of justice by increasing the likelihood that the jury will ascertain the truth about the cause of the accident.

5. Notice

[The notice requirement is held satisfied.]

Vacated and remanded with directions.

UNITED STATES v. SPOSITO

United States Court of Appeals, First Circuit
106 F.3d 1042 (1997)

Torrvella, C.J..

[To obtain Defendant Sposito's conviction for gambling violations, the Government relied in part on a transcript of the testimony of Louis Padova, who had testified at an earlier trial involving a separate set of gambling offenses by Arthur Marder. Padova had testified that Marder had told him that he (Marder) was paying everyone — the implication being that Marder paid off local politicians to protect his illegal video poker business using Sposito as a go-between. The statement did not name Sposito directly. At Sposito's trial, Padova refused to testify even under a grant of immunity. The transcript would not have been admissible under the former testimony exception because Sposito had no opportunity to cross-examine, but the trial court admitted it under the residual exception, finding it relevant to a material fact and more probative on the point for which it was offered than other evidence. Here, Sposito argues that residual-exception evidence must be "more probative" of a "material" or ultimate fact, claiming that the material fact was whether Marder was paying politicians, not what Marder said to Padova. The Court of Appeals rejects this argument.

In ruling on the question, the trial court found "that the testimony relates to a material fact whether Arthur Marder was indeed paying off politicians to obtain protection for his video poker machine business in Revere. If that fact is proven, it increases the likelihood that he was paying off those politicians through Mr. Sposito." The court also found that "the testimony of Padova is more probative on the point of what Arthur Marder said to Padova than any other testimony the Government can procure."]

Rule 804(b)(5) requires that:

(A) the statement is offered as evidence of a material fact;

(B) the statement is more probative on the point for which it is offered than any other evidence which the proponent can procure through reasonable efforts; and

(C) the general purposes of these rules and the interests of justice will best be served by admission of the statement into evidence.

Reading the first two subparagraphs together, defendant argues, requires that (B) be read as if it included the words "of material fact" after the word "point." Thus, the defendant alleges that the district court [*i.e.*, the trial court] erred by not directing its inquiry to the "question of whether Marder's statement to Padova was more probative on the issue of whether Marder was paying off politicians than any other available testimony."

We begin, as always, with an examination of the plain language of the rule. Subsection (B) requires only that the statement be more probative on "the point for which it is offered." The subparagraph does not include the words "of material fact" as advocated by defendant. The drafters of Rule 804(b)(5) separated the "material fact" element of the test found in subparagraph (A) from the "more probative" element of subparagraph (B). Were the rule intended to have the meaning advocated by defendant, it could have been written with much greater clarity. As written, however, the plain language of the rule does not require that the issue on which the statement is most probative be a material fact; it requires only that it be most probative on the point "for which it is offered."

The statement is more probative on that point of evidence — what Marder told Padova — than any other evidence that the government could procure through reasonable efforts.

Defendant, perhaps recognizing that the language of the rule is not favorable to his argument, turns to legislative history. He points to language in the Senate Report to the effect that the residual hearsay exception should be used rarely. Our own examination of the legislative history, however, reveals that the inclusion of the residual hearsay exception was intended for cases, such as the one before us, that "have guarantees of trustworthiness equivalent to or exceeding the guarantees reflected by the [other Rule 804(b)] exceptions, and to have a high degree of [probativeness]."

In order to illustrate the type of evidence that the Senate Committee felt should be admitted but that may not fall within one of the other hearsay exceptions, the Senate Report cited *Dallas County v. Commercial Union Assurance Company*, 286 F.2d 388 (5th Cir.1961). S. Rep. No. 1277. At issue in that case was the cause of the collapse of the Dallas County Courtroom clock tower. [T]he insurers sought to introduce a newspaper article from 1901 describing a fire that had occurred in the courtroom in that year. The court admitted the evidence despite the fact that it was not characterized "as a 'business record,' nor as an 'ancient document,' nor as any other readily identifiable and happily tagged species of hearsay exception."

Under defendant's construction of the residual hearsay exception, however, the newspaper article in *Dallas County* would not be admissible. The story was not more probative on the point of [the ultimate issue of causation] than any other evidence. It was, however, more probative than any other evidence that the insurers could provide on the question of whether there had been a fire.

Finally, we turn to the policies served by the residual hearsay exception. These can be summarized as follows:

1. To provide sufficient flexibility to permit the courts to deal with new and unanticipated situations.

2. To preserve the integrity of the specifically enumerated exceptions.

3. To facilitate the basic purpose of the Federal Rules of Evidence: truth ascertainment and fair adjudication of controversies.

It is our view that these objectives are best served by rejecting defendant's proposed construction of 804(b)(5).

Defendant-appellant [also] claims that the admission of Padova's testimony was erroneous because the district court failed to analyze each part of the testimony in order to determine each part's reliability. In support of his claim, defendant cites *Williamson v. United States*, 512 U.S. 594 (1994), in which the Supreme Court ruled that, for the purposes of Rule 804(b)(3), which governs statements against interest, the word "statement" refers to a single remark. "The district court may not just assume for purposes of Rule 804(b)(3) that a statement is self-inculpatory because it is part of a fuller confession." Defendant would have us apply the same definition of "statement" to Rule 804(b)(5) and, under such a definition, he argues that the district court failed to analyze each part of the testimony.

The district court does not appear to have engaged in a sentence-by-sentence analysis of the testimony, as would be required by *Williamson*. The indicators of reliability that the district court used, however, are not specific to any portion of the testimony and would apply to every statement therein, implying that there is no error with respect to the reliability of the testimony. Specifically, the district court stated that "Mr. Padova testified at the Marder trial under oath, he was immunized and, therefore, had an incentive to tell the truth in order to avoid prosecution for perjury. He testified based upon personal knowledge." The judge also noted that "he was vigorously cross-examined by Mr. Duggan, the defense counsel."

There was, therefore, no plain error in the assessment of the reliability of the testimony.

With respect to subparagraphs (A)-(C) of Rule 804(b)(5), however, not every sentence of the testimony is admissible. For example, not every sentence in that testimony can be said to have been offered as evidence of a material fact. For this reason, assuming, arguendo, that *Williamson* applies, the district court's ruling was erroneous. The error was not, however, "plain." [Since this issue was raised for the first time on appeal, and there is no plain error, there is no reversible error.]

NOTES AND QUESTIONS

(1) *Trustworthiness Generally. See United States v. Fredericks*, 599 F.2d 262 (8th Cir. 1979) (evidence excluded in part because of lack of trustworthiness, because witness was girlfriend of defendant's brother); *Robinson v. Shapiro*, 646 F.2d 734 (2d Cir. 1981) (time lapse between event and statement as factor of

trustworthiness concerning evidence of conversation between repair crew foreman and building superintendent upon returning to accident scene after the construction accident, as to its cause). *See also Kirk v. Raymark Indus., Inc.*, 61 F.3d 147 (3d Cir. 1995) (interrogatory response of codefendant who had settled was not trustworthy).

(2) *Corroboration as it Relates to Trustworthiness.* A few cases suggest that corroboration of the facts related in the out-of-court statement can help indicate "trustworthiness" as the catchall hearsay exception uses that term. But most decisions agree with *Huff, supra* (suggesting that such corroboration cannot be considered — that, like other hearsay exceptions, there must be something inherent in the statement or the circumstances of making the statement that indicates trustworthiness).

(3) *What other Factors may Constitute "Trustworthiness?"* Trustworthiness sometimes is in the eyes of the beholder. What is your assessment of the following decisions? Be prepared to argue both sides.

(a) Defendant's brother is arrested for possession with intent to distribute cocaine. He testifies in his own suppression hearing that he directed defendant, who has not yet been charged, to purchase the toolbox (which contained the drugs) and arrange for the drug delivery. Defendant is then arrested. When his brother refuses to testify, the above testimony is offered pursuant to the catchall (not former testimony because the defendant could not cross-examine his brother). *See United States v. Clarke*, 2 F.3d 81 (4th Cir. 1993) (affirming admission), *cert. denied*, 510 U.S. 1166 (1994). *But see* § 11.03[B].

(b) Sister of defendant was stopped by police for driving the getaway car shortly after a robbery. She gave a false address and inconsistent statements about her possession of the car. She had $400 in her purse. After being given *Miranda* warnings and learning that other officers were making further arrests, she agreed to cooperate. She indicated that she had been awakened by her brother and others who came to her house, handled money, and gave her money and the car to go shopping. At trial, despite a grant of immunity, she refused to testify. *See United States v. Roberts*, 844 F.2d 537 (8th Cir.) (affirming admission under catchall, but recognizing that statement was not reliable enough to be against her penal interest), *cert. denied*, 488 U.S. 867 (1988). *But see* § 11.03[B].

Are these decisions based on a view of sibling loyalty? Would the results have been different if the declarant had not been related to the defendant?

(4) *Trustworthiness of Children.* In *United States v. Harrison*, 296 F.3d 994 (10th Cir. 2002), *cert. denied*, 537 U.S. 1134 (2003), in granting wide deference to the trial judge's finding that a child molestation victim's out-of-court accusations were trustworthy, the court said:

> [C]onsistency in the declarant's statements is not the sort of external corroboration barred from consideration. In our view, the consistency of C.V.'s three [earlier] statements [aside from her recantation] is a strong indicator of the trustworthiness of her statement.

The court also cites the extreme specificity and peculiarity of her accounts. The child in question in the case was fourteen when she made the statement alleging abuse that had happened more than four years earlier, and had a possible motive to lie. Is consistency by children always a factor supporting reliability? Review *Tome* in § 8.01[C]. Is consistency a factor that would support admission if the declarant were an adult?

(5) *Can a Statement by an Unavailable Declarant be More Probative than Live Testimony? Workman v. Cleveland-Cliffs Iron Co.*, 68 F.R.D. 562 (N.D. Ohio 1975), held that an unsworn statement (given on the day of the accident) by an accident victim (now dead) to an attorney for the defendant (who now offers it) was not more probative on the point than other evidence where there were other witnesses to the accident. Would this result be different if the witnesses testified contrary to the statement? In child abuse cases, judges often admit statements pursuant to the catchall, whether or not the child also testifies. *See United States v. Shaw*, 824 F.2d 601 (8th Cir. 1987) (upholding admission of statement, although child testified at length concerning incident), *cert. denied*, 484 U.S. 1068 (1988).

(6) *The Notice Requirement.* Failure to give adequate notice also can defeat the introduction of hearsay under the catchall. *See United States v. Pelullo*, 964 F.2d 193 (3d Cir. 1992) (lack of notice not harmless error). However, many courts are quite flexible in interpreting the notice provision. *See United States v. Iaconetti*, 540 F.2d 574 (2d Cir. 1976), *cert. denied*, 429 U.S. 1041 (1977) (holding that five days' notice given at trial satisfies rule, even though rule seems to say pretrial notice).

(7) *"Near Misses:" Hearsay that Almost, but Not Quite, Qualifies Under Other Exceptions.* One strategy for limiting the availability of the catchall for hearsay is found in cases refusing to admit "near misses," i.e., hearsay that does not quite fit a traditional hearsay exception. *See In re IBM Peripheral E.D.P. Devices Antitrust Litig.*, 444 F. Supp. 110 (N.D. Cal. 1978). Having rejected a contention that evidence is admissible under Fed. R. Evid. 804(b)(1) (former testimony), the court turned to the contention that Fed. R. Evid. 804(b)(5) (catchall) (now 807) applies:

> [The Rule] was intended to allow the courts a certain amount of discretion in admitting hearsay where there are equivalent circumstantial guarantees of trustworthiness. However, it is unlikely that Congress meant this exception to be used to circumvent its own restriction of another exception.

Judge Becker popularized this view in *Zenith Radio Corp. v. Matsushita Elec. Indus. Co.*, 505 F. Supp. 1190 (E.D. Pa. 1980). However, on appeal of *Zenith* the Third Circuit rejected the "near miss" concept because it "puts the federal evidence rules back into the straightjacket from which the residual exceptions were intended to free them." *In re Japanese Elec. Prods. Antitrust Litig.*, 723 F.2d 238, 302 (3d Cir. 1983), *rev'd on other grounds*, 475 U.S. 574 (1986).

Most other circuits also have refused to adopt a ban on near misses. For example, *United States v. Laster*, 258 F.3d 525 (6th Cir. 2001), decided that "the phrase 'specifically covered' [by another hearsay exception] [as that phrase is used in Rule 807] means only that if a statement is *admissible* under one of the [803 or 804] exceptions, such subsection should be relied upon instead of the residual exception." Would this mean that if another hearsay exception specifically excluded a particular kind of statement, the statement is not "specifically covered" by another hearsay exception, with the result that it could be admitted under Rule 807? Even if there were no special, unanticipated indicator of trustworthiness on the facts, and the only trustworthiness factor relied upon is the one the drafters found insufficient? For example, suppose it is argued that former testimony by a now unavailable witness (given in a proceeding under oath subject to perjury law, *but where there was no opportunity to cross-examine*) has a sufficient guarantee of trustworthiness to be admitted under Rule 807 simply because it was given at a proceeding under oath subject to perjury law, notwithstanding that the drafters of Rule 804(b)(1) specifically seem to have excluded such a statement from the former testimony exception. Is such a statement (because it is not rendered admissible by 804(b)(1)) not "specifically covered" by 804(b)(1)? Could we argue that such a statement *is* indeed "specifically covered" by 804(b)(1) (because it is specifically excluded) and therefore cannot be admitted under 807? Or would 804(b)(1) need to say in so many words "such a statement is excluded" or, even stronger, "is inadmissible"? Can you think of a hearsay exception that says such a thing? For example, Rule 803(3) or 803(8)? Would *Laster* still think, *even in that instance*, that the statement is *still not* "specifically covered" by the other hearsay exception (because not admissible under it) and thus is still admissible under the catchall?

In *People v. Katt*, 662 N.W.2d 12 (Mich. 2003), the Michigan Supreme Court stated: "We agree with the majority of the federal courts and conclude that a hearsay statement is 'specifically covered' by another exception for purposes of [the Michigan catchall, worded much the same], only when it is admissible under that exception. Therefore, we decline to adopt the near-miss theory as part of our method for determining when hearsay statements may be admissible under [the catchall]."

See also United States v. Fernandez, 892 F.2d 976 (11th Cir. 1989) (no *per se* exclusion of grand jury testimony). In *United States v. Carlson*, 547 F.2d 1346 (8th Cir. 1976), the Eighth Circuit affirmed admission against the criminal defendant of statements by a grand jury witness who refused to testify at trial. The court focused on the fact that the declarant had been under oath at the time of making the statements, and that when informing the trial judge of his refusal to testify later, the declarant stated he had told the truth to the grand jury. *See also United States v. West*, 574 F.2d 1131 (4th Cir. 1978) (trustworthiness found in deceased declarant's grand jury testimony offered against the criminal defendant because close supervision of his activities as undercover informant rendered deception of agents "substantially impossible"). What about the Congressional intent that grand jury statements are admissible only if the witness is also present at the trial, manifest in Fed. R. Evid. 801(d)(1)(A), and that this can be dispensed with only where the former proceeding involved cross-examination (which a grand jury does not), manifest in Fed. R. Evid. 804(b)(1)? *See also United States v. Deeb*, 13 F.3d 1532 (11th Cir. 1994), *cert. denied*, 513 U.S. 1146 (1995) and *United States v. Shaw*, 69 F.3d 1249 (4th Cir. 1995) (admitting testimony from previous trials of co-conspirators that was not former testimony due to absence of opportunity for cross-examination by defendant). But some of these specific decisions of admissibility against the criminal defendant in this note, though possibly good law under Rule 807, may now be overridden by the new Confrontation clause jurisprudence under *Crawford*. See Chapter 11.

Other near misses that have been permitted under the residual exception include prior inconsistent statements not under oath (*United States v. Marshall*, 856 F.2d 896 (7th Cir. 1988)); child hearsay not fitting excited utterances (*United States v. Ellis*, 935 F.2d 385 (1st Cir.) (social worker's testimony concerning child's play with anatomically correct dolls), *cert. denied*, 502 U.S. 869 (1991)); and business and official records without sufficient foundation or within the law enforcement exclusion (*United States v. Nivica*, 887 F.2d 1110 (1st Cir. 1989) (Mexican bank records), *cert. denied*, 494 U.S. 1005 (1990)); *United States v. Blackburn*, 992 F.2d 666 (7th Cir.) (computer printouts (of lensometer readings for eyeglasses) created at FBI's request), *cert. denied*, 510 U.S. 949 (1993).

For a discussion of safety codes and standards prepared by industries, governments, or organizations formed for the purpose of promoting safety that also might fit Fed. R. Evid. 803(18), see *Johnson v. William C. Ellis & Sons Iron Works, Inc.*, 604 F.2d 950 (5th Cir.), *reh'g denied in part and granted in part*, 609 F.2d 820 (5th Cir. 1979).

Are there other examples of near misses qualifying under the catchall in the cases and notes in this chapter? Is there a distinction between relying, in a near miss situation, on the trustworthiness factors that don't quite make it under the standard exception and relying on additional case-specific, unforeseen factors?

(8) *Admitting Opinion Polls Under the Catchall.* The catchall also has been used to admit evidence of the results of surveys or polls, of the type found in *Zippo Mfg. Co. v. Rogers Imports, Inc.*, 216 F. Supp. 670 (S.D.N.Y. 1963) (treating question as one of whether evidence is hearsay in first place, and whether it is within state of mind exception, and holding it admissible on both grounds) and in *Baumholser v. Amax Coal Co.*, 630 F.2d 550 (7th Cir. 1980) (treating matter as one of whether such a poll may be proper basis for expert opinion testimony, another good road for admitting such evidence). These cases appear *supra* at § 7.03 and § 5.04, respectively. If the poll or survey was conducted with proper polling techniques by people with proper training, the evidence frequently comes in under the "catchall." In fact, *Zippo* mentions in support of its opinion (admitting the evidence) that proper polling techniques and trained personnel were in fact employed, and mentions the extreme inconvenience of calling to the stand the hundreds of persons questioned by the pollsters. Thus, it was in part a precursor of the "catchall" exception, with its twin requirements of special trustworthiness of and necessity for the evidence. Other rules also may be involved, such as Fed. R. Evid. 401–403 and 702–703.

(9) *Exceptional Circumstances.* Is there any limitation on the rule to "exceptional circumstances"? *See, e.g., United States v. American Cyanamid Co.*, 427 F. Supp. 859 (S.D.N.Y. 1977):

> The Government argued at the trial, that the hearsay exception of Fed. R. Evid. 803(24) [now 807] was meant to apply only in exceptional cases. This argument is based on a reading of the Senate Judiciary Committee Report which limits the application of this section to exceptional cases. Neither the Rule, nor the cases in this Circuit interpreting the Rule, however, impose any express limitation concerning exceptional cases. To every criminal defendant, his own case is exceptional. [The Rule] establishes sufficient express criteria which must be satisfied before an item of hearsay will be

> admissible. Since the exhibits listed above conform to these criteria, they should be received. There is no requirement that the court find a case to be "exceptional," whatever that means, in order to receive any evidence. To imply such a provision, as suggested by the Judiciary Committee, *supra*, would bring into each trial the foot of the Chancellor, an historical enemy of our liberties.

There are other cases that disagree.

(10) *Catchall Admittance as Harmless Error: An Oxymoron?* Does it make sense to cite harmless error to affirm a conviction where hearsay was erroneously admitted under the catchall, since one of the criteria of the catchall is that the evidence is more probative than other evidence the proponent can procure? *See United States v. Trenkler*, 61 F.3d 45 (1st Cir. 1995) (harmless error to admit evidence from computerized database of bombings and arson incidents).

(11) *Should There Even be a Residual Hearsay Exception Like This and if so, Should it be Broad or Narrow?* On the question whether there should be a residual or "catchall" hearsay exception and what strictures it should have, see Testimony of P. Rothstein, Hearings, Rules of Evidence, Committee on the Judiciary, U.S. Senate, 93d Cong. 2d Sess., on H.R. 5463 (Federal Rules of Evidence), June 4 and 5, 1974, p. 215, particularly at pp. 266–267, 270–275. This was at a period immediately prior to the enactment of the Federal Rules of Evidence when Congress was debating the catchall issue. The testimony contributed to the subsequent narrowing of the original position of the draft rules.

For articles critiquing the use of the catchalls and suggesting that they have the potential to turn the hearsay ban into a discretionary rule, see Raeder, *A Response to Professor Swift: The Hearsay Rule At Work: Has It Been Abolished De Facto by Judicial Discretion*? 76 Minn. L. Rev. 473, 507 (1992); *Confronting the Catchalls*, 6 CRIM. JUST. MAG. 30 (Summer, 1991), and *The Effect of the Catchalls on Criminal Defendants: Little Red Riding Hood Meets the Hearsay Wolf and Is Devoured*, 25 LOY. L.A. L. REV. 925 (1992). There also is the opposing view, which is that the exception works properly when considering its purposes, and is not unusual in light of our history of common-law creation of and evolution of new hearsay exceptions. There is even an argument that it is needed when the other hearsay exceptions are codified and cannot be easily expanded for deserving evidence as they could at common law.

(12) *The Evolution of Ad Hoc Exceptions at Common Law, Resembling the Catchall.* Although prior to 1994 Indiana had not yet adopted the Federal Rules of Evidence or a similar state version, the Indiana courts indulged in reasoning similar to that indulged by the drafters of the Federal Rules of Evidence to arrive at rulings on occasion very similar to positions of the Federal Rules of Evidence, as have other state courts. See, e.g., *Connell v. State*, 470 N.E.2d 701 (Ind. 1984), wherein the court recognized a new exception to Indiana's hearsay rule similar to Fed. R. Evid. 803(17). The court invoked a process like that embodied in the Federal Rules of Evidence catchall provisions. In the *Connell* case, the defendant was charged with (and convicted of) burglary and robbery. His defense was alibi:

He testified that he was at the residence of Kelly Lynn Beneford at the time of the crime. Beneford testified that appellant was at her residence from 12:30 P.M. to 2:30 P.M. on December 4, 1981, the time of the crime. Also, she testified that she remembered the times because there were cartoons on television.

On rebuttal the State was permitted to introduce as Exhibit H, the television listing for the day in question. This schedule was contained in an issue of the Muncie Star, a newspaper. A police officer sponsor testified that it was the paper for the day, and that it had been procured by him from a reporter for the paper. Appellant objected to the admission of the Exhibit on the grounds that it was hearsay, and the court ruled that it was not hearsay. If the questioned utterance is offered to prove the fact of the utterance and not offered to prove the truth of the facts asserted, then there is no hearsay. The fact of the utterance may safely rest for its evidentiary value upon the credibility of any witness who may have heard or read it and testifies to it in court. The rule guards against fact asserted in an utterance because it rests for its evidentiary value, not upon the credibility of any witness who may have heard it, but upon the actual asserter who is absent from the trial.

The assertions in Exhibit H were not under oath, and those persons who may have made them were not present in court and subject to cross-examination. It is the purpose to which evidence is sought to be put which is at the heart of the application of rules of evidence. It is clear to this court that it was sought to be introduced at trial for the purpose of influencing the jury to infer from the lack of scheduled cartoons, that cartoons were not in fact broadcast by the television stations as testified to by the alibi witness Beneford, and that she should not therefore be believed. The exhibit was therefore hearsay, and it was error to permit its introduction unless an exception to the rule justifies the action.

There is good and sound cause upon which to predicate an exception. First: the viewing of television programs is a most common experience, yet there is a superficial simplicity to the process of disproving a particular broadcast by objective and unbiased proof. Second: the television listing is publicly announced and widely disseminated on a daily or weekly basis. Third: there is the widest of successful public reliance on the accuracy of listings. Fourth: their accuracy is dictated by the business interest of newspapers and television stations. Fifth: they are not intended to create evidence for court. Sixth: they are readily available and inexpensive.

The argument against the exception would be that the listings are periodically changed and are inaccurate. In our judgment this factor is no greater than is present upon consideration of market reports published in newspapers, business entries, and public records.

We now hold that the law of evidence reflects an exception to the hearsay rule warranting the introduction of television listings and schedules published in newspapers and periodicals on a regular basis and intended to be relied upon by the public and shown to the satisfaction of the court to be authentic.

§ 10.06 FINAL THOUGHTS ABOUT HEARSAY — BOGUS HEARSAY RULES

One who has an academic interest in evidence and also gets into real-life courts is apt to notice that there is, in common use in the courts, a somewhat astonishing "second body" of evidence principles (not taught in any book or law school) coexisting with or even eclipsing the main body of evidence law.

This second body we call the "Non-Rules of Evidence." As far as research can tell, they cannot be found in written precedent. Yet they are asserted nearly every day in our busier trial courts. They even seem to constitute the mainstay of some judges' and lawyers' repertoires. Mostly they are misconceptions that probably originated in the "back-up-against-the-wall" bluster of some unfortunate lawyer who had run out of legitimate arguments and knowledge. Judges and opposing counsel no doubt were afraid to question the non-rule for fear it really existed. The non-rule usually is based on some legitimate but limited principle that is broadened and blown up, out of all proportion, to form the non-rule.

Let us illustrate with just a few non-rules:

The Presence-of-Client Non-Rule

Attorney: "Your honor, I object on the grounds that what Mr. Smith said out of court as related here by witness Jones is inadmissible hearsay."

The Court
(or opposing counsel): "Wait a minute. Your client was present when he (Smith) said it, wasn't he?"

Attorney: "Yes."

The Court: "Then it's admissible."

The rule implicit in the court's ruling is that "anything said in the presence of the client is admissible" or "is an exception to the hearsay rule." There is no such rule. There is instead a much more limited principle that, where a party to the litigation has on some previous occasion stood mute in the face of and did not deny an accusation (not made by or in the presence of police or the like) and the facts and circumstances indicate that he acquiesced in the facts stated (in effect adopting the statement as his own), a hearsay objection can be surmounted because he is viewed as making an implied statement of acquiescence in the accusation, which would be within the party admissions exception to (or exemption from) the hearsay rule.

The Res Gestae Non-Rule

Attorney: "Your honor, I object. The evidence is hearsay."

Opposing
Attorney: "It's part of the res gestae."

Judge: [Thinking: "Uh-oh. It's Latin."] "Objection overruled."

What is this ubiquitous exception to the hearsay rule for "res gestae"? Loosely, what is meant by that Latin phrase is that the statement is part of the litigated occurrence. There is, strictly speaking, no "res gestae" exception, at least under modern authority. Under that authority, "res gestae" is a loose term that can refer to any of the following hearsay exceptions or exemptions, and better practice would be to refer specifically by name to the particular exception or exemption rather than to "res gestae":

1. Excited utterances;
2. Declarations of present sense impressions;
3. Declarations of bodily feeling;
4. Declarations to physicians;
5. Declarations of state of mind or emotion;
6. Declarations not offered for their truth but rather because they are themselves facts with operative legal consequences (as, e.g., "I agree," offered to establish an oral contract);
7. Various other principles, depending on the whim of the lawyer or particular court.

Frequently, but not always, the out-of-court statement (declaration) under these listed exceptions or exemptions is uttered at, near, during, or as part of the occurrence that is the central focus of the litigation. For this reason, some lawyers and judges are under the erroneous impression that any statement uttered at, near, during, or as part of the litigated occurrence is automatically admissible, and they have elevated that notion to a generalized rule of law.

The Self-Serving Non-Rule

Attorney: "I object and move to strike, your honor. The evidence is self-serving."

Judge: "Sustained. Ladies and gentlemen of the jury, you are to disregard that evidence."

There is no general rule that self-serving evidence is inadmissible. Yet courts and attorneys constantly act as if there were. "Self-serving" is a proper objection only to a declaration that purports to come in through a hearsay rule exception or exemption that depends on the declaration being against interest, as in the case of party admissions or declarations against interest. In some jurisdictions a few other exceptions also may depend on that status. In addition, on occasion a piece of evidence may be so self-serving, or self-serving in such a fashion, that the evidence cannot properly be evaluated by the jury (even with aid from the judge and counsel). Or its slim probative value may be outweighed by factors such as time consumption, prejudice, and the like. In these instances, the evidence might be excluded pursuant to a general power like that codified from the common law in Fed. R. Evid. 403 (ad hoc power of judge to exclude on naked consideration of these factors). But such a situation is rare. More commonly, the self-serving nature of evidence is deemed only to be a matter of weight for the fact-finder to consider.

PROBLEM SET 10E: REVIEW PROBLEMS FOR HEARSAY EXCEPTIONS CHAPTERS — HEARSAY EXCEPTIONS QUIZ.

This quiz is like the hearsay quiz at the end of Chapter 8, but this time you also must consider the exceptions in Fed. R. Evid. 803-804. Some of the examples are not hearsay; others are, and they may or may not fit one or more exceptions. Therefore, the questions are: is it hearsay (considering both the basic definition and exemptions); if so, which exception(s), if any, apply; and why? Do not consider the Confrontation Clause at this point.

(1) Before a controlled cocaine buy, Officer Lauren Norder copied the serial numbers of the buy money in her handwriting on a tiny yellow Post-It Note, while looking at the bills in the field. The serial numbers were too long and numerous to memorize, but Officer Norder proposes now to offer or to read the Post-It Note to the jury to show that the serial numbers of the buy money were the same as those on the bills recovered from the defendant.

(2) Same as (1) except that Officer Norder has died, and the prosecution offers to have the police chief, who did not participate in any of the events involved in this case but who has care, custody, and control of the case documents, offer or read the Post-It Note.

(3) Same as (1), except that the Post-It Note is offered in a disciplinary proceeding, in which Officer Norder is accused of having neglected her duty by failing to make any record of the serial numbers. She offers the note to prove that the allegation is false and that she did make such a record.

(4) Plaintiff in a civil negligence case offers testimony of bystander A about a declaration by bystander B, whose whereabouts are now unknown. Bystander A would testify that B shouted, promptly after the loud and violent crash the accident produced, "The [defendant's] Buick entered the intersection against a red light!"

(5) Same as (4), except that, instead of A's testimony, plaintiff offers a police report made by Officer Lauren Norder that incorporates A's repetition of B's statement, which Officer Norder learned from speaking to A the day after the accident. The sponsoring witness is the case officer, Ima Kopp, who has care, custody, and control of the case documents on behalf of the police department.

(6) In a civil case for obtaining credit by fraud, the plaintiff Bank offers financial statements given to its loan officer, which the Bank intends to prove are false. The loan officer identifies the documents and testifies that the defendant personally gave them to him.

(7) In the case involved in (6) above, the Bank also offers a report by the same loan officer, stating that the Bank was relying on the financial statements in the course of making the loan. Such a report is a uniform step in the Bank's processing of its loans and is written contemporaneously with the other loan documents by the responsible loan officer. Offered to prove the Bank's reliance.

(8) Same as (7), except that the report is offered solely to show that the bank followed its usual procedures by generating such a report in processing this loan.

(9) Same as (7), except that the report is offered by the defendant because it contains alleged exculpatory material in the form of a statement by the loan officer that defendant "informed me that his statements are only approximate." Offered by defendant to show that the defendant did so inform the loan officer.

(10) In a personal injury suit, Doctor Bluster testifies that plaintiff told him he now has radiating pain down his leg and has had such pain for two years (which is the duration of time since the accident in controversy). Doctor Bluster never treated the plaintiff but rather examined him solely to make a diagnosis of his leg injuries for the purpose of testifying in this suit. Offered to prove the radiating pain and its duration.

(11) Same as (10), except that Doctor Bluster also offers to repeat diagnostic findings orally reported to him by plaintiff's treating physician, who personally observed the reported symptoms while treating plaintiff.

(12) In a wrongful death case, plaintiff offers to testify that her deceased husband told her a few minutes before the accident that he wasn't in any hurry and planned to take his time in driving to the office that morning. Offered to show that decedent was not speeding.

(13) In case (12), testimony of a bystander that promptly after the accident the decedent staggered out of his car, obviously with fatal injuries, and stammered out: "Tell my wife . . . I love her," whereupon he lost consciousness. Offered by plaintiff wife to prove affection, as an issue related to damages.

(14) Same as (13), except that decedent also blurts out, "I was driving . . . slowly . . . ." Offered to disprove contributory negligence on decedent's part.

(15) Same as (13) and (14), except that the evidence is offered to show decedent was conscious for at least some period of time after the accident, as relevant to recovery of damages for his conscious pain and suffering.

(16) Same as (13) through (15), except it is discovered that the "accident" was staged, the "deceased" actually is alive, the plaintiff wife sent half the money recovered in the "wrongful death" case to him in Brazil, and there is a document in wife's handwriting that appears to be an advance plan for the entire hoax. In wife's federal criminal trial for mail fraud, the prosecution seeks to have the bystander testify about the pretend-decedent's (husband's) statements after the accident, to show how the crime was committed.

(17) In the case in (16), the prosecution also offers a signed but unsworn confession made by the husband to Brazilian authorities during efforts by U.S. authorities for his extradition, in which he said: "I want to clear my conscience. My wife and I together staged that accident and fraudulently concocted the wrongful death suit." Offered against wife in her trial for mail fraud, to prove her participation.

(18) In the case in (16) and (17), the husband gave a deposition in a civil suit by the Federal Deposit Insurance Corporation, an entity created by the United States, which is successor to the civil claim for the funds at issue. The deposition was given in Brazil under questioning by an Assistant United States Attorney and recorded, with the witness sworn by an official court reporter appointed for the purpose by

the federal judge hearing the civil suit. The deposition contains the husband's testimony that "I concocted and completed the sham accident and the entire fraud by myself, and my wife had nothing to do with it." Offered by wife in her defense during her mail fraud trial.

(19) After introduction of the deposition testimony in (18), the Government offers the husband's Brazilian confession in (17) to impeach his deposition testimony. The judge gives a limiting instruction confining the jury's use of the confession solely to evaluation of husband's credibility.

(20) Same as (19), except that the judge grants the Government's request that there be no limiting instruction, so that the jury also may consider husband's confession as substantive evidence against wife.

(21) In a personal injury suit, to prove the severity of damages, a "day in the life" videotape is offered by the plaintiff that shows the severely injured plaintiff performing everyday tasks with difficulty.

(22) Same as (21), except that the videotape contains portions in which plaintiff describes what she is doing and how it differs from before she was injured.

(23) In a rape prosecution, testimony is offered that the defendant fled the country for seven years.

(24) In a murder case, to prove self-defense, the defendant offers testimony by a defense witness that he told the defendant the victim was a notorious gang member who was out to get the defendant.

(25) In a personal injury suit brought against Joe because his dog allegedly bit a child (Janice), Janice's parents offer evidence of Joe's statement to a friend that "I'm very upset because Janice's parents told me that my dog bit Janice."

Chapter 11

CONSTITUTIONAL CONSIDERATIONS

CONFRONTATION, DUE PROCESS, AND OTHER DOCTRINES

§ 11.01 INTRODUCTION[1]

(1) *The Relationship Between the Constitutional Requirement of Confrontation and the Hearsay Rule.* The hearsay rule is concerned with statements made out-of-court, because the maker of the statement could not be contemporaneously subjected to courtroom safeguards such as face-to-face meeting, open display, oath, perjury penalties, and cross examination, often refered to collectively as "confrontation." The Confrontation Clause of the Constitution guarantees a criminal accused "the right to . . . be confronted with the witnesses against him." Are hearsay declarants whose out-of-court words are used against a criminal defendant "witnesses against" the defendant for purposes of the Confrontation Clause? As you will see from the cases in this chapter, the Clause bears a relationship to the hearsay rule since the two doctrines share some overlapping concerns and values. But the Confrontation Clause is not identical to the hearsay rule. You will need to understand for yourself from reading the cases more precisely what the relationship is.

(2) *Beyond the Hearsay Rule: Confrontation Also Guarantees a Certain Format for In-Court Witness Testimony, Protects the Scope of Cross-Examination of Such a Witness, and Helps Prevent Prejudice in a Joint Trial.* In addition to the matters in note (1) just above, the Confrontation Clause implicates issues that transcend the concerns of the hearsay rule. It also protects a criminal defendant's right to cross-examine adverse witnesses who appear at trial. For example, in *Olden v. Kentucky*, 488 U.S. 227 (1988), the defendant's theory was that the prosecution's principal witness had "concocted" her testimony that she was raped to protect her relationship with her boyfriend, but the trial judge excluded evidence about that interracial relationship as prejudicial. The Supreme Court reversed under the Confrontation Clause because the evidence was significant on the issue of the complainant's bias.

The Confrontation Clause also limits efforts to screen frightened witnesses on the stand from having to see the accused eye-to-eye. *See, e.g.*, *Coy v. Iowa*, 487 U.S. 1012 (1988) and *Maryland v. Craig*, 497 U.S. 836 (1990), *infra*. And the Clause prevents some kinds of evidence admissible against one defendant (e.g., that particular defendant's confession) from prejudicially affecting other defendants in a joint trial. *See Bruton v. United States*, 391 U.S. 123 (1968), *infra*. The relationship

[1] Study Guide Reference: Evidence in a Nutshell, Chapter 8:V.

between confrontation and hearsay, however, is one of the most interesting aspects of the Clause, and it is the major focus here.

(3) *Other Constitutional Doctrines: The Due Process and Compulsory Process Clauses.* The Due Process Clause is a more general guarantee of minimum fairness and can make the exclusion of important criminal defense evidence a constitutional violation, whether or not the evidence has anything to do with cross examination or impeachment. But in some cases it may bear a relationship to the Confrontation Clause. For example, sometimes the exclusion of evidence offered by the defendant to impeach or to cross-examine may violate the Due Process Clause. *See Chambers v. Mississippi*, 410 U.S. 284 (1973), *infra*, which found a due process violation where a defendant was prohibited by state hearsay and impeachment rules from introducing the out-of-court confession (to the crime in question) of a third party who testified on the stand to the contrary. But, under Due Process, even if the evidence had not been related to impeachment or cross examination — that is, even if the confessor had not testified — the result probably would have been similar.

The Compulsory Process Clause gives the criminal defendant the right "to have compulsory process for obtaining witnesses in his favor." This accords a right to subpoena and introduce significant exculpatory evidence. In some cases, this right complements the Confrontation Clause in that if the prosecution does offer hearsay without producing the declarant for cross examination, compulsory process enables the defendant herself to produce the declarant for examination unless the declarant is unavailable. This right has sometimes been argued to be a reason for relaxing the confrontation-clause obligation of the prosecution to confront defendant with a declarant whose words the prosecution wants to use against the defendant.

Ultimately, these rights are often referred to collectively as the defendant's "right to present a defense." *See Holmes v. South Carolina*, 547 U.S. 319 (2006), *infra*, and *Washington v. Texas*, 388 U.S. 14 (1967). However this right-to-defend is not unlimited. It extends only to "fundamental principle[s] of justice." *See Montana v. Egelhoff*, 518 U.S. 37 (1996), *supra* at § 2.04, as well as *Holmes*. *See generally* IMWINKELRIED & GARLAND, EXCULPATORY EVIDENCE: THE ACCUSED'S CONSTITUTIONAL RIGHT TO INTRODUCE FAVORABLE EVIDENCE (3d ed. 2004).

§ 11.02 CONFRONTATION CLAUSE APPLIED TO OUT-OF-COURT STATEMENTS BY TESTIFYING DECLARANTS

UNITED STATES v. OWENS

United States Supreme Court
484 U.S. 554 (1988)

SCALIA, JUSTICE.

[At defendant Owens' trial for assault with intent to commit murder, the victim, Foster, could not remember, because of amnesia from his injuries, seeing his assailant, or seeing any hospital visitors except the FBI agent who interviewed him, or whether any visitor had suggested that Owens was the assailant. He did, however, remember identifying to the agent Owens's photo as being that of his assailant. Owens objected to Foster's testimony because Foster's lack of memory made effective cross-examination impossible. The Supreme Court, per Justice Scalia, upheld the admissibility of Foster's testimony.] [This portion of the opinion deals with the Confrontation Clause challenge to its admissibility. The portion dealing with the hearsay challenge appears in § 8.01[D], *supra*.]

In *Delaware v. Fensterer*, 474 U.S. 15 (1985) (per curiam), we determined that there was no Confrontation Clause violation when an expert witness testified as to what opinion he had formed, but could not recollect the basis on which he had formed it . . . .

Our opinion noted that a defendant seeking to discredit a forgetful expert witness is not without ammunition, since the jury may be persuaded that "his opinion is as unreliable as his memory.". . . It is sufficient that the defendant has the opportunity to bring out such matters as the witness' bias, his lack of care and attentiveness, his poor eyesight, and even (what is often a prime objective of cross-examination) the very fact that he has a bad memory . . . . Indeed, if there is any difference in persuasive impact between the statement "I believe this to be the man who assaulted me, but can't remember why" and the statement "I don't know whether this is the man who assaulted me, but I told the police I believed so earlier," the former would seem, if anything, more damaging and hence give rise to a greater need for memory-testing, if that is to be considered essential to an opportunity for effective cross-examination . . . .[There is no guarantee that cross-examination will be effective.] The weapons available to impugn the witness' statement when memory loss is asserted will of course not always achieve success, but successful cross-examination is not the constitutional guarantee. They are, however, realistic weapons, as is demonstrated by defense counsel's summation in this very case, which emphasized Foster's memory loss and argued that his identification of respondent was the result of the suggestions of people who visited him in the hospital.

Our constitutional analysis is not altered by the fact that the testimony here involved an out-of-court identification that would traditionally be categorized as hearsay . . . . We do not think that a constitutional line drawn by the Confrontation Clause falls between a forgetful witness' live testimony that he once believed this defendant to be the perpetrator of the crime, and the introduction of the witness' earlier statement to that effect.

PROBLEM 11A: APPLYING OWENS GENERALLY TO CONFRONTATION ISSUES REGARDING TESTIFYING WITNESSES.

Crawford v. Washington, 541 U.S. 36 (2004), reiterated general language found in other cases that when the declarant appears for cross-examination at trial, the Confrontation Clause places no constraints at all on the use of his prior testimonial statements. Presumably these expressions assume the opportunity at trial was for constitutionally sufficient cross examination. After these cases, including *Owens*, can a Confrontation Clause violation ever exist when the declarant is a witness at trial? What of the provision in some states that a child can testify, sometimes not under oath, without any finding of competency, in child sexual abuse cases? If a child is virtually mute or unable to give intelligible answers, is mere presence all that is required to satisfy the Confrontation Clause? What if a witness doesn't even remember as much as the witness in *Owens*? Would a cardboard cutout placed on the witness stand do as well?

§ 11.03 CONFRONTATION CLAUSE APPLIED TO STATEMENTS BY NONTESTIFYING DECLARANTS

[A] Intertwining Hearsay and Confrontation Clause Analysis: The *Roberts* Era

OHIO v. ROBERTS
United States Supreme Court
448 U.S. 56 (1980)

BLACKMUN, JUSTICE.

This case presents issues concerning the constitutional propriety of the introduction in evidence of the preliminary hearing testimony of a witness not produced at the defendant's subsequent state criminal trial.

Roberts was charged with forgery of a check in the name of Bernard Isaacs, and with possession of stolen credit cards belonging to Isaacs.

A preliminary hearing was held in Municipal Court. The prosecution called several witnesses, including Mr. Isaacs. Respondent's appointed counsel [called the Isaacs' daughter, Anita] as the defense's only witness. Anita Isaacs testified that she knew respondent, and that she had permitted him to use her apartment for several days while she was away. Defense counsel questioned Anita at some length and attempted to elicit from her an admission that she had given respondent checks and the credit cards without informing him that she did not have permission to use them. Anita, however, denied this.

[F]ive subpoenas for four different trial dates were issued to Anita at her parents' Ohio residence. The last three carried a written instruction that Anita should "call before appearing." She was not at the residence when these were executed. She did not telephone and she did not appear at trial.

Respondent took the stand and testified that Anita Isaacs had given him her parents' checkbook and credit cards with the understanding that he could use them. Relying on Ohio Rev. Code Ann., which permits the use of preliminary examination testimony of a witness who "cannot for any reason be produced at the trial," the State, on rebuttal, offered the transcript of Anita's testimony.

Asserting a violation of the Confrontation Clause the defense objected. The trial court conducted a voir dire hearing as to its admissibility. Amy Isaacs [i.e., Anita's mother], the sole witness at voir dire, was questioned by both the prosecutor and defense counsel concerning her daughter's whereabouts. Anita, according to her mother, left home for Tucson, Ariz., soon after the preliminary hearing. About a year before the trial, a San Francisco social worker was in communication with the Isaacs about a welfare application Anita had filed there. Through the social worker, the Isaacs reached their daughter once by telephone. Since then, however, Anita had called her parents only one other time and had not been in touch with her two sisters. When Anita called, some seven or eight months before trial, she told her parents that she "was traveling" outside Ohio, but did not reveal the place from which she called. Mrs. Isaacs stated that she knew of no way to reach Anita in case of an emergency. Nor did she "know of anybody who knows where she is." The trial court admitted the transcript into evidence. Respondent was convicted on all counts.

The Court of Appeals of Ohio reversed. [The Supreme Court reverses the reversal, as follows:]

The Sixth Amendment's Confrontation Clause, made applicable to the States through the Fourteenth Amendment provides: "In all criminal prosecutions, the accused shall enjoy the right to be confronted with the witnesses against him." If one were to read this language literally, it would require, on objection, the exclusion of any statement made by a declarant not present at trial . . . . But, if thus applied, the Clause would abrogate virtually every hearsay exception, a result long rejected as unintended and too extreme.

[T]he Clause was intended to exclude some hearsay. Moreover, underlying policies support the same conclusion. [T]he Clause reflects a preference for face-to-face confrontation at trial, and that "a primary interest secured by [the provision] is the right of cross-examination." [The Court here refers to ways that cross-examination and confrontation insure reliability, including, among others, that it is difficult to lie about someone you are facing. Prof. Wigmore is quoted, to the effect that cross-examination "is the greatest legal engine ever invented for the discovery of truth."] . . .

The Court, however, has recognized that competing interests, if "closely examined," may warrant dispensing with confrontation at trial . . . .

[H]earsay rules and the Confrontation Clause are generally designed to protect similar values, and stem from the same roots . . . .

In sum, when a hearsay declarant is not present for cross-examination at trial, the Confrontation Clause normally requires a showing that he is unavailable. Even then, his statement is admissible only if it bears adequate "indicia of reliability." Reliability can be inferred without more in a case where the evidence falls within a firmly rooted hearsay exception. In other cases, the evidence must be excluded . . . .absent a showing of particularized guarantees of trustworthiness.

[In the present case,] the opportunity to cross-examine at the preliminary hearing — even absent actual cross-examination — satisfies the Confrontation Clause.

Counsel's questioning clearly partook of cross-examination as a matter of form. His presentation was replete with leading questions, the principal tool and hallmark of cross-examination. In addition, counsel's questioning comported with the principal purpose of cross-examination: to challenge [the witness's truthfulness].

Anita's unwillingness to shift the blame away from respondent became discernible early in her testimony. Yet counsel continued to explore the underlying events in detail. He attempted, for example, to establish that Anita and respondent were sharing an apartment, an assertion that was critical to respondent's defense at trial and that might have suggested ulterior personal reasons for unfairly casting blame on respondent. At another point, he directly challenged Anita's veracity by seeking to have her admit that she had given the credit cards to respondent to obtain a television. When Anita denied this, defense counsel elicited the fact that the only television she owned was a "Twenty Dollar old model."

[R]espondent's counsel was not significantly limited in any way in the scope or nature of his cross-examination.

We are also unpersuaded [by the argument that Anita] was not personally available for questioning at trial . . . . [nor by the argument that defendant had a different lawyer at trial from the one at the preliminary hearing] . . . .

[The] guarantees of trustworthiness [are] in the accouterments of the preliminary hearing itself; [not] the inherent reliability or unreliability of [the witness and her] story.

. . . .Since there was an adequate opportunity to cross-examine [the witness], and counsel availed himself of that opportunity, the transcript bore sufficient indicia of reliability and afforded the trier of fact a satisfactory basis for evaluating the truth of the prior statement.

Our holding that the Supreme Court of Ohio erred in its "indicia of reliability" analysis does not fully dispose of the case, for respondent would defend the judgment on an alternative ground. The State, he contends, failed to lay a proper predicate for admission of the preliminary hearing transcript by its failure to demonstrate that Anita Isaacs was not available to testify in person at the trial.

The basic litmus of Sixth Amendment unavailability is established: [A] witness is not unavailable for purposes of the exception to the confrontation requirement unless the prosecutorial authorities have made a *good-faith effort* to obtain his presence at trial . . . .

Given these facts, the prosecution did not breach its duty of good-faith effort. To be sure, the prosecutor might have tried to locate by telephone the San Francisco social worker with whom Mrs. Isaacs had spoken many months before and might have undertaken other steps in an effort to find Anita. One, in hindsight, may always think of other things. Nevertheless, the great improbability that such efforts would have resulted in locating the witness, and would have led to her production at trial, neutralizes any intimation that a concept of reasonableness required their execution.

In *Barber [v. Page]*, the Court found an absence of good-faith effort where the prosecution made no attempt to secure the presence of a declarant incarcerated in a federal penitentiary in a neighboring State. There, the prosecution knew where the witness was, procedures existed whereby the witness could be brought to the trial, and the witness was not in a position to frustrate efforts to secure his production. Here, Anita's whereabouts were not known, and there was no assurance that she would be found in a place from which she could be forced to return to Ohio.

[Reversed.]

[Justices Brennan, Marshall, and Stevens dissented, on the grounds that "reasonable efforts" required that the state do more than it did to locate Anita Isaacs.]

NOTES ON SUPREME COURT CASES INTERPRETING *ROBERTS*

Roberts' reliability analysis and linkage to hearsay exceptions has been overruled by *Crawford, infra*, but its requirement (and definition) of unavailability (and probably its definition of what is an adequate former opportunity to cross examine) still play a role even after *Crawford* and are still good law. Therefore, some cases dealing with unavailability pursuant to the *Roberts* regime are included in this series of notes even though they are pre-*Crawford*. Some other *Roberts*-era cases in these notes have continuing vitality because they deal with confrontation areas that are probably not changed by *Crawford*, such as those shielding vulnerable victims who testify from full face-to-face cross examination. Some other cases, however, are included not because they continue to be viable, but because they shed light on the results of *Roberts* for your background.

(1) *Cases Applying or Refining Roberts Generally.* After *Roberts*, the Court decided a number of cases interpreting the two prongs of *Robert's* general approach: unavailability and reliability. Reliability was satisfied if the hearsay exception was "firmly rooted," and the cases examined a number of hearsay exceptions to see which ones were "firmly rooted". If the firmly rooted hearsay exception did not require unavailabilty, the uavailability requirement of *Roberts* would not be applied, these cases suggested.

A fact-specific *Roberts* reliability determination was required in cases where the hearsay was admitted through ad hoc or newer hearsay exceptions. A frequent complaint about this approach was its tendency to encourage the expansion of "firmly rooted" hearsay exceptions to eliminate the need for any separate Confrontation Clause analysis. This was particularly an issue in child abuse cases, where courts broadly interpreted hearsay exceptions for excited utterances and medical statements.

Under *Roberts*, as a practical matter, confrontation usually only became a difficult issue if the hearsay was introduced via ad hoc or newer hearsay exceptions such as those expressly permitting trustworthy hearsay, child hearsay, or declarations against penal interest. For example, *Idaho v. Wright*, 497 U.S. 805 (1990), rejected the admission of statements by a young child sexual abuse victim to an examining pediatrician under a state residual provision patterned after FRE 807 as a violation of the Confrontation Clause. The Court left open whether a showing of unavailability would be required by the Confrontation Clause to use this exception, because the child was incapable of communicating with the jury, rendering her unavailable. *Wright* noted that the exception was ad hoc, and did "not share the same tradition of reliability that supports the admissibility of statements under a firmly rooted hearsay exception." Therefore, a finding of "particularized guarantees of trustworthiness" was required, based on a "totality of the circumstances" surrounding the making of the statement that rendered the declarant particularly worthy of belief. The following factors were identified as relating to reliability of a child's statement: spontaneity and consistent repetition; mental state of the declarant; use of terminology unexpected of a child of similar age; and lack of motive to fabricate.

By contrast, in *White v. Illinois*, 502 U.S. 346 (1992), out-of-court statements of a young child victim of sexual abuse made under similar circumstances were admitted through two hearsay exceptions that were viewed as "firmly rooted": excited utterances (under a rule like FRE 803(2)) and statements for purposes of diagnosis and treatment (like FRE 803(4)). This was considered to pass constitutional muster (apparently regardless of availability or unavailability, since these hearsay exceptions did not require unavailability). Looking at these two cases, and others at the time, one concludes, with some justification, that the constitutional decision under the *Roberts* regime often hinged on what hearsay exception the state trial judge chose to use to admit the evidence.

See generally Raeder, *Hot Topics in Confrontation Clause Cases and Creating a More Workable Confrontation Clause Framework Without Starting Over*, 21 QUINNIPIAC L. REV. 1013 (2003); Raeder, *White's Effect on the Right to Confront One's Accuser*, 7 CRIM. JUST. MAG. 2 (Winter, 1993).

(2) *Justice Thomas' Alternative Basis for the Result in White: Is the Confrontation Clause Confined to "Formalized" Testimonial Substitutes?* Justice Thomas, joined by Justice Scalia, concurred in *White*, by proposing a "narrower" view of the Confrontation Clause: "The federal constitutional right of confrontation extends to any witness who actually testifies at trial, but the Confrontation Clause is implicated by extrajudicial statements only insofar as they are contained in formalized testimonial materials, such as affidavits, depositions, prior testimony, or confessions." His reason: The historical record cannot justify Confrontation Clause jurisprudence banning hearsay broadly. "It was this discrete category of testimonial materials that was historically abused by prosecutors, . . . and under this approach, the Confrontation Clause would not be construed to extend beyond the historical evil to which it was directed."

The majority rejected this position, "which would virtually eliminate [the Confrontation Clause's] role in restricting the admission of hearsay testimony," because it "is foreclosed by our prior cases." But the majority did not dispute Justice Thomas's historical analysis. *See Crawford* and its progeny *infra*, particularly *Williams*, for how this analysis fares when the *Roberts'* reliability test is rejected. As our notes following *Williams* indicate, his view may have some viability.

(3) *What Constitutes Good Faith Efforts to Produce a Witness?* Although *Crawford*, *infra*, rejects *Roberts'* reliability test, proving unavailability appears still to be required before courtroom confrontation can be dispensed with in certain cases. Whether unavailability for these constitutional purposes will be defined and decided exactly the same way as under Fed. R. Evid. 804(a) remains to be seen, but

the policy behind the requirement seems somewhat analogous. The constitutional "unavailability" portion of the decision in *Ohio v. Roberts*, reproduced in this chapter *supra*, would still seem to be good law in situations where unavailability is required under *Crawford*, as would *Barber v. Page*, 390 U.S. 719 (1968), requiring as a constitutional matter that the State must make a diligent effort to produce a declarant incarcerated in a federal prison in a neighboring State. *Mancusi v. Stubbs*, 408 U.S. 204 (1972) may also still be good law in this respect, although it is more problematic. *Mancusi* distinguished, on the one hand, cases where, in the Court's view, it would be reasonable to require due diligence to find and produce the witness (such as cases where the witness is somewhere in the United States, cases like *Barber*, where the witness is incarcerated in a federal prison in another state, and cases where a party could resort to legal process in a sister state where the witness resides), from, on the other hand, cases like *Mancusi*, where the witness had left the country. In the latter, it would be unreasonable to mandate constitutionally the use of any diligence to find and produce, the Court holds in *Mancusi*.

More recently, *Hardy v. Cross*, 132 S. Ct. 490 (2011), rejected a challenge to the introduction of prior testimony of A.S., a complaining witness who had been cross examined during the defendant's previous trial. The defense claimed the prosecution had not made a good faith effort to obtain the witness' presence at the defendant's retrial because she had not been subpoenaed, despite her avowed fear of him. In a *per curiam* decision, the Court noted that "[w]e have never held that the prosecution must have issued a subpoena if it wishes to prove that a witness who goes into hiding is unavailable for Confrontation Clause purposes, and the issuance of a subpoena may do little good if a sexual assault witness is so fearful of an assailant that she is willing to risk his acquittal by failing to testify at trial."

(4) *Does a Trial Court Really Have the Capacity to Make a Meaningful Finding of Unavailability for a Child Witness Based on Projections of Future Harm?* Consider the following argument in Crump, *Child Victim Testimony, Psychological Trauma, and the Confrontation Clause: What Can the Scientific Literature Tell Us?*, 8 St. John's J. Legal Comment. 83, 95–97 (1992):

> [I]t is scientifically unsound to imagine that a judge, psychotherapist, or anyone else can predict the long-term effects, into adulthood, of vigorously cross-examining an abused child. For example, among the adult conditions caused by childhood sexual abuse are delinquency, drug abuse, and a condition known as "borderline personality disorder." Borderline personality, in particular, has been shown in very recent years to be heavily correlated with childhood sexual abuse. However, the factors that combine to "cause" borderline personality in one abused child, and that fail to produce this disorder in another, are unknown and probably unknowable . . . . Moreover, "[i]nformation on the long-term effects of sexual abuse is extremely limited, and no systematic longitudinal data on childhood victims of sexual abuse exist.". . . The factors probably include genetic determinants. It is far-fetched to assume that a judge would inquire into the genetic makeup of an abused child in order to determine whether she could testify without effects lasting into adulthood, but . . . that is precisely what the individualized model of necessity would call upon the judge to do.

> Taken to its extreme, the individualized necessity approach is analogous to deciding to expose a child to a carcinogen unless the child can prove that she, individually, will contract cancer because of that particular exposure. The problem is that some exposed persons will contract cancer, others will not, and all that can be said with confidence is that exposure to carcinogens is correlated with cancer. [T]he same is true of cross-examination about child abuse. [T]he severity of resulting disorders cannot be made the basis of accurate *individual* predictions regarding the affected children's adulthood.
>
> In fact, since denial and repression are part of the pathology of child abuse, it is precisely those children who *least* appear to suffer ill effects who may, ironically, be *most* at risk. In other words, if the child "seems" to be "tough," "strong," or able to endure what defendant in *White* called "adversarial testing," the explanation may be that the child actually is suffering from denial or repression of the effects of abuse. Instead of being among those most likely to survive the "adversarial testing" intact, . . . this "tough" child actually may be among those *most* likely to be harmed.
>
> Thus, there is great danger that such a finding of individualized necessity would be diametrically opposed to reality.

Does this reasoning have merit, and if so, how does it affect findings of unavailability when children do not testify?

(5) *Does the Compulsory Process Clause Reduce the Need for an Unavailability Requirement? White*, supra, note (1), admitting the hearsay, relies for its result, in part, on the Compulsory Process Clause. If the prosecution uses hearsay without presenting the declarant, the defendant has the constitutional right to subpoena the declarant just as the State can — using compulsory process. The likely result will be either that the declarant will testify or that efforts to compel testimony will demonstrate unavailability. Under this analysis, arguably it does not matter whether the State can demonstrate unavailability, because it is obligated under the Compulsory Process Clause, at the defendant's behest, to demonstrate it — or to supply the testimony. There will remain some cases in which the defendant does not want the live testimony; in that event, the *White* approach merely avoids exploiting the child witness by repeatedly demanding her testimony. Is this argument persuasive? Or does it ignore the Confrontation Clause, which is an independent provision? *Cf.* Crump, *supra* at 99-103 (suggesting, however, that on request, the child witness should be called by the court without the jury being informed of the defendant's subpoena, so that the presentation of a reluctant child is done in a way that avoids prejudice to defendant). *See also* Raeder, *White's Effect on the Right to Confront One's Accuser*, 7 CRIM. JUST. MAG. 2 (Winter 1993).

(6) *Eye-to-Eye Confrontation Issues where Witness is Present: The Coy and Craig Cases.* The Confrontation Clause also is concerned with the requirement of face-to-face confrontation of witnesses who are presented. Simplistically, this value sometimes is expressed in terms of requiring witnesses to "look the accused in the eye." For example, in *Coy v. Iowa*, 487 U.S. 1012 (1988), the trial judge protected the child victim-witness in a sexual assault case by setting up a one-way screen that prevented her from having to face the defendant in an open courtroom. The

Supreme Court reversed the conviction. It held that such a procedure perhaps could be used only upon a *particularized* showing that it was necessary to avert a risk of harm to the individual child, not a generalized assumption about children generally. In *Maryland v. Craig*, 497 U.S. 836 (1990), the trial judge allowed a child witness to testify via closed circuit television, so that not only the need for the child to face the defendant could be avoided, but the courtroom setting as well. The Court upheld this procedure because it was predicated on a *particularized* showing of necessity (likely harm to this specific child) that conformed to the requirements of *Coy*. The protective procedure in *Coy* and *Craig* (a one-way screen in *Coy*; and a one-way video hookup combined with a two-way audio hookup in *Craig*) were the functional equivalents of each other, and infringed only one small aspect of the bundle of rights we associate with confrontation: Only the witness' view of the defendant was eliminated; but the defendant, lawyers, judge and jury, could see the witness, the witness and all these participants could hear one another, and all questions by both attorneys could be directly put to and answered by the witness. Would the Court allow a bigger infringement of the confrontation bundle of rights, for similar or other policy reasons like those invoked in *Craig*? Was *Craig* an important infringement? Does the witness viewing the defendant tend to scare a witness off of a truthful story, or a false story? Which effect preponderates? Is there empirical evidence on this? Do such questions about what promotes the truth, really matter to the question before the court in the two decisions, or was the question before the court merely a question of what "confront" in the constitutional provision means? See *Crawford*, immediately *infra*, on all these questions in a slightly different context. Would *Crawford* change *Coy* or *Craig* in any way? Because *Crawford* appears hostile to balancing tests, *Craig's* continuing viability has been challenged in several cases, so far unsuccessfully. The Court recently denied *certiorari* in *Rose v. Michigan*, which argued that *Craig* should be overruled.

Do these decisions (*Coy* and *Craig*) make sense in light of (1) the relative importance of facial confrontation as compared to other confrontation values such as cross-examination, demeanor, and oath, (2) the difficulty of evaluating the particularized "risk" of harm to an individual child for the long-term future (*see* note (4) just above), and (3) the interests of the defendant?

The Court did not discuss in either *Coy* or *Craig* the possibility that the mere presence of the screen or hookup could imply guilt to the jury by suggesting that protection of the child from trauma or from the defendant was needed.

See generally Raeder, *Distrusting Young Children Who Allege Sexual Abuse: Why Stereotypes Don't Die and Ways to Facilitate Child Testimony*, 16 Widener L. Rev. 239 (2010).

[B] Rejecting *Roberts:* The Testimonial Approach to the Confrontation Clause

[1] The Seminal Case: Relying on Alleged Historic Analysis To Discern What the Framers Intended

CRAWFORD v. WASHINGTON
Supreme Court of the United States
541 U.S. 36 (2004)

JUSTICE SCALIA delivered the opinion of the Court.

I

On August 5, 1999, Kenneth Lee was stabbed at his apartment. Police arrested petitioner later that night. After giving petitioner and his wife Miranda warnings, detectives interrogated each of them twice. Petitioner eventually confessed that he and Sylvia had gone in search of Lee because he was upset over an earlier incident in which Lee had tried to rape her. The two had found Lee at his apartment, and a fight ensued in which Lee was stabbed in the torso and petitioner's hand was cut.

The State charged petitioner with assault and attempted murder. At trial, he claimed self-defense. Sylvia did not testify because of the state marital privilege, which generally bars a spouse from testifying without the other spouse's consent. *See* Wash. Rev. Code Section 5.60.060(1) (1994). In Washington, this privilege does not extend to a spouse's out-of-court statements admissible under a hearsay exception, *see State v. Burden*, 120 Wash. 2d 371 (1992), so the State sought to introduce Sylvia's tape-recorded statements to the police as evidence that the stabbing was not in self-defense. Noting that Sylvia had admitted she led petitioner to Lee's apartment and thus had facilitated the assault, the State invoked the hearsay exception for statements against penal interest, Wash. Rule Evid. 804(b)(3) (2003).

Petitioner countered that, state law notwithstanding, admitting the evidence would violate his federal constitutional right to be "confronted with the witnesses against him." Amdt. 6. According to our description of that right in *Ohio v. Roberts*, it does not bar admission of an unavailable witness's statement against a criminal defendant if the statement bears "adequate 'indicia of reliability.' " To meet that test, evidence must either fall within a "firmly rooted hearsay exception" or bear "guarantees of trustworthiness." The trial court here admitted the statement on the latter ground, offering several reasons why it was trustworthy: Sylvia was not shifting blame but rather corroborating her husband's story that he acted in self-defense or "justified reprisal"; she had direct knowledge as an eyewitness; she was describing recent events; and she was being questioned by a "neutral" law enforcement officer. The prosecution played the tape for the jury and relied on it in closing, arguing that it was "damning evidence" that "completely refutes [petitioner's] claim of self-defense." The jury convicted petitioner of assault.

We granted certiorari to determine whether the State's use of Sylvia's statement violated the Confrontation Clause.

II

The Sixth Amendment's Confrontation Clause provides that, "[i]n all criminal prosecutions, the accused shall enjoy the right . . . to be confronted with the witnesses against him." We have held that this bedrock procedural guarantee applies to both federal and state prosecutions . . . . As noted above, *Roberts* says that an unavailable witness's out-of-court statement may be admitted so long as it has adequate indicia of reliability — i.e., falls within a "firmly rooted hearsay exception" or bears "particularized guarantees of trustworthiness." Petitioner argues that this test strays from the original meaning of the Confrontation Clause and urges us to reconsider it.

[The opinion's lengthy historical background discussion of the origins of the Confrontation Clause is omitted. One point made in this portion of the opinion is that the requirement of confrontation in ancient England was in part the product of popular dissatisfaction with the conviction and ultimate execution for treason of Sir Walter Raleigh on evidence of extra-judicial statements made to authorities by one Cobham who did not testify and who later recanted.]

III

This history supports two inferences about the meaning of the Sixth Amendment.

First, the principal evil at which the Confrontation Clause was directed was the civil-law [i.e., European] mode of criminal procedure, and particularly its use of ex parte examinations as evidence against the accused. It was these practices that the Crown deployed in notorious treason cases like Raleigh's; that the Marian statutes invited; that English law's assertion of a right to confrontation was meant to prohibit; and that the founding-era rhetoric decried. The Sixth Amendment must be interpreted with this focus in mind.

Accordingly, we once again reject the view that the Confrontation Clause applies of its own force only to in-court testimony, and [we reject] that its application to out-of-court statements introduced at trial depends upon "the law of Evidence for the time being." . . . This focus also suggests that not all hearsay implicates the Sixth Amendment's core concerns. An off-hand, overheard remark might be unreliable evidence and thus a good candidate for exclusion under hearsay rules, but it bears little resemblance to the civil-law abuses the Confrontation Clause targeted. On the other hand, ex parte examinations might sometimes be admissible under modern hearsay rules, but the Framers certainly would not have condoned them.

The text of the Confrontation Clause reflects this focus. It applies to "witnesses" against the accused — in other words, those who "bear testimony." 1 N. Webster, An American Dictionary of the English Language (1828). "Testimony," in turn, is typically "[a] solemn declaration or affirmation made for the purpose of establishing or proving some fact." *Ibid.* An accuser who makes a formal statement to government officers bears testimony in a sense that a person who makes a casual remark to an acquaintance does not. The constitutional text, like the history underlying the common-law right of confrontation, thus reflects an especially acute concern with a specific type of out-of-court statement.

Various formulations of this core class of "testimonial" statements exist: "ex parte in-court testimony or its functional equivalent — that is, material such as affidavits, custodial examinations, prior testimony that the defendant was unable to cross-examine, or similar pretrial statements that declarants would reasonably expect to be used prosecutorially," Brief for Petitioner 23; "extrajudicial statements . . . contained in formalized testimonial materials, such as affidavits, depositions, prior testimony, or confessions," *White v. Illinois*, 502 U.S. 346, 365 (1992) (THOMAS, J., joined by SCALIA, J., concurring in part and concurring in judgment) . . . .; "statements that were made under circumstances which would lead an objective witness reasonably to believe that the statement would be available for use at a later trial," Brief for National Association of Criminal Defense Lawyers et al. as Amici Curiae 3. These formulations all share a common nucleus and then define the Clause's coverage at various levels of abstraction around it. Regardless of the precise articulation, some statements qualify under any definition — for example, ex parte testimony at a preliminary hearing.

Statements taken by police officers in the course of interrogations are also testimonial under even a narrow standard. Police interrogations bear a striking resemblance to examinations by justices of the peace in England. The statements are not sworn testimony, but the absence of oath was not dispositive. Cobham's examination was unsworn, yet Raleigh's trial has long been thought a paradigmatic confrontation violation . . .

In sum, even if the Sixth Amendment is not solely concerned with testimonial hearsay, that is its primary object, and interrogations by law enforcement officers fall squarely within that class.

The historical record also supports a second proposition: that the Framers would not have allowed admission of testimonial statements of a witness who did not appear at trial unless he was unavailable to testify, and the defendant had had a prior opportunity for cross-examination. The text of the Sixth Amendment does not suggest any open-ended exceptions from the confrontation requirement to be developed by the courts. Rather, the "right to be confronted with the witnesses against him," Amdt. 6, is most naturally read as a reference to the right of confrontation at common law, admitting only those exceptions established at the time of the founding. As the English authorities above reveal, the common law in 1791 conditioned admissibility of an absent witness's examination on unavailability and a prior opportunity to cross-examine . . . .

Most of the (common law) hearsay exceptions covered statements that by their nature were not testimonial — for example, business records or statements in furtherance of a conspiracy. We do not infer from these that the Framers thought exceptions would apply even to prior testimony . . . .

V

Although the results of our decisions have generally been faithful to the original meaning of the Confrontation Clause, the same cannot be said of our rationales. *Roberts* conditions the admissibility of all hearsay evidence on whether it falls under a "firmly rooted hearsay exception" or bears "particularized guarantees of trustworthiness." This test departs from the historical principles identified above in two respects. First, it is too broad: It applies the same mode of analysis whether or not the hearsay consists of ex parte testimony. This often results in close constitutional scrutiny in cases that are far removed from the core concerns of the Clause. At the same time, however, the test is too narrow: It admits statements that do consist of ex parte testimony upon a mere finding of reliability. This malleable standard often fails to protect against paradigmatic confrontation violations.

Where testimonial statements are involved, we do not think the Framers meant to leave the Sixth Amendment's protection to the vagaries of the rules of evidence, much less to amorphous notions of "reliability.". . . To be sure, the Clause's ultimate goal is to ensure reliability of evidence, but it is a procedural rather than a substantive guarantee. It commands, not that evidence be reliable, but that reliability be assessed in a particular manner: by testing in the crucible of cross-examination. The Clause thus reflects a judgment, not only about the desirability of reliable evidence (a point on which there could be little dissent), but about how reliability can best be determined.

The *Roberts* test allows a jury to hear evidence, untested by the adversary process, based on a mere judicial determination of reliability. The Raleigh trial itself involved the very sorts of reliability determinations that *Roberts* authorizes. In the face of Raleigh's repeated demands for confrontation, the prosecution responded with many of the arguments a court applying *Roberts* might invoke today: that Cobham's statements were self-inculpatory, that they were not made in the heat of passion, and that they were not "extracted from [him] upon any hopes or promise of Pardon.". . . [T]he problem was that the judges refused to allow Raleigh to confront Cobham in court, where he could cross-examine him and try to expose his accusation as a lie.

Dispensing with confrontation because testimony is obviously reliable is akin to dispensing with jury trial because a defendant is obviously guilty. This is not what the Sixth Amendment prescribes.

The legacy of *Roberts* in other courts vindicates the Framers' wisdom in rejecting a general reliability exception. The framework is . . . unpredictable . . . .

Reliability is an amorphous, if not entirely subjective, concept. There are countless factors bearing on whether a statement is reliable; the nine-factor balancing test applied by the Court of Appeals below is representative. Whether a statement is deemed reliable depends heavily on which factors the judge considers and how much weight he accords each of them. Some courts wind up attaching the same significance to opposite facts. For example, the Colorado Supreme Court held a statement more reliable because its inculpation of the defendant was "detailed," [cite], while the Fourth Circuit found a statement more reliable because the portion implicating another was "fleeting," [cite]. The Virginia Court of Appeals found a statement more reliable because the witness was in custody and charged with a crime (thus making the statement more obviously against her penal interest), *see* . . . , while the Wisconsin Court of Appeals found a statement more reliable because the witness was not in custody and not a suspect, *see* . . . . Finally, the Colorado Supreme Court in one case found a statement more reliable because it was given "immediately after" the events at issue, [cite] while that same court, in another case, found a statement more reliable because two years had elapsed, [cite].

The unpardonable vice of the *Roberts* test, however, is not its unpredictability, but its demonstrated capacity to admit core testimonial statements that the Confrontation Clause plainly meant to exclude. Despite the plurality's speculation in *Lilly* that it was "highly unlikely" that accomplice confessions implicating the accused could survive *Roberts*, courts continue routinely to admit them. One recent study found that, after *Lilly*, appellate courts admitted accomplice statements to the authorities in 25 out of 70 cases — more than one-third of the time . . . . Courts have invoked *Roberts* to admit other sorts of plainly testimonial statements despite the absence of any opportunity to cross-examine. *See* . . . (plea allocution showing existence of a conspiracy); . . . (grand jury testimony); . . . (prior trial testimony); . . . .

To add insult to injury, some of the courts that admit untested testimonial statements find reliability in the very factors that make the statements testimonial. As noted earlier, one court relied on the fact that the witness's statement was made to police while in custody on pending charges — the theory being that this made the statement more clearly against penal interest and thus more reliable. Other courts routinely rely on the fact that a prior statement is given under oath in judicial proceedings.

Roberts' failings were on full display in the proceedings below. Sylvia Crawford made her statement while in police custody, herself a potential suspect in the case. Indeed, she had been told that whether she would be released "depend[ed] on how the investigation continues." In response to often leading questions from police detectives, she implicated her husband in Lee's stabbing and at least arguably undermined his self-defense claim. Despite all this, the trial court admitted her statement, listing several reasons why it was reliable. In its opinion reversing, the Court of Appeals listed several other reasons why the statement was not reliable. Finally, the State Supreme Court relied exclusively on the interlocking character of the statement and disregarded every other factor the lower courts had considered. The case is thus a self-contained demonstration of *Roberts*' unpredictable and inconsistent application.

Each of the courts also made assumptions that cross-examination might well have undermined. The trial court, for example, stated that Sylvia Crawford's statement was reliable because she was an eyewitness with direct knowledge of the events. But Sylvia at one point told the police that she had "shut [her] eyes and . . . didn't really watch" part of the fight, and that she was "in shock." The trial court also buttressed its reliability finding by claiming that Sylvia was "being questioned by law enforcement, and, thus, the [questioner] is . . . neutral to her and not someone who would be inclined to advance her interests and shade her version of the truth unfavorably toward the defendant." The Framers would be astounded to learn that ex parte testimony could be admitted against a criminal defendant because it was elicited by "neutral" government officers. But even if the court's assessment of the officer's motives was accurate, it says nothing about Sylvia's perception of her situation. Only cross-examination could reveal that.

The State Supreme Court gave dispositive weight to the interlocking nature of the two statements — that they were both ambiguous as to when and whether Lee had a weapon. The prosecutor obviously did not share the court's view that Sylvia's statement was ambiguous — he called it "damning evidence" that "completely refutes [petitioner's] claim of self-defense." We have no way of knowing whether the jury agreed with the prosecutor or the court. Far from obviating the need for cross-examination, the "interlocking" ambiguity of the two statements made it all the more imperative that they be tested to tease out the truth.

We readily concede that we could resolve this case by simply reweighing the "reliability factors" under *Roberts* and finding that Sylvia Crawford's statement falls short. But we view this as one of those rare cases in which the result below is so improbable that it reveals a fundamental failure on our part to interpret the Constitution in a way that secures its intended constraint on judicial discretion.

We have no doubt that the courts below were acting in utmost good faith when they found reliability. The Framers, however, would not have been content to indulge this assumption. They knew that judges, like other government officers, could not always be trusted to safeguard the rights of the people; the likes of the dread Lord Jeffreys [a particularly autocratic, harsh and despised chief judge in the 17th Century] were not yet too distant a memory. They were loath to leave too much discretion in judicial hands. *Cf.* U.S. Const., Amdt. 6 (criminal jury trial); Amdt. 7 (civil jury trial); *Ring v. Arizona*, 536 U.S. 584, 611-612 (2002) (Scalia, J., concurring). By replacing categorical constitutional guarantees with open-ended balancing tests, we do violence to their design. Vague standards are manipulable, and, while that might be a small concern in run-of-the-mill assault prosecutions like this one, the Framers had an eye toward politically charged cases like Raleigh's — great state trials where the impartiality of even those at the highest levels of the judiciary might not be so clear. It is difficult to imagine *Roberts*' providing any meaningful protection in those circumstances.

Where nontestimonial hearsay is at issue, it is wholly consistent with the Framers' design to afford the States flexibility in their development of hearsay law — as does *Roberts*, and as would an approach that exempted such statements from Confrontation Clause scrutiny altogether. Where testimonial evidence is at issue, however, the Sixth Amendment demands what the common law required: unavailability and a prior opportunity for cross-examination. We leave for another day any effort to spell out a comprehensive definition of "testimonial." Whatever else the term covers, it applies at a minimum to prior testimony at a preliminary hearing, before a grand jury, or at a former trial; and to police interrogations. These are the modern practices with closest kinship to the abuses at which the Confrontation Clause was directed.

[Reversed and remanded.]

CHIEF JUSTICE REHNQUIST, with whom JUSTICE O'CONNOR joins, concurring in the judgment: . . .

In choosing the path it does, the Court of course overrules *Ohio v. Roberts*, a case decided nearly a quarter of a century ago. *Stare decisis* is not an inexorable command in the area of constitutional law, *see Payne v. Tennessee*, 501 U.S. 808, 828 (1991), but by and large, it "is the preferred course because it promotes the evenhanded, predictable, and consistent development of legal principles, fosters reliance on judicial decisions, and contributes to the actual and perceived integrity of the judicial process," *id.* And in making this appraisal, doubt that the new rule is indeed the "right" one should surely be weighed in the balance. Though there are no vested interests involved, unresolved questions for the future of everyday criminal trials throughout the country surely counsel the same sort of caution. The Court grandly declares that "[w]e leave for another day any effort to spell out a comprehensive definition of 'testimonial.' " But the thousands of federal prosecutors and the tens of thousands of state prosecutors need answers as to what beyond the specific kinds of "testimony" the Court lists, is covered by the new rule. They need them now, not months or years from now. Rules of criminal evidence are applied every day in courts throughout the country, and parties should not be left in the dark in this manner.

NOTES AND QUESTIONS

(1) *Introductory Note on Crawford's Rejection of Roberts.* First, it should be remembered that the Confrontation Clause comes into play only when a jurisdiction's evidence rules allow a piece of evidence to come in *against a criminal defendant*, and not when it comes in against the prosecution or in a civil case. Second, to be admissible, an out-of-court statement must survive *both* the jurisdiction's hearsay rule (through some hearsay exception or exemption the jurisdiction has provided) *and* the federal constitution's Confrontation Clause, as well as any additional protections that might be provided in the constitutions of individual states. Third, the Confrontation Clause apparently does not apply to out-of-court statements not offered for the truth of the matter stated in them. (In an aside not reproduced here, *Crawford* comments that the confrontation clause does not prevent even "testimonial" statements if they are offered for "purposes other than establishing the truth of the matter asserted," citing *Tennessee v. Street*, 471 U.S. 409 (1985)). None of these fundamental propositions has been changed by *Crawford.*

However, *Crawford* does significantly change what the Confrontation Clause demands concerning out-of-court hearsay statements where the declarant does not testify and the statement is offered for its truth. The Court attempts to define a class of "testimonial" out-of-court defendant-inculpatory statements (including, perhaps among others, officially garnered statements, like statements to police, grand jury statements, affidavits, testimony at other trials or proceedings, etc.) that are the special focus of the historical Confrontation Clause (like, most famously, the abuses committed by the prosecution in the Sir Walter Raleigh case), and says that even if they come within a hearsay exception (like declarations against interest, excited utterances, etc.) or are otherwise deemed reliable, they may not come into evidence unless the witness is unavailable and there was an earlier opportunity to cross-examine. Questions will no doubt arise in the future, about whether such a former opportunity to cross-examine was sufficient for confrontation clause purposes. Some of these questions will be very like the "similar motive" questions, etc., that arise under Fed. R. Evid. 804(b)(1) (the former testimony hearsay exception). Whether they will be resolved exactly the same way remains to be seen, but the policy objectives seem quite analogous in the two areas.

(2) *What Is "Testimonial"?* The Court in *Crawford* leaves open what it means by "testimonial" — or at least leaves the outer edges of it vague — saying that the Court will define the concept more completely over time. But it seems that "testimonial" has in part to do with either (1) whether government (or law enforcement like police) was involved (to what extent and with what subjective or objective purpose is unclear) in obtaining it; or (2) whether the declarant knows (or declarants in general would know) that he may be making evidence against someone (or, perhaps that the information is relevant to an investigation); or (3) both.

Crawford may, on first blush, *seem* to affect statements admitted against a criminal defendant pursuant to the former testimony hearsay exception (Rule 804(b)(1)) because that testimony was garnered at or taken at an *official proceeding*, but such testimony, though clearly "testimonial," would be acceptable under the Confrontation Clause because the former testimony hearsay exception requires *unavailability* and earlier *cross-exam opportunity*, and thus complies with *Crawford*, provided that the definition of these terms is the same in the two contexts (hearsay exception and confrontation).

The "former witness statement" exemption from the hearsay rule (Rule 801(d)(1), even (d)(1)(A), inconsistent statements made at an official proceeding), though in some situations embracing "testimonial" statements, would not be affected by *Crawford* because under these evidentiary rules the witness is on the stand for cross-examination at the present proceeding, even if not at the earlier proceeding.

Crawford is in considerable measure anti-prosecution, because it restricts (nearly absolutely) "testimonial" hearsay statements' offered against the criminal defendant — they can no longer be justified as within a firmly rooted hearsay exception or as being otherwise reliable. However, to the extent that all confrontation-clause scrutiny is removed from non-testimonial hearsay statements (rather than still applying the *Roberts*-based test to them we assume), then there is a pro-prosecution aspect to this as well, because previously, under *Roberts*, these non-testimonial hearsay statements were subject to confrontation-clause scrutiny (they had to be within a firmly rooted hearsay exception or be otherwise reliable) as an additional exclusionary filter even if they survived the jurisdiction's hearsay rule through a hearsay exception provided by the jurisdiction. If this confrontation-clause scrutiny is removed from them, a state could let them in quite freely if the state wants too — could abolish its hearsay rule, or riddle it with all kinds of odd non-firmly-rooted hearsay exceptions, which would survive the Confrontation Clause so long as the hearsay statement admitted is non-testimonial.

(3) *Was Roberts Unpredictable? If So, Isn't Crawford Unpredictable Too?* The *Crawford* opinion criticizes the *Roberts*-based test for being unpredictable: What is "firmly rooted"? What is "reliable"? How reliable is reliable? But remember, the *Crawford* test has something that is also going to be difficult or subjective to define (although probably not *as* subjective): What is "testimonial"? Probably not testimonial in the *Crawford* sense is a statement made by a declarant to a friend (especially if made before any crime has been committed) where declarant does not consciously know he (declarant) may be providing evidence or something useful to an investigation. Nor, in all likelihood, is an excited utterance if made unaware of its implications, at least when not made to or overheard by someone with a governmental connection. But what if police electronically eavesdrop on such statements? Must there be an interrogation? Must the statement have been gotten in some kind of *formalized* setting/proceeding? Or, alternatively, is the keystone that declarant is consciously aware of making evidence against someone? Or aware of relevance to an investigation? Or that a reasonable person would be aware? Or that the police or reasonable police would be aware? While there are certain core statements that would be testimonial under all of these variants, each variant adds a different category of statements. Some spread the periphery of the concept of "testimonial" farther than others. By "testimonial", the Court is aiming to outlaw statements like those used against Sir Walter Raleigh. But how "like"?

(4) *Is Justice Scalia's History Selective? Is It in Fact Inaccurate?* Some scholars believe Justice Scalia "cherry picked" the history he wished to follow and that some of it is even inaccurate. *See, e.g.*, David Crump, *Overruling* Crawford v. Washington: *Why and How*, 88 NOTRE DAME L. REV. 115 (2012); John R. Grimm, Note, *A Wavering Bright Line: How* Crawford v. Washington *Denies Defendants a Consistent Confrontation Right*, 48 AM. CRIM. L. REV. 185 (2011).

One interesting thing the Court missed in its analysis, is that there was another piece of hearsay used against Raleigh than Lord Cobham's government garnered statement. Raleigh was also convicted on the basis of the vague statement, apparently mere speculation, rumor, and opinion, of a boatman in Spain (who apparently had no relation whatsoever to any of the people involved), made to a random English traveler, who also had no connection with the events other than to be called as a witness against Raleigh to recount the boatman's statement that the boatman thought the English King would never be crowned, but would be killed, if Raleigh had anything to do with it. Would the reforms that ultimately led to the confrontation clause be concerned with this evidence, too, as well a Lord Cobham's government garnered statement against Raleigh that is mentioned as fundamental to those concerns in *Crawford*?

This hearsay of the boatman would not fit easily into the outlawed "testimonial" category defined in *Crawford*.

(5) *Crawford Focuses on Case Specific Facts Rather than Hearsay Categories.* While *Crawford* holds that certain categories of hearsay may not usually be testimonial, e.g., business records and coconspirator statements, even these categories may arguably contain testimonial statements, e.g. if made to agents of government for evidentiary or investigative purposes. For example, certain forensic reports are offered as business records. As mentioned in note (1), above, statements

within recognized hearsay exceptions are no longer insulated from a confrontation challenge just because they fit within a firmly rooted hearsay exception, but must be analyzed individually on the particular facts of the case to determine if they are testimonial. Does this change of approach mean that trials will be longer, and admissibility determinations less predictable?

(6) *When are the Residual Exception and Other Ad Hoc Hearsay Exceptions Unusable Against Criminal Defendants After Crawford?* Before *Crawford*, the residual exception was commonly used to admit against criminal defendants grand jury testimony of unavailable declarants, even though in most jurisdictions there is no opportunity for the defendant to be represented or to examine or cross-examine anyone at the grand jury. *Crawford* specifically identifies such statements as testimonial. What about hearsay exceptions allowing trustworthy hearsay in child abuse, domestic violence and elder abuse cases? Would these statements be admissible?

(7) *Can Dying Declarations be Testimonial?* One of *Crawford's* footnotes (omitted above) discussed the fact that dying declarations were admitted at common law even when they were testimonial. The Court concluded: "We need not decide in this case whether the Sixth Amendment incorporates an exception for testimonial dying declarations. If this exception must be accepted on historical grounds, it is *sui generis*." Does this undermine the Court's testimonial approach? Whether there is such a *sui generis* constitutional exception for dying declarations, and whether it has the same shape as the dying declarations exception in the FRE (Rule 804 (b)(2)) remains to be seen.

Justice Scalia's statement that dying declarations were a *sui generis* exception to exclusion has been described as "flatly wrong." David Crump, *supra*, at 127.

(8) *Crawford is Not Retroactive.* The Supreme Court decided that *Crawford* is not retroactive to cases already final on direct review. *See Whorton v. Bockting*, 549 U.S. 406, 409 (2007). As a result, many cases that admitted clearly testimonial hearsay statements pursuant to hearsay exceptions like declarations against penal interest and others, as being reliable or within firmly rooted hearsay exceptions pursuant to *Roberts*, in violation of *Crawford*, will not be reviewed, even though *Crawford* questioned the reliability of many of these statements, decried the subjectivity involved in the determination of trustworthiness, and declared that firm-rootedness does not matter. *Whorton* also contains language that seems to confirm that the *Roberts* analysis does not have any continuing vitality even as to non-testimonial hearsay, even when such hearsay is totally unreliable and not within any firmly rooted hearsay exception (but such unreliable hearsay possibly might be subject to a Due Process analysis).

(9) *Did Crawford Improperly Fail to Consider Established Criteria for Departing from Stare Decisis (and Would Those Criteria Have Led to the Opposite Result)?* One criticism of *Crawford* is that the Supreme Court has well-established criteria for overruling a prior case or departing from *stare decisis*, and Justice Scalia never analyzed or even mentioned those criteria in overruling *Roberts*.

(10) *Should Crawford Be Overruled? (In Fact, Has It Been Overruled?)* One of the authors of this casebook has written as follows. His conclusions are not

necessarily shared by the other two, but should be considered by the student. After reading the remainder of the cases in this chapter, you can reach your own conclusions:

> The stars are aligned today for the overruling of *Crawford v. Washington*. Although Justice Scalia's opinion in that Confrontation Clause case omitted analysis of most of the recognized factors justifying its sharp departure from *stare decisis*, by now those factors have developed in a way that justifies departure from *Crawford* itself. For example, even commentators who support the apparent goal of that decision, namely, broad exclusion of evidence on Confrontation Clause grounds, describe *Crawford* and its progeny as unstable. The underpinnings of the decision are dubious and, in some instances, provably wrong. *Crawford* has led to a series of decisions by closely divided Courts that have left important issues heavily discussed but unresolved. To reach decisions that make sense after *Crawford*, the Justices have resorted to transparent judicial fudging. In summary, the *Crawford* approach is neither faithful to the Constitution nor workable. And by now, remarkably, a majority of the Court is united in rejecting that approach and preferring differing alternatives that easily could be reconciled and that would produce results more congruent with the purposes of the Confrontation Clause.

David Crump, *Overruling* Crawford v. Washington: *Why and How*, 88 NOTRE DAME L. REV. 115 (2012) (collecting other generally uncomplimentary commentaries about *Crawford* in a footnote). There are other scholars who praise *Crawford*.

You may agree or disagree with Prof. Crump's assessment after reading the cases that have followed *Crawford*, contained in this chapter. The case Prof. Crump believes may reflect a majority who seem to *sub silentio* (but not expressly) reject *Crawford* is *Williams v. Illinois*, reproduced later in this chapter — although he admits it is not clear that it does.

After reading the subsequent cases in this chapter, ask yourself whether you think the Justices, by deciding *Crawford* the way they did, have painted themselves into a corner from which they are seeking to escape.

[2] The Domestic Violence Context: Filling in Some Unanswered Questions

DAVIS v. WASHINGTON

Supreme Court of the United States
547 U.S. 813 (2006)

Justice SCALIA delivered the opinion of the Court, in which Chief Justice ROBERTS and Justices STEVENS, KENNEDY, SOUTER, GINSBURG, BREYER AND ALITO, joined. Justice THOMAS filed an opinion concurring in the judgment in part and dissenting in part.

I

The relevant statements in *Davis v. Washington* [the first case we consider in this joint appeal] were made to a 911 emergency operator on February 1, 2001. When the operator answered the initial call, the connection terminated before anyone spoke. She reversed the call, and Michelle McCottry answered. In the ensuing conversation, the operator ascertained that McCottry was involved in a domestic disturbance with her former boyfriend Adrian Davis, the petitioner in this case:

"911 Operator: Hello.

"Complainant: Hello.

"911 Operator: What's going on?

"Complainant: He's here jumpin' on me again.

"911 Operator: Okay. Listen to me carefully. Are you in a house or an apartment?

"Complainant: I'm in a house.

"911 Operator: Are there any weapons?

"Complainant: No. He's usin' his fists . . . .

"911 Operator: Okay, sweetie. I've got help started. Stay on the line with me, okay?

"Complainant: I'm on the line.

"911 Operator: Listen to me carefully. Do you know his last name?

"Complainant: It's Davis.

"911 Operator: Davis? Okay, what's his first name?

"Complainant: Adrian . . . .

"911 Operator: Okay. What's his middle initial?

"Complainant: Martell. He's runnin' now."

As the conversation continued, the operator learned that Davis had "just r[un] out the door" after hitting McCottry, and that he was leaving in a car with someone else. McCottry started talking, but the operator cut her off, saying, "Stop talking and answer my questions."

The State charged Davis with felony violation of a domestic no-contact order. The State's only witnesses were the two police officers who responded to the 911 call. Both officers testified that McCottry exhibited injuries that appeared to be recent, but neither officer could testify as to the cause of the injuries. McCottry presumably could have testified as to whether Davis was her assailant, but she did not appear. Over Davis's objection based on the Confrontation Clause of the Sixth Amendment, the trial court admitted the recording of her exchange with the 911 operator, and the jury convicted him.

In *Hammon v. Indiana* [the second case we consider in this joint appeal] police responded late on the night of February 26, 2003, to a "reported domestic disturbance" at the home of Hershel and Amy Hammon. They found Amy alone on the front porch, appearing " 'somewhat frightened,' " but she told them that " 'nothing was the matter,' " She gave them permission to enter the house, where an officer saw "a gas heating unit in the corner of the living room" that had "flames coming out of the . . . partial glass front. There were pieces of glass on the ground in front of it and there was flame emitting from the front of the heating unit."

Hershel, meanwhile, was in the kitchen. He told the police "that he and his wife had 'been in an argument' but 'everything was fine now' and the argument 'never became physical.' " By this point Amy had come back inside. One of the officers remained with Hershel; the other went to the living room to talk with Amy, and "again asked [her] what had occurred." Hershel made several attempts to participate in Amy's conversation with the police, but was rebuffed. The officer later testified that Hershel "became angry when I insisted that [he] stay separated from Mrs. Hammon so that we can investigate what had happened." After hearing Amy's account, the officer "had her fill out and sign a battery affidavit." Amy handwrote the following: "Broke our Furnace & shoved me down on the floor into the broken glass. Hit me in the chest and threw me down. Broke our lamps & phone. Tore up my van where I couldn't leave the house. Attacked my daughter."

The State charged Hershel with domestic battery and with violating his probation. Amy was subpoenaed, but she did not appear at his subsequent bench trial. The State called the officer who had questioned Amy, and asked him to recount what Amy told him and to authenticate the affidavit. Hershel's counsel repeatedly objected to the admission of this evidence. Nonetheless, the trial court admitted the affidavit as a "present sense impression," and Amy's statements as "excited utterances" that "are expressly permitted in these kinds of cases even if the declarant is not available to testify."

II

Our opinion in *Crawford* set forth "[v]arious formulations" of the core class of " 'testimonial' " statements, ibid., but found it unnecessary to endorse any of them, because "some statements qualify under any definition," *id.* at 52. Among those, we said, were "[s]tatements taken by police officers in the course of interrogations," ibid.; see also id. at 53. The questioning that generated the deponent's statement in *Crawford* — which was made and recorded while she was in police custody, after having been given *Miranda* warnings as a possible suspect herself — "qualifies under any conceivable definition" of an " 'interrogation'." We therefore did not define that term, except to say that "[w]e use [it] . . . in its colloquial, rather than any technical legal, sense," and that "one can imagine various definitions . . . , and we need not select among them in this case." The character of the statements in the present cases is not as clear, and these cases require us to determine more precisely which police interrogations produce testimony.

Statements are non-testimonial when made in the course of police interrogation under circumstances objectively indicating that the primary purpose of the interrogation is to enable police assistance to meet an ongoing emergency. They are testimonial when the circumstances objectively indicate that there is no such ongoing emergency, and that the primary purpose of the interrogation is to establish or prove past events potentially relevant to later criminal prosecution.

III

The question before us in *Davis*, then, is whether, objectively considered, the interrogation that took place in the course of the 911 call produced testimonial statements. A 911 call, [unlike a police interrogation,] and at least the initial interrogation conducted in connection with a 911 call, is ordinarily not designed primarily to "establis[h] or prov[e]" some past fact, but to describe current circumstances requiring police assistance.

The difference between the interrogation in *Davis* and the one in *Crawford* is apparent on the face of things. In *Davis*, McCottry was speaking about events as they were actually happening, rather than "describ[ing] past events." Sylvia Crawford's interrogation, on the other hand, took place hours after the events she described had occurred. Moreover, any reasonable listener would recognize that McCottry (unlike Sylvia Crawford) was facing an ongoing emergency. Although one might call 911 to provide a narrative report of a crime absent any imminent danger, McCottry's call was plainly a call for help against a bona fide physical threat. Third, the nature of what was asked and answered in *Davis*, again viewed objectively, was such that the elicited statements were necessary to be able to resolve the present emergency, rather than simply to learn (as in *Crawford*) what had happened in the past. That is true even of the operator's effort to establish the identity of the assailant, so that the dispatched officers might know whether they would be encountering a violent felon. And finally, the difference in the level of formality between the two interviews is striking. *Crawford* was responding calmly, at the station house, to a series of questions, with the officer-interrogator taping and making notes of her answers; McCottry's frantic answers were provided over the phone, in an environment that was not tranquil, or even (as far as any reasonable 911 operator could make out) safe.

We conclude from all this that the circumstances of McCottry's interrogation objectively indicate its primary purpose was to enable police assistance to meet an ongoing emergency. She simply was not acting as a witness; she was not testifying . . . .

This is not to say that a conversation which begins as an interrogation to determine the need for emergency assistance cannot, as the Indiana Supreme Court put it, "evolve into testimonial statements" once that purpose has been achieved. In this case, for example, after the operator gained the information needed to address the exigency of the moment, the emergency appears to have ended (when Davis drove away from the premises). The operator then told McCottry to be quiet, and proceeded to pose a battery of questions. It could readily be maintained that, from that point on, McCottry's statements were testimonial, not unlike the "structured police questioning" that occurred in *Crawford*. Through *in limine* procedure, [courts] should redact or exclude the portions of any statement that have become testimonial, as they do, for example, with unduly prejudicial portions of otherwise admissible evidence. Davis's jury did not hear the complete 911 call, although it may well have heard some testimonial portions. We were asked to classify only McCottry's early statements identifying Davis as her assailant, and we agree that they were not testimonial.

Determining the testimonial or non-testimonial character of the statements that were the product of the interrogation in *Hammon* is a much easier task, since they were not much different from the statements we found to be testimonial in *Crawford*. It is entirely clear from the circumstances that the interrogation was part of an investigation into possibly criminal past conduct — as, indeed, the testifying officer expressly acknowledged. There was no emergency in progress; the interrogating officer testified that he had heard no arguments or crashing and saw no one throw or break anything. When the officers first arrived, Amy told them that things were fine, and there was no immediate threat to her person. When the officer questioned Amy for the second time, and elicited the challenged statements, he was not seeking to determine (as in *Davis*) "what is happening," but rather "what happened." Objectively viewed, the primary, if not indeed the sole, purpose of the interrogation was to investigate a possible crime — which is, of course, precisely what the officer should have done.

It is true that the *Crawford* interrogation was more formal. It followed a *Miranda* warning, was tape-recorded, and took place at the station house. While these features certainly strengthened the statements' testimonial aspect — made it more objectively apparent, that is, that the purpose of the exercise was to nail down the truth about past criminal events — none was essential to the point. It was formal enough that Amy's interrogation was conducted in a separate room, away from her husband (who tried to intervene), with the officer receiving her replies for use in his "investigat[ion]." What we called the "striking resemblance" of the *Crawford* statement to civil-law ex parte examinations is shared by Amy's statement here. Both declarants were actively separated from the defendant — officers forcibly prevented Hershel from participating in the interrogation. Both statements deliberately recounted, in response to police questioning, how potentially criminal past events began and progressed. And both took place some time after the events described were over. Such statements under official interrogation are an obvious substitute for live testimony, because they do precisely what a witness does on direct examination; they are inherently testimonial.

Although we necessarily reject the Indiana Supreme Court's implication that virtually any "initial inquiries" at the crime scene will not be testimonial, we do not hold the opposite — that no questions at the scene will yield non-testimonial answers. We have already observed of domestic disputes that "[o]fficers called to investigate . . . need to know whom they are dealing with in order to assess the situation, the threat to their own safety, and possible danger to the potential victim." *Hiibel*, 542 U.S. at 186. Such exigencies may often mean that "initial inquiries" produce non-testimonial statements. But in cases like this one, where Amy's statements were neither a cry for help nor the provision of information enabling officers immediately to end a threatening situation, the fact that they were given at an alleged crime scene and were "initial inquiries" is immaterial.

IV

Respondents in both cases, joined by a number of their amici, contend that the nature of the offenses charged in these two cases — domestic violence — requires greater flexibility in the use of testimonial evidence. This particular type of crime is notoriously susceptible to intimidation or coercion of the victim to ensure that she does not testify at trial. When this occurs, the Confrontation Clause gives the criminal a windfall. We may not, however, vitiate constitutional guarantees when they have the effect of allowing the guilty to go free. But when defendants seek to undermine the judicial process by procuring or coercing silence from witnesses and victims, the Sixth Amendment does not require courts to acquiesce. While defendants have no duty to assist the State in proving their guilt, they do have the duty to refrain from acting in ways that destroy the integrity of the criminal-trial system. We reiterate what we said in *Crawford*: that "the rule of forfeiture by wrongdoing . . . extinguishes confrontation claims on essentially equitable grounds." That is, one who obtains the absence of a witness by wrongdoing forfeits the constitutional right to confrontation.

We affirm the judgment of the Supreme Court of Washington in No. 05-5224. We reverse the judgment of the Supreme Court of Indiana in No. 05-5705, and remand the case to that Court for proceedings not inconsistent with this opinion.

NOTES AND QUESTIONS

(1) *Are Most 911 Calls Admissible After Davis?* The primary purpose test appears to require fact specific analysis even for excited utterances. Does *Davis* ensure that most 911 calls will be admitted? The early trend after *Davis* appeared to favor admission of 911 calls, particularly in domestic violence cases. (In such cases, victims frequently do not testify, so the extrajudicial evidence is often sorely needed.) *See generally* Raeder, *History Redux: The Unheard Voices of Domestic Violence Victims, A Comment On Aviva Orenstein's Sex, Threats and Absent Victims, Res Gestae*, FORDHAM ONLINE J. (May 2011), available at http://fordhamlawreview.org/articles/history-redux-the-unheard-voices-of-domestic-violence-victims-a-comment-on-aviva-orenstein-s-em-sex-threats-and-absent-victims-em; Raeder, *Domestic Violence Cases After Davis: Is the Glass Half Empty or Half Full*, 15 BROOK. J.L. & POL'Y 759 (2007).

(2) *Justice Thomas' Critique of the Primary Purpose Test.* Justice Thomas' view expressed in a concurrence called the *Davis* standard unworkable and as unpredictable as the *Roberts* reliability test. He would require "formalized dia-

logue" before something can be called "testimonial" — which would exclude most informal or volunteered statements to law enforcement from any Confrontation Clause scrutiny. After *Davis* can informal statements to police officers be testimonial? Can formal ones be non-testimonial? What about formal and informal statements to individuals employed by the government in non-law-enforcement jobs, such as social workers or doctors? Would the standard be different for doctors depending on whether they are employed by the state? What is "formal"? After *Davis*, does formality play any role? (Remember, *Crawford* seemed to make it a significant factor.) Does there have to be an "interrogation"? What qualifies as an "interrogation?" Is it different than Thomas' "formalized dialogue"?

(3) *What Does Davis' "Objectively Determined Primary Purpose Test" Mean?* Whose purpose (police or declarant) is significant (even if objectively determined)? Suppose they appear to have different purposes or each to have mixed purposes? Are their *actual* purposes (as opposed to objective appearances of their purpose) irrelevant? For example, imagine that a domestic violence survivor talks excitedly to police officers in order to secure her own safety from the perpetrator, while the police officers' undisclosed aim is to address a crime. The ambiguity of this situation is one of the difficulties after *Crawford.*

Suppose the *actual* intent was to implicate defendant but on an objective view that did not appear? Conversely, is there still room to argue that in some circumstances statements are testimonial if an objective observer would reasonably believe the statement would be available for use at a later trial, even if in fact this was not so or was not the purpose of the police and/or was not the purpose of the declarant? In what kind of case would it matter if an objective test, rather than an *actual* primary purpose test is employed? Would "objective" mean a reasonable declarant; or reasonable police officer; or reasonable outside observer? How much of the particular perspective, experience, or circumstances of the actual participants is to be taken into account under an objective test?

What if police were not involved? After *Davis* can the Confrontation Clause be invoked if the circumstances did not have some type of governmental involvement?

(4) *How Should Statements of Children be Evaluated*? Some prosecutors argue that because young children do not understand criminal investigations, prosecutions, and trial practice, none of their out-of-court statements can have the necessary purpose to make them testimonial even if made to police. Do you agree? Does *Crawford* or *Davis* predict how child abuse cases will be handled, when the child is incompetent or refuses to testify, but where there are out-of-court statements of the child to physicians, other medical personnel, baby sitters, welfare workers, parents, or police, implicating the defendant? *See generally* Raeder, *Comments on Child Abuse Litigation in a "Testimonial" World: The Intersection of Competency, Hearsay and Confrontations After Davis*, 82 IND. L.J. 1009 (2007).

If an incompetent or not very competent child is permitted to testify, does that satisfy the Confrontation Clause? What does an opportunity to cross-examine mean in the context if a very young child who cannot respond very well to questions? Does *Owens* (supra, § 11.02) shed any light on this?

(5) *Does Roberts Still Apply to Non-testimonial Hearsay?* Assuming this was still in doubt, did *Davis* sound the death knell for any Confrontation Clause scrutiny for non-testimonial hearsay statements when it noted (in a passage not reproduced above) that: "[i]t is the testimonial character of the statement that separates it from other hearsay that, while subject to traditional limitations upon hearsay evidence, is not subject to the Confrontation Clause"? Do you see any other statements in *Davis* relevant to this question? Although a few courts evaluated non-testimonial hearsay under the criteria of *Roberts* and its progeny after *Davis*, most commentators and decisions find that after *Davis* (and particularly after our next case, *Bryant*) no federal Confrontation Clause scrutiny is required for non-testimonial hearsay. Does this mean that unreliable hearsay is admissible if non-testimonial? (The Due Process Clause might keep it out, but only in extreme cases.)

Though in federal cases *Roberts* may be gone even for non-testimonial hearsay statements, the states are free to interpret their own Confrontation Clauses to be more protective of the criminal defendant than the federal clause. Thus, even if the federal clause is held inapplicable to non-testimonial hearsay statements, state constitutions could be construed to subject such statements to a *Roberts*-type or other type confrontation clause analysis. In a similar vein, state courts could reject, for state constitutional purposes, federal decisions (even U.S. Supreme Court decisions) that they feel confine the definition of "testimonial" too much. In other words, states could cast the state net of protections for the criminal defendant broader than the federal net (but not narrower). However, either of these additional state protections would apply only in state prosecutions, unlike the federal protection, which applies to state and federal prosecutions.

(6) *Could a Court Sensibly Have Reached the Opposite Result in Both Davis and Hammon?* Was Amy (in *Hammon*) really more tranquil than McCottry (in *Davis*)? The difference in tranquility is arguably a good part of the reason for the difference between the two results. The more tranquil situation is more likely focused on gathering evidence (which makes the statement testimonial) than on resolving an emergency (which makes the statement non-testimonial). The Court seems to describe the atmosphere as tranquil in *Hammon*. So presumably Amy was focused on supplying evidence, which is a testimonial purpose, rather than concerned with an emergency. But arguably Amy was *not* so tranquil. Amy was injured, with the defendant still present, trying to intervene, interrupting, and facing the police officers. The defendant was Amy's husband, with whom she would have to deal in future. The Indiana Supreme Court recognized her stress when it found her statement to be an excited utterance. Arguably, this was not a tranquil situation. On the other hand, in *Davis*, McCottry, who made the 911 call, was, in the U.S. Supreme Court's view, focused on an emergency, which is not a testimonial purpose. Was she in a state less tranquil than Amy, thus more focused on resolving an emergency? Maybe not: McCottry, unlike Amy, was safe; McCottry's assailant was gone ("he's runnin"), unlike the situation with Amy. So, maybe the opposite result should have been reached than was reached in the two cases. Are determinations of this kind inherently unpredictable?

[3] Other Types of Emergencies: Filling in Some More of the Puzzle

MICHIGAN v. BRYANT

Supreme Court of the United States
131 S. Ct. 1143 (2011)

Justice SOTOMAYOR delivered the opinion of the Court.

At respondent Richard Bryant's trial, the court admitted statements that the victim, Anthony Covington, made to police officers who discovered him mortally wounded in a gas station parking lot. A jury convicted Bryant of, *inter alia*, second-degree murder. On appeal, the Supreme Court of Michigan held that the Sixth Amendment's Confrontation Clause, as explained in our decisions in *Crawford* v. *Washington* and *Davis* v. *Washington*, rendered Covington's statements inadmissible testimonial hearsay, and the court reversed Bryant's conviction. We granted the State's petition for a writ of certiorari to consider whether the Confrontation Clause barred the admission at trial of Covington's statements to the police. We hold that the circumstances of the interaction between Covington and the police objectively indicate that the "primary purpose of the interrogation" was "to enable police assistance to meet an ongoing emergency." *Davis*, 547 U.S., at 822. Therefore, Covington's identification and description of the shooter and the location of the shooting were not testimonial statements, and their admission at Bryant's trial did not violate the Confrontation Clause. We vacate the judgment of the Supreme Court of Michigan and remand.

I

Around 3:25 a.m. on April 29, 2001, Detroit, Michigan police officers responded to a radio dispatch indicating that a man had been shot. At the scene, they found the victim, Anthony Covington, lying on the ground next to his car in a gas station parking lot. Covington had a gunshot wound to his abdomen, appeared to be in great pain, and spoke with difficulty. The police asked him "what had happened, who had shot him, and where the shooting had occurred." Covington stated that "Rick" [i.e. Bryant] shot him at around 3 a.m. He also indicated that he had a conversation with Bryant, whom he recognized based on his voice, through the back door of Bryant's house. Covington explained that when he turned to leave, he was shot through the door and then drove to the gas station, where police found him.

Covington's conversation with the police ended within 5 to 10 minutes when emergency medical services arrived. Covington was transported to a hospital and died within hours. The police left the gas station after speaking with Covington, called for backup, and traveled to Bryant's house. They did not find Bryant there but did find blood and a bullet on the back porch and an apparent bullet hole in the back door. Police also found Covington's wallet and identification outside the house.

At trial, which occurred prior to our decisions in *Crawford* and *Davis*, police officers who spoke with Covington at the gas station testified about what Covington had told them. The jury returned a guilty verdict on charges of second-degree murder, being a felon in possession of a firearm, and possession of a firearm during the commission of a felony.

II

The Confrontation Clause of the Sixth Amendment states: "In all criminal prosecutions, the accused shall enjoy the right . . . to be confronted with the witnesses against him." [This is binding on both state and federal prosecutions.] . . .

[After *Crawford*,] the Court in *Davis* v. *Washington* and *Hammon* v. *Indiana* took a further step to "determine more precisely which police interrogations produce testimony" and therefore implicate a Confrontation Clause bar. We explained that when *Crawford* said that

> interrogations by law enforcement officers fall squarely within [the] class' of testimonial hearsay, we had immediately in mind (for that was the case before us) interrogations solely directed at establishing the facts of a past crime, in order to identify (or provide evidence to convict) the perpetrator. The product of such interrogation, whether reduced to a writing signed by the declarant or embedded in the memory (and perhaps notes) of the interrogating officer, is testimonial. *Davis*, 547 U.S., at 826.

We thus made clear in *Davis* that not all those questioned by the police are witnesses and not all "interrogations by law enforcement officers," are subject to the Confrontation Clause.

Davis and *Hammon* were both domestic violence cases . . . .

To address the facts of both cases, we expanded upon the meaning of "testimonial" that we first employed in *Crawford* and discussed the concept of an ongoing emergency. We explained:

> Statements are nontestimonial when made in the course of police interrogation under circumstances objectively indicating that the primary purpose of the interrogation is to enable police assistance to meet an ongoing emergency. They are testimonial when the circumstances objectively indicate that there is no such ongoing emergency, and that the primary purpose of the interrogation is to establish or prove past events potentially relevant to later criminal prosecution. *Davis*, 547 U.S., at 822.

Examining the *Davis* and *Hammon* statements in light of those definitions, we held that the statements at issue in *Davis* were nontestimonial and the statements in *Hammon* were testimonial. We distinguished the statements in *Davis* from the testimonial statements in *Crawford* on several grounds, including that the victim in *Davis* was "speaking about events *as they were actually happening*, rather than 'describ[ing] past events,' " that there was an ongoing emergency, that the "elicited statements were necessary to be able to *resolve* the present emergency," and that the statements were not formal. In *Hammon*, on the other hand, we held that, "[i]t is entirely clear from the circumstances that the interrogation was part of an investigation into possibly criminal past conduct." There was "no emergency in progress." The officer questioning Amy "was not seeking to determine . . . 'what is happening,' but rather 'what happened.' " It was "formal enough" that the police interrogated Amy in a room separate from her husband where, "some time after the events described were over," she "deliberately recounted, in response to police questioning, how potentially criminal past events began and progressed." Because her statements "were neither a cry for help nor the provision of information enabling officers immediately to end a threatening situation," we held that they were testimonial.

. . . Whether formal or informal, out-of-court statements can evade the basic objective of the Confrontation Clause, which is to prevent the accused from being deprived of the opportunity to cross-examine the declarant about statements taken for use at trial . . . . When, as in *Davis*, the primary purpose of an interrogation is to respond to an "ongoing emergency," its purpose is not to create a record for trial and thus is not within the scope of the Clause. But there may be *other* circumstances, aside from ongoing emergencies, when a statement is not procured with a primary purpose of creating an out-of-court substitute for trial testimony. In making the primary purpose determination, standard rules of hearsay, designed to identify some statements as reliable, will be relevant. Where no such primary purpose exists, the admissibility of a statement is the concern of state and federal rules of evidence, not the Confrontation Clause.

Deciding this case also requires further explanation of the "ongoing emergency" circumstance addressed in *Davis*. Because *Davis* and *Hammon* arose in the domestic violence context, that was the situation "we had immediately in mind (for that was the case before us)." 547 U.S., at 826. We now face a new context: a nondomestic dispute, involving a victim found in a public location, suffering from a fatal gunshot wound, and a perpetrator whose location was unknown at the time the police located the victim. Thus, we confront for the first time circumstances in which the "ongoing emergency" discussed in *Davis* extends beyond an initial victim to a potential threat to the responding police and the public at large. This new context requires us to provide additional clarification with regard to what *Davis* meant by "the primary purpose of the interrogation is to enable police assistance to meet an ongoing emergency."

III

To determine whether the "primary purpose" of an interrogation is "to enable police assistance to meet an ongoing emergency," *Davis*, 547 U.S. at 822, which would render the resulting statements nontestimonial, we objectively evaluate the circumstances in which the encounter occurs and the statements and actions of the parties.

The Michigan Supreme Court [here] correctly understood that this inquiry is objective. *Davis* uses the word "objective" or "objectively" no fewer than eight times in describing the relevant inquiry.

An objective analysis of the circumstances of an encounter and the statements and actions of the parties to it provides the most accurate assessment of the "primary purpose of the interrogation." The circumstances in which an encounter occurs — *e.g.*, at or near the scene of the crime versus at a police station, during an ongoing emergency or afterwards — are clearly matters of objective fact. The statements and actions of the parties must also be objectively evaluated. That is, the relevant inquiry is not the subjective or actual purpose of the individuals involved in a particular encounter, but rather the purpose that reasonable participants would have had, as ascertained from the individuals' statements and actions and the circumstances in which the encounter occurred.

. . . The existence of an ongoing emergency is relevant to determining the primary purpose of the interrogation because an emergency focuses the participants on something other than "prov[ing] past events potentially relevant to later criminal prosecution." *Davis*, 547 U.S., at 822. Rather, it focuses them on "end[ing] a threatening situation." *Id.*, at 832. Implicit in *Davis* is the idea that because the prospect of fabrication in statements given for the primary purpose of resolving that emergency is presumably significantly diminished, the Confrontation Clause does not require such statements to be subject to the crucible of cross-examination.

This logic is not unlike that justifying the excited utterance exception in hearsay law. Statements "relating to a startling event or condition made while the declarant was under the stress of excitement caused by the event or condition," Fed. Rule Evid. 803(2) . . . . An ongoing emergency has a similar effect of focusing an individual's attention on responding to the emergency.

[The court below . . . employed an unduly narrow understanding of "ongoing emergency" . . . .

[W]hether an emergency exists and is ongoing is a highly context-dependent inquiry. *Davis* and *Hammon* involved domestic violence, a known and identified perpetrator, and, in *Hammon*, a neutralized threat. Because *Davis* and *Hammon* were domestic violence cases, we focused only on the threat to the victims and assessed the ongoing emergency from the perspective of whether there was a continuing threat *to them.*

Domestic violence cases like *Davis* and *Hammon* often have a narrower zone of potential victims than cases involving threats to public safety. An assessment of whether an emergency that threatens the police and public is ongoing cannot narrowly focus on whether the threat solely to the first victim has been neutralized because the threat to the first responders and public may continue. An emergency posed by an unknown shooter who remains at large does not automatically abate just because the police can provide security to his first victim.

The Michigan Supreme Court also did not appreciate that the duration and scope of an emergency may depend in part on the type of weapon employed. The court relied on *Davis* and *Hammon*, in which the assailants used their fists, as controlling the scope of the emergency here, which involved the use of a gun . . . . If Hershel [the husband in *Hammon*] had been reported to be armed with a gun, however, separation by a single household wall might not have been sufficient to end the emergency.

The Michigan Supreme Court's failure to focus on the context-dependent nature of our *Davis* decision also led it to conclude that the medical condition of a declarant is irrelevant . . . . But *Davis* and *Hammon* did not present medical emergencies . . . . Thus, we have not previously considered, much less ruled out, the relevance of a victim's severe injuries to the primary purpose inquiry.

Taking into account the victim's medical state does not, as the Michigan Supreme Court below thought, "rende[r] non-testimonial" "all statements made while the police are questioning a seriously injured complainant." The medical condition of the victim is important to the primary purpose inquiry to the extent that it sheds light on the ability of the victim to have any purpose at all in responding to police questions and on the likelihood that any purpose formed would necessarily be a testimonial one. The victim's medical state also provides important context for first responders to judge the existence and magnitude of a continuing threat to the victim, themselves, and the public . . . .

[A] conversation which begins as an interrogation to determine the need for emergency assistance" can "evolve into testimonial statements." This evolution may occur if, for example, a declarant provides police with information that makes clear that what appeared to be an emergency is not or is no longer an emergency or that what appeared to be a public threat is actually a private dispute. It could also occur if a perpetrator is disarmed, surrenders, is apprehended, or, as in *Davis*, flees with little prospect of posing a threat to the public. Finally, our discussion of the Michigan Supreme Court's misunderstanding of what *Davis* meant by "ongoing emergency" should not be taken to imply that the existence *vel non* of an ongoing emergency is dispositive of the testimonial inquiry. As *Davis* made clear, whether an ongoing emergency exists is simply one factor — albeit an important factor — that informs the ultimate inquiry regarding the "primary purpose" of an interrogation. Another factor the Michigan Supreme Court did not sufficiently account for is the importance of *informality* in an encounter between a victim and police. Formality is not the sole touchstone of our primary purpose inquiry because, although formality suggests the absence of an emergency and therefore an increased likelihood that the purpose of the interrogation is to "establish or prove past events potentially relevant to later criminal prosecution," *Davis*, at 822, informality does not necessarily indicate the presence of an emergency or the lack of testimonial intent. Cf. *id.*, at 826 (explaining that Confrontation Clause requirements cannot "readily be evaded" by the parties deliberately keeping the written product of an interrogation informal "instead of having the declarant sign a deposition"). The court below, however, too readily dismissed the informality of the circumstances in this case in a single brief footnote and in fact seems to have suggested that the encounter in this case was formal. As we explain further below, the questioning in this case occurred in an exposed, public area, prior to the arrival of emergency medical services, and in a disorganized fashion. All of those facts make this case distinguishable from the formal station-house interrogation in *Crawford*.

In addition to the circumstances in which an encounter occurs, the statements and actions of both the declarant and interrogators provide objective evidence of the primary purpose of the interrogation . . . .

As the Michigan Supreme Court correctly recognized, *Davis* requires a combined inquiry that accounts for both the declarant and the interrogator. In many instances, the primary purpose of the interrogation will be most accurately ascertained by looking to the contents of both the questions and the answers. To give an extreme example, if the police say to a victim, "Tell us who did this to you so that we can arrest and prosecute them," the victim's response that "Rick did it," appears purely accusatory because by virtue of the phrasing of the question, the victim necessarily has prosecution in mind when she answers.

The combined approach also ameliorates problems that could arise from looking solely to one participant. Predominant among these is the problem of mixed motives on the part of both interrogators and declarants. Police officers in our society function as both first responders and criminal investigators. Their dual responsibilities may mean that they act with different motives simultaneously or in quick succession . . . .

Victims are also likely to have mixed motives when they make statements to the police. During an ongoing emergency, a victim is most likely to want the threat to her and to other potential victims to end, but that does not necessarily mean that the victim wants or envisions prosecution of the assailant. A victim may want the attacker to be incapacitated temporarily or rehabilitated. Alternatively, a severely injured victim may have no purpose at all in answering questions posed; the answers may be simply reflexive. The victim's injuries could be so debilitating as to prevent her from thinking sufficiently clearly to understand whether her statements are for the purpose of addressing an ongoing emergency or for the purpose of future prosecution . . . .

IV

As we suggested in *Davis*, when a court must determine whether the Confrontation Clause bars the admission of a statement at trial, it should determine the "primary purpose of the interrogation" by objectively evaluating the statements and actions of the parties to the encounter, in light of the circumstances in which the interrogation occurs. The existence of an emergency or the parties' perception that an emergency is ongoing is among the most important circumstances that courts must take into account in determining whether an interrogation is testimonial because statements made to assist police in addressing an ongoing emergency presumably lack the testimonial purpose that would subject them to the requirement of confrontation. As the context of this case brings into sharp relief, the existence and duration of an emergency depend on the type and scope of danger posed to the victim, the police, and the public . . . .

We first examine the circumstances in which the interrogation occurred. The parties disagree over whether there was an emergency when the police arrived at the gas station. Bryant argues, and the Michigan Supreme Court accepted, that there was no ongoing emergency because "there . . . was no criminal conduct occurring. No shots were being fired, no one was seen in possession of a firearm, nor were any witnesses seen cowering in fear or running from the scene." Bryant, while conceding that "a serious or life-threatening injury creates a medical emergency for a victim," further argues that a declarant's medical emergency is not relevant to the ongoing emergency determination.

In contrast, Michigan and the Solicitor General explain that when the police responded to the call that a man had been shot and found Covington bleeding on the gas station parking lot, "they did not know who Covington was, whether the shooting had occurred at the gas station or at a different location, who the assailant was, or whether the assailant posed a continuing threat to Covington or others.". . .

The police officers who spoke with Covington at the gas station testified that Covington did not tell them what words Covington and Rick had exchanged prior to the shooting. What Covington did tell the officers was that he fled Bryant's back porch, indicating that he perceived an ongoing threat. The police did not know, and Covington did not tell them, whether the threat was limited to him. The potential scope of the dispute and therefore the emergency in this case thus stretches more broadly than those at issue in *Davis* and *Hammon* and encompasses a threat potentially to the police and the public.

This is also the first of our post-*Crawford* Confrontation Clause cases to involve a gun. The physical separation that was sufficient to end the emergency in *Hammon* was not necessarily sufficient to end the threat in this case; Covington was shot through the back door of Bryant's house. Bryant's argument that there was no ongoing emergency because "[n]o shots were being fired," surely construes ongoing emergency too narrowly. An emergency does not last only for the time between when the assailant pulls the trigger and the bullet hits the victim. If an out-of-sight sniper pauses between shots, no one would say that the emergency ceases during the pause. That is an extreme example and not the situation here, but it serves to highlight the implausibility, at least as to certain weapons, of construing the emergency to last only precisely as long as the violent act itself, as some have construed our opinion in *Davis*.

At no point during the questioning did either Covington or the police know the location of the shooter. In fact, Bryant was not at home by the time the police searched his house at approximately 5:30 a.m . . . .

We reiterate, moreover, that the existence *vel non* of an ongoing emergency is not the touchstone of the testimonial inquiry; rather, the ultimate inquiry is whether the "primary purpose of the interrogation [was] to enable police assistance to meet [the] ongoing emergency." *Davis*, 547 U.S., at 822. We turn now to that inquiry, as informed by the circumstances of the ongoing emergency just described. The circumstances of the encounter provide important context for understanding Covington's statements to the police. When the police arrived at Covington's side, their first question to him was "What happened?" Covington's response was either "Rick shot me" or "I was shot," followed very quickly by an identification of "Rick" as the shooter. In response to further questions, Covington explained that the shooting occurred through the back door of Bryant's house and provided a physical description of the shooter. When he made the statements, Covington was lying in a gas station parking lot bleeding from a mortal gunshot wound to his abdomen. His answers to the police officers' questions were punctuated with questions about when emergency medical services would arrive. He was obviously in considerable pain and had difficulty breathing and talking. [Testimony of various officers cited here.] From this description of his condition and report of his statements, we cannot say that a person in Covington's situation would have had a "primary purpose" "to establish or prove past events potentially relevant to later criminal prosecution." [*Davis*]. For their part, the police responded to a call that a man had been shot. As discussed above, they did not know why, where, or when the shooting had occurred. Nor did they know the location of the shooter or anything else about the circumstances in which the crime occurred. The questions [the officers] asked – "what had happened, who had shot him, and where the shooting occurred," were the exact type of questions necessary to allow the police to " 'assess the situation, the threat to their own safety, and possible danger to the potential victim' " and to the public, *Davis*, including to allow them to ascertain "whether they would be encountering a violent felon," *Davis*, 547 U.S., at 827. In other words, they solicited the information necessary to enable them "to meet an ongoing emergency." *Id.* . . . .

Nothing in Covington's responses indicated to the police that, contrary to their expectation upon responding to a call reporting a shooting, there was no emergency or that a prior emergency had ended. Covington did indicate that he had been shot at another location about 25 minutes earlier, but he did not know the location of the shooter at the time the police arrived and, as far as we can tell from the record, he gave no indication that the shooter, having shot at him twice, would be satisfied that Covington was only wounded. In fact, Covington did not indicate any possible motive for the shooting, and thereby gave no reason to think that the shooter would not shoot again if he arrived on the scene. As we noted in *Davis*, "initial inquiries" may "*often* . . . produce nontestimonial statements." The initial inquiries in this case resulted in the type of nontestimonial statements we contemplated in *Davis*.

Finally, we consider the informality of the situation and the interrogation. This situation is more similar, though not identical, to the informal, harried 911 call in *Davis* than to the structured, station-house interview in *Crawford*. As the officers' trial testimony reflects, the situation was fluid and somewhat confused: the officers arrived at different times; apparently each, upon arrival, asked Covington "what happened?"; and, contrary to the dissent's portrayal, *post*, at 7-9 (opinion of Scalia, J.), they did not conduct a structured interrogation. The informality suggests that the interrogators' primary purpose was simply to address what they perceived to be an ongoing emergency, and the circumstances lacked any formality that would have alerted Covington to or focused him on the possible future prosecutorial use of his statements.

Because the circumstances of the encounter as well as the statements and actions of Covington and the police objectively indicate that the "primary purpose of the interrogation" was "to enable police assistance to meet an ongoing emergency," *Davis*, 547 U.S., at 822, Covington's identification and description of the shooter and the location of the shooting were not testimonial hearsay. The Confrontation Clause did not bar their admission at Bryant's trial.

[Vacated and remanded.]

Scalia, J., dissenting.

Today's tale — a story of five officers conducting successive examinations of a dying man with the primary purpose, not of obtaining and preserving his testimony regarding his killer, but of protecting him, them, and others from a murderer somewhere on the loose — is so transparently false that professing to believe it demeans this institution. [The police obviously knew they had a victim who might die, and they wanted to preserve his evidence for trial.] . . . But reaching a patently incorrect conclusion on the facts is a relatively benign judicial mischief; it affects, after all, only the case at hand. In its vain attempt to make the incredible plausible, however — or perhaps as an intended second goal — today's opinion distorts our Confrontation Clause jurisprudence and leaves it in a shambles. Instead of clarifying the law, the Court makes itself the obfuscator of last resort. Because I continue to adhere to the Confrontation Clause that the People adopted, as described in *Crawford*, I dissent.

[Justice GINSBURG filed a dissent agreeing essentially with Justice SCALIA but adding that if the point had been raised, the statement might have qualified for the sui generis exception to confrontation, if there is such an exception (presumably, meaning dying declarations). Justice THOMAS concurred in the majority judgment that the victim"s statement was admissible, but on different grounds: that the victim's statement did not have sufficient formality and solemnity to qualify as testimonial.]

NOTES AND QUESTIONS

(1) *Are Hearsay Statements Testimonial Only if Made to Law Enforcement?* A footnote (omitted above) in *Bryant* noted that *Davis* considered 911 operators to be agents of law enforcement. However, *Bryant* like *Davis* reserved the question whether and when statements made to someone other than law enforcement personnel are testimonial.

Justice Scalia's dissent in *Bryant* relies on *King v. Brasier*, 1 Leach 199, 200, 168 Eng. Rep. 202, 202–03 (K.B. 1779). That case appears to reject a child hearsay statement to her mother made after the child was sexually assaulted, which statement was attempted to be repeated by the mother on the stand in court against the assaulter. The mother was a private citizen who had no ties to law enforcement. *Davis* also referred favorably to the same case in a portion we have not reproduced. Does this all suggest that even statements to *non*-law-enforcement people can be testimonial and inadmissible under the Confrontation Clause? Under what conditions might they be testimonial?

Another equivocal clue concerning the status of statements made to persons other than law enforcement officers appeared in *Crawford*. In parts of its discussion, which we redacted, *Crawford* seemed to countenance the result of the pre-*Crawford* case of *Idaho v. Wright*, 497 U.S. 805 (1990), which excluded (on then-fully-extant *Roberts* Confrontation-Clause grounds) unreliable hearsay of a child to a private doctor. Some early commentators on *Crawford* assumed this was a non-testimonial statement, but that *Crawford* felt that non-testimonial hearsay is still subject to federal Confrontation Clause regulation pursuant to a continuing *Roberts* test for non-testimonial statements (a theory that is apparently no longer viable after indications like those in *Davis* and *Bryant* that *Roberts* does not continue). But other commentators suggested that maybe the child's statement was deemed *testimonial* by *Crawford* because it was made to a doctor *selected* by the police, even though the doctor was not exactly law enforcement personnel.

(2) *Are Some Hearsay Exceptions More Likely to be Non-Testimonial than Others? Bryant* mentions that excited utterances are excepted from hearsay because their reliability depends on excitement which eliminates the possibility of

fabrication, and compares such utterances to ongoing emergencies, noting they have a "similar effect of focusing an individual's attention on responding to the emergency." In view of this, can excited utterances be testimonial? Under what conditions? Were the statements in *Hammon* that were found testimonial, excited utterances?

Bryant also includes a lengthy footnote (deleted above) that reaffirmed dicta in other cases about types of hearsay that are ordinarily non-testimonial:

> Many other exceptions to the hearsay rules similarly rest on the belief that certain statements are, by their nature, made for a purpose other than use in a prosecution and therefore should not be barred by hearsay prohibitions. See, e.g., Fed. Rule Evid. 801(d)(2)(E) (statement by a co-conspirator during and in furtherance of the conspiracy); 803(4) (Statements for Purposes of Medical Diagnosis or Treatment); 803(6) (Records of Regularly Conducted Activity); 803(8) (Public Records and Reports); 803(9) (Records of Vital Statistics); 803(11) (Records of Religious Organizations); 803(12) (Marriage, Baptismal, and Similar Certificates); 803(13) (Family Records); 804(b)(3) (Statement Against Interest); see also *Melendez-Diaz v. Massachusetts*, 129 S. Ct. 2527 (2009) ("Business and public records are generally admissible absent confrontation not because they qualify under an exception to the hearsay rules, but because — having been created for the administration of an entity's affairs and not for the purpose of establishing or proving some fact at trial — they are not testimonial"); *Giles v. California*, 554 U.S., at 376 (noting in the context of domestic violence that "[s]tatements to friends and neighbors about abuse and intimidation and statements to physicians in the course of receiving treatment would be excluded, if at all, only by hearsay rules"); *Crawford*, 541 U.S., at 56 ("Most of the hearsay exceptions covered statements that by their nature were not testimonial — for example, business records or statements in furtherance of a conspiracy").

Can hearsay statements received under these exceptions ever be testimonial? Conversely, *Bryant's* text reaffirmed *Crawford's* dicta that prior testimony at a preliminary hearing, before a grand jury or at a former trial are testimonial.

Is it still true that *Crawford* un-linked hearsay rule exceptions from the Confrontation Clause?

In view of its discussion of excited utterances, has the opinion in *Bryant* returned in some degree to the *Robert's* analysis?

Are there other portions of the *Bryant* opinion that seem to hark back to and perhaps re-introduce a reliability approach? Is this fundamentally inconsistent with the testimonial approach of *Crawford?* Where will it lead?

(3) *Combined Approach for Determining Primary Purpose. Bryant* emphasizes that statements and actions of both the declarant and the questioners must be evaluated in determining the primary purpose. *Bryant* thus disavows some implications in *Davis* which had caused confusion about whether the inquiry prescribes examination of one participant to the exclusion of the other. Justice Thomas argues that many statements have a dual purpose, one of which is

testimonial. He does not view the combined primary purpose test as providing any guidance for determining which purpose prevails in the Confrontation Clause analysis. Do you agree?

(4) *Does Bryant Answer Questions Left Open By Davis and Earlier Cases?* Refer again to our notes (3) and (4) following *Davis*, supra, concerning the vagaries of the "objectively determined primary purpose test". Are the questions there answered by *Bryant?*

Does *Bryant* shed light on whether a statement can be testimonial if there is no interrogation? On whether law enforcement personnel must be involved? On whether a testimonial statement must be accusatory?

(5) *What is the Role of Due Process in a Testimonial Approach?* A footnote in *Bryant* explicitly identifies the Due Process Clauses of the Fifth and Fourteenth Amendments as constituting a further bar to admission of, for example, very unreliable hearsay or other fundamentally unfair evidence, citing *Montana v. Egelhoff*, 518 U.S. 37, 53 (1996) (plurality opinion) and *Dutton v. Evans*, 400 U.S. 74, 96–97 (1970) (Harlan, J., concurring in result) ("[T]he Fifth and Fourteenth Amendments' command that federal and state trials, respectively, must be conducted in accordance with due process of law" is the "standard" by which to "test federal and state rules of evidence").

[4] Affidavits, Certifications, Reports, and Other Expert Issues in the Forensic Context

MELENDEZ-DIAZ v. MASSACHUSETTS
Supreme Court of the United States
557 U.S. 305 (2009)

SCALIA, JUSTICE delivered the opinion of the Court.

The Massachusetts courts in this case admitted into evidence affidavits reporting the results of forensic analysis which showed that material seized by the police and connected to the defendant was cocaine. The question presented is whether those affidavits are "testimonial," rendering the affiants "witnesses" subject to the defendant's right of confrontation under the Sixth Amendment.

In 2001, Boston police officers received a tip that a Kmart employee, Thomas Wright, was engaging in suspicious activity. The informant reported that Wright repeatedly received phone calls at work, after each of which he would be picked up in front of the store by a blue sedan, and would return to the store a short time later. The police set up surveillance in the Kmart parking lot and witnessed this precise sequence of events. When Wright got out of the car upon his return, one of the officers detained and searched him, finding four clear white plastic bags containing a substance resembling cocaine. The officer then signaled other officers on the scene to arrest the two men in the car — one of whom was petitioner Luis Melendez-Diaz. The officers placed all three men in a police cruiser.

During the short drive to the police station, the officers observed their passengers fidgeting and making furtive movements in the back of the car. After depositing the men at the station, they searched the police cruiser and found a plastic bag containing 19 smaller plastic bags hidden in the partition between the front and back seats. They submitted the seized evidence to a state laboratory required by law to conduct chemical analysis upon police request.

Melendez-Diaz was charged with distributing cocaine and with trafficking in cocaine in an amount between 14 and 28 grams. At trial, the prosecution placed into evidence the bags seized from Wright and from the police cruiser. It also submitted three "certificates of analysis" showing the results of the forensic analysis performed on the seized substances. The certificates reported the weight of the seized bags and stated that the bags "[h]a[ve] been examined with the following results: The substance was found to contain: Cocaine." The certificates were sworn to before a notary public by analysts at the State Laboratory Institute of the Massachusetts Department of Public Health, as required under Massachusetts law.

Petitioner objected to the admission of the certificates [on Confrontation Clause grounds].

The jury found Melendez-Diaz guilty. He appealed, contending, among other things, that admission of the certificates violated his Sixth Amendment right to be confronted with the witnesses against him . . . .The [Mass. Courts sustained the conviction.] We granted certiorari . . .

There is little doubt that the documents at issue in this case fall within the "core class of testimonial statements." Our description of that category mentions affidavit twice. The documents at issue here, while denominated by Massachusetts law "certificates," are quite plainly affidavits: "declaration[s] of facts written down and sworn to by the declarant before an officer authorized to administer oaths." Black's Law Dictionary . . . . The fact in question is that the substance found in the possession of Melendez-Diaz and his codefendants was, as the prosecution claimed, cocaine — the precise testimony the analysts would be expected to provide if called at trial. The "certificates" are functionally identical to live, in-court testimony, doing "precisely what a witness does on direct examination." *Davis v. Washington.*

Here, moreover, not only were the affidavits " 'made under circumstances which would lead an objective witness reasonably to believe that the statement would be available for use at a later trial,' " *Crawford*, but under Massachusetts law the sole purpose of the affidavits was to provide "prima facie evidence of the composition, quality, and the net weight" of the analyzed substance, Mass. Gen. Laws, ch. 111, § 13. We can safely assume that the analysts were aware of the affidavits' evidentiary purpose, since that purpose — as stated in the relevant state-law provision — was reprinted on the affidavits themselves.

In short, under our decision in *Crawford* the analysts' affidavits were testimonial statements, and the analysts were "witnesses" for purposes of the Sixth Amendment. Absent a showing that the analysts were unavailable to testify at trial and that petitioner had a prior opportunity to cross-examine them, petitioner was entitled to " 'be confronted with' " the analysts at trial. *Crawford.*

We must assure the reader of the falsity of the dissent's opening alarum that we are "sweep[ing] away an accepted rule governing the admission of scientific evidence" that has been "established for at least 90 years" and "extends across at least 35 States and six Federal Courts of Appeals." (Opinion of Kennedy, J.).

The vast majority of the state-court cases the dissent cites in support of this claim come not from the last 90 years, but from the last 30, and not surprisingly nearly all of them rely on our decision in *Ohio v. Roberts* or its since-rejected theory that unconfronted testimony was admissible as long as it bore indicia of reliability . . . .

[The remainder of the majority opinion, which attempts to rebut the dissenting opinion, is discussed in the notes below.]

This case involves little more than the application of our holding in *Crawford*. The Sixth Amendment does not permit the prosecution to prove its case via *ex parte* out-of-court affidavits, and the admission of such evidence against Melendez-Diaz was error. We therefore reverse the judgment of the Appeals Court of Massachusetts and remand the case for further proceedings not inconsistent with this opinion.

THOMAS, JUSTICE, concurring.

I write separately to note that I continue to adhere to my position that the Confrontation Clause is implicated by extrajudicial statements only insofar as they are contained in formalized testimonial materials, such as affidavits, depositions, prior testimony, or confessions.

KENNEDY, J., with whom CHIEF JUSTICE ROBERTS, JUSTICE BREYER, and JUSTICE ALITO join, dissenting.

The Court sweeps away an accepted rule governing the admission of scientific evidence. Until today, scientific analysis could be introduced into evidence without testimony from the "analyst" who produced it . . . . It is remarkable that the Court so confidently disregards a century of jurisprudence. The immediate systemic concern is that the Court makes no attempt to acknowledge the real differences between laboratory analysts who perform scientific tests and other, more conventional witnesses — "witnesses" being the word the Framers used in the Confrontation Clause.

Crawford and *Davis* dealt with ordinary witnesses — women who had seen, and in two cases been the victim of, the crime in question . . . . But *Crawford* and *Davis* do not say that anyone who makes a testimonial statement is a witness for purposes of the Confrontation Clause, even when that person has, in fact, witnessed nothing to give them personal knowledge of the defendant's guilt . . . .

Consider how many people play a role in a routine test for the presence of illegal drugs. One person prepares a sample of the drug, places it in a testing machine, and retrieves the machine's printout — often, a graph showing the frequencies of radiation absorbed by the sample or the masses of the sample's molecular fragments. See 2 P. Giannelli & E. Imwinkelried, Scientific Evidence § 23.03 (4th ed. 2007) (describing common methods of identifying drugs, including infrared spectrophotometry, nuclear magnetic resonance, gas chromatography, and mass spectrometry). A second person interprets the graph the machine prints out — perhaps by comparing that printout with published, standardized graphs of known drugs. *Ibid.* Meanwhile, a third person — perhaps an independent contractor — has calibrated the machine and, having done so, has certified that the machine is in good working order. Finally, a fourth person — perhaps the laboratory's director — certifies that his subordinates followed established procedures.

It is not at all evident which of these four persons is the analyst to be confronted under the rule the Court announces today. If all are witnesses who must appear for in-court confrontation, then the Court has, for all practical purposes, forbidden the use of scientific tests in criminal trials. As discussed further below, requiring even one of these individuals to testify threatens to disrupt if not end many prosecutions where guilt is clear but a newly found formalism now holds sway.

It is possible to read the Court's opinion, however, to say that all four must testify. Each one has contributed to the test's result and has, at least in some respects, made a representation about the test. Person One represents that a pure sample, properly drawn, entered the machine and produced a particular printout. Person Two represents that the printout corresponds to a known drug. Person Three represents that the machine was properly calibrated at the time. Person Four represents that all the others performed their jobs in accord with established procedures.

And each of the four has power to introduce error. A laboratory technician might adulterate the sample. The independent contractor might botch the machine's calibration. And so forth. The reasons for these errors may range from animus against the particular suspect or all criminal suspects to unintentional oversight; from gross negligence to good-faith mistake. It is no surprise that a plausible case can be made for deeming each person in the testing process an analyst under the Court's opinion.

[T]the range of other scientific tests that may be affected by the Court's new confrontation right is staggering. See, *e.g., Comment, Toward a Definition of "Testimonial": How Autopsy Reports Do Not Embody the Qualities of a Testimonial Statement*, 96 Cal. L. Rev. 1093, 1094, 1115 (2008) (noting that every court post-*Crawford* has held that autopsy reports are not testimonial, and warning that a contrary rule would "effectively functio[n] as a statute of limitations for murder") . . . .

It is difficult to confine at this point the damage the Court's holding will do in other contexts. Consider just two — establishing the chain of custody and authenticating a copy of a document . . . .

The iron logic of which the Court is so enamored would seem to require in-court testimony from each human link in the chain of custody. That, of course, has never been the law.

In any number of cases, the crucial link in the chain will not be available to testify and so the evidence will be excluded for lack of a proper foundation.

Consider another context in which the Court's holding may cause disruption: The long-accepted practice of authenticating copies of documents by means of a certificate from the document's custodian stating that the copy is accurate. See, *e.g.*, Fed. Rule Evid. 902(4) (in order to be self-authenticating, a copy of a public record must be "certified as correct by the custodian"); Rule 902(11) (business record must be "accompanied by a written declaration of its custodian"). Under one possible reading of the Court's opinion, recordkeepers will be required to testify.

. . . The Confrontation Clause is not designed, and does not serve, to detect errors in scientific tests. That should instead be done by conducting a new test. Or, if a new test is impossible, the defendant may call his own expert to explain to the jury the test's flaws and the dangers of relying on it. And if, in an extraordinary case, the particular analyst's testimony is necessary to the defense, then, of course, the defendant may subpoena the analyst.

. . . [No] purpose [of confrontation] is served by the rule the Court announces today. It is not plausible that a laboratory analyst will retract his or her prior conclusion upon catching sight of the defendant the result condemns. After all, the analyst is far removed from the particular defendant and, indeed, claims no personal knowledge of the defendant's guilt. And an analyst performs hundreds if not thousands of tests each year and will not remember a particular test or the link it had to the defendant.

As matters stood before today's opinion, analysts already spent considerable time appearing as witnesses in those few cases where the defendant, unlike petitioner in this case, contested the analyst's result and subpoenaed the analyst. By requiring analysts also to appear in the far greater number of cases where defendants do not dispute the analyst's result, the Court imposes enormous costs on the administration of justice.

Setting aside, for a moment, all the other crimes for which scientific evidence is required, consider the costs the Court's ruling will impose on state drug prosecutions alone. In 2004, the most recent year for which data are available, drug possession and trafficking resulted in 362,850 felony convictions in state courts across the country. [Citation.] Roughly 95% of those convictions were products of plea bargains, which means that state courts saw more than 18,000 drug trials in a single year.

The analysts responsible for testing the drugs at issue in those cases now bear a crushing burden. For example, the district attorney in Philadelphia prosecuted 25,000 drug crimes in 2007. Assuming that number remains the same, and assuming that 95% of the cases end in a plea bargain, each of the city's 18 drug analysts will be required to testify in more than 69 trials next year. Cleveland's district attorney prosecuted 14,000 drug crimes in 2007. Assuming that number holds, and that 95% of the cases end in a plea bargain, each of the city's 6 drug analysts (two of whom work only part time) must testify in 117 drug cases next year.

[T]he FBI laboratory at Quantico, Virginia, supports federal, state, and local investigations across the country. Its 500 employees conduct over one million scientific tests each year. The Court's decision means that before any of those million tests reaches a jury, at least one of the laboratory's analysts must board a plane, find his or her way to an unfamiliar courthouse, and sit there waiting to read aloud notes made months ago.

The Court purchases its meddling with the Confrontation Clause at a dear price, a price not measured in taxpayer dollars alone. Guilty defendants will go free, on the most technical grounds, as a direct result of today's decision, adding nothing to the truth-finding process. The analyst will not always make it to the courthouse in time. He or she may be ill; may be out of the country; may be unable to travel because of inclement weather; or may at that very moment be waiting outside some other courtroom for another defendant to exercise the right the Court invents today.

[T]he Clause refers to a conventional "witness" — meaning one who witnesses (that is, perceives) an event that gives him or her personal knowledge of some aspect of the defendant's guilt.

In keeping with the traditional understanding of the Confrontation Clause, this Court in *Dowdell* (1911) rejected a challenge to the use of certificates, sworn out by a clerk of court, a trial judge, and a court reporter, stating that defendants had been present at trial. Those certificates, like a copyist's certificate, met every requirement of the Court's current definition of "testimonial." In rejecting the defendants' claim that use of the certificates violated the Confrontation Clause, the Court in *Dowdell* explained that the officials who executed the certificates "were not witnesses against the accused" because they "were not asked to testify to facts concerning [the defendants'] guilt or innocence."

On a practical level, today's ruling would cause less disruption if the States' hearsay rules had already required analysts to testify. But few States require this. At least sixteen state courts have held that their evidentiary rules permit scientific test results, calibration certificates, and the observations of medical personnel to enter evidence without in-court testimony. The Federal Courts of Appeals have reached the same conclusion in applying the federal hearsay rule. The modern trend in the state courts has been away from the Court's rule and toward the admission of scientific test results without testimony — perhaps because the States have recognized the increasing reliability of scientific testing. It appears that a mere six courts continue to interpret their States' hearsay laws to require analysts to testify. [Cites to appendices, deleted here, throughout.]

In an unconvincing effort to play down the threat that today's new rule will disrupt or even end criminal prosecutions, the Court professes a hope that defense counsel will decline to raise what will soon be known as the Melendez-Diaz objection. There is no authority to support the Court's suggestion that a lawyer may shirk his or her professional duties just to avoid judicial displeasure. This Court has recognized the bedrock principle that a competent criminal defense lawyer must put the prosecution to its proof.

In further support of its unlikely hope, the Court relies on the [fact that] nearly 95% of convictions are obtained via guilty plea and thus do not require in-court testimony from laboratory analysts. What the Court does not consider is how its holding will alter these statistics. The defense bar today gains the formidable power to require the government to transport the analyst to the courtroom at the time of trial. Zealous counsel will insist upon concessions: a plea bargain, or a more lenient sentence in exchange for relinquishing this remarkable power.

[End of opinion. Appendices deleted.]

NOTES AND QUESTIONS

(1) *General Description of Decision.* During the state-court's drug trial of Mr. Melendez-Diaz, the prosecution introduced certificates of state laboratory analysts stating that material seized by police and connected to petitioner was cocaine. As required by Massachusetts law, the certificates were sworn to before a notary public and were submitted as prima facie evidence of what they asserted. The Supreme Court held that the certificates were testimonial and their admission violated the defendant's Sixth Amendment right to confront the witnesses against him as defined by *Crawford.* As a result, the chemist ("analyst") must testify, unless that individual is unavailable and there had been a previous opportunity for cross examination.

Speaking broadly, the decision, including the portions redacted above, may be summarized as holding (a) analysts' certificates of analysis were affidavits within the core class of testimonial statements covered by the Confrontation Clause; (b) analysts were not removed from coverage of the Confrontation Clause on the theory that they were not "accusatory" witnesses; (c) analysts were not removed from coverage of the Confrontation Clause on the theory that they were not conventional witnesses; (d) analysts were not removed from coverage of the Confrontation Clause on the theory that their testimony consisted of neutral, scientific testing; (e) certificates of analysis were not removed from coverage of the Confrontation Clause on the theory that they were akin to official and business records; and (f) defendant's ability to subpoena analysts did not obviate the state's obligation to produce analysts for cross-examination.

The decision could reach all manner of expert and other information recorded in all kinds of government reports, in addition to those from chemists. Prosecutors have argued that the decision will result in many cases being dismissed and at a minimum it will be extremely costly to hire the number of analysts necessary to testify.

The *Melendez-Diaz* decision in *dicta* not reproduced above, approved "notice and demand" statutes that require defendants to request (within a given time after pre-trial notice by the prosecution of proposed prosecution use at trial of a forensic report) that the forensic witness be called by the prosecution to testify at trial. If the defendant does not so request, the confrontation objection to the report is waived. The dictum gave no further guidance about the constitutionality of statutes that required something more by the defendant, such as good cause.

The decision was 5-4, with Justice Scalia writing for the majority. Justice Kennedy's dissent complained that the word "testimonial" does not appear in the constitution. Instead, the relevant language is "witness against," which in his view, applies to lay witnesses not to "neutral" experts.

Melendez-Diaz was acquitted at his retrial. However, the media reported that the result was not based on issues concerning the report, but about whether he possessed the drugs in question.

(2) *Rebutting the Dissent.* Justice Scalia spends most of the majority opinion trying to rebut the views of the dissenters. The following are his rebuttal points (the arguments being rebutted are given here in italic headings):

(a) *Declarant was not an accusatory witness* There is no support for the proposition that the analysts are not subject to confrontation because they are not "accusatory" witnesses, in that they do not directly accuse petitioner of wrongdoing; rather, their testimony is inculpatory only when taken together with other evidence linking petitioner to the contraband.

(b) *Declarant was not a conventional witness* The claim that the analysts should not be subject to confrontation because they are not "conventional" (or "typical" or "ordinary") witnesses of the sort whose ex parte testimony was most notoriously used at the trial of Sir Walter Raleigh does not exclude them from confrontation scrutiny. The dissent provides no support for limiting confrontation to witnesses who observe the crime or any human action related to it.

(c) *There was no interrogation* It does not matter that that the statements in the report were not provided in response to interrogation, since "[t]he Framers were no more willing to exempt from cross-examination volunteered testimony or answers to open-ended questions than they were to exempt answers to detailed interrogation."

(d) *Declarant was not recounting historical events* There is no difference, for Confrontation Clause purposes, between testimony recounting historical events, which are "prone to distortion or manipulation," and the testimony at issue here, which the dissent claims is the "resul[t] of neutral, scientific testing." "This argument is little more than an invitation to return to our overruled decision in Roberts, which held that evidence with "particularized guarantees of trustworthiness" was admissible notwithstanding the Confrontation Clause."

(e) *Science is neutral evidence* 'Nor is it evident that what respondent calls 'neutral scientific testing' is as neutral or as reliable as respondent suggests. Forensic evidence is not uniquely immune from the risk of manipulation. According to a recent study conducted under the auspices of the National Academy of Sciences, '[t]he majority of [laboratories producing forensic evidence] are administered by law enforcement agencies, such as police departments, where the laboratory administrator reports to the head of the agency.' And '[b]ecause forensic scientists often are driven in their work by a need to answer a particular question related to the issues of a particular case, they sometimes face pressure to sacrifice appropriate methodology for the sake of expediency.' A forensic analyst responding to a request from a law enforcement official may feel pressure — or have an incentive — to alter the evidence in a manner favorable to the prosecution."

"Confrontation is designed to weed out not only the fraudulent analyst, but the incompetent one as well. Serious deficiencies have been found in the forensic evidence used in criminal trials."

"This case is illustrative. The affidavits submitted by the analysts contained only the bare-bones statement that '[t]he substance was found to contain: Cocaine.' At the time of trial, petitioner did not know what tests the analysts performed, whether those tests were routine, and whether interpreting their results required the exercise of judgment or the use of skills that the analysts may not have possessed."

" '[T]here is wide variability across forensic science disciplines with regard to techniques, methodologies, reliability, types and numbers of potential errors, research, general acceptability, and published material.' " National Academy Report (also discussing problems of subjectivity, bias, and unreliability of common forensic tests such as latent fingerprint analysis, pattern/impression analysis, and toolmark and firearms analysis)."

(f) *Report is like common law business records and official records* Despite the dissent's characterization of the affidavits as "akin to the types of official and business records admissible at common law," they do not qualify as traditional official or business records, and even if they did, their authors would be subject to confrontation nonetheless because they were prepared for use at trial. "The analysts' certificates — like police reports generated by law enforcement officials — do not qualify as business or public records for precisely [this] reason. See Rule 803(8) (defining public records as "excluding, however, in criminal cases matters observed by police officers and other law enforcement personnel")."

(g) *Compulsory process is sufficient* "The [defendant's] ability to subpoena the analysts pursuant to state law or the Compulsory Process Clause is no substitute for the right of confrontation. Unlike the Confrontation Clause, those provisions are of no use to the defendant when the witness is unavailable or simply refuses to appear." "More fundamentally, the Confrontation Clause imposes a burden on the prosecution to present its witnesses, not on the defendant to bring those adverse witnesses into court."

(h) *Decision imposes huge burden on prosecutors and law enforcement* The Confrontation Clause cannot be ignored to accommodate the necessities of trial and the adversary process.

"Perhaps the best indication that the sky will not fall after today's decision is that it has not done so already. Many States have already adopted the constitutional rule we announce today, while many others permit the defendant to assert (or forfeit by silence) his Confrontation Clause right after receiving notice of the prosecution's intent to use a forensic analyst's report. Despite these widespread practices, there is no evidence that the criminal justice system has ground to a halt in the States that, one way or another, empower a defendant to insist upon the analyst's appearance at trial."

States can still employ notice-and-demand statutes, which will ease the burden and allow case management. These statutes require the prosecution to provide notice to the defendant of its intent to use an analyst's report as evidence at trial, after which the defendant is given a period of time in which he may object to the admission of the evidence absent the analyst's appearance live at trial. The defendant always has the burden of raising his Confrontation Clause objection; notice-and-demand statutes simply govern the time within which he must do so. States are free to adopt procedural rules governing objections.

Further easing the burden, the defense will often stipulate to the nature of the substance in the ordinary drug case. "It is unlikely that defense counsel will insist on live testimony whose effect will be merely to highlight rather than cast doubt upon the forensic analysis. Nor will defense attorneys want to antagonize the judge or jury by wasting their time with the appearance of a witness whose testimony defense counsel does not intend to rebut in any fashion."

Which side convinces you? Identify the points above that are essential to the Confrontation Clause analysis. Why are the other points discussed in such detail?

(3) *Who Is It Who Must Testify*? The decision seems to proceed on the basis that the analyst who analyzed the substance is also the person who wrote the certificate/affidavit. He is the person who must testify. But the decision left unclear who must testify when more than one person is involved in the analysis and report. The majority indicates in language we have not reproduced that the absence of some witnesses may go to weight, rather than admissibility, but how is this determined?

What if the writer of the certificate/affidavit is, say, the director of the lab, and had nothing to do with the analysis itself, but is merely reporting what he got from his underling, the real analyst? Will his testimony do? Cf. our next principal case below, *Bullcoming.*

What happens when the analyst is no longer employed by the department, moves away or dies? Can someone else interpret the report, or must the analysis be redone? If the latter, what happens when the evidence is no longer available? These problems can arise is cases where, for example, there is a cold hit years after the crime, based on a DNA analysis done at the time of the crime; or where there is a retrial in a prosecution and the original forensic analysis was not subject to cross-examination; or where there was an original autopsy some time ago, the medical examiner who did it now cannot be found or has died, and the evidence cannot be re-tested because it has perished. In the last example, does the decision mean as a practical matter there is a de facto statute of limitations on murder? (In most jurisdictions the law has no actual statute of limitations on murder.)

Should a "report" that merely sends raw data be treated differently? *People v. Brown*, 918 N.E.2d 927 (N.Y. 2009) held that machine-generated raw data, graphs, and charts of DNA characteristics of the male specimen isolated from the victim's rape kit, was non-testimonial. Do you agree?

(4) *Affects Many Kinds of Forensic Evidence*. The decision affects a broad range of scientific and technological evidence in criminal cases — almost everything the "CSI" people do that they would write reports about: *e.g.*, DNA analysis, alcohol tests (e.g. blood, breath, and urine tests in DUI cases), ballistics, narcotics (identity of substances seized, or presence in the body, etc.), autopsies, etc. Psychological reports would also be covered. Can you think of others?

(5) *Public or Private Labs*. Does it make any difference whether the analyst in *Melendez-Diaz* works for a government lab or a private lab? Or whether the lab is truly independent?

(6) *Non-Adversarial/Routine Records Exception?* The decision may suggest that there is a routine records (or non-adversarial records) exception to the Confrontation Clause, the way there is such an exception under some decisions to the exclusion of law enforcement records contained in FRE 803(8) (public records)

discussed *supra*, § 9.07, note (3) following *Beech Aircraft v. Rainey*. *Melendez-Diaz* mentions in portions we have deleted that business and public records are generally admissible since they are usually created for the "administration of an entity's own internal affairs." Several deleted footnotes contain similar expressions potentially exempting from "testimoniality" hearsay statements dealing with such things as the "normal course of equipment maintenance," "matters of internal administration," etc. Are these "exemptions" going to present as many problems of uncertainty and unpredictability of definition as previous confrontation jurisprudence under *Roberts*?

(7) *Can the Problem of Melendez-Diaz Be Easily Avoided*? Is confrontation satisfied if the State provides by statute that the defense has the right to call to the stand, *at state expense*, the analyst who wrote the certificate/affidavit, rather than requiring the prosecution itself to call the analyst? This question seems to have been answered by *Melendez-Diaz*, in its discussion that defendant's right to Compulsory Process does not defeat his right to Confrontation.

But nevertheless the Supreme Court, immediately after deciding *Melendez-Diaz*, granted certiorari to answer the question in *Briscoe v. Virginia*, 557 U.S. 933 (2009). Perhaps the Court granted certiorari so it could simply and clearly say "we decided that already." It was possible, however, that, with a new Justice, Sonya Sotomayor, replacing Justice David Souter (who signed onto the majority opinion in *Melendez-Diaz*, a 5-4 decision), the statements in *Melandez-Diaz* on this point might have been modified or interpreted away. Instead, after oral argument in *Briscoe* the Court decided not to decide *Briscoe* and remanded it for consideration in light of the holding in *Melendez-Diaz*, raising speculation that the dissenters were not able to gain an additional vote.

Of the two disadvantages of relying on the Compulsory Process Clause to the exclusion of the Confrontation Clause mentioned by Justice Scalia (see note (2)(g) immediately supra), does the state *paying* for production of the witness by defendant, alleviate them both? Would they both be alleviated by payment *and* a rule that if the witness is unavailable (e.g., dead), compulsory process could not substitute for the right to confrontation? How would that work?

If the right to compulsory process excused non-production of witnesses by the prosecution, would the prosecution *ever*, in *any* kind of case, forensic or otherwise, have to produce any witnesses, or could the prosecution just gather witnesses' out-of-court statements and convict on the basis of those? Could this be done even for the eyewitness in a murder case?

Even if the availability to the defense of compulsory process does not generally excuse non-production of witnesses by the prosecution in these forensic cases, might the availability to the defense of compulsory process play a role in deciding that some lesser analysts in a chain of analysts producing a report need not be produced? Or that a properly qualified expert or knowledgable lab supervisor of the test or report might be an acceptable surrogate witness for the analyst(s)?

BULLCOMING v. NEW MEXICO

Supreme Court of the United States
131 S. Ct. 2705 (2011)

Ginsburg, J., delivered the opinion of the Court, except as to Part IV and footnote 6.[2]

In *Melendez-Diaz v. Massachusetts*, 557 U.S. 305 (2009), this Court held that a forensic laboratory report stating that a suspect substance was cocaine ranked as testimonial for purposes of the Sixth Amendment's Confrontation Clause. The report had been created specifically to serve as evidence in a criminal proceeding. Absent stipulation, the Court ruled, the prosecution may not introduce such a report without offering a live witness competent to testify to the truth of the statements made in the report.

In the case before us, petitioner Donald Bullcoming was arrested on charges of driving while intoxicated (DWI). Principal evidence against Bullcoming was a forensic laboratory report certifying that Bullcoming's blood-alcohol concentration was well above the threshold for aggravated DWI. At trial, the prosecution did not call as a witness the analyst who signed the certification. Instead, the State called another analyst who was familiar with the laboratory's testing procedures, but had neither participated in nor observed the test on Bullcoming's blood sample. The New Mexico Supreme Court determined that, although the blood-alcohol analysis was "testimonial," the Confrontation Clause did not require the certifying analyst's in-court testimony. Instead, New Mexico's high court held, live testimony of another analyst satisfied the constitutional requirements.

The question presented is whether the Confrontation Clause permits the prosecution to introduce a forensic laboratory report containing a testimonial certification — made for the purpose of proving a particular fact — through the in-court testimony of a scientist who did not sign the certification or perform or observe the test reported in the certification. We hold that surrogate testimony of that order does not meet the constitutional requirement. The accused's right is to be confronted with the analyst who made the certification, unless that analyst is unavailable at trial, and the accused had an opportunity, pretrial, to cross-examine that particular scientist.

---

[2] Ed. note: Part IV briefly dismisses objections that requiring analysts to testify imposes an undue burden on law enforcement. It notes in this regard that constitutional rights cannot depend on convenience, that many states and prosecutors do produce the analyst, that there can be re-testing if the original analyst is gone, that there are notice-and-demand statutes easing the burden, that cases often settle before trial, that defendants often find it in their interests to stipulate to admission of the reports rather than insist on the witness, and that proper scheduling and task assignments can alleviate the problem. Footnote 6 of the opinion re-affirms the ***Davis/Bryant*** primary purpose test and that business and public records, unlike the present record, often are not testimonial because they are made in order to deal with internal administration of the entity rather than to prove facts at trial. It is interesting to speculate why Part IV and footnote 6 did not attract a majority.

I

Because Bullcoming refused to take a breath test, the police obtained a warrant authorizing a blood-alcohol analysis. Pursuant to the warrant, a sample of Bullcoming's blood was drawn at a local hospital. To determine Bullcoming's blood-alcohol concentration (BAC), the police sent the sample to the New Mexico Department of Health, Scientific Laboratory Division (SLD). In a standard SLD form titled "Report of Blood Alcohol Analysis," participants in the testing were identified, and the forensic analyst certified his finding.

SLD's report contained in the top block "information . . . filled in by [the] arresting officer." *Ibid.* (capitalization omitted). This information included the "reason [the] suspect [was] stopped" (the officer checked "Accident"), and the date ("8.14.05") and time ("18:25 PM") the blood sample was drawn. *Ibid.* (capitalization omitted). The arresting officer also affirmed that he had arrested Bullcoming and witnessed the blood draw. The next two blocks contained certifications by the nurse who drew Bullcoming's blood and the SLD intake employee who received the blood sample sent to the laboratory.

Following these segments, the report presented the "certificate of analyst," completed and signed by Curtis Caylor, the SLD forensic analyst assigned to test Bullcoming's blood sample. Caylor recorded that the BAC in Bullcoming's sample was 0.21 grams per hundred milliliters, an inordinately high level. Caylor also affirmed that "[t]he seal of th[e] sample was received intact and broken in the laboratory," that "the statements in [the analyst's block of the report] are correct," and that he had "followed the procedures set out on the reverse of th[e] report." Those "procedures" instructed analysts, inter alia, to "retai[n] the sample container and the raw data from the analysis," and to "not[e] any circumstance or condition which might affect the integrity of the sample or otherwise affect the validity of the analysis." Finally, in a block headed "certificate of reviewer," the SLD examiner who reviewed Caylor's analysis certified that Caylor was qualified to conduct the BAC test, and that the "established procedure" for handling and analyzing Bullcoming's sample "ha[d] been followed."

SLD analysts use gas chromatograph machines to determine BAC levels. Operation of the machines requires specialized knowledge and training. Several steps are involved in the gas chromatograph process, and human error can occur at each step.

Caylor's report that Bullcoming's BAC was 0.21 supported a prosecution for aggravated DWI, the threshold for which is a BAC of 0.16 grams per hundred milliliters, § 66-8-102(D)(1). The State accordingly charged Bullcoming with this more serious crime.

The case was tried to a jury in November 2005, after our decision in *Crawford v. Washington*, 541 U.S. 36 (2004), but before *Melendez-Diaz*. On the day of trial, the State announced that it would not be calling SLD analyst Curtis Caylor as a witness because he had "very recently [been] put on unpaid leave" for a reason not revealed. A startled defense counsel objected. The prosecution, she complained, had never disclosed, until trial commenced, that the witness "out there . . . [was] not the analyst [of Bullcoming's sample]." Counsel stated that, "had [she] known that the analyst [who tested Bullcoming's blood] was not available," her opening, indeed, her entire defense "may very well have been dramatically different." The trial court overruled the objection, and admitted the SLD report as a business record. The jury convicted Bullcoming of aggravated DWI . . . .

While Bullcoming's appeal was pending before the New Mexico Supreme Court, this Court decided *Melendez-Diaz*. In light of *Melendez-Diaz*, the New Mexico Supreme Court acknowledged that the blood-alcohol report introduced at Bullcoming's trial qualified as testimonial evidence . . . . Nevertheless, for two reasons, the court held that admission of the report did not violate the Confrontation Clause.

First, the court said certifying analyst Caylor "was a mere scrivener," who "simply transcribed the results generated by the gas chromatograph machine." Second, SLD analyst Razatos, although he did not participate in testing Bullcoming's blood, "qualified as an expert witness with respect to the gas chromatograph machine." "Razatos provided live, in-court testimony," the court stated, "and, thus, was available for cross-examination regarding the operation of the.. machine, the results of [Bullcoming's] BAC test, and the SLD's established laboratory procedures."

We granted *certiorari* to address this question: Does the Confrontation Clause permit the prosecution to introduce a forensic laboratory report containing a testimonial certification, made in order to prove a fact at a criminal trial, through the in-court testimony of an analyst who did not sign the certification or personally perform or observe the performance of the test reported in the certification. Our answer is in line with controlling precedent: As a rule, if an out-of-court statement is testimonial in nature, it may not be introduced against the accused at trial unless the witness who made the statement is unavailable and the accused has had a prior opportunity to confront that witness. Because the New Mexico Supreme Court permitted the testimonial statement of one witness, *i.e.*, Caylor, to enter into evidence through the in-court testimony of a second person, *i.e.*, Razatos, we reverse that court's judgment.

II

The State in the instant case never asserted that the analyst who signed the certification, Curtis Caylor, was unavailable. The record showed only that Caylor was placed on unpaid leave for an undisclosed reason. Nor did Bullcoming have an opportunity to cross-examine Caylor. *Crawford* and *Melendez-Diaz*, therefore, weigh heavily in Bullcoming's favor. The New Mexico Supreme Court, however, although recognizing that the SLD report was testimonial for purposes of the Confrontation Clause, considered SLD analyst Razatos an adequate substitute for Caylor. We explain first why Razatos' appearance did not meet the Confrontation Clause requirement. We next address the State's argument that the SLD report ranks as "nontestimonial," and therefore "[was] not subject to the Confrontation Clause in the first place."

The New Mexico Supreme Court held surrogate testimony adequate to satisfy the Confrontation Clause in this case because analyst Caylor "simply transcribed the resul[t] generated by the gas chromatograph machine," presenting no interpretation and exercising no independent judgment. Bullcoming's "true 'accuser,'" the court said, was the machine, while testing analyst Caylor's role was that of "mere scrivener." Caylor's certification, however, reported more than a machine-generated number.

Caylor certified that he received Bullcoming's blood sample intact with the seal unbroken, that he checked to make sure that the forensic report number and the sample number "correspond[ed]," and that he performed on Bullcoming's sample a particular test, adhering to a precise protocol. He further represented, by leaving the "[r]emarks" section of the report blank, that no "circumstance or condition . . . affect[ed] the integrity of the sample or . . . the validity of the analysis." These representations, relating to past events and human actions not revealed in raw, machine-produced data, are meet for cross-examination . . . .

The potential ramifications of the New Mexico Supreme Court's reasoning, furthermore, raise red flags. Most witnesses, after all, testify to their observations of factual conditions or events, *e.g.*, "the light was green," "the hour was noon." Such witnesses may record, on the spot, what they observed. Suppose a police report recorded an objective fact — Bullcoming's counsel posited the address above the front door of a house or the read-out of a radar gun. Could an officer other than the one who saw the number on the house or gun present the information in court — so long as that officer was equipped to testify about any technology the observing officer deployed and the police department's standard operating procedures? As our precedent makes plain, the answer is emphatically "No."

The New Mexico Supreme Court stated that the number registered by the gas chromatograph machine called for no interpretation or exercise of independent judgment on Caylor's part. We have already explained that Caylor certified to more than a machine-generated number. In any event, the comparative reliability of an analyst's testimonial report drawn from machine-produced data does not overcome the Sixth Amendment bar. This Court settled in *Crawford* that the "obviou[s] reliab[ility]" of a testimonial statement does not dispense with the Confrontation Clause. 541 U.S., at 62 (Clause "commands, not that evidence be reliable, but that reliability be assessed in a particular manner: by testing [the evidence] in the crucible of cross-examination"). Accordingly, the analysts who write reports that the prosecution introduces must be made available for confrontation even if they possess "the scientific acumen of Mme. Curie and the veracity of Mother Teresa." *Melendez-Diaz*.

Recognizing that admission of the blood-alcohol analysis depended on "live, in-court testimony [by] a qualified analyst," the New Mexico Supreme Court believed that Razatos could substitute for Caylor because Razatos "qualified as an expert witness with respect to the gas chromatograph machine and the SLD's laboratory procedures." But surrogate testimony of the kind Razatos was equipped to give could not convey what Caylor knew or observed about the events his certification concerned, *i.e.*, the particular test and testing process he employed. Nor could such surrogate testimony expose any lapses or lies on the certifying analyst's part. Significant here, Razatos had no knowledge of the reason why Caylor had been placed on unpaid leave. With Caylor on the stand, Bullcoming's counsel could have asked questions designed to reveal whether incompetence, evasiveness, or dishonesty accounted for Caylor's removal from his work station. Notable in this regard, the State never asserted that Caylor was "unavailable"; the prosecution conveyed only that Caylor was on uncompensated leave. Nor did the State assert that Razatos had any "independent opinion" concerning Bullcoming's BAC. See Brief for Respondent 58, n. 15. In this light, Caylor's live testimony could hardly be typed "a hollow formality.". . .

In short, when the State elected to introduce Caylor's certification, Caylor became a witness Bullcoming had the right to confront . . . .

III

We turn, finally, to the State's contention that the SLD's blood-alcohol analysis reports are nontestimonial in character, therefore no Confrontation Clause question even arises in this case. *Melendez-Diaz* left no room for that argument.

Distinguishing Bullcoming's case from *Melendez-Diaz*, where the analysts' findings were contained in certificates "sworn to before a notary public," the State emphasizes that the SLD report of Bullcoming's BAC was "unsworn." [T]he absence of [an] oath [i]s not dispositive' in determining if a statement is testimonial.

Here, as in *Melendez-Diaz*, a law-enforcement officer provided seized evidence to a state laboratory required by law to assist in police investigations, N.M. Stat. Ann. § 29-3-4 (2004). Like the analysts in *Melendez-Diaz*, analyst Caylor tested the evidence and prepared a certificate concerning the result of his analysis. Like the *Melendez-Diaz* certificates, Caylor's certificate is "formalized" in a signed document, *Davis*, 547 U.S., at 837, n. 2 (opinion of Thomas, J.), headed a "report." Noteworthy as well, the SLD report form contains a legend referring to municipal and magistrate courts' rules that provide for the admission of certified blood alcohol analyses . . . .

[Part IV, which is not part of the majority opinion, is omitted. It attempts to rebut the argument that this decision would impose an undue burden on the prosecution.]

[*Reversed and Remanded.*]

[Justices Thomas and Kagan concurred in the result, and in the opinion in part. Justice Sotomayor concurred in the result and in part with the opinion, in a separate opinion quoted from, below. Justice Kennedy wrote a dissent, outlined below, in which Chief Justice Roberts and Justices Breyer and Alito joined.]

NOTES AND QUESTIONS

(1) *Formality.* Justice Thomas' vote was key to forming the majority opinion holding that the unsworn certificate was testimonial. Why do you think the certificate was formal enough to satisfy his view of "formality"? Is it enough to be signed? Must there also be some attestation by the signer that it is true or accurate?

(2) *Unanswered Questions.* Justice Sotomayor's concurrence in *Bullcoming* focused on issues (immediately below) which were not raised in the case but were

likely to arise in later cases. Some of these issues were subsequently further addressed in *Williams v. Illinois, infra.* Justice Sotomayor's concurrence in *Bullcoming* said, in part:

> First, this is not a case in which the State suggested an alternate purpose, much less an alternate primary purpose, for the BAC report. For example, the State has not claimed that the report was necessary to provide Bullcoming with medical treatment.
>
> Second, this is not a case in which the person testifying is a supervisor, reviewer, or someone else with a personal, albeit limited, connection to the scientific test at issue. The court below also recognized Razatos' total lack of connection to the test at issue.
>
> Third, this is not a case in which an expert witness was asked for his independent opinion about underlying testimonial reports that were not themselves admitted into evidence. See Fed. Rule Evid. 703 (explaining that facts or data of a type upon which experts in the field would reasonably rely in forming an opinion need not be admissible in order for the expert's opinion based on the facts and data to be admitted). We would face a different question if asked to determine the constitutionality of allowing an expert witness to discuss others' testimonial statements if the testimonial statements were not themselves admitted as evidence.
>
> Finally, this is not a case in which the State introduced only machine-generated results, such as a printout from a gas chromatograph. The State here introduced Caylor's statements, which included his transcription of a blood alcohol concentration, apparently copied from a gas chromatograph printout, along with other statements about the procedures used in handling the blood sample.

The case excerpted immediately below, *Williams v. Illinois*, arguably may answer some of the questions left open here, and it should be considered for that purpose. On what *Bullcoming* did and did not decide, see generally Coleman & Rothstein, *Grabbing the Bullcoming by the Horns: How the Supreme Court Could Have Used* Bullcoming v. New Mexico *to Clarify Confrontation Clause Requirements for CSI-type Reports*, 90 NEB. L. REV. 502 (2011).

(3) *Dissent.* The argument of the dissenters in *Bullcoming* relies partly on the burden to law enforcement, including a 71% increase between 2008 and 2010 in the number of subpoenas for New Mexico analysts' testimony in impaired-driving cases, and experiences in several other jurisdictions. How do these considerations affect the Confrontation Clause analysis? As Justice Kennedy pointed out, "[u]p to 40 analysts" may be involved in processing a single sample inside a state's testing laboratory: people who perform technical functions (not just couriers), but the opinions do not clarify how many will suffice at trial.

The dissent also characterizes the certifying analyst's role as "no greater than that of anyone else in the chain of custody." Do you agree?

Finally, the dissenters argue that *Bullcoming*, by rejecting such scientific reports, may actually foster reliance on less reliable evidence (for example, eye-witnesses). Therefore, Justice Kennedy calls for either a wholesale rejection of *Crawford*, or a refusal to extend *Melendez-Diaz.* How likely is it that the current Court will reject the testimonial approach in the near future?

(4) *Primary Purpose Test.* How is the primary purpose test used in analyzing the certificate in *Bullcoming*? Was there any rationale for creating the certificate other than an evidentiary one?

In light of *Davis, Bryant, Melendez-Diaz* and *Bullcoming*, are medical and psychological reports that are at least in part motivated by treatment concerns likely to be considered non-testimonial? What factors might be considered? In what kind of cases is this likely to be an issue? Many jurisdictions have specially trained and certified nurses (sometimes called by the acronym SANE) who work with police and whose job it is to both aid the medical treatment of sexual assault victims and obtain evidence such as traces for rape kits. Are statements to them by victims "testimonial"? Will each portion of statements to them need to be specially examined to ascertain the particular predominant purpose (as between the two purposes) of that particular portion? Are *reports* by such nurses "testimonial"? Again, will this depend on a close assessment of particulars?

In these and other cases, there is likely to be a lot of uncertainty, unpredictability, and litigation, about what is genuinely an exempt statement for purposes of medical treatment.

(5) *Which of Many Participants Must Testify*? Did *Bullcoming* provide any guidance about who in a chain of participating analysts must testify to satisfy Confrontation? Justice Ginsburg for the majority, you will notice, speaks of "the analyst who signed the certification" as the witness who should have been present but was not. But the logic of the opinion may require more if there is a chain of analysts (or, the signature may not be important at all). Again, the majority opinion seems to be assuming the analyst who did the work and who signed the report are one and the same and others were not involved in the analysis or report. The opinion does not say what the case would be and who should come forward if more people were involved in the process. Are some of these people discretionary with the prosecutor depending upon how strongly she wants to establish the chain of custody (as long as there is the minimum required to satisfy evidentiary authentication requirements — see Section 12.01[D] infra)? Can the prosecutor if she wishes use a certificate attesting to the where the sample tested came from, or to accuracy and calibration of the testing device? Are these subject to Confrontation Clause analysis, or simply governed by a jurisdiction's rules concerning evidence? Cf. Note (7) below.

Does Justice Sotomayor's second hypothetical case (see note (2) supra, involving testimony by a person who reviewed or supervised the process) suggest that there might be one witness who could be a satisfactory surrogate for all of the analysts?

(6) *Scrivener Exception?* Do the second through fifth paragraphs under heading II of Justice Ginsburg's majority decision above leave some room for a "mere scrivener" or "copyist" exception to the confrontation requirement, even though she feels the exception would not apply in *this* case because the report did more than merely transcribe machine results?

(7) *Is the Federal Authentication Rule Unconstitutional? United States v. Wittig*, 333 F. Supp. 2d 1048 (D. Kan. 2004), upholds a challenge to the procedure set forth in Rule 902(11) of the Federal Rules of Evidence, which permits authentication of business records to be established by certification in lieu of live testimony. The court held that the prosecution could not use a certificate, and instead needed a live witness, to attest to the facts that a document met the requirements of the business records hearsay exception (i.e., the facts that the document was prepared in the regular course of business at or near the time of the transaction, etc.), even though Rule 902(11) itself permitted the certificate to be so used. The underlying business records themselves were not made with any evidentiary or investigative use in mind, but purely for commercial business purposes, though they in fact turned out at trial to be incriminating to defendant when combined with other evidence. Thus, these underlying business records were not testimonial. Was the decision that the authentication certificate was testimonial correct?

The Supreme Court has approved an amendment to Fed. R. Evid. 803(10) (absence of a public record) and sent it to Congress to be effective December 1, 2013 unless disapproved or altered by Congress. It includes a "notice and demand" procedure providing that if the defendant fails to make a timely pretrial demand to produce a witness, a certification under Rule 902 will be admissible. A "notice and demand" procedure has been referred to favorably in the Supreme Court's decisions under *Crawford* and such procedure presumably would eliminate Confrontation Clause violations caused by the introduction of a certificate, if it were viewed as testimonial. The rule admits the certificate under the following conditions:

> . . . in a criminal case, a prosecutor who intends to offer a certification provides written notice of that intent at least 14 days before trial, and the defendant does not object in writing within 7 days of receiving the notice — unless the court sets a different time for the notice or the objection.

This amendment raises a number of questions. Probably the most significant issue, however, is whether defense attorneys will decline to demand the witnesses in appreciable numbers of cases, rather than putting the Government to its proof. In *Bullcoming*, the dissenters were understandably skeptical of this possibility.

WILLIAMS v. ILLINOIS

Supreme Court of the United States
132 S. Ct. 2221 (2012)

ALITO, JUSTICE.[3]

In petitioner's bench trial for rape, the prosecution called an expert [from the state police lab] who testified that a DNA profile produced by an outside laboratory, Cellmark, matched a profile produced by the state police lab using a sample of

---

[3] The opinions in this case have been very heavily redacted here because of their extraordinary length. Deletions have not been flagged, but significant ones are mentioned in our notes following the case. — Eds.

petitioner's blood. On direct examination, the expert testified that Cellmark was an accredited laboratory and that Cellmark provided the police with a DNA profile. The expert also explained the notations on documents admitted as business records, stating that, according to the records, vaginal swabs taken from the victim [Ms. L.J.] were sent to and received back from Cellmark. The expert made no other statement that was offered for the purpose of identifying the sample of biological material used in deriving the profile or for the purpose of establishing how Cellmark handled or tested the sample. Nor did the expert vouch for the accuracy of the profile that Cellmark produced. Nevertheless, petitioner contends that the expert's testimony violated the Confrontation Clause as interpreted in *Crawford*.

Petitioner's main argument is that the expert went astray when she referred to the DNA profile provided by Cellmark as having been produced from semen found on the victim's vaginal swabs. But both the Illinois Appellate Court and the Illinois Supreme Court found that [any out-of-court] statement [that may be involved here in what Cellmark sent] was not admitted for the truth of the matter asserted [in it], and it is settled that the Confrontation Clause does not bar the admission of such statements [that are not offered for their truth]. See *Crawford* n. 9 (citing *Tennessee v. Street*, 471 U. S. 409 (1985)). For more than 200 years, the law of evidence has permitted the sort of testimony that was given by the expert in this case. Under settled evidence law, an expert may express an opinion that is based on facts that the expert assumes, but does not know, to be true. It is then up to the party who calls the expert to introduce other evidence establishing the facts assumed by the expert. While it was once the practice for an expert who based an opinion on assumed facts to testify in the form of an answer to a hypothetical question, modern practice does not demand this formality and, in appropriate cases, permits an expert to explain the facts on which his or her opinion is based without testifying to the truth of those facts. See Fed. Rule Evid. 703. That is precisely what occurred in this case, and we should not lightly swee[p] away an accepted rule governing the admission of scientific evidence. [Justice Alito here notes that since this was a trial to the judge without a jury, the judge could be expected to understand the limited not-for-truth role of the Cellmark report, and seems to recognize the possibility thaqt the limitation may not have been clearly enough articulated had this been a trial to a jury.]

We now conclude that this form of expert testimony does not violate the Confrontation Clause because that provision has no application to out-of-court statements that are not offered to prove the truth of the matter asserted. When an expert testifies for the prosecution in a criminal case, the defendant has the opportunity to cross-examine the expert about any statements that are offered for their truth. Out-of-court statements that are related by the expert solely for the purpose of explaining the assumptions on which that opinion rests are not offered for their truth and thus fall outside the scope of the Confrontation Clause. Applying this rule to the present case, we conclude that the expert's testimony did not violate the Sixth Amendment.

As a second, independent basis for our decision, we also conclude that even if the report produced by Cellmark had been admitted into evidence, there would have been no Confrontation Clause violation. The Cellmark report is very different from the sort of extrajudicial statements, such as affidavits, depositions, prior testimony, and confessions, that the Confrontation Clause was originally understood to reach. The report was produced before any suspect was identified. The report was sought not for the purpose of obtaining evidence to be used against petitioner, who was not even under suspicion at the time, but for the purpose of finding a rapist who was on the loose. And the profile that Cellmark provided was not inherently inculpatory. On the contrary, DNA profile is evidence that tends to exculpate all but one of the more than 7 billion people in the world today. The use of DNA evidence to exonerate persons who have been wrongfully accused or convicted is well known. If DNA profiles could not be introduced without calling the technicians who participated in the preparation of the profile, economic pressures would encourage prosecutors to forgo DNA testing and rely instead on older forms of evidence, such as eyewitness identification, that are less reliable. See *Perry v. New Hampshire*, 565 U. S. ___, 132 S. Ct. 716 (2012). The Confrontation Clause does not mandate such an undesirable development. This conclusion will not prejudice any defendant who really wishes to probe the reliability of the DNA testing done in a particular case because those who participated in the testing may always be subpoenaed by the defense and questioned at trial.

Even if the Cellmark report had been introduced for its truth, we would nevertheless conclude that there was no Confrontation Clause violation. The Confrontation Clause refers to testimony by "witnesses against" an accused. Both the noted evidence scholar John Henry Wigmore and Justice Harlan interpreted the Clause in a strictly literal sense as referring solely to persons who testify in court, but we have not adopted this narrow view. It has been said that "[t]he difficulty with the Wigmore–Harlan view in its purest form is its tension with much of the apparent history surrounding the evolution of the right of confrontation at common law." *White v. Illinois* (THOMAS, J., concurring). "[T]he principal evil at which the Confrontation Clause was directed," the Court concluded in *Crawford*, "was the civil-law mode of criminal procedure, and particularly its use of *ex parte* examinations as evidence against the accused." "[I]n England, pretrial examinations of suspects and witnesses by government officials 'were sometimes read in court in lieu of live testimony.' " The Court has thus interpreted the Confrontation Clause as prohibiting modern-day practices that are tantamount to the abuses that gave rise to the recognition of the confrontation right. But any further expansion would strain the constitutional text.

The abuses that the Court has identified as prompting the adoption of the Confrontation Clause shared the following two characteristics: (a) they involved out-of-court statements having the primary purpose of accusing a targeted individual of engaging in criminal conduct and (b) they involved formalized statements such as affidavits, depositions, prior testimony, or confessions. In all but one of the post-*Crawford* cases in which a Confrontation Clause violation has been found, both of these characteristics were present. See *Bullcoming* (certified lab report having purpose of showing that defendant's blood-alcohol level exceeded legal limit); *Melendez–Diaz* (certified lab report having purpose of showing that substance connected to defendant contained cocaine); *Crawford* (custodial statement made after *Miranda* warnings that shifted blame from declarant to accused). The one exception occurred in *Hammon v. Indiana*, which was decided together with *Davis v. Washington*, but in *Hammon* and every other post-*Crawford* case in which the

Court has found a violation of the confrontation right, the statement at issue had the primary purpose of accusing a targeted individual . . . .

The Cellmark report is very different [from the statement in *Hammon*]. It plainly was not prepared for the primary purpose of accusing a targeted individual. In identifying the primary purpose of an out-of-court statement, we apply an objective test. We look for the primary purpose that a reasonable person would have ascribed to the statement, taking into account all of the surrounding circumstances.

[Conviction upheld.]

THOMAS, J. concurring in judgment.

I agree with the plurality that the disclosure of Cellmark's out-of-court statements through the expert testimony of Sandra Lambatos did not violate the Confrontation Clause. I reach this conclusion, however, solely because Cellmark's statements lacked the requisite "formality and solemnity" to be considered " 'testimonial' " for purposes of the Confrontation Clause. As I explain below, I share the dissent's view of the plurality's flawed analysis.

The threshold question in this case is whether Cellmark's statements were hearsay at all. As the Court has explained, "[t]he [Confrontation] Clause . . . does not bar the use of testimonial statements for purposes other than establishing the truth of the matter asserted." See *Crawford v. Washington*, n. 9 (citing *Tennessee v. Street*, 471 U. S. 409, 414 (1985)). Here, the State of Illinois contends that Cellmark's statements — that it successfully derived a male DNA profile and that the profile came from L. J.'s swabs — were introduced only to show the basis of Lambatos' opinion, and not for their truth. In my view, however, there was no plausible reason for the introduction of Cellmark's statements other than to establish their truth.

The plurality's assertion that Cellmark's statements were merely relayed to explain "the assumptions on which [Lambatos'] opinion rest[ed]," ante, at 3, overlooks that the value of Lambatos' testimony depended on the truth of those very assumptions.

The plurality's contrary conclusion may seem of little consequence to those who view DNA testing and other forms of "hard science" as intrinsically reliable. But see *Melendez-Diaz*, supra, at 318 ("Forensic evidence is not uniquely immune from the risk of manipulation"). Today's holding, however, will reach beyond scientific evidence to ordinary out-of-court statements. For example, it is not uncommon for experts to rely on interviews with third parties in forming their opinions. See, *e.g.*, *People v. Goldstein*, 6 N. Y. 3d 119 (2005) (psychiatrist disclosed statements made by the defendant's acquaintances as part of the basis of her opinion that the defendant was motivated to kill by his feelings of sexual frustration).

I have concluded that the Confrontation Clause reaches " 'formalized testimonial materials,' " such as depositions, affidavits, and prior testimony, or statements resulting from " 'formalized dialogue,' " such as custodial interrogation. Applying these principles, I conclude that Cellmark's report is not a statement by a "witnes[s]" within the meaning of the Confrontation Clause. The Cellmark report lacks the solemnity of an affidavit or deposition, for it is neither a sworn nor a certified declaration of fact. Nowhere does the report attest that its statements accurately reflect the DNA testing processes used or the results obtained. The report is signed by two "reviewers," but they neither purport to have performed the DNA testing nor certify the accuracy of those who did. And, although the report was produced at the request of law enforcement, it was not the product of any sort of formalized dialogue resembling custodial interrogation.

KAGAN, J., dissenting [joined by Justices Scalia, Ginsburg, and Sotomayor].

Some years ago, the State of California prosecuted a man named John Kocak for rape. At a preliminary hearing, the State presented testimony from an analyst at the Cellmark Diagnostics Laboratory — the same facility used to generate DNA evidence in this case. The analyst had extracted DNA from a bloody sweatshirt found at the crime scene and then compared it to two control samples — one from Kocak and one from the victim. The analyst's report identified a single match. As she explained on direct examination, the DNA found on the sweatshirt belonged to Kocak. But after undergoing cross-examination, the analyst realized she had made a mortifying error. She took the stand again, but this time to admit that the report listed the victim's control sample as coming from Kocak, and Kocak's as coming from the victim. So the DNA on the sweatshirt matched not Kocak, but the victim herself. See Tr. in No. SCD110465 (Super. Ct. San Diego Cty., Cal., Nov. 17, 1995), pp. 3–4 ("I'm a little hysterical right now, but I think . . . the two names should be switched"), online at http://www.nlada.org/forensics/for_lib/Documents/1037341561.0/JohnIvanKocak.pdf (as visited June 15, 2012, and available in Clerk of Court's case file). In trying Kocak, the State would have to look elsewhere for its evidence.

Our Constitution contains a mechanism for catching such errors — the Sixth Amendment's Confrontation Clause . . . .

Under our Confrontation Clause precedents, [the present case, *Williams*] is an open-and-shut case. The State of Illinois prosecuted Sandy Williams for rape based in part on a DNA profile created in Cellmark's laboratory. Yet the State did not give Williams a chance to question the analyst who produced that evidence. Instead, the prosecution introduced the results of Cellmark's testing through an expert witness who had no idea how they were generated. That approach — no less (perhaps more) than the confrontation free methods of presenting forensic evidence we have formerly banned [see e.g. *Bullcoming* where at least the witness presented was from the same lab] — deprived Williams of his Sixth Amendment right to "confron[t] . . . the witnesses against him."

The Court today disagrees, though it cannot settle on a reason why. Justice Alito, joined by three other Justices, advances two theories — that the expert's summary of the Cellmark report was not offered for its truth, and that the report is not the kind of statement triggering the Confrontation Clause's protection. In the pages that follow, I call Justice Alito's opinion "the plurality," because that is the conventional term for it. But in all except its disposition, his opinion is a dissent: Five Justices specifically reject every aspect of its reasoning and every paragraph of its explication. See ante, at 1 (Thomas, J., concurring in judgment) ("I share the dissent's view of the plurality's flawed analysis"). Justice Thomas, for his part, contends that the Cellmark report is nontestimonial on a different rationale. But no other Justice joins his opinion or subscribes to the test he offers.

That creates five votes to approve the admission of the Cellmark report, but not a single good explanation. The plurality's first rationale endorses a prosecutorial dodge; its second relies on distinguishing indistinguishable forensic reports. Justice Thomas's concurrence, though positing an altogether different approach, suffers in the end from similar flaws. I would choose another path — to adhere to the simple rule established in our decisions, for the good reasons we have previously given. Because defendants like Williams have a constitutional right to confront the witnesses against them, I respectfully dissent from the Court's fractured decision.

NOTES AND QUESTIONS

(1) *Williams' Relationship to Justice Sotomayor's Bullcoming Concurrence.* Does *Williams* answer or address any of the open questions Justice Sotomayor raised in her concurrence in *Bullcoming?* (These questions are set forth in note (2) following *Bullcoming* immediately preceding our reproduction of the *Williams* case supra.) For an interesting debate on the issues raised by *Williams* published just prior to the decision, see Coleman & Rothstein, *Williams v. Illinois and the Confrontation Clause: Does Testimony by a Surrogate Witness Violate the Confrontation Clause?*, appearing at http://publicsquare.net/williams-v-illinois-and-the-confrontation-clause-part-1, and at Georgetown Scholarly Commons, Georgetown Law Faculty Publications and Other Works, *Paper 740* (2011).

(2) *Justice Alito's Plurality Decision in Williams* was described as follows by Prof. Rothstein in informal materials when the decision was first handed down:

> A. Justice Alito's Rationale No. 1. In this part of his opinion, he says the information from the outside lab (the report)(Cellmark) was in the nature of a hypothetical put to the on-the-stand expert. In other words, the prosecutor essentially asked "Assuming this is the profile from the vaginal swab, does it match what your lab took from the defendant?" "Yes." Or, put another way, the witness's answer just itself was built on a hypothetical assumption, even if the exact question wasn't asked.
>
> So then it is up to the fact-finder to decide whether the assumed hypothetical facts are true. The on-the-stand expert has not said anything about whether the assumed facts are true, which is what would invoke the confrontation clause having to be applied to the Cellmark analyst(s). Thus the report is not being used for the truth of the matter asserted in it.
>
> So far, Alito makes a certain degree of sense. But then, if he is correct in this, there is no support at all for the expert opinion — no evidence to support a finding by the fact-finder that the hypothetical facts are true — and the expert's opinion should be stricken. On this point, Alito says [in a portion of the plurality opinion we have not reproduced], yes there is evidence to support the hypothetical facts — the circumstantial evidence that the police sent a sample swabbed from the victim to Cellmark, a DNA

profile came back, and it exactly matched the defendant, the guy the victim testifies did it.

The trouble with this, though, is that this circumstantial evidence itself depends on the truth of Cellmark's implied statement that "this profile comes from a sample" or "from the sample you sent." What if Cellmark just made up the profile? (Can we get around this by invoking the "coincidental traces" doctrine expressed in *Bridges*, supra, § 7.03? Maybe, maybe not.)

A better answer Alito could have made at this point would have been, *not* that the circumstantial evidence supports the truth of the hypothetical facts, *but that the question whether the hypothetical facts could be found true by the factfinder is not before us. You didn't raise a Due Process claim. And even if you did, overall there is enough evidence of guilt to convict, i.e., the victim's testimony. Normally in the absence of a viable Due Process claim we leave it to the state court to decide sufficiency of evidence.* Alito does say this, but he also goes on to say the questionable stuff about circumstantial evidence supporting the hypothetical facts.

Also I am not sure that the overall sufficiency of evidence of guilt (the victim's testimony) is an answer to a Due Process claim that important evidence of guilt was admitted that shouldn't have been admitted.

B. Justice Alito's Rationale #2. Relying on the confrontation clause's phrase "witness *against* the accused", he says since there was no suspect at the time Cellmark did its test and report, there is no way the report is testimonial, because it was not specifically *against* the accused. This would be like a person on the street being interviewed about something ("What kind of cars were in the parking lot") that later becomes significant when they catch a suspect for a crime (who is found to have a car matching a description of one of the many cars the witness had described) — becomes significant in placing defendant in the town where the parking lot was, near the time and place of the crime. But at the time of the on the street interview, the cars information had no specific significance. This also makes some degree of sense (maybe).

Do you agree with this analysis by Professor Rothstein of the plurality opinion in *Williams?*

(3) *Lengthy Fractured Decision. Williams* consists of 4 opinions totaling nearly 100 pages, much of which we have redacted. Justice Alito's plurality opinion including its reasoning was joined by the Chief Justice, Justice Kennedy, and Justice Breyer. Justice Thomas concurred that the evidence was constitutionally admissible and thus concurred in the judgment which upheld William's conviction (which was for aggravated criminal sexual assault, aggravated robbery, and aggravated kidnapping). But he had a different reason for the admissibility (his reason was the informality of the report) than the plurality, rejecting all the reasons given by the plurality. (Justice Breyer, in addition to concurring with the plurality, also wrote a separate concurrence suggesting that the case should be set for reargument to consider how the Confrontation Clause applies more generally to crime laboratory reports and technicians statements in them.) Justice Kagan wrote

a dissent, joined by Justices Scalia, Ginsburg, and Sotomayor. These dissenters rejected the reasons given by the plurality and the reasons given by Justice Thomas, sticking to a pure *Melendez-Diaz* view requiring the appearance of the analyst reponsible for a report whose contents gets before the factfinder regardless of how the contents of the report came before the factfinder (as the basis of an expert's opinion or more directly) and regardless of whether the report targets an individual or not. Justice Thomas's approach, relying on formality/infomrality, rejects the dissenters entire approach. *So there is no theory achieving five votes, though there was a cobbling together of disparate theories commanding five votes for constitutional admissibility.* For this reason, a number of commentators say there is no "holding" of the case.

Focusing on the second-to-last paragraph of the Justice Alito's plurality opinion as reproduced above, one of the authors of this casebook, Professor Crump, reads the *Williams* set of decisions quite differently. See if you agree with him:

> A single theory that replaces Crawford does appear to be shared by five justices, even though it is expressed in opinions that disagree in other respects. Justice Thomas and the plurality made up a majority that, in fact, agreed upon the single most basic feature of both opinions: an insistence that exclusion under the Confrontation Clause extends only to "formalized" or "solemn[ ]" out-of-court declarations that are generated by the state as evidence. In fact, one can argue that the Court now has overruled Crawford's wholesale exclusion of testimonial evidence — in *Williams*, sub silentio, by a majority that excludes only the narrower category of manufactured statements. An explicit opinion discarding the old regime would be preferable, but perhaps the reality that *Crawford* has been overruled already exists. If the evidence is not "formal" apparently, five Justices would regard it as immune from the Confrontation Clause. Isn't this the single "reason why" that the dissenters claim is absent?

Prof. Rothstein believes the last sentence of that second-to-last paragraph of Justice Alito's plurality opinion that Prof. Crump focusses on, refutes Prof. Crump's argument. Under that sentence, a statement that targets an individual is testimonial whether formal or not. *[The notes in this series will proceed NOT on the basis of Prof. Crump's reading.]*

(4) *Report Not Used for Truth of the Matter Asserted: Ground # 1 of the Plurality Decision Finding Non-Testimoniality.* Although the conviction was affirmed, there were 5 votes finding that the report was used for the truth of the matter asserted in it even though the report was not itself technically introduced in evidence. (The four dissenters plus Justice Thomas.) In contrast, the four votes in the plurality believe it was *not* used for the truth of the matter asserted, and therefore was *not* testimonial, but they were able to pick up Justice Thomas' vote as a fifth vote that it was not testimonial, which he cast on a different ground, that it was not testimonial because of its informality.

(5) *"Targeted Individual" (or "Non-Adversarial Record") Test: Ground #2 of the Plurality Decision Finding Non-Testimoniality.* The plurality includes an expanded definition of testimonial statements:

> The Clause refers to testimony by witnesses against an accused, prohibiting modern-day practices that are tantamount to the abuses that gave rise to the confrontation right, namely, (a) out-of-court statements having the primary purpose of accusing a targeted individual of engaging in criminal conduct, and (b) formalized statements such as affidavits, depositions, prior testimony, or confessions.

Part (a) of this definition seems new to these cases and appears to add a new wrinkle to the primary purpose test, which previously seemed only to require contemplation that the information might be used in an investigation or legal proceeding, not against any particular person. In applying this new wrinkle here, the plurality finds the report was not testimonial because at the time it was compiled, Williams was not a suspect in the rape:

> The primary purpose of the Cellmark report, viewed objectively, was not to accuse petitioner or to create evidence for use at trial. When the ISP lab sent the sample to Cellmark, its primary purpose was to catch a dangerous rapist who was still at large, not to obtain evidence for use against petitioner, who was neither in custody nor under suspicion at that time.

Both Justices Thomas and Kagan (and the three other dissenters for whom Kagan wrote) expressly rejected the "targeted individual" requirement. This addition to the test currently lacks a fifth vote. Would it severely limit what statements are subject to Confrontation Clause protection? For example, would all DNA cold hits be excluded? Would a major number of statements garnered from citizens by police trying to solve crimes, be excluded? Does it seem to expand the time allotted for "emergencies" in *Davis* and *Bryant*? Under the plurality, what would be required/sufficient to make a forensic-type report non-testimonial under the "targeted individual" theory? 1. Keeping the lab in the dark about the suspect? Would that only work with an independent lab? 2. Not having a suspect? Defendant not suspected yet? Defendant not a suspect in ANY crime? 3. No crime yet committed at time of the report or test? An example of the last might be routine reports of the particular chemical profile of each batch of fertilizer produced by factories, for possible use in identification of source if a fertilizer-based terrorist bombing does eventually occur. Or similar recordations of bullet lead compositions at the production point, or of gun barrel striations that mark bullets as they pass through, or of the genetic composition of bio-agents as they are produced, all in case they are ever used in a crime, so they could then be traced to source. Would another example be routinely kept DNA profiles or fingerprints, of all prisoners, for later use if and when other crimes occur after the prisoners' release?

Is this "targeted individual" requirement reminiscent of the "routine, non-adversarial records" exception to the ban on law enforcement records we studied under Rule 803(8) (public records hearsay exception)? See § 9.07 supra, note (3) following *Beach Aircraft Corp. v. Rainey*.

(6) *Did Justice Thomas and the Dissenters Dismiss the Not-for-Truth Conclusion Too Quickly?: Remembering Bridges v. State (in the Hearsay Chapter).* Cellmark's DNA pattern matched Williams's either because of an amazing (impossible) coincidence — or else, it was non-hearsay. Cellmark "knew" the DNA it reported. In this respect, *Williams v. Illinois* is remarkably similar to *Bridges v.*

State, which we saw in the hearsay chapter. In that case, Sharon's description of the defendant's room, to which she was abducted, showed her knowledge of the room. It was not relevant, however, for its description of the room, but for its match to the actual room, which was proved by other evidence. In *Williams*, Cellmark's description of the unknown DNA that it tested was not relevant for its description, but only because it matched Williams's DNA, which was shown by other evidence.

How could Cellmark have known how to report the DNA pattern of the unknown, which miraculously matched Williams's? Undoubtedly, you have thought: well, the Illinois authorities could have been sneaky, and they could have told Cellmark's personnel about Williams's precise DNA pattern and asked them to match it. But this conspiratorial inference seems far-fetched — how could Cellmark engage in the widespread kind of conspiracy that would be required, and handle thousands of DNA samples credibly, and stay in business? This inference, in any event, is a matter for cross examination, if anything, and would not prevent a finding by a preponderance that the evidence is not hearsay. Furthermore, this conspiratorial possibility also follows *Bridges*, where the evidence was not hearsay. Conceivably, Sharon could have learned about the room she described from an earlier visit, or from a conspiracy between her and police officers, but it seems unlikely, just as it does in *Williams*. A law of evidence driven by admissibility determinations founded on inferences of that kind would make it difficult to admit any kind of scientific evidence. Do you agree?

(7) *What Should a Prosecutor Do Now?* Suppose you are a prosecutor with a lab report that you want to use as part of the basis for the opinion of a qualified expert who did not participate in its making, rather than produce the reporting analyst herself. Would the following be good advice?:

> A. **If the trial is to a jury rather than a judge**, (i) make sure the facts found in the report are clearly and explicitly in the form of a hypothetical question to the expert (". . . if such and such facts are true, what would be your opinion . . .") and then (ii) be sure you have some evidence that those facts are true, which may be nothing more than showing that such-and-such sample was sent to the lab and the lab sent back a report showing such-and-such profile. (iii) Be sure the judge gives a jury instruction that the particular facts you have used from the report "are purely hypothetical and not offered for their truth but merely as a basis for the expert's opinion, i.e. they are assumptions he has made which he feels if true lead to the opinion he is giving; if they are not proved up by other evidence, the opinion is worthless."
>
> *If you have a report that was made in circumstances where the defendant was not at the time a "targeted individual," none of the above is necessary.*[4]
>
> These two paragraphs above embody two different approaches: the "hypothetical-with-proof-of-the-hypothetical-facts" approach; and the "not-a-targeted- individual" approach. The trial judge in ruling on admissibility will understand that either of these two approaches would pick up four

[4] In this situation, the report itself would be directly admissible, whether or not an expert was used.

votes (the plurality) if the case got to the Supreme Court. But you need a fifth vote.[5] *To get a fifth, you will also have to be sure the report is not "formal."* This will pick up Justice Thomas' vote as a fifth vote. Be sure there is no evidence that you did something special to make a report that normally is formal, informal, since Justice Thomas says he will be alert to whether the informality is in "bad faith". It is unclear what kind of showing might demonstrate "bad faith". It seems easy to evade the Confrontation Clause under Justice Thomas' "formality" test.

B. **If the trial is to a judge rather than a jury**, the same advice applies but it need not be made so clear that the facts in the report are hypothetical only — the expert can frankly base his opinion on the report, and the judge will understand that the facts in the report are in the nature of a hypothetical that need to be proved.

C. In all events, the expert witness must not be a *mere conduit* for the hearsay findings of those doing the test and making the report. This means that in addition to being qualified, the expert witness must have done some independent analysis or work of her own contributing to her opinion.

D. An alternative route to any of this *may* be to have a lab supervisor who had something to do with the testing and report, present the report. (See Justice Sotomayor's second case scenario in note (2) following *Bullcoming* supra.)

E. If the report is at the same time both (1) informal (so Justice Thomas will vote for admissibility) and (2) does not target an individual (so the four plurality justices will vote for admissibility), the expert-witness route to admissibility of the report's contents is not necessary and the report can come in directly because five justices are voting that the report itself is non-testimonial in the first place (though for different reasons), and therefore the prosecutor does not have to resort to showing that a non-testimonial use is being made of it, i.e., a use that involves illuminating an expert witness's basis rather than establishing the report's truth.

F. If the report is formal (so Justice Thomas would vote for inadmissibility), Thomas would join the four *Williams* dissenters (who felt the report information is always inadmissible based on a pure reading of *Melendez-Diaz* regardless of formality/informality, and regardless of whether the report is the basis of expert testimony, and regardless of whether it targets an individual, all of which tests they thought were completely bogus), and there is nothing the prosecutor can do to get the evidence in — the expert route will not get it in (because Justice Thomas and the four dissenters felt that route is entirely bogus) nor will arguing that it does not target an individual get it in either (even if it truly does not target an individual) because Justice Thomas and the four dissenters felt that the "targeting" test is also a bogus approach and that targeting makes no difference — the evidence is inadmissible regardless of targeting.

---

[5] This is because there are nine justices on the Supreme Court, so five would be a majority.

Thus, if the report is *formal*, the evidence will be constitutionally inadmissible, regardless of any of these other things. So, in that particular instance (where the report is formal), Justice Thomas's vote (Justice Thomas' formality/informality test) is absolutely controlling.

If the report is *informal* (as in the actual *Williams* case) so that Justice Thomas would say it is constitutionally admissible, his vote is not entirely controlling: he must pick up four more votes for admissibility. The four *Williams* dissenters in no event will vote for admissibility (since they take a pure *Melendez-Diaz* approach). So Thomas's only hope to accomplish constitutional admissibility in this situation is to pick up the four in the *Williams* plurality. But if (unlike in *Williams*) the report does not target an individual and the expert route has not been used properly in the trial court (so that neither of the conditions is present that made the evidence in *Williams* admissible in the eyes of the plurality), the four plurality votes for admissibility drop away, Thomas stands alone, and the evidence is constitutionally inadmissible.

If the report was not composed for law enforcement purposes, such as a report of a medical or mental examination made for a private patient solely for treative purposes, that later becomes relevant in a prosecution, the Confrontation Clause would not be implicated.

How would an autopsy report as to cause of death, where no criminality is yet suspected, and there is no particular person targeted, be treated?

(8) *California Seems to Follow Justice Thomas's View.* Since *Williams*, Justice Thomas' view has found favor in California. Objective statements of fact in an autopsy report were too informal to be testimonial in *People v. Dungo*, 286 P.3d 442 (Cal. 2012) (Query: Do autopsy reports necessarily target an individual?) Similarly, in *People v. Lopez*, 286 P.3d 469 (Cal. 2012), notations linking the defendant's name to a blood sample in a laboratory report on blood alcohol concentration (BAC) were not formal enough to be considered testimonial where the notation was labeled "FOR LAB USE ONLY." Does this show that Prof. Crump (see note (3) supra) is right?

(9) *Was the Plurality Just Looking For a Way to Overrule Melendez-Diaz Without Actually Doing it?* Notice that the plurality in *Williams* are the dissenters in *Melendez-Diaz.* So they don't think these forensic reports violate the Confrontation Clause, even if introduced directly without the expert, whether or not they target an individual. Suppose in *Williams* the facts were slightly different so that the plurality could invoke neither of its two rationales (outlined supra, note (2)). Do you think the justices in the plurality would have come up with yet another theory why the report did not violate the Confrontation Clause — for example, that Cellmark was an independent lab and was quite reliable; and/or that on the facts there was no realistic possibility the DNA profile that came back to the police was faked, mistaken, switched, or obtained from some other sample or source of Williams's DNA? (In a portion of *Williams* that we have not reproduced, these factors are mentioned by the plurality in passing as a kind of practical support for but not necessarily a rationale for the admissibility result reached.) This would mean that in a future case, even without the two rationales for admissibility given

by the plurality in *Williams*, if the report is informal (thus satisfying Justice Thomas's requirement for admissibility), and reliable in this fashion, the report *itself* (whether targeting an individual or not) would be constitutionally admissible even without an expert (there being five votes for admissibility, four on reliability grounds, and one on the informality grounds). Has the *Roberts* reliability criterion been resurrected? Is there anything else, in any other of these cases after *Crawford*, that suggests it has been?

CRAWFORD REVIEW PROBLEMS 11B: WHAT MAKES SOMETHING SAID OUT-OF-COURT "TESTIMONIAL"?

Consider the following problems in the light of *Crawford and its progeny*:

(1) *Undercover Investigation.* In an embezzlement prosecution of Fred Embezzle, a pizza deliveryman, the government wishes to put on the witness stand, Martin Undercover, a police informant who has been on the regular payroll of the police department for a number of years. Undercover proposes to testify that, as part of the embezzlement investigation, he, Undercover, pretending to be just an ordinary citizen, was looking for Fred Embezzle so he could have him arrested for the embezzlement, and, pursuant to his search, wound up at a very expensive restaurant and club, called *Mon Ami Billionaire*, frequented only by wealthy playboys and playgirls. Undercover will further testify that he pretended to strike up a casual conversation with the bartender, Joe Bartender, and, in a seemingly innocent off-the-cuff way, steered the conversation to the subject of family. Undercover's testimony will continue, to the effect that at an appropriate moment in this conversation about family, Undercover indicated to Bartender that he (Undercover) incidentally happened to have some pictures of his family in his wallet. Undercover will testify that at that point in the conversation he showed Bartender pictures of a fake "family", among which was a picture of Fred Embezzle. When Bartender asked him who that was, Undercover said it was a picture of his brother, and then added "Why? Do you know him?" Bartender responded that Embezzle had just been in the club less than an hour ago. Discuss admissibility.

(2) *Variations.* Would it make any difference if Undercover were wearing a police uniform? If Bartender thought Undercover was looking for a witness? If Bartender knew Undercover was police but Bartender's disclosure that Fred Embezzle had been in the club came up in innocent conversation before any crime was known of by the police? Or was even committed? (Assume Bartender's disclosure happens accidentally to be relevant at the trial for the crime — say, for example, to show that Fred Embezzle was probably in town the day of the embezzlement.) Suppose the same facts as the last two sentences, but Bartender did not know of any police connection on the part of Undercover. Make any difference? In any version of this problem, does it matter if Bartender's statement was volunteered without questioning or manipulation? In other words, would it make any difference, under any version of this problem, whether Bartender volunteered, as a passing casual remark, the information about Fred Embezzle's presence in the club, instead of being questioned or prompted to do so? What if Bartender wanted to incriminate Embezzle? In general, does it matter whether the police initiate getting a statement, or the declarant initiates it?

(3) *Statement Overheard by but Not Made to Police Officer.* Review the problem entitled ***PROBLEM 8B: "YOU WENT THROUGH A RED LIGHT!"*** in § 8.02 [C], *supra*, and assume the approaching police officer overhears the bystander. Could the bystander's statement to Jones be testified to (by the policeman) for its truth in a criminal prosecution of Jones for running the red light?

(4) *Dying Declaration to Police Officer Made Under Questioning.* (a) Reconsider the problem (1) in the series entitled ***PROBLEM 10C: VARIOUS ASPECTS OF DYING DECLARATIONS*** in § 10.03, *supra.* How does *Crawford* and its progeny affect admissibility there, if at all? (b) While it is not entirely clear, *Crawford* and some of the other cases indicate without deciding that dying declarations might have a special historical exemption from the Confrontation Clause, even when they are testimonial. Does this exemption depend on the idea that declarant is not thinking of making evidence (perhaps like a 911 call) or rather on some notion that, by killing the declarant, the defendant has forfeited his right to object to the fact that declarant is not present to be confronted — since defendant produced that state of affairs? In other words, is it a concept something like Fed. R. Evid. 804(b)(6) (forfeiture by wrongdoing), except, perhaps, that the killing was not done necessarily specifically to render declarant unavailable as a witness? If this is the basis of the exemption for dying declarations from the Confrontation Clause, how is the exemption affected by the fact that dying declarations under Fed. R. Evid. 804(b)(2) has altered the common law requirements for dying declarations, by removing the requirement that the declarant actually be dead, so long as declarant is unavailable for *some* reason, whether or not that reason is the fault of the defendant? How is it affected by the fact that under the 804(b)(2) defendant need not have inflicted the believed deadly wound (or other cause) and may be on trial for something entirely unrelated?

(5) *Interview in I.R.S. Offices Years Later where Declarant Not Aware of Significance.* Review the note numbered (2) entitled *Lack of Awareness that the Statement is Against Interest*, in § 10.04 [A], *supra* (the *Filesi* case). Would that evidence be admissible under the Confrontation Clause (assuming the hearsay rule exception had been revised so as not to require knowledge)?

(6) *Can a Predecessor-in-Interest Preserve a Criminal Defendant's Confrontation Rights?* Under Fed. R. Evid. 804(b)(1) (hearsay exception for former testimony), in a *civil case*, a party cannot claim a lack of opportunity to cross examine if a predecessor-in-interest of his who had a similar motive, had the opportunity. Could 804(b)(1) be amended to apply the same rule to criminal cases, as some states provide? Is the rule in those states unconstitutional? The Supreme Court Draft of the Federal Rules of Evidence (changed by Congress before enactment) had an even broader provision — anyone, whether technically a predecessor-in-interest or not, who had a similar interest and motive, was sufficient, in both civil and criminal cases. Would this be constitutional?

(7) *California's Hearsay Exception for Threats of Infliction of Injury.* In 1996, California adopted the following hearsay exception (Cal. Evid. Code § 1370):

§ 1370. Threat of Infliction of Injury

(a) Evidence of a statement by a declarant is not made inadmissible by the hearsay rule if all of the following conditions are met:

(1) The statement purports to narrate, describe, or explain the infliction or threat of physical injury upon the declarant.

(2) The declarant is unavailable as a witness pursuant to Section 240.

(3) The statement was made at or near the time of the infliction or threat of physical injury. Evidence of statements made more than five years before the filing of the current action or proceeding shall be inadmissible under this section.

(4) The statement was made under circumstances that would indicate its trustworthiness.

(5) The statement was made in writing, was electronically recorded, or made to a law enforcement official.

Subsection (b) of this law provides three nonexclusive factors for assessing trustworthiness (litigation motive, bias, and corroboration) and subsection (c) requires advance notice to the opponent.

Although the exception is not so limited, this hearsay exception reflected California's experience with victims of continued abuse, particularly in domestic situations. For example, in the trial of O.J. Simpson, the prosecution offered a number of statements by the murder victim, Nicole Brown Simpson, about repeated threats and assaults she suffered from the defendant. Some statements were recorded, some written, and some offered through lay or police witnesses orally. Questions: (a) To what extent would the California Code admit these hearsay statements? (b) Is this admittance wise and appropriate? (c) Does this exception survive *Crawford?* Would it survive *Roberts?* Does it have to satisfy both tests? *See* Raeder, *Domestic Violence, Child Abuse, and Trustworthiness Exceptions After Crawford*, 20 A.B.A. CRIM. J. 24 (2005), expanded at 71 BROOK. L. REV. 311 (2005); Lininger, *Prosecuting Batterers After Crawford*, 91 VA. L. REV. 747 (2005). A somewhat similar hearsay exception for "statements of elder or dependent adult victims of abuse" who are deceased or incapacitated, and unavailable to testify, contained in Cal. Evid. Code § 1380, has been rejected by several courts, as unconstitutional after *Crawford*.

(8) *Interplay of Fed. R. Evid. 803(8) (Public Records) and Crawford.* (a) Reconsider the problem entitled ***PROBLEM 9H: POLICE OFFICERS' OR INSURANCE REGULATORS' REPORTS IN DIFFERENT CASE SETTINGS*** that is at the end of § 9.07 (hearsay exception for public records), *supra.* Would *Crawford* affect the admissibility of any of the report material in that problem under any of the alternatives there? (b) In note (3) following *Beech Aircraft v. Rainey* in § 9.07 (hearsay exception for public records), *supra*, it is indicated that some courts have fashioned a "routine records" doctrine allowing into evidence against the criminal defendant some otherwise forbidden law enforcement records

under the rule — primarily those that were compiled as a routine matter under non-adversarial circumstances and not in connection with the particular case. Has this "routine records" doctrine been imported into the Confrontation Clause? Only in connection with the public records exception to the hearsay rule? Or more broadly, in connection with any and all otherwise testimonial statements?

(9) *Autopsy Reports.* Given the current split by the Justices in their view of whether and when forensic reports are testimonial or not, give the best arguments on each side on how to categorize autopsy reports.

(10) *Scientific Machines.* Can a printout from a lab apparatus be introduced in evidence to prove the data on the printout? Can a report of the data shown on the printout be introduced assuming the report does nothing other than transcribe verbatim what the machine printout said, with no interpretation or other information such as how the machine was calibrated, what was put into the machine, etc.? Could it be argued in that case, that the person who transcribed the printout data into the report is a mere scrivener rather than a witness and does not need to be subject to confrontation?

(11) *Co-Conspirator Statements.* Would the out-of-court statement in *Bourjaily*, supra, § 8.02[F] be admissible under the Confrontation Clause? Would it if the theory of the offer were not the co-conspirator exemption from the hearsay rule, but rather that the statement was part of the crime of conspiracy, i.e., one of the overt acts fostering the objectives of the conspiracy, that is a needed element of the crime of conspiracy?

§ 11.04 CONFRONTATION CLAUSE APPLIED TO STATEMENTS BY NONTESTIFYING CODEFENDANTS

BRUTON v. UNITED STATES

United States Supreme Court
391 U.S. 123 (1968)

Brennan, Justice

[Defendant Bruton was joined for trial with a codefendant, Evans. Evans had made a confession implicating Bruton. The trial court ruled that the confession could be admitted into evidence, with the trial judge instructing the jury to disregard it as to defendant Bruton. This procedure was allowed under the authority of *Delli Paoli v. United States*, 352 U.S. 232 (1957). The Supreme Court majority in *Bruton* (accepting, as a given, that under evidence law the evidence was inadmissible against Bruton) saw this as a denial of Bruton's right to confrontation under the Sixth Amendment to the Federal Constitution. Mr. Justice Brennan delivered the Court's opinion.]

The basic premise of *Delli Paoli* was that it is "reasonably possible for the jury to follow" sufficiently clear instructions to disregard the confessor's extrajudicial statement that his codefendant participated with him in committing the crime. If it were true that the jury disregarded the reference to the codefendant, no question would arise under the Confrontation Clause, because by hypothesis the case is treated as if the confessor made no statement inculpating the nonconfessor. But since *Delli Paoli* was decided this Court has effectively repudiated its basic premise. Plainly, the introduction of Evans' confession added substantial, perhaps even critical, weight to the Government's case in a form not subject to cross-examination, since Evans did not take the stand. Petitioner thus was denied his constitutional right of confrontation.

Delli Paoli assumed that this encroachment on the right to confrontation could be avoided by the instruction to the jury to disregard the inadmissible hearsay evidence. But, as we have said, that assumption has since been effectively repudiated.

NOTES AND QUESTIONS

(1) *What Result if Both Defendants in a Joint Trial Confess and the Confessions are "Interlocking"? Lee v. Illinois*, 476 U.S. 530 (1986). In *Lee*, the prosecution perhaps had an argument for distinguishing *Bruton*, in that both defendants confessed, not just one, and the confessions "interlocked" or corroborated each other on many details. Lee's confession, however, diverged from her codefendant's in crucial respects, by reducing her participation in planning, facilitating, and premeditating the crime. The trial judge, in a bench trial, relied substantively on the codefendant's confession in these respects. The Court, per Justice Brennan, reversed: the codefendant's confession implicating Lee was presumptively unreliable as evidence against her, and the congruence or interlock did not supply the missing indicia of reliability.

(2) *What Result if the Two Confessions Interlock but the Jury is Instructed to Disregard the Other Confession as to a Codefendant who Repudiates his Confession? Cruz v. New York*, 481 U.S. 186 (1987). This case presented another variation: both defendants in a joint trial had confessed and the confessions interlocked as to many details, but Cruz repudiated his confession. The trial judge admitted both confessions but instructed the jury to disregard the codefendant's confession when judging Cruz's guilt. The Court, per Justice Scalia, reversed and remanded for reconsideration of the indicia of reliability of the codefendant's confession. That confession was not rendered inconsequential in light of Cruz's own confession, as the lower courts had reasoned; instead, it "confirm[ed]" Cruz's, which was "enormously damaging." The interlocking rather was related to a different theory: that the codefendant's confession actually was reliable enough to be admitted against Cruz as evidence. But the lower courts had not considered this theory, and hence the remand.

(3) *What Result if the Codefendant's Confession is Redacted so that it Does Not Refer Directly to the Defendant, but it can be Construed Together with Other Evidence to Implicate Him? Richardson v. Marsh*, 481 U.S. 200 (1987). This case presented yet a third variation. The codefendant's confession was redacted so that it did not directly mention the defendant, Marsh. It still could have been construed as implicating her, but only by consideration of other testimony. The trial judge gave an instruction to disregard the confession in considering Marsh's guilt. The

Court, per Justice Scalia, upheld this procedure: "Where the necessity of such linkage is involved, it is a less valid generalization that the jury will not obey the instruction to disregard the evidence." Are these three decisions — *Lee*, *Cruz* and *Marsh* — all persuasively justified, and are they consistent?

(4) *Replacing the Defendant's Name with a "Symbol or Neutral Pronoun."* *Marsh* left open "the admissibility of a confession in which the defendant's name has been replaced with a symbol or neutral pronoun." Decisions of lower courts immediately subsequent to *Marsh* were split on this issue. Some follow the "contextual" or "evidentiary linkage" approach which finds a denial of confrontation whenever the confession tends to inculpate the defendant in light of other evidence. In contrast, others use a "facial implication" doctrine to permit a joint trial by simply replacing the defendant's name with a neutral pronoun. A third view looks to whether the redacted confession compels a directly inculpating inference against the defendant. *Gray v. Maryland*, 523 U.S. 185 (1998), held that the *Bruton* rule — prohibiting introduction during a joint trial of the confession of a non-testifying codefendant that names he defendant as the perpetrator — also extends to redacted confessions in which the name of the defendant is replaced by a black space, the word "deleted," or a similar symbol. The Court distinguished *Richardson v. Marsh*, 481 U.S. 200 (1987), as follows:

> *Richardson* must depend in significant part upon the kind of, not the simple fact of, inference. *Richardson's* inferences involved statements that did not refer directly to the defendant himself and which became incriminating "only when linked with evidence introduced later at trial." 481 U.S., at 208. The inferences at issue here involve statements that, despite redaction, obviously refer directly to someone, often obviously the defendant, and which involve inferences that a jury ordinarily could make immediately, even were the confession the very first item introduced at trial . . .
>
> Nor are the policy reasons that *Richardson* provided in support of its conclusion applicable here. *Richardson* expressed concern lest application of *Bruton's* rule apply where "redaction" of confessions, particularly "confessions incriminating by connection," would often "not [be] possible," thereby forcing prosecutors too often to abandon use either of the confession or of a joint trial.

The Court also made clear that *Bruton* applies to nicknames or other identifying characteristics of the accused.

(5) *Is Bruton Still Viable if the Codefendant's Statement is Admissible Against the Defendant?* Does *Crawford* affect the *Bruton* doctrine? Bruton was charged with armed postal robbery and his codefendant's confession was made to a postal inspector. What if the declaration against interest is made to someone not employed by the government? In *Bruton*, the confession did not satisfy any hearsay exception (declarations against penal interest was not recognized under evidence law at the time). Would the Federal Rules of Evidence (as interpreted in *Williamson* § 10.04[B], *supra*) make the confession admissible as a declaration against penal interest? Does that matter? Several cases now explicitly hold that *Bruton* only applies to testimonial statements. *See, e.g.*, *State v. Usee*, 800 N.W.2d 192 (Minn. Ct.

App. 2011); *United States v. Figueroa-Cartagena*, 612 F.3d 69 (1st Cir. 2010).

§ 11.05 WAIVER OF CONFRONTATION RIGHT: EXCEPTION FOR FORFEITURE BY WRONGDOING AND F.R.E. 804(b)(6)[6]

Read Federal Rule of Evidence 804(b)(6), "Statement Offered Against a Party That Wrongfully Caused the Declarant's Unavailability." (formerly titled "Forfeiture by Wrongdoing")

What if a criminal defendant deliberately kills all of the witnesses against him to prevent their testimony? They may have made statements to the police or to a grand jury, but admittance of these statements would be precluded for most witnesses by the hearsay rule and the Confrontation Clause under *Crawford*. To avoid allowing a person to profit from such wrongdoing, a new exception to the hearsay rule was added to the Federal Rules of Evidence, Rule 804(b)(6). Earlier in this volume where hearsay exceptions were discussed, we deferred consideration of Fed. R. Evid. 804(b)(6) even though in the Federal Rules of Evidence it is on the list of hearsay exceptions. We deferred because of the kinship that rule has to waiver of Confrontation Clause rights. The rule was added to the Federal Rules to parallel a growing body of cases in the constitutional confrontation area.

Rule 804(b)(6) punishes those who wish to *object* to an otherwise objectionable hearsay declaration that is not within any other hearsay exception, if they have wrongfully procured the declarant's unavailability in order to prevent declarant's testimony. It should not be confused with the last paragraph of Rule 804(a)(definition of unavailability), which punishes *offerors* of hearsay (which hearsay *is* within an 804(b) hearsay exception) if they have wrongfully procured the declarant's unavailability. The provision we are discussing at this point in our text, *i.e.*, Rule 804(b)(6), prevents *the objector from objecting* to hearsay. In contrast, the 804(a) provision prevents the *offeror from offering* hearsay (under 804(b)). The misconduct that engenders the punishment is somewhat similar in both: wrongfully procuring unavailability of the declarant for purposes of preventing testimony.

The exception under Rule 804(b)(6), however, raises some difficulties. How should it apply when the defendant's misconduct is not a serious crime such as murder but merely consists of doing nothing when a witness says, "I've received this subpoena and I think I'm going to arrange to be absent"? (The Rule admits the evidence when the defendant has "acquiesced" in the wrongdoing.) What if the case hasn't arisen yet and the declarant's role as a potential witness is unclear? (Of course no subpoena would be mentioned.) Note that the evidence of the defendant's action or inaction also may be unclear; the judge then makes a finding about admissibility from circumstantial evidence. Will there always have to be a hearing before the judge? May the witness's unavailability and the defendant's misconduct be proved to the jury in addition to the statement itself? (A line of case law about spoliation of evidence suggests that the answer is yes.)

---

[6] Study Guide Reference: Evidence in a Nutshell, Chapter 10:III at "Hearsay Exception for Wrongfully Causing Declarant's Unavailability" F.R.E. 804(b)(6)."

In a criminal case, when employed against defendant, the forfeiture by wrongdoing provision is constitutional under the Confrontation Clause even though it deprives the defendant of his right to confrontation. There a principle of waiver of Confrontation Clause rights that is analogous to Rule 804(b)(6).

NOTES AND QUESTIONS

(1) *Relationship of Forfeiture Rules and Constitutional Constraints.* In *United States v. Houlihan*, 92 F.3d 1271 (1st Cir. 1996), the district court admitted portions of hearsay statements made by George Sargent on the theory that the government had shown by clear and convincing evidence that those defendants conspired to kill Sargent at least in part for the purpose of preventing him from cooperating with the police, and that such actions were tantamount to a knowing waiver of their confrontation rights.

Houlihan and Nardone argued that the waiver-by-misconduct doctrine, even if good law, should not be employed because Sargent was not an actual witness — no charges had been lodged against Houlihan or Nardone at the time of Sargent's murder, and no grand jury had as yet been convened — but at most a turncoat cooperating with the police. Thus, they could not have been on notice that they were waiving a trial right. The First Circuit found this argument unpersuasive, noting "although the reported cases all appear to involve actual witnesses, we can discern no principled reason why the waiver-by-misconduct doctrine should not apply with equal force if a defendant intentionally silences a *potential* witness."

Houlihan and Nardone also argued that even if they waived their confrontation rights, the district court should not have admitted Sargent's hearsay statements because they were tinged with self-interest (having been made in police custody with a stiff sentence for distributing large quantities of narcotics in prospect) and therefore lacked "circumstantial guarantees of trustworthiness." Fed. R. Evid. 804(b)(5) [the "catchall" hearsay exception, now in Rule 807]. On the facts of the case, the appellate court found that the misconduct waived not only their confrontation rights but also their hearsay objections, thus rendering a special finding of reliability superfluous.

(2) *Crawford's and Davis' View of Forfeiture (Waiver of Confrontation Rights). Crawford* contains the following sentence concerning forfeiture:

> For example, the rule of forfeiture by wrongdoing (which we accept) extinguishes confrontation claims on essentially equitable grounds; it does not purport to be an alternative means of determining reliability. *See Reynolds v. United States*, 98 U.S. 145, 158-159, 25 L.Ed.244 (1879).

Similarly, *Davis* expanded this discussion:

> [W]hen defendants seek to undermine the judicial process by procuring or coercing silence from witnesses and victims, the Sixth Amendment does not require courts to acquiesce. While defendants have no duty to assist the State in proving their guilt, they do have the duty to refrain from acting in ways that destroy the integrity of the criminal-trial system.

> We take no position on the standards necessary to demonstrate such forfeiture, but federal courts using Federal Rule of Evidence 804(b)(6), which codifies the forfeiture doctrine, have generally held the Government to the preponderance-of-the-evidence standard. State courts tend to follow the same practice. Moreover, if a hearing on forfeiture is required, *Edwards*, for instance, observed that "hearsay evidence, including the unavailable witness's out-of-court statements, may be considered."

(3) *Federal Rule of Evidence on Forfeiture and the Constitutional Doctrine: Are They Co-Extensive? Open Questions on What They Require.* Does the constitutional waiver rule mirror the hearsay forfeiture rule? Is the "wrongdoing" required in both cases limited to technical witness tampering? Is causing a person not to testify at trial sufficient "wrongdoing" or is some action necessary to produce unavailability? Suppose only persuasion is used? Or calling to the attention of a witness, the witness' privilege not to testify? Or urging the witness to assert privilege? Would it matter if there really *is* such a privilege available to the witness?

(4) *Intent to Impede Justice.* After *Davis*, a number of courts held that the defendant forfeited the right to confrontation in murder cases where a hearsay statement of the victim was offered by the prosecution, without requiring that there have been intention by the defendant to procure the absence of a witness. Some commentators asserted this result was contrary to the history of forfeiture. *See* Flanagan, *Confrontation, Equity, and the Misnamed Exception for "Forfeiture" by Wrongdoing*, 14 WM. & MARY BILL RTS. J. 1193 (2006) (arguing that intent has always been required). In *Giles v. California*, 554 U.S. 353 (2008), the Supreme Court adopted the historical approach and rejected the view that forfeiture could occur merely because the murder rendered the victim unavailable to testify. But there are still several possibilities regarding what intent will suffice: Intent to render the witness unavailable for (a) this proceeding, (b) a related proceeding (how directly related?), or (c) an unrelated proceeding. Does the following passage from *Giles* contain any clues on this question?:

> Acts of domestic violence often are intended to dissuade a victim from resorting to outside help, and include conduct designed to prevent testimony to police officers or cooperation in criminal prosecutions. Where such an abusive relationship culminates in murder, the evidence may support a finding that the crime expressed the intent to isolate the victim and to stop her from reporting abuse to the authorities or cooperating with a criminal prosecution — rendering her prior statements admissible under the forfeiture doctrine. Earlier abuse, or threats of abuse, intended to dissuade the victim from resorting to outside help would be highly relevant to this inquiry, as would evidence of ongoing criminal proceedings at which the victim would have been expected to testify.

What if a defendant intends to kill one witness to prevent him from testifying (in (i) the present case or (ii) another case) and accidentally kills another potential witness. Can he raise an objection to the out-of-court statements of the second witness or has he forfeited that right? For some thoughts about proving forfeiture, see Raeder, *Thoughts About Giles and Forfeiture in Domestic Violence Cases*, 75

Brook. L. Rev. 1329 (2010) and *Being Heard After Giles, Comments on the Sound of Silence*, 87 Tex. L. Rev. 105 (2009).

Is there a reason to treat forfeiture under 804(b)(6) any differently than under the Confrontation Clause in this regard?

(5) *Forfeiture in Domestic Violence Cases.* While *Davis*, *supra* at § 11.03, refused to treat domestic violence differently from other cases in its testimonial analysis, the decision recognized that "[t]his particular type of crime is notoriously susceptible to intimidation or coercion of the victim to ensure that she does not testify at trial." What is required to find forfeiture in this context? *Giles*, supra note (4), arose in the domestic violence context. While the majority opinion, authored by Justice Scalia, did not create an exception for domestic violence cases, it noted that statements to friends and neighbors could be admitted subject to hearsay rules. Similarly:

Where such an abusive relationship culminates in murder, the evidence may support a finding that the crime expressed the intent to isolate the victim and to stop her from reporting abuse to the authorities or cooperating with a criminal prosecution — rendering her prior statements admissible under the forfeiture doctrine. Earlier abuse, or threats of abuse, intended to dissuade the victim from resorting to outside help would be highly relevant to this inquiry, as would evidence of ongoing criminal proceedings at which the victim would have been expected to testify. This is not, as the dissent charges, post, at 2708, nothing more than "knowledge-based intent." 128 S. Ct. 2693.

Does this mean that forfeiture be presumed if a history of domestic violence is present despite the absence of any specific evidence of the defendant's purpose or intent? Davis suggested, without deciding, that the preponderance of the evidence standard would be appropriate for deciding forfeiture.

(6) *Dying Declaration Redux.* Reconsider once again the problem entitled ***PROBLEM 10C: VARIOUS ASPECTS OF DYING DECLARATIONS*** in § 10.03, *supra.* Would the principle of waiver (or forfeiture) affect the constitutional (or evidentiary) analysis of that problem?

§ 11.06 OTHER CONSTITUTIONAL RIGHTS OF DEFENDANTS THAT LIMIT APPLICATION OF EVIDENTIARY RULES: HEARSAY AND BEYOND[7]

CHAMBERS v. MISSISSIPPI

United States Supreme Court

410 U.S. 284 (1973)

MR. JUSTICE POWELL delivered the opinion of the Court.

Petitioner, Leon Chambers, was tried by a jury in a Mississippi trial court and convicted of murdering a policeman. [C]ertiorari was granted, to consider whether petitioner's trial was conducted in accord with principles of due process under the Fourteenth Amendment. We conclude that it was not.

[Two Woodville policemen (Forman and Liberty) entered a local bar and poolhall to arrest a youth named Jackson. A hostile crowd gathered to prevent it. Reinforcements came. Guns were drawn. Shots rang out.] Forman was looking in a different direction when the shooting began, but immediately saw that Liberty had been shot several times in the back. Before Liberty died, he turned around and fired both barrels of his riot gun into an alley in the area from which the shots appeared to have come. The first shot scattered the crowd standing at the face of the alley. [The second] hit one of the men in the crowd as he ran down the alley. That man was Leon Chambers.

Officer Forman could not see from his vantage point who shot Liberty or whether Liberty's shots hit anyone. One of the deputy sheriffs testified at trial that he was standing several feet from Liberty and that he saw Chambers shoot him. Another deputy sheriff stated that, although he could not see whether Chambers had a gun in his hand, he did see Chambers "break his arm down" shortly before the shots were fired.

Chambers was subsequently charged with Liberty's murder. He pleaded not guilty and has asserted his innocence throughout.

The story of Leon Chambers is intertwined with the story of another man, Gable McDonald. McDonald, a lifelong resident of Woodville, was in the crowd on the evening of Liberty's death. McDonald agreed to make a statement to Chambers' attorneys, who maintained offices in Natchez. Two days later, he appeared at the attorneys' offices and gave a sworn confession that he shot Officer Liberty.

One month later, at a preliminary hearing, McDonald repudiated his prior sworn confession. He testified that [Rev. Stokes, his wife's friend] had persuaded him to confess that he shot Liberty. He claimed that Stokes had promised that he would not go to jail and that he would share in the proceeds of a lawsuit that Chambers would bring against the town of Woodville. On examination by his own attorney and on cross-examination by the State, McDonald swore that he had not been at the scene when Liberty was shot but had been down the street drinking beer in a cafe

---

[7] Study Guide Reference: Evidence in a Nutshell, Chapter 8:VI.

with a friend, Berkley Turner. When he and Turner heard the shooting, he testified, they walked up the street and found Chambers lying in the alley. He, Turner, and Williams took Chambers to the hospital. The local justice of the peace accepted McDonald's repudiation and released him from custody. The local authorities undertook no further investigation of his possible involvement.

Chambers' case came on for trial in October of the next year. At trial, he endeavored to develop two grounds of defense. He first attempted to show that he did not shoot Liberty. Only one officer testified that he actually saw Chambers fire the shots. Although three officers saw Liberty shoot Chambers and testified that they assumed he was shooting his attacker, none of them examined Chambers to see whether he was still alive or whether he possessed a gun. Indeed, no weapon was ever recovered from the scene and there was no proof that Chambers had ever owned a .22-caliber pistol. One witness testified that he was standing in the street near where Liberty was shot, that he was looking at Chambers when the shooting began, and that he was sure that Chambers did not fire the shots.

Petitioner's second defense was that Gable McDonald had shot Officer Liberty. He was only partially successful, however, in his efforts to bring before the jury the testimony supporting this defense. Sam Hardin, a lifelong friend of McDonald's, testified that he saw McDonald shoot Liberty. A second witness, one of Liberty's cousins, testified that he saw McDonald immediately after the shooting with a pistol in his hand. In addition to the testimony of these two witnesses, Chambers endeavored to show the jury that McDonald had repeatedly confessed to the crime. Chambers attempted to prove that McDonald had admitted responsibility for the murder on four separate ocassions, once when he gave the sworn statement to Chambers' counsel and three other times prior to that occasion in private conversations with friends.

In large measure, he was thwarted in his attempt to present this portion of his defense by the strict application of certain Mississippi rules of evidence. Chambers asserts in this Court that the application of these evidentiary rules rendered his trial fundamentally unfair and deprived him of due process of law.

At trial, after the State failed to put McDonald on the stand, Chambers called McDonald, laid a predicate for the introduction of his sworn out-of-court confession, had it admitted into evidence, and read it to the jury. The State, upon cross-examination, elicited from McDonald the fact that he had repudiated his prior confession. McDonald further testified, as he had at the preliminary hearing, that he did not shoot Liberty, and that he confessed to the crime only on the promise of Reverend Stokes that he would not go to jail and would share in a sizable tort recovery from the town.

At the conclusion of the State's cross-examination, Chambers renewed his motion to examine McDonald as an adverse witness. The trial court denied the motion, stating: "He may be hostile, but he is not adverse in the sense of the word, so your request will be overruled."

Defeated in his attempt to challenge directly McDonald's renunciation of his prior confession, Chambers sought to introduce the testimony of the three witnesses to whom McDonald had admitted that he shot the officer. The State objected to the admission of this testimony on the ground that it was hearsay. The trial court sustained the objection.

As a consequence of the combination of Mississippi's "party witness" or "voucher" rule and its hearsay rule, [Chambers] was unable either to cross-examine McDonald or to present witnesses in his own behalf who would have discredited McDonald's repudiation and demonstrated his complicity. Chambers had, however, chipped away at the fringes of McDonald's story by introducing admissible testimony from other sources indicating that he had not been seen in the cafe where he said he was when the shooting started, that he had not been having beer with Turner, and that he possessed a .22 pistol at the time of the crime. But all that remained from McDonald's own testimony was a single written confession countered by an arguably acceptable renunciation. Chambers' defense was far less persuasive than it might have been had he been given an opportunity to subject McDonald's statements to cross-examination or had the other confessions been admitted.

The right of an accused in a criminal trial to due process is, in essence, the right to a fair opportunity to defend against the State's accusations. The rights to confront and cross-examine witnesses and to call witnesses in one's own behalf have long been recognized as essential to due process.

Chambers was denied an opportunity to subject McDonald's damning repudiation and alibi to cross-examination. He was not allowed to test witness' recollection, to probe into the details of his alibi, or to "sift" his conscience so that the jury might judge for itself whether McDonald's testimony was worthy of belief.

In this case, petitioner's request to cross-examine McDonald was denied on the basis of a Mississippi common-law rule that a party may not impeach his own witness. The rule rests on the presumption — without regard to the circumstances of the particular case — that a party who calls a witness "vouches for his credibility."

The "voucher" rule, as applied in this case, plainly interfered with Chambers' right to defend against the State's charges.

We need not decide, however, whether this error alone would occasion reversal since Chambers' claimed denial of due process rests on the ultimate impact of that error when viewed in conjunction with the trial court's refusal to permit him to call [the] other witnesses. Each would have testified to the statements purportedly made by McDonald, on three separate occasions shortly after the crime, naming himself as the murderer. The State Supreme Court approved the exclusion of this evidence on the ground that it was hearsay.

A number of exceptions have developed over the years to allow admission of hearsay statements made under circumstances that tend to assure reliability and thereby compensate for the absence of the oath and opportunity for cross-examination. Among the most prevalent of these exceptions is the one applicable to declarations against interest — an exception founded on the assumption that a person is unlikely to fabricate a statement against his own interest at the time it is made. Mississippi recognizes this exception but applies it only to declarations against pecuniary interest. It recognizes no such exception for declarations, like

McDonald's in this case, that are against the penal interest of the declarant. *Brown v. State*, 99 Miss. 719, 55 So. 961 (1911).

This materialistic limitation on the declaration-against-interest hearsay exception appears to be accepted by most States in their criminal trial processes . . . ., although a number of States have discarded it. Declarations against penal interest have also been excluded in federal courts under the authority of *Donnelly v. United States*, 228 U.S. 243, 272-273 (1913) [approving exclusion of a confession of a third party not connected with nor related in any way to defendant that the third party himself had committed the murder defendant was charged with (even though the confession seemed to have some corroboration)], although exclusion would not be required under the newly proposed Federal Rules of Evidence. Exclusion, where the limitation prevails, is usually premised on the view that admission would lead to the frequent presentation of perjured testimony to the jury. It is believed that confessions of criminal activity are often motivated by extraneous considerations and, therefore, are not as inherently reliable as statements against pecuniary or proprietary interest . . . .

The hearsay statements involved in this case were originally made and subsequently offered at trial under circumstances that provided considerable assurance of their reliability. First, each of McDonald's confessions was made spontaneously to a close acquaintance shortly after the murder had occurred. Second, each one was corroborated by some other evidence in the case — McDonald's sworn confession, the testimony of an eyewitness to the shooting, the testimony that McDonald was seen with a gun immediately after the shooting, and proof of his prior ownership of a .22-caliber revolver and subsequent purchase of a new weapon. The sheer number of independent confessions provided additional corroboration for each. Third, whatever may be the parameters of the penal-interest rationale, each confession here was in a very real sense self-incriminatory and unquestionably against interest . . . . Finally, if there was any question about the truthfulness of the extrajudicial statements, McDonald was present in the courtroom and was under oath. He could have been cross-examined by the State, and his demeanor and responses weighed by the jury . . . .

Few rights are more fundamental than that of an accused to present witnesses in his own defense . . . . Although perhaps no rule of evidence has been more respected or more frequently applied in jury trials than that applicable to the exclusion of hearsay, exceptions tailored to allow the introduction of evidence which in fact is likely to be trustworthy have long existed . . . . The testimony rejected by the trial court here bore persuasive assurances of trustworthiness and thus was well within the basic rationale of the exception for declarations against interest. That testimony also was critical to Chambers' defense. In these circumstances, where constitutional rights directly affecting the ascertainment of guilt are implicated, the hearsay rule may not be applied mechanistically to defeat the ends of justice.

Reversed and Remanded.

NOTES AND QUESTIONS

(1) *How Broad are the Opposing Implications of Chambers and Montana v. Egelhoff, 518 U.S. 37 (1996)?* Reread *Egelhoff, supra* at § 2.04[B], upholding an instruction to the jury, in accordance with Montana Code § 45-2-203, that it was forbidden to consider Egelhoff's "intoxicated condition . . . in determining the existence of a mental state which is an element of the offense." The Court noted that the hearsay rules "prohibit the introduction of testimony which, though unquestionably relevant, is deemed insufficiently reliable." Although *Egelhoff* is not a hearsay case, it has implications that apply to all defensive evidence. Do you agree with Justice Scalia's characterization in *Egelhoff* of *Chambers* as an "exercise in highly case-specific error correction" and not establishing a broader principle about a defendant's right to present "critical evidence" that is reliable? If this analysis is followed in later decisions, when, if ever, will defendants be able to use due process to trump evidentiary rules prohibiting the introduction of reliable hearsay (or other evidence) that is significant to their theory of the case? Fed. R. Evid. 804(b)(3) (declarations against interest hearsay exception) includes declarations against penal interest that exculpate the accused only if clearly corroborated. Does this comply with *Chambers*?

(2) *What if, in Egelhoff, the Judge had Excluded All Evidence of Intoxication?* The trial judge in *Egelhoff* permitted the evidence of intoxication to be used on another theory than that defendant lacked the specific intent to take a life: i.e., the jury was allowed to consider that the evidence was relevant to defendant's contention that he was too drunk to have physically committed the crime (unable to physically point the gun and pull the trigger). Could the trial judge have prohibited any mention of intoxication altogether, for any purpose?

(3) *O.K. to Exclude Defense Evidence of Alternative Perpetrators.* In *United States v. McVeigh*, 153 F.3d 1166 (10th Cir. 1998), *cert. denied*, 526 U.S. 1007 (1999), the court upheld the exclusion of evidence of alleged alternative perpetrators, noting that "the exclusion of evidence can result in a fundamentally unfair trial only if the excluded evidence was so 'material' that it would have created 'reasonable doubt that did not exist without the evidence.' " Is this the same standard as proposed by *Egelhoff?* Is "*would* have" an unusually stringent standard? *Cf. People v. Primo*, 753 N.E.2d 164 (N.Y. 2001) (rejecting as test of admissibility, a test that requires a "clear link" between the third person and the crime, if such test means anything other than the standard Rule 403 kind of calculus that New York applies to all other evidence). The limits of this doctrine are discussed in *Holmes v. South Carolina*, 547 U.S. 319 (2006), *infra*.

UNITED STATES v. SCHEFFER

United States Supreme Court
523 U.S. 303 (1998)

JUSTICE THOMAS announced the judgment of the Court.

This case presents the question whether Military Rule of Evidence 707, which makes polygraph evidence inadmissible in court-martial proceedings, unconstitutionally abridges the right of accused members of the military to present a defense. We hold that it does not.

In March 1992, respondent Edward Scheffer, an airman stationed at March Air Force Base in California, volunteered to work as an informant on drug investigations for the Air Force Office of Special Investigations (OSI). His OSI supervisors advised him that, from time to time during the course of his undercover work, they would ask him to submit to drug testing and polygraph examinations. In early April, one of the OSI agents supervising respondent requested that he submit to a urine test. Shortly after providing the urine sample, but before the results of the test were known, respondent agreed to take a polygraph test administered by an OSI examiner. In the opinion of the examiner, the test "indicated no deception" when respondent denied using drugs since joining the Air Force.

On April 30, respondent unaccountably failed to appear for work and could not be found on the base. He was absent without leave until May 13, when an Iowa state patrolman arrested him following a routine traffic stop and held him for return to the base. OSI agents later learned that respondent's urinalysis revealed the presence of methamphetamine.

Respondent was tried by general court-martial on charges of using methamphetamine, failing to go to his appointed place of duty, wrongfully absenting himself from the base for 13 days, and, with respect to an unrelated matter, uttering 17 insufficient funds checks. He testified at trial on his own behalf, relying upon an "innocent ingestion" theory and denying that he had knowingly used drugs while working for OSI. On cross-examination, the prosecution attempted to impeach respondent with inconsistencies between his trial testimony and earlier statements he had made to OSI.

Respondent sought to introduce the polygraph evidence in support of his testimony that he did not knowingly use drugs. The military judge denied the motion, relying on Military Rule of Evidence 707, which provides, in relevant part:

(a) Notwithstanding any other provision of law, the results of a polygraph examination, the opinion of a polygraph examiner, or any reference to an offer to take, failure to take, or taking of a polygraph examination, shall not be admitted into evidence.

A defendant's right to present relevant evidence is not unlimited, but rather is subject to reasonable restrictions. . . . *Rock v. Arkansas*; *Chambers v. Mississippi*. A defendant's interest in presenting such evidence may thus " 'bow to accommodate other legitimate interests in the criminal trial process.' " *Rock, supra*, at 55; accord *Michigan v. Lucas*, 500 U.S. 145 (1991). As a result, state and federal rulemakers have broad latitude under the Constitution to establish rules excluding evidence from criminal trials. Such rules do not abridge an accused's right to present a defense so long as they are not "arbitrary" or "disproportionate to the purposes they are designed to serve." Moreover, we have found the exclusion of evidence to be unconstitutionally arbitrary or disproportionate only where it has infringed upon a weighty interest of the accused. *See Rock, supra,* at 58; *Chambers, supra,* at 302.

Rule 707 serves several legitimate interests in the criminal trial process. These interests include ensuring that only reliable evidence is introduced at trial, preserving the jury's role in determining credibility, and avoiding litigation that is collateral to the primary purpose of the trial. The rule is neither arbitrary nor disproportionate in promoting these ends. Nor does it implicate a sufficiently weighty interest of the defendant to raise a constitutional concern under our precedents.

State and federal governments unquestionably have a legitimate interest in ensuring that reliable evidence is presented to the trier of fact in a criminal trial. Indeed, the exclusion of unreliable evidence is a principal objective of many evidentiary rules. *See, e.g.,* Fed. Rule Evid. 702; Fed. Rule Evid. 802; Fed. Rule Evid. 901; *see also Daubert v. Merrell Dow Pharmaceuticals, Inc* . . . .

The contentions of respondent and the dissent notwithstanding, there is simply no consensus that polygraph evidence is reliable. To this day, the scientific community remains extremely polarized about the reliability of polygraph techniques . . . .

This lack of scientific consensus is reflected in the disagreement among state and federal courts concerning both the admissibility and the reliability of polygraph evidence. Although some Federal Courts of Appeal have abandoned the per se rule excluding polygraph evidence, leaving its admission or exclusion to the discretion of district courts under *Daubert,* at least one Federal Circuit has recently reaffirmed its per se ban . . . and another recently noted that it has "not decided whether polygraphy has reached a sufficient state of reliability to be admissible.". . . Most States maintain per se rules excluding polygraph evidence. New Mexico is unique in making polygraph evidence generally admissible without the prior stipulation of the parties and without significant restriction. *See* N. M. Rule Evid. § 11-707. Whatever their approach, state and federal courts continue to express doubt about whether such evidence is reliable . . . .

The approach taken by the President in adopting Rule 707 — excluding polygraph evidence in all military trials — is a rational and proportional means of advancing the legitimate interest in barring unreliable evidence. Although the degree of reliability of polygraph evidence may depend upon a variety of identifiable factors, there is simply no way to know in a particular case whether a polygraph examiner's conclusion is accurate, because certain doubts and uncertainties plague even the best polygraph exams. Individual jurisdictions therefore may reasonably reach differing conclusions as to whether polygraph evidence should be admitted. We cannot say, then, that presented with such widespread uncertainty, the President acted arbitrarily or disproportionately in promulgating a *per se* rule excluding all polygraph evidence.

The three of our precedents upon which the Court of Appeals principally relied, *Rock v. Arkansas*, *Washington v. Texas*, and *Chambers v. Mississippi*, do not support a right to introduce polygraph evidence, even in very narrow circumstances. The exclusions of evidence that we declared unconstitutional in those cases significantly undermined fundamental elements of the accused's defense. Such is not the case here.

In *Rock*, the defendant, accused of a killing to which she was the only eyewitness, was allegedly able to remember the facts of the killing only after having her memory hypnotically refreshed. Because Arkansas excluded all hypnotically refreshed testimony, the defendant was unable to testify about certain relevant facts, including whether the killing had been accidental. In holding that the exclusion of this evidence violated the defendant's "right to present a defense," we noted that the rule deprived the jury of the testimony of the only witness who was at the scene and had firsthand knowledge of the facts. Moreover, the rule infringed upon the accused's interest in testifying in her own defense — an interest that we deemed particularly significant, as it is the defendant who is the target of any criminal prosecution. For this reason, we stated that an accused ought to be allowed "to present his own version of events in his own words."

In *Washington*, the statutes involved prevented co-defendants or co-participants in a crime from testifying for one another and thus precluded the accused from introducing his accomplice's testimony that the accomplice had in fact committed the crime. In reversing Washington's conviction, we held that the Sixth Amendment was violated because "the State arbitrarily denied [the accused] the right to put on the stand a witness who was physically and mentally capable of testifying to events that he had personally observed.". . .

In *Chambers*, we found a due process violation in the combined application of Mississippi's common law "voucher rule," which prevented a party from impeaching his own witness, and its hearsay rule that excluded the testimony of three persons to whom that witness had confessed. *Chambers* specifically confined its holding to the "facts and circumstances" presented in that case; we thus stressed that the ruling did not "signal any diminution in the respect traditionally accorded to the States in the establishment and implementation of their own criminal trial rules and procedures." *Chambers* therefore does not stand for the proposition that the accused is denied a fair opportunity to defend himself whenever a state or federal rule excludes favorable evidence.

Rock, *Washington*, and *Chambers* do not require that Rule 707 be invalidated, because, unlike the evidentiary rules at issue in those cases, Rule 707 does not implicate any significant interest of the accused. Here, the court members heard all the relevant details of the charged offense from the perspective of the accused, and the Rule did not preclude him from introducing any factual evidence. Rather, respondent was barred merely from introducing expert opinion testimony to bolster his own credibility. Moreover, in contrast to the rule at issue in *Rock*, Rule 707 did not prohibit respondent from testifying on his own behalf; he freely exercised his choice to convey his version of the facts to the court-martial members. We therefore cannot conclude that respondent's defense was significantly impaired by the exclusion of polygraph evidence. Rule 707 is thus constitutional under our precedents.

[This opinion only contains those sections of the decision which reflect the views of a majority of the justices — Eds.]

NOTES AND QUESTIONS

(1) *Lone Dissent in Scheffer.* Justice Stevens dissented asserting that the Court's "holding rests on a serious undervaluation of the importance of a citizen's constitutional right to present a defense to a criminal charge and an unrealistic appraisal of the importance of the governmental interests that undergird the Rule."

(2) *What is Left of the Defendant's Right to Present a Defense?* Do *Scheffer* and *Egelhoff* severely limit an accused's right to present a defense, or are both cases merely very specific exceptions to the general right?

HOLMES v. SOUTH CAROLINA

Supreme Court of the United States
547 U.S. 319 (2006)

Justice Alito delivered the opinion of the Court.

This case presents the question whether a criminal defendant's federal constitutional rights are violated by an evidence rule under which the defendant may not introduce proof of third-party guilt if the prosecution has introduced forensic evidence that, if believed, strongly supports a guilty verdict.

86-year-old Mary Stewart was beaten, raped, and robbed in her home. She later died of complications stemming from her injuries. Petitioner was convicted by a South Carolina jury of murder and he was sentenced to death. Upon state postconviction review petitioner was granted a new trial. At the second trial, the prosecution relied heavily on the following forensic evidence:

"(1) [Petitioner's] palm print was found just above the door knob on the interior side of the front door of the victim's house; (2) fibers consistent with a black sweatshirt owned by [petitioner] were found on the victim's bed sheets; (3) matching blue fibers were found on the victim's pink nightgown and on [petitioner's] blue jeans; (4) microscopically consistent fibers were found on the pink nightgown and on [petitioner's] underwear; (5) [petitioner's] underwear contained a mixture of DNA from two individuals, and 99.99% of the population other than [petitioner] and the victim were excluded as contributors to that mixture; and (6) [petitioner's] tank top was found to contain a mixture of [petitioner's] blood and the victim's blood."

In addition, the prosecution introduced evidence that petitioner had been seen near Stewart's home within an hour of the time when, according to the prosecution's evidence, the attack took place.

As a major part of his defense, petitioner attempted to undermine the State's forensic evidence by suggesting that it had been contaminated and that certain law enforcement officers had engaged in a plot to frame him. Petitioner's expert witnesses criticized the procedures used by the police in handling the fiber and DNA evidence and in collecting the fingerprint evidence. Another defense expert provided testimony that petitioner cited as supporting his claim that the palm print had been planted by the police.

Petitioner also sought to introduce proof that another man, Jimmy McCaw White, had attacked Stewart. At a pretrial hearing, petitioner proffered several witnesses who placed White in the victim's neighborhood on the morning of the assault, as well as four other witnesses who testified that White had either acknowledged that petitioner was " 'innocent' " or had actually admitted to committing the crimes. One witness recounted that when he asked White about the "word . . . on the street" that White was responsible for Stewart's murder, White "put his head down and he raised his head back up and he said, well, you know I like older women." According to this witness, White added that "he did what they say he did" and that he had "no regrets about it at all." Another witness, who had been incarcerated with White, testified that White had admitted to assaulting Stewart, that a police officer had asked the witness to testify falsely against petitioner, and that employees of the prosecutor's office, while soliciting the witness' cooperation, had spoken of manufacturing evidence against petitioner. White testified at the pretrial hearing and denied making the incriminating statements. He also provided an alibi for the time of the crime, but another witness refuted his alibi.

The trial court excluded petitioner's third-party guilt evidence citing *State v. Gregory* (S.C. 1941) . . . . Citing both *Gregory* and its later decision in *State v. Gay* (S.C. 2001), the State Supreme Court held that "where there is strong evidence of an appellant's guilt, especially where there is strong forensic evidence, the proffered evidence about a third party's alleged guilt does not raise a reasonable inference as to the appellant's own innocence.". . . [T]he court held that petitioner could not "overcome the forensic evidence against him to raise a reasonable inference of his own innocence." We granted certiorari.

"[S]tate and federal rulemakers have broad latitude under the Constitution to establish rules excluding evidence from criminal trials." *United States v. Scheffer*. This latitude, however, has limits. "Whether rooted directly in the Due Process Clause of the Fourteenth Amendment or in the Compulsory Process or Confrontation clauses of the Sixth Amendment, the Constitution guarantees criminal defendants 'a meaningful opportunity to present a complete defense.' " This right is abridged by evidence rules that "infring[e] upon a weighty interest of the accused" and are " 'arbitrary' or 'disproportionate to the purposes they are designed to serve.' " *Scheffer* (quoting *Rock v. Arkansas*).

This Court's cases contain several illustrations of "arbitrary" rules, i.e., rules that excluded important defense evidence but that did not serve any legitimate interests. In *Washington v. Texas* (1967), state statutes barred a person who had been charged as a participant in a crime from testifying in defense of another alleged participant unless the witness had been acquitted. As a result, when the defendant in *Washington* was tried for murder, he was precluded from calling as a witness a person who had been charged and previously convicted of committing the same murder. Holding that the defendant's right to put on a defense had been violated, we noted that the rule embodied in the statutes could not "even be defended on the ground that it rationally sets apart a group of persons who are particularly likely to commit perjury" since the rule allowed an alleged participant to testify if he or she had been acquitted or was called by the prosecution.

A similar constitutional violation occurred in *Chambers v. Mississippi*. A murder defendant called as a witness a man named McDonald, who had previously confessed to the murder. When McDonald repudiated the confession on the stand, the defendant was denied permission to examine McDonald as an adverse witness based on the State's " 'voucher' rule," which barred parties from impeaching their own witnesses. In addition, because the state hearsay rule did not include an exception for statements against penal interest, the defendant was not permitted to introduce evidence that McDonald had made self-incriminating statements to three other persons. Noting that the State had not even attempted to "defend" or "explain [the] underlying rationale" of the "voucher rule," this Court held that "the exclusion of [the evidence of McDonald's out-of-court statements], coupled with the State's refusal to permit [the defendant] to cross-examine McDonald, denied him a trial in accord with traditional and fundamental standards of due process."

Another arbitrary rule was held unconstitutional in *Crane v. Kentucky* (1986). There, the defendant was prevented from attempting to show at trial that his confession was unreliable because of the circumstances under which it was obtained, and neither the State Supreme Court nor the prosecution "advanced any rational justification for the wholesale exclusion of this body of potentially exculpatory evidence."

In *Rock v. Arkansas*, this Court held that a rule prohibiting hypnotically refreshed testimony was unconstitutional because "[w]holesale inadmissibility of a defendant's testimony is an arbitrary restriction on the right to testify in the absence of clear evidence by the State repudiating the validity of all post-hypnotic recollections." By contrast, in *United States v. Scheffer*, supra, we held that a rule excluding all polygraph evidence did not abridge the right to present a defense because the rule "serve[d] several legitimate interests in the criminal trial process," was "neither arbitrary nor disproportionate in promoting these ends," and did not "implicate a sufficiently weighty interest of the defendant."

While the Constitution thus prohibits the exclusion of defense evidence under rules that serve no legitimate purpose or that are disproportionate to the ends that they are asserted to promote, well-established rules of evidence permit trial judges to exclude evidence if its probative value is outweighed by certain other factors such as unfair prejudice, confusion of the issues, or potential to mislead the jury. *See, e.g.*, Fed. Rule Evid. 403. Plainly referring to rules of this type, we have stated that the Constitution permits judges "to exclude evidence that is 'repetitive . . . , only marginally relevant' or poses an undue risk of 'harassment, prejudice, [or] confusion of the issues.' " *Crane* (quoting *Delaware v. Van Arsdall* (1986)). *See also Montana v. Egelhoff* (terming such rules "familiar and unquestionably constitutional").

A specific application of this principle is found in rules regulating the admission of evidence proffered by criminal defendants to show that someone else committed the crime with which they are charged. See, e.g., 41 C.J.S., Homicide § 216 (1991) ("Evidence tending to show the commission by another person of the crime charged may be introduced by accused when it is inconsistent with, and raises a reasonable doubt of, his own guilt; but frequently matters offered in evidence for this purpose are so remote and lack such connection with the crime that they are excluded"); 40A Am. Jur. 2d, Homicide § 286 (1999) ("[T]he accused may introduce any legal evidence tending to prove that another person may have committed the crime with which the defendant is charged . . . . [Such evidence] may be excluded where it does not sufficiently connect the other person to the crime, as, for example, where the evidence is speculative or remote, or does not tend to prove or disprove a material fact in issue at the defendant's trial". Such rules are widely accepted, and neither petitioner nor his amici challenge them here. In *Gregory*, the South Carolina Supreme Court adopted and applied a rule apparently intended to be of this type, given the court's references to the "applicable rule" from Corpus Juris and American Jurisprudence.

In *Gay* and this case, however, the South Carolina Supreme Court radically changed and extended the rule. In *Gay*, after recognizing the standard applied in Gregory, the court stated that "[i]n view of the strong evidence of appellant's guilt — especially the forensic evidence . . . the proffered evidence . . . did not raise 'a reasonable inference' as to appellant's own innocence." Similarly, in the present case, as noted, the State Supreme Court applied the rule that "where there is strong evidence of [a defendant's] guilt, especially where there is strong forensic evidence, the proffered evidence about a third party's alleged guilt" may (or perhaps must) be excluded.

Under this rule, the trial judge does not focus on the probative value or the potential adverse effects of admitting the defense evidence of third-party guilt. Instead, the critical inquiry concerns the strength of the prosecution's case: If the prosecution's case is strong enough, the evidence of third-party guilt is excluded even if that evidence, if viewed independently, would have great probative value and even if it would not pose an undue risk of harassment, prejudice, or confusion of the issues.

Furthermore, as applied in this case, the South Carolina Supreme Court's rule seems to call for little, if any, examination of the credibility of the prosecution's witnesses or the reliability of its evidence. Here, for example, the defense strenuously claimed that the prosecution's forensic evidence was so unreliable (due to mishandling and a deliberate plot to frame petitioner) that the evidence should not have even been admitted. The South Carolina Supreme Court responded that these challenges did not entirely "eviscerate" the forensic evidence and that the defense challenges went to the weight and not to the admissibility of that evidence. Yet, in evaluating the prosecution's forensic evidence and deeming it to be "strong" — and thereby justifying exclusion of petitioner's third-party guilt evidence — the South Carolina Supreme Court made no mention of the defense challenges to the prosecution's evidence.

Interpreted in this way, the rule applied by the State Supreme Court does not rationally serve the end that the *Gregory* rule and its analogues in other jurisdictions were designed to promote, i.e., to focus the trial on the central issues by excluding evidence that has only a very weak logical connection to the central issues. The rule applied in this case appears to be based on the following logic: Where (1) it is clear that only one person was involved in the commission of a particular crime and (2) there is strong evidence that the defendant was the perpetrator, it follows that evidence of third-party guilt must be weak. But this logic depends on an accurate evaluation of the prosecution's proof, and the true strength of the prosecution's proof cannot be assessed without considering challenges to the reliability of the prosecution's evidence. Just because the prosecution's evidence, if credited, would provide strong support for a guilty verdict, it does not follow that evidence of third-party guilt has only a weak logical connection to the central issues in the case. And where the credibility of the prosecution's witnesses or the reliability of its evidence is not conceded, the strength of the prosecution's case cannot be assessed without making the sort of factual findings that have traditionally been reserved for the trier of fact and that the South Carolina courts did not purport to make in this case.

The rule applied in this case is no more logical than its converse would be, *i.e.*, a rule barring the prosecution from introducing evidence of a defendant's guilt if the defendant is able to proffer, at a pretrial hearing, evidence that, if believed, strongly supports a verdict of not guilty. In the present case, for example, the petitioner proffered evidence that, if believed, squarely proved that White, not petitioner, was the perpetrator. It would make no sense, however, to hold that this proffer precluded the prosecution from introducing its evidence, including the forensic evidence that, if credited, provided strong proof of the petitioner's guilt.

The point is that, by evaluating the strength of only one party's evidence, no logical conclusion can be reached regarding the strength of contrary evidence offered by the other side to rebut or cast doubt. Because the rule applied by the State Supreme Court in this case did not heed this point, the rule is "arbitrary" in the sense that it does not rationally serve the end that the *Gregory* rule and other similar third-party guilt rules were designed to further. Nor has the State identified any other legitimate end that the rule serves. It follows that the rule applied in this case by the State Supreme Court violates a criminal defendant's right to have " 'a meaningful opportunity to present a complete defense.' " *[Vacated and remanded.]*

NOTE

Is Holmes Another Atypical case? Does *Holmes* provide additional arguments for defendants who want to admit evidence otherwise prohibited by statutes or rules, or is it an extreme example, not likely to provide support in more typical cases?

Chapter 12

WRITINGS AND EXHIBITS

ADDITIONAL REQUIREMENTS OF AUTHENTICATION (F.R.E. ARTICLE IX), BEST EVIDENCE (F.R.E. ARTICLE X), AND COMPLETENESS (F.R.E. ARTICLE I, RULE 106)

§ 12.01 AUTHENTICATION[1]

Read Federal Rules of Evidence 901, "Authenticating or Identifying Evidence" and 903, "Subscribing Witness's Testimony."

[A] Documents and Signatures

ALEXANDER DAWSON, INC. v. NATIONAL LABOR RELATIONS BOARD

United States Court of Appeals, Ninth Circuit
586 F.2d 1300 (1978)

PER CURIAM.

Alexander Dawson, Inc. (the company) petitioned for review of an order of the National Labor Relations Board.

The company contends that it was error for the Board to find that it had unlawfully refused to hire applicants Dunkle, Hardson, Walters, Chandler, Mighell, Lewman and Russo, since the finding was based solely on what it argues were improperly admitted, unauthenticated job application forms. These applicants did not testify at the hearing but application forms completed in their names were admitted into evidence . . . .

The ALJ [Administrative Law Judge] found the documents to be admissible under Rule 901(a) of the Federal Rules of Evidence.

The issue for the trial judge under Rule 901 is whether there is prima facie evidence, circumstantial or direct, that the document is what it is purported to be. If so, the document is admitted in evidence. It then remains for the trier of fact to make its own determination of the authenticity of the admitted evidence and the

---

[1] Study Guide Reference: Federal Rules of Evidence, Chapter 11:I; IV; and Chapter 3:II at "Illustration of the Balancing; Offering Replications: Results of Experiments that Attempt to Recreate Litigated Event or Portion Thereof; Reenactments; Simulations; Models; Photos; Graphic Representations."

weight which it feels the evidence should be given.

The ALJ's finding was based on the similarity of the challenged applications to those filed by applicants who testified and authenticated their own applications. He also noted that the company did not present any evidence to contradict this prima facie evidence of authenticity and did not attempt to prove the applications were fraudulently prepared.

The company challenges this basis of authentication, which it terms "authentication by similarity of underlying form," urging there is no such concept. We disagree. The content of a document, when considered with the circumstances surrounding its discovery, is an adequate basis for a ruling admitting it into evidence.

. . . It was reasonable for the ALJ to conclude that since all the applications appeared to come from the same source and were on the same form, and since the majority were conceded to be authentic applications for employment, a prima facie case of authenticity was established as to the seven remaining documents.

UNITED STATES v. CHIN

United States Court of Appeals, Second Circuit
371 F.3d 31 (2004)

McLaughlin, Circuit Judge.

Tin Yat Chin was convicted of one count of impersonating a federal officer and three counts of tax evasion after a jury trial. To support his claim that he was misidentified before and at trial, Tin Yat Chin proffered customer copies of credit card transaction receipts as part of an alibi notice. The district court excluded the receipts as unauthenticated under Fed. R. Evid. 901.

[W]e hold that the receipts were authenticated and admissible as non-hearsay, and the erroneous exclusion was not harmless.

Twenty-seven witnesses, primarily victims and their relatives and others with business connections to the swindler, testified at trial. Eleven victims and their relatives identified Tin Yat Chin as the swindler. However, [there were problems with some of the identifications].

Based on perceived weaknesses in the witnesses' identifications at trial, Tin Yat Chin energetically pressed his central defense theory: misidentification.

. . . Tin Yat Chin responded with an alibi notice and moved *in limine* to admit into evidence copies of credit card transaction receipts, allegedly bearing his signature, showing that he was in a Queens, New York, P.C. Richard & Sons store and a Queens Key Food supermarket at the time Government witnesses would testify that he was in China. A collection of receipts, including the P.C. Richard's receipt, dated July 7, and the Key Food receipts, dated July 8, 10, and 26, were produced by Tin Yat Chin's wife while Tin Yat Chin was detained in a federal correctional facility pending trial. At the time of his arrest, Tin Yat Chin had on his person a September 2001 Key Food receipt similar to the ones from July 1999.

. . . However, the district court excluded the receipts as unauthenticated under Fed.R.Evid. 901 and therefore refused to admit them under any other evidentiary rationale.

Specifically, the court held that "[Tin Yat Chin's] proffer fail[s] to provide a rational basis for concluding that the receipts are in fact customer copies of records of purchases made on particular dates at particular stores by [Tin Yat Chin]." The court . . . emphasized, in particular, that "[Tin Yat Chin] offers no evidence by any witness or any document that can establish that . . . his signature was placed on them at the time and place he proffers.". . .

The Government concedes the receipts were generated at the times and places designated on the receipts. Thus, the parties have narrowed their authenticity dispute down to whether Tin Yat Chin himself signed the receipts at the times and places indicated. There may be questions about the ultimate reliability of the receipts as proof of Tin Yat Chin's alibi, but the district court applied an unreasonably high standard for their authentication under Rule 901.

A district court has broad discretion to determine whether a piece of evidence has been properly authenticated. *United States v. Tropeano*, 252 F.3d 653, 661 (2d Cir. 2001).

Rule 901 provides that "[t]he requirement of authentication or identification as a condition precedent to admissibility is satisfied by evidence sufficient to support a finding that the matter in question is what its proponent claims." Fed. R. Evid. 901(a). Rule 901 "does not erect a particularly high hurdle," and that hurdle may be cleared by "circumstantial evidence." *United States v. Dhinsa*, 243 F.3d 635, 658–59 (2d Cir. 2001). The proponent is not required "to rule out all possibilities inconsistent with authenticity, or to prove beyond any doubt that the evidence is what it purports to be." *United States v. Pluta*, 176 F.3d 43, 49 (2d Cir. 1999). Rule 901's requirements are satisfied "if sufficient proof has been introduced so that a reasonable juror could find in favor of authenticity or identification." *Id.*

Once Rule 901's requirements are satisfied, " 'the evidence's persuasive force is left to the jury' " *Dhinsa*, 243 F.3d at 658 (quoting *United States v. Ortiz*, 966 F.2d 707, 716 (1st Cir. 1992)). . . [T]he other party then remains free to challenge the reliability of the evidence, to minimize its importance, or to argue alternative interpretations of its meaning, but these and similar other challenges go to the weight of the evidence — not to its admissibility.

The evidence that the receipts were signed by Tin Yat Chin at the times and places where they were generated is contradicted by testimony of Government witnesses who place him in China in July 1999. Another person, such as Tin Yat Chin's wife, a co-holder of the credit card, may have signed the originals which, having been destroyed, can no longer be compared to the copies bearing Tin Yat Chin's signature. Alternatively, store employees may have permitted Tin Yat Chin's wife either to complete the transactions without a signature or to separate the yellow copies and affix her signature to the merchant's copy, allowing her husband to sign the customer copies at a later date. These doubts about the ultimate reliability of the receipts, however, do not justify their exclusion under Rule 901's minimal standards for authentication.

The combined proffered testimony of: (1) Tin Yat Chin's wife (that she had not made the purchases), (2) the store managers (regarding their transaction practices), and (3) a handwriting expert (identifying Tin Yat Chin's signature) was sufficient to satisfy Rule 901's authentication requirements.

The district court also questioned, in particular, the authenticity of the July 7, 1999, P.C. Richard & Sons receipt. The accompanying charge card receipt lacked a date, and "[m]ost significantly, the expiration date of the charge card imprinted on the . . . sales slip is '11/99,' but the expiration date handwritten on the charge card receipt bearing defendant's signature is '9/00.' " Because the discrepancy between expiration dates was not raised by the Government or the district court during pre-trial argument on the motion *in limine*, Tin Yat Chin had no opportunity to explain it. In any event, these discrepancies alone — which may have been explained as a clerical error — do not alter our conclusions about the admissibility of the P.C. Richard & Sons receipt, nor are they relevant to the July 8, 10, and 26, Key Food receipts.

The Government and the district court all but concede that, had the receipts been authenticated, they would have been admissible as non-hearsay. They tended to show that a person referring to himself as "Tin Yat Chin" signed receipts on the dates and times in question, laying a foundation for the testimony of Tin Yat Chin's wife, store managers, and a handwriting expert to support Tin Yat Chin's alibi.

NOTES AND QUESTIONS

(1) *Authentication Only Requires Prima Facie Showing.* In *United States v. Goichman*, 547 F.2d 778 (3d Cir. 1976), the issues involved the determination of a tax deficiency using the net worth method. The net worth method aims to show that the defendant was spending more money than his reported income could support. Defendant William Goichman objected to the trial court's admission of a document entitled "History of Children's Assets" for the purpose of showing that the children's assets were purchased by Goichman. An IRS agent found the document in a state court clerk's office, in which court there had been an equity divorce support proceeding, *William A. Goichman v. Beverly Goichman*, in which the present defendant (William Goichman) claimed to have provided the funds for these assets. The "History" was a two-page unsigned document. The state court clerk certified the document as being from the original record. The Court of Appeals stated:

> Appellant correctly contends that the certification on the document does not govern its admissibility. It is well-settled that "no certified copy whatever may be used where the original record itself is not admissible under the rules of evidence for the purpose in hand." . . .
>
> What appellant overlooks is that the showing of authenticity is not on a par with more technical evidentiary rules, such as hearsay exceptions, governing admissibility. Rather, there need be only a prima facie showing, to the court, of authenticity, not a full argument on admissibility . . . .
>
> Here there was sufficient evidence to let the jury consider the relevance and weight of the document. It was certified as being part of the docket

> record in the prior Montgomery County support proceeding; it referred to children having the same first names as did Goichman's; the contents are corroborated (as pertaining to Goichman) by Goichman's complaint in that Montgomery County proceeding, exhibit 639, which was correctly attributed to appellant, and by bank statements as well. In sum, the document was supported by a prima facie showing of authenticity.

(2) *Authentication Compared to Business Records Foundation.* Frequently the same facts may be necessary to *authenticate* and to *establish the requisites for the business records exception to the hearsay rule.* For example, suppose a letter was offered, purportedly from the files of a lienholder company, stating to some third party "today we orally released the lien" (assume that the lienholder company is not a party to the lawsuit, only the question of misrepresentation to the lender being in issue). *Authentication* is needed to tie the letter to the lienholder, i.e., to show that the lienholder authored it. (Assume the person who allegedly signed is not present or available.) Additionally, there must be proof it is a record *of that company* in its *regular course of business* to survive the hearsay rule. Suppose an *affidavit* of a custodian of company files is offered, stating facts that would do both jobs (business records and authentication). An affidavit technically is inadmissible evidence. Could it be received to establish the requisites for the business records exception? (Who is the "decider" as to whether those requisites are made out?) Can the affidavit be received to *authenticate*? (Who is the ultimate "decider" on *that*? Who is the initial "decider"?) See the excellent discussion in *Zenith Radio Corp. v. Matsushita Elec. Ind. Co.*, 505 F. Supp. 1190 (E.D. Pa. 1980), containing a thorough exploration of many issues concerning business records and authentication. Some aspects of *Zenith* were reversed *sub nom. In re Japanese Electronics Products Litigation*, 723 F.2d 238 (3d Cir. 1983), but the discussion still is very viable. *See also Matsushita Elec. Ind. Co. v. Zenith Radio Corp.*, 475 U.S. 574 (1986).

Revisit *State v. Blake*, reproduced at § 9.06 (business records exception to the hearsay rule), supra. There were several things that needed to be authenticated. What were they? What methods recognized in Rule 901 were implicitly employed in that case to autheticate them?

(3) *Do Rule 901(b)'s Illustrations Require More than the Quantum of Evidence Needed to Satisfy Rule 901(a)?* Is there a conflict between Fed. R. Evid. 901(a) and (b)? Fed. R. Evid. 901(a) seems to say that what is required is a quantum and quality of evidence that would justify a reasonable person concluding that the purported signatory actually signed the document. But Fed. R. Evid. 901(b), with its illustrations, seems to require more than that. For example, if (b) were not present, wouldn't a judge be led by the language of (a) alone to hold that when a signature says "John Jones," a jury may decide, even without any other evidence, whether the document *was* signed by John Jones or not? Wouldn't a reasonable person in everyday life assume that it was? (Or is this not everyday life?) But the purport of (b) is that the judge is not to do this. The problem comes up where nothing in (b) fits the case, and the judge must rely on (a) to decide if there is sufficient authenticating evidence. (It also comes up in interpreting how much is required under (b).) Doesn't *Dawson, supra*, require very little? Is the fact that it was the company's files significant?

In view of what has just been said, how would you solve the following: A typewritten note, unsigned, which cannot be traced to a particular typewriter or printer, is found in a desk used 60 percent of the time by Smith and 40 percent of the time by others. Does this satisfy the authentication threshold required to tie the note to Smith? (Assume there are no other authenticating circumstances.)

(4) *What Quantum of Proof is Needed to Demonstrate Authenticity of an Exemplar?* In *United States v. Mangan*, 575 F.2d 32 (2d Cir.), *cert. denied*, 439 U.S. 931 (1978), Kevin and Frank Mangan were convicted of filing income tax returns for fictitious persons, claiming refunds. The Government's handwriting expert used as exemplars of Frank Mangan's handwriting (as the basis for his opinion that Frank wrote the fictitious returns) the body of two of his federal income tax returns and forms contained in Frank Mangan's personnel file, which were written mostly in block capitals, as were the fictitious returns. Although no witness testified that these were indeed written by Frank Mangan, the judge permitted them to be used as exemplars because of the statutory presumption (IRC § 6064) of the genuineness of the signatures on tax returns, the similarity of these signatures to those in the IRS personnel files (Frank was an employee of the IRS), the fact that the papers in the personnel file were of the sort that normally would be filled out by the employee, and the similarity of the material in block capitals on the returns and on the personnel forms. The court held that the exemplars were sufficiently authenticated. Fed. R. Evid. 901 treats the genuineness of an exemplar no differently than that of the writing in dispute. In contrast, California requires that the judge find the exemplar to be genuine before submitting it to the jury for comparison (Cal. Evid. Code § 1417).

(5) *Familiarity of a Lay Witness, with the Questioned Handwriting.* In *Hall v. United Ins. Co. of America*, 367 F.3d 1255 (11th Cir. 2004), a representative's affidavit provided insufficient foundation for affiant's conclusion that the signature on a termination of a life insurance policy was not the insured's. The decision discussed the interplay between Rule 901(b)(2), which allows non-expert opinion testimony about the genuineness of handwriting evidence based on sufficient familiarity, and Rule 701, which allows lay opinion testimony that is rationally based on personal perceptions. The affidavit stated that she (Hall, the affiant) became familiar with Bobby's (the purported signer's) handwriting over the course of thirty years, having seen him "write, [having] received correspondence from him, and [having] helped him review documents which he executed in my presence." She asserted that the signature on the waiver did not appear to be his. In the court's view, Hall's affidavit did not provide the proper foundation detailing how her familiarity with Bobby's handwriting was obtained:

> While witnessing the disputed signature is not required, *see, e.g., United States v. Tipton*, 964 F.2d 650, 655 (7th Cir. 1992), we conclude that the lay witness must provide more detailed information regarding any "correspondence," "documents," or the like, relied upon to establish familiarity. Such instruments must be identified with particularity . . . . Hall has provided no detailed information regarding either the instruments relied upon to garner familiarity with Bobby's handwriting or her relationship with him. Accordingly, we cannot say that the district court's decision to strike Hall's affidavit was an abuse of discretion.

Because Hall could not demonstrate sufficient familiarity, the district court held that the affidavit did not satisfy Rule 701 because her opinion "would not be rationally based on her own perceptions." Do you agree, or is the court imposing too high a threshold?

(6) *Failure to Identify Author Not Necessarily a Bar to Authentication.* The defendants in *United States v. Wilson*, 532 F.2d 641 (8th Cir.), *cert. denied*, 429 U.S. 846 (1976), were convicted of conspiracy to distribute heroin. In discussing whether the trial court erred in admitting against defendant two notebooks and their contents, despite the fact that the government did not know the identity of the author, the court said:

> [T]he contents of these notebooks refer to activities (in this case, drug trafficking) and are characterized by a code of which only someone connected with the transactions would have known. The writer uses nicknames of individuals and the code term "buttons" which the informant had testified were heroin capsules. The writer was obviously familiar with the procedures used by the defendants in their drug operations. Although the precise identity of the declarant is unknown, we think there was at least a prima facie showing that the declarant was a member of the drug conspiracy charged in the indictment.
>
> Moreover, there is other evidence which corroborates the authenticity of the notebooks. The books were found in an apartment which the informant said both "Punkin" and Brenda (two of the defendants) frequented, and in which drugs were sold. The apartment had an unusual hole in its door fitting the informant's description and a known co-conspirator was found there at the time of the raid. The informant further testified that the defendants' drug transactions were recorded in notebooks. This evidence in our view provides a prima facie showing of authenticity of the notebooks. This showing could have been, but was not, countered by any evidence from defendants that the documents were forged or otherwise not what the government claimed.

What was being authenticated in this case: that a particular author wrote the writing, or that it was issued in connection with a particular "business?"

(7) *Ancient Documents.* Authentication as an "ancient document" is well recognized. *See, e.g., West v. Houston Oil Co. of Texas*, 120 S.W. 228 (Tex. Civ. App. 1909):

> The reasons for this rule are: (1) After such a long lapse of time, ordinary testimonial evidence from those who saw the document's execution or knew the handwriting or heard the party admit its execution is practically unavailable and a necessity always exists for resorting to circumstantial evidence; and (2) the circumstance of age or long existence of the document, together with its proper custody, its unsuspicious appearance, and perhaps other circumstances, suffice, in combination, as evidence to be submitted to the jury.

Fed. R. Evid. 901(b)(8) only requires twenty years for a document to be considered "ancient." *Cf.* Rule 803(16). A number of states, such as California and

Texas, still adhere to the common law requirement of 30 years. *E.g.*, Cal. Evid. Code § 1331.

(9) *Is there a Relationship Between Authentication and Hearsay?* Can the entire problem of authentication be viewed as a hearsay problem? When a signature on a letter or other document purports to be that of "John Jones," isn't it an out-of-court statement (by an out-of-court declarant) asserting "This is John Jones'signature?" If any step in the use that is sought to be made of that letter or document depends (i.e., if its relevance depends) on the signature in fact being John Jones' signature, then the assertion is being offered as true, is it not?

LORRAINE v. MARKEL AMERICAN INSURANCE COMPANY

United States District Court, District of Maryland
241 F.R.D. 534 (2007)

Grimm, Chief United States Magistrate Judge.

Plaintiffs/Counter-Defendants Jack Lorraine and Beverly Mack bring this action to enforce a private arbitrator's award finding that certain damage to their yacht, *Chessie*, was caused by a lightning strike that occurred while *Chessie* was anchored in the Chesapeake Bay. Defendant/ Counter-Plaintiff Markel American Insurance Company ("Markel") likewise has counterclaimed to enforce the arbitrator's award, which, in addition to concluding that certain damage to *Chessie*'s hull was caused by lightning, also concluded that the damage incurred was limited to an amount of $14,100, plus incidental costs. Following discovery, Plaintiffs moved for summary judgment, and Defendants filed a response in opposition and cross motion for summary judgment. I denied without prejudice both motions for the reasons discussed more fully below.

BACKGROUND

It is difficult for the Court to provide the appropriate background to the underlying arbitration in this case because, as will be discussed in greater detail below, neither party has proffered any admissible evidence to support the facts set forth in their respective motions. The scope of the arbitration agreement is the basis of this litigation. The final agreement states, in relevant part,

> "The parties to this dispute . . . have agreed that an arbitrator shall determine whether certain bottom damage in the amount of $36,000, to the Yacht CHESSIE was caused by the lightning strike occurring on May 17, 2004, or osmosis, as claimed by [Markel]."

The arbitrator issued his award. . . . In it, he held that some, but not all, of *Chessie*'s hull damage was caused by lightning. This award forms the basis for the present litigation. . . .

SUMMARY JUDGMENT STANDARD

Summary judgment is appropriate when there exists no genuine issue as to any material fact and a decision may be rendered as a matter of law. If the party seeking summary judgment demonstrates that there is no evidence to support the nonmoving party's case, the burden shifts to the nonmoving party to identify specific facts showing that there is a genuine issue for trial. [T]he evidentiary materials submitted must show facts from which the finder of fact reasonably could find for the party opposing summary judgment. Moreover, to be entitled to consideration on summary judgment, the evidence supporting the facts set forth by the parties must be such as would be admissible in evidence. Unsworn, unauthenticated documents cannot be considered on a motion for summary judgment.

THE FEDERAL ARBITRATION ACT

. . . The question before the Court is whether the arbitrator exceeded his authority under the arbitration agreement by assigning a value to the damages attributable to the lightning strike that was less than the $36,000 claimed by Plaintiffs. If the answer is yes, then the court can vacate, remand, or modify the award. If the answer is no, then the court must grant Defendant's motion to confirm the award. . . .

Here, I find that the language of the arbitration agreement is ambiguous; it could be read either to permit the arbitrator to determine the amount of damage to *Chessie*, or to limit his authority to determining only whether the claimed damages were caused by the lightning strike. Under normal circumstances, the Court would look to the documentary evidence provided by the parties, which in this case includes the arbitration agreement, award, and copies of e-mail correspondence between counsel, ostensibly supplied as extrinsic evidence of the parties' intent with regard to the scope of the arbitration agreement. In this case, however, the admissibility problems with the evidence presented are manifest. First, none of the documentary evidence presented is authenticated by affidavit or otherwise. Next, most of the facts relevant to the contract negotiations at issue have been provided by counsel *ipse dixit*, without supporting affidavits or deposition testimony. The evidentiary problems associated with the copies of e-mail offered as parol evidence likewise are substantial because they were not authenticated, but instead were simply attached to the parties' motions as exhibits.

Because neither party to this dispute complied with the requirement that they support their motions with admissible evidence, I dismissed both motions without prejudice to allow resubmission with proper evidentiary support. I further observed that the unauthenticated e-mails are a form of computer generated evidence that pose evidentiary issues that are highlighted by their electronic medium. Given the pervasiveness today of electronically prepared and stored records, as opposed to the manually prepared records of the past, counsel must be prepared to recognize and appropriately deal with the evidentiary issues associated with the admissibility of electronically generated and stored evidence. Although cases abound regarding the discoverability of electronic records, research has failed to locate a comprehensive analysis of the many interrelated evidentiary issues associated with electronic evidence. Because there is a need for guidance to the bar regarding this subject, this opinion undertakes a broader and more detailed analysis of these issues than would be required simply to resolve the specific issues presented in this case. It is my hope that it will provide a helpful starting place for understanding the challenges associated with the admissibility of electronic evidence.

ADMISSIBILITY OF ELECTRONICALLY STORED INFORMATION

It has been noted that "[t]he Federal Rules of Evidence . . . do not separately address the admissibility of electronic data." . . . However, "the Federal Rules of Evidence apply to computerized data as they do to other types of evidence." Fed.R.Evid. 102 contemplates that the rules of evidence are flexible enough to accommodate future "growth and development" to address technical changes not in existence as of the codification of the rules themselves. Further, courts have had little difficulty using the existing rules of evidence to determine the admissibility of ESI, despite the technical challenges that sometimes must be overcome to do so. *See, e.g., In re F.P.* . . . ("Essentially, appellant would have us create a whole new body of law just to deal with e-mails or instant messages. . . . We believe that e-mail messages and similar forms of electronic communications can be properly authenticated within the existing framework of [the state rules of evidence].").

The process is complicated by the fact that ESI [i.e., electronically stored information] comes in multiple evidentiary "flavors," including e-mail, website ESI, internet postings, digital photographs, and computer-generated documents and data files.

Whether ESI is admissible into evidence is determined by a collection of evidence rules that present themselves like a series of hurdles to be cleared by the proponent of the evidence. Failure to clear any of these evidentiary hurdles means that the evidence will not be admissible. Whenever ESI is offered as evidence, either at trial or in summary judgment, the following evidence rules must be considered: (1) is the ESI **relevant** as determined by Rule 401 (does it have any tendency to make some fact that is of consequence to the litigation more or less probable than it otherwise would be); (2) if relevant under 401, is it **authentic** as required by Rule 901(a) (can the proponent show that the ESI is what it purports to be); (3) if the ESI is offered for its substantive truth, is it **hearsay** as defined by Rule 801, and if so, is it covered by an applicable exception (Rules 803, 804 and 807); (4) is the form of the ESI that is being offered as evidence an **original** or **duplicate** under the original writing rule, of if not, is there admissible secondary evidence to prove the content of the ESI (Rules 1001-1008); and (5) is the probative value of the ESI substantially outweighed by the danger of **unfair prejudice** or one of the other factors identified by Rule 403, such that it should be excluded despite its relevance. Preliminarily, the process by which the admissibility of ESI is determined is governed by Rule 104, which addresses the relationship between the judge and the jury with regard to preliminary fact finding associated with the admissibility of evidence. Because Rule 104 governs the very process of determining admissibility of ESI, it must be considered first.

Preliminary Rulings on Admissibility (Rule 104)

The relationship between Rule 104(a) and (b) can complicate the process by which ESI is admitted into evidence at trial, or may be considered at summary judgment. The rule states, in relevant part: [quoted]

When the judge makes a preliminary determination regarding the admissibility of evidence under Rule 104(a), the Federal Rules of Evidence, except for privilege, do not apply. Therefore, the court may consider hearsay or other evidence that would not be admissible if offered to the jury, and "hearings on preliminary matters need not be conducted with all the formalities and requirements of a trial." Accordingly, the trial judge may make preliminary determinations in chambers or at a sidebar conference in court.

The following types of preliminary matters typically are determined by the judge under Rule 104(a): whether an expert is qualified, and if so, whether his or her opinions are admissible; existence of a privilege; and whether evidence is hearsay, and if so, if any recognized exception applies.

The interplay between Rule 104(a) and 104(b) can be a bit tricky, which is illustrated by the manner in which evidence, whether ESI or "hard copy," must be authenticated under Rule 901(a). Authentication under Rule 901 is viewed as a subset of relevancy, because "evidence cannot have a tendency to make the existence of a disputed fact more or less likely if the evidence is not that which its proponent claims." Accordingly, "[r]esolution of whether evidence is authentic calls for a factual determination by the jury and admissibility, therefore, is governed by the procedure set forth in Federal Rule of Evidence 104(b) 'relating to matters of conditional relevance generally.' " In essence, determining whether ESI is authentic, and therefore relevant, is a two step process. First, "[b]efore admitting evidence for consideration by the jury, the district court must determine whether its proponent has offered a satisfactory foundation from which the jury could reasonably find that the evidence is authentic." Then, "because authentication is essentially a question of conditional relevancy, the jury ultimately resolves whether evidence admitted for its consideration is that which the proponent claims." As the Fourth Circuit summarized this process: "Although the district court is charged with making this preliminary determination, because authentication is essentially a question of conditional relevancy, the jury ultimately resolves whether evidence admitted for its consideration is that which the proponent claims. Because the ultimate resolution of authenticity is a question for the jury, in rendering its preliminary decision on whether the proponent of evidence has laid a sufficient foundation for admission the district court must necessarily assess the adequacy of the showing made before the jury." . . .

With respect to this two step process, the Fourth Circuit went on to state: "[a]n in camera hearing addressing authenticity does not replace the presentation of authenticating evidence before the jury; the district court must revisit this issue at trial. Thus, even though the district court may have ruled during an in camera proceeding that the proponent had presented sufficient evidence to support a finding that [the evidence] was authentic, evidence that would support the same ruling must be presented again, to the jury, before the [evidence] may be admitted."

. . .

In short, there is a significant difference between the way that Rule 104(a) and 104(b) operate. Because, under Rule 104(b), the jury, not the court, makes the factual findings that determine admissibility, the facts introduced must be admissible under the rules of evidence. *See, e.g., United States v. Safavian*, 435 F.Supp.2d 36, 41-42 (D.D.C.2006) (trial judge relied on proffers of government lawyers about facts learned by FBI agents during their investigation to make preliminary determination that e-mails were admissible, but cautioned that at trial the government would have to call witnesses with personal knowledge of facts and not rely on FBI agents' testimony about what others had told them regarding the origin of the e-mails); Saltzburg at § 901.02[5] ("In order for the trier of fact to make a rational decision as to authenticity [under Rule 104(b)], the foundation evidence must be admissible and it must actually be placed before the jury if the Judge admits the evidence").

It is important to understand this relationship when seeking to admit ESI. For example, if an e-mail is offered into evidence, the determination of whether it is authentic would be for the jury to decide under Rule 104(b), and the facts that they consider in making this determination must be admissible into evidence. In contrast, if the ruling on whether the e-mail is an admission by a party opponent or a business record turns on contested facts, the admissibility of those facts will be determined by the judge under 104(a), and the Federal Rules of Evidence, except for privilege, are inapplicable.

Relevance (Rules 401, 402, and 105)

The first evidentiary hurdle to overcome in establishing the admissibility of ESI is to demonstrate that it is relevant, as defined by Federal Rule of Evidence 401, which states: [quoted]

Clearly, facts that tend to prove essential elements of the causes of action and affirmative defenses asserted in the pleadings are "of consequence to the litigation," as are facts that tend to undermine or rehabilitate the credibility of the witnesses who will testify. So too, however, are background facts that, although they may not prove elements of the claims and defenses, and may not even be disputed, nonetheless routinely are admitted to help the fact finder understand the issues in the case and the evidence introduced to prove or disprove them. It is important to recognize that relevance is not a static concept; evidence is not relevant or irrelevant, occupying some rigid state of all or nothing. Instead, "[r]elevancy is not an inherent characteristic of any item of evidence but exists only as a relation between an item of evidence and a matter properly provable in the case." Fed.R.Evid. 401 advisory committee's note. As recognized by Federal Rule of Evidence 105, evidence may be admissible for one purpose, but not another, or against one party, but not another. Therefore, it is important for the proponent of the evidence to have considered all of the potential purposes for which it is offered, and to be prepared to articulate them to the court if the evidence is challenged. This point is particularly significant, as discussed below, when considering hearsay objections, where disputed evidence may be inadmissible hearsay if offered for its substantive truth, but admissible if offered for a reason other than its literal truth.

In assessing whether evidence is relevant under Rule 401, it also is important to remember that there is a distinction between the admissibility of evidence, and the weight to which it is entitled in the eyes of the fact finder, as Rule 104(e) instructs. Fed.R.Evid. 104(e) states: "[Rule 104] does not limit the right of a party to introduce before the jury evidence relevant to weight or credibility [of evidence that has been admitted by an adverse party]."

To be relevant, evidence does not have to carry any particular weight — it is sufficient if it has "any tendency" to prove or disprove a consequential fact in the litigation. Whether evidence tends to make a consequential fact more probable than it would be without the evidence is not a difficult showing to make. "To be relevant it is enough that the evidence has a *tendency* to make a consequential fact even the least bit more probable or less probable than it would be without the evidence. The question of relevance is thus different from whether evidence is *sufficient* to prove a point." . . .

The Federal Rules of Evidence are clear: evidence that is not relevant is never admissible. Fed.R.Evid. 402. Once evidence has been shown to meet the low threshold of relevance, however, it presumptively is admissible unless the constitution, a statute, rule of evidence or procedure, or case law requires that it be excluded. Thus, the function of all the rules of evidence other than Rule 401 is to help determine whether evidence which in fact is relevant should nonetheless be excluded. Fed.R.Evid. 402 advisory committee's note ("Succeeding rules [in Article IV of the rules of evidence] . . . in response to the demands of particular policies, require the exclusion of evidence despite its relevancy.").

Establishing that ESI has some relevance generally is not hard for counsel. Articulating all of what may be multiple grounds of relevance is something that is important, though not as frequently done as it should be. Accordingly, evidence that might otherwise be admitted may be excluded because the proponent put all his or her eggs in a single evidentiary basket, which the trial judge views as inapplicable, instead of carefully identifying each potential basis for admissibility. That was not the problem in this case, however, because the e-mail and other documentary evidence attached as exhibits to the summary judgment motions are relevant to determining the scope of the arbitration agreement between the parties, and therefore this evidence meets the requirements of Rule 401. Assuming, as is the case here, the proponent of ESI establishes its relevance and concomitant presumptive admissibility, the next step is to demonstrate that it is authentic. It is this latter step that the parties in this case omitted completely.

Authenticity (Rules 901-902)

In order for ESI [electronically stored evidence] to be admissible, it also must be shown to be authentic. Rule 901(a) defines what this entails: "[t]he requirement of authentication or identification as a condition precedent to admissibility is satisfied by evidence sufficient to support a finding that the matter in question is what its proponent claims." As already noted, "[a]uthentication and identification represent a special aspect of relevancy. . . . This requirement of showing authenticity or identity falls into the category of relevancy dependent upon fulfillment of a condition of fact and is governed by the procedure set forth in Rule 104(b)." Fed.R.Evid. 901 advisory committee's note.

A party seeking to admit an exhibit need only make a prima facie showing that it is what he or she claims it to be. This is not a particularly high barrier to overcome. For example, in *United States v. Safavian*, the court analyzed the admissibility of e-mail, noting, "[t]he question for the court under Rule 901 is whether the proponent of the evidence has 'offered a foundation from which the jury could reasonably find that the evidence is what the proponent says it is . . .' The Court need not find that the evidence is necessarily what the proponent claims, but only that there is sufficient evidence that the *jury* ultimately might do so."

[T]he inability to get evidence admitted because of a failure to authenticate it almost always is a self-inflicted injury which can be avoided by thoughtful advance preparation. *See, e.g.*, *In re Vee Vinhnee* (proponent failed properly to authenticate exhibits of electronically stored business records); *United States v. Jackson* (proponent failed to authenticate exhibits taken from an organization's website); *St. Luke's Cataract and Laser Institute PA v. Sanderson* (excluding exhibits because affidavits used to authenticate exhibits showing content of web pages were factually inaccurate and affiants lacked personal knowledge of facts); *Rambus v. Infineon Tech. AG* (proponent failed to authenticate computer generated business records); *Wady v. Provident Life and Accident Ins. Co. of Am.* (sustaining an objection to affidavit of witness offered to authenticate exhibit that contained documents taken from defendant's website because affiant lacked personal knowledge); *Indianapolis Minority Contractors Assoc., Inc. v. Wiley* (proponent of computer records failed to show that they were from a system capable of producing reliable and accurate results, and therefore, failed to authenticate them).

In *In re Vee Vinhnee*, the court addressed the authentication of electronically stored business records. It observed "[a]uthenticating a paperless electronic record, in principle, poses the same issue as for a paper record, the only difference being the format in which the record is maintained. . ." However, it quickly noted "[t]he paperless electronic record involves a difference in the format of the record that presents more complicated variations on the authentication problem than for paper records. Ultimately, however, it all boils down to the same question of assurance that the record is what it purports to be." The court did conclude, however, that "it is becoming recognized that early versions of computer foundations were too cursory, even though the basic elements covered the ground," before exercising a demanding analysis of the foundation needed to authenticate a paperless business record and lay the foundation for the business record exception to the hearsay rule, ultimately ruling that a proper foundation had not been established, and excluding the evidence. *See also* Manual for Complex Litigation ("In general, the Federal Rules of Evidence apply to computerized data as they do to other types of evidence. Computerized data, however, raise unique issues concerning accuracy and authenticity. Accuracy may be impaired by incomplete data entry, mistakes in output instructions, programming errors, damage and contamination of storage media, power outages, and equipment malfunctions. The integrity of data may also be compromised in the course of discovery by improper search and retrieval techniques, data conversion, or mishandling. The proponent of computerized evidence has the burden of laying a proper foundation by establishing its accuracy. The judge should therefore consider the accuracy and reliability of computerized evidence, including any necessary discovery during pretrial proceedings, so that challenges to the evidence are not made for the first time at trial").

Although courts have recognized that authentication of ESI may require greater scrutiny than that required for the authentication of "hard copy" documents, they have been quick to reject calls to abandon the existing rules of evidence when doing so. For example, in *In re F.P.*, the court addressed the authentication required to introduce transcripts of instant message conversations. In rejecting the defendant's challenge to this evidence, it stated:

> "Essentially, appellant would have us create a whole new body of law just to deal with e-mails or instant messages. The argument is that e-mails or text messages are inherently unreliable because of their relative anonymity and the fact that while an electronic message can be traced to a particular computer, it can rarely be connected to a specific author with any certainty. Unless the purported author is actually witnessed sending the e-mail, there is always the possibility it is not from whom it claims. As appellant correctly points out, anybody with the right password can gain access to another's e-mail account and send a message ostensibly from that person. However, the same uncertainties exist with traditional written documents. A signature can be forged; a letter can be typed on another's typewriter; distinct letterhead stationary can be copied or stolen. We believe that e-mail messages and similar forms of electronic communication can be properly authenticated within the existing framework of PaR.E. 901 and Pennsylvania case law . . . We see no justification for constructing unique rules of admissibility of electronic communications such as instant messages; they are to be evaluated on a case-by-case basis as any other document to determine whether or not there has been an adequate foundational showing of their relevance and authenticity."

Indeed, courts increasingly are demanding that proponents of evidence obtained from electronically stored information pay more attention to the foundational requirements than has been customary for introducing evidence not produced from electronic sources.

In general, electronic documents or records that are merely stored in a computer raise no computer-specific authentication issues. If a computer processes data rather than merely storing it, authentication issues may arise. The need for authentication and an explanation of the computer's processing will depend on the complexity and novelty of the computer processing. There are many states in the development of computer data where error can be introduced, which can adversely affect the accuracy and reliability of the output. Inaccurate results occur most often because of bad or incomplete data inputting, but can also happen when defective software programs are used or stored-data media become corrupted or damaged.

The authentication requirements of Rule 901 are designed to set up a threshold preliminary standard to test the reliability of evidence, subject to later review by an opponent's cross-examination. Factors that should be considered in evaluating the reliability of computer-based evidence include the error rate in data inputting, and the security of the systems. The degree of foundation required to authenticate computer-based evidence depends on the quality and completeness of the data input, the complexity of the computer processing, the routineness of the computer operation, and the ability to test and verify results of the computer processing.

Determining what degree of foundation is appropriate in any given case is in the judgment of the court. The required foundation will vary not only with the particular circumstances but also with the individual judge.

Obviously, there is no "one size fits all" approach that can be taken when authenticating electronic evidence, in part because technology changes so rapidly that it is often new to many judges.

Although Rule 901(a) addresses the requirement to authenticate electronically generated or electronically stored evidence, it is silent regarding how to do so. Rule 901(b), however, provides examples of how authentication may be accomplished. It states: [quoted]

The ten methods identified by Rule 901(b) are non-exclusive. . . *See also United States v. Simpson*, 152 F.3d 1241, 1249 (10th Cir.1998) (evaluating methods of authenticating a printout of the text of a chat room discussion between the defendant and an undercover detective in a child pornography case).

When faced with resolving authentication issues for electronic evidence, courts have used a number of the methods discussed in Rule 901(b), as well as approved some methods not included in that rule.

Rule 901(b)(1).

This rule permits authentication by: "[t]estimony that a matter is what it is claimed to be." This rule contemplates a broad spectrum including testimony of a witness who was present at the signing of a document. . . . "[I]n recognition of the proponent's light burden of proof in authenticating an exhibit . . . the 'knowledge' requirement of Rule 901(b)(1) is liberally construed. A witness may be appropriately knowledgeable through having participated in or observed the event reflected by the exhibit." [Citation.] Courts considering the admissibility of electronic evidence frequently have acknowledged that it may be authenticated by a witness with personal knowledge. *United States v. Kassimu* (ruling that copies of a post office's computer records could be authenticated by a custodian or other qualified witness with personal knowledge of the procedure that generated the records); *St. Luke's* ("To authenticate printouts from a website, the party proffering the evidence must produce 'some statement or affidavit from someone with knowledge [of the website] . . . for example [a] web master or someone else with personal knowledge would be sufficient.' "); *Safavian* (noting that e-mail may be authenticated by a witness with knowledge that the exhibit is what it is presented as); *Wady* (sustaining objection to affidavit of plaintiff's witness attempting to authenticate documents taken from the defendant's website because the affiant lacked personal knowledge of who maintained the website or authored the documents). Although Rule 901(b)(1) certainly is met by the testimony of a witness that actually drafted the exhibit, it is not required that the authenticating witness have personal knowledge of the making of a particular exhibit if he or she has personal knowledge of how that type of exhibit is routinely made.

> "Oftentimes a witness need not be familiar with specific exhibits to be sufficiently knowledgeable to authenticate or identify them. Business records and records of government agencies, for example, are frequently authenticated by witnesses who have never seen the specific records that comprise the exhibits and know nothing about the specific information they contain. Their authentication is accomplished when a witness identifies the exhibits as documents of a type that the organization typically develops, and testifies about the procedures the organization follows in generating, acquiring, and maintaining documents of that type, and explains the method by which the specific exhibits were retrieved from the organization's files. Similarly, exhibits that are automatically produced upon the occurrence of specified events may be authenticated by the testimony of persons with knowledge of the system or process that results in the production of the exhibit." [Weinstein]

It is necessary, however, that the authenticating witness provide factual specificity about the process by which the electronically stored information is created, acquired, maintained, and preserved without alteration or change, or the process by which it is produced if the result of a system or process that does so, as opposed to boilerplate, conclusory statements that simply parrot the elements of the business record exception to the hearsay rule, Rule 803(6), or public record exception, Rule 803(8).

Rule 901(b)(3).

This rule allows authentication or identification by "[c]omparison by the trier of fact or by expert witnesses with specimens which have been authenticated." Interestingly, the rule allows either expert opinion testimony to authenticate a questioned document by comparing it to one known to be authentic, or by permitting the factfinder to do so. Obviously, the specimen used for the comparison with the document to be authenticated must be shown itself to be authentic. This may be accomplished by any means allowable by Rule 901 or 902, as well as by using other exhibits already admitted into evidence at trial, or admitted into evidence by judicial notice under Rule 201. Although the common law origin of Rule 901(b)(3) involved its use for authenticating handwriting or signatures, it now is commonly used to authenticate documents, and at least one court has noted its appropriate use for authenticating e-mail. *Safavian* (E-mail messages "that are not clearly identifiable on their own can be authenticated . . . by comparison by the trier of fact (the jury) with 'specimens which have been [otherwise] authenticated' — in this case, those e-mails that already have been independently authenticated under Rule 901(b)(4).").

Rule 901(b)(4).

This rule is one of the most frequently used to authenticate e-mail and other electronic records. It permits exhibits to be authenticated or identified by "[a]ppearance, contents, substance, internal patterns, or other distinctive characteristics, taken in conjunction with circumstances." The commentary to Rule 901(b)(4) observes "[t]he characteristics of the offered item itself, considered in the light of circumstances, afford authentication techniques in great variety," including authenticating an exhibit by showing that it came from a "particular person by virtue of its disclosing knowledge of facts known peculiarly to him," or authenticating "by content and circumstances indicating it was in reply to a duly authenticated" document. Use of this rule often is characterized as authentication solely by "circumstantial evidence." Courts have recognized this rule as a means to authenticate ESI, including e-mail, text messages and the content of websites. *See United States v. Siddiqui* (allowing the authentication of an e-mail entirely by circumstantial evidence, including the presence of the defendant's work e-mail address, content of which the defendant was familiar with, use of the defendant's nickname, and testimony by witnesses that the defendant spoke to them about the subjects contained in the e-mail); *Safavian* (same result regarding e-mail); *In re F.P.* (noting that authentication could be accomplished by direct evidence, circumstantial evidence, or both, but ultimately holding that transcripts of instant messaging conversation circumstantially were authenticated based on presence of defendant's screen name, use of defendant's first name, and content of threatening message, which other witnesses had corroborated); *Perfect 10, Inc. v. Cybernet Ventures, Inc.* (admitting website postings as evidence due to circumstantial indicia of authenticity, including dates and presence of identifying web addresses).

One method of authenticating electronic evidence under Rule 901(b)(4) is the use of "hash values" or "hash marks" when making documents. A hash value is: "A unique numerical identifier that can be assigned to a file, a group of files, or a portion of a file, based on a standard mathematical algorithm applied to the characteristics of the data set. The most commonly used algorithms, known as MD5 and SHA, will generate numerical values so distinctive that the chance that any two data sets will have the same hash value, no matter how similar they appear, is less than one in one billion. 'Hashing' is used to guarantee the authenticity of an original data set and can be used as a digital equivalent of the Bates stamp used in paper document production." . . .

Hash values can be inserted into original electronic documents when they are created to provide them with distinctive characteristics that will permit their authentication under Rule 901(b)(4). Also, they can be used during discovery of electronic records to create a form of electronic "Bates stamp" that will help establish the document as electronic. This underscores a point that counsel often overlook. A party that seeks to introduce its own electronic records may have just as much difficulty authenticating them as one that attempts to introduce the electronic records of an adversary. Because it is so common for multiple versions of electronic documents to exist, it sometimes is difficult to establish that the version that is offered into evidence is the "final" or legally operative version. This can plague a party seeking to introduce a favorable version of its own electronic records, when the adverse party objects that it is not the legally operative version, given the production in discovery of multiple versions. Use of hash values when creating the "final" or "legally operative" version of an electronic record can insert distinctive characteristics into it that allow its authentication under Rule 901(b)(4).

Another way in which electronic evidence may be authenticated under Rule 901(b)(4) is by examining the metadata for the evidence. Metadata, "commonly described as 'data about data,' is defined as 'information describing the history, tracking, or management of an electronic document.' *The Sedona Guidelines: Best Practice Guidelines & Commentary for Managing Information & Records in the Electronic Age* defines metadata as 'information about a particular data set which describes how, when and by whom it was collected, created, accessed, or modified and how it is formatted (including data demographics such as size, location, storage requirements and media information).' Technical Appendix E to the *Sedona Guidelines* provides an extended description of metadata. It further defines metadata to include 'all of the contextual, processing, and use information needed to identify and certify the scope, authenticity, and integrity of active or archival electronic information or records.' Some examples of metadata for electronic documents include: a file's name, a file's location (e.g., directory structure or pathname), file format or file type, file size, file dates (e.g., creation date, date of last data modification, date of last data access, and date of last metadata modification), and file permissions (e.g., who can read the data, who can write to it, who can run it). Some metadata, such as file dates and sizes, can easily be seen by users; other metadata can be hidden or embedded and unavailable to computer users who are not technically adept." *Williams v. Sprint/United Mgmt. Co.*; Federal Judicial Center, *Managing Discovery of Electronic Information: A Pocket Guide for Judges*, Federal Judicial Center (defining metadata as "[i]nformation about a particular data set or document which describes how, when, and by whom the data set or document was collected, created, accessed, or modified . . ."). Recently revised Federal Rule of Civil Procedure 34 permits a party to discover electronically stored information and to identify the form or forms in which it is to be produced. A party therefore can request production of electronically stored information in its "native format," which includes the metadata for the electronic document. Because metadata shows the date, time and identity of the creator of an electronic record, as well as all changes made to it, metadata is a distinctive characteristic of all electronic evidence that can be used to authenticate it under Rule 901(b)(4). Although specific source code markers that constitute metadata can provide a useful method of authenticating electronically stored evidence, this method is not foolproof because, "[a]n unauthorized person may be able to obtain access to an unattended computer. Moreover, a document or database located on a networked-computer system can be viewed by persons on the network who may modify it. In addition, many network computer systems usually provide for a selected network administrators to override an individual password identification number to gain access when necessary." . . . [*S*]*ee also Fennell v. First Step Designs, Ltd.* (discussing how metadata markers can reflect that a document was modified when in fact it simply was saved to a different location). Despite its lack of conclusiveness, however, metadata certainly is a useful tool for authenticating electronic records by use of distinctive characteristics.

Rule 901(b)(7).

This Rule permits authentication by "Evidence that a writing authorized by law to be recorded or filed and in fact recorded or filed in a public office, or a purported public record, report, statement, or data compilation, in any form, is from the public office where items of this nature are kept." The commentary to Rule 901(b)(7) recognizes that it applies to computerized public records, noting that "[p]ublic records are regularly authenticated by proof of custody, without more. [Rule 901(b)(7)] extends the principle to include data stored in computers and similar methods, of which increasing use in the public records area may be expected." To use this rule the "proponent of the evidence need only show that the office from which the records were taken is the legal custodian of the records." . . . This may be done by "[a] certificate of authenticity from the public office; [t]he testimony of an officer who is authorized to attest to custodianship, [or] the testimony of a witness with knowledge that the evidence is in fact from a public office authorized to keep such a record." . . . Examples of the types of public records that may be authenticated by Rule 901(b)(7) include tax returns, weather bureau records, military records, social security records, INS records, VA records, official records from federal, state and local agencies, judicial records, correctional records, law enforcement records, and data compilations, which may include computer stored records.

Courts have recognized the appropriateness of authenticating computer stored public records under Rule 901(b)(7) as well, and observed that under this rule, unlike Rule 901(b)(9), there is no need to show that the computer system producing the public records was reliable or the records accurate. For example, in *United States v. Meienberg*, the court rejected defendant's challenge to the admissibility of a law enforcement agency's computerized records. Defendant argued that the only way they could be authenticated was under Rule 901(b)(9), through proof that they were produced by a system or process capable of producing a reliable result. Defendant further argued that the records had not been shown to be accurate. The appellate court disagreed, holding that the records properly had been authenticated under Rule 901(b)(7), which did not require a showing of accuracy. The court noted that any question regarding the accuracy of the records went to weight rather than admissibility. 263 F.3d at 1181. Thus, a decision to authenticate under Rule 901(b)(7), as opposed to 901(b)(9) may mean that the required foundation is much easier to prove. This underscores the importance of the point previously made, that there may be multiple ways to authenticate a particular computerized record, and careful attention to all the possibilities may reveal a method that significantly eases the burden of authentication.

Rule 901(b)(9).

This Rule recognizes one method of authentication that is particularly useful in authenticating electronic evidence stored in or generated by computers. It authorizes authentication by "[e]vidence describing a process or system used to produce a result and showing that the process or system produces an accurate result. This rule was "designed for situations in which the accuracy of a result is dependent upon a process or system which produces it." Fed.R.Evid. 901(b)(9) advisory committee's note. *See also* Weinstein ("Computer output may be authenticated under Rule 901(b)(9).. . . When the proponent relies on the provisions of Rule 901(b)(9) instead of qualifying the computer-generated information for a hearsay exception, it is common for the proponent to provide evidence of the input procedures and their accuracy, and evidence that the computer was regularly tested for programming errors. At a minimum, the proponent should present evidence sufficient to warrant a finding that the information is trustworthy and provide the opponent with an opportunity to inquire into the accuracy of the computer and of the input procedures."); *In re Vee Vinhnee* ("Rule 901(b)(9), which is designated as an example of a satisfactory authentication, describes the appropriate authentication for results of a process or system and contemplates evidence describing the process or system used to achieve a result and demonstration that the result is accurate. The advisory committee note makes plain that Rule 901(b)(9) was designed to encompass computer-generated evidence . . ."). In *Vinhnee*, the court cited with approval an eleven-step foundational authentication for computer records. . . . Although this foundation is elaborate, and many courts might not be so demanding as to require that it be followed to authenticate computer generated records, the fact that one court already has done so should put prudent counsel on notice that they must pay attention to how they will authenticate computer generated records, and that they should be prepared to do so in a manner that complies with the Federal Rules of Evidence and any governing precedent. The price for failing to do so may be, as in *In re Vee Vinhnee*, exclusion of the exhibit.

Rule 902.

In addition to the non-exclusive methods of authentication identified in Rule 901(b), Rule 902 identifies twelve methods by which documents, including electronic ones, may be authenticated without extrinsic evidence. This is commonly referred to as "self-authentication." The rule states: [quoted]

The obvious advantage of Rule 902 is that it does not require the sponsoring testimony of any witness to authenticate the exhibit-its admissibility is determined simply by examining the evidence itself, along with any accompanying written declaration or certificate required by Rule 902. The mere fact that the rule permits self-authentication, however, does not foreclose the opposing party from challenging the authenticity. Because Rule 104(b) applies in such cases, the exhibit and the evidence challenging its authenticity goes to the jury, which ultimately determines whether it is authentic. Some of the examples contained in Rule 902, such as Rule 902(3) (foreign public documents), 902(4) (certified copies of public records), 902(8) (acknowledged documents), 902(11) (certified copies of domestic records of a regularly conducted activity), and 902(12) (certified foreign records of regularly conducted activity), do require a certificate signed by a custodian or other qualified person to accomplish the self-authentication.

Although all of the examples contained in Rule 902 could be applicable to computerized records, three in particular have been recognized by the courts to authenticate electronic evidence: 902(5) (official publications); 902(7) (trade inscriptions); and, 902(11) (certified domestic records of regularly conducted activity). The first, Rule 902(5), provides: "(5) Official publications. Books, pamphlets, or other publications purporting to be issued by public authority."

The rule "[dispenses] with preliminary proof of the genuineness of purportedly official publications . . . [but] does not confer admissibility upon all official publications; it merely provides a means whereby their authenticity may be taken as established for purposes of admissibility." Fed.R.Evid. 902(5) advisory committee's note. This means that, to be admissible, the proponent may also need to establish that the official record qualifies as a public record hearsay exception under

Rule 803(8). Although the rule is silent regarding the level of government that must authorize the publication, commentators suggest that the list includes the United States, any State, district, commonwealth, territory or insular possession of the United States, the Panama Canal Zone, the Trust Territory of the Pacific islands, or a political subdivision, department, officer, or agency of any of the foregoing.

In *Equal Employment Opportunity Commission v. E.I. DuPont de Nemours and Co.*, the court admitted into evidence printouts of postings on the website of the United States Census Bureau as self-authenticating under Rule 902(5). Given the frequency with which official publications from government agencies are relevant to litigation and the increasing tendency for such agencies to have their own websites, Rule 902(5) provides a very useful method of authenticating these publications. When combined with the public records exception to the hearsay rule, Rule 803(8), these official publications posted on government agency websites should be admitted into evidence easily.

Rule 902(7) provides that exhibits may be self-authenticated by "[i]nscriptions, signs, tags, or labels purporting to have been affixed in the course of business and indicating ownership, control, or origin." As one commentator has noted, "[u]nder Rule 902(7), labels or tags affixed in the course of business require no authentication. Business e-mails often contain information showing the origin of the transmission and identifying the employer-company. The identification marker alone may be sufficient to authenticate an e-mail under Rule 902(7)." [Weinstein]

Rule 902(11) also is extremely useful because it affords a means of authenticating business records under Rule 803(6), one of the most used hearsay exceptions, without the need for a witness to testify in person at trial. It provides: [quoted]

This rule was intended to "[set] forth a procedure by which parties can authenticate certain records of regularly conducted activity, other than through the testimony of a foundation witness." Fed.R.Evid. 902(11) advisory committee's note. Unlike most of the other authentication rules, Rule 902(11) also contains a notice provision, requiring the proponent to provide written notice of the intention to use the rule to all adverse parties and to make available to them the records sufficiently in advance of litigation to permit a fair opportunity to challenge them. Because compliance with Rule 902(11) requires the proponent to establish all the elements of the business record exception to the hearsay rule, Rule 803(6), courts usually analyze the authenticity issue under Rule 902(11) concomitantly with the business record hearsay exception.

Finally, Rule 901(b) makes clear that the ten examples listed are illustrative only, not exhaustive. In ruling on whether electronic evidence has been properly authenticated, courts have been willing to think "outside of the box" to recognize new ways of authentication. For example, they have held that documents provided to a party during discovery by an opposing party are presumed to be authentic, shifting the burden to the producing party to demonstrate that the evidence that they produced was not authentic. *Perfect 10*, 213 F.Supp.2d at 1153-54 (finding that exhibits of website postings had been properly authenticated for three reasons, including that certain of them had been provided to the plaintiff by the defendant during discovery).

In *Telewizja Polska USA*, the court embraced a non-traditional method of authentication when faced with determining whether exhibits depicting the content of the defendant's website at various dates several years in the past were admissible. The plaintiff offered an affidavit from a representative of the Internet Archive Company, which retrieved copies of the defendant's website as it appeared at relevant dates to the litigation though use of its "wayback machine." The "wayback machine" refers to the process used by the Internet Archive Company, www.archive.org, to allow website visitors to search for archived web pages of organizations. The defendant objected, contending that the Internet Archive was not a reliable source, and thus the exhibits had not been authenticated. The court disagreed, stating:

> "Federal Rule of Evidence 901 'requires only a prima facie showing of genuineness and leaves it to the jury to decide the true authenticity and probative value of the evidence.' Admittedly, the Internet Archive does not fit neatly into any of the non-exhaustive examples listed in Rule 901; the Internet Archive is a relatively new source for archiving websites. Nevertheless, Plaintiff has presented no evidence that the Internet Archive is unreliable or biased. And Plaintiff has neither denied that the exhibit represents the contents of its website on the dates in question, nor come forward with its own evidence challenging the veracity of the exhibit. Under these circumstances, the Court is of the opinion that [the affidavit from the representative of the Internet Archive Company] is sufficient to satisfy Rule 901's threshold requirement for admissibility."

Additionally, authentication may be accomplished by the court taking judicial notice under Rule 201 of certain foundational facts needed to authenticate an electronic record. Judicial notice could be a helpful way to establish certain well known characteristics of computers, how the internet works, scientific principles underlying calculations performed within computer programs, and many similar facts that could facilitate authenticating electronic evidence.

Authentication also can be accomplished in civil cases by taking advantage of Fed.R.Civ.P. 36, which permits a party to request that his or her opponent admit the "genuineness of documents." Also, at a pretrial conference, pursuant to Fed.R.Civ.P. 16(c)(3), a party may request that an opposing party agree to stipulate "regarding the authenticity of documents," and the court may take "appropriate action" regarding that request. Similarly, if a party properly makes his or her Fed. R. Civ. P. 26(a)(3) pretrial disclosures of documents and exhibits, then the other side has fourteen days in which to file objections. Failure to do so waives all objections other than under Rules 402 or 403, unless the court excuses the waiver for good cause. This means that if the opposing party does not raise authenticity objections within the fourteen days, they are waived.

The above discussion underscores the need for counsel to be creative in identifying methods of authenticating electronic evidence when the facts support a conclusion that the evidence is reliable, accurate, and authentic, regardless of whether there is a particular example in Rules 901 and 902 that neatly fits.

Finally, any serious consideration of the requirement to authenticate electronic evidence needs to acknowledge that, given the wide diversity of such evidence, there is no single approach to authentication that will work in all instances. It is possible, however, to identify certain authentication issues that have been noted by courts and commentators with particular types of electronic evidence and to be forearmed with this knowledge to develop authenticating facts that address these concerns.

E-mail

Perhaps because of the spontaneity and informality of e-mail, people tend to reveal more of themselves, for better or worse, than in other more deliberative forms of written communication. For that reason, e-mail evidence often figures prominently in cases where state of mind, motive and intent must be proved. Indeed, it is not unusual to see a case consisting almost entirely of e-mail evidence. There are many ways in which e-mail evidence may be authenticated. [E]-mail messages may be authenticated by direct or circumstantial evidence. An e-mail message's distinctive characteristics, including its contents, substance, internal patterns, or other distinctive characteristics, taken in conjunction with circumstances may be sufficient for authentication.

Printouts of e-mail messages ordinarily bear the sender's e-mail address, providing circumstantial evidence that the message was transmitted by the person identified in the e-mail address. In responding to an e-mail message, the person receiving the message may transmit the reply using the computer's reply function, which automatically routes the message to the address from which the original message came. Use of the reply function indicates that the reply message was sent to the sender's listed e-mail address.

The contents of the e-mail may help show authentication by revealing details known only to the sender and the person receiving the message.

E-mails may even be self-authenticating. Under Rule 902(7), labels or tags affixed in the course of business require no authentication. Business e-mails often contain information showing the origin of the transmission and identifying the employer-company. The identification marker alone may be sufficient to authenticate an e-mail under Rule 902(7). However, the sending address in an e-mail message is not conclusive, since e-mail messages can be sent by persons other than the named sender. For example, a person with unauthorized access to a computer can transmit e-mail messages under the computer owner's name. Because of the potential for unauthorized transmission of e-mail messages, authentication requires testimony from a person with personal knowledge of the transmission or receipt to ensure its trustworthiness. *See, e.g.*, *Siddiqui*, 235 F.3d at 1322-23 (E-mail may be authenticated entirely by circumstantial evidence, including its distinctive characteristics); *Safavian*, 435 F.Supp.2d at 40 (recognizing that e-mail may be authenticated by distinctive characteristics 901(b)(4), or by comparison of exemplars with other e-mails that already have been authenticated 901(b)(3)); *Rambus*, 348 F.Supp.2d 698 (E-mail that qualifies as business record may be self-authenticating under 902(11)); *In re F.P.*, 878 A.2d at 94 (E-mail may be authenticated by direct or circumstantial evidence).The most frequent ways to authenticate e-mail evidence are 901(b)(1) (person with personal knowledge), 901(b)(3) (expert testimony or comparison with authenticated exemplar), 901(b)(4) (distinctive characteristics, including circumstantial evidence), 902(7) (trade inscriptions), and

902(11) (certified copies of business record).

Internet Website Postings

Courts often have been faced with determining the admissibility of exhibits containing representations of the contents of website postings of a party at some point relevant to the litigation. Their reaction has ranged from the famous skepticism expressed in *St. Clair v. Johnny's Oyster and Shrimp, Inc.* —

> "Plaintiff's electronic 'evidence' is totally insufficient to withstand Defendant's Motion to Dismiss. While some look to the Internet as an innovative vehicle for communication, the Court continues to warily and wearily view it largely as one large catalyst for rumor, innuendo, and misinformation. So as to not mince words, the Court reiterates that this so-called Web provides no way of verifying the authenticity of the alleged contentions that Plaintiff wishes to rely upon in his Response to Defendant's Motion. There is no way Plaintiff can overcome the presumption that the information he discovered on the Internet is inherently untrustworthy. Anyone can put anything on the Internet. No web-site is monitored for accuracy and *nothing* contained therein is under oath or even subject to independent verification absent underlying documentation. Moreover, the Court holds no illusions that hackers can adulterate the content on *any* web-site from *any* location at *any* time. For these reasons, any evidence procured off the Internet is adequate for almost nothing, even under the most liberal interpretation of the hearsay exception rules found in Fed.R.Evid. 807. Instead of relying on the voodoo information taken from the Internet, Plaintiff must hunt for hard copy back-up documentation in admissible form from the United States Coast Guard or discover alternative information verifying what Plaintiff alleges."

— to the more permissive approach taken in *Perfect 10* [where] the court noted that a "reduced evidentiary standard" applied to the authentication of exhibits purporting to depict the defendant's website postings during a preliminary injunction motion. The court found that the exhibits had been authenticated because of circumstantial indicia of authenticity, a failure of the defendant to deny their authenticity, and the fact that the exhibits had been produced in discovery by the defendant. The court declined to require proof that the postings had been done by the defendant or with its authority, or evidence to disprove the possibility that the contents had been altered by third parties.

The issues that have concerned courts include the possibility that third persons other than the sponsor of the website were responsible for the content of the postings, leading many to require proof by the proponent that the organization hosting the website actually posted the statements or authorized their posting. *See United States v. Jackson* (excluding evidence of website postings because proponent failed to show that sponsoring organization actually posted the statements, as opposed to a third party); *St. Luke's* (plaintiff failed to authenticate exhibits of defendant's website postings because affidavits used to authenticate the exhibits were factually inaccurate and the author lacked personal knowledge of the website). One commentator [Joseph] has observed "[i]n applying [the authentication standard] to website evidence, there are three questions that must be answered explicitly or implicitly. (1) What was actually on the website? (2) Does the exhibit or testimony accurately reflect it? (3) If so, is it attributable to the owner of the site?" The same author suggests that the following factors will influence courts in ruling whether to admit evidence of internet postings:

> "The length of time the data was posted on the site; whether others report having seen it; whether it remains on the website for the court to verify; whether the data is of a type ordinarily posted on that website or websites of similar entities (e.g. financial information from corporations); whether the owner of the site has elsewhere published the same data, in whole or in part; whether others have published the same data, in whole or in part; whether the data has been republished by others who identify the source of the data as the website in question?"

Counsel attempting to authenticate exhibits containing information from internet websites need to address these concerns in deciding what method of authentication to use, and the facts to include in the foundation. The authentication rules most likely to apply, singly or in combination, are 901(b)(1) (witness with personal knowledge) 901(b)(3) (expert testimony) 901(b)(4) (distinctive characteristics), 901(b)(7) (public records), 901(b)(9) (system or process capable of producing a reliable result), and 902(5) (official publications).

Text Messages and Chat Room Content

Many of the same foundational issues found encountered when authenticating website evidence apply with equal force to text messages and internet chat room content; however, the fact that chat room messages are posted by third parties, often using "screen names" means that it cannot be assumed that the content found in chat rooms was posted with the knowledge or authority of the website host. One commentator [Saltzburg] has suggested that the following foundational requirements must be met to authenticate chat room evidence:

> "(1) [e]vidence that the individual used the screen name in question when participating in chat room conversations (either generally or at the site in question); (2) [e]vidence that, when a meeting with the person using the screen name was arranged, the individual . . . showed up; (3) [e]vidence that the person using the screen name identified [himself] as the [person in the chat room conversation]; evidence that the individual had in [his] possession information given to the person using the screen name; (5) [and] [e]vidence from the hard drive of the individual's computer [showing use of the same screen name]."

Courts also have recognized that exhibits of chat room conversations may be authenticated circumstantially. For example, in *In re F.P.*, the defendant argued that the testimony of the internet service provider was required, or that of a forensic expert. The court held that circumstantial evidence, such as the use of the defendant's screen name in the text message, the use of the defendant's first name, and the subject matter of the messages all could authenticate the transcripts. Similarly, in *United States v. Simpson*, the court held that there was ample circumstantial evidence to authenticate printouts of the content of chat room discussions between the defendant and an undercover detective, including use of the e-mail name of the defendant, the presence of the defendant's correct address in the messages, and notes seized at the defendant's home containing the address, e-mail address and telephone number given by the undercover officer. Likewise, in *United States v. Tank*, the court found sufficient circumstantial facts to authenticate chat room conversations, despite the fact that certain portions of the text of the messages in which the defendant had participated had been deleted. There, the court found the testimony regarding the limited nature of the deletions by the member of the chat room club who had made the deletions, circumstantial evidence connecting the defendant to the chat room, including the use of the defendant's screen name in the messages, were sufficient to authenticate the messages.

Based on the foregoing cases, the rules most likely to be used to authenticate chat room and text messages, alone or in combination, appear to be 901(b)(1) (witness with personal knowledge) and 901(b)(4) (circumstantial evidence of distinctive characteristics).

Computer Stored Records and Data

Given the widespread use of computers, there is an almost limitless variety of records that are stored in or generated by computers. [It has been] observed [that] "[m]any kinds of computer records and computer-generated information are introduced as real evidence or used as litigation aids at trials. They range from computer printouts of stored digital data to complex computer-generated models performing complicated computations. Each may raise different admissibility issues concerning authentication and other foundational requirements." The least complex admissibility issues are associated with electronically stored records. "In general, electronic documents or records that are merely stored in a computer raise no computer-specific authentication issues." Weinstein. That said, although computer records are the easiest to authenticate, there is growing recognition that more care is required to authenticate these electronic records than traditional "hard copy" records.

"Computerized data," however, raise unique issues concerning accuracy and authenticity. Accuracy may be impaired by incomplete data entry, mistakes in output instructions, programming errors, damage and contamination of storage media, power outages, and equipment malfunctions. The integrity of data may also be compromised in the course of discovery by improper search and retrieval techniques, data conversion, or mishandling. The proponent of computerized evidence has the burden of laying a proper foundation by establishing its accuracy.

The judge should therefore consider the accuracy and reliability of computerized evidence. . . . [As Prof. Imwinkelreid has noted]:

> "In the past, many courts have been lax in applying the authentication requirement to computer records; they have been content with foundational evidence that the business has successfully used the computer system in question and that the witness recognizes the record as output from the computer. However, following the recommendations of the

Federal Judicial Center's *Manual for Complex Litigation*, some courts now require more extensive foundation. These courts require the proponent to authenticate a computer record by proving the reliability of the particular computer used, the dependability of the business's input procedures for the computer, the use of proper procedures to obtain the document offered in court, and the witness's recognition of that document as the readout from the computer."

Two cases illustrate the contrast between the more lenient approach to admissibility of computer records and the more demanding one. In *United States v. Meienberg*, the defendant challenged on appeal the admission into evidence of printouts of computerized records of the Colorado Bureau of Investigation, arguing that they had not been authenticated because the government had failed to introduce any evidence to demonstrate the accuracy of the records. The Tenth Circuit disagreed, stating: "Any question as to the accuracy of the printouts, whether resulting from incorrect data entry or the operation of the computer program, as with inaccuracies in any other type of business records, would have affected only the weight of the printouts, not their admissibility." *See also Kassimu* (To authenticate computer records as business records did not require the maker, or even a custodian of the record, only a witness qualified to explain the record keeping system of the organization to confirm that the requirements of Rule 803(6) had been met, and the inability of a witness to attest to the accuracy of the information entered into the computer did not preclude admissibility); *Sea-Land Serv., Inc. v. Lozen Int'l* (ruling that trial court properly considered electronically generated bill of lading as an exhibit to a summary judgment motion. The only foundation that was required was that the record was produced from the same electronic information that was generated contemporaneously when the parties entered into their contact. The court did not require evidence that the records were reliable or accurate).

In contrast, in the case of *In re Vee Vinhnee*, the bankruptcy appellate panel upheld the trial ruling of a bankruptcy judge excluding electronic business records of the credit card issuer of a Chapter 7 debtor, for failing to authenticate them. The court noted that "it is becoming recognized that early versions of computer foundations were too cursory, even though the basic elements covered the ground." The court further observed that:

"The primary authenticity issue in the context of business records is on what has, or may have, happened to the record in the interval between when it was placed in the files and the time of trial. In other words, the record being proffered must be shown to continue to be an accurate representation of the record that originally was created. . . . Hence, the focus is not on the circumstances of the creation of the record, but rather on the circumstances of the preservation of the record during the time it is in the file so as to assure that the document being proffered is the same as the document that originally was created."

The court reasoned that, for paperless electronic records:

"The logical questions extend beyond the identification of the particular computer equipment and programs used. The entity's policies and proce-

> dures for the use of the equipment, database, and programs are important. How access to the pertinent database is controlled and, separately, how access to the specific program is controlled are important questions. How changes in the database are logged or recorded, as well as the structure and implementation of backup systems and audit procedures for assuring the continuing integrity of the database, are pertinent to the question of whether records have been changed since their creation."

In order to meet the heightened demands for authenticating electronic business records, the court adopted, with some modification, an eleven-step foundation proposed by Professor Edward Imwinkelried:

> "1. The business uses a computer. 2. The computer is reliable. 3. The business has developed a procedure for inserting data into the computer. 4. The procedure has built-in safeguards to ensure accuracy and identify errors. 5. The business keeps the computer in a good state of repair. 6. The witness had the computer readout certain data. 7. The witness used the proper procedures to obtain the readout. 8. The computer was in working order at the time the witness obtained the readout. 9. The witness recognizes the exhibit as the readout. 10. The witness explains how he or she recognizes the readout. 11. If the readout contains strange symbols or terms, the witness explains the meaning of the symbols or terms for the trier of fact."

Although the position taken by the court in *In re Vee Vinhnee* appears to be the most demanding requirement for authenticating computer stored records, other courts also have recognized a need to demonstrate the accuracy of these records. *See, e.g.*, *State v. Dunn* (Admissibility of computer-generated records "should be determined on the basis of the reliability and accuracy of the process involved."); *State v. Hall* ("[T]he admissibility of the computer tracing system record should be measured by the reliability of the system, itself, relative to its proper functioning and accuracy.").

As the foregoing cases illustrate, there is a wide disparity between the most lenient positions courts have taken in accepting electronic records as authentic and the most demanding requirements that have been imposed. If it is critical to the success of your case to admit into evidence computer stored records, it would be prudent to plan to authenticate the record by the most rigorous standard that may be applied. If less is required, then luck was with you.

The methods of authentication most likely to be appropriate for computerized records are 901(b)(1) (witness with personal knowledge), 901(b)(3) (expert testimony), 901(b)(4) (distinctive characteristics), and 901(b)(9) (system or process capable of producing a reliable result).

Computer Animation and Computer Simulations

Two similar, although distinct, forms of computer generated evidence also raise unique authentication issues. The first is computer animation, the display of a sequence of computer-generated images. The attraction of this form of evidence is irresistible, because:

> "when there is no movie or video of the event being litigated, a computer animation is a superior method of communicating the relevant information to the trier of fact. Absent a movie or video, the proponent might have to rely on static charts or oral testimony to convey a large amount of complex information to the trier of fact. When the proponent relies solely on oral expert testimony, the details may be presented one at a time; but an animation can piece all the details together for the jury. A computer animation in effect condenses the information into a single evidentiary package. In part due to television, the typical American is a primarily visual learner; and for that reason, in the short term, many jurors find the animation more understandable than charts or oral testimony. Use of an animation can also significantly increase long-term juror retention of the information." [Imwinkelreid.]

The second form of computer generated evidence is a computer simulation. "Computer generated evidence is an increasingly common form of demonstrative evidence. If the purpose of the computer evidence is to illustrate and explain a witness's testimony, courts usually refer to the evidence as an animation. In contrast, a simulation is based on scientific or physical principles and data entered into a computer, which is programmed to analyze the data and draw a conclusion from it, and courts generally require proof to show the validity of the science before the simulation evidence is admitted." . . .

Courts generally have allowed the admission of computer animations if authenticated by testimony of a witness with personal knowledge of the content of the animation, upon a showing that it fairly and adequately portrays the facts and that it will help to illustrate the testimony given in the case. This usually is the sponsoring witness. *State v. Sayles* (state's expert witness had knowledge of content of shaken infant syndrome animation and could testify that it correctly and adequately portrayed the facts that would illustrate her testimony); *Hinkle v. City of Clarksburg* (holding that a computer-animated videotaped recreation of events at issue in trial is not unduly prejudicial if it is sufficiently close to the actual events and is not confused by the jury for the real life events themselves); *Friend v. Time Mfg. Co.* ("The use of computer animations is allowed when it satisfies the usual foundational requirements for demonstrative evidence. 'At a minimum, the animation's proponent must show the computer simulation fairly and accurately depicts what it represents, whether through the computer expert who prepared it or some other witness who is qualified to so testify, and the opposing party must be afforded an opportunity for cross-examination.' "); *People v. Cauley* (holding that, "[a] computer animation is admissible as demonstrative evidence if the proponent of the video proves that it: 1) is authentic . . .; 2) is relevant . . .; 3) is a fair and accurate representation of the evidence to which it relates; and 4) has a probative value that is not substantially outweighed by the danger of unfair prejudice . . ."); *Clark v. Cantrell* ("[A] party may authenticate a video animation by offering testimony from a witness familiar with the preparation of the animation and the data on which it is based . . . [including] the testimony of the expert who prepared the underlying data and the computer technician who used that data to create it." (citation omitted)). Thus, the most frequent methods of authenticating computer animations are

901(b)(1) (witness with personal knowledge), and 901(b)(3) (testimony of an expert witness).

Computer simulations are treated as a form of scientific evidence, offered for a substantive, rather than demonstrative purpose. The case most often cited with regard to the foundational requirements needed to authenticate a computer simulation is *Commercial Union v. Boston Edison*, where the court stated:

> "The function of computer programs like TRACE 'is to perform rapidly and accurately an extensive series of computations not readily accomplished without use of a computer.' We permit experts to base their testimony on calculations performed by hand. There is no reason to prevent them from performing the same calculations, with far greater rapidity and accuracy, on a computer. Therefore . . . we treat computer-generated models or simulations like other scientific tests, and condition admissibility on a sufficient showing that: (1) the computer is functioning properly; (2) the input and underlying equations are sufficiently complete and accurate (and disclosed to the opposing party, so that they may challenge them); and (3) the program is generally accepted by the appropriate community of scientists."

The *Commercial Union* test has been followed by numerous courts in determining the foundation needed to authenticate computer simulations. For example, in *State v. Swinton*, the court cited with approval *Commercial Union*, but added that the key to authenticating computer simulations is to determine their reliability. In that regard, the court noted that the following problems could arise with this type of computer evidence: (1) the underlying information itself could be unreliable; (2) the entry of the information into the computer could be erroneous; (3) the computer hardware could be unreliable; (4) the computer software programs could be unreliable; (5) "the execution of the instructions, which transforms the information in some way-for example, by calculating numbers, sorting names, or storing information and retrieving it later" could be unreliable; (6) the output of the computer-the printout, transcript, or graphics, could be flawed; (7) the security system used to control access to the computer could be compromised; and (8) the user of the system could make errors. The court noted that Rule 901(b)(9) was a helpful starting point to address authentication of computer simulations. *See also Bray v. Bi-State Dev. Corp.* (citing *Commercial Union* and ruling that authentication properly was accomplished by a witness with knowledge of how the computer program worked, its software, the data used in the calculations, and who verified the accuracy of the calculations made by the computer with manual calculations); *Kudlacek v. Fiat* (citing *Commercial Union* and holding that computer simulation was authenticated by the plaintiff's expert witness). Thus, the most frequent methods of authenticating computer simulations are 901(b)(1) (witness with personal knowledge); and 901(b)(3) (expert witness). Use of an expert witness to authenticate a computer simulation likely will also involve Federal Rules of Evidence 702 and 703.

Digital Photographs

Photographs have been authenticated for decades under Rule 901(b)(1) by the testimony of a witness familiar with the scene depicted in the photograph who testifies that the photograph fairly and accurately represents the scene. Calling the photographer or offering exert testimony about how a camera works almost never has been required for traditional film photographs. Today, however, the vast majority of photographs taken, and offered as exhibits at trial, are digital photographs, which are not made from film, but rather from images captured by a digital camera and loaded into a computer. Digital photographs present unique authentication problems because they are a form of electronically produced evidence that may be manipulated and altered. Indeed, unlike photographs made from film, digital photographs may be "enhanced." Digital image "enhancement consists of removing, inserting, or highlighting an aspect of the photograph that the technician wants to change." Edward J. Imwinkelried, *Can this Photo be Trusted?*, Trial, October 2005, at 48. Some examples graphically illustrate the authentication issues associated with digital enhancement of photographs:

> "[S]uppose that in a civil case, a shadow on a 35 mm photograph obscures the name of the manufacturer of an offending product. The plaintiff might offer an enhanced image, magically stripping the shadow to reveal the defendant's name. Or suppose that a critical issue is the visibility of a highway hazard. A civil defendant might offer an enhanced image of the stretch of highway to persuade the jury that the plaintiff should have perceived the danger ahead before reaching it. In many criminal trials, the prosecutor offers an 'improved', digitally enhanced image of fingerprints discovered at the crime scene. The digital image reveals incriminating points of similarity that the jury otherwise would never would have seen." *Id.*

There are three distinct types of digital photographs that should be considered with respect to authentication analysis: original digital images, digitally converted images, and digitally enhanced images.

An original digital photograph may be authenticated the same way as a film photo, by a witness with personal knowledge of the scene depicted who can testify that the photo fairly and accurately depicts it. If a question is raised about the reliability of digital photography in general, the court likely could take judicial notice of it under Rule 201. For digitally converted images, authentication requires an explanation of the process by which a film photograph was converted to digital format. This would require testimony about the process used to do the conversion, requiring a witness with personal knowledge that the conversion process produces accurate and reliable images, Rules 901(b)(1) and 901(b)(9) — the later rule implicating expert testimony under Rule 702. Alternatively, if there is a witness familiar with the scene depicted who can testify that the photo produced from the film when it was digitally converted, no testimony would be needed regarding the process of digital conversion.

For digitally enhanced images, it is unlikely that there will be a witness who can testify how the original scene looked if, for example, a shadow was removed, or the colors were intensified. In such a case, there will need to be proof, permissible under

Rule 901(b)(9), that the digital enhancement process produces reliable and accurate results, which gets into the realm of scientific or technical evidence under Rule 702. *Id.* Recently, one state court has given particular scrutiny to how this should be done. [*State v. Swinton*, reproduced elsewhere in this chapter, is discussed here.]

Because the process of computer enhancement involves a scientific or technical process, one commentator [Imwinkelried] has suggested the following foundation as a means to authenticate digitally enhanced photographs under Rule 901(b)(9): (1) The witness is an expert in digital photography; (2) the witness testifies as to image enhancement technology, including the creation of the digital image consisting of pixels and the process by which the computer manipulates them; (3) the witness testifies that the processes used are valid; (4) the witness testifies that there has been "adequate research into the specific application of image enhancement technology involved in the case"; (5) the witness testifies that the software used was developed from the research; (6) the witness received a film photograph; (7) the witness digitized the film photograph using the proper procedure, then used the proper procedure to enhance the film photograph in the computer; (8) the witness can identify the trial exhibit as the product of the enchantment process he or she performed. . . . [I]t is probable that courts will require authentication of digitally enhanced photographs by adequate testimony that it is the product of a system or process that produces accurate and reliable results. Fed.R.Evid. 901(b)(9).

In this case, neither plaintiffs nor defendants provided any authenticating facts for the e-mail and other evidence that they proffered in support of their summary judgment memoranda — they simply attached the exhibits. This complete absence of authentication stripped the exhibits of any evidentiary value because the Court could not consider them as evidentiary facts. This, in turn, required the dismissal, without prejudice, of the cross motions for summary judgment, with leave to resubmit them once the evidentiary deficiencies had been cured.

Hearsay (Rules 801-807)

[The portion of the opinion dealing with hearsay and the business records exception to the hearsay rule, as applied to electronically stored and digital information, is reproduced *supra* in the section of this book dealing with the business records exception to the hearsay rule.]

The Original Writing Rule, Rules 1001-1008

The next step in evaluating the admissibility of electronic evidence is to analyze issues associated with the original writing rule, which requires an original or duplicate original to prove the contents of a writing, recording or photograph unless secondary evidence is deemed acceptable. *See* Fed.R.Evid. 1001-08. The best way to understand the rule is to appreciate its structure. Rule 1001 contains the key definitions that animate the rule: "original," "duplicate," "writing," "recording," and "photograph." The substantive requirements of the original writing rule are succinctly provided by Rule 1002, which mandates that "[t]o prove the content of a writing, recording, or photograph, the original writing, recording, or photograph is required, except as otherwise provided in these rules or by Act of Congress." It is

Rule 1002 that gives the rule its modern name, the "original writing rule," as it requires the original to prove the contents of a writing, recording or photograph, except as excused by the remaining rules in Article X of the rules of evidence. As will be seen, the key to the rule is to determine when "the contents" of a writing, recording or photograph actually are being proved, as opposed to proving events that just happen to have been recorded or photographed, or those which can be proved by eyewitnesses, as opposed to a writing or recording explaining or depicting them. Rule 1003 essentially provides that duplicates are co-extensively admissible as originals, unless there is a genuine issue as to the authenticity of the original, or the circumstances indicate that it would be unfair to admit a duplicate in lieu of an original. *People v. Huehn* (duplicates of computer generated bank records admissible to the same extent as an original absent unfairness or lack of authenticity). Because of Rule 1003, duplicates are more often admitted into evidence than originals. Rice at 192 ("As a practical matter, Fed.R.Evid. 1003 has eliminated best evidence objections. Copies from the pages of books, treatises, and the other papers are now introduced in place of the entire volume because photocopies of originals are now admissible as if they were the original."). Rule 1004 is the primary rule that identifies when secondary evidence is admissible. As a practical matter, "secondary evidence" is any proof of the contents of a writing, recording or photograph other than an original or duplicate. Examples include testimony from the author of the writing, or someone who read it, earlier drafts, copies, or an outline used to prepare the final. Rule 1005 describes how to prove the contents of public records, since it is obvious that something other than the original must be used. Rule 1006 permits introduction into evidence of written or testimonial summaries of voluminous writings, recordings or photographs, provided the original or duplicates from which the summaries were prepared were made available to the adverse party at a reasonable time in advance of trial for examination or copying. Thus, Rule 1006 is an example of secondary evidence. Rule 1007 allows the proof of the contents of a writing, recording or photograph by the deposition or testimony of a party opponent, without having to account for the nonproduction of the original. This is another form of secondary evidence. The final rule in Article X of the Federal Rules of Evidence is Rule 1008. It is a specialized application of Rule 104(b) — the conditional relevance rule — and sets forth what must happen when there is a dispute regarding whether there ever was a writing, recording, or photograph, or when there are conflicting versions of duplicates, originals, or secondary evidence offered into evidence. In such instances, as in Rule 104(b), the jury decides the factual dispute.

Traditionally the rule has been referred to as the "Best Evidence Rule," which is a misleading title. The rule is more accurately is referred to as the "Original Writing Rule" because it does not mandate introduction of the "best" evidence to prove the contents of a writing, recording or photograph, but merely requires such proof by an "original," "duplicate" or, in certain instances, by "secondary evidence" — any evidence that is something other than an original or duplicate (such as testimony, or a draft of a writing to prove the final version, if no original or duplicate is available).

It has been acknowledged that the original writing rule has particular applicability to electronically prepared or stored writings, recordings or photographs. One respected commentator [Weinstein] has observed:

> "Computer-based business records commonly consist of material originally produced in a computer (e.g. business memoranda), data drawn from outside sources and input into the computer (e.g. invoices), or summaries of documents (e.g. statistical runs). The admissibility of computer-based records 'to prove the content of a writing' is subject to the best evidence rule set out in Rule 1002. The rule generally requires the original of a writing when the contents are at issue, except that a 'duplicate' is also admissible unless a genuine issue is raised about its authenticity. A duplicate includes a counterpart produced by 'electronic re-recording, which accurately reproduces the original.' Courts often admit computer-based records without making the distinction between originals and duplicates."

When analyzing the original writing rule as it applies to electronic evidence, the most important rules are Rule 1001, containing the definitions; Rule 1002, the substantive original writing rule; Rule 1004, the "primary" secondary evidence rule; Rule 1006, the rule permitting summaries to prove the contents of voluminous writings, recordings and photographs; and Rule 1007, allowing proof of a writing, recording or photograph by the admission of a party opponent.

Rule 1001 states: [quoted]

It is apparent that the definition of "writings, recordings and photographs" includes evidence that is electronically generated and stored. . . . It further is clear that under Rule 1001(3) the "original" of information stored in a computer is the readable display of the information on the computer screen, the hard drive or other source where it is stored, as well as any printout or output that may be read, so long as it accurately reflects the data. *Laughner v. State* (ruling that content of internet chat room communications between defendant and undercover police officer that officer "cut-and-pasted" into a word processing program were originals under state version of original writing rule). Moreover, if a computer record accurately reflects the contents of another writing, and was prepared near the time that the original writing was prepared, it may qualify as an original under Rule 1001.

> "In today's commercial world, a single transaction often generates successive entries of the same information in separately prepared writings. Though the purposes of these separate records may be different, a computerized business record, prepared simultaneously with or within a reasonable time period of the written record, and containing the same or similar information, would appear to be no less an 'original' than a handwritten record. However, it seems equally clear that where a written record, prepared prior to the computer record, contains a more detailed and complete description of the transaction than that contained in the computer record, the proponent of the evidence should be required to produce the more detailed record, or account for its nonproduction under F.R.E. 1004. Similarly, where a computerized record appears to be nothing more than a summary of a more detailed written record, the written record should be produced except where the requirements of F.R.E. 1006 have been satisfied." [Citation omitted].

Finally, as already noted, as a result of Rule 1003, the distinction between duplicates and originals largely has become unimportant, as duplicates are co-extensively admissible as originals in most instances.

Once the definitions of the original writing rule are understood, the next important determination is whether the rule applies at all. Rule 1002 answers this question. It provides: "To prove the content of a writing, recording, or photograph, the original writing, recording, or photograph is required, except as otherwise provided in these rules or by Act of Congress." As the advisory committee's note to Rule 1002 makes clear:

"Application of the rule requires resolution of the question whether contents are sought to be proved. Thus an event may be proved by non-documentary evidence, even though a written record of it was made. If, however, the event is sought to be proved by the written record, the rule applies. For example, payment may be proved without producing the written receipt which was given. Earnings may be proved without producing books of account in which they are entered. Nor does the rule apply to testimony that books or records have been examined and found not to contain any reference to a designated matter. The assumption should not be made that the rule will come into operation on every occasion when use is made of a photograph in evidence. On the contrary, the rule will seldom apply to ordinary photographs. . . . On occasion, however, situations arise in which contents are sought to be proved. Copyright, defamation, and invasion of privacy by photograph or motion picture falls into this category. Similarly, as to situations in which the picture is offered as having independent probative value, e.g. automatic photograph of bank robber, photograph of defendant engaged in indecent act."

Whether the content is at issue is determined on a case-by-case basis. For example, proof that someone is married may be made by the testimony of a witness to the ceremony. The marriage license is not required. However, the rule applies if the only proof of the marriage is by the record itself. Similarly, someone who heard a politician give a speech may testify to what was said without the video recording of the speech, because the content of the recording is not at issue. In contrast, if the only way to prove the content of the speech is by the video, because there are no witnesses available to testify, the rule would apply to the video recording.

Rule 1002 also does not apply when an expert testifies based in part on having reviewed writings, recordings or photographs, because Rule 703 allows an expert to express opinions based on matters not put into evidence. . . . Finally, when the contents of writings, recordings or photographs merely are collateral to the case, meaning they are not "closely related to a controlling issue" in a case, Rule 1002 does not apply, and secondary evidence may be used to prove their contents. Fed.R.Evid. 1004(4). In contrast, proving legal transactions, such as wills, contracts, and deeds commonly do involve the best evidence rule because the documents themselves have the central legal significance in the case.

An example of when the original writing rule did apply to electronic evidence is *Laughner v. State*. Laughner was charged with attempted child solicitation. To prove the crime, the state offered printouts of instant message chats between the defendant and an undercover police officer posing as a thirteen year old boy. The police officer "cut-and-pasted" the text of the text messages from the internet chat room into a word processing program, and the printouts that were introduced into evidence were prepared from that program. The defendant objected (citing the state version of the original writing rule, which was identical to the federal version), arguing that the printouts were not the "original" of the text of the chat room communications. The appellate court agreed that the state was proving the content of a writing, and that the original writing rule required an original, but found that the printout was an original, reasoning:

> "Evidence Rule 1002, the 'best evidence' rule, requires an 'original' in order to prove 'the content' of a writing or recording. However, Evidence Rule 1001(3) provides that when 'data are stored in a computer or similar device, any printout or other output readable by sight, shown to reflect the data accurately is an 'original.' According to [the police officer] he saved the conversations with Laughner after they were concluded, and the printout document accurately reflected the content of those conversations. Therefore, the printouts could be found to be the 'best evidence' of the conversations [between the defendant and the officer]."

It is important to keep in mind that failure to properly object to the introduction of evidence in violation of the original writing rule likely will result in a waiver of the error on appeal. *State v. Braidic* (Defendant was convicted of rape and other sex offenses with minor. At trial, victim's mother testified, without objection, to content of chat room text messages between defendant and victim. Appellate court noted applicability of original writing rule to require original to prove the contents of the chat room records, but found that defense counsel's failure to object did not constitute ineffective assistance of counsel). Counsel need to insure that a timely objection is made to attempts to prove the contents of electronic writings, recordings or photographs in violation of the original writing rule.

Rule 1004 identifies four circumstances in which secondary evidence may be introduced instead of an original. The rule provides: [quoted]

The first example [originals lost or destroyed in good faith] may be particularly suited for electronic evidence. Given the myriad ways that electronic records may be deleted, lost as a result of system malfunctions, purged as a result of routine electronic records management software (such as the automatic deletion of e-mail after a set time period) or otherwise unavailable means that the contents of electronic writings may have to be proved by secondary evidence. Indeed, at least one court has recognized that the "tenuous and ethereal nature of writings posted in internet chat rooms and message boards means that in all likelihood the exceptions [to the original writing rule that permit secondary evidence] would . . . [apply]." *Bidbay.com, Inc. v. Spry*; *People v. Huehn* (holding that trial court did not abuse discretion in admitting computer generated bank records that contained listing of ATM transactions prepared by another company that bank retained to process ATM transactions. The court noted that the Colorado version of Rule 1004(1) permitted secondary evidence of the records provided they were not lost or destroyed in bad faith.

Additionally, Rule 1004 permits proof of the contents of a writing, recording or photograph by secondary evidence when the proponent of the evidence is unable to obtain an original through use of legal process, or when the original is in the possession or control of an adverse party that has actual or inquiry notice of the contents that the proponent intends to introduce the evidence. In the later circumstance, as the advisory committee's note to Rule 104(3) points out, "[a] party who has an original in his control has no need for the protection of the [original writing] rule if put on notice that proof of contents will be made. He can ward off secondary evidence by offering the original."

Finally, Rule 1004(4) permits proof of the contents of writings, recordings of photographs by secondary evidence if they relate to "collateral matters," defined as "not closely related to a controlling issue" in the case. The advisory committee's note to Rule 1004(4) candidly acknowledges that this is a nebulous standard, stating "[w]hile difficult to define with precision, situations arise in which no good purpose is served by production of the original." *See also* Weinstein ("[t]he distinction between controlling and collateral issues can be an exasperating one. The term 'collateral' is elusive and vague. It cannot be defined conceptually, only pragmatically: balancing the importance of the document against the inconvenience of compelling its production, is the rule worth enforcing?") An example illustrates. A doctor testifying as an expert in a personal injury case can testify that she is licensed to practice medicine in a state without having to produce the license itself. However, if a defendant is charged with practicing medicine without a license, his testimony alone that he has a license from the state will not be accepted, as the license is closely related to a controlling issue in the case.

Rule 1006 recognizes another source of secondary evidence to prove the contents of writings, recordings, or photographs, stating: [this rule, allowing summaries, charts, and calculations, is quoted]

The advisory committee's note recognizes that Rule 1006 is one of necessity, as the "admission of summary of voluminous books, records, or documents offers the only practicable means of making their contents available to judge and jury." A number of observations may be made about the use of summaries under Rule 1006. First, as the rule expressly states, the writings, recordings or photographs to be summarized must be voluminous [or complicated]. Second, although the rule is silent on the nature of the summary, the prevailing view is that it may be either written, or testimonial. Weinstein ("[s]ummary evidence need not be an exhibit, but may take the form of a witness's oral testimony."). Third, the majority view is that the summaries themselves constitute the evidence of the contents of the materials summarized, rather than the underlying writings, recordings or photographs. Fourth, if the summaries are accepted as the evidence of the materials summarized, they function as the equivalent of a special exception to the hearsay rule. Fifth, the writings, recordings and photographs that are summarized must be made available to the adverse party for examination or copying reasonably in advance of the use of the summary, a requirement that originates from Rule 1006 itself, regardless of whether the adverse party has served a request for production of documents under Fed.R.Civ.P. 34. Sixth, the underlying materials from which the summaries are made must themselves be admissible into evidence.

Because the production of electronically stored information in civil cases frequently is voluminous, the use of summaries under Rule 1006 is a particularly useful evidentiary tool, and courts can be expected to allow the use of summaries provided the procedural requirements of the rule are met. *See, e.g.*, *Wapnick v.*

Comm'r of Internal Revenue (holding that summaries of voluminous computer records were admissible under Rule 1006 even though they were prepared in anticipation of litigation, because the underlying documents had been admitted into evidence and reasonably had been made available to the opposing party to inspect).

Rule 1007 identifies another, though little used, way in which secondary evidence may be used to prove the contents of electronically prepared or stored information. It provides that "[c]ontents of writings, recordings, or photographs may be proved by the testimony or deposition of the party against whom offered or by that party's written admission, without accounting for the nonproduction of the original."

On its face this rule is limited to admissions by a party opponent regarding the content of a writing, recording or photograph. Use of the word "admission" refers to any of the types of admissions covered by Rule 801(d)(2), which includes admissions by a representative, agent, employee or co-conspirator that meets the requirements of Rule 801(d)(2) for each of these types of admissions. It does not require that any showing be made that the writing, recording or photograph is lost or otherwise unavailable. Further, the rule expressly limits the types of admissions that may be used to prove the contents of writings, recordings or photographs to those obtained during in court testimony, during a deposition, or by the adverse party's written admission. An adverse party's answers to federal rule of civil procedure Rule 33 interrogatories or a Rule 36 request to admit the genuineness of documents would meet the provisions of Federal Rule of Evidence 1007 regarding a "written admission."

[D]espite the limitation in Rule 1007 to testimonial or written admissions of a party opponent, a non-testimonial oral admission by a party opponent would still be admissible as secondary evidence to prove the contents of a writing, recording or photograph under Rule 1004 if the writing, recording or photograph was lost of destroyed, absent bad faith, beyond the reach of court ordered production, in the possession, custody of control of the adverse party, or if the writing, recording or photograph was not closely related to a controlling issue in the litigation.

Rule 1008 is the last of the rules in Article X of the rules of evidence. It states: [quoted]

This rule is a specialized application of Rule 104(b), and it allocates responsibility between the trial judge and the jury with respect to certain preliminary matters affecting the original writing rule. Under the rule, the trial judge determines: whether originals have been lost or destroyed under Rule 1004(1), as well as all issues relating to the appropriateness of the proponent's efforts to search for the lost original; whether or not the original is obtainable by judicial process, under Rule 1004(2); whether the original is in the possession, custody or control of the opposing party under Rule 1004(3); and whether the writing, recording or photograph relates to a collateral matter, which removes it from the reach of the original writing rule.

Rule 1008 identifies three issues that are questions for the jury, however: (1) whether the writing, recording or photograph ever existed in the first place; (2) whether some other writing, recording, or photograph that is offered into evidence is in fact the original; and (3) whether "other" (i.e., secondary) evidence of contents correctly reflects the content of the writing, recording or photograph. Given the challenges that often are associated with the authentication of electronically created or stored evidence, it is not unlikely that there will be disputes of fact regarding whether an electronic writing ever existed in the first place, if the original cannot be produced and secondary evidence is offered, or when different versions of the same electronic document are offered into evidence by the opposing parties.

In summary, when counsel intend to offer electronic evidence at trial or in support of a motion for summary judgment they must determine whether the original writing rule is applicable, and if so, they must be prepared to introduce an original, a duplicate original, or be able to demonstrate that one of the permitted forms of secondary evidence is admissible. In this case, counsel did not address the original writing rule, despite its obvious applicability given that the e-mail exhibits were closely related to a controlling issue and they were proving the contents of the e-mails themselves.

The final evidentiary issue that must be considered in determining whether electronic evidence will be admitted is whether the probative value of the evidence is substantially outweighed by the danger of unfair prejudice, as proscribed under Rule 403 of the Federal Rules of Evidence.

Balancing Probative Value Against the Danger of Unfair Prejudice Under Rule 403

After evaluating the issues associated with relevance, authenticity, hearsay, and the original writing rule, the final step to consider with regard to electronically prepared or stored evidence is the need to balance its probative value against the potential for unfair prejudice, or other harm, under Rule 403 of the Federal Rules of Evidence. This rule states: [quoted]

Rule 403 recognizes that relevance alone does not ensure admissibility. A cost/benefit analysis must often be employed. Relevant evidence may be excluded if its probative value is not worth the problems that its admission may cause. The issue is whether the search for truth will be helped or hindered by the interjection of distracting, confusing, or emotionally charged evidence.

A determination of whether evidence should be excluded under Rule 403 falls within the those made by the court under Rule 104(a), but it is used sparingly. Generally, "[i]f there is doubt about the existence of unfair prejudice, confusion of issues, misleading, undue delay, or waste of time, it is generally better practice to admit the evidence, taking necessary precautions of contemporaneous instructions to the jury followed by additional admonitions in the charge." [Weinstein].

[C]ourts are particularly likely to consider whether the admission of electronic evidence would be unduly prejudicial in the following circumstances: (1) When the evidence would contain offensive or highly derogatory language that may provoke an emotional response. *See Monotype Corp.* (Finding that trial court properly excluded an email from a Microsoft employee under Rule 403 that contained a "highly derogatory and offensive description of . . . [another company's] type director."); (2) When analyzing computer animations, to determine if there is a substantial risk that the jury may mistake them for the actual events in the litigation, *Friend v. Time Manufacturing Co.* ("Therefore, the question is simply whether the animation accurately demonstrates the scene of the accident, and whether the probative value is substantially outweighed by the danger of unfair prejudice, confusion of the issues, or misleading the jury, or by considerations of undue delay, waste of time, or needless presentation of cumulative evidence."); *State v. Sayles* (Appellate court found no error in trial court's admission of computer animation slides showing effects of shaken infant syndrome, finding that trial court properly considered state version of Rule 403, and admitted evidence with a cautionary instruction that the evidence was only an illustration, not a re-creation of the actual crime); (3) when considering the admissibility of summaries of voluminous electronic writings, recordings or photographs under Rule 1006, Weinstein ("Summary evidence is subject to the balancing test under Rule 403 that weighs the probative value of evidence against its prejudicial effect"); and (4) in circumstances when the court is concerned as to the reliability or accuracy of the information that is contained within the electronic evidence, *St. Clair v. Johnny's Oyster and Shrimp Inc.* (Court expressed extreme skepticism regarding the reliability and accuracy of information posted on the internet, referring to it variously as "voodoo information". Although the court did not specifically refer to Rule 403, the possibility of unfair prejudice associated with the admissibility of unreliable or inaccurate information, as well as for confusion of the jury, makes Rule 403 a likely candidate for exclusion of such evidence).

If a lawyer is offering electronic evidence, particularly computer animations, that may draw a Rule 403 objection, he or she must be prepared to demonstrate why any prejudice is not unfair, when measured against the probative value of the evidence. In this case, counsel did not address whether Rule 403 was implicated with respect to the electronic evidence attached to their summary judgment memoranda.

Conclusion

In this case the failure of counsel collectively to establish the authenticity of their exhibits, resolve potential hearsay issues, comply with the original writing rule, and demonstrate the absence of unfair prejudice rendered their exhibits inadmissible, resulting in the dismissal, without prejudice, of their cross motions for summary judgment. The discussion above highlights the fact that there are five distinct but interrelated evidentiary issues that govern whether electronic evidence will be admitted into evidence at trial or accepted as an exhibit in summary judgment practice. Although each of these rules may not apply to every exhibit offered, as was the case here, each still must be considered in evaluating how to secure the admissibility of electronic evidence to support claims and defenses. Because it can be expected that electronic evidence will constitute much, if not most, of the evidence used in future motions practice or at trial, counsel should know how to get it right on the first try. The Court hopes that the explanation provided in this memorandum order will assist in that endeavor.

[The portion of the opinion dealing with hearsay and the business records exception to the hearsay rule, as applied to ESI is reproduced *supra* in the section of this book dealing with the business records exception to the hearsay rule.]

[B] Voice Identification

Read Federal Rule of Evidence 901(b)(5) and (6), Authentication of Voices and Authentication of Telephone Conversations. The provisions here specifically refer to voice authentication. This does not mean that other of the authentication provisions cannot be used to authenticate a voice.

UNITED STATES v. VITALE

United States Court of Appeals, Eighth Circuit
549 F.2d 71, *cert. denied*, 431 U.S. 907 (1977)

Per Curiam.

[The defendant was convicted of distributing controlled substances.]

Officer Zinselmeier testified that on August 12, 1976, he placed a telephone call to the residence of one Peggy Lindsay. A female voice answered. After the court sustained defense counsel's objection of lack of a proper foundation for testimony about the phone call, Zinselmeier testified that he had spoken with appellant [Juanita Vitale] on at least three occasions (two of which were face-to-face meetings), that he could identify appellant's voice, and that the voice on the other end of the phone was appellant's. The district court then overruled defense counsel's lack of foundation objection. Zinselmeier testified that the first call was followed by a second call during which the same female voice identified herself as Juanita Vitale, arranged to sell Zinselmeier dilaudid at a restaurant parking lot, and gave a physical description of herself and the car in which she would go to the parking lot. One hour later appellant, who matched the physical description given in the phone call and who was riding in the car described in the phone call, met Zinselmeier in the designated parking lot and sold him the substance later identified as dilaudid.

Appellant alleges that evidence about the telephone conversations should have been excluded because no proper foundation was laid. The essence of this allegation is that Zinselmeier had not spoken to appellant prior to the phone call and could not identify her voice then.

Rule 901(a) of the Federal Rules of Evidence provides that the requirement of authentication is met where there is "evidence sufficient to support a finding that the matter in question is what its proponent claims." Rule 901(b)(5) allows for identification of a voice "by opinion based upon hearing the voice at any time under circumstances connecting it with the alleged speaker." In the Notes of the Advisory Committee to Rule 901(b)(5), the Committee stated: "[T]he requisite familiarity may be acquired *either before or after* the particular speaking which is the subject of the identification, . . . (emphasis added)." In the instant case, Officer Zinselmeier testified that he had spoken with appellant personally on two occasions and could identify her voice. This clearly seems to meet the standards of admissibility.

Furthermore, identity may be proven by circumstantial evidence. Appellant's presence at the parking lot designated during the second phone call, matching the physical description given on the phone, and riding in the car described on the phone is strong evidence that she is the party with whom Zinselmeier spoke.

NOTE

Identification May Be Sufficient Even if It Does Not Fit Any Illustration in Rule 901 (b). See United States v. Alessi, 638 F.2d 466 (2d Cir. 1980):

> Ferrara claims that the court erred in admitting against him the testimony of Milton Freedman regarding telephone conversations with a person named "Corky" in which Freedman arranged cash purchases of [the fraudulently obtained] airline tickets at a discount. He argues that the conversations were not authenticated as prescribed by Rule 901, Fed. R. Evid. The claim is meritless.
>
> The phone number called by Freedman was listed in the name of Ferrara's wife at their residence. At trial Freedman identified Ferrara as "Corky" and further testified to meeting Ferrara, known as "Corky," at Kennedy Airport where Freedman paid him for the tickets. Thereafter he arranged further purchases of tickets by telephone with Ferrara in the same manner, mailing money to Ferrara and receiving airline tickets in return.
>
> This authentication of Ferrara's voice was adequate. The illustrations in Rule 901(b)(6) are just that, illustrations, and not limitations on methods of identification that may be used.

See also United States v. Sliker, 751 F.2d 477 (2d Cir. 1984), *cert. denied*, 470 U.S. 1058 (1985), in which the judge admitted the tape based on his comparison of the voice on the tape with that of the witness testifying, and the jurors authenticated the tapes by making the same comparison.

UNITED STATES v. ESPINOZA

United States Court of Appeals, Fourth Circuit
641 F.2d 153, *cert. denied*, 454 U.S. 841 (1981)

Staker, District Judge.

Joseph Jesse Espinoza, appellant here, and J-E Enterprises, Inc. (J-E), were jointly convicted [of transporting] obscene films and magazines.

Espinoza's defense was that he could not be guilty of the charges, because throughout the [relevant] period [1976–77] he was [no longer] involved in or with J-E's business operations . . . . Espinoza claims that the court erred by permitting witness Holdren [owner-operator of Kip's discount store, which stocked some of J-E's pornography] to testify to his telephone conversations with Espinoza, arguing that since Holdren had never met him, Holdren could not identify him as the person with whom Holdren spoke at J-E. [Holdren testified that he had never met him and that if he saw him at trial he would not know him.]

Holdren testified that he communicated by telephone with J-E on at least four occasions, always speaking with "Joe," concerning ordering, pricing and shipping adult materials and kiddie porn, some of those conversations having been initiated by him and some by J-E; that two of those conversations dealt with kiddie porn; that when Holdren called J-E, a lady would answer the telephone, Holdren would ask for "Joe" and a man would get on the telephone and say, "This is Joe"; and that in one of the those conversations with Joe, he ordered kiddie porn from J-E as a result of which kiddie porn was shipped to Kip's Discount from J-E by Greyhound Bus.

Holdren could not pinpoint the exact dates upon which he talked with Joe; however, a telephone company statement rendered to Kip's Discount was admitted into evidence and showed charges for calls made on November 2 and 3, 1976, from Kip's Discount to a California telephone number shown to be that of J-E on J-E's invoices rendered to Kip's Discount. Two of those invoices bore Espinoza's fingerprints, as testified to by an expert witness. One of the two, invoice 4002, listed several items as having been sold and shipped by J-E to Kip's Discount, including the item "bulbs," which Holdren testified "checked out [as against the merchandise actually received by Kip's Discount from J-E under that invoice] to be kiddie porn." Also admitted into evidence was Kip's Discount's cancelled check signed by Holdren, written to J-E in payment of invoice 4002 and identifying that invoice on the face of the check.

Witness Ganley, a member of the Los Angeles Police Department Administrative Division, Pornography Unit, identified Espinoza at trial and testified that he had J-E's warehouse under surveillance for two months during the period from the fall of 1976 to and including the spring of 1977, during which he saw Espinoza enter and leave the warehouse regularly.

The admissibility of Holdren's testimony identifying Espinoza as the person with whom he spoke by telephone is governed to some extent by Rules 901(a) and 104(b) of the Federal Rules of Evidence. Under the provisions thereof, it was not requisite to the admissibility of Holdren's testimony that it be sufficient itself to support a finding that it was Espinoza to whom Holdren spoke by telephone; Holdren's testimony was properly admissible, under the provisions of Rule 104(b), "upon, or subject to, the introduction of [other] evidence sufficient to support a finding of the fulfillment of the condition," that is, other evidence which would be sufficient to support a finding that Espinoza was the person to whom Holdren spoke by telephone, the establishment of the identity of Espinoza as that person being requisite to the relevancy of Holdren's testimony . . . .

Here, the evidence of Espinoza's response to Holdren's telephoned order to J-E for kiddie porn almost certainly identifies Espinoza as the "Joe" to whom Holdren spoke in that conversation: Holdren communicated to J-E, by speaking with "Joe," Holdren's order for kiddie porn, in response to which kiddie porn was shipped from J-E to Holdren (Kip's Discount) along with J-E's invoice therefore listing the kiddie porn thereon as "bulbs," per Holdren's testimony, and Holdren paid J-E the amount of that invoice by his check. These facts, standing alone, perhaps would not be sufficiently probative of Espinoza's identity, as the "Joe" to whom Holdren communicated the order and as a person involved in J-E's response to that order, to permit Holdren's testimony to the telephone conversation to be sufficiently relevant to remain before the jury as to Espinoza. But given the additional evidentiary fact that the invoice rendered by J-E to Holdren for the kiddie porn bore the fingerprint of Espinoza, then compelling evidence existed tending not only to establish that Espinoza had a personal role in the making of J-E's response to

Holdren's order, thereby sufficiently identifying him as the "Joe" to whom Holdren spoke in the telephone conversation in which he made that order . . . .

Affirmed.

NOTES AND QUESTIONS

(1) *Does Rule 901 Require Something More than is Suggested by Conditional Relevancy in Rule 104(b)?* In a footnote attached to its discussion of the relationship between Fed. R. Evid. 104 and Fed. R. Evid. 901, the court in *Espinoza* repeats the oft-quoted Advisory Committee statement under Fed. R. Evid. 901(a), which we have seen in other cases and which is fundamental to both Fed. R. Evid. 104 and Fed. R. Evid. Article IX, that "the requirement of showing authenticity or identity falls in the category of relevancy dependent upon fulfillment of a condition of fact and is governed by Rule 104(b)." Examples of such facts determining relevancy are that the voice in *Espinoza* was in fact Espinoza's; that the signatures, in the other cases in this section, were genuine; or that a weapon offered is indeed the weapon used in the robbery or murder. But isn't the evidence relevant (under the liberal test of Fed. R. Evid. 401) even without the proof required by Fed. R. Evid. 901? Isn't it slightly more likely a signature purporting to be mine is mine than if it did not purport to be mine, all other things being equal, including an absence of information on whose it is? The same could be said of a voice purporting to be mine. It could even be said of a voice purporting to be "Joe": that it is slightly more likely to be Joe Espinoza's than if it had purported to be "Frank," all other things being equal. And a knife is slightly relevant, in a case where a knife was used, even without proof it is the same knife used in the crime, is it not? *Cf.* Rothstein, *Intellectual Coherence in an Evidence Code*, 28 Loy. L.A. L. Rev. 1259, 1265–70 (1995).

If all of this is so, what does it do to the whole scheme of Fed. R. Evid. 104? What does it do to the whole scheme of Fed. R. Evid. 901? What does it do to Wigmore's belief repeated and adopted in that same Advisory Committee Note, that the authenticity rules express "an inherent logical necessity" implicit in the requirement of relevance — that the evidence is not relevant unless the authenticity rules are complied with?

(2) *Can You Avoid Identifying the Caller by Calling it Circumstantial Evidence?* Consider *United States v. Brown*, 603 F.2d 1022 (1st Cir. 1979):

> Defendant-appellant, John T. Brown, appeals from a jury conviction of stealing sixteen [rare] birds [from the air freight at Logan airport].
>
> Based on the evidence, the jury could find beyond a reasonable doubt that appellant overheard conversations [at a pet store] relative to the [prospective] arrival of the birds at Delta's air freight terminal. There was evidence from which it could find that appellant decided to steal the birds and that he called Delta to confirm the shipment and ascertain the shipping charges. There is little question that appellant went to the airport and picked up a box there. [Appellant challenges the admission of testimony that an unidentified male telephoned the Delta air freight terminal.]

> Appellant misunderstands the reason for the admission of the phone call. The question of voice identification was not in issue. There was testimony by Proulx [a cohort of appellant] that appellant made a phone call prior to the trip to the airport. Witness Morris [a Delta employee] was properly allowed to testify that, prior to the time the birds were picked up, he received a phone call from an unidentified male inquiring about the shipment and that he responded by giving the shipping charges . . . . The phone call, although not critical by itself, was another link in the chain of circumstantial evidence tending to prove that appellant stole the birds. The identity of a person making a phone call can be proven by circumstantial evidence. It was not error to admit the testimony as to the phone call received at the Delta air freight terminal inquiring about the shipment of birds.

Is this decision correct? Does it contain the seeds of destruction of the authentication requirement? Can you think of an alternative ground for the decision?

NOTES ON AUDIO RECORDING

(1) *Introduction.* In the above cases, the relevant conversations are recounted, rather than introduced via a tape or other recording thereof. The only problem in those cases is whether the person in the conversation could be reliably identified, i.e., a problem of authentication of the voice (which seemed to belong to so-and-so). Frequently, however, the conversation is introduced through a tape recording played for the jury. Additional problems concerning the accuracy of the tape may arise. Thus, a particular tape recording may involve both the law of authentication of the voice and the law that has evolved to help assure the accuracy of the tape recordings that are played for the jury. What Federal Rules of Evidence would be involved in judicial measures to insure accuracy? Questions of clarity and meaning also may be more complicated. What rule(s) would be involved in this determination? (We assume for the moment that any hearsay problem is taken care of and that the recording was not illegally obtained, which involves consideration of laws such as state and federal regulation of electronic surveillance, eavesdropping and wiretapping, and state and federal constitutional provisions.) In addition, there may be a separate problem of insuring not only that the recording is of the voice of the relevant person, but that it is actually what was said at the relevant time and place, for example where the case is a prosecution for entering into an illegal transaction such as a narcotics "buy," a bribe, or making a threat. Sometimes this problem is conceived of as a second authentication problem: authenticating that the recording is of the actual conversation. The voice may authentically be that of the defendant, but it may have been recorded at another time and place, or the tap may be made of pieces pasted together from other times and places. A sampling of cases involving tape recordings follows:

(2) *Commonsense Approach to Establishing the Foundation for Tape Recordings. United States v. Moss*, 591 F.2d 428 (8th Cir. 1979):

> The fundamental requirements for the admission of evidence obtained by electronic surveillance are set out in *United States v. McMillan.* [The

> *McMillan* requirements are: (1) The recording device was capable of taping the conversation now offered in evidence. (2) The operator of the device was competent to operate the device. (3) The recording is authentic and correct. (4) No changes, additions or deletions have been made in the recording. (5) The recording has been preserved in a manner that is shown to the court. (6) The speakers are identified. (7) The conversation elicited was made voluntarily and in good faith, without any kind of inducements.] Here, the very fact of the existence of the tape recordings establishes that the recording devices were capable of picking up sounds. Furthermore, both Dempsey and Smith reviewed the recordings and testified that the tapes accurately and fully portrayed their conversations with the defendant. [T]he Government sufficiently complied.

(3) *Unintelligibility of Tape Recordings.* On occasion, when tapes are being played before the jury, portions of the recording will be inaudible. The general rule is that the court must determine whether the inaudible portions are "so substantial as to make the rest more misleading than helpful." *See United States v. Carbone*, 798 F.2d 21 (1st Cir. 1986). The court's ultimate ruling is discretionary.

(4) *Authentication and Admissibility of Transcripts.* Particularly in cases involving lengthy excerpts from surveillance tapes, one or both of the parties may offer transcripts for the jury to follow along as they listen. The transcript, unlike the tape, usually identifies the names of the people talking and often clarifies what they are saying. How should the transcripts be authenticated, and can they be taken into the jury room? *See United States v. Onori*, 535 F.2d 938 (5th Cir. 1976), comparing the use of a transcript as a guide to the use of "expert" testimony for other types of authentication issues. *Onori* concludes that disputes about the transcripts are to be treated as other authentication questions, resulting in the possibility of two disputed versions being submitted to the jury. Typically the court will instruct the jury that the tapes are the primary evidence and any conflict between what the jurors hear and the transcripts must be resolved in favor of what they hear.

[C] Self-Authentication

Read Federal Rule of Evidence 902, "Evidence That Is Self-authenticating."

UNITED STATES v. CARRIGER

United States Court of Appeals, Sixth Circuit
592 F.2d 312 (1979)

Lively, Circuit Judge.

The defendant was convicted by a jury of evading income taxes for the year 1971. The jury acquitted him of the same charge for 1972. The government sought to prove by the net worth method that Carriger substantially understated his taxable income on the returns which he filed for each of the taxable years for which he was indicted.

The ground urged for reversal is that the district court erred in excluding evidence by which the defendant sought to attack the accuracy of the prosecution's opening net worth calculation and analysis of 1971 income. In his opening statement counsel for Carriger stated that the defense would show that the defendant's brother paid large amounts of money to the defendant in 1971 and that two promissory notes dated in 1970 were evidence that his brother owed the defendant $24,000.

The promissory notes were first offered during the testimony of an attorney who had represented the defendant's brother and had seen the notes in his office, probably in 1971. Though the witness stated that he was familiar with Vernon Carriger's signature, he was not permitted to testify that the signature on the two notes appeared to be that of Vernon Carriger. The notes were next offered as exhibits during the testimony of another attorney who stated that he represented Vernon Carriger for seven or eight years and had also represented the defendant in tax matters. The witness testified that he was able to recognize the signatures of Vernon Carriger and the other signer of the note, Valada Mason. The witness was not permitted to testify that the signatures on the notes were those of Vernon Carriger and Valada Mason because the district court concluded that there was "no foundation at all" for such testimony. Following this ruling the witness testified that he had seen both signers of the two notes sign their names hundreds of times. He was then permitted to identify the signatures on the notes as those of Vernon Carriger and Valada Mason.

In overruling Carriger's motion for a new trial the district court held that "the promissory notes were properly excluded since no foundation was laid for their admission into evidence." In its brief the government equates this language with a holding that the notes were excluded for lack of authentication. Rule 901, Fed. R. Ev., provides in part as follows: [(a) and (b)(1) and (2) quoted]. The note of the Advisory Committee appended to Rule 901 states, "Authentication and identification represent a special aspect of relevancy." This comment ties Rule 901 to Rule 104(b), Fed. R. Ev., which deals with the admission of evidence where relevancy depends upon fulfillment of a condition of fact. Under this rule the district court was required to make a preliminary determination of whether there was sufficient evidence "to support a finding that the matter in question is what its proponent claims." Rule 901(a), *supra*. The requirement of the illustration in Rule 901(b)(2), *supra* [nonexpert opinion] was clearly satisfied by the testimony of the witness who was familiar with the handwriting and signatures of both signers of the notes.

The government argues that exclusion of the notes from evidence was proper because defendant failed to present testimony of a witness with knowledge "that a matter is what it is claimed to be." Rule 901(b)(1), *supra*. This argument echoes the statement of the district court that testimony concerning the underlying transaction was required to make the notes admissible. Actually the notes were sufficiently identified as promissory notes by their production and no further authentication was required by reason of an applicable provision for self-authentication in Rule 902(9), Fed. R. Ev.: [self-authentication of items purporting to be commercial paper]. The Advisory Committee Note and the Report of the House Committee on the Judiciary indicate that "general commercial law" refers to the Uniform Commercial Code. Under Uniform Commercial Code § 3–307 mere production of a note is prima facie evidence of its validity and of the holder's right to recover on it.

In *United States v. Goichman*, 547 F.2d 778, 784 (3d Cir. 1976), the court stated:

> Once a prima facie case [of authenticity] is made, the evidence goes to the jury and it is the jury who will ultimately determine the authenticity of the evidence, not the court. The only requirement is that there has been substantial evidence from which they could infer that the document was authentic.

We conclude that the district court erred in requiring further authentication of the promissory notes. Actually, no testimony was required to establish the genuineness of the signatures on the notes. In effect UCC § 3–307 creates a presumption that commercial paper offered in evidence is authentic and Rule 902 dispenses with a requirement of extrinsic evidence for admissibility. By requiring proof of the underlying transaction as a condition for admission the district court denied the defendant the benefit of the rule. Of course, admission of the notes would not have established their genuineness or the existence of an indebtedness conclusively. As the Advisory Committee note states, "in no instance is the opposite party foreclosed from disputing authenticity." In effect the district court required the defendant to prove that the notes were genuine and that a debt existed, whereas only a prima facie showing was required to make them admissible.

The judgment of the district court is reversed, and the cause is remanded for a new trial.

UNITED STATES v. TROTTER

United States Court of Appeals, Eighth Circuit
538 F.2d 217, *cert. denied*, 429 U.S. 943 (1976)

Stephenson, Circuit Judge.

Appellant contends the trial court erred in receiving in evidence the certified, exemplified, and authenticated Indiana registration records of the Indiana Bureau of Motor Vehicles showing that the stolen vehicle in issue was last registered in the name of Frank W. Tweedy, Muncie, Indiana. Initially, appellant contends the exhibit was not relevant since it is not a crime to drive an automobile which is registered to another person. The contention is devoid of merit. The exhibit tended to show that appellant did not own the vehicle and further that it was owned by a person who lived in Muncie, Indiana. Both facts corroborated appellant's confession that he stole the vehicle in Muncie and were therefore relevant. Appellant's further contention that the exhibit was not admissible because not shown to be a record kept, recorded or copied in the normal course of business is likewise without merit. The exhibit included a photocopy of the certificate of registration, attested to and certified by the Commissioner of the Bureau of Motor Vehicles of the State of Indiana, the custodian of such records, together with the certificate of the governor of Indiana that the attached attestation and certificate was executed by the duly appointed, qualified and acting Commissioner of the Bureau of Motor Vehicles of the State of Indiana and custodian of the records therein. The documents executed by the governor and the commissioner contained the seals of their respective offices. The documents were executed in full compliance with Fed. R. Evid. 902(1).

[*Affirmed.*]

NOTES AND QUESTIONS

(1) *Relationship between Self-Authentication of Affidavit and Hearsay Exception for Absence of Official Record.* In *United States v. M'Biye*, 655 F.2d 1240 (D.C. Cir. 1981), the defendant was accused of falsely claiming on a loan application that he was employed by the United Nations. The issue on appeal was the admission of an affidavit executed by the Chief of Personnel at the relevant U.N. agency stating that a search of the relevant records had been done and had revealed no record of defendant having been employed by the U.N. The Court of Appeals held that the U.N. and its agencies satisfy the threshold requirement of Fed. R. Evid. 803(10) (hearsay exception for self-authenticated certificate [affidavit] or testimony, as to absence of public record) in that they are "public offices or agencies." As to the reference to Fed. R. Evid. 902 requirements contained in Fed. R. Evid. 803(10), requiring that the affidavit be on the list in Fed. R. Evid. 902 of "self-authenticating documents," the Court found the affidavit fit squarely within Fed. R. Evid. 902(8) (self-authenticating status of documents acknowledged by notary public), since the affidavit was executed and sworn to before a New York notary public. In contemplating Fed. R. Evid. 902(8), consider that a notary certificate only states that a person purporting to be the affiant appeared before the notary and signed and swore, under legal penalty, to the truth of all recitals contained in the document. The certificate does not state either (a) that the person appearing in fact was who he or she claimed to be, or (b) that, in fact, the recitals are true. How reliable, then, in terms of trustworthiness, is a notarial certificate? The court held the affidavit admissible.

The court also discusses whether provisions of Fed. R. Evid. 902 other than Fed. R. Evid. 902(8) could be used to satisfy Fed. R. Evid. 803(10)'s requirement that the affidavit be self-authenticating under Fed. R. Evid. 902. Reiterating that Fed. R. Evid. 902 lists documents for which no independent evidence of authenticity is required for admissibility, the court examines Fed. R. Evid. 902(2), which declares that domestic documents not under seal can be self-authenticating in certain circumstances. The court holds this does not cover the present affidavit because Fed. R. Evid. 902(2), by reference to other provisions, requires that the affidavit be signed by an officer of an American jurisdiction, and the U.N. does not qualify as such. Nor is the affidavit within Fed. R. Evid. 902(3) (foreign public documents complying with certain procedures), the court holds, since the U.N. is not a "foreign public" agency.

Query: If the search of the records by the U.N. official had revealed a record that Mr. M'Biye was indeed an employee of the U.N., could Mr. M'Biye have introduced an affidavit from the official to that effect, to establish the employment? If not, why is an affidavit to the opposite effect allowed, as in the *M'Biye* decision itself?

(2) *Is Rule 902 Simply a "Presumption of Authenticity?"* Fed. R. Evid. 902, in an earlier draft, was entitled "Presumption of Authenticity." Does that better convey the meaning? Is that all that any authentication means? In other words, when we say a document has been "authenticated" within the meaning of Article IX,

or that Article IX has been complied with, do we merely mean there is a rebuttable presumption of genuineness or authenticity?

(3) *Authentication of Business Records.* Fed. R. Evid. 902(11) and (12), assigned *supra* at the head of this subsection, are relatively new provisions added to allow convenient laying of a foundation — i.e. by means of a certificate rather than having a witness come to the stand — for records to qualify under the hearsay exception for business records. Consider the following in connection with these provisions:

(a) Are these provisions (902(11) and (12)) concerned solely with authentication? Authentication of what? That the principal document being offered, to which the certificate attaches, issued from the business? Isn't more involved than that? For example, what about that document's preparation, maintenance, and normal use? Is that "more" really in the province of "authentication?"

(b) What about authentication of the *certificate* (called a *"declaration"* in the provisions)? Is there any provision that *that* is self-authenticating? Or is that implied? Or is there another authentication rule taking care of that? Or is it left in limbo? In addition to authentication of the authorship of the certificate, is a hearsay exception needed to assure the accuracy of the facts stated in the certificate? Aren't there a number of such facts, in addition to merely that the business document to which the certificate is attached issued from the business? (*See* paragraph (a) of this note, immediately above, indicating there are such facts.)

(c) Does the certificate itself *have* to comply with the hearsay rule and the authentication requirement, in order to come in before the judge to establish the admissibility of the business document to which it is attached? *See* Rule 104(a).

(d) Why are these provisions (902(11) and (12)) in a rule entitled "Self-Authentication," when they deal with neither "self" (because the business record requires a certificate) nor mere "authentication" (for the reasons suggested above)?

(e) Will these provisions prove dubious in certain circumstances, in light of *Crawford's* testimonial approach to constitutional confrontation (*see* Chapter 11, *supra*)? Is the certificate in essence an affidavit stating facts sworn to before a public official, which *Crawford* condemns? Or does the confrontation clause not apply when the facts stated are received on a preliminary question (the admissibility of evidence)? *See United States v. Wittig*, *supra*, § 11.03[B].

(f) Is there a practical problem concerning what the jury is to make of the business record if (for any of the reasons suggested in paragraphs (b), (c), or (e) of this note above) the certificate that accompanies the business record is admitted only before the judge on the question of admissibility of the business record and there is no witness to tell the jury what the business record is, where it came from, nor how it was prepared?

(4) *Self-Authentication Does Not Solve All Hearsay Problems.* In *United States v. One 1968 Piper Navajo Twin Engine Aircraft*, 594 F.2d 1040 (5th Cir. 1979), an airplane used for smuggling drugs was seized by the U.S. The owners claimed it had been stolen at gunpoint from them and used for smuggling by bandits. The owners thus tried to get the plane back from the government. They offered (in translation) a signed statement given by the plane's Mexican pilot to Mexican authorities that the plane had been stolen from him and a Mexican deposition of someone to whom the pilot had told the same story (also in translation). These were offered in advance of trial in a motion to admit them pursuant to Fed. R. Evid. 902(3) (certain foreign documents are self-authenticating.) In response to the motion, the government stipulated to their authenticity under that rule. The court holds that filing a motion pursuant to Fed. R. Evid. 902(3) "pertains only to dispensing with extrinsic evidence of the documents' authenticity as a condition precedent to their admissibility. A motion made under it is not sufficient to put the opponent on notice that the proponent means to offer it in evidence" pursuant to the catchall hearsay exception, formerly in Fed. R. Evid. 803(24) [now Fed. R. Evid. 807]. Thus, the pretrial notice required by the catchall exception was lacking. No other hearsay exception was available either. Thus, the documents were inadmissible. The stipulation only dispensed with authentication requirements. The documents still were hearsay:

> Although the government has stipulated to the authenticity of this document pursuant to Rule 902(3), Fed. Rules of Evid., it contends that the document is nonetheless hearsay in that the declarant was not subject to cross-examination at the time the statement was made and did not testify at trial. Claimant argues that satisfaction of Rule 902 authenticity requirements renders hearsay precautions irrelevant. The court cannot accept claimant's position, however, as authentication is a separate requirement from the hearsay rules. "Merely because a document is authenticated does not mean it is admissible. It may, for example, need to meet the hearsay requirements if it is offered to prove the truth of assertions made in it."

[D] Chain of Custody

UNITED STATES v. COFFMAN

United States Court of Appeals, Tenth Circuit
638 F.2d 192 (1980), *cert. denied*, 451 U.S. 917 (1981)

DOYLE, CIRCUIT J.

[Defendants were convicted of possession of LSD].

Defendants have argued that the police lab allowed evidence, consisting of plastic bags filled with LSD-saturated pieces of blotter paper [purchased from and seized from defendants], to be tested for fingerprints before the blotter paper was tested for LSD, [and thus] that the chain of custody was broken. They also maintained that a real possibility exists that the blotter paper became adulterated while in the custody of the police lab. The testimony concerning the custody of the bags while out of the police lab was not allowed because the witness was inadvertently not endorsed as a government witness. The case of *United States v. Aviles*, 623 F2d 1192 (7th Cir. 1980), said:

> The standard for the admission of exhibits into evidence is that there must be a showing that the physical exhibit being offered is in substantially the same condition as when the crime was committed. This determination is to be made by the trial judge and may not be overturned but for a clear abuse of discretion.

This court in *United States v. Freeman*, 412 F2d 1181 (10th Cir. 1969) said:

> The matters relating to the chain of possession of the tablets from agent Bullock to the chemist and back relate only to the weight to be given the testimony of the chemist. In the final analysis, the verdict depended on whether the jury believed agent Bullock or the defendant. The matter of credibility is for the jury, not for the appellate court.

Finally, Judge Finesilver [the trial judge in the present case] made findings on this question also:

> [T]he chain of custody has been established substantially in this case, and while the safeguards were not foolproof, we find that there was a reasonable probability that they are in the same form as they were when they initially were obtained by the officers in question. We are satisfied that from the totality of all the evidence, considering the nature of the articles, the circumstances surrounding the preservation and the custody of the drugs or the substances, the likelihood of any meddlers or unlikelihood of any tampering, that the overwhelming evidence supports the admissibility in evidence of the substances in question and that the chain of custody has been established. We are satisfied there is no evidence of any adulteration or misidentification or any irritants or any contamination of the Exhibits, or that they have been confused with anything or with any other Exhibits that were examined. Further, we are satisfied that reasonable steps were taken to insure the integrity of the substances, and that the chain of custody has been established to our satisfaction.

Affirmed.

UNITED STATES v. THOMAS

U.S. Air Force Court of Military Review
38 M.J. 614 (1993)

Johnson, Senior J.

[Thomas was convicted of possessing drug paraphernalia, among other offenses. At trial, a paper bag containing the paraphernalia was received in evidence. Defense counsel did not object to the exhibit, although apparently the only foundation testimony was the seizing government agent's statement that it looked like the bag of paraphernalia seized from Thomas, on the basis of its general appearance. On appeal, Thomas argued that his attorney's failure to object constituted ineffective assistance of counsel. The appellate court briefly rejected this argument on the ground that this foundation was sufficient to make the exhibit admissible.]

Sergeant Thomas' complaint that his counsel [was ineffective because he] failed to object to admission of the drug paraphernalia is not supported by the record. The items in question (a small brown paper bag containing [baggies and straws with cocaine residue and other items]) are sufficiently unique in their general appearance and in their unusual association together that there was adequate foundation to admit them into evidence without formal proof of their chain of custody after seizure by government agents. [Rule] 901(b)(4).

Affirmed.

NOTES AND QUESTIONS

(1) *"Minor" Breaks in Chain Only Affect Weight. See also United States v. Pasha*, 751 F.2d 377 (3d Cir. 1984) (small gap in chain of custody of cocaine seized from defendants, involving substance's transportation from police narcotics unit to laboratory, does not require exclusion of trial testimony that substance seized by police was same substance tested in laboratory), *cert. denied*, 469 U.S. 1214 (1985); *United States v. Clark*, 732 F.2d 1536 (11th Cir. 1984) (use of lock seal bags by FBI established chain of custody sufficient to support admissibility of drugs seized from defendant; failure to identify evidence custodian who received lock seal bag in mail did not break chain of custody; only affected weight of evidence, not admissibility); *United States v. Shackleford*, 738 F.2d 776 (7th Cir. 1984) (in prosecution for possessing unregistered explosives, no error in admitting exhibits of copper pipe and putty substance purportedly found at defendant's residence; although investigating officer failed to place identifying tags on items, government established chain of custody for them through testimony of two other officers who were at defendant's residence when search took place; any discrepancies in chain of custody affected only weight of the exhibits, not admissibility). *See generally* Gianelli, *Chain of Custody and the Handling of Real Evidence*, 20 Am. Crim. L. Rev. 527 (1983).

(2) *Effect of O.J. Simpson Case.* Do you think the widely publicized O.J. Simpson case may affect the attitude toward chain of custody expressed in several preceding cases, such as the trial judge's view in *Coffman, supra*?

Compare another high profile case, *In re Exxon Valdez*, 270 F.3d 1215 (9th Cir. 2001), involving the asserted liability of the Captain (Hanzelwood) and the owner (Exxon Corp.) for a massive oil spill in Alaska, when a tanker ship ran aground:

> Exxon and Hazelwood moved *in limine* to exclude evidence of a .061% blood alcohol level in samples taken eleven hours after the *Exxon Valdez* ran aground on Bligh Reef. Expert testimony was offered to show that if he still had that much alcohol in his blood eleven hours later, he must have been deeply under the influence when he [finally] abandoned the bridge to the third mate. The district court, despite noting "remarkable mishandlings" of the blood samples, denied the motion *in limine*. Its reasons were that any change in the blood from bad storage would have been observed and noted by the laboratory technicians, and that the evidence on chain of

custody regarding sealed tubes with Hazelwood's name and social security number on them was good enough so that reasonable jurors could conclude that the tubes contained Hazelwood's blood. Hazelwood argues on appeal that because of improper storage and because of a discrepancy between the color of the stoppers in the evidence log and the lab notes, the evidence should not have been admitted.

We review evidentiary rulings for abuse of discretion. The authentication of evidence is "satisfied by evidence sufficient to support a finding that the matter in question is what its proponent claims." The district court properly exercised its discretion according to the correct standard, which is whether "a reasonable juror could find" that the tested specimens were Hazelwood's.

Was the issue more than whether this was the blood of Hazelwood? Was there also a question of whether the alcohol in the specimen was in the original? In the same amount? Were there chemical changes? Were they purposely or accidentally introduced? Are these also authentication (identification) questions? If not, what are they? Isn't "remarkable mishandlings" more than a mere break in the chain affecting credibility or weight before the jury?

[E] Photographs, Videotapes, and the Like

AVERHART v. STATE

Indiana Supreme Court

470 N.E.2d 666 (1984), *cert. denied*, 471 U.S. 1030 (1985)

Pivarnix, J.

[Defendants were charged with murder arising out of a bank robbery in which a police officer was killed by gunfire in a shootout with the robbers as they attempted their escape.]

An automatic camera in the bank photographed the scene during the perpetration of this robbery. No photographer operated it. It was activated by an employee who pushed a button at his station. The officer responsible for the camera equipment stated it had been checked earlier that morning and it had in it unexposed film ready to be used if the camera was activated. Admissibility of photographs is basically a matter of the sound discretion of the court and will not be disturbed unless an abuse of discretion can be clearly shown. Witness Mavis Reeves examined the photographs produced by the automatic camera and was able to identify a large number of them as truly and accurately depicting what she saw. Evidence produced at trial showed the film in the camera was unexposed before the robbery and the camera was inspected and found to be in working order. There also was clear testimony as to the retrieval and chain of custody of the film. This is not denied by defendants. Unrefuted testimony indicated the method used to process and print the films, and further showed they had not been retouched or altered. The testimony of Mavis Reeves, an eyewitness to the event, confirmed that the parts of the events she saw corresponded to the tale that was shown by the photographs.

There were, of course, occurrences during the robbery revealed by the photographs that were outside her range of view. Under all of these circumstances it was not necessary that all and each of the photographs be supported by testimony of a witness that the photograph is an accurate representation of the witness' observation. The photographs were admissible not only as demonstrative evidence but as substantive evidence under the silent witness theory. In this regard it is held that the photographs speak for themselves when, as here, there is a strong showing of the photographs' competence and authenticity coupled with showing that they were not retouched or altered. An examination of the photographs shows that they clearly depict the interior of the bank and shows the activities of persons during the robbery, including employees and the three perpetrators. There was ample supporting testimony here authenticating the photographs. Therefore, the ruling of the trial court admitting the photographs into evidence was proper.

NOTES AND QUESTIONS

(1) *No Need for Photographer.* It is often argued that a photograph introduced to show some relevant scene must be authenticated by showing that it was taken by a competent photographer and by accounting for its whereabouts between the taking and the introduction into evidence (the "chain of custody"), and that an expert must testify that there were no relevant distortions resulting from camera angle, lighting, etc. However, it is now well settled in most jurisdictions that this is not required (although it may do the trick), at least not as a matter of authentication or identification, if there is someone who viewed the scene under the relevant conditions (whether that person is connected with the taking of the photo or not) who looks at the photo before or during the trial and testifies that it is an accurate representation of the scene as the witness saw it. The matters mentioned in the first sentence of this Note, however, may affect the weight the fact-finder will ascribe to the photograph and even may be required as a matter of Fed. R. Evid. 403 in certain cases where there may be some special reason to be suspicious about the photograph for one of those reasons.

For a knowledgeable discussion of factors involved in photographic accuracy, see Houts, Photographic Misrepresentation (1964). A graphic illustration of the difference between a scene shot with a camera with a short focal length lens and precisely the same scene shot from the same position with a long focal length lens appears at pp. 5–46 to 5–49, figures 54 and 55, in that book. One of those two photos, reproduced there, makes it painfully evident that the car merging into oncoming traffic had considerable distance and time to make it safely, whereas the other photo makes the opposite equally painfully evident, i.e., that there was not enough room or time to make it before being hit by the oncoming car. Yet in reality the distances and positioning of the cars in both were exactly the same, and both are pictures of the same event. (The referenced pages are worth looking at.) Are these matters of authentication and identification, or of some other rule or rules? Which is the "true" representation? Probably plaintiff and defendant saw it differently. How should the judge decide admissibility of such photos and the jury evaluate them? Do you suppose digital photography provides even more opportunities for this sort of things?

(2) *"Day in the Life" Videos.* In personal injury litigation, plaintiffs often produce "Day in the Life" videotapes or discs showing how traumatic injuries have affected the ability of the plaintiff to do even simple tasks. What foundational questions are implicated? Defendants sometimes offer surreptitiously taken "Day in the Life" videos that show active and unimpaired activities of the plaintiff.

Regarding videotapes and videodiscs generally, see FEDERAL TRIAL GUIDE, Ch. 65, *Demonstrative Evidence* (Matthew Bender); JOSEPH, MODERN VISUAL EVIDENCE (current Supp); Comment, *Truth, Lies, and Videotape: Are Current Federal Rules of Evidence Adequate?* 21 SW. U. L. REV. 1199 (1992).

(3) *Technology can Affect Authentication.* Fed. R. Evid. 901(b)(9) (authentication by process or system) was in part designed to cover a case like *Averhart, supra.* In *Averhart* itself, much more was shown (perhaps to enhance weight) than would be needed merely to authenticate. In fact, several different methods of authentication were employed together.

Advances in technology can implicate authentication questions. For example, computer technology can be used to alter photographs in ways that are difficult to tell just by looking at the picture. Enhancement and enlargement of photographs and creating still photographs from videotape now are common. These techniques typically require expert testimony in order to establish a proper foundation.

STATE v. SWINTON

Supreme Court of Connecticut
847 A.2d 921 (2004)

KATZ, J.

The defendant, Alfred Swinton, appeals from the judgment of conviction, rendered after a jury trial, of one count of murder.

[T]he defendant challenges the admissibility of two separate, but related, pieces of evidence: first, photographs of a bite mark on the victim's body that were enhanced using a computer software program known as Lucis, and second, images of the defendant's teeth overlaid, or superimposed, upon photographs of the bite mark that were made through the use of Adobe Photoshop, another computer software program.

[I. Computer Enhancements: Admissible]

At trial, the state presented several images of the bite marks that were computer enhancements of a photograph taken at the victim's autopsy. The enhancements were created through the use of a software program called Lucis. The state introduced the enhancements through Major Timothy Palmbach, overseer of the division of scientific services in the state department of public safety. Palmbach has a master's degree in forensic science, and extensive experience in the forensic field. Palmbach had obtained the original photographs for the purpose of enhancement from Karazulas [a police dentition expert]. Because the state police did not possess the equipment necessary to generate the digitally enhanced photographs, Palmbach produced the computer enhanced photographs at Lucis' manufacturer's offices. Palmbach explained that Lucis was developed for "scientific applications," but that experts had used it in forensic settings.

Palmbach explained how the Lucis program works:

> [I]t allows us to see image detail that we normally couldn't see. [A] normal photograph . . . has many layers of contrast in it. Your average photograph is going to have around 255 layers of contrast in it. [O]ur eyes are only capable of perceiving 32 layers . . . . So our eyes see very, very little of actually what's present inside of the image itself. [O]ur eye perceive . . . the major contrast differences . . . . So this program allow[s] us to make a selection of a particular range of contrast . . . . And by . . . narrowing [the] band of contrast layers down, we increase the image detail. So we reduce the amount of layers that we're looking at. We're not getting rid of them . . . . [T]he result is the picture's got tremendous detail . . . .

With the use of a laptop computer, Palmbach demonstrated to the jury exactly how the original bite mark photograph had been enhanced . . . . Palmbach testified several times that nothing was added to or removed from the photograph by the enhancement process . . . .

Although much of Palmbach's testimony concerned how the Lucis program worked, he was not qualified as an expert in computer programs, generally, or in Lucis specifically, nor was he qualified as a programmer. Palmbach testified that he was not aware of how the computer makes the distinction as to how many layers there are in an image, or what the algorithm is, or how the algorithm actually sorts the layers. Palmbach testified that Lucis did not create any artifacts in its enhancement process.

On appeal, the defendant argues that the evidence at issue resembles composite photographs, and therefore, should be governed under a similar standard. With respect to composite photographs, "[t]he moving party must present witnesses with firsthand knowledge of how the composite was prepared and of how accurately it portrays that which it is intended to depict." [Case.] The defendant also claims that because this evidence actually was created by and through the use of a computer, it is computer generated evidence, and thus entails additional foundational requirements.

The state argues, to the contrary, that the Lucis enhanced photographs are mere "reproductions" of the photograph of the bite mark, and that their admissibility therefore should be governed by the foundational standard for photographs. Under that standard, all that is required is that a photograph be introduced through a witness competent to verify it as a fair and accurate representation of what it depicts . . . ..The state further argues that a photographer's in-court testimony is not required for the admission of a photograph [Case] and therefore, the computer programmer's testimony is not required in this instance . . . .

We do not agree with the state's proposition that the enhanced photographs in the present case are like any other photographs . . . . We note that "[d]igital images are easier to manipulate than traditional photographs and digital manipulation is more difficult to detect." After the photographs were put in a digital format, they were enhanced, a process which can also introduce manipulation or alteration of the original image. [U]nlike other types of enhancement wherein the original and the enhanced product could easily be inspected visually for distortion, or dissimilarity, the images in this case involve a bite mark, which, because it actually is composed of multiple smaller marks, is not so easily inspected. Odontological matching depends on millimeters.. . . .Other types of enhanced evidence, such as videotapes, may be more amenable to visual inspection because they are larger in scale.

[C]ases in Connecticut that give rise to the question of the admissibility of computer generated evidence involve the admissibility of computerized business records. In *American Oil Co. v. Valenti* the court adopted a general rule, requiring "testimony by a person with some degree of computer expertise, who has sufficient knowledge to be examined and cross-examined about the functioning of the computer." [T]he court cautioned, "[c]omputer machinery may make errors because of malfunctioning of the hardware, the computer's mechanical apparatus. Computers may also, and more frequently, make errors that arise out of defects in the software, the input procedures, the data base, and the processing program . . . . In view of the complex nature of the operation of computers and general lay unfamiliarity with their operation, courts have been cautioned to take special care to be certain that the foundation is sufficient to warrant a finding of trustworthiness and that the opposing party has full opportunity to inquire into the process by which information is fed into the computer." [T]he court did not require the computer programmer, or even the person who had entered the information into the computer, to testify, because the reliability of the records was extrinsically established. Routinely prepared records are well recognized exceptions to the hearsay rule, because their regular use in the business of the company insures a high degree of accuracy. In the case before us, such reliability has not been extrinsically established . . . .

In *Nooner v. State* the Arkansas Supreme Court upheld a ruling in a pretrial hearing that "so long as the process leading to the duplicate videotape and enhanced photographs was explained to the jury," they could be introduced as evidence [and] the court allowed the enhancements because their reliability was attested to by multiple witnesses who all "meticulously described their role in the enhancement process." . . . Additionally, the court noted that there was no evidence of distortion [or additions, deletions, or changes] in the enhancements . . . .

What is consistent, in [the] cases, is that the technician or analyst who testified was the person who had engaged in the enhancement process and was capable of testifying in specific detail as to the process . . . . [T]his standard does not dictate that the only person capable of such expertise is the programmer of the software . . . .

Rule 901(b)(9) of the Federal Rules of Evidence [to which we can look for guidance] provides [for] authentication or identification [by] a process or system . . . . [The] rule requires sufficient evidence to authenticate both the accuracy of the image and the reliability of the machine producing the image.

. . . This standard [can be] satisfied by evidence that (1) the computer equipment is accepted in the field as standard and competent and was in good working order, (2) qualified computer operators were employed, (3) proper procedures were followed in connection with the input and output of information, (4) a reliable software program was utilized, (5) the equipment was programmed and operated correctly, and (6) the exhibit is properly identified as the output in question . . . . *Commercial Union Ins. Co. v. Boston Edison Co.* (conditioning admissibility on sufficient showing that: "[1] the computer is functioning properly; [2] the input and underlying equations are sufficiently complete and accurate [and disclosed to the opposing party, so that they may challenge them]; and [3] the program is generally accepted by the appropriate community of scientists"). . . .

We note that [r]eliability problems may arise through or in: (1) the underlying information itself; (2) entering the information into the computer; (3) the computer hardware; (4) the computer software (the programs or instructions that tell the computer what to do); (5) the execution of the instructions, which transforms the information in some way — for example, by calculating numbers, sorting names, or storing information and retrieving it later; (6) the output (the information as produced by the computer in a useful form, such as a printout of tax return information, a transcript of a recorded conversation, or an animated graphics simulation); (7) the security system that is used to control access to the computer; and (8) user errors, which may arise at any stage. . . .

[W]e conclude that the state laid an adequate foundation for the Lucis enhancements of the bite mark photograph. First, Palmbach testified that the computer equipment is accepted as standard equipment in the field . . . . Second, it was established that a qualified computer operator produced the enhancement. Palmbach's testimony clearly demonstrated that he was well versed in the Lucis program.. . . . Additionally, Karazulas, an odontological expert, was with Palmbach throughout the process and was able to aid him in determining when the image was appropriately enhanced for forensic comparison . . . .

Third, the state presented evidence that proper procedures were followed in connection with the input and output of information. Palmbach testified regarding the process of the digitization of the image — wherein a photograph is transformed into pixels; — and how [he] then had used the Lucis software to select comparable points of contrast and array them into layers . . . how the Lucis program then diminished certain layers in order to heighten the visual appearance of the bite mark . . . . he even demonstrated the enhancement process to the jury. Palmbach compared the enhanced photographs with the unenhanced photographs in front of the jury. Palmbach testified: "Lucis does not remove any pixels. It is only selecting to show you the range that you've asked for. Every one of those pictures and every bit of that contrast is still present in the enhanced portion . . . . It's just that we're diminishing some and bringing others forward . . . just for viewing purposes. But every bit of that information is still present."

Fourth, the state adequately demonstrated that Lucis is a reliable software program . . . . Palmbach testified that unlike other computer programs such as Adobe Photoshop, [Lucis] does not even have image editing features . . . Although Palmbach testified that he was not aware of the error rates regarding the Lucis program, he stated that he was aware of Lucis' marketing papers and an article that had been written concerning Lucis, both of which claimed that the program was artifact free, which would contribute greatly to a low error rate. Additionally,

Palmbach personally tested Lucis' accuracy by making a known exemplar using a bite mark made by Karazulas on his own arm and then subjecting it to enhancement.

Although Palmbach admitted that the algorithm itself was programmed by someone who "knows a lot more about computers" than he did, our review of the record reveals that Palmbach had sufficient knowledge of the processes involved in the enhancement to lay a proper foundation . . . .

[II. Photoshop Overlays: Not Admissible]

Through Karazulas, the state offered overlays, created with the use of Adobe Photoshop, which superimposed images of the defendant's dentition over photographs of the bite mark. Karazulas had extensive training and experience in the study of bite mark identification, and was admitted as an expert in the field of forensic odontology. He testified that bite mark identification is based upon the recognition of unique characteristics of the person whose teeth had left that mark . . . .

[After making extensive comparisons that he described] Karazulas engaged in a series of steps that eventually led to the creation of the Adobe Photoshop overlays at issue. First, he made a wax impression using the plaster molds taken of the defendant's teeth. Karazulas then placed the upper and lower molds of the defendant's teeth onto a copy machine and printed out an image from these molds. Next, placing paper over that image, and holding it over a lighted surface, he manually traced out the biting edges of the teeth. That tracing was then photocopied onto a clear piece of acetate, producing a transparent overlay depicting the edges of the defendant's dentition.

Karazulas then had both enhanced and unenhanced photographs of the bite mark, as well as tracings of the defendant's dentition, scanned into a computer. Because he was not familiar with Adobe Photoshop, Karazulas secured the assistance of Gary Weddle, a Fairfield University chemistry professor, to scan these images and create the overlays by using the computer program to superimpose the defendant's dentition over the bite mark. Karazulas [watched and] instructed Weddle not to alter the original images in creating the overlays.

. . . Weddle created a number of overlays. First, there are overlays, such as state's exhibits 117 and 166, which are tracings of the defendant's dentition superimposed over cropped photographs of the bite mark, both enhanced and unenhanced. Second, there are overlays composed of images of the defendant's actual teeth superimposed over photographs of the bite mark. This type of overlay, as depicted in state's exhibits 118 through 121, as well as state's exhibit 164, was created by: scanning portions of the molds taken of the defendant's teeth to create state's exhibit 115; directing the computer software to isolate the upper layers of the occlusal edges of the molds from the images contained in state's exhibit 115; applying a process to the images of the teeth whereby the teeth became less opaque and more transparent; and lastly, superimposing the image of the translucent teeth over various photographs of the bite mark. Karazulas concluded that the defendant had bitten the victim's breasts. [He pointed out to the jury the matching features in detail on the exhibits.]

[T]he state [argues] that, because the exhibits used to create the overlay — the photographs of the bite mark and the tracings or molds of the defendant's teeth — were authenticated properly, the overlay itself, as a product of the two, was authenticated as well. In addition, the state claims that the overlays created by Adobe Photoshop are the equivalent of what could be seen if a tracing of the defendant's teeth manually were placed over a photograph of the bite mark.

The defendant claims that, "the computer was used to create a picture which did not exist before," and that "[a] dramatic new technique was used to create the single most important piece of evidence offered . . . ."

Karazulas recognized his own limitations as a witness with respect to the Adobe Photoshop evidence. He admitted that he had "no skill or experience" with Adobe Photoshop. When asked whether the computer bent the image in some respects in order to account for the curvature of a three-dimensional object, such as a breast, when the computer is actually superimposing one two-dimensional flat image onto another, Karazulas responded that he did not think that the computer could do so, but stated: "I'm not an expert in it, but I think we [can] get somebody who knows computers, they can explain that.". . .

Without a witness who satisfactorily can explain or analyze the data and the program, the effectiveness of cross-examination can be seriously undermined, particularly in light of the extent to which the evidence in the present case had been "created." Karazulas lacked the computer expertise to provide the defendant with this opportunity . . . .

We conclude that, based on the standards discussed in this opinion, the trial court improperly admitted the Adobe Photoshop overlays.

NOTES AND QUESTIONS

(1) *Expert Testimony Issue. Swinton* mentions *Daubert* (treated in § 6.02[A], *supra*) in a brief cryptic passage we have deleted indicating that defendant invoked *Daubert* in his appellate argument. The court does not make clear, however, how *Daubert*, which applies in Connecticut, relates to the questioned evidence, saying only what we have reproduced above, and that bite-mark identification is an accepted science. Nevertheless, doesn't *Swinton* effectively turn the authentication question into a *Daubert* issue? Authentication is determined by reference to the Rule 104(b) standard. Is reliability for *Daubert* purposes determined by the judge under Rule 104(a)? Can Rule 901(b)(9) be reconciled with the 104(b) standard?

(2) *Commercially Available Photo Programs.* Many readers of this book have probably used Adobe Photoshop. Should a commercially available program need the same level of foundation as a specially designed one-of-a-kind process or software?

(3) *Effect of Official Guidelines Regarding Imaging.* On digitized photographs and other imaging technologies, in 1999 an F.B.I. sponsored Scientific Working Group on Imaging Technologies ("SWGIT") published "Definitions and Guidelines for the Use of Imaging Technologies in the Criminal Justice System." Since that

time, the group has published several additional recommendations. How does this affect the authentication question? The *Daubert/Frye* issue?

(4) *Other Issues in Swinton. Swinton* ultimately holds that the error regarding admission of the overlays was harmless, primarily because Karazulis' other testimony of identification of the bite mark, not dependent on the overlay, was admissible and there was much other evidence both that the defendant had left the bite-mark and of guilt. The decision also discusses whether the defendant's difficulty at trial in attacking the overlay evidence (because it was based on Weddle's input, who was not available for cross-examination) made the overlay's admission a confrontation-clause violation under either the state or the federal constitution, or merely an evidentiary error. What difference does this make? Would the harmless error analysis be different? The court ultimately concludes that the error in admission of the overlay evidence did not rise to the level of a constitutional violation because defendant had other substantial ways to challenge the testimony, including, *inter alia*, cross-examination of Karazulis and showing the extent to which the overlays did not match defendant's dentition. Therefore, under state decisions, the error was harmless unless it was more probable than not that it affected the result. Could this be squared with *Crawford* and its progeny in Chapter 11, *supra*? Other trial errors alleged by the defendant are also discussed in the *Swinton* decision. In the end, *Swinton* affirms the conviction.

[F] DEMONSTRATIONS, ANIMATIONS, AND SIMULATIONS[2]

UNITED STATES v. GASKELL

United States Court of Appeals, Eleventh Circuit
985 F.2d 1056 (1993)

Birch, Circuit J.

Gaskell argues that Dr. Mittleman's demonstration of shaken baby syndrome using a rubber infant mannequin was irrelevant and unfairly prejudicial. "As a general rule, the district court has wide discretion to admit evidence of experiments conducted under substantially similar conditions." The burden is on the party offering a courtroom demonstration or experiment to lay a proper foundation establishing a similarity of circumstances and conditions. Although the conditions of the demonstration need not be identical to the event at issue, "they must be so nearly the same in substantial particulars as to afford a fair comparison in respect to the particular issue to which the test is directed." Further, experimental or demonstrative evidence, like any evidence offered at trial, should be excluded "if its probative value is substantially outweighed by the danger of unfair prejudice, confusion of the issues, or misleading the jury." Fed. R. Evid. 403.

In the presence of the jury, the government proposed that Dr. Mittleman should use the doll "to demonstrate the amount of force which would be necessary to cause

---

[2] *See also Swinton*, immediately *supra*; *Lorraine*, Section 12.01, *supra*.

[Kristen's] injuries[.]" Moreover, the demonstration was conducted during a segment of Dr. Mittleman's testimony concerning the degree of force required to produce the fatal injuries. The conditions of the demonstration, offered for this purpose, were not sufficiently similar to the alleged actions of the defendant to allow a fair comparison. As noted by defense counsel in her objection, due to differences in the weight of the doll's head as well as the flexibility and length of the doll's neck, a considerably greater degree of force was required in order to produce the head movement characteristic of shaken baby syndrome. As the party offering the evidence, the burden was on the government to show that the conditions of Dr. Mittleman's demonstration were sufficiently similar to the circumstances of Kristen's death to afford a fair comparison. Based on the differences enumerated by defense counsel, the government failed to meet this burden. Dr. Mittleman admitted that the doll's neck was stiffer than that of a seven-month-old infant and that this would affect the degree of force necessary to move the head in the required fashion. Dr. Mittleman explained that his presentation was based on a demonstration of shaken baby syndrome by a police officer whose knowledge was derived from the confession of a father in an unrelated case. [T]he government did not establish that Dr. Mittleman's hearsay knowledge of this unrelated case provided any reliable or accurate basis upon which to draw conclusions regarding Kristen's death. Further, although Dr. Mittleman repeatedly shook the doll before the jury, he was unable to state the number of oscillations required to produce Kristen's injuries. The conditions of the demonstration were thus substantially dissimilar; the government failed to establish that either the degree of force or the number of oscillations bore any relationship to the defendant's actions. Although the presentation did illustrate the path of movement of an infant's head during shaken baby syndrome, this phenomenon could have been demonstrated with equal effectiveness by a direct manipulation of the doll's head, as suggested by defense counsel at sidebar.

Whatever slight probative value that inhered in the demonstration was overwhelmed by its unfairly prejudicial effects. The sight of an adult male repeatedly shaking a representation of an infant with the degree of force necessary to manipulate the doll's head in the required fashion was likely to form a strong impression upon the jury. This prejudicial effect was magnified by the fact that the outcome of this trial hinged upon whether the jury believed that the degree of injury suffered by Kristen could support Gaskell's testimony that he inflicted the fatal injuries in a panicked attempt to revive her. By displaying a greater degree of force than the level required to produce shaken baby syndrome in a seventh-month-old infant and by arbitrarily selecting a number of oscillations, the demonstration tended to implant a vision of Gaskell's actions in the jurors' minds that was not supported by any factual basis for the demonstration. We are thus persuaded that, under Rule 403, the unfairly prejudicial nature of the demonstration outweighed any probative value.

Reversed.

BRAY v. BI-STATE DEVELOPMENT CORPORATION

Missouri Court of Appeals, Eastern District, Division Two
949 S.W.2d 93 (1997)

CRANE, P.J.

[A pedestrian who was injured while stepping off a curb in a parking garage sued the operator of the garage for failure to adequately light the area. On appeal from a defense verdict, the court held that the operator's expert had laid sufficient foundation for the validity of the computer software that produced a chart depicting light intensity levels.]

Exhibit I was produced for litigation with a computer and graphically depicts the result of computations made with a computer. An adequate foundation includes proper authentication of such computer-generated evidence. The function of computer programs like the program used in this case "is to perform rapidly and accurately an extensive series of computations not readily accomplished without use of a computer." Just as experts may base their testimony on calculations performed by hand, they may perform the same calculations using a computer. Admissibility of computer simulations is governed by the standard applicable to results of experiments.

Whether a proper foundation has been established is primarily a question addressed to the sound discretion of the trial court. Missouri courts have not laid out specific foundational requirements for computer-generated evidence of this nature. We, therefore, survey cases from other jurisdictions to see what general principles have developed.

We begin with *Commercial Union* in which the Massachusetts Supreme Court enunciated the following guidelines to establish a foundation to authenticate computer-generated evidence. The court conditioned admissibility on a sufficient showing that:

> (1) The computer is functioning properly;
>
> (2) The input and underlying equations are sufficiently complete and accurate (and disclosed to the opposing party, so that they may challenge them);
>
> (3) The program is generally accepted by the appropriate community of scientists.

Commercial Union, 591 N.E.2d at 168. Two other states have expressly used these guidelines. Courts have not required the first requirement of the *Commercial Union* guideline that the computer be functioning properly, to be affirmatively shown in the absence of any challenge thereto.

With respect to the second *Commercial Union* guideline, cases generally require that the accuracy of the input be established. However, the relevant technical or scientific community's use of or reliance on such software has been held sufficient to establish the accuracy of the software.

The second guideline contains a parenthetical requirement of pretrial disclosure. Pretrial disclosure gives the opposing party an adequate opportunity to raise objections by motion in limine and to prepare for cross-examination and rebuttal. Pretrial disclosure also reduces the need for more exacting foundational requirements. Exclusion of evidence for lack of pretrial disclosure is within the trial court's discretion.

The third *Commercial Union* guideline, general acceptance, derives from the *Frye* case [see *Frye v. United States*, 293 F. 1013, 1014 (D.C. Cir. 1923) in § 6.01, *supra*].

Other state courts have considered the sufficiency of a foundation to authenticate computer-generated evidence using similar criteria. In *People v. McHugh*, 124 Misc.2d 559, 476 N.Y.S.2d 721, 723 (Sup. 1984), the court ruled that a computer reenactment of a car crash may be admitted into evidence if it is relevant to a possible defense, fairly and accurately reflects the oral testimony, and aids the jury's understanding of the issue.

Finally, we note that Rule 901(b)(9), Fed. R. Evid., for authentication of a process, includes computer-generated evidence. The above cases and authority demonstrate that, while *Commercial Union* provides a helpful starting point to analyze questions of sufficiency of foundation, its three guidelines standing alone do not precisely reflect what courts in fact require or consider sufficient to establish a sufficient foundation. However, there is a developing consensus, as shown by the cases and authorities cited herein, which agrees on how the accuracy of computer-generated evidence can be established and gives a trial court sufficient parameters to exercise its discretion in this area without the need for a precise formula.

The trial court did not err in admitting Exhibit I over the objection to foundation based on a challenge to the validity of the software.

Affirmed.

HINKLE v. CITY OF CLARKSBURG

United States Court of Appeals, Fourth Circuit
81 F.3d 416 (1996)

RUSSELL, CIRCUIT J.

[The jury found for the defendants in a civil rights action.]

At trial, Alexander Jason, a Forensic Animation Technologist, testified for the Appellees to a version of the shooting that was based on his interpretation of the evidence and was consistent with the police officers' testimony. To illustrate Jason's testimony, Appellees introduced a computer-animated videotape. The videotape depicted Wilson's apartment complex, the officers' position in relation to the open door to Wilson's apartment, and a step-by-step account of the incident. It showed an animated version of Officer Lake on the stairwell outside the apartment aiming his gun toward Wilson, who was moving toward the open door. It depicted Wilson raising his shotgun toward the doorway, Officer Lake firing the fatal shot, Wilson's body spinning around from the force of the shot, and his shotgun discharging into the stuffed chair in the back of the room. It then showed how the officers' version of the event was consistent with the physical evidence by concluding with a depiction of the trajectory of Officer Lake's bullet in-line with the wounds to Wilson's forearm, chest, back, and the bullet hole in the wall of the room.

Appellants assign as error the district court's denial of their motion in limine to suppress this evidence. Appellants contend the videotape was inadmissible because it was experimental evidence that attempted to recreate the events but failed to reflect conditions substantially similar to those existing at the time of the shooting.

Typically, demonstrations of experiments used to illustrate principles forming an expert's opinion are not required to reflect conditions substantially similar to those at issue in the trial. We have, however, recognized the unique problems presented by the introduction of videotapes purporting to recreate events at the focus of a trial. We [have] noted the potential prejudicial effect of such evidence because the jury viewing a recreation might be so persuaded by its life-like nature that it becomes unable to visualize an opposing viewpoint of those events. Hence, we established a requirement that video taped evidence purporting to recreate events at issue must be substantially similar to the actual events to be admissible.

Obviously, the requirement of similarity is moderated by the simple fact that the "actual events" are often the issue disputed by the parties. Nonetheless, to the extent the conditions are not a genuine trial issue, they should be reflected in any videotaped recreation. In *Gladhill*, for instance, the plaintiff crashed his car into a utility pole. He sued General Motors in a products liability action, contending that the brakes were faulty. The parties agreed that at the time of the accident it was night, and plaintiff was driving down a hill at a sharp curve in the road when he struck the utility pole. General Motors introduced a videotaped recreation of the accident that was conducted at a test facility on a flat, straight, asphalt surface in daylight by an experienced driver. We rejected the use of this videotape, holding that "when the demonstration is a physical representation of how an automobile behaves under given conditions, those conditions must be sufficiently close to those involved in the accident at issue to make the probative value of the demonstration outweigh its prejudicial effect."

We have not previously applied the requirement of "substantial similarity" to computer-animated videotapes that purport to recreate events at issue in trial. We fail to see a practical distinction, however, between a real-life recreation and one generated through computer animation; both can be a particularly powerful recreation of the events. Nonetheless, we need not explicitly decide this issue because we are satisfied the jury here fully understood this animation was designed merely to illustrate Appellees' version of the shooting and to demonstrate how that version was consistent with the physical evidence. The district court carefully instructed the jury on this point:

> [T]his animation is not meant to be a recreation of the events, but rather it consists of a computer picture to help you understand Mr. Jason's opinion

> which he will, I understand, be giving later in the trial. And to reenforce the point, the video is not meant to be an exact recreation of what happened during the shooting, but rather it represents Mr. Jason's evaluation of the evidence presented.

Although there is a fine line between a recreation and an illustration, the practical distinction "is the difference between a jury believing that they are seeing a repeat of the actual event and a jury understanding that they are seeing an illustration of someone else's opinion of what happened." The jury understood that the very thing disputed in this trial was the condition under which the shooting occurred. In light of this fact and the court's cautionary instruction, there was no reason for the jury "to credit the illustration any more than they credit the underlying opinion."

We are convinced Appellants suffered no undue prejudice as a result of this computer animation, and we will not disturb the broad discretion afforded trial judges in this area. In reaching this holding, however, we are not unmindful of the dramatic power of this type of evidence; hence, we encourage trial judges to first examine proposed videotaped simulation evidence outside the presence of the jury to assess its foundation, relevance, and potential for undue prejudice.

Affirmed.

NOTES AND QUESTIONS

(1) *Courts Vary Regarding Foundation for Demonstrations. Compare Gaskell with Powell v. State*, 487 S.E.2d 424 (Ga. Ct. App. 1997) (state was not required to show similarity in head and neck strength, control, and movement between doll and child as part of foundation for admission of demonstration of shaking baby, even though doll's legs came off during demonstration).

(2) *Foundation for Computer Animations and Out-of-Court Experiments Shown on Videotape. Hinckle* indicates that not only is the videotape subject to a foundational showing, but so is the underlying demonstration, whether it be a re-creation or an illustration.

(3) *Rule 403 Redux.* This section revisits some of the principles that are treated in Chapter 2 (particularly §§ 2.03 and 2.06) concerning prejudice. The extent to which the foundation shows the same or substantially similar conditions, affects the determination about prejudice versus probative value and the other counterweights.

[G] Electronic Communications

UNITED STATES v. LEBOWITZ

676 F.3d 1000 (11th Cir. 2012)

A jury convicted Adam Wayne Lebowitz of producing child pornography in violation of 18 U.S.C. § 2251(a) and (e), and of attempting to entice a child to engage in unlawful sexual activity in violation of 18 U.S.C. § 2422(b). After examining each issued raised by Lebowitz on appeal, we affirm his convictions and sentences.

When K.S. was 15 years old, he registered for a MySpace account. For MySpace profiles to be viewable by the public, the user must attest to being over the age of 21. K.S. desired such a profile, so he falsely claimed he was 21 years old on the registration form. K.S. then created an on-line profile that suggested his age was either 17 or 18 years old. On October 25, 2006, Lebowitz, whose MySpace profile identified himself as a 47–year–old doctor, sent a message to K.S. via his MySpace account, saying: "that's a great pic of you hitting the [base]ball. [G]ot any more pics of you playing?" Lebowitz provided K.S. with his contact information, and the two engaged in on-line chats and exchanged e-mails. The chats were sexual in nature, and Lebowitz sent K.S. nude photographs of himself. In one of these initial chats, K.S. told Lebowitz he was 15 years old.

[K.S. mother discovered the messages. She contacted the county sheriff's department and agreed to let K.S continue communicating with Lebowitz in order to "determine his intentions." These "intentions" developed into a planned sexual encounter. Sheriff's officers arrested Lebowitz at the planned location. A later search disclosed evidence of Lebowitz's intentions as well as a video of Lebowitz engaging in sexual acts with teenage males. One of these was located and he testified in addition to K.S. The excerpt that follows was concerned with authentication and best evidence issues regarding a printout made by K.S. of communications with Lebowitz.]

Lebowitz argues that the district court abused its discretion by admitting into evidence printouts of internet chat conversations between K.S. and Lebowitz. This court reviews a district court's evidentiary rulings for abuse of discretion. The factual findings underlying those rulings are reviewed for clear error.

Lebowitz argues that admission of the printouts violated the authentication requirement in Federal Rule of Evidence 901. To authenticate a document, Rule 901 only requires a proponent to present "sufficient evidence to make out a prima facie case that the proffered evidence is what it purports to be." [Case.] After meeting the prima facie burden, the evidence may be admitted, and the ultimate question of authenticity is then decided by the jury. A district court has discretion to determine authenticity, and that determination should not be disturbed on appeal absent a showing that there is no competent evidence in the record to support it. Evidence may be authenticated through the testimony of a witness with knowledge. [Case citing Fed.R.Evid. 901(b)(1)].

Here, K.S. testified that he had printed out the chats and that the printouts submitted into evidence accurately reflected the chat messages. K.S. also told the jury he could not remember certain aspects of how the printouts were created. However, [a]ppellate courts reviewing a cold record give particular deference to credibility determinations of a fact-finder who had the opportunity to see live testimony. We find that the district court did not clearly err by finding K.S. credible. Accordingly, the Government met its prima facie burden under Rule 901, leaving the ultimate question of authenticity for the jury.

Lebowitz also argues that the admission of the printouts violated the best evidence rule because the printouts did not accurately reflect the data stored in

K.S.'s computer. *See* Fed.R.Evid. 1001–1004. Rule 1002 requires introduction of an original document. Rule 1001(3) defines "original" to include a printout of computer data shown to accurately reflect that data. Accuracy of the printout is a preliminary question of admissibility to be determined by the judge. Fed.R.Evid. 104(a) & 1008. Here, the district judge credited K.S.'s testimony concerning the accuracy of the printouts, and we defer to that credibility determination. The district judge did not clearly err by admitting the printouts as originals.

NOTES AND QUESTIONS

(1) *Processing That Alters the Evidence Requires More.* If the exhibit is enhanced or otherwise changed, it requires a predicate explaining the processing. See the section above on animations.

(2) *Authentication of the Authorship of E-Mail. See, e.g., United States v. Siddiqui*, 235 F.3d 1318 (11th Cir. 2000), *cert. denied*, 533 U.S. 940 (2001), which found the following foundation sufficient:

> In this case, a number of factors support the authenticity of the e-mail. The e-mail sent to Yamada and von Gunten each bore Siddiqui's e-mail address "*msiddiquo@jajuar1.usouthal.edu*" at the University of South Alabama. This address was the same as the e-mail sent to Siddiqui from Yamada as introduced by Siddiqui's counsel in his deposition cross-examination of Yamada. Von Gunten testified that when he replied to the e-mail apparently sent by Siddiqui, the "reply-function" on von Gunten's e-mail system automatically dialed Siddiqui's e-mail address as the sender. The context of the e-mail sent to Yamada and von Gunten shows the author of the e-mail to have been someone who would have known the very details of Siddiqui's conduct with respect to the Waterman Award and the NSF's subsequent investigation. In addition, in one e-mail sent to von Gunten, the author makes apologies for cutting short his visit to EAWAG, the Swiss Federal Institute for Environmental Science and Technology. In his deposition, von Gunten testified that in 1994 Siddiqui had gone to Switzerland to begin a collaboration with EAWAG for three or four months, but had left after only three weeks to take a teaching job. Moreover, the e-mail sent to Yamada and von Gunten referred to the author as "Mo." Both Yamada and von Gunten recognized this as Siddiqui's nickname. Finally, both Yamada and von Gunten testified that they spoke by phone with Siddiqui soon after the receipt of the e-mail, and that Siddiqui made the same requests that had been made in the e-mail. Considering these circumstances, the district court did not abuse its discretion in ruling that the documents were adequately authenticated.

Would authentication have been established, if any of the above facts were eliminated? Which are key to authentication?

See also, on this whole subsection, the *Lorraine* case, *supra*, Section 12.01.

§ 12.02 BEST EVIDENCE RULE: REQUIREMENT OF ORIGINAL DOCUMENT[3]

Read Federal Rules of Evidence 1001, "Definitions"; 1002, "Requirement of Original"; 1003, "Admissibility of Duplicates"; 1004, "Admissibility of Other Evidence of Contents"; 1005, "Public Records"; 1006, "Summaries"; 1007, "Testimony or Written Admission of a Party"; and 1008, "Functions of Court and Jury."

INTRODUCTION

The "Best Evidence Rule" (or, more properly, the "Original Documents Rule") can be tricky. So, by way of introduction, we provide the following explanatory notes and illustrations of the basic parameters of the rule:

(1) *No General "Best" Evidence Rule.* There is no *general* rule of evidence that the best available evidence of a fact is required to prove the fact. (In other words, in most instances you may prove what you need to prove, either with the best evidence available to you or with some inferior evidence; it is your choice.) Such a rule, i.e., one requiring the best available evidence, applies only to proving the contents of a writing or items analogized to writings. (The concept behind such a rule may, however, play some role in the fashioning of some other rules, such as the hearsay rule, and rulings based on a balancing of probativeness, prejudice and time. Of course, the failure to produce the best evidence available to you may affect the weight the trier-of-fact ascribes to your case.) *See generally* Nance, *The Best Evidence Principle*, 73 Iowa L. Rev. 227 (1988).

The limited nature of the best evidence rule is pointed out cogently in *Hocking v. Ahlquist Bros., Ltd.*, Eng. Rep. 1944, King's Bench Div., 120 (Viscount Caldecote, C.J.). In that case, in proving a claim that certain articles of civilian clothing (in particular a blue striped suit) were manufactured by defendant in violation of regulations prescribing trouser width and the number of waistcoat buttons, pockets, and straps, it was contended that the articles (the suit) themselves had to be produced in evidence, rather than the oral testimony of the inspector who saw them. The court rejected that contention.

In *United States v. Duffy*, 454 F.2d 809 (5th Cir. 1972), the court holds that the best evidence rule was not applicable to require the production of a shirt (with its laundry mark) rather than testimony that the shirt was found in the incriminatory car and bore the laundry mark "DUF" (presumably linking Duffy with the crime). The ground is that the government was not attempting to prove the contents of a *writing*. (Do you agree?) How would this evidence fare under the federal rules relating to best evidence and authentication? *Cf. United States v. Snow*, 517 F.2d 441 (9th Cir. 1975) (attempt to introduce into evidence briefcase connected with crime because it bore initials of defendant; hearsay objection; what about *authentication* objection; how should it be handled under the Federal Rules of Evidence?)

In *Duffy*, the court, quoting from McCormick, summarizes the policy justifications for the best evidence rule:

---

[3] Study Guide Reference: Evidence in a Nutshell, Chapter 11:II.

> (1) [P]recision in presenting to the court the exact words of the writing is of more than average importance, particularly as respects operative or dispositive instruments, such as deeds, wills and contracts, since a slight variation in words may mean a great difference in rights. (2) [T]here is a substantial hazard of inaccuracy in the human process of making a copy by handwriting or typewriting, and (3) as respects oral testimony purporting to give from memory the terms of a writing, there is a special risk of error, greater than in the case of attempts at describing other situations generally. In the light of these dangers of mistransmission, accompanying the use of written copies or of recollection, largely avoided through proving the terms by presenting the writing itself, the preference for the original writing is justified.

(2) *Rule Does Not Apply to Collateral Matters. Farr v. Zoning Bd. of Appeals*, 95 A.2d 792 (1953), points out some other limits on the rule. Plaintiff brought suit to prevent the zoning board from allowing a liquor store to operate. In order to do so, plaintiffs had to be Manchester taxpayers and voters. Admission of their testimony "that they are Manchester taxpayers, landowners and electors" was challenged. The property title documents (deeds) or town registry presumably were alleged to be the best evidence. The court held:

> The best evidence rule "applies when the issue of title or ownership is directly involved, and not when it is collaterally involved, in which case a prima facie right of ownership may be established by parol evidence from one qualified to speak." As Wigmore points out, "ordinarily where the terms of a document are not in actual dispute, it is inconvenient and pedantic to insist on the production of the instrument itself." Furthermore, if testimony as to ownership upon a collateral issue is disputed, it can easily be contested. This the defendant made no attempt to do. The question of title was only collaterally involved in the present case, because the decision of the case would not conclusively determine whether the plaintiffs were the owners of the properties concerning which they testified. Abundant authority supports the court's ruling in allowing the testimony to prove ownership. For like reasons, the court properly admitted the testimony of the plaintiffs that they were also taxpayers and electors.

Notice there are several reasons given in this passage, all limitations on the rule. (Was the oral testimony really offered to evidence the *contents of a writing* in the first place? If not, the court did not have to get into a discussion of the best evidence rule at all.) Fed. R. Evid. 1004(4) continues the rule about "collateral" issues, expressed in the above quotation, by exempting from the best evidence (original documents) rule evidence offered on issues that are "not closely related to a controlling issue." *See United States v. American Tel. and Tel. Co.*, 498 F. Supp. 353 (D.D.C. 1980).

(3) *If the Absence of the Original is Excused, Oral Testimony is Permitted, because there are No "Degrees" of Secondary Evidence.* In *Baroda State Bank v. Peck*, 209 N.W. 827 (1926), the bank claimed that since the defendant had sent the bank a letter authorizing a certain agent to incur debt with the bank for defendant's account, the defendant owed the amounts so incurred. The bank introduced a copy

of the letter (presumably a copy that was made by someone at the bank by retyping; the bank cashier did not know who retyped it or much about it, except he expressed a kind of confidence that it probably was accurate; query if there is a hearsay and business records problem here that went unnoticed). The original was lost: the cashier testified that he had the original, delivered it to the bank's attorney, and that when trial came, it could not be found. He said that in his presence the attorney unsuccessfully searched his safe, all the files in the law firm's office, and every piece of stationery in the bank. Against objection, this was held sufficient proof of loss to warrant introduction of the copy by the bank. It was held error to instruct that the jury could find liability if they found it to be a substantially correct (rather than exact) copy. (The court noted that the evidence of accuracy, above, was very weak; that defendant was stopped by the rules of evidence from showing another version (*see* below); and that, had objection been more specifically addressed to failure to prove the exactitude of the copy, the copy may have been excluded on that ground. Query: what more could defendant do?)

The defendant was prevented from orally testifying to his version of the letter (which he claimed did not grant authority) by application of the "American Rule" variety of the best evidence rule. Under it, if an original is lost, but the party has a copy, he must prove the writing by the copy other than by oral testimony. Here, the defendant testified he had made a copy (presumably handwritten) of the letter and sent off the original; that the copy was in the possession of his attorney in Chicago; and that he had not brought it because he presumed the original would be used. The oral testimony was not received because the preferred form of secondary evidence of the writing, namely the copy, was available to him. (If the same standard of unavailability were applied to him as to the bank above, would his copy here be unavailable to him? If so, the American Rule would allow the next best form of secondary evidence that is available to him to be used, i.e., his oral testimony. Is there a lesson to both sets of lawyers in this case respecting their practices concerning documents?) The appellate decision reverses this point and adopts the so-called "English Rule" (later adopted by the Federal Rules of Evidence), under which there are no degrees of secondary evidence: the copy and the oral testimony, both secondary evidence of the contents of the original, are considered equal, and either is freely admissible if the original is unavailable, without any further showing of unavailability. The oral testimony may be used without showing the copy is unavailable.

(4) *Copies as Originals.* A lurking problem in best evidence cases is that often what appears to be a copy is in fact the document alleged to have the legal effect under the substantive contract or property law (or other body of substantive law), and therefore is in legal contemplation the *original*, for purposes of the best evidence rule. For example, if a copy of the contract is the one that is signed, rather than the ribbon copy (original typed copy), then the contract (and the "original" for purposes of best evidence) is the signed copy, in a suit on the contract. If the typed ribbon copy and several other copies all were signed, they all would have force as "originals" and all would be considered, under the best evidence rule in this kind of case, to be originals (sometimes called "duplicate originals," which is confusing terminology because of the other use of the word "duplicate" in the Federal Rules of Evidence). This principle can have some very subtle ramifications. But it will be

helpful if you always ask: which copy is it that is alleged to be the legally effective document having legal consequences in this particular case?

(5) *Best Evidence Distinguished from Authentication.* The distinction between the best evidence rule and the rule requiring authentication is illustrated by the following, from *McGowan v. Armour*, 248 F. 676 (8th Cir. 1918) (the defendant is Mrs. McGowan):

> Plaintiff in error relies mainly upon two groups of assignments challenging rulings as to the admissibility of evidence.
>
> The first relates to an alleged letter written by defendant to plaintiff's husband. Plaintiff testified that she found the letter in her husband's pocket during his temporary absence from the room; that he returned just as she was finishing reading it, snatched it from her hand, and tore it up, throwing part of it into the wastebasket, and part of it out of the window. There was sufficient proof to show that the letter had been destroyed so as to make secondary evidence of its contents admissible, provided only that the letter itself, if it had been present in court, would have been admissible. The only evidence as to the genuineness of the letter as a document written by defendant consists in the statement of plaintiff that she thought she would know defendant's writing, and her statement that the name at the end of the letter was Mrs. M.E. McGowan. The plaintiff did not testify that the letter was in Mrs. McGowan's handwriting, or that the signature was hers. Without any further proof, and over an objection which clearly challenged the foundation which had been laid, plaintiff was permitted to testify to the contents of the letter. This was clearly erroneous. A letter does not prove itself. In order to make it evidence it must be shown either to have been written by the person against whom it is produced, or by some one authorized to act in his behalf. Nothing of this kind was shown in respect to the letter in question. Receiving this proof was therefore error, and it was highly prejudicial in its character.

In addition, both authentication and best evidence are distinguishable from other rules of evidence (all of which also are applicable to writings), such as the hearsay rule, character rule, rules against evidence of insurance, compromise, or corrective measures, etc. This is important because a stipulation, motion, request, offer, objection, ruling, etc., relating to best evidence or authentication does not cover other rules of evidence. So be careful. Also, it is often thought that a stipulation, motion, objection, etc., relating to authentication also relates to best evidence (or the reverse), which usually is not the case. So again, the attorney must be careful.

MEYERS v. UNITED STATES

United States Court of Appeals, District of Columbia Circuit
171 F.2d 800, 84 U.S. App. D.C. 101 (1948), *cert. denied*, 336 U.S. 912 (1949)

MILLER, CIRCUIT JUDGE.

[Prosecution against Meyers for Meyers' counselling of Lamarre to commit perjury. The prosecution sought to establish the content of Lamarre's testimony before a Senate subcommittee. A transcript of the stenographic record of Lamarre's testimony was available, but the committee's counsel was permitted to recount orally the substance of Lamarre's testimony.]

William P. Rogers, chief counsel to the senatorial committee, who had examined Lamarre before the subcommittee and consequently had heard all the testimony given by him before that body, was permitted to testify as to what Lamarre had sworn to the subcommittee. [The transcript was introduced later.]

The dissenting opinion asserts it was reversible error to allow Rogers to testify at all as to what Lamarre had said to the subcommittee, on the theory that the transcript itself was the best evidence of Lamarre's testimony before the subcommittee.

That theory is, in our view, based upon a misconception of the best evidence rule. As applied generally in federal courts, the rule is limited to cases where the contents of a writing are to be proved. Here there was no attempt to prove the contents of a writing; the issue was what Lamarre had said, not what the transcript contained. The transcript made from shorthand notes of his testimony was, to be sure, evidence of what he had said, but it was not the only admissible evidence concerning it. Rogers' testimony was equally competent, and was admissible whether given before or after the transcript was received in evidence. Statements alleged to be perjurious may be proved by any person who heard them, as well as by a reporter who recorded them in shorthand.

As we have pointed out, there was no issue as to the contents of the transcript and the government was not attempting to prove what it contained; the issue was what Lamarre actually had said. Rogers was not asked what the transcript contained but what Lamarre's testimony had been.

After remarking, ". . . there is a line of cases which holds that a stenographic transcript is not the best evidence of what was said. There is also a legal cliche that the best evidence rule applies only to documentary evidence," the dissenting opinion asserts that the rule is outmoded and that "the courts ought to establish a new and correct rule." We regard the principle set forth in the cases which we have cited as being, not a legal cliche, but an established and sound doctrine which we are not prepared to renounce.

Affirmed.

PRETTYMAN, CIRCUIT JUDGE (dissenting).

I do not know why an appellate court should perpetuate a rule clearly outmoded by scientific development. I know that courts are reluctant to do so. I recognize the view that such matters should be left to Congress. But rules of evidence were originally judge-made and are an essential part of the judicial function. I know of no reason why the judicial branch of Government should abdicate to the legislative branch so important a part of its responsibility.

The rationale of the so-called "best evidence rule" requires that a party having available evidence which is relatively certain may not submit evidence which is far less certain. The law is concerned with the true fact, and with that alone; its procedures are directed to that objective, and to that alone. It should permit no procedure the sole use of which is to obscure and confuse that which is otherwise plain and certain.

We need not venture into full discussion of all the principles involved. As between two observers of an event, the law will not accept the evidence of one and exclude that of the other, because the law cannot say which is more accurate. But as between a document itself and a description of it, the law accepts the former and excludes the latter, because the former is certain and the latter is subject to many frailties. So as between the recollection of the parties to a contract evidenced by a writing and the writing itself, the law rejects the former and accepts the latter. To be sure, the writing may be attacked for forgery, alteration or some such circumstance. But absent such impeachment, the writing is immutable evidence from the date of the event, whereas human recollection is subject to many infirmities and human recitation is subject to the vices of prejudice and interest. Presented with that choice, the law accepts the certain and rejects the uncertain. The repeated statement in cases and elsewhere that the best evidence rule applies only to documents is a description of practice and not a pronouncement of principle. The principle is that as between human recollections the law makes no conclusive choice; it makes a conclusive choice only as between evidence which is certain and that which is uncertain.

It may be remarked at this point that the transcript in the case at bar is a document, not challenged for inaccuracy or alteration. It possesses every characteristic which the most literal devotee of established rules of evidence could ascribe to written evidence of a contract as justification for preference of such writing over the recollection of the parties.

In my view, the court iterates an error when it says that the best evidence rule is limited to cases where the contents of a writing are to be proved. The purpose of offering in evidence a "written contract" is not to prove the contents of the writing. The writing is not the contract; it is merely evidence of the contract. The contract itself is the agreement between the parties. Statutes such as the statute of frauds do not provide that a contract be in writing; they provide that the contract be evidenced by a writing, or that a written memorandum of it be made. The writing is offered as evidence of an agreement, not for the purpose of proving its own contents.

* * *

From the theoretical point of view, the case poses this question: Given both (1) an accurate stenographic transcription of a witness's testimony during a two-day hearing, and (2) the recollection of one of the complainants as to the substance of that testimony, is the latter admissible as evidence in a trial of the witness for perjury? I think not. To say that it is admissible is to apply a meaningless formula and ignore crystal-clear actualities. The transcript is, as a matter of simple, indisputable fact, the best evidence. The principle and not the rote of the law ought to be applied.

NOTE

Did Meyers Argue the Wrong Objection on Appeal? In *Meyers*, the defense did not receive until the beginning of trial the more than 300 pages of the transcripts containing the Lamarre testimony claimed to be perjurious. Rogers, a well-respected public official, testified as the government's first witness, detailing the "substance" of Lamarre's earlier testimony in the words of the indictment. The defense objected to this manner of proceeding as being "preposterously unfair" and moved to strike all of Rogers' direct testimony as to what Lamarre's testimony had been, claiming he was "interpreting" Lamarre, not recounting his words. The trial judge denied this motion. The defense reserved the right to cross-examine Rogers later (due to its recent receipt of the transcript). However, when counsel later attempted to show that the totality of Lamarre's testimony negated a perjurious interpretation, the court sustained the government's objection that this was improper cross-examination. Similarly, objections to questions construing Lamarre's words were sustained because the transcript "speaks for itself." Yet the jury would have to read a significant portion of the transcript to determine if Roger's recollection of the "substance" was correct. Do you think the jurors did that? Did the defense press the wrong issue on appeal? In addition, was there another objection to Roger's testimony that could have been made in the trial court?

UNITED STATES v. BENNETT

United States Court of Appeals, Ninth Circuit
363 F.3d 947 (2004)

[Chandler, a Customs officer, testified that the global positioning satellite (GPS) display data on defendant's boat revealed that the boat had traveled from Mexican waters.]

First, the GPS display Chandler saw was a writing or recording because, according to Chandler, he saw a graphical representation of data that the GPS had compiled about the path of Bennett's boat. *See* Fed.R.Evid. 1001(1). Second, Chandler never actually observed Bennett's boat travel the path depicted by the GPS. Thus, Chandler's testimony concerned the "content" of the GPS, which, in turn, was evidence of Bennett's travels. Fed. R. Evid 1002. At oral argument, the government admitted that the GPS testimony was offered solely to show that Bennett had come from Mexico. Proffering testimony about Bennett's border-crossing instead of introducing the GPS data, therefore, was analogous to proffering testimony describing security camera footage of an event to prove the facts of the event instead of introducing the footage itself.

This is precisely the kind of situation in which the best evidence rule applies. *See, e.g., L.A. News Serv. v. CBS Broad. Inc.*, 305 F.3d 924, 935 (9th Cir. 2002) ("We think that Fox's report of what he saw on the label . . . was inadmissible under the best evidence rule."), *amended by* 313 F.3d 1093 (9th Cir. 2002); *see also* 14 Am. Jur. Proof of Facts 2d 173 § 14 (1977) ("The reported cases show that proponents of computer-produced evidence occasionally founder on the best evidence rule by presenting oral testimony based on the witness' review of computer printouts without actually introducing the printouts themselves into evidence.") (citing *State v. Springer*, 283 N.C. 627, 197 S.E.2d 530 (N.C. 1973)). Yet the government did not produce the GPS itself — or a printout or other representation of such data, *see* Fed. R. Evid 1001(3) — which would have been the best evidence of the data showing Bennett's travels. Instead, the government offered only Chandler's GPS-based testimony about an event — namely, a border-crossing — that he never actually saw.

"[O]ther evidence" of the contents of a writing, recording or photograph is admissible if the original is shown to be lost, destroyed or otherwise unobtainable. Fed.R.Evid. 1004. But the government made no such showing. When asked on cross-examination to produce the GPS or its data, Chandler simply stated that he was not the GPS's custodian. He further testified that "there was no need to" videotape or photograph the data and that he had nothing other than his testimony to support his assertions about the GPS's contents. Moreover, the government has not offered any record evidence that it would have been impossible or even difficult to download or print out the data on Bennett's GPS. On the record before us, the government is not excused from the best evidence rule's preference for the original. We therefore hold that Chandler's GPS-based testimony was inadmissible under the best evidence rule.

NOTES AND QUESTIONS

(1) *Figuring Out When the Contents of the Writing are Being Proved.* Concerning the best evidence rule, it is easy to become confused as to whether "contents of a writing" are being proved, which is the only situation to which the rule applies. This confusion arises, for example, where a plaintiff in a personal injury action is attempting to testify to his medical expenses, or where, in a business litigation, profits, expenses, etc., are sought to be shown by oral testimony. Are the bills, books or records required, and is the oral testimony excluded? The amounts to be proved are not "contents of a writing," unless the testimony is based not on direct knowledge but knowledge of these documents. The problem arises wherever something is reflected both in a document and in some other way, especially when the document seems the easiest and most direct reflection. For example, where a person might have to prove that he or she is a licensed physician, nurse, accountant, broker, etc., must the license be produced? Or may the person testify to having passed the exams and registering and practicing as a doctor (or to "being a duly authorized physician")?

The point is, if both the document and the oral testimony are evidence of an underlying fact and are independent of one another (i.e., the testimony is not based on knowledge of the document, but is directly reflective of knowledge of the underlying fact, e.g., that certain money was paid out), the oral testimony is not "evidence of the contents of" the document.

Even if the content is being proven, such as an x-ray, can a doctor explain the results without the x-ray being admitted into evidence? Isn't this permitted by Fed. R. Evid. 703? Why doesn't Rule 703 apply in *Bennett?* Is there also a Rule 702 (*Daubert*) issue?

(2) *Tape Recordings Not being Proven when a Person Testifies to Directly Hearing a Conversation that also was Taped.* In *United States v. Rose*, 590 F.2d 232 (7th Cir. 1978), *cert. denied*, 442 U.S. 929 (1979), a prosecution for transportation of stolen goods, the government's principal "evidence" was some tape recordings (which they had lost and could not produce at trial!) of some incriminating telephone conversations of defendant obtained by legal surveillance. The court held that whether or not the government presently had the tapes or lost them through negligence, the telephone conversations and their contents could be established by oral testimony of the informer and agents who had listened in on those conversations, since the " 'so-called best evidence rule,' codified and expanded to cover recordings and photographs in Fed. R. Evid. 1001 and 1004, requires only that a party seeking to prove the contents of a document introduce the original document or explain why it cannot be produced. In the case at bar, the government sought to prove the contents of a conversation, not the contents of a tape recording. Consequently, the 'best evidence rule' is inapplicable." Query: (a) If the agents were testifying about what the *tape* said, or knew what the conversation said only from listening to the tape, would the result have been different? (b) Could defense counsel make any argument to the jury about the loss of the tape, on the facts of the case as they actually were (not as modified in (a))? Should the judge instruct the jury on inferences that may arise from such loss? Should the government be able to adduce evidence explaining the loss?

See also United States v. Bourne, 743 F.2d 1026 (4th Cir. 1984) (agents can testify to directly hearing conversation and its contents without offering into evidence tape that was made, because government wants to prove contents of conversation directly heard, not contents of tape).

UNITED STATES v. GERHART

United States Court of Appeals, Eighth Circuit
538 F.2d 807 (1976)

Gibson, Chief Judge.

Gerhart appeals from his jury conviction of knowingly making a material false statement on a loan application.

In connection with [the] loan application, defendant presented the bank with photocopies of two checks [payable to him] but the amount on the photocopy of check No. 106 was illegible. The figures were altered or smudged so as to read "$54,822.40", rather than "$4,822.40." [H]e told the bank that check No. 106 had mistakenly been sent to the IRS [rather than to him].

An officer of the bank, Charles M. Stinson, thereafter contacted the IRS and inquired as to the whereabouts of check No. 106. The IRS answered that no such check had been received. Thereafter, on request of Special Agent Robert Smith of the Iowa Department of Public Safety, Mr. Stinson surrendered the photocopies of both checks, but first, as a precaution, made a second photocopy of each of them. Subsequently, the Iowa agency misplaced the original photocopies. Thus, at trial the Government introduced the second photocopy of check No. 106 that was made by the bank. Bank officer Stinson and Special Agent Smith testified that they had viewed both the first and second photocopies and that, with the exception of some handwriting not seen by the jury, the exhibited copy accurately reproduced the original photocopy of the check.

Under the new Federal Rules of Evidence, though proof of the contents of a writing requires production of the original document, secondary evidence is admissible if the original has been lost. Fed. R. Ev. 1004(1). The defendant does not dispute this principle and does not challenge the adequacy of the Government's showing that the original photocopy had been lost. Rather, he contends that a further prerequisite to the admission of secondary evidence is a clear and convincing showing of its trustworthiness and that no such showing was made.

The defendant's contentions are entirely without merit. A clear showing of trustworthiness need not be made to admit secondary evidence of the contents of a writing.

[Fed. R. Evid. 1004], essentially a restatement of the common law, excuses production of the original of a writing if one of the enumerated conditions is satisfied. The rule recognizes no degrees of secondary evidence and in this respect is probably a departure from the rule found in the majority of American jurisdictions. Thus, once an enumerated condition of Rule 1004 is met, the proponent may prove the contents of a writing by any secondary evidence, subject to an attack by the opposing party not as to admissibility but to the weight to be given the evidence, with final determination left to the trier of fact. On the other hand, the new rules allocate to the court preliminary questions such as authenticity, lack of an original and whether the proponent has presented a sufficient foundation so that a "reasonable juror could be convinced" that the secondary evidence correctly reflects the contents of the original. [S]ee Fed. R. Ev. 104, 901(a), 1008. Contrary to defendant's assertions, no "clear and convincing evidence of authenticity and accuracy" is required for admission.

In the instant case, the Government was merely required to demonstrate preliminarily, to the satisfaction of the court, that the original photocopy was lost, that the proffered photocopy was what it purported to be and that it accurately reflected the contents of the original photocopy. This the Government achieved through the testimony of Mr. Stinson and Special Agent Smith. The district court's implicit preliminary findings are supported by the record and admission of the exhibit in evidence was by no means an abuse of the district court's discretion.

The judgment of the district court is affirmed.

NOTES AND QUESTIONS

(1) *Originals and Duplicates.* Note that in this case, the "original" for purposes of the original documents rule was the document alleged to constitute the fraudulent act, which incidentally was itself a photocopy: the photocopy given to the bank. The question in the case concerned copies of that document. *See also United States v. Rangel*, 585 F.2d 344 (8th Cir. 1978), a conviction for knowingly and fraudulently demanding that a debt due from the United States be paid by virtue

of a false instrument. Rangel, an employee of the United States Environmental Protection Agency, submitted three vouchers to the E.P.A. requesting reimbursement for lodging costs incurred in conjunction with three business trips. To each voucher he allegedly attached a photocopy of the customer's copy (customer's receipt) of a credit card sales slip as documentation for lodging expenses incurred. Rangel challenged the admissibility of the photocopies because they were not the "original" altered customer's receipts and therefore did not constitute the "best evidence." The court disagreed:

> The government had to prove the contents of the photocopy of the altered receipt since the photocopy, not the altered receipt, was identified as the document Rangel had submitted to support his demand for payment. Thus the photocopies were admitted as originals. However, even if the photocopies are considered to be duplicates, as xerox copies may be, they would also be admissible, since Rangel did not raise a genuine issue concerning their authenticity. [Fed. R. Evid. 1001(4), 1003.]

(2) *Certified Copies of Public Records. United States v. Rodriguez*, 524 F.2d 485 (5th Cir. 1975), *cert. denied*, 424 U.S. 972 (1976), applies Fed. R. Evid. 1003 to permit a photocopy of a car title to be admitted as a duplicate to prove defendant owned the car in which marijuana was found. The court also states an alternative reason for admissibility on the facts:

There is still another basis for admitting the duplicate certificate. Vehicle registration is a matter of public record. Federal Rule of Evidence 1005 provides that: "[t]he contents of an official record may be proved by copy, certified as correct in accordance with Rule 902 [self-authentication] or testified to be correct by a witness who has compared it with the original."

(3) *Excusing Absence of the Original*. In *United States v. Marcantoni*, 590 F.2d 1324 (5th Cir.), *cert. denied*, 441 U.S. 937 (1979), an officer, Detective Brodesser, wrote down the serial numbers of two $10 bills, but when he returned with a warrant for the bills, they were missing. The defendants argued that Fed. R. Evid. 1004 required the Government to introduce the two bills in evidence and that the officer's testimony was secondary evidence of the contents of the bills and not admissible because the Government failed to establish any of the conditions for the admissibility of secondary evidence specified by Fed. R. Evid. 1004. The Court disagreed:

> We have no difficulty in concluding that, under the circumstances of this case, the trial judge would have been authorized to find, under section (1) of the rule, that the two bills were "lost or [had] been destroyed." Surely, the Marcantonis could not have contended that the unavailability of the bills was the product of Government "bad faith." The trial judge could also have found, under section (2) of the rule, that "[n]o original [could] be obtained by any available judicial process or procedure." Even assuming that the Marcantonis were amenable to a subpoena directing the production of the bills at trial, we think it unrealistic to expect that they would have readily produced the two instruments that would have made the Government's case against them complete. In short, the Government was not required to go through the motion of having a subpoena issued, served and returned

> unexecuted in order to establish, under section (2), that the bills were unobtainable.
>
> As for section (3) of the rule, a legitimate argument can be made on this record that the Marcantonis were "put on notice" that the serial numbers of the two $10 bills "would be a subject of proof" at the trial, and that, having not produced them at trial, the Marcantonis could not object to the use of Brodesser's notes. In sum, although the trial judge, in overruling the Marcantonis' best evidence objection, should have announced the predicate to admissibility he found to have been established under Rule 1004, his decision to receive the evidence was correct.

Would calling the officer's notes past recollection recorded get around the best evidence problem? *See United States v. Cambindo Valencia*, 609 F.2d 603 (2d Cir. 1979) (upholding admission of recorded notation of telephone number written in another document that was lost), *cert. denied*, 446 U.S. 940 (1980). Wouldn't the officer's recorded note, which would be read to the jury, still be secondary evidence of the contents (serial numbers) on the money? Alternatively, if his notes were used merely to refresh his recollection, isn't his testimony secondary evidence? Even if he testifies from recollection and does not need his notes at all, at any time, to remind him, isn't his testimony secondary evidence of what's on the money?

(4) *"Inscribed Chattels."* In *Marcantoni*, in note (3), *supra*, the court assumed that serial numbers on currency were subject to the best evidence rule. Compare this to *Duffy*, in the introductory notes to this section, where a laundry mark was not considered to be a writing. Courts vary as to when the best evidence rule applies to what commentators call "inscribed chattels." Often the determining factors are the feasibility of bringing the original to court (digging up a tombstone or taking down a highway billboard) and the complexity of the writing. Is a photograph a "duplicate" in these circumstances?

(5) *Does the Original Exist?* Suppose one party alleges there never was an original. Indeed, suppose that is the basic dispute in the case, e.g., a contract action in which defendant alleges there never was a contract (writing). Plaintiff claims there was, adduces evidence tending to show he made a diligent search and couldn't find it, and offers to testify to what it said. Can he? Must there be some independent evidence that there ever was such a document? Consider the following passage from *Vigano v. Wylain, Inc.*, 633 F.2d 522 (8th Cir. 1980):

> This case is an action for breach of contract with federal jurisdiction based on diversity of citizenship. The three plaintiffs, Robert Vigano, Greers Ferry Builders, Inc., and Robert J. Hines allege they were distributors of modular homes produced by the Continental Homes Division of defendant Wylain, Inc., and that Wylain's wrongful termination of their distributorship agreements caused each of them serious financial loss. After a four day trial, the jury awarded plaintiffs damages totaling $82,500.
>
> At trial, neither Vigano nor Greers Ferry was able to produce a copy of the Independent Distributorship Agreement executed by an officer of Wylain. Vigano testified that he never received such a document from Wylain. Greers Ferry was unable, despite a diligent search of their records,

> to produce their copy of the document. These circumstances differ from those of plaintiff Robert J. Hines, who did not testify to signing such an agreement. In essence, however, the claims of Vigano and Hines are the same since neither could or did allege a completed written contract. Rather, they alleged an oral agreement pursuant to the terms of the Independent Distributorship Agreement. Greers Ferry, on the other hand, alleged a written contract which was lost or misplaced.
>
> Wylain argues the trial court erred in admitting parol proof of the written agreement alleged by Greers Ferry. Secondary proof of a written contract is essentially a problem coming under the Best Evidence Rule, Rule 1002 et seq. of the Federal Rules of Evidence, not the Statute of Frauds. This rule is merely one expressing a preference for the original document. If the original cannot be produced because lost or destroyed, the proponent's case is not necessarily lost. Rule 1004 allows "other evidence" in such an event. The defendant need not, of course, admit the existence of such an agreement in order to allow such proof. Any suggestion to this effect in Wylain's brief is clearly to be rejected as it would defeat the purpose of the rule.

(6) *The Judge has the Final Word.* In *Seiler v. Lucasfilm, Ltd.*, 808 F.2d 1316 (9th Cir. 1986), *cert. denied*, 484 U.S. 826 (1987), the plaintiff claimed that the "Imperial Walkers" made famous in the film "The Empire Strikes Back" infringed his copyright for "Garthian Striders." After a lengthy hearing, the trial judge excluded the plaintiff's reconstructed drawings, finding that the best evidence rule applied in the plaintiff's copyright infringement case and that the plaintiff had destroyed the originals in bad faith. Seiler appealed, arguing that Fed. R. Evid. 1008 required the judge to submit to the jury the issue of whether the reconstructions correctly reflected the contents of the destroyed originals. The court said:

> In the instant case, the condition of fact which Seiler needed to prove was that the originals were not lost or destroyed in bad faith. Had he been able to prove this, his reconstructions would have been admissible and then their accuracy would have been a question for the jury. In sum, admissibility of the reconstructions was dependent upon a finding that the originals were not lost or destroyed in bad faith.

Do you agree?

UNITED STATES v. JOHNSON

United States Court of Appeals, Ninth Circuit
594 F.2d 1253, *cert. denied*, 444 U.S. 964 (1979)

Choy, Circuit Judge.

At the trial the government sought to prove that [appellants] had been involved in an elaborate land sale fraud involving Thunderbird Valley corporation, of which appellants were major stockholders. The government maintained that Thunderbird Valley used the same lots as security on two or more instruments without telling the creditors of other claims against the lots.

A jury found appellants guilty.

[A]ppellants contended that the 16 instances of double assignment revealed in the government's case-in-chief were inadvertent. [T]he government [questioned] Mr. Harbert, a postal inspector, about a summary he had made of records seized from the offices of the Thunderbird Valley corporation. This summary purported to establish that Mr. Harbert found 80 double assignments out of 260 files of transactions perused. When this questioning began, defense counsel immediately objected.

The government then observed that it had sent defense counsel notice of its intent to use summaries. The court ascertained that counsel for each defendant had received that notice. Then the following colloquy took place:

MR. GAYNES: My objection is based on the fact that the exhibits of what you're making summaries out of, you have to have some kind of foundation as to the trustworthiness of the documents, somehow, that they're business-related or business records and then you can make summaries of proper foundation — if you show a proper foundation as to business records. We don't know whether these business records — . . .

THE COURT: You had an opportunity to look. That's the problem, though, and evidently you didn't. You didn't care to.

The district court erred in not requiring the proponent of the summary to establish a foundation. It was incorrect to suggest that the opponents had the burden of determining that a foundation was lacking.

The government invoked Fed. R. Evid. 1006. We hold that under this Rule the proponent of the summary must establish that the underlying materials upon which the summary is based are admissible in evidence.

The purpose of Rule 1006 is to allow the use of summaries when the volume of documents being summarized is so large as to make their use impractical or impossible; summaries may also prove more meaningful to the judge and jury. Such a rationale imports that instead of using a summary, the proponent of the summary could introduce the underlying documents upon which the summary is based.

Moreover, requiring the proponent to show the admissibility of the underlying materials is necessary to protect the integrity of the Federal Rules. In the instant case, the government argued that notification of opposing counsel obviated the need to show that the underlying materials fell within an exception to the hearsay rule. We do not believe that Congress intended that counsel could abrogate other restrictions on admissibility — like the hearsay rule — by the use of summaries; we cannot read Rule 1006 as preempting the other Rules.

Finally, Congress placed Rule 1006 not in the Article of the Federal Rules dealing with exceptions to the hearsay rule, Article VIII, but rather in the Article dealing with "Contents of Writings, Recordings and Photographs," Article X. While the government argues that this Article X Rule abrogates the hearsay limitations of Article VIII, the Article X provisions more properly deal with the "best evidence" problems arising from the use of materials other than originals. *See* Fed. R. Evid.

1002. And when Congress intended to provide an exception to the hearsay rule for materials which it also exempted from the best evidence rule in Article X, it did so by a provision in Article VIII. For example, Rule 1005 provides that public records may be proved with other than the original under some circumstances. Rules 803(8), (9), (10), however, provide the hearsay exception for various types of public records. Similarly, Rule 1007 allows the use of secondary materials to prove the contents of testimony or a written admission of a party. But Rule 801(d)(2) provides that admissions are not subject to the hearsay rule. In claiming that Rule 1006 provides an exception from both the best evidence rule for summaries and the hearsay rule for the underlying materials, the government (and the district court) misapprehended this congressional scheme.

We conclude that the proponent of a summary must demonstrate the admissibility of the underlying writings or records summarized, as a condition precedent to introduction of the summary into evidence under Rule 1006.

The government argues that even if the proponent of a summary must demonstrate that the underlying materials are admissible, such a requirement was met here; thus the district court's failure to articulate such a requirement was harmless error.

The government argues first that "if the records viewed are identified as being in the general control of the defendant, the normal foundation for business records is not necessary." The government appears to be arguing that such records would constitute admissions excluded from the hearsay rule by Fed. R. Evid. 801(d)(2).

Assuming arguendo that such records would constitute admissions, the testimony relied upon by the government does not show that the records were "in the general control" of any of the appellants. At best that testimony established that the files of the 260 transactions had been taken from the offices of Thunderbird Valley and one witness referred to them as "corporate records." This testimony also does not demonstrate that the documents fell within the business record exception to the hearsay rule. *See* Fed. R. Evid. 803(6).

Reversed and the cases remanded.

NOTES AND QUESTIONS

(1) *How do the Hearsay and Expert Testimony Rules Affect the Admission of Summaries?* Consider the following, which is virtually the entire decision in *Nichols v. Upjohn Co.*, 610 F.2d 293 (5th Cir. 1980):

> Lee Nichols brought this product liability suit in diversity, alleging he suffered permanent loss of vision in his right eye after taking the prescription drug "Motrin." Nichols sought to impose liability on the manufacturer, The Upjohn Company, contending that the warnings provided were inadequate and that the advertising contained misrepresentations of material facts.
>
> Plaintiff also attacks two evidentiary rulings. In the first the court allowed defendant's witness, Dr. Samuel Stubbs to testify about the

contents of investigative reports contained in the 94,000 page New Drug Application filed by Upjohn with the Food and Drug Administration in connection with Motrin. Plaintiff objected that the testimony was hearsay and not the best evidence.

We find no error in the admission of Dr. Stubbs' testimony. Federal Rule of Evidence 1006 allows courts to admit summaries of voluminous documents provided the documents themselves are made available to other parties. The New Drug Application is obviously a voluminous document and it is undisputed that plaintiff's counsel was given the opportunity to examine, and indeed did examine, this 300 volume application. Plaintiff's argument fails.

The second evidentiary ruling under attack also arose during the course of the testimony of Doctor Stubbs, as he was asked questions relative to eye complaints received by the defendant Upjohn concerning Motrin. Defendant's Exhibit No. 6 was a document which listed the eye complaints received. Plaintiff's objection to the exhibit was "The records from which the document was prepared are not available, and it is hearsay. This is the first time I have ever seen this document." However, it is undisputed that the documents from which the exhibit had been prepared had been made available to the plaintiff for examination prior to trial. The exhibit was admissible under Rule 1006, Federal Rules of Evidence.

Finding no merit in the four points of error, the judgment of the district court is affirmed.

What about *Johnson's* requirement that the underlying documents must be admissible? Are the underlying documents here inadmissible hearsay? If not, why not? Because they are not offered for their truth? Or are within a hearsay exception? Suppose they were inadmissible hearsay. Would the fact that an expert made the summary overcome this objection because of Fed. R. Evid. 703? Would Fed. R. Evid. 703 be usable to dispense with the obligation in Fed. R. Evid. 1006 to make the underlying documents available? If they were the objector's own documents, would that alone vitiate the obligation, or must specific portions and documents that are relied on still be identified?

(2) *When Summaries are Not Admissible. See United States v. Seelig*, 622 F.2d 207 (6th Cir.), *cert. denied*, 449 U.S. 869 (1980), a prosecution of a pharmacy operator for dispensing narcotics ("Schedule V substances") in an amount that appeared to be more than reasonably attributable to normal sales:

Appellants object to the admission of exhibits 210, 211, and 212, which are summaries made by Kopp [a government investigator] from exhibits 1 through 165 [i.e., business sales records of the pharmacy and similar records required to be filed or kept on prescriptions] showing high volume purchasers [from appellant's pharmacy] and the dates when they purchased a schedule V substance. Appellants claim these were irrelevant and prejudicial, since they show a total of 1,409 sales, of which only 32 were mentioned in the indictment. Rule 1006, Fed. R. Evid., provides that the contents of voluminous writings, recordings, or photographs which cannot

> be conveniently examined in court may be presented in the form of a chart, summary, or calculation. In *United States v. Scales*, 594 F.2d 558 (6th Cir.), *cert. denied*, 99 S. Ct. 2168 (1979), this court held the admission of a summary chart of 161 underlying exhibits was proper. Although the underlying writings could possibly have been examined [by the jury on its own], the use of the summary was permitted under Rule 1006 as comprehension of the voluminous exhibits would have been difficult and certainly inconvenient. The facts summarized were objective and were stated in a neutral way. The chart was found to be accurate and authentic. Finally, the trial court had given a limiting instruction that the chart was not evidence but was only an aid in evaluating the evidence. In the present case, the underlying documents were numerous and inconvenient to examine. Appellants do not object to the accuracy of the summaries. They do object to the failure to give a limiting instruction, but the record does not show they asked for such an instruction. [The court also holds that the greater number of narcotics sales shown on the chart than charged in the indictment may be justified on the issue of intent, and anyway the chart shows nothing more than the underlying exhibits (perhaps that is where the objection should have been directed).]
>
> The admission of [another chart, comparing this pharmacy's narcotic sales to other pharmacies', referred to as] the sales comparison chart was error. The underlying records on which they were based were not exhibits nor were they made available to appellants. The only records of these other stores examined by Dempsey were the schedule V sales. There was no attempt to compare the stores in terms of total sales. Sergeant Dempsey was not an expert witness. He admitted he was not an economist, statistician, or real estate appraiser. The chart could not therefore be admitted under the exception for the bases of opinion testimony by experts. He did not know if his allegedly comparable stores operated the same hours. The two Seelig stores were located near a freeway. He testified that he picked, apparently at random, six stores from each area, then did not use two whose volume seemed too low. The record does not show these other stores were the same size, covered the same marketing area, were open the same hours, had pharmacists on duty at all times, had the same access to the public, or, most importantly, charged the same prices — all of which could have significantly affected the volume of sales. Thus, the sales comparison chart is simply irrelevant for failure to establish the comparability of the other stores.

What resulted in the sales comparison chart being inadmissible: the inadmissibility of the underlying documents, the failure to make them available, or the unfairness of the comparisons? Are these each sufficient grounds? What rules govern each? Suppose the chart had columns headed "Unreasonable Amount of Narcotics" and "Reasonable Amount of Narcotics" for each pharmacy, including defendant's, and had check marks in them? Does Fed. R. Evid. 403 come into play? Are exhibits 210, 211, and 212 really governed by Fed. R. Evid. 1006 when the underlying documents are in evidence (as they were)? What other rule or rules might have been invoked? *See also United States v. Samaniego*, 187 F.3d 1222 (10th

Cir. 1999), which reversed a conviction for drug-related charges where a significant part of the agents' testimony focused upon summaries he made of subpoenaed telephone records. None of the underlying telephone records were admitted into evidence, and the government did not establish any business record foundation for the underlying documents.

UNITED STATES v. EVANS

United States Court of Appeals, Fifth Circuit
572 F.2d 455, *cert. denied*, 439 U.S. 870 (1978)

HILL, CIRCUIT JUDGE.

[The defendants were charged in a sixteen-count indictment of fraud in the operation of a student loan collection operation for the federal government. They allegedly appropriated some of the money and misreported amounts collected and expenses. The court described the number of documents the government used in the case as "too numerous to count" and they numbered in the thousands.]

Appellants Gent and Tate contend that the district court erred in permitting the government case-agent, a Special Agent of the F.B.I., to testify regarding his analysis of some of the evidence. The obvious answer to this is that appellants have mischaracterized the nature of this testimony. The evidence did not consist of data compilations by the F.B.I. Special Agent, but was a summarization of evidence admitted at trial. All of the information referred to in his testimony was before the jury in the form of documentary exhibits and/or testimony of other witnesses pertaining to specific events. Appellants are acutely aware that the documentary evidence in this case was voluminous. They were provided with complete access to all the documents prior to trial. If the evidence was already introduced, then it was certainly "produced in court." In fact, during the course of the trial the appellants were furnished with copies of critical documents upon request. The record also establishes that the court properly charged the jury that the charts and summaries were not evidence, and their purpose was merely explanatory. The jury was instructed to disregard any summaries not comporting with the evidence. There was no error in the procedure followed. [H]is testimony was admissible pursuant to Rule 1006, Federal Rules of Evidence, which provides that summaries of voluminous documents may be presented, provided that the documents themselves are made available to opposing parties. *United States v. Smyth*, 556 F.2d 1179 (5th Cir. 1977), *cert. denied*, 434 U.S. 862 (1977).

Affirmed.

NOTES AND QUESTIONS

(1) *Questions Based on Evans.* Suppose the documents, though admissible, were not actually put into evidence, but instead a summary of them of some kind was sought to be used.

(a) Would the government's making the entire class of documents available at the time of trial en masse without further specificity be enough to satisfy the availability requirement of Fed. R. Evid. 1006?

(b) As a general proposition, should it make any difference as to the amount of time required to be given to the opponent of a summary to examine the underlying documents, and to the specificity required to be supplied, that the documents are in some way connected with the business of the opponent of the summary? Or that they are business documents of the proponent?

(c) Would it make any difference to the above that the underlying documents are in evidence? Consider that in *Evans* masses of documents were dumped into evidence that were never individually presented, never individually considered by the jury, never individually addressed, and never individually displayed with opportunity for individual objection, and the appellate court upholds the trial court's discretion to proceed this way in a mass documents case.

The full *Evans* decision is a study in how large groups of documents (mostly written or computerized business records) can be admitted by the government apparently with a generalized foundation being laid for many of them all at once. The appellate court faults the defendant for not specifically objecting to those individual ones he found objectionable. Apparently the court believes he had sufficient access beforehand to pick them out.

(2) *Oral Summaries by Experts.* On oral summaries by experts and visual charts, broadly putting together the evidence that has been introduced in the case, *see United States v. King*, 616 F.2d 1034 (8th Cir.), *cert. denied*, 446 U.S. 969 (1980), a willful tax evasion case:

> Ms. Jane Sweet was called as a summary witness by the government. She is an I.R.S. agent, trained as a certified public accountant . . . . The testimony of a summary witness may be received so long as she bases her summary on evidence received in the case and is available for cross-examination.
>
> The government offered several organizational charts, prepared by Ms. Sweet, for the different projects which were discussed. Where charts which fairly summarize the evidence are used as an aid in understanding the testimony already introduced and the witness who prepared the charts is subject to cross-examination with all documents used to prepare the summary, the use of charts is proper. Evidential use of such summaries rests within the sound discretion of the trial judge, whose action in allowing their use may not be disturbed by an appellate court except for an abuse of discretion. We find no such abuse.

(3) *Summaries Based on Information Found in Computer Discs.* In *United States v. Foley*, 598 F.2d 1323 (4th Cir. 1979), *cert. denied*, 444 U.S. 1043 (1980), the defendants complained that the base data for one chart was never made available to them:

> The chart was compiled from data contained in machine-readable "diskettes" provided by the multiple listing service. The diskettes were not

> made available to defendants, but a computer print-out of the information they contained was and the diskettes themselves only contained data that was provided to defendants themselves by their multiple listing service in the normal course of business. The computer print-outs qualify as duplicates of the diskettes within the meaning of Rule 1006. Fed. R. Evid. 1001(4). In any event, defendants conceded that substantial out-of-state funds were used to purchase houses they brokered. Thus, the admission of the chart, if erroneous, would seem to be harmless error.

If the diskettes had contained millions of pieces of information from years of doing business, some of the information being relevant to this case but much being relevant to thousands of other business transactions, stored in an order totally different from that in the summaries, and the selection and retrieval of the information for the summaries had required the design of a special program to pick out, order, and process the information (although not beyond the power of any competent programming firm to do), would it be enough for the government to supply the defendants with all the diskettes or a printout of all information on the diskettes in the order it appears on the diskettes? Would that be enough if the diskettes were not those of defendant's own records? Suppose the complicated diskettes are in fact diskettes from the computers of the party who is offering the summary.

(4) *Dangers Posed by Summaries in Criminal Cases.* In *United States v. Scales*, 594 F.2d 558 (6th Cir.), *cert. denied*, 441 U.S. 946 (1979), although the court upheld the admission of an exhibit that summarized the indictment and part of the government's proof, it observed:

> The danger of permitting presentation of a summary of some of the evidence in a criminal case is plain. The jury might rely upon the alleged facts in the summary as if these facts had already been proved, or as a substitute for assessing the credibility of witnesses. This danger has led to the requirement of "guarding instructions" to the effect that the chart is not itself evidence but is only an aid in evaluating the evidence. Even with such instructions, a summary may still be considered as too conclusory or as emphasizing too much certain portions of the government's case, or as presenting incompetent facts. Trial courts may take care that such unfair summaries are not presented to juries.

REVIEW PROBLEM 12A: WHAT ARE THE ADVANTAGES AND DISADVANTAGES OF THE LIBERALIZED AUTHENTICATION AND BEST EVIDENCE RULES?

The liberalizations of Articles IX (Authentication and Identification) and X (Best Evidence) in the Federal Rules of Evidence as compared with the common law (and here we are talking about all types of applications) seem to be part of a larger pattern in the Federal Rules of Evidence to take burdens or tasks off the party offering evidence (that is, the burden to show that the evidence is admissible) and shift the burden or task to the party opposing the evidence (that is, the burden to show that the evidence is inadmissible or weighs little). It seems to be felt that under modern discovery, this no longer is unfair and indeed is economical, since acceptability should not have to be shown in cases where there is no indication there is anything wrong with the evidence. Thus, Fed. R. Civ. P. 26(a)(3) provides that objections to previously disclosed documents or other exhibits, including summaries, must be made prior to trial or they will be waived, with the exception of objections to relevancy and prejudice (Fed. R. Evid. 401 and 403). Do you think these reforms are good or bad?

§ 12.03 COMPLETENESS[4]

Read Federal Rule of Evidence 106, "Remainder of or Related Writings or Recorded Statements."

BEECH AIRCRAFT CORP. v. RAINEY

United States Supreme Court
488 U.S. 153 (1988)

Brennan, Justice.

[Rainey brought a products liability action against Beech for the death of his wife, a pilot, who died in a plane crash in which her student pilot also was killed. At trial, Beech claimed the accident occurred because of pilot error.]

Respondents also contended on appeal that reversal was required because the District Court improperly restricted the cross-examination of plaintiff Rainey by his own counsel in regard to the letter Rainey had addressed to Lieutenant Commander Morgan. We agree with the unanimous holding of the Court of Appeals en banc that the District Court erred in refusing to permit Rainey to present a more complete picture of what he had written to Morgan.

We have no doubt that the jury was given a distorted and prejudicial impression of Rainey's letter. The theory of Rainey's case was that the accident was the result of a power failure, and, read in its entirety, his letter to Morgan was fully consistent with that theory. While Rainey did discuss problems his wife had encountered the morning of the accident which led her to attempt to cancel the flight, and also agreed that her airplane had violated pattern integrity in turning left prematurely, the thrust of his letter was to challenge Morgan's theory that the crash had been caused by a stall that took place when the pilots turned sharply right and pitched up in attempting to avoid the other plane. Thus Rainey argued that Morgan's hypothesis was inconsistent with the observations of eyewitnesses, the physical findings in the wreckage, and the likely actions of the two pilots. He explained at length his theory of power failure and attempted to demonstrate how the various pieces of evidence supported it. What the jury was told, however, through the defendants' direct examination of Rainey as an adverse witness, was that Rainey had written six months after the accident (1) that his wife had attempted to cancel the flight, partly because her student was tired and emotionally drained, and that "unnecessary pressure" was placed on them to proceed with it; and (2) that she or

---

[4] Study Guide Reference: Evidence in a Nutshell, Chapter 11:III and IV.

her student had abruptly initiated a hard right turn when the other aircraft unexpectedly came into view. It is plausible that a jury would have concluded from this information that Rainey did not believe in his theory of power failure and had developed it only later for purposes of litigation. Because the court sustained defense counsel's objection, Rainey's counsel was unable to counteract this prejudicial impression by presenting additional information about the letter on cross-examination.

The common-law "rule of completeness," which underlies Federal Rule of Evidence 106, was designed to prevent exactly the type of prejudice of which Rainey complains. In its aspect relevant to this litigation, the rule of completeness was stated succinctly by Wigmore: "[T]he opponent, against whom a part of an utterance has been put in, may in his turn complement it by putting in the remainder, in order to secure for the tribunal a complete understanding of the total tenor and effect of the utterance." 7 J. Wigmore, Evidence in Trials at Common Law § 2113, p. 653 (J. Chadbourn rev. 1978). The Federal Rules of Evidence have partially codified the doctrine of completeness in Rule 106.

In proposing Rule 106, the Advisory Committee stressed that it "does not in any way circumscribe the right of the adversary to develop the matter on cross-examination or as part of his own case." Advisory Committee's Notes on Fed. Rule Evid. 106. We take this to be a reaffirmation of the obvious: that when one party has made use of a portion of a document, such that misunderstanding or distortion can be averted only through presentation of another portion, the material required for completeness is ipso facto relevant and therefore admissible under Rules 401 and 402. The District Court's refusal to admit the proffered completion evidence was a clear abuse of discretion.

While much of the controversy in this suit has centered on whether Rule 106 applies, we find it unnecessary to address that issue. Clearly the concerns underlying Rule 106 are relevant here, but, as the general rules of relevancy permit a ready resolution to this litigation, we need go no further in exploring the scope and meaning of Rule 106.

Reversed.

NOTES AND QUESTIONS

(1) *Application of the Rule of Completeness in a Criminal Case.* See *United States v. Walker*, 652 F.2d 708 (7th Cir. 1981), in which the court reversed a conviction for extortion under color of official right because the defendant was prohibited from having the government read portions of the defendant's examination at a prior trial in conjunction with the parts of the defendant's testimony read into evidence by the government. The defendant did not testify at the retrial:

> Federal Rule of Evidence 106 codifies the common law rule of completeness. The portions sought to be admitted (1) must be relevant to the issues and (2) only those parts which qualify or explain the subject matter of the portion offered by the opponent need be admitted. *United States v. McCorkle* [511 F.2d 482 (7th Cir.), *cert denied*, 423 U.S. 826 (1975)].

We find that the excluded testimony satisfies the standard enunciated in *United States v. McCorkle, supra*, because substantial portions were both relevant to specific elements of the government's proof and explanatory of the excerpts already admitted. For instance, some of the excluded testimony probed Walker's intent and developed his allegation that his participation in the July 7th meeting was innocent.

The Advisory Committee's Note indicates that Rule 106 is primarily designed to affect the order of proof. "The rule is based on two considerations. The first is the misleading impression created by taking matters out of context. The second is the inadequacy of repair work when delayed to a point later in the trial." Consequently, the trial judge's exercise of discretion under the rule should involve the weighing of the adequacy of the "repair work" necessary to correct any potentially misleading impression caused by an incomplete presentation against "the waste of time and attention and the unfairness involved in blunting the proponent's presentation of his case when everything is required to be read at one time."

In criminal cases where the defendant elects not to testify, as in the present case, more is at stake than the order of proof. If the government is not required to submit all relevant portions of prior testimony which further explain selected parts which the government has offered, the excluded portions may never be admitted. Thus there may be no "repair work" which could remedy the unfairness of a selective presentation later in the trial of such a case. While certainly not as egregious, the situation at hand does bear similarity to [f]orcing the defendant to take the stand in order to introduce the omitted exculpatory portions of [a] confession [which] is a denial of his right against self-incrimination. [T]he government's incomplete presentation may have painted a distorted picture of Walker's prior testimony which he was powerless to remedy without taking the stand.

Walker's entire testimony constituted only twenty-eight pages. The government read approximately fourteen of these pages into evidence. Forcing the government to include the remainder would not have seriously disrupted the prosecution's case. [T]he government's efforts to [conduct a fair trial] should be at least as active as its zeal to secure convictions.

The potential unfairness to the defendant, by contrast, was substantial. Because Walker chose not to testify at the second trial, the government's selective presentation of his prior testimony resulted in the total exclusion of Walker's testimony explaining the parts admitted, not just a delay in the introduction of the remaining parts. This result penalizes Walker for failing to testify at his second trial.

Any inconvenience to the court caused by the introduction of the remaining testimony would have been minimal. At trial, the government attorneys read the selected portions to the jury with one attorney assuming the role of the defendant and the other taking the part of the examiner. The additional time necessary for them to have read the remaining pages would have been inconsequential.

(2) *How Broad is the Rule of Completeness?* Fed. R. Evid. 106 has potential use in connection with a wide variety of documents of whatever kind, portions of which have been introduced for whatever purpose, whether they are like deeds and contracts, which have direct effect under the substantive law; or government reports, business records, party admissions, recorded recollections, etc., originally introduced under some exception to or exemption from the hearsay rule as recountings of relevant fact; or statements introduced for impeachment or used to refresh recollection; or deposition transcripts; etc. Might the rule be used to require introduction of other letters in a series? Other files?

To what, besides writings, does Fed. R. Evid. 106 apply? Tape recordings? Films? Videotapes? Photographs? Electronic computer tapes, discs, or memories? Conversations? Oral statements? Do conversations and oral statements need to be made concrete in tape or transcript to be subject to the rule, or is it enough that they are testified to by anyone who heard them? Is the definition of "writing" under Fed. R. Evid. 106 coextensive with the definition under Fed. R. Evid. 1001?

(3) *Does the Doctrine Require Admission of Otherwise Inadmissible Evidence?* Suppose that the remainder that is being offered under Fed. R. Evid. 106, for completeness or to put the previously introduced portion into context, is a portion that violates some rule of evidence such as the hearsay rule, the character rule, the insurance rule, the rule against compromise offers or safety measures, the attorney-client or work-product privilege, other privilege, etc.? Can Fed. R. Evid. 106 still be used to get it in? Is such evidence offered "for the truth of the matter asserted"?

(4) *Combination of Some Principles in Last Three Notes. See United States v. Fredericks*, 599 F.2d 262 (8th Cir. 1979) (affirming exclusion of statement made during subsequent interview as hearsay). In *Fredericks*, a prosecution for assault with a dangerous weapon (a gun), the defendant claimed he fired at an oncoming automobile in self-defense. Statements made by one of the automobile's passengers (who was unavailable) were introduced into evidence against him. These statements (made at the time of the alleged assault) were, "He has a gun," and "Let's get the hell out of here; he's going to kill us." Fed. R. Evid. 106 did not permit the admission of another statement of the same passenger, made during a subsequent interview with a police officer, that a second passenger said, prior to the shooting, "Let's run over [defendant]," when no other statement from that interview had been introduced. Do you agree with this result? Even if Fed. R. Evid. 106 does not apply, are there other rules or doctrines that one might argue to admit this evidence?

Chapter 13

PRIVILEGES

RECOGNITION OF OTHER CONCERNS (F.R.E. ARTICLE V, RULE 501)

§ 13.01 INTRODUCTION[1]

Read Federal Rule of Evidence 501, "Privilege in General."

(1) *Privilege versus Truth.* Because privileges conflict with the obligation of every person to give testimony, they are viewed as an impediment to finding the truth.[2] Therefore, the law has been hostile to recognizing any privilege, except to the extent that it furthers greater societal goals. The justifications for privilege often combine instrumental and humanistic rationales. The instrumental purposes are highly practical, based on the assumption, for example, that individuals will not reveal necessary information or obtain needed assistance without a guarantee of confidentiality. Humanistic rationales rest on the importance of such values as privacy, autonomy, and dignity. The following criteria have been influential in evaluating whether a privilege based on confidentiality of communications is warranted (8 WIGMORE, EVIDENCE § 2285 (McNaughton rev. 1961)):

> (1) The communications must originate in confidence that they will not be disclosed.
>
> (2) This element of confidentiality must be essential to the full and satisfactory maintenance of the relation between the parties.
>
> (3) The relation must be one which in the opinion of the community ought to be sedulously fostered.

---

[1] Study Guide Reference: Evidence in a Nutshell, Chapter 5:I;II.

[2] With some exceptions, privileges ordinarily cover testimony, documents, objects, recordings, etc., revealing the privileged information. It is important to realize that, in general, in the absence of a privilege, testimony or other evidence a court requires to resolve a controversy is compellable. Compellability is thus the "background" or "default" position. If, in the absence of a privilege, a person refuses to testify or give evidence despite a proper subpoena or court order to do so that is not quashable on other grounds, he or she may be held in contempt of court and jailed or fined perhaps continuously until the evidence is given.

If a communication, say between lawyer and client, or husband and wife, or doctor and patient, or clergyman and parishioner, is what is covered by a privilege, evidence of the communication will be inadmissible, but the facts related in the communication ordinarily are not. Thus, a person may not be asked "What did you tell your [lawyer, spouse, doctor, or clergyman] happened in the incident you were involved in"; but may be asked "what happened in the incident you were involved in?"

(4) The injury that would inure to the relation by the disclosure of the communication must be greater than the benefit thereby gained for the correct disposal of the litigation.

These criteria are useful in assessing whether a court having power to do so will create or expand the interpretation of a recognized privilege. In addition, they have influenced the creation of exceptions to privileges. In most instances, since most of these privileges are not "qualified" privileges, the Wigmore criteria are used *not* to assess the interest served by privilege versus the desirability of disclosure *in the particular case*, but rather to assess the wisdom of creating a *categorical* privilege (for example, a psychotherapist-patient privilege), a categorical expansion of a privilege, or a categorical exception to a privilege.

It has been said that "Truth, like all other good things, may be loved unwisely — may be pursued too keenly — may cost too much." *Pearse v. Pearse*, 63 Eng. Rep. 950, 957 (1846). Privileges embody that philosophy. The Wigmore criteria are intended to help with the determination of when the cost is too much. Can you think of other areas of the law than privilege, where the quote from *Pearse* might be applicable?

Congress in particular, in enacting the Federal Rules of Evidence for federal courts, had difficulty in deciding just when the pursuit of truth "cost too much" and privilege should be accorded. In the end, Congress punted, and left the matter to the federal courts as something to be gradually explicated, or to state law, depending on the nature of the case.

After a highly acrimonious debate in Congress, the detailed proposed federal rules defining particular privileges and procedures governing them were rejected in favor of Fed. R. Evid. 501, which made federal privilege law dependent on "the principles of the common law as they may be interpreted . . . in the light of reason and experience." But Rule 501 provides that in civil cases "with respect to an element of a claim or defense as to which state law supplies the rule of decision," privilege is dictated by state law. Thus, the vast majority of diversity cases will be governed by state privilege law, and this result is considered by some as a recognition that privilege law really is substantive in nature, rather than evidentiary. In general, state privilege law is quite developed because it controls the behavior of individuals outside the courtroom and therefore embodies policy concerns that should be explicitly recognized in order to be effective. The bifurcated treatment of state and federal privilege law in Rule 501 can produce tension, especially when state and federal claims are joined in federal court, requiring the judge to decide which privilege law trumps or whether both policies can be accommodated. When reading this chapter, compare the results reached under the evolving common law with those dictated by specific rules and assess the relative advantages and disadvantages of flexibility over certainty in the realm of privileges. Also ask yourself (where the facts invite it): what does the possibility of loss of privilege in a federal action do to the state's policy of encouraging the communication?

(2) *Third Person's Privilege versus Criminal Defendant.* Some of the following materials pose the question of what is to be done when a third person's privilege would seem to bar criminal defendants from obtaining evidence to defend them-

selves. This has come up not only with respect to journalist privilege and some of the "less ordinary" privileges, but can come up under such "ordinary" privileges as husband-wife, physician-patient, and attorney-client as well. *E.g.*, *United States v. Brown*, 634 F.2d 819 (5th Cir. 1981) (government witness's wife asserts spousal privilege and bars defendant from obtaining material to impeach witness; privilege sustained). Compare the discussion of rape shield provisions in § 3.03[A]. *See also* Chapter 11, particularly § 11.06, discussing Confrontation, Due Process, and Compulsory Process. *See generally* Comment, *Defendant vs. Witness: Measuring Confrontation and Compulsory Process Rights Against Statutory Communications Privileges*, 20 Stan. L. Rev. 935 (1978); Imwinkelried & Garland, Exculpatory Evidence (2d ed. 1995).

In *Pennsylvania v. Ritchie*, 480 U.S. 39 (1987), pursuant to the Due Process Clause, the Court required an *in camera* inspection of statements alleging child abuse that were in the possession of the government despite the existence of a qualified statutory privilege. *Ritchie* indicated that evidence favorable to the accused and material to guilt or punishment must be disclosed to the defendant, and a retrial is necessary if such evidence probably would have changed the outcome of the trial. Courts have interpreted *Ritchie* narrowly. *See, e.g.*, *People v. Hammon*, 938 P.2d 986 (Cal. 1997) (defendant did not have Sixth Amendment right to have court review, *in camera*, privileged records sought from complainant's private psychologists prior to trial). This issue has become more significant with the expansion of privileges for psychotherapists, social workers, rape counselors and domestic abuse workers. *See, e.g.*, Cal. Evid. Code § 1035 (Sexual Assault Victim-Counselor Privilege) and Cal. Evid. Code § 1037 (Domestic Violence Victim-Counselor Privilege). Would it matter if the privilege blocking access was absolute rather than qualified in determining whether the defendant's constitutional rights trumped the conflicting statutory privilege? Think about the matters raised in this paragraph as you consider each of the selected privileges addressed in this chapter.

(3) *Proceedings where Privileges Apply.* Privileges govern only disclosability *in court*, albeit at any stage of the proceedings, including in most jurisdictions as to most privileges not only the trial itself, but also discovery, grand-jury proceedings, preliminary examinations, and hearings before the judge on the admissibility of a piece of evidence.[3] Privileges do not govern disclosure out of court; nor do they, at least not *per se*, govern what may be subpoenaed in a criminal investigation,[4] or seized in an otherwise justified search by the government.[5] But there may be other

---

[3] However, where the admissibility question before the judge relates to privilege, the allegedly privileged material may be receivable before the judge to some extent (and perhaps only *in camera*) at least if there is some indication it might not be privileged. One reason given for this is that the material is not really privileged material at that point, because the determination of privilege has not yet been made. *See Zolin, infra*, under attorney-client privilege.

[4] *See* Slobogin, *Subpoenas and Privacy*, 54 DePaul L. Rev. 805 (2005).

[5] Nor are Congressional investigations or hearings necessarily governed by privilege law, unless it is constitutional law, such as the Fifth Amendment privilege against self-incrimination, or the Congressional body has adopted its own rules tracking privileges. Nevertheless, Congress has usually respected the privileges that would apply in court. In a criminal case, government out-of-court infringement of the private attorney-client relationship, such as listening to confidential communications between a criminal defendant and his lawyer, has been thought, at least in some circumstances, to violate the constitutional

law governing these matters that may track privilege concepts. For example, subpoenas for material or witnesses will ordinarily be suppressed if the material would be privileged if attempted to be introduced in court, or if it appears the only purpose for subpoenaing the witness is to get information that would be privileged under the law of privileges applicable in court. Similarly, some privilege concepts may be applied to limit government seizures pursuant to criminal investigations.[6] Ethical or standard-of-care violations may occur if a professional breaches confidentiality out of court (with certain exceptions), and that may result in disciplinary action or tort malpractice suits. Though the concepts in such situations draw heavily on privilege law, they are not technically a matter of privilege law and are not necessarily co-terminous with it.

Similarly, the Freedom of Information Act, 5 U.S.C.A. § 552, governs disclosure of governmental information to the public, as opposed to disclosure in court. The latter kind of disclosure is the province of privilege law. The Freedom of Information Act generally commands that governmental information be made available to the public, but with exceptions covering such things as certain law enforcement, investigative, and private personnel records. The contours of these exceptions have had influence on courts in shaping a number of governmental privileges that accord secrecy in court analogous to the secrecy provided in the public arena by the Freedom of Information Act exceptions. For it would make little sense to privilege (and thus forbid to the court), information that is made available to the public (because outside a Freedom of Information Act exception). After all, a court ordinarily has *greater* need for information than the public. And, anyway, if information is available to the public, it may be a practical impossibility to keep it out of court. However, the reverse is not necessarily true: Something *withheld* from the public (pursuant to a Freedom of Information Act exception) should not necessarily be withheld (pursuant to privilege) from a court, because, again, a court would ordinarily have greater need for the information than the public. So, while a particular Freedom of Information Act exception may bear a relationship to a particular governmental in-court privilege, the two are not necessarily congruent.

It is important to realize, as you go through the privilege cases and materials in this chapter, that there may be rules of evidence other than privilege that affect the particular allegedly privileged piece of evidence, as well. For example, every time an allegedly privileged communication is sought to be introduced into evidence, there is usually also a hearsay problem, although in some instances there may be a

---

Sixth Amendment Right to Counsel, even though the evidence gained is not used in court (and thus it is not technically "privilege" that is in issue). But some doubt has been cast on this proposition of late in terrorism cases. *See* Ruzenski, *Balancing Fundamental Civil Liberties and the Need for Increased Homeland Security: The Attorney-Client Privilege After September 11th*, 19 St. John's J. Legal Comment. 467 (2005); *cf.* Clare, *We Should Have Gone to Med School: In the Wake of Lynne Stewart, Lawyers Face Hard Time for Defending Terrorists*, 18 Geo J. Legal Ethics 651 (2005). In general, in accord with the notion that privilege governs only disclosure in court, there is no "fruit of the poisonous tree" doctrine for other than constitutional privileges. And, also in accord with this notion, in many jurisdictions, at least as to most privileges, there cannot be a privilege objection to the introduction into evidence of a previous voluntary out-of-court statement made by the other party to the privileged relationship — even if the statement would be privileged if attempted to be made in court.

[6] *See Klitzman, Klitzman & Gallagher v. Krut*, 744 F.2d 955 (3d Cir. 1984) (seizure improperly infringed on attorney-client privilege and work-product protection).

hearsay exception available on the facts. The materials at this point in the book deal only with the privilege problem.

(4) *Sources of Privilege Law.* The Congressionally rejected privilege rules referred to above included nine specifically codified privileges. They included privileges for (1) statutorily required reports where the statute accorded privilege, (2) lawyer-client communications, (3) psychotherapist-patient communications, (4) adverse spousal testimony, (5) communications to clergymen, (6) the tenor of a person's political vote, (7) trade secrets, (8) secrets of state and other official information, and (9) the identity of informers to law enforcement and legislative investigative committees. The provisions also included some general across-the-board prescriptions on (a) waiver of privilege, (b) the effect of disclosure under compulsion or without opportunity to claim privilege, and (c) the permissibility of comment on or drawing inferences from a claim of privilege. The nine privileges and three general provisions were part of what was called the "Supreme Court Draft" (also known as the "Proposed Rules") of the entire Federal Rules of Evidence. This draft was introduced in and then altered by Congress in a number of respects, including *inter alia* deletion of the specific privilege rules, before the final Congressional enactment of the Federal Rules of Evidence as a whole.

The rejected draft had been carefully crafted by a distinguished Advisory Committee and approved by the Supreme Court, albeit without the Court's detailed consideration of each rule. For the most part, the rejection of the draft's detailed privilege rules reflected not so much a disapproval of the merits of the specific rules, but more a desire to accord flexibility, to foster further development of privilege law, and to recognize state privilege law in federal diversity cases. Thus, current Fed. R. Evid. 501, the only rule on privilege law in the enacted Rules, replaces all the detailed privilege rules. As you can see, it provides two sources of privilege law in federal courts: the judge is referred to either evolving common law principles or to state law, depending on the kind of case.[7]

In contrast to federal law, privileges in state law tend to be specifically codified in statutes, but often with a heavy overlay of case interpretation influenced by a particular privilege's common-law roots, if any. On the other hand, some state courts stick very closely to the statutory language, regardless of any common law roots.

In the materials that follow in this chapter, we reproduce examples of privilege provisions, but only as a framework for your thinking. Our examples will usually be drawn from the Supreme Court Draft or the Uniform Rules of Evidence (a body of rules approved for state use by the National Conference of Commissioners on Uniform State Laws and the American Bar Association). The Uniform Rules are based on and are very similar to the Supreme Court Draft. But in some respects the Uniform Rules are more developed.

As indicated, the rejection of the Supreme Court Draft privilege rules was not necessarily on the merits, but merely at least in part a preference for more elastic provisions. Thus, the Uniform Rules' and the Supreme Court Draft's privilege provisions tend to influence the formation or interpretation of both federal and state

[7] There are also many federal statutes and regulations establishing privileges in particular regulatory areas, which are largely beyond the scope of this book.

law, but they are not necessarily definitive. Some states have expressly adopted the Uniform Rules, the Draft Federal Rules, or something similar. Others have their own distinct privilege law. Federal courts, in fashioning privilege law under the phrase "the principles of the common law as they may be interpreted . . . in the light of reason and experience" in current Rule 501, tend to utilize, in a non-binding advisory way, the privilege provisions of the Uniform Rules and the Supreme Court Draft, as well as the positions of scholars and jurisdictions around the country to the extent there is reasonable consensus. Or at least the *Supreme Court* has, on a few occasions. The Supreme Court's conception of wise social policy also played a role on these occasions, as seems to be called for by the rule. In this connection, it is important to note that the phrase in Rule 501 does not bind one to a static reading of what the common law was at a given point in history, but uses more expansive words: "principles" of the common law, "interpreted" in the "light of reason and experience", suggesting that — while the starting point may be history and the common law — the broader policies underlying the common law, and modern experience, together with independent reasoning, should also be operative. Evolution through a common law *process* seems to be what is contemplated and invited. Lower federal courts have been reluctant to evolve privilege law in this way, looking instead to the Supreme Court to do it if it is to be done. For a long time, the Supreme Court was also reluctant. But some have seen a change in the Supreme Court's attitude, beginning with *Trammel* (*infra*, under husband-wife privilege) and accelerating in *Jaffee* (*infra*, under psychotherapist and social worker privilege). They predict that this signal from the Supreme Court may embolden lower courts. There has not, however, been a rush in this direction as yet, either by the Supreme Court or the lower federal courts.

We make no attempt to cover all evidentiary privileges in this book. Rather, we have selected the ones we think most important and instructive. The effort has been to expose you to a representative sample of privilege issues of a kind that should equip you to confront even those that have been omitted.

For more about privilege law, see ROTHSTEIN & CRUMP, FEDERAL TESTIMONIAL PRIVILEGES (2d ed. 2012–13, updated yearly); Broun, *Giving Codification a Second Chance — Testimonial Privileges and the Federal Rules of Evidence*, 53 HASTINGS L.J. 769 (2002); Imwinkelried, *An Hegelian Approach to Privileges Under Federal Rule of Evidence 501: The Restrictive Thesis, The Expansive Antithesis, and the Contextual Synthesis*, 73 NEB. L. REV. 511 (1994); Rothstein, *The Proposed Amendments to the Federal Rules of Evidence*, 62 GEO. L.J. 125 (1973).

§ 13.02 ATTORNEY-CLIENT PRIVILEGE: EXAMINATION OF SOME ISSUES COMMON TO MANY PRIVILEGES[8]

Uniform Rules of Evidence (as Amended 1999) [Recommended Model Provisions for States: Not Part of the Federal Rules]:[9]

Rule 502. Lawyer-Client Privilege

(a) **Definitions.** In this rule:

(1) **"Client" means a person**[10] for whom a lawyer renders professional legal services or who consults a lawyer with a view to obtaining professional legal services from the lawyer.

(2) A communication is "confidential" if it is not intended to be disclosed to third persons other than those to whom disclosure is made in furtherance of the rendition of professional legal services to the client or those reasonably necessary for the transmission of the communication.

(3) "Lawyer" means a person authorized, or reasonably believed by the client to be authorized, to engage in the practice of law in any state or country.

(4) "Representative of the client" means a person having authority to obtain professional legal services, or to act on legal advice rendered, on behalf of the client or a person who, for the purpose of effectuating legal representation for the client, makes or receives a confidential communication while acting in the scope of employment for the client.

---

[8] Study Guide Reference: Evidence in a Nutshell, Chapter 5:III.

[9] The Uniform Rule's attorney-client privilege is quite similar to the analogous "Supreme Court Draft" Rule ("Proposed Rule") in many respects but the Uniform Rule incorporates the U.S. Supreme Court's *Upjohn* decision (reproduced *infra*), broadening the corporation's privilege beyond communications involving members of the control group, whereas the Supreme Court Draft, coming before *Upjohn*, left the matter open. See the definition of "representative of the client" in the Uniform Rule, which is missing from the draft Federal Rule. Several states still restrict the privilege to the control group, but federal law now uniformly does not. The Supreme Court Draft also did not confine the joint client consultation situation described as privileged in (b)(3) to "pending actions," and did not have the exception (d)(7) relating to government attorney-client privilege. Actual law concerning these two matters on which the provisions differ is unsettled on the state and federal level. A number of states have adopted Uniform Rule 502.

Uniform Rules 510 through 511, like their counterparts in the Supreme Court Draft Federal Rules ("Proposed Rules"), are meant to be applicable to privileges more generally, not just attorney-client privilege.

[10] By virtue of definitional provisions elsewhere in the Uniform Rules, the word "person" as used in this privilege includes a public officer, corporation, association, or other organization or entity, either public or private.

(5) "Representative of the lawyer" means a person employed, or reasonably believed by the client to be employed, by the lawyer to assist the lawyer in rendering professional legal services.

(b) General rule of privilege. A client has a privilege to refuse to disclose and to prevent any other person from disclosing a confidential communication made for the purpose of facilitating the rendition of professional legal services to the client:

(1) between the client or a representative of the client and the client's lawyer or a representative of the lawyer;

(2) between the lawyer and a representative of the lawyer;

(3) by the client or a representative of the client or the client's lawyer or a representative of the lawyer to a lawyer or a representative of a lawyer representing another party in a pending action and concerning a matter of common interest therein;

(4) between representatives of the client or between the client and a representative of the client; or

(5) among lawyers and their representatives representing the same client.

(c) Who may claim privilege. The privilege under this rule may be claimed by the client, the client's guardian or conservator, the personal representative of a deceased client, or the successor, trustee, or similar representative of a corporation, association, or other organization, whether or not in existence. A person who was the lawyer or the lawyer's representative at the time of the communication is presumed to have authority to claim the privilege, but only on behalf of the client.

(d) Exceptions. There is no privilege under this rule:

(1) if the services of the lawyer were sought or obtained to enable or aid anyone to commit or plan to commit what the client knew or reasonably should have known was a crime or fraud;

(2) as to a communication relevant to an issue between parties who claim through the same deceased client, regardless of whether the claims are by testate or intestate succession or by transaction inter vivos;

(3) as to a communication relevant to an issue of breach of duty by a lawyer to the client or by a client to the lawyer;

(4) as to a communication necessary for a lawyer to defend in a legal proceeding an accusation that the lawyer assisted the client in criminal or fraudulent conduct;

(5) as to a communication relevant to an issue concerning an attested document to which the lawyer is an attesting witness;

(6) as to a communication relevant to a matter of common interest between or among two or more clients if the communication was made by any of them to a lawyer retained or consulted in common, when offered in an action between or among any of the clients; or

(7) as to a communication between a public officer or agency and its lawyers unless the communication concerns a pending investigation, claim, or action and the court determines that disclosure will seriously impair the ability of the public officer or agency to act upon the claim or conduct a pending investigation, litigation, or proceeding in the public interest.

* * *

Rule 510. Waiver of Privilege

(a) Voluntary disclosure. A person upon whom these rules confer a privilege against disclosure waives the privilege if he or his predecessor while holder of the privilege voluntarily discloses or consents to disclosure of any significant part of the privileged matter. This rule does not apply if the disclosure itself is privileged.

(b) Involuntary disclosure. A claim of privilege is not waived by a disclosure that was compelled erroneously or made without an opportunity to claim the privilege.

Rule 511. Comment upon or Inference from Claim of Privilege; Instruction

(a) Comment or inference not permitted. A claim of privilege, whether in the present proceeding or upon a previous occasion, is not a proper subject of comment by judge or counsel. No inference may be drawn from the claim.

(b) Claiming privilege without knowledge of jury. In jury cases, proceedings must be conducted, to the extent practicable, so as to facilitate the making of claims of privilege without the knowledge of the jury.

(c) Jury Instruction. Upon request, any party against whom the jury might draw an adverse inference from a claim of privilege is entitled to an instruction that no inference may be drawn therefrom

[A] Basic Privilege

AMERICAN NATIONAL WATERMATTRESS CORP. v. MANVILLE

Alaska Supreme Court
642 P.2d 1330 (1982)

BURKE, JUSTICE.

Florence Manville was injured when she was pinned beneath her waterbed after it rolled off its pedestal. Manville filed an action against ANWC [manufacturer] and Pendley [dealer] for her injuries on theories of negligence, breach of warranties, and strict liability.

ANWC presently appeals from the final judgment.

I. Should the trial court have ordered Manville to produce her interview with her attorneys' employee?

Within a few days after the accident, Manville contacted her present attorneys for legal advice. Since two of the firm's attorneys were then in trials, the firm sent its full-time employee, Chuck Ward, to interview Manville so that they "could provide her with legal advice and possible legal assistance in regard to that accident." It is undisputed that Ward was not an attorney.

Ward interviewed Manville in her hospital room and tape recorded a portion of his conversation with her. This tape recording was transcribed and delivered to the firm's attorneys. The firm subsequently accepted Manville's case.

During discovery, defendants learned of the existence of Manville's statement and requested its production. Manville refused, claiming the document was privileged.

ANWC and Pendley then moved for an order to compel production. After oral argument, the trial court denied the motion.

On appeal, ANWC again asserts that Manville's statement was not protected. [We hold] her statement is protected from discovery by the attorney-client privilege as a confidential communication from Manville to her attorneys through their agent.

Civil Rule 43(h)(2) provided the basis for the attorney-client privilege:

> An attorney shall not, without the consent of his client, be examined as to any communication made by his client to him, nor as to the attorney's advice given thereon, in the course of the attorney's professional employment.

As this court has noted: "The purpose of the attorney-client privilege is to promote the freedom of consultation of legal advisors by clients by removing the apprehension of compelled disclosure by the legal advisors." However, this desire to promote the consultation of attorneys through the use of the attorney-client privilege must be balanced against the need for the discovery of facts. As we have stated: "Given our commitment to liberal pre-trial discovery, it follows that the scope of the attorney-client privilege should be strictly construed in accordance with its purpose."

This court has never directly ruled on the question of whether a statement of facts given by a prospective client to an attorney's agent is protected by the attorney-client privilege. For analysis, this issue may be more conveniently broken into three subissues.

A. Was Manville a "client" entitled to the protection of the attorney-client privilege, where she made the questioned communication in an attempt to obtain legal advice, but the attorney had not yet accepted her case?

While Civil Rule 43(h)(2) and our own case law are silent on this issue, the statement of the attorney-client privilege embodied in the new Evidence Rules contains a clear answer which, although not in effect at the time of trial, is persuasive. Evidence Rule 503(a)(1) sets out the following definition of a "client" for the purposes of the attorney-client privilege: "A client is a person who is rendered professional legal services by a lawyer, or who consults a lawyer with a view to obtaining professional legal services."

The language is clarified in the Commentary: "The definition of 'client' extends the status of client to one consulting a lawyer preliminarily with a view to retaining him, even though actual employment does not result."

In addition, it is clearly the universal common-law rule that such "[c]ommunications in the course of preliminary discussion with a view to employing the lawyer are privileged though the employment is in the upshot not accepted."

As stated by one court, the reason for such a rule is that "no person could ever safely consult an attorney for the first time with a view to his employment if the privilege depended on the chance of whether the attorney after hearing his statement of the facts decided to accept the employment or decline it."

Manville was seeking an attorney to prosecute her case. Manville qualified as a "client."

B. Was Manville's statement protected by the attorney-client privilege where it was made to an employee of her attorney, rather than the attorney himself?

Again, Civil Rule 43(h)(2) and Alaska case law do not address this issue. However, new Evidence Rule 503(b) sets out the general rule of privilege:

> A client has a privilege to refuse to disclose and to prevent any other person from disclosing confidential communications made for the purpose of facilitating the rendition of professional legal services to the client, (1) between himself or his representative and his lawyer or *his lawyer's representative*, or (2) between his lawyer and *the lawyer's representative.* [Emphasis added.]

Rule 503(a)(4) provides a definition of "representative of a lawyer": "A representative of the lawyer is one employed to assist the lawyer in the rendition of professional legal services."

The Commentary states: "The definition of 'representative of the lawyer' recognizes that the lawyer may, in rendering legal services, utilize the services of assistants in addition to those employed in the process of communicating." [E]ven in the absence of the "representative of the lawyer" language, the attorney-client privilege would protect confidential client communications to the attorney's employee who is used simply as a conduit for communication.

[T]he common-law privilege extended to laymen who are necessary intermediaries between attorney and client.

In this case, the investigator was an employee and agent of the attorney who was acting as a conduit for the transmission of information from the client to her attorney.

C. Is Manville's statement of the facts of the accident protected by the attorney-client privilege, where no legal points were discussed during the interview?

ANWC maintains that only raw facts [were discussed].

The privilege under Civil Rule 43(h)(2) included "any communication made by his client to him in the course of the attorney's professional employment." The current Evidence Rule 503(b) provides that "communications made for the purpose of facilitating the rendition of professional legal services to the client" are protected. Neither of these formulations lend support to ANWC's contention that legal points must be discussed. If the communication is either "in the course of" the attorney's professional employment or "facilitates" the rendition of legal services, it is protected.

In addition, the very heart of the common-law privilege was to protect the facts given by the client to his attorney. The privilege was based on the necessity that an attorney have the full disclosure of the facts from his client. Indeed, the now generally recognized application of the privilege to communications from the lawyer to the client is but an extension of the original essence of the privilege as a protection of only the client's factual communications to his attorney.

[*Affirmed, except for damages computation error.*]

NOTES AND QUESTIONS

(1) *What Procedures Govern the Judge's Privilege Determinations?* In *United States v. Zolin*, 491 U.S. 554 (1989), in the context of deciding whether a communication fell within the crime-fraud exception to attorney-client privilege, the Court held that a judge could employ an *in camera* review of the allegedly privileged information in reaching a decision about whether the information truly was privileged. *Zolin* rejected the argument that the communication could not be considered because Fed. R. Evid. 104(a) prohibits reference to privileged information in making preliminary fact determinations. The Court found no reason to treat

the communication as presumptively privileged in deciding its admissibility. In contrast, some states restrict a judge's ability to see the allegedly privileged material. *See, e.g.*, Cal. Evid. Code § 915.

In discussing the threshold showing that must be demonstrated before permitting *in camera* review of an allegedly privileged communication, *Zolin* noted that:

> A blanket rule allowing *in camera* review as a tool for determining the applicability of the crime-fraud exception would place the policy of protecting open and legitimate disclosure between attorneys and clients at undue risk . . . . In fashioning a standard for determining when *in camera* review is appropriate, we begin with the observation that *in camera* inspection . . . is a smaller intrusion upon the confidentiality of the attorney-client relationship than is public disclosure . . . .We therefore conclude that a lesser evidentiary showing is needed to trigger *in camera* review than is required ultimately to overcome the privilege. Before engaging in *in camera* review to determine the applicability of the crime-fraud exception, the judge should require a showing of a factual basis adequate to support a good faith belief by a reasonable person, that *in camera* review of the materials may reveal evidence to establish the claim that the crime-fraud exception applies. Once that showing is made, the decision whether to engage in *in camera* review rests in the sound discretion of the district court. The court should make that decision in light of the facts and circumstances of the particular case, including, among other things, the volume of materials the district court has been asked to review, the relative importance to the case of the alleged privileged information, and the likelihood that the evidence produced through *in camera* review, together with other available evidence then before the court, will establish that the crime-fraud exception does apply. The district court is also free to defer its *in camera* review if it concludes that additional evidence in support of the crime-fraud exception may be available that is not allegedly privileged, and that production of the additional evidence will not unduly disrupt or delay the proceedings.

In camera review is not limited to questions of the crime-fraud exception to attorney-client privilege, but can arise when evaluating the applicability of any questions concerning any privilege.

Some states presume the confidentiality of a communication, placing the burden of establishing its nonconfidentiality on the opponent of the claim of privilege. *See, e.g.*, Cal. Evid. Code § 917.

(2) *Can an Observation be a Communication?* Are observations of an attorney privileged as communications? The answer depends on whether these observations are confidential. In other words, dress or other attributes that can be seen by the world at large are not privileged, but observations that are confidential, such as an attorney going to a location specified by the client and seeing physical evidence, are privileged. However, the privilege is lost to the extent that an attorney interferes with potential physical evidence. *See People v. Meredith*, 631 P.2d 46 (Cal. 1981) (although observation of wallet was protected, removing or altering it was not).

(3) *Can Accountant-Client Documents Fall within the Attorney-Client Privilege?* There is no general accountant-client privilege (and no accountant work-product privilege) in federal privilege law, unlike the law of many states, which contains an accountant privilege of some sort. See *United States v. Arthur Young & Co.*, 465 U.S. 805 (1984), holding there is no accountant communications or work-product privilege covering "tax accrual work papers" of an accountant. However, communications between an accountant and client sometimes can be brought within the attorney-client or attorney work-product privilege. *See Eglin Federal Credit Union v. Cantor, Fitzgerald Sec. Corp.*, 91 F.R.D. 414 (N.D. Ga. 1981):

The defendants also contend that plaintiff waived its attorney-client privilege . . . by turning confidential documents over to his accountant. If the accountant is consulted in connection with the client's obtaining legal advice, the privilege extends to cover confidential documents in the accountant's possession. If the documents were turned over to the accountant for reasons totally unrelated to seeking legal advice, the accountant is viewed as an unrelated third party and the attorney-client privilege as to these formerly confidential documents is waived. As the court understands the facts in this case, the board minutes produced by plaintiff's former accountants had been turned over to them for the purpose of conducting plaintiff's annual audit and not for reasons relating to the obtaining of legal advice [so turning them over did not waive privilege as to related board minutes.] The board minutes which plaintiff has claimed are privileged are those at which a representative of plaintiff's current outside accountants was present to assist board and legal counsel in understanding transactions relevant to this lawsuit. The accountant was, therefore, present not as an unrelated third party but as an expert assisting client and attorney. Defendants have argued that these same documents were routinely made available to the accountants for audit purposes. Plaintiff has not presented any evidence that these minutes were edited or that some other precaution was taken to protect the confidential communications contained within these minutes before turning them over to the accountants for audit purposes. The burden of persuasion rests on the party opposing discovery. Plaintiff has in this instance failed to carry its burden. In this regard, the court specifically rejects plaintiff's contention that accountant-client privileges recognized under Georgia and Florida law are applicable in this federal question case. *Couch v. United States*, 409 U.S. 322, 335 (1973). The defendants' motion to compel production of documents on this ground is granted.

In 1998, Congress enacted 26 U.S.C. § 7525 to accord an accountant's privilege covering communications to federally authorized tax practitioners (who are often accountants) in any noncriminal tax proceedings in Federal court brought by or against the United States. The underlying premise was that clients should not be disadvantaged by obtaining advice from accountants, when a disclosure of the same information to a lawyer, performing the same service as the accountant, would be privileged. However, this does not act as a general accountant-client privilege. *See United States v. Frederick*, 182 F.3d 496 (7th Cir. 1999), *cert. denied*, 528 U.S. 1154 (2000).

(4) *Does the Privilege Survive the Client's Death?* On this question, the recent decisions seem to distinguish two situations: (1) where the question in the case

involves the meaning or interpretation of the dead client's will, it is held that the testator would have wanted what he told his lawyer (relating to the drafting of the will), to be disclosed after death (although not during his life), in order to best effectuate the testator's intent, at least where the case is a will-contest case; and (2) other cases.

In *Swidler & Berlin v. United States*, 524 U.S. 399 (1998), the Independent Counsel who was appointed to look into wrongdoing on the part of U.S. President Bill Clinton sought a grand-jury subpoena to obtain the notes of the private attorney of Presidential Advisor Vince Foster, relating to conversations the attorney and Vince Foster had before Foster committed suicide. The Independent Counsel asserted that the death of the client terminated any attorney-client privilege. The lower court held that, when the client dies, because of the reduced interest on the side of privilege, the privilege becomes "qualified," that is, it gives way where great need for disclosure is shown — as where attorney-client information will be the sole practicable source of evidence in an important criminal investigation, as alleged in this case. This is because a client in speaking to his lawyer has less concern about confidentiality after death than during life, and will be less inclined to hold back because of fear of disclosure after death, even though there may be *some* concern about after-death disclosures since reputation and family could still be harmed at that point. In fact, Foster's attorney has said that Foster specifically asked if his conversation with the attorney would be privileged if Foster later passed away. The Supreme Court in *Swidler & Berlin* held that the attorney-client privilege survives, in a non-qualified fashion, the death of the client:

> The great body of this caselaw supports, either by holding or considered dicta, the position that the privilege does survive in a case such as the present one. Given the language of Rule 501, at the very least the burden is on the Independent Counsel to show that "reason and experience" require a departure from this rule.
>
> The Independent Counsel contends that the testamentary exception supports the posthumous termination of the privilege because in practice most cases have refused to apply the privilege posthumously. He further argues that the exception reflects a policy judgment that the interest in settling estates outweighs any posthumous interest in confidentiality. He then reasons by analogy that in criminal proceedings, the interest in determining whether a crime has been committed should trump client confidentiality, particularly since the financial interests of the estate are not a stake.
>
> But the Independent Counsel's interpretation simply does not square with the caselaw's implicit acceptance of the privilege's survival and with the treatment of testamentary disclosure as an "exception" or implied "waiver." And the premise of his analogy is incorrect, since cases consistently recognize the rationale for the testamentary exception is that it furthers the client's intent.
>
> Commentators on the law also recognize that the general rule is that the attorney-client privilege continues after death. Undoubtedly, as the Independent Counsel emphasizes, various commentators have criticized this

rule, urging that the privilege should be abrogated after the client's death where extreme injustice would result, as long as disclosure would not seriously undermine the privilege by deterring client communication. But even these critics clearly recognize that established law supports the continuation of the privilege and that a contrary rule would be a modification of the common law.

Despite the scholarly criticism, we think there are weighty reasons that counsel in favor of posthumous application. Knowing that communications will remain confidential even after death encourages the client to communicate fully and frankly with counsel. While the fear of disclosure, and the consequent withholding of information from counsel, may be reduced if disclosure is limited to posthumous disclosure in a criminal context, it seems unreasonable to assume that it vanishes altogether. Clients may be concerned about reputation, civil liability, or possible harm to friends or family. Posthumous disclosure of such communications may be as feared as disclosure during the client's lifetime.

Finally, the Independent Counsel, relying on cases such as *United States v. Nixon*, 418 U.S. 683, 710 (1974), and *Branzburg v. Hayes*, 408 U.S. 665 (1972), urges that privileges be strictly construed because they are inconsistent with the paramount judicial goal of truth seeking. But both *Nixon* and *Branzburg* dealt with the creation of privileges not recognized by the common law, whereas here we deal with one of the oldest recognized privilege in the law. And we are asked, not simply to "construe" the privilege, but to narrow it, contrary to the weight of the existing body of caselaw.

It has been generally, if not universally, accepted, for well over a century, that the attorney-client privilege survives the death of the client in a case such as this. While the arguments against the survival of the privilege are by no means frivolous, they are based in large part on speculation — thoughtful speculation, but speculation nonetheless — as to whether posthumous termination of the privilege would diminish a client's willingness to confide in an attorney. In an area where empirical information would be useful, it is scant and inconclusive. Rule 501's direction to look to "the principles of the common law as they may be interpreted by the courts of the United States in light of reason and experience" does not mandate that a rule, once established, should endure for all time. But here the Independent Counsel has simply not made a sufficient showing to overturn the common law rule embodied in the prevailing caselaw. Interpreted in the light of reason and experience, that body of law requires that the attorney-client privilege prevent disclosure of the notes at issue in this case.

(5) *The Argument that the Client's Death Should Affect Privilege.* In *Swidler & Berlin*, one contention of Independent Counsel was that, because the privilege would have to give way if it covered material necessary to a *criminal defendant's defense* (a proposition, we might add, that is not clear in the law), the privilege is obviously a qualified privilege, and therefore should have to give way when, on the other side of the coin, a *prosecutor* needs the information in a criminal investigation.

At least, Independent Counsel argued, both these qualifications on the privilege should obtain when the client has died. This is because the client's interest in confidentiality after death is muted. Therefore the prosecutor's (or criminal defendant's) need is more persuasive. The Supreme Court did not accept this argument but did not indicate whether or not the privilege, either before or after death, would have to give way if the criminal defendant needed it to give way. That question was left open. The Court saw it as a fundamentally different problem. (Perhaps this was because privilege comes up against defendant's constitutional rights in that case.) The Court also suggested that a qualified communications privilege is little better than no privilege from the standpoint of promoting communications. To be encouraged to communicate, a person needs to know with certainty whether privilege will apply.

(6) *Would the Privilege have Given Way if a Criminal Defendant Needed the Privileged Information in Order to Defend?* The case of *State v. Macumber*, 544 P.2d 1084 (Ariz. 1976) came up in connection with the argument in *Swidler & Berlin* that the privilege gives way if a *criminal defendant* needs the information to defend himself, at least after the death of the client. In *Macumber* a third person who was deceased by the time of defendant's trial apparently confessed to his lawyers that he (not defendant) committed the murders defendant was on trial for. The family of the confessor, as heirs of the privilege, asserted the privilege on behalf of the confessor. The *Macumber* court held that the privilege does not give way even in this situation. The conviction was reversed on other grounds (improper exclusion of expert evidence offered by the defense) and a new trial ordered. A concurring opinion took issue with the ruling that attorney-client privilege prevails, setting forth some of the facts:

> The nature of the defense evidence was contained in an offer of proof. Essentially, the evidence was expected to show that a third person, now deceased, had admitted in 1968 to two attorneys that he had committed the dual murders with which the defendant was charged. At the time of the admission the third person was being tried in federal court for an unrelated murder which occurred in the same general vicinity as the murders in this case. The two lawyers were involved in the defense of the third party for the unrelated murder. Subsequently the third party died.
>
> When the attorneys learned that the defendant was being charged with the murders which their former client claimed to have committed, they sought and received an informal opinion from the Committee on Ethics of the State Bar which advised the attorneys that the privilege of attorney-client did not apply to prevent them from disclosing the information to the defense, prosecution, and court. The attorneys, upon receiving the advice of the Ethics Committee, disclosed their information to the defense and prosecution, but the trial judge ruled the information privileged and not admissible.
>
> The information which the attorneys possess is material and relevant to the defense, and while it was excluded solely on the basis of the attorney-client privilege, it is necessary to examine whether the evidence would have been inadmissible on other grounds. Historically, out-of-court confessions

of third persons of crimes tending to exonerate the accused have been excluded from the declaration-against-interest hearsay exception. *See, e.g., Donnelly v. United States*, 228 U.S. 243 (1913). However, relying on the dissent in *Donnelly* (Holmes, J.) a substantial number of states have abandoned this rule in criminal cases. Our Court of Appeals, in [1966] recognized that a declaration against penal interest does fall within the declaration-against-interest hearsay exception, although in that case it was only called upon to rule upon it in a civil action. In [1970] our Court of Appeals recognized the applicability of the declaration-against-penal-interest exception to the hearsay rule in a criminal case but noted that the facts in that case did not show sufficient circumstantial probability of trustworthiness surrounding the declaration to justify its admission into evidence.

Although this Court has not specifically ruled on the extent of the hearsay exception, it must be acknowledged that the decisions of our Court of Appeals have declared the rule in Arizona to be that the declaration-against-interest exception includes declarations against penal interest. In addition, and more fundamentally, the United States Supreme Court in *Chambers v. Mississippi* (1973) has ruled that it is a violation of due process for a state rule of evidence to preclude the admission of reliable hearsay declarations against penal interest when such evidence is offered to show the innocence of an accused.

Although the offered testimony should have been admissible under the hearsay exception, the trial court refused to admit it on the grounds that the subject matter was privileged. As the majority point out, the attorney-client privilege has been held to survive the death of the client. Whether the rule should be followed in a case such as this or an exception created would require an extended discussion not called for in a specially concurring opinion. The real problem is whether the privilege can survive the constitutional test of due process.

It is basic that an accused has the right to present a defense to a criminal charge, and, to accomplish this right, accused has the right to compel the attendance of witnesses and the right to present their testimony. *Washington v. Texas*, 388 U.S. 14 (1967). Even a claim of privilege may have to give way when faced with the necessity by the accused to present a defense. *Roviaro v. United States*, 353 U.S. 53 (1957) (informer's privilege). The problem of balancing competing interests, privilege versus a proper defense, is a difficult one, but the balance always weighs in favor of achieving a fair determination of the cause.

A state's rules of evidence cannot deny an accused's right to present a proper defense. *Chambers v. Mississippi, supra.* In the case at issue the interest to be protected by the privilege would seem to be at an end because of the client's death.

When the client died there was no chance of prosecution for other crimes, and any privilege is merely a matter of property interest. Opposed to the property interest of the deceased client is the vital interest of the

> accused in this case in defending himself against the charge of first degree murder. When the interests are weighed, I believe that the constitutional right of the accused to present a defense should prevail over the property interest of a deceased client in keeping his disclosures private. I would allow the defendant to offer the testimony of the attorneys concerning the confession of their deceased client.

You have in this book both *Chambers* (*supra* § 11.06) and a subsequent U.S. Supreme Court decision, *Egelhoff* (*supra* § 2.04[B]) bearing on the due process question. Does *Egelhoff* shed any light on the constitutional problem raised by the *Macumber* concurrence? In *Macumber* itself, however, the question was subsequently rendered moot because the family, by the time of the retrial, had waived the privilege; but the judge then held that the confession (also repeated, it turned out, by the confessor to his psychiatrist) was inadmissible hearsay because of insufficient surrounding guarantees of trustworthiness to bring it within the state's declarations-against-penal-interest hearsay exception. The defendant was again convicted, and this time the conviction was affirmed. 582 P.2d 162 (Ariz. 1978). The U.S. Supreme Court refused to review the case.

Subsequently, a remarkably similar case arose, again involving a deceased third party's privileged confession (including an express exoneration of defendant) to the third party's attorney, of the very murder that defendant was being tried for. But this court decided that the privilege falls. Allowing privilege to prevail, as the lower court had done, was held to have violated defendant's right to defend himself under the due process clause. It rendered his trial "fundamentally unfair," and therefore unconstitutional, under *Chambers*. *Morales v. Portuondo*, 154 F. Supp. 2d 706 (S.D.N.Y. 2001) (also holding that the state's hearsay rule had an exception that embraced the confessor's statements). Do you think this case would have come out differently if the client had not died?

Surprisingly, cases involving this issue, either before or after the death of the client, are quite rare and the law is in conflict. The same is true with respect to most other privately held privileges, too. Would a "dangerous client" exception to the privilege make the problem easier? *See infra*, § 13.02[E], note (4).

See generally Ciepluch, *Overriding the Posthumous Application of the Attorney-Client Privilege: Due Process for a Criminal Defendant*, 83 Marq. L. Rev. 785 (2000).

(7) *No Law Student Privilege.* In *Dabney v. Investment Corp. of America*, 82 F.R.D. 464 (E.D. Pa. 1979), the issue was whether the attorney-client privilege extended to confidential communications made by defendant company to a third-year law student (and other such communications made to him later when he became a law school graduate not yet admitted to the bar) who was in defendant company's employ and was subsequently admitted to the bar and employed by defendant as an in-house attorney. The court held that, notwithstanding the belief of the client company (defendant) that he was a qualified though as yet unlicensed professional legal advisor, the privilege was inapplicable (at least unless he was working under the supervision of a licensed attorney, as would be a not-yet-licensed associate of a law firm). The court stated that to find otherwise "would permit the claiming of the privilege not simply where one party to a conversation is an attorney

whose professional advice is sought, but in virtually any situation where legal confidences are exchanged, [and] would poorly serve the purpose of the privilege which is to provide the freedom of consultation that is essential to full and effective legal representation." It made no difference that the company had a regular house counsel during part of the period, because he did not directly supervise the student (or, later, the graduate).

[B] Corporate Setting

UPJOHN CO. v. UNITED STATES

United States Supreme Court
449 U.S. 383 (1981)

JUSTICE REHNQUIST delivered the opinion of the Court.

[Petitioner pharmaceutical company's (Upjohn's) general counsel, Thomas (who also was Vice President and Secretary) was told by its independent accountants that subsidiaries apparently were making payments to foreign governments to secure their business. Thomas, together with outside counsel and the Chairman of the Board, decided to conduct an internal investigation. The attorneys prepared a questionnaire over the Chairman's signature and sent it to all foreign area and general managers, stating that management had asked General Counsel to conduct such investigation into the amount and nature of any such payments. It said the investigation was to be kept highly confidential from anyone other than employees who might have useful information. Responses were to be sent to Thomas. Thomas and outside counsel also interviewed many Upjohn officers and employees. Thereafter Upjohn voluntarily submitted its preliminary findings to the SEC, disclosing certain questionable payments, with a copy to the IRS, which then began an investigation to determine the tax consequences. The IRS issued a summons demanding all responses to the questionnaires and all notes of the interviews. The company refused disclosure on grounds of attorney-client and work-product privilege. The lower court denied protection.]

Federal Rule of Evidence 501 provides that "the privilege of a witness shall be governed by the principles of the common law as they may be interpreted by the courts of the United States in light of reason and experience." The attorney-client privilege is the oldest of the privileges for confidential communications known to the common law. Its purpose is to encourage full and frank communication between attorneys and their clients and thereby promote broader public interests in the observance of law and administration of justice. The privilege recognizes that sound legal advice or advocacy serves public ends and that such advice or advocacy depends upon the lawyer being fully informed by the client. "The lawyer-client privilege rests on the need for the advocate and counselor to know all that relates to the client's reasons for seeking representation if the professional mission is to be carried out." *Fisher v. United States*, 425 U.S. 391, 403.

[W]e recognize the purpose of the privilege to be "to encourage clients to make full disclosure to their attorneys." Admittedly complications in the application of the privilege arise when the client is a corporation, but this Court has assumed that the privilege applies when the client is a corporation.

The court of appeals, however, considered the application of the privilege in the corporate context to present a "different problem," since the client was an inanimate entity and "only the senior management, guiding and integrating the several operations can be said to possess an identity analogous to the corporation as a whole." 600 F.2d, at 1226. The first case to articulate the so-called "control group test" adopted by the court below reflected a similar conceptual approach:

> [I]f the employee making the communication, of whatever rank he may be, is in a position to control or even to take a substantial part in a decision about any action which the corporation may take upon the advice of the attorney, then, in effect, *he is (or personifies) the corporation*. [Citation.]

Such a view, we think, overlooks the fact that the privilege exists to protect not only the giving of professional advice to those who can act on it but also the giving of information to the lawyer to enable him to give sound and informed advice. The first step in the resolution of any legal problem is ascertaining the factual background and sifting through the facts with an eye to the legally relevant.

In the case of the individual client the provider of information and the person who acts on the lawyer's advice are one and the same. In the corporate context, however, it will frequently be employees beyond the control group as defined by the court below — "officers and agents responsible for directing [the company's] actions in response to legal advice" — who will possess the information needed by the corporation's lawyers. Middle-level — and indeed lower-level — employees can, by actions within the scope of their employment, embroil the corporation in serious legal difficulties, and it is only natural that these employees would have the relevant information needed by corporate counsel if he is adequately to advise the client with respect to such actual or potential difficulties.

The control group test adopted by the court below thus frustrates the very purpose of the privilege by discouraging the communication of relevant information by employees of the client to attorneys seeking to render legal advice to the client corporation. The attorney's advice will also frequently be more significant to noncontrol group members than to those who officially sanction the advice, and the control group test makes it more difficult to convey full and frank legal advice to the employees who will put into effect the client corporation's policy.

The narrow scope given the attorney-client privilege by the court below not only makes it difficult for corporate attorneys to formulate sound advice when their client is faced with a specific legal problem but also threatens to limit the valuable efforts of corporate counsel to ensure their client's compliance with the law. In light of the vast and complicated array of regulatory legislation confronting the modern corporation, corporations, unlike most individuals, "constantly go to lawyers to find out how to obey the law," particularly since compliance with the law in this area is hardly an instinctive matter, *see, e.g., United States v. United States Gypsum Co.*, 438 U.S. 422, 440, 441 (1978) ("the behavior proscribed by the [Sherman] Act is often difficult to distinguish from the gray zone of socially acceptable and economically justifiable business conduct").

The test adopted by the court below is difficult to apply in practice, though no

increased certainty

abstractly formulated unvarying "test" will necessarily enable courts to decide questions such as this with mathematical precision. But if the purpose of the attorney-client privilege is to be served, the attorney and client must be able to predict with some degree of certainty whether particular discussions will be protected. An uncertain privilege, or one which purports to be certain but results in widely varying applications by the courts, is little better than no privilege at all. The very terms of the test adopted by the court below suggest the unpredictability of its application. The test restricts the availability of the privilege to those officers who play a "substantial role" in deciding and directing a corporation's legal response. Disparate decisions in cases applying this test illustrate its unpredictibility. *Compare, e.g., Hogan v. Zletz* (control group includes managers and assistant managers of patent division and research and development department) with *Congoleum Industries, Inc. v. GAF Corp.* (control group includes only division and corporate vice-presidents, and not two directors of research and vice- president for production and research).

The communications at issue were made by Upjohn employees to counsel for Upjohn acting as such, at the direction of corporate superiors in order to secure legal advice from counsel. As the magistrate found, "Mr. Thomas consulted with the Chairman of the Board and outside counsel and thereafter conducted a factual investigation to determine the nature and extent of the questionable payments *and to be in a position to give legal advice to the company with respect to the payments.*" Information, not available from upper-echelon management, was needed to supply a basis for legal advice concerning compliance with securities and tax laws, foreign laws, currency regulations, duties to shareholders, and potential litigation in each of these areas. The communications concerned matters within the scope of the employees' corporate duties, and the employees themselves were sufficiently aware that they were being questioned in order that the corporation could obtain legal advice. The questionnaire identified Thomas as "the company's General Counsel" and referred in its opening sentence to the possible illegality of payments such as the ones on which information was sought. A statement of policy accompanying the questionnaire clearly indicated the legal implications of the investigation. The policy statement was issued "in order that there be no uncertainty in the future as to the policy with respect to the practices which are the subject of this investigation." It began "Upjohn will comply with all laws and regulations," and stated that commissions or payments "will not be used as a subterfuge for bribes or illegal payments" and that all payments must be "proper and legal." Any future agreements with foreign distributors or agents were to be approved "by a company attorney" and any questions concerning the policy were to be referred "to the company's General Counsel." This statement was issued to Upjohn employees worldwide, so that even those interviewees not receiving a questionnaire were aware of the legal implications of the interviews. Pursuant to explicit instructions from the Chairman of the Board, the communications were considered "highly confidential" when made, and have been kept confidential by the company.

The court of appeals declined to extend the attorney-client privilege beyond the limits of the control group test for fear that doing so would entail severe burdens on discovery and create a broad "zone of silence" over corporate affairs. Application of the attorney-client privilege to communications such as those involved here, however, puts the adversary in no worse position than if the communications had never taken place. The privilege only protects disclosure of communications; it does not protect disclosure of the underlying facts by those who communicated with the attorney:

> The protection of the privilege extends only to *communications* and not to facts. A fact is one thing and a communication concerning that fact is an entirely different thing. The client cannot be compelled to answer the question, "What did you say or write to the attorney?" but may not refuse to disclose any relevant fact within his knowledge merely because he incorporated a statement of such fact into his communication to his attorney. *City of Philadelphia v. Westinghouse Electric Corp.*, 285 F. Supp. 830, 831 (ED Pa. 1962).

Here the government was free to question the employees who communicated with Thomas and outside counsel. Upjohn has provided the IRS with a list of such employees, and the IRS has already interviewed some 25 of them. "Discovery was hardly intended to enable a learned profession to perform its functions . . . on wits borrowed from the adversary."

Needless to say, we decide only the case before us, and do not undertake to draft a set of rules which should govern challenges to investigatory subpoenas. Any such approach would violate the spirit of FRE 501. *See* S. Rep. No. 93-1277, 93d Cong., 2d Sess, 13 ("the recognition of a privilege based on a confidential relationship . . . should be determined on a case- by-case basis"). While such a "case-by-case" basis may to some slight extent undermine desirable certainty in the boundaries of the attorney-client privilege, it obeys the spirit of the Rules. At the same time we conclude that the narrow "control group test" sanctioned by the court of appeals in this case cannot, consistent with "the principles of the common law as . . . interpreted . . . in light of reason and experience," FRE 501, govern the development of the law in this area.

Our decision that the communications by Upjohn employees to counsel are covered by the attorney-client privilege disposes of the case so far as the responses to the questionnaires and any notes reflecting responses to interview questions are concerned. The summons reaches further, however, and Thomas has testified that his notes and memoranda of interviews go beyond recording responses to his questions. To the extent that the material subject to the summons is not protected by the attorney-client privilege as disclosing communications between an employee and counsel, we must reach the ruling by the court of appeals that the work-product doctrine does not apply to [tax investigative] summonses. (The following discussion will also be relevant to counsel notes and memoranda of interviews with the seven former employees [who were also interviewed as part of the same investigation] should it be determined that the attorney-client privilege does not apply to them.)

The government concedes, wisely, that the court of appeals erred and that the work-product doctrine does apply to IRS summonses. This doctrine was announced by the Court over 30 years ago in *Hickman v. Taylor*, 329 U.S. 495 (1947). In that case the Court rejected "an attempt, without purported necessity or justification, to secure written statements, private memoranda, and personal recollections prepared or formed by an adverse party's counsel in the course of his legal duties." The Court noted that "it is essential that a lawyer work with a certain degree of privacy" and reasoned that if discovery of the material sought were permitted much of what is now put down in writing would remain unwritten. An attorney's thoughts, heretofore inviolate, would not be this own. Inefficiency, unfairness and sharp practices would inevitably develop in the giving of legal advice and in the preparation of cases for trial. The effect on the legal profession would be demoralizing. And the interests of the clients and the cause of justice would be poorly served.

The "strong public policy" underlying the work-product doctrine has been substantially incorporated in Federal Rule of Civil Procedure 26(b)(3).[7]

As we stated last Term, the obligation imposed by a tax summons remains "subject to the traditional privileges and limitations." Nothing in the language of the IRS summons provisions or their legislative history suggests an intent on the part of Congress to preclude application of the work-product doctrine. [T]he Federal Rules of Civil Procedure are applicable to summons enforcement proceedings. While conceding the applicability of the work-product doctrine, the government asserts that it has made a sufficient showing of necessity to overcome its protections. The magistrate apparently so found. The government relies on the following language in *Hickman:*

> We do not mean to say that all written materials obtained or prepared by an adversary's counsel with an eye toward litigation are necessarily free from discovery in all cases. Where relevant and nonprivileged facts remain hidden in an attorney's file and where production of those facts is essential to the preparation of one's case, discovery may properly be had . . . . And production might be justified where the witnesses are no longer available or may be reached only with difficulty.

The government stresses that interviewees are scattered across the globe and that Upjohn has forbidden its employees to answer questions it considers irrelevant. The above-quoted language from *Hickman*, however, did not apply to "oral statements made by witnesses presently in the form of [the attorney's] mental impressions or memoranda." As to such material the Court did "not believe that any showing of necessity can be made under the circumstances of this case so as to justify production. If there should be a rare situation justifying production of these matters, petitioner's case is not of that type." Forcing an attorney to disclose notes and memoranda of witnesses' oral statements is particularly disfavored [by *Hickman*] because it tends to reveal the attorney's mental processes, 329 U.S. at

---

[7] This provides, in pertinent part:

> A party may obtain discovery of documents and tangible things otherwise discoverable under subdivision (b)(1) of this rule and prepared in anticipation of litigation or for trial by or for another party or by or for that other party's representative (including his attorney, consultant, surety, indemnitor, insurer, or agent) only upon a showing that the party seeking discovery has substantial need of the materials in the preparation of his case and that he is unable without undue hardship to obtain the substantial equivalent of the materials by other means. In ordering discovery of such materials when the required showing has been made, the court shall protect against disclosure of the mental impressions, conclusions, opinions, or legal theories of an attorney or other representative of a party concerning the litigation.

513 ("what he saw fit to write down regarding witnesses' remarks"); *id.*, at 516-517 ("the statement would be his [the attorney's] language, permeated with his inferences") (Jackson, J., concurring).

Rule 26 accords special protection to work product revealing the attorney's mental processes. The Rule permits disclosure of documents and tangible things constituting attorney work product upon a showing of substantial need and inability to obtain the equivalent without undue hardship. This was the standard applied by the magistrate. Rule 26 goes on, however, to state that "[i]n ordering discovery of such materials when the required showing has been made, the court shall protect against disclosure of the mental impressions, conclusions, opinions or legal theories of an attorney or other representative of a party concerning the litigation." Although this language does not specifically refer to memoranda based on oral statements of witnesses, the *Hickman* court stressed the danger that compelled disclosure of such memoranda would reveal the attorney's mental processes. It is clear that this is the sort of material the draftsmen of the Rule had in mind as deserving special protection. *See* Notes of Advisory Committee ("The subdivision . . . goes on to protect against disclosure the mental impressions, conclusions, opinions, or legal theories . . . of an attorney or other representative of a party. The *Hickman* opinion drew special attention to the need for protecting an attorney against discovery of memoranda prepared from recollection of oral interviews. The courts have steadfastly safeguarded against disclosure of lawyers' mental impressions and legal theories . . .").

Based on the foregoing, some courts have concluded that *no* showing of necessity can overcome protection of work product which is based on oral statements from witnesses. Those courts declining to adopt an absolute rule have nonetheless recognized that such material is entitled to special protection.

We do not decide the issue at this time. It is clear that the magistrate applied the wrong standard when he concluded that the government had made a sufficient showing of necessity to overcome the protections of the work-product doctrine. The magistrate applied the "substantial need" and "without undue hardship" standard articulated in the first part of Rule 26(b)(3). The notes and memoranda sought by the government here, however, are work product based on oral statements. If they reveal communications, they are, in this case, protected by the attorney-client privilege. To the extent they do not reveal communications, they reveal the attorneys' mental processes in evaluating the communications. As Rule 26 and *Hickman* make clear, such work product cannot be disclosed simply on a showing of substantial need and inability to obtain the equivalent without undue hardship.

While we are not prepared at this juncture to say that such material is always protected by the work-product rule, we think a far stronger showing of necessity and unavailability by other means than was made by the government or applied by the magistrate in this case would be necessary to compel disclosure. [W]e think the best procedure with respect to this aspect of the case would be to remand the case for such further proceedings in connection with the work-product claim as are consistent with this opinion.

[Reversed and remanded for further proceedings.]

NOTES AND QUESTIONS

(1) *Determining Who the Client is for Purposes of the Privilege. Upjohn* is a case where the identity of who may speak for (make communications for) the client must be determined to see if the information is privileged at all. For the colorful facts behind the communications at issue in *Upjohn*, see Rothstein, *Upjohn v. United States: The Story of One Man's Journey to Extend Lawyer-Client Confidentiality and the Social Forces that Affected It*, in EVIDENCE STORIES (2006).

In *Schwartz v. Broadcast Music, Inc.*, 16 F.R.D. 31 (S.D.N.Y. 1954), plaintiff, an individual songwriter, had confidential communications with the attorney for the American Society of Composers, Authors, and Publishers (ASCAP), seeking legal advice. The court, stating that "each individual member of the association is a client of the association's lawyer," held that plaintiff, a member of the association, could invoke the attorney-client privilege to resist disclosure of the conversations.

In some cases, the information is privileged, but the question is who has the ability to raise or waive the privilege. For example, the United States Supreme Court has held that the trustee of a corporation in bankruptcy has the power to waive the corporation's attorney-client privilege with respect to prebankruptcy communications. *Commodity Futures Trading Comm'n v. Weintraub*, 471 U.S. 343 (1985). The Court emphasized that the trustee after bankruptcy exercises most of the powers formerly exercised by management and has a duty to ferret out possible mismanagement and fraud by the former management that may have led to the bankruptcy. Thus, the power to raise or waive privilege has passed from management, where it formerly resided, to the trustee.

Garner v. Wolfinbarger, 430 F.2d 1093 (5th Cir. 1970), *cert. denied*, 401 U.S. 974 (1971), held that shareholders may penetrate the corporation's privilege in certain circumstances when good cause is shown.

In *Upjohn*, could the employee raise the privilege if the corporation wished to cooperate with the government and waive the privilege? Does this cast doubt on the whole rationale of *Upjohn*?

As to former employees, see Becker, *Discovery of Information and Documents from a Litigant's Former Employees: Synergy and Synthesis of Civil Rules, Ethical Standards, Privilege Doctrines, and Common Law Principles*, 81 NEB. L. REV. 868 (2003).

(2) *Futher Issues Arising in a Corporate Setting: The Lawyer Who Wears Many Hats; Public Filings.* In *S.E.C. v. Gulf & Western Indus., Inc.*, 518 F. Supp. 675 (D.D.C. 1981), Joel Dolkart served as outside general counsel to Gulf & Western for sixteen years. During the relevant time he also wore several other hats, serving as a Gulf & Western corporate director and secretary and as a member of its pension advisory committee. As a partner in the New York-based law firm of Simpson Thacher & Bartlett, he primarily devoted his attention and time to Gulf & Western affairs. Simpson Thacher commenced an investigation of suspicious and questionable withdrawals by Dolkart from the law firm's (and Gulf & Western's)

financial account. The embezzlements were immediately reported to the authorities and a New York County grand jury charged Dolkart. Dolkart agreed to cooperate with the county prosecutors and the Securities & Exchange Commission concerning information he alleged he had concerning misconduct by officers in various prominent corporations in exchange for the prosecutor recommending that his sentence be reduced to a term of probation.

The defendants claimed that the Commission "pursued Dolkart and affirmatively induced him to breach the attorney-client privilege, thus obtaining an insider's view of Gulf & Western that only its principal lawyer could provide." In discussing the privilege, the Court said that:

> The privilege applies only if (1) the asserted holder of the privilege is or sought to become a client; (2) the person to whom the communication was made (a) is a member of the bar of a court, or his subordinate and (b) in connection with this communication is acting as a lawyer; (3) the communication relates to a fact of which the attorney was informed (a) by his client (b) without the presence of strangers (c) for the purpose of securing primarily either (i) an opinion on law or (ii) legal services or (iii) assistance in some legal proceeding, and not (d) for the purpose of committing a crime or tort, and (4) the privilege has been (a) claimed and (b) not waived by the client.

In denying the claim of privilege, the Court noted that the burden is on the party claiming the privilege to show that the consultation was professional and confidential and that a blanket assertion of privilege is unacceptable. Thus, because of Dolkart's many roles and the large amount of time he spent at Gulf & Western's offices, it could not be assumed that all of his discussions with corporate officials involved legal advice. Similarly, evidence was not presented that the advice in question was confidential at the time it was given or that confidentiality had since been maintained. The Commission contended that the advice about the purchase of Bangor Punta securities was given by a number of people and widely disseminated. Also, the discussions regarding the litigation terms in the tender offer documents, the fraudulent schedule 13D, and the antitrust considerations on the proposed A&P tender offer allegedly took place in the presence of a third party. Moreover, some of the challenged information was revealed in publicly filed documents. "Communications revealed to unessential third parties or contained in public documents are not even colorably privileged."

Compare In re Ford Motor Co., 110 F.3d 954 (3d Cir. 1997), holding minutes of a "Policy and Strategy Committee" privileged and noting:

> Certainly, the ultimate decision reached could be characterized as a business decision, but the Committee reached that decision only after examining the legal implications of doing so. Even if the decision was driven principally by profit and loss, economics, marketing, public relations, or the like, it was also infused with legal concerns, and was reached only after securing legal advice. At all events, disclosure of the documents would reveal that legal advice.

(3) *Are Governmental Lawyers Protected by Attorney-Client Privilege?* On the general subject of the attorney-client privilege as it applies to government lawyers, see Lawry, *Who Is the Client of the Federal Government Lawyer?*, 37 FED. B.J. 61 (1978). The Supreme Court Draft (unenacted but influential, at least on uncontroversial points) of the Federal Rules of Evidence (Rule 503: Attorney-Client Privilege) handled the matter simply by including "public officers" and "public organizations"in the list of persons and organizations who could be "clients" (i.e., in the definition of "client"). The 1974 Uniform Rules of Evidence (adopted by a number of states), which in most respects conformed to the Federal Rules of Evidence or the Supreme Court Draft thereof, have an additional provision (substantially continued in the current Uniform Rule) as well:

> There is no lawyer-client privilege as to a communication between a public officer or agency and its lawyers unless the communication concerns a pending investigation, claim, or action and the court determines the disclosure will seriously impair the ability of the public officer or agency to process the claim or conduct a pending investigation, litigation, or proceeding in the public interest.

The matter of attorney-client privilege for government bodies was obscure at common law. Authority was scarce. What little federal authority there was seemed to deny privilege to public officers and agencies, although not uniformly. The scarce state authority was conflicting but seemed more favorable to privilege. However, *In re Grand Jury Subpoena Duces Tecum*, 112 F.3d 910 (8th Cir.), *cert. denied*, 521 U.S. 1105 (1997), narrowly interpreted the existence and scope of this privilege by holding that the Bill Clinton White House could not invoke any form of governmental attorney-client privilege to withhold potentially relevant information from a grand jury. The case arose after the death of White House Deputy Counsel Vincent Foster and the discovery of records from the First Lady's former law firm in the White House residence area. Lawyers representing the Office of the President held a series of meetings with Hillary Rodham Clinton and her personal counsel concerning her activities in connection with these matters. A federal grand jury investigating potential crimes related to the Whitewater Development subpoenaed the notes of the lawyers for the Office of the President. The Office of the President resisted by relying on attorney-client privilege and the work product doctrine.

The Court of Appeals held that neither the privilege nor the work product doctrine applied. The court reasoned that lawyers for a governmental entity do not have the same kind of interest as private corporate lawyers would in detecting and preventing misconduct by agents or employees, since a governmental entity like the Office of the President cannot itself be held criminally liable. This conclusion, coupled with the concern that a privilege for communications between government attorneys and government employees suppressing information about crimes would disserve the public interest in exposing governmental wrongdoing, tipped the balance against the privilege. The court also held that, even if the privilege existed for the Office of the President, the Office of the President did not have a sufficient "common interest" with Mrs. Clinton in her private capacity to extend a joint-consultation privilege to cover communications with her. Finally, said the court, the work product doctrine was inapplicable because the notes were not prepared in anticipation of litigation. The Office of the President petitioned the Supreme Court for a writ of *certiorari*, and Professor Rothstein wrote an *amicus curiae* brief on behalf of a number of law professors. *Certiorari* was denied at 521 U.S. 1105 (1997).

In *In re Bruce R. Lindsey*, 158 F.3d 1263 (D.C. Cir. 1998), the court, mirroring the reasoning of much of the Eighth Circuit decision above in this note, held that the White House Counsel may not invoke government attorney-client privilege to protect communications made to him by President Bill Clinton when disclosure is sought by a federal grand jury, apparently regardless of whether the communications involved the giving of legal advice, since the discovery of wrongdoing in government is paramount. The court also held that it follows that there can be no "common interest" attorney-client privilege either, covering matters shared between White House Counsel and the President's private attorney, and thus the President's privilege with his private attorneys might be abrogated to that extent by lack of confidentiality, except insofar as White House Counsel was acting as an intermediary between the President and the President's private attorney (although litigation strategy and certain other matters do not qualify for this intermediary principle). It is not clear what role is played by the fact that the particular communications might be regarded as being on a "personal" legal matter. *See also In re Witness Before Special Grand Jury 2000-2*, 288 F.3d 289, 293–94 (7th Cir. 2002) (no privilege between state officeholder and state government lawyer in federal criminal investigation). For a different view upholding such a privilege in a grand jury context, see *In re Grand Jury Investigation*, 399 F.3d 527 (2d Cir. 2005). *See generally* Radson & Waratuke, *The Attorney-Client and Work Product Privileges of Government Entities*, 30 Stetson L. Rev. 799 (2001).

(4) *Federal Work-Product Immunity.* On the work-product doctrine in federal court mentioned in *Upjohn*, even in civil cases where state privilege law is employed, work product still is usually governed by federal law because it is an immunity from discovery found in Fed. R. Civ. Proc. 26(b)(3). *See, e.g., Dunn v. State Farm Fire & Cas. Ins. Co.*, 927 F.2d 869 (5th Cir. 1991). In federal court, work product does not terminate at the end of the litigation in which it is created. *See F.T.C. v. Grolier*, 462 U.S. 19 (1983) (decided in context of Freedom of Information Act).

[C] Effect of Intentional or Unintentional Disclosure (or the Like)

NOTES AND QUESTIONS

(1) *Voluntary Disclosure to Governmental Agencies.* In *Permian Corp. v. United States*, 665 F.2d 1214 (D.C. Cir. 1981), the client had previously disclosed certain communications to the SEC to expedite the issuance of a registration statement, expressly reserving the right to assert confidentiality for other purposes (although this reservation was ambiguous as to whether it meant to preserve confidentiality from other government agencies or merely private parties). In this litigation, the Department of Energy sought those communications. The court held there was a waiver of the attorney-client privilege but not of the work-product privilege. In contrast, a number of courts also have held that work product is waived by such voluntary disclosures. *See Westinghouse Elec. Corp. v. Republic of the*

Philippines, 951 F.2d 1414 (3d Cir. 1991) (surveying case law). Other positions also are found. *See In re Columbia/HCA Healthcare*, 293 F.3d 289, 293–14 (6th Cir. 2002) (exhaustive review of case-law; holding release waived both attorney-client privilege and work product). One oft-cited case for limiting the waiver to the particular agency, in order to promote co-operation with the agency, is *Diversified Indus. Inc. v. Meredith*, 572 F.2d 596 (8th Cir. 1977). *Diversified* is the minority view. Most courts deem disclosure to a particular entity to be a breaking of the confidentiality and therefore a waiver as to all comers.

Which position fosters law enforcement more?

Should the presence of a written statement by or agreement between attorneys before disclosure is made, or a provision in a judicial disposition, that attorney-client privilege is preserved as against third parties, make a difference?

If a court holds that waiver as to a government agency does not waive as to third parties, would it have to hold the same if the initial waiver was not to a government agency, but rather to a private party? If a court holds there is no general waiver in this last situation, could it decline to hold the same where the initial waiver was to a government agency? In which situation is the policy stronger for limiting the waiver? How much of an aid is it to enforcement of the law, to have these initial waivers? What would encourage them?

Government agencies, prosecutors, and other law enforcers often demand waiver of attorney-client privilege as the price of making a deal. If waiver means third parties can also get the information, is the utility of attorney-client privilege dead? *See generally* Buchanan, *Effective Co-operation by Business Organizations and the Impact of Privilege Waivers*, 39 WAKE FOREST L. REV. 587 (2004).

(2) *Waiver by Putting Claim or Defense "In Issue."* A number of cases suggest that if a party to a lawsuit raises a claim or defense that seems to directly put in issue a communication between her and her attorney, she may be taken to have waived the privilege *pro tanto*. This frequently is the case where the party alleges that she acted on advice of counsel. *See, e.g.*, *United States v. Miller*, 600 F.2d 498 (5th Cir.) (where defense is based on good faith reliance on counsel, cross-examiner cannot be prevented from "utilizing the communication itself to get at the truth"), *cert. denied*, 444 U.S. 955 (1979). It also would seem to be the case where the client alleges ineffective assistance of counsel (e.g., to overturn a criminal conviction), or alleges malpractice or ethical breach on the part of the attorney, although waiver in some of these cases also has been justified on the ground there is no confidentiality between the attorney and his or her client, or that it is unfair to allow an attack while allowing the attacker to deprive the attacked person of his or her defense and suppress part of the complete picture. To some extent these cases overlap the principle that forbids disclosure of part while suppressing the remainder that is necessary to put the part in context. (A number of cases also hold that in fee disputes between attorney and client, there is no privilege as to relevant communications that have passed between them. Such a situation involves at least some similar considerations.) *Cf. Shooker v. Superior Court*, 111 Cal. App. 4th 923 (Cal. Ct. App. 2003), holding that a party to the lawsuit's designation of himself as an expert witness on a business deal that is the subject of his lawsuit is not itself an implied waiver of the attorney-client privilege as to meetings he had with his lawyer

concerning the business deal, but waiver can occur when he testifies, depending on the testimony.

(3) *Selective Disclosures Leading to Broader Waiver.* In *Weil v. Investment/Indicators, Research & Management, Inc.*, 647 F.2d 18 (9th Cir. 1981), an investment fund was charged with malfeasance in not registering adequately with the appropriate governmental units. Scienter to defraud and deceive was alleged. During discovery, the Fund disclosed that its counsel had said something to it about the need to register with that governmental unit. The court held that this waived the privilege of the Fund as to all communications with the same counsel on the subject of such registration. The court states that as a general principle voluntary disclosure constitutes a waiver as to all communications on the same subject, regardless of whether such waiver was intended or not. Subjective intent to waive is only one factor; inadvertence of disclosure does not, as a matter of law, prevent waiver in the court's view. Other decisions require that the initial disclosure must be of a significant part. *See, e.g.*, *In re Von Bulow*, 828 F.2d 94 (2d Cir. 1987) (subject matter disclosure not warranted, only disclosure of particular communications in question). *See also In re Keeper of Records (XYZ Corp.)*, 348 F.3d 16 (1st Cir. 2003), holding that the extrajudicial disclosure of attorney-client communications, not thereafter used by the client to gain adversarial advantage in judicial proceedings, cannot work an implied waiver of all confidential communications on the same subject matter. Where there is "subject matter" waiver, what will be regarded as related to the "same subject"?

(4) *Accidental Disclosure During Discovery.* Inadvertent disclosure of privileged documents during discovery has generated substantial litigation, and courts split as to what steps a litigator must take to ensure that privilege is not waived. The problem is at its height in cases involving discovery requests for massive numbers of documents, or massive amounts of information in electronic computerized data bases. The difficulty, trouble, care, delay, and expense of scrutinizing each item to see if it is attorney-client privileged or work-product protected before allowing the other side to have its requested access in discovery can be staggering. *See* Hedges, *A View from the Bench and the Trenches: A Critical Appraisal of Some Amendments to the Federal Rules of Civil Procedure*, 227 F.R.D. 123 (2005), describing several attorney discovery practices meant to cope with the problem: the "claw back" procedure where the inadvertently disclosing attorney attempts to get back the protected material and restore its protection; and the "quick peek" procedure whereby no attempt is made to comb the material beforehand for protected material, but an agreement is struck with the other side (or the judge enters an order to facilitate expeditious discovery) that privilege can be claimed later as to any documents that are privileged if the need arises. The article examines three previous case law views on the "claw-back": (1) that privilege is lost by the disclosure, even though it was inadvertent; (2) that privilege is not lost because disclosure was unintentional or the client did not agree to it; and (3) that privilege is not lost if care was taken both to comb the material before and to promptly seek return after the disclosure. The article further states that under previous law the "quick peek" agreement or judicial order probably cannot preserve privilege as against third parties.

Without answering the question of whether and when privilege is lost, Fed. R. Civ. P. 26(b)(5)(B) now provides that the party accidentally disclosed-to, must, upon being notified, return, destroy, or sequester the material and may not disclose or use it until the claim is resolved.

Recently enacted Fed. R. of Evid. 502 relating to waiver of attorney-client privilege and work-product protection answers some of the questions that were not answered at the time of the article (two paragraphs above) and helps answer whether, when, and to what extent privilege is lost by the kind of disclosure discussed in this note. Inadvertent disclosure waives only to the extent of the document actually disclosed (not related documents). This waiver by inadvertent disclosure takes place only if reasonable care was not employed by the disclosing party to screen for privileged and protected material before the disclosure (or if reasonable care was not taken by that party to promptly retrieve the disclosed material) unless a claw back or quick-peek agreement is entered into between the parties. If such an agreement is not only entered into, but also incorporated into a court order, it also binds other parties than those who agreed; that is, it binds any and all parties in any and all subsequent litigation, state or federal, and they will be barred from claiming that this disclosure destroyed confidentiality and accomplished waiver, which it might otherwise do.

(5) *Refreshing Recollection with Protected Information.* An attorney runs a risk of destruction of privilege if she represents the privilege holder (or if she is the privilege holder) and uses privileged material or a portion of it to prepare a witness or refresh his recollection before or during trial or deposition. Fed. R. Evid. 612 appears to highlight this risk. *See* Rothstein, *Attorneys' Privileges Endangered by Recent Judicial Rulings*, LEGAL TIMES, p. 13 (Jan. 22, 1979). The feeling seems to be that if you are going to make use of material protected by the attorney-client privilege or work-product privilege, you had better be prepared to disclose it for exploration of its influences on the testimony. (As such, it is an "opening the door" or "making the issue" principle, akin to the cases immediately above in these notes.) *See, e.g., Berkey Photo, Inc. v. Eastman Kodak Co.*, 74 F.R.D. 613 (S.D.N.Y. 1977) (principle even applies to preparing experts for depositions, even though that is not technically refreshing memory). This can have profound effect on the way a lawyer prepares her case and (since there are no time limits on the rule) on policies about who within agencies and companies will be given routine access to files. There is some disagreement, however, on the matter of whether there is such waiver. *See, e.g., In Joseph Schlitz Brewing Co. v. Muller & Phipps, Ltd.*, 85 F.R.D. 118 (W.D. Mo. 1980). On the procedural requirements that may be necessary to invoke Fed. R. Evid. 612 when documents used to prepare a witness before a deposition or trial are work-product privileged, see *Sporck v. Peil*, 759 F.2d 312 (3d Cir.), *cert. denied*, 474 U.S. 903 (1985), which requires disclosure only of documents that requesting counsel specifically identifies and that the witness's answers reveal actually have refreshed recollection.

As indicated, questions of waiver also have arisen in the context of furnishing documents to experts. *Compare Bogosian v. Gulf Oil Corp.*, 738 F.2d 587 (3d Cir. 1984) (showing expert work product does not waive privilege even where used to develop expert's opinion), *with Vaughan Furn. Co., Inc. v. Featureline Mfg., Inc.*, 156 F.R.D. 123 (M.D.N.C. 1994) (opinion work-product privilege waived when material is used by expert as basis of trial testimony). Fed. R. Civ. P. 26 now partially codifies the discoverability of materials furnished by a lawyer to an expert, but it only partially addresses these questions.

[D] Joint Defense and Joint Consultation

(1) *Joint Clients Under Uniform Rule 502 and Unenacted Fed. R. Evid. 503.* Rule 503 of the originally proposed but ultimately not enacted "Supreme Court Draft" Federal Rules of Evidence provided:

> (d) *Exceptions.* There is no privilege under this rule:
>
> (5) *Joint clients.* As to a communication relevant to a matter of common interest between two or more clients if the communication was made by any of them to a lawyer retained or consulted in common, when offered in an action between any of the clients

As you can see, Uniform Rule 502(d)(6) reproduced at the head of this section in this book has a very similar provision. In general, the provision represents the law on this matter. The rationale for this exception is that no secrecy exists between the parties at the time of the communication. *See* 8 Wigmore, Evidence § 2312 (McNaughton rev. 1961).

(2) *Protection Against the Outside World.* The privilege applies to block access by everyone except the joint client. *See, e.g., Ohio-Sealy Mattress Mfg. Co. v. Kaplan*, 90 F.R.D. 21 (N.D. Ill. 1980):

> Where two or more persons jointly consult an attorney concerning a mutual concern, "their confidential communications with the attorney, although known to each other, will of course be privileged in a controversy of either or both of the clients with the outside world." . . . Moreover, the joint defense privilege cannot be waived without the consent of all parties to the defense, except in the situation where one of the joint defendants becomes an adverse party in a litigation.

The court in *Ohio-Sealy* explores the exception to the joint defense privilege that obtains where the parties to the joint defense (or joint matter) subsequently become adverse.

Note the slightly more restricted version of the joint privilege in Uniform Rule 502(b)(3), *supra*, at the head of this section, which, atypically, requires a "pending action."

(3) *Antagonistic Interests.* In *Government of the Virgin Islands v. Joseph*, 685 F.2d 857 (3d Cir. 1982), defendant gave a statement to an attorney representing a codefendant, implicating himself and exonerating the codefendant. The statement was admitted at trial against the defendant who gave it, the court holding that the "common defense" principle would apply only where codefendants are joined in a common purpose. The court found that at all times the interests of each were completely antagonistic. *Compare In re L.T.V. Sec. Litig.*, 89 F.R.D. 595 (N.D. Tex. 1981), which also provides a review of many of the attorney-client and work product issues raised in this section.

[E] Crime-Fraud Exception and Other Typically Criminal Issues

IN RE GRAND JURY PROCEEDINGS (MATTER OF JEFFREY FINE)

United States Court of Appeals, Fifth Circuit
641 F.2d 199 (1981)

REAVLEY, CIRCUIT JUDGE.

The United States sought an order from the district court to compel grand jury testimony from attorney Jeffrey Fine. An unnamed client of Fine's, a target of the grand jury investigation, intervened in the proceedings to prevent Fine from being forced to reveal the client's name. The district court granted the motion to compel, and the unnamed target appealed.

[T]he government [wants] to ascertain the ownership of a motor vessel known as the Nordakrum, which was used to smuggle marijuana. The ship was found, scuttled and burning, off the Louisiana coast. The registered owner is "Labol Investments" (Labol).

Fine refused to reveal the name of the client at whose request Labol was formed. The government relied upon the short amount of time that elapsed between the formation of Labol and the purchase of the Nordakrum, as well as the suspicious events surrounding the purchase itself, to show that the formation of Labol was part and parcel of a criminal enterprise that eventuated in the use of the Nordakrum to smuggle marijuana. The district court accepted this as an adequate prima facie showing and granted the motion to compel Fine's testimony.

The attorney-client privilege exists to protect confidential communications between a lawyer and his client on matters that relate to the legal interests of society and the client. But that purpose is not served if the professional relationship is secured to further present or intended illegal activity, regardless of whether the attorney knows his client's true motivations. If there is a prima facie showing that the professional relationship was intended to further a criminal enterprise, the privilege does not exist.

[T]he definition of prima facie contained in BLACK'S LAW DICTIONARY [is] "[s]uch as will suffice until contradicted and overcome by other evidence. [A] case which has proceeded upon sufficient proof to that stage where it will support finding if evidence to contrary is disregarded."

Fine testified at an evidentiary hearing granted by the court that his professional responsibilities for the unnamed client related only to the establishment of Labol and continuing representation as Labol's resident domestic agent. He knew nothing of the purchase of the Nordakrum or its subsequent uses, nor did he have any indication that the vessel actually belonged to Labol. The government introduced no contrary evidence.

The shady circumstances surrounding the Nordakrum's purchase clearly indicate that criminal activity was afoot by the time of that transaction. But there is no connection between purchase of the vessel and the formation of Labol other than the facts that (1) the two events took place within six months of each other and (2) the stranger who purchased the Nordakrum directed that it be registered in the name of Labol. As a matter of law, these two facts alone are inadequate to serve as the basis of a prima facie showing that Labol was initially formed to further a criminal enterprise. These facts may support a strong suspicion, which is often enough for police and prosecutors, but it is not enough for courts. We must vacate the order of the district court.

But that does not entirely dispose of the question whether Fine must testify before the grand jury. It is well established that "[t]he identity of a client is a matter not normally within the privilege, nor are matters involving the receipts of fees from a client usually privileged." The client's name and fee arrangements become privileged communications only if disclosure "would implicate that client in the very criminal activity for which legal advice was sought."[5]

The professional relationship between Fine and his client either was formed to further a criminal enterprise or it was legitimate and independent. Mr. Fine has testified that it was legitimate and independent, and the government has failed to make a contrary prima facie showing. The name of the client and the fee arrangement are not privileged because the evidence is that Mr. Fine was engaged only to form and maintain Labol in a legitimate manner, and no criminal liability threatens the unnamed client for activities pertaining to that legitimate, independent, professional relationship.

NOTES AND QUESTIONS

(1) *Defining the Crime-Fraud Exception and Establishing its Foundation.* In *United States v. Zolin*, 491 U.S. 554 (1989), Justice Blackmun discussed the crime-fraud exception to attorney-client privilege as follows:

> The attorney-client privilege must necessarily protect the confidences of wrongdoers, but the reason for that protection — the centrality of open client and attorney communication to the proper functioning of our adversary system of justice — "ceas[es] to operate at a certain point, namely, where the desired advice refers not to prior wrongdoing, but to future wrongdoing." 8 WIGMORE, § 2298, p. 573 (emphasis in original); see also *Clark v. United States*, 289 U.S. 1, 15 (1933). It is the purpose of the crime-fraud exception to the attorney-client privilege to assure that the "seal of secrecy," *ibid.*, between lawyer and client does not extend to communications "made for the purpose of getting advice for the commission of a fraud" or crime. *O'Rourke v. Darbishire*, [1920] A.C. 581, 604 (P.C.).

---

[5] The Fifth Circuit precedent generally uses broader language, that the name and fee arrangement are privileged if their disclosure would lead to conviction for a criminal offense. But [it] adopted the rationale of the famous Ninth Circuit case, *Baird v. Koerner*, 279 F.2d 623 (9th Cir. 1960) [which relies on narrower Ninth Circuit cases].

Although the Court did not decide the quantum of proof necessary ultimately to establish the applicability of the crime-fraud exception, in footnote 7 it noted that:

> [T]his Court's use in *Clark v. United States*, 289 U.S. 1, 14 (1933), of the phrase "prima facie case" to describe the showing needed to defeat the privilege has caused some confusion. *See* Gardner, *The Crime or Fraud Exception to the Attorney-Client Privilege*, 47 A.B.A.J. 708, 710–711 (1961); Note, 51 BROOKLYN L. REV. 913, 918–919 (1985) ("The prima facie standard is commonly used by courts in civil litigation to shift the burden of proof from one party to the other. In the context of the fraud exception, however, the standard is used to dispel the privilege altogether without affording the client an opportunity to rebut the prima facie showing"). *See also In re Grand Jury Subpoena Duces Tecum Dated September 15, 1983*, 731 F.2d 1032, 1039 (2d Cir. 1984). In using the phrase in *Clark*, the Court was aware of scholarly controversy concerning the role of the judge in the decision of such preliminary questions of fact. *See* 289 U.S., at 14. The quantum of proof needed to establish admissibility was then, and remains, subject to question. *See*, e.g., Maguire & Epstein, *Preliminary Questions of Fact in Determining the Admissibility of Evidence*, 40 HARV. L. REV. 392, 400 (criticizing courts insofar as they "have allowed themselves to be led into holding that only a superficial, one-sided showing is allowable on any admissibility controversy"), 414–424 (exploring alternative rules) (1927); 21 C. WRIGHT & K. GRAHAM, FEDERAL PRACTICE AND PROCEDURE: EVIDENCE § 5052, p. 248 (1977) (suggesting, with respect to the process of proving preliminary questions of fact, that "[p]erhaps it is a task, like riding a bicycle, that is easier to do if you do not think too much about what you are doing"). In light of the narrow question presented here for review, this case is not the proper occasion to visit these questions.

(2) *Complicity of Client and/or Lawyer.* For the crime-fraud exception to apply, the client must know or have reason to know the contemplated course of conduct is a crime under the law. When the client seeks legal advice as to how to accomplish a certain business objective that, under the body of complicated antitrust decisions, turns out to be a violation of the antitrust laws, does the crime-fraud exception apply? Does the exception apply only if the attorney helps the client's plan to break the law? *See In re Grand Jury Proceedings*, 87 F.3d 377 (9th Cir. 1996) (applying exception where lawyer did nothing to assist client).

(3) *Other Typically Criminal Issues: Identity, Fees and Attorney Reporting Statutes.* The cases are anything but consistent on the matter of disclosability of client identity and fees. *See United States v. Liebman*, 742 F.2d 807 (3d Cir. 1984), holding that while the identity of a client normally must be disclosed by the attorney, where, as here, this information, combined with information already known or suspected by the authorities reveals a client communication, the identity is privileged. Contrast *In re Grand Jury Subpoena Duces Tecum (Shargel)*, 742 F.2d 61 (2d Cir. 1984), holding that fee records, and the names of people paying fees for other clients, must be disclosed by an attorney notwithstanding that disclosure would suggest that the clients knew that they had "a criminal problem" and would support an inference of concerted criminal activity.

Along with the tendency of courts to hold that fees and client identity are unprivileged, current federal law requires reporting to the government of any cash transaction or series of related transactions involving over $10,000 cash. This would include lawyers' fees from the client. The lawyer must report such fees and identify the paying client, for example, on IRS Form 8300. Does such reporting violate ethical rules as well as implicating privilege?

Some of the general principles that can be gleaned from the growing body of case law on these interrelated questions are found in *United States v. Sindel*, 53 F.3d 874 (8th Cir. 1995):

> Although the federal common law of attorney-client privilege protects confidential disclosures made by a client to an attorney in order to obtain legal representation, *Fisher v. United States*, 425 U.S. 391 (1976), it ordinarily does not apply to client identity and fee information. *In re Grand Jury Proceedings* (85 Misc. 140), 791 F.2d 663, 665 (8th Cir. 1986); *In re Grand Jury Subpoenas (Anderson)*, 906 F.2d 1485, 1488 (10th Cir. 1990). The various Circuit Courts have, however, identified certain circumstances under which the privilege protects even client identity and fee information. One court has categorized these overlapping "special-circumstance" exceptions as the legal advice exception, the last link exception, and the confidential communications exception. *Anderson*, 906 F.2d at 1488. The legal advice exception protects client identity and fee information when "there is a strong probability that disclosure would implicate the client in the very criminal activity for which legal advice was sought." *Id.* The last link exception, as its name implies, prevents disclosure of client identity and fee information when it would incriminate the client by providing the last link in an existing chain of evidence. *Id.* at 1489. The confidential communications exception, which we have recognized on another occasion, protects client identity and fee information "if, by revealing the information, the attorney would necessarily disclose confidential communications." 85 Misc. 140, 791 F.2d at 665; *see Anderson*, 906 F.2d at 1491. Our decision regarding Sindel's claim of attorney-client privilege therefore must rest upon a determination of whether the information requested by IRS Form 8300 is protected in this case by one of the special-circumstance exceptions. *See United States v. Goldberger & Dubin, P.C.*, 935 F.2d 501, 505 (2nd Cir. 1991) (acknowledging that special circumstances may render privileged the information sought by Form 8300); *United States v. Leventhal*, 961 F.2d 936, 940 (11th Cir. 1992) (recognizing that Form 8300 may trigger an exception to the rules governing the attorney-client privilege); *United States v. Gertner*, 873 F. Supp. 729 (D. Mass. 1995) (holding that under the special circumstances of the case, the information requested by Form 8300 was protected by the attorney-client privilege). After examining Sindel's *in-camera* testimony about his clients' special circumstances, we conclude that he could not release information about the payments on behalf of Jane Doe without revealing the substance of a confidential communication. We do not find any similar constraints upon the disclosure of information about the payments on behalf of John Doe.

> The Missouri Rules of Professional Conduct appear on their face to extend somewhat broader protection to client identity and fee information than does the federal common law of attorney-client privilege. Rule 1.6 provides that a "lawyer shall not reveal information relating to representation of a client unless the client consents after consultation." Rules Governing the Mo. Bar and Judiciary 4, 1.6 (1986). Even assuming arguendo that Rule 1.6 would prohibit disclosure of the information required to complete an IRS Form 8300, Congress cannot have intended to allow local rules of professional ethics to carve out fifty different privileged exemptions to the reporting requirements of 26 U.S.C. § 60501. Thus the Missouri Rules of Professional Conduct do not expand the scope of the exemption beyond what is established by the federal common law of attorney-client privilege.

That "special circumstances" is read narrowly by many courts can be seen in *Lefcourt v. United States*, 125 F.3d 79 (2d Cir. 1997), which rejected the argument accepted in some circuits that incrimination in the current case renders client-identifying and fee information privileged.

In *Sindel*, Mr. Sindel also unsuccessfully argued that application of the reporting statutes to an attorney:

> violates the client's Sixth Amendment right to counsel by inhibiting the ability to retain counsel, discouraging communication between attorney and client, forcing the attorney to act as an agent for the government, and disqualifying counsel of choice. As the Second Circuit accurately points out in *Goldberger & Dubin*, 935 F.2d at 504, the statutory reporting requirements do not prevent a would-be client from hiring counsel. Not only are cash payments not automatically forfeit, but a client is also free to pay counsel in some other manner to avoid being reported to the IRS. By contrast, we recognize the serious Sixth Amendment implications of Sindel's claim that an attorney becomes a *de facto* agent for the government when compelled to offer an opinion as to whether a particular cash payment was a "suspicious transaction," a question added to the January, 1990, version of Form 8300. Sindel used this later version of Form 8300 to consolidate his reporting of the payments made on behalf of Jane Doe. Because we have already determined that the federal common law of attorney-client privilege excuses Sindel from reporting any additional information regarding the Jane Doe payments, however, the constitutionality of the January, 1990, version of Form 8300 is not at issue in this case. Sindel's speculative claim that the reporting requirements would disqualify counsel by allowing prosecutors to subpoena a reporting attorney to testify against a client is likewise not ripe for adjudication. There is thus no Sixth Amendment bar to enforcement of the IRS summons against Sindel.

See generally Comment, *The Attorney-Client Privilege as a Protection of Client Identity: Can Defense Attorneys be the Prosecution's Best Witnesses?: In re Grand Jury Proceedings (Pavlick)*, 21 Am. Crim. L. Rev. 81 (1983).

(4) *California's "Dangerous Client" Exception.* In 1994, California enacted Cal. Evid. Code § 956.5, which provides: "There is no privilege under this article if the

lawyer reasonably believes that disclosure of any confidential communication relating to representation of a client is necessary to prevent the client from committing a criminal act that the lawyer believes is likely to result in death or substantial bodily harm." Among other issues, this provision has supported predictions that attorneys might face *Tarasoff* liability. *See Tarasoff v. Regents of Univ. of Calif.*, 551 P.2d 334 (Cal. 1976) (psychologist liable for consequences of failure to warn prospective victim of potential harm from psychologist's patient). Would this provision have solved the problem of *Macumber, supra*, § 13.02[A], note (6)?

ATTORNEY-CLIENT PRIVILEGE PROBLEM SET 13A.

Consider the following problems in the light of all the principles you have learned in the materials herein on attorney-client privilege:

(1) *The Angry, Unpredictable Divorce Client.* You represent Janet Jones, whose husband John has left her, has taken up residence with another woman with whom he has had a lengthy affair, and has sued Janet for dissolution of the marriage. You recognize that Janet is depressed, angry and unpredictable. She has bought a gun and ammunition because financial pressures have forced her and the children to move to a high-crime district. At one point she confides to you: "I hate my husband so much that I'd like to see him dead." You think there is some appreciable chance of violence by Janet against John. May (or must) you disclose this confidence — if you are located in a State with, or without, this California provision? Consider, among other factors, what is meant by a "reasonable belief" that disclosure is "necessary."

(2) *Get Rid of the Weapon.* Which, if any, of the following communications is admissible, and why? The offense is murder; the punishment, death.

The deceased secured a divorce from appellant [Clark] on March 25, 1952. That night she was killed, as she lay at home in her bed, as the result of a gunshot wound. From the mattress on her bed, as well as from the bed of her daughter, were recovered bullets which were shown by a firearms expert to have been fired by a .38 special revolver having Colt characteristics. Appellant was shown to have purchased a Colt .38 Detective Special some ten months prior to the homicide.

Marjorie Bartz, a telephone operator in the City of San Angelo, testified that at 2:49 in the morning of March 26, 1952, while on duty, she received a call from the Golden Spur Hotel; that at first she thought the person placing the call was a Mr. Cox and so made out the slip; but that she then recognized appellant's voice, scratched out the word "Cox" and wrote "Clark." She stated that appellant told her he wanted to speak to his lawyer, Jimmy Martin in Dallas, and that she placed the call to him at telephone number Victor 1942 in that city and made a record thereof, which record was admitted in evidence. Miss Bartz testified that, contrary to company rules, she listened to the entire conversation that ensued, and that it went as follows:

The appellant: "Hello, Jimmy, I went to the extremes."

The voice in Dallas: "What did you do?"

The appellant: "I just went to the extremes."

The voice in Dallas: "You got to tell me what you did before I can help."

The appellant: "Well, I killed her."

The voice in Dallas: "Who did you kill; the driver?"

The appellant: "No, I killed her."

The voice in Dallas: "Did you get rid of the weapon?"

The appellant: "No, I still got the weapon."

The voice in Dallas: "Get rid of the weapon and sit tight and don't talk to anyone, and I will fly down in the morning."

It was stipulated that the Dallas telephone number of appellant's attorney was Victor 1942.

Appellant contends that the court erred in admitting the testimony of the telephone operator, because the conversation related was a privileged communication between appellant and his attorney.

(Based on *Clark v. State*, 261 S.W.2d 339 (Tex. Crim. App.), *cert. denied*, 346 U.S. 855 (1953).)

(3) *A Client Confidence of Guilt and of Another's Wrongful Conviction and Death Sentence.* Smith, who is not your client, has been convicted of the murder of Green and sentenced to death. Your client, Jones, whom you are representing in a variety of matters relating to his past activities, tells you in confidence: "Smith didn't do that murder. I know, because I'm the one who did it." Is this statement covered by the general scope of the privilege, and if so, is there an exception that allows disclosure? (Note: This problem is designed to illustrate the costliness of privileges, among other matters.)

(4) *What Effect Does the Corporate Privilege Have in Shielding Communications that Officers or Employees Want to Keep Confidential to Protect Their Individual Interests?* Seton Duck, the president of the Last State Bank, consulted the Bank's corporate counsel, attorney Lauren Horder, about bank business, in an effort to complete an ostensibly advantageous economic transaction while avoiding violations of criminal law by either him or the Bank. But the "advantageous" transaction proved to be a very bad investment. It contributed to the failure of the Bank and its takeover by federal bank regulatory authorities (the "FSLIC"). Other evidence made FSLIC authorities suspicious of a crime in the transaction, and a federal grand jury, with the full cooperation of FSLIC, now seeks to obtain evidence from Lauren Horder, the Bank's lawyer, about confidential communications from Seton Duck. Can he, as former president of the Bank, prevent disclosure?

(5) *The Partly Co-Operating Company.* The X Corp. in 2005 is accused of many years of overcharging (since 1995) in the sale of a product whose price is regulated by law. Previous to any government investigation (government investigations were commenced in 2005), X Corp.'s president, who is also its general counsel, went out and interviewed X Corp. salesmen from around the country, to find out what they were charging customers. The first federal agency to investigate was the SEC. The company agrees to co-operate with the SEC and waives attorney-client privilege as to interviews that took place between 1995-2000, but not as to those that took place

between 2000 and 2004. A settlement is reached with the SEC. The IRS has now entered the picture, and is also investigating. The company now wants to assert attorney-client privilege as to the entire set of interviews, and resists a subpoena from the IRS issued to compel the company's president and general counsel to testify to all the interviews. Discuss whether he must testify.

(6) *Gaps in Lawyer-Client Confidentiality.* After reading this entire section, can you list all the situations in which lawyer-client "confidences" may not indeed be held confidential? Should clients be warned about these in advance? *See* Rothstein, *"Anything You Say May Be Used Against You": A Proposed Seminar on the Lawyer's Duty to Warn of Confidentiality's Limits in Today's Post-Enron World*, 76 FORDHAM L. REV. 1745 (2007) (cataloging gaps in confidentiality and suggesting warnings).

§ 13.03 SPOUSAL PRIVILEGES: A FURTHER STUDY IN PRIVILEGE POLICIES, INCLUDING TESTIMONIAL AND COMMUNICATION PRIVILEGES[13]

Uniform Rules of Evidence (as Amended 1999) [Recommended Model Provisions for States: Not Part of the Federal Rules]:[14]

Rule 504. Spousal Privilege

(a) Confidential communication. A communication is confidential if it is made privately by an individual to the individual's spouse and is not intended for disclosure to any other person.

(b) Marital communications. An individual has a privilege to refuse to testify and to prevent the individual's spouse or former spouse from testifying as to any confidential communication made by the individual to the spouse during their marriage. The privilege may be waived only by the individual holding the privilege or by the holder's guardian or conservator, or the individual's personal representative if the individual is deceased.

[13] Study Guide Reference: Evidence in a Nutshell, Chapter 5:IV.

[14] The Uniform Rule on spousal privilege is significantly different from the "Supreme Court Draft" Federal Rule, in that the Uniform Rule has both a marital communications privilege and a criminal-case adverse spousal testimony privilege, whereas the Draft Federal Rule has only the criminal-case adverse spousal testimony privilege (which in itself differs from the Uniform Rule's adverse spousal testimony privilege in that under the Draft Federal Rule both spouses have the privilege). Federal cases under the federal branch of current Fed. R. Evid. 501 accord both privileges; and confine the adverse spousal testimony privilege not only to criminal cases, but to the testifying spouse (that is, only that spouse can raise the privilege; the accused spouse cannot prevent the witness spouse from testifying if the witness spouse wishes to testify against the accused spouse). The law in the states differs from state to state on these points and others. Some states have expressly adopted some version of the Uniform Rule.

(c) Spousal testimony in criminal proceeding. The spouse of an accused in a criminal proceeding has a privilege to refuse to testify against the accused spouse.

(d) Exceptions. There is no privilege under this rule:

(1) in any civil proceeding in which the spouses are adverse parties;

(2) in any criminal proceeding in which an unrefuted showing is made that the spouses acted jointly in the commission of the crime charged;

(3) in any proceeding in which one spouse is charged with a crime or tort against the person or property of the other, a minor child of either, an individual residing in the household of either, or a third person if the crime or tort is committed in the course of committing a crime or tort against the other spouse, a minor child of either spouse, or an individual residing in the household of either spouse; or

(4) in any other proceeding, in the discretion of the court, if the interests of a minor child of either spouse may be adversely affected by invocation of the privilege.

[A] Testimonial Privilege Not to Testify Against One's Spouse (Which Can Include Privilege to Prevent Adverse Spousal Testimony Against One's Self)

TRAMMEL v. UNITED STATES

United States Supreme Court
445 U.S. 40 (1980)

CHIEF JUSTICE BURGER delivered the opinion of the Court.

We granted certiorari to consider whether an accused may invoke the privilege against adverse spousal testimony so as to exclude the voluntary testimony of his wife.

[P]etitioner Otis Trammel was indicted for importing heroin. The indictment also named six unindicted coconspirators, including petitioner's wife Elizabeth Ann Trammel.

According to the indictment, petitioner and his wife flew carrying with them a quantity of heroin. Freeman and Roberts assisted. She was searched, the heroin was discovered, and she was arrested. After discussions with Drug Enforcement Administration agents, she agreed to cooperate with the government.

Prior to trial on this indictment, petitioner moved to sever his case from that of Roberts and Freeman. He advised the court that the government intended to call his wife as an adverse witness and asserted his claim to a privilege to prevent her from testifying against him. At a hearing on the motion, Mrs. Trammel was called as a government witness under a grant of use immunity. She testified that she and petitioner were married [seven months prior to the arrest] and that they remained married. She explained that her cooperation with the government was based on assurances that she would be given lenient treatment. She then described, in considerable detail, her role and that of her husband in the heroin distribution conspiracy.

After hearing this testimony, the district court ruled that Mrs. Trammel could testify in support of the government's case to any act she observed during the marriage and to any communication "made in the presence of a third person"; however, confidential communications between petitioner and his wife were held to be privileged and inadmissible.

At trial, Elizabeth Trammel testified within the limits of the court's pretrial ruling; her testimony, as the government concedes, constituted virtually its entire case against petitioner. He was found guilty.

In the court of appeals petitioner's only claim of error was that the admission of the adverse testimony of his wife, over his objection, contravened this Court's teaching in *Hawkins v. United States*, 358 U.S. 74 (1958). The court of appeals rejected this contention. It concluded that *Hawkins* did not prohibit "the voluntary testimony of a spouse."

The privilege claimed by petitioner has ancient roots. Writing in 1628, Lord Coke observed that "it hath been resolved by the Justices that a wife cannot be produced either against or for her husband." This spousal disqualification sprang from two canons of medieval jurisprudence: first, the rule that an accused was not permitted to testify in his own behalf because of his interest in the proceeding; second, the concept that husband and wife were one, and that since the woman had no recognized separate legal existence, the husband was that one. From those two now long-abandoned doctrines, it followed that what was inadmissible from the lips of the defendant-husband was also inadmissible from his wife.

[I]t was not until 1933 in *Funk v. United States*, 290 U.S. 371, that this Court abolished the testimonial disqualification in the federal courts, so as to permit the spouse of a defendant to testify in the defendant's behalf. [We,] however, left undisturbed the rule that either spouse could prevent the other from giving adverse testimony. The rule thus evolved into one of privilege rather than one of absolute disqualification.

The modern justification for this privilege against adverse spousal testimony is its perceived role in fostering the harmony and sanctity of the marriage relationship. Notwithstanding this benign purpose, the rule was sharply criticized. Wigmore and others suggested a privilege protecting only private marital communications, modeled on the privilege between priest and penitent, attorney and client, and physician and patient.

In *Hawkins v. United States*, the district court had permitted petitioner's wife, over his objection, to testify against him. [The Supreme] Court held the wife's testimony inadmissible [and rejected] the government's suggestion that the Court modify the privilege by vesting it in the witness spouse, with freedom to testify or not independent of the defendant's control.

Hawkins, then, left the federal privilege for adverse spousal testimony where it found it, continuing "a rule which bars the testimony of one spouse against the other unless both consent."

The Federal Rules of Evidence acknowledge the authority of the federal courts to continue the evolutionary development of testimonial privileges in federal criminal trials "governed by the principles of the common law as they may be interpreted in the light of reason and experience." Fed Rule Evid 501. The general mandate of Rule 501 was substituted by the Congress for a set of privilege rules drafted by the Judicial Conference Advisory Committee on Rules of Evidence and approved by the Judicial Conference of the United States and by this Court. That proposal defined nine specific privileges, including a husband-wife privilege which would have codified the *Hawkins* rule and eliminated the privilege for confidential marital communications. In rejecting the proposed rules [Congress wanted] to "provide the courts with the flexibility to develop rules of privilege on a case-by-case basis," and to leave the door open to change.

Since 1958, when *Hawkins* was decided, support for the privilege against adverse spousal testimony has been eroded further. Thirty-one jurisdictions, including Alaska and Hawaii, then allowed an accused a privilege to prevent adverse spousal testimony. The number has now declined to 24. In 1974, the National Conference on Uniform State Laws revised its Uniform Rules of Evidence, but again rejected the *Hawkins* rule in favor of a limited privilege for confidential communications. That proposed rule has been enacted in Arkansas, North Dakota, and Oklahoma — each of which in 1958 permitted an accused to exclude adverse spousal testimony. The trend in state law toward divesting the accused of the privilege to bar adverse spousal testimony has special relevance because the laws of marriage and domestic relations are concerns traditionally reserved to the states. *See Sosna v. Iowa*, 419 U.S. 393, 404 (1975). Scholarly criticism of the *Hawkins* rule has also continued unabated.

Testimony exclusionary rules and privileges contravene the fundamental principle that "the public . . . has a right to every man's evidence." *United States v. Bryan*, 339 U.S. 323, 331 (1950). As such, they must be strictly construed and accepted "only to the very limited extent that permitting a refusal to testify or excluding relevant evidence has a public good transcending the normally predominant principle of utilizing all rational means for ascertaining truth." *Elkins v. United States*, 364 U.S. 206, 234 (1960) (Frankfurter, J., dissenting). Accord, *United States v. Nixon*, 418 U.S. 683, 709, 710 (1974). Here we must decide whether the privilege against adverse spousal testimony promotes sufficiently important interests to outweigh the need for probative evidence in the administration of criminal justice.

It is essential to remember that the *Hawkins* privilege is not needed to protect information privately disclosed between husband and wife in the confidence of the marital relationship — once described by this Court as "the best solace of human existence." *Stein v. Bowman*, 18 Pet. at 223. Those confidences are privileged under the independent rule protecting confidential marital communications. *Blau v. United States*, 340 U.S. 332 (1951). The *Hawkins* privilege is invoked, not to exclude private marital communications, but rather to exclude evidence of criminal acts and of communications made in the presence of third persons.

No other testimonial privilege sweeps so broadly. The privileges between priest and penitent, attorney and client, and physician and patient limit protection to private communications. These privileges are rooted in the imperative need for confidence and trust. The priest-penitent privilege recognizes the human need to disclose to a spiritual counselor, in total and absolute confidence, what are believed to be flawed acts or thoughts and to receive priestly consolation and guidance in return. The lawyer-client privilege rests on the need for the advocate and counselor to know all that relates to the client's reasons for seeking representation if the professional mission is to be carried out. Similarly, the physician must know all that a patient can articulate in order to identify and to treat disease; barriers to full disclosure would impair diagnosis and treatment.

The *Hawkins* rule stands in marked contrast to these three privileges. Its protection is not limited to confidential communications; rather it permits an accused to exclude all adverse spousal testimony. As Jeremy Bentham observed more than a century and a half ago, such a privilege goes far beyond making "every man's house his castle," and permits a person to convert his house into "a den of thieves." It "secures, to every man, one safe and unquestionable and ever ready accomplice for every imaginable crime."

The ancient foundations for so sweeping a privilege have long since disappeared. Nowhere in the common-law world — indeed in any modern society — is a woman regarded as chattel or demeaned by denial of a separate legal identity and the dignity associated with recognition as a whole human being. Chip by chip, over the years those archaic notions have been cast aside so that "[n]o longer is the female destined solely for the home and the rearing of the family, and only the male for the marketplace and the world of ideas." *Stanton v. Stanton*, 421 U.S. 7, 14, 15 (1975).

The contemporary justification for affording an accused such a privilege is also unpersuasive. When one spouse is willing to testify against the other in a criminal proceeding — whatever the motivation — their relationship is almost certainly in disrepair; there is probably little in the way of marital harmony for the privilege to preserve. In these circumstances, a rule of evidence that permits an accused to prevent adverse spousal testimony seems far more likely to frustrate justice than to foster family peace. Indeed, there is reason to believe that vesting the privilege in the accused could actually undermine the marital relationship. For example, in a case such as this, the government is unlikely to offer a wife immunity and lenient treatment if it knows that her husband can prevent her from giving adverse testimony. If the government is dissuaded from making such an offer, the privilege can have the untoward effect of permitting one spouse to escape justice at the expense of the other. It hardly seems conducive to the preservation of the marital relation to place a wife in jeopardy solely by virtue of her husband's control over her testimony.

Our consideration of the foundations for the privilege and its history satisfy us that "reason and experience" no longer justify so sweeping a rule as that in *Hawkins*. Accordingly, we conclude that the existing rule should be modified so that the witness spouse alone has a privilege to refuse to testify adversely; the witness may be neither compelled to testify nor foreclosed from testifying. This modification

— vesting the privilege in the witness spouse — furthers the important public interest in marital harmony without unduly burdening legitimate law enforcement needs.

Here, petitioner's spouse chose to testify against him. That she did so after a grant of immunity and assurances of lenient treatment does not render her testimony involuntary. Accordingly, the district court and the court of appeals were correct in rejecting petitioner's claim of privilege, and the judgment of the court of appeals is affirmed.

Affirmed.

NOTES AND QUESTIONS

(1) *Sham and Common-Law Marriages. See United States v. Saniti*, 604 F.2d 603 (9th Cir.), *cert. denied*, 444 U.S. 969 (1979), affirming the trial court's finding (as a preliminary question of fact) that a marriage was sham (and thus there was no adverse spousal testimony privilege). The trial judge found that although the marriage was valid for marriage-law purposes, it was entered into in order to obtain the privilege. (The federal branch of Fed. R. Evid. 501 was involved.) *See also United States v. Byrd*, 750 F.2d 585 (7th Cir. 1984), holding that communications made during a married couple's permanent separation are excluded from the marital communications privilege.

What of common-law marriage? *See United States v. Lustig*, 555 F.2d 737 (9th Cir. 1977), *cert. denied*, 434 U.S. 1045 (1978), finding no privilege where the state in which the couple resided did not recognize common-law marriage. Do you think the court would do the same in the case of a gay marriage or civil union?

(2) *Is There A Crime-Fraud Exception to Spousal Privilege? See In re Grand Jury Empanelled Oct. 18, 1979*, 633 F.2d 276 (3d Cir. 1980):

> Ruth Malfitano appeals from an order of the district court holding her in contempt for refusing to answer questions before a federal grand jury empanelled to investigate an alleged attempt by [her] husband, Samuel Malfitano, and others to secure a loan from the Teamsters Union Pension Fund. The government believes that there was a conspiracy involving [her] husband, other individuals, and several corporate entities to secure this loan by paying a 10% kickback. The appellant is the secretary of five of these corporations, and her husband is the president of the same five.
>
> [T]he appellant appeared before the grand jury and was asked questions. After consulting with her attorney, the appellant refused to answer on the ground of marital privilege. [The court ordered her to testify. Her refusal resulted in jailing.]
>
> The main rationale for the privilege today is that it protects the marriage from discord. The major justification offered by the government for not according appellant the privilege is the fact that she was allegedly involved in the criminal acts of her husband. This position is supported, either by

dictum or holding, in a number of cases [and] rests on a variety of possible premises [as follows].

An initial possibility [is that] it is more likely that the marriage is [already] unstable.

There is nothing in the record or otherwise to indicate that marriages with criminal overtones disintegrate and dissolve. The spouses in fact may be very happy. [T]he witness spouse being the holder of the privilege completely satisfies any [such] concern.

[A] second premise underlying this proposed exception is that such marriages are bad or otherwise not deserving of any protection.

[W]here the marriage is unstable, it should not be endangered further.

We fail to see how the source of that instability, whether it be normal domestic difficulties or the spouses' joint criminal activity, makes any difference. As long as neither state nor federal substantive law attaches [the penalty of dissolution of marriages] to joint crimes of spouses, it is inappropriate to use evidentiary rules to impose such a penalty. The assumption seems to be that because of what may be an isolated criminal act, the marriage has no social value whatsoever. This may not be true. Marriage is a social bond that not only ties the individuals together but also can tie the individuals into certain social norms and behavioral patterns. Thus the marriage may well serve as a restraining influence on couples against future antisocial acts and may tend to help future integration of the spouses back into society.

[I]f courts were able to assess the social utility of particular marriages the proposed exception to the privilege might be justifiable. *Compare United States v. Brown*, 605 F.2d 389, 396 (8th Cir. 1979) (marriage was of short duration and so unstable as to not deserve the protection of the privilege), *cert. denied*, 444 U.S. 972 (1979), *with Ryan v. Commissioner of Internal Revenue*, 568 F.2d 531, 543 (7th Cir. 1977) (marriage was of such long duration and so stable that protection not needed), *cert. denied*, 439 U.S. 820 (1978). Indeed, here we have absolutely no way of knowing what type of marriage appellant and her husband have because there was no inquiry into the question.

[W]e do not think that courts should condition the privilege on a judicial determination that the marriage is a happy or successful one.

Where the spouse does not want to testify, the only way to get her testimony will be to accuse her. This will put pressure on her to testify, perhaps at the expense of her spouse, to protect herself. Given the intimacy of marriage and the fact that conspiracy is a rather flexible concept, it will be quite easy to allege that the spouses are partners. Ironically, the closer the marriage, the more likely it will [so] appear. [T]here will not be much difficulty in asserting that the appellant is involved even though she is not even a target of the grand jury. Thus recognition of an exception where it can be said that both spouses are involved will tend to undermine the marriage precisely in the manner that the privilege is designed to prevent.

> [W]e realize the possibility that the social benefit of the privilege may be minimal and that it could be dispensed with without serious erosion of marriages. Nevertheless, *Trammel* chose not to abolish the privilege but rather to modify it. As long as the privilege remains law, the exceptions to it must be based on verifiable assumptions or on ascertainable factual standards.
>
> The order of the district court finding the appellant in contempt will be reversed.

Not all courts agree. *See, e.g.*, *United States v. Clark*, 712 F.2d 299 (7th Cir. 1983), for a case rejecting spousal privilege for joint participants in crime. *See generally* Rothstein, *A Re-Evaluation of the Privilege Against Adverse Spousal Testimony in the Light of its Purpose*, 12 INT'L & COMP. L.Q. 1189 (1963) (addressed to questions such as strength and social utility of marriage, criminal partnerships, interspousal crimes, and policy of privilege, and also arguing for change (with exceptions) subsequently accomplished by *Trammel* and large number of states). This article was cited in *Trammel* in support of the decision. We have deleted most citations.

PROBLEM 13B: THE TRIAL OF WARREN MOON FOR ALLEGEDLY ASSAULTING FELICIA MOON.

On July 18, 1995, Felicia Moon, married to Minnesota Vikings (formerly Houston Oilers) quarterback Warren Moon, gave a statement to police in which she charged her husband with having struck and choked her until she "saw black and could not breathe." She feared for her life, she said, and she apparently fled in her car with her husband pursuing her at speeds up to 100 m.p.h. Police photographs showed injuries to her face, including scratches and abrasions. Her son Jeffrey also made an emergency telephone call reporting and describing the alleged assault. Under these facts, the State of Texas (where the couple resided) charged Warren Moon with Class A misdemeanor assault and subpoenaed both Felicia and Jeffrey.

Texas Code of Criminal Procedure, article 38.10 (as amended in 1995) provides:

> EXCEPTIONS TO THE SPOUSAL ADVERSE TESTIMONY PRIVILEGE. The privilege of a person's spouse not to be called as a witness for the state does not apply in any proceeding in which the person is charged with a crime committed against the person's spouse, a minor child, or a member of the household of either spouse.

Several months after the event, however, Felicia Moon filed a motion to quash the subpoenas. She declared that she was not a battered woman but was "an independent, strong-minded, college-educated woman who wants the State to stay out of her bedroom." She alleged that her family was singled out because of celebrity status: "Leave me, my privacy and the sanctity of my marriage alone." She denied any coercion or intimidation by her husband. Forcing her son Jeffrey to testify would "damage his fragile emotional health" because he was "extremely devoted to his father." Finally, Felicia stated that she would invoke the Fifth Amendment and refuse to testify anyway, unless granted "full immunity." *See* Muck, *Felicia Moon Wants Subpoenas Dropped*, HOUS. CHRONICLE, § A, at 1, col. 1.

Questions: *(1) Victimless Prosecution.* What chance is there of successful prosecution of Warren without Felicia's testimony? *(2) Testimonial Privilege.* Are there sound policies underlying the privilege of a spouse not to testify involuntarily, and if so, are there overriding policies for abolishing it here? *(3) The Motion to Quash the Subpoenas.* Is there lawful authority for quashing the subpoenas on the privacy and marital sanctity grounds stated in the motion, given the applicable statute above? Note that many jurisdictions that have statutory privileges, including this jurisdiction, make them exclusive, preventing common-law evolution. *(4) The Federal Privilege; Trammel.* What result if the prosecution were in a federal court? (Note that no Supreme Court authority addresses a case precisely like this one.) *(5) Official Discretion.* The District Attorney has wide discretion over initiation of prosecutions or subpoenas. In fact, in this case he predicted that he would not call the son, Jeffrey, as a witness, but stated that he wanted to talk to him. Should the District Attorney exercise discretion to withdraw the subpoenas or decline prosecution here? (Picture a press conference at which a public official justifies such a decision by reference to the college-educated or celebrity status of the participants; consider also whether a fair uniform policy could be devised and applied here.) *(6) The Self-Incrimination Claim.* What do you suppose lies beneath Felicia Moon's claim of the Fifth Amendment? *(7) The Outcome.* The State gave Felicia immunity. She testified under compulsory process. The jury promptly acquitted Warren. Is any of this surprising?

[B] Marital Communications

UNITED STATES v. NEAL

United States District Court, District of Colorado
532 F. Supp. 942 (1982), *aff'd*, 743 F.2d 1441 (10th Cir. 1984), *cert. denied*, 470 U.S. 1086 (1985)

CARRIGAN, DISTRICT JUDGE.

Neal is accused of having robbed the Midland Federal Savings and Loan [in violation of a federal statute]. A female teller assaulted during the robbery died from her injuries a few days later.

[I]n the course of seeking evidence to implicate the defendant in this crime, an FBI agent listened to and tape recorded three telephone conversations between Neal and his wife Marcia. A promise of immunity from prosecution was used to obtain Mrs. Neal's consent to the telephone monitoring and tape recording. In this effort to induce the defendant to incriminate himself, his wife asked him questions suggested to her by the FBI agent. The questions were apparently designed to bait the defendant to respond with incriminating answers.

Defendant Neal, invoking the marital communications privilege, moves to prevent the government from introducing at his trial any evidence of the contents of those three conversations. The parties agree that if the proposed evidence is to be admitted at the trial, it would have to be introduced through one or more of three means: (1) testimony of the defendant's wife, Marcia Neal; (2) testimony of the government agent who listened to the conversations; or (3) playing the tape recordings to the jury.

Pursuant to the parties' joint written request, I have listened to tape recordings of the conversations at issue. In the conversations Mrs. Neal's tone is that of a frightened, dependent wife confiding in her husband her fears that the police are upon her and seeking his advice and reassurance. The husband changed phones during the calls, lowered his voice in an apparent effort to avoid being heard by anyone but his wife, and generally demonstrated great reluctance to respond to his wife's "planted" inquiries. The overall character of the monitored conversations was set by the wife's opening question in the first call when she asked her husband, "Is there somewhere I can talk to you without anybody bothering us?"

I. Issues

The issues presented by this motion are whether the marital communications privilege: (1) precludes testimony by Marcia Neal of her husband's statements to her in the three telephone conversations; (2) prevents any government agent who overheard the conversations from testifying about them; or (3) prohibits introducing the tapes into evidence at trial.

II. Applicable Law

Testimonial privileges in federal courts are governed by FRE 501.

Prior to adoption of Rule 501 in its present form, the Supreme Court had approved and sent to Congress a rule expressly setting out the recognized evidentiary privileges, including that protecting husband-wife communications. The Senate Judiciary Committee, while not including in the Rules the Supreme Court's list of testimonial privileges, took pains to disclaim any intention of disapproving the husband-wife privilege, or the other privileges contained in the Supreme Court's version of the rule. Rather, the Committee expressed in this rule its preference "that the recognition of a privilege based on a confidential relationship . . . should be determined on a case-by-case basis." Thus we must refer to case law.

The Supreme Court has long recognized the common law privilege against disclosure of communications between spouses. In fact, this privilege is the second oldest testimonial privilege recognized at common law.

The essence of the privilege is to protect confidences only . . . . The purpose is to insure subjectively the unrestrained privacy of communication, free from any fear of compulsory disclosure. It follows that if the communication is not intended to be a private one the privilege has no application to it. [Wigmore.]

Marital confidences are considered "so essential to the preservation of the marriage relationship as to outweigh the disadvantages to the administration of justice which the privilege entails." An interspousal communication is presumed to be confidential, although that presumption may be overcome by proof that it was not intended to be private.

Such testimonial privileges, however, [must be strictly construed because of the cost to finding truth].

In carrying out the duty imposed by Rule 501 to consider each case of confidential communication privilege on a case by case basis, courts cannot be oblivious to the effects of their decisions on related privileges. The task before me would be less difficult were I free to apply one rule of evidence law to admit such evidence in emotion-laden murder cases, and a different rule to enforce the privilege in cases involving lesser crimes. Indeed, weighing the public interest in convicting criminals against the public interest in protecting the sanctity of marital privacy against prying government investigators, it may be that more serious crimes should weigh more in the balance, thus justifying application of different rules to different kinds of crime.

Thus, for example, if this issue had arisen in a run-of-the-mill income tax case, it would seem simpler. If, in such a case, the government had promised a wife not to pursue her liability on a joint tax return in exchange for her cooperating to ensnare her husband through phone calls like these, the legal issues might have been seen unobscured by feelings naturally stirred in a murder case. Emotions, however, cause hard cases to make bad law. Absent some contrary guidance from the Supreme Court, I must apply in this case the same rule to be applied in all cases — of all types.

Over at least the past decade, the circle of privacy surrounding each of us has drawn smaller with each new governmental incursion and each new technological advance. Courts have sought to preserve inviolable some small island of privacy as a refuge for the human spirit where government may not intrude. Here the question is whether one such sanctuary, protected by the common law for centuries, shall be breached, rendering the secrets told to wives by husbands fair game for government investigators.

The issue is whether in our free society the government may, by making a deal with one's spouse, invade the confidences of marriage to turn those nearest and dearest into informers. Once the marital confidential communication is breached, other like sanctuaries of testimonial privilege cannot prevail against similar invasions, for they are shielded only by similar evidentiary privileges of no less penetrable nature. Thus, by pre-arrangement with a criminal suspect's priest, minister or rabbi, psychiatrist or other physician, or lawyer, the police could obtain much information of great value in combating crime. The only question is whether the price would be too high.

Because of this tension between society's desire to protect marital privacy and the duty of courts to find the truth, the marital privilege has been strictly limited to communications between persons actually married when the communication took place. Moreover, certain exceptions to the privilege have been recognized. Three of those exceptions must be discussed in relation to this case.

The first exception provides that communications made by a spouse who knows that a third person is present are not protected from disclosure. A spouse who is aware of a third party's presence cannot be said to intend his or her statements only for the other spouse; thus the essence of confidential marital communication is absent. No justification exists, therefore, to prevent anyone present during the conversation from testifying about what either spouse said to the other.

The second exception allows testimony of communications between spouses regarding a future crime, or a crime in progress when the conversation occurs. This exception is rationalized on the ground that the public benefit advanced by protecting marital communication is minimal, if not nonexistent, when spouses exploit their privacy to plan or perform criminal acts.

The third exception allows persons who overhear marital communications to testify about what the spouses said to each other. A number of courts and commentators, however, recognize an exception to this exception when the third party is able to overhear the conversation only through the connivance or treachery of one spouse "setting up" the other. This third exception, and its sub-exception, will be discussed below in greater detail.

III. Specific Applications of the Marital Communications Privilege

A. Whether the wife may testify regarding the conversations

Jake Neal argues that his marital privilege precludes his wife's testifying about what he said in the conversations. The parties agree that Jake and Marcia Neal are presently married, have been married for nearly fifteen years, and were married when the questioned conversations occurred. Nor is there any dispute that, as to his statements, the defendant as the communicator is the holder of the privilege, and that his wife's willingness to testify does not, by itself, abrogate his privilege.

The government contends that Mrs. Neal may testify to the substance of the conversations because: (1) the conversations occurred in the "presence" of a third party, the FBI agent who monitored the call, and (2) the conversations related to present or future crimes, and thus are not protected by the privilege.

I conclude that the "presence-of-a-third-party" exception is inapplicable here. The rationale behind this exception is that a spouse's willingness to speak to the other spouse, knowing that a third party is present, indicates an intent that the communication not be confidential. Here, however, there is no evidence that Mr. Neal, who asserts the privilege, knew that a third party was on the telephone line. Absent some showing that the defendant was aware that someone besides his wife was listening, the government cannot overcome the presumption of confidentiality that attaches to marital communications.

Nothing in the tapes indicates that Mr. Neal knew of the agent's eavesdropping. In fact, his conduct during the conversations strongly indicates that he intended his statements to his wife to be confidential. He kept his voice low and changed telephones, apparently to prevent being overheard by persons near the phone into which he was speaking. Nor is there any indication in the tapes that he suspected his wife had become a government agent.

I find that the government's second argument, relying on the present and future crimes exception, also must fail. My review *in camera* of the tapes indicates that the recorded conversations contain no evidence of either future crimes, or crimes in progress when the conversations took place. Such a connection, however, may not be obvious. For that reason, I do not foreclose the government from offering such evidence if it exists, i.e., if further foundation evidence should place these conversations within the exception here under discussion, they may be admitted. For example, if Mrs. Neal's testimony at the trial establishes a future crime or crime in progress, her testimony may provide the predicate to bring these calls within the exception. [To prevent a mistrial,] the government shall inform defense counsel and the court before it attempts to elicit at trial any evidence of marital communications falling within this exception. In addition, counsel for both sides shall brief this issue in advance of trial so that a prompt ruling can be made in order to minimize trial delays for hearings outside the jury's presence. Of course, all such issues may be raised by motions in limine.

Absent the further foundation just discussed, Marcia Neal may not testify at trial regarding the substance of the telephone conversations between herself and her husband. As stated before, she may testify regarding matters not protected by the marital privilege.

B. Whether federal agents may testify regarding the telephone conversations

Neal contends that the FBI agent or agents who overheard and taped the telephone calls cannot testify about them because the eavesdropping was made possible only by his wife's cooperation, connivance, or betrayal. The government argues [that despite this] its agents should be permitted to testify to what was heard.

The parties agree that most jurisdictions permit a garden variety eavesdropper to testify to conversations between spouses. Although acknowledging that this rule breaches the protection normally accorded marital communications, most courts and commentators reason that excluding an eavesdropper's testimony unreasonably extends the marital communication privilege at the expense of unduly restricting the courts' ability to find the truth.

But this is not an ordinary eavesdropper case. Here Marcia Neal surreptitiously permitted government agents to listen to her three conversations with her husband. Further, she acted as an agent provocateur, baiting her husband with FBI questions calculated to elicit from him incriminating responses. In effect, a suspect was being interrogated by the FBI while he thought he was conversing privately with his wife. The wife's cooperation, purchased by promising her immunity, was essential to the FBI's hearing and recording the husband's admissions. In such circumstances, Neal argues, the FBI agent is no ordinary eavesdropper, but rather an agent of Mrs. Neal through whom she attempts to betray the marital confidences entrusted to her by her husband. Although Mrs. Neal clearly would not be permitted, over her husband's objection, thus to betray his confidences by courtroom testimony, defense counsel argues that she is attempting to accomplish the same purpose indirectly by out-of-court duplicity in permitting the FBI to listen to her husband's marital communications.

There is a paucity of authority in point and the few, mostly old, cases extant are not in agreement. Some courts have permitted the eavesdropper to testify even when one spouse has cooperated in making the eavesdropping possible. Apparently the majority, however, would exclude the testimony of an eavesdropper who learned of a marital confidence through a spouse's betrayal or connivance. The federal authorities that bear on this question seem to support the majority rule, insofar as they support either position.

The rationale for excluding such testimony when one spouse has participated in its acquisition is inherent in the reasons supporting the eavesdropper exception. The law refuses to suppress an ordinary eavesdropper's testimony since that testimony has no effect on one spouse's trust in the other. If an ordinary eavesdropper overhears a marital conversation, neither spouse can blame the other for breaching a confidence, and both are likely to continue imparting confidences, although they might become more cautious. When one spouse actively assists an eavesdropper who is seeking information to use against the other, a quite different situation is presented.

Such connivance, of course, destroys the betrayed spouse's feeling of trust toward his mate. From that point on there can be no real sense of marital privacy, no real sharing of secrets, no real mutual trust, no real marriage in the sense of sharing all. This undermining of mutual trust resulting in destruction of the marriage itself is the evil the rule of privileged communication seeks to prevent.

One who bares his soul in privacy to his wife should not have to fear that, unbeknownst to him, the communicator, his words spoken to his wife are being heard and recorded by the police for later use against him, all without a warrant or any kind of warning to him. Here the better-reasoned cases have weighed the societal value of greater police efficiency against the societal value of marital privacy, and have come down on the side of marriage.

For these reasons (subject to what was said above regarding evidence of future crimes or crimes in progress) no government agent may testify regarding the content of the conversations between Jake and Marcia Neal.

C. Whether the Tape Recordings are Admissible

The government has not contended that the tape recordings are admissible if neither the testimony of Mrs. Neal nor that of the FBI agent is admissible. Whether treated as mere replicas of Marcia Neal's and the agent's proposed testimony, or as a separate government "eavesdropper," the tapes clearly are not admissible.

Accordingly, it is ordered that, absent a further showing, the government may not introduce evidence of the substance of the conversations between the defendant Jake Keller Neal and Marcia Neal, whether by testimony of Marcia Neal or a government agent, or by tape recordings of those conversations.

NOTES AND QUESTIONS

(1) *Charting the Boundaries of Confidentiality.* Can a public act be privileged as confidential? See, e.g., *State v. Robbins*, 213 P.2d 310 (Wash. 1950), finding inadmissible testimony of a wife (divorced from him shortly before trial) that her husband waited in the automobile for her, but finding no error in admission of her testimony that (at the same time) she went to an office in the County-City building

in Seattle and applied for license plates and a certificate of title for a Pontiac automobile, signing "James Driscoll, By (wife) Mrs. June Driscoll" (which were fraudulent names). The Court noted:

> The statement that appellant was waiting outside in an automobile was testimony as to an act of the other spouse, as distinguished from testimony as to an oral or written communication. The privilege established by the statute does not ordinarily extend to testimony regarding the acts of the other spouse. For example, in a prosecution for the crime of rape, a divorced wife was permitted to testify that, on a certain occasion, she discovered her then husband in the act of sexual intercourse with her daughter, the complaining witness. Likewise, in a murder prosecution, a wife was permitted to testify that she discovered her husband dumping some object into a hole in which the deceased's body was found.
>
> However, there are circumstances under which testimony as to an act of the other spouse is clearly protected by the statutory privilege. Where the act is one which would not have been done by one spouse in the presence of, or with the knowledge of, the other but for the confidence between them by reason of the marital relation, testimony as to such act is inadmissible. The rule is stated as follows in 70 C.J. Witnesses: "The term 'communication,' within the meaning of the privileged communication rule, as to husband and wife should be given a liberal construction and is not confined to mere audible communications or conversations between the spouses, but embraces all facts which have come to his or her knowledge or under his or her observation in consequence or by reason of the confidence of the marital relation, and which but for the confidence growing out of it would not have been known. It includes knowledge communicated by an act, which would not have been done by one spouse in the presence of, or within the sight of, the other, but for the confidence between them by reason of the marital relation . . . ."
>
> It might at first be supposed that appellant's act of waiting in an automobile in sight of all on a public thoroughfare, was not an act done in reliance upon the confidence established by the marital relation. He was apparently willing to be seen by the public, including acquaintances who might be passing by. The reason he was not afraid of being seen by the general public, however, was that it was unlikely that this would result in connecting appellant with the transaction then taking place inside the building. But his wife knew why he was waiting there, and was accordingly in a position to disclose appellant's connection with the transaction then in progress. It is obvious that he would not have waited in the automobile had he not relied upon the confidence between them by reason of the marital relation. The testimony of the witness as to appellant's act of waiting was accordingly inadmissible.
>
> We reach a different conclusion with respect to the witness' testimony that she applied for license plates and a certificate of title. Disassociated from her further testimony that her husband was waiting outside in the car, her statement that she made this application was testimony concerning the

> witness' own act. It was not testimony as to a communication between husband and wife.
>
> If the witness had testified that she was authorized by her husband to file the application, that would have been testimony as to a communication. But she did not do so. It is true that the application, which had already been placed in evidence, was signed "James Driscoll, By (wife) Mrs. June Driscoll," and that [the witness] testified that she signed in that manner. From this the jury was undoubtedly expected to conclude, and may well have concluded, that [she] was in fact authorized by her husband. But this would be a conclusion based upon an inference — not upon the witness' direct testimony. She did not testify as to the truth of any representation contained in the application.
>
> We are not willing to extend the rule of privileged marital communications to the point where it is necessary to hold testimony as to a witness' own acts inadmissible if the jury might infer therefrom a communication between husband and wife.

See also State v. Robinson, 376 S.E.2d 606 (W. Va. 1988) (defendant's actions in growing marijuana in presence of his wife were undertaken in reliance on confidentiality of marital relation, and thus wife could not testify about her observations in prosecution of defendant for manufacturing controlled substance).

(4) *Various Tests for Determining what Acts are Privileged. Curran v. Pasek*, 886 P.2d 272 (Wyo. 1994), explains how at least some courts determine whether acts are privileged:

> Courts apply one of two tests in determining whether certain conduct qualifies as a confidential marital communication: the "expectation test" and the "intentions test." The "expectation test" asks whether the conduct was undertaken in reliance on the confidences of the marital relationship, i.e., whether there was an expectation of confidentiality. The "intentions test" asks whether the conduct was intended to communicate a confidential message to the other spouse . . . .
>
> We find the rationale underlying the "intentions test" persuasive and adopt it as the rule in Wyoming. This test treats assertive conduct that is intended to communicate a confidential message from one spouse to another as a confidential marital communication. Conduct that is undertaken in reliance on the confidence of the marital relationship, i.e., with an expectation of confidentiality, is not necessarily considered a confidential marital communication.
>
> The rationale for the intentions test is succinctly characterized in *Hannuksela* as follows: if "the husband is indifferent to the presence of the wife — there is no communication and the marital confidence aspect of the act is likely to be slight. In such cases the privilege should not be allowed to deprive the court of the evidence." The court concluded:
>
> In this case, the acts which Granthum observed and testified about at trial fall into the nonassertive category. She testified she observed that (1)

appellant concealed a shotgun in his jacket, (2) he later had Nelson's keys, instant cash card, and unexplained cash, (3) he unloaded Nelson's belongings from the pickup, (4) he entered a building at Point Douglas Park, and (5) he walked in the woods, along a railroad track, near Gilbert. In the context of the circumstances surrounding each of these events, it is difficult to characterize any of appellant's actions as being assertive in nature. Therefore, we conclude the trial court correctly ruled that the interspousal communication privilege was not applicable to bar Granthum's testimony.

Are the following acts privileged?: A wife's act of placing a gun in a drawer, seen (unbeknownst to her) by her husband (a) where she locks the drawer and takes the only key; (b) where she leaves the drawer unlocked; and (c) where, instead of placing it in a drawer, she places it on the dresser top? Be prepared to argue both ways. Does it make a difference which approach is adopted?

(5) *Testimony of Third Parties Who Overhear Privileged Conversations. Compare Neal* with *Nash v. Fidelity-Phenix Fire Ins. Co.*, 146 S.E. 726 (W. Va. 1929). Plaintiff, Roy Nash, sued the insurance company on a fire policy. The defense of the company was arson. Judgment went for plaintiff, and the defendant company appealed. On this appeal, the court said:

The defendant assigns as error the action of the trial court in rejecting the testimony of Mrs. Roy Nash, who stated that a few days prior to the fire her husband, during the course of a conversation had with her at their home, said: "Before he would let the creditors come in on him and close him out, he would burn the damn thing." She stated that, because of previous discussions had with her husband in this regard, she knew that he had reference to the burning of the store. This conversation took place about 11 o'clock at night while Roy Nash and his wife were in their bedroom preparing to retire. A Miss Blankenship, who was then boarding in the home and clerking in Nash's store, was in a nursery room with the Nash children across the hall, and about 10 feet away. She testified that she heard Nash say [it] in a loud tone of voice. The door of the Nash bedroom was open on this occasion, and Mrs. Nash said she heard Miss Blankenship moving around in the room across the hall.

We are of the opinion that the trial court ruled correctly in excluding the testimony of Mrs. Nash regarding the alleged statement. It was clearly a confidential and privileged communication made by the husband to his wife. Defendant contends, however, that the conversation was not privileged, because it was made in the presence of a third person. An examination of the authorities has failed to reveal a single case in which a wife has been permitted to testify to a conversation taking place between her and her husband in the alleged presence of a third person, unless the husband, in making the communication to his wife, was aware of such presence. It is not shown in the instant case that the husband knew that Miss Blankenship was listening to their conversation. It was late at night, and the statement attributed to him was made in the privacy of his bedchamber.

> However, we are of opinion that the court did rule erroneously in rejecting the testimony of Miss Blankenship. For, even though a conversation between a husband and wife was intended to be confidential, a third person who overheard it, whether his presence was known or not, may testify as to what was said. The rejection of this evidence was prejudicial to the defendant, and is reversible error.

Would the result have been the same in *Nash* if Mr. Nash had been more careful in trying to prevent the third party (Miss Blankenship) from getting access to the communication?

(6) *Does the Presence of Children Break the Privilege?* On the effect of a child of the family having access to an interspousal communication, see *Hopkins v. Grimshaw*, 165 U.S. 342 (1897) (presence of 13- or 14-year-old child did not defeat privilege concerning testimony of spouses, but child (now grown) could testify to overheard statement). Modern cases look to whether the child was old enough to understand the statement or participated in the conversation. If so, the privilege typically is defeated. *See People v. Sanders*, 443 N.E.2d 687 (Ill. App. Ct. 1982).

(7) *Impeachment.* For the general suggestion by at least one view that privileged spousal communications can be used to impeach the communicator's testimony to facts contrary to those stated in the communication, see *United States v. Neal*, 743 F.2d 1441 (10th Cir. 1984) (especially Judge Logan's concurrence), *cert. denied*, 470 U.S. 1086 (1985).

(8) *Should Privilege be Extended to Other Relationships?* Would the rationale of the husband-wife privileges suggest there should be a parent-child privilege? A brother-sister privilege? A friend-friend privilege? A same-sex couple privilege? Only where same-sex marriage is recognized and they have entered into it?

(11) *Is a Statement Made While Committing a Criminal Act Against a Spouse Privileged?* In *People v. Johnson*, 233 Cal. App. 3d 425 (Cal. Ct. App. 1991), *cert. denied*, 503 U.S. 963 (1992), a statement by defendant, made while beating his second wife, that what happened to his first wife would happen to her, was properly admitted in connection with the alleged murder of his first wife. The court found that the "essence of a confidential communication between spouses is that it springs from the confidence which exists between them because of the marital relationship." This public policy consideration would not be served by shielding threats made by one spouse in the course of criminally victimizing the other spouse.

HUSBAND-WIFE PRIVILEGE REVIEW PROBLEM SET 13C.

Consider the following problems in the light of what you have learned about husband-wife privileges:

(1) *Distinction Between the Two Spousal Privileges.* Why, in law and policy, didn't the *other* marital privilege (the adverse spousal testimony privilege) apply in *Neal* (our principal case in subsection [B], Marital Communications, immediately *supra*) and in *Robbins* (in note (3) following *Neal, supra*)?

(2) *Statutory Wording.* In *Robbins*, set forth in note (3) following *Neal, supra*, the jurisdiction's marital privilege statute read:

- A husband shall not be examined for or against his wife without the consent of the wife, nor a wife for or against her husband without the consent of the husband;
- Nor shall either, during marriage or afterwards, without the consent of the other, be examined as to any communication made by one to the other during marriage.
- But these exceptions to the duty to give evidence shall not apply to a civil action or proceeding by one against the other, nor to a criminal action or proceeding for a crime committed by one against the other.

Does this help you answer question (1) above in part? More importantly, bearing in mind among other things, that all privileges are an exception to the principal that all witnesses may be compelled by a court to give evidence, do you see a number of ways in which a literal application of this statute could have very perverse results? Notice also that there is no requirement on the face of the statute requiring that the conversation be "confidential" (or "marital" which some courts deem to mean "confidential"). Could this cause pernicious results?

(3) *Unconventional Relationship.* A and B are joined in a gay civil union ceremony, though they know they are very different sorts of people: A is very "flexible" about obeying the law, whereas B often turns people in for even minor infractions. Some time after their gay civil union, A says, rather shamefacedly, to B (after being told that their friend Frobish's car had been seen with two people inside speeding away from a bank robbery loaded with stacks of money), "I was driving Frobish's car." This is offered, via the on-the-stand testimony of B, against Frobish in a prosecution of Frobish for participating in the scheme to rob the bank. Consider not only the privilege issue, but also whether this could survive the hearsay rule and any other rules of evidence you deem applicable.

§ 13.04 PHYSICIAN-PATIENT PRIVILEGE[15]

(1) *Why Physician-Patient Privilege Has Met with Resistance.* For discussion of the general physician-patient privilege, see Judge Weinstein's decision in *United States ex rel. Edney v. Smith*, 425 F. Supp. 1038 (E.D.N.Y. 1976), *aff'd*, 556 F.2d 556 (2d Cir.), *cert. denied*, 431 U.S. 958 (1977), in which he observed:

> The physician-patient relationship, unlike that of attorney-client, did not give rise to a testimonial privilege at common law; a physician called as a witness had a duty to disclose all information obtained from a patient. In 1828 New York became the first jurisdiction to alter the common-law rule by establishing a statutory privilege. Since that time approximately three-quarters of the states have followed New York's lead and enacted similar statutory provisions.

Legal scholars have been virtually unanimous in their condemnation of these legislative attempts to foster the doctor-patient relationship by rules of exclusion.

---

[15] Study Guide Reference: Evidence in a Nutshell, Chapter 5:V at "Definition of the Physician-Patient Privilege" and "Exceptions and Limits."

They repeatedly argue that while the adverse impact of the privilege on the fact-finding function of the courts is immediate and unquestionable, empirical evidence of the alleged benefits of the privilege is speculative at best and more realistically non-existent. Professor Chafee's well-known criticism is typical:

> The reasons usually advanced for extending the privilege of silence to the medical profession are not wholly satisfactory. First, it is said that if the patient knows that his confidences may be divulged in future litigation he will hesitate in many cases to get needed medical aid. But although the man who consults a lawyer usually has litigation in mind, men very rarely go to a doctor with any such thought. And even if they did, medical treatment is so valuable that few would lose it to prevent facts from coming to light in court. Indeed, it may be doubted whether, except for a small range of disgraceful or peculiarly private matters, patients worry much about having a doctor keep their private affairs concealed from the world. This whole argument that the privilege is necessary to induce persons to see a doctor sounds like a philosopher's speculation on how men may logically be expected to behave rather than the result of observation of the way men actually behave. Not a single New England state allows the doctor to keep silent on the witness stand. Is there evidence that any ill or injured person in New England has ever stayed from a doctor's office on that account?
>
> The same a priori quality vitiates a second argument concerning the evils of compelling medical testimony, namely, that a strong sense of professional honor will prompt perversion or concealment of the truth. Has any member of the numerous medical societies in New England observed such a tendency among New England doctors to commit perjury for the sake of "professional honor"?

Chafee, *Privileged Communications: Is Justice Served or Obstructed by Closing the Doctor's Mouth on the Witness Stand?*, 52 YALE L.J. 607, 609–10 (1943).

Legal practice in the states which have adopted a general medical privilege confirms the criticism of the commentators. Although no state has repealed the privilege once it has been adopted, recognition of its undesirable effects has led to judicial and legislative whittling away so that its scope has been considerably reduced. Numerous nonuniform exceptions have evolved which have rendered the privilege substantially impotent and difficult to administer.

In the federal sphere awareness of these difficulties led the Advisory Committee on the Federal Rules of Evidence to omit any provision for a general physician-patient privilege. It noted that:

> [While] many states have by statute created the privilege, the exceptions which have been found necessary in order to obtain information required by the public interest or to avoid fraud are so numerous as to leave little if any basis for the privilege.

Does the existence of the hearsay exception for statements relating to medical diagnosis and treatment corroborate the point made by Prof. Chaffee that patients don't need an incentive to tell their doctors the complete truth?

(2) *Exceptions to the Physician-Patient Privilege.* Exceptions vary. The Federal Advisory Committee Note (mentioned above) lists some commonly found among the state physician-patient privileges:

> Among the exclusions from the statutory privilege, the following may be enumerated: communications not made for purposes of diagnosis and treatment; commitment and restoration proceedings; issues as to wills or otherwise between parties claiming by succession from the patient; actions on insurance policies; required reports (venereal diseases, gunshot wounds, child abuse); communications in furtherance of crime or fraud; mental or physical condition put in issue by patient (personal injury cases); malpractice actions; and some or all criminal prosecutions. California, for example, excepts cases in which the patient puts his condition in issue, all criminal proceedings, will and similar contests, malpractice cases, and disciplinary proceedings, as well as certain other situations, thus leaving virtually nothing covered by the privilege.

(3) *Critiques of Supreme Court Draft.* The Supreme Court Draft is discussed in Rothstein, *The Proposed Amendments to the Federal Rules of Evidence*, 62 GEO. L.J. 125 (1973). The article argues for a defined set of federal privileges and suggests that there might be some value to minimizing differences between state and federal privilege law. The conclusion is that the Federal Rules of Evidence should contain a general physician-patient privilege. However, federal cases still resist the privilege. *See Patterson v. Caterpillar, Inc.*, 70 F.3d 503 (7th Cir. 1995) (rejecting a general physician-patient privilege). There are, however, also a few federal cases that seem to approve a general doctor-patient privilege. The most that can be said is that federal law on this privilege is inconclusive but leans toward non-recognition.

§ 13.05 PSYCHOTHERAPIST AND SOCIAL WORKER PRIVILEGES[16]

Uniform Rules of Evidence (as Amended 1999) [Recommended Model Provisions for States: Not Part of the Federal Rules]:[17]

---

[16] Study Guide Reference: Evidence in a Nutshell, Chapter 5:V at "Evolution or Adoption of a Psychotherapist Privilege and Its Limits."

[17] The brackets within the rule and its title (that is, within the box) indicate that the drafters mean the various versions of the privilege to be optional with the adopting state. But you will note that some version of mental diagnosis/treatment privilege (either a psychotherapist or a broader mental-health provider privilege) is included in each of the options offered and that it is only the general physician-patient privilege, covering physical diagnosis/treatment, that is truly optional.

Rule 503. [Psychothrapist] [Physician and Psychotherapist] [Physician and Mental-Health Provider] [Mental-Health Provider] — Patient Privilege

(a) Definitions. In this rule:

(1) A communication is "confidential" if it is not intended to be disclosed to third persons, except those present to further the interest of the patient in the consultation, examination, or interview, those reasonably necessary for the transmission of the communication, and persons who are participating in the diagnosis and treatment of the patient under the direction of a [psychotherapist] [physician or psychotherapist] [physician or mental-health provider] [mental-health provider], including members of the patient's family.

[**(2)** "Mental-health provider" means a person authorized, in any State or country, or reasonably believed by the patient to be authorized, to engage in the diagnosis or treatment of a mental or emotional condition, including addiction to alcohol or drugs.]

(3) "Patient" means an individual who consults or is examined or interviewed by a [psychotherapist] [physician or psychotherapist] [physician or mental-health provider] [mental-health provider].

[**(4)** "Physician" means a person authorized in any State or country, or reasonably believed by the patient to be authorized to practice medicine.]

[**(5)** "Psychotherapist" means a person authorized in any State or country, or reasonably believed by the patient to be authorized, to practice medicine, while engaged in the diagnosis or treatment of a mental or emotional condition, including addiction to alcohol or drugs, or a person licensed or certified under the laws of any State or country, or reasonably believed by the patient to be licensed or certified, as a psychologist, while similarly engaged.]

(b) General rule of privilege. A patient has a privilege to refuse to disclose and to prevent any other person from disclosing confidential communications made for the purpose of diagnosis or treatment of the patient's [physical,] mental[,] or emotional condition, including addiction to alcohol or drugs, among the patient, the patient's [psychotherapist] [physician or psychotherapist] [physician or mental-health provider] [mental-health provider] and persons, including members of the patient's family, who are participating in the diagnosis or treatment under the direction of the [psychotherapist] [physician or psychotherapist] [physician or mental-health provider] [mental-health provider].

(c) Who may claim the privilege. The privilege under this rule may be claimed by the patient, the patient's guardian or conservator, or the personal representative of a deceased patient. The person who was the [psychotherapist] [physician or psychotherapist] [physician or mental-health provider] [mental-health provider] at the time of the communication is presumed to have authority to claim the privilege, but only on behalf of the patient.

(d) Exceptions. There is no privilege under this rule for a communication:

(1) relevant to an issue in proceedings to hospitalize the patient for mental illness, if the [psychotherapist] [physician or psychotherapist] [physician or mental-health provider] [mental-health provider], in the course of diagnosis or treatment, has determined that the patient is in need of hospitalization;

(2) made in the course of a court-ordered investigation or examination of the [physical,] mental[,] or emotional condition of the patient, whether a party or a witness, with respect to the particular purpose for which the examination is ordered, unless the court orders otherwise;

(3) relevant to an issue of the [physical,] mental[,] or emotional condition of the patient in any proceeding in which the patient relies upon the condition as an element of the patient's claim or defense or, after the patient's death, in any proceeding in which any party relies upon the condition as an element of the party's claim or defense;

(4) if the services of the [psychotherapist] [physician or psychotherapist] [physician or mental-health provider] [mental-health provider] were sought or obtained to enable or aid anyone to commit or plan to commit what the patient knew, or reasonably should have known, was a crime or fraud or mental or physical injury to the patient or another individual;

(5) in which the patient has expressed an intent to engage in conduct likely to result in imminent death or serious bodily injury to the patient or another individual;

(6) relevant to an issue in a proceeding challenging the competency of the [psychotherapist] [physician or psychotherapist] [physician or mental-health provider] [mental-health provider];

(7) relevant to a breach of duty by the [psychotherapist] [physician or psychotherapist] [physician or mental-health provider] [mental-health provider]; or

(8) that is subject to a duty to disclose under [statutory law].

JAFFEE v. REDMOND

United States Supreme Court
518 U.S. 1 (1996)

JUSTICE STEVENS delivered the opinion of the Court.

After a traumatic incident in which she shot and killed a man, a police officer received extensive counseling from a licensed clinical social worker. [T]he question is whether it is appropriate for federal courts to recognize a "psychotherapist privilege" under Rule 501 of the Federal Rules of Evidence.

I

[Mary Lu Redmond was a police officer of the Village of Hoffman Estates who responded to a "fight in progress" call. At the scene, Redmond testified to immediate reports of a stabbing, to a man waving a pipe, and to Ricky Allen chasing another man with a butcher knife; she testified she drew her revolver when the men ignored her orders, and she shot and killed Allen, she said, when she believed he was about to stab the other man. A hostile crowd gathered before her backup arrived.]

[Ricky Allen's administrator and family ("petitioners") filed a federal suit, asserting § 1983 and state-law claims. They presented testimony contradicting Redmond in several respects, most notably by the claim that Allen was unarmed.]

[During discovery, petitioners learned that Redmond had participated in about 50 counseling sessions with Karen Beyer, a licensed clinical social worker employed by the Village. They sought production of Beyer's notes. Respondents resisted by asserting the existence of a patient- psychotherapist privilege. The trial judge refused to recognize the privilege and ordered discovery. Respondents still refused production, and the trial judge ultimately instructed the jury that since the refusal was without "legal justification," the jury could presume that Beyer's notes were unfavorable to Redmond. The jury returned a verdict for petitioners totaling more than $500,000.]

[The Seventh Circuit reversed. It concluded, for the first time, that "reason and experience," which are the Fed. R. Evid. 501 touchstones for acceptance of a privilege, compelled recognition of the patient-psychotherapist privilege. But the Seventh Circuit qualified the privilege by stating that it would not apply if, "in the interest of justice, the evidentiary need for the disclosure . . . outweighs that patient's privacy interests," a qualification that did not apply in this case because of the number of eyewitnesses and the strength of Officer Redmond's privacy interests. Here, the Supreme Court upholds the Seventh Circuit's reversal, but it justifies and limits the privilege differently.]

II

Rule 501 of the Federal Rules of Evidence authorizes federal courts to define new privileges by interpreting "common law principles . . . in the light of reason and experience." [T]he Senate Report accompanying the 1975 adoption of the Rules indicates that Rule 501 "should be understood as reflecting the view that the recognition of a privilege based on a confidential relationship . . . should be determined on a case-by-case basis." The Rule thus did not freeze the law governing the privileges of witnesses in federal trials at a particular point in our history, but rather directed federal courts to "continue the evolutionary development of testimonial privileges." *Trammel v. United States*, 445 U.S. 40, 47 (1980); see also *University of Pennsylvania v. EEOC*, 493 U.S. 182, 189 (1990).

The common-law principles underlying the recognition of testimonial privileges can be stated simply. " 'For more than three centuries it has now been recognized as a fundamental maxim that the public . . . has a right to every man's evidence. When we come to examine the various claims of exemption, we start with the primary assumption that there is a general duty to give what testimony one is capable of giving, and that any exemptions which may exist are distinctly exceptional, being so many derogations from a positive general rule.' " *United States v. Bryan*, 339 U.S. 323, 331 (1950). *See also United States v. Nixon*, 418 U.S. 683, 709 (1974). Exceptions from the general rule disfavoring testimonial privileges may be justified, however, by a "public good transcending the normally predominant principle of utilizing all rational means for ascertaining the truth." *Trammel.*

III

Like the spousal and attorney-client privileges, the psychotherapist-patient privilege is "rooted in the imperative need for confidence and trust." *Trammel.* . . . Treatment by a physician for physical ailments can often proceed successfully on the basis of a physical examination, objective information supplied by the patient, and the results of diagnostic tests. Effective psychotherapy, by contrast, depends upon an atmosphere of confidence and trust in which the patient is willing to make a frank and complete disclosure of facts, emotions, memories, and fears. [A]s the Judicial Conference Advisory Committee observed in 1972 when it recommended that Congress recognize a psychotherapist privilege as part of the Proposed Federal Rules of Evidence, a psychiatrist's ability to help her patients:

> is completely dependent upon [the patients'] willingness and ability to talk freely. This makes it difficult if not impossible for [a psychiatrist] to function without being able to assure . . . patients of confidentiality and, indeed, privileged communication. Where there may be exceptions to this general rule . . . , there is wide agreement that confidentiality is a *sine qua non* for successful psychiatric treatment.

By protecting confidential communications between a psychotherapist and her patient from involuntary disclosure, the proposed privilege thus serves important private interests.

Our cases make clear that an asserted privilege must also "serv[e] public ends." *Upjohn Co. v. United States*, 449 U.S. 383, 389 (1981). Thus, the purpose of the attorney-client privilege is to "encourage full and frank communication between attorneys and their clients and thereby promote broader public interests in the observance of law and administration of justice." *Ibid.* And the spousal privilege, as modified in *Trammel*, is justified because it "furthers the important public interest in marital harmony." The psychotherapist privilege serves the public interest by facilitating the provision of appropriate treatment for individuals suffering the effects of a mental or emotional problem.[10]

In contrast to the significant public and private interests supporting recognition of the privilege, the likely evidentiary benefit that would result from the denial of the privilege is modest. If the privilege were rejected, confidential conversations between psychotherapists and their patients would surely be chilled, particularly when it is obvious that the circumstances that give rise to the need for treatment will probably result in litigation. Without a privilege, much of the desirable evidence to which litigants such as petitioner seek access — for example, admissions against interest by a party — is unlikely to come into being. This unspoken "evidence" will therefore serve no greater truth-seeking function than if it had been spoken and privileged.

That it is appropriate for the federal courts to recognize a psychotherapist privilege under Rule 501 is confirmed by the fact that all 50 States and the District of Columbia have enacted into law some form of psychotherapist privilege. Because state legislatures are fully aware of the need to protect the integrity of the factfinding functions of their courts, the existence of a consensus among the States indicates that "reason and experience" support recognition of the privilege. In addition, given the importance of the patient's understanding that her communications with her therapist will not be publicly disclosed, any State's promise of confidentiality would have little value if the patient were aware that the privilege would not be honored in a federal court.[13]

[W]e hold that confidential communications between a licensed psychotherapist and her patients in the course of diagnosis or treatment are protected from compelled disclosure under Rule 501 of the Federal Rules of Evidence.

IV

All agree that a psychotherapist privilege covers confidential communications made to licensed psychiatrists and psychologists. We have no hesitation in concluding in this case that the federal privilege should also extend to confidential communications made to licensed social workers in the course of psychotherapy. The reasons for recognizing a privilege for treatment by psychiatrists and psychologists apply with equal force to treatment by a clinical social worker such as Karen Beyer. Today, social workers provide a significant amount of mental health treatment. Their clients often include the poor and those of modest means who could not afford the assistance of a psychiatrist or psychologist, but whose

---

[10] This case amply demonstrates the importance of allowing individuals to receive confidential counseling. [T]he entire community may suffer if police officers are not able to receive effective counseling and treatment after traumatic incidents, either because trained officers leave the profession prematurely or because those in need of treatment remain on the job.

[13] [Petitioner] discounts the relevance of the state privilege statutes by pointing to divergence among the States concerning the types of therapy relationships protected and the exceptions recognized. A small number of state statutes, for example, grant the privilege only to psychiatrists and psychologists, while most apply the protection more broadly . . . . The range of exceptions recognized by the States is similarly varied.

counseling sessions serve the same public goals. Perhaps in recognition of these circumstances, the vast majority of States explicitly extend a testimonial privilege to licensed social workers.

We part company with the Court of Appeals on a separate point. We reject the balancing component of the privilege implemented by that court and a small number of States. [A]s we explained in *Upjohn*, if the purpose of the privilege is to be served, the participants in the confidential conversation "must be able to predict with some degree of certainty whether particular discussions will be protected. An uncertain privilege, or one which purports to be certain but results in widely varying applications by the courts, is little better than no privilege at all."

These considerations are all that is necessary for decision of this case. A rule that authorizes the recognition of new privileges on a case-by-case basis makes it appropriate to define the details of new privileges in a like manner. Because this is the first case in which we have recognized a psychotherapist privilege, it is neither necessary nor feasible to delineate its full contours in a way that would "govern all conceivable future questions in this area."[19]

V

The conversations between Officer Redmond and Karen Beyer and the notes taken during their counseling sessions are protected from compelled disclosure under Rule 501 of the Federal Rules of Evidence.

The judgment of the Court of Appeals is affirmed.

JUSTICE SCALIA, with whom CHIEF JUSTICE REHNQUIST joins as to Part III, dissenting:

The Court has discussed at some length the benefit that will be purchased by creation of the evidentiary privilege in this case: the encouragement of psychoanalytic counseling. It has not mentioned the purchase price: occasional injustice. That is the cost of every rule which excludes reliable and probative evidence — or at least every one categorical enough to achieve its announced policy objective. In the case of some of these rules, such as the one excluding confessions that have not been properly "Mirandized," see *Miranda v. Arizona*, 384 U.S. 436 (1966), the victim of the injustice is always the impersonal State or the faceless "public at large." For the rule proposed here, the victim is more likely to be some individual who is prevented from proving a valid claim — or (worse still) prevented from establishing a valid defense.

Testimonial privileges "*are not lightly created nor expansively construed*, for they are in derogation of the search for truth." *United States v. Nixon* (emphasis added). Adherence to that principle has caused us, in the Rule 501 cases we have considered to date, to reject new privileges, see *University of Pennsylvania v.*

[19] Although it would be premature to speculate about most future developments in the federal psychotherapist privilege, we do not doubt that there are situations in which the privilege must give way, for example, if a serious threat of harm to the patient or to others can be averted only by means of a disclosure by the therapist.

EEOC, 493 U.S. 182 (1990) (privilege against disclosure of academic peer review materials); *United States v. Gillock*, 445 U.S. 360 (1980) (privilege against disclosure of "legislative acts" by member of state legislature), and even to construe narrowly the scope of existing privileges, *see, e.g., United States v. Zolin*, 491 U.S. 554, 568-570 (1989) (permitting in camera review of documents alleged to come within crime-fraud exception to attorney-client privilege); *Trammel, supra* (holding that voluntary testimony by spouse is not covered by husband-wife privilege). The Court today ignores this traditional judicial preference for the truth, and ends up creating a privilege that is new, vast, and ill-defined. I respectfully dissent.

I

[T]he Court makes its task deceptively simple by the manner in which it proceeds. It begins by characterizing the issue as "whether it is appropriate for federal courts to recognize a 'psychotherapist privilege,' " and devotes almost all of its opinion to that question. Having answered that question (to its satisfaction) in the affirmative, it then devotes *less than a page of text* to answering in the affirmative the small remaining question whether "the federal privilege should also extend to confidential communications made to licensed social workers in the course of psychotherapy."

[I]t seems a long step from a lawyer-client privilege to a tax advisor-client or accountant-client privilege. But if one recharacterizes it as a "legal advisor" privilege, the extension seems like the most natural thing in the world. That is the illusion the Court has produced here: It first frames an overly general question ("Should there be a psychotherapist privilege?") that can be answered in the negative only by excluding from protection office consultations with professional psychiatrists (*i.e.*, doctors) and clinical psychologists. And then, having answered that in the affirmative, it comes to the *only* question that the facts of this case present ("Should there be a social worker-client privilege with regard to psychotherapeutic counseling?") with the answer seemingly a foregone conclusion.

The [Rules Advisory] Committee did indeed recommend a "psychotherapist privilege" of sorts; but more precisely, and more relevantly, it recommended a privilege for psychotherapy conducted by "a person authorized to practice medicine" or "a person licensed or certified as a psychologist," which is to say that *it recommended against the privilege at issue here.*

II

To say that the Court devotes the bulk of its opinion to the much easier question of psychotherapist-patient privilege is not to say that its answer to that question is convincing. [E]ffective psychotherapy undoubtedly is beneficial to individuals with mental problems, and surely serves some larger social interest in maintaining a mentally stable society. But merely mentioning these values does not answer the critical question: are they of such importance, and is the contribution of psychotherapy to them so distinctive, and is the application of normal evidentiary rules so destructive to psychotherapy, as to justify making our federal courts occasional instruments of injustice? On that central question I find the Court's analysis insufficiently convincing to satisfy the high standard we have set for rules that "are in derogation of the search for truth."

When is it, one must wonder, that *the psychotherapist* came to play such an indispensable role in the maintenance of the citizenry's mental health? For most of history, men and women have worked out their difficulties by talking to, *inter alios*, parents, siblings, best friends and bartenders — none of whom was awarded a privilege against testifying in court. Ask the average citizen: Would your mental health be more significantly impaired by preventing you from seeing a psychotherapist, or by preventing you from getting advice from your mom? I have little doubt what the answer would be. Yet there is no mother-child privilege.

How likely is it that a person will be deterred from seeking psychological counseling, or from being completely truthful in the course of such counseling, because of fear of later disclosure in litigation? And even more pertinent to today's decision, to what extent will the evidentiary privilege reduce that deterrent? The Court does not try to answer the first of these questions; and it *cannot possibly have any notion* of what the answer is to the second, since that depends entirely upon the scope of the privilege, which the Court amazingly finds it "neither necessary nor feasible to delineate." If, for example, the psychotherapist can give the patient no more assurance than "A court will not be able to make me disclose what you tell me, unless you tell me about a harmful act," I doubt whether there would be much benefit from the privilege at all. That is not a fanciful example, at least with respect to extension of the psychotherapist privilege to social workers. *See* Del. Code Ann., Tit. 24, § 3913(2) (1987); Idaho Code § 54-3213(2) (1994).

Even where it is certain that absence of the psychotherapist privilege will inhibit disclosure of the information, it is not clear to me that that is an unacceptable state of affairs. Let us assume the very worst in the circumstances of the present case: that to be truthful about what was troubling her, the police officer who sought counseling would have to confess that she shot without reason, and wounded an innocent man. If (again to assume the worst) such an act constituted the crime of negligent wounding under Illinois law, the officer would of course have the absolute right not to admit that she shot without reason in criminal court. But I see no reason why she should be enabled *both* not to admit it in criminal court (as a good citizen should), and to get the benefits of psychotherapy by admitting it to a therapist who cannot tell anyone else.

The Court confidently asserts that not much truth-finding capacity would be destroyed by the privilege anyway, since "[w]ithout a privilege, much of the desirable evidence to which litigants such as petitioner seek access . . . is unlikely to come into being." If that is so, how come psychotherapy got to be a thriving practice before the "psychotherapist privilege" was invented? Were the patients paying money to lie to their analysts all those years?

The Court suggests one last policy justification: since psychotherapist privilege statutes exist in all the States, the failure to recognize a privilege in federal courts "would frustrate the purposes of the state legislation that was enacted to foster these confidential communications." This is a novel argument indeed. A sort of inverse pre-emption: the truth-seeking functions of *federal* courts must be adjusted so as not to conflict with the policies *of the States*.

The Court's failure to put forward a convincing justification of its own could perhaps be excused if it were relying upon the unanimous conclusion of state courts in the reasoned development of their common law. It cannot do that, since *no* State has such a privilege apart from legislation.

And the phrase "some form of psychotherapist privilege" covers a multitude of difficulties. The Court concedes that there is "divergence among the States concerning the types of therapy relationships protected and the exceptions recognized." [T]he state laws vary to such a degree that the parties and lower federal judges confronted by the new "common law" have barely a clue as to what its content might be.

III

Turning from the general question that was not involved in this case to the specific one that is: The Court's conclusion that a social-worker psychotherapeutic privilege deserves recognition is even less persuasive. In approaching this question, the fact that five of the state legislatures that have seen fit to enact "some form" of psychotherapist privilege have elected not to extend *any* form of privilege to social workers, ought to give one pause. So should the fact that the Judicial Conference Advisory Committee was similarly discriminating in its conferral of the proposed Rule 504 privilege.

A licensed psychiatrist or psychologist is an expert in psychotherapy — and that may suffice (though I think it not so clear that this Court should make the judgment) to justify the use of extraordinary means to encourage counseling with him, as opposed to counseling with one's rabbi, minister, family or friends. One must presume that a social worker does *not* bring this greatly heightened degree of skill to bear, which is alone a reason for not encouraging that consultation as generously. Does a social worker bring to bear at least a significantly heightened degree of skill — more than a minister or rabbi, for example? I have no idea, and neither does the Court.

Another critical distinction between psychiatrists and psychologists, on the one hand, and social workers, on the other, is that the former professionals, in their consultations with patients, *do nothing but psychotherapy*. Social workers, on the other hand, interview people for a multitude of reasons. Thus, in applying the "social worker" variant of the "psychotherapist" privilege, it will be necessary to determine whether the information provided to the social worker was provided to him *in his capacity as a psychotherapist*, or in his capacity as an administrator of social welfare, a community organizer, etc. Worse still, if the privilege is to have its desired effect (and is not to mislead the client), it will presumably be necessary for the social caseworker to advise, as the conversation with his welfare client proceeds, which portions are privileged and which are not.

[T]he majority of the States that accord a privilege to social workers do *not* do so as a subpart of a "psychotherapist" privilege. The privilege applies to *all* confidences imparted to social workers, and not just those provided in the course of psychotherapy. In Oklahoma, for example, the social-worker-privilege statute prohibits a licensed social worker from disclosing, or being compelled to disclose, "*any information* acquired from persons consulting the licensed social worker in his or her professional capacity" (with certain exceptions to be discussed *infra*). Thus, in Oklahoma, as in most other States having a social-worker privilege, it is not a subpart or even a derivative of the psychotherapist privilege, but rather a piece of special legislation similar to that achieved by many other groups, from accountants, *see, e.g.*, Miss. Code Ann. § 73-33-16(2) (1995) (certified public accountant "shall not be required by any court of this state to disclose, and shall not voluntarily disclose" client information), to private detectives, *see, e.g.*, Mich. Comp. Laws § 338.840 (1979) ("Any communications . . . furnished by a professional man or client to a [licensed private detective], or any information secured in connection with an assignment for a client, shall be deemed privileged with the same authority and dignity as are other privileged communications recognized by the courts of this state"). These social-worker statutes give no support, therefore, to the theory (importance of psychotherapy) upon which the Court rests its disposition.

[T]he Court does not reveal the enormous degree of disagreement among the States as to the scope of the privilege. [I]n adopting *any* sort of a social worker privilege, then, the Court can at most claim that it is following the legislative "experience" of 40 States, and contradicting the "experience" of 10.

But turning to those States that do have an appreciable privilege of some sort, the diversity is vast. In Illinois and Wisconsin, the social-worker privilege does not apply when the confidential information pertains to homicide. In Missouri, the privilege is suspended as to information that pertains to a criminal act, and in Texas when the information is sought in any criminal prosecution, *compare* Tex. Rule Civ. Evid. 510(d) *with* Tex. Rule Crim. Evid. 501 *et seq.* In Kansas and Oklahoma, the privilege yields when the information pertains to "violations of any law," in Indiana, when it reveals a "serious harmful act," and in Delaware and Idaho, when it pertains to any "harmful act." In Oregon, a state-employed social worker like Karen Beyer loses the privilege where her supervisor determines that her testimony "is necessary in the performance of the duty of the social worker as a public employee." In South Carolina, a social worker is forced to disclose confidences "when required by statutory law or by court order for good cause shown to the extent that the patient's care and treatment or the nature and extent of his mental illness or emotional condition are reasonably at issue in a proceeding." The majority of social-worker-privilege States declare the privilege inapplicable to information relating to child abuse. And the States that do not fall into any of the above categories provide exceptions for commitment proceedings, for proceedings in which the patient relies on his mental or emotional condition as an element of his claim or defense, or for communications made in the course of a court-ordered examination of the mental or emotional condition of the patient.

In other words, the state laws to which the Court appeals for support demonstrate most convincingly that adoption of a social-worker psychotherapist privilege is a job for Congress.

NOTES AND QUESTIONS

(1) *Rule 501's "Reason and Experience" Test: What Does it Mean?* The majority relies on such indicia as the degree of dependence of the private relationship on confidentiality, the service to the public interest that this relationship arguably provides, inferences about lack of impact on evidence availability, and the existence and coverage of legislation by the states. Justice Scalia, on the other hand, argues that because of the indeterminacy of the Court's inferences, the paucity of judicial support, and the asserted inappropriateness of relying on diverse state legislation, the issue presents "a job for Congress." Is Justice Scalia correct in arguing that the diffuse basis for decision here should counsel judicial restraint, or did Congress in fact "do the job" when it directed the courts in Fed. R. Evid. 501 to consider privileges under a reason-and-experience standard? In general, should we be suspicious of privileges that have been enacted because of political pressure on legislatures, rather than the slow judicial development associated with common-law privileges? Or should we defer to the states because they have a more direct interest than federal courts in regulating the out-of-court behavior encouraged by privilege law?

For a provocative critique of *Jaffee*, see Raeder, *The Social Worker's Privilege, Victim's Rights, and Contextualized Truth*, 49 Hastings L.J. 991 (Apr. 1998), arguing that the success of the victim's rights movement in state legislatures resulted in the adoption of a federal privilege; comparing the change in public policy from twenty years ago when Representative Hungate voiced concern that opening up privileges resulted in everyone from social workers to piano tuners wanting one; and suggesting that victims view the privilege as an ally in establishing the truth at trial, not as an adversary of truth, because they consider that lawyers will unfairly distort the truth by using privileged material for impeachment, when such statements actually may reflect the tortuous process of coming to terms with a traumatic event before being able to see the event in its true light.

(2) *The Alleged Need for Confidentiality, the Asserted Connection to the Public Interest, and the Inference of Little Impact on Evidence Availability: Is the Majority's Reasoning Persuasive?* The majority relies primarily on mere assertions about the bases for its derivation of the privilege, as opposed to convincing proof. Justice Scalia, however, treats the majority's premises as unknowns, or as false inferences. For example, he points out that psychotherapy thrived before recognition of the privilege, and this fact in turn undermines the inference that the privilege will not affect evidence availability. In fact, as he points out, Texas allows no psychotherapy privilege at all in criminal cases, and yet there is no indication that this has had any impact on psychotherapy in that state — or that patients even are aware of it. Are the majority's inferences justifiable, or does Justice Scalia have a point? But if he does, doesn't much of his reasoning undermine many of the traditional privileges? Would this include the attorney-client privilege? Who has the burden of proof, the majority or dissent?

(3) *Does the Court's Reasoning Undermine the Arguments for a Physician Privilege?* At the beginning of Part III, the Court suggests that physicians — unlike attorneys, spouses and psychotherapists — rely more on objective information and less on patient confidences. Do you agree with this? Is this factor a justification for

nonrecognition of a physician-patient privilege in the federal courts, or would widespread recognition of a physician privilege among the states counteract the argument? Or is the argument just that there is less — but not no--need for a physician privilege?

(4) *A Privilege for Psychiatrists and Psychologists Only, or for All Licensed Mental Health Workers Performing Psychotherapy, or for All Confidences to Social Workers, or Only When the Social Worker is Performing Psychological Services?* Justice Scalia persuasively maintains that social workers as a group are less extensively trained in psychotherapy than some other licensed practitioners — and that they have extensive other functions, such as community welfare, that will require difficult efforts to categorize their communications. The states differ greatly in how they treat social worker confidences. Do these factors justify separate analysis of the claims for a social worker privilege and for a psychiatrist/psychologist privilege, as Justice Scalia argues, or is the majority correct in privileging both for confidences during psychotherapy?

Similarly, the undefined nature of the privilege no doubt will fuel efforts to expand it to rape and domestic violence counselors whose qualifications as mental health providers typically are minimal. *See, e.g.*, Cal. Evid. Code § 1035.8 (Sexual Assault Victim-Counselor Privilege) and Cal. Evid. Code § 1037.5 (Domestic Violence Victim-Counselor Privilege). In the absence of a statute, courts have been reluctant to find such a privilege, particularly because it may impact on a criminal defendant's ability to confront witnesses or present evidence in his own behalf. *See, e.g., In re Pittsburgh Action Against Rape*, 428 A.2d 126 (Pa. 1981) (rape victim's statements to rape crisis counselor are not privileged against rape defendant's discovery in criminal proceedings if they bear on facts of alleged offense); *Murphy v. Superior Court*, 689 P.2d 532 (Ariz. 1984) ("victim assistance caseworker," who talked to rape victim as rape crisis counselor, has no privilege to avoid testifying or being deposed in connection with criminal rape case; defendant in rape prosecution sought deposition or testimony).

An attempt to expand a psychotherapist-type privilege to "confidential" communications among Alcoholics Anonymous members failed in *Cox v. Miller*, 296 F.3d 89 (2d Cir. 2002) and *State v. Boobar*, 637 A.2d 1162 (Me. 1994). *See* Reed, *The Futile Fifth Step: Compulsory Disclosure of Confidential Communications Among Alcoholics Anonymous Members*, 70 St. John's L. Rev. 693 (1996).

(5) *The Biggest Open Question: What are the Exceptions and Limits to the Privilege?* The privilege recognized in *Jaffee* could be extremely narrow, or relatively broad, depending on subsequent lower court decisions narrowing or broading limits and exceptions. For example, if courts were to hold that any confidential communication about a "harmful act" is unprivileged, many if not most communications relevant to litigation will be unprivileged. Some jurisdictions, as Justice Scalia points out, exclude "harmful act" communications from the social worker privilege. The majority's only suggestion of limits (beyond the requirements of psychotherapy, confidentiality, diagnosis or treatment, and licensure) is that "serious threats" to harm someone may not be privileged. A number of states recognize a dangerous patient exception. *See, e.g.*, *Menendez v. Superior Court*, 834 P.2d 786 (Cal. 1992) (finding Menendez brothers met dangerous-patient exception

as to some of their sessions with their psychologist). Does the nondefinition of limits make the privilege so ill-defined, as Justice Scalia suggests, that its adoption is ill-advised?

The Ninth Circuit ruled *en banc* that the federal psychotherapist patient privilege does not contain a "dangerous patient" exception. *See United States v. Chase*, 340 F.3d 978 (9th Cir. 2003), *cert. denied*, 540 U.S. 1220 (2004). To somewhat similar effect is *United States v. Hayes*, 227 F.3d 578 (6th Cir. 2000). *But see United States v. Glass*, 133 F.3d 1356 (10th Cir. 1998).

What would a dangerous patient exception of the kind referred to in the *Jaffee* footnote embrace? Only evidence necessary in a proceeding to commit or imprison the patient to prevent him carrying out the danger he exhibited in the psychotherapeutic session? Or evidence in any kind of case, so long as dangerousness was exhibited in the psychotherapeutic session and the information is relevant, even if the case is not directly related to anything the patient did or the threat he posed? Would the exception apply after the danger the patient exhibited in the psychotherapeutic setting has passed? Would the exception apply in a prosecution or civil suit against the patient for a killing he indicated to his psychotherapist he would commit, but had already committed by the time of the prosecution or civil suit, so disclosure is not necessary for prevention of the killing? Would privilege be lost if the patient threatened only the psychiatrist (and did not carry it out)?

Would privilege be lost for a whole consultation or series of consultations, if one statement exhibits credible dangerousness? What would be required to trigger the exception: general dangerousness, or dangerousness toward a specific person? How dangerous? Only that degree of dangerousness which the standard of care or psychotherapeutic community regards as over and above dangerousness expressed by other patients undergoing similar therapy? Psychotherapists report that patients very often express violent thoughts that are usually just fantasies, although one can never be sure. They also report that expressing and discussing such thoughts are often an important part of the treatment. Would a dangerous patient exception hinder that treatment?

Does any of this have anything to do with the case you probably studied in Torts, *Tarasoff v. Regents of Univ. of Calif.*, 551 P.2d 334 (Cal. 1976) (psychologist liable for failure to warn prospective victim of potential harm from psychologist's patient; psychologist's duty is confined to a situation where patient threatens harm to a specific person, and the duty can require nothing beyond merely warning that person)?

(6) *Custody Battles.* Does deciding the best interests of a child in a custody dispute take precedence over privilege? Courts vary as to whether the mental health of both parents is at issue whenever child custody is being determined. *See generally* Slovenko, *Child Custody and the Psychotherapist-Patient Privilege*, 19 J. PSYCHOL. & LAW 163 (1991).

(7) *Interplay Between a Privilege and Other Statutes.* Policy considerations can be important in evaluating whether a privilege must give way to conflicting statutory mandates. See, e.g., *Minnesota v. Andring*, 342 N.W.2d 128 (Minn. 1984), holding that a state statute requiring health care personnel to report suspected

child abuse, and prohibiting the use of the physician-patient privilege to exclude evidence regarding a child's injuries in child abuse cases, abrogates the medical privilege only as to the identity of the child, the identity of the parent or guardian, the nature and extent of the child's injuries, and the name and address of the reporter; and does not require the disclosure of other information contained in the medical records of a patient father who received treatment at an alcoholic medical center and disclosed information there in connection with sexual abuse of young children to whom he was partially related. The policy of discovering child abuse and identifying the participants required no further waiver.

See also, to similar effect, respecting a psychotherapist-patient or psychologist-patient privilege, *People v. Stritzinger*, 668 P.2d 738 (Cal. 1983), holding that a statute imposing a duty on a psychologist to report possible incidents of child abuse automatically waived the privilege respecting the first counseling session with the sexual abuser, but not the second, since the disclosure of the first session was sufficient to accomplish the purposes of the act, that is, to identify the incident and the participants. Thus, additional matters disclosed in the second counseling session with the defendant abuser were privileged in the defendant abuser's trial for the sexual abuse. The court holds that it is particularly important to encourage patients to come and disclose to psychotherapists, because of the potential danger to the public if they do not seek and get treatment. Today, a large number of states provide that child abuse reporting statutes take precedence over any type of psychotherapist privilege.

(8) *Limited Exceptions in the Original Supreme Court Draft Federal Rule of Evidence on Psychotherapist Privilege.* The Supreme Court draft psychotherapist-patient privilege contained only the following three exceptions:

> *(a) Proceedings for hospitalization.* There is no privilege under this rule for communications relevant to an issue in proceedings to hospitalize the patient for mental illness, if the psychotherapist in the course of diagnosis or treatment has determined that the patient is in need of hospitalization.
>
> *(b) Examination by order of judge.* If the judge orders an examination of the mental or emotional condition of the patient, communications made in the course thereof are not privileged under this rule with respect to the particular purpose for which the examination is ordered unless the judge orders otherwise.
>
> *(c) Condition an element of claim or defense.* There is no privilege under this rule as to communications relevant to an issue of the mental or emotional condition of the patient in any proceeding in which he relies upon the condition as an element of his claim or defense, or, after the patient's death, in any proceeding in which any party relies upon the condition as an element of his claim or defense.

PROBLEM 13D: JAFFEE v. REDMOND ON REMAND: SHOULD THE PRIVILEGE PROTECT THE RELEVANT COMMUNICATIONS, OR SHOULD THE EVOLUTION OF EXCEPTIONS AND LIMITS REQUIRE DISCLOSURE?

As Justice Scalia points out, some states create exceptions for confidential communications to licensed social workers that concern homicide, violations of law, or harmful acts. Are the petitioners free to argue these exceptions to the lower court in *Jaffee v. Redmond* on remand? If so, what limits or exceptions might (or should) the lower courts accept, how should they go about examining the communications to separate out which particular statements during the "about 50" counseling sessions are or are not privileged, and what would be the result. Could the "exceptions" conceivably swallow the rule of privilege?

§ 13.06 OTHER SIMILAR PRIVILEGES[21]

[A] Introduction

Since you now have been introduced to some fairly typical privileges, certain others may be treated more briefly, in many instances merely by reference to cases and materials containing instructive discussion. The present section is concerned with privileges that bear a kinship to those studied in the previous sections of this chapter. A number of privileges that have not yet been examined, however, involve sufficiently distinctive principles that they are reserved for treatment in a subsequent section.

Some of the privileges in the present section are of quite recent origin. These latter privileges in particular, when argued to be a proper subject for judicial adoption, can be an excellent study in the evolution *vel non* of privilege law by development of and analogy to older well-established privileges and principles.

Notice from many of the cases in this section that when courts invoke this common-law process to recognize relatively new privileges, they are reluctant to create an absolute privilege, but qualify it in some way that involves a weighing and balancing of competing factors on the facts of the individual case.

Some of the cases in the present section provide an excellent study in possible conflict between state and federal privilege law and how Fed. R. Evid. 501 operates in such a situation.

---

[21] Study Guide Reference: Evidence in a Nutshell, Chapter 5:VI.

[B] Commonly Found Privileges, and Related Attempts to Extend Them

[1] Clergy-Communicant Privilege

(1) *Scope of the Privilege.* The clergy-communicant privilege has longstanding roots, but scholars disagree as to how far back into the common law it reaches. The privilege was mentioned in dictum in *Totten v. United States*, 92 U.S. 105 (1876), a case dealing with state secrets in which clergy privilege was mentioned in passing by analogy to demonstrate that privilege is not a foreign concept to the law. *Mullen v. United States*, 263 F.2d 275 (D.C. Cir. 1958) examined the clergy privilege's history and concluded that the privilege has a sufficient common law pedigree to allow it to be recognized in federal law. A good statement of the privilege is found in Uniform Rule 505 (1999), which is somewhat similar to the analogous Supreme Court Draft Federal Rule. After defining "cleric" as a "minister, priest, rabbi, accredited Christian Science Practitioner, or other similar functionary of a religious organization, or an individual reasonably believed so to be," Uniform Rule 505 (1999), entitled "Religious Privilege," provides as follows:

> **(b) General rule of privilege.** An individual has a privilege to refuse to disclose and to prevent another from disclosing a confidential communication by the individual to a cleric in the cleric's professional capacity as spiritual adviser.
>
> **(c) Who may claim the privilege.** The privilege under this rule may be claimed by an individual or the individual's guardian or conservator, or the individual's personal representative if the individual is deceased. The individual who was the cleric at the time of the communication is presumed to have authority to claim the privilege but only on behalf of the communicant.

(2) *Modern Authority.* The privilege appears to be widespread, almost universal, in the United States, but it is difficult to come by modern federal cases that find it to be applicable on the facts, whether they are applying state or federal law. *See, e.g., United States v. Webb*, 615 F.2d 828 (9th Cir. 1980) (question whether federal court in this federal-law case will recognize privilege is deferred because, even if it did, no privilege would arise here, since prison guard obviously was present; thus, no confidentiality); *United States v. Gordon*, 655 F.2d 478 (2d Cir. 1981) (privilege, assumed to exist in this federal criminal case, does not apply to communication on business, rather than spiritual, matters); *Seidman v. Fishburne-Hudgins Educational Foundation, Inc.*, 724 F.2d 413 (4th Cir. 1984) (in diversity-jurisdiction wrongful death action, district court properly admitted evidence of confidential communications between plaintiff and priest that were relevant to defendant's claim of contributory negligence; under Virginia law, which controls, privilege belongs to clergy, and priest here did not invoke it). For a recent case surveying case law as to who is the holder of the privilege, see *State v. Szemple*, 640 A.2d 817 (N.J. 1994) (clergy was only holder of privilege under New Jersey privilege law). *See also Mockaitis v. Harcleroad*, 104 F.3d 1522 (9th Cir. 1997) (granting injunction against District Attorney recording or using any confidential communications from inmates

to clerics, but refusing to order destruction of tape where penitent chose to make its contents public).

In the case of *In re Grand Jury Investigation*, 918 F.2d 374 (3d Cir. 1990), the government sought to compel a cleric to testify before a grand jury to statements made in an ostensible family counseling session. Present were a husband and wife, the wife's adult son from a previous marriage, and the son's fiancèe. The court held (1) a privilege exists under the federal branch of Rule 501 (2) to protects communications to members of the clergy in their spiritual or professional capacity (3) by persons seeking spiritual counseling (4) who reasonably expect confidentiality, and (5) the presence of third parties essential to the furtherance of the communication does not vitiate the privilege. The case was remanded for a determination of whether (2), (3), and (4) were satisfied on the facts of this case. *Cf. Morales v. Portuondo*, 154 F. Supp. 2d 706 (S.D.N.Y. 2001) (New York State privilege law interpreted; a "heart to heart" talk with a priest that was not a formal confession was not covered because the Church had determined it was not covered by the confidentiality obligation). Cf. W. Va. Code § 57-3-9 (2005), a clergy privilege that specifically covers "any confession or conversation" and "any communication . . . for the purpose of [reconciling] estranged spouses." Is the policy to re-unite divorced or separated spouses? Do you suppose they accord marital privilege in the situations meant to be covered by this?

(3) *Reporting Child Abuse.* Virtually all states have statutes requiring reporting of child abuse that is learned of. Should clergy have to report child abuse they learn of from communicants? Is it privileged? Doctors are required to report. Are lawyers? Is a requirement to report different from whether something is privileged in court? *See* Mitchell, *Must the Clergy Tell? Child Abuse Reporting Requirements Versus the Clergy Privilege and Free Exercise of Religion*, 71 MINN. L. REV. 723 (1987); Comment, *How Secrets Are Kept: Viewing the Current Clergy-Penitent Privilege Through a Comparison with the Attorney-Client Privilege*, 2002 B.Y.U. L. REV. 489 (2002).

[2] Accountant-Client Privilege

Couch v. United States, 409 U.S. 322 (1973), and *United States v. Arthur Young & Co.*, 465 U.S. 805 (1984), have made clear there is no general federal accountant-client privilege or accountant work product protection. In contrast, a number of states have enacted such privileges. In conflict situations, the federal courts have favored admissibility. *See FDIC v. Mercantile Nat. Bank of Chicago*, 84 F.R.D. 345 (N.D. Ill. 1979) (securities fraud action with state and federal claims, discovery subpoenas for testimony and documents from party's accountant; Illinois law has accountant-client privilege that appears to cover information; same information relevant to state and federal claims; court holds, after recognizing there is no clear workable answer in Fed. R. Evid. 501, that federal law of no privilege applies to whole case); *Wm. T. Thompson Co. v. General Nutrition Corp.*, 671 F.2d 100 (3d Cir. 1982) (similar problem in antitrust area; similar solution). *Cf.* 26 U.S.C. § 7525, discussed in note (3) § 13.02[A], *supra*.

[3] Journalist (Reporter, Newsperson, Newsgatherer, News Media) Privilege

(1) *Scope of the Privilege.* Some form of this privilege exists in almost all states. The provisions are quite varied. For example, California provides:

> A publisher, editor, reporter, or other person connected with or employed upon a newspaper, magazine, or other periodical publication, or by a press association or wire service, or any person who has been so connected or employed, shall not be adjudged in contempt by a judicial, legislative, or administrative body, or any other body having the power to issue subpoenas, for refusing to disclose the source of any information procured while so connected or employed for publication in a newspaper, magazine or other periodical publication, or for refusing to disclose any unpublished information obtained or prepared in gathering, receiving or processing of information for communication to the public.
>
> Nor shall a radio or television news reporter or other person connected with or employed by a radio or television station, or any person who has been so connected or employed, be so adjudged in contempt for refusing to disclose the source of any information procured while so connected or employed for news or news commentary purposes on radio or television, or for refusing to disclose any unpublished information obtained or prepared in gathering, receiving or processing of information for communication to the public.
>
> As used in this subdivision, "unpublished information" includes information not disseminated to the public by the person from whom disclosure is sought, whether or not related information has been disseminated and includes, but is not limited to, all notes, outtakes, photographs, tapes or other data of whatever sort not itself disseminated to the public through a medium of communication, whether or not published information based upon or related to such material has been disseminated.

Somewhat atypically, this provision is part of the California Constitution. Cal. Const. Art. I, § 2(b) (added 1974, amended 1980). Although the privilege — commonly statutory and commonly referred to as the "journalist's" or "reporter's" privilege — varies from state to state, certain general points may be made:

(2) *General Policy Considerations.* The journalist privilege frequently protects the identity of the source and sometimes the information learned therefrom. A few states afford even broader protection. Problems have arisen concerning how a journalist should be defined: does it include radio and television personnel, people who write articles one time only who are not professional journalists, an author of a book, an author of a limited-use unpublished monograph or paper, writers for magazines, contributors to newsletters, contributors to local "rags," bloggers, contributors to films, scholars, researchers, or experimenters writing or reporting results in learned, scientific, or psychological journals? Are there other privileges that would cover some of these?

The theory of most journalist privileges is that the public should be fully and truthfully informed as much as possible; that the press (and perhaps other media) provide information to the public; that the information often is obtained from informers; that informers are timid and reluctant to supply information to journalists — for example, information reflecting adversely on, or revealing wrongdoing on the part of, themselves, their bosses (e.g., in government or business), or someone (like organized crime) who might retaliate in other ways; and that these informers will be less reluctant to supply information if they know their identity will be kept secret. The privilege also is intended to protect one who does inform from reprisals, as a goal in itself; and to preserve his or her future usefulness. The arguments are similar to those underlying the informer-to-police privilege (*infra*).

Against these considerations must be balanced some counter-considerations: some informers (and indeed journalists) may feel freer to report untruths if they know informers' identities will be kept secret and thus the sources never can be identified, checked, sued, prosecuted, or fired. This can lead to public misinformation and damaging falsehoods against individuals and organizations. Also, privilege entails possible loss of evidence.

Debate over whether to adopt a journalist privilege frequently has centered on such questions as: Are the media necessary to watchdog other institutions, principally government and big business? Have the media been performing effectively without a privilege? How does the balance come out on the information-misinformation question raised by the counter-considerations mentioned above? Watergate often is mentioned.

In designing a journalist privilege, other troubling questions have occurred, with various answers: Should the privilege be a qualified privilege, giving way to need for the information, or giving way in certain kinds of important cases? Should there be an exception to the privilege for criminal cases or certain kinds of criminal cases? Should the privilege apply in grand jury proceedings? Perhaps *only* in grand jury proceedings? Should the privilege apply only if the journalist has agreed with, or assured, the informant that there would be confidentiality? There are other questions.

Some courts, including some federal courts, have accorded some incomplete protection in this area by finding, in the concept of constitutional freedom of speech, a rule against *unnecessarily* subpoenaing journalists for information that is obtainable elsewhere or of little use or relevance. Other courts find a similar principle inherent in the law governing the issuance and quashing of subpoenas and other court process. Analogy is drawn to the cases allowing quashing for undue hardship. Sometimes the result is put on the basis of the common-law development allowed by Fed. R. Evid. 501 or the court's inherent or express protective power over discovery processes. (Recent federal law restricting law enforcement searches of newsrooms can be expected to lend strength to these approaches.) With reference to all privileges intended to encourage communications, what effect on such encouragement would a weighing approach have such as we find in these cases, or in the work-product privilege, or in some of the peripheral areas of attorney-client privilege, or in some governmental privileges (*infra*)? Is it worth the price? This approach often is given the name "qualified privilege."

(3) *First and Sixth Amendment Considerations. See Branzburg v. Hayes*, 408 U.S. 665 (1972) (no absolute constitutional First Amendment privilege (at least not on facts) of news reporters to refuse to disclose to grand jury information received from confidential source; there are some constitutional protections, however, and such information must not be sought lightly), cited with approval in *Cohen v. Cowles Media Co.*, 501 U.S. 663 (1991); *United States v. Long*, 978 F.2d 850 (4th Cir. 1992) (reporters who interviewed member of state legislature charged with criminal offense had no qualified privilege under First Amendment against being compelled to testify regarding interviews); *United States v. Cutler*, 6 F.3d 67 (2d Cir. 1993) (in criminal contempt case, treating as dicta Second Circuit test that required disclosure of reporter's notes only upon clear and specific showing that information is highly material and relevant, necessary, or critical to maintenance of claim, and not obtainable from other available sources); *Lewis v. United States*, 517 F.2d 236 (9th Cir. 1975) (federal grand jury investigating bombing of hotel seeks original message sent to radio station by group claiming responsibility; federal prosecution, so California newsman's privilege statute inapplicable; refuses, under federal branch of Fed. R. Evid. 501, to recognize similar privilege because of *Branzburg*, although affirms that new privileges can be recognized in appropriate cases under that rule, and state law can be advisory as to what is good direction for federal law to go).

In *Matter of Farber*, 394 A.2d 330 (N.J.), *cert. denied*, 439 U.S. 997 (1978), a defendant in a state murder prosecution, for defense purposes, sought information (and its sources) obtained by a newsman preparing a story that led to the defendant's murder indictment. The newspaper refused to make the information available even for *in camera* inspection by the judge. *Farber* held that *Branzburg* recognizes no constitutional privilege under the First Amendment, but that the New Jersey newsman's shield statute accords a privilege. However, the Sixth Amendment and New Jersey analogue thereof grant a right to "compulsory process" to a criminal defendant to defend himself; thus, on the facts and preliminary showings of this case, there must be an *in camera* inspection of the allegedly privileged material by the judge to determine a criminal defendant's need for the information and its relevancy, materiality, and availability from other sources. *See also United States v. Cuthbertson*, 630 F.2d 139 (3d Cir. 1980), *cert. denied*, 449 U.S. 1126 (1981) (case like *Farber*, except crime was federal fraud, not state murder, and news show leading to indictment was CBS's "60 Minutes" show; court holds there is a federal common-law *qualified* newsman's privilege covering CBS's taped interviews with informants; thus, showing like in *Farber* is required, even before *in camera* inspection; also, discovery rule allows subpoena to third party only for *admissible evidence*; no showing made that information would be admissible, except perhaps as impeachment of informants, but can't tell *that* until informants actually testify; also, no showing that information (other than as impeachment) was unavailable to criminal defendant by interviewing informants; also discussion of CBS's right to appeal, even though not cited for contempt).

See also Shoen v. Shoen, 48 F.3d 412 (9th Cir. 1995) (libel action; reversing contempt citation of journalist because information was somewhat confidential, requiring disclosure only upon showing that material is unavailable despite exhaustion of all reasonable alternatives, is noncumlative, and clearly is relevant to important issue in case; showing of relevance found lacking); *Zerilli v. Evening News Ass'n*, 628 F.2d 217 (D.C. Cir. 1980) (federal-law civil suit against U.S. Attorney General for leaking information [obtained through wiretap] to press; reporter of story refuses to reveal his source to plaintiff; held: on particular facts, balancing comes out that First Amendment interest in protecting press outweighs interest in disclosure; *Branzburg* cited; criminal cases distinguishable; summary judgment against plaintiff on merits upheld because he (as consequence of decision) had little evidence of who leaked); *Miller v. Transamerican Press*, 621 F.2d 721 (5th Cir. 1980), *cert. denied*, 450 U.S. 1041 (1981) (diversity jurisdiction; libel suit against magazine for saying plaintiff swindled pension fund of which he was trustee; pretrial motion by plaintiff to compel defendant to disclose source; trial court, after *in camera* inspection, ordered defendant to turn over *summaries* of magazine's investigative file, for plaintiff's counsel's eyes only, but not identity of informant; state privilege law applies; federal court sits in Texas, so is Texas law, but includes Texas conflicts law that may or may not point to California, where editorial work done, or Virginia, plaintiff's domicile, or D.C., plaintiff's place of business, rather than Texas; only California has privilege statute; but all, including California, mean to protect reporters only to extent of First Amendment, so no conflict; in case where public figure (plaintiff) must prove malice to win libel case, First Amendment privilege of defendant gives way where information sought is relevant and no alternative way to get it exists; here, informer's identity must be disclosed).

(4) *Recent Case Provides a Good Practical Illustration.* A recent illuminating federal decisions on journalist privilege under the federal branch of Fed. R. Evid. 501 and the U.S. Constitution is *In re Grand Jury Subpoena, Judith Miller*, 438 F.3d 1141 (D.C. Cir. 2005). The court declined to protect the two journalists facing jail in the case for refusing to disclose information relating to their sources. The court held (1) that the First Amendment did not give the reporters a constitutional right to refuse to divulge confidential sources in response to a grand jury subpoena, (2) that even if there was a privilege under federal common law, it is a qualified one, and was overcome by need here, and (3) that no Due Process rights of the reporters were violated when the prosecutor, *ex parte* and *in camera*, made his showings to the judge to overcome the privilege. Of course, the positions of other circuits remain unaffected by this decision unless and until the Supreme Court decides the matter. The background and aftermath of this case — set forth in the following article in the May 28, 2005 New York Times — provide a glimpse into some practicalities in the area:

> Two reporters facing up to 18 months in jail for refusing to testify about their sources gained some unlikely allies yesterday. The attorneys general of 34 states and the District of Columbia filed a brief in the United States Supreme Court supporting the reporters, Judith Miller of THE NEW YORK TIMES and Matthew Cooper of TIME magazine. The brief urged the court to hear the reporters' case and argued that the absence of federal protection for journalists and their sources undermined the laws of the 49 states that do offer protection.
>
> State court judges considering subpoenas for reporters' sources usually balance two competing interests: the importance of the evidence versus the

damage that forcing reporters to talk may do to the flow of information to the public.

The brief took no position on whether Patrick J. Fitzgerald, the federal special prosecutor pursuing the two reporters' testimony, would win or lose under such a standard. But it said the Supreme Court should take the case to establish similar protection in federal cases. That would close a gap, the brief argued. At present, reporters receive widely varying protection depending on whether their testimony about a given interview is sought in state or federal court. As a consequence, the brief said, reporters and sources cannot make agreements in the confidence that state laws will protect them. (Only Wyoming has not addressed the issue.) "In the absence of some kind of federal privilege, our laws could become meaningless," Attorney General W. A. Drew Edmondson of Oklahoma, a Democrat, said in an interview. Attorney General Mark L. Shurtleff of Utah, a Republican, said "In something like this, a majority of A.G.'s asking the Supreme Court to look at this can have an impact." The attorney general of Connecticut joined in the brief; those of New York and New Jersey did not.

The case against the reporters arose from the publication of the identity of a covert C.I.A. operative, Valerie Plame, by the syndicated columnist Robert Novak, who said "two senior administration officials" had told him the information. It can be a crime for government officials to disclose such facts. Mr. Fitzgerald appears to assert that Mr. Cooper, who wrote about Ms. Plame after the Novak column, and Ms. Miller, who never wrote on the subject, have information that may point to criminal conduct by a government official. Mr. Novak's role in Mr. Fitzgerald's investigation remains a mystery.

In February, the federal appeals court in Washington D.C. upheld a trial judge's decision holding the two reporters in contempt and ordering them jailed, but the appeals court panel split three ways on whether federal law recognizes a reporter's privilege to protect confidential sources. A 1972 decision of the Supreme Court, Branzburg v. Hayes, held that the First Amendment did not supply such protection, at least in cases involving grand jury subpoenas. But a rule of evidence adopted by Congress in 1975 authorizes federal courts to recognize new privileges in light of "reason and experience." In the brief filed yesterday, the state attorneys general argued that the breadth and consistency of state protections, many of them relatively recent, satisfied that requirement. The reporters have remained free while the Supreme Court decides whether to hear the case.

Attorney General Shurtleff explained the policy behind the state shield laws. "If you don't have protection, there is going to be a chilling effect and people don't talk," he said. "If people don't talk, the public won't hear important stories." Attorney General Greg Abbott of Texas, a Republican, said in a statement, "A free and open democracy requires a free and open press." Those are arguments and sentiments one is used to hearing from journalists and their lawyers, said Floyd Abrams, who represents Ms. Miller. They have more force, Mr. Abrams said, coming from law enforcement officials. "These are the people who are losing evidence because of shield laws," Mr. Abrams said. "Yet they still come in and say, in effect, that we can live with that."

Theodore J. Boutrous Jr., who represents Mr. Cooper along with Theodore B. Olson, a former United States solicitor general, said the brief filed by the attorneys general might strike a chord with the Supreme Court, which has been concerned with the relationship between the federal government and the states. "The lack of a privilege could undermine, and defeat from a federalism perspective, what the states are trying to protect," Mr. Boutrous said. "The state attorney generals have had a lot of experience with shield laws," Mr. Cooper said, "and they realize they're totally compatible with law enforcement."

Mr. Edmondson, who has been a prosecutor for 20 years, said he had never felt it necessary to subpoena a reporter for information about a source. "There have been times when I have been very curious and would like to know," he said, "but that's insufficient."

Liptak, *State Attorneys General Ask Supreme Court to Hear Two Reporters' Case*, N.Y. TIMES, May 28, 2005.

[4] Researcher Privilege

This privilege is not "commonly found" but is in this subsection because analytically, if it exists, it is a direct extension of the principle involved in the journalist privilege. On researcher privilege, see *Richards of Rockford, Inc. v. Pacific Gas and Elec. Co.*, 71 F.R.D. 388 (N.D. Cal. 1976) (Harvard professor conducts study of electric companies to determine how environmental decisions are made; he and research assistant interview, on pledge of confidentiality, employees of PG&E; includes interview about certain equipment; later, manufacturer of equipment and PG&E in dispute in federal court based on diversity jurisdiction over payment for equipment and whether it works; plaintiff (who seeks payment) subpoenas research assistant, for discovery, to supply interviewees' identities and research notes of interviews (professor and assistant are not parties); held, per Renfrew, J., as matter of federal court's supervisory power over discovery (*not* as matter of privilege under Fed. R. Evid. 501, because that rule would compel applicability of state privilege law, which had no such privilege) that society's interest in free flow of information from sources, for research projects, outweighs, on particular facts, need for disclosure).

See also In re Grand Jury Subpoena dated January 4, 1984 (Brajuha), 750 F.2d 223 (2d Cir. 1984) (rejecting "scholar's privilege" in case where federal grand jury investigating suspicious restaurant fire subpoenaed research notes of Ph.D. candidate who was working as waiter at restaurant; candidate was writing dissertation entitled "The Sociology of the American Restaurant"; court rejected his assertion of privilege to resist supplying information but held open possibility that there might be privilege if he had shown detailed description of nature and seriousness of scholarly study, of methodology employed, of need for assurances of confidentiality to various sources, and of fact that the disclosure requested would seriously impinge on that confidentiality); *Wright v. Jeep Corp.*, 547 F. Supp. 871 (E.D. Mich. 1982) (per Joiner, J; crash researcher — famous professor and research scientist, not party — has no privilege not to testify or supply notes, drafts, and all other material and underlying data that went into his famous study showing lack of crashworthiness of recreational vehicles like Jeeps, sought by defendant in this personal injury action; defendant expecting study to be used by plaintiffs and wanting to be prepared to meet it; since material is highly likely to be relevant, discovery rules do not bar disclosure; nor is there privilege covering academic researchers under privilege law of Michigan, which Fed. R. Evid. 501 requires be applied in this diversity case; while Michigan discovery rules questionably might be of use to professor, federal discovery rules are applicable rules, save as to privilege; court queries whether showing that information was confidential (none made here) would make any difference; court states that since disclosure of informants (sources) is not involved, First Amendment, which is concerned with chilling sources, is not applicable; thus, though there is some balancing to do, balance comes out in favor of disclosure, since chilling on researchers themselves will be slight; invoking subpoena rules addressed to burdensomeness, court notes this famous study may garner many subpoenas to this professor, and thus he is entitled to rather ample remuneration and need not appear beyond his own county).

In *Kaufman v. Edelstein*, 539 F.2d 811 (2d Cir. 1976), a civil federal antitrust suit by government against IBM, the government subpoenaed an unwilling famous expert (from an accounting and management firm) on the structure of the electronics market to testify to the facts of the market structure he already knows, and perhaps give opinions he already has given. No new work was required, nor opinions on new facts. The Court held, in these circumstances, with proper compensation, if relevant, there is no privilege to resist, even if other equally satisfactory experts may be available. The court indicated it might rule otherwise if the expert's fame gets him subpoenaed in too many cases.

[5] Trade Secrets Privilege

Supreme Court Draft Federal Rule of Evidence 508, though unenacted, provides a good statement of the privilege as it exists today:

> A person has a privilege, which may be claimed by him or his agent or employee, to refuse to disclose and to prevent other persons from disclosing a trade secret owned by him, if the allowance of the privilege will not tend to conceal fraud or otherwise work injustice. When disclosure is directed, the judge shall take such protective measure as the interests of the holder of the privilege and of the parties and the furtherance of justice may require.

See, on this privilege, *Wearly v. Federal Trade Comm'n*, 462 F. Supp. 589 (D.N.J. 1978) (federal branch of Fed. R. Evid. 501 adopts Supreme Court Draft Fed. R. Evid. 508 because it was not controversial in Congress and codified common law; rule and common law require balancing of destruction of property interest represented by revelation of trade secret against need for disclosure; protective order limiting material that is to be revealed, and limiting persons to whom and purposes for which it may be revealed, etc., should be entered if there is to be disclosure; holder's disclosure of secret to his attorney, itself privileged under attorney-client privilege, does not destroy confidentiality and hence trade secret privilege; privilege, to achieve its goals — especially this privilege — must apply in all forums, including administrative agencies; otherwise constitutional right not to be deprived of property without due process might be implicated; balancing done; protective orders discussed), *vacated* (on jurisdictional grounds), 616 F.2d 662 (3d Cir.), *cert. denied*, 449 U.S. 822 (1980). *See also* "business strategy" privilege in note (3) in the subsection immediately below.

[C] Privileges Less Frequently Recognized (at Least as Yet)

[1] Privilege Covering Peer Review and Self-Critical Analysis

(1) Peer Review Privileges. The effort to obtain a federal qualified peer review privilege for deliberations and discussions concerning university hiring, promotion, and tenure decisions was derailed by *University of Pa. v. EEOC*, 493 U.S. 182 (1990). This case held that the policies underlying the statute banning discrimination (under which this case was brought), which did not contain any peer review privilege, might be frustrated by the adoption of a privilege that could block disclosure of information relevant to determining if illegal discrimination has taken place. The Court found no historic or statutory basis for the privilege and dismissed any First Amendment claims that the privilege was necessary to ensure academic freedom. The argument in favor of adopting such a privilege is that otherwise discussion will be chilled because the individuals entrusted with making decisions could not rely on the confidentiality of the proceedings. Claims for peer review privileges also arise in litigation concerning denial or termination of physicians from hospital staffs. For the most part, such privileges are statutory rather than judge-made. Are there ways to provide some confidentiality while disclosing the underlying material? Does redaction work?

(2) *Privileges for Critical Self-Analysis.* A separate self-critical analysis or self-evaluation privilege has met with mainly negative reception. In rejecting such a privilege in the public setting, the court in *FTC v. TRW, Inc.*, 628 F.2d 207 (1980), noted:

> The roots of the "self-evaluative" privilege are to be found in *Bredice v. Doctor's Hospital*, 50 F.R.D. 249 (D.D.C. 1970). In *Bredice*, a plaintiff in a malpractice action sought in the course of civil discovery to compel production of the minutes and reports of a hospital medical review committee's investigation of the death of a patient. The court noted that there was an "overwhelming public interest" in having the medical review committee's work proceed on a confidential basis, and found that this interest would be compromised by requiring disclosure of the committee's records. Accordingly, a qualified privilege against disclosure was fashioned to apply in all but "extraordinary circumstances."
>
> Whatever may be the status of the "self-evaluative" privilege in the context of private litigation, courts with apparent uniformity have refused its application where, as here, the documents in question have been sought by a governmental agency. As a general matter this conclusion makes sense

> in light of the roots of the privilege in the public interest, and the strong public interest in having administrative investigations proceed expeditiously and without impediment.
>
> We hold, accordingly, that no "self-evaluative" privilege shields the production of documents from an otherwise valid FTC subpoena.

Similarly, in *Dowling v. American Hawaii Cruises, Inc.*, 971 F.2d 423 (9th Cir. 1992), the court rejected a critical self-analysis privilege for routine internal safety reports. In surveying the literature and case law, *Dowling* concludes that: "The Supreme Court and the circuit courts have neither definitely denied the existence of such a privilege, nor accepted it and defined its scope. Rather, when confronted with a claim of the privilege, they have refused on narrow grounds to apply it to the facts before them."

When, if ever, might investigations and their resulting reports, of the kind discussed in this note and note (1) immediately above, qualify for exclusion under Fed. R. Evid. 407? Might any of the privileges mentioned in note (3) immediately below, qualify?

(3) *Related Business Privileges.* Several courts have recognized a business strategy privilege against disclosure. *See* Rhodes, *The White Knight Privilege in Litigated Takeovers: Leveling the Playing Field in Discovery*, 43 Stan. L. Rev. 445 (1991). A qualified privilege for environmental audit reports also has been recognized. *See* Mazza, *The New Evidentiary Privilege for Environmental Audit Reports: Making the Worst of a Bad Situation*, 23 Ecology L.Q. 79 (1996). However, an "ombudsmen" privilege, first recognized in federal court by *Kientzy v. McDonnell Douglas Corp.*, 133 F.R.D. 570 (E.D. Mo. 1991), has been rejected by the Circuit in which it was decided. *See Carman v. McDonnell Douglas Corp.*, 114 F.3d 790 (8th Cir. 1997).

[2] Privilege to Withhold Information if One's Life is Threatened

A number of commentators have argued for this privilege. *See*, for example Note, 55 B.U. L. Rev. 495 (1975). It is questionable as to whether any court at the present time would recognize this privilege unless a very persuasive case were made. The problem of witness intimidation, which can result in a witness refusing to testify even if no privilege is accorded, or can result in a witness lying or changing his story, is a severe problem. *See* Graham, *Witness Intimidation*, 12 Fla. St. U. L. Rev. 239, 240 (1984) (examining rules and procedures that can help alleviate this problem, such as Fed. R. Evid. 801(d)(1)(A), Fed. R. Evid. 804(b)(1), depositions to perpetuate testimony, Fed. R. Evid. 807, etc.). There may be a *de facto* privilege, if not one in law, in the situation addressed here, because criminal-case witnesses frequently in fact refuse to testify (or they give perjured testimony) when threats against their lives or the lives of loved ones are made to prevent their honest testimony and courts are reluctant to punish them. This is why witnesses (victims) in domestic violence cases are frequently absent. Prosecutors, at least in these cases, are reluctant to compel testimony. Why, do you suppose? In this situation, the normal instinct of prosecutors is to drop the case. Can you say why? Laws and policies in most places now encourage prosecution with other evidence.

[3] Parent-Child Privilege

A parent-child privilege did not exist at common law and is found in a very few state jurisdictions, mostly by statute. There is currently no federal statute according the privilege, and federal case law has been loath to create one. Parent-child privilege bills have been introduced in Congress, but none have gotten very far. Several were introduced as a result of the Monica Lewinsky scandal. Young Monica's mother was subpoened and compelled by Independent Counsel Kenneth Starr to testify before a grand jury investigating Monica's sexual relationship with President Clinton in order to discover whether President Clinton lied under oath about it. The most well-developed federal bill is entitled the "Parent-Child Privilege Act of 1998", H.R. 4286. It attempts to place a specific parent-child privilege in the Federal Rules of Evidence, Article V. It has failed to pass in several Congressional sessions, but it provides a useful model for discussion. The rule proposed reads as follows:

> ***Parent-Child Privilege***
>
> **(a) Definitions** — For purposes of this rule, the following definitions apply:
>
> (1) The term "child" means the son, daughter, stepchild, or foster child of a parent or the ward of a legal guardian or of any other person who serves as the child's parent. A person who meets this definition is a child for the purposes of this rule, irrespective of whether or not that person has attained the age of majority in the place in which that person resides.
>
> (2) The term "confidential communication" means a communication between a parent and the parent's child, made privately or solely in the presence of other members of the child's family or an attorney, physician, psychologist, psychotherapist, social worker, clergy member, or other third party who has a confidential relationship with the parent or the child, which is not intended for further disclosure except to other members of the child's family or household or to other persons in furtherance of the purposes of the communication.
>
> (3) The term "parent" means a birth parent, adoptive parent, stepparent, foster parent, or legal guardian of a child, or any other person that a court has recognized as having acquired the right to act as a parent of that child.
>
> **(b) Adverse Testimonial Privilege** — In any civil or criminal proceeding governed by these rules, and subject to the exceptions set forth in subdivision (d) of this rule —
>
> (1) a parent shall not be compelled to give testimony as a witness adverse to a person who is, at the time of the proceeding, a child of that parent; and
>
> (2) a child shall not be compelled to give testimony as a witness adverse to a person who is, at the time of the proceeding, a parent of that child; unless the parent or child who is the witness voluntarily and knowingly waives the privilege to refrain from giving such adverse testimony.

(c) Confidential Communications Privilege —

(1) In any civil or criminal proceeding governed by these rules, and subject to the exceptions set forth in subdivision (d) of this rule —

(A) a parent shall not be compelled to divulge any confidential communication made between that parent and the child during the course of their parent-child relationship; and

(B) a child shall not be compelled to divulge any confidential communication made between that child and the parent during the course of their parent-child relationship;

unless both the child and the parent or parents of the child who are privy to the confidential communication voluntarily and knowingly waive the privilege against the disclosure of the communication in the proceeding.

(2) The privilege set forth in this subdivision applies even if, at the time of the proceeding, the parent or child who made or received the confidential communication is deceased or the parent-child relationship is terminated.

(d) Exceptions — The privileges set forth in subdivisions (b) and (c) of this rule shall be inapplicable and unenforceable—

(1) in any civil action or proceeding by the child against the parent, or the parent against the child;

(2) in any civil action or proceeding in which the child's parents are opposing parties;

(3) in any civil action or proceeding contesting the estate of the child or of the child's parent;

(4) in any action or proceeding in which the custody, dependency, deprivation, abandonment, support or nonsupport, abuse, or neglect of the child, or the termination of parental rights with respect to the child, is at issue;

(5) in any action or proceeding to commit the child or a parent of the child because of alleged mental or physical incapacity;

(6) in any action or proceeding to place the person or the property of the child or of a parent of the child in the custody or control of another because of alleged mental or physical capacity; and

(7) in any criminal or juvenile action or proceeding in which the child or a parent of the child is charged with an offense against the person or the property of the child, a parent of the child or any member of the family or household of the parent or the child.

(e) Appointment of a Representative for a Child Below the Age of Majority — When a child who appears to be the subject of a privilege set forth in subdivision (b) or (c) of this rule is below the age of majority at the time of the proceeding in which the privilege is or could be asserted, the court may appoint a guardian, attorney, or other legal representative to represent the child's interests with respect to the privilege. If it is in furtherance of the child's best interests, the child's representative may waive the privilege under subdivision (b) or consent on behalf of the child to the waiver of the privilege under subdivision (c).

(f) Non-Effect of this Rule on Other Evidentiary Privileges — This rule shall not affect the applicability or enforceability of other recognized evidentiary privileges that, pursuant to rule 501, may be applicable and enforceable in any proceeding governed by these rules.

IN RE GRAND JURY

United States Court of Appeals, Third Circuit
103 F.3d 1140 (1997)

GARTH, CIRCUIT JUDGE:

[This consolidated appeal determined three different claims of parent-child privilege. In one case, a Virgin Islands federal grand jury subpoenaed the father of an eighteen-year-old son who was the target of a criminal investigation. The father moved to quash the subpoena on the ground that revelation of confidences would destroy his close relationship with his son and prevent him from listening or giving advice to him. In the second case, from Delaware, a mother and sixteen-year-old daughter sought to prevent the daughter's testimony before a grand jury investigating her father's participation in the kidnapping of a woman who had disappeared. The third appeal concerned, in the same case, the father's motion to bar his daughter's testimony. The District Courts denied all claims of parent-child privilege.

[The Court of Appeals affirmed. It first noted that eight federal courts of appeals had rejected the claimed privileges, and state courts overwhelmingly had declined to adopt a common-law privilege. It then turned to the "reason and experience" standard of Fed. R. Evid. 501 as construed in such cases as *Jaffee* and *Trammell*. In *Jaffee*, for example, all of the states had recognized some type of psychotherapist-patient privilege, but here only four states, by statute, had adopted any kind of parent-child privilege. This did not constitute a "consistent body of policy determinations by state[s]" supporting the claimed privilege.

[The court also considered common-law reasoning. Dean Wigmore had set out four required factors for any communications privilege: (1) confidentiality of the communications, (2) the essential nature of confidentiality to the relationship, (3) community opinion that the relationship should be fostered, and (4) injury exceeding the benefit of correct disposition of litigation. The Court concluded that the second and fourth of Dean Wigmore's elements were absent.]

First, confidentiality — in the form of a testimonial privilege — is not essential to a successful parent-child relationship, as required by the second factor.

[I]t is not clear whether children would be more likely to discuss private matters with their parents if a parent-child privilege were recognized than if one were not. It is not likely that children, or even their parents, would typically be aware of the existence or non-existence of a testimonial privilege covering parent-child communications.

Indeed, the existence or nonexistence of a parent-child privilege is probably one of the least important considerations in any child's decision as to whether to reveal some indiscretion, legal or illegal, to a parent. Moreover, it is unlikely that any parent would choose to deter a child from revealing a confidence to the parent solely because a federal court has refused to recognize a privilege protecting such communications from disclosure.

Finally, the proposed parent-child privilege fails to satisfy the fourth condition of the Wigmore test. As explained above, any injury to the parent-child relationship resulting from non-recognition of such a privilege would be relatively insignificant. In contrast, the cost of recognizing such a privilege is substantial: the impairment of the truth-seeking function of the judicial system and the increased likelihood of injustice resulting from the concealment of relevant information.

An even more compelling reason for rejecting a parent-child privilege stems from the fact that the parent-child relationship differs dramatically from other relationships. If, for example, a fifteen year old unemancipated child informs her parent that she has committed a crime or has been using or distributing narcotics, and this disclosure has been made in confidence while the child is seeking guidance, it is evident to us that, regardless of whether the child consents or not, the parent must have the right to take such action as the parent deems appropriate *in the interest of the child.* That action could be commitment to a drug rehabilitation center or a report of the crime to the juvenile authorities. This is so because, in theory at least, juvenile proceedings are undertaken solely in the interest of the child. We would regard it intolerable in such a situation if the law intruded in the guise of a privilege, and silenced the parent because the child had a privilege to prevent disclosure.

[Judge Mansmann, concurring in part and dissenting in part, would have reversed the Virgin Islands decision by recognizing a "limited privilege" for communications by a child to a parent "in the course of seeking parental advice and guidance." The majority responded with an explanation of its conclusion that such a "limited" privilege would be unworkable, and it emphasized that the issue "should be left to Congress."]

NOTES AND QUESTIONS

(1) *Current Federal Law.* While no U.S. Supreme Court case has addressed this privilege, several lower federal courts have, and almost every one that has, has declined to recognize it. Further, no federal court of appeals has recognized it, while nine have expressly rejected. *See*, in addition to *In re Grand Jury* immediately above, *In re Erato*, 2 F.3d 11 (2d Cir. 1993); *In re Grand Jury Proceedings of Doe*, 842 F.2d 244 (10th Cir. 1988); *United States v. Davies*, 768 F.2d 893 (7th Cir. 1985); *Port v. Heard*, 764 F.2d 423 (5th Cir. 1985); *United States v. Ismail*, 756 F.2d 1253 (6th Cir. 1985); *In re Grand Jury Subpoena of Santarelli*, 740 F.2d 816 (11th Cir. 1984); *United States v. Jones*, 683 F.2d 817 (4th Cir. 1982); and *United States v. Penn*, 647 F.2d 876 (9th Cir. 1980). Three federal district courts have recognized the privilege (two of them in a narrow way). *See In re Grand Jury Proceedings, Unemancipated Minor Child*, 949 F. Supp. 1487 (E.D. Wash. 1996) (recognizing

confidential communications privilege but child did not make a sufficient factual showing to claim it); *In re Agosto*, 553 F. Supp. 1298 (D. Nev. 1983) (recognizing confidential communications and adverse testimony privileges); *In re Grand Jury Proceedings (Greenberg)* (recognizing privilege to the extent Jewish faith prevents mother from testifying against daughter), 11 Fed R. Evid. Serv. 579 (D. Conn. 1982). Of these, *Agosto* accords the broadest privilege. Thirty-two-year-old Mr. Agosto claimed that he should not have to testify against his father before a federal grand jury in a tax evasion case. The court agreed with him. It held that parent and child, even adult children, each have both the confidential communication and the adverse testimonial privilege. The court invoked in support the evolutionary language of the federal branch of Rule 501, notions of constitutional familial privacy, and the value to society of fostering a strong and harmonious parental relationship — not only during the child's minority, when he or she needs guidance and integration into society, although that is a crucial benefit, but lifelong. The court noted that forced testimony of this kind has a deleterious and irreparable effect on the relationship by eroding trust, which the court regarded as essential to the relationship. Privilege, the court continued, would have comparatively minimal adverse impact on availability of evidence, since parents and children would probably rather perjure themselves than testify against each other.

(2) *Current State Law.* The states have also been reluctant to recognize privilege in this area. Only four have accorded the privilege by statute. These are Connecticut, Idaho, Massachusetts, and Minnesota.[22] Some New York state courts have created a parent-child privilege by case law. *See, e.g.*, *In re A & M*, 61 A.D.2d 426 (N.Y. App. Div. 1978); *People v. Fitzgerald*, 101 Misc. 2d 712 (N.Y. Cty. Ct. 1979). *See also In re Ryan*, 123 Misc. 2d 854, 855 (N.Y. Fam. Ct. 1984) (conversation between grandmother and minor grandson privileged). Almost all other state courts that have considered the matter have been against judicially creating this privilege if none exists by legislation. *See, e.g.*, *In re Inquest Proceedings*, 676 A.2d 790 (Vt. 1996); *State v. Maxon*, 756 P.2d 1297 (Wash. 1988); *State v. Amos*, 414 N.W.2d 147 (Mich. Ct. App. 1987) (per curiam); *In re* Gail D., 525 A.2d 337 (N.J. Super. Ct. App. Div. 1987); *People v. Dixon*, 411 N.W.2d 760 (Mich. Ct. App. 1987); *State v. Willoughby*, 532 A.2d 1020 (Me. 1987); *Cabello v. State*, 471 So. 2d 332 (Miss. 1985); *De Leon v. State*, 684 S.W.2d 778 (Tex. App. 1984); *In re Frances J.*, 456 A.2d 1174 (R.I. 1983); *Three Juveniles v. Commonwealth*, 455 N.E.2d 1203 (Mass. 1983); *People v. Sanders*, 457 N.E.2d 1241 (Ill. 1983); *State v. Gilroy*, 313 N.W.2d 513 (Iowa

---

[22] The Massachusetts provision prevents only unemancipated minor children from having to testify against their parents in a criminal proceeding and does not include a confidential communications privilege. Mass. Gen. Laws ch. 233, § 20 (2003). Minnesota's contains only a confidential communications privilege, covering those made from a minor child to the parent in both civil and criminal cases, and allowing either to waive the privilege. Minn. Stat. § 595.02(1)(j) (2002). Idaho's contains an adverse testimonial privilege and prohibits parents from being compelled to disclose any communication, confidential or otherwise, made to them by their minor children; and it applies in both civil and criminal proceedings in which the child is a party. Idaho Code § 9-203(7) (2002). Connecticut's permits parents of minors to refuse to testify in juvenile court for or against the accused child regardless of whether any communication involved was confidential. Conn. Gen. Stat. Ann. § 46b-138a (West 2003). Each of these state statutes also provides exceptions to privilege for offenses by the parent or child against one another or any family member.

1981); *Gibbs v. State*, 426 N.E.2d 1150 (Ind. Ct. App. 1981); *In re Terry W.*, 59 Cal. App. 3d 745 (Cal. Ct. App. 1976).

For more arguments concerning parent-child privilege, see Ross, *Implementing Constitutional Rights for Juveniles: The Parent-Child Privilege in Context*, 14 Stan. L. & Pol'y Rev. 85, 99–102 (2003).

[D] Miscellaneous Privileges

(1) *Counselor-Student Privilege.* The North Dakota Century Code contains a counselor-student privilege, enacted in 1969 [N.D. Cent. Code § 31-01-06.1]:

> Counselors shall be immune from disclosing information given by pupils. — For the purpose of counseling in a school system, any elementary or secondary school counselor possessing a valid North Dakota guidance credential from the department of public instruction, and who has been duly appointed a counselor for a school system by its proper authority, shall be legally immune from disclosing any privileged or confidential communication made to such counselor in a counseling interview. Such communication shall be disclosed when requested by the counselee.

(2) *Probation Officer Privilege.* On privilege covering statements made to a probation officer, see *Warren v. United States*, 436 A.2d 821 (D.C. 1981) (local rule of criminal procedure prohibiting use of information in presentence reports; rule not uncommon); *United States v. Holmes*, 594 F.2d 1167 (8th Cir.) (refusing to recognize presentence report privilege under federal branch of Fed. R. Evid. 501), *cert. denied*, 444 U.S. 873 (1979).

(3) *Boss-Secretary Privilege.* At one time, Oregon Rev. Stat. § 44.040(1)(f) provided: "A stenographer shall not, without consent of his or her employer, be examined as to any communication or dictation made by the employer to him or her in the course of professional employment." *United States v. Schoenheinz*, 548 F.2d 1389 (9th Cir. 1977), refused to adopt this as a matter of common law. How do we determine what type of relationships deserve a privilege?

(4) *Legislator Privilege.* In *United States v. Gillock*, 445 U.S. 360 (1980), the Court rejected an evidentiary privilege for state legislators that would bar evidence of legislative acts in federal criminal prosecutions.

(5) *Federal Statutory Privilege.* There are many federal and state statutory privileges peculiar to particular regulatory areas. No attempt is made to track them here. An example will suffice: *Pierce County, Washington v. Guillen*, 537 U.S. 129, 146 (2003), held that 23 U.S.C. § 409 of the Hazard Elimination Program provides an evidentiary privilege for accident reports compiled or collected by state agencies for purposes of applying for federal funds, but not for information compiled or collected for purposes unrelated to funding, and held by agencies not pursuing funding objectives.

§ 13.07 GOVERNMENTAL AND GOVERNMENT-RELATED PRIVILEGES[23]

(1) *Privileges for Required Reports.* Supreme Court Draft Federal Rule of Evidence proposed the following Rule 502, entitled "Required Reports Privileged by Statute":

> A person, corporation, association, or other organization or entity, either public or private, making a return or report required by law to be made has a privilege to refuse to disclose and to prevent any other person from disclosing the return or report, if the law requiring it to be made so provides. A public officer or agency to whom a return or report is required by law to be made has a privilege to refuse to disclose the return or report if the law requiring it to be made so provides. No privilege exists under this rule in actions involving perjury, false statements, fraud in the return or report, or other failure to comply with the law in question.

In the Matter of Grand Jury Impaneled January 21, 1975, 541 F.2d 373 (3d Cir. 1976), addressed the question of whether a person filing records under a state "required records" law providing for qualified confidentiality has a privilege against use of those records in any phase of a federal criminal proceeding. Despite Proposed Rule 502, which would have enacted such a privilege, the Court rejected it because of "the public's interest in law enforcement and in ensuring effective grand jury proceedings."

In re Hampers, 651 F.2d 19 (1st Cir. 1981), found a qualified privilege for state tax return information requested by a federal grand jury. In doing so, it followed the criteria established in *American Civil Liberties Union of Miss. v. Finch*, 638 F.2d 1336 (5th Cir. 1981), asking if the state recognized such a privilege, balancing the federal versus state interest, determining whether the state's asserted privilege is "intrinsically meritorious in our independent judgment," and employing the four Wigmore criteria (see note (1), *supra*, in § 13.01). *Hampers* held that in order to enforce a subpoena in federal criminal investigation, a federal grand jury must proffer reasonable cause to believe that a federal crime has been committed, the information sought will be probative of a matter at issue in the prosecution of that crime, and the same information or equally probative information cannot be obtained elsewhere through reasonable efforts.

For the law on the complicated matter of the disclosability of federal income tax returns, on which there is a special, detailed federal statute, see *United States v. Dean*, 647 F.2d 779 (8th Cir. 1981), *cert. denied*, 456 U.S. 1006 (1982) (independent evidentiary concerns about admitting tax returns as well).

(2) *Identity of Informers Privilege.* Supreme Court Draft Federal Rule of Evidence 510, though unenacted and non-binding, provides a fairly concise and influential statement of the law of informer's identity privilege:

> (a) **Rule of privilege.** The government or a state or subdivision thereof has a privilege to refuse to disclose the identity of a person who has furnished information relating to or assisting in an investigation of a

---

[23] Study Guide Reference: Evidence in a Nutshell, Chapter 5:VII.

possible violation of law to a law enforcement officer or member of a legislative committee or its staff conducting an investigation.

(b) Who may claim. The privilege may be claimed by an appropriate representative of the government, regardless of whether the information was furnished to an officer of the government or of a state or subdivision thereof. The privilege may be claimed by an appropriate representative of a state or subdivision if the information was furnished to an officer thereof, except that in criminal cases the privilege shall not be allowed if the government objects.

(c) Exceptions.

(1) Voluntary disclosure; informer a witness. No privilege exists under this rule if the identity of the informer or his interest in the subject matter of his communication has been disclosed to those who would have cause to resent the communication by a holder of the privilege or by the informerown action, or if the informer appears as a witness for the government.

(2) Testimony on merits. If it appears from the evidence in the case or from other showing by a party that an informer may be able to give testimony necessary to a fair determination of the issue of guilt or innocence in a criminal case or of a material issue on the merits in a civil case to which the government is a party, and the government invokes the privilege, the judge shall give the government an opportunity to show *in camera* facts relevant to determining whether the informer can, in fact, supply that testimony. The showing will ordinarily be in the form of affidavits, but the judge may direct that testimony be taken if he finds that the matter cannot be resolved satisfactorily upon the affidavit. If the judge finds that there is a reasonable probability that the informer can give the testimony, and the government elects not to disclose his identity, the judge on motion of the defendant in a criminal case shall dismiss the charges to which the testimony would relate, and the judge may do so on his own motion. In civil cases, he may make any order that justice requires. Evidence submitted to the judge shall be sealed and preserved to be made available to the appellate court in the event of an appeal, and the contents shall not otherwise be revealed without consent of the government. All counsel and parties shall be permitted to be present at every stage of proceedings under this subdivision except a showing *in camera*, at which no counsel or party shall be permitted to be present.

(3) Legality of obtaining evidence. If the information from an informer is relied upon to establish the legality of the means by which evidence was obtained and the judge is not satisfied that the information was received from an informer reasonably believed to be reliable or credible, he may require the identity of the informer to be disclosed. The judge shall, on request of the government, direct that the disclosure be made *in camera*. All counsel and parties concerned with the issue of legality shall be permitted to be present at every stage of proceedings under this subdivision except a disclosure *in camera*, at which no counsel or party shall be

> permitted to be present. If disclosure of the identity of the informer is made *in camera*, the record thereof shall be sealed and preserved to be made available to the appellate court in the event of an appeal, and the contents shall not otherwise be revealed without consent of the government.

Roviaro v. United States, 353 U.S. 53 (1957), remains the seminal case concerning the nature of the informer's privilege, which as the Court says,

> is in reality the Government's privilege to withhold from disclosure the identity of persons who furnish information of violations of law to officers charged with enforcement of that law. The purpose of the privilege is the furtherance and protection of the public interest in effective law enforcement. The privilege recognizes the obligation of citizens to communicate their knowledge of the commission of crimes to law enforcement officials and, by preserving their anonymity, encourages them to perform that obligation.

As the Court also recognized:

> The scope of the privilege is limited by its underlying purpose. Thus, where the disclosure of the contents of a communication will not tend to reveal the identity of an informer, the contents are not privileged. Likewise, once the identity of the informer has been disclosed to those who would have cause to resent the communication, the privilege is no longer applicable.
>
> A further limitation on the applicability of the privilege arises from the fundamental requirements of fairness. Where the disclosure of an informer's identity, or of the contents of his communication, is relevant and helpful to the defense of an accused, or is essential to a fair determination of a cause, the privilege must give way. In these situations the trial court may require disclosure and, if the Government withholds the information, dismiss the action.

Three situations tend to be distinguished by courts in criminal cases where identity-of-informer privilege is attempted to be asserted by the government: (1) "Probable cause" hearings where an arrest, search, seizure, or warrant is being challenged and the informer is not presented or identified, but an officer states that an informant provided certain information that is set forth (that apparently amounts to probable cause if obtained from a reasonably reliable source) and also states specific factual reasons he has justifying a reasonable belief in the informant's reliability, such as tips that proved to be correct before; (2) situations where an informer does not take the stand at defendant's trial but may be in possession of information that may help the defendant's defense; and (3) situations where the informer testifies against the defendant at trial.

In situation (1), the need for disclosure of identity is the least, because all that must be proved by the government is that the officers had "probable cause" — basically, reasonable grounds — to believe, even if the grounds, though appearing to a reasonable officer to be true, subsequently prove not to be in fact true. Only if the court cannot ascertain this without knowing the identity of the informer, will the identity be required. Situation (2) is the *Roviaro* situation. Here, if the defendant shows sufficient need, identity will have to be revealed. But the defendant is hard pressed to meet this burden, which entails showing that the informer may have important information, because the defendant does not know who the informer is until defendant meets that burden. *Roviaro* suggests what might be a sufficient showing of need. In that case it was held sufficient to show that the informant (a government undercover employee) was the only other participant in and witness to the crime (a private heroin transaction), and that a government witness said the informant denied ever knowing or seeing defendant, and there may have been entrapment. Situation (3) is the one where the constitutional need of the defendant to have the identity is at its greatest. See *Smith v. Illinois*, 390 U.S. 129 (1968), holding that having the witness' identity is part of the constitutional right to confrontation. It is very hard to mount an attack on someone's credibility if you don't know who they are, and the witness' incentive to be truthful might be muted.

Though this privilege is commonly called the "informer's privilege," you will note that it is actually held and exercisable only by the government, not the informer.

(3) *State and Military Secrets Privilege. United States v. Reynolds*, 345 U.S. 1 (1953), establishes that in a civil action in which the government is the defendant, it cannot be forced to disclose state or military secrets even if the plaintiff demonstrates "the most compelling necessity." *See also Black v. United States*, 62 F.3d 1115 (8th Cir. 1995) (invocation given utmost deference and can result in dismissal), *cert. denied*, 517 U.S. 1154 (1996). The boundaries of the doctrine still are unsettled. Supreme Court Federal Rule of Evidence 509, though unenacted and non-binding, provides a fairly concise and influential statement of the privilege for state and military secrets (sometimes simply called the "state secret privilege"), although the draft rule attempts to resolve some issues that are still in dispute today in the law. The rule also includes an "official information" privilege, which we consider in Note (4) later. For now, concentrate on the rule's provisions regarding state (including military) secrets:

Rule 509. Secrets of State and Other Official Information

(a) Definitions.

(1) Secret of state. A "secret of state" is a governmental secret relating to the national defense or the international relations of the United States.

(2) Official information. "Official information" is information within the custody or control of a department or agency of the government the disclosure of which is shown to be contrary to the public interest and which consists of: (A) intra-governmental opinions or recommendations submitted for consideration in the performance of decisional or policymaking functions, or (B) subject to the provisions of 18 U.S.C. § 3500,[24] investigatory files compiled for law enforcement purposes and not otherwise available, or (C) information within the custody or control of a governmental depart-

[24] This is the so-called "Jencks Act," which insulates prior statements of government witnesses in criminal cases against subpoena, discovery, or inspection until the witness has testified on direct examination at the trial but then entitles the defense to production.

ment of agency whether initiated within the department or agency or acquired by it in its exercise of its official responsibilities and not otherwise available to the public pursuant to 5 U.S.C. § 552.[25]

(b) General rule of privilege. The government has a privilege to refuse to give evidence and to prevent any person from giving evidence upon a showing of reasonable likelihood of danger that the evidence will disclose a secret of state or official information as defined in this rule.

(c) Procedures. The privilege for secrets of state may be claimed only by the chief officer of the government agency or department administering the subject matter which the secret information sought concerns, but the privilege for official information may be asserted by any attorney representing the government. The required showing may be made in whole or in part in the form of a written statement. The judge may hear the matter in chambers, but all counsel are entitled to inspect the claim and showing and to be heard thereon, except that, in the case of secrets of state, the judge upon motion of the government, may permit the government to make the required showing in the above form *in camera.* If the judge sustains the privilege upon a showing *in camera,* the entire text of the government's statements shall be sealed and preserved in the court's records in the event of appeal. In the case of privilege claimed for official information the court may require examination *in camera* of the information itself. The judge may take any protective measure which the interests of the government and the furtherance of justice require.

(d) Notice to government. If the circumstances of the case indicate a substantial possibility that a claim of privilege would be appropriate but has not been made because of oversight or lack of knowledge, the judge shall give or cause notice to be given to the officer entitled to claim the privilege and shall stay further proceedings a reasonable time to afford opportunity to assert a claim of privilege.

(e) Effect of sustaining claim. If a claim of privilege is sustained in a proceeding to which the government is a party and it appears that another party is thereby deprived of material evidence, the judge shall make any further orders which the interests of justice require, including striking the testimony of a witness, declaring a mistrial, finding against the government upon an issue as to which the evidence is relevant, or dismissing the action.

The rule provides a concise and convenient focus for thinking about a number of important and complex issues in this area of the law and the law of governmental privilege generally, some of which issues are currently the subject of a conflict of authority:

(i) *The definition of state secret in (a)(1) and the likelihood of danger language in (b).* Do these provisions make it too easy for the government to claim privilege? Note that the "danger" required to be shown is only that

---

[25] This is the Freedom of Information Act, explained *supra* in § 13.01 of this book, to which you should refer at this point.

the material reveals a "secret of state," defined as anything that "relates to" national defense or international relations, presumably in any degree. It is not required that it be shown that there is a danger of *harm* to national defense or international relations. And there is no specification of degree (neither concerning *how much* danger there must be that something will be revealed relating to national defense or international relations, nor *how closely* information must "relate to" national defense or international relations). Can't almost anything be deemed to "relate to" national defense and international relations in some degree, if there is no requirement about how closely it must relate?

Note also that in (a)(1), the rule seems to define "secret of state" by using the phrase "government secret" relating to national defense or international relations. This seems to add nothing more to the requirements than that the government regard it as a secret, that the government has thus far kept it a secret, and that the government now claims privilege for it.

Is the court being asked by the rule to take the word of the government that something is secret, that it involves national defense or international relations, that it will be revealed, that revelation would be harmful to national interests in some important respect and degree, and that the harm is sufficient in kind and degree to outweigh countervailing concerns? Does the rule mean there shall be no independent scrutiny by the court, despite the fact that the rule appears to give the court a role?

Does the requirement that the information be a "government secret" mean that it has to have been "classified"? If it has been marked "classified" by the government, can there be any inquiry into whether it was properly classified?

Do you think government officials tend to over-classify or claim secrecy for illegitimate reasons (e.g., to cover incompetence, prevent embarrassment, or avert liability) as well as legitimate reasons? *Reynolds* itself, *supra*, the leading case on this privilege, is a case in point. In *Reynolds*, personnel were aboard an airplane testing electronic defense equipment for the government, when a fire broke out and many of them perished. Surviving family members sued the government and requested a copy of the government's accident investigation report. At the insistence of the government, that request was ultimately denied by the court on grounds of the state-military secrets privilege. Many years later, when the report was declassified, it was revealed that nothing at all of any importance relating to the allegedly sensitive electronic defense equipment or any other sensitive matter was contained in it. *See* Siegal, *A Daughter Discovers What Really Happened*, L.A. Times, p. A1 (Apr. 19, 2004).

In *E.P.A. v. Mink*, 410 U.S. 73 (1973), the Court held that the propriety of the government's classifying a document "top secret" could not be inquired into by the judge, where the government claimed the document was within the exception or exemption in the Freedom of Information Act for state-military secrets. (*See* § 13.01 *supra* for an explanation of the

Freedom of Information Act.) However, the Freedom of Information Act was subsequently amended to permit such a challenge, and this probably would govern *a fortiori* in the privilege context, although that is not entirely certain.

Now let us look at the other side of the coin. Shouldn't we tend to err on the side of secrecy in these times of terrorism? Do we want a lot of scrutiny and independent judgment by the court? Don't we have to trust the government? Can things really be revealed in court but protected sufficiently by placing them under seal and restricting access? Can judges and lawyers be trusted? Parties? But would it be fair and constitutional to restrict a party's access to information used in court?

Are special security measures really effective? Consider storage in secure locations, introduction of summaries of sensitive information instead of the real information, requiring security clearances for everyone who might see the information. Would summaries be fair? Constitutional?

See the Classified Information Procedures Act, 18 U.S.C. App. 3 describing procedures like those just mentioned for minimizing unnecessary disclosures and leaks in criminal cases where defendants claim (perhaps correctly or nefariously) that if the prosecution goes forward, state or military secrets will have to be disclosed in order for them to defend themselves. This kind of threat is sometimes known as "graymail" by analogy to "blackmail." *See United States v. Moussaoui*, 382 F.3d 453 (4th Cir. 2004) (in prosecution of the so-called 20th hijacker in the Sept. 11 airplane attacks on the N.Y. World Trade Center Twin Towers, procedures of the Act were utilized; decision holds that summaries of statements allegedly showing *Moussaoui* was not involved in plans for the hijacking, for which he could get the death penalty, are allowed to the extent judge finds them to be satisfactory substitutes for the live testimony of persons in custody whom the U.S. claims cannot be produced without jeopardy to national interests; *Moussaoui* ultimately pleads guilty to lesser charges in a plea deal).

Can you think of a better definition of "state secret" and the degree and kind of danger that must be shown, than what is in the rule, to better accommodate the conflicting interests involved? Or is the rule the best we can do in view of what is at stake?

(ii) *Who must make the privilege claim?* Notice that the provision on this in the rule is different for the two privileges addressed by the rule. Why that difference? Does it have to do with political accountability? In *Reynolds* the Secretary of the Air Force asserted the claim, which procedure the Court approved, saying the head of the "executive department" involved must make the claim after "actual personal consideration." The rule says "agency or department." Is this different?

(iii) *May the judge inspect the content of the secret in deciding the privilege claim?* The answer seems to be no, under the rule, even if the inspection is *in camera*, by the judge alone. *Reynolds* is ambiguous.

Reynolds says the trial judge had only to be satisfied that there was a "reasonable possibility that military secrets were involved" (not that they actually were). *Reynolds* further states that the depth of the judge's inquiry on this depends on the strength of the other side's showing of need for the information. But once the judge is satisfied of this reasonable possibility, the privilege applies, with no process of balancing the other side's need for the information against degree of danger to the public interest, no matter how compelling the need. On the particular facts of *Reynolds* itself, the Court holds that the showing of need was not great and therefore only a superficial inquiry concerning the overall circumstances and the broad subject of the report was called for. But then *Reynolds* adds that no matter how compelling the showing of need, once it appears that there is a reasonable possibility a "military secret" might be involved, the privilege "cannot be overcome." It is uncertain whether this means the secret information itself can never be examined by the judge even *in camera*. *E.P.A. v. Mink*, 410 U.S. 73 (1973) held that, in the context of the Freedom of Information Act, which has an exception or exemption specifically for state secrets, see § 13.01 *supra*, the judge could not examine, even *in camera*, "top secret" documents that the government claimed was within the exemption. However, the Freedom of Information Act was subsequently amended, specifically to overrule *Mink*. If the judge may now examine such documents for purposes of Freedom of Information Act requests, which are made by members of the press and the public, it would make little sense to say that the judge may not do so under the privilege where information is needed in court. Nevertheless, the law on this point concerning the privilege is still uncertain.

Why is there a difference between the two privileges covered by the rule on the matter of the judge's inspection of the privileged material itself? Can the judge make a decision on the matters called for by the rule, or on the needs of a criminal defendant or other party, without examining the allegedly secret material? Or are those needs irrelevant? Can they be irrelevant in a criminal case?

(iv) *Who is privy to showings and arguments to the judge on the privilege question?* Is there a difference on this matter, between the two privileges covered by the rule? Why? How can an individual mount an argument against the government's privilege claim if he/she is not privy to the showings made in support of the claim?

(v) *What is the effect on the government's case of the judge properly sustaining the government's privilege claim, in a case to which the government is a party?* This needs to be broken down into (a) a civil case where the government is a party plaintiff, (b) a civil case where the government is a party defendant, and (c) a criminal case. In situations (a) and (c) courts generally hold that the government's case will be dismissed, or at least the factual issue that could have been illuminated (but for the privilege), will be resolved against the government.[26] But in situation (b), there will be no effect at all. Why this difference? Is it explained by the notion that the government can use the privilege as a shield but not a sword? What does that mean? Does this have any analogy under informer's privilege?

Does the rule bear out the three distinctions discussed under number (v)?

The cases of *Totten v. United States*, 92 U.S. 105 (1876), and, more recently, *Tenet v. Doe,* 544 U.S. 1 (2005), reveal that if a court feels that state or military secrets will inevitably be revealed if the suit goes forward, or that state or military secrets are centrally and inextricably intertwined with the subject matter of the litigation, the court may not permit the suit to proceed at all. It will dismiss rather than attempt to determine which particular pieces of evidence should be barred as privileged. Both these cases were suits by private individuals against the government (in *Totten,* against the administration of Abraham Lincoln) for breach of a government contract for the individual's spying services. It was held in both that the suits had to be dismissed because of the extreme sensitivity of the subject of whether or not there was any spy contract. The suit alone, including any assertion, acknowledgment or denial of the contract, would be a state secret. And such secrets would inevitably be revealed in the course of the litigation.[27]

(vi) *What is the effect, under the rule, of the judge properly sustaining the privilege claim, in a case to which the government is not a party?* This situation might involve, for example, a civil suit between a contractor and a subcontractor on a government defense project, say to build a secret nuclear powered spy plane, where the merits of a claim or defense of one of them depends upon some evidence that the government claims is privileged. For example, the evidence might be the specifications for the plane that the government provided to these security-cleared contractors. The sub-contractor for a component part may have interpreted a specification in a way that caused the job to run well over the allotted time, causing the main contractor to lose money. Only the plans can show who was right. But the government claims they are privileged. What happens? The usual result in the courts is that nothing happens: the case proceeds as though the evidence was burned up or the witnesses with the information are dead. *See Bareford v. General Dynamics Corp.*, 973 F.2d 1138 (5th Cir. 1992); *Farnsworth Cannon, Inc. v. Grimes*, 635 F.2d 268 (4th Cir. 1980) (*en*

---

[26] Indeed, even if the government wrongfully insists on privilege and refuses to disclose information the judge quite properly orders disclosed, the extent of the penalty may only be some effect on the government's case, such as dismissing it or resolving issues against it, if the government is a party. There is a judicial reluctance to throw anyone in jail or fine them, in this area. Why do you suppose that is so?

[27] See also *Farnsworth Cannon,* immediately below, indicating that this same principle of dismissal may also apply to cases wholly between private parties involving state-military secrets — for example, a lawsuit between two government contractors on a national defense project — if secrets would necessarily be implicated.

banc). The lawsuit is determined without the evidence. Let the chips fall where they may. But is this fair? One of the parties — perhaps the one who should have won — loses, perhaps only because he couldn't show the plans that would have borne him out. Indeed, he may be wiped out financially by the loss of the suit. And why does he lose? Because the public needed the protection the privilege accords. Should that one contractor have to pay for the public's protection? Shouldn't the public as a whole pay for it? But how would that work?

(vii) *Is the privilege a "qualified" privilege?* A number of privileges are said to be "qualified" in that they give way upon a showing of special need for the evidence by the other side or by the system in the particular case — need in a degree that outweighs the degree of benefit conferred by the privilege on the particular facts. "Need" means the evidence is important evidence, on an important point, in an important kind of litigation, and the substantial equivalent of the evidence cannot be obtained any other reasonable way.

Is the state secrets privilege a qualified privilege? Most courts say "No." Does the rule seem to accord with this? Do you see another sense in which the privilege might be qualified, when you look at the rule, or when you consider some of the above points? In what sense is the *other* privilege in the rule qualified? Is informers' privilege qualified? Presidential privilege? Reporter's privilege? *See* materials *supra* and *infra* on these privileges.

Consider again carefully what is said in our point (iii) above about *Reynolds*. Is the state secrets privilege under *Reynolds* a qualified privilege? Do you think courts might draw different conclusions on this from *Reynolds*?

(4) *Official Information/Deliberative Process Privilege.* In a lawsuit the government attempts to resist disclosure of certain relevant documents in the files of a local office of a government agency. The government concedes that the information contained therein does not rise to the level of a state, military, or diplomatic secret, or a secret relating to international relations, but does claim that up until now the information has been kept confidential within the agency and that disclosure would be adverse to the public interest because the documents contain deliberations and notations by departmental workers and information supplied by citizens; and that these people would feel reluctant to enter into deliberations, make notations, and supply information so freely if they thought these kinds of things could be disclosed. Alternatively, the government feels that disclosure would be against the public interest because the documents constitute a preliminary position paper, a final position not having yet been reached by the office or agency. Disclosure, the government argues, would cause early public debate that might make decision difficult and harden people into positions before all sides are put forward. The documents relate to where the best neighborhood would be to locate a new sewage and garbage landfill. The lawsuit is a civil lawsuit to which the government is not a party. The documents are relevant in the lawsuit because the lawsuit is a private breach-of-contract action against a seller of land who refused to sell after making a contract to do so. The issue is an issue of damages: under the operative law, the

buyer would be entitled to lost profits he might have made on resale or productive use of the land; but the question of whether or not there was any chance of a landfill being located nearby, and the degree of probability thereof, would have a bearing on the expected profitability and uses the buyer could have made of the land. Is the material privileged? Proposed Rule 509(a)(2), reproduced in full above near the beginning of note (3), provided an absolute privilege for "official information," which it defined as:

> information within the custody or control of a department or agency of the government the disclosure of which is shown to be contrary to the public interest and which consists of: (A) intragovernmental opinions or recommendations submitted for consideration in the performance of decisional or policymaking functions, or (B) subject to the provisions of 18 U.S.C. § 3500 [*Jencks* Act], investigatory files compiled for law enforcement purposes and not otherwise available, or (C) information within the custody or control of a governmental department or agency whether initiated within the department or agency or acquired by it in its exercise of its official responsibilities and not otherwise available to the public pursuant to 5 U.S.C. § 552 [Freedom of Information Act].

While you have not studied the Freedom of Information Act, you should try solving the problem anyway, as best you can.

For the official information privilege in action, with informative discussion, including reference to draft Fed. R. Evid. 509, *see In re Franklin Nat'l Bank Sec. Litig.*, 445 F. Supp. 723, *supplemented*, 449 F. Supp. 574 (E.D.N.Y. 1978) (lawsuit concerning financial collapse of very large bank; reports of federal bank examiners not privileged, but summaries and analyses of reports made by various governmental officials are privileged; balancing of competing interests); *Peck v. United States*, 88 F.R.D. 65 (S.D.N.Y. 1980) (in action against federal government for alleged misconduct of FBI, government task force report investigating incident was privileged from plaintiffs, notwithstanding that report was to be submitted to Congress; factors: even if unprivileged, report would not be admissible in evidence and most of facts in report were otherwise available to plaintiffs; also, material furnished by persons under promise of confidentiality deserves special protection under this privilege). On reading these two cases, one gets the impression from the discussion in the first one that there is very little that ever would be privileged, and from discussion in the second one that there is very little that ever would be unprivileged. For a case surveying the case law about what it calls the "deliberative process" privilege and finding it to be a qualified privilege, see *Texaco Puerto Rico, Inc. v. Dep't of Consumer Affairs*, 60 F.3d 867 (1st Cir. 1995). *See also Grand Cent. Partnership, Inc. v. Cuomo*, 166 F.3d 473 (2d Cir. 1999), which held that the deliberative process privilege only applies to federal, not state, agencies under the Freedom of Information Act.

(5) *Executive Privilege.* This privilege, which is of uncertain contours, operates to keep the chief executive (President or perhaps governor) and his oral and written communications and papers, and some of his close advisors and their oral and written communications and papers, out of court, even though none of the other privileges may apply — e.g., no state or military secret, etc., is claimed to be

involved, and the executive does not wish to advance a reason for assertion of privilege (required for the "official information" privilege) — probably only if the documents, communications, etc., to be inquired into are connected with performing or advising or fashioning advice for the President concerning his official business. Related conversations of these persons also will be within the privilege. *In re Sealed Case*, 121 F.3d 729 (D.C. Cir. 1997), notes that the "presidential privilege is rooted in constitutional separation of powers principles and the President's unique constitutional role," and "unlike the deliberative process privilege, the presidential communications privilege applies to documents in their entirety, and covers final and post-decisional materials as well as pre-deliberative ones."

In *United States v. Nixon*, 418 U.S. 683 (1974), the Supreme Court held that the courts in the "Watergate" criminal case (the President was not a defendant) had a need for certain presidential tapes (of his conversations), materials, and written information, and that the need was superior to the President's assertion of his privilege (unsupported as it was by any specific harms, other than general inhibition of communications, that might come from disclosure, such as jeopardy of any state or military secrets). The principle may be broader than merely this particular privilege. The court did not base its decision on any suggestion that the President may have been involved in the illegality.

Courts vary in how broadly they interpret the contours of executive privilege and the principles it espouses. *Compare In re Sealed Case, supra*, which found that the "public interest is best served by holding that communications made by presidential advisers in the course of preparing advice for the President come under the presidential communications privilege, even when these communications are not made directly to the President" *with In re Grand Jury Subpoena Duces Tecum*, 112 F.3d 910 (8th Cir.), *cert. denied*, 521 U.S. 1105 (1997), which held that the White House could not invoke any form of governmental attorney-client privilege to withhold potentially relevant information from a grand jury, and that no common interest existed between the President's wife in her personal capacity and the White House justifying invocation of common-interest doctrine to extend the attorney-client privilege to conversations involving the President's wife, her personal attorney, and attorneys representing the White House.

There may even be a "privilege not to have to claim privilege" residing in the President and Vice President. *See Cheney v. United States Dist. Court*, 542 U.S. 367 (2004) (constitutional separation of powers concept may insulate Vice President from very broad and otherwise legitimate discovery request in a legitimate lawsuit, without the Vice President or his people having to sort through all the documents requested in order to identify those for which he may want to claim executive privilege, if any). *See also In re Lindsey*, 158 F.3d 1263 (D.C. Cir.), *cert. denied*, 525 U.S. 996 (1998), holding that the Deputy White House Counsel could not assert government attorney-client privilege to avoid responding to a grand jury if he possessed information relating to possible criminal violations by the President or his people.

§ 13.08 FIFTH AMENDMENT PRIVILEGE[28]

No attempt is made here to cover the privilege against self-incrimination. The subject usually is covered in courses on criminal law, constitutional law, or criminal procedure. We already have encountered some of its applications. A few case citations are all that will be suggested here. *See*, on the privilege generally, *Malloy v. Hogan*, 378 U.S. 1 (1964) (seminal case; Fifth Amendment is applied to states by Fourteenth Amendment; applicable where disclosure might furnish link in chain of evidence connecting defendant to crime for which he could be prosecuted); *Murphy v. Waterfront Comm'n of N.Y. Harbor*, 378 U.S. 52 (1964) (seminal case concerning immunity and possibility of prosecution by another jurisdiction); *United States v. Balsys*, 524 U.S. 666 (1998) (although *Murphy v. Waterfront Comm'n* held that fear of prosecution by another American jurisdiction is cognizable under the privilege, concern with foreign prosecution is beyond the scope of the Fifth Amendment privilege against self-incrimination); *Schmerber v. California*, 384 U.S. 757 (1966) (taking blood is not testimonial); *Pillsbury Co. v. Conboy*, 459 U.S. 248 (1983) (civil deponent retains privilege when asked to confirm previous immunized testimony so long as deposition testimony is not also immunized); *Pennsylvania v. Muniz*, 496 U.S. 582 (1990) (revealing physical manner in which words are articulated is not testimonial; also permits response to routine booking questions, despite absence of *Miranda* warnings); *Ohio v. Reiner*, 532 U.S. 17 (2001) (defendant can assert Fifth Amendment privilege despite her claim of innocence, since she had reasonable cause to apprehend danger from her answers at trial); *Hiibel v. Sixth Judicial Dist. Court of Nevada, Humboldt County*, 542 U.S. 177 (2004) (suspect's conviction for refusal to identify himself in violation of Nevada's "stop and identify" law, did not violate his Fifth Amendment right against self-incrimination, absent showing that disclosure of his name presented any reasonable danger of incrimination); *McKune v. Lile*, 536 U.S. 24 (2002) (adverse consequences faced by state prisoner for refusing to make admissions required for participation in sexual abuse treatment program were not so severe as to amount to compelled self-incrimination); *Chavez v. Martinez*, 538 U.S. 760 (2003) (because right against self-incrimination does not apply absent the use of the suspect's compelled statements in a criminal proceeding against him, allegations of coercive questioning could not be the basis of a civil action alleging that the officer violated individual's constitutional rights by subjecting him to coercive interrogation after he had been shot by another police officer, since he was not charged with any crime).

The case of *Griffin v. California*, 380 U.S. 609 (1965), is widely cited for the constitutional proposition that in federal and state prosecutions neither judge nor opposing lawyer may invite the jury to draw an adverse inference from a criminal defendant's exercise of his or her Fifth Amendment privilege to stay off the stand. The corollary of *Griffin* is an entitlement to an instruction to the jury not to draw an adverse inference, if the party would want such an instruction (query whether the judge should be able to give one whether wanted or not?). Similarly, *Mitchell v. United* States, 526 U.S. 314 (1999), held that neither defendant's guilty plea nor her statements at plea colloquy functioned as a waiver of her right to remain silent at

[28] Study Guide Reference: Evidence in a Nutshell, Chapter 5:VIII–X; Chapter 6:X at "The Scope of Cross Examination." *See also* Fed. R. Evid. 608(b) last paragraph.

sentencing, and that the sentencing court could not draw any adverse inference from defendant's silence, in determining facts relating to circumstances and details of the crime. In contrast, a witness's assertion, in a civil trial, of the privilege against self-incrimination may be considered by a jury, and inferences may be drawn therefrom, both under the constitution and under the Federal Rules of Evidence, notwithstanding *Griffin* and a provision about privileges in general in the Supreme Court Draft Federal Rules of Evidence and the Uniform Rules. The Uniform Rule provision is reproduced at the beginning of our section on Attorney-Client privilege, *supra. See Baxter v. Palmigiano*, 425 U.S. 308 (1976) (permitting adverse inference in prison disciplinary hearing; establishing general principle for civil cases); *Brink's Inc. v. City of New York*, 717 F.2d 700 (2d Cir. 1983) (adverse inferences permitted against employer for taking of Fifth by both present and former employees).

Concerning subpoenaed records, *compare United States v. Doe*, 465 U.S. 605 (1984) (*Doe I*) (holding that contents of sole proprietor's voluntarily prepared business records are not protected by Fifth Amendment privilege; act of producing such records, however, might be, since it could be both testimonial and incriminating), *with Braswell v. United States*, 487 U.S. 99 (1988) (holding that act-of-production doctrine is not implicated when documents are subpoenaed from corporate custodian, even in one-person corporation). *Braswell* epitomizes the rationale for the Collective Entity Doctrine, which denies any privilege for the records of any type of collective entity, despite the fact that those records may be personally incriminating. The privilege against self-incrimination also does not protect unprivileged preexisting client documents that have been given to an attorney. *Fisher v. United States*, 425 U.S. 391 (1976). Concerning documents, see also *Doe v. United States*, 487 U.S. 201 (1988) (*Doe II*), holding that a "consent directive" form that permits disclosure of foreign bank records was not testimonial because its wording did not require any statement regarding the existence of the account or the Does' control over it, and it did not authenticate the documents produced. In *United States v. Hubbell*, 530 U.S. 27 (2000), the Supreme Court held that immunity granted a defendant in a prior prosecution in exchange for his disclosure of broad categories of documents responsive to a subpoena precluded his subsequent, unrelated prosecution, to the extent that the testimonial aspect of the defendant's act of producing documents was the first, necessary step in discovery of evidence supporting the second prosecution. *Hubbell* applies, in a somewhat complex fact setting, a simpler doctrine (adverted to above) under the privilege against self-incrimination, one that is applicable to other privileges as well, particularly attorney-client privilege. The doctrine is that while certain documents may not themselves be privileged, the act of producing or selecting documents in response to a subpoena or other request, or for other purposes, may itself create a new "message" with new information, that may be privileged — in this case, incriminatory information. For example, producing a document may acknowledge that the document exists, that it is authentic, that you have it and know about it, or that the document is relevant to the subject of the request. But see *Baltimore City Dep't of Social Services v. Bouknight*, 493 U.S. 549 (1990), which denied any act of production privilege that would permit a mother, who had been ordered to produce her child by the Juvenile Court because of fear for the child's safety, to withhold the child pursuant to an argument that producing the child might incriminate her.

When a defendant does not plead insanity or introduce psychiatric evidence at trial, the state's evidence obtained from a court-ordered competency examination to support imposition of the death penalty violates the Fifth Amendment. *See Estelle v. Smith*, 451 U.S. 454 (1981). In *Penry v. Johnson*, 532 U.S. 782 (2001), the Supreme Court distinguished *Estelle v. Smith*, in a habeas corpus context:

> First, the defendant in *Estelle* had not placed his mental condition at issue, whereas Penry himself made his mental status a central issue in both the 1977 rape case and his trials for Pamela Carpenter's rape and murder. Second, in *Estelle*, the trial court had called for the competency evaluation and the State had chosen the examining psychiatrist. Here, however, it was Penry's own counsel in the 1977 case who requested the psychiatric exam performed by Dr. Peebles. Third, in *Estelle*, the State had called the psychiatrist to testify as a part of its affirmative case. Here, it was during the cross-examination of Penry's own psychological witness that the prosecutor elicited the quotation from the Peebles report. And fourth, in *Estelle*, the defendant was charged with a capital crime at the time of his competency exam, and it was thus clear that his future dangerousness would be a specific issue at sentencing. Penry, however, had not yet murdered Pamela Carpenter at the time of his interview with Dr. Peebles.

Chapter 14

JUDICIAL NOTICE

ESTABLISHING OBVIOUS FACTS (F.R.E. ARTICLE II)

§ 14.01 INTRODUCTION

Judicial notice is a doctrine invoked by courts to obviate the necessity of formal proof on a matter. Cogent judicial discussion of the underlying theory is rare, however. For such discussion the reader is referred to several works by Professor Kenneth Culp Davis: 2 ADMINISTRATIVE LAW TREATISE, Ch. 15 (2d ed. 1980), substantially reproduced in DAVIS & PIERCE, ADMINISTRATIVE LAW TREATISE 155 (3d ed. 1994); *Judicial Notice*, 55 COLUM. L. REV. 945 (1955); and *Official Notice*, 62 HARV. L. REV. 537 (1949). *See also* Turner, *Judicial Notice and Federal Rule of Evidence 201 — A Rule Ready for Change*, 45 U. PITT. L. REV. 181 (1983); Davis, *"There is a Book Out. . .": An Analysis of Judicial Absorption of Legislative Facts*, 100 HARV. L. REV. 1539 (1987); Faigman, *"Normative Constitutional Fact-Finding": Exploring the Empirical Component of Constitutional Interpretation*, 139 U. PA. L. REV. 541 (1991); Graham, *Judicial Notice of Adjudicative and Legislative Facts*, 17 CRIM. L. BULL. 241 (1981); Langum, *Uncodified Federal Evidence Rules Applicable to Civil Trials*, 19 WILLAMETTE L. REV. 513, 527–29 (1983). Judicial decisions in the area are more interesting for what they do than for what they say.

There are several categories of judicial notice that can be easily defined but often prove difficult to distinguish in practice. The type governed by Federal Rule of Evidence 201 concerns adjudicative facts, which typically are thought of as the facts establishing the "who, what, why, when and where" of the action. In contrast, legislative facts often are not really even facts at all but the information and opinions that are relied upon by judges when they make law or rules or interpret legal standards. What some call "communicative" and "evaluative" facts are the common-sense principles we use to process information. By shared language we have a picture of a "car" that is different from a "truck" or a "bus." Similarly, while the fact that it was raining on the night of an accident is adjudicative, the "fact" that we know when it rains roads may be slippery or cars may not stop as quickly as usual or without skidding is evaluative. Judicial notice of law also is a well-recognized category. Rule 201's limitation to adjudicative facts does not mean that all notice of other than adjudicative facts is prohibited. Instead, it simply means that any other form of judicial notice is not governed by the restrictions in Rule 201.

§ 14.02 JUDICIAL NOTICE OF ADJUDICATIVE FACTS[1]

Read Federal Rule of Evidence 201, "Judicial Notice of Adjudicative Facts.":

SHAHAR v. BOWERS

United States Court of Appeals, Eleventh Circuit
120 F.3d 211 (1997)

BY THE COURT:

[An attorney sued the Georgia Attorney General, asserting that the Attorney General violated the plaintiff's rights of intimate and expressive association, freedom of religion, equal protection, and substantive due process when the Attorney General withdrew an offer of employment to the plaintiff after he learned of the plaintiff's lesbian "marriage." Summary judgment was entered for the Attorney General. The Court of Appeals, 70 F.3d 1218, affirmed in part and vacated and remanded in part. On a rehearing *en banc*, 114 F.3d 1097, the Court of Appeals affirmed the summary judgement in full and withdrew the order remanding. The plaintiff then petitioned for a rehearing and moved to supplement the record or for a remand to do so. The Court of Appeals here denies the petition and holds that the matter in question was not appropriate for judicial notice.]

Ms. Shahar's petition for rehearing relies, in part, on two recent newspaper articles reporting that former Attorney General Michael J. Bowers has admitted to having an adulterous affair in the past with a woman employed in the Department of Law. She requests that this information become part of the record in this case by judicial notice or by remand to the district court for discovery.

[T]he taking of judicial notice of facts is, as a matter of evidence law, a highly limited process. The reason for this caution is that the taking of judicial notice bypasses the safeguards which are involved with the usual process of proving facts by competent evidence in district court. Courts can take notice of certain facts without formal proof but only where the fact in question is "one not subject to reasonable dispute in that it is either (1) generally known within the territorial jurisdiction of the trial court or (2) capable of accurate and ready determination by resort to sources whose accuracy cannot reasonably be questioned." Fed. R. Evid. 201(b).

For example, the kinds of things about which courts ordinarily take judicial notice are (1) scientific facts: for instance, when does the sun rise or set; (2) matters of geography: for instance, what are the boundaries of a state; or (3) matters of political history: for instance, who was president in 1958. Ms. Shahar asks us to take judicial notice of the conduct of one person, Michael J. Bowers; and she asks us to take judicial notice of conduct which is not his official conduct (an example of his official conduct which might be judicially noticed would be that he issued a particular official opinion on a certain date). She has shown us no case — and we have found none — where a federal court of appeals took judicial notice of the

[1] Study Guide Reference: Evidence in a Nutshell, Chapter 2:I.

unofficial conduct of one person based upon newspaper accounts (or the person-campaign committee's press release) about that conduct.[5] We are not inclined to extend the doctrine of judicial notice as far as Plaintiff-Appellant asks us to take it.[6]

The petition for rehearing is denied.

BIRCH and BARKETT, CIRCUIT JUDGES, and GODBOLD, SENIOR CIRCUIT JUDGE, dissenting:

We dissent from the court's denial of Shahar's motion to supplement the record. Bowers' public statement is relevant to whether his asserted fear of adverse public reaction to perceived sexual misconduct of persons in the Georgia Department of Law was a bona fide reason for terminating Shahar and to whether he acted as a non-discriminatory decisionmaker in the Shahar matter.

Judicial notice is obviously appropriate. The "newspaper account" was not a reporter's conclusion or a statement by a third party; it was a statement by Bowers admitting his conduct and asking forgiveness for it. The statement was made through Bowers' political campaign headquarters and was published nationwide by newspapers, radio, television, and magazines of national circulation. Surely, this court can know the content of a statement that is relevant, accurate because made by Bowers himself, and known to millions. Moreover, in light of the fact that "Attorney General Baker and Bowers have no objection to the Court's including the proffered information in the record of this case," Response of Attorney General Thurbert E. Baker and Former Attorney General Michael J. Bowers, we fail to see why the court refuses to do so.

NOTES AND QUESTIONS

(1) *Judicial Notice of Existence of Documents versus their Truth.* Often courts draw distinctions between taking judicial notice of the existence of a document and taking notice of the truth of its content. This frequently occurs when judicial proceedings from other courts are being noticed, because the contents of the court records often contain disputed facts. *See Kramer v. Time Warner, Inc.*, 937 F.2d 767 (2d Cir. 1991).

(2) *Timing of Notice.* Fed. R. Evid. 201(f) permits notice at any stage of the

---

[5] We stress that we are not asked merely to take judicial notice of the fact that the media has reported "X" or the fact that a press release says "X." We are asked to know "X."

The dissent mentions a statement "made by Mr. Bowers." The only pertinent statement before us which might be said to have been made by Mr. Bowers is a written press release on "Bowers for Governor" letterhead. The statement is unsworn, unsigned, and speaks neither of "adultery" nor of other sexual conduct; it does use words like "involved with" and "relationship." Whatever people in general may wish to infer for themselves from this release, the statement lays no foundation for a federal court's taking judicial notice that Mr. Bowers has committed adultery or fornication.

[6] We do not accept this proposition to be part of the law of evidence: that information — a "fact" which is an improper subject of judicial notice — automatically becomes a proper subject of judicial notice if no party objects to the "fact" and that, therefore, an appellate court is bound to take judicial notice of the "fact."

proceedings. Here the notice was requested on appeal. In civil cases, notice can contradict the pleadings in situations where the procedural rules do not allow reference to outside materials, such as in challenges to the complaint for failure to state a claim. *See Solis-Ramirez v. United States Dep't of Justice*, 758 F.2d 1426 (11th Cir. 1985) (Fed. R. Civ. Proc. 12(b)(6)).

PROBLEM 14A: CAN YOU GET FOOD POISONING FROM THE E. COLI BACTERIA AFTER PROPERLY COOKING BEEF?

Plaintiff brings a suit against his local food market claiming that he became violently ill after eating a hamburger made with beef he bought there. His complaint alleges that his sickness resulted from the beef being contaminated with e. coli bacteria. The plaintiff testifies in his deposition that he cooked the beef at the proper temperature until it was no longer pink inside before eating it. Defendant moves for summary judgment, and asks the court to take judicial notice that properly cooking hamburger at a sufficient temperature kills the e. coli bacteria. Is this the sort of fact that can be judicially noticed? At this stage of the proceeding? If notice is taken of this fact, does it automatically result in summary judgment being granted?

§ 14.03 SPECIAL CONSIDERATIONS CONCERNING JUDICIAL NOTICE OF ADJUDICATIVE FACTS IN CRIMINAL CASES

UNITED STATES v. HAWKINS

United States Court of Appeals, Fourth Circuit
76 F.3d 545 (1996)

Per Curiam.

Cassius Hawkins appeals his conviction for criminal contempt. Finding that the trial court committed reversible error, we vacate the judgment of conviction and remand for a new trial.

Since this was a proceeding before a judge who had not personally witnessed the contempt in question, Judge Maxwell was required to find that the elements of criminal contempt had been established by the evidence at the hearing before him.

The evidence against Hawkins at the hearing consisted of the Assistant United States Attorney's identification of Hawkins as the same person who had been recalcitrant and had uttered obscenities before Chief Judge Stamp and a copy of the transcript from the trial before Chief Judge Stamp. The identity of Hawkins, which is an element of the crime of contempt, was shown solely by unsworn testimony [The Assistant United States Attorney was not placed under oath]. Hawkins' counsel objected that identity had not been proven, and contended the Assistant United States Attorney's unsworn statement should not have been considered.

The government argues that the error in admitting the identification testimony was harmless, because even without the identification testimony, identity could have been established by judicial notice (a) that proceedings before the court had proceeded in a regular manner, and (b) that in the course of regular proceedings, the proper incarcerated defendant generally is brought before the court. However, judicial notice of Hawkins' identity or of the regularity of the proceedings was, in fact, neither requested by the government, nor taken *sua sponte* by Judge Maxwell. See *United States v. James*, 987 F.2d 648, 651 (9th Cir. 1993) (overturning robbery conviction on grounds of insufficient evidence, and refusing to find harmless the government's failure to prove one element of the crime, where judicial notice of the existence of the unproven element was not requested or taken at trial). In *United States v. Burroughs*, 564 F.2d 1111, 1116 n. 7 (4th Cir. 1977), we affirmed the entry of a judgment of acquittal, finding that a federal nexus was an element of the crime and no evidence of a federal nexus was introduced at trial. In so holding, we reasoned that "we will not take judicial notice on appeal of an unproven essential element of a criminal offense." *Id.* at 1116 n. 7; *see also, Glover v. Cole*, 762 F.2d 1197, 1200 n. 6 (4th Cir. 1985) ("Judicial notice is an inappropriate device for remedying a failure of proof.").

Moreover, we believe that the identity of a defendant may not be proven by judicial notice in the manner proposed by the government. Clearly, Hawkins' identity is not a fact generally known in West Virginia, nor is it capable of determination by resort to sources whose accuracy cannot reasonably be questioned.

Identity is an element of every criminal offense, and one that is frequently and quite reasonably disputed. The unsworn statement of government counsel in this case does not eliminate reasonable dispute. *See United States v. Wilson*, 631 F.2d 118, 120 (9th Cir. 1980) (overturning, on grounds of insufficient evidence, a conviction for bail-jumping, and holding that the district court could not take judicial notice that the defendant had been out of custody for seven days as claimed by the prosecutor in an unsworn statement). If judicial notice that proceedings had been regular and that regular proceedings generally bring the correct defendant to the court were sufficient to establish identity, the government would no longer have to prove the identity of defendants, and an innocent defendant could conceivably be convicted of crimes committed by another. *Cf. In re Mundorff*, 8 F.R.D. 7, 8 (D.Or. 1948) ("The Clerk cannot take judicial notice of [the identity of a defendant's] signature. If a defendant comes into court here, his identity can be either admitted by him or proven. But [one] cannot know that some one is not masquerading as a defendant in order to save the real culprit."). Accordingly, the erroneous admission of government counsel's unsworn identification testimony was not harmless.

UNITED STATES v. JONES

United States Court of Appeals, Sixth Circuit
580 F.2d 219 (1978)

ENGEL, CIRCUIT JUDGE.

Appellee William Allen Jones, Jr. was convicted by a district court jury of illegally intercepting telephone conversations of his estranged wife and of using the contents of the intercepted communications. The proofs at trial showed only that the telephone which Jones had tapped was furnished by South Central Bell Telephone Company. Other than this fact, the government offered no evidence to show that South Central Bell was at the time a "person engaged as a common carrier in providing or operating . . . facilities for the transmission of interstate or foreign communications." 18 U.S.C. § 2510(1).

Following the jury verdict of guilty on three of the five counts of the indictment, Jones' counsel moved the court for a new trial on the ground that the government had altogether failed to prove that the wire communication which the defendant tapped came within the definition of Section 2510. Upon a careful review of the evidence, United States District Judge Frank Wilson agreed and entered a judgment of acquittal. The government has appealed.

. . . [W]as the proof that the tapped telephone was installed and furnished by "South Central Bell Telephone Company," without more, sufficient to enable the jury to find as a matter of fact that South Central Bell was a common carrier which provided facilities for the transmission of interstate or foreign communications [, a required element of the statute]? The government contends that, construing that evidence in the light most favorable to it, these facts could be permissibly inferred by the jury without any other proof. The government's argument is essentially twofold. First, it urges that South Central Bell's status may reasonably be characterized as a fact within the common knowledge of the jury and that no further record evidence was necessary. Failing that, the government urges that such a fact is the proper subject of judicial notice which may be taken at any stage of the proceeding, including appeal, under Federal Rule of Evidence 201.

The government's first argument finds some support in 9 WIGMORE ON EVIDENCE § 2570. Similarly, the legislative history of the Federal Rules of Evidence indicates that, even in criminal cases, "matters falling within the common fund of information supposed to be possessed by jurors need not be proved." Advisory Committee Note. . . .

While the issue is not without difficulty, we are satisfied that South Central Bell's status as a "common carrier . . . providing . . . facilities for the transmission of interstate . . . communications" is a fact which, if to be established without direct or circumstantial proof, must be governed by the judicial notice provisions of the Federal Rules of Evidence.

The government did not at any time during the jury trial specifically request the district court to take judicial notice of the status of South Central Bell. Neverthe-less, it relies upon the provisions of Rule 201 [d] which state that "(j)udicial notice may be taken at any stage of the proceeding." It is true that the Advisory Committee Note [to that provision] indicates that judicial notice is appropriate "in the trial court or on appeal.". . . There is, however, expressly in Rule 201 [f] a critical difference in the manner in which the judicially noticed fact is to be submitted to the jury in civil and criminal proceedings:

> Instructing jury. In a civil action or proceeding, the court shall instruct the jury to accept as conclusive any fact judicially noticed. In a criminal case, the court shall instruct the jury that it may, but is not required to, accept as conclusive any fact judicially noticed.

> Thus . . . judicial notice of a fact in a civil case is conclusive while in a criminal trial the jury is not bound to accept the judicially noticed fact and may disregard it if it so chooses. . . .

As enacted by Congress [which expressly inserted the provision regarding the special criminal instruction], Rule 201 plainly contemplates that the jury in a criminal case shall pass upon facts which are judicially noticed. This it could not do if this notice were taken for the first time after it had been discharged and the case was on appeal. We, therefore, hold that Rule 201[d], authorizing judicial notice at the appellate level, must yield in the face of the express congressional intent manifested in 201[f] for criminal jury trials. To the extent that the earlier practice may have been otherwise, we conceive that it has been altered by the enactment of Rule 201.

[Acquittal affirmed.]

NOTE

Right to Trial by Jury. The Uniform Rules of Evidence, Rule 201(g), provides that the jury is instructed that it must accept the noticed fact in both civil and criminal cases. This has been adopted by a number of states, including California. Do you think judicial notice of adjudicative facts against criminal defendants that is binding on the jury would violate the constitutional requirement of trial by jury? *See United States v. Mentz*, 840 F.2d 315 (6th Cir. 1988), reversing a conviction because the jury was instructed in a bank robbery case that banks were insured by the Federal Deposit Insurance Corporation, where federal jurisdiction is an element of the offense. More importantly the reader should see the recent U.S. Supreme Court cases declaring that former "sentencing factors" that judges used to increase sentences, must now be proved to and found by the jury beyond a reasonable doubt (like all facts of the case) under the constitution. *Apprendi v. New Jersey*, 530 U.S. 466 (2000); *United States v. Booker*, 543 U.S. 220 (2005); *Ring v. Arizona*, 536 U.S. 584 (2002).

§ 14.04 JUDICIAL NOTICE OF LEGISLATIVE FACTS

UNITED STATES v. GOULD

United States Court of Appeals, Eighth Circuit
536 F.2d 216 (1976)

GIBSON, CHIEF JUDGE.

Defendants [in this prosecution for importing or exporting a Schedule II controlled substance] contend that the District Court erred in improperly taking judicial notice and instructing the jury that cocaine hydrochloride is a Schedule II controlled substance. Defendants contend that evidence should have been presented on the subject of what controlled substances fit within Schedule II for the purpose of establishing a foundation that cocaine hydrochloride was actually within that schedule. Schedule II controlled substances, for the purpose of the Controlled Substances Import and Export Act, include the following:

> Coca leaves and any salt, compound, derivative, or preparation of coca leaves, and any salt, compound, derivative, or preparation thereof which is chemically equivalent or identical with any of these substances, except that the substances shall not include decocainized coca leaves or extraction of coca leaves, which extractions do not contain cocaine or ecgonine. 21 U.S.C. § 812 (1970); *see* 21 C.F.R. § 1308.12 (1975).

At trial, two expert witnesses for the Government testified as to the composition of the powdered substance removed from Ms. Kenworthy's platform shoes at the Miami airport. One expert testified that the substance was comprised of approximately 60 percent cocaine hydrochloride. The other witness stated that the white powder consisted of 53 percent cocaine. There was no direct evidence to indicate that cocaine hydrochloride is a derivative of coca leaves. In its instructions to the jury, the District Court stated:

> If you find the substance was cocaine hydrochloride, you are instructed that cocaine hydrochloride is a Schedule II controlled substance under the laws of the United States.

Our inquiry on this first assignment of error is twofold. We must first determine whether it was error for the District Court to take judicial notice of the fact that cocaine hydrochloride is a Schedule II controlled substance. Secondly, if we conclude that it was permissible to judicially notice this fact, we must then determine whether the District Court erred in instructing the jury that it must accept this fact as conclusive.

The first aspect of this inquiry merits little discussion. In *Hughes v. United States*, 253 F. 543, 545 (8th Cir. 1918), *cert. denied*, 249 U.S. 610 (1919), this court stated:

> It is also urged that there was no evidence that morphine, heroin, and cocaine are derivatives of opium and coca leaves. We think that is a matter of which notice may be taken. In a sense the question is one of the definition or meaning of words long in common use, about which there is no obscurity, controversy, or dispute, and of which the imperfectly informed can gain complete knowledge by resort to dictionaries within reach of everybody. Common knowledge, or the common means of knowledge, of the settled, undisputed, things of life, need not always be laid aside on entering a courtroom.

It is apparent that courts may take judicial notice of any fact which is "capable of such instant and unquestionable demonstration, if desired, that no party would think of imposing a falsity on the tribunal in the face of an intelligent adversary." IX J. Wigmore, Evidence § 2571. The fact that cocaine hydrochloride is derived from coca leaves is, if not common knowledge, at least a matter which is capable of certain, easily accessible and indisputably accurate verification. *See* Webster's Third New International Dictionary 434. Therefore, it was proper for the District Court to judicially notice this fact.

Our second inquiry involves the propriety of the District Court's instruction to the jurors that this judicially noticed fact must be accepted as conclusive by them. Defendants, relying upon Fed. R. Ev. 201[f], urge that the jury should have been instructed that it could discretionarily accept or reject this fact.

It is clear that the reach of rule 201 extends only to adjudicative, not legislative, facts. Fed. R. Ev. 201(a). Consequently, the viability of defendants' argument is dependent upon our characterization of the fact judicially noticed by the District Court as adjudicative, thus invoking the provisions of Rule 201[f]. . .

The precise line of demarcation between adjudicative facts and legislative facts is not always easily identified. Adjudicative facts have been described as follows:

> When a court . . . finds facts concerning the immediate parties — who did what, where, when, how, and with what motive or intent — the court . . . is performing an adjudicative function, and the facts are conveniently called adjudicative facts. Stated in other terms, the adjudicative facts are those to which the law is applied in the process of adjudication. They are the facts that normally go to the jury in a jury case. They relate to the parties, their activities, their properties, their businesses. 2 K. Davis, Administrative Law Treatise § 15.03.

Legislative facts, on the other hand, do not relate specifically to the activities or characteristics of the litigants. A court generally relies upon legislative facts when it purports to develop [or create] a particular law or policy and thus considers material wholly unrelated to the activities of the parties. Legislative facts are ordinarily general and do not concern the immediate parties. . . .

Legislative facts are established truths, facts or pronouncements that do not change from case to case but apply universally, while adjudicative facts are those developed in a particular case. Applying these general definitions, we think it is clear that the District Court in the present case was judicially noticing a legislative fact rather than an adjudicative fact. Whether cocaine hydrochloride is or is not a derivative of the coca leaf is a question of scientific fact applicable to the administration of the Comprehensive Drug Abuse Prevention and Control Act of 1970. . . .

It is clear to us that the District Court took judicial notice of a legislative, rather than an adjudicative, fact in the present case and rule 201 is inapplicable. The District Court was not obligated to inform the jury that it could disregard the judicially noticed fact. In fact, to do so would be preposterous, thus permitting juries to make conflicting findings on what constitutes controlled substances under federal law.

Affirmed.

UNITED STATES v. HERNANDEZ-FUNDORA

United States Court of Appeals, Second Circuit
58 F.3d 802, *cert. denied*, 515 U.S. 1127 (1995)

MAHONEY, CIRCUIT JUDGE.

[The defendant was convicted of assault within the special maritime and territorial jurisdiction of United States concerning an assault that occurred in a federal correctional facility. He contended that the district court erred in removing the jurisdictional element of his offense from the jury's consideration.]

The court charged the jury that:

> [T]he Government must prove the alleged assault took place within the special maritime and territorial jurisdiction of the United States. This simply means that the alleged assault must have occurred in any lands reserved or acquired for the use of the United States and under the exclusive or concurrent jurisdiction thereof. I charge you now that [Raybrook] is a place that falls within the territorial jurisdiction of the United States. Therefore, if you find beyond a reasonable doubt that the acted [sic] alleged occurred at [Raybrook], the sixth element of the offense has been met.

Thus, the court removed from the jury's consideration the issue whether Raybrook was within the special maritime and territorial jurisdiction of the United States, but reserved for the jury the question whether the assault occurred at Raybrook.

This approach is consistent with prior cases in this circuit. In *United States v. Jones* the defendant was convicted after a jury trial of theft within the special territorial jurisdiction of the United States in violation of 18 U.S.C. § 661. The theft occurred at a Veterans Administration hospital in West Haven, Connecticut. The trial court charged the jury that the hospital was within the special territorial jurisdiction of the United States, and that the jury should determine whether the theft occurred at the hospital. Responding to the defendant-appellant's argument that the jurisdictional issue had been improperly taken from the jury, we held that "the district court properly determined this question as a matter of law and submitted to the jury the question of whether the offense was committed on land determined by the court to be within the special territorial jurisdiction of the United States." We concluded that "the court's instruction correctly left the factual element — the locus of the crime — to the jury, while reserving the question of law — whether the federal government had accepted jurisdiction — to itself."

These authorities clarify that while courts may take judicial notice of either legislative or adjudicative facts, only notice of the latter is subject to the strictures of Rule 201. Although Rule 201 is frequently (albeit erroneously) cited in cases that involve judicial notice of legislative facts, we recognize the importance of this distinction and its clear basis in Rule 201(a) and the advisory note thereon. We therefore conclude that the jurisdictional issue in this case is premised upon a determination of legislative, rather than adjudicative, facts to which Rule 201, including 201 [f], is inapplicable.

NOTES AND QUESTIONS

(1) *Are the Facts in Gould and Hernandez-Fundora Really Legislative?* Is designating these facts as legislative simply a way for these courts to evade the mandate of Fed. R. Evid. 201(f), because its application would have resulted in a reversal for insufficient evidence with the result that the defendant could not have been retried (because of double jeopardy)? *Gould* viewed as preposterous allowing the jury to disregard the pharmacologically unimpeachable fact that cocaine hydrochloride is derived from coca leaves. But couldn't this be said of any notice of adjudicative fact under Rule 201 as well? Aren't they always unimpeachable by definition? Yet Rule 201(f) allows the jury to ignore the fact in criminal cases. Furthermore, are legislative facts always indisputable? *Hernandez-Fundora* decides that the facts are legislative, but relies on some cases we have deleted that (if you read them) call this judicial notice of law. Some commentators make a distinction between proving where the crime occurred and the legal significance of that proof. In other words, once the place is established, jurisdiction is proper because it is the judge's role to determine its legal significance.

A countervailing argument is that in a criminal trial the jury should have the right to ignore even uncontroverted and incontrovertible facts in reaching a verdict. Doesn't this preserve the jury's right to render a totally irrational verdict? *See United States v. Piggie*, 622 F.2d 486 (10th Cir.), *cert. denied*, 449 U.S. 863 (1980), criticizing Rule 201(f) for mandating an instruction in a criminal case that a jury may find that transportation between New York City and Newark, New Jersey, is not interstate; and for indicating that "in the morning when the judge tries a civil case the world is round. That afternoon when he tries a criminal case the world is flat." *Piggie* states that it would be "absurd" to say that Fort Leavenworth is not in federal territorial jurisdiction. The case holds that it was harmless error not to give the Rule 201(f) instruction on it, and the right to jury trial could not be infringed just because the jury did not get to consider it. *But see* Carter, *"Trust Me, I'm a Judge": Why Binding Judicial Notice of Jurisdictional Facts Violates the Right to Jury Trial*, 68 Mo. L. Rev. 649 (2003).

(2) *Some of the Cases Referred to in Hernandez-Fundora Treat Jurisdiction as an Adjudicative Fact. Hernandez-Fundora* cites *Canal Zone v. Burjan Villarreta*, 596 F.2d 690 (5th Cir. 1979), with approval. However, this case treated jurisdiction as an adjudicative fact, finding no problem in taking notice on appeal because the trial below was argued to a judge, not a jury. However, the court noted that the constitutional right to *confrontation* does not prevent judicial notice of adjudicative facts being taken on appeal under the rule because the noticed facts are indisputable. (Does *Crawford, supra*, § 11.03[B], change this interpretation of constitutional confrontation?)

It proceeded to take judicial notice as follows: The court (remember, this is the appellate court, where it is unusual to receive documents other than briefs and the court record) received maps of the Canal Zone showing the boundaries of the Zone.

The maps were certified by the Chief of Surveys of the Panama Canal Company to be true and accurate. (Would they have been admissible evidence under the rules of evidence? Do they have to be, in order to be admitted for judicial notice purposes either below or in the Court of Appeals as was done here?) The appellate court took judicial notice of the maps as "sources whose accuracy cannot reasonably be questioned" under the rule, and accepted the boundaries of the Canal Zone as indicated on the maps. Since X Street was shown on the maps as being within the borders of the Canal Zone, the court took judicial notice, based on the maps and the testimony of victim #1, that offense #1, which occurred on X Street, took place within the Canal Zone. Thus jurisdiction was proper as to that offense. As to offense #2, since one of the blocks it may have occurred on was shown on the maps to be within the Canal Zone and another of the blocks was shown on the maps to be outside the Canal Zone, the court refused to take judicial notice that there was jurisdiction over this offense, and reversed this conviction.

In *United States v. Anderson*, 528 F.2d 590 (5th Cir.), *cert. denied*, 429 U.S. 837 (1976), also referenced in *Hernandez-Fundora*, defendant was convicted of assault with intent to murder "within the territorial jurisdiction of the United States." The prosecutor proved at trial that the assault took place at the Federal Corrections Institution in Tallahassee, Florida. The trial judge took judicial notice "that the Federal Corrections Institution at Tallahassee, Florida is within the territorial jurisdiction of the United States on lands acquired and reserved for the use of the United States and under the exclusive jurisdiction thereof." He then instructed the jury "you may and are allowed to accept that fact as fact proven before you just as though there had been evidence to that effect before you." The jury found jurisdiction and convicted defendant. The appellate court approved the trial court's action, saying that the matter was properly noticed under Rule 201, and specifically confirmed his instruction under Rule 201(f), which provides that in a criminal case the jury should be instructed that it "may, but is not required to" accept the noticed fact.

(3) *Use of Judicial Notice of Fact for Making Rules, Interpretations, and Constitutionality Determinations.* The Brandeis Brief submitted to the Supreme Court in *Muller v. Oregon*, 208 U.S. 412 (1908), is a prime example of social science evidence, not introduced in the record, being explicitly used by courts in their rule-making functions and their interpretation of law. In that brief, then-attorney Brandeis marshaled empirical social science evidence to convince the court that it was constitutional to limit female laundry workers to working ten hours per day. However, the Supreme Court has not necessarily been consistent in deciding when to rely on materials outside the record nor correct in its assessment of empirical evidence. *See generally* Faigman, *"Normative Constitutional Fact-Finding": Exploring the Empirical Component of Constitutional Interpretation*, 139 U. PA. L. REV. 541 (1991). Often-cited examples illustrating these issues are *Ballew v. Georgia*, 435 U.S. 223 (1978), and *Williams v. Florida*, 399 U.S. 78 (1970), where the Court's treatment of empirical evidence concerning the six-person jury was lambasted by commentators, and *McCleskey v. Kemp*, 481 U.S. 279 (1987), where the Court refused to take notice of studies indicating the disproportionate numbers of blacks being sentenced to capital punishment.

Given modern technology, the role of "Google" searches in supplying missing evidence has started to be noted in cases. Are there any limitations on a judge's use of search engines? Justice Brown of the California Supreme Court wrote a biting dissent on this subject in *People v. Mar*, 52 P.3d 95 (Cal. 2002):

> We are a court of review. The question for review here was whether the judgment of conviction must be overturned because defendant was required to wear a stun belt, and the answer is, we should have affirmed the judgment because no prejudice was shown. Full stop. The question in this case was not whether stun belts pose serious medical risks for persons with heart problems or other medical conditions, nor was it whether the current design of the stun belt could be improved upon. There is absolutely no evidence in the record bearing on these questions. In the absence of such evidence, we had two choices. We could have deferred to the Legislature, which can make law after hearing from distinguished experts on all sides of controversial issues. Or we could have waited for a case that raised these questions on an adequate record. Instead, the majority, rushing to judgment after conducting an embarrassing Google.com search for information outside the record, has tied the hands of the Legislature, to the likely peril of judges, bailiffs, and ordinary citizens called upon to do their civic duty.

Is this a question of judicial notice?

(4) *Judicial Notice of Scientific Technology.* In *United States v. Beasley*, 102 F.3d 1440 (8th Cir. 1996), *cert denied*, 520 U.S. 1246 (1997), the Court indicated that in the future, DNA analysis using PCR technology would be admitted without any hearing concerning the science:

> This Court has already taken judicial notice of the reliability of the general theory and techniques of DNA profiling, and specifically the use of the restriction fragment length polymorphism (RFLP) procedure. . . . The PCR method, however, has not previously been reviewed by this Court. Thus, the District Court appropriately held an evidentiary hearing under standards announced in *Daubert* to determine whether the PCR method is reliable and whether the proffered DNA evidence would be admitted.
>
> [W]e believe that the reliability of the PCR method of DNA analysis is sufficiently well established to permit the courts of this circuit to take judicial notice of it in future cases. In every case, of course, the reliability of the proffered test results may be challenged by showing that a scientifically sound methodology has been undercut by sloppy handling of the samples, failure to properly train those performing the testing, failure to follow the appropriate protocols, and the like.

Not all courts agree, as discussed in detail in § 6.04, *supra*.

(6) *Should there be Rules Governing the Taking of Notice of Legislative Facts?* Assume a court is asked to create a new exception to the husband-wife privilege. The court feels that if the exception is made, it will have a very marginal effect on marital harmony or on the willingness of spouses to communicate. For that reason, the court is inclined to create the exception pursuant to the "reason and experience" standard of Fed. R. Evid. 501. Do you suppose the fact that the effects on marital

harmony and willingness to communicate will be marginal would be beyond reasonable dispute, and generally known or readily and accurately ascertainable through use of sources whose accuracy cannot reasonably be questioned, as provided by Fed. R. Evid. 201? Should proof have to be taken on the matter? Should the court be free to create the exception based on its own perception that the effects will be marginal even if reasonable people differ on that? Could the law function if such judgments were subject to the strict standards imposed by Fed. R. Evid. 201 before judicial notice may be taken? Can you identify cases in the chapter on privileges, in which judicial notice of just this sort of matter, subject to reasonable differences of opinion and not generally known (nor ascertainable through use of sources of relatively indisputable accuracy), was taken in order to advance, develop, change, or interpret the law? Does Fed. R. Evid. 201 purport to apply to this kind of matter?

§ 14.05 OTHER TYPES OF NOTICE

(1) *Administrative Hearings: Notice as a Rule of Convenience, Rather than a Rule of Caution. See Banks v. Schweiker*, 654 F.2d 637 (9th Cir. 1981) (notice expressly taken by Administrative Law Judge, in administrative Social Security hearing, of kind of advice agency workers give applicants in a certain situation). Upon a challenge to this Administrative Law Judge's taking of notice, the court holds that in Fed. R. Evid. 201(b) the drafters of the Federal Rules of Evidence adopted a "rule of caution," requiring that the noticed facts be "not subject to reasonable dispute." The court raises the question as to whether such extreme caution was still warranted after the draft of Fed. R. Evid. 201(e) was altered to provide for a right to a hearing to challenge the noticed fact, a right not in the original draft. At any rate, for administrative proceedings that are not under the Federal Rules of Evidence, the court adopts a "rule of convenience" and does not require reasonable indisputability. Under this expanded concept of official notice, the ALJ's own knowledge of something that would be useful is sufficient; neither the reasonably indisputable criterion nor the regulation of source (generally known in the community or ascertainable by reasonably unquestionable sources) of Rule 201, applies. The court notes that some cases do apply the rigors of Rule 201 to official notice even though Rule 201 does not apply directly. The court states, however, that since the scope of official notice is thus expanded over judicial notice, it is doubly important to be sure that the right to challenge the noticed fact is safeguarded. *Compare with Banks* the case of *United States v. Bourque*, 541 F.2d 290 (1st Cir. 1976) (matter of whether or not Internal Revenue Service ever loses tax returns is not appropriate matter for notice).

(2) *Does Banks (Note (1) supra) Really Involve an Adjudicative Fact?* In the actual case, the Administrative Law Judge's notice of agency personnel practice was taken by him in his capacity as fact-finder, to resolve a hotly contested factual issue. Is the fact officially noticed in *Banks*, then, really an "adjudicative fact" within Rule 201's meaning, thus requiring (if 201 applied) reasonable indisputability in order to take notice? Don't jurors (let alone judges) ordinarily utilize such facts or notions in evaluating credibility? Aren't they often peculiar to the experience of the particular juror — e.g., a juror has had certain experiences with a police officer, minister, or Social Security agent, which the juror uses to evaluate this police officer's,

minister's, or agent's testimony, or to evaluate the likelihood of a story that reports they acted a certain way? Does the litigant get to confront those notions? Would it make sense to require them to be reasonably indisputable? Is it possible to give a litigant an opportunity to argue every "experiential" proposition a juror utilizes in evaluating a witness or story? Does this suggest that the Administrative Law Judge in *Banks* made a mistake by articulating his? If he merely found the claimant's story "incredible based on my experience of human affairs and what is a likely and what an unlikely story, in the light of human motives and how people behave," would there have been any problem?

(3) *Notice of Statutes and Content of Federal Register. United States v. Coffman*, 638 F.2d 192 (10th Cir. 1980), *cert. denied*, 451 U.S. 917 (1981), is a case factually somewhat similar to *Gould*, reproduced at the beginning of § 14.04, *supra*. The trial judge in *Coffman* instructed the jurors that if they find the substance found on defendants to be LSD, then defendant was in possession of a controlled substance that is on the schedule as a matter of law. Defendant complained that there was no evidence that LSD was on the schedule, either at the time of the offense or at any other time. Indeed, defense counsel had argued to the jury before the instructions that the government had failed to prove that LSD was on the schedule. The appellate court upheld the trial judge on slightly different grounds than in *Gould*. The court holds that the trial judge is allowed to take judicial notice of statutes and of the contents of the Federal Register (44 U.S.C. § 1507). It is not entirely clear from the opinion why the Federal Register is mentioned, but apparently it is in regulations authorized under the statute that LSD is interpreted as being included on the statutory schedule. Thus, the decision is put on the basis that judicial notice of law (not legislative fact) is outside the scope of Rule 201. The court also adds that since it is abundantly clear that LSD is on the schedule, even if the instruction were error under Fed. R. Evid. 201(f), it would not be plain error. Thus it would not be cognizable on appeal since there was no request for a 201(f)-type instruction at trial. It is unclear whether defendant objected at trial to the instruction that was given. Such objection, or even defendant's counsel's argument to the jury, could be considered to preserve the point for appeal if the court were sympathetic.

(4) *Do the Existing Distinctions Provide a Usable Framework for Judges?* Are the distinctions among judicial notice of adjudicative fact (covered by Fed. R. Evid. 201), judicial notice of legislative fact (not covered by Fed. R. Evid. 201), judicial notice of evidence-evaluative fact as in note (2) above (not covered by Fed. R. Evid. 201), and judicial notice of law (not covered by Fed. R. Evid. 201) too abstruse to be administered practicably by average judges in the hurly burly of trial? (Are they too elusive for you?) (*Coffman*, note (3) immediately *supra*, in the course of the decision, remarks on the difficulty.) And what about the distinction between official notice (administrative notice) (rule of convenience) and judicial notice (rule of caution), in note (1) supra. Does this further confuse the situation?

(5) *Judicial Notice of Law Generally.* For perhaps more straightforward cases involving judicial notice of law, which is not within Fed. R. Evid. 201, see the following cases:

United States v. Atwell, 71 F.R.D. 357 (D. Del. 1976): A federal statute prohibits possession, transportation, etc., of a firearm by one convicted of a felony (defined in the same statute) under any state or federal law. The court judicially noticed the text of the statute of Maryland under which defendant had previously been convicted to determine whether the Maryland provision met the definition of a felony. The court found that it did, and defendant was convicted under the federal firearm statute. The court holds judicial notice of law to be outside Fed. R. Evid. 201, and thus the procedural protections of that rule do not apply. The rule applies only to adjudicative facts, the court states, and points to the Advisory Committee Note as particularly instructive on the meaning of that term.

Using the same doctrine to seemingly different effect is *Campbell v. Mincey*, 413 F. Supp. 16 (N.D. Miss. 1975), *aff'd*, 542 F.2d 573 (5th Cir. 1976): Plaintiff brought an action against a hospital for refusing her admittance in connection with the birth of her son. She claimed violation of Mississippi statutes imposing duties on the hospital. The relevant statute required hospitals to obey "rules, regulations, and standards" promulgated by the Mississippi Hospital Care Commission. Since there was no proof of the content of any of these rules, regulations, or standards, the court held that plaintiff failed to sustain her burden of proof, and stated that state regulations are beyond the scope of judicial notice provided for in Fed. R. Evid. 201. [Would the result have been the same if Rule 201 had applied?] Under the law relating to notice of law and regulations, it is frequently said by courts that the law of another jurisdiction must be proved, but there may be some liberality concerning how it may be proved, and it may not have to be proved to the jury. (In the absence of proof, some courts will assume the law is the same as the law of the court's home jurisdiction, if there is any on the matter.) Is this the same thing as taking judicial notice? Does judicial notice require a source for the information? Is *Mincey* really different from *Atwell*? Is a statute book good evidence of the law?

(6) *Political Facts.* In *Ivezaj v. I.N.S.*, 84 F.3d 215 (6th Cir. 1996), the court takes judicial notice of persecution of Albanians by the Serbs, saying that notice of changed political circumstances in a foreign country is appropriate in immigration cases. On occasion, questions involving the political status of a country may be established by representations made by State Department officials.

(7) *New Forms of Judicial Notice?* In *United States v. Salinas*, 611 F.2d 128 (5th Cir. 1980), the question at a suppression hearing was the legality of a search of suitcases at a border patrol checkpoint located seven miles south of Falfurrias, Texas, made without probable cause. The search uncovered marijuana, which defendant was attempting to suppress. The legality of the search depended on whether it occurred at the "functional equivalent" of the border, because then it did not need to be accompanied by probable cause. The trial court took judicial notice that this checkpoint was the functional equivalent of the border based on two other federal trial court decisions that had discussed the mobile Falfurrias checkpoints. The trial court in the present case found (on evidence introduced) that the facts of the present checkpoint were not significantly different from the checkpoints found to be functional equivalents of the border in those cases.

The Court of Appeals upheld the trial judge, stating "It is not required that the underlying facts concerning a particular checkpoint location be proved over and over again in each case arising out of the same checkpoint location, so long as such facts remain unchanged." Was what the trial judge did in *Salinas* really a matter of judicial notice? The Court never mentioned Fed. R. Evid. 201. Is that significant? What type of fact is this?

In *United States v. Hitsman*, 604 F.2d 443 (5th Cir. 1979), a large part of the evidence against defendant in this methamphetamine (an illegal drug) manufacturing case was that someone with the courses defendant Perkins had taken in college could well manufacture methamphetamine. Perkins challenged the admission of a copy of his college transcript by the government. The trial court admitted the transcript without any sponsoring witness pursuant to Fed. R. Evid. 803(24) (now Rule 807), the general trustworthiness hearsay exception, and found it to be a self-authenticating document under Fed. R. Evid. 901 and 902. It took judicial notice of the existence of the college and found that it was normal for a college to make such a record in the course of its operations and that the exhibit had the indicia of being an authentic copy, since it bore a seal above the registrar's signature. No error was found in its admission.

Does the approach to judicial notice in *Hitsman* permit a complete evasion of any or all of the other rules of evidence? Is it a different type of judicial notice than the other categories already mentioned?

§ 14.06 LIMITS OF JURY OR JUDGE USING FACTS IN THEIR PERSONAL EXPERIENCE TO "EVALUATE" EVIDENCE

(1) *Background Knowledge of Jurors.* Suppose a jury disbelieves an auto-accident defendant's story because it doesn't square with their idea of how long it takes to stop a car going approximately 30 m.p.h. on a clear day. Does the defendant have to be informed of what each juror believes about stopping distances at 30 m.p.h., and have a chance to respond? Does it even matter whether the jury is right or wrong? Does a juror's notion on this have to meet the "reasonably indisputable" standard? Jurors come to the courtroom with their own perspectives and experience. It is well recognized that "[j]uries are free to use their common sense and apply common knowledge, observation, and experience gained in the ordinary affairs of life when giving effect to the inferences that may reasonably be drawn from the evidence." *United States v. McAfee*, 8 F.3d 1010 (5th Cir. 1993). *See generally* Mansfield, *Jury Notice*, 74 Geo. L.J. 395 (1985). See also the discussion in *Jones*, § 14.03, *supra*.

(2) *Finding Out About Jurors' Backgrounds.* If counsel are concerned about a juror's special knowledge or background, the way to address this issue is through *voir dire* questions and the use of peremptory challenges to exclude jurors for any reason other than racial or gender discrimination. However, there will always be problems associated with the judge not giving enough latitude to lawyers to ferret out all of the background information that they desire, or with jurors not being totally candid, not understanding the questions, or lying. In *McDonough Power Equip., Inc. v. Greenwood*, 464 U.S. 548 (1984), the Court noted that "to invalidate the result of a three-week trial because of a juror's mistaken, though honest, response to a question, is to insist on something closer to perfection than our judicial system can be expected to give." To obtain a retrial, "a party must first

demonstrate that a juror failed to answer honestly a material question on *voir dire*, and then further show that a correct response would have provided a valid basis for a challenge for cause." *See* Crump, *Peremptory Challenges After* McDonough Power Equipment, Inc. v. Greenwood: *A Problem of Fairness, Finality, and Falsehood*, 69 Or. L. Rev. 741 (1990).

Similarly, *Rivera v. Illinois*, 556 U.S. 148 (2009), held that the erroneous denial of a peremptory challenge on grounds that it was discriminatory on gender grounds was not a structural error rendering the defendant's trial fundamentally unfair. As a result reversal was not required, even though the female juror who was not excused served as foreperson of the jury that found defendant guilty of first degree murder.

(3) *Juror Misconduct by Obtaining Outside Information.* Although jurors can use their background information to evaluate the evidence, they cannot affirmatively obtain outside information to assist them once the trial has started. For example, California Jury Instruction 1.00.5 provides that:

> You must decide all questions of fact in this case from the evidence received in this trial and not from any other source. You must not make an independent investigation of the facts or the law or consider or discuss facts as to which there is no evidence. This means, for example, that you must not on your own visit the scene, conduct experiments, or consult reference works for additional information.

Thus, a juror's going to the site of an accident for an unauthorized view would be prohibited, while their previous knowledge of the location would not. However, jury deliberations usually are not otherwise open to attack. The rules concerning impeachment of jury verdicts are very restrictive in order to ensure finality of verdicts, encourage open and frank deliberations, and discourage after-the-fact harassment of jurors. For example, Fed. R. Evid. 606(b) limits impeachment to the question of "whether extraneous prejudicial information was improperly brought to the jury's attention or whether any outside influence was improperly brought to bear upon any juror." *See Tanner v. United States*, 483 U.S. 107 (1987) (refusing to permit impeachment based on alcohol and drug use by jurors during trial), reproduced and discussed along with Rule 606(b) at § 4.02[D] *supra*.

(4) *Judicial Knowledge versus Judicial Notice.* In *Government of the Virgin Islands v. Gereau*, 523 F.2d 140 (3d Cir. 1975), *cert. denied*, 424 U.S. 917 (1976), the defendant challenged, in a post-trial motion, a jury verdict against him in a murder case. His grounds were that outside information was brought to the attention of the jury. At the hearing on the motion, a juror testified that the matron in charge of the jury (a court official) had told the juror certain extra-judicial information about the case. The matron testified that the conversation did not take place. The trial judge decided the motion against the defendant because the judge believed the matron rather than the juror. He believed the matron expressly on the grounds that this particular matron was known by the judge to be "grateful for the opportunity to earn extra income as a jury matron." The appeals court said:

> We do not consider these credibility findings to lack adequate support in the record. However, we do hold that the trial judge's reliance on his

personal, subjective belief about the needs and motives of Matron Foye was an improper ground for rejecting Cappin's concededly credible testimony.

In basing his fact-finding on personal knowledge, the trial judge was, in effect, taking judicial notice of extra-record, adjudicative facts. *See generally* K. Davis, *An Approach to Problems of Evidence in the Administrative Process*, 55 Harv. L. Rev. 364, 406–07 (1942). "With respect to judicial notice of adjudicative facts, the tradition has been one of caution in requiring that the matter be beyond reasonable controversy." Advisory Committee's Notes to Fed. R. Evid. 201(b); *cf.* Fed. R. Evid. 201(a). A second hallmark of facts properly the subject of judicial notice is that they be either matters of common knowledge or "capable of immediate and accurate determination by resort to easily accessible sources of indisputable accuracy. . . ." *Weaver v. United States*, 298 F.2d 496, 498 (5th Cir. 1962); 9 Wright & Miller, *supra*, § 2410 at 339. Facts possessing these characteristics are entitled to be considered by a judge without first being proved through the routine processes of introducing evidence. The necessary cachet is not, however, bestowed merely by a judge's knowledge of a particular fact.

"There is a real but elusive line between the judge's personal knowledge as a private man and these matters of which he takes judicial notice as a judge. The latter does not necessarily include the former; as a judge, indeed, he may have to ignore what he knows as a man, and contrariwise. . . . It is therefore plainly accepted that the judge is not to use from the bench, under the guise of judicial knowledge, that which he knows only as an individual observer outside of court. The former is in truth 'known' to him merely in the fictional sense that it is known and notorious to all men, and the dilemma is only the result of using the term 'knowledge' in two senses. Where to draw the line between knowledge by notoriety and knowledge by personal observation may sometimes be difficult, but the principle is plain." J. Wigmore, Evidence, § 2569 at 539–40 (3d ed. 1940).

It is apparent that the trial judge's knowledge about Matron Foye falls into this latter category of personal knowledge and, therefore, does not qualify for judicial notice. It follows that the trial judge erred in rejecting Cappin's testimony on the ground stated. Similarly untenable is the trial judge's finding that juror Torres could not have heard any rumors while she was resting in the judge's chambers, since that finding was based solely on the judge's personal knowledge of the soundproofing in his chambers.

Suppose the judge in the present case had merely relied on the general belief that a person in the matron's position would "be grateful." Isn't that what fact-finders are supposed to do in judging credibility? Aren't they instructed to decide who is telling the truth by considering, among other things, what squares with their experience? The Court of Appeals also faults (on similar grounds) the trial judge's additional finding that another juror could not have heard any rumors while she was resting in the judge's chambers, despite her testimony to the contrary. The trial judge so found expressly because he personally knew of the soundproofing in his chambers. Query: Is this a less disputable, more objective fact, capable of ready ascertainment?

(5) *Additional Reasons for Reversals Based on Judge's Out-of-Court Observations.* In *Vaughn v. Shelby Williams of Tennessee, Inc.*, 813 S.W.2d 132 (Tenn. 1991), a nonjury workers' compensation action, the issue was how disabled the plaintiff was from a back injury suffered in the course and scope of his employment. The doctor assessed an impairment rating of 25 percent and urged the plaintiff to seek vocational rehabilitation because he could not return to his previous employment, which involved repetitive bending and lifting. When the case was tried, the trial judge awarded 80 percent permanent partial disability to the body as a whole plus temporary total disability benefits. In its memorandum opinion, the court stated: "As to this particular defendant, the court had an opportunity to observe him on one occasion about a week before the trial, on another occasion at the Morristown Mall, and at another time in the parking lot, and, of course, during the trial. You can't always tell how disabled a person is by just observing him; anyway, this man looks and walks a little better than death warmed over." The award was based upon the medical and vocational proof and "general observations of the Plaintiff." The appeals court reversed the award, and remanded for a new trial before a different judge:

> [A] judge is not to use from the bench, under the guise of judicial knowledge, that which he knows only as an individual observer outside of the judicial proceedings. Judicial knowledge upon which a decision may be based is not the personal knowledge of the judge, but the cognizance of certain facts the judge becomes aware of by virtue of the legal procedures in which he plays a neutral role.
>
> Significantly, a judge is not permitted to make an investigation of a case, even an inadvertent one, off the record and then base a holding on the information obtained incident thereto. Moreover, when a judge becomes a source of evidence, appellate courts are put in an awkward position, in that the character of the evidence obtained through private inquiry or observation, as well as its probative value, is not shown in the record, making an evaluation of the information on appeal difficult, if not impossible.
>
> [B]y observing a party outside of the judicial proceedings and then basing a decision on those observations, the judge becomes a source of evidence, in effect, a witness. Rule 605 clearly prohibits a judge presiding over a trial from serving as a witness, and for good reason. Perhaps the most obvious one is that the system of justice does not appear to be impartial if the judge charged with the duty of adjudicating the litigation also acts as a source of evidence. Additionally, when the trial judge becomes a source of information, the parties may not be willing to cross-examine vigorously the judge whose goodwill is perceived to be important to the outcome of the case. Worse yet, the parties may not even get the opportunity to cross-examine the judge to begin with.
>
> Finally, at no point prior to or during the trial did the trial court advise either counsel that he had previously observed the Plaintiff on three occasions separate and apart from any judicial proceeding. The parties were denied the opportunity to cross-examine the judge or offer rebuttal proof to the judge's "testimony" that he had seen the Plaintiff on three

prior occasions and that the Plaintiff "looks and walks a little better than death warmed over." Without the opportunity to cross-examine, the Defendant was unable to verify the judge's identification of the Plaintiff as the person he saw at the mall and in the parking lot.

(6) *Other Instances of Judges Taking Judicial Notice of Personal Knowledge.* In *1.70 Acres v. State*, 935 S.W.2d 480 (Tex. App. 1996), the court remarked:

> Although such variables as a vehicle's speed, road construction or repairs, weather, traffic, or accidents may be matters in someone's personal knowledge, they are not necessarily matters subject to judicial review. Personal knowledge is not judicial knowledge, and a judge may personally know a fact of which he cannot take judicial knowledge. Using the test of "verifiable certainty," we conclude that the court below could not take judicial notice of a ten minute time span to drive an alleged distance of 9.2 miles.

Matter of Estate of Friedli, 473 N.W.2d 604 (Wis. Ct. App. 1991), held that a judge who personally knew the author of a letter offered in evidence in a will contest could not properly take judicial notice of the author's sense of humor in interpreting the evidentiary value of the letter.

Similarly, in *United States v. Lewis*, 833 F.2d 1380 (9th Cir. 1987), the trial judge was not entitled to rely on his personal experience in concluding that a confession given by defendant, a heroin addict, shortly after she returned from surgery and was awakened from general anesthesia, was involuntary and therefore inadmissible before the jury. At the admissibility hearing, the trial judge stated: "You are not accountable for what you do or say for quite a number of hours after you come out of a general anesthetic. So I cannot find that a person who is both withdrawing from heroin and coming out from under a general anesthetic and is under arrest and confronted by FBI agents is in a position to make a voluntary and knowing statement at that time."

In reversing, the appeals court started with the "obvious principle" that the trial judge in this matter was not a competent witness to Lewis' condition. The judge presiding at the trial may not testify in that trial as a witness. (Fed. R. Evid. 605). Moreover, this judge also lacked personal knowledge of Lewis' condition. (Fed. R. Evid. 602). As to the claim that the trial judge had taken judicial notice of the facts, the court remarked that there was no announcement that notice was being taken so as to accord a party the opportunity to be heard as to its propriety. The appeals court further observed that:

> The trial judge's reliance in the instant matter on facts known to him from his personal experience, denied the government the opportunity to test the basis for the court's opinion concerning the effect of an anesthetic on a person's freedom of choice through the usual methods that assure trustworthiness in our adversarial system of justice. The prosecutor was denied the opportunity to contrast the nature of the illness or injury suffered by the judge with Lewis' abscessed shoulder, the amount of anesthesia administered to each, or the actual statements made by the judge which others characterized as "incredible" with the responses made

> by the defendant in this matter. Lewis' statements on October 21, 1986 were not "incredible" nor unresponsive. Instead, her answers demonstrated her capacity to understand what was said to her and to respond truthfully.

In *Lewis*, the trial judge was rendering a legal decision based on his finding of fact. Why is this treated differently from jurors using their experience in deliberation? If anything, here the government lawyer could point out the difficulties with the judge's conclusions at the hearing. In contrast, lawyers cannot correct erroneous impressions of jurors used in deliberations, nor can they impeach the verdict based on those erroneous impressions. Do we expect more from judges than jurors in their fact-finding roles? Would the appellate court have ruled differently if the judge hadn't given his reason for finding the confession involuntary, but had said his decision was based on all of the circumstances surrounding the giving of the confession?

Chapter 15

BURDENS AND PRESUMPTIONS

TILTING THE PLAYING FIELD (F.R.E. ARTICLE III)

§ 15.01 BURDENS OF PROOF: PREREQUISITE TO UNDERSTANDING PRESUMPTIONS[1]

(1) *General Principles.* There are two separate burdens in every case: the burden of production (going forward with the evidence) and the burden of persuasion. In civil cases, these burdens initially may be set on either party, usually based on considerations of convenience, public policy, fairness, and access to evidence, among other things. In criminal cases, placing burdens on defendants is constrained by constitutional principles such as the presumption of innocence and the requirement that the prosecution prove each of the elements of its case beyond a reasonable doubt. (However, as an aside you should note that, even in criminal cases, preliminary fact determinations by the judge for purposes of evidentiary admissibility are not subject to being proved beyond a reasonable doubt. *See, e.g.*, *Bourjaily v. United States*, 483 U.S. 171 (1987) (preponderance).)

The burden of production on a particular issue is met by providing enough evidence that a reasonable juror could find in favor of the party. Sometimes this concept is conveyed by saying that the party has made a "prima facie" case, but this terminology is fraught with uncertainty because of the absence of agreement as to its actual meaning. While satisfying the burden of production is all that is required to get to the jury, it is only if the jury is persuaded by the appropriate standard (preponderance, clear and convincing, or beyond reasonable doubt) that the party with the burden of persuasion on the issue prevails. When the evidence is in equipoise, equally balanced, the party with the burden of persuasion loses.

(2) *Getting to the Jury. Smith v. Rapid Transit, Inc.*, 58 N.E.2d 754 (Mass. 1945), was a case brought against a bus company. Plaintiff's evidence at trial showed that at 1:00 a.m. on February 6, 1941, when driving an automobile on Main Street, Winthrop, in an easterly direction toward Winthrop Highlands, she observed a bus coming toward her, which she described as a "great big, long, wide affair." The bus, which was proceeding at about forty miles an hour, "forced her to turn to the right," and her automobile collided with a "parked car." The plaintiff was coming from Dorchester. The department of public utilities had issued a certificate of public convenience or necessity to the defendant for three routes in Winthrop, one of which included Main Street, and this was in effect in February, 1941. There was another

[1] Study Guide Reference: Evidence in a Nutshell, Chapter 2:II. A more extensive treatment is found in a previous edition of the *Nutshell*, the second edition (1981), Chapter 2.

bus line in operation in Winthrop at that time but not on Main Street. According to the defendant's timetable, buses were scheduled to leave Winthrop Highlands for Maverick Square via Main Street at 12:10 a.m., 12:45 a.m., 1:15 a.m., and 2:15 a.m. The running time for this trip at that time of night was thirty minutes. In affirming the grant of directed verdict for the defendant, the court found that:

> The ownership of the bus was a matter of conjecture. While the defendant had the sole franchise for operating a bus line on Main Street, Winthrop, this did not preclude private or chartered buses from using this street; the bus in question could very well have been one operated by someone other than the defendant. [I]t is "not enough that mathematically the chances somewhat favor a proposition to be proved; for example, the fact that colored automobiles made in the current year outnumber black ones would not warrant a finding that an undescribed automobile of the current year is colored and not black; nor would the fact that only a minority of men die of cancer warrant a finding that a particular man did not die of cancer." The most that can be said of the evidence in the instant case is that perhaps the mathematical chances somewhat favor the proposition that a bus of the defendant caused the accident. This was not enough. A "proposition is proved by a preponderance of the evidence if it is made to appear more likely or probable in the sense that actual belief in its truth, derived from the evidence, exists in the mind or minds of the tribunal notwithstanding any doubts that may still linger there."

Contrast *Evans & Co. v. Astley* [1911] A.C. 674, 678 (British House of Lords, per Earl Loreburn, L.C.):

> It is, of course, impossible to lay down in words any scale or standard by which you can measure the degree of proof which will suffice to support a particular conclusion of fact. The applicant must prove his case. This does not mean that he must demonstrate his case. If the more probable conclusion is that for which he contends, and there is anything pointing to it, then there is evidence for a Court to act on. Any conclusion short of certainty may be miscalled conjecture or surmise, but Courts, like individuals, habitually act upon a balance of probabilities.

§ 15.02 CIVIL PRESUMPTIONS[2]

Read Federal Rules of Evidence 301, "Presumptions in Civil Cases Generally" and 302, "Applying State Law to Presumptions in Civil Cases."

(1) *Caution Regarding Scope of Coverage.* Presumptions have been described as "the slipperiest member of the family of legal terms." 2 McCORMICK ON EVIDENCE § 342 (4th ed. 1992). The word is used in a variety of contexts, with inconsistent meanings and results, and has generated both extensive litigation and extensive

[2] Study Guide Reference: Evidence in a Nutshell, Chapter 2:III at "Mandatory and Permissive Presumptions" and "Evidence Rebutting the Presumed Fact" and "Presumptions Under the Federal Rules." A more extensive treatment is found in a previous edition of the *Nutshell*, the second edition (1981), Chapter 2.

literature. This chapter is simply meant to familiarize the reader with the general principles concerning presumptions. An in-depth treatment of this subject is beyond the scope of an introductory evidence course. *See generally* Allen, *Presumptions in Civil Actions Reconsidered*, 66 Iowa L. Rev. 843 (1981).

(2) *Introduction to Presumptions and their Effects.* A presumption may be described as a rule of law that states that once fact A (the "basic fact") is established (to the satisfaction of the jury or as a matter of law by indisputable or overwhelming evidence), fact B (the "presumed fact" or "elemental fact") must be taken as established, at least if there is no evidence of non-B. If the presumption is the familiar one that delivery of a letter is presumed from proper mailing, proper mailing is fact A (the basic fact) and delivery is fact B (the presumed or elemental fact). A presumption can have effect on the jury, or on the court in its deliberations over whether to direct a verdict or finding.

In some jurisdictions (e.g., New York) another species of rule is distinguished from true presumption. This is a rule that holds that fact B may be, but need not be, found by the trier of fact upon proof of fact A (again where there is no evidence of non-B). If the rule about mailing and delivery were of this sort, rather than the other sort, then proof of proper mailing, in the absence of any evidence of nondelivery, would merely make a jury question on the issue of delivery, rather than require a finding of delivery.

New York, like some other states, calls rules of this latter sort "inferences" or "presumptions of fact." In some states they may be called "permissive" presumptions. Rules of the other type are called, in New York, "presumptions," "true presumptions" or "presumptions of law." Elsewhere they may be called "mandatory" (not "conclusive") presumptions.

Suppose that plaintiff, normally having the burden on the issue of delivery, relies on the presumption of delivery from mailing (assume it is a true mandatory presumption), and she establishes mailing (say for simplicity's sake she establishes it as a matter of law by overwhelming undisputed evidence), and defendant introduces nothing tending to show nondelivery. Plaintiff gets a directed verdict or directed finding of delivery. Thus far, courts are agreed that this is the effect of a true mandatory presumption.

But suppose defendant introduces evidence of nondelivery: the testimony, for example, of her mail room clerk that he does not remember receiving the letter and that he probably would remember if he had received it. It is in this situation, where there is evidence of non-B (evidence against the presumed fact), that courts have differed over what effect, if any, is to be given a presumption.

(3) *Questions Useful in Analyzing Presumptions.* The above material makes it clear that there are two important questions to ask yourself about any presumption:

> (a) What effect does the presumption have in the absence of any evidence of non-B (i.e., any evidence contrary to the presumed fact)? In other words, does it have the mandatory effect or the permissive effect? That is, is it a "true presumption" or an "inference," to use one phraseology?

(b) What effect does the presumption have in the presence of evidence of non-B?

In answering these two questions, one should think separately about the presumption's effect on the judge in deciding burden of production issues, and its effect on instructions to the jury for their use in deciding whether the burden of persuasion is satisfied.

For illustrative purposes, let us examine three from among the many views as to what the effect of a presumption in situation (b) should be. Incidentally, each of these views can find support in the language of some decisions even within a single state. There is little consistency of language even among decisions dealing with the same presumption. The three views are:

(a) The presumption [and any commonsense notion underlying the presumption? doubtful] disappears from the case and plays no further role upon the introduction of the defendant's evidence of non-B. The case is to be determined exactly as if it never existed. Under the strongest version of this view, in our hypothetical case above, there would be a directed verdict, or directed finding of non-delivery against the plaintiff (at least if the jury believes the mailroom clerk and the common-sense notion is also removed).

(b) The presumption (and any commonsense notion underlying it) continues in the case even after the introduction of defendant's evidence of non-B; its role thereafter is as follows: the judge may take it into account in determining motions for directed findings or verdicts; and the jury is instructed that they may weigh it against the contrary evidence. It does not accomplish any shift of the burden of persuasion. In our hypothetical case, under this view, the issue of delivery would go to the jury with an instruction that mailing can mean delivery. (An alternate view to this one omits the instruction to the jury.)

(c) The presumption continues in the case and shifts the burden of persuasion. In our hypothetical, the defendant would, under this view, have the burden of proving nondelivery by a preponderance of the evidence. Her evidence on this score is quite weak, although it probably would raise a jury issue. Under the jury instruction that would be given, that the burden to persuade by a preponderance is on her, it is unlikely that the jury would find in her favor on the issue.

(4) *Policy-Based Presumptions.* Suppose, instead of the commonsense type presumption of delivery from mailing, we have a non-commonsense type presumption (e.g., the presumption that testator drew his will with knowledge of antilapse law [a statutory provision designating who takes if a named beneficiary dies], if you think that is a non-commonsense presumption). Do any of the three views expressed in Note (3), *supra*, make more (or less) sense when applied to this presumption than they did when applied to the commonsense mailing-delivery presumption? (Fact A would be the making of the will by the testator, fact B that he had knowledge of the law.)

McNULTY v. CUSACK
Florida District Court of Appeal
104 So. 2d 785 (1958)

ALLEN, ACTING CHIEF JUDGE.

This is an appeal from a final judgment in a negligence action, entered after a directed verdict for plaintiff as to liability. Annie B. Cusack sued F. Jerome McNulty as the result of a rear-end collision between a car driven by plaintiff and another driven by defendant. Defendant's car ran into the rear of plaintiff's car at an intersection.

We state the principal question involved here as follows:

> Whether the showing of a rear-end collision and the circumstances under which it occurred, in the absence of explanation, gives rise to a presumption of negligence so as to authorize a directed verdict, or whether it only gives rise to an inference of negligence sufficient for presentation to the jury.

There is a split of authority on whether or not a rear-end collision, coupled with circumstances under which it occurs, gives rise to an inference or a presumption of negligence. The following authorities hold that a presumption arises and that the burden of going forward with the evidence is on the person who ran into the preceding car from the rear: [citations from various states].

The Rhode Island court, in the case of *Douglas v. Silvia* [180 A. 359 (1935), which is in the group of cases last cited above], said:

> [P]roof of a rear-end collision makes a prima facie case of negligence against the driver of the car in the rear. This does not mean, however, that the driver of an automobile which is following another is to be held liable under all conditions and irrespective of existing circumstances. When a prima facie case is made out by proving that the plaintiff was damaged in a rear-end collision, the duty of going forward with evidence of due care falls upon the defendant. If the testimony then shows a conflict of evidence from which different conclusions may reasonably be drawn by ordinarily prudent persons, then the question becomes one of fact for the jury to determine under proper instructions from the court. The burden of proof in such a case still remains with the plaintiff.

The case of *Harvey v. Borg*, 1934, 218 Iowa 1228, 257 N.W. 190, 193, indicates the logic of those cases which hold that only an inference of neglect arises from the fact that a rear-end collision occurred and, therefore, it becomes a matter for the jury.

In *Harvey v. Borg*, *supra*, the Supreme Court of Iowa said:

> It is universally agreed that no inference of negligence arises from the mere fact that a collision occurred. A collision of two motor vehicles might result without negligence upon the part of the operator of either of them. The facts and circumstances surrounding the occurrence must be considered. It is certainly the general rule that a truck driven by a careful and

> prudent driver would not ordinarily crash with the rear of a forward moving vehicle of any kind. The inference recognized in such cases is by no means conclusive and may be readily dissipated by an explanation on the part of the party causing the injuries by evidence in the usual way. Appellant [sic] did not see fit to offer any explanation or to present testimony in their behalf. Appellee made out a prima facie case of negligence, and, in the absence of explanation on the part of defendant or of other evidence, an issue was presented for the jury.

The record shows that the sole testimony as to negligence in the [present] case was that of the plaintiff. After the plaintiff rested, the defendant also rested, so there was no explanation on the part of the defendant of his actions of crashing his car into the rear-end of plaintiff's car.

We, therefore, have the testimony of the plaintiff that she had stopped her car at a street intersection where the traffic light showed red and was waiting for the light to change to green, that while still sitting there, the defendant's car crashed into the back of her car; and in addition, that the defendant rushed up and apologized to her and when she stated to him that he had wrecked her car, he remarked that that could be fixed.

Was there sufficient evidence before the court to create a presumption of negligence on the part of the defendant so as to require him to go forward with testimony to show that he was not legally at fault in crashing into the back of plaintiff's car? We agree with the circuit judge that the facts above stated created a presumption of negligence and not an inference of negligence and that, in the absence of an explanation from the defendant, a verdict should have been directed by the lower court in favor of the plaintiff. We think the court could take judicial notice of the fact that it was the duty of both the plaintiff and the defendant to stop at the intersecting street when a traffic light was showing red. In this day of heavy motor traffic all over the nation, the youngest or the most careless motorist knows that it is negligence to go through a red light. In addition, the rules of the road would require the defendant, as he approached the intersection, to have his car under control so that he would not drive into the rear-end of a motorist obeying traffic signals by waiting for the red light to turn green. If the defendant had a justifiable reason for not observing traffic rules, then it was his duty to go forward with the evidence to show that he was not negligent and thus, permit the case to go to a jury for the jury's determination on conflicting theories or facts.

The judgment is affirmed.

NOTES AND QUESTIONS

(1) *Was a Directed Verdict Appropriate?* How could a verdict be directed in the principal case, even if fact B (negligence) necessarily follows from fact A (rear-end collision)? Fact A (rear-end collision) does not have to be accepted by the jury, does it? Isn't credibility always for the jury to decide? Couldn't reasonable people always disagree as to credibility of a witness? Shouldn't the jury be given the opportunity to disbelieve plaintiff's testimony that she was hit by defendant from behind?

Shouldn't they at least be given that freedom where the witness has an interest? Or do you suppose it wasn't disputed by defendant in the pleadings? Is his silence at trial the same thing?

(2) *Rationales Favoring the Use of Presumptions. Watkins v. Prudential Ins. Co.*, 173 A. 644 (Pa. 1934), listed the following policy reasons for creating presumptions:

> They are either (1) a procedural expedient, or (2) a rule of proof production based upon the comparative availability of material evidence to the respective parties, or (3) a conclusion firmly based upon the generally known results of wide human experience, or (4) a combination of (1) and (3). The presumption as to the survivorship of husband and wife meeting death in a common disaster is a procedural expedient. It is not based upon extensive data arising from human experience. An unexplained absence for seven years raises the presumption of the death of the absentee upon the expiration of the last day of the period. This also is a procedural expedient — an arbitrary but necessary rule for the solution of problems arising from unexplained absences of human beings. An example of (2) is the rule requiring persons on trial for doing certain acts which are illegal if done without a license to produce evidence that they belong to a class privileged by license. The following are examples of (3): (a) An envelope properly addressed and stamped will reach the addressee if the latter is alive; (b) a child born during the wedlock of its parents is legitimate; (c) a person who drives across a railroad crossing will show due care. If the driver is killed at such a crossing, the presumption that he showed due care shifts the burden of proof to the party who defends the action on the ground of the victim's want of care. (In this example, the presumption of the victim's due care is merely the converse of the statement that the burden of proof rests on the asserter of the victim's negligence.) A presumption that a debt is paid after a lapse of a definite long period of time is both a procedural expedient (1) and a conclusion based on the results of wide human experience (3).

The court omits at least one entry most would add to the list of reasons for presumptions. See the following:

> [N]otions, usually implicit rather than expressed, of social and economic policy incline the courts to favor one contention by giving it the benefit of a presumption, and correspondingly handicapping the disfavored adversary. A classic instance is the presumption of ownership from possession, which tends to favor the prior possessor and to make for stability of estates. McCormick, Evidence § 968 (3d ed. 1984).

The court's omission may be unintentional.

HINDS v. JOHN HANCOCK MUTUAL LIFE INSURANCE CO.

Supreme Judicial Court of Maine
155 A.2d 721 (1959)

WEBBER, JUSTICE.

Plaintiff is beneficiary of an insurance policy covering the life of his late father, Donald Hinds. The policy provides for payment of a death benefit of $9,000 and, in addition thereto, of a like sum in the event the death of the assured should be due to bodily injuries sustained solely through "violent, external and accidental means." Suit was brought in behalf of plaintiff, a minor, by Emily Hinds, his mother and legal guardian. It is not disputed that the death of the assured being shown, the plaintiff is entitled to recover the ordinary death benefit of $9,000. The jury, however, awarded double indemnity as reflected by a verdict of $18,000. Issues are raised both by general motion and exceptions.

In the case of *Cox v. Metropolitan Life Ins. Co.*, 139 Me. 167, 28 A.2d 143, involving suit on a policy covering accidental death, our court recognized that the burden of proving accident rested upon the claimant throughout the trial and never shifted. The distinction is clearly made in *Watkins v. Prudential Ins. Co.*, 1934, 315 Pa. 497, 173 A. 644, 649, as between suits on insurance policies like the one here sued on, which insure against death as a result "of bodily injuries effected solely through external, violent and accidental means" and suits on those policies which insure against death but which contain a proviso avoiding the policy "if the insured dies by his own act." As the court there pointed out, in the former situation the plaintiff has the unremitting burden of proof as to accident, whereas in the latter situation the plaintiff need only prove death while the defendant has from the inception the burden of proof as to suicide which is there raised as an affirmative defense. So in the case before us, the death of the insured person by violent and external means was conceded. The defendant by its pleadings having raised the issue, it remained for the plaintiff to prove by a fair preponderance of the whole evidence that those means were also accidental.

The plaintiff in the first instance was aided by the so-called presumption against suicide. This presumption stems from and is raised by our common knowledge and experience that most sane men possess a natural love of life and an instinct for self-protection which effectively deter them from suicide or the self-infliction of serious bodily injury. It is commonly recognized that there is an affirmative presumption of death by accidental means which arises under appropriate circumstances from the negative presumption against suicide. Whether and to what extent the presumption persists in the face of contrary evidence is a matter of great and even decisive importance in the instant case.

Although a small minority of states adhere to an opposite view, it is now almost universally held that disputable presumptions are not themselves evidence nor are they entitled to be weighed in the scales as evidence. Rather are they recognized as "rules about evidence." They may be distinguished from inferences in that an inference is permissible, whereas a presumption is mandatory. They compel a finding of the presumed fact in the absence of contrary evidence. They perform the office of locating the burden of going forward with evidence, but having performed that office they disappear in the face of countervailing evidence.

The minority view that the presumption is itself evidence or has evidentiary weight has its adherents among the courts, some of which have felt constrained to that result by judicial interpretation of applicable statutes. No statute exists in Maine declaring that disputable presumptions are themselves evidence.

A far more difficult and troublesome question arises in determining what quantum or quality of evidence is required to cause a rebuttable presumption to disappear. Conversely, to what extent will such a presumption persist in the face of contrary evidence? And who is to evaluate that evidence, the trial judge or the jury? It is at this point that courts have gone their several ways and too often semantics have been substituted for logic. On the one hand is the risk that the jury may be confused by instructions relating to presumptions and may misapply them, especially by according to presumptions artificial evidentiary weight in the scales which they do not possess. On the other hand is the concern expressed by many writers of opinion and texts that if the presumption be regarded purely as a procedural tool in the hands of the trial judge, he will have in effect usurped the province of the jury as factfinder in determining the weight and credibility of such evidence as tends to negative the presumed fact. Efforts to reconcile these two desirable objectives have produced both compromise and confusion.

Many courts have adopted what is usually referred to as the Thayer theory of rebuttal which provides that disputable presumptions (other than the presumption of legitimacy) fall as a matter of law when evidence has been introduced which would support a finding of the non-existence of the presumed fact. This rule has the virtue of uniformity and won approval in the American Law Institute, Model Code of Evidence, Rules 703 and 704. In the foreword of the Model Code, Professor Edmund M. Morgan, the reporter and a recognized authority in the field of evidence and procedure, makes this excellent analysis of the several views (page 55):

> As to the other consequences of the establishment of the basic fact, save only the basic fact of the presumption of legitimacy, the opinions reveal at least eight variant views, of which the following are the most important:
>
> 1. The existence of the presumed fact must be assumed unless and until evidence has been introduced *which would justify a jury in finding the non-existence of the presumed fact.* When once such evidence has been introduced, the existence or non-existence of the presumed fact is to be determined exactly as if no presumption had ever been operative in the action; indeed, as if no such concept as a presumption had ever been known to the courts. *Whether the judge or the jury believes or disbelieves the opposing evidence thus introduced is entirely immaterial.* In other words, the sole effect of the presumption is to cause the establishment of the basic fact to put upon the party asserting the non-existence of the presumed fact the risk of the non-introduction of evidence which would support a finding of its non-existence. This may be called the *pure Thayerian rule*, for if he did not invent it, he first clearly expounded it.

2. The existence of the presumed fact must be assumed unless and until evidence has been introduced which would justify a jury in finding the non-existence of the presumed fact. When such evidence has been introduced, the existence or non-existence of the presumed fact is a question for the jury unless and until *"substantial evidence" of the non-existence of the presumed fact has been introduced. When such substantial evidence has been introduced, the existence or non-existence of the presumed fact is to be decided as if no presumption had ever been operative in the action.* Thus if the basic fact, by itself or in connection with other evidence, would rationally support a finding of the presumed fact, the existence or non-existence of the presumed fact is a question for the jury; if the basic fact is the only evidence of the presumed fact and would not rationally justify a finding of the presumed fact, the judge directs the jury to find the non-existence of the presumed fact. *Unfortunately the cases which support this rule do not define substantial evidence: it is certainly more than enough to justify a finding; sometimes it seems to be such evidence as would ordinarily require a directed verdict.*

3. *The existence of the presumed fact must be assumed unless and until the evidence of its non-existence convinces the jury that its non-existence is at least as probable as its existence.* This is sometimes expressed as requiring evidence which balances the presumption.

4. The existence of the presumed fact must be assumed unless and until the jury finds *that the non-existence of the presumed fact is more probable than its existence.* In other words the presumption puts upon the party alleging the non-existence of the presumed fact both *the burden of producing evidence and the burden of persuasion of its non-existence.* This is sometimes called the "Pennsylvania rule."

Professor Morgan and his distinguished colleague, Professor John M. Maguire, have never concealed their preference for some form of the fourth of the foregoing variants which would involve the shifting of the burden of persuasion at least as to certain classifications of presumptions, if not as to all. *See* MAGUIRE ON EVIDENCE, COMMON SENSE AND COMMON LAW, page 187; Model Code of Evidence, page 57; MORGAN, SOME PROBLEMS OF PROOF, page 81; Morgan, *Presumptions and Burden of Proof*, 47 HARV. L. REV. 59; Morgan and Maguire, *Looking Backward and Forward at Evidence*, 50 HARV. L. REV. 909, 913. This concept was finally approved by both the American Bar Association and the American Law Institute in 1954 and appears as Rule 14 of the Uniform Rules of Evidence promulgated by the National Conference of Commissioners on Uniform State Laws. That rule is as follows:

Rule 14. Effect of Presumptions. Subject to Rule 16, and except for presumptions which are conclusive or irrefutable under the rules of law from which they arise, (a) if the facts from which the presumption is derived have any probative value as evidence of the existence of the presumed fact, the presumption continues to exist *and the burden of establishing the non-existence of the presumed fact* is upon the party against whom the

> presumption operates, (b) if the facts from which the presumption arises have no probative value as evidence of the presumed fact, the presumption does not exist when evidence is introduced *which would support a finding of the non-existence of the presumed fact*, and the fact which would otherwise be presumed shall be determined from the evidence exactly as if no presumption was or had ever been involved. Jones on Evidence, 5th Ed., Vol. 4, page 1903 (see Comment, page 1904). [Eds. note: The Uniform Rule was subsequently substantially revised.]

Amid so much confusion, there is the natural temptation toward over-simplification. Nevertheless, if the presumption is to be a useful procedural tool in the hands of the trial court, relative simplicity is a desirable goal. In the article in 47 Harv. L. Rev. 59 already cited, Professor Morgan has made a thorough and helpful analysis of this troublesome problem. As he points out, rebuttable presumptions have been created "(a) to furnish an escape from an otherwise inescapable dilemma or to work a purely procedural convenience, (b) to require the litigant to whom information as to the facts is the more easily accessible to make them known, (c) to make more likely a finding in accord with the balance of probability, or (d) to encourage a finding consonant with the judicial judgment as to sound social policy." Although the purposes for which presumptions are raised might properly and logically affect the method of their rebuttal, the writer, while suggesting that they should be permitted to shift the burden of persuasion, sees no serious or insurmountable objection to the establishment of a single procedural rule that a disputable presumption persists until the contrary evidence persuades the fact-finder that the balance of probabilities is in equilibrium, or, stated otherwise, until the evidence satisfies the jury or factfinder that it is as probable that the presumed fact does not exist as that it does exist. We view the adoption of such a rule as a practical solution of a confusing procedural problem. In establishing the vanishing point for presumptions, it provides more certainty than do the varying definitions of "substantial countervailing evidence." It has also the virtue of reserving to the factfinder decisions as to veracity, memory, and weight of testimony whenever they are in issue. In essence, the proposed rule recognizes that when an inference has hardened into a presumption compelling a finding in the absence of contrary evidence, it has achieved a status which should not vanish at the first "tapping on the window pane." It recognizes that "surely the courts do not raise such a presumption merely for the purpose of making the opponent of the presumption cause words to be uttered." We agree with Mr. Morgan that our objective should be to devise a "simple, sensible and workable" plan for the procedural use of disputable presumptions and are satisfied that the suggested rule achieves that end.

Such a rule gives to the presumption itself maximum coercive force short of shifting the burden of persuasion. Although we are keenly aware that there is severe criticism by respected authority of the widely accepted rule that the burden of persuasion on an issue never shifts, that rule has been thoroughly imbedded in the law of this state. An unbroken line of judicial pronouncements to this effect are to be found in our opinions. We would be most reluctant to make a radical change in the accepted rule unless forced to do so by some compelling logic. We feel no such compulsion here. Logic compels the conclusion that a mere procedural device is not itself evidence. But beyond that there seems to be a certain amount of judicial latitude which permits the court to determine how a disputable presumption, necessarily artificial in its nature, can best perform a useful function in forwarding the course of a trial. As already noted, it seems pointless to create a presumption and endow it with coercive force, only to allow it to vanish in the face of evidence of dubious weight or credibility. Neither does it seem to us necessary, in order to bring some order out of chaos, to overrule all precedent and permit the presumption to shift the burden of persuasion from him who first proposes the issue and seeks to change the status quo. These considerations prompt us to adopt the foregoing rule which seems to us a satisfactory middle course.

In our review of many opinions on this subject, we have discovered no more careful or accurate an analysis than is contained in a dissenting opinion by Mr. Justice Traynor appearing in *Speck v. Sarver*, 128 P.2d [Cal.] at pages 19, 22. Endorsing the view which we take of the effect of rebuttable presumptions as the "sounder one," he states: "Once such evidence (contrary to the presumed fact) is produced and believed, the jury should weigh it against any evidence introduced in support of the facts presumed and decide in favor of the party against whom the presumption operates if it believes that the non-existence of the facts is as probable as their existence. Nothing need be said about weighing the presumption as evidence."

With respect to the presumption against suicide in particular, Mr. Justice Taft concurring in *Carson v. Metropolitan Life Ins. Co., supra* [165 Ohio St. 238, 135 N.E.2d 263], said: "There may be instances where the only evidence produced or introduced to rebut the presumption against suicide is evidence which the jury may quite properly disbelieve in exercising its function as trier of the facts and judge of the credibility of witnesses. In such an instance, if the rule is as broadly stated as is suggested then incredible evidence or evidence having no weight whatever could be effective in making the presumption against suicide disappear. Obviously, that would be unreasonable.

"There may therefore be instances where it will be necessary for the trial court to mention the presumption against suicide in charging a jury, even though it is erroneous to advise the jury that that presumption may be weighed as evidence."

The rule for which we have expressed preference does not, as we interpret it, mean that the persistence or disappearance of a disputable presumption may never be resolved as a matter of law. Whenever no countervailing evidence is offered or that which is offered is but a scintilla, or amounts to no more than speculation and surmise, the presumed fact will stand as though proven and the jury will be so instructed. On the other hand, when the contrary evidence comes from such sources and is of such a nature that rational and unprejudiced minds could not reasonably or properly differ as to the non-existence of the presumed fact, the presumption will disappear as a matter of law. Where proof of the presumed fact is an essential element of the plaintiff's case, he would suffer the consequence of a directed verdict. Such would ordinarily be the result, for example, when evidence effectively rebutting the presumption is drawn from admissions by the plaintiff, evidence from witnesses presented and vouched for by the plaintiff, or from uncontroverted physical or documentary evidence. [Thus, on the evidence here, the court holds, the presumption of accidental (non-suicidal) death was as a matter of law rebutted (and thus dropped from the picture entirely) by *plaintiff's own evidence*, which showed that death was caused by a gun pressed to the right temple and a horizontal bullet trajectory. Since there was nothing else indicating any non-suicidal (accidental) cause, plaintiff receives a sum of only $9000.]

NOTES AND QUESTIONS

(1) *Principal Case. Hinds* has been cited as the leading case adopting the approach that the presumption exists until the factfinder decides that the nonexistence of the fact is as likely as its existence. The current presumption rule in Maine shifts the burden of persuasion.

(2) *Should Presumptions Affect Burden of Production or Persuasion? Hinds* mentions Rule 704 of the Model Code of Evidence as finalized in 1942. It provides that:

> (1) . . . when the basic fact of a presumption has been established in an action, the existence of the presumed fact must be assumed unless and until evidence has been introduced which would support a finding of its non-existence.
>
> (2) . . . when the basic fact of a presumption has been established in an action and evidence has been introduced which would support a finding of the non-existence of the presumed fact the existence or non-existence of the presumed fact is to be determined exactly as if no presumption had ever been applicable in the action.

This adopts Professor Thayer's "Bursting Bubble" view of presumptions: that they are a procedural tool that disappears when the presumption is rebutted by the appropriate degree of evidence. Fed. R. Evid. 301 has been said to adopt this approach in federal civil actions not otherwise provided for by an Act of Congress. (Do you agree?) As to state claims, Fed. R. Evid. 302 (before restyling in 2011) applied state law to presumptions "respecting a fact which is an element of a claim or defense as to which state law supplies the rule of decision." Thus, in most diversity cases, presumptions of intermediate facts will be governed by Fed. R. Evid. 301 (affecting only burden of production?), but the more important presumptions affecting an *element* of the claim or defense will be governed by state law. (The restylers unwittingly removed the word "element", suggesting that state law governs whether an element or an intermediate fact is being proved. But the restylers have professed that their intention was not to change any result or ruling, so the unwitting deletion could be argued to have no effect.)

In contrast, the position of the current Rule 301 of the Uniform Rules of Evidence is that "a presumption imposes on the party against whom it is directed the burden of proving the nonexistence of the presumed fact is more probable than its existence." In other words, the presumption affects the burden of persuasion, not simply the burden of producing evidence.

States, even those whose evidence rules are generally patterned on the Federal Rules of Evidence, adopt highly individual approaches to whether and how particular presumptions affect the burden of production or persuasion. As a result, this is one area where generalities are of little help in solving an actual problem based in a specific jurisdiction. Only a perusal of the local law will suffice, and even then the answer may be unclear or may vary with the context.

(3) *Federal Cases: Determining if Congress Provided Otherwise.* Fed. R. Evid. 301 excepts from its coverage not only criminal cases, but civil cases for which Congress has provided some different effect for the particular presumption involved. Questions arise as to whether this means "expressly provided" or whether policy implications of, or regulations under, the statute suffice. For an example of such a law engendering a complex scheme of presumptions and burden shifting, see discussion in *Texas Dep't of Community Affairs v. Burdine*, 450 U.S. 248 (1981), concerning the nature of the evidentiary burden placed upon the defendant in an employment discrimination suit brought under Title VII of the Civil Rights Act of 1964, 42 U.S.C. § 2000 et seq. (after the plaintiff has proved a prima facie case of discriminatory treatment by a preponderance of the evidence, the burden shifts to the defendant to articulate some legitimate, nondiscriminatory reasons for the challenged employment action; if defendant carries this burden, the plaintiff must have an opportunity to prove by a preponderance that the reasons offered were a pretext for discrimination; citing *McDonnell Douglas Corp. v. Green*, 411 U.S. 792 (1973)). *Burdine* held that the burden that shifts to the defendant to rebut the presumption of discrimination is a burden of production, not persuasion. Is this any different from Fed. R. Evid. 301? The Court does not appear to refer at all to Fed. R. Evid. 301, but rather relies upon statutory and other policies.

(4) *Conflicting Presumptions.* What happens when two presumptions clash? For example, in *Atkinson v. Hall*, 556 A.2d 651 (Me. 1989), a paternity case, a presumption that a child born or conceived during marriage is legitimate conflicted with the presumption that the results of blood tests are valid. The test showed that the father was the defendant in this paternity case, not the husband. The court found no error in discarding the competing presumptions and instructing the jury simply that the mother must prove her case by a preponderance. Maine has a provision governing conflicts that requires the court to apply the presumption founded on weightier considerations of policy and logic. If there is no such presumption, both presumptions shall be disregarded. This is somewhat similar to the approach of the current Uniform Rule 301, which states that neither presumption applies when considerations of policy are of equal weight.

An example of conflicting presumptions of unequal weight would be the presumption of the validity of a marriage and the presumption of the continuation of a marriage. The classic example is the widow who claims her share of her husband's property by proving that they got married, while her adversary then proves that previous to that marriage she was married to another man. Particularly given the frequency of remarriages, the latter presumption is simply a shortcut for proof, while the former is based on policies favoring legitimacy and inheritance.

PROBLEM 15A: HOW DO PRESUMPTIONS REALLY WORK IN COURT?

The question at trial is whether the plaintiff gave notice to her insurance company in a timely manner as required by her policy. If so, the insurance company is liable for the plaintiff's damages; if not, the insurance company is off the hook. The evidence at trial concerning the giving of notice consists of plaintiff's testimony that she wrote a letter containing the necessary information, put it in an 8 x 11 inch yellow envelope with her supporting documentation, addressed it to the insurance company, affixed the proper amount of postage, and mailed the envelope by placing it in a mailbox on June 1. The insurance company's office is located in the same city where the plaintiff resides. To be effective, notice was required to be received by July 1. There is a statutory presumption in the jurisdiction that if a letter is properly addressed and mailed, it is received, unless rebutted by evidence of nondelivery.

Assume that the above information is the only evidence on this issue. What court ruling or instruction is the plaintiff entitled to at the end of the case? What happens if the insurance company calls a mailroom clerk who testifies that he does not remember seeing any large yellow envelope being delivered during the month of June. Is the plaintiff entitled to an instruction on the statutory presumption? Does the answer depend on whether the jurisdiction is governed by Fed. R. Evid. 301, rather than a rule that shifts the burden of persuasion? Even in a jurisdiction that shifts only the burden of production, would any evidence, regardless of how suspect, defeat the presumption?

§ 15.03 CRIMINAL PRESUMPTIONS[3]

COUNTY COURT OF ULSTER COUNTY v. ALLEN

United States Supreme Court
442 U.S. 140 (1979)

JUSTICE STEVENS delivered the opinion of the Court.

A New York statute provides that, with certain exceptions, the presence of a firearm in an automobile is presumptive evidence of its illegal possession by all persons then occupying the vehicle.

Four persons, three adult males (appellants) and a 16-year-old girl (Jane Doe, *who is not an appellant here*), were jointly tried on charges that they possessed two loaded handguns, a loaded machinegun, and over a pound of heroin found in a Chevrolet in which they were riding when it was stopped for speeding on the New York Thruway. The two large-caliber handguns, which together with their ammunition weighed approximately six pounds, were seen through the window of the car by the investigating police officer. They were positioned crosswise in an open

---

[3] Study Guide Reference: Evidence in a Nutshell, Chapter 2:III at "Criminal Presumptions and Their Restriction by the Constitution." A more extensive treatment can be found in an earlier edition of the *Nutshell*, the second edition (1981), Chapter 2.

handbag on either the front floor or the front seat of the car on the passenger side where Jane Doe was sitting. Jane Doe admitted that the handbag was hers. The machinegun and the heroin were discovered in the trunk after the police pried it open. The car had been borrowed from the driver's brother earlier that day; the key to the trunk could not be found in the car or on the person of any of its occupants, although there was testimony that two of the occupants had placed something in the trunk before embarking in the borrowed car. The jury convicted all four of possession of the handguns and acquitted them of possession of the contents of the trunk.

Counsel for all four defendants objected to the introduction into evidence of the two handguns, the machinegun, and the drugs, arguing that the State had not adequately demonstrated a connection between their clients and the contraband. The trial court overruled the objection, relying on the presumption of possession created by the New York statute. Because that presumption does not apply if a weapon is found "upon the person" of one of the occupants of the car, the three male defendants also moved to dismiss the charges relating to the handguns on the ground that the guns were found on the person of Jane Doe. The trial judge twice denied it, concluding that the applicability of the "upon the person" exception was a question of fact for the jury.

At the close of the trial, the judge instructed the jurors that they were entitled to infer possession from the defendants' presence in the car. He did not make any reference to the "upon the person" exception in his explanation of the statutory presumption, nor did any of the defendants object to this omission or request alternative or additional instructions on the subject.

Defendants filed a post-trial motion in which they challenged the constitutionality of the New York statute as applied in this case. The challenge was made in support of their argument that the evidence, apart from the presumption, was insufficient to sustain the convictions.

[The New York Court of Appeals decided that the application of the presumption in this case is unconstitutional.]

In this case, the Court of Appeals undertook the task of deciding the constitutionality of the New York statute "on its face." Its conclusion that the statutory presumption was arbitrary rested entirely on its view of the fairness of applying the presumption in hypothetical situations — situations, indeed, in which it is improbable that a jury would return a conviction or that a prosecution would ever be instituted. . . .

Inferences and presumptions are a staple of our adversary system of factfinding. It is often necessary for the trier of fact to determine the existence of an element of the crime — that is, an "ultimate" or "elemental" fact — from the existence of one or more "evidentiary" or "basic" facts.

The value of these evidentiary devices, and their validity under the Due Process Clause, vary from case to case, however, depending on the strength of the connection between the particular basic and elemental facts involved and on the degree to which the device curtails the factfinder's freedom to assess the evidence independently. Nonetheless, in criminal cases, the ultimate test of any device's constitutional validity in a given case remains constant: the device must not undermine the factfinder's responsibility at trial, based on evidence adduced by the State, to find the ultimate facts beyond a reasonable doubt.

The most common evidentiary device is the entirely permissive inference or presumption, which allows — but does not require — the trier of fact to infer the elemental fact from proof by the prosecutor of the basic one and which places no burden of any kind on the defendant.

. . . Because this permissive presumption leaves the trier of fact free to credit or reject the inference and does not shift the burden of proof, it affects the application of the "beyond a reasonable doubt" standard only if, under the facts of the case, there is no rational way the trier could make the connection permitted by the inference. . . .

A mandatory presumption is a far more troublesome evidentiary device. For it may affect not only the strength of the "no reasonable doubt" burden but also the placement of that burden; it tells the trier that he or they must find the elemental fact upon proof of the basic fact, at least unless the defendant has come forward with some evidence to rebut the presumed connection between the two facts. In this situation, the Court has generally examined the presumption on its face to determine the extent to which the basic and elemental facts coincide. To the extent that the trier of fact is forced to abide by the presumption, and may not reject it based on an independent evaluation of the particular facts presented by the State, the analysis of the presumption's constitutional validity is logically divorced from those facts and based on the presumption's accuracy in the run of cases. It is for this reason that the Court has held it irrelevant in analyzing a mandatory presumption, but not in analyzing a purely permissive one, that there is ample evidence in the record other than the presumption to support a conviction.

Without determining whether the presumption in this case was mandatory, the Court of Appeals analyzed it on its face as if it were. In fact, it was not, as the [highest New York court] had earlier pointed out.

The trial judge's instruction made it clear that the presumption was merely a part of the prosecution's case, that it gave rise to a permissive inference available only in certain circumstances, rather than a mandatory conclusion of possession, and that it could be ignored by the jury even if there was no affirmative proof offered by defendants in rebuttal. The judge explained that possession could be actual or constructive, but that constructive possession could not exist without the intent and ability to exercise control or dominion over the weapons. He also carefully instructed the jury that there is a mandatory presumption of innocence in favor of the defendants that controls unless it, as the exclusive trier of fact, is satisfied beyond a reasonable doubt that the defendants possessed the handguns in the manner described by the judge. In short, the instructions plainly directed the jury to consider all the circumstances tending to support or contradict the inference that all four occupants of the car had possession of the two loaded handguns and to decide the matter for itself without regard to how much evidence the defendants introduced.

Our cases considering the validity of permissive statutory presumptions such as the one involved here have rested on an evaluation of the presumption as applied to the record before the Court. None suggests that a court should pass on the constitutionality of this kind of statute "on its face." It was error for the Court of Appeals to make such a determination in this case.

As applied to the facts of this case, the presumption of possession is entirely rational. Notwithstanding the Court of Appeals' analysis, respondents were not "hitchhikers or other casual passengers," and the guns were neither "a few inches in length" nor "out of [respondents'] sight." The argument against possession by any of the respondents was predicated solely on the fact that the guns were in Jane Doe's pocketbook. But several circumstances — which, not surprisingly, her counsel repeatedly emphasized in his questions and his argument — made it highly improbable that she was the sole custodian of those weapons. . . .

. . . [T]he case is tantamount to one in which the guns were lying on the floor or the seat of the car in the plain view of the three other occupants of the automobile. In such a case, it is surely rational to infer that each of the respondents was fully aware of the presence of the guns and had both the ability and the intent to exercise dominion and control over the weapons. The application of the statutory presumption in this case therefore comports with the standard laid down . . . in *Leary* [*v. United States*, 395 U.S. 6 (1969)], for there is a "rational connection" between the basic facts that the prosecution proved and the ultimate fact presumed, and the latter is "more likely than not to flow from" the former.

Respondents argue, however, that the validity of the New York presumption must be judged by a "reasonable doubt" test rather than the "more likely than not" standard employed in *Leary*. Under the more stringent test, it is argued that a statutory presumption must be rejected unless the evidence necessary to invoke the inference is sufficient for a rational jury to find the inferred fact beyond a reasonable doubt. Respondents' argument again overlooks the distinction between a permissive presumption on which the prosecution is entitled to rely as one not necessarily sufficient part of its proof and a mandatory presumption which the jury must accept even if it is the sole evidence of an element of the offense.

In the latter situation, since the prosecution bears the burden of establishing guilt, it may not rest its case entirely on a presumption unless the fact proved is sufficient to support the inference of guilt beyond a reasonable doubt. But in the former situation, the prosecution may rely on all of the evidence in the record to meet the reasonable-doubt standard. There is no more reason to require a permissive statutory presumption to meet a reasonable-doubt standard before it may be permitted to play any part in a trial than there is to require that degree of probative force for other relevant evidence before it may be admitted. As long as it is clear that the presumption is not the sole and sufficient basis for a finding of guilt, it need only satisfy the test described in *Leary*.

The permissive presumption, as used in this case, satisfied the *Leary* test. And, as already noted, the [highest New York court] has concluded that the record as a whole was sufficient to establish guilt beyond a reasonable doubt.

The judgment is reversed.

NOTES AND QUESTIONS

(1) *Language Associated with Presumptions.* Note the use of terminology in *Ulster.* Mandatory Presumptions are distinguished from Permissive Presumptions. This may not be precisely the same permissive-mandatory dichotomy we used above in connection with civil cases. But for the moment we will overlook this.

The word presumption might be thought only to apply to mandatory statements (if A is proven, you *must* find B). In other words, aren't permissive presumptions simply *inferences*, rather than true presumptions? Aren't they more akin to a judge commenting on the evidence or lawyers telling the jurors in argument that they *may* find a link between A and B? Most inferences are made by the jurors in evaluating the evidence without any instruction from the court. Many civil cases do not call permissive presumptions "presumptions" at all. Because *Ulster* adopted for both kinds, the "presumption" terminology, followed in later cases, all discussion of presumptions should conform to its definitions, at least in criminal cases. If "presumption" was a word generally used in civil cases only for mandatory presumptions when Fed. R. Evid. 301 was adopted, then perhaps Fed. R. Evid. 301 (which expressly covers only civil "presumptions") may not be applicable to presumptions that are permissive. Courts are divided on this.

(2) *Mandatory Presumptions (Unlike the Ulster Permissive Presumption) Must be Evaluated for Rationality on the Basis of the Range of Imaginable Cases Without Regard to the Evidence in the Particular Case and Thus may be Invalid Even if They Provide Rational Inferences in the Particular Circumstances of the Case.* In a lengthy footnote in *Ulster*, the Court uses *Leary v. United States*, 395 U.S. 6 (1969), to illustrate that mandatory presumptions are evaluated facially to determine their constitutionality. In that case, Dr. Timothy Leary, a professor at Harvard University, was stopped by customs inspectors in Laredo, Texas, as he was returning from the Mexican side of the international border. Marijuana seeds and a silver snuffbox filled with semirefined marijuana and three partially smoked marijuana cigarettes were discovered in his car. He was convicted of having knowingly transported marijuana that he knew had been illegally imported into this country in violation of 21 U.S.C. § 176a. That statute included a mandatory presumption: "possession shall be deemed sufficient evidence to authorize conviction unless the defendant explains his possession to the satisfaction of the jury." Leary admitted possession of the marijuana and claimed that he had carried it from New York to Mexico and then back (so that the wasn't importing or knowingly transporting imported stuff, which was required for there to be commission of this crime). *Ulster* says of *Leary:*

> Mr. Justice Harlan for the Court noted that under one theory of the case, the jury could have found direct proof of all of the necessary elements of the offense without recourse to the presumption. But he deemed that insufficient reason to affirm the conviction because under another theory the jury might have found knowledge of importation on the basis of either direct evidence or the presumption, and there was accordingly no certainty that

the jury had not relied on the presumption. The Court therefore found it necessary to test the presumption against the Due Process Clause. Its analysis was facial. Despite the fact that the defendant was well educated and had recently traveled to a country that is a major exporter of marijuana to this country, the Court found the presumption of knowledge of importation from possession irrational. It did so, not because Dr. Leary was unlikely to know the source of the marijuana, but instead because "a majority of possessors" were unlikely to have such knowledge. Because the jury had been instructed to rely on the presumption even if it did not believe the Government's direct evidence of knowledge of importation (unless, of course, the defendant met his burden of "satisfying" the jury to the contrary), the Court reversed the conviction.

(3) *No Presumptions Permitted in Criminal Cases that Shift the Burden of Persuasion on Elements of the Crime.* In *Francis v. Franklin*, 471 U.S. 307 (1985), a jury instruction stating that the "acts of a person of sound mind and discretion are presumed to be the product of a person's will, but the presumption may be rebutted" was held to violate due process. In reaching this conclusion, the Court said:

> When combined with the immediately preceding mandatory language, the instruction that the presumptions "may be rebutted" could reasonably be read as telling the jury that it was required to infer intent to kill as the natural and probable consequence of the act of firing the gun unless the defendant persuaded the jury that such an inference was unwarranted. The very statement that the presumption "may be rebutted" could have indicated to a reasonable juror that the defendant bore an affirmative burden of persuasion once the State proved the underlying act giving rise to the presumption. . . . [T]he challenged language undeniably created an unconstitutional burden-shifting presumption with respect to the element of intent.

(4) *A Fortiori, No Conclusive "Evidentiary" Presumptions on Elements in Criminal Cases. Sandstrom v. Montana*, 442 U.S. 510 (1979), seems to hold broadly that conclusive presumptions on elements are unconstitutional in a criminal case. In *Sandstrom*, the jury was told that "[the] law presumes that a person intends the ordinary consequences of his voluntary acts." Because the jurors were not told they had a choice, "a reasonable juror could have easily viewed such an instruction as mandatory," creating an irrebuttable presumption of intent, which was an element of the crime. (Note that mandatory is used here to mean conclusive or irrebuttable). *Accord Carella v. California*, 491 U.S. 263 (1989) (invalidating, as conclusive, presumptions that intent to commit theft by fraud is presumed from retaining rental car beyond 20 days after written demand, and that person wilfully failing to return rental vehicle after 5 days from lease expiration is presumed to embezzle vehicle.) *Sandstrom* also says that the presumption would be unconstitutional even if the jury only understood it to shift a burden of persuasion to defendant (by a preponderance or beyond a reasonable doubt).

(5) *But Conclusive Presumptions Are Permissible in Criminal Cases When They are "Substantive Definitions of Law."* Can a seemingly conclusive presump-

tion ever survive a due process challenge in a criminal case? Yes, when it is really a permissible redefinition of the substantive law. For example, *People v. Dillon*, 668 P.2d 697 (Cal. 1983) upheld the conclusive presumption (of "malice" normally required for the crime of murder) established by California's felony murder rule (i.e., the rule that death inflicted in the course of committing another felony is murder). Justice Mosk explained:

> [W]e start with the indisputable fact that if the effect of the felony-murder rule on malice is indeed a "presumption," it is a "conclusive" one. It does not simply shift to the defendant the burden of proving that he acted without malice . . .; rather, in a felony-murder prosecution the defendant is not permitted to offer any such proof at all. Yet it does not necessarily follow that he is denied the presumption of innocence with regard to an element of the crime, as in *Sandstrom*. We are led astray if we treat the "conclusive presumption of malice" as a true presumption; to do so begs the question whether malice is an element of felony murder. And to answer that question, we must look beyond labels to the underlying reality of this so-called "presumption."
>
> . . . [T]o say that (1) the prosecution must also prove malice in felony-murder cases, but that (2) the existence of such malice is "conclusively presumed" upon proof of the defendant's intent to commit the underlying felony, is merely a circuitous way of saying that in such cases the prosecution need prove only the latter intent. In Wigmore's words, the issue of malice is therefore "wholly immaterial for the purpose of the proponent's case" when the charge is felony murder. In that event the "conclusive presumption" is no more than a procedural fiction that masks a substantive reality, to wit, that as a matter of law malice is not an element of felony murder.
>
> The "substantive statutory definition" of the crime of first degree felony murder in this state does not include either malice or premeditation: "These elements are eliminated by the felony-murder doctrine, and the only criminal intent required is the specific intent to commit the particular felony."

Is this doctrine consistent with the other cases and notes in this section? Are there any limits to the doctrine? Does it contain the seeds of destruction of the constitutional requirement that crimes must be proven to the jury beyond a reasonable doubt? *Compare Mullaney v. Wilbur*, 421 U.S. 684 (1975) ("malice aforethought" required for murder, which is the opposite of "heat of passion" reducing murder to manslaughter, cannot be presumed and therefore presumption instruction to jury effectively imposing burden of persuasion by a preponderance on that issue on defendant is unconstitutional), *with Patterson v. New York*, 432 U.S. 197 (1977) (defendant charged with murder; placing affirmative defense on defendant to prove "extreme emotional disturbance" to reduce the offense to manslaughter was constitutionally permissible). Can these cases be reconciled?

TABLE OF CASES

[References are to pages]

A

A. & M., In re 852
A. L. Williams Corp. v. Faircloth. 80; 99; 282
Abel; United States v. 44; 203; 204
Adams v. Chevron U.S.A., Inc. 159
Adkins v. Brett. 444
Agosto, In re 852
Air Disaster at Lockerbie Scotland, In re. 515
Ake v. Oklahoma. 313
Alberico; State v.. 323
Albert; United States v.. 51
Alcalde; People v. 453, 454
Alessi; United States v. 709
Alexander Dawson, Inc. v. NLRB. 667
Alford v. United States 188; 205; 208
Alksnis; People v.. 31
Allen; United States v.. 175
Altkrug v. William Whitman Co. 380
Alvarado; United States v. 233
Amador-Galvan; United States v. 336
Amaechi; United States v.. 223
American Civil Liberties Union of Miss. v. Finch 854
American Cyanamid Co; United States v.. 567
American Nat'l Watermattress Corp. v. Manville . 71; 770
American Tel. & Tel. Co; United States v. . 419; 738
American Universal Ins. Co. v. Falzone. 261
Amerson; United States v.. 555
Amos; State v.. 852
Anderson v. Charles 411
Anderson v. Morrow. 129
Anderson; United States v. 43
Anderson; United States v.. 880
Andrews v. Neer 177
Appeal of (see name of party)
Application of (see name of party)
Apprendi v. New Jersey 875
Arcoren v. United States. 328
Arenson v. Skouras Theatres Corp 417
Armstead v. State. 309; 313
Arthur Young & Co; United States v. 774; 838
Asplundh Mfg. Div. v. Benton Harbor Eng'g. . .244
Atkinson v. Hall 904
Atwell; United States v. 883
Audibert v. Michaud. 186
Ault v. International Harvester Co. 161
Averhart v. State 721
Aviles; United States v. 719
Awkard v. United States 116

B

Bah; United States v.. 120
Bailey; United States v. 558
Bains v. Cambra 449
Baird v. Koerner 795
Baker v. Elcona Homes Corp.. 509
Ball; State v.. . . . . .64; 73
Ballew v. Georgia 880
Ballou v. Henri Studios, Inc. 47
Balsys; United States v. 866
Baltimore & O. R. Co. v. Schultz. 238
Baltimore City Dep't of Social Services v. Bouknight. 867
Bank of China, New York Branch v. NBM LLC. 246
Banks v. Schweiker 882
Bankston; United States v.. 368
Barber v. Page 526; 583
Barefoot v. Estelle 323; 330
Bareford v. General Dynamics Corp 862
Baroda State Bank v. Peck. 738
Barrett v. State 328
Barrett; United States v.. 195
Bauman v. Volkswagenwerk Aktiengesellschaft . . 72
Baumholser v. Amax Coal Co. 567
Baxter v. Palmigiano. 867
Beasley; United States v.. 881
Beck v. Norris 180
Beech Aircraft Corp. v. Rainey. 430; 508; 757
Beechum v. United States 190
Beechum; United States v.. . . . . .86; 190
Belisle; State v.. 112
Bemis v. Edwards 437
Benedetto; United States v.. 88
Benfield; United States v. 521
Bennett; United States v.. 743
Berkey Photo, Inc. v. Eastman Kodak Co. . 476; 792
Berman Enterprises, Inc. v. Local 333, United Marine Div. International Longshoremen's Ass'n. . . .73
Biggers v. Tennessee. 404
Bill v. Farm Bureau Life Ins. Co.. 61
Black v. United States. 857
Blackburn v. United States. 481; 567
Blackburn; United States v. 481; 567

[References are to pages]

Blackwell v. Franzen. 230
Blake; State v. 495
Blau v. United States. 804
Bogosian v. Gulf Oil Corp. 476; 792
Bohannon v. Pegelow 239
Boller v. Cofrances. 189
Bombard v. Ft. Wayne Newspapers, Inc. 466
Bonds; United States v.. . . . . .295, 296
Bonnett; United States v.. 195
Boobar; State v. 833
Booker; United States v.. 875
Boone; United States v. 551, 552
Borawick v. Shay. 182
Bordeaux; United States v.. 125
Borrelli; United States v.. 243
Bourjaily v. United States 69; 420; 891
Bourne; United States v.. 745
Bourque; United States v.. 882
Bowden v. McKenna 51
Bowe; United States v. 57
Boyd; United States v.. 322
Branzburg v. Hayes. 776; 841
Braswell v. United States 867
Bray v. Bi-State Dev. Corp. 731
Bredice v. Doctors Hospital, Inc. 846
Bridges v. State. 383
Brink's Inc. v. City of New York 867
Briscoe v. Virginia 624
Brown v. Southeastern Pa. Transp. Auth. (In re Paoli R.R. Yard PCB Litig.) 296
Brown v. State 657
Brown; People v.. 623
Brown; United States v.. 230
Brown; United States v.. 265
Brown; United States v.. 454
Brown; United States v.. 514
Brown; United States v.. 711
Brown; United States v.. 763
Brown; United States v.. 807
Bruce R. Lindsey, In re 789; 865
Bruton v. United States. 575; 647; 664
Bryan; United States v.. . . . . .804; 825
Bueno-Sierra v. United States 504
Bueno-Sierra; United States v.. 504
Bullcoming v. New Mexico 625
Burch; United States v. 165
Burden; State v. 586
Burns; State v.. 133
Burroughs; United States v.. 873
Bushaw v. United States. 193
Byrd; United States v.. 806

C

C. F. W. Constr. Co. v. Travelers Ins. Co.. 142
Cabello v. State. 852
Cain; United States v.. 441
Calhoun v. Baylor 420
California v. Green 393; 464
Calvert; United States v.. . . . . .75; 80; 214
Campbell v. Mincey 884
Canal Zone, Government of v. Burjan 879
Canton v. Kmart Corp.. 438
Capital Marine Supply, Inc. v. M/V Roland Thomas II. 481
Capital Traction Co. v. Hof. 18
Carbone; United States v.. 713
Carella v. California 910
Carlsen v. Javurek 213
Carlson; United States v.. 566
Carman v. McDonnell Douglas Corp.. 847
Carriger; United States v.. 713
Carson v. Metropolitan Life Ins. Co. 902
Carter v. Hewitt 32; 211
Castillo; United States v.. 256
Castro-Ayon v. United States 393
Castro-Ayon; United States v.. 393
Caudle; United States v.. 188
CBS, Inc. v. Democratic Nat'l Comm.. 39
Cestnik; United States v.. 507
Chambers v. Mississippi. . .67; 180; 193; 576; 654; 660
Chapple; State v.. 226
Charley; United States v.. 289
Charter v. Chleborad. 166
Chase; United States v. 834
Chavez v. Martinez. 866
Chavous v. State 504
Chein v. Shumsky 258
Chemical Leaman Tank Lines, Inc. v. Stevens . . 500
Cheney v. United States Dist. Court. 865
Chestnut v. Ford Motor Co 442
Chevere; United States v. 107
Ciccarelli v. Gichner Sys. Group, Inc. 551
City of (see name of city)
Clark v. State. .800
Clark v. Stewart 149
Clark v. United States 795, 796
Clark; United States v.. 720
Clark; United States v.. 808

[References are to pages]

Clarke; United States v. 564
Clay v. Johns-Manville Sales Corp.. 534
Clifford v. Commonwealth. 238
Close v. United States 523
Coffman; United States v. 718; 883
Cohen v. Cowles Media Co.. 841
Coleman v. Home Depot, Inc 515
Collins; People v.. 356
Colon Osorio; United States v. 247
Colorado v. Connelly. 421
Commercial Union Ins. Co. v. Boston Edison Co.. 731
Commodity Futures Trading Comm'n v. Weintraub 786
Commonwealth v. (see name of defendant)
Conduct of (see name of party)
Connell v. State 568
Connor v. State. 541
Contractor Utility Sales Co. v. Certain-Teed Products Corp.. 412
Cooper; United States v.. 127
Cordery; United States v. 433
Couch v. United States. 774; 838
County Court of Ulster County v. Allen 905
Cox v. Metropolitan Life Ins. Co 898
Cox v. Miller. .833
Coy v. Iowa. 575; 584
Craft; United States v.. 29
Crandell v. United States 20
Crawford v. Washington. 577; 586; 613; 626
Crawford v. Worth 254
Creaghe v. Iowa Home Mut. Casualty Co. 366
Cree v. Hatcher. 222
Crisp; United States v.. 338
Cromedy; State v.. . . . . .229; 337
Crowder; United States v.. 108
Cruz v. New York 648
Cruz; United States v.. 256
Cruz; United States v.. 355
Cueto; United States v. 232
Cunningham; United States v.. 93
Curran v. Pasek. 816
Curtis; United States v.. 60
Cuthbertson; United States v.. 841
Cutler; United States v. 195
Cutler; United States v. 841

D

Dabney v. Investment Corp. of America 779
Dallas County v. Commercial Union Assurance Company 562
Daubert v. Merrell Dow Pharmaceuticals, Inc.. .267; 269; 284; 286
Davies; United States v.. 851
Davis v. Alaska 188; 205; 209
Davis v. Washington 597
Dawson v. Delaware 107
De Leon v. State 852
De Marines v. KLM Royal Dutch Airlines 380
Dean; United States v.. 854
Deaver v. Hickox. 247
Deeb; United States v.. 566
Delaware v. Fensterer 577
Delli Paoli v. United States 647
Demasi v. Whitney Trust & Sav. Bank 543
Dennis v. United States 535
DeShay; State v.. 256
Dhinsa; United States v.. 669
Diaz; United States v.. 517
Dickerson v. United States. 404
DiDomenico; United States v.. 320
Dillon; People v.. 911
Dinitz; United States v. 213
Distaff, Inc. v. Springfield Contracting Corp . . . 515
District Attorney's Office for the Third Judicial District v. Osborne 314
Diversified Indus. Inc. v. Meredith 790
Dixon; People v.. 852
Dixon; United States v. 328
Doe v. United States. 867
Doe; United States v.. 867
Donnelly v. United States 657; 778
Donoho; People v.. 134
Dorian; United States v.. 157
Dorsey; United States v.. 337
Double Admissibility. United States v. Jackson. .441
Douglas v. Silvia. 895
Dowling v. American Hawaii Cruises, Inc.. . . . 847
Dowling v. United States 88; 133
Downing; United States v.. 226
Doyle v. Ohio. 194; 411
Drackett Products v. Blue. 58
Drake v. State 91
Drapeau; United States v.. 122
Dravecz; Commonwealth v.. 410
Drogoul; United States v.. 523
Dubose v. State. 313
Duffy; United States v.. 737

[References are to pages]

Dungo; People v.. 643
Dunkle; Commonwealth v.. 332
Dunn v. State Farm Fire & Cas. Ins. Co. 789
Duran Samaniego; United States v. 445; 522
Dutton v. Evans 614

E

E.P.A. v. Mink 859; 861
Edney, United States ex rel. v. Smith 819
Edwards; United States v. 473
Eglin Federal Credit Union v. Cantor, Fitzgerald Sec. Corp.. 774
Eldredge v. Barton 408
Elkins v. United States. 804
Ellis; United States v. 567
Elmer v. Fessenden. 445
Engel v. United Traction Co 29
Envirex, Inc. v. Ecological Recovery Assocs.. . .141
Erato, In re. .851
Escobar; People v.. 137
Espinoza; United States v.. 709
Estelle v. McGuire 89; 158; 329
Estelle v. Smith. 868
Estes; United States v.. 221
Evans v. Greyhound Corp 154
Ewoldt; People v. 87
Ex rel. (see name of relator)
Exxon Valdez, In re 720

F

F.P., In the Interest of 690
F.T.C. v. Grolier 789
Falsetta; People v.. 134
Farnsworth Cannon, Inc. v. Grimes 862
Farr v. Zoning Bd. of Appeals. 738
Federal Deposit Ins. Corp. v. Mercantile Nat'l Bank. 838
Federal Trade Com. v. TRW, Inc.. 846
Fernandez; United States v. 566
Ferrara v. Galluchio 368
Figueroa-Cartagena; United States v. 650
Figueroa-Lopez; United States v. 245
Filesi v. United States 543
Fine, In re Grand Jury Proceedings in Matter of. 794
Fisher v. United States 780; 797; 867
Fitzgerald; People v.. 852
Flecha; United States v.. 408
Flenory; United States v. 43
Foley; United States v.. 755
Ford Motor Co., In re 787
Foster; United States v. 256
Foster; United States v. 354
Fox v. Dannenberg. 257
Fraley v. Rockwell Int'l Corp 511
Frances J, In re. 852
Francis v. Franklin. 910
Franklin v. Skelly Oil Co.. 510
Franklin Nat'l Bank Sec. Litigation, In re 864
Frederick; United States v.. 774
Fredericks; United States v. 563; 760
Freeman; United States v.. 719
Friedli, Matter of Estate of 889
Frost; United States v.. 430
Frye v. United States 266; 269; 717; 732
Funk v. United States 803

G

Gabe; United States v.. 469
GAF Corp; United States v.. 413
Gail D., In re. 852
Garner v. State 379
Garner v. Wolfinbarger. 786
Gaskell; United States v.. 729
Gastiaburo; United States v.. 323
General Elec. Co. v. Joiner. 44; 274; 298, 299
Gerhart; United States v.. 745
Gertner; United States v.. 797
Gibbs v. State. 853
Gichner v. Antonio Troiano Tile & Marble Co. . 542
Gilbert v. California 403
Giles v. California. 613; 652, 653
Gillespie; United States v.. 329
Gillock; United States v.. . . . . 828; 853
Gilmore; United States v.. 25
Gilroy; State v.. 852
Girod; United States v.. 199
Glass; United States v.. 834
Glasser v. United States 422
Glover v. Cole .873
Goichman; United States v. 670; 715
Goldade v. Wyoming. 469
Goldberger & Dubin, P.C; United States v. . 797, 798
Goldstein; People v.. 635
Gomez; People v.. 520
Gonzalez; People v. 351
Gorby v. Schneider Tank Lines, Inc. 242
Gordon v. United States 220
Gordon; United States v.. 837

[References are to pages]

Gould; United States v. 875
Government of (see name of government)
Grady; United States v. 514
Grand Cent. Partnership, Inc. v. Cuomo 864
Grand Jury Impaneled January 21, 1975, In re. . 854
Grand Jury Investigation, In re 789
Grand Jury Investigation, In re 838
Grand Jury Proceedings (Greenberg), In re. . . . 852
Grand Jury Proceedings, In re. 796
Grand Jury Proceedings, In re. 797
Grand Jury Proceedings, In re. 850
Grand Jury Proceedings of Doe, In re. 851
Grand Jury Proceedings, Unemancipated Minor Child. 851
Grand Jury Subpoena Duces Tecum, In re 796
Grand Jury Subpoena Duces Tecum, In re 865
Grand Jury Subpoena Duces Tecum (Shargel), In re 796
Grand Jury Subpoena, In re 844
Grand Jury Subpoena, Judith Miller, In re 842
Grand Jury Subpoena of Santarelli, In re. 851
Grand Jury Subpoenas (Anderson), In re 797
Gray v. Maryland. 649
Grecinger; State v. 231; 328
Green; United States v. 233
Greenwood v. Boston & M. R.R. 139
Greer v. Miller 411
Greer; United States v.. 195
Griffin v. California 866
Grinnage; United States v.. 310
Guardia; United States v. 134
Guetersloh v. C.I.T. Corp 12
Gulf States Utilities Co. v. Ecodyne Corp.. 52

H

Haakanson v. State. 156
Hadden v. State. 332
Haimowitz; United States v.. 231
Hale; United States v. 411
Hale; United States v. 515
Hall v. United Ins. Co. of America 672
Hamilton v. Huebner. 436
Hammann v. Hartford Accident & Indem. Co.. . . 95
Hammon; People v. 763
Hampers, In re 854
Hancock v. Dodson 517
Hankey; United States v.. 355
Hankins v. Civiletti. 190
Hansen; State v. 439
Hanson v. Johnson. 373
Hardy v. Cross 583
Harris v. New York. 193
Harris; United States v. 256
Harrison; United States v.. 564
Harvey v. Borg 895
Harvey; United States v.. 207
Havens; United States v.. 193
Hawkins v. United States 803
Hawkins; United States v.. 872
Hayes; United States v. 514
Hayes; United States v. 834
Hazelwood School District v. United States . . . 143
Headley v. Tilghman 157; 256
Hearst; United States v.. 88
Hedman; United States v. 477
Heinz; State v.. 207
Heller v. Shaw Industries, Inc.. . . . . 283, 284
Henderson v. United States. 12
Hensel; United States v.. 379
Hermanek; United States v. 355
Hernandez; People v.. . . . . 110; 157; 482
Hernandez-Fundora; United States v. 878
Herzberg; United States v.. 212
Hester v. BIC Corp. 241
Hickman v. Taylor 783
Hicks; United States v.. 336
Hiibel v. Sixth Judicial Dist. Court of Nevada, Humboldt County. 866
Hilyer v. Howat Concrete Co 441
Hinchliffe; State v.. 113
Hinds v. John Hancock Mut. Life Ins. Co.. . . . 898
Hinkle v. City of Clarksburg. 732
Hirschman v. People. 116
Hitsman; United States v. 885
Ho v. Michelin N. Am., Inc.. 291
Hodas v. Davis. 471
Hodge v. United States. 131
Holmes v. South Carolina 576; 658; 662
Holmes v. United States. 853
Holmes; United States v.. 853
Hoosier; United States v.. 410
Hopkins v. Grimshaw 818
Houlihan; United States v.. 651
House Moving v. Workmen's Compensation Appeal Bd.. 444
Houston Oxygen Co. v. Davis. 439
Hubbell; United States v. 867
Huddleston v. United States. 82

[References are to pages]

Hudson; United States v. 195
Huff v. White Motor Corp. 556
Hughes v. United States 876
Hungerford; State v. 337
Hunt; State v. .411
Hurd; State v. .180

I

Iaconetti; United States v. 425; 565
IBM Peripheral EDP Devices Antitrust Litig., In re. 534; 565
Idaho v. Wright. 581; 612
Ideal Food Products Co. v. Rupe 253
In Matter of (see name of party)
In re (see name of party)
In the Interest of (see name of party)
Inadi; United States v. 369
Ingram v. McCuiston. 250
Inquest Proceedings, In re 852
Interest of (see name of party)
International Paper Company v. United States . . 255
Ismail; United States v. 851
Ives; United States v. 31
Ivezaj v. I.N.S. 884
Iwakiri; State v. 180

J

J.Q.; State v. 331
Jackson v. United States 439
Jackson; United States v. 34; 45
Jackson; United States v. 125; 230
Jackson; United States v. 378
Jackson-Randolph; United States v. 74
Jaffee v. Redmond 824
James v. Illinois 194
James; People v. 456
James; United States v. 873
Janus v. Akstin 406
Japanese Elec. Prods. Antitrust Litig., In re.565; 671
Jenkins v. Anderson 194; 411
Jinro America Inc. v. Secure Investments, Inc. . 354
John Deere Co. v. May 155
John Hancock Mut. Life Ins. Co. v. Dutton. . . .241
Johnson v. Gulick 145
Johnson v. Lutz. 498; 500
Johnson; People v. 818
Johnson v. William C. Ellis & Sons Ironworks, Inc. 75; 567
Johnson, Roberts ex rel. v. Galen of Virginia, Inc 232
Johnson; United States v. 749
Joint E. & S. Dist. Asbestos Litig, In re 295
Jones v. State 81
Jones; United States v. 286
Jones; United States v. 851
Jones; United States v. 873
Joseph Schlitz Brewing Co. v. Muller & Phipps, Ltd. 792
Joy; United States v. 437

K

Kannankeril v. Terminix Int'l, Inc. 283
Kansas v. Ventris 194
Karnes; United States v. 23
Karsun v. Kelley 146
Katt; People v. 566
Kaufman v. Edelstein 845
Keeper of Records (XYZ Corp.), In re 791
Keiser; United States v. 124
Kelly; People v. 268
Kentucky v. Stincer 176
Kientzy v. McDonnell Douglas Corp 847
Kilarjian v. Horvath. 57; 74
Kilbourne; United States v. 74, 75
Kim; United States v. 558
Kimberlin; United States v. 183
Kime; United States v. 336
King; United States v. 755
Kirk v. Raymark Indus., Inc. 564
Kitchen v. Robbins. 406
Klitzman, Klitzman & Gallagher v. Krut 764
Knight; United States v. 53
Kramer v. Time Warner, Inc 871
Krone; State v. .354
Kulling v. State 91
Kumho Tire Co. v. Carmichael 276

L

L.A. News Serv. v. CBS Broad., Inc. 743
L.T.V. Sec. Litig., In re 793
Lane v. State. 99
Lane; Unites States v. 51
Lang; United States v. 526
Larson; United States v. 133
Laster; United States v. 565
Lauzon v. Senco Products 350

[References are to pages]

Lawrence; State v. 38
Leahy; People v. 268
Leake v. Hagert 366
Leary v. United States 908, 909
Lebowitz; United States v. 734
Lechoco; United States v. 430
Lee v. Illinois. 648
Lefcourt v. United States. 798
Lego v. Twomey 421
Leichtman; United States v. 94
Leonard; People v. 313
Leventhal; United States v. 797
Levin v. United States 139
Lewis v. United States. 841
Lewis; United States v. 889
Lexington Ins. Co. v. Western Pa. Hosp. 379
Liebman; United States v. 796
Lindh; United States v. 76
Linthicum v. Richardson. 144
Lippay v. Christos 419
Little Fay Oil Co. v. Stanley. 405
Littlewind; United States v. 187
Lloyd v. American Export Lines, Inc. 529
Loetsch v. New York City Omnibus Corp. 382
Lombardi; People v. 520
Long v. State. .74
Long; United States v. 256
Loper v. Andrews 508
Lopez; People v. 643
Lorraine v. Markel Am. Ins. Co. 482; 674
Los Robles Motor Lodge, Inc. v. Department of Alcoholic Beverage Control 367
Lovato; State v. 216
Lovejoy v. United States. 466
Lovett; People v. 437
Lowery v. Maryland 555
Lubbock Feed Lots, Inc. v. Iowa Beef Processors, Inc. 242
Luce v. United States 222
Luck v. United States. 218, 219
Lui; United States v. 256
Lustig; United States v. 806
Lynch; United States v. 195

M

M.B.A.F.B. Federal Credit Union v. Cumis Ins. Soc. 185
M'Biye; United States v. 716
MacDonald; United States v. 62
Macumber; State v. 777; 779; 799
Mahlandt v. Wild Canid Survival & Research Center, Inc. 407
Mahone v. Lehman. 370
Malfitano, Appeal of. 806
Malloy v. Hogan 866
Mancusi v. Stubbs 583
Mangan; United States v. 73; 672
Manney v. Housing Authority 250
Mar; People v. 881
Marcantoni; United States v. 747
Marcus; United States v. 11
Marler; United States v. 262
Marshall v. State. 34
Marshall; United States v. 567
Martinez; United States v. 308
Martinez; United States v. 311
Maryland v. Craig 575; 585
Maryland Casualty Co. v. Therm-O-Disc 350
Master Key Antitrust Litig., In re 534
Matlock; United States v. 421
Matsushita Elec. Indus. Co. v. Zenith Radio Corp. 565; 671
Matter of Estate of (see name of party)
Matthews; State v. 540
Maxon; State v. .852
Mazyak; United States v. 373
McAfee v. Travis Gas Corp. 373
McAfee; United States v. 885
McCandless v. United States 29
McCleskey v. Kemp 880
McClure v. Koch. 250
McClure; United States v. 234
McConnell; People v. 94
McCorkle; United States v. 758, 759
McDonald; People v. 227; 336
McDonnell Douglas Corp. v. Green. 904
McDonough Power Equip., Inc. v. Greenwood. .885
McGinty v. Motor Truck Equipment Corp 373
McGowan v. Armour. 740
McHugh; People v. 732
McKee v. Jamestown Bakery Co. 498
McKeon; United States v. 413
McKune v. Lile. 866
McNulty v. Cusack. 895
McPartlin; United States v. 480
McQueen v. Garrison 180
McRae; United States v. 74
McVeigh; United States v. 658
Meienberg; United States v. 686
Melendez-Diaz v. Massachusetts . 613, 614; 625; 635

[References are to pages]

Melton v. Dallas County Child Welfare Unit. . . .444
Melville v. American Home Assurance Co.. 515
Mendelsohn v. Sprint/United Mgmt. Co.. 44
Mendoza; United States v.. 551
Menendez v. Superior Court. 833
Mentz; United States v. 875
Meredith; People v. 773
Merkouris; People v.. 454
Metropolitan St. Ry. v. Gumby 533
Meyer v. United States. 141
Meyers v. United States 740
Meza; United States v.. 196
Mezzanatto; United States v.. 163
Miami Herald Pub. Co. v. Tornillo 39
Michael H, In re 177
Michelson v. United States 111; 113; 119
Michigan v. Bryant. 604
Michigan v. Lucas 130; 659
Miller v. Mullin 289
Miller v. Poretsky 143
Miller v. Transamerican Press 842
Miller v. United States. 790
Miller; United States v. 790
Minnesota v. Andring 834
Miranda v. Arizona. 827
Miranda; United States v. 243
Mitchell v. United States. 866
Mockaitis v. Harcleroad 837
Monarch Fed. Sav. & Loan Ass'n v. Genser . . . 481
Monotype Corp. PLC v. Int'l Typeface Corp. . . .481
Montana v. Egelhoff 66; 576; 614; 658
Montiel v. City of Los Angeles 515
Mooney v. Holohan 133
Moore v. State 539, 540
Moore; United States v. 411
Morales v. Portuondo. 779; 838
Morales; United States v. 323
Moran v. Pittsburgh-Des Moines Steel Co.. 510
Moreno; People v.. 94
Morgan v. Consolidated Rail Corp 368
Morgan; People v. 301
Morgan; United States v.. 419
Morlang; United States v. 201
Morrison; United States v.. 526
Morvant v. Construction Aggregates Corp.. 233
Moskowitz; United States v.. 552
Moss; United States v. 712
Mound; United States v.. 133
Moussaoui; United States v.. 860
Mukhtar v. California State University, Hayward.289
Mullaney v. Wilbur. 911
Mullen v. United States 837
Muller v. Oregon. 880
Mundorff, In re. 873
Murphy v. Superior Court 229; 833
Murphy v. Waterfront Comm'n of N.Y. Harbor. .866
Murphy; State v.. 129
Mutual Life Ins. Co. v. Hillmon 450, 451
Myrick v. Lloyd 417

N

Nacchio; United States v. 293
Nachtsheim v. Beech Aircraft Corp 196
Napier; United States v.. 438
Nash v. Fidelity-Phenix Fire Ins. Co 817
Neal; United States v. 809; 818
New England Mut. Life Ins. Co. v. Anderson . . 534
New York Foreign Trade Zone Operators; United States v.. 502
Newkirk v. Commonwealth 331
Newsome v. McCabe. 336
Newsome; State v.. 393
Nichols v. Upjohn Co 751
Nick; United States v. 463, 464
Nickels; United States v.. 177
Nivica; United States v.. 567
Nix v. Whiteside 174
Nix v. Williams. 421
Nixon; United States v. . . . 422; 776; 804; 825; 865
Norris v. Baxter Healthcare Corp.. 293
Nulf v. International Paper Co. 189; 191

O

O'Conner v. Commonwealth Edison Co.. 286
O'Gee v. Dobbs Houses, Inc. 463; 465
O'Malley; United States v.. 402
Oates; United States v.. 513
Ohio v. Reiner 866
Ohio v. Roberts. 464; 578
Ohio-Sealy Mattress Mfg. Co. v. Kaplan 793
Ohler v. U.S.. 222
Oil Spill by The Amoco Cadiz, In re 515
Old Chief v. United States . . . 44; 47; 99; 108; 151
Olden v. Kentucky 128; 575
One 1968 Piper Navajo Twin Engine Aircraft; United States v.. 718
Onori; United States v.. 713
Orozco; United States v.. 514
Orrico; United States v. 393

[References are to pages]

Ortiz; United States v. 669
Osborne v. United States. 224
Owens; United States v. 393; 400; 576

P

Palmer v. Hoffman 502; 512
Palmer v. Peyton 404
Parr v. United States 102
Pasha v. United States 720
Pasha; United States v.. 720
Patterson v. Caterpillar, Inc.. 821
Patterson v. East Texas Motor Freight Lines . . . 151
Patterson v. New York. 66; 911
Payne v. Tennessee. 592
Peck v. United States. 864
Pekelis v. Transcontinental & W. Air Inc.. 502
Pelster v. Ray. 262
Peltier; United States v.. 92
Pelullo; United States v. 504; 565
Penn; United States v.. 851
Pennsylvania v. Muniz. 866
Pennsylvania v. Ritchie 763
Penry v. Johnson. 868
Pent-R-Books, Inc; United States v.. 507
People v. (see name of defendant)
Perez-Perez; United States v. 214
Perfect 10, Inc. v. Cybernet Ventures, Inc. . 487; 688
Perkins; State v.. 21
Permian Corp. v. United States 789
Perricone v. Kansas City S. R. Co.. 523
Perry v. New Hampshire. 634
Petrov; United States v.. 43
Philadelphia v. Westinghouse Electric Corp. . . . 783
Phillips; People v. 158; 329
Pierce County, Washington v. Guillen. 853
Piggie; United States v.. 879
Pillsbury Co. v. Conboy 866
Pineda-Torres; United States v. 256
Pittsburgh Action Against Rape, In re. 833
Plaza; United States v.. 342
Plessy v. State 538
Plumb v. Curtis 74
Pluta; United States v.. 669
Pointer v. Klamath Falls Land & Transp. Co. . . 251
Pointer v. Texas 188
Pollack; United States v.. 234
Pollard v. Metropolitan Life Ins. Co 42
Ponca, Village of v. Crawford. 262
Pooler; State v.. 97
Pooshs v. Phillip Morris USA, Inc.. 315
Pope, State ex rel. v. Superior Court 127
Port v. Heard. 851
Portuondo v. Agard. 231
Potts v. Florida. 351
Powell v. State. 734
Prime; United States v.. 340
Primo; People v.. 658
Pruitt v. State. 299
Pungitore; United States v.. 256

Q

Qualley v. Clo-Tex Int'l, Inc.. 424
Quercia v. United States. 18
Quezada; United States v.. 514

R

Ramada Dev. Co. v. Rauch 162
Rambus, Inc. v. Infineon Techs. AG. 690
Ramirez v. State 355
Rangel; United States v.. 746
Ranieri; State v. 185
Rankin v. Brockton Public Market 416
Raulie v. United States. 413
Ray; United States v.. 216
Rebbe; United States v.. 165
Red Lion Broadcasting Co. v. FCC. 39
Rendini; United States v.. 467
Renville; United States v.. 468
Reyes v. Missouri P. R. Co.. 138
Reynolds v. United States 651
Reynolds; United States v.. 377
Reynolds; United States v. 857
Richards of Rockford, Inc. v. Pacific Gas and Elec. Co.. 844
Richardson v. Marsh 648, 649
Riley; United States v.. 504
Riley; United States v.. 551
Ring v. Arizona. 591; 875
Rivera v. Illinois 886
Rivera; United States v.. 256
Roach; United States v.. 174
Robbins; State v.. 814
Roberts; United States v.. 131
Robinson v. Fort Dodge Limestone Co.. 418
Robinson v. Mandell. 339
Robinson v. Shapiro 563
Robinson; State v.. 816

[References are to pages]

Robinson; United States v. 22
Robinson; United States v. 41
Rock v. Arkansas. 179
Rodriguez v. State. 34
Rodriguez v. State. 91
Rodriguez v. State 311
Rodriquez; United States v. 184
Rodriguez; United States v. 747
Rose; United States v.. 745
Rouse; United States v. 332
Roviaro v. United States 778; 856
Rudberg; United States v.. 231
Rudzinski v. Warner Theatres, Inc. 414
Ruiz-Troche v. Pepsi Cola. 284
Rutland; United States v.. 340
Ryan v. Commissioner of Internal Revenue. . . .807
Ryan, In re 852

S

S.E.C. v. Gulf & Western Indus., Inc 786
Saada; United States v.. 430
Safavian; United States v. 678; 690
Safeway Stores, Inc. v. Combs 368
Sahin v. Maryland 126
Salerno; United States v.. 535
Salinas; United States v.. 884
Sallins; United States v.. 369
Samaniego; United States v.. 753
Sampol; United States v.. 178
San Antonio Traction Co. v. Cox 152
Sanders; People v.. 818
Sanders; People v.. 852
Sanders; United States v.. 481
Sandstrom v. Montana. 68; 910
Saniti; United States v.. 806
Santos; United States v.. 419
Santos; United States v.. 441
Sawyer; United States v.. 514
Scales; United States v.. . . . . .753; 756
Scheffer; United States v.. . . . . . . .275; 297; 659
Schmerber v. California 866
Schnapp; United States v.. 196
Schoenheinz; United States v.. 853
Schwartz v. Broadcast Music, Inc. 786
Scott; State v.. 310
Scott; United States v.. 352
Scout; United States v.. 125
Sea-Land Service, Inc. v. Lozen Int'l, LLC.411; 419; 481
Sealed Case, In re 865
Seamster; United States v. 223
Seelig; United States v.. 752
Seidman v. Fishburne-Hudgins Educational Foundation, Inc.. 837
Seiler v. Lucasfilm, Ltd 749
United States v. Williams 473
Senak; United States v.. . . . . .213; 474
Sesay; United States v.. 448
Seschillie; United States v.. 233
Setser; United States v.. 201
70 Acres v. State. 889
Shackleford; United States v.. 720
Shahar v. Bowers. 870
Shain, In re. .841
Shaw v. United States 565
Shaw; United States v.. . . . . .565; 566
Shepard v. United States. 454
Sheptur v. Procter & Gamble Distributing Co.. .252; 253
Sherrod v. Berry. 42
Shoen v. Shoen. 841
Shooker v. Superior Court. 790
Shoupe; United States v.. 202
Siddiqui; United States v. 690; 736
Simmons; United States v.. 213
Simmons; United States v.. 256
Simpson; United States v.. 682
Sindel; United States v.. 797
Sirico v. Cotto 252
Sledge v. State 454
Slifka v. Johnson. 417
Smith v. Illinois 857
Smith v. Ithaca Corp. 509
Smith v. Ohio Oil Co 75
Smith v. Rapid Transit, Inc 891
Smith v. Roe 137
Smith; United States v.. 219
Smith; United States v.. 227
Smith; United States v.. . . . . .262; 272
Smith; United States v.. 336
Smith; United States v.. 436
Smith; United States v.. 512
Smyth; United States v.. 754
Sneed; State v.. 358
Snow; United States v.. 737
Snyder; United States v.. 177
Solis-Ramirez v. United States Dep't of Justice . 872
Sosna v. Iowa. 804

[References are to pages]

Southland Sod Farms v. Stover Seed Co 350
Sparr & Green v. Wellman. 406
Sporck v. Peil. 476; 792
Sposito; United States v.. 561
Spreigl; State v. 131
Springer; State v.. 743
Sprint/United Mgmt. Co. v. Mendelsohn. 43
Stagl v. Delta Airlines, Inc. 258
Standafer v. First Nat'l Bank of Minneapolis . . . 37
Standard Oil Co. of California v. Moore 499
Stanton v. Stanton 805
Starzecpyzel; United States v.. 340
State v. (see name of defendant)
State ex rel. (see name of relator)
Steer v. Little. 187
Stevenson v. Stewart 30
Stewart v. People 29
Stoll; People v.. 329
Stone; State v. 157
Stone; United States v.. 351
Stovall v. Denno 403
Strickland v. Davis. 407
Strickland Transp. Co. v. Ingram 185
Stritzinger; People v.. 835
Sumner; United States v.. 133
Susemiehl v. Red River Lumber Co. 405
Sutton; United States v. 517
Swallow; State v.. 156
Swidler & Berlin v. United States. 775
Swinton; State v.. 723
Szemple; State v.. 837

T

Takoma Park Bank v. Abbott 169
Talley v. State 34
Tampa Bay Shipbuilding & Repair Co. v. Cedar Shipping Co., Ltd. 247
Tanner v. United States. 182; 886
Tarasoff v. Regents of Univ. of Calif.. . . . .799; 834
Tassell; People v. 87
Tassin v. Sears Roebuck 286
Taylor v. Baltimore & O. R. Co. 503
Telfaire; United States v.. 227
Tenet v. Doe 862
Tenn. Laborers Health & Welfare Fund v. Columbia/HCA Healthcare Corp. (In re Columbia/HCA Healthcare Corp. Billing Practices Litig.) 790
Tennessee v. Street 592; 633; 635
Terry W., In re 853
Texaco Puerto Rico, Inc. v. Dep't of Consumer Affairs. 864
Texas Dep't of Community Affairs v. Burdine . . 904
Thevis v. United States 230
Thevis; United States v.. 230
Thomas, In Interest of. 474
Thomas; United States v. 553
Thomas; United States v. 719
Thompson; United States v.. 51
Thorp; State v.. 237
Three Juveniles v. Commonwealth 852
Tin Yat Chin; United States v.. 668
Tipton; United States v. 672
Tolisano; State v.. 377
Tome v. United States 393
Totten v. United States. 837; 862
Townsend v. State 326
Trammel v. United States. 802; 825; 828
Tran Trong Cuong; United States v.. 262
Trascher v. Territo 540
Trenkler; United States v. 568
Tropeano; United States v.. 669
Trotter; United States v. 715
Truman; United States v.. 388
Turquitt; United States v. 213
Turvey; State v.. 403
Tyus v. Urban Search Management 282; 330

U

U.S. v. (see name of defendant)
United States v. (see name of defendant)
United States, In re 232
United States Gypsum Co.; United States v. . . . 781
Universal Rehab. Servs. Inc; United States v. . . . 55
University of Pennsylvania v. EEOC. .825; 827; 846
Upjohn Co. v. United States. 780; 825
Usee; State v.. .649

V

Valle; United States v.. 319
Van Dyk; People v.. 475
Van Wyk; United States v. 341
Van Gaasbeck; People v.. 115
Vargas; United States v.. 436
Varlack v. S.W.C. Caribbean, Inc 232
Vaughan Furn. Co., Inc. v. Featureline Mfg., Inc.792
Vaughn v. Shelby Williams of Tennessee, Inc . . 888
Veach's Adm'r v. Louisville & I. Ry. Co 543
Vega; United States v.. 552

[References are to pages]

Velez; United States v.. 165
Verduzco; United States v.. 354
Vigano v. Wylain, Inc 748
Vik; United States v.. . . . . 128; 230
Village of (see name of village)
Virgin Islands, Government of the v. Gereau. . . 886
Virgin Islands, Government of the v. Joseph . . . 793
Virgin Islands, Government of v. Petersen 207
Virgin Islands, Government of the v. Roldan. . . 126
Virginia Ry. & Power Co. v. Burr. 238
Vitale; United States v.. 708
Von Bulow, In re. 791

W

W.C.L., Jr. v. People. 468
W.L.; State v.. .331
Wade; United States v.. 403
Wainwright v. Greenfield. 411
Walden v. City of Chicago. 317
Walker; United States v.. 758
Ward; United States v.. 177
Warren v. United States 519; 853
Washington v. Texas 180; 576; 778
Washington; United States v.. 24
Watkins v. Prudential Ins. Co.. . . . . 897, 898
Watkins v. Telsmith, Inc.. 285
Watson; United States v.. 323
Watts v. Delaware Coach Co 506
Wearly v. Federal Trade Com.. . . . . 845; 846
Weaver v. United States 887
Webb; United States v.. 837
Weil v. Investment/Indicators, Research & Management, Inc.. 791
Weiss v. La Suisse Societe D'Assurances Sur La Vie. 167
Welch; United States v.. 336
West v. Houston Oil Co.. 673
West; United States v.. 566
Westinghouse Elec. Corp. v. Republic of the Philippines 789
Whitaker v. Keough 418
White v. Illinois. 582; 584; 588
White v. Zutell 501; 503
Whittey; State v.. 302
Whorton v. Bockting. 595
Wicker v. McCotter 180
Widrick; Commonwealth v.. 229
Williams v. Anderson 143
Williams v. Board of Regents of University System 33
Williams v. Florida. 880
Williams v. Illinois. 632
Williams v. State. 90
Williams v. United States 207
Williams; United States v.. 272
Williams; United States v.. 369
United States v. Williams 473
Williamson v. United States 544; 563
Willoughby; State v.. 852
Wilson v. Clark. 259
Wilson v. State 258; 362
Wilson v. Volkswagen of America, Inc.. 140
Wilson; United States v.. 222
Wilson; United States v.. 673
Wilson; United States v.. 873
Winship, In re. 68
Witness Before the Special Grand Jury 2000-2, In re 789
Wittig; United States v.. 632
Wm. T. Thompson Co. v. General Nutrition Corp.. 838
Wolak v. Spucci 130
Woods; State v.. .196
Woods; United States v.. 97
Woods; United States v.. . . . . 504; 517
Workman v. Cleveland-Cliffs Iron Co. 565
Worley; United States v.. 555
Wright v. Jeep Corp.. 844

Y

Yakobov; United States v.. 515
Yarbrough; United States v.. 117
Yates v. Bair Transport, Inc.. . . . . 497; 505
Yates; United States v. 19
Yildiz; United States v.. 419
Young v. James Green Management, Inc.. 419
Young v. State Farm Mutual Automobile Insurance Co 367
Young Bros., Inc. v. United States. 481
Young Brothers, Inc; United States v.. 480
Young; United States v.. 328

Z

Zaccaria; United States v.. 191
Zalimas; People v.. 474
Zarintash; United States v.. 186
Zeidman; United States v.. 505
Zenith Radio Corp. v. Matsushita Elec. Indus. Co.. . . . . .565; 671

[References are to pages]

Zenni; United States v.. 377
Zerilli v. Evening News Ass'n. 842
Zipkin; United States v.. 43
Zippo Mfg. Co. v. Rogers Imports, Inc . . . 385; 567
Zolin; United States v. 772; 795; 828

TABLE OF STATUTES

[References are to pages]

CALIFORNIA
CALIFORNIA STATUTES

Evidence Code

Sec.	Page
352	134
403	424
769	201
770	201
870	243
915	773
917	773
956.5	798
1035.	763
1035.8.	833
1037.	763
1037.5.	833
1108	88; 134
1109.	137
1150.	184
1201.	201
1230.	555
1235.	201
1250.	453
1331.	674
1370.	645
1380.	646
1417.	672

CONNECTICUT

Connecticut General Statutes

Sec.	Page
46b-138a	852

DELAWARE

Delaware Code

Tit.:Sec.	Page
24:3913(2)	829

IDAHO

Idaho Code

Sec.	Page
9-203(7).	852
54-3213(2)	829

KENTUCKY

Kentucky Revised Statutes

Sec.	Page
510.145.	128

MASSACHUSETTS

Massachusetts General Laws

Ch.:Sec.	Page
111:13.	615
233:20	852

MICHIGAN

Michigan Compiled Laws

Sec.	Page
338.840.	831

MINNESOTA

Minnesota Statutes

Sec.	Page
595.02(1)(j).	852

MISSISSIPPI

Mississippi Code

Sec.	Page
73-33-16(2).	831

[References are to pages]

MONTANA

Montana Code

Sec.	Page
45-2-203	66; 658

NEW MEXICO

New Mexico Statutes

Sec.	Page
29-3-4	629

NEW YORK

New York Civil Practice Law and Rules

Sec.	Page
4518	498

NORTH DAKOTA

North Dakota Century Code

Sec.	Page
31-01-06.1	853

OREGON

Oregon Revised Statutes

Sec.	Page
44.040(1)(f)	853

TENNESSEE

Tennessee Code

Sec.	Page
59-1033	300

WASHINGTON

Washington Revised Code

Sec.	Page
5.60.060(1)	586

WEST VIRGINIA

West Virginia Code

Sec.	Page
57-3-9	838

FEDERAL STATUTES, RULES, AND REGULATIONS

United States Constitution

Amend.	Page
amend.:1	39; 107; 841–843; 845, 846
amend.:4	193, 194
amend.:5	62; 190; 193; 202; 230; 389; 535; 552; 555; 614; 763; 808, 809; 866–868
amend.:6	5; 128; 130; 174; 176; 180; 188; 194; 205; 209, 210; 332; 365; 401; 423; 442; 449; 464; 512; 514, 515; 521; 526; 546; 551, 552; 556; 566; 572; 575–584; 586–596; 598; 601–616; 618–625; 627–640; 642, 643; 645; 647, 648; 650, 651; 653; 661; 663; 717; 763; 798; 841
amend.:7	591
amend.:8	370
amend.:14	67; 107; 134; 137; 178; 579; 614; 654; 663; 866
art.:I:2(b)	839
art.:III:	404

United States Code

Title:Sec.	Page
5:552	764; 858; 864
18:111	24
18:111(a)(1)	122
18:111(b)	122
18:113(c)	106
18:113(f)	105
18:661	878
18:921(a)(20)	100
18:922(g)(1)	99, 100
18:924(c)	106
18:1114	24
18:1153	105, 106
18:1960	120
18:2113(a)	203

[References are to pages]

United States Code—Cont.

Title:Sec. Page
18:2113(d) 203
18:2251(a) 734
18:2251(e) 734
18:2422(b) 734
18:2510(1) 874
18:3500 . . . . . 857; 864
18:3502 404
18:3509 . . . . . 176; 536
18:3510 234
18:3593 234
18:Appendix:3 860
18:Appendix:1202(a)(1) 24
21:176a 909
21:812 876
21:841(a)(1) 108
23:409 853
26:6064 672
26:7525 . . . . . 774; 838
26:60501 798
42:269(b) 511
42:1983 178
42:2000 904
44:1507 883

Code of Federal Regulations

Title:Sec. Page
21:1308.12 876

Federal Rules of Appellate Procedure

Rule Page
35(a)(2) 133

Federal Rules of Civil Procedure

Rule Page
12(b)(6) 872
26 . . . . . 246; 793
26(a)(3) 757
26(b)(3) 784; 789
26(b)(5)(B) 792
32 526
32(a) 527
32(a)(3) 526

Federal Rules of Civil Procedure —Cont.

Rule Page
56 18

Federal Rules of Criminal Procedure

Rule Page
6(e) 536
16 246
16(a)(1)(E) 246
23(a) 106
26.2 476

Federal Rules of Evidence

Rule Page
53 766
62 . . . . . 766; 821
64 481
74 377
80 481
102 . . . . . 46; 136; 186; 438
103 . . . . . 9; 11; 13; 413
103(a)(2) 167
104 . . . . . 9; 69, 70; 175; 424; 711; 746
104(a) 69; 84; 298; 421; 424; 542; 736; 772
104(b) 70; 85; 542; 710
105 . . . . . 18; 24, 25; 85; 371
106 . . . . . 3; 429; 757, 758; 760
201 . . . . . 271; 869, 870; 874; 882–885
201(a) 877; 887
201(b) 870; 882; 887
201(e) 882
201(f) 871; 877; 879; 883
301 . . . . . 892; 903–905; 909
302 903
401 . . 27; 29; 32; 35, 36; 40; 43; 45; 53–55; 57; 60; 65; 69; 73; 75; 161; 711; 757
401 to 402 . . . . . 77; 400
401 to 403 . . . . . 56; 84; 567
402 . . . . . 27; 29; 32; 35; 40; 43; 100; 213; 392

[References are to pages]

Federal Rules of Evidence—Cont.

Rule **Page**

403 . 4; 7; 29; 33; 40–43; 45; 47; 50; 53; 55; 57; 60; 64–66; 69, 70; 73–75; 87; 93; 100; 104; 132–134; 137; 161; 167; 169, 170; 177; 186, 187; 196; 206; 213, 214; 230; 295; 297; 322; 369; 380; 392; 400; 430; 515; 571; 664; 722; 729; 753; 757
404 . . . 33; 79; 97; 131; 158; 214
404 to 405 . . . 110; 151
404(a). . . .111; 118; 120; 157; 517
404(a)(1) . . . 118; 207
404(a)(2) . . . 123, 124
404(a)(2)(A) . . . 125
404(b). . .46; 79, 80; 82, 83; 87–90; 93, 94; 96; 99; 101; 105; 108; 110; 131, 132; 137; 142, 143; 154
404(b)(2). . . .95
405 . . . 79; 99; 118; 126; 131
405(a) . . . 118; 120; 124; 207; 517
406. . . .138, 139; 141
407. . . .158; 160, 161; 847
408 . . . 162
410 . . . 163, 164
411. . . .165, 166; 170
412. . . .127–130
413. . . .130–133; 137
413 to 415 . . . 134
414 . . . 133
501 . . 761, 762; 765, 766; 780; 783; 801; 804; 806; 810; 824; 826, 827; 832; 836; 838; 840–842; 844, 845; 850; 853; 881
502 . . . 792
503 . . . 788; 793
508 . . . 845
509 . . . 857; 864
510 . . . 854
601. . . .174; 176–179
602 . . . 184; 889
603 . . . 177
605 . . . 182; 889
606(b) . . . 183, 184; 886
607 . . . 191; 193
608. . . .126; 207; 211; 230
608(a). . . .118; 224, 225; 230; 517
608(b). . . .211; 214–217; 222; 430
609. . . .25; 207; 218, 219; 222–224
609(a)(2) . . . 221, 222
609(b). . . .221
609(d). . . .211
610 . . . 178; 207

Federal Rules of Evidence—Cont.

Rule **Page**

611 . . . 18; 186; 232
611(a) . . . 186, 187; 196; 232
611(b). . . .189, 190
611(c). . . .187
612 . . . 476; 792
613. . . .194–196
613(a). . . .202; 400
613(b) . . . 195, 196; 199; 208
615. . . .231–233
615(1). . . .232
615(2). . . .232, 233
615(3). . . .232, 233
701 . . . 4; 239, 240; 246; 441
702 . . 227; 246; 250; 253, 254; 268; 273, 274; 276; 282; 287; 307; 310; 314, 315; 320; 335; 342; 660
702 to 703 . . . 567
703 . . . 233; 259–262; 630; 633; 744; 752
703 to 705 . . . 467
704 . . . 242; 319
704(b). . . .321; 323
706 . . . 298, 299
801 . . . 379; 426
801(a). . . .365; 410
801(a)(1) . . . 545
801(a)(2). . . .377
801(b). . . .365
801(c). . . .365; 371; 410
801(d)(1) . . . 201; 387
801(d)(1)(A) . . . 196; 389; 391; 393; 566; 847
801(d)(1)(B). . . .230; 394; 398; 400
801(d)(1)(C) . . . 378; 401
801(d)(2). . . .404; 410; 413; 424; 751
801(d)(2)(E). . . .420; 613
802. . . .401, 402; 660
803. . . .429; 443; 513; 516
803(1) . . . 430; 437, 438; 441; 443
803(2) . 378; 430; 433; 437; 441; 443; 463; 582; 607
803(3) . . . 444; 447; 465; 522
803(4). . . .458, 459; 465–467; 469, 470; 582
803(5). . . .470; 473; 514
803(6) . 477; 479–481; 498; 504, 505; 508; 513–515; 751
803(7). . . .505
803(8). . . .419; 507, 508; 514, 515; 623; 646
803(8)(B) . . . 513, 514
803(8)(C) . . . 508; 530
803(10) . . . 515; 632; 716

[References are to pages]

Federal Rules of Evidence—Cont.

Rule	Page
803(16)	517
803(17)	517; 568
803(18)	508; 517; 567
803(21)	517
803(22)	517
803(24)	157; 378; 400; 514; 556; 567; 718; 885
803 to 804	572
803(C)	513, 514
804	429
804(2)	527
804(a)	519; 527; 582
804(a)(1)	527
804(a)(2)	392; 527; 537
804(a)(3)	527; 542
804(a)(4)	521
804(a)(5)	523
804(a)(5)(B)	528
804(b)	392; 527; 556
804(b)(1)	527; 529, 530; 534, 535; 565, 566; 593; 645; 847
804(b)(2)	595; 645
804(b)(3)	447; 544; 552, 553; 555; 658
804(b)(5)	514; 556; 565; 651
804(b)(6)	645; 650; 652
805	429
806	423; 430
807	157; 400; 469; 514; 532; 556; 581; 718; 847
901	51; 660; 667–669; 672; 709; 711; 714; 735; 885
901(6)	708
901 to 104(b)	714

Federal Rules of Evidence—Cont.

Rule	Page
901(a)	667; 669; 671; 708; 710, 711; 746
901(b)	671
901(b)(1)	735
901(b)(5)	708
901(b)(8)	517; 673
901(b)(9)	723; 725; 732
902	713; 716; 885
902(1)	715
902(2)	716
902(3)	716; 718
902(4)	618
902(8)	716
902(9)	714
902(11)	504; 632; 717
902(12)	504; 717
1001	737; 745; 760
1001(1)	743
1001(3)	744
1001(4)	747; 756
1001 to 1004	736
1002	743; 749, 750
1003	747
1004	744–747
1004(1)	746
1004(4)	738
1005	747
1006	186; 750; 752–755
1008	736; 746; 749

INDEX

[References are to sections.]

A

ATTORNEY-CLIENT PRIVILEGE (See PRIVILEGES, subhead: Attorney-client privilege and examination of issues common to many privileges)

AUTHENTICATION OF WRITINGS AND EXHIBITS (See WRITINGS AND EXHIBITS, subhead: Authentication)

B

BOGUS HEARSAY RULES
Generally . . . 10.06

BURDENS AND PRESUMPTIONS
Burdens of proof as prerequisite to understanding presumptions . . . 15.01
Civil presumptions . . . 15.02
Criminal presumptions . . . 15.03

C

CHARACTER EVIDENCE
"Action in conformity," specific acts offered to prove . . . 3.01[A]
Bad acts, other . . . 3.01[C]
Habit versus character . . . 3.04
Opinion and reputation evidence
  Generally . . . 3.02
  Action in conformity, not related to . . . 3.02[A]
  Allowed to show action in conformity . . . 3.02[B]
  Not related to action in conformity . . . 3.02[A]
Other transactions, similar occurrences, and profiles . . . 3.05
Sexual crimes and related offenses, character in cases of
  Complainant's sexual character, conduct, or propensity . . . 3.03[A]
  Extending admissibility of propensity evidence beyond sexual offenses . . . 3.03[C]
  "Rape shield" and similar state rules, restricted admissibility under Rule 412's . . . 3.03[A]
  Rules 413-415; broader admissibility of defendant's other conduct or propensity in sexual cases
    Generally . . . 3.03[B]
    General principle of Rules 413-415 . . . 3.03[B][1]
    Rule 403 and Constitution, interplay with . . . 3.03[B][2]

CHARACTER EVIDENCE—Cont.
Specific-acts evidence, contours of exclusion of
  Probativity of depends on human tendency to repeat; must not be characterized as character or propensity reasoning
    Generally . . . 3.01[B][1]
    Revisiting evidence recognized as propensity evidence . . . 3.01[B][3]
  Probativity of does not depend on human tendency to repeat; not character or propensity reasoning . . . 3.01[B][2]

COMPETENCY AS PREREQUISITE FOR WITNESS TESTIMONY (See WITNESS TESTIMONY, subhead: Competency as prerequisite for)

CONFRONTATION CLAUSE OF CONSTITUTION (See CONSTITUTIONAL CONSIDERATIONS, subhead: Confrontation Clause)

CONSTITUTIONAL CONSIDERATIONS
Generally . . . 11.01
Confrontation Clause
  Nontestifying codefendants, applied to statements by . . . 11.04
  Nontestifying declarants, applied to statements by
    Intertwining hearsay and Confrontation Clause analysis from *Roberts* era . . . 11.03[A]
    Roberts, rejecting (See subhead: Rejecting *Roberts*: testimonial approach to Confrontation Clause)
    Testimonial approach to Confrontation Clause (See subhead: Rejecting *Roberts*: testimonial approach to Confrontation Clause)
  Out-of-court statements by testifying declarants, applied to . . . 11.02
  Waiver of rights under; relation to exception for forfeiture by wrongdoing (Rule 804(b)(6)) . . . 11.05
Rejecting *Roberts*: testimonial approach to Confrontation Clause
  Affidavits, certifications, reports, and other expert issues in forensic context . . . 11.03[B][4]
  Domestic violence context: filling in unanswered questions . . . 11.03[B][2]
  Emergencies types: filling in puzzle . . . 11.03[B][3]
  Forensic context, affidavits, certifications, reports, and other expert issues in . . . 11.03[B][4]
  Framers intended, relying on alleged historic analysis to discern what . . . 11.03[B][1]
  Relying on alleged historic analysis to discern what framers intended . . . 11.03[B][1]
  Seminal case . . . 11.03[B][1]

[References are to sections.]

CONSTITUTIONAL CONSIDERATIONS—Cont.
Rights of defendants that limit application of evidentiary rules, constitutional . . . 11.06
Roberts, rejecting (See subhead: Rejecting *Roberts*: testimonial approach to Confrontation Clause)
Sexual crimes and related offenses, broader admissibility of defendant's other conduct or propensity in . . . 3.03[B][2]
Testimonial approach to Confrontation Clause (See subhead: Rejecting *Roberts*: testimonial approach to Confrontation Clause)

CROSS-EXAMINATION (See WITNESS TESTIMONY, subhead: Cross-examination)

D

***DAUBERT* DECISION** (See SCIENTIFIC AND PROBABILISTIC EVIDENCE, subhead: *Daubert* decision)

E

EVIDENCE (GENERALLY)
Character evidence (See CHARACTER EVIDENCE)
Classroom versus real world . . . 1.01[A]
Courtroom scenario and basic procedures
  Admitted evidence . . . 1.02[B]
  Excluded evidence . . . 1.02[B]
  Jury trial, evidence rules relating to all events and stages of . . . 1.02[C]
  Offers and objections . . . 1.02[A]
Development of evidence law . . . 1.01[B]
Impartiality, judicial . . . 1.03
Judge's conduct of trial, limit on . . . 1.03
Key concepts of evidence law . . . 1.01[B]
Limiting instructions to jury . . . 1.04
Relevant evidence (See RELEVANT EVIDENCE)
Scientific and probabilistic evidence (See SCIENTIFIC AND PROBABILISTIC EVIDENCE)
Witness testimony (See WITNESS TESTIMONY)
Writings and exhibits (See WRITINGS AND EXHIBITS)

EXHIBITS (See WRITINGS AND EXHIBITS)

EXPERT WITNESSES
Opinion testimony (See OPINION TESTIMONY, subhead: Expert opinion)
Psychology, mental health, social sciences, and related fields . . . 6.05[A]

H

HEARSAY
Generally . . . 7.01[A]
Basic hearsay, elements of . . . 7.01[B]
Constitutional considerations and (See CONSTITUTIONAL CONSIDERATIONS)
Elements of basic hearsay . . . 7.01[B]
Exceptions not requiring showing of unavailability
  Generally . . . 9.01

HEARSAY—Cont.
Exceptions not requiring showing of unavailability—Cont.
  Business records . . . 9.06
  Excited utterances and present sense impressions . . . 9.02
  Medical diagnosis or treatment, statements for purposes of . . . 9.04
  Miscellaneous other hearsay exceptions . . . 9.08
  Past recollection recorded, "present memory refreshed" distinguished from
    Generally . . . 9.05
    "Present memory refreshed" . . . 9.05[B]
    Recorded recollection . . . 9.05[A]
  Present mental, emotional, or physical condition, declarations of . . . 9.03
  Present sense impressions, excited utterances and . . . 9.02
  Public records . . . 9.07
Exceptions requiring showing of unavailability of declarant
  Bogus hearsay rules . . . 10.06
  "Catchall" or residual exception . . . 10.05
  Declarations against interest
    Generally . . . 10.04
    Pecuniary and proprietary interests, declarations against . . . 10.04[A]
    Penal interest, declarations against . . . 10.04[B]
  Defining unavailability of declarant . . . 10.01
  Dying declarations . . . 10.03
  Former testimony . . . 10.02
Exemptions from hearsay rule
  Admissions of party
    Generally . . . 8.02; 8.02[A]
    Adoptive admissions . . . 8.02[C]
    Authorized to speak for principals, admissions by agents . . . 8.02[D]
    Basic doctrine . . . 8.02[B]
    Co-conspirator statements . . . 8.02[F]
    Unauthorized agents or employees about matters within their scope, admissions by . . . 8.02[E]
  Former statements of presently testifying witnesses
    Generally . . . 8.01; 8.01[A]
    Consistent statements . . . 8.01[C]
    Inconsistent statements . . . 8.01[B]
    Statements of identification . . . 8.01[D]
Out-of-court words (or conduct) stating or revealing declarant's state of mind . . . 7.03
Statements implied from words or conduct . . . 7.02

J

JUDICIAL NOTICE
Generally . . . 14.01
Adjudicative facts, of
  Generally . . . 14.02
  Criminal cases, in . . . 14.03

[References are to sections.]

JUDICIAL NOTICE—Cont.
Jury or judge using facts in their personal experience to "evaluate" evidence, limits of . . . 14.06
Legislative facts, of . . . 14.04
Other types of notice . . . 14.05

O

OPINION TESTIMONY
Expert opinion
Common-law tradition . . . 5.02
Expansion of admissibility of (otherwise inadmissible) facts and data considered by expert, based on . . . 5.04
Federal Rules of Evidence, reform of common law by . . . 5.03; 5.04
Scientific evidence . . . 6.05[A]
Who are experts and to what may they testify . . . 5.03
Lay opinion
Common-law restrictions . . . 5.01[A]
Federal Rules of Evidence, under . . . 5.01[B]

P

PRESUMPTIONS (See BURDENS AND PRESUMPTIONS)

PRIVILEGES
Generally . . . 13.01
Accountant-client privilege . . . 13.06[B][2]
Attorney-client privilege and examination of issues common to many privileges
Generally . . . 13.02
Basic privilege . . . 13.02[A]
Corporate setting . . . 13.02[B]
Crime-fraud exception and other typically criminal issues . . . 13.02[E]
Intentional or unintentional disclosure (or the like), effect of . . . 13.02[C]
Joint defense and joint consultation . . . 13.02[D]
Clergy-communicant privilege . . . 13.06[B][1]
Fifth Amendment privilege . . . 13.08
Governmental and government-related privileges . . . 13.07
Journalist privilege . . . 13.06[B][3]
Miscellaneous privileges . . . 13.06[D]
Parent-child privilege . . . 13.06[C][3]
Peer review and self-critical analysis, privilege covering . . . 13.06[C][1]
Physician-patient privilege . . . 13.04
Psychotherapist privilege . . . 13.05
Researcher privilege . . . 13.06[B][4]
Spousal privileges (See SPOUSAL PRIVILEGES)
Trade secrets privilege . . . 13.06[B][5]
Withhold information if one's life is threatened, privilege to . . . 13.06[C][2]

PROBABILISTIC EVIDENCE (See SCIENTIFIC AND PROBABILISTIC EVIDENCE)

R

RELEVANT EVIDENCE
Generally . . . 2.01
Character evidence (See CHARACTER EVIDENCE)
Counterweight to
Character evidence as (See CHARACTER EVIDENCE)
Formalistic logic used to determine relevance . . . 2.02
Judge's role under Rule 104 . . . 2.05
Materiality or probative value, "overriding" Rules 401-403 by re-characterizing underlying components of
Concepts of materiality and probative value, review of . . . 2.04[A]
Possible re-characterization . . . 2.04[B]
Other transactions, similar occurrences, and profiles . . . 3.05
Rule 403 as (See subhead: Rule 403 as counterweight to)
Settlement matters (compromise, offers to compromise, withdrawn pleas, and related matters)
Civil cases . . . 3.07[A]
Criminal cases; guilty pleas and plea negotiations . . . 3.07[B]
Subsequent remedial measures . . . 3.06
Emerging patterns or quasi-rules in application of Rule 403 factors
Other emerging categories . . . 2.06[B]
Pretrial experiments . . . 2.06[A]
Formalistic logic used to determine relevance . . . 2.02
Insurance, evidence indicating or suggesting . . . 3.08
Judge's role under Rule 104 . . . 2.05
Materiality or probative value, "overriding" Rules 401-403 by re-characterizing underlying components of
Concepts of materiality and probative value, review of . . . 2.04[A]
Possible re-characterization . . . 2.04[B]
Other transactions, similar occurrences, and profiles . . . 3.05
Rule 403 as counterweight to
Generally . . . 2.03
Judicial options other than admissibility/inadmissibility, Rule 403 providing . . . 2.03[B]
Limits on Rule 403, potential . . . 2.03[C]
Structure and operation of Rule 403 . . . 2.03[A]
Settlement matters (compromise, offers to compromise, withdrawn pleas, and related matters)
Civil cases . . . 3.07[A]
Criminal cases; guilty pleas and plea negotiations . . . 3.07[B]
Subsequent remedial measures . . . 3.06

[References are to sections.]

S

SCIENTIFIC AND PROBABILISTIC EVIDENCE
Daubert decision
Generally . . . 6.02; 6.02[A]
Application to experts other than "scientific" . . . 6.02[B]
"Fit" and "reliability" factors under *Daubert-Kumho*, evaluation of . . . 6.02[C]
Procedures for deciding *Daubert/Kumho* issues . . . 6.02[D]
DNA . . . 6.04
Forensic evidence other than DNA in criminal cases
Fingerprinting . . . 6.06[B]
Handwriting . . . 6.06[A]
Miscellaneous evidentiary challenges . . . 6.06[C]
Frye standard, traditional . . . 6.01
Mathematical probability evidence . . . 6.07
Mental health (See subhead: Psychology, mental health, social sciences, and related fields)
Minor premise, test properly conducted as . . . 6.03
Psychology, mental health, social sciences, and related fields
Charged crime, inadmissibility of opinions on mental elements of . . . 6.05[B]
Child abuse cases, psychological testimony in . . . 6.05[D]
Expert opinion relevance and reliability of . . . 6.05[A]
Inadmissibility of opinions on mental elements of charged crime . . . 6.05[B]
Perception and memory in adults . . . 6.05[E]
Post-traumatic stress disorder, related syndromes, and related evidence . . . 6.05[C]
Rule 704(b) . . . 6.05[B]
Rule 702 testimony by experts, current test under (See subhead: *Daubert* decision)
Social sciences (See subhead: Psychology, mental health, social sciences, and related fields)
Test properly conducted as minor premise . . . 6.03

SEXUAL CRIMES (See CHARACTER EVIDENCE, subhead: Sexual crimes and related offenses, character in cases of)

SPECIFIC-ACTS EVIDENCE (See CHARACTER EVIDENCE, subhead: Specific-acts evidence, contours of exclusion of)

SPOUSAL PRIVILEGES
Generally . . . 13.03
Adverse spousal testimony against one's self, privilege to prevent . . . 13.03[A]
Marital communications . . . 13.03[B]

SPOUSAL PRIVILEGES—Cont.
Testimonial privilege not to testify against one's spouse . . . 13.03[A]

W

WITNESS TESTIMONY
Bias . . . 4.07
Competency as prerequisite for
Dead Man's Statutes or rules . . . 4.02[B]
General competency rules . . . 4.02[A]
Hypnotically refreshed testimony . . . 4.02[C]
Judges and jurors . . . 4.02[D]
Convictions . . . 4.09
Credibility issues, miscellaneous . . . 4.12
Cross-examination
Bias, to show . . . 4.07
Form of questions in . . . 4.03
Misconduct not resulting in conviction, regarding . . . 4.08
Prior inconsistent statements, regarding . . . 4.06
Right to . . . 4.04[A]
Scope of . . . 4.04[B]
Direct examination, form of questions in . . . 4.03
Eyewitness testimony . . . 4.11
Impeachment . . . 4.05
Misconduct not resulting in conviction, inquiries regarding . . . 4.08
Opinion testimony (See OPINION TESTIMONY)
Personal knowledge as prerequisite for . . . 4.02[E]
Presenting . . . 4.01
Prior inconsistent statements . . . 4.06
Reputation and opinion evidence of character for lack of veracity . . . 4.10
Sequestration of witnesses . . . 4.13

WRITINGS AND EXHIBITS
Authentication
Generally . . . 12.01
Animations . . . 12.01[F]
Chain of custody . . . 12.01[D]
Demonstrations, animations, and simulations . . . 12.01[F]
Documents and signatures . . . 12.01[A]
Electronic communications . . . 12.01[G]
Photographs, videotapes, etc. . . . 12.01[E]
Self-authentication . . . 12.01[C]
Signatures . . . 12.01[A]
Simulations . . . 12.01[F]
Voice identification . . . 12.01[B]
Best evidence rule . . . 12.02
Completeness . . . 12.03
Original documents, requirement of . . . 12.02